THE MORAL ORDER

THE MORAL ORDER

AN INTRODUCTION TO THE HUMAN SITUATION

RAOUL NAROLL

With the editorial assistance of Frada Naroll

SAGE PUBLICATIONS
Beverly Hills / London / New Delhi

For Frada, Lifelong Collaborator

Without her help, this book never would
have gotten off the ground

Without her help, its author never
would have, either

For information address:

SAGE Publications, Inc.
275 South Beverly Drive
Beverly Hills, California 90212

SAGE Publications India Pvt. Ltd.
C-236 Defence Colony
New Delhi 110 024, India

SAGE Publications Ltd
28 Banner Street
London EC1Y 8QE, England

Printed in the United States of America

Library of Congress Cataloging in Publication Data

Naroll, Raoul.
    The moral order.

    Bibliography: p.
    Includes index.
    1. Social ethics.   2. Social values.   3. Social
problems.   I. Title.
HM216.N33   1982   170   82-19204
ISBN 0-8039-1916-6
ISBN 0-8039-1917-4 (pbk.)

FIRST PRINTING

Contents

PART II: MORALNETS AND SOCIAL ILLS

Figures

Tables

Foreword

While I have been turning over the human situation in my mind for more than forty years, I only began work on the study of it seriously in 1971. True, when I was in the army in 1942, I tried to do the thing out of my head in about twenty thousand words—but that was preposterous. And after that war, I spent nearly two years trying to do it systematically out of a set of the 1910 edition of the *Encyclopedia Britannica;* that, too, was preposterous. But I used up two reams of paper in successive drafts of outlines.

I wound up my outlining with a concern for the setting of the human situation in history—in cosmological, paleontological, archeological, as well as historical history. I went back to UCLA to work on a Ph.D. in history, on comparative method and on the rise of civilization. The *Outline of Anthropology* by Jacobs and Stern sent me to Hobhouse, Wheeler, and Ginsburg's classic worldwide comparative study of cultural evolution among small-scale societies. Ralph Beals told me about George Peter Murdock, and so I began my lifelong concern with holocultural studies—general tests of theories through worldwide statistical comparisons of small-scale societies. Meanwhile, my history teachers got me into classical source criticism, and that was to lead me later to data quality control.

I also learned a lesson from my doctoral thesis. Not from anything I discovered about the human situation there, but from what I was taught by the dead. My problem as a graduate student needing a Ph.D. degree was to bring my unconventional interests in broad-scale comparative history to terms that would make sense to my understanding, tolerant, and helpful but conventionally specialized history teachers. To that end, I chose to study the Federal Convention of 1787—the authors of the U. S. Constitution. The debates there ranged far over the comparative history of Western civilization and its classical Mediterranean ancestor.

I began by viewing the work of that convention as an essay in political theory—an attempt at a general solution to the problem of federal government. Following the thinking of Carl Van Doren in *The Great Rehearsal*, I wanted to learn from these men how we could design a proper constitution for a world federation. But the message that came through from delegate after delegate all that hot summer of 1787 was clear: Never mind theory; never mind Locke and Montesquieu. We have all read them. Now forget them. Our job is to write a constitution that will suit our own people. One that they will come to love. One that is as close to what they are already used to as possible. "Experience must be our only guide," said one. "Reason may mislead us."

So I came to realize in later years, as I pondered over the lessons of 1787, the central message to be taken from those most successful of constitution writers: Writing a constitution is not an exercise in political theory. It is an exercise in cultural anthropology. The constitution has to rest firmly on the ideological and political and moral culture of the people. The delegates of 1787 would not have been surprised to see their constitutional model fail when it was copied again and again in Latin America. "We weren't writing a constitution for ex-Spaniards," they would have said, "we were writing one for ex-Englishmen."

I abandoned as foolish my dream of devoting my life to the design of a world government. I now believe that such a government will not be designed; it will be an organic growth. If a successful convention produces one, it will be one like that of 1787, a convention of well-educated, practical politicians—not one of anthropological or political theorists. The authors of such a constitution will work as far as possible—as did the men of 1787—with the political, moral, social, and economic order as they find it. They will hammer out only those shifts and compromises that are necessary to convert a weak confederation like that of eighteenth-century Switzerland into a workable one—as the Swiss did in 1848 when they adapted the U.S. Constitution of 1787 to their own similar situation and needs.

So if scholars like me are to help such politicians convert the Charter of the United Nations into a working world system—as the men of 1787 transformed a feeble American union under the Articles of Confederation into an effective nation—we must rather seek to transform the moral and social and political culture of mankind.

I see that effort as a chief task of the social sciences. And my leading task in my study of the human situation is to survey the work of the social scientists to see how far along all of us have come.

The catalysts that sent me back to my study of the human situation in 1971 were two. One of them was the student strike at my university in 1970. The other was Ward Goodenough's request that I review the findings of holocultural studies for the *American Anthropologist*. By the time the students struck the State University of New York at Buffalo, that manuscript, "What Have We Learned from Cross-Cultural Surveys?" was in his hands.

When the strikers took over the campus, David Hays organized a peace patrol and asked me to serve as its chief of staff. My training at the Camp Ritchie Military Intelligence school in 1945 had taught me how to keep up a situation map and present a formal estimate of the situation: What is our task? Exactly what force does the enemy have and where does he have it? What force do we have and where do we have it? What can the enemy do to us? What can we do to the enemy?

So, I set about to estimate the situation. We Peace Patrollers were accepted as neutrals, like the Red Cross. Everyone would talk to us: the strike leaders, the campus police, the university administration, and the leaders of the Buffalo community anxiously watching the trouble at their university. What I found to my shock was that nobody was watching that situation as a whole, systematically estimating the campus situation. The pamphlet we Peace Patrollers put out, objectively looking at each of the demands on the striker's list, was the most popular thing we did. It met a need felt by all the parties to the dispute.

The strike ended. Calm returned to the campus. There was no longer a campus situation for anyone to have to estimate. But there was still a worldwide human situation to estimate. No one had been estimating the campus situation. And no one was estimating the worldwide human situation, either.

True, the United Nations puts out triennially a document on the social situation of the world. It tries to survey the needs and problems of the world, country by country. But it does not try to look at the human situation as a whole. It does not consider core values; it takes them for granted. It does not offer any worldwide social indicator reviews—no scoreboards, as I call them. It does not try to review the state of social science critically, does not consider what we already know and what we need to learn about our problems. It does not offer any proposals for further tests of theory to improve our understanding of the world's problems. Nor does it make a systematic attempt to propose specific programs of action to cope with these problems.

But those five elements constitute my idea of a proper estimate of what I call the *socionomy*—that is, the current human situation as a whole. I call those elements the Five Steps. And so in 1971 I set out to put together such an estimate. I began by listing the problems that seemed to concern the public today. My two associates—my wife, Frada, and my assistant, Enid Margolis— helped me. Together, we drew up a preliminary list of about forty such problems.

I began working on problems of home and family. (I dropped drug abuse from the list because too little was known about it.) By the time I had drafted chapters on the structure of the Five Steps, and on personal problems reflected by mental illness, alcoholism, suicide, and family problems, a pattern had emerged. There is an underlying cause that seems to explain a large part of these problems, and there is also an underlying body of theory about that cause. I call it *moralnet* theory. (By a moralnet, I mean a primary group that serves as a normative reference group. The archetypical moralnets are the extended family or the primeval hunting band.) In its simplest form, moralnet theory is as old as Confucius and Moses. It is often discussed today by family sociologists like Bronfenbrenner. But what neither Moses nor Confucius could know—and what neither Bronfenbrenner nor Empey nor any other sociologist of moralnets today realizes either—is how large a number of rigorous theory tests now support moralnet theory.

The central impediment here is the information explosion. The knowledge business is completely out of hand. Neither Bronfenbrenner nor Empey nor anyone else keeps up with the relevant sociological and psychological and anthropological literature. No one can. No one can possibly keep up even with the literature on alcoholism alone—hundreds of books and thousands of articles come out around the world every year. It is even harder to keep up with the suicide literature. Probably Empey knows the literature on juvenile delinquency as well as anyone; but even he finds it necessary to confine his reading largely to studies of American delinquency—not because he thinks that British or French or Russian juvenile delinquency is a different kind of problem, but because he does not have the time to study them all.

There have been at least two previous systematic efforts in the last 25 years to review the whole of social science. But each of these defined its task solely as reviewing the theories—the ideas. I am defining my task as reviewing and evaluating theory test results—quite another matter. Theory and theory tests are two different things entirely. The one is a survey of thought. The other is a survey of research findings. So this effort is an extension of my 1970 paper, "What Have We Learned from Cross-Cultural Surveys?" That paper looked at research findings. It assumed that *learning* something about human behavior means testing a theory against data. "Experience must be our only guide," as they said in 1787, "reason may mislead us." In other words, clever theory illustrated by selected impressive, suitable examples does not constitute learning. Only rigorous tests of theory against actual events—research—constitute learning.

So the first half of this book is about socionomic method—about how to estimate the human situation. About how to find out where we stand and what we can do about it. And the last half of the book applies that method—the Five Steps—to the problems of personal and family troubles. And sees as the foundation of a world order and so a happy human situation a moral order grounded on the Five Steps and the moralnet. For the moralnet is not only the key to a happy family and personal life. It is the foundation of public morality, and so the foundation of a moral, social, political, and economic world order.

The creation of such a world order is, I believe, the deepest historical task of our times. A stable human world order means a stable, managed world ecology—the world as mankind's park. Such a world order would constitute the fifth great breakthrough of biological evolution (nearly a thousand million years after the fourth, the development of effective multicelled macroorganisms).

Such a world order might well set the stage for the sixth great breakthrough—which might well require another thousand million years—the colonization and organization of the outer disk of our galaxy. But I do not talk about the role of the moral order in human destiny in this book. Nor do I apply here the Five Steps to the problems of the larger society—problems of economics or politics. These indeed are tasks for a proper study of the human situation. But they are not addressed in this introductory volume, *The Moral Order*.

What *The Moral Order* does address are ten personal and family problems: mental illness, alcoholism, suicide, family disorganization, child abuse, juvenile delinquency, neglect of old people, sex roles, divorce, and sexual frustration. I believe that application of the Five Steps to these problems today might well reduce their rate of incidence in a country like the United States by at least 10 percent within ten years—at a savings of billions of dollars per year, not to speak of savings in heartache and heartbreak.

So here is my reading of that part of the human situation dealing with personal and family problems. Here is my estimating model—the Five Steps. Here is my theoretical model—the moralnet.

—Raoul Naroll
State University of New York at Buffalo

Notes

Jacobs and Stern (1947); Hobhouse, Wheeler, and Ginsberg (1965); Murdock (1937, 1949); and Simmons (1945) were my introduction to holocultural studies.

Naroll (1953) and Van Doren (1965) on the Federal Convention of 1787; it was John Dickinson who appealed to experience in preference to reason there, on August 15.

On the Swiss Constitution of 1848, see Dierauer (1913-1917:V: 769). On the findings of holocultural studies, see Naroll (1970a).

Bronfenbrenner (1976) cries alarm about the American family; Empey (1978) reviews American youth crime.

Bernier and Yerkey (1979: 31-45) on information overload.

Alcoholism literature overload: private communication from Mark Keller, long the director of CAAAL.

Two earlier attempts to review and summarize the findings of social science are Handy and Kurtz (1963); Berelson and Steiner (1964).

The information overload makes it certain that I have ignored much important evidence for this book—even though I followed the reviews of expert specialists wherever I could. Furthermore, despite what seems to me immense care, I may have occasionally garbled what I did read. If the book nevertheless finds favor with the public, I will want to do a revised edition. To that end, I would publicly thank by name those who write me about my errors or oversights. I would be especially thankful for copies of papers or reviews of books that test theories bearing on my work. Write me at the Department of Anthropology, State University of New York, Buffalo, NY 14261. In begging the indulgence of a tolerant public for my failings, I hope that with all its imperfections, this book still makes a persuasive case for its two main ideas: (1) that the Five Steps can provide a workable foundation for a worldwide moral order, and (2) that weakened moralnets mean trouble.

Introduction

1.1 THE THREE SISTERS AND THE HUMAN SITUATION

"If only we could know!" says Olga Sergeyevna Prozorov, as the last curtain falls on Chekhov's play, *Three Sisters.*

Despite the troubles she and her sisters endure, Olga still hopes for a better world. The play ends, you remember, as word comes that Lieutenant Tusenbach has been killed. The skeptical lieutenant had been the last hope of a happy marriage for any of the sisters. Irina, his fiancee, sobs an attempt at self-comfort:

"There will come a time when everybody will know why, for what purpose there is all this suffering, and there will be no more mysteries."

Olga agrees. "For those who shall live after us," she says as she holds her sister's head to her breast, "our suffering will be transformed into joy. Happiness and peace will reign on earth, and for those who live now, they will have a good word and blessings."

Olga feels her sister's loss of a lover the more, since she has never had one of her own. She would have taken any decent man as a husband, even an old or ugly one. But no one had asked her. So she soothes her sister:

"The band is playing so cheerfully and joyously—maybe if we wait a little longer, we shall find out why we live, why we suffer. . . . Oh, if we only knew! If only we knew!"

Years before, in the second act of the play, their sister Masha also had asked about the meaning of life: "I think man ought to have faith or ought to seek a faith, or else his life is empty, empty. . . . To live and not to understand why cranes fly; why children are born; know what one is living for or else it is all nonsense and waste."

Colonel Vershinin, Masha's lover, would have agreed. He is no happier than the three sisters. Trapped like Masha in a bad marriage, and now departing with his regiment for distant Poland, he bids the sisters farewell with words of hope

Author's Note: See Notes at the end of each chapter for sources, asides, explanations and elaborations on the text. In the vignettes that introduce many chapters, names of living persons have been changed; other appropriate names from the society in question have been substituted.

for mankind. As though in this wreck of their lives they can find some consolation in the vague future.

"Life is heavy to bear," the colonel says. "Many of us consider that it is a blind alley, hollow and hopeless, and yet, we must admit that it becomes each day more luminous, easier, and everything leads us to believe that the time will not be far off when it will be entirely enlightened."

Earlier in the play, Irina's lover argues with Masha's about human prospects. Vershinin, as we see, looks for steady progress. Tusenbach, on the contrary, looks only for continued suffering.

"In two or three hundred years," says Vershinin when first we meet him, "life on earth will be unimaginably beautiful, amazing, astonishing."

"It seems to me," says Vershinin again, later on, "that little by little, everything on earth will be transformed, and is already being transformed under our very eyes. In two or three hundred years, or maybe in a thousand years—it doesn't matter how long exactly—life will be different. It will be happy. Of course, we shan't be able to enjoy that future life, but all the same, what we're living for now is to create it. That's the goal of our life, and you might say that's the only happiness we shall ever achieve."

"Not only after two or three hundred centuries," says Tusenbach, "but in a million years, life will still be as it was; life does not change, it remains forever, following its own laws, which do not concern us, or which, at any rate, you will never find out. Migrant birds, cranes, for example, fly and fly and whatever thoughts, high or low, enter their heads, they will still fly and not know why or where. They fly and will continue to fly, whatever philosophers come to life among them; they may philosophize as much as they like, only they will fly."

Tusenbach thus thought there was no answer to Olga's question, no way of guessing why we live, what the overall pattern is, what the meaning of the human situation is. Vershinin, along with millions of others in that heyday of simple optimism, thought in terms of simple progress to an ever happier life—though he himself was miserable. I think I see another sort of pattern emerging.

1.2   AN OFFHAND SKETCH OF THE COSMIC SITUATION

The human situation may perhaps best be understood in terms of cosmology. If there is a meaning to human history, it may well be found there. Every moral order needs an image of human history, of human destiny. Every moral order offers *some* kind of answer to Olga Prozorov. That of a scientific moral order is to be found in cosmology. Our cosmological destiny has, I think, been widely misunderstood. As I see it, we are not, as some say, doomed to perish with the sun in about 5 billion years. Nor, in my opinion, are we doomed to await either a later, final universal catastrophe in the big crunch of a closed universe, or else a later, final dissolution into a sort of thin, cold soup of an open universe. I think most astronomers fail to allow for the impact of intelligent life on cosmic dynamics 5 or 10 billion years hence.

Mankind in its present form emerged only within the last 100,000 years from the natural selection process that has been developing ever more intelligent forms of animal life. But manlike creatures have been around for at least 3 million years. Until 5,000 or 10,000 years ago, all mankind lived in small hunting bands, and survived by fishing and collecting plants and hunting animals, large and small. Only in the past 5,000 or 10,000 years have people lived in settled towns or villages, eating food from their farms or animal herds.

If we take the last 5,000 years of human history broadly, a thousand years at a time, we see a process of the rise and fall of empires as the most prominent and conspicuous pattern. These empires have been getting larger and larger. Only within the last 200 years has it clearly been in the power of a successful military state to create a world empire embracing all mankind. Now in the United Nations we may have in embryo a world federation—to make such an empire unnecessary.

At the same time, there has been an accelerating growth of knowledge and understanding. That process has immensely speeded up in the last 500 years of our own Western civilization. And with the development of science and the industrial revolution, speeded up still further in our own time. It is often remarked that more professional scientists are alive today than ever lived at all before the twentieth century. Both these trends—toward world government and toward behavioral science—point to a coming world order.

In *The Moral Order* I begin my attempt to review the present state of understanding of the human situation, to estimate how close we are to establishing that stable ideological, social, economic, political, and cultural world order. The creation of such a stable world order, then, would constitute the end of the current stage of the evolution of life on earth and, I conjecture, the beginning of the next—the colonization of our galaxy. With the last stage being the long-term management of our galaxy to ensure the survival of our seed and culture forever—whatever the bent of the universe.

The processes that produced the present order of the universe as a whole, that gave rise to life on earth originally, that have governed its biological evolution, and that now govern cultural evolution, are fundamentally but three. Two everywhere and a third at the heart of life. These three processes are all well known to science, but two of them lack suitable names. I speak of the *servomechanism*, the *natural selection process*, and the *self-reinforcing process*. I call these the *servo*, the *darwin*, and the *snowball*. (The last two terms are my coinings. See the Glossary at the back of the book for definitions of all technical or unusual words. I mark those I had to coin for this book with asterisks there.)

The *servomechanism* is a basic device of life, much used also in human culture. Many naturally occurring servomechanisms are called *homeostatic systems*. The central idea of the servomechanism is that of a control system. In a servomechanism, some entity can possibly exist in a variety of states with respect to some characteristic. One of those states is specified as a goal. A mechanism is provided for measuring the state of the controlled entity, for comparing that state with the designated goal, and for taking action to change the state to accord with the goal, should it depart from it. There is nothing mystical or vague about servomechanisms. They guide ships, airplanes, and spacecraft. And they guide plants and animals, families and councils, and armies. The science of control systems is known as *cybernetics*. In this present volume I describe a cybernetic model of the mind as well as a cybernetic model of the moral order—the Five Steps.

The cybernetic approach to a philosophy of science and a philosophy of morals offers among other things simple, concrete, specific, and operational definitions of such philosophical problems as the nature of knowledge (epistemology), the meaning of cause and effect, the nature of reality (ontology), the distinction between mind and body, the meaning of chance (probability), and the nature of instinct in human behavior. Such cybernetic definitions turn up later in this present work (Chapters 4, 6, and 7).

The *darwin*, or natural selection process, as Donald T. Campbell has pointed out, applies in a wide variety of situations—not merely in the biological process leading to the origin of new species. A natural selection process, or darwin, then, is any process of blind variation and selective retention. It is through natural selection that some clumps of matter, occurring through chance collisions, form the nucleus of stars and galaxies—for when by chance a large clump occurs, that clump tends to be preserved through gravity. In his description of the chemical evolution process of Stage One of the evolution of life on earth, Dickerson describes such darwins as tending to produce and retain elements of the life system. Chance merely gets the process started; it is some selection and retention principle that leads to increasing order, to decreasing entropy. Within human culture there are many darwins that people themselves have created: civil service examinations, elections, markets in which firms compete for existence, civilizations in which state systems compete militarily and diplomatically for survival. Science itself is a darwin, in which the selection method is scientific theory testing and the critical review of such theory tests by other scientists. Some darwins are relatively mild, kind, and gentle; others are harsh and cruel.

The third fundamental dynamic process at work managing the universe as a whole, the evolution of life, and the evolution of culture, is the *snowball*. By a snowball I mean a self-reinforcing process. One exists whenever it is true that the more of something an entity already has, the more it is likely to get still more. The rich get richer while the poor get children. The larger a star or a galaxy, the more powerful its gravity and hence the more likely it is to get even larger, by attracting stray, wandering bits of matter. The more dominant a species, the more likely it is to crowd out rivals and so become even more dominant. Thus mankind now is no longer subject to rivalry from other species. We have crowded them out already. Suppose the baboons or the chimpanzees were following a path of cultural evolution like that which led to our triumph. We'd shoot them down long before they ever became a threat.

It is this model of cultural evolution that I would offer to the Olga Prozorovs of this world, rather than the old one of steady, gradual progress. Cultural evolution through increasingly powerful (and sometimes ruthless) servos. Cultural evolution through blind variation and selective retention by a dozen different sorts of darwins, operating at once. Cultural evolution through the snowballing of ideologies, of social orders, of political and economic orders. These processes *can* be relatively gentle—though all change is painful. Or they can be quite cruel. The paroxysms of our own century, with its tens of millions of cruel deaths in wars and revolutions, are but symptoms and aspects of this process.

But as I shall argue at greater length in the next chapter, if mankind survives at all, and if a stable world order is at all possible, then sooner or later, if only by the mere operation of chance, it must be inevitable. And such an order, by regularizing, regulating, organizing, and managing all these interrelated servos, darwins, and snowballs, might well make life far more pleasant in many ways than it has been these last 5,000 years. Though perhaps less interesting, less exciting.

Mankind, then, seems to be in the throes of travail—in the midst of a painful labor. The spasms that mark that process are agonizing. And the pain and suffering go on. That process may well not end gradually, with the pain gradually lessening. Instead, as in childbirth, it may well end suddenly, in one last spasm that produces a stable world order.

Is such an order, given the best of luck, within reach today? In the lifetime of people born now? If we cannot be sure it is, neither can we be sure it is not. As I said in the Foreword, there is such a flood of behavioral science that no one is keeping track of it. No one is watching the whole of our knowledge about ideological, social, political, and economic order. Perhaps the review I begin here may suggest the chief elements of a feasible model of a stable world order. Certainly this first volume, on the moral order, offers grounds for optimism rather than pessimism.

True, there are still risks of utter disaster. An all-out atomic war might not only kill off billions of us; it might conceivably make life impossible for large land animals by destroying the protective barrier of ozone in the upper atmosphere that shields us from the killing ultraviolet rays of the sun. Or conceivably we might in some way disturb the earth's delicate climatic balance, might trigger a heating or cooling snowball that could freeze or roast us to death. Not until that stable world order arrives will we be out of danger. The race between cultural evolution and universal catastrophe is still on.

1.3   SOCIONOMICS AS META-IDEOLOGY

For humankind to take charge of our earth, we must first take charge of ourselves. As Western scientific humanists have been assuming for the past 300 years, I assume here that all men and women are brothers and sisters—that the moral order is a world order embracing and caring for all people. To take charge of ourselves, we must all agree on some common values, some common principles, some common policies for mankind at large. A set of such values, principles, and policies organized into a single system constitutes an ideology. Christianity, Islam, and Buddhism long have offered all mankind a vision of a worldwide moral order. Socionomics, I suggest, can in many ways play the part that traditional religions have played in seeking to guide human affairs.

Alston, a philosopher of religion, has set forth the key elements or components of traditional religions. These are founded on beliefs in powerful supernatural beings, gods. They distinguish between sacred and profane objects. They embody ritual acts focused on sacred objects. They offer a moral code sanctioned by the gods. They evoke characteristically religious feelings that tend to be aroused in the presence of sacred objects and during the practice of ritual, and that are associated with the gods. They make use of prayer and other forms of communication with the gods. They offer a world view—a general picture of the world as a whole and the place of the individual therein. More or less they seek to organize a person's life based on that world view. They create social groups bound together by these first eight elements.

I see socionomics as a scientific discipline to be used in and by all the behavioral sciences, as a synthesizing and controlling part of their work. I see it as a means by which the work of behavioral science can furnish mankind at large with a common ideology to guide its affairs.

As a scientific discipline, of course, socionomics would have nothing to do with a belief in supernaturals. As a scientific discipline, socionomics would not interfere with freedom of thought or freedom of research. It would depend for its effect on the maturity of behavioral science itself. Any suggestion that socionomic orthodoxy was interfering with freedom of thought through threat of punishment of scientists would be a sign of serious weakness. The central idea of socionomic control is control by power of the ideas and evidence of a mature science—power whose leading validation is the very freedom of all people, scientists, and laypersons alike, to dissent, with no other penalty than being thought a fool and laughed at.

I would, however, imagine that most of the other elements of traditional religions would one way or another take form, someday—if and when socionomics becomes a mature science, displaying to all its power to predict and control public affairs, shelter the weak, comfort the afflicted, tidy up the economy and the polity, and most important of all, keep the peace. So I would look for the development of rituals, for a sense of the sacred, for the arousal of feelings of awe and reverence. But later on, when socionomics has matured. First the scientific findings, then the successful applications, then the moral code; and the feelings of awe and the reverential rituals last.

I have nothing more to say about socionomic awe, reverence, or rituals. My business here is rather with the state of mankind and the state of behavioral science, seen from the viewpoint of a scientist and a methodologist.

This search for unity amid diversity and for discipline amid freedom means that socionomics cannot be an ideology, but only a *meta-ideology*. That is to say, socionomics as such may not go beyond core values to insist on the validity of any specific laws of public policy or private morality. Socionomics is not a theory; it is a method. It may only posit a scientific paradigm about the means through which socionomists might hope to establish policy and morality. Through the power of scientific evidence, public opinion must reach that state of consensus and moral concern which translates the findings of socionomists into that policy and that morality. It is the evidence that must prevail, not the socionomist.

As I have said, I define socionomics as the science of the socionomy—the study of the human situation at large. The principles of scientific research I have in mind are those now generally governing behavioral science. If I here approach the socionomic task from the cybernetic point of view, that is only because as a scientist I consider it the most helpful one. Whether the cybernetic approach or some other ultimately prevails—or whether the cybernetic approach merely forms part of a larger paradigm—depends on the evidence as it appears.

Behavioral science, however, has largely kept to a value-free study of human affairs, while socionomics itself is value laden. The analogy here is with medicine. On the one hand, medical science seeks coldly to describe the nature of the human body and its ailments. On the other hand, it seeks to use that knowledge to help people; doctors swear the value-laden Hippocratic oath, which begins by promising above all never intentionally to do harm. We must divorce ourselves from our moral attitudes when we are collecting data and testing theories about natural laws—and those activities are our main business. Nevertheless, the Five Steps of socionomics embody value-free observation and value-free theory testing in a larger value-laden process that begins with core values and ends with policy recommendations.

Those five steps, as you may recall, are (1) establish core values, (2) check scoreboards, (3) survey theory tests, (4) plan further studies, and (5) cope with troubles now.

Steps 1 and 5 are value laden. Steps 2, 3, and 4 are largely value free. Pure scientists can work at ease on Steps 2, 3, or 4—whatever their values and whatever their policy views. Indeed, values and policies only get in the way of the work of these central steps and need to be laid aside for the time being while people are at work on them. But given the value canons of Step 1, the policies of Step 5 follow from the value-free work of the central steps.

For example, consider the links between divorce and suicide. As we shall see in Chapters 9 and 15, the link is well established. It is a fact that among both individuals and cultures, the more divorce, the more suicide. Whether we think divorce and suicide are good, bad, or indifferent things, that link remains a fact. Further, though the evidence is not quite overwhelming, it strongly tilts in support of a natural law that calls divorce a cause and suicide an effect. That law would say: If you want to decrease suicides, and divorce is frequent, decrease divorces. To convert that natural law to a moral law making divorce a conditional or absolute evil requires some value assumptions about suicide, as well as some further information about possible side effects and tradeoffs involved in restricting divorce. The key point, then, is that value-free behavioral science announces a natural law about divorce and suicide. Value-laden socionomics must set that finding in a larger context and apply its value assumptions to produce a moral law, a public policy.

The whole discipline of socionomics breaks down into two distinct and but loosely related parts. The first of these is the larger picture of the human situation as set in the very long run—in the cosmic scale. I have just briefly sketched that picture as I now see it, and propose to devote the next work in my study of the human situation to filling that sketch out. The second part of the discipline of socionomics is the application of the Five Steps to the human situation here and now. And it is with this second part that the present volume is concerned.

The Five Steps of socionomics merely formalize and make a system out of studies and viewpoints already common among behavioral scientists. None of these steps is new. None is in itself controversial. That is to say, there is nothing controversial about looking for core values or in stating value assumptions; there is much controversy about which values ought to have priority. There is nothing controversial about using social indicators to measure the current state of the human situation; there is much controversy about the present accuracy of those indicators. Again, there is nothing controversial about reviewing the scientific literature in an attempt to learn what we know about this or that, nor is there anything controversial about embodying a methodological critique in that review; there may be some controversy about the specific findings of any given review. Again, there is nothing controversial about concluding a review of theory with a call for further research; there may often be controversy about the most fruitful research path to follow. Finally, there is nothing controversial about basing public policy on the findings of behavioral science where those findings are clear and unequivocal; there may often be controversy about the validity and implications of any particular set of findings. So the Five Steps of socionomics, as a paradigm, simply combine into a formal whole five elements that taken separately are already familiar parts of behavioral science. That whole, however, is greater than the sum of its parts. Separated, the parts cannot provide a moral order to guide mankind. Joined together, they can.

What is novel, then, is my call for a synthesizing discipline in which one person takes on all five tasks. Whoever does that with respect to even a single social problem is thus practicing socionomics. But as I try to do here, someone must also put together, as best he or she can, the whole human situation, in all its parts.

Part One of this book is a review of the Five Steps. In Chapter 2, I review Step 1 on establishing core values. I begin that chapter, like all others, with a vignette that seeks to arouse readers' interest, as well as to illustrate by an ethnographic or historical example the main topic of the new chapter.

I then review variations in value orientations in cultures around the world and survey the evolution of value orientation in human history. Here, as elsewhere in the book, I look where I can at historical and archeological records, but depend for my main thrust on comparative ethnology. The evolution of values orientations here—as of other things later in the book—is inferred from the worldwide comparative study of recent small-scale societies. (By a small-scale society I mean a speech community without any cities.) The validity of inferring past history from present ethnography has often been questioned. All peoples have equally long histories. The recent culture of no single human society offers an adequate picture of the culture of its own ancestors —much less a picture of the culture of ours. This book is not the place to deal with such problems of inference about the past. Let me just say here that I depend on two propositions generally uncontested by anthropologists: First, I take it that for the past 50,000 years at least, mankind has had no genetic variations that have led to any important behavioral differences among human populations. All such differences, on the contrary, reflect only learned culture patterns. Second, I take it that 25,000 years ago, there were no large-scale societies—all human societies then were small scale. There were no cities or large towns in those days. A large body of systematic research has shown that the world around, a great many cultural traits tend to go with settlement size. Indeed, the size of the largest settlement in any speech community may well be the best overall index of its societal complexity or level of cultural evolution. Among those other cultural traits I point out in Chapter 2 are certain elements of values orientation. And that is how I vaguely infer the broad history of values orientation from a comparative worldwide ethnographic study of recent small-scale societies.

I next consider the core values of the core values—how such values are to be established. There are three possibilities to look at. First, there is the argument that a stable world order is inevitable, if mankind survives at all. This argument breaks down into two parts: (a) if only through trial and error, a stable world order must sooner or later emerge from the constantly changing unstable world order that now exists; and (b) whatever value system happens to dominate that stable world order must itself also have the quality of stability in order for the order it animates likewise to be stable. Second, there is the argument that from the nature of the human mind, of the human nervous system, certain social and cultural values are implied. Third, there is the observation that the core values of European scientific humanism, whatever their ultimate merits or ultimate destiny, are in fact shared by most leaders in the world today—including most people at all likely to read this book. I suspect that ultimately all three of these approaches may point to the same final set of core values. But for the time being, I arbitrarily assume or posit those familiar European humanistic values. So I rest my values argument on the banal; to my readers, my values assumptions ought to seem familiar, trite, and obvious—however strange, unfamiliar, and unwelcome they might have seemed to other people at other times or with other cultural traditions.

Here are the familiar values on which socionomics as I practice it rests: (1) *peace*—a stable, universal order for all mankind; (2) *humanism*—scientific empiricism as our way of knowing, and mankind's earthly happiness as our goal; (3) *decency*—the brotherhood and sisterhood of all mankind, which means justice for the strong and compassion for the weak; (4) *progress*—defined as increasingly powerful knowledge obtained through individual liberty and cultural variety, to encourage wide diversity under the law.

In Chapter 2, finally, I consider the measurement of the value orientations of mankind—both with respect to what people profess to value and to what they actually honor through their behavior.

In Chapter 3 I deal with Step 2. I focus on measuring the actual attainment of goals set by core values. Chapter 3 is a chapter on social indicators— scoreboards. It is concerned with two chief problems—norms and accuracy. With respect to norms, I argue for the selection from time to time of the single nation with the best quality of life as an overall model country for all scoreboards—including those in which it does comparatively poorly. I also argue for the establishment of a minimal worldwide range of variation needed to preserve variety for continued progress. With respect to accuracy, I review the main sources of error in national statistics and the chief techniques for improving their quality.

In Chapter 4 I deal with Step 3; it is a chapter on reviewing theory tests, and thus on scientific method. I offer a cybernetic model of truth and knowledge. Its epistemology rests on the view that the task of the mind is to build a model of the world outside the mind—a model that is continually tested by prediction and control. Hence the ultimate test of scientific method is not a logical one but a cybernetic one—the ability of that method to lead to successful prediction and control of the world outside the mind.

My chief concern in Chapter 4 is to review specific behavioral science methods of theory testing. I review evidence for three pervasive biases of the unscientific mind and so show the need for methods of the quantitative, rigorous sort associated with behavioral science as a research style. I discuss four fundamental research strategies—three of them behavioral and the fourth humanistic—and argue for a triangulation approach using all four strategies in turn to test the same theories. Finally, I propose a crude theory trust meter as a formal measure of the application of triangulation to the testing of specific theories.

In Chapter 5 I briefly consider two techniques that assist behavioral scientists to perform both Step 4 and Step 5—to *plan further studies* and to *cope with trouble now*. These techniques are concerned with the mechanics of the communication process rather than with its fundamental nature. The first technique is the new THINCS system for formally reviewing and assessing scientific research reports and so communicating what problems remain to be studied and what conclusions lead plainly to policy recommendations. The second technique is an age-old one: I make a brief plea for clear writing, for plain talk.

In Chapters 2 through 5 I thus propose the Five Steps for socionomists to follow so that behavioral science can produce a scientific ideology and a moral order for all mankind. What scientific basis do these Five Steps themselves possess? What is *their* validation as a paradigm? They can have no other validation than their ability to help mankind predict and control our affairs. Therefore, in the second part of this book, in Chapters 6 through 15, I apply the Five Steps to a set of specific social problems. These problems offer a working test of the Five Steps themselves. I hope that the present state of knowledge, set forth in Part Two of this book, will already tend to persuade the reader of the value of the Five Steps as they shed light on the moral order and on the moralnets that maintain it. I also hope that the study plans and policy recommendations I offer there will lead to research and to action that will snowball into large improvements in the future worldwide scoreboards—as suicide, alcoholism, mental illness, child battering, juvenile delinquency, and divorce rates go down. If such research and action do indeed happen in response to the kind of thing I try to do here, then and only then will socionomics have its validation. Then and only then will socionomics be a mature science.

1.4   WEAKENED MORALNETS MEAN TROUBLE

In Part Two of this work, accordingly, I deal with moralnets and their effect on ten prominent social problems: mental illness, alcoholism, suicide, disrupted family ties, child abuse, juvenile delinquency, neglect of old people, sex role discrimination (sexism), divorce, and sexual frustration. This focus on weakened moralnets is a particularly good test of the Five Steps of socionomics. We now know much about the link between weakened moralnets as causes and these personal and family problems as effects. We also have a body of theory on how to strengthen moralnets. That body of theory is ripe for testing in half a dozen different ways. Success in those tests would let socionomics endorse new social policies about strengthening moralnets. Then comes the final test. Will those policies, by strengthening natural and surrogate families, lead to impressive new readings? To lower rates of mental illness? Lower rates of alcoholism? Lower rates of suicide? To better care of the aged and so to lower suicide rates for old people? To less child abuse? Less juvenile delinquency? Less divorce? If they do, I repeat, then we would have a mature socionomics. These tests can be made now—made locally, on a small scale, at small cost.

Any such successful program of testing and using moralnet theory also offers another benefit. It tests a general theory of value transmission as set forth in Part Two of this book. That theory points the way to transmitting economic, political, and ideological values as well as those governing personal and family life. Thus Part Two does indeed present a general model of the moral order—how morality is to be established and how maintained.

In each chapter of Part Two I conclude with a sketch of a cost-benefit analysis on the topic of that chapter. I try to guess the costs of the research studies and policy recommendations made in the chapter and the benefits that might thus accrue. Of course, no benefits can be guaranteed; that is why pilot studies are first needed. And of course, the cost estimates are not rigorous or trustworthy; I lacked the time and resources to do a proper job. These, then, are estimates of orders of magnitude rather than realistic budgets.

Furthermore, the estimates of benefit are made from the point of view of an administrator, a political leader, or a budget officer. I deal only with manifest benefits, whose results show up clearly and unmistakably for the whole world to see, in the form either of reducing the administrator's costs or increasing the revenues by providing public support for the program.

The body of moralnet theory from which such results can be hoped for is neither strange nor novel. In its fundamentals it is as old as Moses and Confucius. The main point of Part Two is not to introduce startling new theories of social disorder. Rather it is to review a huge amount of high-quality behavioral science research that shows how right Moses and Confucius were in their concern for family ties: Weakened moralnets mean trouble. I do not say that no one has heard of these theories before. I do say that no one has put together in one place before even a half or a quarter of the hard evidence that supports the moralnet theory.

I begin my review of moralnet theory in Chapter 6 by setting forth the cybernetic model of the mind—the mind as an intricate set of mental programs that manages thousands of intricate sets of mental and neuro servomechanisms. That model points toward social and family life, including marriage, as a kind of instinctive behavior. That model points to rituals, ceremonies, fine arts, and literature—especially literature—as the means by which the culture programs a moral order into the human mind. The focus of the chapter is on moralnets. I define a moralnet as a primary group—the largest primary group that serves as a person's normative reference group. Thus I tap into a large body of theory and research by sociologists and social psychologists who have long studied these groups as transmitters of morality.

In Chapters 7, 8, and 9 I look at three manifestations of psychological disorder—mental illness, alcoholism, and suicide. For each, in turn, the Five Steps are applied. Thus, I do not confine my attention to weakened moralnets but consider also what other causal influences may lead to these troubles. With some kinds of mental illnesses, for example, there can be no doubt that susceptibility is hereditary, genetic. There are also clear indications of genetic predispositions toward alcoholism, and much reason to suspect that many sick old people commit suicide as a realistic solution to hopeless and painful illness— quite apart from the strength or weakness of their moralnet ties. Still, I cannot claim that these chapters ended as I envisioned them when I began—as unbiased reviews of all the evidence on the causes and treatment of the three problems. Rather, when I began to see in my preliminary drafts the weakened moralnet pattern so prominent throughout the realm of personal and family problems, my mind latched onto that theory. Latched hard. So in my revisions I have surely tended to overemphasize it. For the evidence, as you will see for yourself in these chapters, is truly overwhelming. Whatever other things may tend to make for mental illness, for alcoholism, and for suicide, weakened moralnets are likely to aggravate or increase the strain, and a sudden breakdown of a moralnet tie is likely to trigger their onset.

Chapter 10 is a general review of family theory from an anthropological point of view. However, I give little attention to the pet topics of traditional kinship theory—kinship algebra, as some people call them. The studies of Lévi-Strauss and others on unilateral cross-cousin marriage, or the semantic analyses of kinship terminology by the componential analysts, tell us nothing about the role of the family as the normal moralnet. And that is what Chapter 10 is about. So I am interested in the social instinct as it tends to build human families, and argue that in the absence of other cultural schemes, the extended bilateral kindred is the natural, or instinctive, human family type (but by no means necessarily for that reason any better, or more "moral," than any other type). I also argue that marriage—pair bonding—is instinctive among human beings, as it is among many other species of birds and mammals. The main thrust of this chapter is that the family is the instinctive and so the easiest and cheapest way to build human moralnets, and that the family is the natural and so the easiest and cheapest way for the larger culture to transmit its moral order to the young. I close with Jane Howard's ten untested but plausible policies for strengthening family ties—and call for research to test them.

In the next three chapters I review the social problems of three age groups: young children, adolescents, and old people. For young children, the leading social problem is child abuse. And child abuse in turn is largely linked to weakened moralnets. That is to say, it is parents with weakened ties to *their* extended families who tend to become child abusers. For adolescents, the weaker the ties to parents and school, the more likely are the boys or girls to get into trouble. Especially the boys—for most juvenile delinquents are boys. And what is more to the point, youth crime is almost invariably a social event; the youth does not go wrong alone, but as a member of an antisocial moralnet, an informal or formal gang. The evidence on weakened moralnet theory with respect to both child abuse and youth crime is strong. Each of these fields of study has its schools of thought, but those schools that most emphasize formal and rigorous theory testing are the ones that give the most weight to weakened moralnets. For old people, the evidence on moralnets is poor; in general, there are few studies of rigor or quality on the social problems of old people; social geriatrics is a much-neglected field whose body of tested knowledge is slim indeed. But what evidence there is does support weakened moralnet theory. Further, there is reason to believe that weakened ties between grandparents and grandchildren not only sadden the elders but deprive the young of one of the main traditional conduits of moral order.

I close by surveying the findings on sex role discrimination, on sexual frustration, and on divorce. There is a clear conflict between those moral codes popular among many Western intellectuals in the past twenty years and the implications of moralnet theory. In its most extreme form, the emphasis on self-realization by each person as the highest moral norm has broken up families—or prevented their formation in the first place—and so deprived growing children not only of their grandparents and extended family but even of one of their parents. Against the ideal of the free soul—realizing the inner self and be damned to the rest of the world—moralnet theory offers the model of the *mensch*, the real human being, the person who knows his or her place in society, who knows and does his or her duty. Moralnet theory stresses personal duty.

With respect to sex roles, in Chapter 14 I review the traditional division of labor between the sexes. That pattern made the mother the key member of the family moralnet, the link between children and other elders. That pattern was made the more necessary by a high infant mortality rate, which demanded many pregnancies of every childbearing woman if the population was to hold its own. The greatly lowered infant mortality rate now means that a woman can spend so much less time and energy bearing children. Thus she can have so much more time for other things. But patterns of sex role discrimination have also reflected patterns of wealth distribution and political and military control. I conclude Chapter 14 by pointing to the equal access of women to property, education, and politics as the key to their equal status in society; I view the great feminists of the nineteenth century as the women who won the key battles for the liberation of their sex from male dominance.

In Chapter 15 I deal with the related problem of sexual frustration. There is a wide range of variation among small-scale societies in the scope of restrictions on sex life, and that range has been studied rigorously by many holoculturalists. Theory needs to distinguish sharply between taboos against premarital and extramarital sex. It is one thing to tell unmarried young people to remain virgins. It is another thing to tell married people to be faithful to their spouses. The widespread restrictions on premarital sex in large-scale societies have been linked to property rights. But the restrictions on extramarital sex may well have something to do with avoiding divorce. The evidence of Chapter 15 supports sexual freedom for unmarried people—as long as the woman does not get pregnant. But the evidence on divorce, as on single-parent families, comes down hard against divorce without remarriage—indeed, against single-parent families in general. And for that reason, there is some support for restricting extramarital sex because it tends to lead to divorce. It is, however, not the fact of divorce itself but the failure to remarry—the production by divorce of a single-parent household—that is the key sexual problem of married life. The theoretical model of marriage offered here is that of an arrangement encouraged by instinct and sustained by sexual satisfactions. In Chapter 15 I emphasize the importance of sex life as a major cementing force in marriage and look to a harmonious sex life as one important link between husband and wife that tends to hold them together and so to avoid divorce. I also recall the importance of a common cultural background and common values as preconditions of marriage. Firm and stable marriage is seen as a central moral value. Where marriage breaks down, prompt remarriage after divorce seems to mend the damage. Premarital sex is seen as harmless if it does not lead to pregnancy, and as a positive good if it later helps young people make a good sexual adjustment within marriage. The sex drive then is seen as a powerful social force for good or evil. Sex is good if it helps build and sustain stable marriages, bad if it tends to lead to children growing up in single-parent homes.

In Chapter 16, the conclusion, I review the status of weakened moralnet theory both in itself and as a validator of the Five Steps of socionomics. The evidence that weakened moralnets mean trouble, set forth in Part Two, is summarized. But my main concern in Chapter 16 is to set forth a systematic model of moralnet theory and a systematic plan for testing that theory. We know beyond a reasonable doubt that weakened moralnets mean trouble. But we do not know so well how we can strengthen moralnets to avoid trouble or to cope with it. In Chapter 16 I set forth twelve specific elements of a strong moralnet. I call for a triangulation strategy. I propose five specific research designs to test the theory that links those twelve elements to moralnet strength. The proposals of Chapter 16 look toward a mature science of socionomics. And the proposals of Chapter 16 aim to make socionomics the basis of a moral order for all mankind.

Notes

1.1   *The Three Sisters and the Human Situation*

The English text of *The Three Sisters* is from Chekhov (1929), Chekhov (1951), or Tchekov (n.d.).

1.2   *An Offhand Sketch of the Cosmic Situation*

On cosmology, I think most astronomers fail to allow for the impact of intelligent life on cosmic dynamics 5 or 10 billion years hence. I am following *Scientific American* (1977), Kaufman (1979), and Silk (1980).

On biological evolution, I am following the September 1978 special issue of *Scientific American*. On human paleontology, I also used Johanson and Edey (1981) and Leakey and Lewin (1978). And I have been strongly influenced by Lovejoy (1981), although I think he overlooks the importance of the extended family and the band. The !Kung San model I discuss in Chapter 10 might well be 3 or 4 million years old.

I defer my review of evidence on the cultural evolution of mankind to my next book, *Painful Progress*, where it is my main topic. There, too, I plan to devote a chapter each to servos, darwins, and snowballs. In the meantime, on servos, see the works cited in these notes for Section 6.2, as well as Kuhn (1974); on darwins, see Campbell (1965, 1970); and on snowballs, see Naroll (1980).

On a long-term trend toward world government, see Hart (1948), Naroll (1967), and Marano (1973).

The seven stages in the evolution of life on and from earth:

(1) The chemical evolution of the anaerobic bacteria took place about 3.5 billion years ago.
(2) The evolution of photosynthetic bacteria took place about 2.4 billion years ago.
(3) The evolution of the eukaryotic cell took place about 1.4 billion years ago.
(4) The evolution of multicelled macroorganisms took place about 800 million years ago.
(5) The evolution of a world ecology under control of a worldwide human society seems to be occurring now (???).
(6) The organized colonization of the Milky Way galaxy to be completed within the next 1 billion years to come, conceivably in association with other intelligent civilizations from other stars (???).
(7) The physical control of the galaxy to make it an eternally stable and safe home to be completed within the next 10 billion years to come (???).

First four stages, from Schopf (1978).

1.3   Socionomics as Meta-Ideology

On traditional religions, see Alston (1963). Myrdal (1968: I: 57-69), Lasswell and Kaplan (1950: 55-73), Lasswell and Holmberg (1969: 354-359), and Bobrow (1974: 12) offer formal systems of value premises generally similar to mine of Chapter 2.

The Hippocratic oath: "The regimen I adopt shall be for the benefit of my patients . . . and not for their hurt or for any wrong" (Singer, 1946).

On the link between settlement size and cultural scale, see Naroll (1970a: 1244, 1973: 335f.) and Levinson and Malone (1980: 37).

Part One:

The Five Steps of Socionomics

Step 1: Establish Core Values

2.1 SHARP-HORN DANCES FOR REVENGE

Who are the five men? They hang from the lodge poles on buffalo hide ropes. Each man is fastened to the rope from which he dangles by a skewer that pierces the flesh of his chest or his shoulder. We are in a Sun Dance lodge of the Crow Indians in the southern part of what is now Montana, about 1865.

The women are singing; the *dancer*, though hungry, thirsty, and weary, still dances. The *doll owner* still holds the *doll*. The dancer's eyes look steadily at the doll's face. Only there can he see his vision. Only if he sees his vision will the singers stop singing. Only then may he stop dancing. Only then may the hanging men end their torment.

Sharp-horn, the dancer, had begun the ceremony in the usual way, some weeks before. The camp herald had walked among the tipis one morning.

"There will be a big buffalo hunt," called the herald. "Everyone get ready."

Sharp-horn's mind had been made up before. Since the day the Cheyenne killed No-shinbone. No-shinbone and Sharp-horn had raided a Cheyenne horse herd. The Cheyenne ambushed them, and a rifle ball went through No-shinbone's brain. The image of his dying friend stuck in Sharp-horn's mind. He would purge that thought. He would be a Sun Dancer.

Sharp-horn wanted to have buffalo tongues for all who took part and all who watched. A thousand tongues would not be too many. So Sharp-horn waited for word of a really large buffalo herd. Waited until the herald announced the hunt. Then Sharp-horn said to the chief:

"Do not give away any of the buffalo tongues to the children. Save them all for me!"

The chief passed the word. The herald went through the camp once more. This time he called a message no Crow had heard for nearly four years.

"Save all the tongues. He is going to cut ankles."

More important than the buffalo tongues was the doll owner. Sharp-horn needed a doll owner as his dance father. The power to bring Sharp-horn the vision he needed lived in the sacred doll—the vision that would lead him to his revenge.

There were only a few dolls among the Crow: one man knew of six, another of only four. They were treasured. The anthropologist Robert Lowie, in 25 years among the Crow, saw only two. Sharp-horn went to Red-eye, a powerful

126375

41

medicine man with a widely respected doll. Sharp-horn took a straight pipe to Red-eye. Red-eye smoked it. Thus Red-eye agreed to take charge of the ceremony.

Sharp-horn had to have a special kilt, made of specially sanctified deerskin by a virtuous woman—a chaste wife. Such women were not easy to find. If any woman shammed the role, she would bring bad luck on the camp, and her lover would be likely to expose her. There were many more details to be arranged.

But finally they were ready to start. Good singers went to Sharp-horn's tipi. Red-eye, the doll owner, dressed Sharp-horn in his special kilt, skunk skin regalia, and eagle plumes. Then Red-eye and his wife painted Sharp-horn with white clay. People carried the sacred cedar and the sacred buffalo skulls from Sharp-horn's tipi to the Sun Dance lodge.

Then at last the Sun Dance started. It went on for three days of hunger, thirst, and exhaustion for Sharp-horn. Three days of hanging from skewered flesh for Grey-bull, Crazy-head, White-hip, and Young-crane. (One-eye's skewer had torn loose from his chest the second day. By the laws of the Sun Dance, his ordeal was then at an end.) Three nights of dull sleep in special beds.

It was only on the fourth day that Sharp-horn, his dazed eyes still fixed on the doll face, his weary mind ready for hallucination, saw his vision. He stopped dancing. He said as plainly as he could:

"I think it will be well. I shall have revenge!" The ceremony was over. The hanging men were released, the people went home; Red-eye gathered the ritual objects and put them away. The Sun Dance lodge was left to rot. The consummation of the ceremony came later—when Sharp-horn killed his Cheyenne on a war party.

I have told you here only a very small part of what Red-eye needed to know to stage the Sun Dance properly. And though they called it a Sun Dance, and they worshipped the sun, yet the sun had little to do with the ceremony. The ceremony had to do with revenge. Its manifest purpose was to aid Sharp-horn to avenge the death of No-shinbone. But I believe that the ceremony had a deeper meaning and see it as a great hymn in praise of the greatest thing in life to the Crow people—war.

2.2   VALUES ORIENTATION AROUND THE WORLD

2.2.1   Variations in Values Orientation

The social values of the Crow Indians, as underscored by their greatest rite, the Sun Dance, thus differ widely from our own. I look at the values of European scientific humanism on which this work rests as merely one of a large number of alternate ways of ordering life. I note the sudden rise and spread of those values. Their sudden wide success is even more spectacular as a historical event than the explosive spread of Islam from Arabia in the hundred years after the death of the Prophet.

But the fact that they have spread so quickly does not make them right. Yet, even so, on them I must depend. All I can do now is to offer my readers an appeal to the banal. My core values will seem trite and obvious to nearly all who read my book, for nearly all of my readers will be as steeped as I am in the values of European humanism. Yet of course there will be those who do not find them banal at all and do not agree with them. Such people I would expect to find in the theological seminaries of New York as well as in those of Qom in Iran or in schools of Zen or Yoga. And my anthropological colleagues would expect their graduate students to make short work of any pretense that the values of European humanism have on their face any claim to eternal truth.

In presenting the ideas of this book to my undergraduate classes, however, I find that many students persist in hearing what they want to hear, despite all my disclaimers. They believe what I take pains to deny—that the core values on which I rely are cultural universals. Of course, every anthropologist and sociologist, every cross-cultural psychologist, knows they are not.

The core values of this book make little sense to members of most small-scale societies, whose ethics and concerns extend not to all mankind but only to those who speak their own language and so share their own culture. Did not our own American frontiersmen say: "The only good injun is a dead injun"? And how many of these people would have replied, "The only good white man is a dead white man"?

The ideals of medieval Europe were far different indeed from the ideals of modern European humanism. On the one hand, medieval Europe in its churches believed that the present happiness of mankind was a thing of little consequence; what really mattered was the eternal life of the soul in the hereafter. On the other hand, medieval Europe in its castles and manorial halls believed in the glories of warfare above all other things. Peace was but a time to prepare for war.

True, our modern ideal of brotherhood was a leading element of medieval Christianity—as it was of Islam and Judaism. And so charity for the poor played a larger role in western Eurasia than in India or China. But to the Greek and Roman forebears of Western culture, on principle, the poor were no concern of the rich. And it was not at all clear whether a slave was even a real human being.

Modern humanistic Europe looks to an ideal future and seeks to attain it through rational progress. In contrast, traditional Confucian China looked to an ideal past when former kings, through their virtuous conduct, inspired the people to a good life. Confucius did not seek progress; to restore the past was his highest goal. Hinduism and Buddhism do not seek anything; they fix the minds of believers on the endless chain of reincarnation. Their ideal goal is to escape that chain entirely; these faiths turn their backs on the real world—past, present, and future alike.

So modern humanism is more like medieval Europe than medieval China with respect to the ideal of brotherhood. However, the ideal of variety in modern humanism is at home in tolerant medieval India and China—but very uncomfortable indeed among the heretic-hunters of orthodox medieval Christianity, Judaism, and Islam alike.

Thus values have varied around the world. In offering my core values, I do so fully aware that my audience is not a random sample of all mankind. Rather, it is only my own in-group at large.

While the Sun Dance was a hymn of revenge to the Crow, it meant something quite different to their enemies, the Cheyenne. Like that of the Crow, the economic system of the Cheyenne was much dependent on the buffalo hunt. Their social class and political systems were similar. But their view of the nature of life greatly differed. To the Cheyenne, the Sun Dance was a hymn of world renewal. Through it, the dancers made the whole world grow. Dorsey says: "When they use the bone whistle, they are happy like the eagle."

Values are part of culture. They vary with culture. Culture—shared, learned patterns of behavior—is a great kaleidoscope. It rearranges similar sets of components into an infinite variety of individual patterns. Later in this book we look at the wide range of variation in mental illness—from societies in which suicide is unknown to societies in which it is rife, for example. We also look at the wide range of variation of family lifestyles: varying modes of family organization, treatment of children, adolescents, old people, and women (by the always dominant men). In later books I hope to look at the wide range of variation in level of civilization, from the simplest hunting bands to the most complex industrial civilizations, as well as to look at varying solutions to economic and political problems.

When we travel in foreign lands we notice cultural differences right away. Language hits us first and hardest. And we still are apt to notice differences in dress—though not so many as formerly. We notice differences in building styles. These are only superficial and easy to see. But it is hard to notice the subtle, hidden, pervasive differences in the orientation system of a culture, the built-in cues and biases that help the people of that culture find their way through life. Especially their way through their *social* life. The orientation system of a culture consists of its conceptual system and its value system, its way of perceiving and interpreting the world. That system is chiefly embedded in the culture's language—but it pervades everything. The study of cultural differences in perception has become a special field of cross-cultural psychology. There have been hundreds of well-designed psychological studies measuring such differences. The wealth of careful measurements of variations in culture has been thoroughly reviewed in the six volumes of *The Handbook of Cross-Cultural Psychology* edited by Triandis. Volume 5 includes a chapter by Zavalloni; she presents the findings of dozens of careful studies showing wide variations around the world from culture to culture in basic notions of what is right and wrong, what is good and bad.

As an example of the kind of evidence Zavalloni reviews, let us look at one of the best known and most penetrating studies—the work of F. Kluckhohn and Strodtbeck. They studied five diverse communities near Gallup, New Mexico: the Ramah Navajo, the Zuñi, a Spanish-American village, a Mormon town, and a group of American farmers—homesteaders or Texans. Kluckhohn and Strodtbeck wished to measure differences in fundamental world views among these people. For this they had to design a questionnaire; each question had to be translated in such a way that it meant the same thing in four languages: English, Spanish, Zuñi, and Navajo. Each language has its own way of looking at life, its own vocabulary. The words do not necessarily match in meaning from one language to another. For example, take the simple matter of color. There are the so-called six basic colors: red, orange, yellow, green, blue, and purple.

Now translate: "The sky is blue but the grass is green" into Spanish, Zuñi, and Navajo. In Spanish, the sky is *azul*, but the grass is *verde*. In Zuñi, the sky is *lhil lanna*, but the grass is *lashena*. In Navajo, the sky is *dotl'ish*, but the grass is also *dotl'ish*, the same word.

Don't the Navajo see any difference between the color of the sky and the grass? They do. Give them swatches of colored cloth to sort and they will sort them the same way that Zuñi, Spanish-Americans, or homesteaders sort them. But to the Navajo, sky blue and grass green are two shades of *dotl'ish*, as turquoise and navy are two shades of *blue* to us. So blue is not an absolute thing, but a way to sort out a group of shades or hues.

Translate the word "aunt" into the Crow language. Or for that matter, into Julius Caesar's Latin. Impossible. Julius Caesar had no aunt. Instead he had his mother's sister, his *consobrina*. And he had his father's sister, his *amita*, another relative altogether. His *amita* was his fellow clanswoman and belonged to his Julian clan. But his *consobrina* belonged to his mother's clan and so was more of an outsider. The Crow call their father's sister, their *amita*, *basbaxia*. Her daughter is also a *basbaxia*, and her daughter, and *her* daughter. Each language then has its own system of classifying reality; that system is embodied in its word definitions. We call such systems as a group *emic* systems. Until anthropologists started comparative studies that tried to get outside their own native emic systems, these were the only systems of human thought. But when anthropologists began to study kin terms comparatively, they found that of the thousands of emic systems in existence—of the hundreds thoroughly analyzed—only eight basic kinds of distinctions were ever involved. In color terms, as far as we know, there are usually but two kinds of distinctions made—at most three. English green differs from English blue by *hue*—by position on the light spectrum. English pink differs from English red by *brightness*—by how much color there is.

Terms discovered or coined by anthropologists to name the key distinctions of a topic of meaning, a semantic domain, are called *etic* concepts. "Aunt" is an English emic concept in the semantic domain of kin terms; "blue" is an English emic concept in the semantic domain of color terms. "Sex of relative," "collaterality," and "generation" are the three etic ideas found in English "aunt;" "hue" is the one etic idea found in English "blue." If I speak of my aunt you know by that kin term that the relative I am talking about is a woman, not a man, you know she is a collateral (side) relative rather than a direct ancestor or descendant, and you know that she is one generation older. If I tell you my aunt is wearing a blue dress you know where the hue of her dress comes on the color spectrum, but you do not know anything about its brightness.

Kluckhohn and Strodtbeck were trying to do something far more difficult than to translate such emic ideas as "aunt" and "blue" from English into Navajo. They were dealing neither with emic nor with etic concepts, but with a third kind — *theoric*. By a theoric concept I mean a concept developed by social scientists in order to test theories cross-culturally. Theoric concepts need to be defined in etic terms.

Kluckhohn and Strodtbeck translated basic value orientations by using simple, practical everyday situations that all people in that dry country face, trying to make a living from the land. Their model posits five fundamental kinds of differences in lifestyle and world view. The answers they got to their questions from hundreds of people in all communities clearly showed four kinds. For example, they studied the world view of the people as to the relationship of man to nature. Should man submit in subjection to nature? Should he seek harmony with nature? Or should he seek mastery over nature? Navajo south of Gallup feel that people should seek harmony with nature. Texans feel people should master nature.

Kluckhohn and Strodtbeck further posited a range of variation in the basic attitude of a culture toward human nature. Is man basically good or evil? Or a mixture of the two? Or neutral? And is this aspect of man's character mutable or immutable?

Third, is the salient time to which man should direct his attention the past, the present, or the future?

Fourth, is mankind most significant and meaningful in respect to doing or to being?

Fifth, are the most important social relations those arranged linearly, as in lines of authority? Or arranged collaterally, with respect to the mutuality of relationships between people seen as essentially equal? Or are they individualistic, each man for himself, each woman for herself?

Kluckhohn and Strodtbeck did *not* find significant differences among their five cultures with respect to attitudes about the basic nature of man. But they did find clear and significant differences with respect to time orientation, to doing or being, and to social relationships. Caudill and Scarr asked the Kluckhohn-Strodtbeck questions of many Japanese, as did Sutcliffe of many Palestinian Arab peasants. The care with which these people worked in choosing their samples, standardizing their questions, and measuring their results gives me confidence in their findings.

We see that among the groups studied, Texans, Mormons, and Japanese tend to think in terms of man mastering and controlling nature; Zuñi and Navajo tend to think in terms of man bringing himself into harmony with nature. Spanish-Americans and Palestinian peasants tend to think in terms of man submitting to nature.

Texans and Mormons tend to think more of the future than of the present or past. The other groups tend to think more of the present than of the future. Zuñi and Navajo tend to think more of the past than of the future; the others more of the future than of the past.

Spanish-Americans tend to think more of being than of doing. Palestinians tend to think about equally of each. Texans, Mormons, Zuñi, and Navajo tend to think more in terms of doing than of being.

Zuñi and Navajo tend to think of their social relations collaterally—as an organization of equals. Spanish-Americans, Texans, Mormons, and Japanese tend to think of them individually, each person for himself or herself.

These results may apply only to the communities sampled. But I predict that they would hold up, for older people at least, in other communities of the same ethnic group. A careful study of Colombian leaders found that the older they were, the less likely they were to agree with the "modern" attitudes revealed by Kluckhohn and Strodtbeck's Texans and Mormons. And Sutcliffe found among Palestinians that the more educated the person, the more "modern" his or her attitudes tended to be. So these attitudes are changing.

These tests show that the man-nature relationship is an important dimension of human value orientation. They do not, however, in any way explain the differences in these attitudes. I would ask, for example, if the Spanish *conquistadores* who settled New Mexico two or three hundred years ago had an equally submissive attitude toward nature. And if not, what led their descendants to change?

My study of the human situation—like all of behavioral science—has its value premises. My values for this work, as I have said, are those I share with almost anyone who is likely to look at it. They are the chief values of European humanism.

Table 2.1 sets forth my value premises. They are, I repeat, supposed to be banal. In applying Step 1 throughout the book, I reduce the values problem to the banal. It is banal to say that acute alcoholics are sick, that suicides are unhappy, and that beating children to death is bad for their health. In my study of the human situation I establish core values by reducing the value component of the problem to some value element that modern educated people—European humanists—take for granted.

Peace. I see human destiny as governed in the long run by a natural selection process in human culture working toward a stable moral world ecology. I see that stable state as the great garden of the earth's people, the happy outcome of our sufferings on the way from the primeval hunting band to that utopian end. Such a viewpoint is implicit in the idea of progress that underlies the modern philosophies of both Marxism and liberalism.

Such a viewpoint is also implicit in the now banal ideal of world peace. Even before World War I, world peace as an ideal had attained wide currency in Western culture. The horrors of the two great wars of our century have made that ideal a banal goal indeed. But world peace in a tightly linked world is unthinkable without some system of world law. If such a system lasts—if world peace lasts—then by definition we have a stable world order. The measure of

TABLE 2.1   Value Premises of My Study of the Human Situation

This work is dedicated to the building for all mankind of a just and stable world order of healthy, happy, peaceful, and free people, enlightened by science and enriched by a wide variety of cultures–a wide variety of local and personal values and ways of life.

Peace

- Universality–a scheme for all mankind.
- Order–an orderly way of life for all mankind, with disputes settled by process of law rather than by violence.
- Stability–a stable world order for all mankind, with change occurring peacefully, under the law.

Humanism

- Scientific empiricism as our way of knowing.
- Mankind's happiness as our goal (pleasure).

Decency

- Brotherhood and Sisterhood (justice to the strong; kindness to the weak).
- Health both of mind and body.

Progress

- Wisdom–powerful knowledge through scientific research.
- Variety–individual liberty and local autonomy to encourage wide diversity under the law.

stability and order is peace; if there are no licit deadly quarrels between moralnets or states, if the law is enforced without killing people, and if this state of affairs prevails the world around, then we have a stable human world order. For my study of the human situation that goal is the ultimate value.

Humanism. Humanism makes people the measure. To the humanist, what can be known is what people can learn through their senses—the epistemology of empiricism, as the philosophers call it. To the humanist, the ultimate good is the happiness of mankind—the greatest good for the greatest number. (Philosophers, of course, call this point of view hedonism or utilitarianism.) Empiricism is the fundamental canon of science. And utilitarianism is actually the foundation of such philosophical systems of ethics as those by Moore and Hourani and of several recent value systems proposed by Laswell, Holmberg, and other social scientists. The humanistic ethic is not a selfish one. Its measure of good is the welfare of mankind at large; it puts the mind of the individual to thinking about the happiness of others—rather than about his or her own.

Decency. The ideal of decency extends the brotherhood and sisterhood of the primeval foraging camp to all mankind. In the camps of most foragers men and women should help each other; the families at their separate fires should help each other. The strong should help the weak; the rich should help the poor; mensches—proper people—should keep the peace; and people should do what they can to cheer the sad and heal the sick. The camp should be a community—

and yet people should own their own clothes, tools, and household goods. The balance between common good and private good should be delicate and subtle.

Progress. I define progress as powerful knowledge—knowledge that helps men and women control the world. If they are decent men and women, they can use powerful knowledge to make a decent world of it. For me, progress consists of science and technology—including social and psychological technology. I take it that progress in general and science in particular are natural selection processes, proceeding through blind variation and selective retention. Hence, other things being equal, the more cultural variation, the more progress. Other things being equal, the more personal liberty and local autonomy, the better.

2.2.2   Evolution of Values Orientation

Most of the core values of Table 2.1 are on the spread over the long term. If we take human history a thousand years at a time, a general pattern shows up. The spread of universality as a value is particularly clear. While many elements of religion spread widely by diffusion, each small-scale society not in touch with large-scale ones typically has its own religion. Often the peace community does not extend beyond the local group.

But as Toynbee suggests, a leading tendency in the history of the large-scale societies of the old world was to develop universal churches. By a universal church I mean a religious community whose members invite all mankind to join them. Typically, such universal churches grow out of narrower ones. Christianity and Islam—two of the most successful universal churches—took their roots in Judaism—whose high God originally was no more than the special god of the Hebrews. To the orthodox, Hinduism is confined to the land of India; to cross the seas is to defile oneself. But out of Hinduism grew Buddhism, whose message, too, was offered to all mankind. European humanism always embraced all mankind. Marxism bids the workers of all the world to unite. Liberalism invites all mankind to do so.

Monotheism is a metaphor betokening universality. If only one god exists, then all mankind must be a single community in the eyes of that god. And if that god is the source of morality, then all men are bound into a single fellowship of duty. The studies of Swanson have shown clear if crude correlation between the level of cultural evolution on the one hand and these elements of theology on the other: the larger the scale of the society, the more likely it is to believe in a high god. And the more likely it is to think of that god as saying what is right and wrong or good and bad and as punishing the evil people and rewarding the good.

European humanism has had a shorter history. Though it looked to classic Greece for learning, it added to the Attic wit and Attic salt of skepticism the Hebrew passion for social justice and human happiness as preached by Isaiah and above all by Jesus of Nazareth. It is hard to find a nation today whose leaders are not in one way or another European humanists—whether Marxists or liberals. (At this writing, the Ayatollah Khomeini reminds us that Montaigne and Descartes have not yet utterly triumphed, however.)

From ancient Greece Europe learned to gain wisdom through science. From ancient Israel Europe learned that the task of morality is to spread the fellowship of the hunting camp through all mankind. European humanism blended the two. Similar messages, of course, can be found in other cultural traditions: Confucian philosophy, for example, is founded on the study of history and teaches that all men are brothers and that unjust rulers are to be punished by dethronement. But no other version is as clear and insistent as Europe's. European science and technology helped spread humanism around the world. And nothing is more instructive about the intellectual power of that humanism than its firm hold today on countries like India and China—with such rich and subtle religious and philosophical traditions of their own. As an idea, European progress reached a climax in the days just before World War I. Then it seemed to most people that progress was inevitable—that every day in every way things *were* getting better and better.

The horrors that followed the two world wars and the great revolutions of our time have broken the faith of many in that progress. As I write, nearly as banal as the idea of progress itself is the response: "What progress? Are the death camps of Hitler and Stalin and Pol Pot progress? Is the atom bomb progress?"

But in this work I reaffirm the value of progress—Hitler or no Hitler, Stalin or no Stalin, Hiroshima or no Hiroshima. I take for granted that the process of cultural evolution is a process of blind variation and selective retention—a process of painful, unsteady, and erratic progress. Further, I look at all the changes of the last 10,000 years as a single process still under way. That mankind at large is today any happier than the !Kung San of the Kalahari, I would not wish to say. (Although I take note that the !Kung too are leaving their foraging life to work for Boer and Tswana wages.)

Measured by manifest signs of unhappiness, I suppose that mankind at large can only expect a clear advantage over our foraging ancestors when, as, and if we at last attain a stable, just world order. So with respect to long-term tendencies toward progress, I can only point out that such a world order now is seen by practical men as a practical possibility. Practical men only began talking about world peace as a practical possibility within the last 100 years. It is a new thing.

2.3   STEP 1: CORE VALUES OF THE CORE VALUES

The scientific problem of values theory is the problem of getting from *is* to *ought*. I submit that the solution to that problem lies in what seems another matter entirely—that of world order. *I* may as author be dedicated to the ideal of a stable and just world order; *you* as reader may or may not agree. But quite apart from what you or I might think *ought to be*, let us consider instead what *is to be*. The question of whether there is or is not to be stable world order is largely a question of whether there *can be* one. Suppose for the sake of argument such a thing is indeed possible. We live now in an *unstable* world order, in which all men are linked by political, economic, and intellectual ties. We are all plugged into these networks. Given the technology we have, does anyone suppose that this world order will dissolve and vanish?

But the terms of intercourse that govern this world order are clearly unstable. The political and economic systems both between and within nations are in a state of constant change. Furthermore, a survey of the history of large-scale societies shows that the great regional orders of the past—orders that existed over large subcontinents throughout the past 3,000 to 5,000 years—likewise were unstable. They never settled down for long. They lasted a few centuries at the most.

If we judge by the history of civilizations so far, then, what we can expect is a cycle of consolidation and disintegration of world empires. Such has been the general pattern of the history of higher civilizations. I have elsewhere offered evidence suggesting that we can expect a consolidation into some kind of a world government within the next few hundred years—if we go by that oft-repeated pattern of the past.

The founders of any such world state would probably seek to make it permanent. Most founders of empires do. If one ever succeeds, then the cycle ends, and ends forever. The number of trials may be infinite. The number of required successes is just one. If, through the comparative study of the rise and fall of empires, we can learn to understand the causes of their instability, then perhaps we can also learn how to avoid that fate. Or perhaps some founder of a world state might just happen on a solution.

The key point is, we have a natural selection process at work here—a darwin. The forces of consolidation are likely to lead to attempt after attempt to produce a stable world order. (Have we not in our own time seen the League of Nations followed by the United Nations?) Let these attempts fail as often as they may; still other attempts will be made—one way or another. This process of trial and error in seeking for a stable world order is the process that is to be—that exists now—whether or not we like it. The one thing that Adolf Hitler and Franklin Roosevelt and Winston Churchill and Josef Stalin all had in common was that each had a dream of a stable world order.

A truly stable world order would have to provide for gradual and orderly adaptation and change. It would have to be an intellectual and moral order as well as a political and economic and military order. Suppose that such a thing is possible. Well then, sooner or later, one of these trials is likely to succeed. The stronger socionomics becomes, the more likely it is that a stable world order will become understood and the sooner it can be expected to be introduced. This proposition does not assert that a stable world order is necessarily good—only that it is widely desired, especially by rulers who aspire to control the whole system. For if we are to control our affairs, we must be able, one way or another, to control the world order. A stable world order—a peaceful world—is a world under control. Many philosophers and theologians and poets and artists and men of letters may not want a world under control. But most rulers do—because control is their business. That again is an *is*, not an *ought*.

So what we have already begun and certainly are to continue is a series of attempts of one kind or another to establish lasting world peace—to establish a stable world order of one kind or another. And such attempts may be expected to continue, whether we like them or not, until one at last succeeds. Such is the implication of the assumption that a stable world order is possible at all when we look at the world as it has become in our day.

The certainty of a stable future world order is my fundamental value premise—and it is a premise about what *is* to be, not a premise about what *ought* to be.

The validity of humanist values must in the long run depend on their stability as core values of a world order. If these core values are inconsistent with the stability of a world order, they are doomed.

If these core values are consistent with the stability of a world order but not required for it, then we humanists are in a contest. And badly as we have mismanaged things in the twentieth century, we still look like winners. When, as and if we win the contest, the process of history that led to the establishment of a stable world order based on humanist core values will have been the process that converted *is* to *ought* for all mankind.

But suppose a Hitler or a Stalin or a Napoleon beats us to it. Suppose that the outcome of World War III or World War IV or World War V is a totalitarian world empire. For us humanists that would be a dreadful nightmare. As humanists, of course, we would want to do all we can to prevent such a catastrophe. But if the worst happens, we may well after all in time get another chance.

In my next book I hope to offer evidence tending to support the theory that a totalitarian world empire would not be stable—would collapse and fall apart within a few hundred years. And then the cycle would begin again. If our humanist core values are not merely consistent with the stability of a world order but, as I suspect, essential to it, then that fact—if it is a fact—would convert our humanist values from *ought* to *is*. Elsewhere, later, I plan also to offer evidence tending to support that model. For the present, since it is obvious that a stable world order based on our humanistic values has in fact not been established, we can only take our values as assumptions.

The passage in values theory from *is* to *ought* is in the last analysis not a problem for philosophers but rather one for future comparative historians. So far we have not had any semblance of a stable world order. When, as and if we get one—as I believe we shall—the problem then becomes whether it will be a temporary or a permanent one. And the empirical reference in terms of which that problem could best be studied would be the comparative frequency of civil wars and disturbances in such a future state with those in ancient empires like the Roman Empire or the Han or Ming dynasties of China. True, these ancient empires controlled far less land than the whole surface of the globe. But they faced problems of internal peace with far weaker tools of control than a world empire would have today. Word of trouble to the capital, or orders in response, moved by relays of horsemen. Troops to keep order marched about thirty kilometers (twenty miles) a day. So they are not unreasonable benchmarks with which to compare the stability of any future world order.

My point is that five centuries of profound world peace, free of all deadly public quarrels, would create a strong presumption that the core values of world order had come to stay. And my guess is that the only world order able to pass such a test would be a humanistic one.

2.4   STEP 2: SCOREBOARDS OF THE CORE VALUES

I offer here two kinds of measures of value orientation around the world. The first comes from a study of the hopes and aspirations of mankind by the Gallup International Research Institutes. It measures the values reflected in the minds of the people interviewed in a worldwide sample survey. The second is an index to the particular scoreboards planned for my study of the human situation; these scoreboards measure value attainments, country by country.

The results of the Gallup study are set forth in Table 2.2. That study was part of a wider one. It did not take information from any of the Communist countries or from the Middle East, but in a crude sort of way may be taken as a measure of the attitudes of the rest of the world. (It is in the sampling design that this study falls short. Otherwise, I find it admirable. See the Notes.)

The entry for each line in Columns A through E of Table 2.2 is the average (median) percentage of the countries or country groups listed. Gallup reports regional totals as well as the results for some of the countries in the region. For example, the total for Western Europe includes data not only from the four nations specified, but for the European Economic Community as a group, for the three Benelux countries as a group, for the four Scandinavian countries as a group, and for Switzerland, Austria, Spain, Portugal, Greece, and Ireland as well. The total for Sub-Saharan Africa includes data from eleven such countries.

Gallup's arrangement heavily emphasizes countries of European cultural heritage. That emphasis is greatest in Column A but remains strong in Column B. So Columns C, D, and E break up the findings into three major cultural heritages—Europe, Sub-Saharan Africa, and East Asia. Thus important contrasts show up. Compare, for example, Columns C and D—European cultural heritage and Sub-Saharan African cultural heritage. While only 42 percent of the Europeans are concerned with getting more money on the average, 84 percent of the Sub-Saharan Africans are. Since the European heritage countries by and large are rich, while the Sub-Saharan African countries are poor, this contrast is, of course, just what we might have expected. But look at lines 6 and 7. The peoples of European heritage are far more concerned about the general economic and political situation than are the peoples of Sub-Saharan Africa; they are also more concerned about doing better at their work.

Each of the lines in the table is a summary of a class of responses that includes mention of:

- *Line 1*—personal character as self-development, improvement, emotional stability and maturity, acceptance by others, and achievement of a sense of personal worth.

TABLE 2.2   The Hopes of Mankind, 1974-1976

The numbers represent the median percentage of people questioned who mentioned these things when asked about their wishes and hopes for the future. The percentages add up to well over 100% because people often mentioned more than one thing.

Hopes	*A*	*B*	*C*	*D*	*E*
(1) To improve my personal character	8.5	11.0	9.5	6.0	2.0
(2) To keep healthy and enjoy myself	32.0	31.0	35.5	24.0	8.0
(3) To have more money	44.0	45.0	42.0	84.0	66.0
(4) To do better at my work	17.5	16.0	18.0	6.0	18.0
(5) To see my family thrive	33.5	33.0	33.5	43.0	33.0
(6) To see general economic conditions get better	2.5	1.0	3.0	1.0	—
(7) To see general political conditions get better	8.0	7.0	8.0	—	—
(8) To improve the social situation	4.0	3.5	4.0	1.0	1.0
(9) To serve others	2.0	2.0	2.0	1.0	2.0
(10) To see a better world	8.0	7.5	8.0	—	—
(11) To keep things as they are	4.0	4.0	4.0	1.0	2.0

SOURCE: Gallup International Research Institutes (1977: 95-110).
A: all Gallup report categories including totals.
B: all Gallup report category totals.
C: Gallup report categories in European Cultural Heritage (including totals).
D: Gallup report total in Sub-Saharan African Cultural Heritage.
E: Gallup report categories in East Asian Cultural Heritage.
NOTE: The Gallup report categories are: U.S.A. (Total), Canada (Total), Western Europe (Total), U.K., France, W. Germany, Italy, E.E.C., Benelux, Scandinavia, Latin America (Total), Brazil, Mexico, Sub-Saharan Africa (Total), Far East (Total), India, Japan, Australia. Latin America and Australia were included in Table 2.2 as belonging to the European Cultural Heritage, as well as North America and Europe proper.

- *Line 2*—personal well-being as health, recreation, travel, leisure time, and a happy old age.
- *Line 3*—personal or family wealth as wealth in general standard of living, family home or garden, modern conveniences, security, own business, or own land.
- *Line 4*—the work situation as success, good job, congenial work, and employment—that is, any job at all.
- *Line 5*—all other family situations—that is, those not connected with family wealth or family work, such things as a happy family life, children, family health, and welfare of relatives.
- *Line 6*—the general economic situation in contrast to that of the respondent or his or her family—nearly all of these spoke of economic stability.
- *Line 7*—the general political situation—nearly all of these spoke of freedom.
- *Line 8*—the general social situation—nearly all of these spoke of social justice.
- *Line 9*—service to others, including references to religion, morality, and public service—nearly all of these spoke of a desire to be useful to others.

- *Line 10*—a better world, references to the international world situation—nearly all of these spoke of world peace.
- *Line 11*—to keep things as they are—references to maintaining the status quo.

This table, then, reflects the leading concerns of a large part of the world's peoples. Nearly all are concerns stated where public content or discontent is not deemed a state secret—for the eyes and ears of the rulers only. Nearly all are concerns stated where people are not afraid to complain openly if they are dissatisfied.

Table 2.2 measures the concerns people express when interviewed. It is thus a subjective measure of mankind's hopes. Table 2.3 sets forth a plan by which I hope in time to measure actual value orientations in another way—objectively. Table 2.3 lists forty specific measures of core value attainments. Eight of these are set forth in the present work, *The Moral Order*. The rest are planned for future volumes. These forty specific measures show the extent to which mankind by its efforts is demonstrating concern for the core values—or lack of concern.

Table 2.2 then looks at what people *say*. Table 2.3 looks at what they actually *do*.

2.5 STEP 3: TESTS OF THEORIES OF CORE VALUES

I know of no such tests whatever. Most behavioral scientists have tried to work in a value-free mental framework. At most, they have made explicit some such value premise as peace or health or kindness. In fact, of course, all have always assumed scientific empiricism as a way of knowing. But they have generally sought to pursue the understanding of human behavior for its own sake. No one has tested any theory to explain the causes of variation in values orientations.

2.6 STEP 4: FURTHER STUDIES OF CORE VALUES

One research task seems urgent. How much of the cold war of the 1950s and 1960s arose out of differences in basic value orientations between Americans and Russians? How much out of confusion in their basic concepts, their emics of social order and social justice?

As a more general and fundamental task, we need an extension of the work of people like Kluckhohn and Strodtbeck. Can we get an inventory of basic value etics? Can we get the dimensions of value terms as thoroughly as four generations of students of kinship have given us the dimensions of kin term analysis? We need rigorous measurements in these dimensions of the world's leading cultures of all their people, not just their college students.

The most urgent action goal I see about cultural concepts and values is simply to get the message across. Writers like Ruth Benedict and Margaret Mead have gotten that message across to much of the English-speaking world—the message that barbarians are not necessarily benighted and that exotic and

TABLE 2.3   Specific Measures of Core Values

Core Value	Scoreboard
Peace	Mass Killer Weapon Stockpile
Peace	General Civil Strife Level
Peace	Warfare Level
Order*	Friendship Net
Order	Regularity of Succession
Order	Productivity
Order	Savings
Order	Crime
Order	Proportion of Prisoners
Order	Proportion of People Executed
Pleasure	Job Satisfaction
Pleasure	General Quality of Life
Pleasure	Per Capita Gross National Product
Pleasure	Leisure Time
Brotherhood	Unemployment
Brotherhood	Labor Union Strength
Brotherhood	Minimum Wages
Brotherhood	Income Distribution
Brotherhood	Interethnic Conflict
Brotherhood	Social Welfare Budget
Brotherhood	Civil Strife as Special Protest
Brotherhood	Graft as Exploitation
Brotherhood	Sex Discrimination
Brotherhood	Trade Balances ("Imperialism")
Brotherhood	Child Abuse
Brotherhood	Youth Stress
Brotherhood	Elders' Stress
Brotherhood	Treatment of Prisoners
Health	Life Expectancy
Health	Mental Illness
Health	Population Density
Health	Suicide
Health	Divorce
Health	Alcoholism
Health	Ecological Balance
Progress	State of Natural Science
Progress	State of Social Science
Progress	Illiteracy
Variety	Number of Languages
Variety	Censorship

*See also scoreboards for General Civil Strife Level, Warfare Level, Divorce, Alcoholism, and Ecological Balance—these measure Order as well as Peace or Health.

NOTE: Universality is implicitly measured by the Warfare scoreboard; Stability is measured by the Warfare and Civil Strife scoreboards; Empiricism is measured by the State of Natural and Social Sciences scoreboards.

goods-poor primitive cultures have rich cultural treasures. Claude Lévi-Strauss has gotten it to the French. But relativity of art styles and philosophies of life is one thing. Relativity of basic social values like political freedom and economic justice is quite another. For a decent world order, I take it, the problem is to seek a set of core values that the whole human community can agree on—and to teach the world to tolerate variety in the rest. So we need a body of studies developing and testing models that explain changes in values systems.

2.7   STEP 5: COPING WITH VALUES ORIENTATION

If we scientific humanists want to win a large following among the public, I submit, we have only to produce through our science a manifest increase in public happiness. The heart of the matter is plain. Never mind whether Walter Reed's scientific papers were lively and readable or dull and cryptic. When his findings led to control methods that stopped yellow fever, first in Havana, then in New Orleans, and a third time in Laredo, the word about mosquitoes got around. In 1890, the question of how yellow fever spread was as lively a scientific controversy as you could find anywhere. By 1910, the argument was all over.

Our thing, too, can snowball once we get it started, just as medical research has snowballed. The more successes we have, the more bright young men and women we will recruit and the more funds we will have to support their work. And the more successes they in turn will bring us.

2.8   COSTS AND BENEFITS OF VALUES RESEARCH

Values research seems chiefly a task for the academy. In itself, it is a branch of pure science. I see no immediate fiscal payoff. As a practical matter, most people in public life today pay lip service to these core values already. A theoretical demonstration raising their philosophical standing would not seem likely to coax more money from the taxpayers. Not in comparison with a program where the potential money payoff is quick and clear and big, one likely to help reduce crime in the streets or alcoholism or drug abuse promptly.

Notes

2.1   Sharp-horn Dances for Revenge

Lowie (1935: 297-326) gives the standard scenario for a Crow Sun Dance rather than a description of a particular dance. So while all personal names and ceremonial details come straight out of Lowie, the story as a whole is imaginary.

2.2.1   Variations in Values Orientation

I do not offer any documentation for my statements about the major philosophical systems: Humanism, as expressed in the philosophy of Europe's eighteenth-century rationalism—the ideas of the Enlightenment; traditional Christianity, Buddhism, Hinduism, Islam; ancient Greece and Israel. I do not document the values of the primeval foraging cultures—those of modern foraging peoples vary widely around the world. Yet I believe the common set of hunting camp attitudes I set forth are typical, even if not by any means universal. An example of how difficult such a thorough description of major philosophical systems would be is the illuminating essay by Hourani (1976) on the rationalist strain in medieval Islam. These comments of mine, then, on historical and comparative philosophy must be excused as *obiter dicta*. I do document rigorous studies of cross-cultural psychologists that demonstrate that our humanist values are far from universal. But I make no claim in this chapter to any scientific showing of their superiority; I only speculate about two possible lines of future study or experience that might conceivably solve the problem I make no claim to have solved. My position, then, is simple: I do not justify these values, but only acknowledge them. And note that I expect most of my readers to take them for granted and to deem them banal.

On the Sun Dance of the Cheyenne, see Hoebel (1960: 11).

The Dorsey quote is from Hoebel (1960: 11).

Zavalloni (1980) is a review article of variations in values. See also Hofstede (1980) and Segall (1979: 136-179).

For a study of five communities, see Kluckhohn and Strodtbeck (1961). Other applications of the Kluckhohn-Strodtbeck scale: Japan (Caudill and Scarr, 1962); Old Order Amish (Egeland, 1967); Colombia (Webber et al., 1974); Jordanian Palestinians (Sutcliffe, 1974); Albuquerque Anglo and Hispanic teachers and school custodians (Jackson, 1973); and several studies of Alberta Indian groups, reviewed in Friesen (1974).

On color terms, see Berlin and Kay (1969: 78, 99, 103, 119, and 126).

On utilitarianism, Moore (1959) renounces and abjures hedonism and utilitarianism and all their works, but the manner in which he does so seems to me tedious hairsplitting. He finds that the love of beautiful things, the love of good people and the absence of pain are the basic ethical goods. For me, beautiful things are those that give one of life's greatest pleasures—that is what makes them beautiful and contrariwise, pleasures *are* things of beauty. The existence of a social instinct implies a dependence on other people, and good people are those who help give others pleasure. Pain is negative pleasure. But the central point to bear in mind is that Moore is talking about a personal ethic, and I am talking about a social value. He supposes that people will, or should, guide their behavior by a pursuit of the good and an avoidance of the evil. I suppose that people tend to do what other people expect them to do; that the locus of value lies in what is good for society, not what is good for an individual per se; but yet that society needs to bind individuals to it by serving their personal good. Moore denies and abjures hedonism and utilitarianism. But I say that no matter how much he protests, he remains a hedonist, seeking pleasure as the highest good, and a utilitarian, seeking to maximize pleasure for all mankind.

On utilitarianism, see Hourani (1956).

Utilitarianism is the underlying presumption of core value systems proposed by such behavioral scientists as Lasswell and Holmberg (1969), Bobrow (1974), Myrdal (1968:I: 57-69), and Kelman (1977).

2.2.2   Evolution of Values Orientation

I can offer no formal documentation for my statement that each small-scale society not in touch with a large-scale one typically has its own religion. However, ethnographers of small-scale societies generally take this view for granted. Lowie (1948), for example, begins his general treatise on primitive religion with chapters on the Crow, Ekoi, and Bakua religions—three small-scale societies. When he describes Polynesian religion—that of an entire culture area—he begins (p. 75) by referring to "many local peculiarities."

On universal churches, see Toynbee (1939: 79, 1957: 76-143). Toynbee is not a rigorous historian but a literary artist, dealing in image and metaphor. If you consider religion and myths as metaphors for reality, then Toynbee, whether he knows it or not, is suggesting that universal churches seek to embrace all mankind.

For the relation between societal scale on the one hand and (1) belief in a high god and (2) belief that God punishes evil and rewards good on the other, see Swanson (1960: 153-174) and Textor (1967: FC 426, 428, 429).

On the recent decay of the independent foraging way of life among the !Kung San, see Lee (1979: 401-431).

We can trace the efforts of practical statesmen to establish world peace from the Hague Conference of 1899 and 1907, through the League of Nations of 1919, to the United Nations of 1945.

2.3   *Step 1: Core Values of the Core Values*

In saying that all mankind is now linked into a single system, I neglect a few thousand tribesmen in the Amazon and Orinoco jungles and the New Guinea highlands—few and getting fewer every year.

Unstable regional orders—the regional cycles of the rise and fall of empires—are systematically reviewed in Naroll (1967), where the probability of a future world empire and problems of internal control of ancient empires are likewise reviewed.

Hitler dreamed vaguely of a world made stable under the leadership of Germany's Thousand Year Reich; the Hitler Youth sang: *Heute gehoert uns Deutschland/Morgen die ganze Welt.* (Today Germany belongs to us, tomorrow the whole world.) Roosevelt and Churchill dreamed of a world at peace under the United Nations. Stalin dreamed the Marxist dream that one day when all the world is Communist and the class struggle is ended, civil strife would end; and with capitalism ended, warfare would end.

2.4   *Step 2: Scoreboards of the Core Values*

Gallup International Research Institutes (1977) did not and could not conduct anything like a truly worldwide representative sample of mankind at large. Sub-Saharan Africa, Oceania, and Latin America were sampled only sketchily; the Communist world, the Middle East, and Southeast Asia not at all. But where they did sample, their skillfully designed questionnaire and staff of experienced professional interviewers give us a trustworthy picture of the state of public opinion.

2.6   *Step 4: Further Studies of Core Values*

The message of cultural relativism was spread through the scholarly community of the English-speaking world by Franz Boas, A. R. Radcliffe-Brown, and Bronislaw Malinowski, whose students to the third and fourth generation dominate the teaching of anthropology there. (For example, I studied with Ralph Beals, who studied with Robert Lowie, who studied with Boas.) Claude Lévi-Strauss seems to be having a like influence among Francophones, where he plays a leading part not only in the scholarly but also the literary world.

2.7   *Step 5: Coping with Values Orientation*

On Walter Reed and yellow fever, see Kelly (1907).

Step 2: Check Scoreboards

3.1   THE VIEW FROM THE HEIGHTS OF OSLO

Nils Retterstøl, director of the Gaustad Mental Hospital on the heights overlooking Oslo, is one of Scandinavia's leading students of suicide. He wants to know if Norway's suicide rate is really less than half that of Sweden. Or do the Swedes just keep more accurate records? Frada and I interviewed Retterstøl in the summer of 1979 because we wondered about that, too. Retterstøl has argued that in many other measures of social troubles as well, Norway does much better than the other Scandinavian countries. And my work on the quality of life—set forth later in this chapter—led me to consider Norway the world's happiest country—and so a model for the rest. But its statistics are, in general, less accurate than those of Sweden.

Retterstøl belongs to a group of Scandinavian scientists who want to verify or correct those statistics on suicide. Frada and I interviewed experts on cause-of-death statistics and suicide in both Oslo and Stockholm. We now believe that the Norwegian suicide statistics in particular are *more* accurate than the Swedish ones—not *less*—because the results of the autopsies of Norwegian pathologists are kept confidential, while those of the Swedish pathologists are made public. Swedish pathologists, whenever they can, class probable suicides as "intent doubtful"—which puts them into the UN's *homicide* column. Sweden, with twice Norway's population, has nearly *fifteen* times as many violent deaths with uncertain intent. If all these deaths were in fact suicides, Sweden's suicide rate for 1977 would go up from 20 to 27 per 100,000.

The Norwegian scientific community offers a number of theories to explain the advantage Norway enjoys over other Scandinavian countries in respect to rates of suicide, crime, and drug abuse. Milbrath reviewed these guesses for me: (1) Norwegians place a higher value on nature and outdoor sports than do their fellow Scandinavians. (2) Norwegian life is slower paced, more leisurely. (3) Norwegians take more holidays and usually spend them with their extended families. (4) Norwegians take public affairs more seriously. (5) Norwegians are more future oriented, do a better job of long-range planning. After discussing with Retterstøl and other Norwegian scientists the moralnet theories set forth later in this book, I would add (6) Norwegian extended family life is more strongly maintained (in part perhaps because Norwegians retain a greater degree of traditional piety).

But the whole case for taking Norway as a model country depends on the accuracy of its national statistics—and while they are not especially bad in quality, neither are they especially good. Rather, compared to other rich countries without censorship, they are only about average, as we shall see.

3.2   SCOREBOARDS AROUND THE WORLD

The oldest continuing tradition of taking censuses is that of China. Censuses were also taken by the ancient Israelites, Assyrians, and Romans. Regular census taking began in Quebec as early as 1665. It has been continuous and fairly accurate for over 200 years in both Sweden and Japan. Not until the nineteenth century did that practice spread to most of the world. And only in the present century have careful probability sampling methods given us trustworthy sample surveys nationwide. Needless to say, such surveys greatly increase the statistical information available.

3.3   STEP 1: CORE VALUES AND SCOREBOARDS

3.3.1   Why Keep Scoreboards at All?

The need seems obvious. If we are ever to bring our affairs under control, we must first know how those affairs stand. Accurate worldwide scoreboards give us a bonus. They permit scientists to run quasi-experiments that offer large returns at little costs. If we can measure changing and varying scores on the problems we are trying to bring under control, we can compare the better with the worse countries to test theories about what underlying causes make the difference. So by comparing suicide rates with divorce rates, country by country, we may see strong support for the theory that divorce tends to cause suicide—that by decreasing divorce rates we can thereby decrease suicide rates.

Basing public policy on broad national scoreboards troubles many people because these measures oversimplify. More than 20,000 people every year kill themselves in the United States alone. Each of these 20,000 people had a painful story. Psychologists, social workers, and clergy have the task of dealing with each such person who has exhibited suicidal tendencies and of considering that person's special case. Yet studies of such people have made it plain that the root cause of most suicides among physically healthy people is loneliness. That finding not only helps society form its moral standards, its customs, and its laws—it also helps guide those very psychologists, social workers, and clergy in their work with individuals. We do not have to choose between the individual approach and the mass approach. Both approaches have their place. Both are vital.

In the use of national statistics as scoreboards to guide national policy there is what we might call the lamppost fallacy. It is exemplified by the drunk who one night looked for his lost coin under the lamppost rather than in the dark, where he had lost it, because there was more light there. A major economic problem in many Communist countries, for example, arises from their tendency to set production quotas by the things most easily measured. So iron foundries produce the heaviest articles rather than those most needed, in order to meet their annual tonnage quotas. This trap can, of course, be avoided by seeking other, better scoreboards, The annual profit and loss statement also is an easily measured scoreboard. Production for the market with an eye toward maximizing profits tends to produce articles most in demand. A common variant of this trap is that of teaching to the test; here the teacher aims the lesson at passing the achievement test rather than at learning the things whose mastery the test is supposed to measure.

I submit this book as a whole in evidence that the use of worldwide scoreboards in the Five Steps helps mankind manage its affairs and solve its problems. But the book also is evidence that the task is hard. The workers must be many, and skilled, and devoted. The years must be many and long. Indeed, it is not a business of years but of generations.

3.3.2   Why Follow a Model Country?

To run a control system, it is not enough to have feedback through scoreboards. We must also have a clearly stated goal. The ideal goal for most scoreboards at first seems obvious. If the thing measured is good, then the more the better; if bad, the less the better. The difficulty arises when we consider the problem of tradeoffs. Again and again in this book, for example, I call attention to the tradeoff between extended family ties and growth of national wealth. As many countries grow wealthier, family ties become looser, and it may well be that thus the rates of mental illness, alcoholism, suicide, child abuse, and juvenile delinquency increase.

In my whole study of the human situation I propose to look at some forty or so scoreboards. For all we know, each of these may well have a tradeoff problem with every other. We do not know what most of these tradeoffs are, much less how to measure them. If we naively ignore these tradeoffs and proceed to try to maximize everything, we may well get the results that are *easiest* to obtain at the expense of those that are most *important*. We may well be trying to spend, in effect, 200 percent or 300 percent of our income. But no one today has the slightest idea of how to measure or even estimate all these tradeoffs.

There is, however, a simple solution to the tradeoff problem—used by industrial control systems engineers. On a factory assembly line, robots may be doing complex mechanical tasks. Many such robots are control systems hierarchies seven levels deep. Calculating the changing optimum goal settings at each level is a formidable problem. The engineers, however, neatly bypass it. The robots are controlled by computers. Such a computer can be set into the LEARN mode. In the LEARN mode, the computer does not control its robot; rather, it observes and records and remembers that robot's performance. So the engineer sets his computer to LEARN. He walks the robot by hand through the task. And thus the computer observes and remembers the changing goal settings at all seven levels as the robot does its task.

In the same way, by observing the most successful countries, we can take their scoreboard readings as guides or models. We thus know that the model we are following is feasible. And we also know that all the *hidden* tradeoffs—all those we do not know about—have been worked out in practice through trial and error.

However, this method will work only if we take all our goals from those of a single country at a single point in time. It will not work if we shop around for each scoreboard separately. We take the country with the best overall score, across the board, as a model for *all* its scoreboards—including those in which it does comparatively poorly. Thus it will often happen that some other country will seem by comparison with the model to have "too little" of something bad or "too much" of something good.

For example, in Table 3.4 we see that Spain's suicide rate is only about half that of Norway's. In one sense, then, we could say that Spain's suicide rate is "too low." By our way of measuring things, Spain's overall way of life is indulging in a luxury it cannot afford—it is sparing its people much of the stress that leads to suicide, but only at the cost of inflicting on them other and presumably even greater stresses. If Spain were doing better than Norway, not only with respect to our measures of mental health like suicide, but also with respect to our other measures of quality of life, then it would replace Norway as our model country. In that case Spain's suicide rate would replace Norway's as our model.

Needless to say, choosing Norway as our model country for the time being does not mean we suppose that country to have attained the ideal tradeoff solution for all times and all places and all groups within nations. To begin with, we expect variation both between and within countries, to allow for varying circumstances and changing times. And, for all we know, there might in time come to be two or three rival model countries—all of which attain similar levels of happiness but by different means and with different tradeoffs. So far, however, no such pattern has appeared. Norway's rivals in Table 3.4 all share much the same values, much the same general political, economic, and social philosophy.

3.3.3   Why Measure Deep Chance Risk?

We would not, however, want to make too much of small differences between the score of the model country and those of other countries. We would expect small differences to occur by chance alone. Furthermore, what we may think of as "chance" depends on our point of view. When we consider the affairs of a nation, the vicissitudes of life of any one person are chance variations. This person lives and that person dies; this person is promoted, that person is fired; this couple marries, that couple divorces. There are millions of such events and they all average out. It is only the averages that constitute the events from a national point of view. So what is a chance event for a nation may be a carefully planned and fully controlled event from the point of view of a particular person within that nation.

The year-to-year changes in things like suicide rates within a single country may well reflect events that from that country's point of view are discrete and theoretically manageable. Perhaps a bad harvest, involvement in war with a neighbor, an economic depression. Such events we might well call assignable causes and so look at the variation from year to year within a single country as not owing to chance at all when it is associated with such things.

To the extent, however, that such events may be viewed as naturally occurring from time to time within this country or that, then from a worldwide point of view, they *would* be considered as chance events. That they happen this year rather than next year or in this country rather than in that one might be considered a chance event.

From the point of view of the historian of one such country, such events might well be considered historical accidents. Other such accidents might well include, for example, the quality of leadership that the country enjoys—the health or illness of its leaders and the particular events of party or court politics that might lead to this or that policy being adopted this or that year.

In this book I look at variation from the worldwide point of view rather than from the point of view of a single country. From the worldwide point of view, the suicide rate of Norway is one single event rather than millions of people deciding not to commit suicide and hundreds of other people, instead, deciding to do so.

The chance risk of particular historical accidents affecting the statistics of particular countries from year to year I call shallow chance risk. But I am interested rather in what I call deep chance risk. The chance risk here is the risk that differences between two countries do not reflect any deep underlying and long-term social and cultural patterns, but instead reflect only historical accidents.

3.3.4 Why Set a Safe Minimum Worldwide Variation?

Like many other theorists, I hold that progress—cultural evolution—is a natural selection process, a result of blind variation and selective retention. I have elsewhere published evidence supporting the view that the chief selection factor in this process is cultural borrowing. Throughout human history, innovation has been rather rare. For most cultures in human history, progress has come not from innovation but from borrowing. One culture has an innovation; it takes hold; and then other cultures copy it. In his study of creativity, Kroeber shows that innovation cannot be simply a function of the chance birth of particularly creative individuals; rather, it must be understood in terms of the receptivity or lack of receptivity of a given culture at a given time. The more cultures there are, the more variety there is to cultural and social settings, and so the better chance an innovation has of being not only proposed but accepted in some culture or other. Further, the greater the variety of cultures around the world, the greater the chance that some culture will already have a trait that new circumstances cause to become useful to mankind at large.

So it would be a mistake to call for all the world to imitate a guide like Norway as closely as possible. Or even in respect to my forty scoreboards. Other things being equal, the more that nations vary, the better.

Social scientists have not often measured variation from an evolutionary point of view. To do so we need a measure that is relative to the average. Students of biological evolution have long been using one—the Coefficient of Evolutionary Variation (CEV). I use it on my worldwide scoreboards wherever I can. The CEV is simply the standard deviation, expressed as a percentage of the mean. So, for example, in Table 9.3 the mean rate of suicide among 25 nations is 12.21. The standard deviation of those rates is 7.187; its CEV = (100 x 7.187)/12.21 = 59%. If we want to ask how much variation we need in social or cultural traits for natural progress, we can most handily ask that question by asking what should be the proper CEV.

What is the proper CEV of worldwide evolutionary variation? How much play should we allow in our goals? I hold that we must be careful not to tighten that play too much—for then we might stifle progress. I can imagine a future when the world could become safe and comfortable and stable, a future when the chief problems are to keep people cheerful and amused. In such a future world, the preservation of some variety among the world's cultures might become a serious problem.

For now, whatever problems mankind may face, lack of variety is clearly not one of them. I have figured the CEVs for some 55 leading social, economic, and political measures of national life, taken from Taylor and Hudson's measures. Their CEVs range from a low of 22 percent to a high of 549 percent, with a median of 105 percent.

Biologists have long been measuring a wide variety of such characteristics of plants and animals as length, area, and volume of parts of the body. Yablokov has collected and studied many hundreds of these measurements; in them, a CEV greater than 15 percent is a wide one—the median comes closer to 10 percent—and one over 100 percent is enormous. So we hardly need to worry today about lack of cultural variety in mankind at large. In the next hundred years we need to limit that variety and bring all the nations of the world reasonably close to Norway's present quality of life.

To sum up, scoreboards can serve as guides to help mankind attain its core values. To do so they need to follow a model country that can set a reasonable and practical standard for other countries. Scoreboards need a working measure of the chance risk that the differences between the model country and any other merely reflects a transient historical accident and so can be complacently ignored, or that instead the risk is likely to reflect some deep-seated and underlying cultural or social pattern requiring reform. And scoreboards need a standard of worldwide minimum variation, which would give warning if mankind at large is becoming *too* much alike to permit continued worldwide progress.

TABLE 3.1   Availability of Death Statistics

Region	Percentage of the Population for Which Death Reports Are Made		
	Number of Deaths	*Causes of Death*	*Infant Deaths*
Europe	100%	99%	100%
North America	98%	98%	98%
Oceania	89%	81%	87%
Africa	72%	17%	56%
Asia	68%	11%	30%
South America	51%	51%	51%
All Mankind	78%	32%	53%

SOURCE: United Nations, World Health Organizations (1976b: VII).

3.4   STEP 2: SCOREBOARDING THE SCOREBOARDS

"Who watches the watchmen?" asked the ancient Romans.

What we need are secondary scoreboards on the primary scoreboards themselves, measuring their accuracy. And when we have those to our satisfaction, then we need tertiary scoreboards on the accuracy of the secondary scoreboards.

I began this chapter with a report of the accuracy of suicide statistics in Norway and Sweden. There are, of course, many sources of error in national statistics. Some of the more important are: (1) sheer ignorance—as when the family physician ascribes death to heart disease although he really has no idea why the patient died, but heart disease is the vogue diagnosis of the day; (2) laziness—as when a census taker fills out a form with imaginary data because that is less trouble than conducting an interview; (3) carelessness—as when that census taker writes down a person's age as "37" instead of "73"; (4) self-interest—as when teenagers deny on a questionnaire ever having stolen anything because they fear that to admit a theft might get them into trouble with police, teachers, or parents; (5) personal kindness—as when a Swedish pathologist classes an overdose of sleeping pills as "intent doubtful" to protect the widow and orphans, although that pathologist, in fact, believes the death was a suicide.

With so many sources of error, if we are to base public policy on national statistics, we need some trustworthy measure of those errors. In this book, I rely much on national statistics on the causes of death. Consider, then, Table 3.1; it reports the share of the world's peoples whose deaths are reported either from actual certificates or from sample surveys. This then is a measure of how many deaths are diagnosed at all, directly or indirectly—however well or poorly.

A formal measure of the quality of cause-of-death statistics is given by the World Health Organization (WHO). The World Health Assembly has a standard classification of causes of death, and member nations are asked to prepare their death certificates and compile their death statistics accordingly. That classification offers two categories for the convenient use of doctors who do not know why their patients die. Category A 136 calls these deaths "senility"; category A 137 calls them "ill-defined and unknown causes." These categories are almost never used by professionally trained forensic pathologists or others skilled in diagnosis. Therefore, their frequency of use is taken as a rough measure of the quality of medical judgment that goes into cause-of-death statistics. Table 3.2 sets forth the results.

By the yardstick of this table, our model country, Norway, falls short of our ideal. (Though in this respect its record is currently improving.)

Hungary, Romania, and Finland are the leaders of Table 3.2. Honorable mention goes to Sweden and the United Kingdom. At the other extreme, the weakest countries are Thailand, the Dominican Republic, El Salvador, and Honduras.

Statistics on economics are at least as variable in quality as those on cause of death. Over a quarter of a century ago, the U. S. Office of Statistical Standards of the Bureau of the Budget published a "Memorandum on International Statistics," whose findings you can see in Table 3.3. For example, 6 of 9 African countries have statistics of the least accurate sort, compared to only 1 of the 21 countries in Europe and Oceania. Compare them with those in Table 3.2.

In this book, in the chapters concerned, I review important sources of error in public statistics on mental illness, alcoholism, suicide, child battering, and juvenile delinquency.

3.5   STEP 3: REVIEWING SOCIAL INDICATOR METHODS

3.5.1   Controlling Scoreboard Data Quality

How easy it is to be dazzled by plausible but tricky numbers—there are lies, damn lies, and statistics. And yet how easy it is to lose sight of urgent and precious data because they are so fuzzy!

On the one hand, the person who would take metropolitan crime statistics in the United States at face value is easily gulled. Victimization studies have shown that often only half of all robberies get reported. On the other hand, no one doubts for a moment that crime rates are much higher in New York than in London or Tokyo—because the reported differences are so huge that even a 50 percent error rate cannot begin to account for them. Similarly, on the one hand national mental health statistics and national economic statistics of all kinds have been shown by careful and detailed studies often to miss their mark widely. A 10 percent error would be a small one here; a 50 percent error would be high but not surprising. On the other hand, no one doubts that Belgium is a richer country than Bangladesh, or Norway than Niger, or Canada than Campuchea. The meaningful patterns of correlations between national statistics of many different kinds offer strong evidence that—whatever sorts of errors and biases

TABLE 3.2 Unexplained Deaths Scoreboard

Country	Unexplained Deaths[a]	Chance Risk
Above Indicated Range		
Thailand	52.9	.0460
Dominican Republic	38.7	.0843
El Salvador	32.4	.1156
Honduras	30.2	.1302
Nicaragua	27.3	.1537
Yugoslavia[b]	24.5	.1824
Venezuela	22	.2147
Egypt	21.8	.2176
Jordan	21.5	.2221
Ecuador	19.9	.2483
Paraguay	19.4	.2574
Mauritius	18.5	.2750
Panama	17.8	.2898
Guadeloupe[c]	17.6	.2943
Portugal[b]	15.9	.3364
Surinam	12.5	.4506
Mexico	12.4	.4548
Philippines	11.4	.4996
Within Indicated Range		
Greece[b]	11	
Kuwait	10.9	
Singapore	10.4	
Colombia	10.1	
Peru	9.1	
Hong Kong[c]	8.7	
Poland	8.5	
Belgium[b]	8.4	
Chile	8.2	
France[b]	7.6	
Costa Rica	7.6	
Bulgaria	6.3	
Uruguay	6.2	
Japan[b]	6.1	
Spain[b]	6	
Norway[b]	5.2	MODEL COUNTRY
Luxembourg[b]	4.8	
Barbados	4.5	
Israel	4.4	
Trinidad and Tobago	4	
Netherlands[b]	3.9	
Germany (West)[b]	3.8	
Italy[b]	3.3	
Puerto Rico[c]	3.2	

(continued)

TABLE 3.2 (Continued)

Country	Unexplained Deaths[a]	Chance Risk
Below Indicated Range		
Denmark[b]	2	.4111
Ireland[b]	1.7	.3362
Austria[b]	1.7	.3362
USA[b]	1.5	.2849
Iceland[b]	1.5	.2849
Switzerland[b]	1.3	.2331
Czechoslovakia	1.2	.2072
Australia	.9	.1314
Canada[b]	.8	.1074
Northern Ireland[bc]	.6	.0632
England and Wales[bc]	.6	.0632
New Zealand	.5	.0440
Sweden[b]	.4	.0274
Scotland[bc]	.4	.0274
Romania	.2	.0051
Finland	.2	.0051
Below Extreme Range		
Hungary	.1	.0007

SOURCE: United Nations, World Health Organization (1978). Worldwide averages and spreads of 59 countries reporting (lognormal distribution):[d] mean of the natural logarithms: 1.57; median: 6.30; range: 52.80; SD: 1.467; CEV: 93.17%. Worldwide averages and spreads of 23 OECD countries reporting (lognormal distribution): mean of the natural logarithms: 0.99899; median: 3.30; range: 24.10; SD: 1.16256; CEV: 116.37%; skew: −0.02; kurtosis: 0.86.

a. Percentage of deaths given as due to either ill-defined or unknown causes.
b. Member of the Organization for Economic Cooperation and Development (OECD).
c. United Nations reporting unit; not an independent nation.
d. See Glossary for meanings of worldwide measures.
SD = standard deviation of natural logarithms.
CEV = coefficient of evolutionary variation.

the statistics on things like national productivity, mental hospitalization, homicide, and suicide rates may reflect—it is not possible to explain their differences and their linkages except by supposing that in considerable part these statistics are also measuring what they are supposed to measure! From these patterns I would estimate that national statistics of the sort used in the scoreboards of this book—taken from the 22 Organization for Economic Cooperation and Development (OECD) countries—are subject overall to error of the order of something like 30 percent. In other words, in those countries the scoreboards taken all together measure something like 70 percent of what they are supposed to measure. True, we could and should do much better than that. But, we can now make excellent use of data even this fuzzy—as I try to show in this book.

Just as Tolstoy (or anyone else) could never learn exactly what happened to this regiment or that at the battle of Austerlitz, we can never hope to get truly

TABLE 3.3   Accuracy of International Statistics about 1956
            (in the opinion of U.S. Office of Statistical Standards)

Region	For 64 Countries around the World				
	Strongest	*Strong*	*Weak*	*Weakest*	*Total*
Africa	0	1	2	6	9
North America	2	1	5	3	11
South America	0	2	4	2	8
Asia	0	2	5	8	15
Europe and Oceania	15	3	2	1	21
Total	17	9	18	20	64

SOURCE: Morgenstern (1963: 279).

accurate data on public statistics. We can never hope to measure national productivity as accurately as physicists measure the speed of light or chemists measure the composition of a substance. But, just as Tolstoy and everyone else easily learned the main facts about Austerlitz—who won, who lost, and what sort of a peace treaty followed—so we can now use public statistics as I do in this book, to offer broad general guidance on public policy.

They would, of course, be much more useful if we could reduce their overall error rate from something like 30 percent to something like 5 percent—to about that of good quality ethnographic field reports. There are no less than six specific methods of measuring the trustworthiness of public statistics. Systematic use of all these to detect patterns of error can, I submit, lead to enough improvements in collection and estimation methods to attain, in time, that goal of 95 percent accuracy. These six methods of measuring trustworthiness are listed below.

(1) *Seek convergent validity.* Measure the same kind of thing in fundamentally different ways, with entirely different and independent sources of error. For example, does a therapeutic community for juvenile delinquents like Silverlake really bring down the arrest rate of its inmates? Or does it just teach them how to avoid getting caught? Or how to win more lenient treatment from police and parole officers? We would be wise not to trust the arrest rate reports alone. But if compared to a control group over many years, these boys on the average not only had much lower arrest records, but also earned much higher salaries from well-established firms, were much more often promoted in military service, and were much more often elected to public office—then we could begin to trust those arrest rate reports.

(2) *Require good audit trails and independent audits*, as accountants do with money.

(3) *Check the statistics internally for consistency*, as demographers do with census records. The twenty-year-olds of this decade are the thirty-year-olds of the next decade. Do they keep their stories straight ten years later?

(4) *Check related figures externally.* As Morgenstern points out, French statistics of exports to England should jibe with English statistics of imports from France—but often they do not.

(5) *Use the control factor method of data quality control* to determine the presence or absence of *systematic* patterns of bias in data errors. Rummel, for example, has found such patterns in national statistics related to the wealth of a country and to

its political freedom: The poorer the country and the more censorship, the more likely that its statistics reflect systematic error. It seems likely that the percentage of deaths ascribed to vague or ill-defined causes will also prove a useful control factor.

(6) *Use the control factor method* to detect *random* error. Where two scoreboards are in fact highly correlated, then the less the random error, the higher the apparent correlation.

So some of us may need to be less gullible. Others may need to be less skeptical. But all of us may need to be more careful.

3.5.2   Selecting a Model Country

The model country is the one with the best overall quality of life. One way to choose that country would be to measure the general satisfaction with life and to pick the country in which people seem to be happiest. Gallup tried to do just that—and came up with Scandinavia as the happiest corner of the world; there only 4 percent of his respondents said they were "not too happy"; 95 percent called themselves either "fairly happy" or "very happy." Within Scandinavia, Allardt found Norway and Sweden the happiest by this standard: there, only 3 percent of his respondents said they were "unhappy." Sweden has an edge on Norway in Allardt's findings: Of the 95 percent who called themselves "happy," 41 percent of the Swedes against 35 percent of the Norwegians called themselves "very happy"; and of the 3 percent who called themselves "unhappy," rather more Norwegians than Swedes called themselves "very unhappy."

To rely on these subjective responses alone, however, is risky. One might well ask whether Scandinavians *really* are less happy than people in other countries, or only are more likely to present a cheerful face to strangers who come around asking personal questions. So an entirely different and objective approach would be safer—especially if the objective results checked with the subjective ones.

It is such an objective approach that I have used in this study. And with my entirely different methods I reach much the same conclusions about Scandinavia as Gallup. I chose twelve particular scoreboards as measures of six of the core values discussed in Chapter 2—the six readily measurable ones: health, brotherhood, wisdom, peace, order, and variety. I constructed from these twelve a single index number, set forth in Table 3.4. I obtained that overall quality of life index by averaging standard scores of each of the twelve scoreboards. Following the example of Smith in his study of quality of life among cities in the United States, I weighted each of these scoreboards equally. That is plainly begging an important question—and I hope in later works to deal with it more effectively. (I chose not to follow the example of Liu and Anderson, who weighted their variables according to their relative importance in the opinion of respondents, because I wanted a purely objective measure to compare with the purely subjective measures of Gallup and Allardt.)

TABLE 3.4 Choosing Our Model Country

Nation	Physical Health Index[a]	Mental Health Index[b]	Brotherhood Index[c]	Progress Index[d]	Peace Index[e]	Order Index[f]	Variety Index[g]	Quality of Life Index
Norway	589	565	550	550	537	550	563	550
Sweden	616	422	539	591	537	543	544	542
Netherlands	587	581	551	482	475	550	560	541
Canada	496	529	492	564	533	517	540	524
Ireland	581	490	559	434	537	523	–	521
Germany (West)	471	465	525	535	537	541	511	512
Denmark	557	381	488	531	537	521	529	506
USA	450	529	412	620	459	370	535	483
Luxembourg	267	541	590	392	537	462	–	465
Finland	394	323	505	497	537	507	535	464
Spain	461	615	418	348	537	543	228	450
Israel	529	557	412	561	190	376	455	440

SOURCES:

a. Life expectancy (United Nations, Department of Economic and Social Affairs, Statistical Office [UNDESA], 1970).

b. Suicide rate (United Nations, World Health Organization [UNWHO], 1976b); mental hospital admission rates (UNWHO, 1976a).

c. Social Security benefits as percentage of per capita GNP (United Nations, International Labor Organization, 1972); child-beating deaths (UNWHO, 1976b); age-specific suicide rates (UNWHO, 1976b).

d. Per capita GNP for 1972 (Newspaper Enterprise Association, 1972: 587); per capita contributions to science, 1967-1970 (Taylor and Hudson, 1972: 295ff., 322ff.).

e. Foreign war deaths, 1945-1965 (Singer and Small, 1972: 260ff., 389ff.).

f. Homicides (UNWHO, 1976b); civil strife deaths, 1948-1967 (Taylor and Hudson, 1972: 11f.).

g. Press freedom rating (Taylor and Hudson, 1972: 51ff.).

NOTE: These twelve nations were chosen from all the others for the completeness of their public statistics on these indexes, but Norway scores higher than any omitted nation on personal happiness as seen by its people.

This choice, of course, is a choice only for the time being. Every five or ten years, I would want to take another look. I wanted to make this choice only among nations that seem to keep full and accurate national statistics. Otherwise, I might be choosing the nation that is more adept at hiding its bad news. And my individual meter goals might be far off. I could find only twelve nations with substantially complete public statistics of my indices.

I made my choice of a model country on the basis of only twelve of my forty meters. I selected those that seem salient, those on which we seem to have fairly good data, those where our goal seems clear. Thus I left out measures of literacy and formal education because they did not seem to help choose among the leading nations. Had I included them, they would only have confirmed and strengthened my choice. I left out population density because I am not at all clear what the goal should be. I left out unemployment rates and crime rates because data on them either could not be had at all, or if they could, were too inaccurate for use. In other words, I left out measures that seemed to me redundant, irrelevant, or not well reported.

The twelve nations that qualify for consideration as guide lands on the strength of adequacy and relative completeness of their statistical information are Canada, Denmark, Finland, West Germany, Iceland, Israel, Luxembourg, Netherlands, Norway, Spain, Sweden, and the United States. To begin with, I ruled out every nation that failed to account for at least 90 percent of its deaths; in other words, I disqualified all that attributed more than 10 percent of their deaths as due to unexplained symptoms or ill-defined causes. That selection criterion reduced my list of candidates to only 35. That list was then reduced to those twelve by cutting out all nations whose data on mental hospital admissions or on causes of death were incomplete.

I converted all raw scores on the meters to standard scores. In this way, I could meaningfully average the scores of the meters. Finally, I changed the signs (from – to + or from + to –) on meters of things that are bad; for example, I gave a suicide rate one standard deviation below the average of the twelve a standard score of +1.0. (My core values, of course, give me the standards of good and bad.)

Table 3.4 shows the results. Norway was overall the clear winner, with Sweden and the Netherlands nearly tying for second place. All index numbers on Table 3.4 come from the formula: $500 + 100Z$, where Z is the standard score. For example, a suicide rate one standard deviation below the mean would have an index score of 600.

- In this way the *physical health index* comes from the reported life expectancy rates.
- The *mental health index* comes from the average of the standard scores of (1) the reported suicide rates and (2) the reported mental hospital admission rates.
- The *brotherhood index* comes from the average of the standard scores of three statistics: (1) the ratio of social security benefits to per capita gross national product, (2) the reported homicide rate for victims one to four years of age—taken as a measure of child batterings, and (3) the ratio of the reported suicide rate for people 65 to 74 years of age to that of people 25 to 34 years of age—taken as a measure of treatment of the aged.

TABLE 3.5   Balance among Model Country Candidates

PROPOSITION: *Norway is not only the highest scoring nation, but the best balanced among the four leaders.*

Nation	Standard Deviation of Standard Scores of 12 Meters	Standard Deviation of Standard Scores of 7 Core Value Indexes
Norway	34	17
Sweden	79	61
Netherlands	51	45
Canada	38	25

SOURCE: Table 3.4.

NOTE: Measure of balance of each nation is the standard deviation (SD) of that nation's set of standard scores. The lower the standard deviation, the less these scores tend to vary one from another.

- The *progress index* comes from the average of the standard scores of two statistics: (1) per capita gross national product, the usual measure of the wealth of a nation, and (2) the per capita ratio of contributions to world scientific scholarship.
- The *peace index* comes from the reported per capita deaths from combat in foreign wars from 1945 to 1965.
- The *order index* comes from the average of the standard scores of two statistics: (1) the reported rate of death from homicide, and (2) the reported per capita rate of deaths in civil strife—civil wars, riots, and the like.
- The *variety index* comes from the standard score of a measure of freedom of the press. Freedom of the press is a direct measure of the free flow of a variety of ideas and reports. So the spread of change within a society is made easy, and the society is also more readily exposed to new ideas from outside. Details on the exact definition of these meters and on my sources of data are in the notes.
- The *Quality of Life Index* is simply the average of the preceding seven.

In this way, I have chosen Norway as my model country. Furthermore, Norway not only is the nation with reportedly the best overall average on my twelve meters; of the four leading nations on my list it is also the best balanced. The variance of its standard scores among the twelve meters is the least. In other words, Norway not only does best on the average overall, but it comes the nearest to doing fairly well on every individual meter—avoiding extremes (see Table 3.5).

3.5.3   Measuring Deep Chance Risk

By chance risk I mean so-called—misnamed—statistical significance. The chance risk scores on my scoreboards measure the probability of getting by chance through random sampling error from a certain imaginary world a result whose difference from that of the model country—Norway—in either direction is at least as unusual as the result in question. In my imaginary world, these two countries are but two among thousands of others. All of these thousands have scores normally distributed (following the bell curve) with a mean equal to Norway's score and a standard deviation equal to that found among the 22 actual countries forming the OECD, about the year 1970. There is, in fact, no such imaginary world. But I submit that if the probability thus measured is rather large, it would nevertheless be prudent to consider it unlikely that the country measured differs markedly from Norway. Differs, that is to say, in its fundamental, deep-seated, and long-term culture in ways subject to public management or control. Whereas if the probability thus measured is rather small, it would on the contrary, I submit, be prudent to consider such differences likely.

Where the probability thus measured is at least one-half, I class the score as "within the indicated range" and do not give any chance risk values. However, where the probability thus measured is less than .0027—less than 27 chances in 10,000—I class the score as "extremely high" or "extremely low." (As a general rule, a score will fall beyond the extreme range only when it falls on the opposite side of the OECD mean from that of the model country—here Norway.)

Given the applicability of my statistical model, where a score is within the indicated range, the preponderance of evidence favors letting things be—the indicated range is the complacency range. But extremely high or extremely low scores qualify under widely used standards of industrial quality control as clearly demanding attention. Here if a score is on the bad side, we may say with confidence, "This situation is intolerable; something has *got* to be done." If a score is on the good side, we can say with equal confidence, "Never mind if cutting some budget or other hurts this; it is plainly a luxury we cannot afford."

The scores between the extreme range and the indicated range are scores that may be rather likely to reflect a manageable problem that deserves attention (and time and money), but do not do so as plainly as to cause an industrial engineer controlling the quality of electrical fuses to demand a change in production methods. So these in-between scores are in the negotiation range, in which expected costs must be balanced against hoped-for benefits.

My statistical model fits best if there is a normal distribution within the 22 OECD countries. So on each scoreboard I give two standard measures of normality—a skewness measure and a kurtosis measure. The value of the S test of normality listed there gives the chance risk of skewness; the K test gives the chance risk of kurtosis (details in Appendix E).

3.5.4   Fixing a Minimum Worldwide Variation

I turn now to the rationale of constructing my imaginary universe using the variance of the OECD nations. In measuring deep chance risk, I seek to distinguish fundamental differences between cultures from superficial differences within cultures. (This is not the place to open up the difficult problem of what is a culture—where one culture stops and the next one starts.)

It is enough for our present purpose to take as a standard of underlying cultural variation the one obtaining during the model decade described below among the 22 nations of the OECD. This procedure, in effect, takes as an arbitrary cutting point for underlying cultural differences such differences as would distinguish any one country in the OECD from at least eleven others. Thus it looks toward differences greater than those usually distinguishing such similar neighbors as Spain from Portugal, or England from Ireland, or Norway from Denmark, or West Germany from Austria—substantial differences.

The problem here is to determine for all scoreboards a range of variation about the model country—an ideal minimum variation—within which cultural variation should be encouraged from country to country, in order to ensure lasting progress.

The wide range of CEVs among those 53 political and social indicators I spoke of earlier supports Yablokov's view that one cannot fix some minimum proper value for the CEV in general. Instead, that value needs to be considered separately, scoreboard by scoreboard.

Furthermore, we also need to think about what tradeoffs there may be among the scoreboards. By considering variation among all the scoreboards at a single point in time, we avoid the risk that worldwide variation of one scoreboard may be affected by worldwide variation of another related one.

At what point should planners begin to worry about the narrowing of worldwide variation on each scoreboard? I suggest a simple rule of thumb. Time enough to worry about worldwide variation growing too small when that variation falls below the CEV among the 22 OECD countries during the good times prevailing from 1965 to 1974. The general rate of progress among mankind at large during this decade, in comparison to human progress before the industrial revolution, was frantically fast. During that decade more than half the innovations were coming from this group of 22—I have marked the countries of this group on all scoreboards. Their contribution alone made for a faster rate of progress than would be required for mankind at large, if mankind at large enjoyed the level of peace, freedom, and prosperity that then prevailed among these 22.

Of course, serious problems still remain. So if some future decade displays a better overall score on all our core values, with progress still continuing, we might well want to substitute that future decade as the future source of our minimum variation CEVs (but see Appendix F).

3.6   STEP 4: FURTHER STUDIES OF SCOREBOARDS

The needs are obvious. We want our scoreboards to be sensitive measures of our social problems. We especially need good proxy measures for problems whose victims—or exploiters—have strong motives for hiding the facts. But most of all we need to work on the accuracy of our scoreboards. In Section 3.5.1, I reviewed six methods of doing so.

3.7   STEP 5: COPING WITH SCOREBOARDS

Enlisting the support of the academics, the governments, and the general public seems to me best attained by successfully applying scoreboards as part of a Five Step program to cope with a key social problem. Consider, for example, measuring juvenile delinquency—and recidivism—more accurately as part of a program to reduce that delinquency by finding and correcting its causes. Accurate and sensitive scoreboards would be essential to show that indeed such a program had succeeded. If it did succeed, the payoff of scoreboard work would be plain.

3.8   COSTS AND BENEFITS OF KEEPING SCOREBOARDS

If a Five Step program works, the benefits attained will far outweigh the costs of the scoreboards. Scoreboarding costs would become as routine a necessary charge as bookkeeping and accounting costs are in modern businesses.

Notes

3.1   *The View from the Heights of Oslo*

On the findings of forensic pathologists concerning suicide and the contrast between Norwegian privacy and Swedish publicity about them, I interviewed Bjørnar Olaisen of the Institute of Forensic Medicine, Rikshospitalet, Oslo, and Jan Lindberg of the National Forensic Medicine Station at the Karolinska Institute in Stockholm. I am indebted to Anna-Marie Bolander, of the Central Statistical Bureau, Stockholm, whose manuscript studies called my attention to the significant patterns of classification of "Deaths of Uncertain Intent"—a set of statistics that fully supports Jan Lindberg's statements. Holan and Haakonsen (1979) report that in 1977, 75.9 percent of all deaths in Norway took place with medical attention during the last illness, 14.2 percent were autopsied, and the remaining 9.9 percent were less confidently explained. Retterstøl's findings on suicide in Norway in particular and in Scandinavia in general are set forth in Retterstøl (1972, 1975, 1978). Swedish statistics on suicides and deaths of uncertain origin are from Sweden (1979: 192); on population, from Sweden (1978: 32). Norway's statistics are from Norway (1978: 6, 43).

Lester Milbrath, an expert on the study of the quality of life, has spent much time in Norway, both in teaching and research; his list of theories was a personal communication. The only rigorous support I know of for any of these theories is in Fuchs et al. (1977), which I discuss at length in Chapter 10; their findings show Norway with the strongest family structure in Scandinavia and moreover with an outstandingly favorable tradeoff between family strength and social pathology.

3.2   *Scoreboards around the World*

For a history of population counts, see Hollingsworth (1969: 63-108).
For a history of sample surveys, see Parten (1950: 5-13).

3.3   *Step 1: Core Values and Scoreboards*

On the use of LEARN mode to program industrial robots, see Albus and Evans (1976).

3.3.4   *Why Set a Safe Minimum Worldwide Variation?*

On creativity as a function of culture pattern rather than of mere individual genius, see Kroeber (1944). On the predominant importance of diffusion rather than independent invention in explaining similarities between cultures, see the literature reviewed in Naroll and Wirsing (1976: 193-194).

On cultural borrowing as the principal selection mechanism in cultural evolution, see Naroll and Wirsing (1976).

The 53 CEVs consisted of all the scoreboards in Taylor and Hudson (1972) for which these authors furnished means and standard deviations.

Yablokov (1974: 44-76) sums up variations in CEV; at page 196 he quotes a passage from I. Schmalhausen, pointing out how widely CEVs of the same materials vary, depending on whether we measure their length, their surface, or their volume.

3.5   Step 3: Reviewing Social Indicator Methods

The reporting units on the scoreboards of this book follow the practice of the UN agencies from which I take my data. Normally, of course, each unit is a member nation, but many variants occur; the United Kingdom often reports its major constituent units separately: England and Wales, Scotland, Northern Ireland, Isle of Man, and Channel Islands. Similarly, we often get separate reports for Puerto Rico, Guadeloupe, Martinique, Okinawa, and Namibia. With respect to the spelling of the names of these units, again I follow the most recent version used by the United Nations.

Rossi and Gilmartin (1980) is a good introduction to the compilation of social indicators; Gilmartin et al. (1979) is a bibliography; and Grant (1978) offers a plan for using social indicators as scoreboards to guide public policy.

In 1971, the OECD had 22 members: See entry for OECD in the Glossary for a list of them.

No one understood better than Tolstoy the difficulty of reconstructing accurately the events of a battle (see Tolstoy, 1942). I have reviewed these difficulties in a minor essay about a minor battle in the American Civil War (Naroll, 1952).

On the serious distortions in U.S. crime statistics revealed by victimization studies, see Penick and Owens (1976: 134-140). On errors in economic statistics, see Morgenstern (1963). On the severe distortions in mental health rates derived from mental hospital admission rates, see Eaton and Weil (1955), Srole et al. (1962: 240-250), and Dohrenwend and Dohrenwend (1969: 174-175).

My guess of 70 percent as a plausible minimum overall accuracy rate for scoreboards among the 22 OECD nations was taken from a multiple regression analysis I am analyzing for later publication (prepared by Celia Ehrlich and Hilary Shreter); it has as a dependent variable the subjective quality of life, as measured by Gallup International Research Institutes (1977), Allardt (1973), and Easterlin (1974). For 31 nations, we examined 13 variables, including the two measures of systematic error validated by Rummel (1970b); we found a raw multiple correlation of .84, supposedly meaning that 70 percent of the variance is explained. (But corrected multiple r-bar is only a little over .50.)

On convergent validity, see Campbell and Fiske (1959).

On internal consistency, see Taeuber (1968: 364).

On external consistency, see Morgenstern (1963).

On data quality control, see Naroll (1962a), Rummel (1970b), Rohner, DeWalt, and Ness (1973), and Naroll, Michik, and Naroll (1980: 496-498).

On the use of control factors to measure random error, see Witkowski (1978), Kang (1981).

3.5.2   Selecting a Model Country

On subjective quality of life, see Gallup International Research Institutes (1977: 139, question 9), Allardt (1973: 119, question 50), Campbell, Converse, and Rodgers (1976), and Milbrath (1972). On the construction of an objective quality of life index, see Smith (1973), and Liu and Anderson (1979).

STEP 3: Review Theory Tests

4.1   KAMANGA TAKES A BRIDE

Kamanga was planning to marry Semini. She was an attractive woman, sensible and hardworking. But how can a man really know a woman until he lives with her? So Kamanga did what the Azande of the Sudan often do when they are puzzled or in doubt. He consulted the poison oracle; he had a certain amount of poison administered to a chicken in a series of doses—just enough so that sometimes the bird would die, sometimes live. As soon as Ongosi gave the bird the first dose, Kamanga began to question the oracle. He spoke to the poison that the bird had swallowed:

"Poison oracle, that woman I intend to marry, is she my wife? Will we make a homestead together? Will we count the years together? Now, listen to me, poison oracle, if so, kill the bird."

"Poison oracle, if it is not true, if she is not my wife, if we will not make a homestead together, if we will not count the years together, spare the bird—now listen to me, poison oracle, if so, let it live."

After the second dose, the bird went into a spasm of agony and it died. So it had answered "yes." It had predicted that Semini would be Kamanga's bride.

But that was only half the work. Ongosi and Kamanga went through the procedure again with a second bird. This time, however, Kamanga inverted his instructions to the poison. This time, if the marriage was to take place, the poison must spare the bird. This time, if the marriage was *not* to take place, the poison must kill the bird. Kamanga harangued the poison at length, admonishing it to speak the truth and promising to praise it should it do so. Indeed, this second bird lived. So Kamanga had his answer. He would marry Semini.

The anthropologist Evans-Pritchard, who tells us about these oracles, used them himself from time to time. "I always kept a supply of poison for the use of my household and neighbors," he said, "and we regulated our affairs in accordance with the oracle's decisions. . . . I found this as satisfactory a way of running my home and affairs as any other I know of."

A Dutch spinner of sea tales, who had sailed many miles on all sorts of ships, advised aspiring sea captains that one of their duties would be to serve as oracle. To the skipper come all his officers with any problem they cannot solve, and they demand immediate decision. The cook, the bosun, the engineer—if they are baffled, it is the skipper next to God who must take the responsibility and decide for them, says Jan de Hartog. No matter if, as it is so often the case, the inquirer knows more about the problem than the captain. It is not advice they seek, but decision—an oracle. Hartog's advice: Give a firm, prompt decision, and stick by it. Best way, he says with a wink, is to give those questions serial numbers and answer "yes" to the even ones and "no" to the odd ones. By the time they get to you, the pros and cons have been weighed in the inquirer's mind to such an extent that he can no longer decide on merit; he wants someone to choose for him from two equally valid decisions. Flipping a coin would work as well. But a coin flip lacks emotional comfort. The Azande are sure that their oracle never fails, and they use it for all manner of difficult questions. They are comforted by knowing that in this way they have made the best decision they can. Similarly, the skipper keeps his method of decision to himself; his officers shift the burden onto his shoulders and so are relieved of self-reproach or blame if things then go wrong.

Polanyi points out that the Azande's faith in poison oracles does not differ essentially from the faith of Londoners in Western science. People often need an oracle, and science is often a good one. Londoners and Azande alike are simply taking on faith what they have been taught and what everyone else believes.

The Azande have a belief system that includes a rationale to deal effectively with apparent contradictions that might disturb it. The Azande, in fact, *encourage* skepticism about particular oracle seances or acts of magic or witchcraft. They are quite ready to look for evidence that any particular seance was faulty—if, for example, Semini had changed her mind after all and refused to marry Kamanga, though the oracle had assured him they were destined to wed. Perhaps someone present had broken one of the taboos on whose faithful observance the success of the oracle depends. Perhaps the poison had been contaminated by the touch of a woman. Perhaps the ritual had been bungled. Consequently, any informal experiments that tend to discredit the whole oracle cult would be attacked by the Azande on the grounds that the failure of the trial merely shows that in one way or another it has been wrongly performed. And a hard science like chemistry, too, must blink away inconsistencies and contradictions within its own body of theory and data, as Polanyi produces instances to show.

Science has other limits, as well. No amount of scientific study of the sociology or social psychology of marriage could have helped Kamanga choose a bride. When a man is in doubt about that, all the advice we scientists can offer is to choose a woman of like cultural heritage. Beyond that, a poison oracle is today as good a way as any to help him make up his mind. Scientifically, as good as a flip of a coin—but psychologically a great deal better, if the man, like everyone else he knows, has been taught from an early age to trust the oracle. Indeed, just as placebos have been shown by experiment after experiment to have much power to relieve symptoms or indeed cure illnesses, so belief in poison oracles or in any other myth system often serves many purposes. (I shall have more to say about the good done by faith in myths in Chapter 6.) Perhaps Kamanga and Semini's belief in the poison oracle convinces them that they are destined "to count the years together"; it might help cement their marriage by leading them to come to terms with its problems—because they know from the oracle that they are going to stay together. Such comforts are presently denied them by science.

The very insistence by social scientists on rigor of proof and skepticism makes them slow to decide on weighty questions. Indeed, there is little advice social scientists can give today with the confidence that medical men have in their diagnosis, prognosis, and treatment of infectious diseases.

Granted all this, science nevertheless is not just another self-contained belief system—not just another oracle—any more than *homo sapiens* is just another species of animal. Like *homo sapiens* as a species in competition with others, I submit, a mature scientific paradigm has the power to push aside and crowd out almost any other rival oracle. That power comes from its ability to outperform its rivals by offering not only a better way to *predict* the future, but also a better way to *control* it.

In comparing the closed system of scientific rationale with the similarly closed systems of other faiths like the Azande faith in the poison oracle, there is one key point, then, to bear firmly in mind. The advantage of scientific method over other methods appears, problem by problem, only when a successful paradigm to deal with that problem has come from that method. That advantage is *not* a superiority in rigor of fundamental logic. Like other methods, the method of science requires that the devotee accept its premises on faith, and it provides that devotee with convenient formulae to dismiss inconvenient contradictions or inconsistencies. The advantage of scientific method lies, rather, in its nature as an open system, a natural selection process, institutionalizing skepticism, welcoming change in belief but institutionalizing the means by which that change occurs. I submit that if the science oracle, in fact, could predict successful marriages for the Azande better than the poison oracle, the Azande would stop using the poison oracle for that purpose.

Western medicine began to displace Chinese medicine in Japan more than 200 years ago. It was not the superior elegance of its logic that caused Japanese physicians like Sugita Gempaku to buy expensive Western medical textbooks; it was the fact that when a man was cut open, these oracles predicted better than the Chinese oracles what his insides looked like.

Western medical science today is, of course, much more powerful in its ability not only to predict but also to control the disorders of the human body. The Azande poison oracle presumably changed much less in that time. For although that poison oracle doctrine contains ample means to defend itself against such an inconsistent observation as a failure of a predicted marriage, it does not contain a means to correct itself by changing its model of the world—and so to improve its ability to predict and control. Western medical science does. If an inconsistency arises between the Azande poison oracle predictions and observations, the poison oracle *must* explain that awkward fact away. The key contrast in logic between London scientists and Azande poison oracle mystics, then, is the fact that scientists are more likely than mystics to change their model to fit their observations, less likely to use logical reasoning to defend the model against their observations.

For logic is the servant of every science, not its master. The master of any science, I repeat, is the test of the scientist's ability to model successfully the world outside the mind—to predict and control it. Thus it is that physics can go along for generations holding two logically contradictory theories of light—the wave theory and the particle theory. The wave theory fits some data and can be used effectively to control some phenomena. The particle theory fits other data and can be used effectively to control other phenomena. Physics will not consider its task done until one day it somehow resolves that logical contradiction. But in the meantime, logical rigor takes second place to successful modeling.

4.2   BEHAVIORAL SCIENCE IN THE WORLD TODAY

"The world we live in," writes Paul Johnson, a former editor of *The Statesman*, "is a woefully discouraging place to those who still believe that well-meaning intellects can solve any of its problems." Johnson, in the pages of the *New York Times Sunday Book Review*, was reviewing the life of Tawney, a great English historian. His piece spoke of Tawney's youth at Oxford on the eve of World War I. There, in those days, brilliant young men like Tawney took for granted that through high ideals and fine scholarship they could solve the problems of mankind. Now to men like Tawney and Johnson, superb scholarship meant reading widely in theory, in history, and in the humanities; it meant thinking hard with a powerful mind about what they read; and it meant writing their resultant thoughts out, along with the facts and ideas that these thoughts drew on. Read hard and well. Think hard and well. Write hard and well. Such were the disciplines of superb scholarship. Beyond this formula, there was no method except for viewing the original sources of the facts they used—the first-hand reports—with a skeptical eye. This classic method of nineteenth-century literary scholarship indeed has failed us, as Johnson says.

The Paul Johnsons of this world are not reading the behavioral science literature, needless to say. It is too technical, it is too carelessly and turgidly written, and there is far, far too much of it for any one person to cope with. But the last half of my book surveys much of that literature. I offer it as evidence that behavioral science *is* getting somewhere. In another new book with a like message—a vast amount of hard evidence on a topic I do not have space for—Fisher and Greenberg review *hundreds* of rigorous tests of the theories of Sigmund Freud and find that these studies taken together strongly support several of Freud's leading theories, but strongly discredit several others. For example, Freud's theory on the origin of the paranoid delusion is in—but his theory of the fundamental nature of dreams as wish fulfillments is out.

Science is a branch of humanism and begins as that very literary scholarship Johnson despairs of. But each branch of science, each specialty, must gradually over the centuries develop and refine its own paradigm.

Behavioral science is a style of social science; it looks toward rigorous (and usually quantitative) tests of theory—tests like those reviewed in Part Two of this book. Few Marxists are behavioral scientists—but some are—Leeuwe, for example. Few historians are behavioral scientists—but some are—Vern L. Bullough, for example. Many economists, political scientists, and cultural anthropologists these days are behavioral scientists, although many others are not. Most sociologists and social psychologists are. (It becomes hard to classify social scientists who favor rigorous quantitative methods for describing the world but casual humanistic methods for explaining it—a point of view common among cultural anthropologists and economists.)

While most literary humanists like Paul Johnson have given up on producing a social science, we behavioral scientists have not. On the contrary, we continue to believe that our efforts will in time lead to a ripening of many social science paradigms.

Yet social scientists are far from satisfied with the state of their affairs. Anthropologists, sociologists, social psychologists, political scientists, economists, and geographers alike complain of the uncertainties troubling their disciplines. None of these scholarly disciplines would claim to be a mature science in the same sense that chemistry, physics, astronomy, or genetics are mature sciences. On the other hand, they are closer to being mature sciences than are mere rhetorical disciplines like literary criticism, astrology, Marxism, history, or theology. Mature sciences, like rhetorical disciplines, are attempts to apply the basic tools of classic Greek philosophy to a body of knowledge—they seek to understand what people observe with their senses through the use of disciplined thought.

Clearly mature sciences can be distinguished from clearly rhetorical disciplines by the following signs: (1) In a mature science there is usually general agreement on what Thomas Kuhn calls its "paradigm." The paradigm of a science states the problems on which it works—that is, the questions it seeks to answer, the riddles it seeks to solve. That paradigm also sets forth in some detail and with some rigor the way in which proposed solutions are to be tested. Changes in that paradigm take place only in response to rigorous observations that show that the new paradigm fits the data better than the old did. Fundamental changes in the paradigms of rhetorical disciplines, in contrast, occur merely through changes in the interests of the scholars—often in response to change in the climate of opinion.

(2) Proposed changes in the paradigms of a rhetorical discipline often lead to fission into rival schools of thought, each of which maintains that it holds the "truth" while its rival is in "error." Proposed changes in the paradigms of a mature science do not lead to such fission. While disputes as often arise in mature sciences as they do in rhetorical disciplines, rivals in scientific disputes agree on the nature of the studies needed to resolve the disputes, and both sides suspend final judgment until such studies are made. When matters are under dispute, all rivals agree that their viewpoints are tentative, pending further research. Mature scientists, then, at any given time tend to agree widely on what constitutes the "truths" of their science and agree on the manner in which that

canon of "truths" may be changed. That is to say, a falsifiability test mechanism is, in effect, specified in some detail.

(3) In a mature science the fundamental elements of the current paradigm have been used to predict events more accurately than could be done without it.

(4) In a mature science those elements of its paradigm that are capable of human control are submitted to tests involving human control of the outcome—so that the experimenter does not merely predict the outcome, but causes it to occur.

(5) In a mature science the model set forth in terms of the fundamental paradigm leads to implications of public policy—pure science leads to applied science; a mature science has proved itself by helping mankind control its world. Applied science makes manifest important benefits in everyday life that validate for the population at large the credentials of the scientists, and of their science, their "truth." Astronomy led to celestial navigation; the observations of the moons of Jupiter led to a means for precise determination of longitude; Charles II of England justified the Greenwich observatory to his people, *not* because it would lead to the advancement of science, but because it would help English mariners find their way over the sea.

The great weakness of social science today, as I see it, is our too-heavy reliance on mere associations. Mere linkages. Mere correlations. Almost all the tests reviewed in this book have been nothing more. I look for a breakthrough to scientific maturity for us when through *purpose tests*—tests of ability to control—we check out a powerful theory with a clear policy message. And when that message is heeded—that policy adopted—and it succeeds. Such an event would seem likely to produce another scientific revolution for Thomas Kuhn to look at.

So social science needs more tests. But purpose tests are ethically sensitive. And often expensive. The best way for pure social science to join the mature sciences, then, may well be through the back door. Through applied experiments rather than through pure ones. In social science, then, perhaps we may see a reversal of the direction of the flow of knowledge between the pure and the applied branches. In the natural sciences we expect the great breakthroughs to come from the pure scientists, and from them flow to the applied. But in social science, because of the difficulty of making purpose tests in the laboratory or in the field, the flow of knowledge may run the other way—with the great breakthroughs coming from applied sciences and going from them to the pure scientists of the academy.

4.3   STEP 1: CORE VALUES OF BEHAVIORAL SCIENCE

Modeling the world outside the thinker's own mind, then, is the main task of science. Indeed, according to Jerison, that is the main task of the brain of all vertebrates. Jerison thinks that the great leaps in the ratio of brain weight to body weight that characterize the evolution of the brain over the past several hundred million years took place to give the brain more powerful means to make such models. The cybernetic model of the mind sees it as primarily a control system—a means by which an animal can control itself and its environment well enough to survive long enough to have children who likewise will so survive. Science is an artificial method of improving that process. Its fundamental core values, then—as I have already said again and again—are the ability of its models to help people predict and control the world outside the thinker's own mind.

For me, epistemology is not a logical problem at all. By its nature, once the mind ever finds that its model fails to predict or lead to control of the world outside, it can no longer have any absolute confidence or certainty about that world; and an attempt to cope with epistemology through logic alone, mathematics alone, without observations, is as empty as an attempt to cope with physics through mathematics alone. Mathematics and logic alone may be essential tools, but they can do nothing alone, unaided by observation. For me, the problem of epistemology is that of science writ small, the problem of the individual testing his or her model of the outside world by attempting to predict and control that world. Consider how well you can predict your breakfast when you see it on the table before you, and how well you can control it by seeking food you prefer and avoiding food you dislike. *That* for me, is the problem of epistemology; and through prediction and control, we can reduce our personal doubts about that model—with respect to everyday trivia or with respect to the best tested propositions of science—to negligibly small probabilities of error.

So to a scientist, the questions raised about the ultimate nature of reality by Eastern mystics—by devotees of Yoga or Zen Buddhism, for example—are quite beside the point. These mystics seek primarily to comfort the thinker's own mind. They dismiss the world outside their own mind as illusion—as a dream. We scientists do not dispute that point with them. Mystics are not concerned with the world outside their own minds; they do not seek to predict or control it. They are not in competition with science; they are pursuing other riddles than ours, with other models.

To deal with the world outside our own minds with the powerful brain that we human beings have been given by our evolutionary past, we can use the methods of observation and reasoning that are, so to speak, "wired in" by our genes. Such a procedure goes by the name of common sense. Cultural systems draw heavily on common sense. They also preserve the common sense of our ancestors through custom, by incorporating through trial and error ways of life that have proved successful in coping with the world, and so in aiding survival.

But human common sense is a fallible tool for modeling, subject to many errors. The weaknesses of common-sense judgments have been much studied in past decades by psychologists. They show that common sense tends to go wrong in at least three fundamental ways. And these three ways are all sources of error that behavioral science—unlike humanistic scholarship—has disciplines to avoid. More on these three modeling fallacies a little later in this chapter.

Science tries to be logical—although, as I have said, logic is our servant, not our master. Behavioral science contrasts with other styles of social science in the way it seeks formal models that are logically coherent and consistent and tests them with the aid of mathematical statistics. Mathematics, I submit, is by far the most successful application of formal logic to scientific modeling. But, as we have seen when we looked at the Azande poison oracle, science relies not on rigorous demonstration, but rather on approaching truth as a limit. By gradually refining and improving our model, even though we may never get it perfect, we gradually make it resemble reality more and more closely. Even though from time to time our predictions may still continue to fail, they fail less and less often. Even though our efforts to apply science to control our affairs may also continue to fail from time to time, they, too, fail less and less often. The concept of limits, so powerful in mathematics, has then its use here, too, in our concepts of truth and reality. Consider this familiar mathematical example—the infinite series. We define the infinite series:

$$f(x) = .5 + .5^2 + .5^3 + \dots$$

And we say that this series approaches 1 as a limit as N goes to infinity. That is to say, no matter how many more terms we add, the sum of this series will never quite reach 1—it will always fall short of it by a certain amount. But that discrepancy may be as tiny as we like—the more terms we add, the smaller it gets. At some point or other, for practical purposes, the difference becomes negligible. And using this kind of series, mathematicians prove able to solve many difficult problems they cannot handle otherwise.

So in science we build models; we test models; we change models when our tests turn up wrong; and if our science is maturing, then by our fundamental values of ability to predict and control, we approach certainty as a limit. Our errors grow fewer and fewer, smaller and smaller.

Here, then, we have the link between the world of model-building imagination inside the philosopher's mind and the world of reality outside the mind that the model seeks to resemble. Through prediction of future perceptions—or even better, through control of future perceptions—the world of the mind tests its model of the world of reality. Hence the profound importance of the wording of the title of Power's book on the human sensorimotor system: *Behavior, the Control of Perception.*

Our concept of truth then is a stochastic one—that is to say, we do not claim absolute certainty about our model, but only some degree of probability that it will fit. So the more mature a science, the higher the probability that its predictions will check out, that the controls it designs will succeed.

For this reason, we may think of the goal of science as reducing the probability of error—of reducing the ratio of doubt to trust. (In Section 4.5.3, "A Theory Trust Meter," I offer a crude and rough measure of that ratio with respect to some leading theories of social ills.)

As Donald T. Campbell has pointed out, science approaches truth by means of a natural selection process. Science is a darwin, a process of blind variation and selective retention. The variation in the process comes from a large number of scientists working independently in complete intellectual freedom on a problem. New disputes about theory or method within a science are signs of health, then—as long as in the course of a generation or two these disputes tend to get resolved. For it is in the systematic selection among rival theories by means of a battery of theory tests that science progresses and matures. *Old disputes, then, are a sign of immaturity and weakness.* Finally, through codification in theory reviews, manuals, and textbooks—through the creation of its own written tradition—a science retains permanently those theories that have been selected. (A new technique for improving selection and retention—the THINCS process—is described in Section 5.2.)

Whether we merely try to predict or whether we also try to control, two central concepts are *cause* and *chance*. The successful application of these concepts to any model constitutes a leading task of science, and so they are among its core values. Cause and chance are not really two distinct concepts at all, but two sides of the same coin. Chance is negative cause. What we explain by assigning causes, we explain; what remains unexplained, we call chance. A chance effect is best defined as the combined net result of a very large number of very small causes. Science can hope to explain large causal influences; it can hope to explain moderate ones; but where a very large number of very small ones are at work, science cannot explain; it can only describe.

But chance, too, has its laws. They have been exhaustively studied by mathematical statistics. So while the work of chance cannot be explained, it can be predicted—with a precisely defined doubt/trust ratio—predicted by the so-called measure of statistical significance—more about this a little later.

Chance, then, I define (following Duncan) in terms of cause. I say that any given effect may result from a few assignable causes or from many unassignable ones—and those many unassignable ones I collectively call chance. What is an assignable cause?

The cybernetic model of the mind offers a ready definition for the idea of cause and effect. That definition disagrees with those offered by such classical philosophers as David Hume and Bertrand Russell or such social scientists as Rudolph Rummel. These others see in cause-and-effect relationships no more than mere association—or association plus sequence, with effects following causes. But common sense disagrees. Every autumn the leaves fall off the hardwood trees here in upstate New York. Soon after, the rivers and lakes freeze; a spectacular ice bridge forms at the foot of Niagara Falls. Neither Hume nor Russell nor Rummel *really* want to say that falling leaves cause the ice bridge to form—though the correlation is perfect and the sequence is invariable. But the point is, you cannot make a river freeze by knocking the leaves off the trees along its banks. You can make it freeze only by lowering its temperature.

The idea of cause and effect is a key element in the design of a servomechanism, a control system. A cause-and-effect relationship is one of potential control. A causes B if it is true that by controlling A I can thereby control B. We all first learn to use our minds to control our bodies—especially our limbs. Then, as we grow older, we learn to use our limbs to control such other things as light switches, thermostats, and steering wheels, which themselves let us control still other things, like lights, room temperatures, and automobiles. As we learn, we constantly seek cause-and-effect relationships— those through which by controlling something we already know how to manage (our "cause") we thereby become able to control something else, something new (our "effect"). Mastering cause-and-effect relationships, then, is a prominent part of normal growth.

To explain something, then, is to describe it in such a way as to distinguish assignable causes from one another and from chance effects and so to link the potentially controllable related parts into a system. Thus Copernicus and Kepler described the solar system; Newton explained it. When a system has been well described, we can predict its future behavior. When it has been explained, we can control it.

What we cannot control, we must leave to chance. The role of chance in scientific observation is commonly measured by means of so-called tests of statistical significance. The nature of these tests is widely misunderstood. There are a number of them, but all have a common underlying logic. They all ask whether the observation you actually got is the sort of thing you would have expected to get by chance alone. Thus they measure the risk that from your observations you have learned nothing—have found no pattern. And so they should be called tests of "chance risk"—and that is what I call them.

The mechanism of chance invoked commonly is the chance error involved in random sampling. Now random sampling is a method of selection carefully arranged so that chance and chance alone does the picking. To eliminate all systematic influences—all assignable causes—is not easy, and unwary samplers often go astray. So fixing on random sampling error as the chance process in question is sensible. But purely random errors in observation and measurement, as well as purely random influences on the things observed, would often have a similar effect. In any case, the key point to bear firmly in mind is that if the mathematical model of the chance risk test seems to fit the data, then we have no reason to believe that we have learned anything further about it. In the jargon of such tests, we then "accept the null hypothesis"—the hypothesis that there is no underlying pattern at all, only chance noise that mimics one.

Hence if an observation fails the chance risk test, it makes no sense to ask whether, in fact, the sample concerned was really random—or whether it was a sample at all—or whether the other conditions of the mathematical model have been met. When the observation fails the test, these questions do not matter at all. If you have failed chemistry, you cannot graduate. So it does not matter whether or not you have also failed some other requirement for your degree— your physical education courses, perhaps, or your course in state history.

A failed chance risk test says that there is a good chance—a high probability—that you have found no pattern at all. That you have found only noise. If the results are "statistically significant" at the 5 percent level, that means you would expect to do as well as you did by chance alone in 5 percent of random samples from a patternless universe. That fact remains true whether or not you took a random sample—or any kind of sample at all. The chance risk result is in the subjunctive mode, not the indicative. It does not say you actually took a random sample from a patternless universe. It tells you the odds that you would have found as much pattern as you did *if you had* taken such a sample.

Chance risk tests, then, are important. They should always be used, regardless of the kind of sampling methods involved. Only if you pass chemistry does it matter whether you meet your other degree requirements. Only if you pass the chance risk test does it matter whether perhaps sampling bias or systematic measurement error might explain that fact. Remember—*no* successful chance risk test fits the mathematical model of the test. The whole point of the test is to establish the implausibility of that model as an explanation of the observed results.

But as Morrison and Henkel remind us, successful chance risk tests do not in themselves prove that the findings have any importance. Their common name, "statistical significance tests," has led to widespread misunderstanding. If there is any real pattern at all, however trivial and petty, then we can always expect impressively low chance risk in a study simply by increasing the number of cases we observe. A failed chance risk test—one with a high probability—always tells us something important, something we would rather not have heard. It always tells us that so far we have learned nothing at all, because we have done no better than we could expect to have done by chance alone. But a successful chance risk test tells us only that we have found *some* kind of pattern. Whether that pattern is the one we are looking for—or whether it results from some other causal influences we have ignored, or whether from a systematic error in our research methods—remains to be seen.

The measurement of chance elements in the phenomena studied is, then, a core value of science, because science, in seeking potential control, seeks causes—and chance risk tests measure the probability of *uncontrol*.

Thus science has these core values: It seeks to test models of the world outside the mind of the scientist in order that people may discern systematic patterns of sequence and causation in them, and thus know how to use those models to predict and control events in that world. But the core values of science go beyond goals, to method. The model of scientific research that we scientists take on faith—encouraged by our successes in prediction and control, but undiscouraged by our failures—is a meta-model, a model on how to build models. It has four axioms that, taken together, define the process and distinguish it from other kinds of knowledge. Science is empirical, skeptical, systematic, and theoretical.

Being *empirical* means accepting as data only information obtained by the ordinary observation of the senses. No arcane, mysterious, divine, mystical, or intuitive messages are received. (Which is not to deny scientists the privilege of playing their hunches in deciding what to observe.)

Being *skeptical* means that anything and everything is open to doubt and subject to question. The opinions of learned scientists, the pronouncements of powerful rulers, the ancient wisdom handed down from time immemorial, the utterances of inspired prophets or holy scriptures—none of these is beyond question. Consequently, science is never finished, since any scientific finding can always be challenged by new evidence. Of course, for most people, a given science is evaluated as a whole according to its success at prediction and control. Beyond that, mature sciences are largely taken on faith, and the authority of eminent scientists is heeded by the public. Even scientists take nearly all of their own science on faith. Skepticism takes over fully only when scientists are at their research—with respect to the problem they study. And skepticism is at its height when scientists hear the research reports of their fellow scientists. Hence Ralph Gerard's dictum: "A scientist is a person who takes a quarrelsome interest in his colleagues' work."

Being *systematic* means classifying observations in some orderly way; this task leads to system in science—taxonomies and sets of concepts created by scientists to make sense of the data. And it means also seeking system in nature, looking for structure and pattern there.

Being *theoretical* means seeking the underlying patterns of sequential and causal relationships that link the elements of the science. A social scientist, then, is a person who studies human society and culture *empirically, skeptically, systematically,* and *theoretically*—on the assumption that if enough of us do this long enough, mankind will thereby learn how to predict and control its affairs.

In practice, a science grows through five processes. Most individual scientists take their discipline as a whole pretty much as they find it, while working intensively only on one or two of these processes, on some small part of the science. But a science often takes a giant leap forward when a leader states its paradigm in a general treatise. The confrontation of general theoretical models by systematic observations is the heart of any science—and it is such a general confrontation that I attempt in this book.

In the growth of science, (1) observation, (2) classification, (3) logical and mathematical analysis, (4) insight, and (5) generalization all play their part. I trust that the reader of this book will have no trouble finding examples of these five processes in the studies I review.

4.4   STEP 2: BEHAVIORAL SCIENCE SCOREBOARDS

It would be useful to measure the maturity of particular social science disciplines by formal and objective scoreboards. I know of none at all. We could measure *consensus* by listing topics of controversy that occupied earlier generations and seeing the extent to which older controversies have been settled. In cultural anthropology a century ago, two leading ones were the measurement of level of cultural evolution and the rival explanations for worldwide similarities in human culture—independent invention versus diffusion. Now both these problems are resolved.

We could measure the absence of consensus another way, by seeking for long-time, well-established rival schools of thought. What are the leading controversies in each discipline? How long have they been in existence? How much agreement is there on the kind of evidence through which they could be resolved? How much willingness is there to suspend judgment while waiting for that evidence? What sorts of predictions does the science lead to? How frequently are they successful? What arenas of public affairs are managed or controlled with the aid of the science in question? How successfully?

4.5   STEP 3: THEORY TEST REVIEW METHOD

4.5.1   Intuition versus Science

Scientific theory tests are needed to guard against at least three fundamental biases or distortions in the human mind—a counting bias, a matching bias, and a latching bias. These distortions tend to warp our perceptions and judgments in the same way that curved mirrors in an amusement park warp and distort our faces and figures. As many rigorous controlled experiments reviewed by Nisbett and Ross have shown, this analogy is often apt. The three fundamental biases can produce as grotesque a monster of reality as the trickiest of curved mirrors:

- *Counting bias*: The most salient type is thought the most frequent.
- *Matching bias*: The most salient pattern is thought the most meaningful.
- *Latching bias*: The most familiar idea is thought the truest.

At bottom, all three fundamental biases stem from a single source and follow a single principle: Heed the salient, heed that which is easiest to grasp. I submit that this salience principle seems so deeply ingrained in our thought processes because it is by far the most efficient for dealing with the swarm of minor decisions in everyday life. As a quick-and-dirty, rough-and-ready guide it usually suffices, and we usually have neither the time nor the need to do a better job of thinking through the situation. The difficulty, however, lies in the fact that because this salience principle is so deeply ingrained, we tend to stick to it even when we *do* have both the time and the need.

The experiments reviewed by Nisbett and Ross display with varying degrees of confidence 21 specific features that lend salience to a thing (see Table 4.1). I have grouped these 21 features into four sets. Each of the four sets of saliency has been demonstrated to lead to fallacies—demonstrated by and large beyond any reasonable doubt, at least with respect to experimental subjects of modern culture. Furthermore, Nisbett and Ross also produce anecdotes showing the operation of these same principles in warping practical judgments in daily life. Let us consider the three fundamental biases in turn, and see in each of them the power of the salient in warping the judgment.

The counting bias. The counting bias or so-called *availability* heuristic—the rule that the most salient type tends to be judged the most frequent (or most likely)—has been shown often by many researchers. For example, Kahneman and Tversky gave subjects a list of names of public figures. There was exactly the same number of men's names as women's names on their list. However, they

TABLE 4.1   Salient Things: The Things That Are Easiest to Grasp

Things most likely to be noticed

- Most often seen
- Most easily seen
- Most dramatic
- Most brightly colored
- Moving rather than still
- Most distinctive (standing out from the background)
- Present rather than absent
- Known first hand rather than second hand
- Said in the active rather than the passive voice

Things most easily remembered

- Most tinged with feeling
- Most familiar
- Most typical
- Associated with what is already on our minds

Most emphatic things, not only most easily noticed, but also most easily remembered

- Most concrete, least abstract
- Pictures rather than words
- Most desirable
- Most dangerous
- Most personal

Patterns most easily configured

- Simplest explanations
- Closest match of
    - Origin to outcome
    - Antecedent to consequent
    - Cause to effect
- Personal character of the actor rather than the situation of the scene

deliberately listed women who were fairly famous but men who were not so famous. The subjects were asked whether the list contained the names of more men or more women. They replied "more women." They had previously heard the names of the more famous women more often than those of the less famous men.

Again, subjects judged that the letter "r" turned up more often as the first letter of a word (as in *red*) than as the third letter (as in *sprint*). In fact, it is the other way around; but the subjects were students who often looked up things in dictionaries, encyclopedias, indexes—and there they almost always were looking for the first letter of a word rather than for the third.

Nisbett and Ross give two anecdotes of this bias from everyday life. These take the form that the blunderer gives as much weight to a few salient instances as to a great many pallid ones. Thus we are told that members of Congress will give as much weight to the first-hand report of a single neighbor about the mileage he gets on his Ford or Chevy as to boring statistical tables and reports coming from the engineers who have carefully tested hundreds of cars. And we are told that Supreme Court Justices give as much heed to a few vivid case histories of the reactions of this or that criminal to the threat of capital punishment as they do to the reports of hundreds or even thousands of cases of murder—again presented in boring, pallid statistical tables and reports.

Nisbett and Ross review many other experiments showing this counting bias—this general tendency to judge how common or likely a thing is by its salience, instead of by a count of occurrences. For example:

Experimental subjects thought there were more people over six feet tall (183 centimeters) on a list of names and heights with many people over six feet, eight inches (203 centimeters) than there were on another list with exactly the same number of six-footers, but none over six feet, two inches (188 centimeters). Subjects estimated that deaths from fire are more frequent than deaths from drowning, and accidental deaths more frequent than deaths from stroke; in fact, it is decidedly the other way about, but fires and accidents get more play in the media than drownings and strokes. Subjects tended to consider behavior more frequent if it was more like their own, and less frequent if it was less like their own. But people tend to associate with others having like habits and tastes, and so see more of their own kind of people.

Then there is the halo effect—so familiar to academics: Across a wide variety of activities, subjects overestimate the importance of their own contributions. In a formal study of a sample of ten American university departments, department chairmen tended to rate the prominence of their own department unduly high— though they were reasonably good judges of the prestige of other departments in their discipline. They overestimated the importance of the behavior they saw the most of.

The matching bias. Even more widespread and devastating in its practical effects than the counting bias is the matching bias. This is the so-called *representativeness* heuristic—the tendency of the mind to form a mental pattern. The human mind loves to jump to conclusions, to find the class by matching a salient feature of the class to a salient feature of the item, to find the origin or antecedent or cause by matching a salient feature of that to a salient feature of the supposed outcome or consequent or effect.

Thus whales are called fish because they have fishlike fins and tails. Thus not only experimental subjects but also practicing clinical psychologists tend to link certain suggestive responses in the famous Rohrschach ink-blot test to homosexuality even though, in fact, there is no connection. For example, if in a certain ink-blot a male patient sees women's clothing, clinical psychologists and experimental subjects alike consider this a sign of homosexual leanings, though in fact it is no such thing. Thus the Azande think that fowl droppings are a cure for ringworm because the two look alike; thus not so many years ago, European doctors thought turmeric a cure for jaundice because the tell-tale symptom of jaundice is the skin color turning yellow, while turmeric, too, is a bright yellow.

And thus experimental subjects explain behavior as the result of the *situation* when they cannot see the actors in a staged scene—but explain exactly the same behavior as the result of the personal qualities of the *actors* when they *can* see them.

In the studies they reviewed, Nisbett and Ross show that this matching bias turns up in all sorts of other subtle and intricate ways. The general principle is that the more salient but less relevant feature of the situation tends to be seized upon at the expense of the less salient but more relevant—and this despite the fact that the mind is indeed well aware of both. Never mind base rate, never mind proportions, never mind the important things that did *not* happen; just match the salient effect or outcome with the salient feature of the antecedent situation to find the cause or source.

The latching bias. Neither the counting bias nor the matching bias, I submit, has nearly the devastating effect on human affairs as the latching bias. Nisbett and Ross show that once the jaws of the mental idea trap close on an idea, it takes great power to release it. Once an intuitive paradigm is set to solve a problem, that paradigm will be followed, despite glaring evidence that it does not work. New evidence bearing on a point already decided tends to firm up the decision, no matter which way that evidence goes. The mind wants to stick to first impressions, no matter what comes later, to hang onto old theories, even if it turns out they were adopted on bad evidence.

After showing the great strength of intuitive paradigms in experiments with rats, cats, dogs, and pigeons, Nisbett and Ross review two similar—if not so blatant—results with people. In one experiment, subjects drew cards from a deck in competition with another person. Now obviously, the shrewdness or stupidity of the opponent could have nothing to do with the outcome. Yet consistently, subjects would bet more money on the outcome if they were playing against an actor behaving stupidly than if they were playing against an actor exuding an air of confidence and skill. Again, in another experiment, people were sold lottery tickets for one dollar each. Some were simply handed a ticket from the stack; others were allowed to take their pick. Just before the lottery, the experimenters bought the tickets back from the subjects. Those who had been given no choice sold them for an average of only $1.96, while those who had been allowed to take their pick held out for an average of $8.67—more than four times as much.

People are following intuitive strategies here that usually work well elsewhere in situations where they now obviously do not fit. Usually it makes sense to have more confidence when playing against a fool than when playing against a self-confident person—but not when all you are doing is cutting cards. Usually it makes sense to have more confidence in an outcome when you play some part in controlling it than when you are a mere helpless spectator—but not when all you are doing is picking out a lottery ticket. "Don't confuse me with facts, my mind's made up."

Controlled experiments with student subjects showed time and again that people tend to stick to first impressions, no matter what comes later. An early classic experiment by Asch was replicated and confirmed by many later investigators. Asch asked two groups of subjects to evaluate a John Smith. Asch told Group One that John was an intelligent, industrious, impulsive, critical, stubborn, and envious man—all these things. Asch told Group Two that John was an envious, stubborn, critical, impulsive, industrious, and intelligent man—the same things, but told in reverse order. Group One liked John better than Group Two did. "Don't confuse me with facts, my mind's made up."

In like manner, other experimental subjects watching a target person solve multiple-choice questions rated him higher if he did well at first but poorly thereafter, than if he did poorly at first but well thereafter—even though both targets ended up getting exactly half the questions right, half wrong. "Don't confuse me with facts, my mind's made up."

An even stronger test of the firmness of first impressions came in the "fire fighter" experiment. There were two groups of subjects: both were given two and only two alleged "case reports" (fictions invented by the experimenters) linking supposed results of a paper-and-pencil "risk preference" test to later success as a fire fighter. One group was thus induced to believe that risk takers make good fire fighters; the other group was thus induced to believe that they make poor ones. The experimenters then showed their hands. They told the subjects that they were but one of two groups and that the other group had been in like manner told exactly the contrary. That it was all pretense and sham. No matter. After hearing how they had been tricked, each group persisted in maintaining its opposite opinion about risk taking and fire fighters. "Don't confuse me with facts, my mind's made up."

Two groups of Stanford students were selected according to their previous views on capital punishment. One group was in favor of executing murderers; the other group was against doing so. Both groups were given exactly the same pair of purported "studies" on the effectiveness of this policy. The two "studies" were of quite different research design and yielded opposite results. Each group thought the study whose outcome favored their previous views was the better research design. Other groups were given only one study. If it favored their views, they reported them strengthened; but if it opposed their views, they reported little or no change.

I do not have nearly enough space for all of the evidence in Nisbett and Ross on the latching bias—and they in turn present but a sampling of the evidence they have seen. "There is a rich research literature," they say,

> that shows the operation of a variety of encoding and decoding biases that favor confirmation of prior hypotheses or beliefs over disconformation. There is good evidence, for instance, that people tend to recognize the *relevance* of confirming cases more readily than that of disconfirming ones, and therefore tend to *search for* such cases in evaluating their hypotheses.

These three biases alone—the counting bias, the matching bias, and the latching bias—are enough to explain the well-settled fact that crude and oversimplified statistical or actuarial formulas tend to predict the future better than do experts, with all their vast scope of intuitive understanding and feeling for the whole patterns. Nisbett and Ross cite study after study showing how badly predictions based on expert judgments fare. Clinical psychologists predicting patient recovery, stockbrokers predicting the growth of corporations, college admissions officers predicting the performance of students, personnel managers predicting the success of people they hire—all these experts do worse by following their judgments than by following the scores on a few attributes known to be associated with outcomes.

4.5.2   Research Methods and Strategies

The great merit of any scientific method is that by imposing a formal discipline, it controls these natural human mental biases and forces the mind to look beyond the salient to the hidden or merely unnoticed governing pattern or system. Table 4.2 sets forth a checklist of methods of inference that social scientists have developed. These methods systematically protect the social scientist from the most common sources of salience bias. It is the task of socionomics to review theory tests with those human mental biases and these scientific safeguards clearly in mind. It seems to me that most social scientists, thinking about research strategy, are strongly sensitive to the strengths of their own usual research strategy and to the weaknesses of all others. My own bias here, of course, favors the hologeistic strategy—the testing of theories by means of worldwide correlations. But in this section, and indeed throughout this book, I shall be arguing for the triangulation approach (also called universalist or multiple strategy). In Part Two of this book I offer evidence in support of it. The leading proponents of that approach have been Donald T. Campbell, Quincy Wright, Richard Snyder, David C. McClelland, and Ronald Rohner. We hold that usually no one research strategy is good enough to test a social science theory. The socionomist who examines a social science theory needs to look for tests of that theory in three or four varying research strategies. For as I shall presently show, each strategy has serious flaws—but the several strategies dovetail, with the strengths of one covering the weaknesses of another.

In the best of all possible worlds, the realms of systematic scientific study of human affairs would be neatly distributed both by topic and research strategy among the several social science disciplines. In fact, social science is not managed. It tends to be governed in its interests and efforts and concentrations by fads and fashions. Donald T. Campbell's classic paper on the fish-scale model of specialization at once presents a clear statement of the problem and offers a hypothetical but seldom-followed solution.

The problem is that every major discipline tends to be dominated by a small number of research microparadigms. Each such paradigm selects a small problem—commonly a worthy one—and attacks it by a particular method—commonly a useful one. Six or twelve of these microparadigms constitute what, in effect, almost everyone in the discipline is doing. Major professors training new doctoral candidates tend to produce replications of themselves who study the same problem with the same methods.

TABLE 4.2   Behavioral Science Research Methods*

Description: Object—Pattern

- ● Primary Observation
  - — Journalistic reporting of participant observation
  - — Geographical mapping
  - — Archeological digging
  - — Artifact collecting
  - — Structured reconnaissance
    - • Observational checklist
    - • Formal interview
    - • Questionnaire
    - • Experiment
- ● Secondary Description
  - — Literary scholarship
    - • Bibliography
    - • Source criticism
  - — Compilations of structured interviews
  - — Structured collections (e.g., *Ethnographic Atlas*)

Analysis: Object—Control

- ● Forms of Inquiry
  - — Seek the salient (literary essays)
  - — Formal modeling
    - • Functional
    - • Structural
    - • Mathematical
    - • Statistical
  - — Control Variables
    - • Rival causes in the real world
    - • Observational biases
    - • Inferential biases
    - • Proxy measures
- ● Forms of Inference
  - — Formal logic
    - • Syllogisms
    - • Mathematics
    - • Symbolic logic (including Boolean algebra)
  - — Statistical counting
    - • Case definition
    - • Variable (trait) definition
  - — Statistical inference
    - • Sampling bias control
    - • Independence of cases
    - • Stratification
  - — Control design
    - • Informal trial
    - • Formal experiment
    - • Formal quasi-experiment
      - — Matrix analysis
      - — Synchronic designs
      - — Diachronic designs

(continued)

TABLE 4.2 (Continued)

- Cross-cultural comparison
  - Problems of field research
    - Entree
    - Rapport
    - Context familiarity
  - Problems of comparative study
    - Emic-etic-theoric conceptualization
    - Emic equivalence
- Historical inference
  - Archeology
  - Diffusion: age and area
  - Holocultural worldwide evolution

Quality Control: Object–Checking

- Confrontational Stance
  - Should be tentative
  - Experiment or study should permit clear discredit as well as clear support
  - Series of studies as a whole should do likewise
- Data Quality Control
  - Check for systematic error
  - Check for random error
  - Check for independent replication
  - Check secondary works for page citations as vouchers
- Check for Cross-Cultural Validity
  - Modes of cross-cultural research
    - Restricted
      - Concomitant variation
      - Cross-cultural psychology
    - Hologeistic
      - Holocultural
      - Holonational
      - Others
- Triangulation

---

*Methods to be used separately or in almost any combination. See Glossary for definitions of terms.

Consequently, only a few of the leading problems in each social science get systematic attention. Consider, for example, the problem of the rise and fall of civilization. Its study is frowned on by professional historians because they are expected to specialize in particular periods of particular cultures, using literary methods. A few sociologists, anthropologists, or social psychologists have worked on it, but nowhere is it considered a proper focus of concern.

I do not have space here to survey the present and past fashions of the several social science disciplines, nor to review the technical problems that the elements of social science research methods set forth in Table 4.2 are designed to solve. However, in the Notes to this section there is a bibliography of some of the leading surveys of social science research methods. I review here thirteen

TABLE 4.3   Some Research Strategy Tradeoffs

		Strategies		
Tradeoffs	*Essay*	*Sample Survey*	*Archival Analysis*	*Formal Experiment*
(1) Pinpointing Causes	bad	fair	good	very good
(2) Persuasiveness	bad	fair	fair	good
(3) Scope	good	bad	fair to good	bad
(4) Unobtrusiveness	good	fair	good	bad to very bad
(5) Quality Control	bad	good	good	good
(6) Payoff per Work Hour	good	fair to bad	fair to bad	fair to bad
(7) Objectivity in Description	bad	good	good	good
(8) Objectivity in Analysis	bad	good	good	good
(9) Sensitivity	fair	good	bad	good
(10) Accuracy	bad	fair	fair	good
(11) Relevance	good	good	bad	fair
(12) Galton's Problem	bad	fair	good	fair
(13) Peculiarities	salience bias	equivalence problem	unit definition	Hawthorne effect

leading task dimensions and contrast the strengths and weaknesses of the four chief social science research traditions with respect to each of these. All I have space enough to offer are some illustrative contrasts. To survey the subject adequately would require another book at least as long as this one.

Table 4.3 sums up the chief strengths and weaknesses of the four chief research strategies. The *essay* is the characteristic strategy of the humanist tradition; the *sample survey*, the *archival analysis*, and the *formal experiment* constitute the three chief modes of the behavioral science tradition. The essay is a literary discussion of a problem. It becomes a social science research method when the author systematically but informally collects evidence supporting the views he argues. Essays are completely in the grip of all three major salience baises. These biases explain why two investigators writing about the same body of data so often reach contradictory findings. Behavioral scientists, too, write essays. This book is an essay, as are almost all other *reviews* of research using the three behavioral science strategies. Only a few, such as the THINCS studies described in Chapter 5, are reviews that are *themselves* controlled archival analyses.

Some essayists systematically try to resist the effects of the three salience biases by consciously seeking all evidence bearing on their problem—evidence tending to discredit the theory they are arguing, as well as that tending to support it. I began this present book over ten years ago, without any theoretical model for Part Two. The weakened moralnet model that now dominates it emerged by itself from the theory tests I reviewed. I did search for evidence supporting causes of social ills other than weakened moralnets. But ever since the weakened moralnets model took shape in my mind I certainly have been biased in its favor. Hence, this work remains an essay.

A well-done *sample survey*, in contrast, systematically controls for salience biases of all three kinds. By a sample survey I mean a social science description or theory test that takes its data from a structured oral or written interview. A well-done survey controls for bias in the selection of people to be interviewed through formal probability sampling methods, for matching bias by formal correlations, for salience biases in the minds of the interviewees through questions specially designed to that end. And it controls for latching bias (1) by using "naive" interviewers—those unaware of the theory being tested; (2) by wording the interview protocol in such a way as not to suggest a particular answer; and (3) by counting the responses through formal tallying— nowadays usually done by a computer. The power of the sample survey to overcome salience bias is attested by its wide use today in politics and industry to determine the state of public opinion.

Archival analyses are as able as sample surveys to control for salience bias. By an archival analysis I mean a social science description or theory test that takes its data from some body of written literature. Examples include studies of census data, studies drawing on existing archives of sample surveys, hologeistic studies (including holocultural, holonational, and holohistorical studies—see glossary), and THINCS theory test reviews. While sample surveys are primary sources, archival analyses are secondary sources. A well-done archival analysis controls for bias by some kind of formal protocol in the selection of sources to be analyzed. One example: the Probability Sample of the Human Relations Area Files. It controls for counting bias in specific data by a code book—a document that plays the part of an interview schedule or a questionnaire. It controls for matching and latching biases in the same way as a sample survey—through correlations for matching bias and use of naive coders for latching bias.

A *formal experiment* in social science divides its human subjects into at least two groups, each of which receives a different treatment. By manipulating the contrasting treatments, a successful formal experiment causes contrasting responses in its subjects. In Section 4.5.1, I reviewed a set of formal experiments to detect salience biases. The controls for experimenter and subject bias in well-conducted formal experiments are similar to those in sample surveys and archival analyses.

Table 4.3, then, sets forth the tradeoffs among the thirteen task dimensions for each of the four research strategies:

Task 1: Pinpointing Cause

Literary description, I hold, whether of historical periods or of ethnographic scenes, is powerless to solve any but the most trivial and obvious problems of causal analysis. The functional analyses of anthropologists like Radcliffe-Brown and Malinowski are but speculations. The great stumbling block for analyzing the causal factors in any given historical period or any single culture at a single point in time is that everything is linked to everything else. There is no way to disentangle relevant factors from irrelevant ones.

In this respect sample surveys and archival studies offer a power of causal analysis of intermediate strength. True, correlations do not show causal direction and may merely reflect the common influence of some third "lurking" variable. But in hologeistic studies, with survey traits objectively coded from worldwide samples of cultures at all levels of development, irrelevant variables can be expected to drop out, to be uncorrelated. And in contrast to sample surveys within a given country, a far wider range of variation in the relevant variables can be expected. Sequence can be studied to see if supposed causes tended to precede supposed effects. Further, certain kinds of multivariate analysis often permit inferences about causal direction.

However, formal experiments directly test cause/effect theories by directly controlling the supposed cause and then looking to see if the supposed effect responds as the theory expects. This great power is their chief virtue. And it is a great virtue. For only through understanding causality can we attain control.

Task 2: Persuasiveness

I mean by persuasiveness the ability to resolve disputes and so produce consensus. Essays, being cast in the most salient images and structures, may superficially seem persuasive on first reading. But a group of scholars reading essays of opposite views in a dispute are likely to form into rival schools of thought rather than to reach consensus. Quasi-experimental studies (sample surveys and archival analyses), because of their controls on salience biases, are likely to accumulate results in a single direction and so in time to lead, if slowly and painfully, to agreement. For example, I expect the quasi-experimental studies in Part Two of this book—so numerous and so harmonious—to produce consensus on the theory that weakened moralnets are one frequent cause of social ills. Nevertheless, because they rely chiefly on correlations and are subject to plausible rival theories, quasi-experiments are far slower and weaker than true formal experiments in producing consensus.

Conceding this, however, it is well to remember that until the first artificial satellite, the "sputnik," was put into orbit, there was never any *experimental* evidence for the soundness of the Copernican theory of the solar system. Nor is there today any experimental evidence that tobacco smoking causes cancer. Nor any experimental evidence for the "big bang" theory of the universe, nor for the evolution of species. All these theories have gained acceptance the more slowly because they lacked direct experimental evidence, yet all prevail in their respective sciences today.

Task 3: Scope

Few social science theories explain as much as 80 or 90 percent of the variance in the effects they study. For most theory tests, to explain 25 percent of the variance is useful; to explain 50 percent is impressive. And all this without considering whether the causal direction linking supposed causes with the supposed effect is properly understood. Hence, literary description of the historical, ethnographic, political, economic, social, or cultural scene remains a vital component of socionomics. For such a description ranges over the entire scene, free of the blinders of rigorous research design. If through academic freedom a wide variety of people with a wide variety of viewpoints exchange comments, we can hope to discern neglected variables—neglected because of the latching biases of the social scientists.

Archival research, too, enjoys a broad scope. Only through archival research can theories about the general course of human history be rigorously tested. Look at the cycle of the rise and fall of empires; that takes on the average about 200 years. Look at the rise of civilization from its origins in hunting and gathering bands; that has so far taken about 10,000 years, and is still going on; it can only be studied by the archival comparisons of archeological and ethnographic reports. Look at the intermittent bursts of intellectual and artistic creativity in which the greatest achievements of the human mind occur. These bursts, these "florescences" as Kroeber calls them, take generations to form and they occur at intervals of centuries—we are in one now. They can only be studied by comparative archival studies. Look at Sorokin's work on the frequency of foreign and civil wars. These too, vary greatly in intensity over cycles that last for centuries; such cycles exist; they can only be studied archivally.

Task 4: Unobtrusiveness

Social science research is about people. But people need privacy; and people have rights. Even such innocent experiments as those on salience bias have been attacked as unethical because they can leave permanent imprints on the minds of their subjects. Remember, for example, how the Stanford experiments on attitudes toward capital punishment strengthened and deepened the subjects' preexisting views. At the other extreme, experiments on whole societies shock the conscience of every decent human being—as, for example, the Nazi experiments on improving the breed of mankind by slaughtering millions of Jews and Slavs, the Stalinist experiments on agricultural production that killed off other millions, and Pol Pot's experiments on redesigning Cambodian society that killed off 10 or 20 percent of its people.

With horrors like these in mind, we see how sharply ethics must hedge the use of formal experiments to test broad political, economic, and social theories. Whenever human subjects are put in any way at risk of harm, ethics forbids experiments—unless the subjects freely consent. The ancient Hippocratic code of medical ethics begins in effect by commanding: "First of all, do no harm." Risky experiments contravene the core value of brotherhood that today forms part of the moral consensus of mankind.

Sample surveys are far less obtrusive. After all, respondents annoyed by a mailed questionnaire can always throw it into the wastebasket and a too-prying interviewer can be put off with quick and superficial fibs. Still, there is a limit to the patience of the public.

Library books and museum collections, however, are infinitely patient. They never get annoyed at being looked at or questioned; reading or viewing them does no one harm.

Task 5: Quality Control

Every research strategy is full of scientific risks—traps and inherent biases that tend to lead the unwary investigator into error. The great strength of the three behavioral science strategies is that they lend themselves to formal—if tedious and expensive—methods of controlling the work so as either to get rid of these biases entirely, or if not, then to measure and report them, as a warning.

For example, look at data error. What is a "fact"? And how do we know a fact is a fact? Classical methods of historical scholarship have ways to test the trustworthiness of sources: Compare a number of reports. Look at the internal plausibility of sources. Do they keep their stories straight? But while in this way traditional historians can indeed improve the quality of their facts, they have no comparable method of seeing whether systematic factual error nevertheless systematically biases their overall findings. Nor do they have any way of distinguishing random error—which merely tends to obscure all patterns—from systematic error—which often tends, rather, to create false patterns, ghosts that can lead us into the darkness. In contrast, sample surveys and archival analysis alike have powerful methods for measuring systematic error—and so for exorcising these ghosts—as well as other methods for measuring random error. And not only can formal experimenters use like methods to measure error, but to a considerable extent they can also cancel out the effects of any error by randomly assigning treatments to subjects. What holds true for data error also hold true for sampling error and for errors in classification and coding by the observers.

But you may ask why historians, for example, could not use like methods to control *their* work. They could, of course, and some are already beginning to do so. But historians who use formal sampling methods to select their data and formal quality controls to measure their error are no longer essayists; they have transformed themselves into archival analysts.

Task 6: Payoff per Work Hour

Here the problem is to test theories as quickly and cheaply as possible. The elaborate apparatus of behavioral science theory testing needed to rule out common sources of error is expensive. It raises the cost of theory testing. Here the use of archival correlations often permits quick and fairly objective theory tests. (I list in the notes some common sources of archival data.) Such tests are, of course, but tentative. If successful, they warrant more expensive, less cost effective but less risky studies. Cost effectiveness reaches its nadir for many socionomic problems in the controlled experiment. Where the supposed cause is a public policy that involves much of the society, one that needs hundreds of years to work its full effects and whose cost of error is paid in the blood, sweat, toil, and tears of millions of suffering people—then for most of us, controlled experiments on such a policy cost too much for us to stomach.

In most behavioral science research there is a sharp tradeoff between quality control and cost effectiveness. The stricter the quality control, the more costly the study. However, archival research using precoded or partly precoded data can offer the best of both worlds. For example, the holoculturalists using the Probability Sample of the Human Relations Area Files (HRAF) and its HRAFLIB set of computer programs can run many strict quality controls for trifling costs—because the controls have already been built into the data archive and punched onto the computer cards. The investigator also may make use of a large number of precoded variables and so may need to add only a few new ones.

Task 7: Objectivity of Description

Here the problem is to observe and record significant information without regard to the salience of the events observed or the latched biases of the observer. Consider, for example, a historian—who disclaims as unattainable any attempt at objectivity—wishing to show that Hitler was (or was not) the chief cause of World War II. Here we have literary description at its worst. However well trained and however sincere and honest, such a historian chiefly tends to notice and to present data that are salient because they fit his thesis; such a work suffers severely from the latching bias. Historians who, on the contrary, try to be objective still suffer substantially from such a bias. It is not good intentions such historians lack; it is a systematic and unbiased method for selecting relevant data.

The other extreme in objectivity is to be found in formal experiments or in archival analyses or sample surveys, where the data are collected and coded by naive coders who are purposely kept ignorant of the theory being tested by the study. Here their attention is directed by their protocol—questionnaire, code book, or experimental plan—to the data relevant to the theory being tested; but they are given no cues as to what sorts of results are expected or hoped for by the director of research. True, the protocol directs their attention exclusively to the elements of behavior that the director supposes are relevant to the problem. The remedy for *that* bias is to encourage a large number of independent studies of the problem by a wide variety of investigators.

Furthermore, there are overall research strategies that will reveal the failure of an investigator to look at all relevant variables. Consider a multiple correlation design; assume that we know the direction of cause and effect between the independent and dependent variables. Then the multiple correlation measures the total amount of variance explained and the total amount not explained. Further, research directed at eliciting regular patterns—if it considers all relevant variables—can lead to substantially accurate prediction. Research aimed at some practical problem in controlling human affairs—if it does its job properly—should lead to successful control of the problem. Failures of prediction and control show that some relevant variable has been overlooked. Hence the director's bias in the selection of variables for observation, too, is ultimately subject to control.

Task 8: Objectivity of Analysis

Humanistic historians arrange their material according to the salience of the patterns that attract their attention. And these patterns, in turn, are wide open to the three salience biases: the counting, matching, and latching biases. No wonder, then, that humanistic historians so often disagree on their analysis of the same body of data. Formal statistical tests, accompanied by the safeguards listed in Table 4.2, are the best protection the human mind now has against these salience biases. The behavioral science approach then—whether through sample survey, archival analysis, or formal experiment—has as a main strength its relative freedom from salience bias in analysis.

Task 9: Sensitivity

By sensitivity I mean the ability of a method to detect fine shadings of variation in the things it observes. Here sample surveys and controlled experiments are strong. Ingenious investigators have often shown how able they are to elicit subtle responses from human subjects, or from hungry rats running experimental mazes, for that matter. Perceptive essayists are less able to make fine distinctions here, because they do not control in any way the behavior of their subjects; but they are free to look widely at freshly observed scenes. Archival analysis, in contrast, must somehow make do with whatever information comes to hand, must often use proxy measures to estimate crudely what a sample survey or an experiment can measure exactly.

Task 10: Accuracy

The conditions are most conducive for accurate observation, free from random or systematic error, in the formal experiment. As I remarked earlier, all three behavioral science strategies can use systematic quality control to detect and measure error; but formal experiments can reduce systematic error or even get rid of it entirely by randomly assigning treatments to subjects. In contrast, the methods of source criticism open to traditional humanistic scholarship apply chiefly to particular observations and do not generalize to the conclusions reached by a set of observations.

Task 11: Relevance

Pure science is not concerned with relevance. To a pure scientist, the anatomy of a flea is as interesting and important as the anatomy of a human being. But, as Senator Proxmire reminds us, the more relevant a social science research problem is to the interests and needs of the public, the more likely is the study of that problem to get attention by students and finance committees. On the score of relevance, I submit, essays can most easily and directly point a study in the direction of public interest. Sample surveys, too, can readily address such topics. Formal experiments are more severely restricted. Archival analysis by its nature deals with information that is at best out of date and often is about that which is not only long ago but also far away.

Task 12: Galton's Problem

The few people who have ever heard of Galton's Problem think of it as a technical difficulty in hologeistic research, but it needs to concern all social scientists. It arose as a counting problem, a problem of independence of cases in statistical analysis. In 1889, at a now famous meeting of the Anthropological Institute in London, Edward Tylor read a paper about avoidance practices. He looked at some 350 small-scale societies to test a theory of the relationship between avoidance practices and rules of descent. But in the discussion that followed, Francis Galton asked about Tylor's counts. How many of these tribes constituted independent trials of Tylor's theory? Did not the spread of culture through borrowing and migration confound his statistics by reduplicating the same customs many times on his list?

I submit that the problem is more general than mere statistical analysis. The problem gets at the broad tendency of culture patterns to spread, and at the wide ramifications of influence among superficially unrelated culture traits. Who would have supposed, for example, that John Calvin's theology of predestination might well have had a great deal to do with the industrial revolution in England if Tawney had not pointed out the possible connection?

Clearly, then, the repeated association of supposed cause with supposed effect in society after society, country after country, family after family, or person after person *may* only reflect the joint spread of two culture traits from a common source. That source can be an ancient and widespread cultural tradition, or a more recent and narrow religious cult, or a style of living like that of seventeenth-century Paris or twentieth-century America.

This possible confounding effect, I submit, might well be the more dangerous and subtle if it took the form of a catalyst. Trait A may indeed cause Trait B, but only in the presence of the widely diffused Trait C. So far, only hologeists have developed formal methods of controlling for Galton's Problem—that is, of directly measuring the influence of cultural diffusion on the relationship between other variables. In sample surveys and formal experiments, the investigators, in effect, seek to control for Galton's Problem when they try to measure or stratify by or randomize the influence of such frequent sources of common cultural background as social class or birthplace or native language. However, when all the subjects of an experiment or all the respondents of a survey belong to the same cultural tradition—and that tradition is shared by the scientists themselves—the biases and distortions of a common culture are likely to go undetected.

The wider the variety of cultures studied, the less likely are they to reflect a common cultural catalyst. And the easier it is to measure diffusion *in general* by means of autocorrelations. Archival analysis, then, is the method par excellence for coping with Galton's Problem. Cross-cultural replication of sample surveys or formal experiments also offers protection. In contrast, essayists usually ignore this problem entirely, but even if aware of it, lack any means to cope with the counting bias that Galton's Problem imposes on the undisciplined mind.

Task 13: Strategic Peculiarities

By strategic peculiarities I mean problems peculiar to one of the four chief strategies. Each has its own special weakness, from which the others are free.

Essays are grievously subject to all three salience biases, as I have already said many times.

Sample surveys that move from one culture to another—or even from the middle-class academic subculture to other subcultures of the scientists' own society—suffer from the problem of equivalence in concepts. One way or another, the result of the survey depends on its respondents all answering the same question. The survey depends on all respondents understanding that question in the same way. But questions must be framed in words; they must be put in emic terms. And emics vary drastically from culture to culture. As we have seen, you cannot ask a Navajo woman straightforwardly whether she prefers a blue skirt or a green one, because both colors are *dotlish* in Navajo. And *democratic* means something very different in Russian from what it means in English. (Hologeistic archival studies avoid this problem entirely by working with theoric concepts, as I explained in Chapter 2.) Campbell and LeVine once sought to translate a questionnaire on ethnocentrism into a hundred different languages, mostly languages of small-scale societies chosen the world around. They sought to check the solutions to the equivalence problem by back translation. They had plenty of money to pay for this kind of work. But the task proved too difficult; they gave up at last.

Comparative archival analysts often face special problems in defining their units of study. This problem is acute, for example, in trying to fix the boundaries of many cultures. The most commonly used delimiter is language; but languages often fade and blur into one another like the colors of a rainbow. Among peasant dialects, for example, there is no real boundary between German and Dutch, or between Italian and French, or between Spanish and Portuguese. But anthropologists are far from agreeing that language is the best delimiter. Some would rather use political systems, or economic adaptations, or religion, or historical tradition. And so it goes.

In formal experiments, the peculiar problem is the so-called Hawthorne effect. By that I mean the special effect of the experimental setting on the work of employees chosen as subjects. The experts speak of the startling things that happened in Chicago at the Hawthorne plant of the Western Electric Company between April 1927 and June 1929. Industrial psychologists there were trying to measure experimentally the effects of varying work tempos: changes in rest periods and length of work day and work week. They set up a special work group of five women to assemble electrical relays. These women previously had been working in a large factory room, part of a group of a hundred women whose pay had depended on the output of the entire hundred. Now they were formed into a special group of only five women. Some were friends already. They now were given much special attention, both by experimenters and by higher management. After hours, they sometimes met at parties they themselves planned. Furthermore, their pay now depended only on the output of the five alone. They formed into a tightly knit work team and their output rose dramatically—no matter what the experimenters did to their rest periods and work schedules. The scientists were puzzled at this rise. Only after the experiment was over did the scientists realize how badly they had designed their study. Only then did they realize how much these other factors had affected the issue. The setting of the experiment itself had affected the result far more than the variables the experimenters thought they were testing. We have here a clear analogy to the problem of the placebo effect in medical experiments. Tell the patients you are giving them a new experimental drug and some of them will, in fact, benefit, even if that drug is nothing but a sugar pill. The Hawthorne effect, like the placebo effect, is good for the subjects but bad for the experimenter.

4.5.3   A Theory Trust Meter

In Part Two of this book I try to make a formal estimate of the doubt/trust ratio on the tests of some leading theories about moralnets by using a Theory Trust Meter. This meter is but a rough and crude measure—it is objective, but it is not unbiased in its design and it is not very sensitive. Still, I think it does help contrast theories that have fairly wide support through multiple strategies with those that have only narrow support. Theories that do better than 50 percent by this meter, I suggest, are among the more trustworthy theories of behavioral science.

See, for example, Figure 9.1; the doubt/trust ratio theory being measured is: "Loss of or damage to moralnet links tends to cause suicide." The trust ratio here is 47 percent. That ratio, I repeat, must not be taken too seriously—it is but a rough-and-ready count. The meter primarily emphasizes causal analysis and scope. The three dials represent three successively more rigorous levels of causal analysis. The *association tests* show correlations; the *sequence tests* show correlations for which sequence has been established between the variables either by time lagging or by causal matrix analysis. Time lagging may be established either by experimental design—where the supposed effect is measured later, while the supposed cause is measured earlier—or it may be established by implication, as here for suicide: correlations between marital status and suicide count as sequence tests because the marital status, from the nature of things, must *precede* the suicide. Causal matrix analysis is a method by which a set of correlations among three or more variables can be analyzed to show that some of the variables seem more likely effects, while others seem more likely causes.

The *purpose tests* show the results of either formal controlled experiments or informal unstructured trials. Purpose tests are those in which the experimenters seek by their intervention to cause the desired effect to occur.

The four quadrants in which each dial is divided refer to four levels of scope. The upper left quadrant deals with archival tests that range over all known human cultures—holocultural studies. The upper right quadrant deals with archival or sample survey tests that range over a worldwide sample of at least ten modern nations. The lower left quadrant deals with sample survey, archival, or experimental tests that focus on a narrow sample of local communities or of individuals. The lower right quadrant deals with archival or sample survey tests that focus on the United States as a whole within the last generation. This last quadrant is intended to test the application of the theory to the author's own home culture, in order to measure relevance. People in other societies, of course, need to substitute a review of like tests on their own society for this lower right quadrant. (There is, for example, some reason to question whether the theory of Figure 9.1 holds good for Nigeria—though it clearly does for most other cultures around the world.)

Within each quadrant, I have classified the theory tests at hand into three classes.

Class I: Essays. Essays I have not counted at all; their lack of control over salience bias makes them useless as theory tests, though valuable often as theory proposers.

Class II: Weak Behavioral Science Tests. Nearly all studies in the upper two quadrants are archival tests; nearly all those in the lower two quadrants are sample surveys, formal experiments, or informal experimental trials (like Alcoholics Anonymous). I classify archival tests as weak if they do not use formal probability sampling, data quality control, and formal tests for Galton's Problem. I classify sample surveys as weak if they do not use formal probability sampling. (I would also have liked to check for formal data quality control, but found it impractical.) I class experiments as weak if they are informal trials rather than formal controlled experiments.

One weak test in any quadrant gets one pie slice. More than one weak test gets two pie slices.

Class III: Strong Behavioral Science Tests. This class then embraces formal controlled experiments, sample surveys using probability sampling, and archival tests using probability sampling, formal data quality control, and formal tests for Galton's Problem

One strong test in any quadrant gets two pie slices. So, for all three pie slices in a quadrant to be lightened, there must be at least two tests—at least one of them a strong test.

Furthermore, note that a purpose test is by that fact itself also a sequence test and an association test. So one weak purpose test gets one pie slice in each of three quadrants—counts triple that of a weak association test. Similarly, one strong sequence test gets two pie slices in each of the association and sequence dials—for a total of four.

In Figure 9.1, for example, we have one strong holocultural study (Naroll, 1969) and two weak ones (Krauss, 1966; Krauss and Krauss, 1968). These all count as sequence tests, because later suicides are linked with earlier weaknesses in social ties, and so the holocultural quadrant is all lightened for both sequence tests and association tests—giving us six pie slices. Durkheim (1951) counts as one weak sequence test; Dublin (1963) counts as one weak association test—weak because it is a correlation between suicide rates and homicide rates; and so we get a total of three pie slices in the holonational quadrant. A large group of strong social disruption studies—for example, Bolin et al. (1968); Breed (1963, 1967)—linking suicide with predisposing social factors, give us pie slices in the local/individual quadrant. Dublin's report of suicide rates among the divorced in the United States gives us one weak sequence test in the U. S. quadrant—for a total of 17 pie slices out of a possible 36, giving a theory test ratio of 47 percent.

4.6   STEP 4: FURTHER STUDIES OF THEORY TEST METHOD

In my view, the brightest prospect for behavioral science research method lies in reviewing the success or failure of practical applications of well-tested social science theories. Part Two of this book, for example, reviews the linkage between weakened moralnets and social ills. From this review, I believe, weakened moralnets emerge as one of the main causes of these social ills. In other words, if evil beings wished to further increase these ills, they could do so by further weakening moralnet ties. If instead, angels wished to decrease these ills, they could do so by strengthening moralnet ties. (Needless to say, however, I do not suppose that weakened moralnets are the *only* causes, nor do I suppose that sufficiently strengthening moralnet ties alone could rid us of these ills altogether.)

I find this theoretical model supported by a very large number of association tests, by a sprinkling of sequence tests, and by a few purpose tests. It seems to me that we need more purpose tests to pin down specific applications of this theory to specific social ills.

Controlled experiments might well help. But these experiments might require many years. And the experiments on social ills run into the Winnie Mae problem.

"Go right ahead, Winnie Mae," said the school superintendent to the teacher, who happened to be his cousin, "Just fix it up." "Just fix it up," meant just doctor the records, just cheat on the experiment.

So Winnie Mae moved four nonreaders and a fifth child who badly needed dental care into the Follow Through class from a control group class. In the Follow Through class the children would get special help. In the control classes they would not. Winnie Mae was not interested in testing theories of education. She was interested in helping children.

Perhaps, then, it might often be safer as well as more humane to institute sets of therapeutic programs and to monitor their successes. The principle of comparison between experimental and control groups might be loosely preserved by matching communities or such installations as mental hospitals and comparing, for example, the suicide rate in the programs with those in matched scenes that lack them. Would a program of artificial moralnets like Alcoholics Anonymous for those who had threatened or attempted suicide decrease the suicide rate among its participants?

Archival reviews of the reports of such therapeutic programs from many countries around the world might, then, constitute the most rigorous feasible test of the theory that weakened moralnets cause suicide and that strengthened moralnets tend to protect people from suicide. In this way applied science could feed back theory tests to pure social science.

4.7   STEP 5: COPING WITH THEORY TEST METHOD

Most social scientists, as I have said, tend to use but a single research strategy and to suffer more or less severe halo effect bias—being keenly aware of the strengths of the strategy they use and the weaknesses of the ones they do not use. However, a few leaders have long been urging the importance of applying a variety of strategies to the same problem. I mentioned Quincy Wright, David McClelland, and Ronald Rohner as making conspicuous use of the triangulation approach. (Rohner's work seems to me especially fruitful; I review it in detail in Chapter 11.)

Look once more at Table 4.3. I have just reviewed it, line by line. Does that table not show us that no one research strategy is enough? That usually, a test of any general theory by as many of these methods as possible is the ideal way?

Notes

4.1   Kamanga Takes a Bride

On the Azande poison oracle, I follow Evans-Pritchard (1937), Part Three, Chapter 1, especially p. 298. Personal names changed.
On the oracle of the "skipper next to God," see Hartog (1966: 537).
Polanyi (1970: 337-341) compares Azande faith in poison oracles and Western faith in science.
On the eighteenth-century introduction of Western medicine to Japan, see Sugita (1942).
On the use by physicists of two logically contradictory theories of the nature of light, see Swenson (1967: 669).

4.2   Behavioral Science in the World Today

On Tawney, see Johnson (1973).
On rigorous tests of Freud's theories, see Fisher and Greenberg (1977); also Silverman (1967, 1972, 1975a, 1975b, 1976) and Silverman, Bronstein, and Mendelsohn (1976).
For examples of their work as behavioral scientists, see Leeuwe (1970) and Naroll, Bullough, and Naroll (1974)—Bullough was chiefly responsible for the European studies in that latter work.
Kuhn (1962) on scientific revolutions presents the concept of a paradigm though not the contrasts between a mature and an immature paradigm I submit here.

4.3   Step 1: Core Values of Behavioral Science

My presentation of cybernetic epistemology derives from the model of the mind set forth in Section 6.2, from Jerison (1973: 17-25), from my earlier published views on stochastic epistemology (Naroll, 1973), and especially from Donald T. Campbell (1970, 1974) and Skagestad (1981) on epistemological naturalism.
On the infinite series, I follow Smail (1953: 461).
On control of perception, see Powers (1977).
On science as a natural selection process, see Campbell (1970).
On chance as negative cause and on chance versus assignable causes, see Duncan (1959: 316).
On cause/effect as a purposeful relationship, see Naroll (1964, 1968, 1976, 1980).
Hume (1961: Book I, Part III, Section 2): "Of probability, and on the idea of cause and effect." Russell (1945: 664-674) reviews Hume's thought and gives his own views. Rummel (1970a: 25) quotes Hume with approval, but presents measurement of association through factor analysis as a means of uncovering causes. Rummel specifically rejects as fuzzy such popular connotations of the term as "to bring about," "to produce an effect," or "to influence." Use of the servo model adds the servo goal—its reference signal—to the notions of sequence and association without loss of precision. Goals can be measured whenever variables can be: a goal is simply a stipulated desired state of the dependent variable.

Earlier discussion of the importance of purpose or goal in defining the cause/effect relationship include Naroll (1964: 690f., 1968: 245), Cohen and Naroll (1970: 5), Köbben (1970), and Burgers (1975).

I invite the reader to compare my treatment of the cause/effect relationship with that in Nisbett and Ross (1980: 113f.). Their six tests of a cause/effect relationship do not, in fact, distinguish events of potential control from mere associations; they all boil down to a high correlation from a representative sample of the universe. Notice, however, that the specific examples Nisbett and Ross give do tend to be situations in which not only sequence but also potential control is, in fact, present. I submit that though they do not realize it, they share the intuitive understanding of cause/effect as potential control that I here argue for.

On "statistical significance," see Morrison and Henkel (1971) and my review thereof (Naroll, 1971a). Ralph Gerard's dictum—a remark at the General Systems Seminar, Center for Advanced Study in the Behavioral Sciences, 1954-1955.

4.4   Step 2: Behavioral Science Scoreboards

On the measurement of cultural evolution, see Naroll (1970a: 1242ff.) and Levinson and Malone (1980: 31ff.). See Driver (1970, 1973) on cultural diffusion.

4.5.1   Intuition versus Science

In this entire section I follow Nisbett and Ross (1980). What I call the counting bias, they call the "availability heuristic"; what I call the "matching bias," they call the "representativeness heuristic"; and what I call the "latching bias," they call "theory maintenance." The two heuristic labels seem to have been bestowed by Kahneman and Tversky, to whom many of the more striking findings in this section are due.

Page	Key element of experiment	Experimenter(s)
74	Names of public figures	Kahneman and Tversky
19-23	First and third letters	Tversky and Kahneman
79f.	Congressmen and Justices	Undocumented anecdotes
74f.	Six-footers	Rothbart et al.
75	Deaths from fire, drowning, accident, and stroke	Slovic, Fischhoff, and Lichtenstein
76	Frequency of behavior like one's own	Ross, Greene, and House
—	Halo effect of over-estimating prominence of own departments	Caplow and McGee (1958: 103-105)
95f.	Rohrschachs and homosexuality	L. J. and J. P. Chapman
116	Azande and ringworm	Evans-Pritchard
116	Jaundice and turmeric	J. S. Mill (essay)
125	Situation versus personal qualities of actors	Taylor and Fiske
105	Rats, cats, dogs, pigeons	Garcia et al.; Seligman; Testa
135f.	Drawing cards	Langer
136	Lottery tickets	Langer
173	Intelligent . . . stubborn	Asch
185	Fire fighters	Anderson, Ross, and Lepper
170	Capital punishment	Lord, Ross, and Lepper

Nisbett and Ross (1980: 181) on the latching bias literature; they cite the review thereof by Wason and Johnson-Laird (1965).

Nisbett and Ross (1980: 140f.) on predictions of clinical psychologists, stockbrokers, college admissions officers, and personnel managers. They cite the literature reviews of Slovic and Lichtenstein (1971) and Dawes and Corrigan (1974).

Political scientists have recently been using these salience bias models to explain seemingly irrational behavior by political leaders. See Snyder and Diesing (1977), Jervis (1976), and Jungermann and Zeeuw (1977).

4.5.2 Research Methods and Strategies

The term "triangulation," of course, comes from navigation and from surveying—by taking a bearing on two or three distant objects you can locate yourself on the map. Conspicuous applications of triangulation include Wright (1942), McClelland (1961), Rohner (1975), and Rohner and Rohner (1980). Eloquent advocates include Snyder and Robinson (1961) and Campbell (1969).

Table 4.2: The Glossary contains definitions of all terms in this table not defined in the *American Heritage Dictionary of the English Language*. The term "matrix analysis" refers to the inference of causal direction from the study of a set of correlations, sometimes of repeated observations to measure change over time. On synchronic analysis (without passage of time) see Boudon (1967) and Blalock (1964). On diachronic analysis—especially the cross-lagged panel technique—see Kenny (1979).

On the fish-scale model, see Campbell (1969).

For a far more comprehensive review of general social science method than the brief sketch I offer here, see Bohrnstedt (1980) and especially McInnis and Scott (1975), who also offer an excellent bibliography of bibliographies.

For anthropology—Naroll and Cohen (1970) cover field and holocultural method. See also Schweizer (1978b), Brim and Spain (1972), Pelto (1970), and Naroll, Michick, and Naroll (1980).

For demography—Wolfenden (1954).

For economics—Theil (1971, 1978), Johnston (1972), and Malinvaud (1970).

For geography—McInnis and Scott (1975: 68-70) have a comprehensive bibliography.

For history—The classic exposition of classical historical method is reviewed from a behavioral science point of view in Naroll (1962a: 8ff.), and in Naroll, Bullough, and Naroll (1974: xli-xliii). As far as I know, nothing has superseded such works as Bernheim (1908), Langlois and Seignobos (1898), and Hockett (1955).

For political science—Przeworski and Teune (1970) and Gurr (1972).

For social psychology—Lindzey and Aronson (1968), Triandis et al. (1980), Cook and Campbell (1979), Rosenthal (1966).

For sociology—Etzioni and Dubow (1970), Miller (1977), Webb, Campbell, Schwartz, and Sechrest (1966), Cochran (1963), Parten (1950), United Nations, DESA (1972), Rossi and Freeman (1982).

For introductory statistics—Blalock (1972), Thomas (1976); for advanced statistical theory—Kendall and Stuart (1958).

From the point of view of Table 4.3, dividing research methods of behavioral science into essays, sample surveys, archival analysis and formal experiments:

For study methods compiling essays in history, see Langlois and Seignobos (1898), Bernheim (1908), and Hockett (1955). In ethnography, see Naroll and Cohen (1970: Parts III and IV).

For sample surveys, see the references under political science, social psychology, and sociology above.

For archival research, see Naroll and Cohen (1970: Parts IV-VII), Naroll, Bullough, and Naroll (1974), Naroll, Michik, and Naroll (1980), Gurr (1972), and the references above under demography, geography, and history.

For controlled experiments, see Rosenthal (1966), Lindzey and Aronson (1968: Vol. 2), and Brown and Sechrest (1980).

Miller (1977: 97-123) inventories data archives. The most useful collectanea are those of the Inter-University Consortium for Political and Social Research, and of the Human Relations Area Files. The headquarters of the former is at the University of Michigan; and the address of the latter is Box 2054, Yale Station, New Haven, CT 06520. The latter offers ethnographic primary sources on over 300 societies around the world; sets of this archive, either in paper or on microfilm, are found in more than 200 libraries and museums around the world. For demographic or cross-national research, the publications of the UN Department of Economic and Social Affairs are essential.

Tylor's classic (1889) paper, with Galton's comments, is reprinted in Moore (1961: 1-25).

For the equivalence problem in comparative emic studies, especially cross-cultural sample surveys, see Berry (1980).

On the Ethnocentrism project of Campbell and LeVine, see Campbell (1981: 476f.) I served briefly as a consultant on that project and received informal verbal progress reports from both Campbell and LeVine over the years.

On the Hawthorne effect, it is important to read the original report by Roethlisberger, Dickson, and Wright (1939) on the Relay Assembly Test Room. There seems to be a great deal of misleading mythology about this classic study among social scientists who only know it from the summaries of others. The key point is that, all unwittingly, these experimenters organized their subjects into a strong moralnet. The difficulty went far beyond the mere fact that those subjects knew they were taking part in an experiment.

4.5.3   A Theory Trust Meter

On the inferences of causal relationships from correlational matrices, see Boudon (1967), Blalock (1964), and Kenny (1979).
For documentation on Figure 9.1, see Chapter 9.

4.6   Step 4: Further Studies of Theory Test Method

On Winnie Mae and the Superintendent, see Travis (1976: 73).

5

Steps 4 and 5: Plan and Cope

5.1   FINLAY'S THEORY

"It is with a great deal of pleasure that I hasten to tell you that we have succeeded in producing a case of yellow fever by the bite of a mosquito." So wrote Major Walter Reed to his wife. Yellow fever was a killer. In the United States alone, during the 1700s and 1800s, it killed more than 100,000.

In 1898 the United States had an army in Cuba to fight the Spaniards. Yellow fever had hit again. Scientists were still arguing how yellow fever spread. Some said by the bedding and clothes of the sick people, by the contamination of their black vomit, or by their feces. Some said by contaminated baggage or merchandise. And some said by an insect. Carlos J. Finlay of Havana had been arguing since 1881 that it spread by a mosquito. Finlay said that the blood of an infected patient carried the infection inside the mosquito, and that infection was passed on to a healthy person when the mosquito bit again.

But Finlay offered little evidence, and that poor, to support his theory. He stated the theory well. But he supported it poorly, so hardly anyone took it seriously or tried to protect people against yellow fever by attacking the mosquitoes, which Finlay said were passing it on. Finlay suspected a type then called *Stegomyia fasciata*, a mosquito easy to spot from the four silvery stripes on its back.

Reed, a trained research scientist, was the army surgeon who knew most about fevers. And he thought Finlay was right. So Reed and Carroll, his assistant, set up what proved to be perhaps the most famous controlled experiment in all medical history. They built two frame houses, fourteen by twenty feet, exactly alike with certain purposeful exceptions. The windows and doors of both were thoroughly screened to keep mosquitoes *out* of one, and *in* the other. They set up a hospital camp around these houses; no one was permitted to enter or leave except three immune men who had already gotten the disease and so could not get it again or carry it in their bloodstream to infect others. No one would get yellow fever unless Walter Reed and his colleagues gave it to him, which they proceeded to try to do.

One of the huts was the stink hut. Only two tiny windows, purposely kept stuffy, with little fresh air. Furnished with sheets, pillowslips, and blankets lately soiled with the black vomit, urine, and feces of men in the throes of yellow fever.

Cooke, Folk, and Jernigan slept in that hut, in those bedclothes, for twenty nights. They stayed healthy.

The other hut was the clean hut. Plenty of fresh air through the screened windows, plenty of clean clothing and bedding. Five men stayed there. On December 5, 1900, at 2:00 P.M., five mosquitoes were allowed to bite John R. Kissinger. These five mosquitoes had all previously fed on a yellow fever patient—two of them 15 days previously; a third, 19 days; the other two, 22 days. Three days, nine and one-half hours later, about midnight, December 8, Kissinger came down with a chill that proved to be the beginning of a severe case of yellow fever. And the next day Reed wrote his wife that letter.

In 1900, there were 308 cases of yellow fever in Havana. In 1901, informed by Reed's work, they cleaned up the mosquitoes there. The next year, 1902, there was not a single case; these experiments led immediately to a determined fight against the Stegomyia mosquitoes. Further, all known yellow fever patients were kept in screened rooms, so that no mosquitoes could get at them.

In 1905 a yellow fever epidemic hit New Orleans and the health authorities went after the mosquitoes. In a few weeks they stopped that epidemic. Before Reed did his work, people knew that hot weather, soiled clothing and bedding, nearness to someone sick with yellow fever, and mosquitoes, all were linked with yellow fever. Reed's work showed that yellow fever was caused by the bite of an infected mosquito, not by the other things.

With Reed's information, yellow fever could be controlled by keeping Stegomyia mosquitoes away from people who had the disease. With a theory of cause and effect, properly tested, it was possible to set up a good social servo. And when that servo worked, it tested the cause/effect theory even further. Those who were still a little skeptical about Reed's work ceased to doubt after mosquito control stopped yellow fever in Havana, Laredo, and New Orleans.

Such dramatic successes in stopping mass killers brought the power of the new medical science forcefully to the eyes of the public. Nothing is more dramatic—more salient—than so sudden and sweeping a victory. Social scientists are not likely to walk so easy a path to public respect and support. Most of our findings lack the crispness and assurance of Reed's controlled experiments. Most of our practical applications lack the drama, suspense, conflict, excitement, and triumph of a successful battle against a yellow fever epidemic.

Our problem is communication, reaching the public with our message. And worse than that, reaching each other. The two tasks, of planning further studies and inducing the public to cope with trouble now—Steps 4 and 5 of our paradigm—are served by two communication devices. One of these, the THINCS propositional inventory, is a new invention. The other—literary skill— is at least as old as Homer and the book of Judges and probably as old as language itself.

5.2   THE THINCS PROPOSITIONAL INVENTORY

THINCS stands for a device to deal with the information overload that now hampers all scientific research. Chemists, they say, now find it easier to check out a new compound by doing a fresh experiment than by searching the immense chemical literature to see what results others may have already had. In the field of alcoholism research alone, hundreds of new books and thousands of new papers are published worldwide ever year. Who then keeps up with the field of alcoholism research as a whole? No one, I assure you, no one.

Early in its development of the THINCS system the Human Relations Area Files tested whether the experts were keeping up with the scientific literature on alcoholism. Levinson, using a specially cross-indexed archive of abstracts of that literature, focused narrowly on the topic of social factors in the treatment of alcoholism. He looked at over ninety reports of behavioral science studies— sample surveys or formal experiments; he found that through replication by a number of high-quality clinical experiments there were some firm findings about these factors. Should an alcoholic under treatment be hospitalized or left at home for out-patient treatment? The answer—at least for English-speaking patients—has been demonstrated beyond any reasonable doubt (see Chapter 8). But two major reviews of the literature on alcoholism commissioned by the U.S. government and compiled by leading experts in the field knew nothing about it. The mass of literature is so great that the experts simply overlooked this work.

The great merit of a THINCS study is that it clearly divides theories into three groups.

(1) Those theories so well tested that they constitute adequate guides for public policy. In other words, with these theories we can take Step 5, Cope with Trouble Now.

(2) Those theories so thoroughly discredited that they do not deserve further attention. Not merely do they not serve as guides to public policy, but they do not need any further study. These are the theories to be discarded.

(3) Those theories that enjoy some support, but which still need more work. These theories, then, direct us to Step 4, Plan Further Studies.

Appendix B gives an example of a THINCS propositional profile. The heart of a THINCS study is a set of these profiles. In each one the reviewer systematically evaluates a specific behavioral science theory test, using a full checklist of methods of study. He then asks: Does the test seem to support the theory? Has the test design taken every known precaution against every known source of error? When a theory has been supported by a variety of high-scoring tests and has plainly been discredited by none, the THINCS reviewer puts it into Group 1—as a policy guide. If it is supported by only one or two tests—and these low scoring—or if results as a whole are ambiguous, then the reviewer puts it into Group 3, for further study. If it is plainly discredited by many low-scoring tests or by a few high-scoring ones, the reviewer puts the theory into Group 2, the reject pile.

The collection of propositional profiles constitutes the archival study of theory tests, which is the heart of a THINCS study. However, all such studies should also produce an essay reviewing the findings of the archival study. Four THINCS studies now exist—all funded and published by the Human Relations Area Files. The THINCS method was devised by me and Hesung Koh, and was developed by a team at the Department of Anthropology of the State University of New York (SUNY) at Buffalo, led by Levinson, under my general direction; important contributions were made by Horan, Margolis, and Perkins.

The four THINCS studies that have been done so far—the first three of them under my guidance—are:

(1) *Guide to Social Theories*, by Levinson et al. This is a substantially complete review of all holocultural theory tests, on whatever topic. The findings of this review were set forth in a book-length essay by Levinson and Malone.
(2) *Guide to Theories of Economic Development*, by Clark. This is a broad review of holonational tests of theories on how to make poor countries richer. The review essay setting forth these findings is Clark's doctoral dissertation at SUNY, Buffalo.
(3) *Guide to Theories of Homicide*, by Horan. This is a broad review of tests of selected theories on homicide. Again, the review essay setting forth her findings is Horan's doctoral dissertation at SUNY, Buffalo.
(4) *Guide to Alcoholism Treatment Research: Volume 1, Behavioral Medicine/Behavior Modification*, by Levinson et al. There is no accompanying review essay, but the introduction contains a comprehensive summary of findings, briefly listed in Section 8.5.4.

Two recent surveys of theory tests in international affairs constitute less ambitious systematic and objective theory test reviews. McGowan and Shapiro inventory, describe, and evaluate 118 tests of theory about foreign policy. Their work, however, fails to sum up its findings plainly and clearly. Most of the propositions lead to inconclusive results, not surprisingly. However, McGowan and Shapiro did find something solid—four independent and well-conducted studies all showing that the larger a nation, the more warlike. This finding is buried. The introduction, conclusion, and the evaluations all chiefly speak to method rather than findings. The body of a THINCS review must be method, but every such study needs a clear summary that classifies theories into those clearly supported, those clearly rejected, and those in doubt. And these theories should be paraphrased in plain talk. Jones and Singer have another compendium, containing abstracts of 158 studies testing theories in international politics. They do not, however, systematically evaluate method. Nor do they decide which propositions we can now trust, which we must reject, and which remain in doubt.

5.3   PLAIN TALK

The results of social science theory tests usually are reported in densely written, hard-to-decipher technical articles. Most scientific journals want their contributions written in difficult jargon; editors will often reject a paper written in plain English *because* it is written in plain English. Requiring that books and papers on social science be written in *plain talk* would serve two purposes: (1) It would protect us against those who dress up thin ideas in pretentious clothes and so deceive the busy reader who lacks time to decipher them. (2) It would lessen the information overload by making it easier for us to read the work of others.

Make no mistake about it, however. Plain talk is not easy to write. Often, the easier it is to read, the harder it is to write; to write in plain talk takes about twice as long as to write in social science jargon. Furthermore, as it stands now, a scientific paper written in plain talk and published in a journal addressed to the general reading public is not only twice as hard to write. It often only counts half as much—or less than half as much—when committees and deans review a scholar's record for promotion or tenure at a university.

The rules of plain talk have long been known to popular writers and editors. Flesch's book, *The Art of Readable Writing*, is a classic guide. Use short and familiar words. Talk directly to the reader. Speak in salient images—those that strike the mind and stick there. Use short sentences. I have tried to make this book an example; if it reaches my colleagues with its calls for further research, the plain talk I have tried to use here may help them plan further studies (Step 4). If it reaches the public with its message on strengthening moralnets, the plain talk I have tried to use may well help people thus cope with trouble now (Step 5).

Notes

5.1   Finlay's Theory

On the *Stegomyia* mosquito (now renamed *Aedes*), on the other affairs of Walter Reed, and on the fight against yellow fever in Havana and New Orleans, I follow Kelly (1907: 111-113, 132f., 135-153, 185).

5.2   The THINCS Propositional Inventory

Levinson's mini-THINCS on social factors in the treatment of alcoholism was an internal HRAF report, done under my supervision.
The four THINCS studies: Levinson (1977a), Levinson (1981), Clark (1981), Horan (n.d.).
The monographic essay reviewing the results of a THINCS study is Levinson and Malone (1980). Clark and Horan are, at this writing, in the final stages of revision of their doctoral theses.
McGowan and Shapiro (1973) inventory theory tests on the comparative study of foreign policy; Jones and Singer (1972) on international politics.

The information overload obscures also the work of those of us who are specially trying to cope with it. Not until this book's final revision had gone to the publisher did I become aware of a major breakthrough in resolving sets of apparently conflicting research findings. I mean meta-analysis. It turns out that unless relationships are very high indeed, such conflicts are only to be expected, but their resolution proves not particularly difficult. Using these meta-analysis methods in THINCS studies would much strengthen them whenever theory tests on a single topic are many in number but inconsistent in result (see Glass, McGaw, and Smith, 1981, and Hunter, Schmidt, and Jackson, 1982).

5.3   Plain Talk

The manuals on writing plain English that I have found most useful are Flesch (1974), Fowler and Fowler (1931), Strunk and White (1979), and Perrin (1950).

Mead (1949, 1953) and Levine (1982) offer models for the effective presentation of data and theory, including abundant documentation, without sacrifice of clarity.

Part Two:
Moralnets and Social Ills

 Certain Normative

Reference Groups,

Here Called Moralnets

Tristan da Cunha is a lonely island in the South Atlantic. The nearest neighbors of Tristaners live 2400 kilometers (1500 miles) away. And there is not much in Tristan, only one small village and a few fields and pastures. But almost all the exiles from Tristan made their way back.

Tristaners are chiefly descended from European sailors and women of mixed European, African, and Asiatic descent; their faces would not seem strikingly foreign in an English seaport. They speak at home a kind of English no more different from the standard than the Lowland Scottish of Robert Burns. They read and write standard English well enough for their needs. They belong to the Church of England. Their family life is much like that of the English.

Their bleak island is a submarine volcano, rising steeply 5500 meters (18,000 feet) from the ocean floor. Late in September 1961, the island began to quiver with earthquakes. Then the volcano erupted. An earth bubble rose like a boil on the mountain slope not far above the island's one village. After it burst, spitting out hot rock and cinders in masses, the inhabitants had to leave the island.

The British navy took them to England, some 264 of them. The British people welcomed them, settled them together in a block of comfortable apartments and found them good-paying jobs. Suddenly the Tristaners had traded a sparse, hand-to-mouth living for the rich marketplaces of England—and money enough. Suddenly they had traded their tiny social world for a varied modern city, with television and newspapers.

They did not like what they found. On the surface, the culture shock of the change would not have seemed too great. Especially since English public sympathy for their plight had been keen and so they had been made more comfortable than millions of the English themselves. And the Tristaners proved able workers, who gave their employers satisfaction. They were law-abiding folk, who had no trouble with the police.

But the Tristaners found that life in England had lost its savor. At home in Tristan, the semiweekly movie had been a source of excitement; everyone came who could. But in England, where they could go to the movies or watch television every day, they took no joy in it.

Work that had seemed so satisfying in Tristan seemed dull in England. In Tristan, men and women alike did their own work, were their own bosses. In England, if they worked for wages, they had to take orders from others. In Tristan, doors had no locks. There were no police. Crime was unknown. In England, a Tristaner was mugged and savagely beaten. The deed shocked them all profoundly. They feared to go out at night. They felt besieged as they huddled behind locked doors and curtained windows. In lonely Tristan, people felt the warmth of rich human society. In crowded England, though dwelling near by one another as companions still, people felt lonesome. Within two years, 262 of them had gone back, and only about a dozen stayed behind in England.

But the tale is not yet told. One family among the returning band viewed with dismay the sight of their burned-out home. At the last minute, after all, they changed their minds and returned to England. The others found the first two years of return hard. Homes and livestock had been plundered; the potato crop failed; and only savings from their English exile wages tided them over. Three years after the return, ten more families, totaling 35 people, left Tristan again for England.

Here they were visited by Munch—of all social scientists, the one who knows the Tristaners best, both at home on Tristan and in their English exile. To his astonishment, Munch learned that these returners were again unhappy in England, and that most of them were going *back again to Tristan.* Munch ends his book with these words:

> One very intelligent housewife among the emigrants remarked not once but several times that "here in England there is no one to talk to." Oh, yes, she talked to her neighbors, and some of them were very nice; they even went for walks together, visited in each other's homes, with an occasional game of bridge, or the men would go to the pub together. "But it isn't the same."

> From my conversations with this young woman I gathered that most of the Tristan Islanders in England were lonely in the midst of the constant stream of humanity that surrounded them. And the more sensitive among them felt sorry for the English because they realized that they, too, were lonely, perhaps without even knowing it. There was no lack of friendly relationships and conversations across the garden gate; but they were hollow, empty, superficial. They were not *personal* relationships comparable to the ones that permeate the Tristan community, expressed and reinforced by a constant exchange of gifts and services. They lacked the warmth, the involvement, commitment, and concern that can only be found in a small community where everybody has grown up together, where all know each other from childhood. This is something that the congested urban community, with all its togetherness and all its freedom of voluntary association, may have lost forever, to the extent that some of us will never partake of it and do not even know that it could exist.

> The recent emigrants from Tristan da Cunha had never before experienced anything like it. The last time they were in England, they had been together among themselves. Now they were strangers, extremely lonesome, in a lonely crowd.

What were these personal relationships that Munch thinks so important? They were the pattern of shared work that dominates the Tristan way of life. Tristaners rarely buy or sell things to each other or hire each other's labor; they prefer to work in small friendship groups. People work together and share the product or take turns helping each other.

Because one man often belongs to four or five different sets of work gangs, the whole island is bound together in a network of these mutual aid groups. Said one Tristaner:

> No, the people on Tristan, they's jus' like one family and they live happy and one help the h'other, and if I's out in my farm and doin' my potatoes, and someone's finish' his'n, he'll come along an' give me a hand, an' the next day he got something to do, I go 'n' give *him* a hand, so we all help 'nother. On Tristan they's jus' like brothers 'n' sisters.

To belong to such a network feels good. Good enough to work hard for it. Good enough to trade rich England for poor Tristan da Cunha. And once people get such a network going, they are likely to produce and sustain a moral order to maintain it.

6.2   THE CYBERNETIC MODEL OF THE MIND

In this chapter, I present a model of the human moral order. My model supposes that man is a social animal, that there is a universal human instinct for living in social groups. My model supposes that these human social groups require complicated sets of rules to operate, and that these rules are learned, not innate. Mankind long ago must have solved the problem not only of how to teach young people these rules—so they know what is expected of them—but also how to motivate them to follow the rules, even when it hurts. I here present a model of how such moral orders are transmitted and enforced by human cultures.

The model has a psychological base. That base is in turn another model, an emerging model of the human mind developed by students of control systems, computers, and information theory. The literature on that cybernetic model is vast. The details as they have now been elaborated are far too technical to discuss here. I have tried to set forth a systematic summary in my Foreword to Hays's *Cognitive Structures.* If you find these ideas both new and intriguing and would like to read further, I commend the book by Peterfreund and Schwartz. If you really want to come to grips with the model in fine and full detail—and have months to study them—the books by Bowlby, by Powers, and by Hays are difficult but essential.

Other models of the mind in common use are not nearly so general as the cybernetic model. Powers suggests how conventional stimulus-response conditioned learning theory can be reconciled with the cybernetic model. Bowlby and Peterfreund and Schwartz similarly deal with Freudian theory. Peterfreund and Schwartz also treat Piagetian learning theory in cybernetic terms. In my Foreword to Hays, I review the evidence bearing on the validity of the cybernetic model; it seems to me that its main elements are strongly supported, but the detailed analyses of Powers and of Hays still require much further study.

For the study of moralnet theory, I draw on four key elements of the cybernetic model: (1) the control system, or servo, (2) the program, (3) the hierarchy, or stack, and (4) the structure of memory.

The central idea of the whole model is that of the control system—the servomechanism, or *servo*. A servo is a device for keeping something at a desired state. A full understanding of any servo calls for a look at its fourteen elements. But here let me just set forth the four most important ones: (1) a thing to be kept under control by being kept at (2) a specified state, a goal, (3) a system for measuring and reporting the actual state of that thing, and (4) a system for acting on the thing to bring it into agreement with the goal when, as, and if needed. For example, a room heater with a thermostat is a familiar servo. The temperature of the room is the thing to be kept under control. The thermostat setting specifies the goal. The thermometer built into the thermostat measures the actual temperature of the room. The heater warms the room if it is too cold, but only when needed (the room will not get too hot).

The cybernetic model of the mind supposes that the mind as a whole is a complex system of thousands upon thousands of such servos.

One of the most important ways servos are organized is into *programs*. Programs are plans for behavior, organized in sequences, often with many decision points and repetition loops built in. Programs may include many servos. But each program is a device for accomplishing the goal of a high-order servo. Human mental programs are seen as analogous to computer programs, but vastly more complex.

Both servos and programs may be organized further into *hierarchies*. Higher-order servos bring the things they control into line with their goals by changing the goals of lower-order servos. Lower-order programs are subroutines that may frequently be called up by a variety of higher-order programs. Thus a subroutine for running may be called by a program for playing baseball: (a) in a subroutine for running between the bases or (b) in a subroutine for running to catch a fly ball. A subroutine for driving a car (itself consisting of an intricate set of subroutines) would be called up to take me to wherever I happen to want to drive my car today.

Programs are not learned by the mind the way most computers are programmed. However, human learning does resemble the way a few are. Programmable calculators, for example, put the computer in LEARN mode and then cause the computer to remember the successive steps of the program that the programmer "walks" the computer through. That is, the computer is not merely told what to do, but actually caused to do it in some other way than by a program, meanwhile remembering the experience. Animals, including people, acquire new programs—that is, learn—by keeping *all* experiences temporarily in short-term memory while permanently remembering those few new experiences that prove especially rewarding or punishing. Because this procedure is rather clumsy, learning experiences generally need to be repeated if the thing being learned is at all complex. It takes practice to make perfect.

Memory in this model is a complex system with many tasks and varying organization. Yet human memory, like computer memory, has a twofold function. The same memory apparatus can hold data or can hold program. Data are information about the state of the world outside the mind. Program is a plan of behavior for the organism. Since program is memory of past interaction between the organism and the environment, the learning process consists of data becoming program.

However, according to Hays, there is considerable segregation in the human mind between memory-as-data and memory-as-program. Hays classifies human memory into two main components: *systemic memory* and *programmatic memory*. Systemic memory is where we store data about facts, about concepts—here we keep our map of the world outside the mind. Programmatic memory is where we keep our memory for controlling operations. But since we control operations by remembering them, it is also where we keep our memory of episodes; linguistic memory is part of programmatic memory. Thus my memory of how to pronounce the English world "apple" is stored in a certain part of the linguistic section of my programmatic memory. My memory of how to write that same word is stored in another such section. My memory of how to type it in a third. But the meaning of that word—the linking of that distinctive English sound or printed word with a certain kind of fruit is found in another part of the mind (and brain) entirely—in systemic memory. It is there that spoken "apple," written "apple"—and German *Apfel* and French *pomme* and Spanish *pomo*—are all tied together with the memories for the look and feel and taste and smell of apples. And linked to information about the apple orchards of western New York and the apple tree in my garden and the price of apples in the local supermarket—and apple pie and applesauce.

Following Bowlby, in the discussion that follows I link the concept of instinct with the servo goal. The key point here is that an instinct is an innate goal whose means of attainment is not innate but learned. Furthermore, I consider the role of culture themes in organizing the systemic memory of a culture. Then, too, I consider the role of tales and ceremonies in providing surrogate or artificial experiences that work in programmatic memory in a way analogous to actual experiences. Implicit in the whole discussion is the culture as a superordinate hierarchical level, organizing both the servos and the programs of the individual culture bearers.

6.3   THE HUMAN SOCIAL INSTINCT

The economist Adam Smith thought that people had an instinct for trading, an innate tendency to exchange goods and services. "It is common to all men," he argued, "and to be found in no other race of animals." Certainly, among the migratory hunting and gathering bands known to anthropologists, the trading pattern of the Tristaners is usually the rule. The hunting and gathering territory is held in common by the band. When a large animal is taken, the meat is divided among the hunters according to fixed rules. Each of them in turn shares his part with certain relatives or friends to whom he may feel under obligation; and *they* in turn have *their* friends; and so it happens that everyone in the band is eating meat. But each person thinks of his act as making a gift to a relative or friend—as we do at Christmas or birthdays or bar mitzvahs or weddings.

The natural condition of mankind—the environment in which people evolved over millions of years as ground apes—seems clearly to have been the environment of such a hunting band. A group of perhaps five to twenty families, sharing a territory and the food in it. They banded together also against predators—the men with their spears against teeth and claws of the great cats. One man or woman alone might not give such beasts much of a fight, but ten or fifteen spearmen would be more than a match.

While other ground apes band together for protection, only families and bands of human hunters systematically do so to take and share food. Was Adam Smith right about there being an innate propensity, an instinct, for trading things among people? In general, do people have an innate propensity, or instinct, for social behavior? Are people innately social animals? Or is social behavior purely something that we learn as part of our culture?

The concept of instinct has been out of favor for the past two generations. Lately, however, there has been a revival of interest among behavioral scientists, led by Bowlby and Wilson among others. (Though they still shy away from the word *instinct*, as people were shying away from the term "cultural evolution" in the 1930s and 1940s.) It helps if we think of an instinct not as an innate sequence of specific behaviors like breathing or swallowing or copulating or defecating—but only as an innate *goal.* No behavioral scientist today doubts that the overwhelming majority of human behavior is learned as part of culture. The only question we are arguing is whether such leading components of culture as kinship and trade and morals have a genetic base.

On the one hand, there are innate programs for breathing or swallowing or copulating or defecating. Such fixed action patterns presumably dominate the behavior of insects, fish, or frogs, but are comparatively unimportant among mammals—especially among people. On the other hand, there are, I suggest, innate goals—vague wishes or desires—stored presumably in systemic memory. It is such innate vague wishes, desires, or yearnings that I call instincts. Note that a fixed action pattern involves not only a goal but a specific sensorimotor program to achieve the goal. But an instinct is only a goal, only a need, only a yearning. It is for each of us *to learn how* to still that yearning, to meet that need, to attain that goal. To learn perhaps from trial and error, perhaps from our culture.

So I see culture as an elaborate set of programs for us to achieve certain innate goals, or instincts—such as eating and drinking, finding a mate (the fixed action pattern program for copulation does not get triggered until the courtship is far along), learning as much as we can about the world we live in. For we higher primates are all curious animals.

The main idea of this section is that moral behavior among people is a kind of instinctive behavior. I believe that the moral order is a necessary outgrowth of the social network, and that the building of social networks by people is an instinct found among all human populations everywhere. So I am not suggesting a theory of genetic differences among individual human beings, or human groups, or human races. I am suggesting a theory of human nature. I am suggesting that human beings, like chimpanzees and gorillas, but unlike orangutans and gibbons, are innately biased to tend to associate in bands of dozens of members. I am also suggesting that people, like gibbons but unlike other apes, are also innately programmed to associate in family groups. So the innately biased human arrangement is a band of several families—a two-level social organization.

And I am not suggesting that this bias produces a fixed action pattern and so a compulsion; I am only suggesting that this bias is a genetically transmitted goal, or desire, and so only a tendency. I am not saying anything at all about the relative genetic superiority or inferiority of any people compared to any other. While all racist theories are genetic theories of behavior, not all genetic theories of behavior are racist. We must not allow our proper horror at the abuses of racist theories to censor and silence the study of the biological elements of human behavior.

But if most of our human behavior is so plainly learned, how can we tell instincts from learned goals? How can a human instinct theory be tested? Since an instinct is only one goal among many competing for the mind's attention, we cannot expect instinctive behavior to be universal. And that fact makes a human instinct theory still harder to test. There seem to be at least five tests any theory of human instinct needs to pass, wherever they apply, before that theory has any claim to scientific standing.

First, the goal in question should be found in all cultures. Even if not all people pursue the goal, much less attain it, that goal should universally be seen as something generally desired by the inner person—by the "animal nature" in man, as many people would say.

Second, the theory demands that in cultures where the attainment of the goal is rare, although no natural obstacles exist in the environment, stress should be laid on the teaching of the young to avoid, reject or repress the goal—as middle-class young ladies of Victorian England were often taught that it was not nice to think about sex. Where the culture conflicts with the goal, the test calls for there to be strain and stress. So absence of the behavior called for by the instinct in a culture is a valuable test of any instinct theory; in such a culture, devices to block off that goal should loom high.

Third, the theory demands that where usually reaching the goal is especially hard, people should strive for it all the harder, and not lightly or easily give it up.

Fourth, the theory demands that among hunting and gathering bands with only crude tools, reaching that goal should have clear survival value. The hypothetical gene for that goal should enjoy a clear advantage in its competition for survival over rival genes that do not fix such a goal.

Fifth, the blocking of a person from reaching such a goal should usually be painfully frustrating. That frustration should produce manifest symptoms of mental stress.

What can we say with respect to these five tests about the theory that human beings are innately social animals—that they have an instinct to live in bands or social groups?

First, hardly any human beings live alone and no culture teaches them to, as a regular or normal thing. Nearly all people live in small family households, at least, if not in larger groups. Most people complain of feeling sad and lonely when they are away from a group for a considerable time.

Second, since there are no cultures in which attainment of the goal of living in social groups is rare, we cannot see whether such cultures teach the young to avoid other people.

Third, in cultures where people commonly live in small, isolated family groups, they do indeed go to great trouble and take great pains to assemble from time to time in larger groups. In contrast to gibbons, human families hardly ever keep within private territories from which other people are rigidly excluded. Gibbon families keep entirely to themselves, and never socialize or forgather with other families. But human families who wander in small foraging units in hard country share their foraging territories with others and regularly arrange to come together in larger groups whenever food supplies permit. All cultures from time to time have social gatherings of many nuclear families.

Fourth, the human migratory hunting band is indeed a successful adaptation to ground ape life on the African savannah. As I have already remarked, men band together to hunt large animals, then share the meat—not only among themselves, but with the women and children. And men band together to fight off large cats or other predators. They not only protect themselves but also their women and children. Meanwhile, women gather plant food and small, slow game and share what they gather not only with their children but also with the men. That plan of social organization—into bands of several food-sharing nuclear families—is found among almost all hunting and gathering peoples living without riding horses or large fishing boats and independently of farmers or herdsmen, on territory with moderate to rich supplies of game and plant food.

Two exceptions to the pattern of friendly food sharing among primeval hunting bands have been the subject of special monographs—the Siriono of Bolivia and the Ik of Uganda. Neither of these societies was well adapted to its environment; each had recently been uprooted. Both Siriono and Ik were farmers as well as foragers. The absence of food sharing among these people went along with severe hunger for most; these were societies in trouble, not societies well adapted to their environments.

Technically, the exchange of goods and services through informal gifts or Tristan work groups is called *reciprocal exchange*; it prevails at lower levels of cultural evolution (see Table 6.1). Here we see clearly that reciprocal gifts are the usual mode of trade among food-collecting peoples but not among food-producing peoples.

Fifth, students of social separation—of grief and mourning—offer much evidence of severe suffering and mental distress as a direct result of that separation. In Chapter 9, I offer evidence that social separation, isolation, or loneliness of a certain kind is a common cause of suicide. Bowlby offers much evidence that a common cause of mental illness among young children is separation from their mother figure. Both Parkes and Marris offer evidence on the severe stress caused among adults by the loss of loved ones. And indeed, is not grief and mourning at the death of our near and dear something only too familiar to most of us in our own lives?

Rosenblatt, Walsh, and Jackson made a worldwide study of grief and mourning. In almost all cultures, people cry at the loss of their loved ones. Of the 73 societies at all levels of cultural development they looked at, only in Bali did people rarely manifest their grief in this way. People almost always react with crying, but they also usually show fear and anger.

What of the Balinese? Bateson and Mead explain the attitude toward grief and mourning at the death of a loved one in their book on Balinese character. The Balinese feel strongly that any such expressions are unseemly. A central theme of Balinese culture is a deep faith in a strictly scheduled transmigration of souls: The dead are not really dead; they have simply gone away for a while, on schedule; they will be back in the third generation—no sooner, no later; let us not then hint at any doubt about this cherished belief by treating their death as a thing of great moment when it is only a passing phase.

Belo, too, tells us how rigidly the Balinese are ruled by their formal etiquette and rules of decorum. However, she makes clear that the Balinese have strong, warm feelings of attachment to their family and friends. In public, decorum permits friends or relatives of the same sex to fondle and embrace one another—and so they do, much oftener than we do. Likewise, people are free to fondle, caress, and embrace young children in public—and they do, much oftener than we do. So the lack of public expressions of grief at Balinese funerals does not constitute evidence that Balinese feel their losses of loved ones any less than do the rest of mankind.

Lynch has recently looked at the medical consequences of loneliness in the United States. Lonely people—single people, divorced people, widowed people—have almost twice as much heart disease as married people. During the first six months after a spouse dies, the death rate from heart disease is nearly ten times as high among widows and widowers as among married people. Indeed, lonely people in the United States are more likely than married people to die from almost any cause of death at all.

Berkman and Syme watched a random sample of nearly 7,000 people in Alameda County, California. They measured the social networks of these people. They considered not only the number of social connections each person had but how strong they were. Over nine years, those with the weakest ties were

TABLE 6.1   Trade among Collecting Peoples

PROPOSITION: *Gifts tend to be the usual mode of trade among food-collecting people.*

	Usual Mode of Trade	
Food Source	*Gifts*	*Wages, Barter, Sales, or Taxes*
Food Collectors (no farming or herding)	Andamanese (near Malaya) Aweikoma (Brazil) Cheyenne (Western U.S.) Copper Eskimo (Canada) Eyak (Alaska) Klallam (Washington) Eastern Ojibwa (Great Lakes region) Wintun (California) (8)	Semang (Malaya) Ona (Tierra del Fuego) Chukchee (Siberia) Gilyak (Siberia) (4)
Food Producers (some farming or herding)	Callinago (Caribbean) Mataco (Argentina) Orokaiva (New Guinea) Papago (Arizona) Tikopians (Melanesia) Toradja (Celebes) Yagua (Peru) (7)	Amhara (Ethiopia) Araucanians (Chile) Austrians Azande (Zaire) Aztecs (Mexico) Burmese Coyotero Apache (Arizona) Chagga (Tanganyika) Dutch Irish Egyptians Fur (The Sudan) Gond (Central India) Hottentot (Namibia) Ifaluk (Micronesia) Ila (Zambia) Iraqi Italians Kababish (The Sudan) Kafirs (Afghanistan) Kapauku (New Guinea) Kazak (USSR) Koreans Land Dyak (Borneo) Luo (Kenya) Malaita (Solomon Islands) Manga Revans (Polynesia) Mende (Sierra Leone) Mongo (Zaire) Tallensi (Ghana) Thonga (Mozambique) Tiv (Nigeria) Tonga (Polynesia) Turks (Turkey) (34)

SOURCE: Food quest from Murdock (1967: cols. 7-11); mode of trade from Naroll et al. (n.d.).
Correlation: .64.
Chance risk: .003.
N = 53.

more than twice as likely to die as those with the strongest. This relationship held good for both sexes and for all age groups.

Is loneliness the cause, and death the effect? Or instead, are people handicapped in some way simply less likely to form social ties and more likely to die? Studies of illness and death rates among widows all point to a cause/effect relationship. Berkman and Syme cite six different studies—covering among them American, English, and European widows—all showing that bereavement itself tends to be followed immediately by an increase in a variety of symptoms of physical and mental illness, including death.

Three social scientists recently surveyed the United States to learn what aspects of their lives seemed most important to its people. What do North Americans consider the most important elements in their quality of life? Family life came second, right after recreation and before standard of living, work, and saving money. Marriage came fourth. Friendships seventh. Health was only in fourteenth place, religion in fifteenth. North Americans must surely be among the most individualistic, self-reliant—and lonely—people in the world. Yet we too cherish our loved ones and our friends.

6.4   NETWORKS AND MORALS

This innate human longing for society may, in fact, provide an innate mechanism for moral codes and moral world views. Social scientists seem to agree that most people get their moral world views from the social networks of their families, close friends, and work mates. These others, taken together, are variously called a person's *primary group, reference group, significant others,* or *social support network.* All such names look at the moral network from the viewpoint of the individual. But from the viewpoint of the social system, it is the network that produces the moral order. Each individual sees that network as his or her primary group, reference group, set of significant others. But the anthropologist usually sees the group as the leading force and all its individuals as subordinates.

Individuals, then, learn their moral ideas, or norms, or values from a specific social network. To define that network more sharply, consider from the point of view of moral ideas the communication net of the smallest-scale foraging bands—the simplest known human societies. We usually find among such societies a three-level communication system at work transmitting moral ideas and values to the people. The largest communication unit in these simplest of known societies is the speech community, or "tribe." That speech community consists of all those people who speak mutually intelligible dialects. (Often the boundaries of such a unit are fuzzy—but that is another matter.) The people of the tribe or speech community do not form a team or social servo. They seldom if ever deliberately collaborate or forgather to stage ceremonies or for any other common purpose. But they share a common oral literature, a common set of myths, a common set of rites and ceremonies—just as all Jews everywhere share the Passover *seder* ceremony and almost all North Americans share the rite of the family Thanksgiving dinner as a ceremonial meal. And through their common language, their common oral literature, and their common ceremonies they share a common set of concepts, values, ideals, ideas, and attitudes. All this collectively constitutes their ideology. And it is a striking fact that while neighboring speech communities—neighboring tribes—of the simplest foraging peoples are likely to resemble each other rather closely, each nevertheless has its own distinctive ideology, its own religion. In these simplest of human societies, then, the *normative reference group* is the speech community or tribe.

The tribe is organized into bands. Each band is usually a land-owning unit. (In very hard country, in desert or arctic wastes where land is not very valuable, land ownership may be absent entirely.) The band may usually camp together and may indeed be defined simply as a group of people who camp together. Or instead it may only forgather from time to time during the year when food happens to be plentiful at a certain spot. The band enacts ceremonies. The band is a face-to-face community, a primary group; it always share or exchanges food among its members. Everyone knows everyone else, watches everyone else, gossips about everyone else. It is through the band that the moral ideas of the tribe are transmitted, are transformed through gossip from theory to moral pressure. And it is primarily in the band that individuals may gain or lose the esteem or respect of their fellow men and women. To gain and hold esteem, a man or woman must perform skillfully and conscientiously the social roles assigned to him or her by the culture. A person who knows those roles and performs them well—who understands and assumes the full social responsibilities called for by the moral code of his or her people—is said by the Chinese to have *ren*. In Yiddish, such a person is called a "mensch," a *real* person. A mensch, a person with *ren*, gains respect in the eyes of family, friends, and neighbors. And so gains his or her own self-respect.

The band in turn is made up of nuclear families. (These are always linked into extended families—sometimes loosely, sometimes tightly. Indeed, the band may consist of a single extended family.) It is within these families that the most intense effort is made to teach the children proper ideas and attitudes and behavior—and where the strongest reinforcement of proper behavior occurs in terms of praise or blame, as well as in terms of shared food and shelter, and shared love.

In the traditional old world, preindustrial higher civilizations, the highest level of ideology was no longer carried by the tribe—a linguistic group—but by a far wider group, the higher civilization. The higher civilization can be looked at as a large social network—often made up of independent, warring states speaking diverse languages—that shares a common body of written literature. If the tribe is typically a speech community, the civilization is typically a script community. Its literature typically, but not always, embodies a single dominant ideology. So it is the literary tradition that forms the heart of the higher civilization. Our own higher civilization, the Western, grew out of the literary tradition of the medieval Roman Catholic world. Other influential higher civilizations have included the Mesopotamian, Egyptian, Hebrew, Greco-Roman, Hindu, Islamic, and Chinese.

However, in many higher civilizations, including our own, there is a diversity of ideology; there are rival sets of ideological literatures—all written in the same script. In this book, I follow the established practice of social psychologists in speaking of a set of people who share a common ideology as a normative reference group. In our own society today, prominent normative reference groups would include (1) the orthodox religious denominations (for the devout and pious believers) and (2) the liberal humanists, those who no longer accept the divine inspiration of the Bible as a guide to morality (but in fact continue to accept as moral axioms the fundamental social values of the Judeo-Christian tradition embodied therein). Our orthodox religious denominations in turn consist of several sects: half a dozen varieties of Christianity along with some orthodox Jews and Moslems. Likewise, our liberal humanists consist of several sects—the behavioral scientists (of whom I, of course, am one), the literati, and several Marxist sects.

A number of studies by social psychologists of college students and summer campers have shown the influence of such normative reference groups in our society on the kinds of answers such people give when asked questions about proper behavior, about morality. Their attitudes, or attitude changes, in the light of their normative reference groups, were carefully measured. Or in some cases, were the subjects of carefully controlled experiments. These studies all go to show one thing: The more such a person is reminded of his or her social membership in a particular moralnet, the more he or she is likely to profess its values, its ideas.

Other studies tend to show that, when nations and entire civilizations think alike with respect to their value systems in general, riots and civil wars occur less frequently.

Sorokin made a detailed study of the past 2500 years of Western cultural history. His chief concern was the effect of changing value systems on warfare—both foreign and civil. He found that both civil wars and foreign wars are more intense, more widespread, and more deadly at times when values are changing than when values are stable. His work suffers from two major flaws: It masquerades as a general theory of social and cultural dynamics, even though actually it measures only changing values on the one hand and warfare on the other. Second, he presents his essential findings in crude, oversimplified tables and charts, and uses nothing but his gut feeling about these tables and charts to draw the essential links between value change and warfare. If his findings were confirmed, they would show the importance of a stable moral order to a stable world order—but he offered no clear correlations to support this finding.

Banks and Textor looked at three measures of national homogeneity in their compendium of holonational correlations: (1) religion, (2) race—and racial differences generally go with cultural differences, and (3) language. They had one proxy measure of moral order—riots and demonstrations as political factors. They found that riots and demonstrations—mob rule—tended to be more common in more heterogeneous nations, as Table 6.2 shows.

TABLE 6.2   National Homogeneity, Political Demonstrations, and Riots

PROPOSITION: *Modern nations whose people are all alike in religion, race, and language*
tend to have fewer riots or political demonstrations than those with
differing religion, race, or language.

	Riots and Demonstrations Common	Riots and Demonstrations Rare
Homogeneous Nations	Jordan Poland Somalia (3)	Austria Costa Rica Denmark Greece Iceland Ireland Italy Libya Luxembourg Norway Portugal Sweden Tunisia United Arab Republic (Egypt) Uruguay (15)
Heterogeneous Nations	Afghanistan Bolivia Brazil Burma Cambodia Cameroon Central African Republic Ceylon Chad Colombia Congo Dahomey Ecuador El Salvador Ethiopia Gabon Germany, East Ghana Guatemala Guinea Haiti Honduras India Indonesia Iran Iraq Ivory Coast	Australia Belgium Canada Czechoslovakia Finland Germany, West Israel Jamaica Liberia Malagasy Republic Netherlands New Zealand Nicaragua Philippines Switzerland Tanganyika Trinidad United Kingdom (18)

TABLE 6.2 (Continued)

	Riots and Demonstrations Common	Riots and Demonstrations Rare
Heterogeneous Nations	Japan	
	Laos	
	Lebanon	
	Malaya	
	Mali	
	Mauritania	
	Mexico	
	Morocco	
	Nepal	
	Niger	
	Nigeria	
	Pakistan	
	Panama	
	Peru	
	Senegal	
	Sierra Leone	
	South Africa	
	Spain	
	Sudan	
	Syria	
	Thailand	
	Togo	
	Turkey	
	Uganda	
	USSR	
	Upper Volta	
	Vietnam Rep.	
	Yugoslavia	
	Zaire	
	(56)	

SOURCE: Banks and Textor (1963: Finished Characteristic 70/125 Matrix Table).
Correlation (phi coefficient): .49.
Chance risk (Fisher's Exact Test): $< .00001$.
N = 92.
NOTE: See Notes to Section 6.4.

In societies of a larger scale than the foraging band, its social and moral equivalent may sometimes be found in the village, sometimes in the extended family or lineage or clan, sometimes in the religious congregation or military unit or club or sodality or what have you. This unit needs a specific name. I call it the *moralnet*. I define the moralnet with respect to any person as the largest primary group that serves him or her as a part of his or her normative reference group. All human cultures are built as sets of moralnets, then, whether these are hunting bands, farming villages, religious congregations, or whatever.

The crucial role of the moralnet as a whole in transmitting moral ideas and securing moral behavior was first rigorously studied thirty years ago by Carle C. Zimmerman and Lucius Q. Cervantes. They provided us with the first clear empirical measurement of moralnet structure in contemporary urban society. They also provided clear evidence of how important that structure is in maintaining as working social systems the individual nuclear families that make up the moralnet. And what is more to the point, they showed the impact of the ideology communicated by that moralnet on the moral behavior of young people. The main concern of the work of Zimmerman and Cervantes was to contrast moralnets having a single, clear value system with moralnets having diverse and fuzzy value systems. These men did not measure value systems directly. Rather, they measured the general cultural background of the households comprising the moralnet.

Zimmerman and Cervantes studied about 10,000 high school seniors in six large American cities in the 1950s. They found that over 70 percent of the family households of these seniors were linked to five or more other family households. (The links, however, formed overlapping networks—not discrete sets. Call the five friend families of senior X families A, B, C, D, and E. Family A in turn might be linked to families X, D, F, G, and H; Family B in turn might be linked to families X, E, I, J, and K.) More than half of these friendship ties were at least ten years old.

The friend families of which we speak consisted of all those described by the respondent high school seniors as "a family whom their family visits, entertains, and associates with often."

Zimmerman and Cervantes found that the more these five friend families resembled the respondent's own family in general cultural background, the less likely the respondent was to have suffered loss of a parent through divorce or desertion. And the less likely the respondent was to have been arrested by the police. Resemblance was measured in terms of four specific traits: (1) kinship, (2) income, (3) region of origin, and (4) religion.

Zimmerman and Cervantes's findings support moralnet theory. Where the friend-family set presented a solid front of agreement on the norms of behavior, the families tended to avoid divorce, desertion, and juvenile delinquency. Zimmerman and Cervantes also showed the salient importance of agreement on religious beliefs between husband and wife in preserving such families from divorce, desertion, and juvenile delinquency. Common religious beliefs suggest a likelihood of common experiences with religious tales and religious ceremonies; common kinship ties suggest such common experiences of extended family ceremonies as Thanksgiving and Christmas dinners. When kinship and religion are combined, we can expect frequent sharing of common attendance at places of worship.

The findings of Zimmerman and Cervantes with respect to the link between moralnet harmony on the one hand and the frequency of divorce and youth crime on the other have solid support in the work of other investigators. I review much of this in Chapter 15 (on divorce) and in Chapter 12 (on youth crime). We also see, in Chapter 11, that child abuse is less frequent when the parents have strong social ties to friends and relations—in other words, to their moralnets.

Perhaps the best evidence on the importance of moralnets in complex societies comes from the studies of juvenile delinquency in the United States and Great Britain. The evidence is overwhelming that most juvenile delinquents get into trouble in gangs. Empey and Lubeck begin *The Silverlake Experiment* by reviewing no fewer than eleven systematic studies of delinquents that found such boys tended to get into trouble in gangs—not alone. The Gluecks studied 500 delinquents and 500 nondelinquents. Fully 98 percent of the delinquents had companions who were also delinquent. But of the nondelinquents, only 7 percent! Similar findings came from ten other studies of towns in widely scattered parts of the United States, as well as in many parts of Great Britain.

But the question remains whether these associations were the causes or the consequences of a leaning toward crime on the part of youths. Here I think the study by Hirschi is the most helpful one we have so far. He studied about 1300 junior and senior high school students in Richmond, California, a low-income, largely black district on San Francisco Bay, north of Berkeley. Hirschi got information about the students from their school records and from police records; 75 percent of the students he asked filled out a detailed questionnaire about their attitudes and their family and school and friendships.

For various reasons (see the Notes to this chapter), I do not trust Hirschi's findings with respect to those students who denied they had ever committed a delinquent act. Clearly many of these were lying to him. But we learn much if we compare those who admitted just one delinquent act with those who admitted more than one—as I do here in Tables 6.3 through 6.6, tables I extracted from Hirshi's report by omitting his data on students who denied they ever committed any delinquent acts at all.

Table 6.3 shows that the teenage boys and girls Hirschi studied who admitted more than one delinquent act themselves were more likely to have had at least three friends who had been picked up by the police. Those who admitted only one delinquent act were more likely to have had no more than two such friends.

Table 6.4 shows that the boys and girls Hirschi studied who reported being more closely supervised by their mothers were less likely to admit more than one delinquent act. Close ties with mothers seemed to tend to go with less delinquency.

Table 6.5 shows that the boys and girls Hirschi studied who reported being on closer, more intimate terms with their fathers were less likely to admit more than one delinquent act than those who were not in such close touch with their fathers.

Finally, Table 6.6 shows that the boys and girls Hirschi studied whose school records showed better grades in their English courses were less likely to admit more than one deliqnuent act than those who had poorer grades.

Furthermore, the responses of grade in English were checked also against police reports of delinquency. Here, as Table 6.7 shows, the results of Table 6.6 are confirmed and strengthened. Notice that in Table 6.7, none of the

TABLE 6.3   Friendship and Crime

PROPOSITION: *Richmond teenagers who admit to more than one "crime" tend to have more friends who get picked up by the police than those who admit to only one.*

Friends Picked up by the Police

	None	1	2	3	4 or More	Total
Admit Only One Crime	104	44	37	15	62	262
Admit More than One Crime	36	34	21	27	94	212
Total	140	78	58	42	156	474

SOURCE: Hirschi (1969: 99, Table 24).
Correlation (Kendall's tau-b): .38.
Chance risk: $< .000001$.
N = 474.
NOTE: See Notes to Section 6.4.

TABLE 6.4   Supervision and Crime

PROPOSITION: *Richmond teenagers who admit to more than one "crime" tend to have less supervision by their mothers than those who admit to only one.*

Mother Knows Teenager's Whereabouts

	Never	Rarely	Often	Usually	Always	Total
Admit Only One Crime	5	9	61	53	181	309
Admit More than One Crime	6	12	68	50	84	220
Total	11	21	129	103	265	529

SOURCE: Hirschi (1969: 89, Table 18).
Correlation (Kendall's tau-b): .23.
Chance risk: $< .00001$.
N = 529.

information is coming from the boys and girls themselves. The police told Hirschi which boys and girls they had police records on. The school told Hirschi their English grades. The fact that this table strengthens the findings of the boys' and girls' own admissions on delinquencies leads us to trust those admissions.

All these tables tend to show that those boys and girls with the stronger attachments to nondelinquent peers, to parents, and to school were the boys and girls least likely to get into trouble with the police. So they tend to support moralnet theory.

And in Rohner's book about parents who reject their children there is more. Rohner reviews five studies of delinquent boys. Two of these, one by Feshbach and one by Jackson, systematically compare delinquents with normal boys. All

TABLE 6.5   Relationship with Father and Crime

PROPOSITION: *Richmond teenagers who admit to more than one "crime" tend to talk less about things that matter to them with their fathers than those who admit to only one*

	Discusses Important Matters with Father					
	Least Often	Less Often	Sometimes	More Often	Most Often	Total
Admit Only One Crime	17	46	122	66	27	278
Admit More than One Crime	42	36	74	43	6	201
Total	59	82	196	109	33	479

SOURCE: Hirschi (1969: 91, Table 19).
Correlation (Kendall's tau-b): .17.
Chance risk: $< .0001$.
N = 479.

TABLE 6.6   Grades in English and Crime—I

PROPOSITION: *Richmond teenagers who admit to more than one "crime" tend to get lower grades in English than those who admit to only one.*

	Grades in English			
	0-49	50-79	80-99	Total
Admit Only One Crime	56	101	82	239
Admit More than One Crime	63	57	43	163
Total	119	158	125	402

SOURCE: Hirschi (1969: 116, Table 30).
Correlation (Kendall's tau-b): .14.
Chance risk: .004.
N = 402.

five of these reviews report that delinquent boys have weaker ties with their parents than normal boys.

6.5   WORLD IMAGES AND CULTURE THEMES

The transmission of a moral order by a moralnet is no easy matter. I propose, in this and the two following sections, to examine three mechanisms that seem to me and many other anthropologists to play a large part in this task. A moral order is a large complex of rules. And these rules need to be organized intellectually, sorted out in the mind. In this way, whole sets of them can be conveniently and effectively transmitted to the young who are being taught their morals.

TABLE 6.7   Grades in English and Crime—II

PROPOSITION: *Richmond teenagers who have police records of more than one"crime"tend to get lower English grades than those who have only one; and these in turn tend to get lower grades than those who have no police record at all.*

	Grades in English			
	0-49	*50-79*	*80-99*	*Total*
No Police Record	188	284	329	801
One Crime	36	39	18	93
More than One Crime	34	28	14	76
Total	258	351	361	970

SOURCE: Hirschi (1969: 116, Table 30).
Correlation (Kendall's tau-b): .18.
Chance risk: $< .000001$.
N = 970.

Successful ideologies are those that manage to get their moral ideas across to the people of the network of believers—and so more or less to influence the moral conduct of the faithful. Such ideologies presumably develop and spread in natural selection arenas—darwins. The ideas that are most effective in seizing the minds of their believers and also in guiding them into a social system that meets their needs presumably are the ideas that tend to prevail. If these ideas are linked through artistic genius into patterns that best suit the systemic memory, we would expect them to be most likely to succeed.

The cross-cultural evidence suggests that the patterns that are indeed most successful are organized around central cultural themes. By a theme is meant a leading idea used as a spine or bus to organize an ideology through association. In North American culture, for example, a central theme is democracy; in English culture, fair play; in French culture, elegant style; in classical Chinese culture, filial piety.

The importance of culture themes as organizing principles of morality is suggested by several holocultural studies. These show associations between diverse activities whose link or relationship most likely appears to be such a theme.

Take a look at Table 6.8. Sipes found that the more warlike a society, the more aggressive were its sports. Further, he found that in the United States, aggressive sports were stressed more in times of war than in times of peace.

Studies by Swanson, by Spencer, and by Davis show that the theology of a culture tends to reflect its social structure. Monotheism tends to be found in societies with branching authority patterns rising up to a supreme ruler like a pharoah or an emperor. Polytheism is more often found in societies with complex social class systems but without a supreme earthly ruler.

The theme idea is further supported by other holocultural studies. Fischer showed strong associations between art styles and social classes: The fewer the social classes, the simpler the designs. Roberts led a group who found that the more complex a society, the more likely its people were to play a game of strategy rather than a game of physical strength or a game of chance (see Table 6.9).

Finally, Lomax led a group including Ayres and Erickson to study folk dances and folk songs. Here, too, the style of singing and dancing clearly reflects the social structure of the people.

So, it may be that to stick effectively in the mind, a world image needs to be skillfully arranged around central themes. Such themes may well make a world view easier to teach to young children, especially if those themes are presented effectively in art, song, story, and drama. In other words, a successful moral order may have to be itself a work of art.

6.6   TALES, CEREMONIES, FINE ARTS

I suggest that these themes lie at the deepest level of the subconscious mind. And that their organization consists of a small number of central concepts. Such concepts I call the themes of a culture system. The culture is, of course, among other things a device for transmitting this subconscious organization system from mind to mind. In each mind, the theme is the center of a web of associations. It is that web that constitutes the organizational structure of the culture. I see the moral order of a culture as a mental network of associated ideas embodied in a set of tales and ceremonies and art styles. A mental network is shared by a social network of people, and includes not only a conscious portion—an ideology—but an unconscious portion. The unconscious portion is often called metaphorically a *spirit*. I submit that the culture subconsciously transmits this pattern of subliminal associations. I suppose that it does so through its tales, its ceremonies, and its fine arts. The key elements in this transmission system are familiar: first, a culture's stories, or tales; second, its ceremonies; third, its poetry, music, paintings, and carvings. And many people have sensed their functions as transmitters of the orientation system of the culture.

Malinowski taught us the importance of myths as charters. A myth is a story whose implicit function is to set forth the structure of society to make it right and proper. If you believe the myth, you accept the social organization.

The Ona of Tierra del Fuego tell the myth of their culture hero, Kaux. They tell how at the beginning of time he walked all over their island. Then he divided it into 39 tracts of land. He marked out the boundaries—one part for each lineage. And that myth has helped the Ona keep to their lineage boundaries ever since.

However, I wish to speak here of *tales*—any narrative of events, any story whether true or false, whether offered to be believed or only offered to amuse. I take it that systemic memory does not have a quality control system, because

TABLE 6.8   Warlike Societies and Sports

PROPOSITION: *The more warlike a society, the more games of combat.*

	Games of Combat	
	Present	*Absent*
Warlike People	Tibetans Sema Naga (India) Ila (Zambia) Comox (British Columbia) Aztecs (Mexico) Tehuelche (Patagonia) Abipon (Argentina) Timbira (Brazil) Thai (9)	Mundurucu (Brazil) (1)
Unwarlike People	Copper Eskimo (Northern Canada) Tikopia (Melanesia) (2)	Semang (Malaya) Bhil (India) Toda (India) Hutterites (North America) Lapps (Scandinavia) Dorobo (Kenya) Kung (Namibia) Naskapi (Quebec) (8)

SOURCE: Sipes (1973: 69).
Correlation (phi coefficient): .60.
Chance risk: (Fisher's Exact Test): .003.
N = 20.

the art of sifting truth from falsehood is a set of programs in programmatic memory. So if I ask whether you believe there ever really was a girl named Little Red Riding Hood, whether she actually met a wolf on her way to her grandmother's, I expect you to turn that quality control program on. And reply at once, "Of course not." But studies of the effects of subliminal communication lead me to believe that when as a child you heard that tale, your systemic memory nevertheless may well have treated the tale of Little Red Riding Hood as though it really happened. And accordingly, you made notes about the nature of wolves. Moral for little boys and girls: *Don't trust strangers.*

The story of George Washington crossing the Delaware—of Washington at Valley Forge—is also a tale. Of course, I do not believe for a moment in the nursery tale of Little Red Riding Hood, but I am quite sure that Washington really did cross the Delaware that cold Christmas eve, and that he and his army really did winter it through at Valley Forge a year later. Moral for Americans: *By such brave deeds against such great odds was our country founded.*

Boys and girls in the United States hear both those stories. That of Little Red Riding Hood begins "Once upon a time" to signal the fact that the teller does not

TABLE 6.9   Social Complexity and Games of Strategy

PROPOSITION: *The more complex a society, the more games of strategy.*

Complexity Level	Games of Strategy Absent	Present
High	Kababish (Sudan) Rwala (Syria) (2)	Venda (South Africa) Chagga (Tanganyika) Dahomeans Jukun (Nigeria) Koreans Lakher (Assam) Lamba (Zambia) Mbundu (Angola) Siwa (Egypt) Tanala (Madagascar) Vietnamese Yap (Micronesia) (12)
Medium	Ainu (Japan) Alor (Indonesia) Buka (Solomon Islands) Chukchee (Siberia) Gros Ventre (USA) Kwakiutl (Canada) Malekula (New Hebrides) Maricopa (Arizona) Menomini (USA) (9)	Aleut (Alaska) Chewa (Malawi) Masai (Kenya) Nauru (Micronesia) (4)
Low	Hopi (Arizona) Woleaians (Micronesia) Kiwai (New Guinea) Lesu (Melanesia) Murngin (Australia) Navaho (Arizona) Papago (Arizona) Siriono (Bolivia) Wapishana (Guiana) Warrau (Venezuela) Witoto (Colombia) Yaruro (Venezuela) Yungar (Australia) (13)	Baiga (India) Copper Eskimo (Canada) Zuñi (New Mexico) (3)

SOURCE: Games from Roberts, Arth, and Bush (1959: 600); complexity level from Murdock (1967).
Correlation (Kendall's tau-b): .51.
Chance risk (Naroll's Exact Test): $< .001$.
N = 43.

really believe it. That of Washington's deeds comes in history books, to signal the fact that the teller really does. But I suggest that for the construction of the moral order in the minds of little boys and girls, the truth or falsity of these tales is not the important point.

The tales of George Washington and the cherry tree, Washington crossing the Delaware, Washington at Valley Forge are deep in the network of our American moral order because they are tales of a culture hero. Most cultures have such tales. Cultures heroes offer specific models for people to follow. Moses, Confucius, the Charioteer of the Bhagavad Gita, Mohammed, Jesus, St. Francis, Joan of Arc, Henry V at Agincourt, Robert the Bruce, Frederick Barbarossa, Queen Elizabeth the First—all are culture heroes whose tales tell their hearers how to act, what is admirable. Such tales we may well call epics—emotionally satisfying, dramatic tales about a culture hero whose life sets forth a model of a moral order.

We remember tales in programmatic memory. Specifically in linguistic memory—for we remember them as strings of words. Systemic memory, though, is impressed by repetition. The most important thing about a tale in an orientation system—in a moral order—may well be not whether it is true or false, but rather how often it is told, how often it is heard.

A tale is a program whose open purpose is to amuse or instruct, but whose hidden purpose is to impress concepts and associations on systemic memory. The story of Little Red Riding Hood is popular throughout Europe. It comes to North America from Germany. (*Rotkäppchen* is her real name.) And those mothers and fathers who tell it to their young ones must, I think, find it comfortable for their own systemic memories, or else they would not tell it. Little Canadian, English, German, and Dutch children all are likely to hear the story of *Rotkäppchen*. It is one of the stories that makes them modern Europeans.

Culturally speaking, it is the tales we hear in childhood that make us what we are. This central idea came to me from Hays. He got it from Bonheur. Bonheur wrote a book reviewing school text stories from French history and literature. His introduction says: "These are the tales that made us Frenchmen."

The French do *not* read or hear, over and over, the story of George Washington crossing the Delaware or at Valley Forge. They *do* hear and read, over and over, the story of Joan of Arc. They hear of Henry IV—who thought that Paris was worth a mass and who said, as king, that it was his task to put a chicken into every French housewife's pot. "Paris is worth a mass." If you are not a student of French history, you are not likely to make much of that. But most French people understand.

What are the stories that make people Prussians? Prussians were not likely to have heard much about George Washington and Valley Forge nor about Henry IV, Paris, and masses. But they will have heard the story of Prince Friedrich von Homburg at the battle of Fehrbellin. And they will have heard the story of Frederick the Great and the miller of Potsdam. (Details of these stories in the Notes.)

I was chiefly educated in the public schools of Los Angeles, but I spent the eighth grade in Toronto, where we studied Canadian history. We dwelt long and lovingly on the War of 1812. I already knew all about that! I had been through it several times before in Los Angeles. "Don't give up the ship!" "We have met the enemy and they are ours!" And above all, the Battle of New Orleans.

The stories of the War of 1812, along with those of the United Empire Loyalists, are the chief stories that make one a Canadian. I heard all those stories for the first time: the capture of Detroit, brave Brock at Queenston Heights, the shameful loss of the Royal Standard at York, and so on. I kept waiting and waiting for the stories they had told me in Los Angeles—for "Don't give up the ship!" and "We have met the enemy and they are ours!" and Andy Jackson at New Orleans. The first two never came. The third got one throwaway line.

They did not actually lie to us about the War of 1812, either in Los Angeles or in Toronto. But they told us two entirely different groups of stories. All they had to do was make a judicious selection. The stories they told us in Los Angeles helped make me an American. The stories they told us in Toronto would have helped make me a Canadian.

A mature socionomics, I submit, one day may bring together tales of social science studies that, taken together, can justify and sustain the moral foundations of a stable world order. If the best of these tales are retold by literary artists of great skill, in language all can understand, we might then have a set of charter myths resting on the best scientific research rather than on dreams and fantasies. Rituals and ceremonies might then fix on a few dramatic episodes in such tales—episodes, it may be, of only minor and incidental scientific importance. Dramas like *Yellow Jack*—on the research that led to the conquest of yellow fever—might drive home the lesson. A moral order that rests on socionomics does not seem likely to gain and hold the love of the people unless it is enshrined in great works of art echoed and reechoed—in literature, music, dance, and architecture. And especially in ceremonies.

If you want to know what sort of tales make people Christians, Moslems, Buddhists, Hindus, Parsis, or Jews, the answer is plain. Those tales are told in their sacred books—the Old Testament, the New Testament, the Koran, and the Bhagavad-Gita, and the rest. However, those tales are not just told in sacred books. They are told and retold weekly in sermons, read and reread nightly in the homes of the pious, and enacted and reenacted yearly in the great ceremonial cycles.

Consider Spicer's study of the Yaqui of Sonora. Spicer was especially struck by two facts about the Yaqui. First, that they had suffered much more than most of their neighbors from trouble with the Mexican government. For years, a guerilla war had raged between the Yaqui and the Mexican army. Hundreds of Yaqui fled as refugees to Tucson, Arizona. Hundreds more were sent as captives to plantations in distant parts of Mexico. Second, that the Yaqui, despite this suffering, kept their value system—their way of life—more tenaciously than neighbors and close relatives like the Pima or the Mayo.

Spicer looked for a central unvarying element in their culture to explain this tenacity of values. He believes he found it in their ceremonial cycle. He believes he found a like tenacity in the culture of the Jews. Though spread wide over the world, harried and hunted and persecuted, the Jews have kept up their value system, their way of life. He thought that they, too, owed the survival of their way of life to their ceremonial cycle.

I submit that we can better understand the role of such ceremonies in transmitting the moral order if we view them as belonging to the topmost level of a four-level intellectual structure:

- Level 1: The central values of a culture, embodied in its themes.

- Level 2: The set of governing laws, rules, or customs that created the social order. These rules are justified by rationales that rely on the central values.

- Level 3: Governing tales. These may be wholly truthful. They may be distorted accounts of actual events. Or they may be imaginary. But they must be dramatic. They must be works of art. They must absorb the interest of the hearers. These tales embody the central values, the culture themes.

- Level 4: First, a ceremonial cycle emphasizes central events in the governing tales. The ceremonies call the tales to mind. Subliminally, the ceremonies insist on the truth of key elements in the tales, however fantastic they may seem. The ceremonies may not themselves lay much stress on the core values or on the rationale or even on the themes. But they do lay stress on dramatic incidents in the governing tales. Second, the thematic elements of the central values are echoed in ways no one yet understands—in child training patterns, in art styles, and in general life-styles.

I take it that this complex structure is evolved through trial and error. Because each individual element of it—each culture trait—tends to be memorable. Subliminally or consciously. And because a selection snowball of traits begins. As these traits are linked by association, if you remember any, it is easier to remember the others. And finally, that the whole complex gets to be cherished. Because it comforts the mind, through meeting a need for a coherent model of the social order. And because it tends to produce a social order that in practice more or less tends to work; it tends to feed the members, shelter them, lead them toward love and friendship, and protect them from their enemies.

I take it that if the system works more or less, the mind, seeking its own comfort, will be happy to distort reality in order to produce a glow of success around the mental network that provides the moral order. By suppressing from consciousness the memory of failures and shortcomings of the system. By highlighting its successes. The latching bias, hard at work. And this process of reality distortion—this myth making—helps make a creaky system work a little better.

Art styles, in ways we poorly understand, symbolize the fundamental structures of our value systems. An eloquent analysis of the importance of the circle as a symbol to the Oglala Dakota was given by one of them to Walker:

> The Oglala believe the circle to be sacred because the great spirit caused everything in nature to be round except stone. Stone is the implement of

destruction. The sun and the sky, the earth and the moon are round like a shield, though the sky is deep like a bowl. Everything that breathes is round like the stem of a plant. Since the great spirit has caused everything to be round mankind should look upon the circle as sacred, for it is the symbol of all things in nature except stone. It is also the symbol of the circle that makes the edge of the world and therefore of the four winds that travel there. Consequently it is also the symbol of the year. The day, the night, and the moon go in a circle above the sky. Therefore the circle is a symbol of these divisions of time and hence the symbol of all time.

For these reasons the Oglala make their *tipis* circular, their camp-circle circular, and sit in a circle at all ceremonies. The circle is also the symbol of the *tipi* and of shelter. If one makes a circle for an ornament and it is not divided in any way, it should be understood as the symbol of the world and of time.

Radin quoted this keen analysis of a central theme in Dakota culture as evidence that red men are as shrewd as white men. Geertz makes the important point that while *one* Oglala saw this pattern clearly and consciously, *most* did not. To most, says Geertz, this meaning would have been intuitively sensed, not consciously interpreted. The circle is a theme—a central ordering principle—in the systemic memory of the mind of Oglala. It got to be that way from the tales the Oglala told, from the ceremonies they enacted, from the very way they built their dwellings and arranged their camps. To a young Oglala, most important things seemed to be in circles.

6.7   CHILD TRAINING AND CULTURE THEMES

I take it that most people learn their morals in childhood. Plainly the thematic tales of a culture work on children when they hear or read them. The ceremonies impress children when they take part. The fine arts also reach and move the feelings of children. And so fine arts help those children learn the themes of a culture.

But one of the most popular topics for holocultural studies has been the fit between specific child-training practices and specific adult ways of life. Levinson and Malone review scores of such studies. Investigators have found links between such things as: beating of children and long menstrual taboos for women, severity of child discipline and complexity of art styles, early weaning of infants and romantic love as a basis for marriage, love-oriented punishment of children and fear of death among adults, physical protection of children and love of gambling among adults, physical tormenting of children and humbling of women.

Consider on the one hand whether mothers carry their infants about with them and the way adults sing their songs. Ayres shows that societies in which most songs have a regular rhythm tend to be societies in which mothers carry their infants. Thus early in life an infant associates the rhythmic sway of walking with the warmth and security of the mother's body. On the other hand, societies in which mothers instead usually keep their infants in a cradle, on a cradleboard, or in a hammock differ in their song styles. There, most songs tend to have an irregular rhythm: The measures vary in length; the accented beats come unevenly.

Ayres was a member of the Lomax group and took her song style codings from them. As part of her work with Lomax, she also found that the musical range of folk songs was linked to the amount of physical stress people place on infants. Tables 6.10 and 6.11 show her findings. Ayres looked at several things as kinds of physical stress on infants: Do the people pierce holes in a baby's nose, ears, or lips? Do they cut off the foreskin of a baby boy's penis or cut off a baby girl's clitoris? Do they cut scars into a baby's skin? Do they stick needles into the baby to inoculate it for a disease? Do they burn the baby with a hot iron to cauterize some hurt? Do they carry out some regular, persistent, and vigorous molding, shaping, or stretching of a baby's head, limbs, or body? Do they knock out one of the baby's teeth? Do they slap it around so badly that it bleeds internally? If they did any of these things before the baby was two years old, then Ayres called that infant stress. Societies in which people thus treat infants are societies in which folk songs tend to vary widely in musical range, from high to low in the musical scale, almost as though they were screaming in pain.

The earliest of these holocultural studies about child training and personality is Whiting and Child's; their book set off a wave of interest and criticism. They wanted to measure the subtle effects of child training practices on the unconscious mind. In our terms, on the thematic structure of systemic memory. So on the one hand, they asked: How early and how suddenly did mothers wean their infants from the breast? How early and how severely did the women toilet train them? Did the older people let children give free reign to their sexual urges—let them fondle themselves and each other as they pleased? How early and how suddenly did people make the children care for themselves self-reliantly, instead of depending on others? How early and how severely did people punish children for disobeying or defying or fighting?

On the other hand, Whiting and Child sought to peep into the hidden places of the adult mind—the adult systemic memory—by looking at their theories of illness. Why did people think they got sick? What did they think would be best to cure them?

Wasn't it ingenious to use theories of illness as a measure of subconscious orientations and attitudes? Of course, in none of the societies studied did the people know anything about microorganisms. So they would only be projecting their own hidden fears in their theories.

How did the study turn out? Mixed. The first and the last did well. Severe weaning went strongly with oral explanations of illness. Severe punishment for aggression went with aggressive explanations of illness. Early stress on self-reliance leaned a little toward a link with dependence explanations of illness—but not enough to mean anything. Sex training and toilet training did not link up at all with illness explanations. If we take the five as a group, we see that Whiting and Child do have something. We would not expect to get a result as striking as that of Table 6.12 even once in a thousand random samples from a universe in which the two things were not linked.

TABLE 6.10   Rhythmic Singing and Carrying Practices

PROPOSITION: *Where mothers usually carry their babies, adults usually sing in regular rhythm.*

	Carry Babies	*Do Not Carry Babies*
Regular Rhythm	Ainu (Japan) Amhara (Ethiopia) Atayal (Taiwan) Azande (Zaire) Bambara (Mali) Chagga (Tanganyika) Goajiro (Colombia) Gond (Central India) Hausa (Nigeria) Jivaro (Ecuador) Lau (Fiji) Murngin (Australia) Samoans (Polynesia) Semang (Malaya) Tanala (Madagascar) Tibetans Tikopia (Melanesia) Tuareg (Sahara) Vietnamese Wolof (Senegal) Yaruro (Venezuela) Yoruba (Nigeria) (22)	Greeks Irish Lapps (Scandinavia) Pomo (California) Shilluk (The Sudan) Yakut (Siberia) (6)
Irregular Rhythm	Aymara (Bolivia) Balinese Koreans Kung (Namibia) Okinawans (Japan) Tarahumara (Mexico) Yaghans (Tierra del Fuego) (7)	Burmese Chukchee (Siberia) Cuna (Panama) Czechs Iroquois (New York) Kazak (USSR) Kurds (Iraq) Malays Maori (New Zealand) Nootka (Canada) Nuer (The Sudan) Papago (Arizona) Quechua (Peru) Salish (Canada) Samoyed (Siberia) Seri (Sonora) Thai Yap (Micronesia) Zuñi (New Mexico) (19)

SOURCE: Ayres (1973: 396).
Correlation (phi coefficient): .52.
Chance risk (Fisher's Exact Test): < .001.
N = 54.

TABLE 6.11 Musical Range and Child Abuse

PROPOSITION: *The earlier in an infant's life the people begin to hurt it on purpose, the wider is the musical range (pitch) of the folk songs those people sing.*

	Before 2 Weeks Old	2 Weeks to 2 Years Old	2 to 6 Years Old	6 to 15 Years Old	Over 15 Years Old
Wide Song Range (N = 10)	Javanese (Indonesia) Burmese Hupa (California) Lau (Fiji Islands)	Yankees (USA) Masai (Kenya) Shilluk (The Sudan) Irish Zuñi (New Mexico) Okinawans (Japan)			
Medium Song Range (N = 19)	Azande (The Sudan) Amhara (Ethiopia) Lakalai (Melanesia) Navaho (New Mexico) Hausa (Nigeria) Salish (British Columbia) Yoruba (Nigeria) Cayapo (Brazil)	Thai (Thailand) Zulu (South Africa) Bambara (Mali)	Chaga (Tanganyika) Tikopia (Melanesia) Ainu (Japan)	Mende (Sierra Leone) Fon (Dahomey) Camayura (Brazil) Semang (Malaya)	Aymara (Bolivia)
Narrow Song Range (N = 18)	Jivaro (Ecuador) Nootka (British Columbia)	Tuareg (Western Sahara) Paiute (Great Basin of North America)	Kurds (Iraq and Iran) Yap (Micronesia) Atayal (Taiwan) Gond (India) Amahuaca (Peru) Yahgan (Tierra del Fuego)	Wolof (Senegal) Witoto (Colombia) Fore (New Guinea) Trumai (Brazil)	Slave Indians (Northwest Canada) Palau (Micronesia) Goajiro (Colombia) Chukchee (Siberia)
Total	14	11	9	8	5

SOURCE: Lomax et al. (1968: 215).
Correlation (Kendall's tau-b): .41.
Chance risk (derived from standard deviation of Kendall's S): $< .001$.
N = 47.

TABLE 6.12   Weaning, Eating, and Illness

PROPOSITION: *Where mothers wean their babies early, adults tend to blame illness*
on something the sick person ate or drank.

	Illness Not Blamed on Food or Drink	*Illness Blamed on Food or Drink*
Early Weaning	Lapps (Scandinavia) Chamorro (Micronesia) Samoans (Polynesia) (3)	Marquesans (Polynesia) Dobuans (Melanesia) Baiga (India) Kwoma (New Guinea) Thonga (Mozambique) Alorese (Indonesia) Chagga (Tanganyika) Navaho (Arizona) Dahomeans Lesu (Melanesia) Masai (Kenya) Lepcha (Sikkim) Maori (New Zealand) Pukapukans (Polynesia) Trobrianders (Melanesia) Kwakiutl (British Columbia) Manus (Melanesia) (17)
Late Weaning	Arapesh (New Guinea) Balinese (Indonesia) Hopi (Arizona) Tanala (Madagascar) Paiute (Oregon) Chenchu (India) Teton Dakota (USA) Flathead (Montana) Papago (Arizona) Venda (South Africa) Warrau (Venezuela) Wogeo (New Guinea) Ontong-Javanese (Polynesia) (13)	Chiricahua (Arizona) Comanche (Texas) Siriono (Bolivia) Bena (Tanganyika) Slave Indians (Canada) Kurtatchi (Melanesia) (6)

SOURCE: Whiting and Child (1953: 156).
Correlation (phi coefficient): .54.
Chance risk (Fisher's Exact Test): $< .001$.
N = 39.

Can we say, then, that early and severe weaning seems to lead the systemic memory to worry about things people eat or drink? Or might it be instead that worrying about things people eat or drink leads to early and severe weaning? Table 6.12 cannot tell us.

Another study of child training styles by Lambert, Triandis, and Wolf found links between treatment of young children and the lifestyles of the gods. Where a

TABLE 6.13   Gods and Nurses Hurting Babies

PROPOSITION: *The gods tend to be dangerous in societies where nurses hurt babies,
but friendly where nurses do not.*

	Nurses Hurt Babies	*Nurses Do Not Hurt Babies*
Dangerous Gods	Alorese (Indonesia)	Andamanese (near Malaya)
	Aymara (Bolivia)	Bena (Tanganyika)
	Chagga (Tanganyika)	Lepcha (Sikkim)
	Chiricahua (Arizona)	Lesu (Melanesia)
	Dahomeans	Manus (Melanesia)
	Kurtatchi (Melanesia)	Wogeo (New Guinea)
	Kwakiutl (Canada)	Yagua (Peru)
	Kwoma (New Guinea)	(7)
	Maori (New Zealand)	
	Navaho (Arizona)	
	Ojibwa (the Great Lakes)	
	Lovedu (South Africa)	
	Siriono (Bolivia)	
	Tenetehara (Brazil)	
	Tepoztlan (Mexico)	
	Thonga (Mozambique)	
	Venda (South Africa)	
	(17)	
Friendly Gods	Arapesh (New Guinea)	Ashanti (Ghana)
	Chamorro (Micronesia)	Chenchu (India)
	Klamath (Oregon)	Cheyenne (Western USA)
	Mbundu (Angola)	Comanche (Texas)
	Ontong-Javanese (Polynesia)	Fijians
	Pukapukans (Polynesia)	Hopi (Arizona)
	Tallensi (Ghana)	Papago (Arizona)
	(7)	Samoans
		Teton Dakota (USA)
		Tikopia (Melanesia)
		Winnebago (Central USA)
		Zuñi (New Mexico)
		(12)

SOURCE: Lambert et al. (1959).
Correlation (phi coefficient): .34.
Chance risk (Fisher's Exact Test): .03.
N = 43.

child's nurse tended also to hurt it, or the gods were usually dangerous, children
were trained early to be independent and self-reliant. But where a child's nurse
was gentle and kind to it, the gods, too, tended to be kindly (see Table 6.13).

In general, however, culture themes might well set up a snowball—a positive
feedback causal system—between child training and adult personality. Each
tends to encourage the other.

I have presented a general model of a moral order—a social and cultural system by which morality is announced, communicated, and maintained among people. That model emphasizes the importance of social ties between people and their moralnets. In Chapter 10, I return to this theme by studying the most important component of the moralnet—often comprising it entirely—the family.

There is a great deal of evidence linking weak moralnets to mental and social ills. In the remaining chapters of Part Two, I look at the causes of nine such problems: mental illness, alcoholism, suicide, child abuse, juvenile delinquency, neglect of the aged, sex role discrimination, divorce, and extramarital parenting. My aim there shall be to apply the Five Steps to each of these problems. Incomplete and partial as it is, this effort constitutes my estimate of the human situation with respect to problems of personal and family life. A leading theme of this review, as I have said, is the great importance to each person of the social ties with the moralnet—either directly or through the nuclear family. Weakened moralnets mean trouble.

Notes

6.1   Once More Back to Tristan

For this story, I relied chiefly on three works by Peter Munch (1964, 1970, 1971). I also used Booy (1957) and Mackay (1963). The ancestry of the Tristaners is traced in Mackay (1963: 69f.); the photographs in these works show that European traits dominate their facial features. According to Mackay (1963: 244), 289 people were evacuated, of whom 264 were native Tristaners. Munch (1964: 375) counts 262 returners. I quote from Munch (1971: 299-300) about their reaction to England. And I follow Munch (1970) on the importance of their social network to their morale, and its role as the chief attraction calling them back to Tristan. Final quote is from Munch (1970: 1309).

6.2   The Cybernetic Model of the Mind

My understanding of the model is set forth in Naroll (1981); it is derived from Hays (1981), Powers (1973), Bowlby (1969, 1973), and Benzon (1978), but I recommend Peterfreund and Schwartz (1971) as preparatory reading.

6.3   The Human Social Instinct

Adam Smith (1970), *Wealth of Nations*, Book I, Chapter 2, alleges an innate tendency for people to trade goods and services.
Trading patterns common among hunting and gathering bands—in Table 6.1 and in Sahlins (1972: 264-267).
The general pattern of the primeval hunting and gathering band is discussed in Lancaster (1975: 78f.), Washburn (1961), and Lee and DeVore (1968).
On instinctive social bonding between mother and child, see Bowlby (1969: 177-361).
On sociobiology, I consider Wilson (1975) weak on human behavior in particular but strong on animal behavior in general.
On the gibbons, see Carpenter (1948). On the social organization of chimpanzees, gorillas, orangutans, and gibbons, see Schaller (1965b).
Almost all hunters and gatherers wander in a territory held communally by many families. A notable exception are the Algonkians in North America, who in recent centuries at least, have had family hunting territories. Speck (1915) argued that this pattern occurred earlier than the fur trade with the French, the Dutch, and the English, but I find Leacock (1954) persuasive in her counter-argument that this Algonkian pattern was a later development, as part of that fur trade.
On Siriono, see Holmberg (1969), and Turnbull (1972) on the Ik.
On grief and mourning, see Bowlby (1969), Parkes (1972), and Marris (1974).
On near universality of weeping at funerals, see Rosenblatt, Walsh, and Jackson (1976: 15).

On Balinese etiquette, attitude toward death, and reincarnation and manifestations of affection, see Bateson and Mead (1942) and Belo (1956: 167-172).

Lynch (1977: 55-8) reviews the literature on higher age-specific death rates of the widowed.

On the strength of social ties and death in Alameda County, California, see Berkman and Syme (1979).

On which aspects of life seem most important to people in the United States today, see Campbell, Converse, and Rodgers (1976: 76).

6.4   Networks and Morals

On the concept of tribe as an ethnic group, see Naroll (1970c: 721-765).

On the delimitation of higher civilizations, see Naroll, Bullough, and Naroll (1974: xxix-xxxvii).

On the development of reference group theory in social psychology, see the Introduction to Hyman and Singer (1968); studies on normative reference groups there are at pages 238-318.

On primary groups, see Cooley (1961).

Social network studies are reviewed by Whitten and Wolfe (1973). The more important studies include Bott (1957), Boissevain (1974), Laumann (1973), Mayer (1961), and Parkin (1969).

Sorokin (1937-1941) on social and cultural dynamics. His conclusions are at III: 375-380, 498.

About Table 6.2, see also Banks and Textor (1963: FC 125/FC66, FC 125/FC 67, FC 125/FC 68, FC 125/FC 69). When Banks and Textor speak of "Interest Articulation by Anomic Groups," they mean the political importance of riots and demonstrations; they are following the thinking of Almond and Coleman (1960: 34).

Zimmerman and Cervantes (1956, especially chaps. 7 and 8, 1960, especially chaps. 3, 5, 6, and 10).

Empey and Lubeck (1971: 34-36) review eleven studies of delinquents, all finding that the delinquents work in gangs, not alone.

I thought Glueck and Glueck (1950) the most impressive of these eleven studies.

Hirschi (1969) is among the best of the juvenile delinquency studies I have seen. (More on these in Chapter 12.) Four lines of further analysis would have made his findings more trustworthy. First, he should have analyzed data comparatively for those boys and girls who he knows are lying about their police records with those who appear truthful. Indeed, a set of measures of response candor might well have been factor analyzed: I have in mind the methods of data quality control proposed in Naroll (1962a, 1970d) and much improved in Rummel (1970b) and Rohner, DeWalt, and Ness (1973). For example, I would have taken admission of a theft of something under two dollars as evidence of candor, and would distrust any boy or girl who denied such a theft. Second, more multiple correlation and linear regression analysis might help us understand better how much of the variance in delinquency (as measured by police records and by self-reporting) is explained when ties to parents, peers, and school are all allowed for. Table 51, at page 156, suggests that the three major sets of social attachments (family, school, peers) together explain only about 25 percent of the variance—assuming that delinquent behavior is the effect and these are the causes, and assuming the data are accurate. Third, the influence of the church or synagogue should also be considered; those ties should be measured and allowed for. Fourth and most difficult, some attempt should be made to determine from among the candid self-reporters whether their first delinquent act preceded or followed their first associations with older delinquent boys or girls.

The study of Zimmerman and Cervantes (1956, 1960) urgently needs replication. But as in a replication of Hirschi's study, more attention needs to be given to quality control of response candor and to getting sequential information on delinquent behavior. Did that behavior occur before or after the moralnet structure was formed?

Notes to Table 6.3 through 6.7. By "crime" in these tables is meant what Hirschi calls a "delinquent act": theft, assault, vandalism. Hirschi's questions are so worded as not always to distinguish serious offenses from peccadillos; therefore, I have put "crime" in quotation marks. All measures of chance risk (statistical significance) are two-tailed probabilities derived from the Standard Error of Kendall's S.

On ties between delinquent boys and parents, see Rohner (1975: 85-88).

Feshback (1970) and Jackson (1950) compare delinquent with normal boys.

6.5   World Images and Culture Themes

Tapp and Kohlberg (1971) offer evidence on the sequence of the learning of moral ideas in modern nations, but they do not investigate the moral network.

On games of combat and warlikeness, see Sipes (1973).

On theology, see Swanson (1960), Spencer (1970), and Davis (1971).

On art styles, see Fischer (1961); Roberts, Arth, and Bush (1959) on games of strategy.

In Table 6.9, societies are coded *high* on complexity if both of the following conditions are met; they are coded *low* if neither condition is met; they are coded of *medium* complexity if only one of the two conditions is met. Condition 1: Political Integration coded as "Minimal State," as "Little State," or as "State." Condition 2: Social Stratification coded as "Hereditary Aristocracy" or as "Complex Stratification."

On folk song styles, see Lomax et al. (1968).

6.6   Tales, Ceremonies, Fine Arts

On the power of subliminal communication, see Key (1974) and Silverman (1976, 1975a, 1975b, 1972).

On myths, see Malinowski (1926).

On Kaux and the Ona, see Gusinde (1931).

Little Red Riding Hood, or *Rotkäppchen*, as every American and European child must know, is a folk tale of a little girl who is almost eaten by a wolf. The wolf had devoured her grandmother and posed in bed as that lady.

Washington, as every American schoolchild knows, by December 1776, had suffered a series of sharp defeats. Most people thought the War for American Independence was over—with the British the victors. On Christmas Eve, during a bitter snowstorm, Washington led his few remaining soldiers to surprise and destroy a large British detachment, thus reviving the hopes of the American revolutionaries.

One year later, at Valley Forge, he held his army together through a bitter winter—a story that is told to point up the moral of determination and faith in the face of discouragement.

No one today credits the tale by an early biographer that Washington as a little boy displayed great virtue in refusing to lie to his father about having cut down a cherry tree. Yet that tale was told to millions of schoolchildren for a hundred years.

Bonheur (1963: 17-18) is a collection of French elementary school tales retold—sometimes irreverently: history, geography, science, and especially literature. It is the common recollection of these tales that Bonheur thinks make the French French: "*Quelques images, quelques récitations, quelques incantations, quelques dictées qui font que, justement, ils sont tous français.*"

Henry of Navarre, the leader of the Protestant movement of predominantly Catholic France, inherited the French throne in 1589. But events proved that as a Protestant he could not hope to rule safely or securely; instead, his succession only continued a bitter civil war. He announced his conversion to Catholicism in 1593. Thus he ended the civil war and became one of France's most admired and respected rulers, providing well for his old Protestant friends.

Prince Friederich von Homburg, as every Prussian who ever saw Kleist's (1964) famous drama well remembers, led the Prussian (then Brandenburger) cavalry at the victory of Fehrbellin in 1675. But the victory proved less fruitful than it might have because the Prince deliberately disobeyed his monarch's order to stand fast and led his cavalry into a premature charge. That monarch, the Great Elector, then condemned him to death. The court was shocked at this cruel sentence against a popular young nobleman, and the army protested. Whereupon the Elector announced that if the Prince deemed his sentence unjust, he would revoke it and grant him a full pardon. The Prince, however, acknowledged the justice of his sentence and went to his death. *Befehl ist Befehl*: Orders are orders.

Kleist's play is fiction. His battle of Fehrbellin is nothing like the battle that actually happened, and his Prince of Homburg is nothing like the actual Prince, who was a middle-aged man in command of the Elector's advance guard, not of his reserve. The Prince did well in the battle and seems to have lived happily ever after, dying at a ripe old age in 1708. Details are in the notes and appendices to Samuel's edition of the play (see Kleist, 1964).

Many stories are told about Frederick the Great, but perhaps the favorite concerns his dealings with the Miller of Potsdam. It is, we are assured, perfectly true. At the height of his reign, after his victory in the Seven Years' War, he laid out a pleasure garden at his palace, *Sans Souci*. Defacing his vista and annoying his ears was an old mill nearby, run by an old miller. Frederick's ministers tried to buy the mill so that they could pull it down. But the miller refused to sell. Frederick himself thereupon sought out the miller and demanded to know his price. The miller still insisted he was not selling.

"Why," said the king to the miller, "if I want to, I can just send my soldiers to pull this old barn down about your ears and not pay you a thing!" And so, of course, he could have. And no dog in Prussia would have dared to bark.

"Oh, no," answered the miller, "not so long as there is a law court in Potsdam!"

And Frederick left the miller without another word. The old miller kept his mill and heard no more about it. The tale was retold many times (see Nelson, 1970: 207). Moral: The people are subject to the king, but the king is subject to the law.

In Los Angeles, the stories they told us about the War of 1812 prominently featured the defeat of the American frigate *Chesapeake*—because its commander's dying words were, "Don't give up the ship." Then Perry at the naval battle of Lake Erie and his victory report: "We have met the enemy and they are ours." And Jackson's defeat of a British army of Peninsular War veterans at the Battle of New Orleans. What they did not tell us was that the British won most of the battles and that our peace negotiators felt they did very well indeed to settle the war without any changes whatever.

In Toronto, on the other hand, they told us of the aftermath of the American Revolution: the saga of the United Empire Loyalists. It was some pages into that story before I realized that these great patriots were none other than the despicable Tories of my Los Angeles history books. They were the first white settlers of Ontario; they wrought well, and Toronto will never cease to praise them. Then the War of 1812: the story of how a small British force under General Brock captured a large American force at Detroit; then the Battle of Queenston Heights, where Brock fell while leading his troops to victory over the invading Americans; then a paragraph or two of mourning on the loss of a Royal Standard to invading Americans at York (now called Toronto). All matters that interested my teachers in Los Angeles not at all.

On the key role of ceremony in preserving both value systems, see Spicer (1954) on the Yaqui and (1971) on the Jews.

The importance of the Jewish ceremonial cycle is reviewed in Zborowski and Herzog (1952: 37-69, 381-402).

The Oglala sacred circle is from Geertz (1970: 327), who got it from Paul Radin, who got it from James Walker, who got it from an Oglala informant.

6.7   Child Training and Culture Themes

Levinson (1977a, 1977b) and Levinson and Malone (1980: 199-106) review holocultural studies on the fit between specific child training procedures and specific adult ways of life.

On song rhythms and child carrying, see Ayres (1973).

On folksong styles and culture, see Lomax et al. (1968).

About the song style codings used in Tables 6.10 and 6.11—I was taught how Lomax coded such songs and consider this coding trustworthy.

On child training and personality, see Whiting and Child (1953).

The data in Table 6.12 that Whiting and Child (1953) needed are not easy to get from ethnographies. Herbert Kelman and Helen Floy Glenn, two of their coders, talked to me afterward about their coding work; they were uneasy about the validity of their codings because they had been pressed to make some decision, no matter how fragmentary the data. But since the coders did not know what Whiting and Child were after, there was usually no particular reason for their work to form a special pattern. It is the ethnographers, not the coders, who are more likely systematically to overestimate weaning age and to underestimate witchcraft importance (Whiting and Child's measure of "fear of others"). More on this problem in Naroll (1970d).

On treatment of the young and nature of the gods, see Lambert, Triandis, and Wolf (1959).

7 Mental Illness

7.1 DR. IHEMBI TREATS A NEUROTIC

Kimbinyi was a sick man. His heart beat rapidly; he had pains in his back, arms, and legs. If he tried to work in his cassava garden, he soon felt too tired to go on. So for long periods he did nothing, but simply shut himself up in his hut.

Then, the anthropologist Turner, who describes his case, told Kimbinyi's people about the celebrated practitioner Ihembi. They begged Turner to fetch Ihembi in his car. Turner brought not only Ihembi but his two assistants. They have different ways with their patients from those of our Western psychiatrists. They use herbs, but Turner doubts if these have much empirical effect on the patient. They use ritual—long ritual—which climaxes in the pretended removal of a stranger's tooth from the body of the patient. Similar sleight-of-hand tricks are a common practice among medicine men the world around. Turner knows the ways of doctors like Ihembi and thinks their methods often work well on neurotic patients. He thinks he knows why and how.

Ihembi and his patient, Kimbinyi, are Ndembu. The Ndembu tribe live in northwest Zambia. Their chief food comes from cassava, though they grow other crops as well, and the men net game in the forests around their small villages. Kimbinyi's village, in which about two dozen people lived in fourteen huts, was split into two rival family groups. The Mbaulu faction, much the larger, lived in a circle around the village meeting house. The Katoyi faction lived off to one side. Kimbinyi lived between the two—he was Katoyi on his father's side, but a Mbaulu on his mother's. Among the Ndembu people, the mother's side is more important. The chieftainship descends in the maternal line—and Kimbinyi had, in fact, a claim to the village chieftainship.

It was not likely that he would get the chieftainship, however. People lacked respect for him. He was a weakling. Furthermore, people said he was impotent. He had had no children, though he was now on his fourth marriage, and his wife, a woman of strong character, openly carried on a love affair with his cousin.

Dr. Ihembi's course of treatment helped Kimbinyi a great deal. A Beverly Hills psychoanalyst would be pleased if a patient with symptoms of like severity showed like improvement. That treatment restored Kimbinyi as an effective member of his village. After it, he worked in his cassava gardens, set traps for game in the forest, traveled long distances to visit friends and relatives, and talked long and animatedly with people who seemed sympathetic. And it would seem that he complained less about pains in his back, arms, and legs. This improvement showed up at once, and when Turner went back to the village a year later, still continued. Kimbinyi seemed to be enjoying life.

Turner believes that organically there had been nothing wrong with Kimbinyi except possibly a little rheumatism—common among the Ndembu. Turner considers this case one of mental illness—neurosis. And in Turner's opinion it is with such illnesses that Ndembu practioners like Ihembi are particularly effective. The ritual they practice is a kind of group therapy. But it is unlike the group therapy found among us in North America today. For the group is not a collection of patients organized to help each other. Rather it is the patient's own natural moralnet. *And the therapist not only treats the patient; he treats the whole moralnet.* In Kimbinyi's case, the whole village.

The Ndembu people, patients and physicians alike, saw Kimbinyi's problems as a combination of spirit possession and witchcraft. Dr. Ihembi hinted that it was partly Kimbinyi's wife and mother-in-law who were bewitching him. But his problem was chiefly with the ghost of a former chieftain, Samalichi, who was afflicting Kimbinyi in a special way—the *ihamba* way. The word *ihamba* is at once the name of a particular medical cult and the name of the evil with which that cult deals. That evil, the *ihamba* evil, is embodied in the upper frontal incisor teeth of certain ancestral spirits—spirits who when alive were mighty hunters with firearms. Hamlet was haunted by his father's spirit. Kimbinyi was haunted in a different way by the spirit of his grandmother's cousin.

The Ndembu believe that the spirit of Samalichi placed his incisor tooth, his *ihamba*, in Kimbinyi's body. There the tooth wandered about, causing pain wherever it went—biting him, as it were. In their eyes the problem was to catch and extract the wandering tooth.

The key point for Turner—the point at which the ancient cult meets modern theory of psychosomatic medicine and moralnet theory—lies in the social element of Ndembu therapy. Ndembu believe it is difficult to find and catch the offending tooth. They believe that only a highly skilled doctor who comes from far away is likely to succeed. (Needless to say, such a doctor could not himself be involved in village quarrels.) They believe further that even such a skilled doctor can succeed only if the villagers all join with him in the ceremony and, under his direction, take part in the treatment.

All must sing when the drum beats—singing is important. Through it the people add their power to that of the therapist. But the people must do something else to help. When the therapist calls on each member of the village in turn, that villager must then declare all the grudges or hard feelings he or she has felt toward the patient. And the patient must in turn make a like avowal of his or her resentments toward the villagers.

For Turner, this airing of grudges is a central element of the whole performance. The physician must persist until the central tensions troubling the moralnet have come out, and he must understand the tensions himself before he starts the ritual. So he begins his course of treatment by interviewing the villagers. Although Dr. Ihembi was a stranger from afar, he was a wise old man who had spent his life learning the intricacies of Ndembu social structure and the histories of their rival family groups. So he knew what to ask. Turner, too, knew the village situation thoroughly, having compiled a genealogy and collected the history of the family disputes for four generations back. He thought that Dr. Ihembi soon gained a grasp of the village social situation, and thus well understood the social tensions that were playing upon Kimbinyi.

During the course of the ritual, the entire village works together to cure the sick person. And by confessing their grudges, they tend to clear the air, to create a new rapport uniting the moralnet in feeling. Turner watched this happen during Kimbinyi's treatment.

But in this case as least, the airing of grudges seems to have brought the village tensions out into the open. The result resembled the lancing of a boil. The people believed that the body of Kimbinyi was healed because Dr. Ihembi removed the biting *ihamba* tooth of the dead spirit. What happened within the year was that this metaphor was acted out in the social life of the village. The "tooth" that had actually been biting the village was the strain between the two rival factions. That "tooth" in fact was pulled. For the Katoyi people all moved away—all but Kimbinyi and his wife. Among the movers was his wife's lover. So all the social tensions were resolved. Had Dr. Ihembi dropped a hint here or there? At one point, he certainly suggested to Kimbinyi that *he* might move away. It begins to look as though Dr. Ihembi functioned not only as a psychotherapist but also as a sociologist. No one had to tell *him* that weakened moralnets mean trouble.

7.2   MENTAL ILLNESS AROUND THE WORLD

By mental illness, I mean a disorder of the mind rather than the body. In the cybernetic model, it is easy to tell the one from the other. The body of a computer is its hardware; the mind of a computer is its software—its programs and its data. A typical computer has a strictly defined body: an inventory of physical components. It may have an infinite variety of software supplied to it. However powerful the hardware, however swift the central processing unit, however capacious and quick of access the memory, a computer can do nothing at all without software. Apply this model to human beings: The "meatware" is the body—the tissue of the nervous system, whose most important part is the brain. But however healthy the body of a child, it cannot live without learning; the software is the mind; it consists of all that has been learned: Learned behavior patterns correspond to computer programs; and learned information—the model of the world outside the mind—corresponds to computer data.

This distinction between mind and body fits well with the general point of view among psychiatrists today. In psychiatry, serious disorders of the mind are usually called psychoses. Psychiatrists classify psychoses as either *organic* (reflecting known or presumed disorders of the body—that is, the nervous tissue or "meatware")—or else *functional* (of the mind alone, existing in bodies that seem healthy, without any known or indicated organic disorder). Organic psychoses then are illnesses of the meatware—the body—reflected in the mind; functional psychoses are of the software—of the mind alone.

In computers, of course, hardware disorders—"bugs"—often produce symptoms or "glitches" in the software. Simple test programs can detect hardware bugs and so distinguish hardware-caused glitches from software-caused ones. Unfortunately, we cannot move people into (and then out of) a warm, caring, satisfying social environment to see if that relieves their mental symptoms. Further, and more important, it is easy for a computer to *unlearn*. Turn the power off, and it is a new-born infant again. So we can always start fresh with new programs and new data, if we want to. But human learning seems largely irreversible; memories may gradually fade but they cannot be erased. So a "mentally ill"—badly programmed—computer may easily be healed by starting over, but there may be no way to help a badly programmed person.

A worldwide study sponsored by the World Health Organization (WHO) has recently shown that psychiatrists know how to identify mental illness fairly consistently in a wide variety of cultures (details in Appendix A).

7.2.1   Range of Variation of Mental Illness

In that WHO study, IPSS as it is called, researchers looked only at people who came to their centers of treatment. Consequently, their work tells us nothing about the epidemiology of mental illness—its relative frequency among the communities served by these mental hospitals. The more that experts look at this point, the less they feel they really know about it. On the one hand, there is a great deal of evidence suggesting wide variation in rates of mental illness among cultures around the world. On the other hand, no one has ever directly measured such variation in a trustworthy way.

That there is indeed variation is suggested by a number of studies. To begin with, as we shall see in Section 7.4, there is wide variation in rates of mental hospital admissions around the world—and indirect evidence suggests that in part this variation must reflect variation in the underlying mental illness rate. Further, there are a number of particular syndromes—like Arctic hysteria, Malay *amok* and *latah*, and the *susto* of Guatemala and Mexico—that are found only in a few particular cultures. Finally, there have been at least eleven well-conducted community surveys of mental illness, and these report widely varying rates. Kato, for example, reporting studies of over 60,000 Japanese, found a prevalence of depressive disorders of only 2 in 10,000, while Sethi and Gupta found a rate of 69 in 10,000 among 500 Indian families. The difficulty is that, unlike the IPSS project, these studies did not follow a standard set of concepts and methods of diagnosis. Hence, for example, we do not know how much these differences reflect differences in what Kato and Sethi notice and call depression—rather than differences in the peoples studied.

With the IPSS study, however, we are confident that at all nine field research centers, standard concepts, methods, and research instruments ensure that substantially the same kind of behavior is being called mental illness. (Even more, we are confident that most of what all nine research centers are calling specifically schizophrenia reports substantially the same sorts of behavior.) But, as I said, here we have no way of knowing what the comparative frequencies of these kinds of behavior are in the communities served by the IPSS centers— because the IPSS looked only at people who came to the centers for treatment. In community studies—like the study of midtown Manhattan by the Srole group, and the study of the Camberwell district of London by the Brown group—there was an astonishingly large number of mentally ill people "in the closet" not getting treatment—and thus not being counted. But because the range in variation of specific symptoms in the IPSS study is so great, it is hard to avoid the conclusion that, at the very least, *symptoms* of mental illness vary greatly from culture to culture.

In Section 7.5 I review evidence tending to show that schizophrenia and depression are often caused by weakened social ties. Since, like other anthropologists, I suppose that the strength of social ties varies greatly from culture to culture around the world, I find it easy to believe that mental illness rates do likewise vary.

7.2.2   Evolution of Mental Illness

The weakened moralnet theory of mental illness predicts that stable, small-scale societies, undisturbed by intrusions that alter their social structure and value systems, would have lower rates of mental illness than modern society—with its weakened family structure and confusion of values. The data we have from community surveys tend to support this model. But as I say, we cannot put much trust in comparing these studies, which were carried out by varying methods and with varying concepts of mental illness.

7.3   STEP 1: CORE VALUES OF MENTAL ILLNESS

Mental health is defined as an essential element of health in the core value system of Chapter 2. So by definition it is good to be mentally healthy and bad to be mentally unhealthy. Mentally ill people may cause social disorder too, and so violate the posited value of order. Finally, it is common for mentally ill people to be sad, or suicidal; and such people at least find life unpleasant.

7.4   STEP 2: MENTAL ILLNESS SCOREBOARD

Table 7.1 shows some cross-national variation in mental hospital admissions. That table is our worldwide mental health scoreboard; it shows the rates for the nineteen countries making full reports. It also shows six other countries making only partial reports, where even these partial reports show that more than 41 people per 10,000 population are being admitted as mental patients each year; by the standards of the nineteen countries with full reports, even these partial

TABLE 7.1   Reported Mental Illness Rate Scoreboard

Country	Reported Mental Illness Rate[a]	Chance Risk
Above the Indicated Range		
Panama	121.1	.0253
Finland	99.5	.0508
Sweden[b]	93.7	.0619
Martinique[c]	80.9	.0979
Isle of Man[c]	71.6	.1392
Bermuda[c]	69.2	.1529
Denmark[b]	63.8	.1894
Iceland[b]	61.7	.2062
Channel Islands[c]	45.2	.4152
Scotland[bc]	44.5	.4282
Within the Indicated Range		
Puerto Rico[c]	37.7	
USA[b]	31.4	
Germany (West)[b]	28.7	
Canada[b]	28.5	
Norway[b]	25.7	MODEL COUNTRY
Portugal[b]	23.1	
Greece[b]	22.5	
Luxembourg[b]	20.2	
Spain[b]	16.4	
Below the Indicated Range		
Netherlands[b]	13.4	.3473
Guatemala	12.8	.3144
Seychelles	8.6	.1141
Turkey[b]	6.3	.0425
Below the Extreme Range		
Burma	1.5	.0000
Tanzania	1.4	.0000

SOURCE: United Nations, World Health Organization (1976b). Worldwide averages and spreads of 25 countries reporting (lognormal distribution):[d] mean of the natural logarithms: 3.27; median: 28.70; range: 119.70; SD: 1.165; CEV: 35.66%. Worldwide averages and spreads of 14 OECD countries reporting (lognormal distribution); mean of the natural logarithms: 3.32185; median: 27.10; range: 87.40; SD: 0.69292; CEV: 20.86%; skew: −0.20; kurtosis: 0.75.

a. Mental hospital admissions per year per 10,000 population.
b. Member of the Organization for Economic Cooperation and Development (OECD).
c. United Nations reporting unit; not an independent nation.
d. See Glossary for meanings of worldwide measures.

SD = standard deviation of natural logarithms.
CEV = coefficient of evolutionary variation.

rates are too high and so suggest too much social strain on the people. For I take it that variations in mental hospital admission rates from country to country largely reflect differences in social or cultural stress in those countries. Such a conclusion seems hard to avoid when we compare the reports from the four

TABLE 7.2   Correlations between Mental Hospitalization Rates*
and Six Traits (among 18 richer nations)

Official Report of	Correlation Level (r)	Chance Risk
Deaths from heart trouble	.72	.003
Deaths from traffic accidents	.57	.018
Calories eaten	.58	.016
Suicides	.50	.038
Alcoholism deaths	.49	.042
Cigarettes smoked	.46	.055

SOURCE: Lynn (1971: 102).
*Mental hospital patients per 1,000 population.

Scandinavian countries. These four countries have similar economies, climates, systems of psychiatric care, and gene pools, Yet Norway has an admissions rate of only 25.7. Denmark's is twice as high—63.8. Sweden's and Finland's are more than three times as high—93.7 and 99.5.

True, mental hospital admissions are notoriously fallible measures of mental illness rates. From culture to culture, from social class to social class, and from family to family, there is much variation in the ability and willingness of a patient's family to deal with mental illness at home. Often the families of mentally disturbed persons can and do cope with them. They keep them quietly in a bedroom away from strangers. They protect and shelter them; they keep their secrets. Then there is much variation in the attitudes and diagnostic habits of physicians. In some societies there may be more socially acceptable paths of deviant behavior open—behavior that is considered sick in one society may not be considered sick in another. Whitmer concluded from a study of hospitalized mental patients that it was not psychosis as such that led to commitment to a mental hospital, but rather "dangerous or unmanageable behavior that threatened the family or the community." These admission rates then must be taken only as an indirect or proxy measure. The midtown Manhattan study investigators found that fewer than one mentally incapacitated person in six (15.6 percent) was actually hospitalized. These findings were based on a carefully conducted random sample of 1,660 interviews from a total population of about 100,000. More than a dozen other studies from all parts of the world have led to parallel findings. So the interesting question about the data in Table 7.1 is not whether they constitute a direct measure of mental health differences. They certainly do not. The question is rather whether they constitute a useful proxy measure. Are such numbers as these of any use whatever in tests of social theory?

Here Table 7.2 tells us a great deal. How may we explain these high correlations? Lynn, who collected them, believes they reflect a common underlying level of anxiety. He may be right. But my point is a simpler one: The factors other than mental illness that affect mental hospitalization rates do not seem to have a like linkage to reports of death from heart trouble, automobile accidents, suicide, or alcoholism. The correlations in Table 7.2 show us that variations in the relative importance of mental hospitalization rates among the richer nations *do* seem to be measuring, among other things, the relative importance of mental illness itself. They do not seem to be mere artifacts of differing attitudes toward mental illness among the people concerned. Mental hospital admission rates, or mental hospital patients per capita, may well offer useful proxy measures of mental health with which to compare the OECD nations, at least.

I do not believe that the mental hospital admission rates in Table 7.1 are accurate measures of mental illness. I do believe that the sources of error involved do *not* explain all of the variation in these admission rates from nation to nation—or even a large part of it. I suppose that a theory of social factors in mental illness can be usefully tested by means of correlations like those in Table 7.2. And I also suppose that nations having mental health care systems like that of Norway—but differing widely from Norway on Table 7.1—differ because, among other things, their mental illness rates differ.

So we cannot take the country by country reports of Table 7.1 at face value. That is why I speak of "reported" rates in the table. But where a country like Sweden has mental hospital admission rates almost *four times* that of its neighbor Norway, it does seem likely that there is much more mental illness in Sweden than in Norway—and not just that in Sweden people with psychic problems are four times as likely to be called mentally ill and sent to a mental hospital.

7.5   STEP 3: TESTS OF THEORIES OF MENTAL ILLNESS

Mental illness often runs in families. For severe schizophrenia at least, we may confidently suppose that a genetic predisposition is at work. Twin studies have shown that identical twins are much more likely to suffer severe schizophrenia than fraternal twins of the same sex. But these same studies also show that this predisposition is only a tendency, not a sentence of madness. About one-third of the severly schizophrenic identical twins had mentally healthy other twins: One-third of the time the same genetic endowment did *not* lead to the same severe schizophrenic result.

Psychosis also displays special biochemical traces in the blood, and often improves after biochemical therapy. These facts have led many to consider mental illness a hereditary or genetic illness. But culture traits, including learned styles of family life, also run in families. And as Bowlby points out, we do not know if the biochemical changes are the root causes of the mental illness, or are only among its intermediate manifestations.

It has long been known that married people enjoy especially low rates of mental illness, whereas people who are separated, divorced, or widowed suffer especially high rates. And the psychiatrist Harry Stack Sullivan long ago pointed to this link as evidence that these marital partings were the cause, and mental illness the effect. But might not the link instead merely be that mentally disturbed people are less likely to marry, and more likely to divorce or separate? Or (less plausibly) more likely to become widowed?

In the past ten years, Sullivan's view has been supported by a series of studies of the link between life events in general and mental illness. In many of these studies researchers looked at life events that took place before the onset of mental illness; many took a mental health census of whole communities, finding that outside mental hospitals, as inside them, married people had lower rates of mental illness; in many of them they distinguished events that the behavior of the patient may have influenced from events that occurred independently of the patient; in many of them they distinguished desirable events from undesirable ones—showing that it was not mere change, but trouble, that tended to lead to mental illness. If we look at any one of these studies we can always find *some* weakness in the research design—but taken together the impact is powerful. We cannot quite declare some cause/effect relationship between weakened moralnets and mental illness "scientifically proved"—supported beyond a reasonable doubt. But from the 22 studies I am about to review, we can confidently suppose such a link among English-speaking people at least—and notice some support for it, as well, among Yoruba Nigerians, Tunisian Arabs, and the Gaelic-speaking islanders of the Scottish Hebrides. English-speaking people may well not be at all unusual in this respect: There is strong worldwide support for a cause/effect relationship between moralnets and suicide (see Chapter 9).

7.5.1   Some Leading Studies of Moralnets and Mental Illness

(1) *Abeokuta*, a Yoruba-speaking city together with a group of surrounding villages in Nigeria, was studied by a team headed by Alexander Leighton. Mental illness was linked with "sociocultural disintegration," as indexed by traits like poverty, secularization, family instability, poor leadership, migration, and "cultural confusion." It replicated the Stirling County study, discussed below.

(2) *Boston Italians* were studied by Mintz and Schwartz. First- and second-generation Italian immigrants in the greater Boston area had lower rates of mental illness if they lived in Italian neighborhoods, higher if elsewhere.

(3) *Boston widows* were studied by Maddison and Walker. Widows who had strong emotional support from friends and relatives suffered less physical and mental illness following loss of husband than those with weak emotional support.

(4) *Camberwell*, a borough of London, England, was studied by Brown and Harris. This is a landmark work. Female mental hospital patients suffering from depression were compared with untreated depression cases and normal controls found in a community sample survey. Depressed women were more likely to have recently suffered the loss of a loved one or other distressing life event than normal women—especially so if they also lacked an intimate, confiding relationship with a husband or lover. Or especially if their mother had died before they were eleven years old. Or if they had small children and little money.

(5) *Canberra*, Australia, was studied by a team headed by Henderson. In two community surveys comparing neurotic people with a matched group of normal controls, the normal people had more and stronger ties with their moralnet than neurotic people.

(6) *Croydon*, a borough of London, England, was studied by Cooper and Sylph. New cases of neurotic illness were compared with a matched control group of mentally healthy patients. The neurotics proved more likely to have recently suffered life crises than the controls.

(7) *Edinburgh*, Scotland, patients were studied by Miller and Ingham. Women who lacked an intimate, confiding relationship with a husband or lover were more likely to suffer mental and physical illness. Findings of the Camberwell study were supported.

(8) *Hertfordshire*, a housing project in a suburb of London, England, was studied by Martin, Brotherston, and Chave. These recently uprooted, transplanted people had higher rates of mental hospitalization than expected from their age, occupation, and marital status.

(9) *Jefferson County*, Arkansas, mental patients were studied by Adler. Marital status was studied at onset of mental illness, rather than upon admission to mental hospital, and controlled for age differences. Married people seemed less likely to become mentally ill than others; divorced people, more likely.

(10) *Leeds*, England, untreated applicants for psychotherapy were studied by Wallace and Whyte. Those who recovered tended to have had a background of more stable marriages and more satisfying group relationships than those who failed to recover.

(11) *Manhattan children* were studied by Gersten, Langner, Eisenberg, and Orzeck. A *prospective* study: That is, psychological adjustment of a community sample of children was measured twice, *five years apart*, and those who got better were compared with those who got worse. Those tended to get worse who in the meantime experienced undesirable life events—especially divorce of parents, death in family, or loss of a close friend. Those tended to get better who in the meantime experienced favorable life events—especially making a new friend.

(12) *Maudsley*, a working-class borough of London, was studied by Roy. Depressed patients were matched with mentally healthy but physically ill ones. The landmark Camberwell study was replicated and confirmed. Loss of mother before age eleven, three or more children at home under age fourteen, lack of a confiding marital relationship, and unemployment were found more frequently among depressed patients than among controls.

(13) *Midtown Manhattan* was studied by a team headed by Srole. In a community sample survey, sophisticated analyses showed the complexity of links between marital status and mental illness. The researchers called for longitudinal studies (that is, studies of change over time), but noted the particularly high prevalence of mental illness among single men and divorced people of both sexes.

(14) *New Haven Change* was a prospective study by Myers, Lindenthal, and Pepper of changing mental health of 720 adults in a community sample of the Connecticut city. They correlated social class with mental illness—the lower the class the more the mental illness. But when life events were controlled, this correlation vanished; however, when social class was controlled, life events remained correlated with mental illness. This finding was later replicated in the Camberwell study, and shows that the oft-reported link between social class and mental illness is explained by the fact that poorer people have more predisposing and disturbing life events than richer ones. Formal evidence thus supports the old saying: "I've been poor and I've been rich and rich is better." But this study had a far more important finding even than that. The subjects were interviewed twice, once in 1967 and again in 1969: The 526 people had at least one important life event in the year preceding at least one of the two interviews. Overall, there was a small but clear link: Those with life events changing for the better were more likely to have their mental health change for the better; those with life events changing for the worse were more likely to have their mental health change for the worse.

However, this was only a *tendency*. The mental health of about half of the people remained stable, regardless of life events. Among the 88 people with the worst change in life events, 19 actually had their mental health *improve*, while 48 had no change. Among the 109 people with the most favorable life events, 16 actually had their mental health get *worse* while 45 had no change.

(15) *New Haven Weeping Wives* was a study by Bullock, Siegel, Weissman, and Paykel; forty depressed women were matched with forty normal controls. The depressed patients had markedly poorer relationships with their husbands than the normal ones. When marital relationships before the onset of depression were compared with those after onset, some aspects got worse after onset but others got better—though overall, the change seemed for the worse. About half of the depressed wives had good marital adjustments before onset, and these tended to blame their sadness on problems outside the marriage.

(16) *New Haven Stress Study* was conducted by Paykel; 185 depressed patients were compared with a normal sample matched for sex, age, marital status, race, and social class. Depressed patients reported *three times* as many disturbed life events as normal controls during the six months preceding interview. The events that turned up more often among depressed patients: (1) increased arguments with spouse, (2) breakup of marriage, (3) changing type of work, (4) death of loved one, (5) illness of loved ones, (6) loved one leaving home, (7) physical illness of patient, (8) major change in work conditions.

(17) *North Uist*, in the Scottish Hebrides, was studied by Brown and Harris as a rural control for their urban Camberwell study. Most people studied were native speakers of Gaelic but were bilingual in English. (Life event data were *not* collected.) Women who were natives of the island and sharers of its dominant culture as crofters and churchgoers had less depression but more anxiety than others there.

(18) *Piedmont* counties of North Carolina and Virginia were studied by Edgerton, Bentz, and Hollister. They used Stirling County instruments and concepts. This community sample survey of a predominantly rural, Baptist population displayed many of the same social correlates of mental illness as are found in hospital admission statistics, thus tending to discredit the theory that in this respect mental hospital admissions are biased samples. Here again, mental illness turned up more frequently among widowed and divorced, less frequently among married. Rural people had significantly higher rates than those living in small towns, a difference presumably reflecting the usual rural pattern in the United States of isolated farm homesteads rather than more neighborly clusters of rural hamlets and villages.

(19) *Saint Louis*, Missouri, was a study by Hudgens of 220 adolescents: 110 of them psychiatric inpatients, 110 patients hospitalized for physical (nonpsychiatric) illness, matched with the psychiatric patients for age, sex, race, and hospital status (whether staff care or private care). The most important finding of this study, however, was happenstance: It turned out that among the 110 normal controls, hospitalized for physical illness, 22 also suffered from depression. Among these 110 controls, prognosis of their *physical* illness was considered as a life event. Further, the parents of all subjects in the study were questioned to see if they had any history of psychiatric disorder. Hudgens divided these normal controls into four groups. Group A had both poor prognosis and poor parentage. Group B had good prognosis but poor parentage. Group C had poor prognosis but good parentage. Group D had both good prognosis and good parentage. Some 50 percent of Group A suffered depression, 27 percent of Group B, 23 percent of Group C, and only 9 percent of Group D. A "good prognosis" means that these physically ailing people were told they could expect to get well, but a poor prognosis means that they were told either that they were going to be permanently disabled or that they were going to die. "Poor parentage" means that at least one of their parents had a history of psychiatric disorder. In other words, people with a history of mental illness in their family were vulnerable to depression if stressed. And while life event stress threatened all, those who were more vulnerable to begin with were more likely to succumb.

(20) *Stirling County*, Nova Scotia, was a landmark study in a team headed by Alexander Leighton. Mental illness was more frequent in "socially disintegrated" communities, those marked by (1) high frequency of broken homes, (2) few and weak associations (churches, clubs), (3) few and weak leaders, (4) few patterns of recreation, (5) high frequency of hostility within the community, (6) high frequency of crime and delinquency, (7) weak and fragmented network of communication. The linkages that had been suggested by studies of mental hospital patients were confirmed by the careful sampling, intensity, and thoroughness of this study. However, the researchers did not attempt to tell whether moralnet weakness was a cause of mental illness, or an effect.

(21) *Sydney*, Australia, was a study by Andrews, Tennant, Hewson, and Vaillant of a representative sample of a suburb. It had parallel results. Life event

stress tended to be followed by poorer mental health—especially among people in vulnerable life situations. The Sidney study pointed to two vulnerability factors: coping style and crisis support. Coping style was measured by a questionnaire that dealt with hypothetical responses to hypothetical problems. Typically, for each problem, six alternate courses of action were offered as possible responses, three of them considered "mature" by the investigators, the other three, "immature." People who selected mature responses to these hypothetical questions were actually less likely to display signs of mental illness than those who selected immature responses. Crisis support was rated according to the number of people the respondent said he or she could turn to for help in trouble. Among those with low stress of life events, mature lifestyle, and high crisis support, only 12.8 percent displayed signs of mental illness, while among those with high stress, immature lifestyle, and low crisis support, 43.3 percent did. Intermediate classes had intermediate rates of signs of mental illness.

(22) *Tunisian Arab* schizophrenics were studied by Ammar and Ledjri. The families of 300 patients were studied—but were not compared with normal controls or the population at large, unfortunately. Practically *one-third* (32.5 percent) of these patients had lost their fathers before they were fifteen years old. (This finding echoes that of the Camberwell and Maudsley studies, pointing to the high proportion of depressed women who had lost their mothers before their eleventh year.)

7.5.2   A Model of Mental Illness Causation

In no one study has a theory of social causation been fully tested, though the Camberwell study comes close. Further, almost all these studies—and all the more rigorous ones—have been done on English-speaking subjects. Yet elsewhere there is clear evidence tending to discredit every remaining rival hypothesis—every remaining weakness of the Camberwell study has been met elsewhere by other studies, which, for other reasons, are weaker and less persuasive than the Camberwell study. Precedent social events linked with subsequent onset of mental illness were looked at in the Camberwell study; treated patients, unhospitalized and untreated mentally ill cases, and mentally healthy controls were compared in a community probability sample survey. A rigorous instrument was used in the Camberwell study—the Present State Examination (PSE) schedule, whose reliability and validity had been widely tested by others—to measure mental illness. And the researchers of the Camberwell study developed and tested for reliability their own instrument for measuring disturbing life events. They carefully distinguished between predisposing circumstances on the one hand and precipitating life events on the other—and measured the linkage of each with mental illness. They also distinguished life events by the degree of influence or control that the subject might have had on them—and so controlled for reverse causation—by classifying the life events into fully independent, partly independent, and not independent, and separately measuring the linkages between the first two classes and mental illness.

Finally, two other investigating teams independently replicated several of Camberwell's central findings and confirmed them.

Is all this not proof positive?

Not quite.

The Camberwell researchers did *not* do a prospective study, and so its dating of onset of mental illness is subject to some doubt. However, in two other studies, which in other ways did not match Camberwell for rigor or thoroughness—namely the Manhattan children study and the New Haven Change study—the researchers *did* do prospective studies and so *did* directly measure change in mental health and link that to intervening life events and *did* reach results similar to Camberwell.

The Camberwell life event model has not been tested on a non-English-speaking population as far as I know. However, purely demographic studies linking mental illnesses with weak moralnets—studies that in themselves do not deal with causal direction at all—show supporting results among the Abeokuta Yoruba and the North Uist Gaelic-speaking Hebridean Islanders; while the study of Tunisian Arabs reports a predisposing factor (early death of father) analogous to one repeatedly found among English women (early death of mother).

The Camberwell researchers studied only women, not men. In the Edinburgh study, where investigators looked only at the role of the intimate confidant as a predisposing factor, both men and women were studied. The findings of the Camberwell study with respect to women—but *not* with respect to men—were confirmed. While the researchers of most of the other life event studies on my list—notably including the two prospective studies—looked at both men and women, they made no distinction between the sexes in reporting their results. We are left then a little up in the air by all the life event studies with respect to the issues raised by the Edinburgh study. In what way do men and women differ in their reactions to life events? However, the less rigorous demographic studies clearly link mental illness in men as well as women to separation and divorce.

Finally, in the Camberwell study no attempt was made to measure genetic influences on mental illness. Since their findings do not pretend to explain all of the variance observed, the results leave the door wide open to the interpretation that genetic as well as social predisposition toward mental illness exists—an interpretation that is supported by the St. Louis study. The key point: There is no conflict between the findings of these 22 studies of social linkages to mental illness and the findings of twin studies that point to genetic predisposition. The genetic studies of severe schizophrenia make a strong case for the proposition that there is *some* genetic predisposition to schizophrenia—*at least* to the extent measured by the higher proportion of concordance in identical twins (69 percent) than in same-sex fraternal twins (18 percent): That difference of 51 percent can hardly be explained away by any environmental model. (A pair of twins are here called *concordant* if they are both mentally ill; *discordant* if only one is.) However, that still leaves ample room for an environmental theory to explain the large percentage of discordant identical twins—31 percent.

Looking at all this evidence together, I find the following model of the causation (etiology) of purely mental illness. We may call this the *Modified Camberwell* model: It follows Brown and Harris, but adds an element of genetic predisposition to their scheme. I confidently suppose that its main elements hold true—though for the reasons just given I do not consider them demonstrated beyond a reasonable doubt.

(1) *Genetic predisposition.* At least in the case of severe schizophrenia. Even here, social predispositon as well as provoking life events presumably play a part as well (thus presumably explaining the high percentage of discordant identical twins).

(2) *Environmental predisposition.* Most of these factors have to do with the statics or current state of moralnet ties. In general, but not invariably, the more such ties and/or the stronger they are, the less the predisposition to mental illness. Social class is *not* in itself a predisposing factor but poorer people are more likely to suffer other predisposing factors or provoking events, at least in English-speaking countries. Brown and Harris distinguish protective factors, which lessen risk, from vulnerability factors, which increase it. But the same items appear on both lists, only turned inside-out. Thus

(a) Loss of mother before age eleven is a vulnerability factor; no loss, a protective factor.
(b) High intimacy with husband is a protective factor; low intimacy, a vulnerability factor.

Other predisposing factors:

(c) Too many children for mother to take care of. (In Chapter 11, I show much other evidence, in addition to mental illness, which indicates that mothers find it hard to care for children without some help; the nuclear family household typical of English-speaking people often makes it hard on working-class mothers who cannot afford household help or nursery schools and who do not have relatives—mothers, sisters—handy to spell them.)
(d) Few or weak social ties with moralnets outside the home (see Canberra, Sydney, Abeokuta, and Stirling County studies).
(e) Cultural dissonance (and so weakness of extended moralnet ties) with neighbors (North Uist, Boston Italian studies).
(f) Immature style for coping with life crises (Sydney study). The mature coping-style elements all respond to problems with some sort of positive action that tends to preserve harmony within the moralnet; the immature coping style elements involve either actions that tend to disrupt harmony or else no action at all—rather mental withdrawal from the situation.
(g) Unemployment.

(3) *Provoking life event.* Only events that are either intrinsically unpleasant or that disrupt moralnet ties have been linked to a worsening of mental health. Those that are pleasant or that strengthen moralnet ties are linked to an

improvement in mental health. Most of these events have to do with a *change* in the state of moralnet ties, and so with their dynamics. They include:

    (a) severe physical illness (especially one from which there is little hope of recovery) of subject, or of subject's spouse or child,
    (b) separation or divorce of subject,
    (c) departure of child,
    (d) unwanted pregnancy or abortion by subject or daughter,
    (e) eviction from home,
    (f) loss of job by subject, spouse, or child,
    (g) discovery of extramarital love affair (of subject by spouse or of spouse by subject),
    (h) failure or problems in school,
    (i) troubles with in-laws,
    (j) stillbirth,
    (k) death of a pet,
    (l) demotion or change to less responsible job.

7.6   STEP 4: FURTHER STUDIES OF MENTAL ILLNESS

Clear final scientific proof of the relationship of moralnet weakness to mental illness—and with it, of the general relationship of mental illness to culture—seems within reach. The findings I have already reviewed tilt the scale of preponderance of evidence sharply (see Figure 7.1). As I have said, we may already confidently suppose that mental illness rates vary from culture to culture and that weakened moralnets tend to cause mental illness, while especially strong ones tend to shelter from it. To raise that "confidently suppose" to "finally conclude" we need to do two things: First, do a holocultural study of mental illness; second, and more important, apply and extend worldwide the methods of the Camberwell study. The IPSS survey should be repeated, using Camberwell methods of community survey to determine true incidence (onset rates) of mental illness, and elaborating the Camberwell methods of life event measurement to seek and verify immediate precedent social causes of that onset. The Canberra measures of moralnet extent should also be used. Finally, for results to be conclusive, a prospective design (like that of the New Haven Change study, for example) must be followed. That is to say, subjects need to be reexamined and reinterviewed after some years have passed so that changes in mental health status can be related to intervening life events. Detailed measurement and analysis of the life event measures need to be made, to establish their reliability and validity across cultures, as was done with the diagnosis of mental illness in the IPSS (see Appendix A).

Needless to say, however, both the Camberwell and the Canberra interview schedules need first to be modified, as was the PSE mental illness schedule, to accommodate varying patterns of kinship and association to be found in places like Moscow, Taipei, Delhi, and Abeokuta.

For example, from the Camberwell study we learn that women living in that part of London tended to be sheltered from the disturbing effects of unhappy life events by a close confiding relationship with a husband or boyfriend. That may

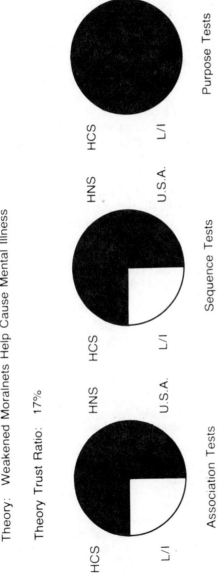

Theory: Weakened Moralnets Help Cause Mental Illness

Theory Trust Ratio: 17%

Association Tests   Sequence Tests   Purpose Tests

SOURCE   L/I: 22 studies reviewed in Section 7.5.1.
NOTE: See *Theory trust meter* in Glossary for a key to this chart, and Section 4.5.3 for the general manner of its composition.
HCS = holocultural test; HNS = holonational test; L/I = local or individual test; U.S.A. = countrywide tests in the United States.

Figure 7.1   Mental Illness Theory Trust Meter

well be a special feature of the culture of English-speaking peoples. Among us, the husband-wife dyad is the central kinship link—the keystone of the moralnet. Other cultures may look elsewhere for the preferred intimate confidants. Among Russians, for example, I have elsewhere suggested the special importance of mother-daughter and sister-sister links. Hsu points to father-son relations among Chinese and mother-son relations among Hindus, as the central kinship dyads. According to the Vassilious, the mother-son relationship is likewise far more important than the husband-wife relationship among modern Greeks. The Tunisian Arab study suggests the special importance of the father-son dyad there.

Investigators also need to measure life events over a fairly long period. Brown and Harris found that with respect to schizophrenia, the 3 weeks preceding onset were critical, but with respect to depression, it was on the average 38 weeks between the provoking life event and the onset of illness. The study of Sacramento, California, patients by Mueller and others looked only at a period four weeks before onset and, after controlling for the social situation in a multiple regression analysis, found no significant difference between patients and normal controls with respect to events independent of the psychological state of the person concerned.

But the most difficult requirement for conclusive demonstration of the causal link between life events and mental illness is the accurate dating both of those events and of changes in mental health. Such a demonstration might perhaps best be performed by a military medical officer, who can arrange for a sizable sample·of people to report regularly to be interviewed—whether or not any changes have taken place in either health or life events since the last interview.

7.7   STEP 5: COPING WITH MENTAL ILLNESS

To reduce the risk of mental illness, these family lifestyles are implied by the studies I have just reviewed:

(1) People—especially women—need to marry someone they can trust with their secret thoughts and fears, someone they can confide in (Camberwell, Edinburgh, New Haven women studies).
(2) People need also to maintain ties of friendship to close friends within the moralnet who will offer them emotional support (Boston widows, Leeds, Manhattan children studies).
(3) People need also to maintain a web of associations with the wider moralnet (Boston Italians, Canberra, North Uist, Stirling County, Abeokuta studies).
(4) If there is a history of mental illness in the family of either parent, the parents should not keep this fact a secret from their children. For in such cases we have evidence of a predisposition toward mental illness—whether from genetic or cultural factors is beside the point. Hence the parents and in time the children in their turn need to take special care to reduce vulnerability by cultivating strong ties with their moralnets. They need to establish strong, intimate confiding relations between parents and children, and between spouses, maintain a strong network of friends, keep a stable job and home. Such a moralnet should not, for

example, be lightly broken by a move to another city merely in order to obtain a better job when the present job is really good enough (St. Louis, twin studies).

(5) People should seek to live in culturally homogeneous neighborhoods (Boston Italians, North Uist studies).

(6) Families should not have children until they can arrange for some kind of help for the mother—perhaps baby sitting, nursery schools, or domestics (Camberwell, Croyden studies; see also Chapter 11).

7.8   COSTS AND BENEFITS OF MENTAL ILLNESS PROGRAMS

Perhaps seven mentally ill people out of eight are already being supported and sustained by their moralnets—their families and loved ones—without the help of professional therapists. The psychiatrists deal only with the tip of the iceberg.

In my view, the general program of family strengthening suggested in Chapter 10—following Jane Howard—with special emphasis, in English-speaking countries at least, on husband-wife rapport, might well be one of the best prophylactics for mental illness. It would also seem to be the cheapest.

But needless to say, we have nothing resembling actual measurements of either costs or benefits of such a program. So my view is but a guess. Fortunately, we are better informed about alcoholism—to which I now turn.

Notes

7.1   *Dr. Ihembi Treats a Neurotic*

The source of this section is Turner (1964). All personal names in it, except for that of Dr. Ihembi, are changed.

The "Mbaulu" faction consisted of the matrilineage of that name; the "Katoyi" faction consisted of the matrilineal descendants of Chief Katoyi (Turner, 1964: 246). Since the Ndembu are matrilineal, Kimbini was, of course, a Mbaulu rather than a Katoyi.

7.2   *Mental Illness around the World*

On the cybernetic model of the mind, see Section 6.2.

7.2.1   *Range of Variation of Mental Illness*

On the IPSS, see United Nations, World Health Organization (1973).

On *pibloktoq* (Arctic hysteria), *latah*, *amok*, and *susto*, see Kennedy (1973: 1152-1165) and Kiev (1972: 65-92). Algonkian *windigo* is evidently a myth—see Marano (1982).

The eleven well-conducted community surveys in mental illness cited in Marsella (1980: 248) include those by Kato, Sethi, and Gupta.

On variations in frequency of symptoms of mental illness between the nation Field Research Centers of the IPSS, see United Nations, World Health Organization (1973: 221f., 229, 230).

After judiciously reviewing the evidence on cross-cultural variation in prevalence of mental illness, Draguns (1980: 134) declines to venture an opinion either way.

While the rigorous evidence is not in, Kiev (1972: 140-163) calls attention to the *apparently* higher frequency of depression in the urban west than elsewhere.

On the Camberwell and Midtown Manhattan studies, see Section 7.5.1 of the chapter text.

7.3   *Step 1: Core Values of Mental Illness*

Judging from the frequency with which extreme depression is itself a clinical symptom, mentally ill people appear often to be profoundly unhappy (see United Nations, World Health Organization, 1973: 221f., 229, 230). Depression turns up not only among suffers from affective psychoses and neuroses, but also among some schizophrenics.

7.4   Step 2: Mental Illness Scoreboard

On the proportion of mentally ill people who are not under treatment, see Srole et al. (1975: 146, 197f., 268) and compare Brown and Harris (1978a) and the community studies inventoried in Marsella (1980: 248).

On commitment to mental hospitals, Whitmer is cited in Srole et al. (1975: 268).

7.5   Step 3: Tests of Theories of Mental Illness

In general, I profited from the reviews of this literature by Draguns (1980), Sanua (1980), Marsella (1979, 1980), and especially Mueller (1980).

On the tendency of mental illness to run in families, see United Nations, World Health Organization (1973: 235).

On studies of schizophrenic twins, see Dohrenwend and Dohrenwend (1969: 34f.).

Bowlby (1980: 261) argues that with biochemical variation, too, as with sociological variation, mere correlation is inadequate proof of causation.

On mental hospital admission rates by marital status, see Adler (1953: 186).

Sullivan's writings had considerable influence on Leighton (1959: 88f.).

Cuvelier (1976) and Roosens (1979) report on a Belgian long-term experiment with mentally ill patients who were billeted in private homes.

7.5.1   Some Leading Studies of Moralnets and Mental Illness

Abeokuta: Leighton, Lambo et al. (1963); Boston Italians: Mintz and Schwartz (1964); Boston widows: Maddison and Walker (1967), Camberwell: Brown and Harris (1978a, 1978b), Tennant and Bebbington (1978); Canberra: Henderson, Byrne et al. (1978), Henderson, Duncan-Jones et al. (1978); Croydon: Cooper and Sylph (1973); Edinburgh: Miller and Ingham (1976); Hertfordshire: Martin et al. (1957); Jefferson County: Adler (1953); Leeds: Wallace and Whyte (1959); Manhattan children: Gersten et al. (1974); Maudsley: Roy (1978); midtown Manhattan: Srole et al. (1975); New Haven Change: Myers et al. (1974); New Haven Weeping Wives: Bullock et al. (1972); New Haven Stress: Paykel (1974); North Uist: Brown and Harris (1978a: 55-56, 249-254); Piedmont: Edgerton et al. (1970); St. Louis: Hudgens (1974); Stirling County: Leighton (1959), Leighton, Harding et al. (1963); Sydney: Andrews et al. (1978); Tunisian Arabs: Ammar and Ledjri (1972).

7.5.2   A Model of Mental Illness Causation

Studies of schizophrenic twins are reviewed by Dohrenwend and Dohrenwend (1969: 34f.).

List of provoking life events is from Brown and Harris (1978a: 160-164), Myers et al. (1974: 196), and Hudgens (1974: 128).

7.6   Step 4: Further Studies of Mental Illness

On the mother-daughter and sister-sister dyad among Russians, see Naroll (1962b). On kinship dyads in general, see Hsu (1972: 509-567). On the mother-son tie among Greeks, see Vassiliou and Vassiliou (1982). On the Sacramento study, see Mueller et al. (1978) and compare Brown and Harris (1978b: 125).

7.8   Costs and Benefits of Mental Illness Programs

A severe criticism of mental hospitals as therapeutic communities is in Jones (1962: 53-73).

Alcohol Use and Abuse

8.1   MUDIDI KILLS HIS FATHER'S BROTHER

Lango brewed the beer that brought his own death. He brewed the beer that his nephew Mudidi had been drinking for six hours before the trouble started. The beer party was a ceremony in honor of a visiting official, the Olugongo. To give such a party in honor of such a visit is the custom among the BaLuyia people of Kavirondo in Kenya. There the trouble came. The Olugongo had brought a gramophone along. His people played music on that gramophone all through the party. Then after six hours, as was BaLuyia custom, each person spoke in praise of himself, and paid some money. By that time the party's host, Lango, had gone to another room to sleep. When Mudidi's turn to boast and to pay came, he paid only ten cents. The Olugongo's policeman called for at least fifty. Mudidi became angry and loud. The Olugongo himself could not quiet him. Finally the noise awakened Mudidi's uncle, Lango. The uncle took Mudidi's drinking reed out of the beer pot and threw it to the ground. Among the BaLuyia, that is an insult. Lango did more. He pushed Mudidi out of the home. So the party of welcome to the Olugongo had been shamed; guests and hosts alike had been humiliated. Lango went back to sleep; he, too, must have been drinking. While he was sleeping, his nephew, angrier than ever, came back and stabbed him to death.

Bohannan studied the records from 1949 to 1954 of 80 similar killings among the BaLuyia. In 27 of these killings, someone had been drinking. And we read of this sort of thing among many peoples around the world. For example, near Lake Superior about the time of the American Revolution, one Indian trader reported the results of a drinking party among the Southern Salteaux, an Ojibwa group. The party lasted four days and four nights. The Whites expected trouble; they collected the Indians' guns, knives, and tomahawks. Even so, the Indians fought among themselves. They killed three men and wounded six.

Among the Bison Horn Gonds of India, murder is common. In about half of the cases that come to court, they say, the murderer killed while drunk on rice beer. One anthropologist looked at a hundred court cases of murder among these Gonds. The judges accepted a plea of drunkenness in nineteen. Goodwin tells about drunkenness among the Western Apache of Arizona. Most of the killings occurred during or following drinking parties. Then the men were likely to pick a fight. These were not the rough-and-tumble brawls so common to

Whites. When the Apache fought he fought to kill. Serious wounds or death were usually the outcome.

As we review the worldwide evidence in this chapter, we find that much of it shows that hard drinking and the trouble it causes often stems from weakened moralnets—from weak or loose ones. You might think that I have picked over that evidence to make my case, like a lawyer preparing his brief. But I did not. I wrote the first draft of this chapter more than five years before I finished the book. When I wrote it, I had no idea of moralnet theory. It was my first drafts of this chapter and of the suicide, child abuse, adolescence, and sex life chapters that sent me to social theory. These drafts sent me to the sociologists and the social psychologists. And they sent me to the primary groups as normative reference groups—or as I call them, moralnets.

8.2   ALCOHOL AROUND THE WORLD

8.2.1   Range of Variation of Alcohol Use and Abuse

I have been citing examples of killings from societies around the world. I could go on all day. And these are usually killings of relatives or friends. Thus they are usually killings that all the local people deem murder. In one early search through the Human Relations Area Files, I found alcohol used in 23 societies. And I found drunken brawling among 16 of these 23. Four other studies had similar findings.

Jellinek defines alcoholism as any use of alcoholic beverages that causes any damage to the individual or society or both. He distinguishes at least five kinds of hard drinking. Type beta is regular, persistent, heavy social drinking without loss of control, without addiction, without inability to abstain, and without periodic bouts of drunken rage. Beta alcoholics pay a price. They may not live as long as other people, or earn as much money. They are not as productive.

Jellinek's type alpha alcoholic seems as much a matter of personal choice as social drinking. Type alpha is habitual drinking to relieve physical or emotional pain, but again without loss of control, without addiction, without inability to abstain, and without periodic bouts of drunken rage.

Three other of Jellinek's types of alcoholism seem more clearly social evils. They seem bad in the eyes of the alcoholics and the people who try to live with them. His type gamma alcoholic involves physiological dependence—physical addiction. Gamma hard drinkers have an insatiable craving and loss of control over their drinking. Type gamma hard drinkers do not drink because they want to; they drink because they have to. Type gamma hard drinking may well be the usual type of alcoholism in English-speaking countries. It is apparently *not* the usual type in most European or Latin American countries, or in most small-scale societies. The growth and influence of Alcoholics Anonymous in English-speaking countries is testimony to the deep distress of many gamma type alcoholics over the loss of control of their drinking habits and their wish to abstain totally.

Jellinek's type delta hard drinking seems simply a more severe form of type gamma; not only do the harder drinkers lose control over their drinking, they cannot abstain even for a day or two. They are addicts, helpless in the face of the pangs of withdrawal symptoms. The French have a high proportion of Jellinek's type delta.

Finally, Jellinek's type epsilon hard drinking consists of what he calls periodical alcoholism. Periodic hard drinkers are usually sober; they drink only from time to time. But when they drink, they really drink. They go on a drinking bout; they release their inhibitions in drunken rage, and often they do much damage to other people. The alcoholic aggression or drunken brawling of the holocultural studies cited below would seem to be largely an example of type epsilon hard drinking.

Another approach to sorting out types of alcoholism was presented by the Factor Study Group. For many years, Bacon, Barry, and Child have been doing powerful holocultural studies. One of these was on alcohol use. For that work they were joined by Buchwald and Snyder. The Factor Study Group looked at nineteen different holocultural measures of the use of alcohol. They classified these measures by means of a factor analysis. They found that all nineteen measures can be well represented by only four basic factors. Each of these basic factors in turn is well represented by a single variable: to study Factor 1, measure the *importance of ceremonial drinking*; to study Factor 2, measure the *frequency of drunkenness*; to study Factor 3, measure the importance of *intensity of hostility* among drunken people; to study Factor 4, measure the amount of *general consumption of alcohol*. Of these four factors, only Factor 2 and Factor 3 directly measure some kind of alcoholic abuse. These four factors look at the social situation; Jellinek's five types look at the individual drinker.

8.2.2   Evolution of Alcohol Use and Abuse

We generally infer cultural evolution patterns as best we can by contrasting the way of life of present-day large-scale societies with present-day small-scale ones. That contrast is clear with respect to alcoholism, but the inference here is highly questionable. The overall pattern of the evolution of hard drinking is not yet clear; but there does seem to have been something like progress. As the English would say, mankind is learning to handle its liquor like gentlemen. The more complex a society, the more likely it is to use alcohol in ceremonies. Presumably, ceremonial drinking is then under better control and less subject to misuse. The more complex a society, the more alcohol its people drink. But frequency of drunkenness and drunken brawling do *not* increase with societal complexity; they decrease (see Table 8.1).

Table 8.1 displays the worldwide pattern of recent centuries. Alcohol may have been in use in the Near East for some 8,000 to 10,000 years, but it seems to have become known in most other places much more recently. And most of the data about simpler peoples in Table 8.1 are about them after Western contact

TABLE 8.1 Complexity of Society and Drunken Brawling

PROPOSITION: *Simple societies have more drunken brawls than complex societies.*

	Pattern of Habitual Drunken Brawling	No Pattern of Habitual Drunken Brawling
Complex Societies	– – –	Azande (The Sudan) Bahians (Brazil) Bemba (Zambia) Kurd (Iraq) Tswana (Botswana) Yakut (Siberia) (6)
Simple Societies	Aweikoma (Brazil) Cagaba (Colombia) Chukchee (Siberia) Ifugao (Philippines) Mataco (Argentina) Murngin (Australia) Ojibwa (Great Lakes Region) Paiute (Southwestern USA) Tarahumara (Mexico) Truk (Micronesia) Warrau (Venezuela) Yaghan (Tierra del Fuego) Zuñi (New Mexico) (13)	Cuna (Panama) Rural Irish Iban (Borneo) (3)

SOURCE: Schaefer (1973: 182; 1978).
Correlation (phi coefficient): −.63.
Chance risk (Fisher's Exact Test): .0011.
N = 22.

had smashed their old way of life. Other than that, we really know nothing about the evolution of alcoholic *addiction* (Jellinek's types gamma and delta).

Another thing. Evidence is mounting that some people can hold their liquor much better than others, and that this is an inborn difference. Goodwin, a leader in these studies, has been working with others both in the United States and in Denmark. His method is to look at sons of alcoholic parents. He compares sons raised by their parents with brothers adopted in infancy by others. In repeated careful studies, he has found that the more often the alcoholic parent had been sent to the hospital because of his or her drinking problems, the more often both kinds of sons were likely to become alcoholics. Social influences varying from family to family within the United States or Denmark did not seem to matter. (But Goodwin and his associates were not looking at moralnet theory. They did not study strength of social ties as such. Their method of carefully matching families may well have kept this factor constant. I would expect that if in our research we held family history of alcoholism constant and varied strength of social ties, we might find results equally striking. More on social ties in Section 8.5.)

Schaefer carried out studies of the rate of alcohol metabolism among Hindu Reddis of Andhra Pradesh, India. He also reviewed several earlier studies of Fenna and Wolff. The samples studied were small. There is no suggestion of overall control of sampling biases. All we can say is that, so far, there is not much support for the firewater myth. That is to say, there is not much support for the idea that some racial groups tolerate alcohol far more poorly than others—that cultural evolution has tended to make people of more complex societies *genetically* better able to hold their liquor than those of less complex societies. Even though important genetic differences between individuals are likely to exist, the evidence linking tolerance for alcohol with cultural evolution seems to point to a cultural rather than a genetic tolerance.

8.3   STEP 1: CORE VALUES OF ALCOHOL USE

Yes, people in most societies deplore the killing of neighbors, friends, or relatives in drunken brawls. However, the use of alcohol is *not* widely deplored by people of small-scale societies. Of 166 small-scale societies around the world, one team of anthropologists found only 14 that disapproved of men *drinking*. Among these same societies, it was possible to rate 83 for the approval of *drunkenness*. Among 43, the people did not seem to disapprove of drunkenness; among 40, they did seem to.

The French present a striking problem in social values here. It seems clear that the widespread regular use of alcohol, especially wine, materially shortens the lives of French people. It is equally clear that any attempt to restrict—or even to talk about restricting—the use of wine stirs up resentment. "Water is for the frogs," they say.

Her candle was burning at both ends, remarked Edna St. Vicent Millay. It would not last her the night. But, she told her foes and her friends, it gave her a lovely light. If the French think they live better with wine and are willing to pay for their fun by an earlier death, that is their affair. In the tradeoff between health and pleasure, they choose pleasure. So they pay taxes on twice as much alcohol per capita as the Americans do—and four times as much as the Norwegians do.

As with the worldwide use of other drugs, we can now say only a little about the worldwide use of alcohol. Like other drugs, alcohol is widely used. Most drinking gives pleasure or relieves pain. Most drinking is considered innocent. Most drinking has not been shown to do more harm than good to the user or others. Nevertheless, it is equally clear that the abuse of alcohol, as of other drugs, often harms many users by decreasing their ability to function, or by inducing mind-impairing addiction. So, to the extent that alcoholism causes physical or mental illness, it contravenes our core value of health. And to the extent that it disrupts family life, and so moralnetting, it contravenes our core value of order. Hologeistic studies do shed some light on the cause and cure of alcohol abuse.

8.4   STEP 2: ALCOHOL USE SCOREBOARD

But neither the Jellinek nor the Factor Study Group type has been used to measure alcoholism nationwide. There are several major measures of alcoholism among modern nations. None of them is satisfactory. Yet all clearly measure people in some kind of trouble. There are statistics on mortality from cirrhosis of the liver. Still, people can get cirrhosis from metal poisoning as well as from drinking wine. Further, people may not get cirrhosis in any consistent way from drinking beer or distilled liquors. However, there is clearly a correlation, country by country and province by province, between alcohol use and cirrhosis deaths. There are also statistics of sorts compiled on deaths from alcoholism. And there are some stray statistics relating alcohol use to crimes of violence and serious accidents.

Lynn found a correlation of .37 between reported rate of alcoholism deaths and reported suicide rate. Unfortunately his sample was too small for this result to claim our confidence, especially since other investigators using other sets of aggregate data found no relationship of consequence.

The best measure we have of alcohol use comes from the tax records of 27 modern nations. That measure is our alcoholism scoreboard (see Table 8.2). Norway again is close to the lead—with only 5.58 liters of tax-paid alcohol drunk per year per person. I would guess that for an adult without undue genetic sensitivity, drinking about six liters a year of alcohol, spread evenly in small doses, might do more good than harm. But as we shall see, in the United States alone, an average of about ten liters a year per person costs something like 15 billion dollars a year in lost working time, accidents, and sickness. And Schaefer, touring Oslo bars, saw many people who were blind drunk. Many Norwegians consider hard drinking the most serious social problem their country faces. Further, Table 8.2 ignores bootleg and home brew. (But home brew is said to be far commoner in Norway than in the United States, for example.) So at best Table 8.2 is only a rough guide to alcoholism around the world, not an accurate measure.

8.5   STEP 3: TESTS OF THEORIES OF ALCOHOLISM

8.5.1   Hard Drinking and Anxiety

Some clinical studies in our own society and in Europe suggest that feelings of anxiety may be one of the major causes of alcohol addiction. Several holocultural studies show that certain kinds of anxiety-provoking situations tend to be associated with heavy drinking within the society as a whole. Horton looked at four proxy measures of anxiety—four situations he thought might provoke strong feelings of anxiety. He looked at insecurity of food supply, disruptive impact of European culture, frequency of sorcery, and warfare. The first two of these four measures proved to be associated with consumption of alcohol. Schaefer found an association between a fifth proxy measure of anxiety—belief in malicious or capricious spirits.

TABLE 8.2   Alcohol Consumption Scoreboard

Country	Alcohol Consumption[a]	Chance Risk
Above Extreme Range		
Portugal[b]	23.43	.0006
France[b]	22.44	.0009
Above Indicated Range		
Germany (West)[b]	14.82	.0196
Belgium[b]	14.36	.0239
Austria[b]	14.08	.0269
Switzerland[b]	13.92	.0289
Italy[b]	13.56	.0338
Australia	13.27	.0384
Spain[b]	12.85	.0462
New Zealand	12.61	.0513
Hungary	12.36	.0573
Czechoslovakia	11.28	.0925
Denmark[b]	10.84	.1124
Canada[b]	10.78	.1154
Netherlands[b]	10.6	.1250
USA[b]	10.48	.1319
United Kingdom[b]	10.16	.1520
USSR	8.85	.2702
Ireland[b]	8.31	.3410
Poland	8.07	.3777
Finland	7.64	.4526
Within Indicated Range		
Japan[b]	7.39	
Peru	7.27	
Sweden[b]	6.97	
Norway[b]	5.58	MODEL COUNTRY
Iceland[b]	4.96	
Below Indicated Range		
Israel	3.25	.1963

SOURCE: Keller and Gurioli (1976). Worldwide averages and spreads of 27 countries reporting (lognormal distribution):[c] mean of the natural logarithms: 2.32; median: 10.78; range: 20.18; SD: 0.431; CEV: 18.55%. Worldwide averages and spreads of 18 OECD countries reporting (lognormal distribution): mean of the natural logarithms: 2.40185; median: 10.81; range: 18.47; SD: 0.41831; CEV: 17.42%; skew: −0.13; kurtosis: 0.78.

a. Average amount of tax-paid alcohol (in liters) consumed per person per year.
b. Member of the Organization for Economic Cooperation and Development (OECD).
c. See Glossary for meanings of worldwide measures.
SD = standard deviation of natural logarithms.
CEV = coefficient of evolutionary variation.

However, the Factor Study Group made the broadest and most systematic test of anxiety theory. Their findings do not indicate that feelings of anxiety are often a root cause of alcoholism. Their strongest finding on anxiety was that associated with toilet training. Classic Freudian theory holds that stressful toilet

TABLE 8.3   Morality and Drunkenness

PROPOSITION: *The stronger the moralnets, the less the drunkenness.*

	Correlation Level	Number of Tribes	Chance Risk
(1) Tribes that indulge their babies more	−.08	63	high
(2) Tribes with several women to mother each baby	−.32	61	$<.05$
(3) Tribes that indulge their children more (after babyhood)	−.02	67	high
(4) Tribes that encourage adults to depend on other people for love and emotional satisfaction	−.38	45	$<.01$
(5) Tribes that encourage adults to depend upon other people for their nonemotional needs	−.48	45	$<.01$
(6) Tribes where people usually eat their meals in groups larger than a single nuclear family	−.30	51	$<.05$

SOURCE: Bacon et al. (1965: 34), and Appendix C.

training of young children is a leading cause of lifelong feelings of anxiety. But the Factor Study Group people found that among societies where toilet training was *more* severe, hard drinking was *rarer*.

Horton's findings can be read as showing a link between hard drinking and anxiety. But they can just as well be read as showing a link between hard drinking and weak moralnets. Food supplies are less secure among hunters and gatherers than among herders and farmers. And the latter likewise tend to have stronger and more elaborate kinship structures. For there is much good evidence on the link between weak moralnets and hard drinking. Let us now have a look at it.

8.5.2   Hard Drinking and Moralnet Strength

Much further light is shed on the causes of alcoholism by the studies of the Factor Study Group. Their most important findings are set forth in Table 8.3. The Factor Study Group focused their attention on the psychological notion of dependency. The more dependency, the less drunkenness. They rate overall indulgence during infancy high in societies in which infants usually are much pampered: People show their love for babies, someone is always at hand to take care of them, they are not deliberately hurt (not spanked, for example) for any reason. This measure, by their theory, should strongly relate to drunkenness. In fact it turns out to have little to do with it.

Line 2 of Table 8.3 is important. The more people there are who help care for a baby in a society, the less drunkenness there is among adults. The key point here is that where nurturance is diffuse in this way, infants feel from the start that there are many people around to care for them. But where nurturance is not diffuse, infants feel from the start that their care depends on the mother—and on her alone.

Line 3 of Table 8.3 concerns the amount of affection children are shown after infancy, and their freedom from physical pain inflicted for any reason by the people who care for them.

Line 4 of Table 8.3 concerns emotional dependence in adulthood. By that, the Factor Study Group mean the extent that the emotional needs of adults are met by others. Societies that meet such needs, they find, are societies with less drunkenness. Compare the first, third, and fourth lines of the table. See how much greater is the correlation with drunkenness on the fourth line than on the first and third. They are telling us something important. They are claiming that the treatment of children is less important than the treatment of adults. This finding conflicts with views of many experts on psychological anthropology.

Line 5 of Table 8.3 deals with instrumental dependence in adulthood. By that, the Factor Study Group mean the extent that the varied needs—other than emotional—of adults are met by their family of associates rather than by themselves acting alone. Such societies, more than any other kind considered here, tend to be societies in which drunkenness is rare. Again, as line 6 shows, societies in which meals tend to be eaten in groups larger than households are likely to be societies with less drunkenness than others.

These findings seem to indicate the type of social situation in which drunkenness is to be expected: (1) Infants tend to look specifically at their mothers alone for loving care rather than at a larger group of relatives, as well. (2) Adults tend to get few manifestations of love from other people. (3) They tend to look primarily to their own solitary efforts for the satisfaction of their other needs. (4) They tend to eat only in household groups, not in larger groups.

Another straw in the wind—from Barry, one of the Factor Study Group. He found a correlation of no less than 77 in 100 between frequency of drunkenness and crying babies. Societies in which babies cry a lot are societies in which grownups drink a lot. What sorts of societies are those in which babies cry a lot? Those in which infants are generally not much indulged.

And where are infants generally not much indulged? In societies with smaller households. Children are indulged the least when the mother has to care for them all by herself. They are indulged a little more when papa is there to help mama. Still more when papa has more than one wife, so the wives can take turns helping each other. Most of all where not only is there papa and mama to pick up baby if it cries, but also grandpa and grandma and uncle and aunt.

Bacon has used another kind of multivariate analysis to measure the relative importance of the traits in Table 8.3 on frequency of drunkenness. Her work assumes that frequency of drunkenness is the combined effect of those four other traits (see Table 8.4).

TABLE 8.4   Frequency of Drunkenness: A Linear Regression

PROPOSITION: *Moralnet strength and pressures for achievement are equally linked to frequency of drunkenness.*

Given that Frequency of Drunkenness (F) is the common *effect.*

Given that these four traits each are contributory *causes*:

(1) pressure on children for personal achievement (P)
(2) diffusion and nurturance of young children among many adults (D)
(3) emotional dependence of adults upon other adults for comfort (E)
(4) instrumental dependence of adults upon other adults, for social or economic support (I)

Then Bacon shows that these four causes taken together explain 46% of the variation in Frequency of Drunkenness in a worldwide sample of 38 tribes—with P alone explaining 21% and the other three traits explaining 25%.

Here is Bacon's equation—an example of linear regression:

$$F = 13.8 + .46P - .45D - .33E - .05I$$

(13.8 is a mathematical constant—the intercept—which tells us nothing about the causes of drunkenness.)

SOURCE: Bacon (1974: 871).

Of the four traits, the most important single cause of drunkenness is pressure on children for personal achievement. Such pressure is shown by applying strict work standards early in life and by punishing children severely for failure to live up to them. In old-fashioned schools in Iran, for example, they taught the young boys to write a beautiful hand. Each day the teacher would review each boy's homework. The teacher would thread a pencil through the boy's fingers, grasp the boy's hand in his, and point out the boy's mistakes. For each mistake, a hard squeeze!

But notice that the other three causes of drunkenness in Table 8.4 are all in one way or another measuring moralnet strength. Thus they support the theory that weakened moralnets mean trouble. Diffusion of nurturance measures the availability of other adults to help a mother care for her babies. Emotional dependence in adulthood measures the emotional ties of people to their moralnets. And instrumental dependence in adulthood measures their social and economic ties.

A like pattern is strongly visible in the work by Davis. In Table 8.5 we see two of his most important findings. Societies with bilateral descent systems tend more often to have much drunkenness than societies with unilineal descent systems. Unilineal descent systems, whether patrilineal or matrilineal, tend to be built up from unilineal extended family households. These households often are linked in larger lineages, clans, or phratries. All these groups are corporate groups; they are family; they commonly tend to live near each other; and they provide each member with a body of relatives he or she can look to for help and

TABLE 8.5   Kin Group and Alcohol

PROPOSITION: *The tighter the kin group, the less drunkenness.*

	Correlation Level[a]	Number of Tribes	Chance Risk[b]
Tribes with bilateral (looser) descent systems rather than with either patrilineal or matrilineal kin groups	.32	67	.007
Monogamous rather than polygamous tribes	.18	71	.15

SOURCE: Davis (1964: 34).
a. Correlations are Kendall's tau-b coefficients of association.
b. The chance risk was computed from Davis's chi-squares using a nomograph (see Wilcoxon, 1949).

support. Societies without extended family households, then, clearly tend to be societies with more drunkenness.

There seems also to be a slight tendency for polygynous families to have less drunkenness than monogamous families. In a polygynous family, husband, and co-wives together provide a larger group of associated adults.

So it forms a pattern. Societies with close-knit households and kin groups—in which broad and diffuse support comes to child and grownup alike from a large set of relatives—tend to be societies with less hard drinking. Those with weak or small kin groups tend to be societies with more hard drinking. Weakened moralnets mean trouble.

A like meaning can be read into the most successful program for treatment of severe alcoholism in the United States: Alcoholics Anonymous. This loosely linked society was founded and developed by amateurs, not by social scientists. But social scientists recognize that it has a better success record than any programs they run. Alcoholics Anonymous works through small local chapters. Each chapter is a moralnet with regular meetings, ceremonies, a clear program of shared values, and strong social and emotional support. And it works.

A series of carefully controlled clinical experiments done in the United States, England, and South Africa provide more evidence. More than a dozen people have done eight distinct studies. Of these, Edwards's is the most persuasive because it is the most careful and thorough. But they all have similar findings. They show that alcoholics who work regularly at the same job for a number of years are more likely to get well than alcoholics who are unemployed or who go from job to job. They show that alcoholics who live with friends or relatives in the same community for a number of years are more likely to get well than those who move about or who live alone or with strangers. They show that alcoholics who have money are more likely to get well than alcoholics who lack it. They show that alcoholics who keep out of trouble with the police are more likely to get well than alcoholics who get arrested. Once again, weakened moralnets mean trouble.

TABLE 8.6   Why We Can Trust the Studies on Social Factors
          in Treatment of Alcoholism

Procedure That Raises Our Trust*	Studies That Used It
(1) Controlled experiment	(1) Edwards: the Kissin group
(2) Replication	(2) The three studies are mutually supportive but not precise replications.
(3) Multivariate analysis	(3) All three
(4) Chance risk tests	(4) Edwards: p = .01; Kissin and Trice groups: p = .05
(5) Naive observers to avoid bias	(5) Trice group
(6) Naive analysts to avoid bias	(6) Edwards; Trice group
(7) Observers systematically trained	(7) All three
(8) Analysts systematically trained	(8) All three
(9) Random sampling	(9) All three
(10) Matched control groups used	(10) All three
(11) Rating scale accuracy tested	(11) Edwards
(12) Double-blind experimental design	(12) None: a weakness

SOURCE: This table is taken from a research proposal by me and David Levinson. The studies in the second column are: Edwards (1970), Kissin et al. (1970), and Trice et al. (1969).
*See Glossary for meanings of technical terms.

A word more about these studies of social factors in the treatment of alcoholism. Levinson looked at the abstracts of 150 such studies. Of these, half (74) proved to be formal theory tests—formal confrontations of theory with data in such a way that if the theory is in fact mistaken, the test seems likely to discredit it. But of these 74, only three proved rigorous enough to trust: one by Kissin, Platz, and Su; one by Trice, Roman, and Belasco; and one by Edwards (see Table 8.6).

In a recent study, the Wolin group looked at the transmission of family rituals—at the strength of family ties. They find that alcoholism often breaks these down and so puts great stress on the children of the family. In other words, we have a snowball: Weakened moralnets mean alcoholism; alcoholism weakens moralnets.

8.5.3   Hard Drinking and the Silver Cord

Davis's thesis tells us even more about drunkenness than about the importance of feelings of social solidarity. In fact, the social solidarity implications of his data did not interest him. Rather, his attention was fixed on another element in the situation—the "silver chord." Clinical studies have led to a theory that the alcoholic typically tends to suffer from maternal overprotection during childhood. This finding seems to be especially applicable to men.

TABLE 8.7 Puberty Rites and Drunkenness

PROPOSITION: *The more puberty rites, the less drunkenness.*

	Correlation Level[a]	Number of Tribes	Chance Risk[b]
Boys' Initiation Rites	.34	44	.02
Segregation of Adolescent Boys	.42	46	.007
Rites for Boys More Important than Rites for Girls	.46	21	.02

SOURCE: Davis (1964: 34).

a. Correlations are Kendall's tau-b coefficients of association.
b. Chance risk was computed from Davis's chi-squares using a nomograph (see Wilcoxon, 1949).

Davis seized on the importance of the diffusion of nurturance correlation (see line 2 of Table 8.3). Societies whose infants look beyond the mother to other people for love and help tend to be societies with less drunkenness than societies whose infants tend to look only to the mother. He sought other characteristics that seemed to him to encourage this diffusion. It was precisely these characteristics of social systems that led him to single them out (see Table 8.3). Certain puberty rites and practices seemed to Davis to help cut the silver chord of attachment between son and mother. He predicted that societies with these rites and practices would have less drunkenness than societies without them. So indeed it proved (see Table 8.7).

However, as Young points out, male puberty rites would seem to make for male solidarity. The hazing lasts only a few days, weeks, or months; but the friendships among the initiates often last a lifetime. The feeling of belonging to a brotherhood of men may well be one of the chief outcomes of these rites. So moralnet theory may explain Davis's findings at least as well as silver chord theory does.

8.5.4 Treatments of Alcoholism

The most rigorous and thorough review of behavioral treatments for alcoholism is Levinson's *Guide to Alcoholism Treatment Research* (see Chapter 5 and Appendix B). He reviews over 200 tests of theories that attempt to treat alcoholism by changing the drinking habits of alcoholics. Of the 200, 19 tests showed that "individualized behavior therapy" clearly works. This approach tailors the treatment to each patient: It involves such things as videotape self-confrontation, role playing, assertiveness training, and electroshock therapy. Another approach works well with alcoholics who are socially stable: These are people who are married and living with their spouses, hold a steady job, and keep out of trouble with the police. This second approach is that of chemical nausea: The alcoholics take a drug that causes them to suffer severe nausea after drinking anything with alcohol in it. Teaching alcoholics to substitute social drinking patterns for alcoholic drinking patterns also has proved successful: Here patients are taught, for example, to sip mixed drinks rather than to gulp neat whiskey or gin. Nine other behavioral treatments have had some preliminary success as well, but need further testing. Still other treatments have been plainly shown to be useless. These things do not work: electrical aversion training, biofeedback, hypnosis, pentathol interviews, relaxation training, social skills training, meditation, and self-confrontation.

8.6   STEP 4: FURTHER STUDIES OF ALCOHOLISM

Most of all, we need good worldwide measures of disabling alcoholism. And good worldwide measures of deaths in which alcohol played an important part. But the United Nations World Health Organization does not now seek such data.

What we do have then from 27 countries are the reports on the total amount of sales of tax-paid alcohol. Those reports do not tell us how much of the alcohol goes into moderate drinking, or how much into alcohol misuse, or how much bootleg or home-brew alcohol people drink.

What do we know about the cause and cure of alcoholism? Hundreds of new books and thousands of new journal articles come out each year the world around. Massive reviews like *Alcohol and Health* try to sum these up. But such reviews are neither complete nor critical. They leave out many studies, and they make no attempt to winnow the few good studies from the many poor ones. Levinson tried an experiment. There are two retrieval systems—two schemes for finding books and papers on alcoholism. The Classified Abstract Archive of the Alcohol Literature (CAAAL) scheme works with punched cards: the National Clearinghouse for Alcohol Information (NCALI) scheme works with a computer. Levinson used these to run down everything he could find on social factors in the treatment of alcoholism. It took 188 hours of work. What he found is set forth in Section 8.5.2. None of those findings was picked up in either edition of *Alcohol and Health*. Nor did any of the later writers, like Edwards, cite all the useful studies by earlier writers.

Levinson found some 44 tested propositions on social factors in the treatment of alcoholism. Based on this sample, he estimates that, in all, there are about 3,000 tested propositions on alcoholism—its measurement, cause, or treatment. What do we know—in any firm, confident way—about the measurement, cause, or treatment of alcoholism? No one knows what we know. Because there are so many, many studies published—most of them untrustworthy. And because no other systematic, objective winnowing of them like HRAF's THINCS project has been done (see Section 5.2).

Genetic factors seem clearly important. But how many people are affected? How can a person tell if he or she is especially vulnerable? How best to treat these people?

Childhood anxieties hanging on into adult life have been much looked into. With what seem to be meager results.

Weakened moralnets do seem to play their part (see Figure 8.1). A theory trust ratio of 50 percent is a good one for current social science. It is, I think, as strong as the evidence that cigarette smoking causes lung cancer.

What should we do next? As I said, we need better yardsticks. Sample surveys of hospital patients and of death certificates could give us high-quality estimates of the incidence and prevalence of alcoholism. Sample victimization surveys would help, too—surveys of the population at large asking people if they have suffered in any way because of the hard drinking of other people. Perhaps of a husband or wife or boss. Perhaps of the driver of the other car in an auto accident.

Only if we have similar hard data on alcoholism from two or three dozen countries can we tell which countries use alcohol best and so learn what laws, policies, or customs make the difference. Such surveys might be run once every two or three years. To do one *carefully* in thirty countries might cost as much as 10 million dollars (based on 1980 dollars).

A thorough review of the thousands of studies already done on alcoholism would be sure to pay off. Such a review probably would turn up something like one or two hundred well tested theories. Such a review would cost only about 250,000 dollars (1980 dollars).

But the most dramatic and decisive results we can hope for might come from a moralnet project like the one I propose in Chapter 16. For a high rate of alcoholism is only one of a set of symptoms of weakened modern moralnets. Only one of several social ills that could be much helped by building better moralnets.

In clinical research, the most urgent task would seem to be to follow up the inconclusive studies on the nine promising but insufficiently tested behavioral therapies reviewed by Levinson. They include contingency management, covert sensitization, systematic desensitization, power motivation training, assertiveness training, self-control training, blood alcohol level discrimination training, fixed interval drinking decision programs, and self-monitoring.

8.7   STEP 5: COPING WITH ALCOHOLISM

The evidence on moralnets leads me to suggest that people who want to avoid trouble with alcoholism for themselves and their children would be wise to build their moralnets. The easiest way for each person to build strong moralnets seems simply to be what we call a good family man or a good homemaker. The family solution to moralnet tending, of course, goes beyond the home itself to the friendship net. Your home needs to be tied in with at least five other friend-family homes, with whom you often meet to share a meal socially. These homes should share your values, your cultural background, and your social status—and many of these families, if possible, should be kinfolk as well. (If your relatives do not share your view of life, your cultural background, and your social status, you might prefer to see more of unrelated friends who do.)

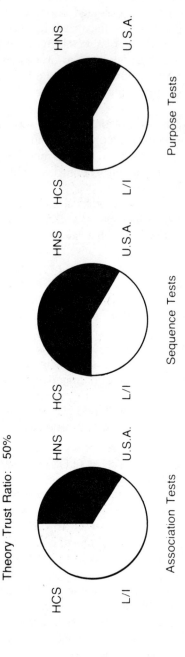

Theory: Weakened Moralnets Increase Alcohol Use

Theory Trust Ratio: 50%

Association Tests · Sequence Tests · Purpose Tests

Figure 8.1 Alcoholism Theory Trust Meter

SOURCES HCS: see Tables 8.3, 8.4, and 8.5; L/I: see Table 8.6; U.S.A.: hundreds of local chapters of Alcoholics Anonymous (see Keller, 1974: 118; Rosenberg, 1971: 78-81).

NOTE: See *Theory trust meter* in Glossary for a key to this chart, and Section 4.5.3 for the general manner of its composition.

HCS = holocultural test; HNS = holonational test; L/I = local or individual test; U.S.A. = countrywide tests in the United States.

If you are unmarried, or divorced, or separated, and can find the time, you would be wise to seek some kind of surrogate family life—perhaps through intense involvement in work or religious or political or recreational groups. If you are raising children as well, they will have a particular need for close family life or its equivalent.

If you are drinking too much and want to quit, faithful attendance at an Alcoholics Anonymous local chapter is presently the course of action most likely to succeed. If you need clinical treatment, then you would be wise to seek an outpatient clinic if you have a steady job and a stable home (five years with both). If not, then you would be wiser to seek admission as a resident patient.

Those who find the rituals of Alcoholics Anonymous uncomfortable or not good enough might well seek out one of the several new methods of behavior change therapies that have lately been shown to help. These are the methods I listed earlier: social skills drinking training, chemical-nausea treatment (which works on the socially stable only), and certain sorts of individualized behavior therapies. Levinson's *Guide* gives details.

8.8 COSTS AND BENEFITS OF ALCOHOLISM PROGRAMS

Building better moralnets, then, seems to me the most urgent task of the struggle against alcoholism—at least in countries like the United States. Not that building better moralnets alone would wipe out alcoholism. But it would richly repay the costs. Alcoholism is the leading public health problem in the United States and many other modern nations—including, it would seem, the USSR. In the United States, its cost is staggering: Policy Analysis, Incorporated, put it at 42.75 *billion* dollars in 1975, compared to another study that put it at 15 billion dollars in 1971. The 1975 cost estimate includes over 19 billion dollars in lost production time. Over 12 billion dollars in health and medical costs. Over 5 billion dollars in motor vehicle accidents. And over 2 billion dollars in violent crimes.

So if better moralnetting could reduce hard drinking by as much as 10 percent in the United States alone in ten years that reduction would be worth 15 billion dollars. And a really good moralnetting program might reduce it not merely by 10 percent, but by as much as 25 percent. (Details in Chapter 16.)

Notes

8.1   Mudidi Kills His Father's Brother

Mudidi case: Bohannan (1960: 162-163)—names changed.
BaLuyia killings: Bohannan (1960: 161).
Ojibwa killings: Long (1904: 93).
Bison Horn Gonds: Grigson (1949: 95) and Elwin (1943: 201-202).
Western Apache killings: Goodwin (1942: 309).

8.2.1   Range of Variation of Alcohol Use and Abuse

Concerning the 16 out of 23 societies that had drunken brawling, see Naroll (1962a: 128). Similar findings in four other studies: Horton (1943: 308f.), Bacon et al. (1965: 104-107), Naroll (1969: 141f.), and Schaefer (1973: 374-379).

On alcoholism types, see Jellinek (1960: 35-41).
Factor Study Group: Bacon et al. (1965: 1-29).

8.2.2   *Evolution of Alcohol Use and Abuse*

On mankind learning to handle its liquor, see Horton (1943: 268-269), Schaefer (1973: 178, 181), and Bacon et al. (1965: 39).
On the introduction of alcohol, see Braidwood et al. (1953).
On genetic factors in alcoholism, see Goodwin et al. (1974), Schaefer (1976, 1979), and the earlier studies these review.

8.3   *Step 1: Core Values of Alcohol Use*

Concerning 43 out of 83 societies that did not disapprove of drunkenness, see Bacon et al. (1965: 108-111).
French attitudes: Jellinek (1960: 23) and Naroll's field notes.
Edna St. Vincent Millay poem: Millay (1922).
Mind-impairing addiction: Blum (1969: 144-153).

8.4   *Step 2: Alcohol Use Scoreboard*

Wine, beer, and spirits related to cirrhosis: Barrett and Franke (1970: 305).
On the link between cirrhosis and alcoholism, see Hyman (1981a, 1981b).
On statistics relating alcohol use to crimes of violence and to serious accidents: For intoxication and automobile accidents, see Strauss (1966: 256) and Waller (1965). For cirrhosis and homicides, see Rudin (1968). For nonmotor vehicle accidents and alcohol use, see Demone and Kasey (1965).
Lynn (1971: 102), Haas (1967: 231-237) and Durkheim (1951: 77-81) found no correlation between rates of death from alcoholism and suicide.

8.5.1   *Hard Drinking and Anxiety*

Review of clinical studies: Schaefer (1973: 5-7) and Tähkä (1966: 30-44).
Proxy measure findings: Horton (1943: 268-275) and Schaefer (1973: 258-259).
On the association between food supplies and subsistence economy, see Field (1962: 53).
On the linkage between societal complexity—or scale—and kinship structure, see Blumberg and Winch (1977).
Comment on alcohol and anxiety: It might be suspected that these correlations are artifacts of a common relationship with societal evolution. But the first-order partial correlation between drunken brawling and malicious-capricious spirits, when controlled for societal complexity, is still .24 (data from Schaefer, 1973: 154).
Factor Study Group: Bacon et al. (1965: 62-77) compare their own findings with those of Horton (1943); their conclusions are on p. 75.

8.5.2   *Hard Drinking and Moralnet Strength*

On baby crying and alcoholism, see Barry (1973: 12); Barry and Paxson (1971: 487) on baby crying and infant indulgence; Whiting (1961: 359) on infant indulgence and household structure.
Bacon (1978: 871) gives a linear regression equation. On kin group ties, see Davis (1964: 34).
My information on Alcoholics Anonymous comes partly from two books written by the organization, and partly from interviews with members of the organization in Buffalo, New York; they were done by two doctoral candidates at the Department of Anthropology of the SUNY University Center there—Susan Horan and Adele Anderson.
The widespread acceptance of Alcoholics Anonymous by therapists and social scientists is reflected in Keller (1974: 118) and in Rosenberg (1971: 78-81).
Levinson's work was part of a three-year unsuccessful effort by HRAF to obtain support from the National Institute of Alcohol Abuse and Addiction for a general THINCS study of alcoholism. The three rigorous studies he found were: Edwards (1970), Kissin et al. (1970), and Trice et al. (1969).
On disrupted family rituals, see Wolin et al. (1980).
The snowball between weakened moralnets and alcoholism was suggested by James M. Schaefer in a personal communication.
Family therapists have tried to treat alcoholism as a family problem: see Burton and Kaplan (1968), Esser (1970), Gleidman (1957), and Meeks and Kelly (1970).

8.5.3   Hard Drinking and the Silver Cord

Concerning the silver cord, see Davis (1964).

For clinical studies of the silver cord theory, see Knight (1937a: 236f., 1937b: 540f., 1938), Tähkä (1966), and McCord and McCord (1960: 35)—all reviewed in Schaefer (1973: 13).

Concerning Table 8.7, Schaefer (1973: 154) got similar results. But one of his coders strongly disagreed with him (pp. 148, 150, 152).

On male puberty rites, see Young (1965).

On treatment research, see Levinson (1981).

8.6   Step 4: Further Studies of Alcoholism

Mark Keller, longtime director of CAAAL, in a private communication, estimates the new publications on alcoholism in all languages, the world around, at 300 new books and 3,700 new articles each year. But only a small proportion of these have reports of confrontational theory tests.

Alcohol and health: see Rosenberg (1971) and Keller (1974).

CAAAL: see Glossary.

NCALI is the National Clearinghouse for Alcohol Information in Rockville, Maryland.

A budget of 10 million dollars for a thirty-country sample survey of alcohol use includes personal interviews, not telephone calls; interviews by professional interviewers, not students; systematic reinterviews to check on the interviewers; quality control questions in the questionnaires to measure respondent bias and candor; random, census-tract sampling; repeated callbacks to find nonrespondents; and a sample size of the order of 1,000 respondents per country.

8.7   Step 5: Coping with Alcoholism

For ways of coping with alcoholism, see Levinson (1981).

8.8   Costs and Benefits of Alcoholism Programs

For proportion of highway deaths associated with drinking on the part of a driver, see Strauss (1966: 256) and Waller (1965).

Costs of alcohol-related problems in 1971 are reviewed in Keller (1974: 37-44).

Terry Bellicha, Director of the National Clearinghouse for Alcohol Information, in a personal communication, cites a study by Policy Analysis, Inc., August 1977, *The Economic Cost of Alcohol Abuse—1975.*

9 Suicide

9.1 TU'IFUA IN A TRAP

Tu'ifua stabbed herself with her older brother's grass knife. She took the knife from its usual place by the kitchen door late one night, when her people were all asleep. They found her in the morning, lying on the floor in a pool of blood. They took her to the hospital. On the way they reproached her for the shame she had brought them. She lingered in the hospital a few hours before she died. Her last word was her husband's name.

"Semisi."

Semisi was waiting outside. When she called for him he came to her bed and knelt beside it. He took her hand in his. But he said nothing. What could he say? He held her hand silently until she died.

Patricia Ledyard, who tells us Tu'ifua's story, was there in Vava'u when it happened. Trained as an anthropologist, she went to the South Sea Islands—to Vava'u in Tonga—as headmistress of a girl's college. She married a Scottish physician who practiced there. It was her husband, Farquhar, who did what little he could for Tu'ifua in the Vava'u hospital. One of Ledyard's neighbors told her the details that brought Tu'ifua to her deathbed in Farquhar's hospital.

Tu'ifua was one of those striking young Polynesian women so admired the world around for their good looks. Her husband, Semisi, was a correspondingly handsome, virile man. They seemed completely happy. Tongans these days are pious Protestants with old-fashioned Protestant ideas of sexual morality. But gossip in Vava'u had not a word to say against Tu'ifua. She was known as a good daughter, a good sister, and a good wife—faithful to her husband and attentive to his needs. They lived above the white sand beach in a fine big house.

Then came Sione. Tongans are always going back and forth to visit their relatives. They stay for weeks and weeks. Sione's aunt lived next door to Tu'ifua; he came to visit his aunt—but he stayed to woo Tu'ifua. We are assured that she gave him no encouragement. But one evening, Sione stumbled into Tu'ifua's kitchen—blind drunk on nearly a quart of gin—just when Tu'ifua was serving Semisi his evening meal. Semisi was tired; he had had a hard day, and he was irritated.

"Who are you and what do you want?" he demanded.

"I am Sione from Kapa and I want Tu'ifua."

In a second, Semisi had Sione by the throat and they brawled, kicking and striking, pounding and choking. Neither Tu'ifua nor Sione's aunt could pull the men apart until they were out of breath.

The fight branded suspicion against Tu'ifua deeply in the mind of everyone— of her husband, of her parents, of her older brother. And Sione began bragging that indeed he *had* slept with her.

So there it was. Ledyard believes Tu'ifua had done nothing amiss. But certainly the suspicion boiling in Semisi's mind made Tu'ifua's married life so unpleasant that she left her husband and went back to her parents. *Their* suspicion and reproaches proved no less unpleasant than her husband's. Well, then, what could she do? She took her older brother's grass knife and stabbed herself.

9.2   SUICIDE AROUND THE WORLD

9.2.1   Range of Variation of Suicide

Ledyard heard of two other local cases of suicide in the five years she lived in Vava'u. One was of a man in a marathon poker game; he lost all his money and all his clothes. It wasn't the loss of wealth that shamed him, says Ledyard; it was that he knew his wife would be very angry with him for staying away so long, and he could not bring himself to face her wrath. So he shot himself. Then there was the lay preacher of Makave. A married man, he was caught having a love affair with a young girl; they told him he was not fit to preach any more sermons; he threw himself to his death from a mango tree.

Looking around the world, we see a wide range of variation in the circumstances and ostensible causes of suicide. Among the Eskimo the struggle for food is bitter and people starve to death in bad winters. Aged Eskimo men walk off to their deaths in the winter cold in order not to be a burden to their families. The Miao of the south China hills need a volunteer once a year to give his life in a great religious ceremony; such a suicide, they feel, greatly benefits his fellow tribesmen. Someone usually offers himself. From many parts of the world we hear stories of girls who kill themselves to avoid being forced into marriages with men they do not like—girls from Fiji, from the Jivaro headhunters of the Ecuadorian jungles, from the Pokot herdsmen of Kenya, from the Toradja villagers of Celebes. Paiute mothers have a way of killing themselves from grief at the death of a child. A Toradja war chief (*tadoelako*) who leads an unsuccessful raid may be reproached on his return by the angry kin of the men killed in the fight; there have been war chiefs who killed themselves from the shame of it. On the island of Truk in Micronesia, people are likely to attempt suicide if they feel rejected and humiliated by their close relatives—even over matters that would seem trifling to us.

In his exhaustive review of the older literature on suicide among small-scale societies, Wisse distinguished nine major categories of reported causes of suicide among such people: (1) material causes such as age, illness, bodily pains, beatings, poverty, hunger; (2) suicides like *suttee* as part of funeral rites; (3) grief at death of a loved one; (4) religious suicide, associated with a belief in immortality, or out of fear of spirits or to propitiate the gods; (5) resentment or

TABLE 9.1   Cultural Evolution and Suicide

PROPOSITION: *There are more suicides at middle levels of cultural evolution*
than at high or low levels.

Level of Cultural Evolution	Societies with Few Suicides	Societies with Many Suicides
(1) Middle	7	13
(2) Low	15	4
(3) High	10	9

SOURCE: Krauss (1970: 163).
Correlation (middle-level cultural evolution with suicide frequency): .25.
Chance risk: $< .03$.
NOTE: Level of association is phi coefficient between means and extremes (line 1 versus sums of lines 2 and 3; chance risk is chi-square of 5.02 with 1 degree of freedom).

despondency at captivity or removal from native country; (6) sexual frustration—either because of rejection or by loss of a love partner, forced marriage, or jealousy at the unfaithfulness of a spouse or lover; (7) an exaggerated sense of personal dignity—shame, injured pride, sense of honor, guilt; (8) sudden impulse when emotionally upset through anger, domestic quarrels, censure, reported "weariness of life from cause of little cogency, trivialities"; (9) revenge.

9.2.2   Evolution of Suicide

Two rival theories of the evolution of suicide have long been current. Both are probably wrong. Von Oettingen, Corre, and Morselli all thought that the smaller scale a society, the *less* suicide it had. People like Zilboorg and Menninger thought that the smaller scale a society, the *more* suicide it had.

But Krauss finds good evidence that the true situation is more subtle. He finds suicide more frequent among small-scale societies at middle levels of cultural evolution (see Table 9.1). Krauss wonders why. I do too.

Among modern nations, by and large the richer the country, the *higher* its suicide rate (see Table 9.2). The Gallup people, however, found that, by and large, the richer the country, the *higher* its quality of life. That is to say, the higher the proportion of its people who told interviewers they felt pleased and satisfied with life. Now suicide is always a rare event—even in Finland, where the rate is so high; even there, only 1 person in 5,000 each year commits suicide. If we guess that for every person who commits suicide, a hundred others may be sad enough to feel like doing so, we still have only one person in fifty affected.

Why does national wealth increase suicide? More on that later on.

If we compare the overall results from the fourteen countries in which at least 90 percent of the people are Roman Catholics with eight other countries in which at least 90 percent of the people are not, we see that the correlation between suicide and wealth in the non-Catholic countries is much higher than in

TABLE 9.2   National Wealth and Suicide

PROPOSITION: *The richer the country, the higher its suicide rate.*

Country	Suicide Rate (1968)*	Per Capita GNP–1963 (in $ US)
Malta	0.3	446
Mexico	1.6	386
Guatemala	2.1	299
Guayana	2.3	259
Mauritius	2.3	303
Ireland	2.5	808
Chile	2.8	324
Costa Rica	3.1	370
Barbados	3.2	414
Greece	3.6	554
Trinidad	4.0	653
Spain	4.5	517
Italy	5.4	954
Netherlands	6.3	1220
Norway	7.0	1564
Iceland	7.4	1719
Israel	7.6	1101
Portugal	9.1	408
New Zealand	9.6	1756
Canada	9.7	2121
Puerto Rico	10.5	982
USA	10.8	3166
Hong Kong	11.6	1689
Luxembourg	12.5	1697
Australia	12.7	1810
Taiwan	13.3	187
Rhodesian (Zimbabwe) Europeans	13.6	212
South African Europeans	14.0	472
Japan	14.1	709
Belgium	15.0	1502
France	15.3	1745
Ceylon	16.9	144
Switzerland	17.3	1996
Denmark	17.8	1689
West Germany	21.3	1639
Finland	21.6	1408
Sweden	21.6	2230
Austria	21.9	1087

SOURCES: Suicide data from UN Department of Economic and Social Affairs (1970: Table 45); GNP data from UN Department of Economic and Social Affairs (1970: Table 183, column headed 1963).
Correlation: .46.
Chance risk: .00026.
N = 38.
*Deaths per 100,000 population.
NOTE: The correlation among eight countries with less than 10% Roman Catholics is all of .78, while among fourteen countries with more than 90% Roman Catholics, it is only .29. Several other studies have correlated like UN statistics on wealth and suicide. That by Barrett and Franke (1970) agrees well with the table. The others agree less closely—but define their variables differently.

the Catholic ones (see notes to Table 9.2). There is a good reason to believe that this lowered correlation is the result of systematic underreporting of suicides in Catholic countries. This marked difference echoes those we find in the famous book on suicide by Durkheim. He explained them by differences in the ritual and tone of Catholic and Protestant churches. But I believe the differences reflect a bias in the reports. Roman Catholics consider suicide a mortal sin; they refuse suicides a religious funeral rite.

Well do I remember the Catholic funeral my wife and I attended in the Tyrolean Alps. That funeral was not an affair for family and friends merely. It was a formal village ceremony. All the parish turned out. They formed a line, in strict ceremonial order, first the young boys, then the grown men, then the young girls of the village—all in white—then the priest and his attendants. They were followed by the coffin, then the immediate family, then the other mourners. Last of all came the village women. There were a hundred people in all, carrying tiny candles. We marched the length of the hamlet to the churchyard. Each in turn bade farewell to the dead girl with a sprinkle of holy water on her coffin.

That girl died from a fall off a mountain rock. Tyrolean Alps are steep and dangerous. Had she thrown herself off that rock, instead of accidentally falling off, there could have been no such ceremony. She could not have been buried in the churchyard. Shamefully, her family would have had to put her away somewhere else. And the gap in the churchyard cemetery would have reminded her family of their grief and shame for the rest of their lives—their family's, and everyone else's. So if a girl is killed by a fall off a rock, not too many awkward questions are likely to be asked by people. Who is to benefit from such an inquiry?

Schneider pursued this line of thought in his study of suicide attempts in Switzerland. Half a century after Durkheim, he found that Swiss Catholic cantons were still reporting consistently fewer suicides than Protestant ones. But he learned from Waldstein that the *accident* rate in the Catholic cantons ran proportionately higher than in the Protestant ones, so that the total rate of suicides plus accidents was about the same. And what is more, the rate of unsuccessful attempts at suicide ran about the same in both. It looks very much as if Durkheim's results reflected a consistent reporting error, not a consistent behavior difference. Catholic countries may well *not* have fewer suicides than non-Catholic ones, but only more suicides registered with the authorities as accidents.

What does such a finding as this do to our confidence in that correlation between suicide rates and wealth? If our rates are so untrustworthy, can we use them at all? There is a statistical paradox here. This evidence of bias does not *decrease* the trustworthiness of that correlation. It actually increases it! This point strikes most people without training in the theory of probability as nonsense. But while we have good reason to suspect that Catholic countries bias their suicide reports down, we have no like reason to suspect their data on wealth. Whatever errors these reports may have are not likely to be church linked. So Catholic countries as such are not likely to differ in the accuracy of their reports on wealth production from Protestant countries. Now if that is so, then we would expect the Catholic suicide reporting bias to lower the correlation between wealth and suicide. By obscuring the suicide data, the Catholic countries obscure the correlation pattern. And so the marked difference in the correlation between Catholic and Protestant countries suggests that the true correlation is closer to the one reported by Protestants than by Catholics. The overall correlation between wealth and suicide rates probably is even higher than Table 9.2 makes it seem to be. That is the paradox.

9.3   STEP 1: CORE VALUES OF SUICIDE

Suicide is far from being universally seen as completely evil. Many cultures approve of it, either in general or at least in stated circumstances. Japanese see suicide as often the dignified and proper way to resolve an intolerable social situation. Among European aristocrats, the sense of honor—of reputation—was keen. If any army officer was caught cheating or stealing by his colleagues, suicide was the best way out. They could not condone the offense, nor could they court-martial the offender and thus put on record the shame of the regiment. So such a man would be left alone in a room with a loaded pistol.

In medieval Europe, on the other hand, suicide was abhorred. Traditionally a suicide was supposed to be buried at a crossroads, not in the consecrated grounds of a churchyard. Indeed, suicide is against the law in many states in our own country; thus technically one who unsuccessfully tries to take his or her life may be prosecuted—although these laws seem to be ignored in recent years.

The vast majority of small-scale cultures take no moral position on suicide either way. They do not consider it either ethically good or ethically evil. For my present purposes, I do not like a social value condemning suicide, nor do I like one requiring or encouraging it. I prefer a culture that makes a suicide a morally neutral act—and one whose commission in no way lets third parties penalize the surviving family of the suicide. Where only the physically healthy are counted, such a set of cultural values would tend to make the reported suicide rate an accurate fever thermometer, measuring emotional despair due chiefly to the loss of warm social ties with the moralnet.

Suicide, needless to say, reflects a situation that contravenes either my core value of pleasure or my core value of health; one way or another, a person who commits suicide is leaving an unpleasant life situation.

There is certainly a wide range of variation from culture to culture in the true rates of suicide. Shaky as our statistics are, we can say that much. On the one hand, consider the Paiutes of Harney Valley in Eastern Oregon. B. Whiting compiled genealogies of this small group. Of a total of some 250 people, no fewer than 23 of them reportedly killed themselves. On the other hand, consider the Ona of Tierra del Fuego. Until the end of the nineteenth century, there were some 2,000 to 4,000 of them. Yet many reporters tell us that the Ona denied ever hearing of anyone committing suicide; the very idea was strange to them. And another people to whom the idea is puzzling are the Kafir of the Hindu Kush. We are told they have no word for suicide in their language. So clearly suicide rates do vary considerably around the world.

Whatever may be the true reasons for these differences from culture to culture, they do reflect one common underlying principle. They show a wide range of variation in the rejection by people of their own cultures. A suicide usually volunteers to die. By that choice, he indicates his lack of contentment with his way of life, his culture. Other things being equal, cultures with higher suicide rates may be considered harder to live in, harder on their own people, more stressful, than cultures with lower suicide rates. So some cultures are better than others.

I take suicide to be an important meter of mental health. As I said, my guess is that for every person who kills him- or herself, there may be hundreds who feel so desperate they sometimes wish they were dead. I review below evidence tending to show that suicides and suicide events tend to be associated with and to follow certain sorts of painful life crises.

9.4   STEP 2: SUICIDE SCOREBOARD

For the comparative study of small-scale societies, a proxy measure of suicide rate seems to be the most useful single measure of culture stress yet available. It is the most useful general worldwide measure, then, of mental health from culture to culture. Discussions of mental illness itself among small-scale societies—not to speak of actual statistics—are still too sparse and scattered and incomplete to be of general, worldwide use.

How can we measure suicide frequency in worldwide studies if reports on suicide rates from small-scale societies are so incomplete? We have a proxy: the relative attention given by ethnographers to suicide (see the test in Table 9.4).

For the worldwide comparative study of modern nations, the measure to be used is, of course, the suicide rate annually reported by each nation to the United Nations. Needless to say, this reported rate is not accurate. Many suicides are disguised as accidents—to save the family from shame or get more insurance money. Driving a car at sixty miles an hour into a concrete pillar is a sure way not only to commit suicide but also to pass off the suicide as an accident. I spoke earlier of systematic underreporting of suicide in Catholic countries. We have to suppose that a certain small number of murders are disguised as suicides. But the high correlations that occur between these worldwide suicide rates and other things like climate and mental hospital admissions show that these reports must covary well with the true rates. For inaccurate reporting of suicide would tend to lower such correlations.

The uses and misuses of worldwide suicide statistics show up well, as we have seen when we compare reports from Roman Catholic countries with those from others. Then we see that Catholic countries do indeed seem consistently to report many fewer suicides than actually occur. But we also have seen that the effect of this bias is to *lower* the worldwide correlations between reported suicide rates and reported national wealth.

Table 9.3 shows the worldwide suicide scoreboard for 1974. Norway's rate may be nearly as accurate as such a thing can be. As I said in Chapter 3, after talking with one of the doctors at a large Oslo hospital who specialized in fixing the cause of sudden deaths there, I believe that the true rate throughout Norway is not more than one-third greater than the rate reported. That rate offers a useful goal for other industrial nations to try for: about 8 suicides per 100,000 population per year. The English-speaking countries fall within the indicated range. It is elsewhere in Scandinavia and in Central Europe that suicide fever runs high. In Section 3.3 I talked about possible explanations of Norway's superior performance with respect to things like suicide.

9.5   STEP 3: TESTS OF THEORIES OF SUICIDE

9.5.1   Weakened Moralnets and Suicide

In trying to explain the higher suicide rates at middle levels of cultural evolution, Krauss looked to see whether social ties were characteristically weaker or less stable at these levels. He found no such relationship. Yet the evidence is strong and clear that unstable social ties do tend to increase the suicide rate.

The most striking instance of this tendency lies in the high rate of suicide among divorced people. A divorcee is much more likely to commit suicide than a widow. So it is not just the loss of the social tie that matters. Some psychoanalysts see the ego defense mechanism of displacement at work here. People may kill themselves because they are angry at themselves. But, argues Karl Menninger, they may also kill themselves because they are angry at *someone else*. They may repress that anger, because it is too painful to face directly, and may displace it by directing it against themselves. There is now strong worldwide evidence to support this view.

Several of us have been testing this theory by looking at the relationship between suicide and what we call "thwarting disorientation situations." Such a situation is one that combines unstable social ties with sources of displaced hostility. We define such a situation as one in which two elements are present. First, a person's social ties are broken or threatened. Second, also at the same time, the break or threat to these social ties comes from some person, some human being—*not* from some impersonal natural force. A widow who understands that she lost her husband from natural causes differs in this respect from a second widow who knows her husband was killed in a war or a brawl. The first woman differs equally from the widow who believes her husband was killed by evil witchcraft. All these women have lost one of their most important relatives—one of their nearest and (presumably) dearest. But the second woman and the third woman have—or think they have—other people to blame

TABLE 9.3 Suicide Scoreboard

Country	Suicide[a]	Chance Risk
Above Extreme Range		
Hungary	33.7	.0000
Above Indicated Range		
Czechoslovakia	23.9	.0097
Finland	21.9	.0238
Austria[b]	21.9	.0238
Sweden[b]	21.5	.0282
Germany (West)[b]	21.3	.0306
Denmark[b]	20.5	.0423
Switzerland[b]	17.3	.1318
France[b]	15.6	.2193
Belgium[b]	15.5	.2255
Australia	15.1	.2516
Luxembourg[b]	14.2	.3177
Japan[b]	14.1	.3257
Iceland[b]	13.2	.4035
Within Indicated Range		
Hong Kong[c]	12	
Poland	11.2	
USA[b]	10.7	
Puerto Rico[c]	10.7	
Uruguay	10.3	
Bulgaria	10.3	
England and Wales[bc]	9.8	
Canada[b]	9.7	
New Zealand	9.6	
Norway[b]	8.1	MODEL COUNTRY
Israel	7.6	
Scotland[bc]	7.5	
Trinidad and Tobago	7.3	
Northern Ireland[bc]	6.6	
Netherlands[b]	6.3	
Italy[b]	5.5	
Spain[b]	4.4	
Below Indicated Range		
Costa Rica	3.1	.4128
Chile	2.8	.3854
Ireland[b]	2.5	.3590
Barbados	1.6	.2870

SOURCE: United Nations Department of Economic and Social Affairs (1975). Worldwide averages and spreads of 35 countries reporting (normal distribution):[d] mean: 12.21; median: 10.70; range: 32.10; SD: 7.187; CEV: 58.87%. Worldwide averages and spreads of 20 OECD countries reporting (normal distribution): mean: 12.31000; median: 11.95; range: 19.40; SD: 6.10548; CEV: 49.60%; skew: 0.18; kurtosis: −0.00.

(notes continued)

TABLE 9.3 NOTES (continued):

a. Suicide rates per 100,000 population per year.
b. Member of the Organization for Economic Cooperation and Development (OECD).
c. United Nations reporting unit; not an independent nation.
d. See Glossary for meanings of worldwide measures.
SD = standard deviation.
CEV = coefficient of evolutionary variation.

for this loss. The first woman blames no one. The second and third woman, then, are examples of victims of thwarting disorientation; the first woman is not.

Table 9.4 shows the worldwide correlations between seven thwarting disorientation situations and a proxy measure of suicide frequency. The measure of suicide itself is the number of words that discuss suicide in the ethnographies consulted. Now obviously the space given to suicide by ethnographers varies from writer to writer, depending on each writer's own feelings, interests, and attitudes. Yet how could these associations possibly be explained that way? The feelings, attitudes, and interests of writers on suicide are hardly likely to be affected by the marriage or divorce rules of the society they study. Even so, their attention to suicide is highly correlated with those rules. Look again at all seven associations. Ask of each: Could these associations reflect variations in author's attitudes or feelings? Hardly. These associations can hardly be explained unless we suppose that authors write more about suicide when there is more suicide to write about. This supposition is supported by the fact that authors who mention more specific cases of suicide tend to write more about suicide than those who mention fewer cases.

I call the kind of suicide considered in Table 9.4 *protest* suicide—voluntary suicide committed in such a way as to come to public notice. This definition leaves out four kinds of suicide: (1) suicides to avoid capital punishment; (2) suicides whose victim is designated by custom (such as *suttee,* a former custom among high caste Hindus, whose widows were expected to burn themselves alive on the funeral pyre of their husbands); (3) suicides disguised as some other kind of death—they lack the element of protest, of publishing, or of calling attention to the suicide's dissatisfaction with his or her way of life; (4) unconscious suicides—people driven by an unconscious death wish may take great and unnecessary risks, and such deaths do not count as protest suicides.

Let us examine Table 9.4. We see there that in societies in which some husbands reportedly beat their wives, ethnographers talk more about suicide than they do in societies in which ethnographers deny that husbands ever beat their wives. Where young people themselves select their husbands and wives, ethnographers talk less about suicide than they do where marriages are arranged for the couple by others. Where men may divorce their wives at pleasure—with or without any reason—ethnographers talk more about suicide than they do where some rules or restrictions limit a man's freedom to divorce his wife. Where people are more afraid of witches or sorcerers, ethnographers talk more about suicide than they do where people are less afraid of witches or

TABLE 9.4   Suicide and Thwarting Disorientation Problems

PROPOSITION: *Ethnographers write more about suicide in societies with thwarting*
                      disorientation problems.

Thwarting Disorientation Problem	Correlation with Suicide Wordage	Chance Risk
Wife Beating	.69	.01
Arranged Marriages	.34	.01
Men's Divorce Freedom	.60	.02
Fear of Witchcraft	.34	.02
Drunken Brawling	.30	.10
Murder	.45	.01
Warfare	.41	.05

SOURCE: Naroll (1963, 1969: 144).

sorcerers. Where people not only take alcoholic drinks but brawl among themselves in their cups, ethnographers talk more about suicide than they do where, although people also take alcoholic drinks, they do not brawl among themselves. Where ethnographers report more than one case of murder (locally unlawful killing), they talk more about suicide than where they report no more than one single murder at most. Finally, we see that in societies in which warfare is comparatively frequent, ethnographers talk more about suicide than they do in societies in which it is comparatively rare.

All seven of these societal traits involve situations that break or threaten social ties to moralnets. Wife beating threatens the social ties between husband and wife; when their children watch, their sense of familial security likewise is threatened. Arranged marriages may break up social ties between courting couples; this situation we already saw leading to suicide of girls among the Pokot of Kenya. Divorce breaks up marriages, needless to say. Where witchcraft is much feared, deaths are commonly blamed on witches; there people often blame loss of a husband or wife or brother or sister or son or daughter on witches. Among small-scale societies, with their small, intimate communities, drunken brawling is usually among people with strong social ties—kinsmen or neighbors.

Thus there seems to be only one plausible single theory to explain all these correlations: Thwarting disorientation situations tend to cause suicides. Table 9.5 shows why. These seven thwarting disorientation measures have little association with each other. This point is crucial. If there were some underlying author interest factor or some societal hostility factor that explained the correlations of Table 9.4, then that fact would require a different kind of Table 9.5 than the one we actually find. If there were some single lurking variable producing the associations of Table 9.4, then we would expect that factor to produce similar associations in Table 9.5. But not so. The average association

TABLE 9.5   Thwarting Disorientation Problems Do Not Tend
                    to Occur Together

Thwarting Disorientation Problem	Average Correlation with the Other 6 Variables
Wife Beating	.11
Arranged Marriages	−.04
Men's Divorce Freedom	.08
Fear of Witchcraft	.01
Drunken Brawling	−.05
Murder	.08
Warfare	.06

SOURCE: Naroll (1969: 144).

NOTE: Average (mean) of all 21 associations between thwarting disorientation problems: .03.

level in Table 9.4 is forty-five out of a possible 100; in Table 9.5, it is only 3. Table 9.4 shows that the thwarting disorientation traits are all related to frequency of attention to suicide, while Table 9.5 shows that, nevertheless, they are largely unrelated to each other. The theory that seven thwarting disorientation traits, all independently of each other, tend to cause suicide and suicide in turn tends to cause people to talk about suicide—predicts a difference in the patterns of Table 9.4 and 9.5 of the sort we find. The rival theory that ethnographers' attitudes lead to their attention both to suicide and to thwarting diorientation—the theory that these numbers are mere reflections of ethnographers' interests—predicts, on the contrary, a similar pattern in Table 9.4 and Table 9.5. So, too, does the rival theory that some underlying factor in the culture—an anxiety factor, for example, or a violence factor—produces both the thwarting disorientation traits and the suicide frequency. The only rival hypothesis that explains the differences between Tables 9.4 and 9.5 as well as mine does is the hypothesis that seven different and independent lurking variables are at work—each of which independently produces a different one of the thwarting disorientation traits along with suicide. Scientists, of course, usually follow the rule of the medieval philosopher Occam: They do not like to multiply hypotheses. Why imagine seven different hidden explanations when the facts before us can be easily explained by a single manifest one?

It is this contrast between Tables 9.4 and 9.5 that makes me confident of two things: First, that our proxy measure is surely measuring suicide rates. Second, that thwarting disorientation situations probably cause suicides.

My confidence is increased by the amount of cross-checking—of replication—that has confirmed these findings. To begin with, there is the work of Krauss. He went behind the seven basic correlations of Table 9.4. These correlations all measured whole societies—characteristics of whole cultures. But, Krauss reasoned, these characteristics all related to sets of specific behaviors, particular kinds of trouble particular people get into. So Krauss went through the sources of data on which Table 9.4 is based. He looked at each suicide case reported there. As to each such case, he asked whether a specific thwarting disorientation situation was also reported. He found a total of 288 suicide cases. Of these, 168 were reportedly committed in the context of thwarting disorientation; 100 others were not. (He could not find enough information to make up his mind about the other 20.)

Much about these seven thwarting disorientation correlations in Table 9.4 has been reported from other worldwide studies. Perhaps the most interesting fact is the correlation between suicide and homicide. That such a correlation exists worldwide among small-scale societies has been confirmed by two other independent studies: those by Palmer and by Lester. (However, among modern nations no such correlation seems to exist; quite the reverse. The more industrialized a nation, the more frequently its women have paying jobs outside the home, and the more frequently *that* happens, the higher the suicide rate, but the lower the homicide rate.)

The correlation between suicide and divorce is one of the most widely tested in all of social science. Durkheim's famous study of suicide emphasized this finding among European nations and provinces within them, toward the end of the last century. The relationship holds good in the United States today; divorced people are more likely to commit suicide than widowed or single people; married people are the least likely.

The correlation between warfare and suicide among modern nations has been confirmed by Haas. By and large, the more warlike nations tend to have higher suicide rates. (Nevertheless, within a given nation, from year to year, suicide rates go down in wartime, up in peacetime.)

Finally, technical studies show that the correlations in Table 9.4 cannot be the result of systematic errors in the sources we studied, nor have the chance risks shown there been distorted by joint diffusion (see Chapter 4 for discussion of this problem).

So these studies point clearly to the weakened moralnet as one of the leading causes of suicide. Lester has recently looked at scores of other studies in the whole field of suicide theory. He looked at studies of predispositions to suicide: genetic, sexual, and cultural predispositions. He looked at the aspects of suicidal personality: suicidal thought processes, suicide as an act of aggression, suicide as a deviant act, and personality correlates of suicide. He looked at the environment of the suicide; the kind of society the victim lives in, the season of the year, the climate.

But none of these theories seemed to Lester as promising as one other group. (A group that included, among others, the thwarting disorientation studies I have just been talking about.) Lester calls them "theories about the social relationships of the suicidal individual." When we look through the studies whose findings so impress Lester, we see that they all deal directly or indirectly with the relationships between a person and his or her moralnet. That is, with his or her small group of intimate social relations—with family, friends, workmates, and peers. Not with his or her relations to the larger society. These studies include several showing that married people have fewer suicides than others, and that people with children have fewer suicides than others. They include many studies showing that suicides often have suffered some form of social disruption either early in childhood or within a few months of their suicide. This finding has since been confirmed by Paykel, Prusoff, and Myers. The Paykel group did a controlled comparison of suicide attempters, depressives, and a sample of the general population of the town. They looked at a broad class of events and found that, among other things, suicide attempts tended to follow undesirable changes in the social field or major changes in family or married life.

The work of Ganzler also deeply impressed Lester. Ganzler compared suicidal subjects with randomly chosen controls. And Ganzler was looking directly at the moralnet idea. He asked his subjects to rate their feelings toward their significant others—their moralnet members. The suicidal people did not get along so well with their moralnets. They clearly felt more isolated than did the normal controls. Ganzler's suicidal people had fewer social contacts than his normal controls. And they declared themselves less satisfied with their social relations than did the normal controls.

Lester did still another follow-up, a worldwide multivariate analysis—a holonational study—on the causes of variation among national suicide rates. He found the most important factor by far to be the birthrate—the higher the birthrate, the lower the suicide rate. Now in part, as he points out, countries with high birthrates are likely to have a smaller proportion of old people. And old people, as we shall see, have especially high suicide rates. But countries with high birthrates are also countries that tend to produce tight moralnets, I suspect. My own mother was one of ten children who lived to grow up. And that set of uncles and aunts provided us cousins with a tight moralnet indeed. So I cannot help wondering to what extent Lester's striking findings about birthrates and suicides may reflect the prevalence of such large families.

But there may be still another explanation. These days the richer the country, the lower the birthrate. And as we have seen, the richer the country, the higher the suicide rate. Adelman and Morris, in their holonational study on economic growth, may well give us the reason for this link. Loose, weak families go along with economic growth. The stronger the family ties, the slower the economic growth.

And why might that be? Adelman and Morris think it has to do with the influence of family structure on investment and on personal incentives. In the large extended families—the strong familial moralnets—of many traditional societies, the fruits of labor are pooled. Such pooling, Adelman and Morris suggest, may well decrease the funds available for investment. At the same time it lessens the individual incentive to work and save, "to get ahead," as we say. Smaller, loose families must rely more on their savings since they can rely less on their relatives. They work harder and save more. Richer countries seem to have weaker family links than poorer ones (more on this in the next chapter). If they do, we have reason enough for the fact that richer countries have more suicides than poorer ones.

So we have a set of links: high birthrates and large, strong families; low suicide rate and slow economic growth. Which comes first, the chicken or the egg? Which causes which? Or is it a snowball—do they all reinforce each other?

It was not only studies like these showing the structural links between moralnets and suicide that impressed Lester. It was other studies looking at the quality of these ties. Not only whether a person has stable social ties with a moralnet, but whether the quality of the relationship with the moralnet is satisfying.

Several studies found that suicidal people were more dependent on others than normal people. More dependent means looking more toward others to make one's decisions—decisions that normal people usually make for themselves. More dependent also means looking more towards others to do the work that normal people usually do for themselves. So more dependent means less able to take care of oneself. The point may well be that when such a dependent person has trouble with the moralnet, the danger of suicide increases.

Take all this evidence together, and the pattern seems clear. Weakened moralnets often lead to suicide.

9.5.2 Other Stresses and Suicide

I do not mean to say that weakened moralnets are the only causes of suicide. Nor do I mean that thwarting disorientation situations are necessarily the chief causes of suicide. There are surely others. Gibbs and Martin have been studying the effect of conflicting social ties on suicide. They predict that suicide frequency will be greater if (and because) more people occupy statuses making incompatible claims on them. Often, a person belongs to more than one moralnet—and his or her loyalties are in conflict. Furthermore, Gibbs and Martin also reason that if two statuses make more incompatible claims on a person, those statuses will tend to be occupied by fewer people. Gibbs and Martin then proceed to test the hypothesis that people in rarely occupied statuses have higher suicide rates than other people. But Gibbs and Martin do not ask whether factors other than status incompatibility make a status unpopular. And in fact two of the most commonly occupied statuses obviously involve serious incompatibilities. The statuses of husband/employee involve conflicting claims on a man's time, loyalties, and energies. The statuses of wife/mother do the same on a woman's time. Thus Gibbs and Martin have an interesting set of correlations, implausibly explained. Yet their findings have been solidly confirmed worldwide with respect to women in the labor force: The higher the proportion of working women, the more suicide.

The study by the Paykel group I spoke of earlier shows a strong link between health problems and suicide. And between trouble with the law and suicide. In

Chapter 13 we will see the overwhelming evidence that aged people have much higher suicide rates than younger ones. Many of these deaths among old people may reflect weakened moralnet ties. But many may also reflect bad health. I would guess both together are at work.

Some recent worldwide work tends to support the old theory that suicide frequency is related to climate or season of the year. Cold, dark times and places tend to encourage suicide, it seems.

9.6   STEP 4: FURTHER STUDIES OF SUICIDE

The suicide rate yardstick needs careful checking. As I said before, suicides are commonly disguised as accidents. Perhaps one randomly chosen "accidental" death out of every hundred might be thoroughly investigated in circumstances in which the privacy of the family is preserved—the findings not published—no names named. If we are to treat the fever, instead of playing tricks with the thermometer, it would be well to do two things about our cause-of-death statistics. First, as in Norway and Sweden today, require that all people who die suddenly, and who are not then under a doctor's care, be autopsied by expert pathologists. Second, as in Norway but not in Sweden, keep that pathologist's findings confidential rather than make them public. These two requirements would do wonders for the accuracy of one of our fever thermometers—the national suicide rate.

The most important theory about the cause of suicide is that illustrated in Figure 9.1. Weakened moralnets cause suicides. As that figure shows, we have overwhelming evidence that suicide tends to occur more often among people with weakened moralnets than among the general population. And because of the nature of things, our evidence shows also that the weakened moralnets come first, and the suicide follows. So we have a case as strong as that linking tobacco smoking and lung cancer. What we do *not* have are any purpose tests— any evidence that people purposefully reduced the suicide rate by strengthening moralnet ties. But I hope that the moralnet trials I propose in Chapter 16 might provide such a test.

We also need to look into the theories of Adelman and Morris about the link between family size and national wealth. A study by Blumberg and Winch confirms this link. But are smaller families a *cause* of growth in national wealth, as they believe? Or only an effect? Or is there a snowball linking the two? How much of a tradeoff is there between smaller family moralnets and national wealth? As yet, I am not aware of any hard answers to these key questions.

More work is needed on the status integration studies of Gibbs and Martin. What are they really measuring? What do their findings really mean? I am intrigued by their correlations, but dissatisfied with their methods of measurement and their linkage between status occupancy and status integration.

Theory: Weakened Moralnets Tend to Encourage Suicide

Theory Trust Ratio: 47%

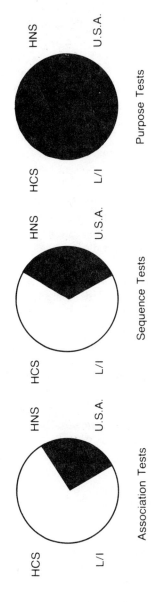

Association Tests Sequence Tests Purpose Tests

SOURCES HCS: Naroll (1969), Krauss and Krauss (1968), and Krauss (1966); HNS: Durkheim (1951) and Lester (1977); L/I: Paykel et al. (1975), Ganzler (1967), and Lester (1970: 97-114); U.S.A.: Dublin (1963: 27).
NOTE: See *Theory trust meter* in Glossary for a key to this chart, and Section 4.5.3 for the general manner of its composition. HCS = holocultural test; HNS = holonational test; L/I = local or individual test; U.S.A. = countrywide tests in the United States.

Figure 9.1 Suicide Theory Trust Meter

9.7   STEP 5: COPING WITH THE SUICIDE RATE

I am not here concerned with treating suicide as a symptom, and so say nothing about suicide clinics. Suicide itself is always a rare event, as I have said before, and so might not itself receive a specially high priority for social concern. Treating would-be suicides without treating the social conditions that drive them to despair is working with the fever thermometer rather than with the fever.

I look at suicide attempts as the tip of the iceberg of loneliness. As I said, I would guess that for every suicide attempter, there may be a hundred unhappy people who are not quite so desperate. (If suicide clinics are active and successful, then I would want to see the United Nations compile reports from them on their caseloads—as their caseloads become a more gentle fever thermometer than the actual suicide rates.)

The evidence I have reviewed points to different policies for developed countries like the United States on the one hand, and for developing countries like India on the other.

Not only the suicide statistics alone, but other indicators collected for Europe by Fuchs, Gaspari, and Millendorfer, and the worldwide holonational study by Adelman and Morris, tell us that economic progress often is paid for by weak moralnets. Rapid industrial growth tends to break up extended families by encouraging nuclear families to move away from home; it also tends to break up the nuclear families themselves by encouraging divorce. (The nesting of a nuclear family snugly within an extended family moralnet may well tend to discourage divorce and so to sustain the nuclear family.)

The prevalent mores among educated people in the 1960s and the 1970s failed to discourage divorce. Yet the evidence linking susceptibility to suicide and the status of the divorced person is overwhelming. That evidence, of course, does not point its finger at the act of divorce but at its consequences. Further, all of the evidence is consistent with the theory that remarriage mends the damage caused by divorce, not only to the divorced people, but also to their children. The evidence in general points more strongly to the importance of maintaining firm, warm, cordial relations within the nuclear family; it also points, if less strongly, to the importance of keeping up like ties with the wider moralnet. That evidence counsels us to value our loves and our friendships—our family ties. It warns us to think about the personal tradeoff—the loneliness cost—when considering a move that uproots family and moralnet ties. And to think not only of the loneliness price that we might have to pay, but the like price our children might have to pay.

Developing countries like India tend to have strong extended family moralnets. These sturdy groups provide the chief economic and political as well as emotional home for their members. Their suicide rates tend, accordingly, to be low. The most conspicuous single victim of extended family systems in traditional societies tend to be the spouses in arranged marriages. Young women who thus move into an extended family household under the control of their mother-in-law tend to be especially vulnerable. The work on thwarting disorientation I reviewed in Section 9.5.1 suggests that arranged marriages may too often serve the interests of the arrangers rather than those of the bride and groom.

9.8   COSTS AND BENEFITS OF SUICIDE PROGRAMS

I have no specific manifest fiscal or political benefits to point to from a lowering of the suicide rate. I would expect that rate, however, to go down as a result of a general policy of moralnet strengthening. And I estimate the manifest benefits of such a general policy in Chapter 16.

Notes

9.1   Tu'ifua in a Trap

Tu'ifua case: Ledyard (1956: 208-220); names have been changed.

9.2.1   Range of Variation of Suicide

Other suicides in Vava'u, Tonga: Ledyard (1956: 210).

Review of range of variation of suicides around the world (Eskimo, Miao, Fiji, Varo, Paiute) are from Naroll (1962a: 61-62, 142-143). See also Adriani and Kruyt (1951: 260f, 420) on the Toradja, and Gladwin and Sarason (1953: 124, 145) on the Trukese and their neighbors.

On the reported causes of suicide, see Wisse (1933: 62); my paragraph comes verbatim from Naroll (1962a: 62).

9.2.2   Evolution of Suicide

On the rarity of suicide among primitive peoples, Steinmetz (1894: 53) reviews the theories of Von Oettingen, of Corre, and of Morselli.

Rejected theories of evolution of suicide: Zilboorg (1937: 23) and Menninger (1938: 43). On cultural evolution and suicide, see Krauss (1970: 163).

I have no evidence to support my guess that for every person who actually commits suicide, a hundred others may sometimes wish to do so; it is just a hunch.

In Table 9.2 the eight non-Catholic countries are: Trinidad, Japan, Denmark, Finland, Iceland, Norway, Sweden, and Barbados; the fourteen Catholic countries are: Mauritius, Costa Rica, Guatemala, Puerto Rico, Chile, Austria, Belgium, Ireland, Italy, Malta, Portugal, Spain, Mexico, and France. Other studies of correlation between GNP and suicide rate are by Quinney (1965), Haas (1967: 232), and Barrett and Franke (1970: 305)—who get a correlation of .37 for 1950 GNP per capita, and one of .52 for 1965 GNP per capita; they cross-lag without result over a fifteen-year lag. Whitt, Gordon, and Hofley (1972) also correlate religion with industrialization. Their results do not agree at all with mine; however, their measure of industrialization is quite different from mine—not GNP per capita, but percentage of males not engaged in agriculture; their dates are different; and their definition of predominant religion is different.

Gallup International Research Institutes (1977: 56f.) assert a correlation between quality of life and economic development, and a scanning of their Personal Happiness response (pp. 139-142) certainly seems to bear them out, but they offer no formal correlation calculations.

Field notes and photographs on the funeral of Anna Luise in Kaunertal, July 8, 1956; details of death in Tiroler Tageszeitung, Innsbruck, July 5, 1956; for more on that village, see Naroll and Naroll (1962).

On the relative frequency of completed and attempted suicides in Switzerland, see Schneider (1954: 90-93); he shows that suicide attempts do not differ proportionately among Catholics and Protestants in Switzerland. He cites the Ph.D. dissertation of E. Waldstein, "Der Selbstmord in der Schweiz" (Basel: Philographischer Verlag, 1934) as the source of the comparison between suicide and accident rates there.

9.3   Step 1: Core Values of Suicide

On the suicide of European aristocrats, such affairs are hushed up, not documented. But for examples, see Magnus (1964: 152f.) and Sayers (1928: 336f.).

Most small-scale societies take no moral position on suicide, according to Wisse (1933: 508-519). I got a similar finding from my War, Stress, and Culture sample; of 51 societies coded for suicide, we could code only 10 on a moral position of approval or disapproval (Naroll, 1970b: trait no. 621). On the extreme frequency of suicide among Harney Valley Paiute and its rarity among Ona and Kafirs, see Naroll (1962a: 144-146).

9.4   Step 2: Suicide Scoreboard

Validity of suicide wordage ratio as a proxy measure is discussed briefly in Section 9.5, but in much more detail in Naroll (1969); see also Lester (1970: 110).

9.5.1   Weakened Moralnets and Suicide

Krauss studies: Krauss (1966), Krauss and Krauss (1968), and Krauss and Tesser (1971).

On displacement of hostility toward others into self-hate: Menninger (1938: 244-250) and Simpson, in Durkheim (1951: 24).

The concept of Protest Suicide is elaborated in Naroll (1962a: 61).

Suicides among Pokot girls to protest arranged marriages: Edgerton and Conant (1964).

Suicide and divorce correlations: Durkheim (1951: 259-276), Dorpat, Jackson, and Ripley (1968), and Dublin (1963: 25-29).

Papago men terrify wives and children when they go on drinking bouts: Naroll, field notes.

Suicide and homicide correlations: Palmer (1965, 1970), Lester (1971, 1974), Barrett and Franke (1970), Quinney (1965), and Hadden and DeWalt (1974); but compare Rudin (1968).

Suicide and warfare correlations: Haas (1964: 44-95) and Dublin (1963: 68-73).

The problems of systematic error and of joint diffusion are discussed as tasks 5 and 12, respectively, of Section 4.5.2. How do these problems bear on the data of Table 9.4? Those data come from my War, Stress, and Culture Sample (Naroll, 1970b). I ran five spatial autocorrelations on my measure of suicide wordage; all proved small and three of the five were negative! Hence we can rule out Galton's Problem as a source of confounding error in that table. Of the 36 data quality control tests I ran on that measure, all but 3 could plausibly be explained as mere chance noise: Only 3 were "statistically significant" at the 5 percent level. There is no way that only three sources of systematic error could explain the contrast between the high correlations of Table 9.4 and the low ones of Table 9.5.

On the social relationships of suicidal individuals, see Lester (1970: 97-114).

On lower suicide rates of married people, see Dublin (1963). On lower suicide rates among parents, see Dublin and Bunzel (1933) and Breed (1966).

On social disruption and suicide, see Bolin et al. (1968), Breed (1963, 1967), Rachlis (1969), Farberow and McEvoy (1966), Murphy and Robins (1967), Robins and O'Neal (1958), Bloom (1967), and Paykel et al. (1975).

On feelings toward their moralnets—their "significant others"—of suicidal people compared to "normal" controls, see Ganzler (1967).

On birthrates and suicide rates, see Lester (1977).

On the relationship between family structure and economic development, see Adelman and Morris (1967: 27f.).

On suicides being more dependent than "normal" people on others, Lester (1970: 112-114) cites: Farberow et al. (1961, 1966), Farberow and McEvoy (1966), Leonard (1967), Lester (1969), Braaten and Darling (1962), and Tabachnick (1961).

Since I finished revising this chapter, two further studies offering more strong evidence in support of the role of weakened moralnets as a cause of suicide have come to hand. Braucht (1979) studied 659 suicide attempts in Denver, Colorado, and got similar results to those by the Paykel group, linking suicide attempts to weakened moralnets, health problems, and legal problems. Sainsbury, Jenkins, and Levey (1980) studied changes in the suicide rate in eighteen European countries between 1961 and 1974. Their analysis is complex; but they found that the most powerful predictors of change in suicide rate were prior changes in the status of women, in anomie (that is, in weakened social ties), and in socioeconomic change—standard of living. They review earlier studies on European countries with parallel findings. Of these, two are particularly striking: Ashford and Lawrence (1976) found that one-person households accounted for as much as 71 percent of the variance in male suicide rates in rural England and Wales beteen 1961 and 1967, and for 48 percent between 1968 and 1971; Lönnqvist (1977) found that over 50 percent of the variance of the changes in suicide rates in Helsinki between 1961 and 1972 were accounted for by changes in social variables—most notably in measures of social disorganization.

9.5.2   Other Stresses and Suicide

On status inconsistency and suicide: Gibbs and Martin (1964), Barrett and Franke (1970), and Hadden and DeWalt (1974).

On health problems, legal problems and suicide: Paykel (1974) and Paykel et al. (1975).

On climate and suicide: Lynn (1971: 126-155) and Robbins, Pelto, and DeWalt (1972).

9.6   Step 4: Further Studies of Suicide

Figure 9.1 summarizes the test results reviewed in Section 9.5. Because the conditions associated with suicide are invariably antecedent to it, I have classed all these tests as sequence tests. In addition, Naroll (1969) offers evidence that the thwarting disorientation complex cannot be the joint product of a single, unknown lurking variable or factor.

Other evidence supports the findings of Adelman and Morris (1967) that smaller families tend to be found among more economically developed nations than among less (see Blumberg and Winch, 1977).

10 The Family

10.1 SUGITA GEMPAKU GOES TO AN AUTOPSY

The body of Aocha Baba was cut up for the physicians by an old *Eta*. In Japan, about 200 years ago, a Japanese medical man could not touch a corpse himself; he had to leave it to a man of that despised caste of menials. The *Eta* showed the doctors all the parts he could. He named the ones he knew: the heart, the liver, the gall-bladder, and the stomach. Dr. Sugita and his colleagues excitedly compared each part of the executed criminal with the drawings in their new Dutch anatomy book. The pictures of human internal organs in this book differed from those in the Chinese anatomy books they had long been using as guides. The doctors had wondered if perhaps Europeans' internal organs differed from those of East Asians. But they saw that Aocha Baba's liver looked like the liver in the Dutch book, not like the livers in the Chinese books. Thus, on that day the study of European medicine in Japan began with the Dutch book of anatomy.

Such books were rare then in Japan, rare and costly. Japanese physicians were modestly paid. Dr. Sugita could not have bought such a book by himself. It would be another hundred years before the Japanese government would pay money for Western knowledge. Where did Dr. Sugita Gempaku find the money for the Dutch anatomy book? He tells us:

> I wanted these books more than anything else in the world. Since I was then too poor to buy them, I brought them to Oka Shinzaemon, the highest official of our clan, and I told him that I simply must have these Dutch books. Shinzaemon then said: "Is it in any way useful to buy and to own them? If it is useful, I will do my best to see that our feudal lord gives you the money for them." "Although the purpose is still not quite clear to me," I answered, "yet one day I will prove to you that it is useful."

> Then one of us, named Sano Kozaemon said: "If you please, try to get him the books. Mr. Sugita would be the last to ask for it, it it were not useful."

So in feudal Japan it was fellow clansmen who backed Dr. Sugita, who made it possible for him to buy his book and thus to revolutionize Japanese medicine. There has been nothing like Japanese clans in Western Europe since Roman times. Indeed, the variety of family organization—of kinship systems—has long fascinated anthropologists.

But though the structure of the family has been one of the most studied of worldwide problems, its functions have been little attended to. It has not been so much ignored as taken for granted. The nuclear family has for most people been the main link to the moralnet. The extended family very often has *been* the moralnet. It is possible to run a good moralnet without using the family as a working part. Possible, yes, but unusual.

In our society, the family often seems weak. Bronfenbrenner has devoted years to the study of the American family. He complains that too often North Americans make the individual instead of the family their center of concern. Too often, he says, the officials and the law treat mother, father, son, and daughter as four individuals instead of one family. Too seldom, he says, do we find here grandmother or grandfather or uncle or aunt living in the home with the family. He is shocked by the number of households in which only one parent lives with the children. Bronfenbrenner blames many of our social ills on this weakening of the family. Infant mortality, school vandalism, serious crime, suicide, poor school work—he blames all of these on the weakened American family moralnet.

Confucius would have agreed. The classical Chinese primer taught as its first lesson: "Filial piety is the origin of morality and the basis of our doctrine."

Books and articles on family life in the United States are almost always written by professional writers or academics. Laws governing family life in the United States are almost always made by professional lawyers and politicians. Such people as these may well not themselves be as likely as most other Americans to maintain strong family ties. They may well move around more, for one thing. For another, their personal values—their philosophies of life—may well tend more often than others to differ from the families that brought them up. However much they respect them, they may no longer really feel at home with them.

So the family attitudes and the images of American family life in the minds of writers and leaders may not be typical of their fellow countrymen. Again I remind you of Zimmerman and Cervantes's study. The most successful households— successful in bringing up their children—proved to be the households that linked up with five other like households of kinfolk. Linked up with extended family moralnets. Note that Zimmerman and Cervantes did *not* define a family's success in terms of money or rank. Instead, they defined success in terms of the mental and social health of the family's children.

I offer more evidence that well-integrated families make for mental and social health—make for moral order. In this chapter I argue for the action of four separate instincts bundling together to reinforce family ties—and so making the extended family the easiest moralnet to build and to keep up. I do not say that it is impossible to build successful moralnets otherwise. Indeed, in Chapter 16 I offer several proposals for building artificial, nonfamilial moralnets where the family breaks down. But these are special remedies for special problems. Best of all is to avoid any need for such remedies by keeping up strong family households and strong extended families.

10.2   FAMILY LIFE AROUND THE WORLD

10.2.1   The Family Instinct

The family is the most common moralnet. Its strength seems firmly grounded in a set of instincts. As I said in Chapter 6, I mean by instinct an inborn goal—a wish, a desire, a liking. Such a goal need not be pursued—such a wish need not be indulged. But other things being equal, people are most comfortable when their instincts are satisfied.

I hold that no less than four instincts are at work supporting human family life:

(1) *The sex instinct.* As Bernard Shaw said, the great advantage of marriage is that it combines a maximum of temptation with a maximum of opportunity.
(2) The *marriage,* or *pair-bonding instinct* (more on that shortly).
(3) The *child-bonding instinct.* In Chapter 6 I described Bowlby's theory of a young child's instinctive attachment to a mother figure. He said nothing about a like attachment instinct within the mother. I know of no scientific tests of the generally held folk view that there is indeed a strong maternal instinct among women—a view I share. The work of Mackey and Day suggests that there is also a somewhat weaker but still palpable paternal instinct among men.
(4) *The general social instinct* I talked about in Chapter 6. Such an instinct would attach people presumably to any human social group with which they are in intimate contact. But if parents and children are instinctively bonded to begin with, then they tend to see a lot of each other while the children are growing. After they become adults, a social bond thus has been created by association. So we would expect extended families to be the most common beneficiaries of social-bonding instincts.

About the pair-bonding instinct among human beings. Obviously, we do not always mate for life: in many societies like our own, divorce is not unusual and casual love affairs are common. Yet there is evidence supporting the theory of a marriage instinct. To begin with, in all societies without exception, marriage is supposed to be the usual way to find a sex partner among mature people, and marriage is supposed also to be a key element in the family residential moralnet. We may call such an arrangement a "normal" marriage.

There are only a few subcultures in which special groups of people run their lives and raise children without normal marriages. Of these subcultures, probably the best known is that of the Nayar of Kerala in South India. Careful study of Nayar sex life provides even stronger support for the theory of a marriage instinct as a main element of family moralnets.

That evidence goes to show that even though for many hundreds of years the Nayars lacked anything like a normal marriage, they nevertheless must have continued to *want* one. The special Nayar household system—which entirely ruled out any kind of meaningful marriage—made sense in the special circumstances in which Nayar men lived for hundreds of years. So that system came to be fully supported by culture—by Nayar values, by Nayar law, and by Nayar property rules. Nevertheless, despite all this cultural support, built up over many centuries, the special Nayar household system entirely vanished within a hundred years after the special circumstance that had given rise to it disappeared (see Appendix D).

10.2.2   Family Structure around the World

How do these four social instincts combine to form larger working family moralnets? The !Kung San of the Kalahari Desert offer a clear example. (The San people resent the name "Bushman," which the White Man has given them, because it so often expresses contempt.) The !Kung live in camps clustered about desert waterholes. Each such camp consists of perhaps one or two dozen people. It is built about a nucleus of close relatives—perhaps a set of brothers and sisters. To this nucleus gets added the husbands and wives of the core members, as a sort of second layer. Then the parents, brothers, sisters, nephews, and nieces of the spouses form a kind of third layer. Their spouses in turn form a kind of fourth layer. And if somehow an aunt or an uncle or a distant cousin shows up, such a person would be welcome.

Camp membership is not stable. People often visit back and forth between waterholes. The web of kinship ties makes it likely that a visitor will turn out to be some kind of distant relative or in-law of someone at the camp. But if not, a visitor who stays on would be adopted as a son or a daughter or a brother or a sister of a camp member. In essence, says Lee, a !Kung camp "consists of kinspeople and affines who have found they can live and work well together."

Where had I heard of something like the !Kung waterhole band structure before? Not in America—but in Britain—among the aristocrats of the Establishment. I recalled my readings on eighteenth-century England. Politics then were dominated by loose alliances of relatives and in-laws, centered around some powerful noble house—like the Bedford faction. Such a network was vaguely called a connection; its membership would build up much like a !Kung waterhole camp. Only the fountain of refreshment would not be a source of water, of course—but a source of public office, of public influence, a center of strings for pulling.

Such a kinship moralnet does not, I submit, have to be planned or organized. Given the four basic instincts that tend toward family, people will come to form one without either plan or instruction.

The bilateral kindred then is a natural kind of moralnet and it is the family system of cultures in many parts of the world—from the Eskimo to the English. However, the kindred is not a corporate group. It cannot thus operate as a landholding group. Nor does it form a natural table of organization for a military force. The !Kung kindred can run a waterhole camp only because in their sparse country land is cheap and labor is dear. Waterhole camps strictly share all food that comes in—like an American kindred at a family picnic. Every new mouth to feed means new pair of hands to gather or to hunt. And the !Kung are not warriors.

Among small-scale societies, the !Kung system of family moralnets is not as common as another system—that of Sugita Gempaku—the patrilineal lineage.

Such a lineage can own farm lands in common, so that the whole extended family can share the work and the harvests. The men of such a lineage can be organized by the scores, hundreds, or even thousands into fighting units. Such lineages often have crests as badges of membership—often have family traditions, legends, distinctive family values—above all, perhaps, family pride.

Consider, for example, the Mapuche of southern Chile. Each Mapuche man and woman belongs to a body of blood relatives on his or her father's side. A Mapuche man traces his father's ancestry through males, from son to father, back four to six generations to the lineage founder. The core of this lineage consists of the living male descendants, who live on its home reservation. These men organize and carry out the traditional Mapuche cultural activities on their reservation. They have common land rights; they help each other at work.

Ideally, the basic unit of Mapuche family life is the extended patrilineal family household. Such a household consists of an older couple, their married sons and unmarried daughters, their sons' wives, and their sons' children. Thus, the lineage would be made up of a number of such households. In past centuries, visitors to the Mapuche reported that such households were the most common form of family life. Today they are not so frequent, although still found now and then. But even today, although Mapuche men found new households when they marry, they usually live near their fathers. In contrast, Mapuche women, today as formerly, always marry husbands who live on other reservations—always away from their parents.

It has been found that among foraging peoples there is a tendency for the family to form bilateral kindreds when the food men bring into camp is roughly equal in importance to that women bring in. However, where the food men bring in is considerably more important than that the women bring in, there is a tendency for the family to form patrilineages more or less like that of the Mapuche. And where, on the contrary, it is the women who bring in most of the food, then we are likely to find a third kind of family structure, the matrilineal system.

The matrilineal family closely resembles the patrilineal family. There is an extended matrilineal family household, there is a matrilineal lineage, and beyond that there are matrilineal clans. The Hopi of northeastern Arizona continue to manage their family life so.

However the matrilineal household or lineage is not the mirror image of a patrilineal one in all respects. The men—not the women—manage both systems. *Matriarchal* societies—where the public officials are predominantly women—exist only in legend. In a matrilineal extended family household, however, it is usually not the women's husbands who manage affairs, but their brothers. In such a household, a child's father is a friendly, but generally un-influential relative, like an English grandfather. The mother's brother or the mother's mother's brother is the man who scolds and praises, who rewards and punishes. A Hopi husband lives with his wife's people; he works their lands; he eats their food; but he never really belongs. When he leaves to visit his own lineage—that of his mother and his sisters—he says, "I am going home now." His moralnet is with his sisters and their children, not with his wife.

Matrilineal societies are common among farming peoples, as well, for other reasons, even where the men do most of the farm work.

10.2.3   Marriage Arrangements around the World

So various cultures have used the principle of descent to build large and effective moralnets. But another natural, instinctive element of family life—the marriage bond—is also often elaborated on by culture in order to strengthen extended family ties. In most societies, marriages mean some kind of formal obligation among kinfolk to pay somebody something. This pattern of marriage gifts often helps build strong family moralnets.

Notice in what differing ways each of the marriage gift systems I am about to describe creates a bond of wealth to help cement the marriage. The couple and often their kinfolk acquire a vested interest in the marriage. If the marriage breaks up, it costs people heavily. We have a folk saying: "When money comes in the door, love flies out the window." But the idea of marriage gifts, on the contrary, is to bring money and love into the marriage together, hand in hand. In the United States today, when a man and woman marry, their friends and relatives usually give them presents. Often the friends of the bride give a party for women only, a shower we call it. Each woman brings the bride a small gift. But at the wedding itself, or soon after, the relatives of the bride and groom often give expensive presents that help the couple start a new household. That is our system now.

The English used to have another way. "Where are you going, my pretty maid?" "I'm going a-milking, sir," she said. "And what is your fortune, my pretty maid?" "My face is my fortune, sir," she said. So runs the old song. And here the word fortune means "dowry." If at all possible, English girls, like girls throughout Europe, brought with them into marriage as much property as their parents could arrange. In the highlands of the Austrian Tyrol in the late 1950s, the dowry was still important among peasant families. Parents sought to provide their daughters not only with clothing but with a complete set of household furnishings: beds, tables, chairs, silver, linen. If a father and mother could not do this, then the daughter set out to earn and save such a dowry for herself. She might need to work five or ten summers as a waitress or a chambermaid at a tourist hotel to do so.

In Greece even today, not only among farming people, but among the educated and wealthy, a girl's dowry is crucial to her marriage. Daughters of shipowners are dowered with tankers. Prosperous middle-class people put a small apartment in the girl's name as her dowry. Poor peasant girls are still expected to bring 1,000 or 2,000 dollars in a bank account with them. The dowry a man could expect with his bride depended on his own rank and wealth. In the 1960s, a university professor might look for 10,000 gold sovereigns—say 100,000 dollars.

So here we have two of the four main systems of marital exchanges—wedding gifts and dowry. The third—the bride wealth or bride price system—is sometimes seen by outsiders as a groom buying a bride. Bride wealth is wealth—money or cattle, for example—given by the groom or his family to the bride's family as part of a marriage contract. In most societies in which a man must find bride wealth to marry, what he buys is a *wife*, not a chattel. His wife may leave him if she feels basely abused—though this may not be easy for her. In many bride price societies, if the husband abuses the wife and she leaves him, he may lose the wealth that he gave her. Among the Thonga of South Africa, for example, if a wife feels mistreated, she is free to go home to her parents. Then her husband must come humbly to her and her parents and beg her to come back. Otherwise, the couple, though still married, are separated. Only if he wishes to divorce her may he claim his *lobolo*, his bride wealth back. If he was in the wrong, he may lose it. "Sometimes," says Junod, "the conclusion of the tale is that the man even loses his *lobolo* money, as a punishment for his bad deed!"

Ogbu surveyed bride wealth in 49 African societies. In 15 of these, a husband got his bride wealth back in case of divorce only if the court found the wife at fault. In most of the remaining 34, all or part of the bride wealth had to be paid back on divorce, no matter who was at fault. The amount usually depended on whether there were children of the marriage and if so, whether they went with the mother or the father. If with the father, he usually forfeited all or part of his bride wealth. Ogbu thinks the primary role of bride wealth in African societies is the support it gives the marriage tie. Requiring a large payment to arrange a marriage makes that marriage an important thing in the eyes of bride and groom alike.

The fourth type of marital exchange system is the affinal exchange. Such a system used to be common in Oceania. From New Guinea to Samoa, Bunzel tells us, the same rule was followed. When a marriage was arranged, debts were thus created on both sides. Payments were made from time to time between the bride's relatives and the groom's relatives as long as the marriage lasted. In Samoa, for example, the man's side gave the woman's side men's goods: wood work, pigs, fish, or other food. The woman's side gave the man's side women's goods: beautiful *tapa* bark cloths and finely woven white mats of pandanus leaves. Such exchanges, too, would seem to create bonds not only between man and wife but between their extended families, and so strengthen their kinship structure.

10.2.4   The Family and Being a Mensch

Hsu, the Chinese-American anthropologist, criticizes Western social science for its myth of the sovereign personality. Hsu was raised in prewar China, imbued with the traditional Chinese feeling for family. But first in Beijing and then in London he studied social anthropology. He sees the world then, as do few other leaders in anthropological thought, from a full understanding of both East and West. And he criticizes us in the West for our faith that the individual human

TABLE 10.1   Relationship between Family Size and Mode of Getting Food

| | How People Get Food in 1137 Societies, Mostly Small Scale | | | | | | |
Family System	Hunting and Gathering Purely	A Little Farming on the Side	Herding	Fishing	Crude Slash-and-Burn Farming	Skilled Dry Farming	Skilled Farming with Irrigation
Large (n = 317)	54%	65%	71%	73%	80%	80%	65%
Small (n = 820)	46%	35%	29%	27%	20%	20%	35%

SOURCE: Blumberg and Winch (1972: 915).
N = 1137.

mind is the master of all things. Far more realistic, say Hsu, is the Chinese concept of *ren*. The key idea of *ren* is absent from the *Oxford English Dictionary*, but has lately crept into American speech from the Yiddish *mensch*. By a mensch or a person with *ren* is meant a proper person, a real human being—one who understands his or her social duties well and sees to it that they are well performed. And of all the social duties a mensch performs, those to his or her family are often the ones of chief importance. A mensch is a person you can count on.

If a family is to be a successful moralnet, its leaders must be mensches. In caring for their family, they have in mind also its links with the larger community. So in large-scale societies mensches are concerned about the family livelihood. And about the family honor—its standing in the larger community. If a family is honored, its members are likely to be well treated by the larger world of its society. So we find families with traditions of public service as well as families with traditions of private wealth and power. In such families, the mensches often devote their lives to keeping up such central elements of family life.

10.2.5   Evolution of the Family

Winch and Blumberg have analyzed family complexity in relation to economic organization. Tables 10.1 and 10.2 show their most important findings. Large, extended family systems are more frequent among small-scale, advanced agricultural societies than among more primitive food production systems. But they grow *less* frequent among the most productive agricultural systems. Among modern nations, the trend is reversed. The more economically developed the nation, the less likely it is to have a large extended family system. Winch and Blumberg then offer a curvilinear hypothesis about the evolution of kinship systems. Among people in small-scale societies, they suggest, the simpler family systems are most likely. At intermediate levels of cultural evolution, systems of large, extended families tend to predominate. But among

TABLE 10.2   Relationship between Family Systems and Industrialization

	Level of Social and Economic Development in 43 Developing Nations		
Family System	Low	Intermediate	High
Extended Family or Clan	100%	60%	12%
Nuclear Family Only	0%	15%	88%

SOURCE: Blumberg and Winch (1972: 917).
Correlation (Goodman and Kruskal's gamma): .88.
Chance risk: $< .001$.

the technologically most advanced societies, there is a strong tendency to return to the simpler family systems. So it is that one of the least complex of societies, the Eskimo, has the same family system as the technologically most advanced countries of Western Europe.

10.3   STEP 1: CORE VALUES AND THE FAMILY

For me the value of the family depends on its value as the foundation of the moral order. That value is an empirical question—a point to be studied, not to be taken for granted. I argue that the family is not only the most common moralnet but inherently the strongest, by reason of its foundation in human social instincts. If so, then it is one of the chief tools by which the core values may in fact govern the way people act. If so, whatever the core vales of a society, it will practice those values better if it expects the family to impart them to the children. I do not mean, however, to deny the importance of other institutions like the school, the church, the club, or the army in sustaining a moral order. I only mean to suggest that these institutions will work best if they share strong family values.

So I rest my study of the family on the working hypothesis that a healthy family system is required to sustain the social order.

10.4   STEP 2: FAMILY STRENGTH SCOREBOARD

We do not have any proper measures of family strength. Table 10.3 is but a fragment. Without a report on Norway, we cannot define our optimal limits.

A second valuable scoreboard—Table 10.4—is even more fragmentary; it has data on only the four Scandinavian countries—taken from a large and carefully conducted sample survey by Allardt. It measures the strength of ties between related households. It shows the proportion of respondents who said they had social visits with relatives *not* members of their own households at least once a week.

TABLE 10.3   Family Life Satisfaction Scoreboard

("Considering everything, how satisfied or dissatisfied are you with your family life?")

Country	Percentage of Respondents Expressing Highest Satisfaction
Brazil	39
USA	38
Australia	34
Canada	28
United Kingdom	25
Mexico	25
Italy	21
France	18
West Germany	17
Japan	8
India	1

SOURCE: Gallup International Research Institutes (1977: 177f.).

10.5   STEP 3: TESTS OF THEORIES OF FAMILY STRENGTH

I know of only one rigorous test of the general theory that family ties make for moral order—the study by Zimmerman and Cervantes I spoke of in Chapter 6 and return to in Chapters 15 and 16. That study, you may recall, showed a clear link between the moral order of high school seniors and their nuclear extended family ties. The high school seniors most successful at staying in school and keeping out of trouble were those living in an intact family, closely linked through regular meetings with five other kin family households having like religion, income, and geographical origin.

In addition to that of the Zimmerman and Cervantes study, scattered through this book are reviews of study after study showing the importance of close social ties in avoiding mental illness, alcoholism, suicide, child abuse, and juvenile delinquency. Hirschi's study of juvenile delinquency pointed directly at strong ties between youth and parent in warding off juvenile delinquency. Glueck and Glueck found that delinquents turn up more often in broken homes than in intact ones. Lester, after reviewing scores of studies of the causes of suicide, concluded that weak social ties was the most important factor. This conclusion was supported, for example, by the link between divorce and suicide found by Durkheim, by Dublin, and by Naroll—and on the links between suicide on the one hand and marriage arrangements and wife beating on the other, in the thwarting disorientation studies of Naroll and of Krauss. The Factor Study Group found household structure a key factor in alcoholism in small-scale societies: The larger the household, the less frequent the abusive drinking. Parents who batter children are likely to be people who lack strong social ties— with their extended families or anyone else. Divorced people, and children of

TABLE 10.4   Moralnet Strength in Scandinavia

Country	Extensive Weekly Family Contacts
Norway	50%
Sweden	50%
Denmark	40%
Finland	39%

SOURCE: Allardt (1973: 120).

divorce, are more likely than married people to show up as mental hospital patients. Indeed, most of the evidence on my central theme that weakened moralnets mean trouble is evidence of links between weak family ties and social pathology.

The results of a recent analysis of family statistics among European countries by Fuchs, Gaspari, and Millendorfer further supports that theory. Figure 10.1 sets forth their main results. Here we see a striking relationship between their family strength indicator and their measure of culture stress. The culture stress measure is an index made from suicide rates, homicide rates, and crime rates. Their family strength index is a set of important variables derived from their factor analysis of nearly a hundred. The main results of that analysis are set forth in Table 10.5.

Factor analysis is a complex mathematical method by which we can define some basic dimension that a set of variables is measuring. The loading of each variable is a measure of its relationship to that basic dimension. The single variable most highly related to the family trouble dimension in Table 10.5 is thus the birthrate among women over 35 years of age. Since it is a negative loading, the analysis points to women who delay motherhood as least likely to belong to troubled families. The four variables that show us we are dealing with a family trouble dimension at all are the two measures of suicide, the measure of homicide, and the divorce rate. Notice how high all four load.

Troubled European families then tend to be those with frequent divorce, a high proportion of married women who work outside the home, a high proportion of births to younger women, and many educated members. Untroubled European families then tend to be those with a high proportion of births to older women, larger families, and large households.

10.6   STEP 4: FURTHER STUDIES OF FAMILY STRENGTH

Again it is urgent for us to get a better measure of family strength among the nations of the world. Sample surveys like the fragmentary Gallup study I mentioned in Section 10.4 need to ask more widely how satisfied or dissatisfied people feel with their family life. We also urgently need worldwide data like those Allardt collected for the four Scandinavian countries on how often people visited relatives *not* part of their households. Put these with the household size data

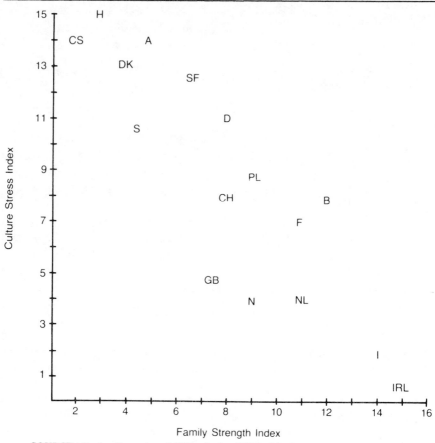

SOURCE   Fuchs, Gaspari, and Millendorfer (1977: 94). Reprinted by permission.
A = Austria; B = Belgium; CH = Switzerland; CS = Czechoslovakia; D = West
Germany; DK = Denmark; F = France; GB = Great Britain; H = Hungary; I = Italy;
IRL = Ireland; N = Norway; NL = Netherlands; PL = Poland; S = Sweden; SF =
Finland.

Figure 10.1 Weak Families Are Linked to Suicide, Homicide, and Crime

already collected by the United Nations, and we would have a working set of
meters on the strength of families as moralnets.

Such data could then be fed into a multivariate analysis—a linear regression,
perhaps—of the causes of cultural stress. The work reviewed here would lead us
to predict that stronger families would exhibit fewer symptoms of culture stress.
A culture stress index could in turn be compiled by combining measures of
things like mental illness, suicide, alcoholism, drug abuse, child battering, and
juvenile delinquency. The results of such studies would be the more impressive,
of course, if we asked this same question in each of the four major domains of
research that I distinguish in my theory trust meters.

TABLE 10.5   European Family Troubles Complex: A Factor Analysis

Loading	Statistic
	Positive Loadings
88	*Divorce rate*
87	Proportion of married women, ages 20 to 30, who work outside the home
85	*Homicide rate*
83	*Birthrate among teenaged mothers
83	*Suicide rate among people aged 15 to 24*
72	Proportion of women who work outside the home
67	*Suicide rate, women over age 65*
65	Proportion of people with higher education
65	*Rate of premature births
62	*Proportion of first-born children—measure of proportion of small families
49	Marriage rate
45	*Proportion of extramarital births
44	*Proportion of divorces that take place within three years of marriage
	Negative Loadings
56	*Proportion of fourth-born children—measure of proportion of large families
59	*Proportion of divorces that take place after 10 years of marriage
62	*Proportion of single men in age group 45 to 64
63	*Average age of women at marriage
63	*People who live in households of five or more members
67	*Proportion of births that take place after the sixth year of marriage
71	*Proportion of births among women over age 35 to those among women under age 35
77	Birthrate among women in the age group 20 to 45
91	*Birthrate among women over age 35

SOURCE: Fuchs et al. (1977).
*Included in the Family Strength Index of Figure 10.1.
Italicized lines are the direct measures of trouble.

Much more could be done by a careful review of culture stress research to cull out findings bearing on this issue. I have reviewed them from the more general point of view of weakened moralnets than from the specific point of view of family strength. And while most of the evidence set forth in my theory trust meter on moralnet strength (see Figure 16.1) is really evidence specifically on family strength, it does not distinguish between ties within the nuclear families and ties with the wider extended family.

We certainly need to follow up the work of Fuchs, Gaspari, and Millendorfer on European family troubles. Is the same complex present elsewhere? Do these patterns hold good worldwide? Does their analysis link some elements peculiar to European peasant lifestyle with other elements that are more universal?

We also need further tests of the theories of the instinctive basis of family life that I have set forth here. For example, institutions similar in certain ways to those of the Nayar are said to occur among the Ashanti of Ghana and the

Menangkabau of Sumatra. If so, can similar cultural pressures be discerned that suppress the hypothetical nuclear family instinct, and do similar signs of strain appear?

The most urgent research task of all is to learn more about what sorts of families tend to be the strongest and most successful. We need a rigorous test of the ten rules for building strong family moralnets proposed by Howard and discussed in the next section.

10.7   STEP 5: COPING WITH WEAK FAMILY TIES

We do not have a set of rigorous findings that would give us all trustworthy counsel on how to build stronger families. The moralnet theory I set forth in Chapter 6 would call for two main things: (1) The cherishing of family ceremonial gatherings. With us, Thanksgiving, Christmas, Easter, and Passover often are the occasions for large family feasts. In the mountains of western Tyrol, each village has its own annual religious festival, when relatives who live outside traditionally come to the village to join their kinfolk in the festivities. In most societies, life crisis rituals of one kind or another tend to be occasions for large family gatherings, as with us at weddings and funerals, at christenings, and at confirmations. (2) A care for family tradition and a cultivation of stories recounting family achievements and sustaining family values.

The best advice I can find on family maintenance is that by Howard in her recent book on families. She did not test out these findings in any scientific way. They simply are her personal impressions—but impressions formed from her work as a family therapist. She sets forth ten ways of life characteristic of good families:

(1) Good families have a family hero—an older member or ancestor in whose achievements all can take pride. (While Howard does not say so, she implies that good families tell each other stories of such a family hero's achievements.)

(2) Good families have a switchboard operator—a communications center—a person who keeps track of all its members and their doings. While Howard does not say so, in the United States today, I suspect that operator usually is a woman rather than a man.

(3) Good families are much to all their members but everything to none. While good families provide all members with a secure base, they encourage each person to develop and foster outside interests and outside work.

(4) Good families are hospitable. They are generous with honorary memberships for friends.

(5) Good families face up to their problems and deal squarely with them, rather than pretend they do not exist.

(6) Good families prize their rituals.

(7) Good families are affectionate.

(8) Good families have a sense of place—a family home. The Germans in song and story and dialect and dress emphasize belonging to a homeland—a *Heimatland*—far smaller and more intimate than Germany or Austria or Switzerland. The homeland of the Tyroleans is Tyrol. The Appenzeller's homeland is not Switzerland but the canton of Appenzell. Howard deplores the fact that in the United States today such feelings of attachment and belonging are rare. Canada seems

to do better: As I said earlier, I certainly sense far more attachment to Ontario on that side of the Niagara than to New York State on this.

(9) Good families are concerned about posterity. They do things that they hope will mean much to their children and grandchildren and great-grandchildren.

(10) Good families honor their elders. They give grandparents an important place in their scheme of things. It is the grandparents who are leading sources of family tradition for the grandchildren, and who support the family values.

Any program for coping with family weakness soon runs into tradeoff problems. I see at least three.

The tradeoff between family instinct and economic progress. On the one hand, the extended family, supported as it seems to be by four instincts would seem to be the best moralnet for most people to cling to. On the other hand, economic development seems at least for a time to snowball extended family weakness: Weak extended families make economic development easier and economic development in turn further tends to weaken extended families. Adelman and Morris found that the greater the per capita wealth produced in a country, the weaker were its extended families. And as I showed in Table 9.2, the greater that wealth, the higher the suicide rate.

I would offer these theories to explain this linkage: First, economic development as a process usually goes with rapid growth of cities. And that growth, in turn, often comes from individuals or married couples moving away from their home towns or home farms to the big city. Second, economic development as a process tends to increase specialization—and people in scarce specialities need to go where their talents are required. Third, economic development as a process tends to go along with the growth of bureaucracies— and these in turn tend to send their officers where they are needed. Countries in which extended families are weak might well then find all three of these tendencies easier to foster, and these tendencies in turn would weaken extended families even further.

What then to do about the instinctive need of people for some sort of warm moralnet—the kind usually offered by extended families?

True, showing that a way of life is instinctive makes it neither right nor inevitable. As Harris is fond of saying, unquestionably by far the strongest human instinct is the *instinct to learn a culture.* So in the many cultural situations in which families cost too much, we may need to think rather of communes or cliques than of families. But even so, if family life meets a number of instinctive needs, then substitute moralnets need to make up for the cost of frustrating those needs. Human instinct ought neither be overvalued nor undervalued.

On the one hand, culture can usually override instinct, and often obviously needs to. Rape may perhaps be instinctive; if so, that makes it neither right nor prudent. Male brawling may be instinctive; that makes it neither right nor prudent. And certainly that same fact makes war neither right nor prudent. People have to curb their sex drives and keep their tempers—instinct or no instinct.

On the other hand, to frustrate an instinct always costs something. Always hurts. So other things being equal, obeying instincts is the way to pleasure. Other things being equal, we ought to do things the instinctive way rather than the artificial way.

True, if family ties get in the way of other important claims of the culture, they must often be loosened. Or untied entirely. And if they are weakened, the culture needs to provide a budget to make good the steep costs in morale and in morals that otherwise show up in higher death rates and higher crimes rates among lonely and demoralized people. A substitute like a well-run monastery or nunnery or army company or labor union local might go far to make good the missing supports that the family normally provides. But we must measure carefully how much such substitutes need to do. How much is enough? So we must compare death rates and crime rates among single people and among isolated nuclear families within such familylike substitutes.

If the economic development tradeoff theory is sound, we then have to ask whether getting rich at the expense of family life is in fact a good bargain. Here is tradeoff problem number one.

Size and structure of the extended family. Tradeoff problem number two is more subtle. It turns up in a worldwide study of grandparents and grandchildren, done by Apple. She found two kinds of cultures. In the first, grandparents and grandchildren typically get along well. Their ties are warm and cosy; friendly equality is the theme. Our own ways offer a good example. But in the second kind of culture, grandparents and grandchildren are typically formal: by our own standards, cold and distant. This contrast, Apple found, was plainly and strongly linked to another one—the grandparents' relationship with the child's parents. If that child's parents as adults are independent of the child's grandparents, then the grandparents and grandchildren are cozy. But if not—if the grandparents have authority over the parents—then grandparents and grandchildren tend to be on more formal terms—colder and more distant. Table 10.6 tells the story.

This story about grandparents and grandchildren may point to a second problem in social planning. The extended family as a moralnet may well be made stronger if it has an economic part to play. If it is something of an insurance agency, something of a business firm. But if so, then its affairs must be managed; the family council may serve as a board of directors, but from day to day someone has to be in charge. So then comes the tug of family authority against individual freedom.

Here is a problem for which worldwide anthropology is well suited. What is the best size of the extended family as a moralnet? What structures are best? And what tasks make such families strong? I have in mind here consequences of moralnet weakness, consequences like crime rates and suicide rates (see Section 16.6.1).

Only through such studies can we hope to know how much harm modern ways have done by tearing down the extended family as they have, how much of an effort we need to make to restore it, to rebuild it, how much instead to build other familylike moralnets to take its place.

TABLE 10.6   Relationship between Grandparents and Grandchildren

PROPOSITION: *Grandparents are friendliest with their grandchildren where the grandparents do not boss those children's parents.*

	Grandparents and Grandchildren on Terms of Friendly Equality	Grandparents and Grandchildren Treat Each Other with Formality
Grandparents have authority over parents	Kurama (Nigeria) Koreans Tallensi (Shana) (3)	Ashanti (Ghana) Moro (Philippines) Koalib (The Sudan) Ibo (Nigeria) Marki Verri Mumuye (Nigeria) Bachama (Nigeria) Yaqui (Mexico) Tanala (Madagascar) Nama Hottentots (Namibia) Cow Creek Seminole (Florida) Atsugewi (California) Jicarilla Apache (Southwestern USA) (12)
Grandparents do not have authority over parents	Tarahumara (Mexico) Saramacca (Guiana) Baiga (India) Bhuiya (India) Burmese Woleaians (Micronesia) Lau Islanders (Fiji) Lesu (Melanesia) Abelam (New Guinea) Mountain Arapesh (New Guinea) Ontong Javanese (Melanesia) Tikopia (Melanesia) Chiricahua Apache (Southwestern USA) Malabu (Nigeria) Kare-Kare (Nigeria) Nyakyusa (Tanzania) Azande (The Sudan) Papago (Southwestern USA) Dakota (Northwestern Plains, USA) Kiowa-Apache (Southwestern USA) Cheyenne (Western Plains, USA) Fox (North-Central USA) Kaska (Northwest Canada) Sanpoil (Northwest USA) Ojibwa (Great Lakes) Oto (Central USA)	Shilluk (The Sudan) Nyima (The Sudan) Ramkokamekra (Eastern Brazil) Lakhers (Assam, India) (4)

(continued)

TABLE 10.6 (Continued)

	Grandparents and Grandchildren on Terms of Friendly Equality	*Grandparents and Grandchildren Treat Each Other with Formality*
Grandparents do not have authority over parents	Lozi (Zambia) Korongo (The Sudan) Dilling (The Sudan) Otoro (The Sudan) Katab (Nigeria) Jukun (Nigeria) (32)	

SOURCE: Apple (1956).
Correlation (phi coefficient): .68.
Chance risk: p < .00001.
N = 51.

Social welfare programs. Such programs, at least in the United States, often seem to administrators easier to manage if, one way or another, aid is channeled to particular family members—such as mothers of young children—even in ways that disrupt family life. Perhaps the mother will be paid an allowance only if she does not live with a man. Nineteenth-century workhouses tended to separate husbands, wives and children. I suspect that such policies may be penny wise but pound foolish—causing as much trouble as they mend.

10.8   COSTS AND BENEFITS OF STRENGTHENING FAMILY TIES

Howard's ten precepts for maintaining good families do not cost money. What they cost is time and trouble and attention by family members to family members—things that are only given freely, never sold. I believe that the payoff, too, will come in the form of warm feelings of content in place of cold feelings of loneliness.

When governments or foundations or corporations draw up their budgets, they could think about (1) supporting well-designed research looking to guide people in their family life, and (2) avoiding harm to family life through misguided welfare programs that weaken family ties. Anything that *can* be done to strengthen family ties and so reduce juvenile delinquency, alcoholism, and mental illness in advanced countries should be done, I think. Where family ties tend to be weak and under stress, a successful program of family building might be one of the best buys a budget officer or a politician could find.

Notes

10.1   Sugita Gempaku Goes to an Autopsy

Sugita Gempaku's memoirs: Sugita (1942: 159-163).
Bronfenbrenner (1976) complains about the decay of the American family.

On the role of grandparents in contrasting family systems, see Apple (1956).
Chinese primer: Hsiao Ching (see Creel, 1948: 39).
Details of the Zimmerman and Cervantes (1956, 1960) studies are in Chapters 7, 12, 15 and 16 of this
book.

10.2.1   The Family Instinct

Five functions usually served by the human family are set forth by Winch (1971: 11f.): (1) reproduction, (2) provision of goods and services, (3) maintenance of order, (4) socialization and education, and (5) maintenance of a sense of purpose.

10.2.2   Family Structure around the World

On !Kung camps, see Lee (1979: 51-76). Concerning eighteenth-century British aristocratic connections resembling !Kung waterhold camps, I know of no specific studies setting forth the
structure. My readings on eighteenth-century politics, from which these comments stem, are set
forth in Naroll (1953: 260-262). I suspect these connections could largely be reconstructed—that
is to say, the specific eighteenth-century network of importance could be set forth in network
tables like Lee's on the !Kung—from a study of the Newcastle manuscripts in the British
museum. And there is a superabundance of memoirs and other correspondence published and
unpublished to fill in the gaps.
Mapuche lineages and households: Faron (1968: 23-27, 28-31) and Cooper (1963: 706-707, 722-724).
Residence rules of foraging peoples depend on division of labor between the sexes: Murdock (1949),
Driver (1956), and especially Ember (1975).
Hopi family life: Thompson and Joseph (1944) and Titiev (1950). "I am going home now" is from
Naroll's field notes.
On the play of male authority and female autonomy among matrilineal societies, see Schlegel (1972).
On main sequence kinship theory, which links changes in residence rules, descent rules, and kinship
terminology, see Murdock (1949), Schneider and Gough (1961), Naroll (1973: 328-330), Levinson
and Malone (1980: 99-116), and Ember and Ember (n. d.).

10.2.3   Marriage Arrangements around the World

Greek dowries: field notes of Raoul and Frada Naroll; Friedl (1962: 53-56). According to *The Econ-
omist* (July 3-9, 1982: "Greece Survey"), the dowry system is still strong in Greece today, but the
Papandreou government is planning new laws to weaken it. The dowry system gives the parents
of the girl much influence over her choice of a husband—perhaps that is the reason *The
Economist* found many women who object to it.
On bride price versus bride wealth, see Gray (1960), Gulliver (1961), and Dalton (1966).
On an abusive husband forfeiting his *lobolo*, see Junod (1912, I: 195-197).
On bride wealth in Africa, see Ogbu (1978).
On affinal exchanges in Oceania, see Bunzel (1938: 388f.).

10.2.4   The Family and Being a Mensch

On being a real person—one with *ren* or *jen*, see Hsu (1971). Rosten (1968: 234) sets forth eloquently
the emic Yiddish concept of *mensch*. So, too, did my grandmother, Martha Soskin.

10.2.5   Evolution of the Family

On the evolution of kinship systems, see Blumberg and Winch (1972).
Table 10.2: The curvilinear evolution hypothesis of Blumberg and Winch (1972) has further support
from Osmond (1969), Sheils (1971), Blitsten (1963), and Goode (1963). See also Nimkoff (1965:
40-44).

10.5   Step 3: Tests of Theories of Family Strength

On family ties and the moral order, see Zimmerman and Cervantes (1956, 1960).
On juvenile delinquency, see Hirschi (1969) and Glueck and Glueck (1950).
On suicide and family ties, see Lester (1970), Durkheim (1951), Dublin (1963), Naroll (1969), and
Krauss (1966).
Factor Study Group: Bacon et al. (1965) on social ties and alcoholism.
Figure 10.1 is taken from Fuchs, Gaspari and Millendorfer (1977: 94). Their Culture Stress Index
("*Sozialpsychologische Belastungsindikatoren*") is made up of their measures of suicide,

homicide, and crime: the first two they derive in turn from the *U.N. Demographic Yearbooks* and the *World Health Statistics Annual* of the World Health Organizaion; their crime rate data are for 1969, and come from a report by Interpol in Paris. The Family Strength Index is their *"Familienindikator,"* whose construction is set forth in detail by them at page 90; this index is excerpted from the longer list of variables of their principal components analysis (p. 60). The monograph by Fuchs, Gaspari, and Millendorfer (1977) is a particularly hard one to work with. However, I think that their work richly repays careful study. Many of their figures depend on the reader recognizing the country abbreviations used in European automobile license plates. But how many North Americans know that SF stands for Finland? Even more difficult are their variable names. These can be tracked down by leafing through the body of their tables in their tabular appendix; they are almost all alphabetically arranged by variable name: Find the table number, go to the table of contents at the beginning of the appendix (no page numbers in the appendix), and there you find the key.

Table 10.5: Fuchs, Gaspari, and Millendorfer (1977) use a principal components analysis (also known as principal axes analysis). On that technique, see Rummel (1970a: 338-345) and Cooley and Lohnes (1962: 151-161).

10.6   Step 4: Further Studies of Family Strength

Fortes, who collected very precise data concerning two Ashanti villages, devotes fourteen pages to residence. "In more than half the marriages, husband and wife prove not to be living together at all. Especially in the beginning, when the marriage is new, each stays in his own compound and they pay each other visits. Sometimes this continues; in other cases either the wife goes to live with the husband . . . or the husband with his wife" (Köbben, 1967: 9).

10.7   Step 5: Coping with Weak Family Ties

Howard (1978) proposes rules to strengthen families.

Adelman and Morris (1967: 217-224) find a negative correlation between economic development and strength of family ties among the least developed modern nations. Among the most highly developed nations, in contrast, they find no correlation at all. But then, how many highly developed nations have strong family moralnets?

I do not know of any formal documentation for Marvin Harris's dictum that mankind's strongest instinct is to learn a culture. But such, I suppose, would be the general opinion of social scientists and sociobiologists today.

On ties between grandparents and grandchildren, see Apple (1956).

Child Abuse

11.1 CACTUS, PEPPER, AND PUDDLES

The Aztecs of Mexico took no nonsense from their young boys. They did not know how to make a child always do as he was told. They did know how to make a child who sometimes didn't, wish that he had! They had a scale of treatments. Many of these are elegantly pictured in a rare set of Aztec paintings—the Codex Mendoza.

Mild treatment: prick the child with a maguey cactus spine. Such a cactus bears thick fleshy arms tapering to firm, sharp needles—like heavy nails. They hurt. Recommended for boys of nine or ten years. If cactus needles do not tame the youngster, then try pepper smoke. Burn red peppers in a fire and hold the child's face in the smoke. Stinging eyes. Paroxysms of nausea. The boys remember that treatment. Recommended for boys of eleven years.

Still not enough? Then lead the boy high into the mountains. Strip him naked. Tie him hand and foot. Dump him in a puddle of water. Then leave him there overnight, alone and wet and shivering in the dark, to think about his elders and the duties he owes them. Recommended for boys of twelve years.

Now the Aztecs were a highly civilized people. When the Spaniards first found them, their central city of Tenochtitlan was about as large as any city in Europe. Their calendar was more accurate than the Julian calendar that Europe then used. They had a rich written literature. And as we shall see, their level of cultural evolution may have been just the trouble. When it comes to treatment of children, as when it comes to warfare, savages are not really savage and barbarians are not really barbaric. Not compared with us.

When it comes to treatment of children, once more we find that moralnets are among the main things to watch. Once more, weakened moralnets mean trouble.

11.2 CHILD ABUSE AROUND THE WORLD

11.2.1 Range of Variation of Child Abuse

Child abuse varies greatly around the world. Of the 58 societies in the War, Stress, and Culture sample, I found information on corporal punishment of children in 40. In 20 of these, ethnographers flatly denied that children were ever punished at all by slaps on the behind, boxes on the ear, serious whippings, thrashings, or beatings. Of the 20 in which some kind of physical punishment was reported, 6 societies inflicted punishment so severe as to create presumption of child battering. By child battering, I mean physical punishment that inflicts visible wounds—severs tissue, causes bleeding, or leaves bruises. Between 1959 and 1964, in one of these six societies, the JoLuo of Kenya, ten men were brought into court for beating or kicking a wife or child to death.

Some idea of the amount of child abuse going on in the United States today comes through a report on my home county of Erie—the city of Buffalo and its suburbs. In 1966, it had just over 1 million people. Some 376 children here are known to have been battered in three years. Most of them displayed bruises or welts. But 10 were burned, 2 had their skulls fractured, 25 had other bones broken, and 1 suffered brain damage. That is 376 children whose injuries were known to the authorities. How many more were there whose hurts never came to light? Erie County experts think that the battering they know about is only the tip of the iceberg. Many respectable societies manage to raise well-behaved children without any kind of physical punishment at all. With a decent world order we should be able to raise children without beating them.

11.2.2   Evolution of Child Abuse

Child abuse is unnatural. All mammals are attached to their young. Parents care for their offspring. Most primates do so especially. Apes do so even more. And mankind is distinguished from all other mammals by the length of time children are dependent on grownups and need their care. Among chimpanzees as among people, adults often care for young other than their own.

So I take it that not only are human children instinctively attached to parents, but human parents are thus bound to children. "I have given suck," said Lady Macbeth, "and know how tender 'tis to love the babe that milks me." By an instinctive attachment, let me say again, I mean an inborn liking, implanted in the brain and there left to compete with other likings—others inborn and others learned.

What evidence would test a genetic theory of parental attachment? I would like proof that such feelings are found among people in all cultures. I would like proof that where—as among the Spartans—ties between parents and young children were hindered by culture, then there would be signs of psychological strain among the parents. I would like proof that in such cultures, people would have to be specially trained not to become *too* attached to their children. I would like proof that where cultural circumstances tended to make it difficult for parents to care for their children—as on Israeli collective farms—parents would make a special effort to be with their children. Finally, I would like proof that such a bonding would tend to be adaptive among bands of ground apes living by their wits on an African savannah; ape children on an African savannah would seem to need adult help to ensure their chances of survival. A formal study of such evidence is yet to be made. But when it is, I predict firm support for that genetic

TABLE 11.1   Cultural Evolution and Parental Acceptance

PROPOSITION: *People who live by food gathering treat their children more warmly than do people who live by herding or farming.*

Trait	Correlation with Foraging Way of Life	Chance Risk
Father part of household	.34	.002
Babies much indulged	.28	.02
Babies' wants attended to	.22	.07
Babies not hurt on purpose	.27	.03
Children much indulged	.21	.07

SOURCE: Textor (1967: FC 51/314, 318, 320, 324, 334).

TABLE 11.2   Cultural Evolution and Obedient Children

PROPOSITION: *Societies at higher levels of cultural evolution are likely to make more demands on children for obedience.*

Measure of Cultural Evolution	Correlation with Demands for Obedience	Chance Risk
Presence of an organized state	.33	.10
Large settlements	.33	.18
Metal working used	.37	.05

SOURCE: Textor (1967: FC 352/71, 81, 86).

theory. As it is, child mortality among hunter-gatherers is high. Perhaps that explains an important finding. By and large, hunting and gathering peoples tend to be more attached to their children, and to treat them more tenderly, than do herding and farming peoples (see Table 11.1). In Rohner's worldwide study of parental feeling toward their children, every single such society treated the children warmly.

Cultural evolution clearly is hard on children. Table 11.2 shows that, in general, larger-scale societies discipline their children more sternly than less advanced ones do. Table 11.3 shows that larger-scale societies are more likely to punish their children physically than are smaller-scale ones. Where physical punishment is allowed, it can easily grow into child battering. With the rise of civilization, punishment of children has tended to become harsher.

11.3   STEP 1: CORE VALUES OF CHILD ABUSE

The core values of child care are health and brotherhood, reinforced by specific human instincts that guide us no less than they guide chimpanzees, gorillas, gibbons or baboons to care for our young.

TABLE 11.3   Child Beating and Cultural Evolution

PROPOSITION: *Societies in which children are punished by beating tend to be larger in scale than do those in which they are not beaten.*

	Social Complexity Index
Child Beating is Reported among:	
Apayao (Philippines)	19
Araucanians (Chile)	30
Burmese	56
Chagga (Tanzania)	27
Egyptians	62
Fur (The Sudan)	31
Gond (Central India)	39
Ifaluk (Micronesia)	24
Italians	81
Kapauku (New Guinea)	29
Klallam (Oregon)	23
Koreans	67
Luo (Kenya)	22
Nahua (Aztecs–Mexico)	58
Ojibwa (Great Lakes, USA and Canada)	29
Ona (Tierra del Fuego)	21
Tallensi (Shana)	36
Tiv (Nigeria)	28
Tonga (Polynesia)	42
Osmanli Turks	77
Average (Mean)	40.3
Child Beating is Denied among:	
Andamanese (Indian Ocean)	14
Araucanians (Chile)	16
Cheyenne (Colorado)	29
Chukchee (Siberia)	23
Copper Eskimo (Northern Canada)	18
Coyotero Apache (Arizona)	18
Drents (Netherlands)	78
Eyak (Alaska)	19
Hottentot (Namibia)	32
Ila (Zambia)	31
Land Dyak (Borneo)	27
Malaita (Melanesia)	33
Mataco (Argentina)	23
Mosquito (Central America)	23
Papago (Arizona)	32
Semang (Malaya)	12
Seniang (Malekula, New Hebrides)	18
Tikopia (Polynesia)	38
Toradja (Celebes)	31
Yagua (Peru)	19
Average (Mean)	26.7

SOURCES: Compiled from Naroll (1970b, 1970c, 1970d); Tatje and Naroll (1970: 778).
So great a difference between these averages either way has a chance risk of .02.
N = 40.

TABLE 11.4   Child Murder Scoreboard

Country	Child Murder[a]	Chance Risk
Above Extreme Range		
Costa Rica	105	.0000
Luxembourg[b]	56.9	.0002
Above Indicated Range		
USA[b]	37	.0196
Japan[b]	28	.0888
France[b]	24.5	.1455
Northern Ireland[bc]	23.8	.1596
Poland	18.9	.2883
Trinidad and Tobago	18.8	.2915
Scotland[bc]	17.8	.3249
Switzerland[b]	16.2	.3833
England and Wales[bc]	16.1	.3871
Australia	15.6	.4067
Hungary	15.3	.4187
Czechoslovakia	13.9	.4776
Sweden[b]	13.6	.4908
Canada[b]	13.4	.4997
Within Indicated Range		
Germany (West)[b]	12.2	
New Zealand	12.1	
Finland	11.3	
Denmark[b]	10.3	
Austria[b]	6.7	
Netherlands[b]	4.2	
Norway[b]	3.8	MODEL COUNTRY
Italy[b]	3.1	
Puerto Rico[c]	0	
Iceland[b]	0	
Barbados	0	

SOURCE: United Nations Department of Economic and Social Affairs (1975: Table 29). Worldwide averages and spreads of 27 countries reporting (normal distribution):[d] mean: 18.46; median: 13.90; range: 105.00; SD: 21.103; CEV: 114.30%. Worldwide averages and spreads of 17 OECD countries reporting (normal distribution): mean: 16.91760; median: 13.60; range: 56.90; SD: 14.22210; CEV: 84.07%; skew: 1.36; kurtosis: −0.00.

a. Homicides per million population of children aged 1 to 4, inclusive.

b. Member of the Organization for Economic Cooperation and Development (OECD).

c. United Nations reporting unit; not an independent nation.

d. See Glossary for meanings of worldwide measures.

SD = standard deviation.
CEV = coefficient of evolutionary variation.

11.4   STEP 2: CHILD ABUSE SCOREBOARD

Barbados, Puerto Rico, and Iceland reported no victims of homicide at all in the age group one to four years. Look at our worldwide scoreboard, Table 11.4. It shows our model country, Norway, with a child-battering murder rate of only four per million people. It shows the United States, with nine times that rate, near the top. It shows the highest rate of all in Costa Rica—105.26 times Norway's rate.

How true is this table? How accurate are these numbers? Only in a country like Sweden, where in some places every sudden death is carefully autopsied, would I trust such reports. But countries like the United States, with child murder rates above normal, cannot hide their shame behind their sloppy statistics: 100 percent of autopsies by well-trained physicians would only push our rates even higher. And there is no reason to suppose that the United States, Japan, and Costa Rica are reporting child murders any more accurately than is Norway, not to speak of more accurately than Sweden, whose reports I do trust, and whose rate is under fourteen.

When we visited Oslo in the summer of 1979, Frada and I interviewed Dr. Bjørnar Olaisen of Oslo's Institute for Forensic Pathology. We asked about Norway's low reported rates of death among battered children. Dr. Olaisen thought Norway's reported rate an accurate one. "We go to meetings," he said. "We hear all these papers on the battered child syndrome in other countries. After all, the symptoms are not hard to spot. Broken bones. Extensive bruises. We look and look for this sort of thing among Norwegian children. We hardly ever find it—and even then it generally turns out to be a child of foreigners."

11.5   STEP 3: TESTS OF THEORIES OF CHILD ABUSE

11.5.1   Parental Acceptance/Rejection Theory and Moralnets

We have no direct worldwide tests of specific theories of child abuse comparable to those on adolescence, old age, or divorce. We do have several worldwide tests by many investigators of general theories of parental acceptance or of child indulgence. It seems safe to assume that child abuse is rare in societies in which parents display much love and concern for their children and usually indulge their needs and wishes. Rather, we expect abuse chiefly in societies in which parents display little love or concern for their children's needs and wishes.

Ronald and Evelyn Rohner give us a carefully controlled test of their theory of the underlying cause of parental rejection; they call this project PAR, for Parental Acceptance or Rejection. Rejecting parents are those whose children find them hostile, aggressive, indifferent, or neglectful; accepting parents are those whose children find them warm, loving, and affectionate.

Table 11.5 shows five factors that seem to cause parents to reject their children. The first three fit together. And tie in firmly with moralnet structure—family structure. Parents tend more often to be cold to their children when there are fewer adults in the home who share the work of child care. No matter how lovable young children may be, they are demanding. A mother will treat her children better when she can get away from them for a while, when the father or another relative is there to spell her.

TABLE 11.5   Why Parents Reject Their Children

Reason for Rejection	Correlation	Chance Risk
No father at home to help	.35	.05
Fathers do not help enough	.40	.005
Grandparents not there to help	*	.04
Children not wanted before birth	.63	.001
Co-wives in same house	.50	.10

SOURCE: Rohner (1975: 113, 114, 115, 118, 269 fn. 19).
*90% of societies accepted children where grandparents are important as socializing agents, N = 16.

Table 11.6 tells the story plainly. The work of Whiting (in Table 11.6) bears out that of the Rohners (in Table 11.5). The world around, parents are warmer to their children when mothers get help in child care from other adults in the home.

From these worldwide findings, I would guess that good day care centers in our cities help mothers and children alike. That children would tend to be rejected less often—battered less often—murdered less often—if their mothers used day care centers for them. But I know of no studies that test this theory.

What happens to children whose parents do not love them? Some wind up in hospitals as battered victims of the parents' fists. A few wind up on slabs in the morgue. But more damage seems to be done to many others who are not mauled or beaten. Just frozen out.

Table 11.7 shows the hidden psychic damage done to the minds of unloved children. They tend to be marred for life. All their lives they tend to think less of themselves, to have less confidence in themselves, to be more dependent on others, and at the same time, to be hostile to others. They need others more but attract them less—a recipe for trouble. They tend to be less emotionally stable, less pleased with the world at large. And less generous and responsible— unpleasant, unhappy people.

The findings of the Rohner PAR project have further support. Nielsen reviewed other work for us. And Nuttal and Nuttal studied warmth of father and mother toward 5,370 students. They found that the more children in the family there are, the less warmth. Minturn and Lambert, in a comparative study of six cultures, found that parents are warmer when there are also grandparents in the home, but colder when there are co-wives and sisters-in-law there. Extended families help when they increase the ratio of adults to children within the household.

Studies of school children in Washington, D.C., by Rohner and by Starkey bear out PAR theory on the effects of parental coldness on children. Starkey found that rejected children had poorer school grades and achievement test scores than accepted children. Rohner found that accepted children were more emotionally responsive, had a brighter world view, had more self-confidence, and were more emotionally stable than rejected children.

TABLE 11.6   Household Size and Child Indulgence

PROPOSITION: *Societies with larger households tend to indulge their babies more than do societies with smaller households.*

	Societies in Which Babies Are Indulged	Societies in Which Babies Are Not Indulged
Societies with *extended family households* (father, mother, brothers, sisters, grandfather, grandmother, uncles, aunts, cousins)	Araucanians (Chile) Cuna (Panama) Hopi (Arizona) Jivaro (Ecuador) Lepcha (Sikkim) Maori (New Zealand) Nauru (Micronesia) Ontong Java (Polynesia) Papago (Arizona) Samoans Tupinamba (Brazil) Winnebago (North-Central USA) Zuñi (New Mexico) (13)	Klamath (Oregon) Tenetehara (Northeast Brazil) (2)
Societies with *polygynous family households* (father, mother, brothers, sisters, mother's co-wives, half-brothers, half-sisters)	Aranda (Australia) Arapesh (New Guinea) Cheyenne (Colorado) Chiricahua Apache (Southwestern USA) Comanche (Southwestern USA) Crow (Montana) Kwoma (New Guinea) Omaha (Missouri Valley, USA) Teton Dakotas (Northern Plains, USA) Wogeo (New Guinea) (10)	Ojibwa (Great Lakes) Paiute (Southwestern Great Basin, USA) (2)
Societies with *nuclear family households* (fathers, mothers, brothers, sisters)	Chamorro (Micronesia) Chenchu (India) Kaska (Northern Canada) Manus (Melanesia) Tikopia (Melanesia) (5)	Alorese (Indonesia) Aymara (Bolivia) Balinese (Indonesia) Ifugao (Philippines) Lamba (Zambia) Navaho (Arizona/New Mexico) Pukapukans (Polynesia) (7)
Societies with *mother-child households* (mother, brothers, sisters only)	Lesu (Melanesia) Kurtatchi (Melanesia) Bena (Tanzania) Chukchee (Siberia) (4)	Ainu (Japan) Ashanti (Ghana) Azande (The Sudan) Chagga (Tanzania) Dahomeans

TABLE 11.6 (Continued)

	Societies in Which Babies Are Indulged	Societies in Which Babies Are Not Indulged
Societies with *mother-child households* (mother, brothers, sisters only)		Ganda (Uganda) Masai (Kenya) Mbundu (Angola) Tanala (Madagascar) Thonga (Mozambique) Venda (South Africa) Western Apache (Arizona) (12)

SOURCE: Computed by R. Naroll from data in Whiting (1961: 359).
Correlation: r = .48.
Chance risk: p < .0001.
N = 55.

Rohner, Roll, and Rohner studied a similar sample of school children in Monterrey, Mexico. They compared their results with others of Rohner's. They found that Mexican children tended to be treated less warmly than Washington children, and tended to differ as predicted by PAR theory. Differences on each of the seven personality traits measured had chance risks under 1 in 1,000.

So the PAR project findings offer further support for the theme of this book: Weakened moralnets mean trouble. A child in difficulty with parents has a troubled moralnet indeed.

11.5.2   Child Abuse and Moralnets

Gelles reviews a variety of theories about the causes of child abuse. Earlier theorists tended to view child battering as the act of a mentally ill person. Gelles points out that little rigorous research supports such a theory. He finds the evidence pointing to social factors more persuasive.

We find some of the same causes of trouble turning up in studies of battered children in the United States and in England. Kotkin made a survey of such studies. She found most of them poorly done. Most such studies, for example, failed to compare the families of battered children with a matched control sample of normal children. But Kotkin did find studies by Gil and by Light that shed clear light on the causes of child battering. Gil looked at every single case of child abuse reported in the United States in the years 1967 and 1968—over 6,000 of them. He defined abuse as the purposeful harming of the child, either by physical assault or by deliberate neglect aimed at hurting the child. Gil looked only at incidents severe enough to be reported to the authorities. So he is talking about children in real trouble.

Because Gil's sample was so large, he could compare these abusing parents with the population of the United States at large. He found that child abusers came disproportionately from poor rather than middle class families, from black rather than white families, from families with many rather than few children,

TABLE 11.7   What Happens to Rejected Children When They Grow Up

	Correlation	Chance Risk
Compared to normal people, they are:		
less proud of themselves.	.40	.005
less self-reliant.	.08	high
more hostile toward other people.	.32	.005
more emotionally dependent on other people.	.41	.01
less emotionally responsive to other people.	.50	.001
less emotionally stable.	.62	.001
less pleased with the world at large.	.29	.025
less generous and responsible.	.41	.05

SOURCE: Rohner (1975: 101).

from families whose father was unemployed rather than employed, from families on welfare rather than from families who were able to support themselves, from families with less rather than more formal education.

But Gil's critics were quick to find fault with his method of study. "Might not your results be wholly misleading? You say that a poor, black, unschooled couple is more likely to abuse children than a middle-class, white, educated couple. But might it not well be that the former is simply more likely to be caught at it? The latter more likely to get away with it?"

Light restudied Gil's data. He used a method of data quality control (see Chapter 4) to see if Gil's critics were right. Light's tests bore out the critics' views about race, poverty, and education. Evidently, poor, black, unschooled people indeed *are no more likely* to abuse their children then are middle-class, white, educated people. Just more likely to get caught.

But Light did find two patterns that stood up under his measures of reporting bias. Child abuse is more probable in American families in which the father is *unemployed*. More probable where the family is *socially isolated*.

So two of the findings of the Gil survey that stood up to data quality control have to do with moralnet structure. More children per American nuclear family means a lower adult/child ratio—and so bears out the worldwide findings of Tables 11.5 and 11.6. Socially isolated American nuclear families have weaker moralnets. It would be helpful to know whether child abusers make less use of day care centers than do other people of like income.

The study of child abuse that seems to have impressed Kotkin most is the work of a British team led by S. M. Smith. He reports the findings of a comparison of the parents of 134 young battered children with the parents of 53 nonabused children of the same age who came to emergency hospitals for help. Table 11.8 shows some of the more striking findings. These seem mostly to bear on the role of moralnets in child abuse, and offer further tests of the worldwide findings of the Rohners and of Whiting. The English child abusers that Smith and his co-workers studied fit the worldwide patterns of child rejection. Child

TABLE 11.8 How Do Child Abusers Differ from Normal Parents?

Trait	Percentage of Child Abusers	Percentage of Normal Parents	Chance Risk
Mothers say they are lonely.	32	10	.01
Mothers have no social activities.	32	5	.01
Mothers say they had no friends as children.	46	16	.001
Mothers say they have *no chance* to get away from the child for a rest.	49	26	.01
Mothers say they like to get away from the child but enjoy it when with it.	50	73	.05
Mothers are not married.	29	6	.01
Children are born out of marriage.	36	6	.001
Fathers do not help mothers take care of children.	21	4	.05
Mothers have "abnormal personalities."	76	14	.001
Fathers have "abnormal personalities."	64	12.5	.001

SOURCE: Smith (1975: 149-172).

abusers tend to have weaker ties with their moralnets. They have less social life now, and had less when they were young children. They are less likely to be married. Mothers get less respite from child care. Fathers help mothers less with child care.

This is not to say that Smith thinks the weakened moralnets are the single most important element in causing child abuse. Abusing parents are emotionally troubled people. That finding is perhaps the most striking. Some of these emotional troubles may in turn be due to weakened moralnets—but the Smith study does not tell us so. Further, abusing mothers may well be less skilled at child care than normal mothers. They are, for example, more likely to pick up a crying child, less likely to know how much crying to expect.

What if child-abusing parents got together to form moralnets like Alcoholics Anonymous—to help each other with their child care problems? Would that reduce child abuse? They have, and it does.

Early in 1970, a Southern California woman put an ad in the paper. "Mothers Anonymous, for moms who blow their cool with their kids, call...." She got more than 200 responses. They call each other for help when they feel stressed. They exchange children. So they get moral support from the moralnet thus created. And they get respite from their children by taking turns baby-sitting for each other. Most of these mothers stop beating their children after about three months in the group.

From this beginning came the Parents Anonymous movement. In 1974, there were 60 chapters; in 1977, 600. Some members join on their own. Others are sent there by the courts. Here then we have what in scientific terms amounts to a quasi-experiment, but one of poor quality. The mothers are self-selected. And there is no control group.

11.6   STEP 4: FURTHER STUDIES OF CHILD ABUSE

The most trustworthy yardstick of child abuse probably is child murder. Especially where, as in parts of Sweden, every sudden death is carefully studied in an autopsy. For children of school age, sample surveys might check child-battering complaints by a victimization survey. That is, school children might be randomly sampled and asked if their parents ever beat them. Or deliberately harm them in other ways.

Figure 11.1 is the theory trust meter for the theme of this chapter: Weakened moralnets increase the number of unloved children. The meter shows solid support for the theory. Which is *not* to say that providing children and their parents with proper moralnets is all we need to do.

Several obvious lines of future research and policy fit together. First, we need to know whether the innate programming of the human computer works against child abuse. We need careful formal tests of the theory of a parental instinct among people. Second, the child murder data in Table 11.4 show that we need a holonational study to correlate these numbers with measures of moralnet structure. And with availability and use of day care centers. Day care centers provide a fine chance to test theory and to help mothers and children. First, do child-abusing parents make less use of day care centers than do normal parents matched for income and occupation? Second, does a program of steering child-abusing parents into day care centers reduce further child abuse? An appropriate test would be to pick 300 abusing couples. Match each with a control sample of normal parents of children of like age. Divide both abusers and controls. Steer group 2 of abusers into Mothers Anonymous. Give remaining controls and abusers comparable attention without, however, doing anything to spell mother or to provide moralnet support. Compare results.

Another line of research seems especially promising. One sees in the press loose claims that a high proportion of convicts in our prisons were abused as children. If we could lower the crime rate twenty years hence by lowering child abuse now, that fact would be of immense importance. And should programs to lower child abuse rates succeed, it would be wise to watch what happens to the crime rate a generation later. Meanwhile, studies comparing convict population with that of the public at large are touchy things. Can we trust the convicts' reports on their childhoods? How many of them have histories of child abuse that became matters of public record at the time? And how do these numbers compare with those from people outside prisons who otherwise resemble convicts with respect to things like education, income of parents, parents' occupation, and ethnic group membership?

11.7   STEP 5: COPING WITH CHILD CARE

If they work, give heavy support in the future to day care centers for all mothers of young children and to Mothers Anonymous, as well, for mothers in trouble for child abuse.

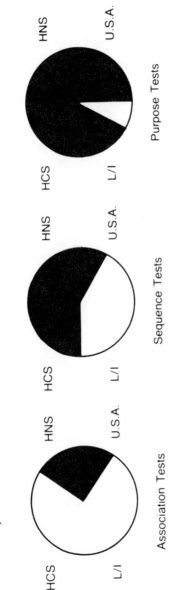

Theory: Weakened Moralnets Tend to Cause Unloved Children

Theory Trust Ratio: 42%

Association Tests

Sequence Tests

Purpose Tests

SOURCES   HCS: Rohner (1975) and Whiting (1961); HNS: taken collectively, Nuttal and Nuttal (1971), Minturn and Lambert (1964), E. Roh-
ner (1980), and Starkey (1980); L/I: Mothers Anonymous movement, see Rohner (1975: 70), Smith (1975), Smith and Hanson (1975), Smith,
Hanson, and Noble (1973, 1974), and Smith Honigsberger, and Smith (1973); U.S.A.: Gil (1968, 1970, 1971, 1974) and Light (1973).
NOTE: See *Theory trust meter* in Glossary for a key to this chart, and Section 4.5.3 for the general manner of its composition.
HCS = holocultural test; HNS = holonational test; L/I = local or individual test; U.S.A. = countrywide tests in the United States.

Figure 11.1   Child Abuse Theory Trust Meter

255

Smith's studies imply that we should consider battering parents as emotionally disturbed people, as people who need help themselves. The fathers often need jobs. And the mothers often need on-the-job training in child care.

From the studies of American child abusers by Gil and by Light, then, as well as from the studies of English child abusers by the Smith group, we find support for the findings of the Rohners and of Whiting. The risk of child abuse presumably would be reduced by improving moralnets, especially by providing the mother with respite from child care and with social life outside the home.

11.8   COSTS AND BENEFITS OF CHILD ABUSE PROGRAMS

What might be the manifest money payoffs of a successful program to reduce child abuse?

If it turned out that child abuse is a large cause of later crime—if abused children are likely to lash back at society by becoming criminals when they grow up—then the payoff through cutting the costs of crime would clearly be large. Other payoffs also seem considerable. Gelles makes a case for some half a million abused children a year in the United States alone. Elmer and Gregg studied all twenty children who turned up as victims of child abuse in twelve years at a certain hospital; they thought that at least five of the twenty were so badly damaged in general that when they grew up they would become public charges. At that rate, child abuse might well be producing 100,000 public charges a year in the United States. That would come to a child abuse bill of about 1 billion dollars per year.

So support for effective programs of research and action on child abuse clearly seems called for. But in Gelles's review of research on child abuse, he offers no convincing evidence that any such program has yet been successful.

Notes

11.1   *Cactus, Pepper, and Puddles*

For the Codex Mendoza of 1553, Plates 58-60, see Clark (1938); and compare Soustelle (1955: 299) and Vaillant (1950: 116f.).

11.2.1   *Range of Variation of Child Abuse*

The War, Stress and Culture codings are set forth in Table 11.3.

Six societies in the War, Stress, and Culture sample with evidence of child battering: Luo, Aztec, Egypt, Fur, Tiv, Burmese. Mean Social Development Index = 43.67 (Tatje and Naroll, 1970: 771).

JoLuo child abuse: Wilson (1960: 189).

Erie County, New York child abuse: Thompson et al. (1971: 14, 107, 119, 145); these statistics cover the 36-month period beginning November 1, 1966. Special county population census of September 1966 is reported in the *Buffalo Evening News Almanac* (1968: 182).

11.2.2   *Evolution of Child Abuse*

On parental attachment in animals, see Wilson (1975: 336-352).

Lady Macbeth's quotation is from Shakespeare's *Macbeth*, Act I, Scene vii.

High infant mortality in small-scale societies: Carr-Saunders (1922: 159-161, 172, 183, 249f.).

On attachment of hunting and gathering peoples to their children being higher than that of herding or farming peoples, see Rohner (1975: 115).

11.4   Step 2: Child Abuse Scoreboard

Our informant on child battering in Oslo: Prosektor Dr. Bjørnar Olaisen, Rettmedisinska Institut, Rikshospitalet, Pilastredet 32, Oslo.

11.5.1   Parental/Acceptance Rejection Theory and Moralnets

My phrasing of the rejection concept is from Rohner (1975: 45). Rohner (1975: 194) defines rejection simply as the absence of warmth and affection for a child by a parent.

I computed the tau-b correlation and chance risk of Table 11.6, using Naroll's (1974a) Exact Test.

On grandparents, co-wives, and sisters-in-law of six cultures see Minturn and Lambert (1964: 260). See Nuttal and Nuttal (1971) on number of children decreasing parental warmth—reviewed in Nielsen (n.d.).

Support for PAR theory in local sample survey studies in Washington, D.C.: Rohner (1980) and Starkey (1980); in Monterrey, Mexico: Rohner, Roll, and Rohner (1980: Tables 1 and 2).

11.5.2   Child Abuse and Moralnets

Gelles (1979: 27-90) reviews child abuse literature.

Kotkin (1976: 20f.) comments on the paucity of theory. Her review was done in preparation for her Ph.D. dissertation in the Department of Psychology at the State University of New York, Buffalo.

Spinetta and Rigler (1972: 296), after reviewing the older literature, conclude that socioeconomic factors "are not of themselves sufficient or necessary causes of abuse." The only attention they give to the weakened moralnet model is their long critique of the work of Gil (pp. 301f.)—but the crucial restudy of Light, which answered their objections, had not yet been published.

The work by Gil and Light is in Gil (1968, 1970, 1971, 1974) and Light (1973).

The work of Smith and his colleagues is in Smith (1975); Kotkin also cites Smith and Hanson (1975), Smith, Hanson, and Noble (1973, 1974), and Smith, Honigsberger, and Smith (1973).

Mothers Anonymous: Rohner (1975: 70). Parents Anonymous: *Newsweek* (October 10, 1977: 114f.).

11.6   Step 4: Further Studies of Child Abuse

Figure 11.1: I consider the work by Rohner, by Light, and by the Smith group strong tests; the others, weak.

11.8   Costs and Benefits of Child Abuse Programs

On the 500,000 abused children in the United States, see Gelles (1979: 75). Elmer and Gregg (1967) are cited in Rohner (1975: 71).

Youth Stress

12.1 THE LION MEN

The Thonga of Lourenco Marques, Mozambique, circumcise their boys eight at a time. The elders take the boys—all between ten and sixteen years old—from the bush school class. Each boy holds a spear. The boys do not know what to expect. Suddenly they are pushed between rows of singing men and are soundly whipped. Each boy is then grabbed by four men. They strip them naked. They sit them down on stones. Eight stones in a row; eight hurt and frightened boys. Facing them are eight other stones; on each facing stone a Lion Man. As the naked boy stares at the mane-covered head of the Lion Man, someone else hits the boy a good whack from behind. The naked boy naturally turns to see who hit him. At that moment they do it. A man quickly and almost painlessly cuts off the top part of the foreskin. But the bottom part takes longer; the knife hurts so much that many boys faint. On these the men throw cold water. They put grass bandages on the sore penises.

Painful initiation rites for teenage boys go on among many societies in all parts of the world. Among many of the natives of Australia, the older men not only cut off the boys' foreskins, they slit the bottom of the penis to its middle all along the whole shaft—subincision. Anthony views this hazing of teenage boys as an elders' plot to intimidate and control them.

To understand the special treatment of young people around the world, we need the concepts of age grades, age sets, and generation sets. An age group is a class of people set apart by, and only by, their relative age (for example, an infant, a child, an adolescent, an adult, an old person). At what age does an infant become a child? Or a child an adolescent? Or an adolescent an adult? Or an adult an elder? Different cultures sort these sequences out differently, just as they sort out the color spectrum differently in coining color terms.

I call an age group an *age grade* if membership in it is formalized. Our own society's system of age groups would become a system of age grades if it were made clear at what point a person is promoted from the status of infant to that of child or from child to adolescent, from adolescent to adult, from adult to elder.

I call an age grade an *age set* if the age grade works together as a team, constituting a social servo. In many small-scale societies, age sets are common.

I call an age set a *generation set* if the criterion of age is relative rather than absolute, having to do with generation differences rather than with differences in date of birth. So that the children of generation set A are defined as generation

set B, even though some members of set B may be older than some members of
set A.

12.2   YOUTH STRESS AROUND THE WORLD

12.2.1   Range of Variation of Youth Stress

This chapter focuses on problems of adolescence. Many cultures offer emic
definitions of age groups that result in some young people being set apart by age
into a group more or less corresponding to the time in the life cycle we call
adolescence. But we can point to two etic concepts that allow us to construct a
theoric concept of our own. The first of these concepts is that of *puberty*—the
physical ability to procreate. Puberty in boys is thus signaled by the first emission
of semen. In girls, it is signaled by the first menstruation. The second of these etic
concepts is that of *marriage*. Marriage is, of course, always a culturally defined
arrangement; it always involves culturally sanctioned rights and duties of family
life. And the timing and manner of marriage varies widely around the world from
culture to culture. Marriage usually, although not always, occurs after the onset
of puberty. So it is useful to define adolescence as the period between the onset
of puberty and the time when a person is deemed ready for marriage.

Thus there are societies in which adolescence so defined does not exist at all.
Among many castes in India, for example, it used to be the rule that girls went
through a marriage ceremony before puberty—and actually began to live with
their husbands as wives with full sexual relations as soon as they began to
menstruate. In many societies, the transition from adolescence, thus defined, to
adulthood is vague and hard to find. Young people may begin having love affairs
as soon as they reach puberty. Marriage may be the expected outcome of a love
affair that settles down into a permanent household. So if the young people like
each other they may start living together. And if they live together for a year or
two, and have a child or two, those facts may constitute their marriage. In such
cultures, then, there are no wedding ceremonies. Marriages are not contracted
at once—by a wedding followed by sexual consummation. Rather, they are
contracted gradually—so that no one can say on what day a couple ceased
merely to be lovers and became instead a married pair.

We can say much about the range of variation of the treatment of adolescents
around the world. But we can say little about the range of variation in the stress
on them. Later in this chapter I say something about variations in painful puberty
rites like those of the Thonga. And about variations in age set structure—in the
way in which adolescents are or are not set aside in separate barracks, or in
which they are or are not otherwise organized into age sets. But I have not found
a systematic review of the variation of stress that these arrangements may or
may not increase.

12.2.2   Evolution of Youth Stress

Again, I have nothing to offer about the evolution of youth stress as such. But I do have something on the evolution of painful puberty rites and on the evolution of age sets.

Precourt's holocultural study on initiation rites finds that public puberty rites tend to occur in tribal societies rather than in chiefdoms. By a tribal society, Precourt means one with common tribe-wide cultural organizations but no central political authority; a chiefdom is a further stage in political evolution in which such authority exists. There measures of cultural evolution were proposed by Service, but he has since repudiated them. They have not been formally validated by correlating them with other measures of societal complexity or scale. However, they strike most people who have studied cultural evolution to be reasonable. Precourt sees such public puberty rites as reflecting a hidden curriculum. Gearing thinks that in formal education systems, the hidden or thematic content is often more important than the open or manifest one. Precourt, Gearing's student, offers evidence that holding puberty rites to initiate young people into adult age grades reveals such a hidden curriculum. In tribal societies, government tends to be more democratic and rigid social class differences less common than they are in chiefdoms. Precourt argues that democratic societies would tend to favor public puberty rites. In a sample of 37 societies, Precourt finds a correlation of .39 (with a chance risk of 3 in 100) supporting that theory.

Textor gives us some glimpses into evolutionary patterns in age groups also. He finds that adolescent age sets are more likely to occur among states than among stateless societies (see Table 12.1).

12.3   STEP 1: CORE VALUES OF YOUTH STRESS

In her classic study on coming of age in Samoa, Mead found that adolescents there lived a far less stressful life than did young people in the United States. Was Samoan culture in this way better than our own?

In building a moral world, ought we to seek a world with as little stress as possible? Should we strive to make life as easy as we can for people? Or might *some* stress be a good thing?

By definition, stress is painful and unpleasant. So our core value of humanism implies that other things being equal, we should indeed strive to make life as easy as we can for people. But there may well be tradeoffs. Many cultures like the Thonga ritually subject their young people to excruciating pain. Some think that this sort of ritual makes life easier for the people in the long run because it trains the young to do their duty. And the well-being of all the people is thought to depend on the performance of their duties. The deepest value of all in our value

TABLE 12.1   Age Sets and States

PROPOSITION: *Age sets are less common in stateless societies than in societies organized into states.*

Linkage	Correlation	Chance Risk
In stateless societies, teenage work groups, play groups, or ceremonial groups are less likely.	.36	.02
In stateless societies, teenagers tend to spend less time in peer group activities.	.24	.09

SOURCE: Compiled from Textor (1967: FC 86/358 and FC 86/365).

system is stable order. If it turns out that stress must be endured to ensure the lasting survival of a stable world order, then it must indeed be endured. For the collapse of a stable world order—returning the world to its present bloody chaos—would itself certainly cost immediate stress again, as it does today.

The value question on youth stress then becomes: Is this stress *really* necessary? In the long run, in the worst of times as well as in the best of times, does this stress *really* save more pain than it costs?

And so, put that way, I hold that the value question becomes banal, as it should be. The problem thus is moved where we want it—it becomes the empirical question of what policies in the long run reduce stress for the most people without being markedly unjust to any.

I do not assume that there ought to be no conflict or tension between adolescents and adults. Not at all. Angry protests by teenagers and young adults often may well do more good than harm; such protests often may call attention to adult failures and social ills. In Western civilization in the last two centuries, people in their teens and twenties frequently have been influential critics and censors of their societies. Presumably, the optimal level of conflict between adolescents and adults would make for the most growth in knowledge through the most searching critique of the human situation with the least suffering in consequence. (However, no one has even begun to study measures of these tradeoffs; we do not have the vaguest notion of what this optimal level might be.)

12.4   STEP 2: YOUTH STRESS SCOREBOARDS

12.4.1   Youth Crime Scoreboard

In the United States, at least, most arrests for murder, assault, and theft are of young men in their late teens and early twenties. We do not deny that adolescent crime may usually be a protest against ugly or nonreciprocal treatment of the young by their elders. And in any case, it is the task of the adults to teach the young moral ways. And to guide them along the right path.

One of the most instructive reports on youth crime is that on the Juvenile Criminal Ratio for the mid-1970s (see Table 16.6). This table shows the percentage of juvenile offenders among all criminals. (It largely reports crimes known to the police only. Since a large number of crimes go unreported, and so unconsidered, in this table any tendency for one country more than another to go easy on juvenile crimes compared with adult ones would, of course, distort and flaw the table.) Norway, our model country, seems to have severe tradeoff problems here; it leads the entire list, with more than 56 percent of offenders juveniles. Nine of the ten countries at the top end of the scale—with the highest proportion of youth crimes—are rich countries. Eight of the ten countries at the bottom of the scale—with the lowest proportion of youth crimes—are poor countries. Adelman and Morris showed that the poorer a country, the stronger its extended family ties. So this table—though shaky in the validity of its data— as far as it can be trusted, certainly supports the view that weakened family ties tend to cause more youth crime.

We should be able to look at youth crime reports from victimization surveys. A victimization survey, of course, is the most accurate measure of crime rates. In such a survey, we interview a random sample. We ask all the people we talk to whether they have been the victims of any crime within the last twelve months. (True, only if the victims have seen the criminals, or if the police have caught them can we know if they are young people or adults.)

Since I cannot give you a good scoreboard, I make do with two fair ones: The Youth Murder Ratio (Table 12.2) and the Youth Suicide Ratio (Table 12.3). Though we do not have good data on young people as murderers, we do have good data on young people as victims of murder. The people most likely to suffer from personal crimes are the young themselves. Victimization studies in the United States show a striking similarity between the age of perpetrators of violent crime and the age of victims of such crime. If like patterns were found in other countries, that finding would greatly heighten our trust in the youth murder ratio as a general measure of youth stress.

We see that the score of our model country, Norway, is quite high. Norway has the second highest youth murder ratio of the 33 countries in our sample. (But remember, this is only a *relative* rate, not an absolute one. The *absolute* rate of deaths from homicide among Norway's youths is less than one-tenth that of youths in the United States.)

12.4.2   Youth Suicide Scoreboard

In our second Youth Stress Scoreboard (Table 12.3) we have the suicide rate among young people compared with that among adults. I trust these numbers. It is true that suicides often go unreported; but I see no reason for reports of youth suicides to differ in this way from reports of adult suicides. Are Catholics less likely to report the suicide of their teenage daughter than of their wife or husband?

TABLE 12.2   Youth Murder Ratio Scoreboard

Country	Youth Murder Ratio[a]	Chance Risk
Within Indicated Range		
Luxembourg[b]	190	
Norway[b]	174	MODEL COUNTRY
Northern Ireland[bc]	154	
Below Indicated Range		
Israel	131	.3403
Scotland[bc]	107	.1373
Germany (West)[b]	102	.1103
Bulgaria	101	.1055
Austria[b]	90	.0625
Belgium[b]	90	.0625
England and Wales[bc]	87	.0537
Italy[b]	84	.0460
Costa Rica	83	.0436
Australia	81	.0392
USA[b]	76	.0298
Finland	76	.0298
Czechoslovakia	76	.0298
Poland	74	.0266
Netherlands[b]	74	.0266
Canada[b]	73	.0251
Japan[b]	71	.0224
New Zealand	69	.0199
Sweden[b]	68	.0188
Ireland[b]	67	.0177
Chile	66	.0166
Denmark[b]	62	.0130
Barbados	58	.0101
Puerto Rico[c]	56	.0089
France[b]	56	.0089
Hungary	48	.0052
Trinidad and Tobago	46	.0045
Spain[b]	42	.0034
Below Extreme Range		
Switzerland[b]	35	.0021
Iceland[b]	0	.0001

SOURCE: United Nations Department of Economic and Social Affairs (1975: Tables 7 and 29B). Worldwide averages and spreads of 33 countries reporting (normal distribution):[d] mean: 80.82; median: 74.00; range: 190.00; SD: 37.835; CEV: 46.82%. Worldwide averages and spreads of 20 OECD countries reporting (normal distribution): mean: 85.10000; median: 75.00; range: 190.00; SD: 45.09280; CEV: 52.99%; skew: 0.78; kurtosis: −0.00.

a. Death rate of adolescents (15-24 years of age) due to homicide expressed as percentage of same rate for people aged 25 to 44.

b. Member of the Organization for Economic Cooperation and Development (OECD).

c. United Nations reporting unit; not an independent nation.

d. See Glossary for meanings of worldwide measures.

SD = standard deviation.

CEV = coefficient of evolutionary variation.

TABLE 12.3   Youth Suicide Ratio Scoreboard

Country	Youth Suicide Ratio	Chance Risk
Above Indicated Range		
Trinidad and Tobago	109	.1819
Israel	105	.2335
Japan[b]	93	.4684
Within Indicated Range		
Chile	91	
Costa Rica	91	
Norway[b]	77	MODEL COUNTRY
Bulgaria	76	
Canada[b]	76	
Czechoslovakia	72	
Switzerland[b]	72	
Australia	71	
Poland	71	
USA[b]	68	
Below Indicated Range		
Italy[b]	64	.4776
Germany (West)[b]	62	.4053
Finland	60	.3380
New Zealand	60	.3380
Northern Ireland[bc]	60	.3380
Iceland[b]	57	.2480
Austria[b]	55	.1962
Scotland[bc]	54	.1729
England and Wales[bc]	51	.1136
Netherlands[b]	50	.0972
France[b]	49	.0826
Sweden[b]	49	.0826
Below Indicated Range		
Barbados	48	.0695
Spain[b]	48	.0695
Puerto Rico[c]	47	.0580
Hungary	44	.0316
Denmark[b]	41	.0155
Luxembourg[b]	41	.0155
Belgium[b]	38	.0067
Below Extreme Range		
Ireland[b]	33	.0011

SOURCE: United Nations Department of Economic and Social Affairs (1975: Tables 7 and 29B). Worldwide averages and spreads of 33 countries reporting (lognormal distribution):[d] mean of the natural logarithms: 4.10; median: 60.00; range: 76.00; SD: 0.296; CEV 7.21%. Worldwide averages and spreads of 20 OECD countries reporting (lognormal distribution): mean of the natural logarithms: 4.00915; median: 54.50; range: 60.00; SD: 0.26036; CEV: 6.49%; skew: 0.01; kurtosis: 0.81.

(notes continued)

TABLE 12.3 NOTES (continued):

a. Death rate of adolescents (15-24 years of age) officially recorded as due to suicide expressed as percentage of same rate for people aged 25 to 44.
b. Member of the Organization for Economic Cooperation and Development (OECD).
c. United Nations reporting unit; not an independent nation.
d. See Glossary for meanings of worldwide measures.
SD = standard deviation of natural logarithms.
CEV = coefficient of evolutionary variation.

Here again, Norway, our model country, scores high: sixth highest of 33 countries. So it would seem that Norway has been less successful in making a good way of life for its young people than for its adults.

Adolescent suicide, we presume, is a reflection of unhappiness. In fact, adolescents are less likely to commit suicide than their elders. Suicide *attempts*, on the other hand, seem to be relatively most frequent among people in their twenties. It is young adults, then, who most often cry for help through suicide attempts.

12.5   STEP 3: TESTS OF THEORIES OF YOUTH STRESS

I know of no one who has offered a general theory of youth stress and proceeded to test it against data. In studies of youth stress, as in so much else, social science has rather tended to investigate a few popular topics. Still, I do find considerable work on three problems that shed light on youth stress: (1) Studies of painful puberty rites like those of the Thonga have tested theories holding that these rites serve a useful purpose; if they do, then such rites may save more stress later on than they cause at the time. (2) A great deal of attention has been paid to adolescent age sets around the world; studies have tested theories that would explain these age sets as means of reducing the stress on youth imposed by the sharp differences between the roles of children and the roles of adults in society. (3) Finally, many studies of juvenile delinquency—youth crime—in modern cities have tested theories that explain such crime as reflections or symptoms of other sorts of stress upon people.

12.5.1   Theories of Painful Puberty Rites

In many societies around the world, the onset of puberty is a formal ceremony signaling that a boy or girl has grown up. In many cultures, these are free of physical pain; but in many others, as among the Thonga, they are painful indeed. What is the purpose of such stressful rites? Are they part of the elders' plot—a device by which the old men keep control of the young? Are they indeed what they have often been called—"bush schools"—in which the young are taught their adult roles? Or are they devices for *reducing* the stress of adolescence by helping the young people think of themselves as adults with adult responsibilities rather than as children?

The Elders' Plot

Here we come to Anthony's theory of the "elders' plot." Is the main function of initiation rites to intimidate the young people, especially the young men, so that the elders can keep control? Is it to inculcate the moral order of the adult world into the minds of the young people, so that, from the point of view of their elders, they will be good boys and girls, not bad ones? Are such rites painful in order to impress on the youth the importance of the elders' moral teachings? Painful puberty rites are common enough, especially for boys. Even if the boys are not circumcised, they are often whipped, starved, or otherwise hazed. Girls, too, often undergo puberty rites. Especially in Africa, these rites may involve cutting off the clitoris. Why are these things done?

For one thing, puberty rites are commonly part of a larger program of events for teenagers that amounts to a kind of school or training course for adult life. The puberty rites of Thonga boys are an example. The older men are the teachers. The chief manifest content of the Thonga course is the memorization of secret ritual formulas. The boys study these every morning. The formulas have no clear bearing on everyday life. The boys also learn to become skillful hunters—though the Thonga live mainly from their food crops and their cattle herds. But in Junod's opinion, the real things the Thonga boys learn from their puberty rites are "obedience, endurance, and manliness."

Neither the elders' plot theory nor the school theory has found much favor with anthropologists. Whiting, Kluckhohn, and Anthony have pointed out that painful puberty rites were associated with long postpartum sex taboos. In many societies, chiefly polygymous ones, a man may not sleep with his wife for a year or more after she gives birth. But the child sleeps with the mother. When a boy is finally displaced by his father, we could expect the child to be keenly resentful. At the onset of puberty, this would supposedly make him dangerous. Hence the painful initiation rites—to cool him off.

The Identity Theory

Other holocultural studies have converged on a different theory—the identity theory. This theory sees puberty rites as dramatizing an adult identity that contrasts greatly with a childhood identity. Put this way, we find much support in a large number of holocultural studies that at first glance seem in conflict. Burton and Whiting looked at infant sleeping arrangements. They found that where boy babies sleep exclusively with their mothers but the family is patrilocal, there are painful puberty rites. Rites like these lead the boy to take on the adult male sex identity. In such societies, there are often two emic concepts for sex identity that seem strange to us. One word means an initiated man. The other word means others: women, girls, and boys.

Where boy babies sleep exclusively with their mothers but the family is matrilocal instead of patrilocal, we find couvade for the fathers in place of painful initiation rites for the sons. In the couvade, a father takes to his bed and pretends to be in labor when his wife is actually in childbirth. The couvade displays a man assuming a woman's identity.

Young offers evidence in Table 12.4 that supports another form of the identity theory—male puberty rites intended to dramatize male solidarity. The more important are exclusive male activities, the more we would expect the grown men to constitute a special moralnet—apart from women and children. And the more need for dramatic initiation rites to orient the minds of the youths. To bring them into line with the special values of the adult male moralnet. Y. Cohen endorses this finding. He offers additional evidence from other kinds of holocultural correlations: Painful puberty rites break the silver cord of dependency between child and family; they shift the child's concept of his own identity. Instead of a boy thinking of himself as his mother's son or his sister's brother, he thinks of himself as a man among the men.

Judith Brown sees female puberty rites as announcements of status change among married women who continue to live in the homes of their mothers. Seen from the girl's point of view, these rites, too, could be thought of as shifting self-image from that of a daughter of the household to that of a matron of the village. Why is such a shift in self-image so important? I would guess it would be so where the moralnet of village matrons has values that differ from those of the unmarried girls.

Perhaps the severest puberty rite in the United States is the boot camp of the Marine Corps. Is the chief purpose of that camp to teach a Marine recruit the skills of a foot soldier? Or is it rather to teach him to think of himself as a *Marine*, with a Marine's attitudes, a Marine's loyalties, a Marine's toughness?

No published holocultural study has tested directly the identity theory of puberty rites. None has directly rated societies by degree of contrast between childhood identity and adult identity. Sex role identity, work role identity, political role identity—all need to be considered. The identity theory would predict the most elaborate and severe puberty rites where the contrast of identity is greatest. The identity theory is a sharper version of Van Gennep's classic theory of rites of passage: The greater the contrast between childhood and adult identities, or images of self, the more change between childhood and adulthood; the more change, the greater a need for a rite to dramatize and intensify it.

12.5.2   Role Jog and Age Sets

What I call teenage *role jog* is what Rohner has called "role discontinuity"—the state of affairs in which the part an adult must play differs widely from the part a child must play. Our own society displays role jog so strikingly that we are apt to think of it as the natural way of things. But in many cultures, young boys make a start at their fathers' work early, young girls at their mothers'. So that as they grow older, they do more of that work, and do it better—but they find that a man's or woman's part is but a larger form of a boy's or girl's.

Among the !Kung San of the Kalahari, for example, young girls help their mothers and other older women with the main things women do—gathering and preparing wild plants for food and caring for babies. Early on, young boys play at

TABLE 12.4 Male Activities and Puberty Rites*

PROPOSITION: *The more prized male activities are, the more elaborate are male puberty rites.*

	No Male Puberty Rites	Simple Male Puberty Rites	Elaborate Male Puberty Rites
Societies without Any Male Activities	Alorese (Indonesia) Araucanians (Chile) Ashanti (Ghana) Chiricahua Apache (Southwestern USA) Copper Eskimos (Canada) French Villagers (Peyrane) Ganda (Uganda) Japanese Villagers (Suye Mura) Koryak (Siberia) Lakher (Assam) Lamba (Zambia) Lapps (Sweden) Lepchas (Sikkim) Malaita (Solomon Islands) Maori (New Zealand) Nahuatl-Speaking Mexican Villagers (Tepoztlan) Mixtec (Mexico) Nyakyusa (Tanzania) Papago (Arizona) Pilaga (Venezuela) Pondo (South Africa) Serbian Villagers (Orasac) Siriono (Bolivia) Tallensi (Shana) Tanala (Madagascar) Trobriand Islanders (Melanesia) Truk Islanders (Micronesia) English-Speaking Farmers (New Mexico) Yagua (Peru) (29)	Jivaro (Ecuador) Ojibwa (Great Lakes) (2)	Azande (The Sudan) (1)

(continued)

TABLE 12.4 (Continued)

	No Male Puberty Rites	Simple Male Puberty Rites	Elaborate Male Puberty Rites
Societies with Modest Male Activities	Navaho (Southwestern USA) (1)	Camayura (Brazil) Fiji Islanders (Tolekau) Ontong Javanese (Melanesia) Samoans (Polynesia) Tiv (Nigeria) (5)	Lesu (New Ireland, Melanesia) (1)
Societies with Prestigeful Males Activities	Egyptian Villagers (Silwa) Bontoc Igorot (Philippines) (2)	Balinese (Indonesia) Cagaba (Colombia) Chagga (Tanzania) Cheyenne (Western Plains, USA) Yap Islanders (Micronesia) (5)	Dahomeans (Dahomey) Hopi (Arizona) Kwakiutl (British Columbia) Kwoma (New Guinea) Nuer (The Sudan) Ooldea (South Australia) Thonga (Mozambique) Timbira (Brazil) (8)

SOURCE: Compiled by the author from Young (1965: 172-173, columns 17 and 22).
Correlation: tau-b = .72.
Chance risk: p = .000001.
N = 54.

*By a male activity is meant one in which women may not take part at all, not even as on-lookers or trade partners.

hunting with toy bows and arrows like their fathers'—maybe starting as a game with the shooting of a large beetle as it crawls across the sand. Early on, their fathers and their older brothers teach them tracking, and in the evening around the campfires the men tell their tales of famous hunts, each story filled with precious hints about the hunting craft.

A !Kung girl grows up when she gets married—but as a wife her duties do not change much from what they were just before. A !Kung boy grows up when he kills a prime meat quarry like an antelope. But such a triumph merely marks his final success at the game he has been playing since he shot his first beetle.

The problem of role jog itself seems to be a very real one. Margaret Mead's famous contrast between the Samoan teenagers who suffer little from role jog and unhappy American ones who suffer much from it echoes clearly elsewhere. Rohner tested role jog theory in a small preliminary study of only fifteen societies. He found a strikingly high correlation—.71, chance risk less than .01—

between the degree of role jog and the stress of life for young men, but no such link at all for young women.

Some people see in this problem of role jog one explanation for a prominent feature of teenage life among many small-scale societies. I speak now of age sets.

Many anthropologists have been struck by the intricacy and subtlety with which many small-scale societies organize their young people into age sets. Sometimes the whole society is so organized and the adolescent age set is merely one of several. (Stewart offers us an elaborate study of the underlying quasi-mathematical elements that often serve to define such sets; the intricacies pose a fascinating intellectual conundrum that he may well have solved.)

One simple way to create an adolescent age set is to house the teenagers separately. Many cultures do so. The Murngin of Arnhem Land live in hunting camps. They circumcise boys between six and eight years of age. Then the boys camp apart from their parents, with the older boys and bachelor men. As the boys grow, they learn that they are not supposed to see too much of women, not to stare at them or show great interest in them. Until the boys get married they live completely apart from their families. Out of the 243 societies around the world in Textor's sample, 41 have like arrangements.

The Manus of the Admiralty Islands live in a fishing and gardening village. They set aside a special house for adolescent boys; the boys spend a good deal of their time there. The old people told Margaret Mead in 1928 that when they were young, warlike raids of Manus youths on neighboring villages were common. The main idea the boys had was to capture a young woman. Such a girl would be kept in the boys' house as a sex slave until her hard life wore her out—usually not many years. Another 54 of those 243 societies in Textor's sample had some such arrangement for partially segregating adolescent boys—although few if any of them had arrangements for a captive prostitute like the Manus. The remaining 148 societies of Textor's worldwide sample did not segregate adolescent boys, but housed them with their parents.

Textor's findings give us a crude test of the theory that segregating teenagers helps make up for the stress of role jog. His computer correlated segregation of adult boys with five indicators of general cultural stress: personal crime, frequent divorce, sadistic treatment of war captives, concern for witchcraft, and drunken brawling. None of the correlations turned up in Textor's printout. It might mean no more than that, among the 243 coded on adolescent segregation, he had too few societies coded on the indicators of general cultural stress—too few for a meaningful test. Or it might mean that such age sets have nothing to do with role jog. But it might perhaps suggest that age sets of this sort do help reduce the pain of role jog.

A more elaborate theory of role jog is that offered by Eisenstadt. Here again we have data that permit only a rough, crude, indirect test. Eisenstadt sees the development of teenage peer groups as a response to adult blocking of teenage progress. He looks for such groups to develop in societies in which the families of teenagers do not arrange for their place in adult life, and also in societies in which that place is provided by the family—but tardily. Finally, Eisenstadt looks for such groups to develop in societies in which the sexual activity of teenagers is blocked or restricted.

We can make a little test of Eisenstadt's theory, thanks to the work of Harley and Textor. Textor based his computer study on Harley's scale of youth age sets. Among societies around the world, apart from courtship groups and school or initiation groups, there are three main kinds of youth age sets. These form a Guttman scale of four types:

Type 1: No youth age sets for leisure, public gatherings, or work. The Siriono of Eastern Bolivia are an example. These people are foragers, and not very good ones. They are almost always hungry. When Siriono boys and girls reach their teens, they are grown up. The girls marry at age eleven or twelve. The boys at twelve are men; they hunt; they marry. Of 55 societies around the world correlated in Textor, eleven lacked adolescent peer groups for play, public gatherings, or work.

Type 2: Youth age sets for leisure, but not for public gatherings or work. The Alorese are an example. There are well-developed play groups for children. These groups include teenagers as well as younger people. Alorese play groups involve many games and toys: squirt guns, hoops, marbles. But they also imitate, and thus prepare for, adult activities. Young Alorese, like our youngsters, "play like we are mamma and papa." Girls play at gathering food and cooking it. Boys play at hunting, at death feasts, at war. Harley classes these Alorese play groups as adolescent peer groups. His definition of a free peer group calls for at least three adolescents and no adults present. Evidently he includes groups of adolescents and younger children; presumably such groups would be dominated by the adolescents. About 23 of those same 55 societies fall into Type 2.

Type 3: Youth age sets for leisure and public gatherings, but not for work. The Papago of Arizona are an example. The teenage girls of a village, most of whom are cousins, make up an informal set or clique. They commonly loiter in the shade of the ramada. They gossip. They make jokes. Sometimes they weave baskets. These days, they look through picture magazines together. At fiestas, the adolescent girls start the dancing; they dance together, without the boys or men, all through the first afternoon. Later the boys and men join them. Of 51 societies around the world, 21 had adolescent peer groups in a setting of public gatherings; and nearly all of these likewise had adolescent peer groups in a setting of play or leisure.

Type 4: Youth age sets for work, for public gatherings, and for leisure. The Samoans are an interesting example. *Aualuma* is the name they give the organization of young women; *aumaga* is the corresponding organization of young men. Each of these groups is a work group, each is a ceremonial group, and each is a leisure-time recreational group. Young people between the ages of about sixteen to thirty belong to these groups; a married couple leaves the group when the man gets his first title. But there are also looser groupings of younger adolescent boys—work groups and play groups without other roles. There are

TABLE 12.5   Extended Families and Age Sets

PROPOSITION: *There is some tendency for youth age sets to be more common where people live in extended family households.*

	Societies with Youth Age Sets in a Setting of Public Gatherings		
	Present	*Absent*	*Total*
Societies with Extended Families	18	18	36
Societies with Independent Families	3	12	15
Total	21	30	51

SOURCE: Textor (1967: FC 362, FC 236).
Correlation: phi = .23.
Chance risk: $p < .10$.
N = 51.

three *etic* concepts in Samoan *aualuma* and *aumaga*: (1) sex of group member, (2) age as entry marker, (3) adult title as entry marker.

Of the 51 societies around the world examined by Textor, 11 had adolescent peer groups in a work setting; all of these had such groups also in a leisure setting and 5 of them in a setting of public gatherings, as well.

The last of Eisenstadt's three theories can be directly tested from Textor's tables. They clearly fail to support it: Premarital sex restrictions do not lead to peer group formation. The first two can be tested only indirectly. The most informative results in Textor are those for Type 3—Peer Groups in Public Gatherings. We find a slight tendency for such peer groups to turn up when the family is the extended type rather than the independent type (see Table 12.5). In other words, these peer groups tend to turn up *more* often in families of a type we would expect to make a place for young men in life—not *less* often, as Eisenstadt's theory predicts.

12.5.3   Causes of Youth Crime

Youth crime—juvenile delinquency—is at once a leading symptom of youth stress and a leading problem of adult society. We know little about juvenile delinquency outside modern nations. While we have much information about age grades, age sets, secret societies, and initiation rites, we do not know whether or not these things help ease the transition. We do not know whether societies with these things have less strain between youths and adults than societies without them.

It would seem that societies with well-organized age sets would have less crime by young people than those without them. It would seem that formal initiation rites during which elders induct the young into such age sets would also tend to make for less crime among young people. It would seem that these institutions have such cultural functions. But we have no anthropological evidence one way or the other.

The studies of juvenile delinquency in our own society are another matter. Empey reviews hundreds of them. And we have helpful reviews by Rohner, by Feshback, and by Rutter. Taken together, these present a wide variety of theories. About two-thirds of the theories reviewed point to some sort of causal link between moralnets and juvenile delinquency—and hold that in one way or another, weakened moralnets make for juvenile delinquency.

Many of the weakened moralnet theories have been tested by controlled comparisons between bad boys and good boys; the sample of good boys was matched for social status and neighborhood with the sample of bad ones. But all such comparative studies known to me have been done either in Britain or the United States. Without worldwide tests, we do not know if these relationships can be expected to continue to hold even in Britain and the United States in the future.

But if the weakened moralnet theories have not been tested worldwide, the other theories have hardly been tested at all. A century ago, Lombroso theorized that criminals were a distinct genetic type. His views are not much heeded today. The models of genetic behavior pattern I set forth in Chapter 6 allow for two kinds of such behavior: (1) fixed action patterns and (2) instincts. Lombroso never supposed that any kind of crime is a fixed action pattern—in which not only the crime but the exact mechanism of its commission is innately established, like swallowing or breathing. An instinct, on the other hand, is by definition a genetically transmitted wish or want whose mode of satisfaction is not innate but learned. No one has offered evidence of any such innate linking. There remains the possibility that a criminal genetic type exists, *distinguished by a weakness of the normal human instinct to be social.*

If there were no evidence to the contrary, such a theory might seem plausible. However, the evidence on juvenile delinquency is strong and clear the other way. Crime by youths is characteristically a social act, not a solitary one. Juvenile delinquents usually work in gangs, not alone. So clearly youth crime is *not* a consequence of any weakened social instinct.

A school of radical sociologists today seeks to explain juvenile delinquency as a consequence of capitalist economic structure. So far, however, no comparative studies of good and bad boys have been done by such sociologists to see if the bad boys tended more than the good boys of the same neighborhood to be victims of capitalist exploitation. Nor has any explanation been given for the frequent occurrence of juvenile delinquency in socialist countries like the Soviet Union and the People's Republic of China.

Tannebaum has another theory. He blames youth crime on law enforcement agencies. He see youngsters engaged in normal pranks being made criminals through arrest and thus through labeling. "Give a dog a bad name," says the proverb, "and he'll soon deserve it." Labeling theory does not, however, explain the correlations reported by two major studies between self-reported youth crimes and the moralnet structure of those youths. According to labeling theory, youngsters without any police record should not differ significantly among themselves with respect to self-reported crimes. The Provo and Silverlake studies of Empey and his associates might seem at first glance to offer some support for labeling theory. Through careful controlled experiments both these studies found that sending youth delinquents to prisons or reform schools made them more likely to commit crimes than paroling them. But all Empey subjects had been equally labeled. All alike had been arrested, tried, and convicted. What made the difference was not the labeling, but the jailing—association with criminal moralnets.

A. Cohen explains youth crime as a result of status frustration. He depends on the fact that most delinquent youths in the United States and Britain come from slum neighborhoods. But Cohen does not explain why some slum neighborhood boys get into trouble with the law while others do not. He does not compare bad boys with good boys from the same slum families to see whether the bad boys feel more frustrated than the good boys. More important, neither Cohen nor anyone else in delinquency research has done comparative studies that look at societies with wide differences in status frustration. Cohen's theory implies that the wider the range of incomes and the more rigid the barriers or boundaries between social classes, the greater the delinquency. I would guess that the world around it is the other way—where class differences are hardest and most rigid, juvenile delinquency is least frequent. Only research can decide.

In contrast to the weakness in the evidence so far adduced in support of these rival theories, many rigorous studies support the moralnet theories I am about to discuss. I repeat, it was the review of some of these studies as I worked on this book that led me to moralnet theory—normative reference groups. I did not begin my review with moralnet theory in mind.

In Section 6.4, I reviewed studies by Zimmerman and Cervantes and by Hirschi that pointed at the importance of moralnet ties in the causation of juvenile delinquency. Zimmerman and Cervantes, as I said there, found the more homogeneous the cultural background of the friend family network of a youth, the less likely he was to have trouble with the police. Hirschi found that the stronger were the youth's ties to family and school, and the weaker his ties to other youths who had police records, the less likely he was to get in trouble with the police.

Table 12.6 sets forth the leading controlled comparisons of moralnet theories of delinquency. Despite this strong evidence, juvenile delinquency programs in the United States do not seem to give enough attention to the moralnet—the family setting—perhaps because no one knows how outsiders can do so.

Meanwhile, theorists dispute which elements of the boys' linkages to their moralnets are the key ones. Shaw and McKay spent many years studying delinquency in Chicago. They carefully mapped the home addresses of all Chicago boys arrested by the police. They found a clear pattern. The closer a boy lived to Chicago's downtown loop section, the more likely he was to get arrested. Certain parts of town were high-delinquency areas. Earlier theorists had used this fact to attribute delinquency to the genes of the ethnic groups who

TABLE 12.6 Weakened Moralnets and Bad Boys

PROPOSITION: *The weaker the moralnets, the more boys turn bad.*

| Controlled Comparisons of Juvenile Delinquents | | The Studies Show How Bad Boys and Good Boys Differed |
Study Source	How Groups Were Matched	
Bowlby (1946)	Bad boys with disturbed good boys	Bad boys had prolonged separation from mothers more often in early childhood.
Friedlander (1949)	Bad boys with disturbed good boys	Bad boys had prolonged separation from mothers more often in early childhood.
Jackson (1950)	(1) Bad boys, (2) neurotic good boys, (3) normal good boys	Bad boys were more detached from parents and less deeply involved in family love than the other two groups
Glueck and Glueck (1950)	Bad boys with good boys matched for age, neighborhood, intelligence test scores, and ethnic origin	Bad boys changed homes oftener; home was more crowded; home was less neat and clean; family income was lower and more often unearned; more people were in the home; fewer *parents* were in the home; parents were more often divorced without remarriage; parents were less affectionate; boys were less emotionally attached to parents; father was less often accepted by boy as role model; boy was more often rejected by brothers and sisters; parental discipline was less often "firm but kindly"; school record was poorer; boy disliked school more; boy was less friendly with schoolfellows; boy was more often truant.
Bandura and Walters (1959)	Bad boys of at least average intelligence from intact, middle-class homes with like good boys	Bad boys received less parental warmth and were more often rejected.
Becker et al. (1959)	(1) Bad boys, (2) disturbed boys, (3) normal boys	Bad boys more often had parents who were maladjusted, under weaker emotional control, and arbitrary with their children.

lived there. But Shaw and McKay showed that the trouble was a characteristic of the *neighborhood*, not the ethnic origin. Over the decades, the ethnic makeup of neighborhoods changed; one group moved out and another took its place. But when ethnic groups moved out of the high-crime neighborhoods, their crime rates dropped.

Shaw and McKay focused on youth gangs in high crime neighborhoods. Such gangs are moralnets; they have a culture of crime. Shaw and McKay explain these findings as a consequence of weakened family moralnets. They see slum areas as characterized by social disorganization: disordered family life, poor schools, weak churches, and a diversity of values. The boys gravitate to the youth gangs and take their values from them instead of from home, church, or school. Shaw and McKay found that 80 percent of the crimes by youths in Chicago were committed by groups.

Theorists argue about which element of this slum situation is most important. Poverty, say the radical sociologists. The total neighborhood culture, say Shaw and McKay. The family-friend network, say Zimmerman and Cervantes. The loss of the mother in early childhood (age one to four years) say both Bowlby and Friedlander. The current ties of the boy to home and school, say Healy and Bronner, and Glueck and Glueck, and Bandura and Walters, and Jackson, and Hirschi.

The wide variety and complexity of the American city slum makes it hard for people to see which of the elements is the most important. Here worldwide studies can help. What we need are measures of juvenile delinquency and measures of the moralnet structures. So far, however, there have been no worldwide studies of juvenile delinquency among small-scale societies. But we do have data on variations around the world in the interactions among youths and their parental homes.

Another key factor in youth crime within North American city slums is the youth gang. There have been many worldwide studies of youth groups among small-scale societies. These could be compared to American city slum gangs.

Could it be that where role jog is great, the formation by society of licit and harmless youth age sets fills a need that *otherwise* the young people supply for themselves by forming illicit and harmful ones? Could it be that where role jog is great, the family moralnet often is distasteful and frustrating—and so a special youth moralnet is needed in its place?

12.6   STEP 4: FURTHER STUDIES OF YOUTH STRESS

The identity theory of puberty rites and the similar but not identical role jog theory of age sets could be tested in a single holocultural study. We would want one set of codes for contrasts between adult and child *identity* concepts and another for contrasts between adult and child role definitions. I predict that societies with sharp identity contrasts would also be societies with sharp role jogs. We would want ratings on the importance, drama, and painfulness of puberty rights; on the importance and degree of elaboration of age sets; on symptons of adolescent stress—like adolescent suicide and adolescent homicide. From them we would get a better reading on whether the greater the contrasts in identity concepts in the roles, the more elaborate are the puberty rites and age sets. And so we would get a better reading on whether puberty rites and age set structures tend to reduce the overall strain on young people, even while being stressful in themselves.

Weakened moralnet theory holds that the stronger the ties of youth to licit moralnets, the less the youth crime (see Figure 12.1). By a licit moralnet, I mean one that teaches its members to obey the laws of the larger society to which it belongs.

Theory: Weakened Licit Moralnets Tend to Cause Youth Crime

Theory Trust Ratio: 25%

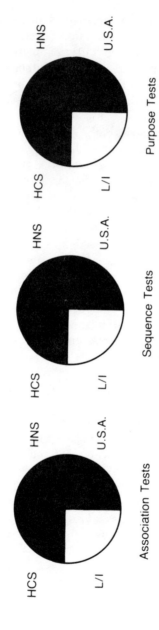

Association Tests Sequence Tests Purpose Tests

SOURCES L/I: Empey and Lubeck (1971) and Empey and Erickson (1972).
NOTE: See *Theory trust meter* in Glossary for a key to this chart, and Section 4.5.3 for the general manner of its composition.
HCS = holocultural test; HNS = holonational test; L/I = local or individual test; U.S.A. = countrywide tests in the United States.

Figure 12.1 Juvenile Delinquency Theory Trust Meter

The weakened moralnet theory of youth crime concerns several moralnets in the modern city: that of the youth's family, that of the school, that of the church, that of criminal street youth gangs, and that of prison inmates. It holds that the tighter are a youth's ties to home, school, and church, the less youth crime. It holds further that the more home, school, and church back each other up, the less the youth crime.

Such a theory predicts markedly less youth crime among religious parochial students in the United States (whether Catholic, Protestant, or Jewish) than among public school students. But the comparison would have to match the religious and public school students for family income and family stability and strength of family ties.

Such a theory can best be tested worldwide. Here are six statements that should be so tested:

(1) The more homogeneous the moral values of a community, the less the youth crime.
(2) The warmer the ties of affection between children and parents, the less the youth crime.
(3) The more homogeneous the moral values of the group of intimate adult friends that youth have, the less the youth crime.
(4) The tighter the social ties of licit youth peer groups, the less the youth crime. (By a licit youth peer group, I mean one that shares the moral values of the adults of its community.)
(5) The tighter the social ties of illicit youth peer groups, the more the youth crime. (By an illicit youth peer group, of course, I mean one that defies the moral values of the adults in its community.)
(6) Other things being equal, the more dramatic the puberty rites, the less the youth crime.

Since youth crime is a striking focal problem of moral order, these tests of youth crime theory would go far toward testing further the fundamental theory of the moral order set forth in this book—normative reference group theory. Or as I call, it moralnet theory.

Economic theories of youth crime might be more readily tested by a holonational study. We may phrase the economic theory of juvenile delinquency thus: The less absolutely wealthy the boys, relative to other boys in their society—the less opportunity they have to rise in the social and economic system—the more the youth crime. There are holonational data about absolute wealth (gross national product per capita) and relative wealth (income distribution). The cost of the test would chiefly lie in collecting data on youth crime and on social mobility.

Labeling theory could be tested by comparing practices in dealing with youthful offenders.

A punishment theory of youth crime could be tested by comparing the certainty of punishment of youthful offenders.

TABLE 12.7   General Model of Juvenile Delinquency Theory

Linear Regression Equation

$$Y = aX_1 - bX_2 - cX_3 - dX_4 + fX_5 - gX_6 - hX_7 + iX_8 + jX_9 + kX_{10} + mX_{11} + e$$

Where:

Y = juvenile delinquency rate

X_1 = heterogeneity of community moral values

a = weight of X_1

X_2 = warmth of ties of affection between children and parents

b = weight of X_2

X_3 = size of intimate adult-friend network

c = weight of X_3

X_4 = tightness of social ties of licit youth peer groups

d = weight of X_4

X_5 = tightness of social ties of illicit youth peer groups

f = weight of X_5

X_6 = dramatic intensity of puberty rites

g = weight of X_6

X_7 = gross national product per capita as measure of absolute wealth of society

h = weight of X_7

X_8 = Gini index of income distribution as measure of relative deprivation.
      (The higher the index, the more unequal the distribution and the greater
      the relative deprivation.)

i = weight of X_8

X_9 = index of social mobility

j = weight of X_9

X_{10} = frequency of labeling of youthful offenders

k = weight of X_{10}

X_{11} = frequency of punishment of youthful offenders

m = weight of X_{11}

e = error factor

NOTE: Needless to say, the purpose of the studies called for is to calculate the weights that measure the relative importance of each of these eleven hypothetical causes of youth crime.

Put these theories together and we have a general model for testing and appraisal. That model has eleven independent variables. It is set forth in Table 12.7.

A set of holocultural, holonational, national, and local studies could solve this equation—find the coefficients a, b, c . . . m that give the relative importance of each of these supposed causes. Then a set of public action programs in country after country around the world based on these studies could give us the practical working proof of theory.

12.7   STEP 5: COPING WITH YOUTH STRESS

The studies of young lawbreakers in the United States and Britain suggest that they are less likely to get in trouble with the law when they come from certain kinds of families. Young people are less likely to get in trouble:

(1) If they live in an *intact home*—in which both father and mother meet with them; if they live in a home with a warm affection between parents and children; if they live in a home in which children talk often with their parents about their lives and their problems; if they live in a home in which father and mother maintain firm but kindly discipline.

(2) If their home family maintains *close ties of friendship with at least five other families*; if these friend families are kinfolk; if these friend families share their religious or philosophical faiths; if these friend families come from the same ethnic and regional backgrounds; and if these friend families have about the same incomes and standards of living as their own.

(3) If father and mother *support the school, its work, and its discipline*; if father and mother help the children with their school work when they need it; if father and mother see that the children do their school work; and if father and mother back up the teachers.

For parents of children who *have* gotten into trouble with the law, I suggest forming a group something like Parents Anonymous. I have in mind a group of concerned parents and their troubled children that meets weekly. (The Toughlove movement builds such self-help clubs.) Such a group might develop much ceremony and ritual—like that of Alcoholics Anonymous. The leaders of such a group might be people now well adjusted but who once had gotten into serious trouble with the law. If Alcoholics Anonymous points the way properly, the success depends on leaders who can tell stories of their own mastering of the central problem the group is formed to face; such leaders should talk about schools and jobs as well as about crime and prisons—talk from personal experience as insiders.

Coping with youth crime is a leading problem in many schools. In recent years, in the United States some 15 percent of urban schools, 6 percent of suburban schools, and 4 percent of rural schools have been seriously affected by student violence. Assaults on teachers and other students in such schools are so common as to suffuse the schools with an atmosphere of dread. Such schools are not simply unlucky ones; they are schools of a certain sort. A survey of much recent research by Ianni and Reuss-Ianni finds that schools are less likely to have serious trouble controlling student violence: if they are not overcrowded but instead hold no more students than they were planned to hold; if they are smaller schools rather than larger ones; if the school principal provides effective educational leadership; if the school principal maintains a firm, fair, and consistent pattern of order for dealing with those who are known to have broken the rules—a pattern in which discipline and sanctions as well as rewards are given out evenhandedly according to the rules, with exceptions rarely if ever made. Further, schools are less likely to have serious trouble controlling student violence: if teachers and students take part in or at least witness the process by which decisions are made, a process followed opening and honestly; if morale is high among faculty, and school spirit is high among students. In other words schools are less likely to have serious trouble controlling student violence if they develop effective moralnets among the faculty and among the students—and the smaller the school, the easier it is to develop such moralnets. But the larger the school, the more diverse its educational offerings can be. So there is a tradeoff between student and faculty morale and richness of curriculum. (And what the optimum size might be, considering both these factors, the Iannis do not say.)

12.8   COSTS AND BENEFITS OF YOUTH STRESS PROGRAMS

A study among small-scale societies of youth crime on the one hand and youth family ties, youth peer groups, and puberty rites on the other offers a fine chance to test theories of juvenile delinquency. A clear test of a theory of youth crime that led to cutting it in half could save billions of dollars a year in the United States alone. In contrast, all of the worldwide research I have proposed—done in the most careful and thorough way—would cost less than ten million dollars.

Even more important would be further experiments of the sort begun by Empey and his colleagues. These indeed seem to me crucial for understanding the moral order. And I have a great deal more to say about tests of moralnet theory in my last chapter.

Notes

12.1   *The Lion Men*

Thonga circumcision: Junod (1912: I: 75-76).
Elders' plot: Anthony (1955).
On informal marriage, see Honigmann (1959: 388).

12.2.2   *Evolution of Youth Stress*

On initiation rites, see Precourt (1975).
On the hidden curriculum, see Gearing and Sangree (1979) and Gearing and Tindale (1973).
Service (1968) repudiates his widely used four-level scale of cultural evolution: band, tribe, chiefdom, and state. No one has ever rigorously applied this system to a worldwide set of data.

12.3   *Step 1: Core Values of Youth Stress*

On Samoan adolescents, see Mead (1949).

12.4.1   *Youth Crime Scoreboard*

A general review of the problem of measuring juvenile delinquency is in Hindelang, Hirschi, and Weis (1981); they focus on the contrast between data from official crime statistics and data from self-reports.

On the strength of family ties in poor countries, see Adelman and Morris (1967).

Concerning adolescent crime statistics in 1968, 76 percent of the arrests for serious crimes reported to the Federal Bureau of Investigation were of people under 25 years of age. Yet people in the 15-to 24-year-old group constitute less than 18 percent of the population; children under 14 are seldom arrested (see United States, Department of Commerce, 1971: 147; United Nations, Department of Economic and Social Affairs, 1970: 168-169).

On the link between the ages of criminals and their victims, see the evidence in Empey (1978: 122-127, 178).

Absolute rate of death from homicide among Norwegian youths 15 to 24 years of age is 2 per 100,000 per year compared to 23.57 in the United States (United Nations, Department of Economic and Social Affairs, 1975: Tables 7, 29B).

12.4.2   Youth Suicide Scoreboard

Adolescent suicide statistics: reported suicide rates for the youth group aged 15 through 19 average 6.61 per 100,000 per year around the world; the rate for all ages is 13.91 per 100,000 per year (see United Nations, World Health Organization, 1962).

On adolescent suicide attempts, see Schneider (1954: 84); compare Farberow and Schneidman (1961: 25).

On measuring suicide in general, see Chapter 9.

12.5.1   Theories of Painful Puberty Rites

On the elders' plot, see Anthony (1955).

On girls' puberty rites, see Judith Brown (1963).

On Thonga rites, see Junod (1912: I: 84f.) for the school theory.

On the influence of the long postpartum sex taboo, see Whiting, Kluckhohn, and Anthony (1958).

On the influence of sleeping arrangements, see Burton and Whiting (1963).

On identity theory, see Young (1965) and Cohen (1964a).

On rites of passage, see Van Gennep (1960).

Schweizer (1978a: 169) constructs a plausible path-analysis model that points to a revised version of the one in Whiting, Kluckhohn, and Anthony (1958) and Whiting (1964). Initiation rites are thus seen as primarily the result of mother-son sleeping arrangements, and secondarily as the result of patrilocality. This model supports identity theory.

12.5.2   Role Jog and Age Sets

On differences of adult and childhood roles, see Rohner (n.d.).

On the !Kung San, see Lee (1979: 235-240).

On Samoa, see Mead (1949).

Stewart (1977) gives an extremely detailed and careful review of age groupings.

On the Murngin, see Warner (1964: 116f.).

On Murngin-like arrangements: Textor (1967: FC 371).

On Manus boys' house prostitutes, see Mead (1953: 118f.).

On segregating adolescent boys, see Textor (1967: FC 370).

The remaining 148 societies that did not segregate adolescent boys are in Textor (1967: FC 148, FC 272, FC 421, FC 441, and FC 477).

On the development of teenage peer groups as a response to adult blocking, see Eisenstadt (1956: 54-55).

On the four-type Guttman scale, see Harley (1963).

On the Siriono lacking peer groups, see Holmberg (1969: 211). For others like the Siriono, see Textor (1967: FC 361-363).

On Alorese leisure groups, see Du Bois (1961: 59-61). For other age sets like the Alorese, see Textor (1967: FC 361-363). On the classification of Alorese play groups, see Harley (1963: 14).

On Papago teenage girls, see Joseph, Spicer, and Chevsky (1949: 151-153). For other age sets like the Papago, see Textor (1967: FC 361-363).

On Samoan adolescent peer groups, see Mead (1949-56).

On peer groups in a work setting, see Textor (1967: FC 361-363).

On a test of the last of Eisenstadt's theories, see Textor (1967: FC 361-363, FC 390).

12.5.3   Causes of Youth Crime

Empey (1978), Rohner (1975: 85-88), Feshback (1970: 213f.), and Rutter (1972) review juvenile delinquency theory.

Lombroso's theories of criminality as the result of genetic predispositions are reviewed in Sutherland
and Cressey (1970: 52-54).

Evidence that teenage criminals usually work in gangs rather than alone is summarized in Section
6.4; see also Empey (1978: 208-213).

The theories of radical sociologists are reviewed in Empey (1978: 369ff.).

On juvenile delinquency, or "hooliganism," in the Soviet Union, see Smith (1976: 209, 218, 458); in
the People's Republic of China, see Leys (1977: 44).

On labeling theory, see Tannenbaum (1938).

Empey (1978: 341-368) reviews labeling theory. Hirschi (1969) and Zimmerman and Cervantes (1960)
link moralnet structure with self-reported juvenile delinquency. On the Provo study, see Empey
and Erickson (1972). On the Silverlake study, see Empey and Lubeck (1971).

On youth crime as status frustration, see Cohen (1955).

On recent public policy toward juvenile delinquency in the United States, see Empey (1978: 525-562).

On geographical locations of juvenile delinquency in Chicago, see Shaw and McKay (1969). They
also find that: (1) Low juvenile crime areas of Chicago are areas of uniform social values among the
residents; high juvenile crime areas are those of value diversity. (2) The family as a moralnet is less
effective in high-crime areas because families are newcomers and do not know the way the city
works, and also because many families there profit from crime by having their criminal members
contribute to family income. (3) High-crime areas are areas with high activity of agencies without local
roots.

On friend-family networks, see Zimmerman and Cervantes (1960), Bowlby (1946), Friedlander
(1949), Healy and Bronner (1936), Glueck and Glueck (1950), Bandura and Walters (1959),
Jackson (1950), and Hirschi (1969).

On the Vice Lord nation, see Keiser (1969).

12.6   Step 4: Further Studies of Youth Stress

Figure 12.1 is based on the studies reviewed in Section 12.1. Of these, Empey and Lubeck (1971) and
Empey and Erickson (1972) were formal, controlled experiments. While Empey's experiments
did not meet their objective, they did show that association with licit moralnets (home or Empey's
experimental groups), rather than commitment to prison and its illicit moralnets, resulted in less
recidivism. A random decision on disposition of delinquents by committing judges made this a
controlled experiment—showing that sending them to prison or reform school increases the
crime rate among young boys.

12.7   Step 5: Coping with Youth Stress

The Toughlove movement is sponsored by the Community Service Foundation, Box 70, Sellersville,
PA 18960; phone: (215) 766-8022.

On violence in schools, see Ianni and Reuss-Ianni (1980).

Old People

13.1 THE SICK OLD SIRIONO WOMAN

The old woman had been left behind without a word when her people moved on. Not even her husband said farewell. Her Siriono band knew she was sick. They thought she was too old to keep up. They saw to her fire; they gave her a calabash of drinking water; they put her personal belongings beside her. And thus they parted. When Allan Holmberg found her bones, they had been stripped clean by the vultures and the ants.

13.2 OLD PEOPLE AROUND THE WORLD

13.2.1 Range of Variation of Treatment of Old People

The world around, old women consistently tend to receive less deference than do old men. Silverman and Maxwell looked at six different ways deference is shown to old people. They found that: (1) Old men were more likely than old women to have a specially good place by the fire set aside for them. And so with all other sorts of good places. (2) Old men were more likely than old women to be served food before other people. Or served better food—choice tidbits. (3) Old men were more likely than old women to be spoken to or about in terms of special deference or honor. (4) Old men were more likely than old women to be favored over others with respect to clothing, grooming, posture, and other gestures or tokens of esteem. (5) Old men were more likely than old women to be taken care of through special services, special care. (6) And old men were more likely than old women to receive special gifts of value.

When people grow old, sick, and weak, they commonly become burdens to themselves as well as to their relatives. Hopi oldsters often complain: "We always looked forward to old age but see how we suffer. It is foolish to look forward to such a time." The poet, Herrick, wrote: "That age is best which is the first, / When youth and blood are warmer; / But being spent, the worse, and worst / Times still succeed the former."

What is to be done with decrepit oldsters? Help them die? Some small-scale societies do. Among the Labrador Eskimo, when an old woman became a burden, people gave her less to eat. Soon she would become too weak to keep on the move, and would fall behind. Then an informal committee of three or four of her male relatives would go back to her on some pretext. They would put her to death; they would tie her corpse with thongs and pile a cairn of stones on top of her. Thus her ghost could not haunt them. Among the Chippewa, there was a ceremony of euthanasia. It began with a feast of dog meat for all. The men smoked the pipe of peace. They sang; they danced; they chanted prayers. At the climax, a son of the oldster killed him with a tomahawk. Most old people too sick or weak to manage, they say, chose to die this way. If one did not, his children might offer to leave him on some small island with a canoe and paddles, bow and arrows, and a drinking bowl, to see if he could feed himself through the frozen winter.

But by and large, small-scale societies around the world take good care of their oldsters and treat them well, as you and I wish to be treated when we grow old. We see this plainly from Simmons's holocultural study of 71 societies (see Table 13.1); by far the greater part of these societies were good to their old people: Either the community usually respected or feared the old ones, or the whole community supported the old people, helping to feed and keep them, or their families supported them. By far the smallest part of these 71 societies abandoned their helpless old or killed them.

13.2.2   Evolution of Treatment of Old People

Sheehan studied worldwide data on treatment of old people from 94 societies. He found a pattern of steadily increasing deference to old people, and power to old people, as societal scale increased. The more complex, the more urban the society, the better off were the old people. But Sheehan looked only at preindustrial societies. He thought that the trend has gone the other way in industrial societies. Sheehan considered his results no more than suggestions and did not give us any counts. So his work will have to be done over again. But slim as it is, it is the best report we have.

13.3   STEP 1: CORE VALUES OF TREATMENT OF OLD PEOPLE

The core values of health, brotherhood, and pleasure all ask of a moral order that it take good care of old people. It seems obvious that in a decent world, old people should be maintained in good health and cheer. But, to be fair (reciprocal) to the younger people who maintain them, it seems obvious also that the elderly should already have earned their way, through their savings or through their earlier care for their children. (Of course, retirement insurance programs and social security programs are types of savings programs.) Finally, it seems obvious that in a decent world, old people should be helped to meet feebleness and death with dignity.

13.4   STEP 2: ELDERS' PROBLEMS SCOREBOARDS

Among small-scale societies, the treatment of the aged varies far more widely than it does among large-scale societies. As we have seen from Simmons's

TABLE 13.1   Treatment of Old People in Small-Scale Societies

Treatment	*Percentage of Societies in Which Such Treatment Is the Usual Rule*
Old men respected or feared	97
Old women respected or feared	82
Community support for old men	62
Community support for old women	59
General family support for old men	93
General family support for old women	86
Old men abandoned (as among Siriono)	26
Old women abandoned (as among Siriono)	35
Old men killed (as among Chippewa)	18
Old women killed (as among Chippewa)	27

SOURCE: Simmons (1945: 245-285; correlation nos. 173, 161, 1, 2, 975, 966, 991, 992, 1087, 1090, 1098, 1099). To read Simmons's table, see his instructions on p. 15. For a number of reasons, Table 13.1 should not be taken too precisely; it doubtless gives the right general idea but may well not be accurate.

study, however, among most small-scale societies the aged are fairly well provided for. Furthermore, among some of them the aged enjoy the most favorable positions in the society. They are treated with deep respect; their wishes are deferred to; they have the wealth and they have the power. Amid so much variation, a good holocultural index of the status of the aged is badly needed. Simmons looked separately at 22 specific points of treatment for old men and women. Many of these could be combined to form an index of treatment of the aged; but Simmons did not do so. Maxwell and Silverman did construct such an index. But of the 24 elements they used, they tell us about only 9.

13.4.1   Suicide Rates

Among most—but not all—modern nations, older people have the highest suicide rates. The rate keeps climbing steadily, decade by decade (see Figure 13.1). I cannot think of any source of error in suicide reporting that could be related to age in such a steady, linear way.

Of course, we cannot assume that all suicides of the very old are to be taken as symptoms of social evils. Old people often kill themselves to end the pain of a fatal illness like cancer.

We have a worldwide scoreboard on suicide by old people. Table 13.2 shows the suicide rate of people over age 65 as a percentage of the rate for people in the prime of life—ages 25 to 44 years. This ratio in the United States comes very close to that of the model country—Norway. In the United States the suicide rate of old people is 131 percent of that of people in their prime; in Norway, it is 120 percent. Contrast those with Israel—where the suicide rate of elders is five times that of people in their prime. Or with Chile, where it is only 64 percent. (And can we believe the report from Barbados—no suicides of old people at all?)

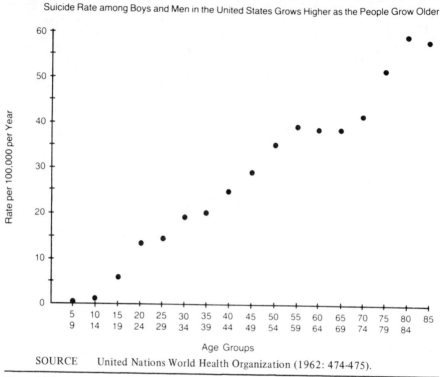

Suicide Rate among Boys and Men in the United States Grows Higher as the People Grow Older

Rate per 100,000 per Year

Age Groups

SOURCE   United Nations World Health Organization (1962: 474-475).

Figure 13.1   Age and Suicide Rates

13.4.2   Murder Rates

We have a second worldwide scoreboard, on murder of old people—Table 13.3. We see the deaths of old people as victims of homicide, stated as a percentage of the like rate of deaths of people in their prime. France reports a fantastically high rate: Old people are more than eight times as likely to be murdered as are people in their prime. Norway, our model country, actually has the second highest such ratio: 177 percent. (Norway may be paying for its general well-being by placing special stress on youths and elders.) The United States in this respect has a ratio well below normal: only 41 percent.

We need two more worldwide scoreboards—to measure income of the old and to measure their degree of participation in the life of their people.

13.5   STEP 3: TESTS OF THEORIES OF THE TREATMENT OF OLD PEOPLE

What factors in the society and culture make for good treatment of the aged? How are they best handled? We see an emerging pattern of issues and evidence.

TABLE 13.2 Elders' Suicide Ratio Scoreboard

Country	Elders' Suicide Ratio[a]	Chance Risk
Above Extreme Range		
Israel	529	.0000
Bulgaria	471	.0001
Above Indicated Range		
Spain[b]	387	.0035
Japan[b]	329	.0224
Italy[b]	303	.0455
Belgium[b]	303	.0455
Netherlands[b]	261	.1232
Luxembourg[b]	248	.1618
Costa Rica	246	.1684
Hungary	241	.1859
France[b]	235	.2087
Trinidad and Tobago	209	.3306
Puerto Rico[c]	200	.3819
Austria[b]	196	.4061
Within Indicated Range		
Czechoslovakia	179	
England and Wales[bc]	168	
Germany (West)[b]	165	
Switzerland[b]	163	
New Zealand	157	
Denmark[b]	156	
Scotland[bc]	137	
USA[b]	131	
Australia	125	
Norway[b]	120	MODEL COUNTRY
Sweden[b]	105	
Finland	102	
Canada[b]	101	
Ireland[b]	93	
Poland	86	
Northern Ireland[bc]	80	
Iceland[b]	71	
Chile	64	
Below Indicated Range		
Barbados	0	.1896

SOURCE: United Nations Department of Economic and Social Affairs (1975). Worldwide averages and spreads of 33 countries reporting (normal distribution):[d] mean: 192.76; median: 165.00; range: 592.00; SD: 116.584; CEV: 60.48%. Worldwide averages and spreads of 20 OECD countries reporting (normal distribution): mean: 187.60000; median: 164.00; range: 316.00; SD: 91.48460; CEV: 48.77%; skew: 0.63; kurtosis: −0.00.

a. Death rate of elders (over 64 years of age) attributed to suicide expressed as a percentage of the same ratio for people aged 25 to 44.
b. Member of the Organization for Economic Cooperation and Development (OECD).
c. United Nations reporting unit; not an independent nation.
d. See Glossary for meanings of worldwide measures.

SD = standard deviation.
CEV = coefficient of evolutionary variation.

TABLE 13.3   Elders' Murder Ratio Scoreboard

Country	Elders' Murder Ratio[a]	Chance Risk
Above Extreme Range		
France[b]	847	.0002
Within Indicated Range		
Norway[b]	177	MODEL COUNTRY
Czechoslovakia	175	
New Zealand	160	
Hungary	153	
Israel	149	
England and Wales[bc]	149	
Italy[b]	142	
Switzerland[b]	141	
Iceland[b]	131	
Trinidad and Tobago	127	
Japan[b]	127	
Chile	126	
Scotland[bc]	124	
Poland	124	
Bulgaria	112	
Austria[b]	110	
Belgium[b]	110	
Denmark[b]	105	
Germany (West)[b]	100	
Netherlands[b]	95	
Costa Rica	88	
Finland	80	
Spain[b]	79	
Sweden[b]	78	
Australia	72	
Below Indicated Range		
Puerto Rico[c]	54	.4889
Canada[b]	54	.4889
Barbados	54	.4889
USA[b]	41	.4442
Northern Ireland[bc]	14	.3591
Luxembourg[b]	0	.3193

SOURCE: United Nations Department of Economic and Social Affairs (1975: Tables 7 and 29, Part B). Worldwide averages and spreads of 32 countries reporting (normal distribution):[d] mean: 128.06; median: 111.00; range: 847.00; SD: 138.324; CEV: 108.01%. Worldwide averages and spreads of 19 OECD countries reporting (normal distribution) mean: 138.10500; median: 110.00; range: 847.00; SD: 177.73700; CEV: 128.70%; skew: 3.55; kurtosis: −0.00.

a. Death rate of elders (over 64 years of age) as a result of homicide expressed as a percentage of the same rate for people aged 25 to 44.

b. Member of the Organization for Economic Cooperation and Development (OECD).

c. United Nations reporting unit; not an independent nation.

d. See Glossary for meanings of worldwide measures.

SD = standard deviation.

CEV = coefficient of evolutionary variation.

Some would explain the treatment of the aged as a simple function of the economic system; but others point to the control of information as a matter of at least equal importance. Then there is a conflict in the theory of withdrawal or disengagement or retirement. Some think old people do best if they withdraw from the hurly-burly of ordinary society; others think that, by and large, they do better if they keep involved as much as they can, as long as they can. First of all, obviously, we need good measures of the status and comfort of the old. If we cannot yet see clearly the resolutions of these issues and the answers to these questions, we can begin to see how they might be resolved and answered.

13.5.1 Economic Support for Old People

Obviously, one way or another, economic support is a crucial point. Table 13.4 tells the story. According to Simmons, where there is general communal sharing of food, old men and women usually get their portion. Where food supply is constant, there usually are food taboos that favor the old. Where there is a system of individual property rights in land, in mining and metals, or in personal debts, then old men—but not old women—usually have vested property rights. Capitalism then tends to provide for prosperous or provident people in their old age.

13.5.2 Information Control by Old People

Many societies tend to reserve certain occupations for the aged. Naturally, these tend to be sedentary occupations requiring little physical strength or vigor. On many islands of the Pacific, the old men sit for hours gossiping and rolling sennit fiber into cords that can be used on the boats. But often, too, the special tasks or crafts of the old are those that need above all knowledge and experience. If people have no books, then perforce their libraries are the minds of their old people. The old men of the society are likely to serve as shamans or magicians; they are healers; they are rainmakers; and they are teachers of these arts. One old Creek Indian, who had become skeptical of his own powers as a rainmaker, nevertheless said to the anthropologist Swanton that rainmaking "was both profitable in supporting many of their helpless old beloved men and very productive of virtue by awing their young people from violating the ancient law."

Maxwell and Silverman studied the relationship between information control by the aged and the treatment received by the aged. They looked at a worldwide sample of 26 societies in the Human Relations Area Files—about 20 of them small-scale societies. They found a high association between the amount of information old people had and the treatment of the aged. They measured information control by a six-level Guttman scale. In ascending order: (1) Old people always took part in social situations involving informal exchange of information. (2) Old people usually consulted with younger adults about important decisions. (3) Old people often also were themselves the decision makers. (4) Furthermore, old people sometime served as entertainers,

TABLE 13.4   Treatment of Aged and Economic System

PROPOSITION: *Treatment of old people in small-scale cultures depends largely on the economic system.*

Particular Economic Feature of Tribe	Particular Treatment of Old People	Correlation	Number of Societies (N)	Chance Risk
Communal sharing of food	Community support of old men	.47	45	.002
Communal sharing of food	Community support of old women	.45	45	.003
Mining and smelting of metals is practiced	Old men have property rights	.43	60	.001
Some system of borrowing and lending	Old men have property rights	.67	39	.0002
Some system of borrowing and lending	Old women have property rights	–.06	39	high

SOURCE: Simmons (1945: 245-285; correlation nos. 1, 2, 51, 52, 73, 76, 81, 82). At this writing, Simmons's data are the best we have; but his work badly needs redoing.

preeminently storytellers or singers in societies without books or theaters. (5) Old people occasionally served as well as arbitrators or judges, to settle disputes among younger adults. And finally, (6) old people occasionally served as teachers of the young. On this scale, decision making and arbitration look like functions of political power as much as they look like functions of information. Still, no doubt the rationale commonly used in both instances is that the oldest and most experienced are therefore the wisest.

In a society that changes slowly rather than quickly; in which *new* techniques and *new* knowledge are rare rather than common; above all, in a society without vast arrays of specialized experts and without any books—there indeed the old people may in fact tend *to be* the best informed and hence the wisest. In any society in which the formulas of economic and political power are complex and subtle and secret, it takes most people many decades to figure them out.

13.5.3   Withdrawal of Old People

In some societies, such as the Samburu Masai, the older men monopolize and manage the levers of power and wealth. But at the opposite extreme, there is the tendency in our own society to withdraw most old people from the arenas of wealth and power and instead to shunt them aside in retirement homes.

Small-scale societies often provide for the special isolation, the withdrawal, of men from women or of adolescent boys or girls from the rest of the people.

Theoretically, there is no reason why they could not make similar provisions for the elderly. They could have a special "old peoples' house" just as some tribes have special "men's houses" or "boys' houses." In fact, as far as I know, the old peoples' home is a specialty of our own modern Western civilization—unknown elsewhere. Perhaps modern medical science is responsible; perhaps only through that science do so many people live into their seventies or eighties. I doubt that the natural laboratory of small-scale societies then has ever conducted so extreme an experiment in withdrawal or disengagement of the old. However, it is common in many societies for elders to retire from the work and responsibilities of the mature.

Reifer is working on a worldwide test of disengagement theory. Her preliminary results split sharply by sex. She finds that keeping old men involved in society by giving them work they can handle does not seem to help their status any. But that for old women, such involvement *does* seem to help.

Cumming and Henry studied old people in Kansas City to test a theory of disengagement. They thought old people would be happier if they withdrew from their society, did not keep up their former social ties, and in general, had less to do with other people. But many other sociologists disagreed. Neugarten and Havighurst looked at old people in several cities not only in the United States but also in Europe. Their findings conflict with those of Cumming and Henry. Neugarten and Havighurst found that old people were happier when they kept up their social ties and contacts as much as they could. For old people too, then, weakened moralnets seem to mean trouble. But, as we shall see, it is the benefits old people may confer on others rather than those they receive from others that may be the more important aspect of this link.

13.5.4   Old People and Moralnets

In the traditional way of life, before the industrial revolution, old people rarely withdrew from the world of the young and those in their prime. They had the key task of serving as moral guides for the moralnet to which most people belonged.

Maxwell has made a study of this role among 45 preindustrial societies. She found old people specially active in three kinds of rituals: life-cycle ceremonies, work-cycle rituals, and power displays. Life-cycle rituals include the ceremonies of birth, of confirmation or puberty, of marriage, and of death. In many societies, one or another of these rituals is the chief ceremony of the culture. Consider the role of the traditional marriage ceremony in Western Europe, the Bar Mitzvah among Jews, the girls' puberty rites among the Cuna of Panama, or the clothes-burning death rites of the Luiseño of Southern California. Maxwell found that in traditional societies, old people were likely to play key parts in such life-cycle rituals as these.

Power-display rituals in traditional societies must serve old people especially well. In such rituals, old people often display their claims to supernatural power. Such claims around the world add up to an impressive list of the supernatural powers often claimed by the old: "I can bring the rain." "Cure the sick." "Speak to the spirits of the dead." "Call spirits from the vasty deep." "Speak to the gods." "Bewitch my enemies, and bring them to their death."

In most of these rituals, the old people serve as moral guides to the moralnet or to the larger community to which it belongs. Since the old usually tend more than the young to favor the traditional ways, they act as a force for stability. They sustain the traditional moral order. But they also often are the last to understand the material power of modern technology—the healing power of modern medicine—the wisdom of modern science.

So we have here one of the most poignant tradeoff problems of the twentieth and twenty-first centuries. On the one hand, breaking up the extended family moralnet releases the young from the influence of the old—so that the young can learn the new wisdom of modern science and technology. It also frees the young to move about the country—wherever the work is. Thus breaking up the extended family moralnets makes for industrial progress.

On the other hand, the shattering of the extended family moralnet along with the shattering of the traditional religious faiths can do much harm to the moral order of modern nations. And to this, as we have seen in earlier chapters, may evidently be charged many suicides, much abuse of drugs and alcohol, much child abuse, and much youth crime.

This traditional pattern of moral leadership by old people has also been studied by Williams; in his book on socialization, he looked at the role of the kin group. He found over and over again in traditional societies a three-part system by which the young were taught their culture by their families: (1) Aunts and uncles often took the part of mothers and fathers; child rearing was the job of the whole extended family, not just that of the parents alone. (2) The kin group was tied together by an ideology; ideas like common descent, totems, life spirits, and supernatural forces backed it up. (3) The chief work of maintaining the moral order was done by the old people, the grandparents; it was the old people who most often told the tales, the charter myths that made sense of the moral order; it was the old people who passed on the ideology itself, the core values. Williams found this three-part system strongly at work among most people of small-scale societies. But among none of the modern ones (see Table 13.5).

13.6   STEP 4: FURTHER STUDIES OF OLD PEOPLE

Social factors among the problems of the elderly have not been well studied by social scientists. In Table 13.6, I offer a general model of theory on the quality of life of old people. This table, of course, states the questions—not the answers. It calls for comparative studies within and between cultures to do two things.

First, the studies need to check the presumed direction of relationship shown by the nine plus signs and two minus signs in Table 13.6. The model supposes that the nine factors (including X_1) preceded by plus signs are good for old people, while the two factors preceded by minus signs are bad for them. I include long life expectancy among the "bads" because I suppose that the better the

(text continues p. 299)

TABLE 13.5 Elders as Moral Guides

PROPOSITION: *In modern industrial societies, old people are no longer moral guides.*

	Old People Were Moral Guides	Elders' Moral Guide System Weakened, But Not Gone	Elders' Moral Guide System Gone
Traditional Small-Scale Societies	Apache (American Southwest)	Abipon (Argentina)	— —
	Arapaho (American Plains)	Ona (Tierra del Fuego)	
	Cheyenne (American Plains)	San Pedro la Laguna (Guatemala)	
	Comanche (Texas)	Warrau (Venezuela)	
	Dakota (American Plains)	Javanese (Indonesia)	
	Eskimos (North American Arctic)	Kiwai (Papua)	
	Flathead (Northwestern USA)	Nauru (Micronesia)	
	Hopi (Arizona)	Nimar Balahis (Central India)	
	Hupa (California)	Koryak (Siberia)	
	Kaska (Northwestern Canada)	Okinawans	
	Klamath (Oregon)	Rajputs (Khalapur, India)	
	Kutenai (British Columbia)	South Slavs, Zadruga (Eastern Europe)	
	Kwakiutl (British Columbia)	Pedi, Bapedi (South Africa)	
	Navaho (Southwestern USA)	Kongo (Zaire)	
	Omaha (American Plains)	Pondo (South Africa)	
	Paiute (American Great Basin)	Thonga (Mozambique)	
	Papago (Southwestern USA)	Tonga (Zambia)	
	Sanpoil (Northwestern USA)	Turkana (Kenya)	
	Slave (Northwestern Canada)	Venda (South Africa)	
	Taos (New Mexico)	(19)	
	Wichita (American Plains)		
	Winnebago (Great Lakes)		
	Zuñi (New Mexico)		
	Camayura (Southwestern Brazil)		
	Jivaro (Ecuador)		
	Kaingang (Eastern Brazil)		
	Sherente (Southwestern Brazil)		

(continued)

TABLE 13.5 (Continued)

	Old People Were Moral Guides	Elders' Moral Guide System Weakened, But Not Gone	Elders' Moral Guide System Gone
Traditional Small-Scale Societies	Siriono (Bolivia) Tenetehara (Northeastern Brazil) Wapishana (Guiana) Witoto (Southeastern Columbia) Yagua (Peruvian Amazon) Ashanti (Ghana) Azande (The Sudan and Zaire) Ganda (Uganda–Baganda) Sotho (Lesotho–Basuto) Bemba (Zambia) Bena (Tanzania) Khoi Bushmen (South Africa) Chagga (Tanzania) Chewa (Malawi) Dahomeans Gusii (Kenya) Kikuyu (Kenya) Lamba (Zambia) Masai (Kenya) Ngoni (Malawi) Nuer (The Sudan) Nyakyusa (Tanzania) Pygmies (Equatorial Africa) Swazi (Swaziland) Tallensi (Ghana) Tanala (Madagascar) Tiv (Nigeria) Tswana (Botswana)		

Traditional Small-Scale Societies

Yoruba (Nigeria)
Zulu (South Africa)
Alor (Indonesia)
Arapesh (Papua, New Guinea)
Arunta (Central Australia)
Balinese (Indonesia)
Chamorro (Micronesia)
Dobuans (Melanesia)
Dusun (Borneo)
Fiji Islanders
Ifaluk (Micronesia)
Ifugao (Philippines)
Ilocos (Philippines)
Kwoma (Papua, New Guinea)
Lesu (Melanesia)
Malaitans (Melanesia)
Malekula (Melanesia)
Manus (Melanesia)
Maori (New Zealand)
Marquesans (Polynesia)
Murngin (Northern Australia)
Ontong-Javanese (Melanesia)
Pukapukans (Polynesia)
Samoans
Tikopia (Melanesia)
Trobrianders (Melanesia)
Trukese (Micronesia)
Ulithians (Micronesia)

(continued)

TABLE 13.5 (Continued)

	Old People Were Moral Guides	Elders' Moral Guide System Weakened, But Not Gone	Elders' Moral Guide System Gone
Traditional Small-Scale Societies	Wogeo (Papua, New Guinea) Yungar (Western Australia) Ainu (Japan) Andaman Islanders (Indian Ocean) Baiga (India) Chenchu (South India) "Deoli" Rajputs (Rajasthan, India) Lakher (Northeastern India) Lepcha (Northern India) Palaung (Burma) Yakut (Siberia) Yukaghir (Siberia) Arab Villagers (Egypt and Palestine) Lapps (Scandinavia) Rif (North Africa) Rwala Bedouin (Syria and Iraq) (99)	---	
Modern Industrial Societies	---	Mexicans (Spanish speakers) Chinese Japanese Puerto Ricans (4)	Americans (Anglos of the USA) English French Germans Israelis Russians (6)

SOURCE: Reconstructed from Williams (1972: 154).
Correlation: tau-b = .59.
Chance risk: < .00001.
N = 128.

TABLE 13.6 General Theoretical Model of Welfare of Old People

$$Y = aX_1 + bX_2 + cX_3 + dX_4 + fX_5 + gX_6 + hX_7 + iX_8 - jX_9 + kX_{10} - hX_{11} + e$$

Where:

Y = Measure of overall quality of life of old people. The suicide ratio of Table 13.2 constitutes an objective measure. A personal happiness rating like that used by Gallup constitutes a subjective measure.

X_1 = Mean income of old people, in terms measuring their purchasing power.

X_2 = Proportion of old people who are active as expert specialists (paid primarily for what they know).

X_3 = Proportion of old people who are in managerial positions in business or government.

X_4 = Proportion of old people who are otherwise employed.

X_5 = General frequency of social contacts enjoyed by old people, with other people of whatever age or degree of kinship. X_5 is a measure of moralnet strength of old people.

X_6 = Specific frequency of social contacts of old people with their kinfolk.

X_7 = Specific frequency of social contacts of old people with other old people.

X_8 = Specific frequency of social contacts of old people with younger people.

X_9 = Withdrawal measure: X_7/X_8.

X_{10} = Proportion of old people who play roles of voluntary moral leadership, for example, in church sodalities.

X_{11} = Life expectancy.

e = Error factor.

---

health care and so the longer that people tend to live, the more ill and frail people with health problems tend to survive.

Second, the studies need to measure the relative importance of each of these supposed welfare factors, and in this way to supply the weights represented by the symbols a, b, c, and so on. Given a body of accurate observations, of course, supplying these weights is a routine task for a home computer.

13.7   STEP 5: COPING WITH THE PROBLEMS OF OLD PEOPLE

When comparative studies of the happiness of old people permit us to supply trustworthy weights for the equation of Table 13.6, public policy goals will become clear. Such studies would guide us in budgeting our resources for the care and comfort of the old. And the success of such policies in raising the measured quality of life of the old in country after country around the world would in turn constitute the best final evidence in support of the theoretical model.

In the meantime, we could do far worse than to find out through sample surveys which of these eleven factors most concerns the old people of each country today. Where do they think that the shoe pinches most?

13.8   COSTS AND BENEFITS OF PROGRAMS FOR OLD PEOPLE

From the payoff point of view the old have a poor claim on public resources. "Stint the old to serve the young" is a fair maxim for tough times. Still, I cannot help but wonder whether studies and programs about sustaining the aged in family settings rather than in institutional ones—studies and programs about making better use of the old people to guide teenagers away from drugs and street crime—might not well produce hard money payoffs.

For even though the old have had their day, our core values bid us care for them. Care about them. But how much more do our core values call on us to care even more for young women in trouble? In many societies, young women never have their chance at all. In many societies, the role of the old people of either sex is not nearly as hard as the role of the young woman. Take the Korea of a hundred years ago. . . .

Notes

13.1   The Sick Old Siriono Woman

Old Siriono woman left to die: Holmberg (1969: 226).

13.2.1   Range of Variation of Treatment of Old People

Old women versus old men: Silverman and Maxwell (1978).
Hopi oldsters: Simmons (1945: 234).
Robert Herrick's poem is: "To the Virgins, to Make Much of Time."
Labrador Eskimo: Turner in Simmons (1945: 232).
Chippewa euthenasia: Skinner in Simmons (1945: 232).

13.2.2   Evolution of Treatment of Old People

On better treatment of old people in more complex traditional societies than in less complex ones, see Sheehan (1976). His data need more sophisticated statistical analysis.

13.4.1   Suicide Rates

In the United States, at least, the steady rise in suicide rates with age is found only among white males; it is absent among white women and among blacks of both sexes (Botwinick, 1978: 32). The physical and psychological problems of aging are better understood than the social ones; these former are well reviewed in Botwinick (1978).

13.5.2   Information Control by Old People

Swanton: in Simmons (1945: 37).
On the relationship between information control by the aged, Maxwell and Silverman (1979) report gamma = .685; chance risk < .01.

13.5.3   Withdrawal of Old People

On the Samburu Masai, see Spencer (1965).
Reifer's (n.d.) correlation on participation by old women had a chance risk of about .09.
On disengagement theory, see Cumming and Henry (1961) and Neugarten and Havighurst (1970); also Botwinick (1978: 62-66).

13.5.4   Old People and Moralnets

Rowland, cited in Botwinick (1978: 37f.), reviews nearly a dozen studies linking bereavement with increase of death rates among the aged. However, neither he nor Botwinick is satisfied that bereavement is the cause and increased death the effect, because the studies they review failed to control for the health of the bereaved. Had these gerontologists been aware of the general studies of bereavement reviewed by me in Section 16.5, perhaps they might have been persuaded—for health of bereaved *was* controlled for there, most persuasively by Berkman and Syme (1979).

On old people and rituals, see Maxwell (1975).

On girls' coming of age rituals among the Cuna, see Stout (1947: 93f.).

The description of Luiseño clothes-burning rituals is from Naroll's field notes.

Table 13.5 is reconstructed from Williams's (1972: 154) table and also from his text. I reluctantly followed Williams's ethnic units, with a single exception—even though I was not happy with treating collectively all the African pygmies, all the Eskimos, all the village Arabs, and all the South Slavs. So long as Williams's practice did not yield a different statistical count than would have come from a focus on a single community of these units, I went along with him. But I dropped the Teton from his list because they are a Dakota group, and Williams had already counted the Dakota. According to the cultunit system I have proposed (Naroll, 1970c), counting the Rwala of Syria and Iraq separately from the Arab villages of Palestine and Egypt is allowed after World War I, because they belong to different nation-states. But all this is merely scholarly fussing. Were the chance risk high, it would really matter; but the chance risk of Williams's results is so small that we could simply drop all these classification problems from his list without disturbing his findings. (Chance risk computed by taking the standard error of Kendall's S, which comes to 6.934 standard deviations.) Another thing: Williams does not supply dates for his units; the China classed as a modern industrial society with a grandparental moral guide system surviving in weakened form was, of course, the China before the Communist revolution. Good hologeistic practice would call for Williams to focus his study of each society on a single community at a single point in time and to take only one such community from each speech community (see Naroll, 1971b).

Men and Women

14.1 DEEP WELLS FOR SAD WOMEN

In Korean villages, as in Chinese ones, the ideal household used to be like that of the Mapuche—an extended patrilineal family. An old woman had a place of dignity; her views on family matters would not be lightly disregarded; she ruled her daughters-in-law with a firm hand. If a girl argued, her husband would usually side with his parents against his wife. Wives who defied their husbands were often beaten until they gave in. The low point in a woman's life came in the early years of her marriage, before she gave birth to sons. That marriage would usually have been arranged by her parents. She might never have seen her husband until her wedding day. If she could not get along with her mother-in-law, perhaps she could persuade her husband to leave his parents' home. If not, she was trapped. Village wells were dark and deep. At night, they were quiet and lonely. A woman who jumped in soon drowned. Many did.

14.2 SEX ROLE DIFFERENCES AROUND THE WORLD

14.2.1 Genetic Differences

Many anthropologists argue that among our prehuman ground ape ancestors, natural selection tended to breed aggressive males but timid females. Our best information leads to the belief that these ancestors lived on mixed savannas—grasslands dotted here and there with trees. Such is the landscape today in those parts of Africa where the earliest human remains have been found. And such was the landscape 2 or 3 millions years ago at Lake Rudolf, one of the oldest known sites of human life. Our ground ape ancestors, Denham argues, would have gone on foot for most of their food into the grasslands, but would have used the trees as nesting places and refuges. When lions roar or leopards cough, it is best for a band of ground apes if the females and young ones scamper off to the trees as fast as they can. Meanwhile, the males should stand their ground, bare their fangs, look fierce, and fight. From the genetic point of view, most adult males are expendable.

Are human female sex hormones programmed to make women gentler? Are human male sex hormones programmed to make men fiercer? As yet we do not

TABLE 14.1   Learning Sex Roles

PROPOSITION: *Girls more often learn to nurture and obey, whereas boys more often learn to work well and be self-reliant.*

	Number of Cultures	Girls Learn More Often	Boys Learn More Often	Both Learn
To take care of younger children	33	82%	0%	18%
To obey elders	69	35%	3%	62%
To be self-reliant	82	0%	85%	15%
To achieve high work standards	31	3%	87%	10%

SOURCE: Barry et al. (1957: 328).

know. Genetically programmed differences in aptitudes or attitudes between the sexes are exceedingly hard to untangle from learned, culturally programmed differences. Boys perhaps may be better at visualizing things in space, for example; but if so, this may be only a consequence of their ranging farther from home than girls do. Certainly, parents around the world tend to teach girls more than boys to be nurturing, to be obedient, to be responsible; they tend to teach boys more than girls to be achieving and self-reliant (see Table 14.1). Do these cultural practices echo and reinforce innately programmed attitudes? Or do they and they alone account for the observed differences in male and female personalities?

Table 14.2 shows that in small-scale societies, men and women usually do different sorts of work. Of the tasks usually done by men, hunting, boat building, fishing, house building, and clearing farm land are all work for which men's greater innate physical strength and greater freedom to move about in harsh conditions would seem to be more suited. Of the tasks usually done by women, weaving, pottery, tailoring, and cooking are all work conveniently done close to home by a pregnant woman tending small children. (But tending and harvesting crops, carrying burdens, carrying water, and grinding grain are hard chores which usually fall to the lot of women.)

The model of instinctive behavior set forth in Section 6.3 can readily be applied to differences in behavior between men and women. That model would hold that men and women do not differ at all in innate aptitudes and skills—except for obvious differences in size and strength—but that instead, they differ innately in their *likings*.

A genetic theory of sex role differences in goal orientation would not, for example, hold that women are innately any less skillful at managing public affairs than men. But it might hold that they are less likely to want to. The careers of Elizabeth I of England and of Catherine the Great of Russia are cases in point here. As young women both were long kept in fear of their lives as expendable pieces on the political chessboard. Both had first-rate minds. Both put those

TABLE 14.2   Men's and Women's Work in Small-Scale Societies

	Only Men Do It	*Either Sex Does It*	*Only Women Do It*
Mostly Male Work			
Hunting	179	13	0
Metal work	78	0	0
Weapon making	122	0	0
Boat building	95	4	1
Wood work	122	5	2
Making musical instruments	47	0	1
Fishing	132	19	7
Herding	46	4	5
House building	118	25	17
Clearing farmland	95	17	18
Mostly Female Work			
Leather work	32	9	35
Tending and harvesting crops	25	35	83
Weaving	21	2	73
Carrying burdens	18	35	77
Pottery	15	6	85
Tailoring	15	8	104
Carrying water	7	5	126
Grinding grain	6	5	127
Cooking	6	9	186

SOURCE: D'Andrade (1966: 177-178).

minds to work at mastering politics as their best hope of survival. So we might have two cases here of cultural preferences overriding innate inclinations.

The evidence seems clear that differences in aggressiveness between the sexes show up very early in life. Table 14.3 shows the work of R. Rohner. By aggressive behavior in this table we mean behavior that is intended to harm, to hurt someone else, to hurt oneself, or to hurt something. Rohner faces the fact that culture has a strong influence on aggressive behavior, even among very young children. On his scale, as this table shows, girls vary in aggressive behavior from a score of 3 to a score of 10; boys from a score of 4 to a score of 12. The variation between cultures, expressed alike in boys and girls, is much greater than the variation between the sexes. Yet that variation persistently shows up in ten of the fourteen societies on the table. In all ten of these societies, the boys were slightly more aggressive than the girls. In none of them were the girls slightly more aggressive than the boys.

Because we have so few societies in the table—only fourteen—the chance risk problem is sharp. How often would we expect differences this great to turn

TABLE 14.3   Aggression among Boys and Girls Aged 2 through 6

PROPOSITION: *Differences in aggression among boys and girls are more closely related to culture than to sex.*

Culture (N = 14)	Aggression Scores	
	Boys	Girls
Boys more aggressive than girls (n = 10)		
Colombians (Mestizos)	12	10
Chamorros (Guam)	10	9
Paiute (Southwestern USA)	10	8
Wogeo (New Guinea)	10	8
Japanese	9	7
Navaho (Southwestern USA)	8	7
Sudanese Arabs	8	4
Potawatomi (North Central USA)	7	6
Manus	7	5
Americans (Anglos of USA)	4	3
Girls more aggressive than boys (n = 0)		
Girls and boys equally aggressive (n = 4)		
Woleaians (Micronesia)	10	10
Sioux (North Central USA)	8	8
Araucanians (Chile)	5	5
Malekula (New Hebrides)	4	4

SOURCES: Rohner (1976: 63); Harvard University Computation Laboratory (1955: 50-51). Chance risk: .001.

up by mere chance—from random sampling error, for example? All ten of the societies in which differences show up are societies where boys are more aggressive than girls. None at all are societies in which girls are more aggressive than boys. The odds that this score of ten to nothing would turn up by chance are less than 1 in 1000.

Denham's ground ape model of innate sex role differences would call for men to be more bold, women to be more cautious. And in fact, in modern nations today, in country after country, we find men more likely to be killed in accidents than women, as Table 14.11 shows.

There are also innate differences in the health risks of the two sexes. Women but not men suffer the risks of childbirth—severe until modern times, but much less so these days. Men suffer increased risk of heart disease and strokes because of the male hormone testosterone.

14.2.2   Range of Variation of Cultural Differences

In Korea, as in all known human societies, it is a man's world. Worldwide, where one sex is freer than the other to arrange marriages, the groom rather than the bride usually has the freer hand. Men tend to have more occupational choices than women in most societies (although less so in the USSR). If women work for wages, they tend to be paid less than men. Most leaders in the world of politics, business, science, learning, and the arts are men. If access to scarce and valued knowledge differs, again it is usually the men who are the scholars. True, men usually risk their health and their lives in warfare far more than women do. But until a hundred years ago, I suspect, for every man who died on the battlefield, a woman died in childbirth. In traditional civilized societies, women almost always were in the hands of male rulers, male judges, male physicians. Among the richer countries today, the role of women comes far closer to that of men than in most earlier societies.

How often do husbands beat or even murder wives? Or wives, husbands? Of the eighteen small-scale societies on which I could find data in my War, Stress, and Culture sample, fourteen permitted wife beating and only four forbade it. (Among at least one of these, the Luo, husbands have been known to beat their wives to death.) Recent studies by Straus, Gelles, and Steinmetz in certain communities in the United States found that as many wives beat their husbands as husbands, their wives. Likewise when it came to murder.

Rohner's study shows that the influence of culture on aggressive behavior in young children is clearly far stronger than that of genetics. He offers fresh support for the basic theory of all anthropology: the dominance of culture over human behavior. In sex roles as in other things, those walking ape ancestors of ours were selected for survival as animals who were first of all learners.

So, we are all learners today. We can *teach* our girls to be much more aggressive than our boys. We can teach them to be alike. But if we want them both to be aggressive, the evidence here says that we will have to encourage the girls a little more than the boys. If we want them both to be gentle, the evidence here says that we will have to discourage the boys' natural bent a little more than that of the girls. And, in fact, equality seems to be the usual pattern. Among adults, the pattern is dramatically different from that among children. As Table 14.4 shows, in most societies the sexes do *not* differ in aggressiveness. And where they do differ, the women are more aggressive than the men in about as many societies as vice versa.

In most societies, then, within the family and the local community, men and women are taught to conform alike to the local standard of aggressiveness, whether high or low. And they conform after the sex hormones of puberty have done their work. What has happened to the ground male ape aggressiveness? Culture has channeled it all into warfare. The women do much of the actual fighting in few cultures. (Of 46 small-scale societies studied by Zelman, women never took part in warfare at all in 30 of the societies, almost never took part in 4, sometimes took part in 5, and always took part in only 1.)

Perhaps the best-known anthropological study of personality differences between men and women is Margaret Mead's *Sex and Temperament in Three*

TABLE 14.4   Adult Aggression

PROPOSITION: *By and large, the world around, neither sex is more aggressive.*

Culture	Aggression Scores	
	Men	Women
Men more aggressive than women		
Colombians (Mestizos)	11	10
Akwe-Shavante (Brazil)	10	9
Tanala (Madagascar)	9	7
Sudanese Arabs	8	4
Araucanians (Chile)	5	4
Eskimos (Alaska)	5	3
Men and women equally aggressive		
Eskimos (Greenland)	10	10
Indians (Brahmins, the highest ranking caste)	10	10
Tukuna (Brazil)	10	10
Indians (Castes ranking below the two highest)	9	9
Alorese (Indonesia)	9	9
Chiracahua Apache (Southwestern USA)	8	8
Tswana (Botswana)	8	8
Chamorros (Guam)	8	8
Chukchee (Siberia)	8	8
Manus (Admiralty Islands)	8	8
Tepoztecans (Mexico)	8	8
Ilocos (Philippines)	7	7
Kwakiutl (Western Canada)	7	7
Paraguayans	7	7
Siriono (Bolivia)	7	7
Andamanese (Indian Ocean)	6	6
Modern Greeks	6	6
Carriacou (West Indies)	4	4
Japanese	4	4
Fijians	2	2
Women more aggressive than men		
Gusii of Kenya	8	9
Indians (Rajputs, second highest caste)	8	9
Trukese (Micronesia)	8	9
Americans (Anglos of the USA)	5	6
Eastern Timbira (Brazil)	2	4

SOURCES: Rohner (1976: 65).

Primitive Societies; in it she makes the point that sex roles are largely the product of culture. Yet even among her peaceful Arapesh, the men were fierce warriors, however mild they were at home in front of women.

A most interesting experiment was made in the African kingdom of Dahomey. There, special regiments of women soldiers used to fight regularly in wars. The Europeans called them the Amazons. And they are the only well-documented case of professional women warriors known to ethnology. What became of their womanhood? Were they sexually aggressive, as professional male soldiers so often seem to be? Or were they repressed? By law, they were all technically wives of the king. But he had thousands of such wives. He did not have sex with his women warriors. And no one else might do so. These women were supposed to be virgins. And if they were caught cheating, as did happen, they were killed.

So there is reason to suppose that we do inherit some small sex role determinants—but that they are too weak to matter very much. Preeminently men are manly and women are womanly because they have learned to be so. And those patterns of manliness and womanliness have evolved and changed with cultural evolution.

Do women by and large work harder than men? We used to say: "Man's work is from sun to sun, but woman's work is never done." One economist a generation ago made a study of the working hours of French married women with salaried jobs. They averaged a total of more than eighty hours of work a week. As much as a moonlighting American man today working at his two full-time jobs. These days, a large proportion of married women have salaried work outside the home. This is probably considerably higher than the proportion of men who hold down two jobs at once—who moonlight.

In most small-scale societies, women do more work than men. In 39 of the 59 societies studied by Zelman, ethnographers said something about the relative amount of work done by the two sexes. Among these, in seven societies it was about the same. In two societies, men did more work than women. In the remaining thirty, women did more work than men. (A difference that great would turn up through random sampling error in less than one sample in a million.)

Men usually rank higher than women, the world around. They usually have higher status, in other words. But the point is a slippery one. We have two recent holocultural studies on women's status in small-scale societies around the world. Zelman's focused on what she called "political and legal status of women." Whyte's tried to deal with status in general—but interestingly enough, paid hardly any attention to political or legal status. Whyte found no fewer than nine other kinds of status that varied independently of each other (details in the Notes). So it is risky indeed to compare the status of men with that of women in general terms. Nevertheless, it seems clear that considering all ten kinds of status—Zelman's one and Whyte's nine—on the average, by and large, men have higher status than women.

As I said, in every culture, men usually rank higher than woman. True, shrewd and powerful rulers like Catherine of Russia, Elizabeth I of England, and

Empress Wu of the T'ang Dynasty have shown how skillfully women can use rank and power. Even so, in Catherine's Russia, in Elizabeth's England, in Wu's China—as in Golda Meir's Israel recently—most high positions were held by men.

Women in most small-scale societies are legally and politically subservient to men. But in more than a few such societies they are equal. Thus Zelman found women holding equal legal status in 20 out of 51 societies. In 12 out of 53 societies, she found that women joined the men in settling disputes within a society—and in one the women alone were the judges. In 4 out of 57 societies, women played a larger part than men in domestic decision making and in 16 others they played an equal part. However, in only 3 out of 58 societies did they play even an equal part in community decision making.

A like pattern holds good for control of wealth. There are many small-scale societies in which women have equal access to wealth, many others in which men have a marked edge over women, but none in which women have an edge over men.

14.2.3   Evolution of Sex Role Differences

Whyte's broad worldwide comparison of small-scale societies found that as cultural evolution progressed, women tended increasingly to suffer five disabilities. The larger scale the society: (1) the less the domestic authority of its women, (2) the less the independent solidarity among women—that is, the less its women tended to form effective social groups composed exclusively of women, (3) the more its women were hampered by unequal restrictions on sexual relations, (4) the more likely it seemed that its men ritualized their fear of women, and (5) the fewer property rights its women enjoyed.

However, Whyte found that the larger scale the society: (1) the more informal influence on its affairs its women had, and (2) the more women tended to participate jointly with males in social activities.

Small-scale societies usually offer women a smaller sphere of occupational choices than they do men. So M. Naroll reports (see Table 14.5). True, her sample is small, but she chose it randomly and the chance risk of sampling error is less than 2 in 100.

The two great revolutions of prehistoric times had a differing effect on women's role. The development of gardening—of digging-stick farming—did not greatly disturb the traditional allocation of food quest roles. Men still were more likely to hunt large animals, while women still were more likely to gather food— even though the food they gathered was the food they themselves planted. Women still were more likely to do the leather work, the pottery, and the basket making. But with the development of intensive plough farming, the men tended to take over the farm work, the leather work, and the pottery—as we learn from White, Burton, and Brudner. Whether this second revolution also tended to narrow women's range of work role choice is not yet clear. In Naroll's small

TABLE 14.5   Work Role Choices for Men and Women

PROPOSITION: *Women have fewer work role choices than men.*

| Society | Occupations Open to | | | Sign |
	Men Only	Women Only	Both Men and Women	
Callinago (West Indies)	3	1	0	+
Mataco (Argentina)	2	3	1	−
Mosquito (Honduras)	2	1	0	+
Gilyak (Siberia)	2	1	0	+
Southern Ojibwa (Midwestern USA)	1	1	0	0
Azande (The Sudan)	7	1	1	+
Kazak (USSR)	8	2	0	+
Hottentots (Southwest Africa)	3	1	0	+
Amhara (Ethiopia)	11	8	5	+
Aztecs (Mexico)	17	9	2	+
Total	58	28	9	

SOURCES: M. Naroll (n.d.); Harvard University Computation Laboratory (1955).
Chance risk (sign test): .02.
NOTE: In eight societies out of nine, the flipped coin turned up "male"—not likely to happen by chance.

sample, she found no pattern linking that range with level of societal complexity. But we need a larger sample to confirm or correct that finding.

Among large-scale societies, Safilios-Rothschild found that women played a wider part in work outside the home at middle levels of industrial growth than at higher or lower levels. At these middle levels, more college graduates were women than at either lower or higher levels. There, too, more lawyers, dentists, architects, teachers, and physicians were women. Nevertheless, nearly everywhere, that larger part was still less than half; men even at middle levels still dominated most professions. There were some striking exceptions: in the United States and Argentina, nearly all the teachers were women; and women rather than men made up more than half the dentists and physicians in Poland and most of the physicians in Italy.

And whatever may be women's work role, they lose fewer children nowadays. Until the sanitary revolution of the nineteenth century transformed the odds in favor of the child, something like half of the children in human societies around the world never grew up. Most of the victims died in their first year. In such a world, reproduction used to claim most of the energy of most women. If societies were to survive—if the human race were to survive—most women had to be pregnant or tending infants through most of their days of strength. Only through fecundity could there be survival.

Finally, in Zelman's study of women's status and power in sixty societies, she found some tendency for women to have lower status as societies became more complex. Textor found the same tendency in his massive compilation of world correlations. The linkage is not strong or clear, but it does seem to be there.

Cultural evolution has brought about a huge increase in the number of work role choices open to people. Men always have had a wider choice than women—but women's choices, too, have broadened along with men's. When machines are first introduced, women play a wider part in the work scene outside the home than they do later on. And finally, over the whole range of cultural evolution, before the medical revolution, women's status had a slight tendency to fall, not to rise—a tendency that over the last hundred years women have been doing something about.

14.3   STEP 1: CORE VALUES OF SEX ROLES

My core values for men and women are reciprocity, or fair play, and health. It is banal these days to say that women should enjoy equal access to the good things of life with men; that women should not, because they are women, be hindered from their chance to learn and earn and from taking part in public affairs; that men should enjoy the same chance at good health and long life as women.

14.4   STEP 2: SEX ROLE STRESS SCOREBOARDS

Perhaps the most critical measure of sexual inequality is the measure of the ability to read and write. As Table 14.6 shows, nearly everywhere today, fewer women than men can write. In Hong Kong, for example, 81 percent of all illiterates are females. (And, as Table 14.6 shows, the probability that our Hong Kong data lack any meaningful differences from Norway's is only about 3 in 10,000. These are the odds that the difference in reports merely reflects random error by the people making the reports, or that the difference merely reflects chance accidents in the actual arrangements of education in Norway and Hong Kong.)

Fewer women than men have a share in running things. As Table 14.7 shows, in our model country, Norway, only 7 percent of the business and government leaders are women. Nearly everywhere else, at least four-fifths of the leaders are men (more about Norway's women a little later).

As I have already said, men are everywhere paid more than women. As Table 14.8 shows, in our model country, Norway, for example, an average male factory workers earns 1.40 kroners for every kroner an average woman earns.

But statistics show that these male advantages go along with other disadvantages. Women live longer than men. More men than women commit suicide (see Table 14.9). More men than women are murdered (see Table 14.10).

TABLE 14.6   Sex Illiteracy Ratio Scoreboard

Country	Sex Illiteracy Ratio[a]	Chance Risk
Above Indicated Range		
Burma	81	.0056
Hong Kong[c]	81	.0056
Greece[b]	80	.0069
Japan[b]	78	.0106
Cyprus	76	.0161
Bulgaria	76	.0161
Yugoslavia[b]	75	.0198
Cambodia	75	.0198
Romania	74	.0242
Korea (South)	72	.0361
Poland	71	.0438
Spain[b]	70	.0531
Ryukyu Islands	70	.0531
Israel	70	.0531
China (Taiwan)	70	.0531
Sri Lanka	69	.0641
Peru	69	.0641
Thailand	68	.0771
Turkey[b]	67	.0925
Singapore	66	.1105
Barbados	66	.1105
Paraguay	65	.1314
Zambia	64	.1558
Mauritius	64	.1558
Jordan	64	.1558
Portugal[b]	63	.1839
Indonesia	63	.1839
Syria	62	.2162
Italy[b]	62	.2162
Hungary	62	.2162
Guyana	62	.2162
Grenada	62	.2162
Malawi	61	.2529
Gabon	61	.2529
Tunisia	60	.2945
Egypt	60	.2945
Bolivia	60	.2945
Uganda	59	.3413
Trinidad and Tobago	59	.3413
Chad	59	.3413
Mexico	58	.3935
Libya	58	.3935
India	58	.3935
Ecuador	58	.3935
Puerto Rico[c]	57	.4513
El Salvador	57	.4513
Algeria	57	.4513

(continued)

TABLE 14.6 (Continued)

Country	Sex Illiteracy Ratio[a]	Chance Risk
Within Indicated Range		
Venezuela	56	
Nepal	56	
Mozambique	56	
Morocco	56	
Iraq	56	
Guatemala	56	
France[b]	56	
Fiji	56	
Chile	56	
Central African Republic	56	
Senegal	55	
Philippines	55	
Namibia	55	
Iran	55	
Colombia	55	
Brazil	55	
Benin	55	
Bahamas	55	
Sudan	54	
Pakistan	54	
Malta	54	
Liberia	54	
Honduras	54	
Haiti	54	
Botswana	54	
Argentina	54	
Sierra Leone	53	
Niger	53	
Nicaragua	53	
Mali	53	
Guinea-Bissau	53	
Dominican Republic	53	
Belgium[b]	53	
Surinam	52	
Costa Rica	52	
Angola	52	
USA[b]	51	
Switzerland[b]	50	
Sweden[b]	50	
Panama	50	
Norway[b]	50	MODEL COUNTRY
Zimbabwe (Rhodesia)	50	
Uruguay	49	
South Africa	49	
Lesotho	49	
Bahrain	48	
Jamaica	45	

TABLE 14.6 (Continued)

Country	Sex Illiteracy Ratio[a]	Chance Risk
Below Indicated Range		
Cuba	44	.4624
Yemen (Southern)	43	.3859
Kuwait	43	.3859

SOURCE: Boulding et al. (1976: Table 46). Worldwide averages and spreads of 97 countries reporting (lognormal distribution):[d] mean of the natural logarithms: 4.07; median: 56.00; range: 38.00; SD: 0.142; CEV: 3.49%. Worldwide averages and spreads of 14 OECD countries reporting (lognormal distribution): mean of the natural logarithms: 4.10361; median: 59.00; range: 30.00; SD: 0.17394; CEV: 4.24%; skew: 0.33; kurtosis: 0.90.

a. Percentage of illiterates who are female. Sex role stress scoreboard 1.
b. Member of the Organization for Economic Cooperation and Development (OECD).
c. United Nations reporting unit; not an independent nation.
d. See Glossary for meanings of worldwide measures.
SD = standard deviation of natural logarithms.
CEV = coefficient of evolutionary variation.

And of course more men than women die in battle. More men than women die in automobile accidents (see Table 14.11). And in other accidents.

14.5   STEP 3: TESTS OF THEORIES OF SEX ROLE DIFFERENCES

14.5.1   The "Male Supremacist Complex"

Schlegel ends her review of sexual stratification with these words: "The emergence of sexual stratification in any society is multidimensional, and the forms it acquires are the unfolding consequences of many different kinds of forces intermingling over time." In other words, she finds no single cause or simple explanation for the fact that women outside the home usually have lower status, less respect than men. Thus, she agrees with Whyte, who, as I said before, found no fewer than nine different independent ways in which women's status varied; and Zelman studied yet another way.

A recent paper by Divale and Harris offered one theory that has angered many women anthropologists. Divale and Harris speak only of people at lower levels of cultural evolution—only of people organized into small bands or simple villages—not about people organized into larger states. They remind us that the ways of life of such people are rigged for men against women. As I said earlier, marriage arrangements usually favor men (see Table 14.12). Women usually leave their parents' home band or village when they marry; that is, residence rules are usually patrilocal or avunculocal, and put the woman at a disadvantage in her marriage. She lives among strangers; her husband lives among his kin. In any dispute, they are likely to back him against her. Polygyny among these people is far more common than monogamy. And as we shall see, women

TABLE 14.7   Sex Managerial Ratio Scoreboard

Country	Sex Managerial Ratio[a]	Chance Risk
Above Indicated Range		
Switzerland[b]	48	.0044
Grenada	43	.0073
Austria[b]	28	.0405
Poland	27	.0460
Guatemala	27	.0460
Malta	21	.1044
France[b]	21	.1044
Germany (West)[b]	20	.1207
Jamaica	18	.1627
USA[b]	17	.1897
Trinidad and Tobago	17	.1897
Hungary	16	.2217
Guyana	16	.2217
Puerto Rico[c]	15	.2599
Colombia	15	.2599
Luxembourg[b]	14	.3056
Denmark[b]	14	.3056
Canada[b]	14	.3056
Belgium[b]	14	.3056
Bahamas	14	.3056
Panama	12	.4256
Nicaragua	12	.4256
New Zealand	12	.4256
Mexico	12	.4256
Dominican Republic	12	.4256
Cambodia	12	.4256
Australia	12	.4256
Within Indicated Range		
Zambia	11	
Peru	11	
Hong Kong[c]	11	
Honduras	11	
Costa Rica	11	
Barbados	11	
Thailand	10	
Sweden[b]	10	
Indonesia	10	
Yugoslavia[b]	9	
South Africa	9	
Sierra Leone	9	
Namibia	9	
Liberia	9	
Greece[b]	9	
El Salvador	9	
Chile	9	
Swaziland	8	

TABLE 14.7 (Continued)

Country	Sex Managerial Ratio[a]	Chance Risk
Within Indicated Range		
United Kingdom[b]	7	
Norway[b]	7	MODEL COUNTRY
Nigeria	7	
Ecuador	7	
Bahrain	7	
Argentina	7	
Venezuela	6	
Portugal[b]	6	
Paraguay	6	
Ireland[b]	6	
Algeria	6	
Zimbabwe (Rhodesia)	5	
Uruguay	5	
Tanzania	5	
Surinam	5	
Nauru	5	
Japan[b]	5	
Iceland[b]	5	
Czechoslovakia	5	
Cyprus	5	
Cuba	5	
Botswana	5	
Angola	5	
Below Indicated Range		
Spain[b]	4	.4082
Singapore	4	.4082
Netherlands[b]	4	.4082
Mauritius	4	.4082
Egypt	4	.4082
Tunisia	3	.2104
Sri Lanka	3	.2104
Ryukyu Islands	3	.2104
Morocco	3	.2104
Iran	3	.2104
India	3	.2104
Ghana	3	.2104
Malaysia (Malaya)	2	.0641
Korea (South)	2	.0641
Pakistan	1	.0040
Libya	1	.0040
Kuwait	1	.0040
Jordan	1	.0040

SOURCE: Boulding et al. (1976: Table 29). Worldwide averages and spreads of 86 countries reporting (lognormal distribution):[d] mean of the natural logarithms: 2.02; median: 9.00; range: 47.00; SD: 0.794; CEV: 39.30%. Worldwide averages and spreads of 20 OECD countries reporting (lognormal distribution): mean of the natural logarithms: 2.33985; median: 9.50; range: 44.00; SD: 0.67656; CEV: 28.91%; skew: 0.43; kurtosis: 0.85.

(notes continued)

usually dislike polygyny. If a man has several wives, they must compete for his favor and attention. He can play one off against the other. Bride price and bride service are common practices that also tend to work against women, in favor of men. True, with his bride price, a man buys a wife, not a slave. She can leave him if she wants to. But often she has nowhere else to go. Often her own people would not welcome her back because then they might have to refund the bride price—a price they may already have spent to buy a wife for her brother. There are, of course, many societies in which neither dowry nor bride price is paid. In these, bride and groom share equally in costs and benefits. But among the simpler societies looked at by Divale and Harris, bride price is the most common mode.

Divale and Harris also argue that the division of labor between the sexes tends to give the drudge work to women, the interesting work to men. In Table 14.2, of the ten kinds of work usually done by men, I would class clearing farm land and herding as drudge work, and the other eight as more interesting: metal work, wood work, hunting, weapon making, boat building, making musical instruments, fishing, and house building. Of the nine kinds of work more often done by women, I would class three as drudge work: carrying burdens, carrying water, and grinding grain; and the other six kinds as more interesting: leather work, tending and harvesting crops, weaving, pottery, tailoring, and cooking. All fourteen kinds of work I class as more interesting are hobbies in our society; none of the five kinds I class as drudge work is.

Yet, we must be careful. We need to look at the social context of each task in each society to see if it is made interesting for the people by embedding it in a ceremony of social pleasures. Consider the task of fetching water—traditionally given to the daughters of the family. Carrying the water itself is no fun. But how about the half hour spent chatting around the well with the other girls of the village?

Again, Divale and Harris remind us that almost everywhere—including in matrilineal societies—the men manage public affairs. They usually control the distribution of power and wealth in the society outside the family. Friedl makes this point in *Women and Men: An Anthropologist's View.* More on that later.

Divale and Harris note, too, that in myth and ritual, men have an edge over women. Though goddesses are many, there are even more gods. Though

TABLE 14.8   Sex Earnings Ratio Scoreboard

Country	Sex Earnings Ratio[a]	Chance Risk
Above Indicated Range		
USA[b]	1.73	.1052
Ireland[b]	1.66	.1934
Luxembourg[b]	1.64	.2274
Within Indicated Range		
United Kingdom[b]	1.5	
Egypt	1.48	
Switzerland[b]	1.47	
Greece[b]	1.44	
Belgium[b]	1.405	
Norway[b]	1.403	MODEL COUNTRY
Germany (West)[b]	1.39	
Finland	1.38	
Iceland[b]	1.32	
Below Indicated Range		
Vietnam	1.27	.4412
Netherlands[b]	1.26	.4058
Denmark[b]	1.186	.1938
Sweden[b]	1.178	.1765
France[b]	1.15	.1241
Australia	1.09	.0510

SOURCE: United Nations International Labor Organization (1972); Martin and Voorhies (1975: 397) from U.S. Census data on "operatives." Worldwide averages and spreads of 18 countries reporting (lognormal distribution):[c] mean of the natural logarithms: 0.32; median: 1.40; range; 0.64; SD: 0.130; CEV: 40.79%. Worldwide averages and spreads of 14 OECD countries reporting (lognormal distribution): mean of the natural logarithms: 0.33542; median: 1.40; range: 0.58; SD: 0.12932; CEV: 38.56%; skew: 0.03; kurtosis: 0.80.

a. Ratio of men's wages to women's wages. Sex role stress scoreboard 3.
b. Member of the Organization for Economic Cooperation and Development (OECD).
c. See Glossary for meanings of worldwide measures.
SD = standard deviation of natural logarithms.
CEV = coefficient of evolutionary variation.

heroines are many, there are even more heroes. Menstrual blood is often shunned. Semen is not. Witches are more widely feared than warlocks. Men's rituals threaten women more often than women's rituals threaten men.

The world around, too, Simmons found that baby boys are preferred to baby girls—two to one—in the small-scale societies he studied. And this bias has resulted in many girl babies being killed. Divale reviewed censuses of small-scale societies while they still were fighting wars and free of foreign influence; among the children under fourteen years of age, he counted 128 boys for every 100 girls.

TABLE 14.9   Sex Suicide Ratio Scoreboard

Country	Sex Suicide Ratio[a]	Chance Risk
Above Extreme Range		
Chile	5.2	.0000
Poland	4.6	.0009
Above Indicated Range		
Puerto Rico[c]	4.3	.0043
Finland	3.9	.0265
Iceland[b]	3.6	.0812
Costa Rica	3.3	.2047
Within Indicated Range		
USA[b]	2.7	
France[b]	2.7	
Czechoslovakia	2.7	
Sweden[b]	2.6	
Switzerland[b]	2.5	
Norway[b]	2.5	MODEL COUNTRY
Ireland[b]	2.5	
Hungary	2.5	
Canada[b]	2.5	
Luxembourg[b]	2.4	
Peru	2.3	
Italy[b]	2.3	
Austria[b]	2.3	
Bulgaria	2.3	
Belgium[b]	2.2	
Australia	2.1	
Below Indicated Range		
Trinidad and Tobago	2	.4279
New Zealand	2	.4279
Germany (West)[b]	1.9	.3415
Denmark[b]	1.7	.2047
Scotland[bc]	1.5	.1129
Netherlands[b]	1.5	.1129
England and Wales[bc]	1.5	.1129
Japan[b]	1.4	.0812
Hong Kong[c]	1.3	.0571
Israel	1.2	.0393
Northern Ireland[bc]	.9	.0112

SOURCE: Calculated by author from United Nations Department of Economic and Social Affairs (1975: Table 28, Part B). Worldwide averages and spreads of 33 countries reporting (normal distribution):[d] mean: 2.45; median: 2.30; range: 4.30; SD: 0.978; CEV: 39.90%. Worldwide averages and spreads of 19 OECD countries reporting (normal distribution): mean: 2.16842; median: 2.30; range: 2.70; SD: 0.63074; CEV: 29.09%; skew: −0.01; kurtosis: −0.00.

a. Ratio of male deaths from suicide to female deaths from suicide. Sex role stress scoreboard 4.
b. Member of the Organization for Economic Cooperation and Development (OECD).
c. United Nations reporting unit; not an independent nation.
d. See Glossary for meanings of worldwide measures.

SD = standard deviation.
CEV = coefficient of evolutionary variation.

TABLE 14.10 Sex Homicide Ratio Scoreboard

Country	Sex Homicide Ratio[a]	Chance Risk
Above Extreme Range		
Northern Ireland[bc]	9	.0010
Above Indicated Range		
Puerto Rico[c]	5.5	.0274
Chile	4.5	.0769
USA[b]	3.3	.2747
Hong Kong[c]	3.3	.2747
Finland	3.3	.2747
Poland	3.1	.3391
Costa Rica	3.1	.3391
Bulgaria	2.8	.4630
Within Indicated Range		
Trinidad and Tobago	2.6	
Peru	2.6	
Italy[b]	2.6	
Israel	2.6	
Sweden[b]	2.4	
Netherlands[b]	2.4	
New Zealand	2.1	
Luxembourg[b]	2.1	
Norway[b]	2	MODEL COUNTRY
Ireland[b]	2	
Germany (West)[b]	2	
Scotland[bc]	1.9	
Czechoslovakia	1.9	
Japan[b]	1.8	
Switzerland[b]	1.7	
Australia	1.7	
Canada[b]	1.6	
Austria[b]	1.6	
Belgium[b]	1.5	
Below Indicated Range		
Iceland[b]	1.3	.3474
France[b]	1.3	.3474
England and Wales[bc]	1.3	.3474
Hungary	1.1	.1922
Denmark[b]	1.1	.1922

SOURCE: United Nations Department of Economic and Social Affairs (1975: Table 28, Part B). Worldwide averages and spreads of 33 countries reporting (lognormal distribution):[d] mean of the natural logarithms: 0.81; median: 2.10; range: 7.90; SD: 0.455; CEV: 56.30%. Worldwide averages and spreads of 19 OECD countries reporting (lognormal distribution): mean of the natural logarithms: 0.67932; median: 1.90; range: 7.90; SD: 0.45848; CEV: 67.49%; skew: 1.90; kurtosis: 0.66.

(notes continued)

TABLE 14.10 NOTES (continued):

a. Ratio of male deaths from murder or war to female deaths from murder or war. Sex role stress scoreboard 5.
b. Member of the Organization for Economic Cooperation and Development (OECD).
c. United Nations reporting unit; not an independent nation.
d. See Glossary for meanings of worldwide measures.
SD = standard deviation of natural logarithms.
CEV = coefficient of evolutionary variation.

He concludes that the missing girls must either have been killed at birth or let die through neglect.

To Divale and Harris, these facts all fit into a single pattern. They explain them all through one single cause—war. They suggest that the male supremacist complex makes women the reward for military bravery. Men are trained to be warriors, and women are trained to docile submission, so they can be awarded as prizes to the war heroes of their bands or villages. However, they offer no evidence on this key point.

In my studies of warfare, I did not actually code separately for access to women as a reward for successful warriors. My hunch is that, while successful warriors do indeed have an advantage here, it is more often through the glamour of their prestige than through their ability to get a woman against her will. Another model that is not unusual, I think, is that of a young man who cannot marry at all until he has proved himself in battle—maybe by bringing home an enemy head.

So while sex may often encourage warriors in small-scale societies, I am not persuaded that it usually does so in the way that Divale and Harris describe. I suspect that there is indeed a link between the importance of warfare in a society and the status of women there; it is not the link that Divale and Harris propose, but another link—that of occupational specialization. The key point about warriors, I suggest, is not that women become their booty—although sometimes no doubt they do. The key point is that warriors are almost always men. In more than 85 percent of all societies. Among more than 90 percent of warriors. So let us turn again to work roles.

14.5.2   Work Roles

Sanday, in a study of only twelve societies, hinted that maybe sex roles were fixed by work shared between the sexes, that women ranked highest when men shared women's work and women shared men's work. Zelman checked Sanday's theory. Table 14.13 spells out the correlations and chance risk levels from Zelman's data. There we see no support at all for Sanday's thesis that equality of work sharing is the main determinant of women's status. On the contrary, it does not seem to matter at all.

TABLE 14.11   Sex Accident Ratio Scoreboard

Country	Sex Accident Ratio[a]	Chance Risk
Above Extreme Range		
Chile	4.8	.0007
Trinidad and Tobago	4.6	.0023
Above Indicated Range		
Costa Rica	4.5	.0041
Puerto Rico[c]	4.3	.0112
Italy[b]	3.7	.1280
Bulgaria	3.7	.1280
Peru	3.6	.1761
Luxembourg[b]	3.4	.3103
Japan[b]	3.4	.3103
Hungary	3.4	.3103
Czechoslovakia	3.3	.3978
Ireland[b]	3.2	.4988
Within Indicated Range		
Austria[b]	3.1	
Switzerland[b]	3	
Poland	2.9	
Northern Ireland[bc]	2.9	
Netherlands[b]	2.9	
Norway[b]	2.8	MODEL COUNTRY
Germany (West)[b]	2.8	
Australia	2.8	
USA[b]	2.7	
Finland	2.7	
Scotland[bc]	2.6	
Canada[b]	2.6	
Belgium[b]	2.6	
Below Indicated Range		
Sweden[b]	2.4	.4988
New Zealand	2.3	.3978
Denmark[b]	2.3	.3978
England and Wales[bc]	2.2	.3103
Israel	2.1	.2365
Hong Kong[c]	2	.1761
Below Extreme Range		
Iceland[b]	1	.0023

SOURCE: Calculated by author from United Nations Department of Economic and Social Affairs (1975: Table 28, Part B). Worldwide averages and spreads of 32 countries reporting (normal distribution):[d] mean: 3.02; median: 2.90; range: 3.80; SD: 0.809; CEV: 26.80%. Worldwide averages and spreads of 18 OECD countries reporting (normal distribution): mean: 2.75556; median: 2.80 range: 2.70; SD: 0.59133; CEV: 21.46%; skew: −1.23; kurtosis: −0.00.

a. Ratio of male deaths in motor vehicle accidents to female deaths in motor vehicle accidents. Sex role stress scoreboard 6.
b. Member of the Organization for Economic Cooperation and Development (OECD).
c. United Nations reporting unit; not an independent nation.
d. See Glossary for meanings of worldwide measures.

SD = standard deviation.
CEV = coefficient of evolutionary variation.

TABLE 14.12   Marriage Arrangements

PROPOSITION: *Marriage arrangements in small-scale societies usually favor men.*

Marriage Arrangement	Societies with Marriage Arrangements Favoring Men	Societies without Marriage Arrangements Favoring Men	Total Number of Societies
Bride price or bride service is usual.[a]	145	110	255
Polygyny is usual.[a]	201	56	257
Polyandry is very rare.[b]	256	1	257
Patrilocality or avunculocality is usual.[a]	169	88	257

SOURCE: Coult and Habenstein (1965: 389, 420, 434).
a. Arrangement favors men.
b. Arrangement favors women.
NOTE: See Notes to Section 14.5.1.

TABLE 14.13   Work Role Sharing and Women's Status

PROPOSITION: *Only the sharing of power roles among men and women is linked with women's status.*

	Correlation with Political and Legal Status of Women	Chance Risk
Nonpower Roles		
Mother helps educate sons	.01	.50
Father helps with baby care	−.06	.63
Father helps care for young children	−.09	.73
Father helps educate daughters	−.19	.88
Men and women share in food getting	−.02	.90
Power Roles		
Value of women compared to men	.41	.001
Women share in settling disputes within the community	.38	.004
Women take part in community decision making	.49	.00007
Women may own land or large animals	.51	.00002

SOURCE: Computed by Horan from Zelman (1974: 221-241).

Rather, in small-scale societies around the world there seem to be four important points linked to women's political and legal status—STATUS:

(1) The general esteem in which women are held—ESTEEM.
(2) The right of women to own land (or in pastoral societies, large animals)—OWNERSHIP.

(3) The right of women to take part in community decision making—GOVERNMENT.

(4) The right of women to take part in settling or judging disputes within the community—JUDGING.

These four other traits are linked not only to women's political and legal status, but to some extent, with each other as well. Simon's method of correlation analysis helps to sort out the causal directions among this web of linkages. His method shows that one such pattern makes the most sense:

(1) OWNERSHIP causes STATUS; STATUS causes GOVERNMENT. If women have the right to own important property, that right tends to lead to high political and legal status for them. And high political and legal status in turn tends to lead to a role for women in community decision making.

(2) ESTEEM and OWNERSHIP both cause STATUS. Not only does the right to own important property tend to lead to high political and legal status for women, but the enjoyment of high general esteem for women does so as well. But, you might ask, might we not as plausibly suppose it the other way around? Would we not expect a high political and legal status to lead not only to property rights but also to build up general esteem? Logically, the answer is yes. But Simon's method of analysis says no. What I have said makes better sense than the other way around because of one simple mathematical fact. STATUS is highly correlated with both ESTEEM and OWNERSHIP. But these two traits are not correlated with each other. It is that pattern of correlations which points to what I have said rather than the other way around.

(3) ESTEEM causes GOVERNMENT; GOVERNMENT causes JUDGING. If women enjoy a high general esteem, that fact tends to give them a part in community decision making; and such a part in general decision making tends in turn to give them a part in settling of disputes.

(4) ESTEEM and OWNERSHIP both cause GOVERNMENT. Women are more likely to play a part in community decision making if they not only enjoy high general esteem, but also have important property rights.

Put these all together, then, and it leads us to focus on property rights and general esteem as leading determinants of the political and legal status of women in small-scale societies. The relative importance of each is given by this formula:

$$\text{STATUS} = .69 + 0.42 \ \text{ESTEEM} + 0.23 \ \text{OWNERSHIP}$$

This formula is a linear regression equation. It comes from Zelman's work on these three traits. It tells us how to predict Zelman's STATUS score from her ESTEEM score and her OWNERSHIP score. It says: (a) multiply Zelman's ESTEEM score by 0.42, (b) multiply Zelman's OWNERSHIP score by 0.23, and (c) add these two and also add 0.69. The total should give you Zelman's STATUS score.

Should give you, I say. Not necessarily *will* give you. Because ESTEEM and OWNERSHIP together only explain 41 percent of that variance in STATUS. There are other important factors that Zelman did not look at. And there is a certain amount of error in all such data as these.

These findings seem to me to be further supported by the history of the women's rights movement in the 1800s. Women demanded property rights; they demanded education; they demanded job access; and they demanded the vote. Raising their level of education raised their general value to society. So did broadening their job access. Success in these fields came first. The vote came after.

In the past, of course, in urban societies, boys used to be offered a far better formal education than girls. And this difference may well have arisen because of the general pattern of division of labor between men and women.

D'Andrade has pointed out that men have tended more to do work involving danger and distance—work that took people away from home (and children)—work that often killed the worker. This finding is supported by the study of work roles by White, Burton, and Brudner. Such work may be more interesting. And it may be more exciting. But where infants and children often die and mothers struggle to raise a family, it confers a survival advantage on a culture if men do the distant and dangerous things. For *culture patterns* are more likely to survive if they provide effectively for a system of raising enough children to keep up the population of the culture bearers.

Clark has evidence supporting the views of many archeologists that the cultural evolution process is a snowball, a positive feedback system. Among the elements in the snowball are military power, political power, and wealth concentration. Men have an edge on these already when the process begins, because they are the warriors. The snowballing process of the positive feedback model of cultural evolution would tend to strengthen their holds on military power, political power, and wealth. And *that* would tend to heighten the division of labor between the sexes—with the men keeping these crucial roles in their own hands.

This model of the processes of cultural evolution is supported by Zelman's smallest space analysis. She looked at 35 traits; these measured cultural evolution, warfare, women's status, division of labor, and sex rituals. In such an analysis, each trait is placed in a cube according to its relationships to the other traits. That is to say, a three dimensional graph is drawn by the Goodman-Lingoe method. The pattern of clustering then tells us what group of traits goes together, and what group of traits lies far apart. In that analysis, women's status and women's esteem lie at the opposite end of the cube from organization of warfare. But organization of warfare clusters together with measures of cultural evolution.

We see this pattern of negative correlation in detail in Table 14.14. By and large, the higher in esteem people hold warfare, the lower in esteem they hold women. So more than half of the thirty societies that hold women in low esteem hold warfare in higher esteem. But of five societies that hold women in high esteem, only one (20 percent) holds warfare in higher esteem. However, Whyte found that the more warlike the society, the greater women's domestic

TABLE 14.14   Warfare and Women

PROPOSITION: *The higher the esteem for warfare, the lower the esteem for women.*

Societies that hold women in . . .	Hold Warfare in Lowest Esteem	Hold Warfare in Low Esteem	Hold Warfare in Moderate Esteem	Hold Warfare in Rather High Esteem	Hold Warfare in Highest Esteem
Low Esteem (30)	Polar Eskimo (Greenland) Tikopia (Western Polynesia) (2)	Lau (Fiji Islands) Papago (Arizona) Thonga (Mozambique) (3)	Ganda (Uganda) Inca (Peru) Marquesans (Polynesia) Monguor (China) Murngin (Australia) Natchez (Southern USA) Nyakyusa (Tanzania) Yakut (Siberia) Yoruba (Nigeria) (9)	Aleuts (Alaska) Fang (Cameroon) Fox (North Central USA) Kiwai (New Guinea) Micmac (Canadian Maritimes) Nambicuara (Brazil) Rwala (Syria) Somali (Somalia and Ethiopia) Thompson (British Columbia) Tlingit (Alaska) Trukese (Micronesia) Waropen (New Guinea) (12)	Coorg (India) Crow (Montana) Winnebago (Central USA) Yanomamo (Brazil) (4)
Moderate Esteem (9)	Dorobo (Kenya) Warao (Venezuela) (2)	Kapauku (New Guinea) Navaho (Southwestern USA) Tallensi (Ghana) (3)	Kachin (Burma) (1)	Burosho (India) Iban (Borneo) Jivaro (Ecuador) (3)	
High Esteem (5)	Semang (Malaya) Yahgan (Tierra del Fuego) (2)	Siriono (Bolivia) (1)	Ifugao (Philippines) (1)	Nuer (The Sudan) (1)	

SOURCE: Computed by Horan from Zelman (1974: 221-241).
Correlation level: r = −.33.
Chance risk: p = .007.
N = 44.

authority—their authority within the household. So, partly we see a weakening of women's status in societies like those of medieval Europe or ancient Rome or Sparta, in which war was the dominant concern of society. Such warlike societies produced a trained, organized, and disciplined band of warriors who fought to gain and hold power at home and abroad. Against such men, women could hope to have a say only by the traditional stereotypic women's ways of soft and gentle insinuation and manipulation and, it may be, pillow talk. But in such societies, warriors were usually away from home and so the women usually ran things at home as her lord and master's chatelaine. These results from worldwide studies of small-scale societies, then, when applied to the warlike scene of medieval and modern Europe—where high rank as well as wealth and power traditionally went to a warrior nobility—should produce just such a male dominance over submissive females as, in fact, we found in the Western world in the 1700s.

But that pattern was shattered in the West by the women's rights movement. To a woman of the 1700s, the remaining disabilities of Western women today—galling though they are—would seem mild. Of these, perhaps the most critical is the attainment of equal access to jobs and equal pay for equal work. For today's woman seems happiest when she can combine marriage with work outside the home.

14.5.3   Love and Marriage

For a traditional woman whose livelihood and career is chiefly that of wife and mother, marriage is the most important event in her life. For woman even more than for man, the right marriage often means a good life, the wrong marriage a hard one. Finding the right man and marrying him was long the chief hope and concern of most young women. Among the 54 societies in the War, Stress, and Culture Sample, 34 left the arrangement of marriages entirely to the couples themselves. Twenty others left these arrangements largely or entirely to other people. Where marriages are arranged by people other than the bridal couple themselves, suicide rates evidently are higher. No proper analysis of this linkage has yet been made. But the young Korean wives who drown themselves to escape an unhappy, arranged marriage have all too many counterparts in other cultures. Pokot girls hang themselves on village trees to protest the grooms their parents choose for them. Jivaro wives often find suicide the easiest way out of their marriages. More study is needed, but I suspect that the world around, where parents arrange marriages, daughters especially are more likely in consequence to kill themselves. No doubt parents and marriage brokers know the ways of the world better than inexperienced young men and women do. But presumably they are not nearly so motivated to choose well for the bride and groom. Arranged marriages often are arranged in the interests of the parents rather than of the bridal couple. And finally, each young woman is the world's leading expert on the kind of man *she* likes, the kind she feels comfortable with.

What accounts for the variation in marriage arrangement customs? Rosenblatt found that free marriage choice most commonly occurs in societies with neolocal residence. Where a bridal couple establish their own household, their parents are less closely affected by the marriage than if the bride is to live with the groom's family, or the groom with the bride's. Further, Rosenblatt found romantic love marriages more common in societies in which babies are weaned suddenly and painfully than in societies in which babies are weaned slowly and gently. He thinks this association results from a greater concern with affection among adults who have been suddenly and painfully deprived of the comforts of nursing as babies. Thus, paradoxically, painful weaning of babies may lead to greater freedom in marriage arrangements.

We have seen that the extended family household system is good for young mothers and small children—by providing the mother with child care help and letting her get away for a rest. But now we see that this same system is hard on these same women as wives—especially as young brides. So here we have a tradeoff problem. What is the best arrangement? No one has yet tried to find an answer.

14.5.4   Polygamy

"Man's love is of man's life a thing apart; 'Tis woman's whole existence." And so it usually was, in the England that Lord Byron knew. In those days, a European woman's usual place was, of course, in the home. Her usual occupation was housewife. Her husband was not only her lover; he was usually her employer and her political leader. To a European woman, the thought of sharing her husband with another woman was disgusting. European law and religion demanded monogamy; if a man kept a mistress, he was quiet about it.

Yet elsewhere, especially in the Moslem world and throughout Africa—but in many other parts of the world as well—men have been allowed to take more than one wife. Where polygamy (many spouses) occurs, it almost always takes the form of polygyny (many wives). The equally logical polyandry (many husbands) is rare; even rarer is group marriage, where more than one husband is simultaneously married to more than one wife.

Polygyny is often seen by Europeans as humiliating to women. Some participants disagree. Many co-wives, we are told, become good friends. Polygyny makes postpartum sex taboos easier; these in turn may somewhat ease the burden of childbearing (and perhaps also of infanticide) on women. Sets of co-wives with their children as half-brothers and half-sisters—polygynous joint families—form households in which babies are more indulged than in nuclear family households. Finally, co-wives can form a kind of labor union local;

when they band together in anger against their man, he must be a strong willed man indeed to stare them down.

However, polygyny seems to work better when co-wives do not share the same dwelling. From society to society, around the world, LeVine noticed that the nearer co-wives live to each other, the more concern there seems to be with witchcraft. He noticed this link first among three societies in western Kenya, and then tested the general theory worldwide.

In many societies, a man is encouraged to take two sisters as co-wives. Such a marriage works more smoothly than if he takes two women who are strangers. The sisters are used to each other and used to living together.

So there are pros and cons. To evaluate polygyny from the woman's point of view we want to know the relationship between polygyny and female suicide— between polygyny and wife beating—between polygyny and divorce. These are questions no anthropologists have yet studied. But Textor found in his worldwide survey that women have a better chance of high status in monogamy than in polygyny. And others have found a clear link between warfare, sex ratio, and polygyny. As Table 14.15 shows, the more men that are killed in battle, the more common is polygyny.

Polygyny is said to flourish most at middle levels of cultural evolution. It is said to be less important among the simpler cultures and among the more complex ones than it is among the middling ones. Why this should be so we do not know. But I suspect that some of the puzzle may be solved if we look more at what people actually do than at what they say. In more complex societies, including our own, men often take second wives—but do not call them that, nor do these wives have any public standing. They are called—or used to be called— mistresses. But if a man keeps a woman permanently, and supports her, then to some anthropologists that is a marriage. And a society in which that sort of thing is a common custom is a polygynous society. If the women keep lovers too, and support them, then it is a polyandrous society. But our tables do not count types of marriages that way.

Finally, there is a strong piece of evidence about the deep-down feeling of women toward polygyny. That evidence fits better with European notions than with Moslem or African ones. It begins to look as though women, when completely free, would exert their influence against polygyny—and toward polyandry. The evidence comes from a study by Schlegel. I now turn to that study.

14.5.5   Focus on Male Authority

Schlegel studied how life in a matrilineal extended family worked out for Hopi women. She analyzed how men manage and control their womenfolk in matrilineal societies. She knew to begin with, of course, that in these as in other societies, it was still a man's world. But she found important variations among matrilineal societies. She focused her attention on the structure of authority

TABLE 14.15   Warfare and Polygyny

PROPOSITION: *The more men killed in battle, the more likely is polygyny.*

	Polygyny Present	Polygyny Absent
Many Men Killed	Aleut (Alaska) Aranda (Australia) Bellacoola (Western Canada) Goajiro (Colombia) Ila (Zambia) Lau (Fiji) Maori (New Zealand) Mapuche (Chile) Mende (Sierra Leone) Murngin (Australia) Nuer (The Sudan) Nupe (Nigeria) Rundi (Ruanda-Urundi) Rwala (Syria) Shilluk (The Sudan) Tiv (Nigeria) Tupinamba (Brazil) Yurok (California) Zuñi (New Mexico) (19)	Delaware (Eastern USA) Samoans (Western Polynesia) Tlingit (Alaska) (3)
Few Men Killed	Chukchee (Siberia) Ngonde (Tanzania) Papago (Arizona) Tallensi (Ghana) Tiwi (Australia) Yokuts (California) (6)	Alorese (Indonesia) Aymara (Bolivia) Callinago (West Indies) Cayapa (Ecuador) Creek (Southeastern USA) Havasupai (Arizona) Ifaluk (Micronesia) Ifugao (Philippines) Khasi (Assam) Lapps (Scandinavia) Lepcha (Sikkim) Marquesans (Polynesia) Majuro (Micronesia) Pekangekum (Ontario) Pukapukans (Polynesia) Tapirape (Brazil) Toda (South India) Trobrianders (Melanesia) Yahgan (Tierra del Fuego) Yao (China) (20)

SOURCES: Ember et al. (1974: 203, 197-206); Osmond (1964: 163); Heath (1958); Sheils (1971).
Corelation level: r = .63.
Chance risk: p = .005.
N = 48.

TABLE 14.16   Husbands against Brothers

PROPOSITION: *In matrilineal societies, women are freest when they can play off husband against brother.*

Women's Problem	Correlation with "Neither-Dominant"	Chance Risk
(1) Wife must defer to husband	−.45	.001
(2) Wife must defer to brother	−.52	.001
(3) Husband must pay bride wealth	−.25	.05
(4) Husband may beat wife severely or publicly humiliate her or allow his friends to beat or rape her	−.49	.001
(5) Brother may threaten or punish his adult, married sister	−.43	.03
(6) Woman has at least some voice in property control	.55	.001
(7) Polygyny practiced	−.38	.025
(8) Polyandry practiced	.24	.06

SOURCE: Schlegel (1972: 59-74).

within housholds. In some matrilineal societies, the husbands were the masters. In others, it was the women's brothers. But in a third type, *neither* was in clear control: husbands had some voice; brothers had some voice. This situation—present, for example, among the Hopi—gives the women of the family their chance to play off husbands against brothers. The goal of the women is not to control the household, but merely to gain autonomy for themselves. For example, among 23 matrilineal societies in which husbands dominated the household, in 19—or 83 percent—the wife had to show special deference to her husband. Among 16 other matrilineal societies, in which the *brothers* dominated the household, in 11—or 69 percent—the woman still had to treat her husband with special deference. But among the 12 matrilineal societies in which neither husband nor brother dominated the household, women treated their husbands with special deference in only one. As line 1 of Table 14.16 shows, the correlation between "Neither-Dominant" and wife deference is −.45; that great a difference would occur by chance less than once in a thousand tries. The wife gets the more favorable treatment in "Neither-Dominant" matrilineal societies right down the table.

Notice especially lines 7 and 8. "Neither-Dominant" societies are less likely to have polygyny and more likely to have polyandry. I assume, of course, that adult women by and large are the best judges of what marriage arrangements are good for themselves. Schlegel thus finds that polygyny clearly tends to be bad for women; polyandry (less clearly) tends to be good.

14.5.6   Spouse Battering

I have already spoken of the studies by Straus, Gelles, Steinmetz, and by others, which indicate that in the United States, husband beating is as common as wife beating—husband murder as wife murder. I know of no comparable worldwide study.

But there is a fascinating fragment from a worldwide study by the Whitings. They studied 55 societies. They were interested in the relationship between physical room arrangements within households on the one hand, and warmth of relations between husband and wife on the other. They found no link between room arrangement and wife beating. Wife beating, they say,

> is associated rather with independent versus extended households. Wife beating tends not to occur in the latter household type, which apparently means that there is safety in numbers. Patricia Draper [1975] has presented evidence corroborating this in her discussion of the frequency of wife beating among the !Kung Bushmen when they move out of their closely spaced camp grounds and settle in nuclear households near Herero villages.

14.6   STEP 4: FURTHER TESTS OF SEX ROLE DIFFERENCES

Our scoreboards show two things plainly. First, that women outside the home have but a small share of power and dignity. It is still largely a man's world there. Second, that women live longer than men. Our scoreboards, however, measure chiefly the richer countries of the West. As usual, we need better data from more countries.

We would also like to have good measures of how women and men fare within the family. What about wife beating? Husband beating? Men are generally stronger than women by nature, of course, and are more likely to be trained as fighters. A wife cannot often put up a fight if her husband beats her. It seems that most do not even try. How many wives are beaten and battered? Most do not complain to the police. So the best way to find out might be through victimization studies, through sample surveys in which people are asked in confidence if they have been victims of crimes. But we do not know how candid women would be in such matters to strange interviewers. A better indication of the extent of wife beating might be the rate at which wives and husbands kill one another—at least among those killings known to the police.

The cultural evolution of sex roles remains a central problem of moral theory. Why are men usually in charge of things? If we seek to understand the past, I think a main line of research ought to study the part women have played—or have not played—in war and in politics. Why have women not done more? Is it indeed because in the past the dominant role of men in warfare has enabled them to seize and hold dominance in politics? And despite Dahomey's Amazons, is there indeed a genetic bias giving men a greater taste for warfare as well as an edge on physical strength?

We should follow up the work set forth in Table 14.14. Here we find a link between women's esteem and women's control of wealth on the one hand with warfare on the other. This table, based on Zelman's data, needs to be checked out on a new sample, with attention to quality control and Galton's Problem; even more important, we need to see if changes in the role of warfare lead to corresponding changes in women's status. Consider societies like Sweden, Switzerland, and Iceland, which have in the past been warlike and then become peaceful. What happened to the esteem in which women were held *after* such a change?

What about women soldiers in our own day? We must look carefully at their branch of service in a modern army. To put a woman into the army does not itself make a fighter of her. It is much more likely to make her a clerk or a telephone operator. But the Russian army in World War I had women in the infantry as fighting foot soldiers. Both the British and the Germans used women to serve anti-aircraft artillery in World War II. Were such women esteemed more highly than other women soldiers?

Such studies of women at war might help us to see why men have tended to control politics in the past. But however it may have been in the past, I suggest that the key to understanding the future lies more in the study of formal education. Why has that too in times past generally been for boys but not for girls?

Again we need to check out Zelman's work on a new sample. Tables 14.13 and 14.14 depend on her work. As Figure 14.1 shows, we can as yet have but little trust in our finding that esteem of women is the main thing in securing them their place in public affairs. We have here a chance for the most powerful of tests of that theory. In the last hundred years, time and again, people have acted on the theory that the status of women can best be raised by educating the girls. They have set up schools and colleges for women, or they have opened men's schools to them. Did they not do so for the very *purpose* we have in mind? To raise the values of women in the public arena, so that they might play a wider part? What has been the result? Has a wider role in public life followed? Have the women thus educated been the women who played the wider part? We can compare the women thus educated with their sisters in the same society at the same time who did not go to school. Such a comparison amounts to a controlled experiment.

But many other women do not yearn so sorely for public standing. They are content to leave the wider world to the men. And still others prefer a compromise—part time as homemaker, part time as professional woman.

So we come to a third study task. What are the true wishes of women for a special life as women? The traditional housewife-helpmate-mother role plainly costs women considerable freedom of movement, in social status, and in power. How important are these things to mental health? Are there compensating

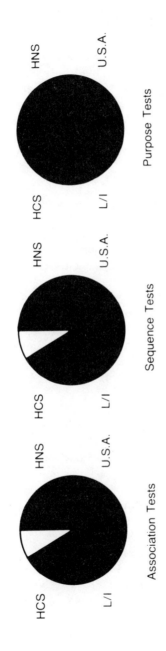

Theory: Women's Status and Public Power Can Best Be Raised by Raising Their Intrinsic Social Value

Theory Trust Ratio: 6%

Association Tests

Sequence Tests

Purpose Tests

SOURCE HCS: Zelman (1974) as analyzed in Section 14.5.2.
NOTE: See *Theory trust meter* in Glossary for a key to this chart, and Section 4.5.3 for the general manner of its composition.
HCS = holocultural test; HNS = holonational test; L/I = local or individual test; U.S.A. = countrywide tests in the United States.

Figure 14.1 Women's Status Theory Trust Meter

335

emotional satisfactions that lead many women to prefer this role to that of a professional or a salaried worker? Can the roles be successfully combined?

Some people suspect that for many women today the ideal role is that of half-time housewife and half-time salaried worker. What proportion of women would prefer this arrangement if it were offered to them? Can it be offered to them more widely and more conveniently?

Perhaps more should be done to encourage men to act as helpmates to women. Husbands of grand opera divas often serve as their business managers—in effect, their helpmates. Perhaps other women doing specially demanding work need like helpmates. In weighing the preferences of men and women for the helpmate role, we must presume that learned cultural attitudes toward sex differences and sex temperaments would lead a greater proportion of women than men to prefer the helpmate role. Are there genetic factors as well?

14.7   STEP 5: COPING WITH SEX ROLE DIFFERENCES

The evidence I have reviewed points to only three specific policies, and these are long taken for granted in most countries today. For English-speaking countries, at least, these findings merely echo the women's rights movement of the 1800s. If political and legal equality of women is to be gained where it is wanting or be maintained where it now exists, it must (1) give women equal access to formal education, in order that their services may be equally needed and so in time equally valued; (2) give women an equal voice in public affairs—in democracies, of course, this means give them the vote; (3) give women equal rights to own and control wealth—equal property rights. Beyond these fundamentals the evidence does not point clearly to any further policy recommendations.

Again and again, in culture after culture, trial and error beat out a common pattern of city life. A pattern that gave men the chief role in the world outside the home and women the chief role inside it. That home, linked with others through kinship and religion, provided the moralnet in which the children learned how to grow into good men and women. Yet, we know that the medical revolution has turned the population problem around. We see crowds of women moving into the world outside the home. Experiments like the Israeli kibbutz and the Soviet day care center show that strong morality can be built in other scenes than the family fireside.

So I do not say that we must not disturb the traditional moral order of the traditional family home. I only say that we must take care of the emotional needs and moral order of the children when we change the social order of their homes. This need to take care brings us to a central research problem of the present volume: the tradeoffs between the small household and the large. An extended family or commune offers much more flexibility in these arrangements. Such families seem likely to be better for young children and young mothers. But worse in many ways for young men and women making their own way in the world. And perhaps worse also for poor nations that wish to grow rich.

14.8   COSTS AND BENEFITS OF SEX ROLE PROGRAMS

In most countries today the public policies I have commended are taken for granted. So I am speaking here chiefly to those planning the economic development of poor countries. The granting of full equality in public affairs to women and the granting of full property rights to them cost the budget nothing. The education of women does cost. But it pays off in several ways: (1) Educated women increase the productivity of the labor force as do educated men. (2) In most developing countries, a leading economic problem is the cost of a high birthrate, which increases the burden on the nation's wealth. Educated women are more likely to obtain work outside the home; their fertility is lowered. (3) A study by Stein of Quechua women in the Peruvian village of Vicos found that the nonliterate women there were more resistant to economic reforms that tended to increase the wealth of the village than were literate ones. I suspect this may be true the world around.

Further research on sex roles cannot as such claim a special priority like that on alcoholism or child battering. However, to the extent that changing sex roles have tended to weaken family life and so moralnet strength, research on that problem may well pay off. In Chapter 16, I sum up the evidence set forth throughout this book on the social costs of weakened moralnets. Rates of alcoholism, child battering, juvenile delinquency, and mental illness clearly rise as a result of weakened moralnets. Sex role research that led to strengthened family moralnets would thus lower the costs of these dreadfully expensive social ills sharply. Lowering the rates of such ills would pay off at something like 100 million dollars a year for each percentage point the rate is lowered in the United States alone.

Notes

14.1   Deep Wells for Sad Women

On troubles of Korean village women in the late nineteenth century, see Moose (1911: 110-111, 232), Saunderson (1894: 305), Griffis (1882: 246, 252), and Ha (1958: 60f.).

14.2.1   Genetic Differences

Denham (1971) models male/female roles on the primeval savanna.

The evidence on the possible genetic bases for sex role differentiation is well reviewed in Leakey and Lewin (1978).

I follow Williams (1967: 203-204) and Luke (1972: 256-257) on the life of Elizabeth I.

On the career of Catherine the Great, see Kluchevsky (1960: Vol. 5).

On selective advantage to timid female and fierce male ground apes, see Denham (1971). Chimpanzees spend much time on the ground, but do not seem very concerned about predators (see Reynolds and Reynolds, 1965: 388; Goodall, 1965: 435).

There has been controversy about Denham's savannah hypothesis. Rowell, cited in Martin and Voorhies (1975: 135), speculates that the savannah may be a recent creation of modern man. But Bonnefille and Carr, two paleobotanists who seem unaware of this controversy, studied plant pollen fossils: Bonnefille (1976: 428) concludes that in the Omo Basin near Lake Rudolph, where some of the earliest known hominid fossils from between two and two and a half million years ago have been found, the "environment . . . was occupied by more or less wooded savanna with some riverine woodland." Carr (1976: 462) agrees, reporting, "grassland, tree/shrub grassland, shrub thicket and shrub steppe"—mixed or mosaic plant growth, predominantly grasslands but with many trees and shrubs scattered about.

Testosterone, the male hormone, shortens men's lives: Woodruff (1978) cites studies by Hamilton and Mestler; they found that castrated men outlived normal men by 13.5 years—and the earlier the castration, the greater the longevity.

14.2.2   Range of Variation of Cultural Differences

See Tables 14.5, 14.6, 14.7, and 14.12 on work role choice, literacy, access to managerial roles, and marriage arrangements; on occupational choice, see Safilios-Rothschild (1971).

Data on wife beating from my War, Stress, and Culture Sample is set forth in Naroll (1969: 140-141). On spouse beating, see Whiting and Whiting (1975) and Straus, Gelles, and Steinmetz (1980); see also the review by Gelles (1979: 91-144).

Rohner's study: see my Table 14.3.

On Dahomean Amazons, see Herskovits (1967).

On Arapesh warfare, see Fortune (1939).

On the working hours of French wives, see Stoetzel (1974: 210, 273).

On the relative amount of work done by men and women, see Zelman (1974: 61).

Here are the nine scales of Whyte (1978); none of these correlate with any other as highly as 0.2:

- DVS 1: Property control scale—5 variables (p. 98).
- DVS 2: Power of women in kinship contests (equals kin power)—4 variables (p. 98).
- DVS 3: Value placed on lives of women (equals value of life)—3 variables (p. 99).
- DVS 4: Value placed on labor of women (equals value of labor)—3 variables (p. 99).
- DVS 5: Domestic authority—3 variables (p. 99).
- DVS 6: Ritualized separation of the sexes (equals ritualized female solidarity)—5 variables, one of which is lack of a belief in general female inferiority. Here Whyte's results do not agree with Zelman's (1974: 101n.). Whyte did not code for female pollution rituals in general, as Zelman did, but only specifically for menstrual taboos (p. 99).
- DVS 7: Control over women's marital and sexual lives (equals control of sex)—4 variables (p. 99f.).
- DVS 8: Ritualized fear of women (equals ritualized fear)—3 variables (p. 100).
- DVS 9: Male-female joint participation (equals joint participation)—3 variables (p. 100).

On sex roles in politics and economics, see Zelman (1974: 199f., 266); on women as warriors (1974: 205, 269), and on wealth control (1974: 214f., 275).

The Empress Wu Hou of T'ang China, who ruled from about 683 to 705, scandalized later Chinese historians by her ruthless treatment of all who stood in her way (see Cordier, 1920: I: 430-432 and Franke, 1961: II: 412-424).

14.2.3   Evolution of Sex Role Differences

On the evolution of sex roles, see Whyte (1978: 172) and M. Naroll (n.d.).

White, Burton, and Brudner (1977) is the most searching analysis of sexual division of labor.

On women entering the labor force, see Safilios-Rothschild (1971) and Collver and Langlois (1962); on women professionals, Safilios-Rothschild (1971). Full information on the role of women in the labor force is in Boulding et al. (1976).

Infant mortality: On the situation today, see Bogue (1969: 584-590). Rates in the poorest countries run as high as 220 per 1,000 births—and this allows nothing for miscarriages or for deaths in childhood after the first year (see also Carr-Saunders, 1922). A sample survey taken in Guinea in 1955 reported that 57.6 percent of all deaths took place among children under fifteen years of age and 32.8 percent of them among infants in their first year (see United Nations, Department of

Economic and Social Affairs, 1970: 594, 618). I take these figures to be typical of mankind until a couple of hundred years ago.

On women's status and power, see Zelman (1977: 624f.); also Textor (1967: FC 277/55, FC 277/96, FC 277/108.)

14.4   Step 2: Sex Role Stress Scoreboards

Rates of attempted suicide are not generally known; all we have are special studies of particular communities. In English-speaking countries, the data at hand suggest that women *attempt* suicide much more frequently than men; if successful and unsuccessful suicide attempts are lumped together as suicidal behavior, then the overall rate of suicidal behavior may well be about the same for each sex (see Farberow and Schneidman, 1961: 25, Dublin, 1963: 10-12). However, in Malmo, Sweden, Dahlgren, cited in Schneider (1954), found no significant difference in sex among suicide attempters, and in Switzerland, rural Vaudois men attempted suicide more often than women; but in urban Lausanne the ratio was reversed, and in Basel, extremely so (Schneider, 1954: 80-82).

I compiled tables on differential mortality between men and women not only on the three causes of death shown in Tables 14.9 through 14.11 (suicide, murder or war, and auto accidents), but also on heart trouble and other accidents, as well as on general life expectancy. All these data came from the United Nations, Department of Social and Economic Affairs (1975: Tables 4 and 28). With respect to life expectancy in modern nations around the world: In the median country, men lived only 92 percent as long as women. With respect to deaths from accidents other than motor vehicle ones, the median death ratio of men to women is 1.6.

14.5.1   The "Male Supremacist Complex"

On the emergence of sexual stratification, see Schlegel (1977: 353).

Divale and Harris (1976) is the scientific paper that sets forth their male supremacist theory; Harris (1977) has a more elaborate, popular presentation of that argument. Fjellman (1979), Newlands (1979), and Kang, Horan, and Reis (1979) have criticized it.

Specifically, Divale and Harris (1976: 527) give 128 for the male-female sex ratio; Divale (1971: 12) gives 138. Divale and Harris rely heavily on shaky data about male-female sex ratios among children, data from which they infer extensive female infanticide.

On the control of wealth and power outside the family, see Friedl (1975: 8f., 135f.).

Note to Table 14.12: The column headed "Societies with Marriage Arrangements Favoring Men" lists the total shown by Coult and Habenstein (1965) at levels 0 or 1 of political organization above the community level. Thus, for example, at page 389 they list a total of 169 such societies with either patrilocal or avunculocal residence. They list 261 societies in all at levels 0 or 1, of which four are not classified, leaving 257 such societies with relevant data on postmarital residence. Of these, 88 have one of the remaining types of postmarital residence: bilocal, neolocal, matrilocal, and duolocal. Bride price, bride service, polygyny, patrilocality, and avunculocality are deemed to be arrangements favoring men, because they appear to me to put men at a bargaining or pressure advantage with respect to their wives in cases of dispute: With bride price or bride service, the husband can claim services owed by him to her; with polygyny, he can play one wife off against another; with patrilocality or avunculocality, his relatives are nearby to back him up, while hers are distant. Polyandry, in contrast, favors women, because here it is the wife who can play off one husband against another.

The data that Divale and Harris (1976) take from Simmons (1945) on preference for boy babies over girl babies agrees with that of a more recent study by Williamson (1976: 99).

14.5.2   Work Roles

On the theory that division of work roles makes for high status, see Sanday (1974: 193).

Linear Regression Equation was computed by me from Zelman's (1974: 221-241) variables no. 76 (Status), no. 45 (Esteem), and no. 125 (Property Rights).

HRAF's TRIADS program was developed by Donald F. Griffiths. He applied a mathematical model developed by Simon (1954) and most elaborately expounded by Boudon (1967). TRIADS works on only three traits at a time. It ignores the influence of a fourth trait on these three. And it assumes that causation goes one way only. I ran this program on nine different combinations of the five mentioned variables—with data taken from Zelman (1974: 182-241), as follows:

- OWNERSHIP (Zelman variable number ZVN 125)
- STATUS (ZVN 76)
- ESTEEM (ZVN 45)
- GOVERNMENT (ZVN 79)
- JUDGING (ZVN 77)

While these runs did not clearly, strongly, and unequivocally support the model set forth in the text, it did enjoy by far the most plausibility. These runs, then, tilt the preponderance of evidence in favor of that model, but do not establish it beyond a reasonable doubt.

On the sexual division of labor, see D'Andrade (1966) and White, Burton, and Brudner (1977).

On cultural evolution, I am following Clark (n.d.).

On smallest space analysis, see Zelman (1977: 727-730).

On women's domestic authority and warfare, see Whyte (1978).

On preference for combining marriage with work outside the home, see Freedman (1978: 99-101).

14.5.3   Love and Marriage

Marriage arrangements and suicide are from my War, Stress, and Culture study (see Naroll, 1969: 140-144).

Pokot girls have a free sex life before marriage, but they frequently end their pleasant youth when they are forced to marry unattractive older men. Then they often hang themselves on village trees in protest, but usually are rescued before they strangle; some, however, perish thus (Edgerton and Conant, 1964: 412-417).

Suicide among Jivaro wives: Naroll (1962a: 148).

Neolocal residence and romantic love: Rosenblatt (1967); phi = .25; p = .02.

Weaning practices and romantic love: Rosenblatt (1966).

14.5.4   Polygamy

Byron: *Don Juan*, Canto I, Stanza 194.

Relative frequency of polygyny and polyandry: Murdock's (1957) World Ethnographic Sample has 132 monogamous societies, 418 polygynous, and only 4 polyandrous ones tabulated (see Coult and Habenstein, 1965: xxii, 420).

On polygyny and witchcraft, see LeVine (1962).

14.5.5   Focus on Male Authority

Matrilineal neither-dominants: Schlegel (1972).

14.5.6   Spouse Battering

See the review of studies in Gelles (1979: 91-144).

On room arrangements and warmth of relationship between husband and wife, see Whiting and Whiting (1975) and Draper (1975).

14.8   Costs and Benefits of Sex Role Programs

On Quechua women of Vicos, see Stein (1975).

End mmm mmm in. 16 galleys

15 The Home

15.1 PALMATTA ASKED FOR TROUBLE

The Kanuri of Northern Nigeria are good Moslems. And like many Moslem men in the old days, the Kanuri men often took more than one wife. The Kanuri say that when two co-wives are married to the same man for a long time, they often become good friends. Cohen tells us about Palmatta, a Kanuri woman who was married to Bukar. Palmatta was lonesome; she wanted a woman to talk to in the home. So Palmatta asked Bukar to take a second wife. Bukar said he did not want a second wife. A second wife would cost a great deal of money. He would have to pay bride wealth. Then there would be the marriage expenses on top of the bride wealth. And Bukar may have felt that one wife to nag and wheedle him was quite enough; for Palmatta nagged and wheedled Bukar now. He gave in. He found a girl named Aisa and he married her. He had to go deeply into debt for the bride wealth and the marriage expenses.

Palmatta was happy with her new friend for several weeks; but within a month she repented. She said that Aisa was not helpful around the house. Aisa was claiming—or getting—more than her share of Bukar's attentions. If Bukar did not divorce Aisa, Palmatta would leave him. Bukar had had enough. He did not divorce Aisa; he divorced Palmatta.

Thanks to her rashness, Palmatta lost her home. By a *home*, I mean a household built around the nuclear family, whether alone or combined into polygamous or extended family groups. So a compound made up of several adjacent dwellings all occupied by a family group constitutes a single home. Such homes are in all cultures the normal place to raise children; and that, I hold, is their leading role.

In this chapter about the home I begin by arguing that human sexual passions combine with other instincts to support family life. But this tendency is not clear or sharp; biologically, we have pair bonding, but it is weaker than among many other species of animals. So we get casual premarital sex—sex without pair bonding. Where premarital sex leads to pregnancy without marriage, a child is not born into a normal home. One of the ways in which homes are broken up is divorce. Divorce in turn may arise from extramarital sex; or it may arise from other causes. Divorce too often leaves children without normal homes. And it also often leaves lonely and frustrated ex-spouses, as well.

Some societies seek to reinforce the link between sex life and family life by restricting sex to marriage. The traditional Judeo-Christian mores call for that way of life, and many people in our society still adhere to that rule, at least as an ideal. But the rule does, of course, lead to tensions between these taboos and sexual passions.

It will be convenient then to deal with these problems in this chapter under two main headings: sexual taboos and divorce. In looking at the former, I also discuss theories linking taboos on sex not to child care but to wealth. However, these links, too, I suggest are links that concern the economic basis of the home. The wealth concerned is wealth that, among other things, helps house and feed and otherwise care for the children.

15.2   HOME BUILDING AND HOME BREAKING AROUND THE WORLD

15.2.1   Sexual Passions and Home Building

Women, like men, are usually in heat—marking us off sharply from our close relatives, the apes. It is true that among many kinds of monkeys and apes copulation can occur at any time of the year. When captive in zoos and laboratories (with nothing much else to do to pass the time), these animals often seem interested in sex the year round. Nevertheless, careful field studies of them in the wild reveal a different story. There, the females have estrous cycles. Sexual activities show marked seasonal variation.

It is clear from this fact that such social primates as chimpanzees and macaques are held together by bonds other than those of sex. I reviewed in Chapter 6 the evidence for a social instinct similarly bonding human groups. Nevertheless, the special characteristics of human sex life have been important in the development of human social life.

Human social organization stands out from that of the other higher social primates in its layered structure. All human societies in effect have organization charts that link smaller social units into larger ones. The nuclear family is indeed found in all human cultures (though not in all subcultures, as we saw in Chapter 10); in other words, there are no known human speech communities in which theoricly normal marriages building theoricly nuclear families are not the emic norm. Nor are there any human cultures in which these nuclear families are not linked by firm social bonds to a set of others, in a band, village, or informal seasonal gathering. These smaller and larger groupings always share or exchange food and other valuables.

Lovejoy recently proposed a model of human origins that looks toward human sexuality and human marriage—with its economic sharing and division of labor—as the crucial adaptive measure that led to the evolutionary success of mankind during the last 5 million years. In the evolutionary struggle, Lovejoy points out that (apart from humans) apes, compared to monkeys, do not fare well. The great-ape system of adaptation has by and large been a failure—an evolutionary backwater. Monkeys are widespread. Apes are rare. Why? The great apes usually find enough food and have few natural enemies. The problem lies precisely in their reproductive system. Apes reproduce very, very slowly. They have few young. Therefore it is crucial for the species that the few young that are born live on so they, too, can become parents in their turn.

Among all the great apes, infants are a burden to their mothers in the mothers' search for food. Strains are considerable. The mother cannot always care for her young properly, or feed them well. At times, she must leave her infant unguarded and alone—and such infants fall easy prey to leopards or hyenas. The death rate among the young is, accordingly, high. That low birth-rate and high death rate among infants and young is the great difficulty for apes. Monkeys breed much more rapidly.

Among humans, the birthrate, too, is very, very low—and often reduced still further through contraception, abortion, and infanticide. According to Lovejoy, the great breakthrough that led to the wide spread of humankind a million or more years ago, long before farming or herding, must have been the evolution of a special human nature—the specific human social instincts that led to the specific human kind of social structure. In Lovejoy's model, human nature is demography. Human nature is a scheme for improving child care, and so for increasing the population.

The main point of human social structure in its evolution over the past 5 or 6 million years has been its special care for women and their children. Husbands help feed their wives; husbands help feed their children; husbands, sisters, mothers, aunts, and cousins help a young woman care for her children. The whole band shares food.

Among chimpanzees, a five-year-old whose mother dies is doomed. Among us, the child's father will look after it and very likely bring home a stepmother. The human father rarely helps much to care for small children, but is likely to be there in an emergency, when the mother's need for help is desperate—precisely the situation when a chimpanzee mother often leaves her child unguarded against predators. Also, while the man's contribution to group subsistence among hunting bands often fails to equal that of the woman's, what he does provide is high in protein and fat content—especially valuable to nursing mothers. Further, the kinship ties cemented by marriage double the network of female relatives on hand to help look out for small children. All this help for mothers reduces the death rate of their children. And compared to the great apes, says Lovejoy, that is the difference that has made all the difference.

In this scheme, sexuality plays its key part in the marriage bond. Regular and frequent sex tends to bond the men to their women and so to encourage their help with the children. But the kinship ties through marriage that hold the band together may be as important as those directly linking man and wife. This ancient need may explain why human genes make for pair bonding, why marriage meets an emotional need, why unmarried people—and especially divorced people—tend to be sad people, as we shall see. Our genes fit the needs of the hunting band.

TABLE 15.1   Pair Bonding and Mother's Food Quest

PROPOSITION: *Where care for their offspring hampers their food quest, animals tend to mate for life.*

	Species	
	Mate for Life	*Do Not Mate for Life*
Mother's care for offspring hampers food quest	wolf yellow-bellied marmot crowned eagle California condor yellow-bellied sapsucker Tasmania native hen quelea dickcissel yellow-eyed penguin oilbird European beaver Mexican jay albatross (13)	Serengeti lion (1)
Mother's care for offspring does not hamper food quest	Alaskan fur seal (1)	giraffe African elephant howler monkey ring-tailed lemur bonnet macaque barren-ground caribou mountain sheep prong-horn antelope mountain gorilla (9)

SOURCE: Ember and Ember (1979).
For all 24 species of birds and mammals:
  Correlation: $r = .83$.
  Chance risk: $p < .002$.
For only the 13 species of mammals, not counting the birds:
  Correlation: $r = .65$.
  Chance risk: $p = .04$.

This model is supported by a cross-species study of animal behavior by the Embers; they found that among birds and mammals, pair bonding (that is, marriage) tends to occur in those species where the mother's care for her offspring tends to hamper her food quest (see Table 15.1).

The erect human posture is one of the oldest hallmarks of mankind. It emerged long before the distinctively human brain. Lovejoy argues that its leading purpose—its leading evolutionary advantage making for its natural selection—may have been the freeing of the hands to carry food home to camp for sharing. But another convenience offered by erect posture is the freeing of the hands and arms to hold our babies. Everyone knows how much babies like to be picked up and held. That liking is clearly innate.

The present chapter, then, examines human sexuality from the social point of view. It looks at sex life as a way to reinforce moralnets. It focuses on two leading problems of human sex life: sex taboos and divorce. If the main point of sex in human nature is to encourage marriage, and so, kin ties, then is there something wrong with sex outside of marriage, after all? If marriage is indeed the central element in human social structure, then divorce must be a central problem.

What link, if any, do sex taboos have on the maintenance of marriage? And what are *their* causes and their consequences? Is divorce indeed an evil? If so, what are its causes and its consequences?

15.2.2 Sex Taboos around the World

We must distinguish three kinds of taboos on sex relations between men and women: (1) incest taboos, which forbid sex between parent and child, or between brother and sister; (2) premarital sex taboos, which forbid sex between unmarried people—typically adolescents; and (3) extramarital sex taboos, which forbid sex by married people with someone other than the spouse.

Although there are a few well-known exceptions for special cases in which certain cultures allow certain favored persons to have sex with or even to marry close relatives, the incest taboo remains universal. No known human society is without incest rules. But the extension of these rules beyond the nuclear family to more distant relatives varies very widely: First cousins who are sexually taboo in one society are preferred marriage partners in another.

Among small-scale societies there is a wide range of variation in attitudes toward both premarital and extramarital sex. While tolerance toward premarital sex is somewhat wider than that toward extramarital sex, both are common. However, taboos of varying degrees of severity are also common (see, for example, Table 15.2).

There is a similar range of attitudes toward homosexuality. Among 42 small-scale societies around the world studied by Broude and Greene, homosexuality was entirely unheard of in 12 percent. It was strongly disapproved of and punished in 41 percent. It was more or less disliked but tolerated in 26 percent. It was calmly accepted in 21 percent.

15.2.3 Evolution of Sex Taboos

It is a striking fact—one repeatedly confirmed in study after study—that there is a clear link between social evolution in general and sexual taboos. The link is somewhat stronger for extramarital than for premarital sex (see Tables 15.3 and 15.4). The larger-scale societies tend to have stricter sex rules, more like those of Victorian England. So it does not appear that human pair bonding is genetically programmed to be strict and exclusive. Rather, I suggest that the ancestral hunting bands of 3 or 4 million years ago may well have had sexual patterns

TABLE 15.2 Sex Life Outside of Marriage

Out of 84 small-scale societies sampled,

43 punish married people who have extramarital sex:

Abipones (Argentina)	Lango (Uganda)	
Ainu (Japan)	Maori (New Zealand)	
Alorese (Indonesia)	Maricopa (Arizona)	
Ashanti (Ghana)	Mataco (Argentina)	
Aymara (Bolivia)	Omaha (Central USA)	
Azande (The Sudan)	Penobscot (Maine)	
Chagga (Tanzania)	Riffians (Morocco)	
Chiricahua (Arizona)	Rwala (Syria and Iraq)	
Creek (Southeastern USA)	Semang (Malaya)	
Crow (Montana)	Seniang (New Hebrides)	
Dobuans (Melanesia)	Swazi (Swaziland)	
Fon (Dahomey)	Taos (New Mexico)	
Ganda (Uganda)	Tehuelche (Argentina)	
Gilbertese (Micronesia)	Thonga (Mozambique)	
Ifugao (Philippines)	Tiv (Nigeria)	
Jivaro (Ecuador)	Tokelau (Polynesia)	
Jukun (Nigeria)	Tolowa (California)	
Kazak (USSR)	Tupinamba (Brazil)	
Khasi (Assam)	Vedda (Sri Lanka)	
Kutenai (Northwestern USA and Canada)	Venda (Lesotho)	
Lakher (Assam and Burma)	Witoto (Peru)	
Lamba (Zimbabwe)	(43)	

41 do not punish married people who have extramarital sex:

Apinaye (Brazil)	Kiowa Apache (Oklahoma)	Murngin (Australia)
Aranda (Australia)	Lapps (Scandinavia)	Nama (Namibia)
Chenchu (India)	Lepcha (Sikkim)	Nandi (The Sudan)
Cheyenne (Colorado)	Lesu (Melanesia)	Naskapi (Labrador)
Choroti (Bolivia)	Lhota Naga (India)	Natchez (Mississippi)
Chukchee (Siberia)	Marquesans (Polynesia)	Papago (Arizona)
Copper Eskimo (Canada)	Marshallese (Micronesia)	Ponapeans (Micronesia)
Cree (Canada)	Masai (Kenya)	Pukapukans (Polynesia)
Dieri (Australia)	Mbundu (Angola)	Purari (Papua)
Dusun (North Borneo)		Siriono (Bolivia)
Gilyak (Siberia)		Tanala (Madagascar)
Hano (Arizona)		Tarahumara (Mexico)
Ila (Zimbabwe)		Tenda (Guinea and Senegal)
Keraki (Papua)		Tenino (Oregon)
		Timbira (Brazil)
		Trobrianders (Melanesia)
		Trukese (Micronesia)
		Zuñi (New Mexico)
		(41)

SOURCE: Textor (1967: FC 393).

TABLE 15.3 Societal Complexity and Sexual Restrictions before Marriage

PROPOSITION: *The more complex the society, the stricter the sex taboos on women before marriage.*

Restrictions	Level of Social Complexity			
	Level 1 Societies	Level 2 Societies	Level 3 Societies	Level 4 Societies
None	Baiga (India) Dobu (Melanesia) Goulborn Islanders (Australia) Kiwai (New Guinea) Mohave (Southwest USA) (5)	Hopi (Arizona) Kikuyu (Kenya) Muria (India) Nyakyusa (Tanzania) Samoans Ulithians (Micronesia) (6)	Thonga (Mozambique) (1)	Balinese (Indonesia) Lepcha (Sikkim) (2)
Weak, Ineffective Taboos	Kwoma (New Guinea) Manus (Melanesia) Orokaiva (New Guinea) (3)	Bambara (Mali) Gusii (Kenya) Ontong Javanese (Melanesia) Tikopia (Polynesia) Trukese (Micronesia) (5)	—	Nupe (Nigeria) Tepoztecans (Mexico) Yadaw (Burma) (3)
Strong, Effective Taboos	Shavante (Brazil) (1)	—	Bemba (Zambia) (1)	Dahomeans Deoli (India) Drageletvsy (Bulgaria) Kabyle (Algeria) Suye Murans (Japan) Taitou (China) (6)

SOURCE: Compiled from Stephens (1972: 11f., Table 3, Columns 8 and 10).
Societal Complexity Levels:
  Level 1: Each local community is autonomous.
  Level 2: Influential regional teams are headed by a chief with no firm legal control over disputes within the chiefdom.
  Level 3: Kingdoms (states) without cities.
  Level 4: States with cities.

Correlation: r = .34.
Chance risk: p = .01.
N = 33.

TABLE 15.4 Societal Complexity and Sexual Restrictions after Marriage

PROPOSITION: *The more complex the society, the stricter the sex taboos after marriage.*

Restrictions	Level of Societal Complexity				
	Level 1 Societies	*Level 2 Societies*	*Level 3 Societies*	*Level 4 Societies*
None	Baiga (India) Kiwai (New Guinea) Mohave (Southwest USA) Orokaiva (Papua) Goulborn Islanders (Australia) (5)	Trukese (Micronesia) Ulithi (Micronesia) Nyakyusa (Tanzania) Marquesans (Polynesia) (4)	— — —	Lepcha (Sikkim) (1)
Weak, Ineffective Taboos	Dobuans (Melanesia) Manus (Melanesia) Kwoma (Papua) Ojibwa (Canada) Kamano (Papua) (5)	Bambara (Mali) Hopi (Arizona) Tikopia (Polynesia) Samoans (Polynesia) (4)	— —	Modjokuto (Java) Nupe (Nigeria) (2)
Strong, Effective Taboos	Shavante (Brazil) (1)	Muria (India) Ontong Javanese (Melanesia) (2)	Bemba (Zambia) (1)	Kabyle (Algeria) Silwa (Egypt) Taitou (China) Deoli (India) Balinese (Indonesia) (5)

SOURCE: Compiled from Stephens (1972: 11, 12. Table 3, Columns 8 and 10).
Societal Complexity Levels:
  Level 1: Each local community is autonomous.
  Level 2: Influential regional teams are headed by a chief with no firm legal control over disputes within the chiefdom.
  Level 3: Kingdoms (states) without cities.
  Level 4: States with cities.

Correlation: r = .40.
Chance risk: p = .006.
N = 30.

much like our own today—marriage the usual sexual outlet, but marriage far from the only one.

What sort of evidence could support such a statement? The surviving pattern of human social instincts, fitted into the Lovejoy model of human demographic adaptation to the crucial problem facing humanity as an animal species—that of child care. Our ancestors of the remote past have left vestiges of their social life implanted in our genes, in the form of our social instincts. The pattern of social instincts suggests that patterns of sexual behavior common among the richer countries in the 1980s—and I mean what the people actually do—may not display any meaningful change from the pattern generally characteristic of our species over the past several million years. Marriage dominates but there is plenty of other play.

15.2.4   Divorce around the World

Our information about divorce in small-scale societies around the world is more meager than our information about sex taboos. Ethnographers often report that divorce is "common" or "frequent" or else that it is "uncommon" or "rare." They seldom give actual statistics. It is easier to get statistics on divorce rules than on divorce frequency. Among 117 small-scale societies around the world studied by Minturn, Grosse, and Haider, the rules made divorce extremely difficult to arrange in about 8 percent, moderately difficult in 18 percent, and easy in 74 percent.

15.2.5   The Evolution of Divorce

Among the 10,000 correlations run by Textor on small-scale societies around the world were several correlating Ackerman's codings of divorce frequency with one measure or another of societal complexity. The result is not clear. The computer did not pick up any linkage between political complexity and divorce frequency. But it did find some small tendency for societies with towns or cities to have less divorce than those without. And although it could compare only eleven societies, it did find a strikingly high linkage between the absence of a formal system of law courts and the frequency of divorce.

15.3   STEP 1: CORE VALUES OF THE HOME

I submit that the central role of sex and marriage in child care continues today in our large, rich cities. Sex builds marriages. Marriages build families. We need the family system as much as ever, but now for different reasons than a million years ago. Today no leopards prowl among us. No wolves or hyenas lurk. If a mother cannot handle her child, some official or other will see that it is fed and sheltered, and seek out a foster home for it. Whatever problems mankind faces today, we are certainly not an endangered species. The odds in favor of any girl born in a country like Norway living long enough to become a mother are very high indeed.

So in our richer countries, at least, it is no longer a question of feeding the babes and keeping them safe. But it is a question of raising them properly, and keeping them out of trouble: keeping them from drug or alcohol addiction, from mental illness, from suicide, from trouble with the police, from being harmfully beaten by their parents, and from harmfully beating their children in their turn.

The value base of this chapter arises out of the findings of earlier chapters. The evidence reviewed earlier in this book has persuaded me, for example, that a single mother, however loving, doing her best by her child but living alone with it, usually has difficulty providing an adequate moralnet. I submit that marriage and the extended family are by far the best tested and most widely used methods of providing an adequate moralnet for growing children and young adults. A second method that also is widely used (if perhaps not with equal success) has been the linking of normal nuclear family households into friendship nets of unrelated but congenial couples. Among the thousands of known human cultures, the Nayar are the only well-studied example of long-standing familial moralnets built without marriage. But Nayar men of fighting age were usually away from home anyway. We do not have any statistics from those old times on Nayar mental illness, drug or alcohol addiction, suicide, child abuse, or crime. And the Nayar themselves dropped the system as soon as the men started staying home regularly.

Sex life is one of our leading pleasures. Hence the moralist who would discourage it has a strong burden of proof to show what harm it does. The tradeoff problem comes for sex outside of marriage. The evidence already reviewed in this book persuades me that premarital sex is bad where it leads to the birth of children who lack a proper moralnet. But to the extent that early sexual experiences prepare people better for a later harmonious sex life within marriage, premarital sex with a healthy partner using effective contraception could be a positive social good.

In this chapter, I evaluate extramarital sex only by asking its effect on the moralnet. Does it tend to lead to divorce? I infer that divorce is a qualified evil. I know of no evidence that shows any permanent harm arising out of divorce not mended by the remarriage of both separating partners. The evidence I am about to review points overwhelmingly to the great harm that divorce does both to the separating spouses and to their children. But the only test I know of that compares divorces leading to permanent broken homes with divorces leading to restoration of normal homes in new marriages clearly supports the theory that it is the broken home—not the mere severance of the marriage—that does the harm.

By *marriage*, I mean a presumably permanent alliance between a man and a woman involving mutal rights of sexual access, mutual economic duties, and mutual responsibilities for the care of the woman's children—an alliance contracted in a manner considered right and proper by the people of the society concerned.

By *divorce*, I mean the permanent dissolution of a marriage in a manner considered right and proper by the people of the society concerned. The divorce-

TABLE 15.5   Divorce and Feelings of General Satisfaction

From a sample of 2150 Americans who were
asked how satisfied they felt.

	Satisfied			*Not Satisfied*		
	Men	*Women*	*Total*	*Men*	*Women*	*Total*
	(in percentages)			*(in percentages)*		
Divorced People (n = 180)	42	33	36	58	67	74
People Who Have Never Been Married (n = 260)	44	55	50	56	45	50
Widowed People (n = 257)	50	56	55	50	44	45
Married People (n = 1453)	66	68	67	34	30	33

SOURCE: Campbell et al. (1976: 398).

prone Kanuri are wise in looking at divorce as a sad event. In the United States, at least, divorced people (if not remarried) tend to be unhappy people. Consider what Campbell, Converse, and Rodgers tell us; they asked Americans about their feelings of happiness or unhappiness—their life satisfaction. Family life and marriage were among the five things people mentioned most as making them happy if good, unhappy if bad. Table 15.5 tells the story. For both men and women, married people are more likely to call themselves happy than unmarried ones. Not only are divorced people much more likely than married people to call themselves unhappy; they are also much more likely than single people or widowed people to do so.

Divorced people are more likely than others to be treated for mental illness. Bloom finds "a growing body of evidence that marital disruption constitutes a severe stress and that the consequences of that stress can be seen in a suprisingly wide variety of physical and emotional disorders." And Bloom was especially impressed by the many studies that Crago reviewed. Again and again, study after study finds that divorced people furnish more than their share of mental hospital patients. Married people furnish less. Widowed people and those who never married fall in between. Table 15.6 tells that story. And in Chapter 7, I reviewed the evidence supporting the view that divorce is the cause, mental illness the effect.

Divorced people are not only more likely to become mental hospital patients; they are more likely to die in auto accidents. A study by McMurray showed that the auto accident rates doubled for people undergoing divorce during the six months before and after the divorce date.

Holmes and Rahe made a general study of stressful events—those likely to make people ill. Not mentally ill, but physically ill. They found eight events especially stressful. Of these, the three most stressful all involved a person losing a wife or a husband: by death, by separation, or by divorce.

Wechsler, Thum, Demone, and Dwinell persuaded Bloom that divorced people are much more likely to need hospital treatment for alcoholism than

TABLE 15.6   Divorce and Mental Illness

PROPOSITION: *Divorced and separated Americans are more prone to mental illness
than others.*

Marital State	Admissions to Mental Hospitals per 100,000 People
Marriages Intact	125
Never Married	340
Widowed	220
Divorced	1465
Married, Separated, and Living Apart	2025

SOURCE: Bloom (1975: 90), taken from the admission rates to mental hospitals in the United
States in 1970.

others. These four writers gave breathalyzer tests to over 6,000 patients who
came for treatment to Massachusetts General Hospital. The 6,000 patients all
came for emergency medical care for something *other than* mental illness,
attempted suicide, or alcoholism—usually for some kind of accident. But
nevertheless, 42 percent of those who were divorced or separated had been
drinking, compared to only 10 percent among the widowers, 19 percent among
the married men, and 24 percent among the single men.

And divorced people are more likely to be murdered than are other people—
among white men in the United States, more than seven times as often.

Thus it is plain that divorced people get into many kinds of trouble more
frequently than do married people. How does divorce affect children? Many
studies have shown that the pain of the family break-up is sharp; children are
hurt and angry. The hurt seems to get worse for about a year, but after two
years, most children seem to have gotten over it. However, children of divorced
families produce more than their share of mental patients and more than their
share of juvenile delinquents.

Several studies have shown that people coming from broken homes are more
likely to suffer mental illness than are other people. Oltman, McGarry, and
Friedman compared 139 mental hospital patients suffering from psychoneurosis
with 230 mental hospital staff members. The sick people were more than twice
as likely to have come from homes broken by divorce as the staff people were.
Chance risk here is less than 1 in 1000.

The study of delinquent boys by the Gluecks may turn out to contain the
really "crucial experiment" on divorce; on the one hand, their careful work
solidly supports the theory that children of divorce are more likely to get into
trouble with the police than those from intact homes. But on the other hand, *the
Gluecks find this true only of children of divorce whose parents did not remarry!*
The Gluecks studied 1,000 boys: 500 of them got into serious trouble with the

TABLE 15.7   Effects of Remarriage on Children

PROPOSITION: *Remarriage of parents seems to mend the moral harm that divorce*
does to children.

	Parents Married/ Both at Home	Parents Never Married/ Separated, Divorced, or Widowed/One Parent Absent	Total
Good Boys[a]	361	133	494
Bad Boys[a]	258	235	493
Total	619	368	987

	At Least One Parent Remarried	Neither Parent Remarried	
Good Boys[b]	23 (76%)	7 (24%)	30
Bad Boys[b]	24 (56%)	19 (44%)	43
Total	47	26	73

SOURCE: Glueck and Glueck (1950: 90).

a. Correlation: $r = .21$.
   Chance risk: $p = < .0000001$.

b. Correlation: $r = .21$.
   Chance risk: $p = .08$.

police—the bad boys; 500 other boys who did not get into serious trouble with the police were matched with the bad boys; they were alike in four ways: (1) race and ethnic background, (2) age, (3) intelligence test scores, and (4) kind of neighborhood. All one thousand boys came from "unwholesome neighborhoods"—slums.

They compared the good slum boys with the bad slum boys to see how they differed. To begin with, 43 of the bad boys came from homes broken by divorce but only 30 of the good boys came from broken homes. We would expect such a difference by chance from a sample this large only 12 times in 100 samples. Table 15.7 shows the whole picture. The Gluecks found 3 children of divorced parents among their 493 delinquent boys for every 2 they found among their matched sample of 494 normal boys. Look at the proportions of children from broken homes in which at least one parent remarried. They are practically identical. Where neither parent remarried, the delinquents outnumber normal boys nineteen to seven—more than two to one. We would expect such a difference by chance in fewer than two tries in a hundred. It is not the divorce as such—or the factors underlying it—that make for delinquent boys. It is the lonely home, apparently.

These findings bear out those of Zimmerman and Cervantes I spoke of in Chapter 6—that high school students who lacked a strong homogeneous moralnet were more likely to get into trouble.

15.4   STEP 2: HOME STRENGTH SCOREBOARDS

Table 15.8 shows the percentages of extramarital births reported for the OECD countries. The quality control problem with this table is serious. Births to couples who are not legally married but who nevertheless live together as man and wife are often counted as extramarital. From our point of view, this count is wrong, and people who live openly together as man and wife are by that fact functionally married. Married couples who live apart—who are separated—are in effect functionally divorced. The more the rate of that counting error varies from country to country, the less useful is a table like this one. Notice, however, that the rate for Sweden is three and a half times that for Norway. I doubt that this difference can be explained away merely as a variation in reporting error; rather, I suspect that, in fact, the true rate is indeed much higher in Sweden than in Norway, just as this table shows.

If marriage is the chief building block of social order and moral order, then the divorce-prone Kanuri must indeed be doing something wrong. The Kanuri must have one of the highest divorce rates. As Table 15.9 shows, the highest trustworthy report of divorce rates is that of the United States. And even in the United States, only about one out of three or four marriages ends in divorce. And many of these are marriages of divorce-prone repeaters.

Table 15.9, our Divorce Scoreboard, shows the model country, Norway, scoring at the median for the 33 countries of 1.2 divorces per 1,000 population per year. The two countries listed whose divorce rates are furthest out of line are the United States and Puerto Rico. Again, this table shows only legal divorces, and fails to count separations that in fact shatter the family home.

15.5   STEP 3: TESTS OF THEORIES OF HOME STRENGTH

15.5.1   Tests of Theories of Sex Taboos

More than forty years ago, Unwin showed the correlation I spoke of above between level of cultural evolution and sexual taboos. He then argued from this correlation that the sex taboos were the *cause* and the rise of civilization the effect—tabooing sexual relations channeled creative sexual energies into other creative activities.

Y. Cohen has another theory to explain these same correlations. He sees premarital sex taboos as a kind of discipline imposed on young people; this discipline helps them become used to another and sterner sort of discipline—that of the authoritative state. Once they are used to that sterner discipline, sex taboos are no longer so important, and can be relaxed.

Still another theory comes from Goody and his colleagues; they have produced some correlations from Europe, Asia, and Africa in support of property control as the cause of civilized sex taboos. Goody points out that male property tends to be transferred differently among settled urban societies with intense agriculture than among small-scale societies. Goody terms the property

TABLE 15.8   Extramarital Births Scoreboard

Country	Extramarital Births[a]	Chance Risk
Above Indicated Range		
Guinea-Bissau	88.7	.0214
Sao Tome	82.4	.0260
Barbados	73.3	.0352
Grenada	72.8	.0358
Panama	71.6	.0373
El Salvador	69.7	.0399
Dominican Republic	66.6	.0446
Guatemala	65.2	.0469
Cape Verde	56.6	.0654
Venezuela	53	.0758
Seychelles	51.8	.0797
Martinique[c]	50.9	.0829
Peru	46.8	.0992
Paraguay	43	.1182
Guadeloupe[c]	42.9	.1188
Bahamas	42.3	.1222
Trinidad and Tobago	41.5	.1270
Guyana	38.6	.1465
Costa Rica	34.7	.1791
Mozambique	34.3	.1830
Uruguay	34.2	.1840
Iceland[b]	34	.1859
Ecuador	32.1	.2062
Sweden[b]	31.4	.2144
Bermuda[c]	28.9	.2473
Argentina	26.4	.2871
Colombia	24.8	.3169
Mexico	21.4	.3952
Chile	19.9	.4377
Puerto Rico	19.2	.4596
Bolivia	19.1	.4628
Within Indicated Range		
Denmark[b]	17.1	
Germany (East)	16.3	
New Zealand	15.8	
Austria[b]	13.8	
USA[b]	12.4	
Canada[b]	12.1	
Australia	9.8	
Bulgaria	9.6	
Norway[b]	9.3	MODEL COUNTRY
Scotland[bc]	9.1	
England and Wales[bc]	8.6	
Channel Islands[c]	8.5	
Isle of Man[c]	8.2	
Finland	7.9	
France[b]	7.8	
Yugoslavia[b]	7.7	

(continued)

TABLE 15.8 (Continued)

Country	Extramarital Births[a]	Chance Risk
Within Indicated Range		
Portugal[b]	7.3	
Hong Kong[c]	6.9	
Germany (West)[b]	6.3	
Hungary	5.7	
Czechoslovakia	5.2	
Below Indicated Range		
Poland	4.8	.4998
Northern Ireland[bc]	4.8	.4998
Luxembourg[b]	4.4	.4451
Switzerland[b]	3.7	.3470
Philippines	3.7	.3470
Djibouti	3.2	.2764
Belgium[b]	3	.2483
Ireland[b]	2.9	.2344
Mauritius	2.8	.2207
Italy[b]	2.5	.1801
Netherlands[b]	2	.1169
Spain[b]	1.5	.0627
Malta	1.2	.0367
Greece[b]	1.2	.0367
Japan[b]	.8	.0123
Israel	.6	.0052
Cyprus	.5	.0029
Below Extreme Range		
Tunisia	.4	.0013

SOURCE: Kurian (1979: Table 28). Worldwide averages and spreads of 70 countries reporting (lognormal distribution):[d] mean of the natural logarithms: 2.48; median: 13.10; range: 88.30; SD: 1.370; CEV: 55.14%. Worldwide averages and spreads of 23 OECD countries reporting (lognormal distribution): mean of the natural logarithms: 1.75903; median: 7.30; range: 33.20; SD: 0.98012; CEV: 55.72%; skew: −0.17; kurtosis: 0.82.

a. Extramarital births (legally defined) as a percentage of total births.
b. Member of the Organization for Economic Cooperation and Development (OECD).
c. United Nations reporting unit; not an independent nation.
d. See Glossary for meanings of worldwide measures.

SD = standard deviation of natural logarithms.
CEV = coefficient of evolutionary variation.

control system among small-scale societies "unilineal devolution"; under it, most male wealth is held by individual men or by lineages, and passes from older man to younger man. In patrilineal or bilateral societies, wealth goes from father to son. In matrilineal societies, it goes from mother's brother to sister's son. Wealth passes from man to man in marital exchanges, too: Bride price goes from the groom and his father and uncles to the bride's father—not to the bride.

TABLE 15.9 Divorce Scoreboard

Country	Divorce[a]	Chance Risk
Above Indicated Range		
USA[b]	4.6	.0468
Puerto Rico[c]	4.3	.0590
Sweden[b]	3.1	.1602
Denmark[b]	2.5	.2774
Hungary	2.4	.3050
Czechoslovakia	2.1	.4076
England and Wales[bc]	2	.4497
Within Indicated Range		
Finland	1.8	
Iceland[b]	1.6	
Canada[b]	1.6	
Scotland[bc]	1.4	
Germany (West)[b]	1.4	
Netherlands[b]	1.3	
Austria[b]	1.3	
Bulgaria	1.3	
Switzerland[b]	1.2	
Poland	1.2	
Norway[b]	1.2	MODEL COUNTRY
New Zealand	1.2	
Australia	1.2	
Belgium[b]	1.1	
Japan[b]	1	
France[b]	1	
Uruguay	.9	
Romania	.8	
Luxembourg[b]	.8	
Israel	.8	
Below Indicated Range		
Barbados	.4	.1040
Trinidad and Tobago	.3	.0402
Northern Ireland[bc]	.3	.0402
Italy[b]	.3	.0402
Costa Rica	.2	.0080
Below Extreme Range		
Peru	.1	.0002

SOURCE: United Nations Department of Economic and Social Affairs (1975: Table 13). Worldwide averages and spreads of 33 countries reporting (lognormal distribution):[d] mean of the natural logarithms: 0.06; median: 1.20; range: 4.50; SD: 0.845; CEV: 1314.40%. Worldwide averages and spreads of 18 OECD countries reporting (lognormal distribution): mean of the natural logarithms: 0.23519; median: 1.30; range: 4.30; SD: 0.67579; CEV: 287.33%; skew: −0.54; kurtosis: 0.69.

a. Divorce rates per 1,000 population per year.
b. Member of the Organization for Economic Cooperation and Development (OECD).
c. United Nations reporting unit; not an independent nation.
d. See Glossary for meanings of worldwide measures.

SD = standard deviation of natural logarithms.
CEV = coefficient of evolutionary variation.

TABLE 15.10   Inheritance by Daughters and Sexual Attitudes

PROPOSITION: *Societies in which girls may get their father's property tend to frown on premarital sex.*

| Societies in which girls . . . | Premarital Sex Restrictions | | |
	Present	Absent	Total
may inherit father's property, get dowries, or both.	56	30	86
may not inherit father's property or get dowry.	70	97	167
Total	126	127	253

SOURCE: Goody (1969: 60).
Correlation level: r = .22.
Chance risk: p < .001.

Among larger-scale societies, in contrast, property transfers follow a pattern Goody calls "diverging devolution." In this system, wealth may pass by inheritance to daughters as well as to sons. And wealth on marriage goes from fathers to daughters in the form of dowries. (True, the husband often controls his wife's dowry. But in large-scale societies dowries are often passed through formal written marriage contracts, containing elaborate provisions for the safeguarding of the dowry. In Greece today, for example, a woman's dowry often remains legally in her name and under her personal control.)

As Table 15.10 shows, there is some correlation between diverging devolution property systems and premarital sex restrictions. Then, too, the correlations between property systems and sex taboos is higher than the correlation between either of these and societal complexity. It begins to look as though premarital sex taboos are at least in part a device by parents to control their wealth. If wealth is to be passed from father to daughter, the father wants to decide whom the daughter will marry. He can do that best or most conveniently if the daughter sleeps alone until she marries. It is old Capulet's money, then, that was at the root of his concern for his daughter's marriage; for money, then, Romeo and Juliet suffered and died. So at least Goody's theory implies.

Far more incisive and impressive are the finds of Rosenblatt, Fugita, and McDowell. Table 15.11 shows what they learned: The more wealth that is transferred on marriage, the tighter the taboo on sex life after bethrothal.

Leeuwe reports an interesting finding, too. He shows that sexual freedom is usually greatest in societies that already have wealth production but do not yet have social classes—societies in which there is little economic pressure on people. And Textor finds a clear link between strict taboos on sex outside of marriage and systems of loans of wealth. And with the keeping of slaves.

TABLE 15.11   Wealth Exchange and Sexual Restrictions

PROPOSITION: *The more wealth that changes hands on marriage, the tighter the sex*
taboos after betrothal.

	Transfer Little or No Wealth at Marriage	Transfer Substantial Wealth at Marriage
Societies in which sex taboos tighten at betrothal	Rotuma (Fiji) (1)	Burmese Chagga (Tanzania) Fang (Cameroon) Ganda (Uganda) Lakher (Assam) Manus (Melanesia) Monguor (China) Siuai (Solomon Islands) Thonga (Mozambique) (9)
Societies in which sex taboos do not change at betrothal	Ainu (Japan) Japanese proper Iban (Borneo) Koreans Trumai (Brazil) Hano Tewa (Arizona) (6)	Ila (Zambia) Lau (Fiji) Lolo (China) Somali (Somalia) (4)
Societies in which sex taboos loosen at betrothal	Lapps (Scandinavia) Merina (Madagascar) Ona (Tierra del Fuego) Tanala (Madagascar) Yokuts (California) (5)	Araucanians (Chile) Mongo (Zaire) (2)

SOURCE: Rosenblatt et al. (1969: 325).
Correlation: tau-b = .49.
Chance risk: p = .01.
N = 27.

So sex taboos seem to loom large where marriage involves the control of wealth. The control of children may also be a factor. Textor finds links between sex taboos and the desire for children, sex taboos and taboos on abortion, sex taboos and postmarital residence rules. Table 15.12 shows his findings.

Working independently on different samples, Zern and Murdock each found a link between kinship structure and sex taboos. Both of these were in the direction of greater concern about premarital sex, where a father's right to control his child linked that child with the kin structure. Murdock, like Textor, found a link between postmarital residence rules and sex taboos. Where a bride comes to live with her husband's people after marriage, premarital sex tends to be tabooed. And where, as is usually the case, such residence rules are linked to patrilineages like those of the Mapuche, a girl who gets pregnant before marriage is more likely to be shamed and disgraced.

TABLE 15.12   Some Things That Textor Learned about Sex Taboos

Finding	Correlation	Chance Risk
Societies that taboo extramarital sex are likely also to be societies that . . .		
permit their people to go into debt—owing money or the like.	.50	.03
have an especially high desire for children.	.35	.05
punish abortion severely.	.43	.05
Societies that taboo all sex for unmarried people are likely also to be societies in which . . .		
at marriage, couples live with or near the parents of the groom rather than of the bride.	.30	.03
at marriage, couples live with or near the relatives of the groom in general.	.30	.003

SOURCE: Textor (1967: FC 393/133; FC 393/282; FC 393/295; FC 389/204; FC 389/210).

Sex taboos tend to go with a long list of other things. Table 15.12 sets forth some of the main findings. But which of these links are the roots and which the branches? Russell has done a factor analysis of these linked traits. (A factor analysis, you may recall, is a method of grouping a large number of interrelated traits into a small number of closely related clusters.) Sex taboos *before* marriage are chiefly linked to his first cluster, his anxiety factor. (In factor analysis, the correlation between any one trait and a given cluster is called the "factor loading"; see Table 15.13).

This cluster of related traits includes many features of early child training studied by Whiting and Child. Their coders often rated these features by hunch or gut feeling. Still, the sex taboo codings come from Murdock's *Ethnographic Atlas* codings, not from these child-training coders. So societies with stricter sex taboos do seem to be societies with frustrated, anxious children. Whether the sex taboos are the causes, the consequences, or the co-consequences of such childhood training remains to be seen. These taboos do not link nearly so strongly with Russell's warfare factor or his cultural evolution factor. Sex taboos *after* marriage—taboos against sex outside it—do have a moderate though not a high link with warfare.

Broude has tested the child care theory of premarital sexual restrictions. She did a multiple regression that also took into consideration social class stratification and cultural complexity. She found that, among 55 societies around the world, these three factors together explained about one-third of the cross-cultural variance in premarital sex restrictions. Of the three, overwhelmingly the most important was the availability of caretakers. Where people other than the mother were readily available to care for young children, premarital sex norms tended to be permissive. Where not, not. That factor alone explained 24 percent of the variance, with only 7 percent explained by the other two factors together.

TABLE 15.13   Sex Taboos and General Anxiety: Russell's Anxiety Factor

Line Number	Variable	Factor Loading
Group 1: Sex Taboos		
(1)	Sex by unmarried people	.60
(2)	Extramarital sex	.40
Group 2: Measures of Anxiety		
(3)	Children are thought to be anxious about being punished for hurting other people.	.75
(4)	Children are thought to be anxious about being punished for sex play.	.71
(5)	Children are thought to be sexually frustrated.	.69
(6)	Children are thought to be anxious about being punished for bad manners.	.66
(7)	Adults seem anxious about sex.	.60
(8)	Children are thought to be especially frustrated when angry, because they fear being punished for hurting other people.	.56
(9)	Babies are thought to be frustrated.	.47
Group 3: A Measure of Cultural Evolution		
(10)	Villages or towns average more than fifty people in size.	.45

SOURCE: Russell (1972: 283-285).

The recent slackening of the pressure of public opinion against premarital sex relations in our own society follows not long after the wide spread of cheap, safe, and reliable contraceptives.

What can we say with confidence about taboos on sex life before marriage? First, that they are the more likely where caretakers for their small children are less easy for mothers to come by. Second, that those taboos are deeply linked to transfers of wealth on marriage. And third, that cultures in which sex taboos are strict are cultures in which people are anxious not only about sex, but also about aggression.

15.5.2   Tests of Theories of Divorce

Why do marriages break up? Rules and practices vary tremendously. In some societies, divorce is not permitted under any circumstances whatever. So it was until recently among the Italians and so it was among the pygmies of the Andaman Islands. In some societies, either partner may end a marriage at will; if either wishes, he or she walks out. Reasons given for divorce range widely. Sometimes divorce is a result of sexual problems: barrenness, impotence,

TABLE 15.14   Divorce and Sterility

PROPOSITION: *Divorce is more frequent in societies in which sterility is more frequent.*

	Separation or Divorce Is Frequent	Separation or Divorce Is Rare	Total Number of Societies
Sterility is high	11	4	15
Sterility is low	3	12	15
Total number of societies	14	16	30

SOURCE: Nag (1962: 203).
Correlation: phi = .53.
Chance risk: $p < .005$.

frigidity (see Table 15.14). Sometimes economic difficulties may be the cause—husbands or wives may not accept their roles or responsibilities.

In the United States, divorce is less likely if the man and woman come from homes that are much alike in religion (or lack of it), alike in income, alike ethnically. And marriages are more likely to last when the man and woman have similar amounts of formal schooling and when they come from the same region of the country. Marriages are stabler when like marries like.

Furthermore, in the United States, as Zimmerman and Cervantes have shown, marriages seem to last longer if the married couple is closely tied in with a set of related "friend families" of like income, religion, and cultural background.

Ackerman extended these findings to a worldwide sample of small-scale societies in the Human Relations Area Files. He looked at 28 societies (see Table 15.15). He, too, found that marriages worldwide are stabler when like marries like. When people married within their local communities, husband and wife were able to keep up their existing family ties. Both husband's people and wife's people were likely to supply friend families for them.

Ackerman wondered what would happen if we combined kinship endogamy with community endogamy, kinship exogamy with community exogamy. (Endogamy, of course, means a rule requiring marriage within the group; exogamy means a rule requiring marriage outside it.) So he looked at the five societies that not only required people to marry locally but also let them marry first cousins. These five he compared with the six other societies in his sample, which not only required people to marry outside their local community but also forbade them to marry either first or second cousins. He found that all five endogamous societies had low divorce rates. Five of the six exogamous societies had high divorce rates. So marked a difference would occur by chance only thirteen times in a thousand, if, in fact, marrying affiliates did not affect the chances of divorce.

Ackerman did not stop there. He carefully studied the one deviant case in that subsample of eleven—the Nyakyusa of Malawi. The Nyakyusa live in

TABLE 15.15   Divorce and Endogamy

PROPOSITION: *Societies whose people marry locally have less divorce than societies whose people marry outsiders.*

	Endogamous Societies[a]	Agamous Societies[b]	Exogamous Societies[c]
Low Divorce Rates	Inca (Peru) Thai (Thailand) Pawnee (Midwestern USA) Burmese Siriono (Bolivia) Kaingang (Brazil) Macassarese (Indonesia) (7)	Iban (Borneo) Pomo (California) Aztecs (Mexico) Andaman Islanders (Indian Ocean) Tubatulabal (California) (5)	Nyakyusa (Tanzania)[d] (1)
High Divorce Rates	Cuna (Panama) Comanche (Midwestern USA) Tarahumara (Mexico) (3)	Ifugao (Philippines) Samoans Chukchee (Siberia) Marquesans (Polynesia) Nambicuara (Brazil) (5)	Lozi (Zambia) Yurok (California) Semang (Malaya) Papago (Arizona) Nootka (British Columbia) Amhara (Ethiopia) Alorese (Indonesia) (7)

SOURCE: Ackerman (1963: 16, Table 1).
Correlation between exogamy and divorce rates: tau-b = .43.
Chance risk: $p = .01$.
$N = 28$.
a. Societies that prefer their people to marry inside their local community.
b. Societies that have no preference about people marrying inside or outside their local community.
c. Societies that prefer their people to marry outside their local community.
d. Even the Nyakyusa tend to marry people they know well and have long associated with.

exogamous communities and they forbid marriage with second cousins; still, their divorce rate is low. But Nyakyusa communities turn out to be very special. They are founded by a group of male adolescents, an age set; these establish a new village near that of their parents. They take their wives from that same parental village. Nyakyusa are polygynous. A Nyakyusa man may not marry his own matrilateral cross-cousin (mother's brother's daughter), but he is encouraged to marry that of his *half-brother's*. His bride is not his own blood relative, but she is his half-brother's first cousin. So a Nyakyusa marriage, too, is a marriage between people who grew up together in the same village and who, furthermore, are closely linked by family ties.

Ackerman made one more test of his affiliation theory. That theory says divorce is less likely when people marry those to whom they are already linked in some other way. As his third test of that theory, Ackerman looked at the custom of the levirate, commonly found in societies with unilineal descent groups. In

TABLE 15.16   Divorce and the Levirate

PROPOSITION: *The Levirate lowers the rate of divorce.*

	Low Divorce Rates	High Divorce Rates
Societies in which a widow marries her husband's brother	Zulu (South Africa) Bhil (India) Lolo (China) Gond (India) Kazak (USSR) Azande (The Sudan) Yoruba (Nigeria) Lepcha (Sikkim) Afghan (9)	---
Societies in which a widow does not marry her husband's brother	Vedda (Ceylon) Mbundu (Angola) Atayal (Formosa) Kikuyu (Kenya) Tikopians (Melanesia) Vietnamese (6)	Lau (Fiji) Ila (Zambia) Yao (Mozambique) Fang (Cameroon) Toda (South India) Zuñi (New Mexico) Omaha (Central USA) Hausa (Nigeria) Khasi (Assam) Bemba (Zambia) Mandan (Central USA) Azande (The Sudan) Ojibwa (Great Lakes) Somali (Somalia) Siwans (Egypt) Mundurucu (Brazil) (16)

SOURCE: Ackerman (1963: 18, Table 3).
Correlation of the Levirate with divorce rate: phi = −.66.
Chance risk: p = .001.
N = 31.

such a society, if a marriage has produced children, the death of a husband while the children are still young may disrupt the lineage relationships as well as the marriage. To maintain the lineage relationships, and to provide the widow and orphans with a husband and father, societies that practice the levirate look for the dead husband's brother (or other suitable lineage mate) to marry the widow. In such a second marriage, the widow is marrying into a family with which she already has close kinship ties. Ackerman expected the divorce rate to be lower in societies with the levirate than in those without it. Table 15.16 shows Ackerman's findings. Again his affiliation theory is supported by his test.

Minturn, Grosse, and Haider asked what social structure had to do with ease of divorce. Table 15.17 shows what they learned. The first lines come as a surprise. I had expected a larger correlation than .18. Many people say that bride

TABLE 15.17   Family Ties and Divorce

PROPOSITION: *Divorce rules are linked to the general structure of the family.*

	Number of Societies	Correlation	Chance Risk
From a worldwide study of 135 societies, divorces are . . .			
harder to get when wealth is exchanged on marriage (as in dowry or bride price).	98	.18	.08
easier to get where people live in extended families than in nuclear families (like ours).	47	.31	.04
harder to get in patrilocal societies than in matrilocal ones.	62	.27	.04

SOURCE: Minturn et al. (1969: 307, Table 3).

price or dowry tends to make marriages more solid, but Minturn, Grosse and Haider found that such practices did not seem to help much. Divorce was easier where people live in large, extended family households. (But such households may offer divorced people and their children a stable home and thus blunt the force of the blow.) And they found divorce harder to arrange in patrilocal societies than in matrilocal ones. This pattern makes some sense where mothers usually keep the children after divorce. Where this is so, divorce would do greater damage to a patrilocal family than to a matrilocal one. If the mother keeps the child, a patrilocal family loses it but a matrilocal family keeps it.

15.5.3   Tests of Theories Linking Sex Taboos and Divorce

Do such cultures as the Toda, which calmly tolerates extramarital sex, tend to have more divorce than those that ban or restrict it? In our own culture, extramarital sex was long one of the most important grounds for divorce in the law courts and no doubt still leads to divorce today. Our folk culture labels extramarital sex "cheating" and deems it humiliating to the other spouse. Traditionally, we define extramarital sex as adultery and make it grounds for public scorn of the other spouse. In Southern European folk humor, the role of the cuckold in effect leads extramarital sex to inflict that humiliation on the husband whose wife loves another.

So the mere linkage of extramarital sex with divorce does not tell us what we need to do. If extramarital sex—being accepted as normal—tends to break up homes and leave spouses and children alone and forlorn, then under our value premises that creates some kind of moral basis for discouraging it. But otherwise, not.

A preliminary report by Broude finds that among small-scale societies around the world, frequent extramarital sex, especially by men, is linked with a high rate of divorce (chance risk less than 1 percent). Broude does not, however distinguish between divorce rates among societies in which extramarital sex is in itself considered a proper reason for divorce and those in which such sex is tolerated. This one study is all the evidence I could find.

15.6   STEP 4: FURTHER STUDIES OF HOME STRENGTH

Let us review the evidence for the human pair-bonding instinct. The preponderance, I submit, already tilts sharply in support of that theory. What further studies are needed to establish the presence of such an instinct beyond a reasonable doubt? In Section 6.2, I proposed five tests for any theory of human instinctive behavior.

Test 1: Is the goal in question found in all human cultures? Answer: clearly yes, without exception—if we define culture as a speech community.

Test 2: Where for some reason a culture tends to frustrate such a goal, are special efforts made to teach the young to repress any "natural" inclinations toward it? The Nayar data need to be studied again from this point of view. What about the training of celibates in religious orders? What attention goes to the discouragement of *marriage* as distinguished from mere *sexual* liaison? (Consider, for example, the concept of a nun as the bride of Christ. Are like concepts found also among Buddhist religious orders?)

Test 3: If attainment of the goal is difficult, then do people tend to make special efforts to achieve it? Here, a systematic review of the evidence is called for. It would be specially helpful to look at occupations in which people must travel and so, like the Nayar, are generally away from home. I think of soldiers, of sailors whether merchant or naval, and of air crews. Do such people characteristically make special efforts to create and support a home, even though they cannot often visit it?

And what about the widespread customs of bride service and bride wealth. Are these not evidence of the strength of a pair-bonding instinct? As far as I know, these customs have not been studied from the man's point of view as a cost of marriage itself rather than as a means of sexual access. What is the correlation between bride price and premarital sex taboos? Is bride price common even where sexual liaisons outside of marriage are easily formed? (Bear in mind that, from the point of view of the Lovejoy thesis, it is the attitudes of the grooms rather than of the brides that are crucial.)

Test 4: What is the adaptive advantage of the supposed instinct among bands of social ground apes? Here the Lovejoy thesis offers the most elaborate model. Further studies of demographic balances among apes on the one hand and simple foraging bands on the other are needed to confirm or correct Lovejoy's findings. A holocultural study of such bands should look not only at demography but also, as specifically as possible, at help given by the other band members to mothers of young children—both in providing food for the mother and in protecting the child from predators. In such a study, we must take heed of the Washburn and Lancaster dictum: Evaluate survival advantage not during normal times but rather during hard times. "During much of the year," Washburn and Lancaster tell us, "many monkeys can obtain food in only three or four hours a day, and under normal conditions, baboons have plenty of time to build the Taj Mahal. The restriction on population, however, is the lean season or atypical year." (Following this dictum, for example, the archeologist Wilson has shown how cultural evolution on coastal Peru was limited in prehistoric times by the seafood available during the occasional especially bad fishing season—perhaps once every ten years—caused by the special warm current called *El Niño*.) How do nursing mothers and their infants fare in foraging bands during times of dearth? Do their husbands really make a difference then? Here the importance of rigorous sampling methods stands out. Well-known hard cases like the Ik and the Siriono are quite atypical, I do assure you.

Test 5: Does the hindering of marriage tend to produce manifest symptoms of mental stress? Gilbert and Sullivan, with tongue in cheek, assure us that blighted affection led to the demise of a certain tom-tit bird. However—also with tongue in cheek—Shakespeare says that men have died, from time to time, and worms have eaten them, but not for love. In Chapter 9, I reviewed the report by Edgerton and Conant on suicide among the Suk of East Africa. Blighted affection there led to girls hanging themselves on trees. How common is this sort of thing? And can we clinically measure less extreme symptoms of emotional stress among frustrated would-be brides and grooms? It would be particularly helpful if a crucial quasi-experiment could investigate specifically the effects of marriage barriers on single people with an active sex life—so that it is specifically the theoretical home-building instinct and not merely the supportive sexual instinct that we measure.

15.6.1   Further Studies of Sex Taboos

Just as the work by Lovejoy and the Embers on pair bonding needs to be followed up to settle firmly the instinct theory of human marriage, so the work by Broude, by Goody, and by Rosenblatt on premarital sex restrictions likewise needs to be continued. Particularly, we need a linear regression analysis like Broude's of romantic love, sexual and aggression anxiety, property transfer, and property inheritance—as well as of accessibility of caretakers, social classes, and societal complexity—to see if we can explain more than Broude's one-third of the worldwide variance of these restrictions.

Even more urgent is the replication and extension of Broude's recent work on the link between extramarital sex and divorce. Ideally, that work would form part of a larger study on the causes and consequences of divorce. We need a high quality, universalist study of divorce like the work of the Rohners on the causes and consequences of parental acceptance of children. That study would also need to pay careful heed to the effect of divorce on remarried people and their children, in contrast to those who fail to remarry. And to causality, to deal directly with the lurking variable issue.

But in general, the role of divorce in leading to social ills like mental illness, alcohol and drug abuse, suicide, child battering, and juvenile delinquency ought to form part of the general work on weakened moralnets. That general work is my main concern in Chapter 16.

If Lovejoy is right, human familial instincts arose through a selection process that gave a survival advantage to those of our ancestors who cared better for mothers and their children. It is these instincts that ultimately tend to govern human sexuality and human marriage. The trust/doubt ratio supporting this aspect of the Lovejoy model leaves much to be desired. If further studies were to offer more support for the Lovejoy model as here presented, and to markedly improve that ratio, then social science would offer a moral guide to sex and family life.

15.6.2   Further Studies of Divorce

In order to lay a firm base for a moral code of sex, marriage, and divorce, the most important kinds of studies, I submit, would be those seeking to demonstrate a clear cause-and-effect link between single-parent households and social pathology. The evidence of correlation between the two is overwhelming. In order to convert a preponderance of evidence into a finding beyond a reasonable doubt, we still need to rule out the rival theory that would explain these links by a lurking variable. The task of a devil's advocate here is to argue that single-parent households are but symptoms of some underlying emotional disorder that leads not only to such single family households (through premarital sex or divorce), but also to alcoholism, suicide, child abuse, and youth crime.

Consider, for example, a comparative study of two kinds of single-family households: (1) those created by divorce and (2) those created by the natural death of one parent. (By natural death I mean a death not the result of human act, whether by intent or by accident.) The devil's advocate predicts that such natural deaths would not lead to an increase in the rate of social pathology among the children so orphaned. On the contrary, the weakened moralnet theory predicts that they *would*. Or consider a study of matched pairs of divorced couples—matching those who remarry with others as similar as possible with respect to emotional maturity and cultural background, but who do not remarry. Best of all would be the successful application of the self-help club approach to single-family households. (More on such clubs in the next chapter.)

15.7   STEP 5: COPING WITH WEAKENED HOMES

We cannot now say the evidence I have just reviewed establishes beyond a reasonable doubt the validity of a certain set of rules governing sex and family life. But I submit that the preponderance of evidence on the broken home tilts in their favor. If that evidence is not yet strong enough to stand up in a common-law criminal prosecution, it is strong enough to decide a civil lawsuit.

That evidence supports six guidelines. People who care for the mental health of themselves and their children would be wise to follow them as best they can.

(1) If unmarried people have sex, they should take care to use safe and effective contraception. (If that advice seems banal, so much the better.)

(2) Ordinarily, unmarried women who nevertheless become pregnant should either have an abortion or else should give the child up for adoption.

(3) Unmarried women should ordinarily be discouraged from trying to raise children alone. Exception: Where an unmarried woman gets pregnant, she might decide to bear and keep the child if she has the support of other relatives, such as her own parents, who offer to make a home for her and her child and so to provide it with a stronger moralnet—especially where a man in the house is a party to the arrangement and thus offers himself as a father figure for the child. This is not to say that in general we know such arrangements are as likely to promote mental health as marriage is—but only to say that the evidence now at hand does not allow us to rule them out.

(4) About extramarital sex, we have only the one study by Broude to support a moral rule—a study whose details at this writing are still unpublished. So the evidence is not yet in. But the straw in the wind points in the direction of faithfulness to avoid divorce.

(5) About divorce: The evidence warns us against it, and so against hasty marriage—likely to lead to divorce. The evidence supports the wisdom of endogamy—of like marrying like. (Such a rule speaks to people most strongly, of course, when they themselves accept and carry on the cultural values and traditions of their parents.) The evidence supports careful weighing of the prospects for remarriage when contemplating divorce, especially if children are involved. The findings of the Gluecks on the effect of remarriage on juvenile delinquency—if confirmed by other studies—might well lead lawgivers and judges to give weight to remarriage prospects in divorce cases.

(6) The model presented here, taken in the context of the evidence on moralnets, says something about homosexuality as well. In a primeval foraging band that faced the demographic problems of our Pliocene ancestors, homosexuals could play a useful part if, one way or another, they helped mothers with their children. The problem then was not how many children were born, but how many grew up. Today, demography is no longer the problem. Mankind at large seems to raise too many children, not too few. Our numbers press against our resources. The central fact about homosexuality is that it does not get women pregnant. Today, that rather argues in its favor than against it. So if 5 or 10 percent of the population prefer to opt out of the breeding pool, that constitutes no problem. The problem, rather, for homosexuals would be to form stable households—as Somerset Maugham or Gertrude Stein did—and to link these into nets of like households.

15.8   COSTS AND BENEFITS OF PROGRAMS TO STRENGTHEN THE HOME

I do not know of a specific program like Alcoholics Anonymous or a therapeutic community that offers any measurable means of reducing either the number of extramarital children or the rate of divorce. There are, of course, professional counselors as well as clergy who seek to discourage both. Unless we can measure the cost of any such program against its effectiveness, we cannot deal with the cost side of the equation. The benefit side, however, seems clear. It seem likely that substantial reductions in the rates of mental illness, alcoholism, drug abuse, and juvenile delinquency would save huge sums in out-of-pocket welfare budgets.

But this is only a part of the general benefit to be gained by a successful program to strengthen moralnets among the richer nations—precisely where moralnets seem weakest. To that general problem I now turn.

Notes

15.1   Palmatta Asked for Trouble

Palmatta case: Cohen (1967: 43-44); the three names used are fictional Kanuri names kindly supplied for my book by Ronald Cohen.
Kanuri divorce statistics: Cohen (1961: 1242).

15.2.1   Sexual Passions and Home Building

On estrus in primates, see Hall (1968: 14f.), Johanson and Edey (1981: 330-336), Eimerl and DeVore (1965: 184f), and Jay (1968: 492).
On the social organization of apes in general, see Schaller (1965b); and on that of the mountain gorilla in particular, see Schaller (1965a) and Schaller and Emlen (1963: 371-373).
On marriage as an evolutionary device, see Lovejoy (1981).
On pair bonding, see Ember and Ember (1979).
The best exposition of Lovejoy's familial theory of erect posture among our hominid ancestors is in Johanson and Edey (1981: 314-340), but the essential demographic data is in Lovejoy (1981).

15.2.2   Sex Taboos around the World

On incest rules in general, see Honigmann (1959: 372f.) and Slater (1959). On the relaxation of the taboo against brother-sister marriage among certain high-ranking Hawaiians, Incas, and ancient Egyptians, see Lowie (1947: 58).
On homosexuality, see Broude and Green (1976: 417).
For a general survey of sexual practices, see Bullough (1976).

15.2.3   Evolution of Sex Taboos

On the link between sex taboos and cultural evolution, see Section 15.5.1.
On child care, see Lovejoy (1981).

15.2.4.   Divorce around the World

On divorce rules, see Minturn, Grosse, and Haider (1969: 312); on divorce rates, see Ackerman (1963: 15).

15.2.5   The Evolution of Divorce

On the evolution of divorce, see Textor (1967:FC 91-101/272; and also FC 272/80 and FC 272/138).
On divorce frequency, see Ackerman (1963).

15.3   Step 1: Core Values of the Home

On the Nayar, see Appendix D.

The Israeli kibbutz is becoming another experiment like that of the Nayar, though not so extreme. In the kibbutz, people marry and visit their children for several hours each day, but otherwise, the nuclear family is vestigial: The married couple room and sleep together, but take their meals and share their work and wealth with the commune. The children live and sleep in the communal day nursery and kindergarten. Thus the kibbutz keeps the nuclear family as a biological and emotional unit, but merges its other roles into the larger communal moralnet. Now in the second generation, this pattern is breaking down. Kibbutz women prefer feminine roles—and actually have fewer masculine skills than those of suburban housewives in the United States. More and more, the women are persuading their men to set up family apartments where they can care for their children (see Tiger and Shephner, 1976; Hazelton, 1977: 154-161).

On the healing effect of remarriage, see Table 15.7.
On life satisfaction, see Campbell, Converse, and Rodgers (1976); also Freedman (1978).
Quote is from Bloom (1975: 89); Crago is cited in Bloom (1975: 89). For more on the proportion of divorced people among the mentally ill, see Blumenthal (1967: 606).
Auto accidents and divorce studies are by McMurray, by Holmes and Rahe, and by Wechsler, Thum, Demone, and Dwinell (cited in Bloom, 1975: 92).
Homicide rate among divorced people: Bloom (1975: 92).
On the initial trauma to children of divorce, see Wallerstein and Kelly (1974, 1975, 1976, 1977) and Kelly and Wallerstein (1976, 1977). On evidence of recovery from this initial trauma, see Luepnitz (1979).
On the high proportion of children of divorce among juvenile delinquents, see Glueck and Glueck (1950: 90-91) and Gregory (1958). On mental patients, see Oltman, McGarry, and Friedman (cited in Gregory, 1958: 439).
On homogeneous moralnets, see Zimmerman and Cervantes (1956, 1960).

15.5.1 Tests of Theories of Sex Taboos

Correlation between level of cultural evolution and tightness of sex taboos: Unwin (1934), Goody (1969), Textor (1967: FC 385/401), Stephens (1972: 13), Cohen (1969), and Prescott (1975).
On transmission of property, sexual freedom, and societal complexity, see Goody (1969, 1976) and Goody, Irving, and Tahany (1970).
For more on sex taboos and wealth, see Rosenblatt, Fugita, and McDowell (1969: 325) and Leeuwe (1970).
On kinship structure and sex taboos, see Murdock (1964) and Zern (1969). For Murdock's correlation between premarital sex taboos and patrilocality, I calculate a tau-b of .22, and a one-tailed chance risk of .001. For Zern's correlation: $r = .36$, and chance risk is less than .05.
On child training, see Whiting and Child (1953).
On sex taboos, see Russell (1972).
Table 15.13: Russell's Anxiety Factor. My correlations come from Russell (1972: 283-285), loadings on rotated factor no. 1. Where I recognized the underlying codings—most of which came from Whiting and Child (1953)—I called the variable by the trait actually coded for, instead of by the label used by the author. For example, line 3 of my table: "Children are thought to be anxious about being punished for hurting other people," comes from Russell's CCS 313, "Agg. Anxiety"—because that is how aggression anxiety was coded; it was a code about punishment of children (Whiting and Child, 1953: 98-102).

Line No. (Table 15.13)	Russell's CCS No.
1	389
2	393
3	313
4	311
5	305
6	308
7	398
8	307
9	302
10	82

All the correlations in my Table 15.13 are positive in sign. I have changed Russell's signs (or reversed his definitions) in order to make his loadings all come out positive. Here my procedure followed two rules: (1) If Russell's signs were negative, I changed them to positive and left it at that. (2) If Russell's signs were positive, I reversed his definition. For example, my line 1 shows a correlation of .60 with the anxiety factor for Premarital Sex Taboos; this number comes from Russell's entry for CCS no. 389 of −602 (Russell omits all leading decimal points from his table). My line 9 comes from Russell's CCS no. 302, "Infant: av. satisfaction"; for that trait, Russell shows a correlation of 465 (i.e., +465). Since the correlation was positive to begin with, and since inverting its definition rather than its sign made Russell's message clearer, I let the sign stand as positive, but changed the label from general *satisfaction* to general *frustration*—frustration, of course, being negative satisfaction.

On premarital sexual restrictions and the child care theory, see Broude (1975: 394, 398) and Barry and Paxson (1971).

15.5.2   Tests of Theories of Divorce

Why are divorced people unhappier than single ones? Perhaps a quatrain from Goethe's *An den Mond* may suggest an answer: "Ich besass es doch einmal/Was so koestlich ist / Dass der Mensch, zu seiner Qual / Nimmer es vergisst." (Once I had the thing which is so precious that, to my sorrow, I can never forget it.)

On lower divorce rates among Americans of homogeneous cultural background, and on friend families, see Zimmerman and Cervantes (1956, 1960).

On divorce and affiliation, see Ackerman (1963).

Table 15.17: Minturn, Grosse, and Haider (1969) report a chi-square of 3.73 for the marital residence correlation in their Table 3, from which I take my third correlation. However, I do not agree; my calculations give a raw chi-square of 4.52, or with Yates's correction, 4.39.

15.5.3   Tests of Theories Linking Sex Taboos and Divorce

On the link between extramarital sex and divorce frequency, see Broude (n.d.). She reports a gamma between male extramarital sex and divorce of .64; of female, .44. The male gamma has a chance risk of less than .01

15.6   Step 4: Further Studies of Home Strength

On marriage and demography among our ancestral apes, see Lovejoy (1981).

On hard times among baboons, see Washburn and Lancaster (1968) cited in Wilson (1981: 93).

On El Niño, see Wilson (1981: 93-120).

On the Siriono, see Holmberg (1969), and Turnbull (1972) on the Ik.

Gilbert and Sullivan's fans remember the tom-tit bird in *The Mikado*; and Shakespeare's remember the jest from *As You Like It*, Act IV, Scene i.

On suicide among the Suk, see Edgerton and Conant (1964).

15.6.1   Further Studies of Sex Taboos

On familial instincts, see Lovejoy (1981).

On pair bonding, see Ember and Ember (1979).

On premarital sex, see Goody (1969).

On the link between extramarital sex and divorce frequency, see Broude (n.d.).

On romantic love, see Rosenblatt (1967) and Rosenblatt, Fugita, and McDowell (1969).

15.7   Step 5: Coping with Weakened Homes

On the link between extramarital sex and divorce frequency, see Broude (n.d.).

On the effect of remarriage on juvenile delinquency (Table 15.7), see Glueck and Glueck (1950: 90f.).

Toward a Worldwide Moral Order

16.1 THE BANNER OF THE THIRTY-FIRST BENGAL

"They'll go too, directly."

The speaker was General Jubal Early of the Army of the Confederate States of America. The scene was the Civil War battlefield of Cedar Creek. The time was October 1864. General Early was pointing to the edge of a wood a thousand yards to the north; there musket fire still sputtered and popped; a remnant of a beaten Union Army was still holding.

"No they won't," said his companion. "That's the Sixth Corps, general. It will not go unless we drive it from the field."

The Sixth Corps was hardly two years old, but it had fought in every major battle of the Army of the Potomac from the Peninsula to Petersburg. Among the soldiers on both sides, the Sixth Corps had a reputation. And rather than lose it, at least one division of that Sixth Corps still stood its dangerous ground and fought.

And the banner of the Thirty-First Bengal. That was the flag before which those Rajput soldiers had taken their oath of allegiance—that the color sergeant would wave in the noise and confusion of battle for the men to see and rally around.

However, the banner of the Thirty-First Bengal disappeared. The British officers could find no hint of what the Rajput soldiers had done with it. It had been riddled with shot at the siege of Bhurtpore in 1805. So torn and tattered by shot and shell that it could no longer be used. For the Thirty-First Bengal had suffered much there. They lost 180 men killed and wounded out of about 400 in two hours of fighting. No one could have asked more of soldiers than the Thirty-First Bengal gave at Bhurtpore. But it proved to be not enough. Despite their valor and their dead, the defenders and the defenses proved too strong. The siege and the assault failed.

Years passed. A generation went by. In 1826, the renamed Thirty-First was once more besieging Bhurtpore—this time as part of a stronger army. This time they took Bhurtpore.

"The troops surged forward to the assault," writes Mason, "through the breaches and into the town, and now it was discovered that the old colors of the Thirty-First had reappeared. The fragments had been secretly preserved as sacred relics by the men who had brought them near the summit of the ramparts under Lord Lake in 1805; their sons brought them out into the light and tied them to the new colors, so that they might redeem by victory the fruitless valor of their fathers."

How did the British manage to instill such loyalty and devotion among the Hindu and Moslem soldiers of their Indian Army? Soldiers of another language, religion, civilization. Who knew nothing of Agincourt, Crecy, Blenheim, or Quebec. Who knew nothing of king or parliament or the rights of Englishmen. Who knew nothing of Christianity's heaven or its hell or of the saving grace of Jesus Christ and the Holy Spirit. Soldiers who knew very much indeed about the cycle of rebirth, the duties of karma, the sacredness of caste, and the beauties of their ancient rituals.

Or how, for that matter, in only two years did service in an army of losers like the Army of the Potomac instill such pride and devotion in the Sixth Corps? How did men come to die for its reputation? Yet die for its reputation men certainly did—as, for example, Ricketts's division did at Spottsylvania.

Or how did the Duke of Wellington put together on the Iberian Peninsula a British army of social misfits—of hard cases and tough characters—to drub the legions of imperial France? "I don't know if they frighten the enemy," said the Duke, of one batch of his recruits, "but they certainly frighten me."

The ability of skilled military officers to weld a body of men quickly into a devoted moralnet gives us hope that such arts could be developed not only for the purposes of war but also for those of peace. If *they* can create a moral order, why can't we?

16.2   MORAL ORDER AROUND THE WORLD

In Section 2.2 I reviewed the history of the great ideological traditions. I noted there that to the typical man in a small-scale society, the moral order embraces only his fellow tribesmen—often only his fellow villagers. But in the last 2,500 years, three religious faiths have spread widely as universal churches—faiths that speak to all mankind—Christianity, Islam, and Buddhism. And the rational humanist ideology of the European enlightenment—whether in the liberal or the Communist version—likewise seeks to embrace all mankind. Today the United Nations embodies these aspirations, and almost all the people of the world are linked in this fraternity of hope.

Around the world, the great ideological systems embodied in the religions of the traditional civilizations have largely lost their authority among most people who have a Western higher education—and that includes the leaders of nearly every nation. Marxism is today the only proposed Western substitute. But *orthodox* Marxism, I suspect, may be no more popular on university campuses around the world than is orthodox Christianity, Islam, or Buddhism. How many

TABLE 16.1   The Grip of Traditional Religious Beliefs

| | *Percentages of People Who Believe . . .* | | | |
Country or Region	*Religion Very Important*	*In Life after Death*	*God Watches, Rewards, and Punishes*[a]	*In Religion in General*[b]
Japan	14	18	25	19
Scandinavia	17	35	28	26.6
West Germany	17	33	36	28.6
France	22	39	37	32.6
United Kingdom	23	43	34	33.3
Australia	25	48	42	38.3
Benelux	26	48	48	40.6
Italy	36	46	56	46
Canada	36	54	49	46.3
Mexico	38	33	70	47
United States	56	69	68	64.3
Brazil	69	53	77	66.3
Sub-Saharan Africa	73	69	86	76
India	86	76	94	85.3

SOURCE: Gallup International Research Institutes (1977: 169-174, Tables 29-31).
a. They believe that God or a universal spirit observes their actions and rewards or punishes them accordingly.
b. Average (mean) of three preceding items.

graduate engineers today really believe that God created the world in six days, as the book of Genesis relates? That God dictated the Koran to Mohammed? That, as Marx and Engels say, the class struggle has been the dominant force in human history?

In neither the Soviet Union nor Saudi Arabia is candor on such matters to be expected from the respondents to a sample survey. However, we do have a report from the Gallup people that gives us more than an inkling of the situation in the 1970s (see Table 16.1).

From this table we see that in France and England, where the philosophy of the European enlightenment took shape about 300 years ago, religious beliefs are of small importance. It is true, as the table shows, that religious beliefs are even less important in Japan than in Western Europe. But we must remember that in China, Japan, Korea, and Vietnam, the traditional moral order rested as much on the secular tradition of Confucian historical studies as on religion.

Perhaps a good hint—a good quick-and-dirty proxy measure—of the relative importance of European secular philosophy around the world is the wearing of Western dress. In how many countries do the young people wear jeans and the heads of states and business leaders wear suits and neckties tailored in the fashion of London, Paris, and New York? And in how many countries do the young people dance to Western music?

The moral order of mankind is in the process of change—that much is plain to see. We are like a sailboat coming about from one tack to the other—the wind is not filling the sails from either side.

In a forum like the United Nations we hear the speakers for nations with the most diverse cultural heritages appealing to many of the core values I follow in the book and set forth in Table 2.1. Even if those appeals were no more than lip service, they would still constitute the beginning of a kind of worldwide moral consensus on what is good for mankind.

As I said, the moral order of the world is coming about. When the sails are full again, might the wind that fills them the world around be the breath of the Five Steps of socionomics?

16.3   STEP 1: CORE VALUES OF A WORLDWIDE MORAL ORDER

The Five Steps offer a flexible and adaptable mode of attainment of a variety of value systems—given only that all share three common goals: peace, order, and tolerance of diversity. In Chapter 2, I set forth a longer list of values on which I rely as a socionomist, the values I use in this book and throughout my studies of the human situation. However, the minimal set of values of a stable worldwide moral order seems to me to include only those three—peace, order, and diversity. Here, the *peace* value requires that all nations abandon war, and that a central authority, perhaps like the Security Council of the United Nations, enforce this taboo. Such a taboo would freeze the boundaries of the nations, much as the boundaries of each of our United States are frozen.

The *order* value requires that every nation attain some kind of stable internal political order, so that civil wars or even riots become a thing of the past. To achieve this value—as some Scandinavian nations may have largely achieved today—presumably requires that a minimal level of social justice and economic efficiency be attained. And manifestly be seen to be attained.

The *tolerance of diversity* value requires that each nation teach and practice tolerance for other nations with differing religious, social, political, and economic ways of life. For without that tolerance, I expect no progress. And without progress, sooner or later there is decay; and with decay, sooner or later collapse. So, no variety, no progress. No progress, no stability. For stability does not mean the absence of change. It means the absence of violent, illegal change. Progress within stability means peaceful change within the law.

Given the attainment of these three values, a stable world order is possible. But this volume is not the place to consider what might be the problems or possibilities of achieving such a goal.

It is enough here to say again what I said in Chapter 2. Given time enough, if a stable world order is possible at all, sooner or later it is inevitable. Whether through sound socionomics and wise planning, or whether instead only through blind trial and error.

16.4   STEP 2: SCOREBOARDS OF MORAL ORDER

I turn now to the measurement of the core values of peace and order. (I take the existence of adequate diversity for granted.) In making public order the measure of the success of a moral order, I do not *here* ask how that order is attained. Many conceivable world orders would buy peace at a price we consider too high, if we heed the core values offered in Chapter 2. Nevertheless, if world peace and civil order are not sufficient conditions for a tolerable world order, they are, I hold, necessary ones—and so I turn now to measure them.

Let us look first at two worldwide scoreboards of war and peace. Table 16.2 ranks the frequency with which nations have been at war during the century and a half from 1816 to 1965. That period begins just at the close of the Napoleonic wars. We see that the nation most frequently at war then was France; other war-prone nations were Great Britain, Turkey, Japan, Spain, Russia, the United States, and Bulgaria.

If we take all wars, great and little, during this century and a half, we find in the tables and charts of Singer and Small only a slight tendency for wars to become either more frequent or more severe in the second half of that period than in the first. However, if we look at the maximums, we see that the worst wars of the twentieth century—the two world wars plus the Chaco war of the 1930s—were of an order of magnitude worse than anything else since Napoleon's day. Thus the battle deaths per million population of the nations involved were huge: 38,235 for the Chaco war, 14,137 for World War I, and 10,912 for World War II.

A prime goal of mankind, I hold, is to reduce these future maximums to zero. In another book I plan to review a large set of rigorous studies showing the tendency of war orientation to snowball. Hence I suspect that nothing is likely to lead socionomists to accept as a proper goal for mankind at large anything less than total and permanent world peace.

A second measure of war and peace is the amount of money spent on defense. We see in Table 16.3 that the nations currently spending the largest share of their wealth on war or the means of war are those in the Middle East. The Communist countries as a group come next, followed by the NATO powers, South Asia, and the Far East. The smallest shares are spent in Oceania and Latin America. A primary goal of mankind is to reduce the future ratios of military budgets to a trifling fraction of their present levels. But here there may be tradeoffs to bear in mind.

A third measure of public order is the frequency of riots and civil disturbances. The tradeoff between freedom from these breakdowns of civil peace on the one hand, and civil liberties on the other, may well prove the deepest test of moral order. A good score on Table 16.4 offers a model only when the nation also enjoys a high level of civil liberties. Here, for example, Norway indeed serves well as a model—for it heads the list in Kurian's rankings of press freedom.

TABLE 16.2   Frequency of Wars Scoreboard (1816-1965)

Country	Frequency of Wars (1816-1965)[a]	Chance Risk
Above Extreme Range		
France[b]	3.34	.0014
Above Indicated Range		
England and Wales[bc]	2.73	.0093
Turkey[b]	2.26	.0319
Canada[b]	2.23	.0343
Spain[b]	1.75	.0983
USSR	1.66	.1173
South Africa	1.55	.1443
Bulgaria	1.41	.1853
Netherlands[b]	1.12	.2964
USA[b]	1.11	.3009
Italy[b]	1.04	.3336
Hungary	1	.3533
Finland	.9	.4057
Bolivia	.79	.4684
Greece[b]	.78	.4744
Romania	.75	.4925
Within Indicated Range		
Yugoslavia[b]	.68	
Mexico	.63	
Belgium[b]	.63	
Brazil	.57	
Argentina	.53	
Paraguay	.51	
Chile	.51	
Peru	.46	
Israel	.28	
Portugal[b]	.22	
Morocco	.19	
Colombia	.19	
Egypt	.17	
Syria	.15	
Lebanon	.13	
Jordan	.13	
Czechoslovakia	.09	
Denmark[b]	.08	
Iraq	.07	
Honduras	.06	
El Salvador	.05	
Norway[b]	.04	MODEL COUNTRY
Iran	.04	
Nicaragua	.03	
Poland	.02	
Guatemala	.02	
Jamaica	0	
Zambia	0	
Yemen	0	

TABLE 16.2 (Continued)

Country	Frequency of Wars (1816-1965)[a]	Chance Risk
Within Indicated Range		
Venezuela	0	
Uruguay	0	
Upper Volta	0	
Uganda	0	
Tunisia	0	
Trinidad and Tobago	0	
Togo	0	
Tanzania	0	
Switzerland[b]	0	
Sweden[b]	0	
Sudan	0	
Somalia	0	
Sierra Leone	0	
Senegal	0	
Saudi Arabia	0	
Rwanda	0	
Panama	0	
Nigeria	0	
Niger	0	
Mauritania	0	
Malta	0	
Mali	0	
Malawi	0	
Luxembourg[b]	0	
Libya	0	
Liberia	0	
Kuwait	0	
Kenya	0	
Ivory Coast	0	
Ireland[b]	0	
Iceland[b]	0	
Haiti	0	
Guinea	0	
Ghana	0	
Germany (West)[b]	0	
Germany (East)	0	
Gabon	0	
Ethiopia	0	
Ecuador	0	
Dominican Republic	0	
Cyprus	0	
Cuba	0	
Costa Rica	0	
Congo	0	
Chad	0	
Cameroon	0	

(continued)

TABLE 16.2 (Continued)

Country	Frequency of Wars (1816-1965)[a]	Chance Risk
Within Indicated Range		
Burundi	0	
Austria[b]	0	
Algeria	0	

SOURCE: Singer and Small (1972: 274-280). Worldwide averages and spreads of 94 countries reporting (normal distribution):[d] mean: 0.33; median: 0.00; range: 3.34; SD: 0.646; CEV: 196.55%. Worldwide averages and spreads of 21 OECD countries reporting (normal distribution): mean: 0.85762; median: 0.63; range: 3.34; SD: 1.03436; CEV: 120.61%; skew: 1.03; kurtosis: −0.00.

a. Mean war months per year: 12.0 = perpetual; 6.0 = partial war.
b. Member of the Organization for Economic Cooperation and Development (OECD).
c. United Nations reporting unit; not an independent nation.
d. See Glossary for meanings of worldwide measures.
SD = standard deviation.
CEV = coefficient of evolutionary variation.

Finally, two scoreboards on crime measure public respect for law as well as it can be: The Murder Ratio Scoreboard (Table 16.5) measures a crime that seems more likely to be reported than most others—and one that in every culture is reprehensible. The Juvenile Criminal Ratio Scoreboard (Table 16.6) measures the strength of family moralnets in raising law-abiding children; it compares the frequency of crimes by youths with crimes by the population at large.

I offer here no formal measures of cultural variety around the world. As I said, I take that for granted. For though we may suffer the want of both peace and order, we certainly do not want for variety in the world today. Not in economics, politics, religion, language, or styles of living.

16.5   STEP 3: REVIEW OF TESTS OF MORAL ORDER THEORY

There are two kinds of moral order theory that I review now. First, theories that link the moral order with public order—that link value systems and moralnets on the one hand with wars, rebellions, and crimes on the other. Second, theories that link weakened moralnets with other social ills like mental illness and suicide. Together these constitute a weakened moralnets model of social disorder (Table 16.7).

In Chapter 6, I reviewed Sorokin's study linking changes in the value system (the ideological order) to the frequencies of both civil and foreign wars. And I showed that riots and civil disturbances were more frequent in culturally diverse countries than in culturally homogeneous ones. In Chapter 12 on youth crime, I reviewed studies linking youth with moralnet ties. In Chapter 5, I reviewed Horan's THINCS study of tests of theories of the causes of murder. She surveyed a broad range of theory tests. She found many studies tending to

(*text continues p. 386*)

TABLE 16.3   Defense Budgets Scoreboard (1975)

Country	Defense Budgets (1975)[a]	Chance Risk
Above Extreme Range		
Egypt	44.29	.0000
Oman	39.41	.0000
Israel	27.69	.0000
Iran	14.19	.0000
Iraq	14.04	.0000
Saudi Arabia	12.83	.0000
Syria	12.82	.0000
Yemen (Southern)	12.19	.0000
Jordan	12.13	.0000
USSR	11.94	.0000
Albania	11.22	.0000
Korea (North)	10.3	.0000
Cambodia	10	.0000
Mongolia	9	.0005
Laos	8.66	.0011
Above Indicated Range		
Nigeria	7.38	.0126
Vietnam	7.04	.0221
China (Taiwan)	6.82	.0311
Somalia	6.64	.0407
Pakistan	6.5	.0498
Greece[b]	6.33	.0630
China (PRC)	6.29	.0665
USA[b]	5.99	.0983
Qatar	5.95	.1033
Turkey[b]	5.4	.1950
Singapore	5.37	.2013
Cuba	5.11	.2626
Yugoslavia[b]	5.09	.2678
Malaysia (Malaya)	5.05	.2784
Korea (South)	5.03	.2838
United Kingdom[b]	5.02	.2865
Portugal[b]	5.01	.2893
Guinea-Bissau	4.9	.3207
Within Indicated Range		
Chad	4.36	
Burma	4.35	
South Africa	4.27	
Zaire	4.17	
Indonesia	4.01	
Germany (East)	4.01	
Yemen	4	
Lebanon	3.88	
France[b]	3.87	
Zambia	3.82	
Chile	3.7	

(continued)

TABLE 16.3 (Continued)

Country	Defense Budgets (1975)[a]	Chance Risk
Within Indicated Range		
Germany (West)[b]	3.6	
Czechoslovakia	3.55	
Netherlands[b]	3.54	
India	3.49	
Congo	3.41	
Sweden[b]	3.38	
Ethiopia	3.37	
Tanzania	3.35	
Uganda	3.29	
Norway[b]	3.26	MODEL COUNTRY
Morocco	3.24	
Bulgaria	3.06	
Thailand	3.03	
Belgium[b]	3.01	
Peru	3	
Zimbabwe (Rhodesia)	2.97	
Bolivia	2.9	
Angola	2.88	
Sudan	2.86	
Italy[b]	2.79	
Hungary	2.7	
Poland	2.69	
Guinea	2.63	
Philippines	2.58	
Denmark[b]	2.58	
Australia	2.58	
Kuwait	2.54	
Cyprus	2.49	
Mauritania	2.47	
Bahrain	2.43	
Uruguay	2.42	
Spain[b]	2.23	
Venezuela	2.17	
Below Indicated Range		
Burundi	2.14	.4977
Guyana	2.06	.4675
Canada[b]	2.02	.4527
Argentina	2	.4455
Switzerland[b]	1.94	.4241
Rwanda	1.92	.4171
Mali	1.91	.4137
Ecuador	1.91	.4137
Algeria	1.89	.4068
Nicaragua	1.82	.3832
New Zealand	1.77	.3669
Upper Volta	1.73	.3542
Paraguay	1.73	.3542

TABLE 16.3 (Continued)

Country	Defense Budgets (1975)[a]	Chance Risk
Below Indicated Range		
Brazil	1.73	.3542
Romania	1.72	.3511
Afghanistan	1.69	.3417
Libya	1.65	.3296
Benin	1.65	.3296
Honduras	1.64	.3266
Senegal	1.59	.3119
Ivory Coast	1.58	.3090
Tunisia	1.57	.3061
Togo	1.53	.2948
Madagascar	1.51	.2893
Finland	1.51	.2893
Cameroon	1.5	.2865
Ireland	1.41	.2626
Kenya	1.39	.2575
Dominican Republic	1.3	.2353
Gabon	1.17	.2056
Ghana	1.16	.2035
Austria[b]	1.15	.2013
Haiti	1.14	.1992
Guatemala	1.13	.1971
El Salvador	1.11	.1929
United Arab Emirates	1.09	.1888
Luxembourg[b]	1.07	.1848
Colombia	.97	.1655
Japan[b]	.94	.1600
Bangladesh	.9	.1530
Sri Lanka	.8	.1363
Sierra Leone	.77	.1316
Mexico	.75	.1285
Liberia	.75	.1285
Malawi	.74	.1270
Nepal	.66	.1154
Jamaica	.64	.1126
Niger	.62	.1099
Malta	.41	.0844
Costa Rica	.37	.0801
Trinidad and Tobago	.26	.0693
Panama	.18	.0622
Mauritius	.18	.0622
Fiji	.15	.0597
Barbados	0	.0484

SOURCE: Kurian (1979: 75f.). Worldwide averages and spreads of 132 countries reporting (normal distribution):[d] mean: 4.28; median: 2.66; range: 44.29; SD: 5.995; CEV: 139.93%. Worldwide averages and spreads of 22 OECD countries reporting (normal distribution): mean: 3.24000; median: 3.14; range: 5.39; SD: 1.65141; CEV: 50.97%; skew: 0.34; kurtosis: 0.00.

a. Defense expenditures as a percentage of GNP.
b. Member of the Organization for Economic Cooperation and Development (OECD).
c. See Glossary for meanings of worldwide measures.

SD = standard deviation.
CEV = coefficient of evolutionary variation.

TABLE 16.4   Civil Disorder Index Scoreboard

Country	Civil Disorder Index[a]	Chance Risk
Above Extreme Range		
Spain[b]	83	.0003
Above Indicated Range		
Italy[b]	58	.0111
South Africa	56	.0142
Iran	51	.0255
Argentina	50	.0286
Portugal[b]	41	.0725
Turkey[b]	37	.1051
Pakistan	33	.1484
Ethiopia	33	.1484
USA[b]	32	.1610
India	30	.1888
China (PRC)	25	.2735
Peru	23	.3138
Israel	23	.3138
France[b]	23	.3138
Colombia	23	.3138
El Salvador	21	.3577
Thailand	20	.3810
Lebanon	19	.4053
Nicaragua	17	.4565
Korea (South)	17	.4565
Philippines	16	.4835
Within Indicated Range		
Japan[b]	15	
Guatemala	15	
United Kingdom[b]	14	
Zimbabwe (Rhodesia)	13	
Sri Lanka	12	
Burma	12	
Mexico	11	
Laos	11	
Angola	11	
Jamaica	10	
Bolivia	10	
Greece[b]	9	
Cambodia	9	
Uganda	8	
Nigeria	8	
Vietnam	7	
Malaysia (Malaya)	7	
Kenya	7	
Bangladesh	7	
Oman	6	
Iraq	6	
Chad	6	

TABLE 16.4 (Continued)

Country	Civil Disorder Index[a]	Chance Risk
Within Indicated Range		
Yemen	5	
Indonesia	5	
Honduras	5	
Egypt	5	
Ecuador	5	
Cyprus	5	
Zaire	4	
Yugoslavia[b]	4	
Panama	4	
Mauritania	4	
Congo	4	
Canada[b]	4	
Australia	4	
Afghanistan	4	
Venezuela	3	
USSR	3	
Tunisia	3	
Romania	3	
Poland	3	
Netherlands[b]	3	
Libya	3	
Comoros	3	
Brazil	3	
Belgium[b]	3	
Uruguay	2	
Sudan	2	
Sierra Leone	2	
Saudi Arabia	2	
Mozambique	2	
Kuwait	2	
Ghana	2	
Germany (West)[b]	2	
Finland	2	
Yemen (Southern)	1	
Syria	1	
Somalia	1	
Seychelles	1	
Niger	1	
New Zealand	1	
Morocco	1	
Maldives	1	
Malawi	1	
Madagascar	1	
Ireland[b]	1	
Haiti	1	
Guinea-Bissau	1	
Guinea	1	
Denmark[b]	1	

(continued)

TABLE 16.4 (Continued)

Country	Civil Disorder Index[a]	Chance Risk
Within Indicated Range		
Czechoslovakia	1	
China (Taiwan)	1	
Benin	1	
Austria[b]	1	
Algeria	1	
Albania	1	
Sweden[b]	0	
Norway[b]	0	MODEL COUNTRY

SOURCE: Kurian (1979: 57). Worldwide averages and spreads of 100 countries reporting (normal distribution):[c] mean: 10.76; median: 4.50; range: 83.00; SD: 14.746; CEV: 137.04%. Worldwide averages and spreads of 20 OECD countries reporting (normal distribution): mean: 16.60000; median: 4.00 range: 83.00; SD: 22.83210; CEV: 137.54%; skew: 1.60; kurtosis: –0.00.

a. Incidents of civil disorder (1975-1978).
b. Member of the Organization for Economic Cooperation and Development (OECD).
c. See Glossary for meanings of worldwide measures.

SD = standard deviation.
CEV = coefficient of evolutionary variation.

support the theory that murderers are more likely than other people to suffer from weakened moralnets (see Appendix G for her findings).

The evidence linking weakened moralnets to human suffering reviewed in Part Two of this book is overwhelming. There can be no doubt that people with weaker moralnets are more likely to suffer other ills as well. This evidence on mental illness, alcoholism, suicide, child battering (where we speak of the moralnet ties of the battering parents), and youth crime can hardly leave any doubt in anyone's mind. Yet there is still more evidence I can cite of other sorts of troubles.

Item: In the Safe School Study conducted by the National Institute of Education, Ianni and Reuss-Ianni found that in the United States in 1978 the smaller schools were safer; they found school spirit stronger in smaller schools. In other words, it is easier to organize a smaller school into a moralnet, with its school traditions and its school values, than a larger one.

Item: Kagan and Levi studied the medical effects of stress. In a comprehensive review of more than 180 medical research reports, they link seven major sources of stress to a number of ailments. The causal role of these stresses they consider as yet unproven but "at a high level of suspicion." First on their list are stresses from family ties—especially from death of a loved one. Other sources of stress that they list from other moralnets are school, religion, work, and housing (overcrowding). Five of their seven stressors involve weakening moralnets of one sort or another, one way or another. Like Brown and Harris on mental illness, Kagan and Levi see the role of these stresses as

TABLE 16.5 Murder Rate Scoreboard

Country	Murder Rate[a]	Chance Risk
Above Extreme Range		
Lesotho	140.81	.0000
Bahamas	22.88	.0000
Guyana	22.21	.0000
Lebanon	20.33	.0000
Iraq	11.94	.0001
Sri Lanka	11.92	.0001
Cyprus	11.11	.0002
Trinidad and Tobago	10.41	.0003
Jamaica	10.25	.0003
USA[b]	9.6	.0004
Kuwait	9.18	.0005
Tanzania	8.98	.0005
Kenya	8.66	.0006
Madagascar	8.14	.0008
Burma	8.06	.0009
Venezuela	7.19	.0014
Netherlands[b]	7.15	.0015
Chile	6.89	.0017
Above Indicated Range		
Jordan	6.06	.0028
Syria	5.52	.0040
Luxembourg[b]	5.25	.0049
Mali	5.02	.0058
Finland	4.88	.0064
Malawi	4.57	.0081
Germany (West)[b]	4.47	.0087
Sierra Leone	4	.0128
Scotland[bc]	3.82	.0149
Libya	3.77	.0156
Egypt	3.45	.0208
India	3.4	.0217
Sweden[b]	3.36	.0226
Austria[b]	3.06	.0301
Italy[b]	2.95	.0336
Singapore	2.77	.0404
Nigeria	2.75	.0413
Australia	2.73	.0421
France[b]	2.7	.0435
Philippines	2.68	.0444
Hong Kong[c]	2.59	.0489
Malaysia (Malaya)	2.49	.0546
Peru	2.44	.0577
England and Wales[bc]	2.24	.0726
Denmark[b]	2.03	.0934
Japan[b]	1.74	.1354
New Zealand	1.51	.1857
Korea (South)	1.33	.2414

(continued)

TABLE 16.5 (Continued)

Country	Murder Rate[a]	Chance Risk
Above Indicated Range		
Zaire	1.19	.2992
Morocco	1.11	.3396
Ivory Coast	1.09	.3508
Within Indicated Range		
Indonesia	.87	
Greece[b]	.87	
Uganda	.83	
Fiji	.71	
Spain[b]	.67	
Norway[b]	.5	MODEL COUNTRY

SOURCE: Kurian (1979: 339). Worldwide averages and spreads of 55 countries reporting (log-normal distribution):[d] mean of the natural logarithms: 1.37; median: 3.77; range: 140.31; SD: 1.049; CEV: 76.48%. Worldwide averages and spreads of 15 OECD countries reporting (log-normal distribution): mean of the natural logarithms: 0.93104; median: 2.95; range: 9.10; SD: 0.83520; CEV: 89.71%; skew: −0.48; kurtosis: 0.79.

a. Murder rate per 100,000 population.
b. Member of the Organization for Economic Cooperation and Development (OECD).
c. United Nations reporting unit; not an independent nation.
d. See Glossary for meanings of worldwide measures.

SD = standard deviation of natural logarithms.
CEV = coefficient of evolutionary variation.

part of a larger pattern of predisposing and protective factors. People with weaker moralnets are less resistant to attacks of disease, and the stress of a blow to the moralnet can trigger an organic ailment to which the victim was already predisposed. Kagan and Levi point specifically to disorders of the digestive tract, thyroid, and heart, and to blood pressure.

There remains the urgent question of the link between weakened moralnets and other ills. That it is one of cause and effect has not yet been plainly demonstrated—any more than the process of the evolution of species or the causal link between tobacco smoking and lung cancer have been. But as with lung cancer, there is strong evidence not only of association but also of sequence.

In the chapters on mental illness and suicide we saw clear evidence that weakened moralnets tend to precede these ills; and in the chapter on alcoholism we saw the impressive results that tend to follow a commitment to Alcoholics Anonymous.

But perhaps the most impressive single study of sequence is that by Berkman and Syme—the random sample of 7,000 people in Alameda County, you may remember. In that study they looked carefully at the strength of the whole moralnet—not just of the nuclear family. First they measured those moralnet ties and then they waited for nine years to see what would happen. And sure

TABLE 16.6   Juvenile Criminal Ratio Scoreboard

Country	Juvenile Criminal Ratio[a]	Chance Risk
Within Indicated Range		
Norway[b]	56.45	MODEL COUNTRY
Australia	39.75	
Below Indicated Range		
Bahamas	37.23	.4369
USA[b]	31.3	.2706
Denmark[b]	30.31	.2454
New Zealand	29.88	.2347
Germany (West)[b]	27.5	.1792
Finland	25.76	.1428
Madagascar	24.97	.1276
Netherlands[b]	24.8	.1245
England[b] and Wales[c]	24.77	.1239
Venezuela	23.74	.1057
Austria[b]	23.6	.1033
Japan[b]	22.9	.0920
Libya	21.32	.0690
Luxembourg[b]	20.13	.0541
Malaysia (Malaya)	17.71	.0304
Peru	17.36	.0277
Chile	14.62	.0116
Cyprus	12.93	.0059
Lesotho	12.89	.0058
Korea (South)	12.57	.0050
Ivory Coast	12.57	.0050
Philippines	11.63	.0032
Below Extreme Range		
France[b]	10.57	.0018
Mali	8.97	.0006
Sierra Leone	8.96	.0006
Greece[b]	7.6	.0002
Trinidad and Tobago	6.99	.0001
Morocco	5.31	.0000
Jamaica	5.25	.0000
Hong Kong[c]	4.72	.0000
Kenya	4.39	.0000
India	4.28	.0000
Kuwait	3.93	.0000
Malawi	3.11	.0000
Nigeria	2.82	.0000
Guyana	2.36	.0000
El Salvador	2.08	.0000
Fiji	1.45	.0000
Burma	1.09	.0000
Egypt	.28	.0000

SOURCE: Kurian (1979: 345). Worldwide averages and spreads of 42 countries reporting (lognormal distribution):[d] mean of the natural logarithms: 2.31; median: 12.73; range: 56.17; SD: 1.125; CEV: 48.59%. Worldwide averages and spreads of 11 OECD countries reporting (lognormal distribution): mean of the natural logarithms: 3.11853; median: 24.77; range: 48.85; SD: 0.53538; CEV: 17.17%; skew: −0.62; kurtosis: 0.70.

(notes continued)

TABLE 16.6 NOTES

a. Percentage of juvenile offenders (mid-1970s) in the population as a whole.
b. Member of the Organization for Economic Cooperation and Development (OECD).
c. United Nations reporting unit; not an independent nation.
d. See Glossary for meanings of worldwide measures.
SD = standard deviation of natural logarithms.
CEV = coefficient of evolutionary variation.

TABLE 16.7   The Weakened Moralnets Model of Social Ills

Causes of Strong Moralnets	*Consequences of Weak Moralnets*
(1) Strong social ties to moralnet	(1) Murder
(2) Emotional warmth from moralnet	(2) Theft and fraud
(3) Economic support from moralnet	(3) Hard drinking—alcoholism
(4) Political support from moralnet	(4) Drug abuse
(5) Cultural homogeneity of moralnet	(5) Suicide
(6) Frequent moral group rituals by moralnet	(6) Brawling
(7) Appealing and memorable charter myths	(7) Wife beating
(8) Plausible ideology	(8) Child battering
(9) Badges or emblems of larger social groups, reinforcing moralnet ideology	(9) Mental illness: neuroses
(10) Promptness of punishment for crime, reinforcing moralnet ideology	(10) Mental illness: psychoses
(11) Probability of punishment for crime, reinforcing moralnet ideology	
(12) Active gossip, shaming those who weaken moralnets	

enough, the weaker the moralnets at the start, the higher the death rates thereafter. Among men and women, old and young, rich and poor, learned and unlettered, smokers and nonsmokers, fat people and thin people, the physically active and the physically passive, the hard drinkers and the abstainers, those with good health care and those with poor, those with good health practices and those with poor, and those whose health was good when the study began as well as those whose health was then poor. Yes, among each of these groups, taken alone, those with weaker moralnet ties were more likely to die than those with stronger ones. Thus Berkman and Syme not only showed sequence but also ruled out nine lurking variables: sex, age, wealth, tobacco, alcohol, exercise, health itself, health care, and health practices.

There is still another large class of studies—those of widowhood—that link an earlier blow to the later occurrence of other sorrows. Parkes compared the health of 44 widows after bereavement with their health before. Widows under the age of 65 with emotional or mental problems visited their doctors three times as often in the six months after their husbands' deaths as before. For physical problems, they went half again as often. Parkes reviewed a wide range of rival hypotheses; it seemed to him very likely that the bereavement itself was the cause of the increase, not only in the mental but also the physical ailments—and in the actual ailments, not just in the frequency of visits to the doctor.

Maddison and Viola used a single, standardized medical questionnaire on matched samples of widows and unwidowed controls in both Boston, Massachusetts, and Sydney, Australia. They, too, found a marked increase in both mental and physical symptoms among the widowed compared to the controls; their report compares the symptoms of several score of ailments, from nervousness and depression through indigestion, vomiting, and weight loss, to diabetes and cancer.

> He first deceased; she for a little tried
> To live without him; liked it not, and died.

Rees and Lutkins tested this poetic thought by a study of death rates among nearly 700 Welsh families. They looked at ties with close relatives: husbands and wives, mothers and fathers, sons and daughters, brothers and sisters. They compared the close relatives of a group of 371 people who died at the start of the study with a matched group of like family clusters who had not suffered a recent death. For the first four years—and especially during the first year—the bereaved group was much more likely to have someone die than the control group. This tendency held good not only among the widowed but also among parents, children, brothers, and sisters. Because most of their subjects were adults, in their work they looked largely at ties among the extended rather than the nuclear family.

In many studies the researchers do look beyond the nuclear family at the full friend-family network: The pioneer study of Zimmerman and Cervantes, discussed once again later in this chapter; the Berkman and Syme Alameda County study just reviewed above; the Mintz and Schwartz study of Boston Italians; the Hertfordshire housing study project; the New Haven Stress study; the North Uist study; and the Sydney study—all reviewed in Chapter 7. In Chapter 8, I showed the role of Alcoholics Anonymous—another study of a wider moralnet. In Chapter 11, I linked neglect or abuse of children to weakness of ties between the nuclear and the extended family. In Chapter 12, I linked youth crime to the peer group moralnet. In Chapter 14, I linked spouse beating to household structure: It was rare in extended family households, common in nuclear family households. In Chapter 15, I showed that divorce was less likely when the couple had like values—and so, one could argue, were more easily linked to the wider moralnet.

Finally, I want to look at Cabot's controlled experiment follow-up. In 1935, Cabot had studied 500 boys, half of whom had been randomly assigned to a five-year treatment program; the other half had been let alone. In 1970 these two groups of men were restudied by McCord. She found that the experimental treatment had not only done no good but had done positive harm. The men who had been the subjects of well-meaning experiments had been injured rather than helped. She believes that the poorer subsequent histories of the experimental group are most likely to be explained by supposing that the treatment disrupted normal moralnets without putting anything else in their place. Dr. Cabot treated individuals, and failed; Dr. Ihembi treated whole moralnets, and succeeded.

Taken together, then, as Figure 16.1 shows, the support for a general weakened moralnets theory is impressive: that weakened moralnets are not merely linked to all those physical, mental, and social ills, but play some direct part in causing them. In other words, if we can strengthen moralnets we can thereby lessen mental illness, alcoholism, suicide, child neglect and child battering, juvenile delinquency, and divorce.

16.6   STEP 4: PLANNING FURTHER STUDIES OF MORAL ORDER THEORY

16.6.1   A Model of Moral Order Theory

The evidence in Figure 16.1 that, in general, weakened moralnets cause social ills seems, then, strong indeed. Still, nothing would be more likely to produce prompt and general consensus among behavioral scientists on this point than some conspicuously successful programs to reduce these ills by strengthening those moralnets.

And while evidence on the effects of weak moralnets is strong, evidence on the means of building strong moralnets is weak. We still cannot be sure why those men carried the banner of the Thirty-First Bengal into Bhurtpore, or why the Sixth Corps stood and fought at Cedar Creek. So I have offered here a general model linking twelve causes of strong moralnets and ten consequences of weak ones and call for triangulation—for five diverse tests of the model (see Table 16.7).

Causes

Cause 1: Moralnets are weaker when people have weaker social ties to them. There is some evidence that suggests that the link between moralnet strength and size, on the one hand, and homicide, on the other, may be curvilinear. It may be that beyond a certain point, moralnets can get too close, too tight, too stifling. So the problem may well be to fix the optimum. What is the ideal size of a moralnet? And how often should the people meet? In their studies of American families, Zimmerman and Cervantes point to an ideal of a *nuclear* family household visiting other such households often—but not to an *extended* family household.

Cause 2: Moralnets are weaker when people get less emotional warmth from them. Warmth of social ties is the key idea of the PAR studies by Rohner and his group discussed in Section 11.4. These studies show that cold treatment of children by parents does much damage. This theory extends the Rohner thought to the whole moralnet—not just to the parents.

Cause 3: Moralnets are weaker when people get less economic support from them. I take it that a moralnet should offer a moral order that includes: a good livelihood, a plan to guide the young into adult roles that meet their material

Theory: In General, Weakened Moralnets Mean Trouble

Theory Trust Ratio: 83%

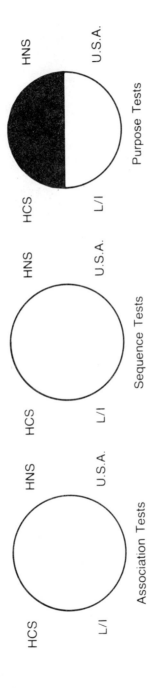

SOURCES   HCS: Figures 8.1, 9.1, 11.1; HNS: Figure 9.1; L/I: Figures 7.1, 8.1, 9.1, 11.1, 12.1; U.S.A.: Figures 8.1, 9.1, 11.1.
NOTE: See *Theory trust meter* in Glossary for a key to this chart, and Section 4.5.3 for the general manner of its composition.
HCS = holocultural test; HNS = holonational test; L/I = local or individual test; U.S.A. = countrywide tests in the United States.

Figure 16.1 Weakened Moralnets Theory Trust Meter

needs and expectations, and an insurance system, the members of which take care of their own.

Cause 4: Moralnets are weaker when people get less political support from them. Political support here is measured as group protection from enemies. An enemy is another person or animal that threatens to harm one's body or to interfere with one's way of life. I take it that the human social order—like that of other social apes—includes an instinctive plan for political support of members by the local group or band, the primeval moralnet.

Cause 5: Moralnets are stronger when people display badges or emblems of their moralnet or of a social group to which it belongs. Here I would count the food taboo of a totemic animal as one such display. Suppose people say they belong to the emu totem, and therefore may never eat emu meat. If their close social ties run to other members of the emu totem, then I would count that as an equivalent of displaying a badge or emblem; but if people say they may not eat pork because it is unclean, then I would not count it.

Cause 6: Moralnets are stronger when people often take part in moral group ceremonies with their fellow members. By a ceremony, I mean a program whose output is merely symbolic, whose output does not in itself help the group gain a livelihood or defend it against its enemies. By a moral ceremony I mean one with strong reminders of events in the charter myths of the moral ideology of the group.

Cause 7: Moralnets are stronger when people have emotionally appealing and memorable charter myths. By a charter myth I mean a tale—or group of tales—that one way or another sets forth and justifies the moral code of the group. Emotional appeal of charter myths could be measured by judges who hear or read the tales but who do not know the homicide rate of the people. If several judges tend to agree, then we would feel confident that they are measuring the same sort of thing. And if their measurements do correlate with murder rate, if this theory is wrong, how else can we explain that linkage?

Memorability of a charter myth could be measured by judges who have never seen or heard the myth before. Let them hear or read the myth. Then test them for recall of its details.

Cause 8: Moralnets are stronger when people have a plausible ideology—a folk theory of morality they trust. The collection of charter myths should contain moral arguments that tend to be supported by the events related in the myth. One widely used device is to tie morality and health: Bad health is a punishment for bad deeds, the Navajo say, for example. Another widely used device is a theory of the afterlife: Bad behavior in this life will be punished in the afterlife, good behavior, rewarded.

Cause 9: Moralnets are stronger when people are culturally homogeneous. This theory holds that moralnet strength comes from like marrying like, like intimately associating with like. But there are two ways to produce cultural homogeneity. One is to make selective choices: In complex, culturally heterogeneous societies, form close social ties only with people of like subcultures. The other is to engender cultural homogeneity through intensive schooling: in schools like West Point, Annapolis, Eton, Harrow, or boot camp, which impose a total set of moral attitudes through stern disciplines. Many initiation rites or bush schools have like patterns of social pressure.

Cause 10: Crime rates are lower when crime is more probably punished.

Cause 11: Crime rates are lower when crime is more promptly punished. These two theories assert that it is promptness and likelihood of punishment, rather than severity, that discourage crime.

Cause 12: Moralnets are stronger where gossip nets are busier. This theory asserts that in cultures in which gossip is encouraged and people meet more often to gossip, the moral codes are more strictly enforced than where people gossip less often—by controlling the frequency of gossip, we can control the moral behavior.

Consequences

I would look for many of these twelve causes of moralnet strength just cited to be linked with at least ten consequences of moralnet weakness. The more a society has of these causes, I submit, the less it will have of the following:

Consequence 1: Murder. Perhaps the easiest serious and universal crime to measure. It is, of course, the local definition of illicit homicide that we must call murder.

Consequence 2: Theft and fraud. Here we must pay attention to emics. It is again the local definition of theft and fraud crimes that we need to go by in this test.

Consequence 3: Hard drinking—alcoholism. (Can be tested only in cultures in which alcohol is used.)

Consequence 4: Drug abuse. (Can be tested only in cultures in which attractive but harmful drugs are available.)

Consequence 5: Suicide.

Consequence 6: Brawling.

Consequence 7: Wife beating. Whatever the moral code of the culture, wives do not like this.

Consequence 8: Child battering. Whatever the moral code of the culture, children do not like this.

Consequence 9: Mental Illness—Neuroses.

Consequence 10: Mental Illness—Psychoses.

In the five subsections that follow, I propose five massive tests of the weakened moralnets model: (1) a holocultural study, (2) a cross-national survey, (3) more friend-family studies, (4) more self-help clubs, and (5) more therapeutic communities.

16.6.2   A Holocultural Study to Test the Model

The most general test of moral theory is holocultural. Small-scale societies, taken all together, have the widest range of variation in moral codes, and the widest range of variation in kinds of ideology, ritual, economic structure, political structure, emotional ties, social ties to moralnets, kinds of badges or emblems of social groups, and patterns of punishment. But what we gain in generality in a holocultural study, we lose in precision, and in relevance to our own problems today. So a holocultural study of moral theory is only the first of five major tests I call for here. Of the ten consequences of immorality I list in Table 16.7, eight have already been coded holoculturally: murder, theft, hard drinking, drug abuse, suicide, brawling, wife beating, and child battering. None of the twelve causes of strong morality I listed has been coded holoculturally before. Not as such. But many related topics have been.

To measure ideology, two things need to be looked at. First, whether the culture includes a complete ideology—a full theory of moral behavior relating one person's behavior somehow to the whole scheme of things. Second, whether people believe and trust that ideology. Holoculturally, the matter of trust might be measured by the local resistance of foreign ideologies—the persistence of local faith.

I predict that these studies will confirm strong links—high correlations— between many of the twelve causes and many of the ten consequences of weakened moralnets. If so, a worldwide set of coordinated field studies could be a logical next step: to compare the weakened moralnets model in twenty or thirty or forty different cultures.

The Hopi of Arizona offer a familiar problem. They are split into traditionalists who want to keep up the old way of thought, and modernists who want to move into the electronic age of the White Man's America. The moralnet model would predict the weakest moralnets among those caught in the middle, those torn between two factions—among those children of traditional homes, for example, who lose respect for the old ways and seek to learn the new. This Hopi situation, so well described by Thompson, is one repeated many times all over the world.

Finally, a set of ethnohistorical studies might also be valuable. Each study needs to begin in a traditional culture with a trustworthy report from fifty or a hundred years ago, on at least one of the model's ten consequences of moralnet weakness. Then, as the traditional culture breaks down—and nearly all *have* broken down, more or less—the incidence of that consequence or symptom of moralnet weakness needs to be measured. Here we look for lag. Does the linkage between decay of ideology and ritual precede, accompany, or follow an increase in the level of the symptom of that decay? Of homicide rate or child beating, for example?

16.6.3   A Cross-National Survey to Test the Model

We need something like the Gallup *Human Needs and Satisfactions* worldwide sample survey, but with a much larger sample. Large enough so that thirty or forty nations can be reported individually, with questions probing the activities of gossip networks. And with supplementary studies of the ideologies of political parties, and studies of promptness and probability of punishment for crime.

Such studies need to use trained local people as interviewers—not graduate students from the Collège de France or Oxford or Berne—to talk to the farm people of Provence or Ayrshire or Valais: In most countries, the farm people still speak their own village dialects; they learn the national literary language in school, but are not really at home in it. After careful training, such local people are the ones used by most of the Gallup affiliates around the world, for they are at home in both languages.

If frequency of mental illness were to form part of this study, then cross-cultural psychiatrists, of course, would have to play a large part in the planning and interviewing. In Chapter 7, I reviewed the methods that have been developed to measure the frequency of mental illness through sample survey interviews in a variety of cultural settings.

16.6.4 More Friend-Family Studies to Test the Model

In Sections 6.4 and 10.5 I spoke of the friend-family study of high school students by Zimmerman and Cervantes. That study takes mere correlation as showing causation. It is merely a study of statistical association. It does not study sequence—not to speak of purpose. As I have said, the friend-family study is the best direct study of moralnets we have. Whatever its weaknesses, this work is way ahead of whatever else is in second place. (True, the Hirschi study of youth crime is far more skillfully done, but he deals only with nuclear family ties, not with friend families.) It is these weaknesses of the Zimmerman and Cervantes study that we need to work on.

Zimmerman and Cervantes found that the high school students they questioned got into the least amount of trouble with the police when their families were linked into a *good* network of friend families. A friend family is another nuclear family that the student's own family household often visits, entertains, and associates with. That *good* network of friend families turned out to consist of at least five families that were all culturally similar to the student's—similar in religious belief, social class, region of origin—that is, from the same part of the United States as the student's family. And finally, similar in family tradition, because they were not merely friends but also relatives—kinfolk.

Zimmerman and Cervantes looked only at boys and girls who stayed in school long enough to become high school seniors. So they called their work a study of *successful* American families. They did not study dropouts. Nevertheless, the strong link between number and homogeneity of friend families on the one hand, and trouble with the police on the other, from so large a sample, deeply impresses me. Especially when I see that—insofar as Hirschi's more careful study checks this one on the importance of family ties—it tells a like story.

Zimmerman and Cervantes contrast the high proportion of divorced families in their sample with the low proportion of such families in the social circles of those who are not themselves divorced. From this fact, they conclude that intact families systematically avoid close ties with divorced ones—and so present a model of a network of intact families to their children.

Zimmerman and Cervantes were pioneers. In my view, no more urgent task faces us today, if we want to build a moral order for mankind, than to redo their work. And do it better. First, we need to contrast "successful" families with "unsuccessful" ones. Compare high school seniors with dropouts. Second, we need to measure sequence with lagged data. Get data on family homogeneity one year. And data on intervening moral trouble the year after. Third, we need to measure many kinds of moral trouble—not only with police, but with divorce among parents, marriage troubles among the high school seniors themselves, drug use, suicide, mental illness, hard drinking, extramarital children.

That divorce and extramarital children are themselves moral troubles is, of course, a theory to be tested. But the findings of Zimmerman and Cervantes lead us to expect that both events tend to produce weak friend-family networks. And the study I now propose should make a point of checking that very fact.

Attention needs to be given in the study to the Zimmerman-Cervantes snowball theory of friend-family network structure. They said that if a family gets into trouble, other families tend to avoid it. So if parents divorce, or a child is picked up by the police, that trouble leads to still more trouble; other friend families tend to drop the family, and its moralnet is further weakened, making further trouble still more likely.

Finally, Zimmerman and Cervantes thought that the pattern they found was purely American. I think, on the contrary, that the moralnet principle is worldwide, a human universal. But I do not doubt that structures of sorts other than informal friendship nets may often supply the moralnet. Indeed, I suspect that the world around, the special friendship net is usually less important than the ordinary kinship net.

Further, any sort of formal extended family structure, such as a lineage, would constitute by the Zimmerman-Cervantes definition a high-quality friend-family net if the people met together often. It would be well to define "often." How often is often? Zimmerman and Cervantes left that to their respondents. A questionnaire of a new friend-family study should also seek a measure of closeness or intimacy between the respondents and their friend families. How warm do they feel toward these people?

Finally, the study needs quality control. Questionnaires should contain built-in checks on the candor of respondents. (For example, ask the respondents if they have ever stolen anything of small value. Or ever done anything against the law. I would suppose that almost all people have, as children, done both. So denials would presumably be false.) Self-reports of trouble with the police should be checked against police records. And respondents should be asked if they have ever been victims of crimes committed by their age mates—so that we can compare victimization data with arrest data. Clearly, this study needs to be replicated in cities and in villages in all parts of the world.

16.6.5   More Self-Help Clubs to Test the Model

I turn now to a special kind of artificial moralnet recently invented in the United States. In Section 8.5.2 I spoke of the great success of Alcoholics Anonymous (AA). While psychiatrists, psychologists, and social scientists have treated alcoholics as individuals, AA treats them as members of a moralnet. It holds open meetings to which families of members are asked to come. But more important, it is a program of building new moralnets of reformed alcoholics. Are these new moralnets the main reason for the success of AA?

I propose a set of analogous trials of similar new moralnets to deal with other social problems. Trials designed as carefully controlled experiments—not only to help the people who are the subjects, but also to test the AA model. I believe that rigorous tests would show whether or not moralnet building on the AA model directly strengthens the moral order.

Just what makes up the AA model? People usually join AA voluntarily. They hear about the organization through friends. And nowadays, also through social workers, therapists, and even through the law courts. (But alas, no one seems to keep track of the dropouts.)

The organization is formed into local chapters, moralnets. All members have a history of hard drinking—people who see themselves as alcohol addicts, feel the effects of the habit as devastating their lives, and urgently wish to break the habit. The groups meet often; one at a Buffalo hospital meets daily. Their meetings offer moral support, fellowship. They begin with an informal chat, often over coffee. Such chats, of course, might well set the scene for gossip about other members.

The formal meeting follows a set pattern. The chair opens the meeting by saying, "Good evening. I'm . . . and I'm an alcoholic." Then all stand and recite together the serenity prayer: "God grant me the courage to change that which needs changing, the strength to accept that which cannot be changed, and the wisdom to know the difference."

The chair then reads the credo: the Twelve Steps and the Three Central Ideas. These set forth the central ideology of the organization. Then follows the main business of the evening, the guest speaker. Such speakers always begin: "My name is . . . and I'm an alcoholic." Their testimonials follow. They tell how they were as unreformed drunks, and what horrible lives they led. They tell how they got the AA word. How at first, they were not interested. Had to hit rock bottom first—be in the depths of despair. Then—often in great detail—their conversion, the turning point. How they came to feel that if their sponsors, the ones who introduced them to AA, could do it, they could do it too. Then how hard it was to give up drinking, but what social and material benefits they have enjoyed since they stopped drinking. The organization's manual for members contains three dozen such testimonial stories.

The AA leaders themselves explain their success by their ideology, their belief system. They hold that for an alcoholic, one drink is always one too many, that an alcoholic can never again touch alcohol. They hold that an alcoholic cannot stop drinking alone, that an alcoholic needs the AA group. And the help of a higher power—of God as each person understands God. This dependence of the alcoholic on the help of God looms large in their teachings.

Finally, they set forth twelve specific steps that make up a program of mental reorientation. These involve the affirmation and practice of simple moral principles. AA presupposes that every person has a set of moral attitudes, attitudes about right and proper relations with other people. So AA's twelve steps involve the people in straightening out (according to their own moral codes) their social dealings with others. They suggest, but do not say in so many words, that the moral wrongs which the alcoholics themselves must point out and right are usually wrongs to others near and dear to them—to others in their other moralnet. So AA emphasizes in a simple but effective way the tending of the moral relationships to the alcoholic's moralnet. AA deftly avoids specifying the nature of the social ties or social duties involved. The alcoholics specify these themselves.

The twelfth step calls on the alcoholic to take active part in the work of AA— in this way to help other alcoholics. This step may be an essential one. It involves the members in the work of the unit, and so makes the unit a cooperative team, working to help other people.

The AA approach has recently been emulated by Parents Anonymous (PA), as I noted in Chapter 11. PA brings child abusers together. They help one another to manage their anger so as to protect their children from it. PA seems to have taken little from AA but the general idea—ritual, ceremony, mythology, and ideology do not seem at all similar. Nor does PA have as impressive a record of success as does AA. Outsiders are not allowed at PA meetings, and publications are sketchy; but what is clear is that here, too, special moralnets are being built.

Families of alcoholics have likewise organized themselves into parallel groups to give each other aid, comfort, and counsel. Such groups seem to reflect some sense that the alcoholic problem is a family problem, not merely an individual problem.

Overeaters Anonymous is another active self-help group.

I now call for a set of community experiments with self-help clubs. The AA experience suggests that like clubs may be powerful tools for dealing with all sorts of other problems. I have in mind here specifically mental illness, suicide, child abuse, the loneliness of old age, and the loneliness of divorce. From the point of view of a scientist who wishes to measure the strength and success of these clubs accurately, it would be best if these experiments were carefully planned. Ideally, the clubs should vary according to an overall experimental design with respect to their cultivation of the theoretical components of a strong moralnet. I set forth a list of twelve such components in Table 16.7. Some clubs should have all twelve of these. Some should deliberately exclude one or more, so that the effectiveness of each of the twelve gets tested. Records need to be kept of the success of the self-help club at coping with the specific moral ill that troubles its members, so that the effectiveness of the specific theoretical components can be measured.

Ideally, for every person who joins a self-help club, another person equally motivated to seek help should be sent instead to some other kind of treatment—to a therapist for counseling, say, so that we have a valid control group against which to measure success.

These tests must be carefully monitored. Particular heed needs to be given to dropouts. How many people give up on the self-help club? (While AA tallies its successes in the tens of thousands, no one seems to have counted its failures.)

It ought not be difficult to vary the theoretical component structure. AA itself clearly embodies only six of my twelve sources of moral strength: (1) It builds strong social ties among the members of the local group. (2) It supplies emotional warmth to its members. (3) It conducts frequent rituals, emphasizing the ideology and core values of the moralnet. (4) It has appealing and memorable charter myths. (5) It has a well-organized and well-presented ideology. (6) It sets a scene for gossip among the members of a local group.

But AA lacks six of my twelve: (1) It does not call for cultural homogeneity within local groups. (2) It offers no economic support to its members. (3) It offers no political support to its members. (4) It does not make use of badges or emblems; there are no lapel pins, paintings, statues, crests, or banners. Finally, (5) promptness of punishment and (6) probability of punishment do not take place; AA does not punish its members at all for "crime"—for drinking alcohol or for failing to follow its twelve steps.

However, the question arises as to the effectiveness of a self-help club organized by outsiders. By people not themselves so troubled. A central fact about AA is that, from beginning to end, and from top to bottom, it is an organization of alcoholics. It was started by alcoholics. It is run by alcoholics. Hospitals, courts of law, social workers may applaud their efforts, but they do not manage them. One of the main appeals of the AA seems to lie in that very fact—that the moral guides are themselves former sufferers.

So if a broad program of self-help clubs is to be instituted, it may well need to be built up by people who qualify through their own experience as full members of the self-help club.

And we ought always to bear in mind that the ideology of the moralnet may turn out to be crucial. Whether that ideology works to comfort the mind, to produce effective social relations, may be a key point. The content of the ideology may be a crucial variable. And so likewise may be the content of the group rituals and the charter myths.

This same warning applies with equal force to the final set of research trials I propose: therapeutic communities.

16.6.6   More Therapeutic Communities to Test the Model

Empey has carried out two grand failures. What he tried to do was hard indeed. And I hope that he has led the way for others to follow. Empey's two failures were his Provo study and his Silverlake study. (In his Provo study he worked with Rabow and Erickson; in his Silverlake study, with Lubeck.) Both studies were controlled experiments, rigorous tests of moralnet theory.

Both these experiments dealt with young people in trouble with the law—in Provo, Utah, and in the Silverlake district of Los Angeles. Working with the courts, Empey was able to arrange a controlled experimental design. He dealt only with people already found guilty and marked for detention. Every third one of these was, in fact, locked up. Every third one was paroled and sent home. These were Empey's two control groups. Every third one was enrolled in one of Empey's experimental groups. The experimental groups were to provide an artificial moralnet—to serve a purpose like the Thirty-First Bengal Infantry. Or the Union Army's Sixth Corps. Only Empey's experimental groups had no larger purpose than to keep its members out of further trouble with the law.

The Provo experimenters tried to find jobs for its group members. The Silverlake experimenters tried to keep them in school. Empey and Lubeck give us a detailed account of the structure of the Silverlake experiment. The moralnet consisted of a home in which the boys lived from Monday through Friday. Weekends they could spend outside with their families if they wished. Every day they went to school. So the Silverlake house was a kind of halfway house.

The experimenters laid down a few simple rules. Boys had to live at the home. They had to go to school. They had to stick to a schedule, rather than to come and go as they pleased. They could not assault anyone. Boys were told that they had to lessen their law-breaking gradually—*not* that they had to stop it all at once.

As I have said, in both these experiments they tried to link the boys with the community by putting them in touch with outside institutions—in the Provo experiment by finding them jobs, in the Silverlake experiment by sending them to a regular outside day school. Each involved a daily meeting of the boys. In each, the boys shared a dwelling and daily meals. So each constituted a social network from which the experimenters hoped the boys would draw their social values. And though the network was made up chiefly of delinquents, and though there seems to have been counseling rather than preaching, Empey hoped that this social network would share the values of the larger society: respect for the law, keeping out of trouble with the police. How did it turn out?

The boys from the experimental groups were compared afterward with the boys from the two control groups—those sent to detention and those paroled to their homes. What was the rate of recidivism among the three groups? How many of each got into trouble with the police again?

There was a clear difference between the boys sent to detention and the other two. The former did worse. Detention did not help; it hurt. But there was no difference between the boys sent to the experimental groups and those paroled to their family homes. Empey's moralnets did not work any better than the moralnets the boys had been used to.

When we contrast Empey's experimental treatment with AA, we notice several sharp differences. First of all, members join AA voluntarily. They begin by declaring that they are sick and want to get well. But Empey's boys were assigned to his treatment by the court; since all three groups were randomly chosen, each presumably had a like proportion of boys who sincerely wanted to change their ways, and of those who did not. So the boys' motivation to reform would be held constant among all three groups, whereas we can assume that with but a few exceptions only people join AA who want to change their drinking habits.

Second, AA offers emotional warmth; the Silverlake design did not. Third, AA offers moral ceremonies, rituals; the Silverlake design did not. Fourth, AA offers an ideology, a theory of the treatment of alcoholism; the Silverlake design did not.

Empey's Provo experiment offered help in finding jobs. And both experiments offered the youth food and lodging. AA offers no economic support.

Once AA developed a history of success, that history became a charter myth. And a central element of AA ritual are testimonies of its members about the strength they get from it.

What I call for here, then, are many trials by many workers to build effective therapeutic communities, halfway houses for juvenile delinquents. Perhaps after awhile the members move out, but return for weekly or monthly reunions. Each trial needs to be only large enough to produce meaningful chance risk tests to compare with control groups. But all must be done, like Provo and Silverlake, with the aid of the courts—which randomly assign boys in trouble to the halfway house, to detention, or to home parole—so that the later police records of all three can be compared.

The difficulties Empey found in his Provo and Silverlake studies warn us not to expect quick or easy success. Certainly the plan needs to meet the legal requirements of the courts and the methodological requirements of the social scientists. But it also needs to meet the leadership requirements of the boys. Perhaps the person in charge ought to have successful experience working with tough kids in the ghettos, or be a former juvenile delinquent with a prison record.

Only trial and error can produce a successful halfway house. But I believe from what I have seen and read of armies that it can be done. Perhaps the theoretical model set forth in Chapter 6 on moralnets might offer us a model for a successful halfway house:

(1) It would be a long-lasting association. It would keep up ties with alumni even after they have settled into good jobs and formed strong moralnets outside it—formed, perhaps, with fellow alumni. It would keep up a gossip network among members and alumni.
(2) It would encourage smaller groups of close friends among its members.
(3) It would encourage emotional warmth among those buddy groups and within the house as a whole. It would be a family.

(4) It would offer economic support in the form of an effective program of job training and placement.
(5) It would offer political support to its members. It would take care of internal troubles itself, and its most severe sanction against members who disturb its order would be expulsion. The supervisors would be in a doctor-patient or an attorney-client relationship with the members.
(6) It would have a badge for the members to wear in public, and would aim to make it a badge of honor. Not a badge of shame. The boys would be constantly reminded that the good police record of the halfway house helps its members and alumni find and hold jobs. So by getting in trouble with the law they would be letting their buddies down.
(7) It would somehow persuade those boys that it is a special house, the best such house in the world. Every well-run army knows that this myth is particularly easy to sell—because the soldiers *want* so much to believe it.
(8) It would have rituals and ceremonies to remind its members of the charter myth—the success stories of its role models, ex-delinquents who made good.
(9) Each house would seek a culturally homogeneous membership, a moralnet where the boys themselves are the carriers of the moral tradition. The Zimmerman-Cervantes study found family moralnets more effective when they were of like religion, ethnic background, dialect, income. Send the boys out to integrated schools and to integrated jobs, but keep their house culturally homogeneous.
(10) The ideology of a halfway house for juvenile delinquents has yet to be written. It needs to be a cogent argument for obeying the law, for community respect, and for self-respect. Embodied, it may be, in a biography of a successful role model. It needs to deal with the rival street ideology, which says that if you are poor and ignorant, crime is the best way to make it.

Perhaps it should emphasize the idea of *expectation*—through some kind of lottery—that committing a crime is drawing a lottery ticket on a life of misery. The odds are that you will not be caught, convicted, and sentenced, but the risk is there, and the convict's life is bleak.

Such to me is the model of an ideal therapeutic community for juvenile delinquents. Far more valuable, of course, would be an authentic account of a real one that actually worked.

16.7   STEP 5: COPING WITH THE MORAL ORDER

This book, as you know, looks to the possibility that a mature behavioral science—expounded and applied through the Five Steps of socionomics—can at last supply all mankind with a common moral order. Such an order, as I see it, might well rest on unity in fundamental moral principles and on a common store of widely accepted, well-tested theories. But within that unity, a wide diversity of political, religious, and economic systems from country to country would seem to me not merely tolerable, but useful. So I neither expect nor hope for a powerful world state, or for any one standard model of law or justice or government, or for one standard system of production or exchange.

Formal theory test reviews like THINCS offer good hope of gaining agreement among socionomists about accepting, rejecting, or suspending judgment on theories of human behavior: psychological theories about the mind and the emotions, sociological theories about the family and the social structure, political theories about the state, geographical theories about human ecology, anthropological theories about human culture, economic theories about systems of production and distribution of wealth.

A successful program of moralnet building that leads to a sharp drop in the scoreboards of social ills might well be the closest thing behavioral scientists can offer to rival the triumphs like the one over yellow fever, which won public support for medical science eighty to a hundred years ago. Some such triumph might well be the next practical step in building that worldwide moral order.

We must not, however, expect great things of our moralnet program on its first trials. How many new models of aircrafts are accepted on their first trials, before the bugs have been worked out? How many computer programs run well the first time? Most complex innovations undergo trial and error before they work right.

Nor can we hope that even the soundest and best-conducted program of moralnet building would stamp out mental illness, alcoholism, suicide, child battering, and youth crime the way the war on mosquitoes stamped out yellow fever. Mosquito bites were the *only* way yellow fever was being spread. But we have no reason to suppose that weakened moralnets are the *only* cause of these social ills.

Yet I submit that we need not cure *everything* by strengthening moralnets. It is enough if we can cure *something*. If we can merely cut way down on youth crime by a program combining moralnet building with job training and job opportunities, it might well be enough to show what behavioral science can do.

Given a body of rigorously tested theories on the causes and consequences of weakened moralnets, we can hope for many small but striking successes. Moralnet theory, I submit, offers an opportunity for successful policy programs now. Psychological problems of mental illness must cope with deep-seated misprogramming of the mind: There is no body of tested theories at hand that gives us good hope of soon producing dramatic improvements in human happiness through psychotherapy. In politics and economics the decisive arenas are so large, the consequences of failure so painful, the intensity of public controversy so high, and above all, the minimum unit required for effective action so large, that early striking successes seem forlorn hopes. But we can go to work on alcoholism, youth crime, suicide, and child battering in any community. We can start modestly with small groups. If at first we fail, few but the specialists will notice. If we score some dramatic successes, we can call in the media. If we have good news here or there, the word will soon spread. Especially if someone reports it in plain talk to begin with, to get the process started.

If successful tests of weakened moralnet theory bring the massive support I hope for, then we may have to guard against the other extreme. We may have to guard against the risk that in future, instead of making too little of our moralnets, we would make too much.

I have already spoken of one cost of stronger moralnets: their tendency to tie people down to particular places. It is precisely the most ambitious people, the future leaders, who are least likely to be willing to be tied down so. And it is harder to start a new mine or factory out in the country if people do not want to move there.

Page Smith says of the colonial New England town: "The town was a little like the girl with the curl in the middle of her forehead. When it was good it was apt to be very, very good (a close approximation of the ideal human group) and when it was bad it was horrid." Very, very good for steady churchgoers who were able to hold their own economically, who had a substantial extended family in the neighborhood, and who shared the dominant values of the town. Horrid for the alcoholics, for the specially dull and the specially bright, for the aberrants— including not only the creative geniuses, the potential writers and artists, but also the neurotics. In all, we must suppose very, very good for those who not only fit the town well but married happily, but horrid for those who married unwisely or unfortunately. Very, very good for those whose work and affairs prospered at least moderately, but horrid for those who fell into debt.

Another cost of stronger moralnets is their tendency to make for ethnic bigotry. The myth that our kind of people are best seems to support moralnets strongly. Generalizing that myth to the way of life of our moralnet gives us ethnocentrism—and ethnocentrics. If our way of life is best, that of others is probably contemptible. Ethnocentrics—who gave us two world wars and Auschwitz. But evidence that moralnets should be culturally homogeneous is not evidence that whole towns, whole districts, whole nations should necessarily be so. There is a tradeoff between civil peace on the one hand and progress through variety on the other. Here the Swiss may offer a useful model of unity amid diversity.

If, mindful of all these tradeoffs, we could lessen social ills by strengthening moralnets through the good use of the Five Steps, would that not help establish socionomics as a tool of behavioral science? Would that not give us confidence in our science? And what might be even more important—would that not give us confidence in ourselves?

Once the Five Steps of socionomics have been demonstrated as a rigorous and effective scientific discipline, might we not hope indeed to make those Five Steps a central theme of a worldwide moral order? Core values, scoreboards, theory test reviews, study plans, and most of all, plans of action to cope with troubles now, to harvest the fruits of our research?

Through that work, then, might we not say something to the spirit of Olga Sergeyevna Prozorov? If through the sufferings of her times and ours we gradually came to understand and cope with problems like those of the three Prozorov sisters, then would not some high purpose have been served by it all?

Notes

16.1   *The Banner of the Thirty-First Bengal*

On the Battle of Cedar Creek, see Naroll (1952).
On the creation of the Sixth Corps of the Army of the Potomac, see Williams (1949: 169).
On the Thirty-First Bengal at Bhurtpore, see Mason (1974).
About Spottsylvania, see Catton (1953: 173).
For the Duke of Wellington's recruits in Spain, see *Penguin Dictionary of Quotations* (1974: 412).

16.4   Step 2: Scoreboards of Moral Order

On a secular trend in war frequency and intensity, 1816-1965, see Singer and Small (1972: 187-201), on casualties, pp. 59-75.

Norway and Sweden added to Table 16.4 with scores of zero. I take this absence from Singer and Small's table to be evidence of no civil disorders, rather than no data.

On cultural heterogeneity, see Kurian (1979: Tables 32-35, 42); also Taylor and Hudson (1972: Tables 2.7, 4.15-4.17).

On the present ample variety of human cultures worldwide, see Section 3.3.4.

16.5   Step 3: Review of Tests of Moral Order Theory

Sorokin (1937-1941), no matter what its author says, is not about social and cultural dynamics in general, but only about the relationship of civil and foreign wars to changes in value systems.

On Safe School Study, see Ianni and Reuss-Ianni (1980: 21G).

On moralnet stress and disease, see Kagan and Levi (1974).

On the Brown-Harris model of mental illness, see Section 7.5.2.

On Alameda County, see Berkman and Syme (1979).

On London widows, see Parkes (1964).

On widows in Boston and Sydney, see Maddison and Viola (1968).

The couplet by Sir Henry Wotton is "Upon the Death of Sir Albert Morton's Wife."

On Welsh family deaths, see Rees and Lutkins (1967).

The restudy of Cabot's boys is in McCord (1978).

While people who belong to religious groups as such are not happier than those who do not, people who have a sense of meaning and direction in their lives are happier than those who lack one (Freedman, 1978: 191-198).

16.6.2   A Holocultural Study to Test the Model

Holocultural codings on the following variables are catalogued in Levinson (1977a)—see there the *Outline of Cultural Materials* index (Vol. II: 145-193), under the following headings: murder, 682; theft and fraud, 685; alcohol abuse, 733; suicide, 762; and see the "Variable Keyword" index (Vol. II: 7-144), under wife beating, brawling, and punishment. Child-beating codings are also found in Table 11.4. Blum (1969) shows that abundant data on drug abuse are available in the ethnographic literature. For several decades Marvin K. Opler and Joshua Bierer edited the *International Journal of Psychiatry*, a rich archive of theory and data on worldwide cultural variations in the concepts, symptoms, and correlates of mental illness. The classic study on the method of taking a mental illness census in an exotic culture is Eaton and Weil (1955).

Again I cite Levinson (1977a) as an index to the many codings on hypothetical causes of moralnet strength as set forth here. On social, political, and economic systems, even the headings are too numerous to review here (see Naroll, 1970a; Levinson, 1977b; and Levinson and Malone, 1980, for reviews; and see Textor, 1967, for many examples). On the remaining variables, in Levinson (1977a), see *Outline of Cultural Materials* index (Vol II.: 145-193), on organized ceremonial, under 796; on ritual, under 788; on mythology and theology, under 773, 775, 776, and 779; on law and justice, in groups 67, 68, 69.

On standards for holocultural research, see Rohner et al. (1978). Examples of page reference citations are in Udy (1959), Naroll (1956, 1962a), Schlegel (1972), and Tatje and Naroll (1970).

On Hopi, see Thompson (1950).

16.6.3   A Cross-National Study to Test the Model

See Gallup International Research Institutes (1977).

16.6.4   More Friend-Family Studies to Test the Model

I have discussed the work of Zimmerman and Cervantes (1956, 1960), and of Hirschi (1969) in Section 6.4.

16.6.5   More Self-Help Clubs to Test the Model

My information on their organization comes from three publications of Alcoholics Anonymous (1955, 1957, 1969) and from reports of visits to meetings of Buffalo chapter groups. Similarly, I consulted three publications of Parents Anonymous (1974, 1975, 1978).

Quotation from "Serenity Prayer" is paraphrased from Alcoholics Anonymous (1955, 1957, 1969).

For Twelve Steps and Three Central Ideas, see Alcoholics Anonymous (1955: 59f.).

On the Al-Anon family groups of family members of alcoholics, see Alcoholics Anonymous (1957: 258, 327).

16.6.6   More Therapeutic Communities to Test the Model

On the Silverlake study, see Empey and Lubeck (1971); Empey and Erickson (1972) on the Provo study.

16.7   Step 5: Coping with the Moral Order

On the good and the horrid, see Smith (1980: 733f.).

Readers who wish to make gifts (deductible from U.S. income tax) for the support of socionomic studies like those called for in this book may send their contributions to: Institute for Cross-Cultural Studies, 4695 Main Street, Amherst, N.Y. 14226. The work of this Institute is presently under the personal direction and control of the author.

Afterword

In this book I argue that the Five Steps of socionomics offer a scientific meta-ideology for a worldwide moral order. I predict that strengthened moralnets will lead to a marked decrease in the rates of mental illness, alcoholism, suicide, child abuse, and youth crime. I offer a model of the methods by which those moralnets might be strengthened. Furthermore, that same model offers a plan of how moral values and attitudes may be effectively taught, in order that the ideals of a culture may in fact be realized in the actual behavior of its people.

However, that model calls for an ideology embedded in an image of human origins and human destiny. In Section 1.2 I offer an offhand sketch of such an image. That sketch suggests that mankind is now in the fifth stage of a seven-stage process—that the chief meaning of human history in the past 5,000 years is in the cultural evolution of a stable human world order that takes charge of our planet. I propose three processes as the main driving forces of that evolution: servos, darwins, and snowballs. I intend to deal with those patterns of cultural evolution in full detail in my next book on the human situation, tentatively titled *Painful Progress*.

No worldwide moral order could take hold that did not offer a coherent and substantially successful plan for ordering mankind's political and economic affairs. It is problems of war and peace; of freedom and order; of honest competent, and responsible government; of economic development; of inflation and unemployment; and, above all, problems of the fair and just distribution of wealth that chiefly concern mankind today. The central problem may well be that of world armament. We need a worldwide arms control and disarmament program to banish the threat of atomic holocaust that might destroy us, and to free 400 billion dollars a year for better uses. To attain that, we need an effective mechanism to keep peace worldwide. These are the main problems, the solution of which would lead mankind to those broad, sunlit uplands Winston Churchill promised us so many years ago. These problems of politics and economics I hope to address in still other works, in time to come.

APPENDIX A

The Diagnosis of

Mental Illness

Psychiatrists have long been unhappy with their set of concepts and diagnostic procedures—all still strongly influenced by the work of Kraepelin 75 years ago. However, the recent worldwide International Pilot Study of Schizophrenia (IPSS) has shown that their procedures and ideas are not without either logic or consistency. (Whether they are also medically *valid* is another matter—outside the scope of this book.)

The IPSS investigators looked at *all* mental illness among about 125 patients in each of nine widely scattered mental hospitals, one such Field Research Center each in England (London), Denmark (Aarhus), Czechoslovakia (Prague), USSR (Moscow Russians), China (Taipei), India (Agra Hindi), Nigeria (Ibadan Yoruba), United States (Washington, DC), and Colombia (Cali).

In each center, the diagnosis of mental health or illness was made through the use of a 360-item clinical check list—*not* a questionnaire—the Present State Examination schedule (PSE). That tool itself had been worked up earlier through international trial and error over eight successive versions; it was further changed after it had been field tested in all nine centers. Translations of it into the local languages were checked by translation back into English. Those who administered it often had to judge whether certain behavior was appropriate or inappropriate in the local cultural context. Their judgments were helped by the fact that the examiner, whether psychiatrist or psychiatric social worker, usually was a native speaker of the local language, familiar with local ways through many years of local residence. (Although not all members of all research staffs knew local ways that well, all such staffs had several psychiatrists and psychiatric social workers who did.)

The same sampling methods, diagnostic procedures, and diagnostic concepts were used in all nine IPSS studies. The investigators in charge at all nine held annual meetings—first for worldwide standardization and later for comparison. Their sampling procedure for selecting patients to study constitutes the best working definition of severe mental illness (psychosis) we have.

To begin with, by definition a mentally ill person is one who has nothing wrong with the nervous tissue—no organic illness. The IPSS investigators began

TABLE A.1   Ten Worldwide Signs of Mental Illness

Confused Thoughts

(1) Delusions*
(2) Hallucinations*
(3) Depersonalization (a state in which one feels that one's body is changed or detached; a state dominated by feelings of unreality and estrangement from self, body, and surroundings)
(4) Other disorders of thinking (for example, experiences of control; derealization)

Confused Emotions

(5) Overwhelming fear
(6) Other disorders of affect (that is, lack of any emotional response at all on the one hand; or, on the other hand, being very happy or very sad without apparent reason)

Confused Behavior

(7) Social withdrawal
(8) Psychomotor disorder
(9) Self-neglect
(10) Other inappropriate and unusual behavior (for example, disregard of social norms, autism)

SOURCE: United Nations, World Health Organization (1973: 109-112).
*Delusions and hallucinations mark functional psychosis if present at all; the others listed do so only if gross or severe—if moderate or mild, they mark neurosis.

by ruling out all patients who seemed to be suffering from any of these organic illnesses: (1) regular abuse of alcohol, (2) regular abuse of drugs acting on the central nervous system, (3) mental disorders attributable to endocrine disorders, (4) mental disorders attributable to metabolic or nutritional disorders, (5) evidence of brain disorder, or of the effects of brain surgery, (6) any other organic psychosis, (7) epilepsy.

The IPSS investigators then looked for ten signs or marks of mental illness among those apparently free from physical disorders of the nervous system. Those ten signs or marks are set forth in Table A.1. To these psychiatrists, a person who has any one of these symptoms is mentally ill.

The IPSS investigators made many tests of reliability of the PSE: They tested it within research centers, by having more than one staff member rate the same patient during the interview and comparing results. They also tested it between research centers, by showing films or videotapes of interviews at the annual meetings of the project; here, each such interview was rated by psychiatrists from all nine centers. For example, a film of the interview of a patient at Ibadan could have been used by psychiatrists from Taipai, Moscow, and all the other centers to prepare a PSE.

There are two distinct questions about the reliability (consistency) of these diagnoses. First, and most important, do these standard criteria work the world around in all cultures if used there by local psychiatrists? In other words, do

TABLE A.2　Local Consistency in Rating Symptoms of Mental Illness (using a single standard diagnostic procedure and symptom schedule)

Center	Correlation
Moscow, USSR	.90
Agra, India	.86
Taipei, China	.82
Prague, Czechoslovakia	.81
London, England	.69
Aarhus, Denmark	.64
Ibadan, Nigeria	.58
Washington, D.C., USA	.54
Cali, Colombia	.53

SOURCE: United Nations, World Health Organization (1973: 126).

Yoruba psychiatrists tend to agree among themselves when applying these standard criteria to Yoruba patients? Do Hindi psychiatrists tend to agree among themselves when applying these standard criteria to Hindi patients? Do Chinese psychiatrists tend to agree among themselves when applying these standard criteria to Chinese patients? Here the Ten Worldwide Signs of Mental Illness listed in Table A.1 do rather well. By and large, Russian, Hindi, and Chinese psychiatrists agree more among themselves than English or American ones—even though the standard examination schedule was originally written in English (see Table A.2). In all nine centers, there is a high local level of agreement on delusions and on experience of control (a thought disorder in which one believes that one's thoughts are controlled by another person or being). There is a moderate local level of agreement on lack of insight, on odd behavior and withdrawal, and on auditory hallucinations (high agreement everywhere but in Washington). These results suggest that the differences in reliability shown in Table A.2 are less a reflection of the vagueness of the IPSS procedures and concepts than of the lack of discipline (equals individual intellectual freedom) of the host culture.

Second, how well do foreign psychiatrists diagnose patients from cultures strange to them? Here the answer is: It all depends. Foreign psychiatrists do nearly as well as local ones in recognizing delusions, hallucinations, and most other disorders of thinking, as well as psychomotor disorders. They do only so-so in recognizing confused emotions or withdrawal. They are no good at all in recognizing lack of insight, disregard for social norms, or neglect of self.

If mental illness is mild, it is usually called neurosis; if severe, functional psychosis. Functional psychosis in turn is almost all classed either as schizophrenia or affective disorder (the latter until recently most often called manic-depressive psychosis). Schizophrenia is by far the more frequent diagnosis—but this fact may conceivably turn out to be a mere artifact of diagnostic style. For psychiatrists lean toward calling the disorder schizophrenia whenever thoughts are seriously disturbed, no matter how much feelings may also be disturbed. By and large, only when feelings are seriously disturbed while thoughts remain clear do they call the illness affective psychosis.

In the IPSS study, the clinicians called 67 percent of all psychoses schizophrenia, 13 percent affective disorder. The project's computer programmers wrote a program, CATEGO, in which they followed the strategy of calling psychosis schizophrenia whenever thoughts are seriously disturbed, regardless of whether or not feelings or behavior are even more seriously disturbed. This program agreed with the clinical diagnosis on the presence or absence of schizophrenia in 70 percent of the patients. Whereas another program, which favored the most severe or widespread disturbance agreed with clinicans on only 62 percent of the patients. (All three agreed on 48 percent of the patients.)

Note

The IPSS report: United Nations, World Health Organization (1973).

APPENDIX B
THINCS Profile Example

PROFILE NUMBER: 0151

MAIN SUBJECT: multifaceted behavioral approach, electrical aversion, behavioral self-control training

PROPOSITION: A multifacted behavioral approach is an effective treatment for alcoholism.

FINDING: " . . . all three groups showed a significant downward drift in consumption during treatment . . . and maintained these gains, with level slopes during follow-up" (Miller 1978: 79)

THEORY: none explicitly stated

RCAS ACCESSION NUMBER: 07803322

MATERIAL TYPE: journal article

LANGUAGE: English

PUBLICATION YEAR: 1978

AUTHOR: Miller, William R.

CITATION: Behavioral Treatment of Problem Drinkers: A Comparative Outcome Study of Three Controlled Drinking Therapies. Journal of Consulting and Clinical Psychology 46: 74-86.

VARIABLE 01: treatment (aversion, self-control, and BAC training)

VALIDITY: manifestly valid

VARIABLE 02: consumption (amount consumed per week as recorded on daily record cards)

VALIDITY: manifestly valid

TREATMENT TYPE: outpatient; electrical aversion in simulated bar; self-control training, BAC discrimination training with electrical aversion, 10 sessions of each

OUTCOME: see finding

SUPPORT: supported

CAUSALITY: management-causal

INSTITUTIONAL AFFILIATION: college/ university

SAMPLE: (n = 46) 32 males, 14 females, mean ages 35.8, 37.3, 11.9, volunteers and court referrals, nonaddicted problem drinkers

RESEARCH DESIGN: multiple-group trial

DATA SOURCES: rating scale

MEASUREMENT INSTRUMENTS: Marlatt Drinking Profile

SCALES: interval

FINANCIAL SUPPORT: see comments

REFERENCES CITED: 0029

STATISTICAL TEST: analysis of variance; .001

COMMENTS: Funding by the Distilled Spirits Council and the Christian Brothers and Hillcrest Vineyards.

PROCEDURES:

SAMPLING: non-probability

ALCOHOLISM TYPE: defined

CONTROL GROUP: no

SUBJECT/CONTROL ASSIGN-
MENT: random

SUBJECT/CONTROL AWARE-
NESS: aware

SUBJECT SELF-SELECTION: no

DATA COLLECTOR TRAINING:
trained

DATA COLLECTOR AWARENESS-
PURPOSE: aware

DATA COLLECTOR AWARENESS-
SUBJECT/CONTROL: aware

PRE-POST DATA COMPARABILITY:
comparable

RELIABILITY: evidence for all data
sources

VERIFICATION OF SELF-REPORTS:
not verified

PERCENT NON-RESPONDERS: 0%

CONTROL OF NON-RESPONDERS:
not applicable

CONTROL OF DROP-OUTS: controlled

CONTROL OF NON-SPECIFIC
EFFECTS: not applicable

REPLICABILITY: replicable

PLANNING: prospective

SOURCE: Levinson (1981: 393-394).

APPENDIX C

Ratings of Adult

Instrumental Dependence

Societies were rated on a scale ranging from a minimum of 11 to a maximum of 28, according to the extent to which the raters judged that adults could ask for and expect help from each other without criticism or other indication of disapproval with respect to satisfying their needs for food, clothing, shelter, transportation, and the like. Such dependence was distinguished from another kind, Emotional Dependence, which was thought of as seeking support from other people in times of crisis, avoiding isolation, seeking security in group contact, and the like (see Bacon, 1974: 865 on these concepts).

Ainu	17	Lesu	20
Aleut	17	Mandan	18
Alorese	11	Maori	21
Aranda	13	Marquesans	18
Arapho	18	Masai	16
Arapesh	18	Mbuti	23
Araucanians	18	Muria	18
Ashanti	17	Nauruans	16
Aymara	15	Navaho	19
Azande	16	Nyakyusa	20
Balinese	23	Ojibwa	11
Basuto	14	Paiute	16
Bechuana	24	Papago	14
Chagga	25	Pukapukans	22
Chenchu	15	Samoans	22
Cheyenne	19	San Pedro	16
Chiracahua	18	Swazi	18
Chukchee	10	Tallensi	17
Comanche	16	Tenetehara	17
Crow	18	Tepoztlan	11
Cuna	25	Teton	17
Hopi	27	Thonga	19
Ifaluk (Woleans)	24	Tikopia	23
Ifugao	11	Trukese	20
Jicarilla	21	Tukuna	17
Kambara (Lau)	24	Turkana	14
Kaska	11	Ulithi	21

Kikuyu	23	Venda	16
Klamath	16	Western Apache	23
Kongo	14	Wichita	15
Koryak	15	Winnebago	18
Kurtachi (Buka)	15	Yagua	19
Kwakiutl	18	Yoruba	18
Kwara	20	Zulu	18
Lepcha	16	Zuñi	21

SOURCE: These ratings were made by Alice Child and Ros Schwartz under the direction of Margaret K. Bacon and Irvin L. Child. They led to the impressively high correlation on Line 5 of Table 8.3, and have not hitherto been published elsewhere. They were furnished for this book through the courtesy of Herbert Barry III.

APPENDIX D
The Nayar Household

This appendix is offered in support of the argument in Section 10.2.1 that human marriage is a kind of instinctive pair bonding, analogous to that found in many other species of birds and mammals—as set forth, for example, in the study by the Embers I discuss in Chapter 15. Since the Nayars of Kerala long lacked any real form of marriage, their case sheds valuable light on this theory.

In Chapter 15, I define marriage as a presumably permanent alliance between a man and a woman involving mutual rights of sexual access, mutual economic duties, and joint responsibilities for the care of the woman's children—an alliance contracted in a manner considered right and proper by the people of the society concerned. In all societies, without exception, such arrangements constitute the normal or ordinary way of creating a nuclear family and in turn such a family in one way or another is linked with others related by birth or marriage to an extended family moralnet.

Such an arrangement was the normal one even in Nara Japan, where, as Kiyama has shown, among many farm families normal marriages did not come into existence until the couples were middle aged. Such an arrangement was the normal one even in Kerala before the British came—the Nayars were always but a small minority of the Malayalam-speaking peoples, and they alone practiced the unusual arrangements I am about to describe.

The Nayars are the only subculture we know of in any detail in which the nuclear family did not exist. That subculture is familiar to anthropologists, thanks to the studies of Gough; I follow her study of the Nayars of Central Kerala along the Malabar Coast of South India. Their *taravād* "marriage" system no longer lives on in Kerala. But it still survived here and there into the twentieth century. So when Gough did her field work in Kerala, in 1947-1949, older informants remembered some women who had continued that system.

The Nayars, until the British conquest, were the military aristocracy of the land. Most of them were able to read and write. Many documents in the Malayalam language survive from earlier times. Arab and European travelers and officials wrote accounts of Nayar sex life for century after century. At least two such accounts come from two colonial officials who lived for many years among the Nayars and knew Malayalam well: Duarte Barbosa and William Logan.

The Malayalam word *taravād* may mean a matrilineal clan; it may mean any of the matrilineal lineages making up such a clan; it may also mean any of the matrilineal extended family households making up such a lineage. But here I use it only in this last sense.

To understand what happened to marriage in Nayar *taravāds*, we must understand what part the Nayars played in the life of Kerala before the English conquest—before about 1800. The Nayars are a caste, or rather, a set of related castes. They generally fit into the scheme of things in Kerala as the Rajputs do in Northern India: traditionally both were castes of landowners, officials, and above all, fighters. Wars were incessant in Kerala; accordingly, Nayar soldiers were usually away from home and it would be a considerable convenience to such a soldier to have a right and proper way to bed a women of his own caste when on his travels. Especially since he could not sleep with a lower-caste woman. On pain of death.

The Nayar *taravād* usually lived in a single house, though sometimes in more than one. It was a matrilineage, up to six generations deep. In its local affairs it was strictly ruled by one of its older men. The *taravād* was typically landlord over considerable estates, farmed by low-caste serfs. So a *taravād* was a family of country squires. Its support came partly from its tenants' crops; partly from the customary services of villagers who in return enjoyed feasting and other perquisites at the *taravād's* expense; and partly from cash through sale of crops in the markets.

When she neared puberty, a *taravād* girl was formally married to a suitable Nayar "husband." They were bedded after the ceremony, and she might indeed then lose her virginity. But after a few days, they parted; and her "husband" had no further rights or duties of any kind beyond an occasional token gift. Thereafter, she was expected to receive lovers, such as pleased her. She might have three or four or even half a dozen liaisons—regular lovers. And if she chose, she might receive as guest for the night any passing gentleman. Lovers made holiday gifts—but not of such value as to make these women professional courtesans. Passing guests were expected to leave a gold coin behind. But such visits were not frequent. It was their brothers who maintained the women, not their bedfellows.

When I say any passing gentleman, I mean any passing Nayar or Brahmin. For her to love anyone of a lower caste meant outcasting. And when she gave birth, she had to find among her lovers a Nayar who would ceremonially acknowledge her child as his. Such a gesture incurred no obligation for child support; it was to their uncles that children looked for support, not at all to their fathers.

A woman's lovers only called on her as visitors; they would pass the night but not move in even for a few days, so they never formed part of the *taravād* household of their mistresses. Their home was with their sisters.

The duties of the women of the *taravād* were not particularly heavy. They cared for the young children. They prepared food (unless the *taravād* was prosperous enough to afford the services of a Nayar or Brahmin cook). They often did the household laundry. And at harvest time, they might help in the fields—but not with planting or weeding. So they had time for their regular lovers as well as for those occasional visiting gentlemen. Such strangers would often be men of standing and consequence. Nayar women had a reputation of never refusing a guest of the proper caste. So it seems that among the Nayar, as among several other well-known societies, sexual favors were among the duties that a well-regulated household owed its guests. "These women," wrote Barbosa, "are very clean, and fare very well, and they consider it a matter of great honour and gallantry and pride themselves greatly thereon, to be able to give pleasure to men, and it is an article of faith with them that every woman who dies a virgin is damned."

Nayar "marriage"—or rather the absence of marriage among them as I would define marriage—thus was well worked into the culture. The system by which Nayar *taravāds* performed all the functions of the family without the aid of husbands lasted over four hundred years. Were human marriage merely a matter of culture, it is hard to see why the Nayar custom should have died out so soon after the English conquest.

But die out it did, within a few generations. Once the British brought peace to Kerala, Nayar men no longer traveled constantly to the wars. By Logan's time, old-fashioned Nayar *taravāds* were already becoming scarce.

"Sometimes a woman accepts the favours of many lovers," he wrote in 1884,

> but this is generally now-a-days scouted by all respectable people, and the fashion is daily becoming more and more prevalent for the woman to leave her ancestral home for that of the husband of her choice, although, as a matter of law, the husband [still] occupies no recognized legal relation involving rights and responsibilities in regard either to his wife or his children.

To change all that was one of the purposes of the Malabar Marriage Commission. Logan himself was a member. The commission made a thorough study of both custom and law, traditional and modern. Logan concluded that the Nayar "marriage" custom arose in the first place to keep the property of the *taravād* in the lineage: To keep a man's children from inheriting his wealth; to reserve it to his sisters' children instead. That inheritance rule was common among many castes in Kerala. What was special before 1800 about the Nayars was not their inheritance rule. It was that the men were generally away from home, where they could not keep an eye on things. "The [Nayar Marriage] custom," says Logan, "had also much to commend it in a society organized as it was then, when the Nayars were the 'protectors' of the State and could seldom, except in old age, settle down to manage their family affairs."

But, in Logan's day, such duties had long ceased. "The martial spirit of the Nayars in these piping times of peace," says Logan,

> has quite died out for want of exercise. The Nayar is more and more becoming a family man. . . . In the days when the Nayar male population were all soldiers . . . the

marital tie was not regarded much . . . but things are changed now that a Nayar usually marries one wife, lives apart with her in their own home, and rears her children as his own also. His natural affections come into play and there is a strong . . . desire for some legal mode . . . for conveying to his children and to their mother all his self-acquired property [instead of letting it go to his sisters and nephews].

The history of Nayar marriage, then, is the history of an experiment in the natural worldwide laboratory of human culture. A system of families built strictly on the blood tie—to the exclusion of husbands. A system supported by much wealth—and by a well codified set of written laws governing the inheritance of property. The customs and the law, the values and the attitudes, went on to Logan's own day, in the 1880s. But in the teeth of custom and law, Nayar men and women set up true marriages in nuclear family households once the men were freed from their former constant life-long pressures of military duties.

That experiment was a rare one—perhaps even a unique one. Its very rareness—together with the disappearance of the old system within a hundred years after the men began to stay at home—is strong support for the theory that the nuclear family as a basic element in family structure has indeed a genetic basis. Strong support for the theory that people, like many other species of birds and mammals, have a pair-bonding instinct.

Notes

Unless otherwise credited, everything I say about Nayar household, kinship, and marriage comes from Gough (1959, 1961), chiefly the latter. People should not try to interpret the earlier writers until they have studied Gough. On the traditional system, Gough chiefly follows Duarte Barbosa in Dames (1918), Buchanan (1807), and Logan (1887)—sources I and my assistant, Susan Horan, carefully compared. It is especially instructive to read Barbosa in the Dames edition, for Dames's copious notes from other early travelers give a real feeling for the strength of the evidence on Nayar "marriage." Gough spent two years in Kerala, but makes no claim to read or speak Malayalam; she says she read Malayalam texts in English translation.

On the survival of traditional Nayar "marriage" into the twentieth century in Travancore, at least, see Dames (1918: 41n.).

Barbosa's field stay and native language familiarity is in Dames (1918: xxxvi). See Logan (1887: 136, Appendix XIV, p. ccxlix) on his own service in Kerala (or Malabar, as it was then called). While I found no explicit claim by Logan to a mastery of the Malayalam tongue, his book is replete with learned little asides about the etymology of particular Malayalam words, and Indian Civil Service officials in his day were required to pass an examination on one of the major languages of India. So it seems unlikely that he would have been appointed Commissioner of Malabar Land Tenures—as he was—unless he had a reading knowledge of Malayalam.

On the term *taravād*, see Gough (1961: 323).

Male Nayar forbidden on pain of death to sleep with a woman of any other caste: Barbosa in Dames (1918: 49) and Buchanan (1807: 412).

Household duties of Nayar women: Gough (1961: 338ff.).

Among the people where sexual hospitality was once well institutionalized are: the Society Islanders (Tahiti, Bora-Bora), many Eskimo groups, and many northern Algonkians of Quebec and Ontario.

Sexual hospitality of Nayar women to high-caste guests: Barbosa in Dames (1918: 54) and Gough (1961: 358).

Quotations on the waning but still surviving traditional "marriage" practices of his day: Logan (1887: 136, 137, 139, 154).

The matrilineal inheritance rules traditionally followed by the Nayar up to Logan's day were called *Marumakkattayam*, and they were followed in two dozen other castes as well (see Logan, 1887: 154f). Compare Logan's list of Nayar subcastes, page 134. As I say in the text, the special thing about the Nayar was not their inheritance system; it was the combination of that system with their unique military duties.

While Gough has done ample justice to the Nayar "marriage" system, which was her chief interest, she treats only sketchily the traditional Nayar political and military role. As these had vanished more than 125 years before Gough went to Kerala, she could hardly have learned much from her informants. But a full account, from Malayalam as well as European documents, would set that marriage system more clearly in its larger context.

APPENDIX E
Computation of Chance Risk
on Worldwide Scoreboards

This is an appendix to Section 3.5.3, "Measuring Deep Chance Risk." I deal here with the strategy and tactics of my computation on worldwide scoreboards of the boundaries of the Indicated and Extreme Ranges, as well as of the individual chance risks of countries outside the Indicated Range.

My computations of chance risk (statistical significance) of individual scores outside the Indicated Range treat each scoreboard as though it were a random sample from an infinitely large Gaussian universe of scores, the mean of which is equal to the score of the Model Country and whose standard deviation is equal to that of the OECD countries in about 1972. (Accordingly, I use the Gaussian distribution rather than Student's t distribution to measure the probability of a given deviation from the stated mean.)

Why use an imaginary rather than an actual observed distribution to measure probabilities? Because I am measuring the departure of particular countries from an ideal model of an ideal world, rather than making real inferences about the real world. The further the Model Country—in this book, Norway—departs from the actual worldwide mean, and the further the OECD 1972 standard deviation departs from the actual worldwide standard deviation, the greater the discrepancies between my ideal world and that real world.

The key point to bear in mind is that although I am using probability models designed for making inferences about a real-world universe by observing a random sample thereof, I am not using those probability models for their originally intended purpose. Instead, I am using an imaginary model of an imaginary world to help us think about the real world. My scoreboard range boundaries and probabilities offer as a guide to policy the mathematics of a situation that would exist if the real world were—as it certainly is not—a random sample from the imaginary universe I have defined. But is it not important that we use a statistical model to which our data in fact conform? Not at all, I submit—not here and not ever. As I argued in Section 4.3, even in a conventional significance test in which indeed we are trying to make inferences about a real universe from a genuine random sample, the whole point of a chance risk test—

of a test of so-called statistical significance—is to discredit the hypothesis that our data can be plausibly explained by the statistical model of the test in use.

I repeat, the range boundaries and chance risk calculations of the scoreboards in this book are not intended as descriptions of the world as it is, but rather of the world as it ought to be: These parameters set forth goals. On every scoreboard, the goal is a world whose countries all have scores within the Indicated Range. That range, in turn, is defined by the score of the Model Country and the variance of the OECD countries at about 1972. I propose that every five or ten years we take another look at the world and whenever appropriate, change our selection of the Model Country—according to some such method as that used in Section 3.5.2. But I propose that we be very slow to change our Model Variance from that established at about 1972 by the OECD countries—changing it no more frequently than perhaps once every hundred years. So where, according to these standards, a country falls within the Indicated Range, I wish to discourage change and to encourage people to keep things as they are. But where, according to these standards, a country falls outside that Indicated Range, then I use the probabilities that are given by my imaginary model as a measure of the urgency of change, to help policy makers set priorities and judge tradeoffs.

Obviously, I am not interested in making any inferences about the state of affairs in my imaginary universe; nor do I wish to be guided by the actual worldwide variance—which now is usually far too great to serve as a model and which in centuries to come, if all goes well, would instead become too small. Chance risk computations are two-tailed, giving the probability of a difference in an observed score from that of the Model Country at least as great as that observed in either direction. I compute chance risk through the use of the following approximation (subject to an error of .00001) derived from Poole and Borchers (1977: 129):

$$F(z) = .5 - R(.4361836t - .1201676t^2 + .937298t^3)$$

where x = raw score
  z = standard score of x
  R = normal ordinate at x
  t = $1/(1 + .33267 |x|)$

Distribution. My imaginary universe is one with a normal distribution—a bell curve. But it is the nature of many social or cultural phenomena to follow a lognormal distribution—especially if they are growing or changing exponentially. (Exponential growth tends to produce allometric relationships among variables, all of which are growing thus at the same time.) Accordingly, whenever I can (and I always could for the scoreboards of this book), I compare the fit of the OECD distribution to a normal and to a lognormal distribution. Where the lognormal fits better, I define my imaginary universe as one with lognormal distribution.

Skewness test. The tests of normality I use are those expounded by Geary and Pearson. My skewness test is their $\sqrt{b}$ statistic: In normal distributions it has a mean of 0. (Duncan calls this statistic γ.) Its standard deviation is a function of sample size; the tables and charts of Geary and Pearson go only to samples as small as 25, but their graph encourages linear extrapolation; for $N = 22$, it should be .45352. The more closely the skewness score approaches zero, the better the fit.

Kurtosis test. My kurtosis test is their *a* statistic. Both mean and standard deviation of that statistic vary among normal distributions according to sample size; Geary and Pearson give values for $N = 21$ and $N = 26$; for a sample of 22, by linear interpolation I get a value of .807516 for the mean and of .043374 for the standard deviation. The closer the kurtosis score of the OECD nations approaches .807516, the better the fit.

I computed these two measures not only of the raw scores, but also of their natural logarithms. As I said, where the OECD logarithms give a better fit than the raw scores, I call the distribution lognormal and report the skew and the kurtosis of the logarithms rather than of the raw scores. Where the results of the skewness test disagree with those of the kurtosis test, I follow the former and ignore the latter. (Had any scores been equal to or less then 0 on the scoreboard, I would have had to ignore all the logarithms of that scoreboard, deal only with the raw scores, and so treat the distribution as normal rather than lognormal. Needless to say, growing things properly measured usually have positive scores—every plant or animal weighs *something*.)

Notes

The contribution of Geary and Pearson (n.d.) to the S and K tests of normality was to compile tables and charts relating their standard deviations (and the mean of the K test) to sample size.

On the S test, see Duncan (1959: 497). Duncan gives a convenient, detailed, and thoughtful summary of the methods of industrial statistical quality control, pioneered in the 1920s and 1930s by W. A. Shewhart. Duncan (1959: 320-322) discusses the use of the three-standard deviation alarm bell. While this is, of course, an arbitrary cutoff point, it now has immense practical support as a plausible signal of a process in so much trouble, that no matter what the cost, it has got to be fixed. The use of that .00135 level of significance will seem eminently reasonable to quality control engineers, but disturbing to social scientists, who are accustomed to thinking of the .05 level as acceptable and the .01 level as almost definitive. Thus, Levine (1982: 161) complains that the author of a study of symptoms among Love Canal victims considered the results not significant, although the chance risk was only .005. The point here is that in social science theory testing, the .05 level grew up as a custom governing the acceptance of a finding as worthy of publication or of theoretical consideration—not as a guide to policy. It costs very little to publish a scientific paper that depends for its validity on a chance risk of 5 percent. But in industrial statistical quality control, as in the Love Canal affair, the issue at stake is often a very large sum of money—hundreds of thousands, even millions, of dollars. So a much more stringent criterion has become customary there: It pays the research scientist to have the null hypothesis discredited—but it pays the employers of the statistical quality control engineer to have it supported. That is why I put the entire range of chance risks between .5 and .00135 in the negotiation range. At Love Canal, for example, it would have paid the Canal residents to discredit the null hypothesis—but it would have paid state taxpayers and federal taxpayers, and the Hooker Corporation stockholders, and the officials who represented them, to support it. Where the results fall within the negotiation range, I submit, the outcome is indeed properly a subject for bargaining between pressure groups—for the political rather than the scientific process.

Poole and Borchers (1977: 129) is my source for Formula 1.

APPENDIX F

Minimum Variation in

a Golden Age

This is a comment on Section 3.5.4, "Fixing a Minimum Worldwide Variation." It speaks then to the concern that mankind's culture might some day become too uniform to permit adequate adaptability and progress.

Future socionomists who carefully study the rate and mode of human progress may well be cautious about easily lowering their minimum variation standards. It is true that if, for example, people were one day to enter a golden age, to attain worldwide the level of happiness now found in Norway, they might feel comfortable with a far slower rate of progress than ours. On the other hand, Kroeber's review of artistic and intellectual creativity has shown it to occur in bursts of one or two centuries, often with fallow intervals of many centuries in between. Innovative breakthroughs seem often to take many hundreds of years to gestate. The pattern of the rise and fall of empires over the past 2,000 years also presents a kind of event that takes hundreds of years to happen. So in a stable golden age, a very long perspective—something like 500 years—would be needed before a future socionomist could safely conclude that mankind has indeed settled down to a comfortably slow but steady rate of progress. If worldwide variety were to drop much below that now prevailing among the 22 OECD nations, it would take that long a golden age to reassure a skeptic that decay might not be setting in.

Notes

On long-term cycles of creativity, see Kroeber (1944).
On cycles of the rise and fall of empires, see Naroll (1967).

APPENDIX G

Weakened Moralnets

and Homicide

by
Susan J. Horan

In *The Moral Order* Naroll presents evidence from empirical tests that weakened moralnets mean juvenile delinquency, mean suicide, mean alcoholism, mean child abuse, mean problems for the aged, and mean problems for divorced people and their children. He recognizes that many of the studies he reviews show correlations and not cause, and he calls for more research, for better research using more advanced statistics, using more controlled experiments, and more worldwide tests.

Many homicide studies give indirect support to Naroll's moralnet theory. For example, Naroll suggests that when people have weak ties to their moralnets, murder will be more frequent. In a study of marital violence, Chimbos (1978) found that the majority of his sample had never received advice or support during their marital problems: 94 percent of these offenders reported cool and distant relationships with their relatives.

Rosenblatt and Greenland (1974) found that only nine of the 22 hospitalized female homicide offenders in their sample had sought help from friends or other helping agents and that few of these offered any aid to these women.

Further support is found in British studies cited by Hood and Sparks (1970), in which delinquency is attributed to problem families with little social control over their children, low standards of child care, and lack of emotional stability. Studies by Humphrey (1978), McCord et al. (1959), Mulvihill and Tumin (1969), Goldstein (1975), and Nye (1958) all report the importance of parental bonds in preventing violence. Moralnet theory postulates that when individuals get less emotional warmth from their moralnets, the homicide rates are higher. Duncan and Duncan (1971), Satten et al. (1960), and Corder et al. (1976) all report

Author's Note: Excerpted by permission from Horan's doctoral thesis, "Theories of Criminal Homicide," pp. 194-196, of August 1981 draft, Department of Anthropology, State University of New York, Buffalo.

childhood physical and psychological abuse to be common among homicide offenders.

Another prediction of moralnet theory is that when individuals do not get economic support from their moralnets, homicide is more frequent. The many epidemiological, demographic, and frustration-aggression studies reported in this thesis all point to the greater number of homicides committed by members of the lower economic class.

One problem with the moralnet theory prediction that homicide rates will be low when individuals belong to culturally homogeneous moralnets is revealed in the studies reviewed in this thesis which found that the homicide rate is high in certain homogeneous subcultures. This could be explained in part by the fact that these subcultures are not totally homogeneous; they are still part of a dominant culture and different moralnets from part of the culture are often in conflict with each other.

Naroll's moralnet theory does seem to be supported by studies from many different disciplines, but a great deal more research is needed. As this thesis has shown, studies are needed that test the moralnet theory worldwide, on primitive societies and on nations; studies are needed that consider and control for individual differences in physiology and psychology; and studies are needed that offer solutions to the problems created by weakened moralnets.

Note

At this writing (July 1982), Horan is still working on her doctoral dissertation, now in its third draft.

Glossary

I have put in this glossary words that are not plainly set forth in *The American Heritage Dictionary of the English Language* (1976). I also include many key words that are defined there in the sense I use them, but which nevertheless are sufficiently technical as to puzzle people who have not studied behavioral science method—terms like *chi-square test* and *standard deviation* and *bus* (in the cybernetic sense). There are a few new terms coined by me especially for this book, and marked here with an asterisk (*).

Affinal relatives. Relatives by marriage rather than by blood; in-laws.

Age-and-area. A method of reconstructing broad patterns of cultural diffusion by comparing the geographical distribution of culture traits with their archeological sequence at a diffusion center.

Age grade. An age group whose membership is formalized so that going from one age group to the next is signaled by a ceremony, such as Bar Mitzvah among Jews.

Age group. A cultural category for sorting people out by age, such as baby, child, adult, senior citizen.

Age set. An age grade whose members act together as a team or social servomechanism, to attain any common goal.

Analyst. In social science, the one who uses a codebook or protocol to classify the reports of an observer, so that these can then be measured statistically.

Antilogarithm. If the number L is the logarithm of X, then X is called the antilogarithm of L.

Association. See Correlation.

Availability heuristic. See Counting bias.

Bell curve. The normal distribution of a random variable about a mean, when plotted on a graph through the methods of analytical geometry, takes the shape of a bell. I use the term to mean that normal distribution; it is the foundation of the theory of mathematical statistics and so is discussed at length in any introductory textbook (see, for example, Thomas, 1976: chap. 7). See also Gaussian integral.

Bilateral descent. A family system in which membership is traced through both fathers and mothers. It is found among most speakers of European languages (including English) in modern times.

Billion. As is customary in North America, I use the term to mean a thousand million, not, as often elsewhere, to mean a million million.

Bride price. See Bride wealth.

Bride wealth. Wealth (in Africa, often cattle) given by the groom or his family to the bride's family as part of a marriage contract.

Bus. In cybernetic theory, a communication spine; a central line of communication set up so that branches can conveniently join it. For example, an electrical circuit, into successive outlets of which we can plug in a radio, a toaster, a television set.

CAAAL. Classified Abstract Archive of the Alcohol Literature, distributed by the Rutgers Center of Alcohol Studies, New Brunswick, New Jersey, 08903.

CEV (Coefficient of Evolutionary Variation). The standard deviation, expressed as a percentage of the mean. It is given by the formula:

$$CEV = 100S/X$$

where S is the standard deviation and X is the mean. The CEV is in wide use among such biologists as Yablokov (1974: 8) to measure evolutionary variation. Such economists as Morgenstern (1963: 256) also use this same concept and call it the *relative deviation*.

*Chance risk. Usually called *statistical significance*, or *significance level*. The probability that a given statistical result (typically a correlation, association, or difference between two or more sets of numbers) might occur by chance through random sampling of a like number of observations from a universe in which no such relationship in fact exists. It also measures simultaneously the probability that the result observed occurred in the real world through the concatenation of a very large number of very small, very weak causal influences. In the scoreboards of this book, chance risk reports the probability that, through chance, a given nation would have a score at least as far from Norway's as the one that given nation has. In Table 7.1, for example, the difference between Finland's mental hospitalization rate of 99.5 and Norway's rate of 25.7 would be expected to occur through chance only 5 times in 100 independent trials.

Chi-square test. A general test of chance risk, of statistical significance; a good approximation of Fisher's Exact Test in fourfold contingency tables when certain conditions are met. It should not be used at all in R × C contingency tables, according to Thomas (1976: 414), if both variables are ranked; instead, Naroll's Exact Test (1974a) or Kendall's S (1962) approximation should be used.

City. A collection of fixed dwellings accommodating at least 25,000 people within ten kilometers of a central point. A society with one or more cities is classed as a large-scale society; one without any cities, as small-scale.

Civilization. A group of cultunits that share a common written literature which they consider to be a major source of wisdom and to which they look for guidance. Such bodies of written literature have been produced only by large-scale societies—though they can, of course, easily be read by people belonging to small-scale ones.

Clan. In kinship theory, a fictitious lineage. A group of people who believe they are a patrilineal lineage, but cannot trace their relationships through actual genealogies, is called a patrilineal clan. This definition is widely used by anthropologists, but the term "clan" is not always used in this way by all.

Concomitant variation study. A comparative, quasi-experimental research design such that either the variables of interest vary while everything else stays constant (Redfield type), or the variables of interest stay constant while everything else varies (Spicer type).

Control variables. In experimental design, variables that are held constant by the experimenter in order to keep them from interfering with the effect of the experimental variables.

Controlled experiment. A test of a theory that treatment A causes result B by applying treatment A to an experimental group while refraining from applying it to a control group. Subjects are randomly assigned to the two groups so that chance risk tests can measure the risk that those choices influence results, and care is taken to see that otherwise the two groups are treated just alike. See also double blind.

Core value. A presumed universal human social value. In a moral worldwide social order, each culture's value system is thought of as consisting of (1) *core* values, which it shares with the rest of mankind, and (2) *outer* values, which are not universal. Liberty and democracy, for example, might be outer values found in North America and Western Europe but not in China or Eastern Europe.

Correlation. A measurement of association or linkage. For example, height is positively correlated with weight, but not perfectly; by and large, the taller a person, the heavier, but not invariably. In a positive correlation between A and B, the more A, the more B. In a negative correlation between A and B, the more A the less B. Perfect positive correlation equals 1.00. (In this book, unless otherwise stated, correlations in fourfold contingency tables are phi coefficients, not Yule's Q; correlations among ranked variables—ordinal matrices—are Kendall's tau-b, not Goodman-Kruskal gammas; others are Pearson product-moment coefficients.)

Counting bias. The fallacious tendency of the mind to overestimate the frequency or typicality of the more salient individuals of a class. Also called *availability heuristic*. See Section 4.5.

Cultunit. A basic culture-bearing unit; a society whose members speak a distinct language, not intelligible to speakers of the language of any other cultunit. Even though they speak the same language, people belong to different cultunits if they belong to different states or if, while belonging to no state at all, they are out of touch with each other.

Culture. In general, behavior learned from a social group and shared with that group. Specifically, the way of life of any particular group, such as the Hopi or the French.

Curvilinear. In mathematical statistics, a regression pattern that tends to follow a curve rather than a straight line. For example, in one model of the cultural evolution of family size, the data points curve like an arch, with high points (most extended families) at middle levels of cultural evolution, but low points (least extended families) at both high and low levels.

Cybernetics. The study of control systems, including the application of information theory, as developed by electrical and mechanical engineers, to the understanding of the nervous system and the mind. Digital computers, servomechanisms, and telephone switches are major sources of cybernetic theory. The word literally means "having to do with steering."

*Darwin. A natural selection arena, in which through blind variation and selective retention, goal oriented change is taking place. See Section 1.2

Data Quality Control (DQC). In holocultural method, a way of analyzing statistical data to see whether they trick the user. DQC catches the false linkage (spurious correlation) produced by systematic errors in the data. Such errors often are made in good faith by well-meaning but unskilled observers. Unsystematic or random errors may also be caught by DQC, but these are also caught by ordinary checking, or by reliability tests.

*Deep chance risk. In contrast to *shallow chance risk*, the probability of fundamental, underlying social and cultural forces or differences affecting national statistical rates from year to year or from country to country.

Deviant case. In a successful statistical correlational test of a theory, it is a case of the class that tends to discredit the theory. In Table. 11.3, for example, the Apayao is a deviant case: Apayao have a low social development index but practice child beating—most societies that practice child beating have high social development indices. The analysis of deviant cases is an important method of deepening understanding and developing new theory.

Dichotomy. A twofold division or classification; everything measured is called A or not-A, male or female, plant or animal, monarchy or republic, New World or Old World.

Diffusion, cultural. The spread of culture traits from one society to another by borrowing, migration, or common cultural heritage. Not to be confused with diffusion of nurturance.

Diffusion of nurturance. A situation in which a human infant tends to be looked after and loved by several older people, rather than by only the mother.

Domain of meaning. See Semantic domain.

Double-blind experimental design. In a blind experimental design, the subjects do not know who is being given the experimental treatment, who is not. To accomplish this purpose, a false but harmless treatment that looks much like the real one must be given to the control group. In a double-blind experiment, those who administer and analyze the treatments also do not know which group is which; only the project director knows.

Emic. A native or folk concept. Each language (except the technical language used by social scientists and philosophers) constitutes a distinct set of emic concepts, which contrasts with etic and theoric concepts.

Empiricism. The scheme of epistemology that holds that people can know only what they observe directly through their senses—what they can see, hear, smell, taste, or touch. It allows me to learn from you by my asking you what you have seen, or heard, or been told by another. But it rules out mystical insights, divine revelations, divinely inspired prophesies, or pronouncements. It demands that the chain of reports on which we rely begin with one from an ordinary person of an ordinary observation.

Epic. In moral theory, an emotionally satisfying dramatic tale about a culture hero whose life sets forth a model of a moral order.

Epistemology. The branch of philosophy that deals with how we know what we know; a particular scheme of knowing.

Ethnographer. One who describes a foreign ethnic group or people.

Ethnography. A description of the way of life of a foreign ethnic group or people. Most ethnographies have been written in European languages by anthropologists, missionaries, or government officials.

Etic. A distinction or key idea in an emic concept. Though there are thousands of sets of emic concepts (such as kin terms or color terms) in any one domain of meaning, we find that very few etic distinctions are involved in each domain. There are less than a dozen used in all the kin term systems known, and not more than three or four— perhaps only two—in all the systems of color terms.

*__Extreme Range__. On the scoreboard tables of this book, the boundary outside which a score plainly calls for public policy changes, since it is manifestly too much different from the score of the model country. I have taken a chance risk of .0027 as the value of this boundary. See Section 3.5.3.

Factor analysis. In mathematics, a method of grouping a large set of interrelated variables into a small number of clusters of interrelationships. The best introduction to this method for social scientists is Rummel (1970a). (However, his suggestion—that the factors produced by factor analysis constitute the underlying causes of a process— derives from his definition of the idea of cause as something to which purpose is irrelevant.)

FC (Finished characteristic). A particular trait or variable in Textor (1967). He numbers these. The body of his work lacks numbered pages; it is arranged by subject trait FC number. To refer to a correlation, refer to its FC number. For example, to find FC 127/FC 213, look first for subject trait FC 127 (page by page); then look line by line on the FC 127 pages for predicate trait FC 213.

Feedback. In a servo, the report of the actual state of the thing under control. In a snowball, the effect of holding a resource which leads to further accumulation of that same resource. Servos are negative feedback systems; snowballs are positive feedback systems.

Fisher's Exact Test. In mathematical statistics, the best measure of chance risk (statistical significance) in fourfold contingency tables (see Thomas, 1976: 291-298).

Five Steps. A five-element system of worldwide morality: (1) core values, (2) scoreboards (social and cultural indicators), (3) theory test evaluations, (4) study plans, and (5) public policies.

FORTRAN. A program language especially adapted to instructing computers to perform mathematically intricate tasks. It was long the computer language most commonly used in the United States on scientific computers.

Fourfold contingency table. A set of four comparisons of two variables. Each variable is cut into two parts, so that any case can have either of two values on either of the two variables—in all, four possibilities (see, for example, Table 12.5).

Galton's problem. In holocultural method, a technical problem in judging worldwide correlations. If cultural diffusion through borrowing, migration, or common cultural heritage multiplies instances of linkage, how many independent cases of correlation do we have? And what is the true magnitude of the correlation?

Gamma coefficient. In mathematical statistics, a measure of association between ordinal variables (see Thomas, 1976: 414-418).

Gaussian integral. In mathematical statistics, the formula in the integral calculus for computing the area under the bell curve (normal or Gaussian distribution) between the mean and any given standard score (here called X):

$$\int_0^X \frac{1}{\sqrt{2\pi}}\, e^{\frac{-x^2}{2}}\, dx$$

where e = 2.71828.

Gini Index of Inequality. A standard measure of the inequality of the distribution of any scarce good, as, for example, distribution of income within a population: If income is equally distributed, then the Gini Index equals 0; if one person gets all the income, and everyone else gets none, then the Gini Index equals 1.0 (see Russett et al., 1964: 237f. for method of calculation).

Guttman scale. In mathematics, an arrangement of several traits (variables, characteristics), each coded as present or absent, such that the presence of later traits in the scale almost always successfully predicts the presence of earlier ones, while the absence of earlier ones almost always successfully predicts the absence of later ones.

Hawthorne effect. The effect that pride and interest in an experiment, by people who are the subjects, have on the outcome of a social experiment (for details, see Roethlisberger, Dickson, and Wright, 1939).

Holocultural index. A measure of some characteristic or variable of a small-scale society in a holocultural study.

Holocultural study. A hologeistic study, the units of which are predominantly small-scale societies without cities; a worldwide cross-cultural survey.

Hologeistic study. A study whose dimensions are worldwide cross-cultural or cross-national (macro-cross-national). Whole nations, societies, or cultures are compared; theories are tested by means of correlations among their characteristics or traits. In such a study a case is a nation, society or culture, and a variable is a characteristic or quality or measurement of a case.

Holohistorical study. A hologeistic study, the units of which are preindustrial societies known from their own written records.

Holonational study. A hologeistic study, the units of which are modern nations; a cross-national or macro-cross-national study.

HRAF. See Human Relations Area Files.

HRAFLIB. A collection of computer programs for holocultural studies distributed by the Human Relations Area Files.

HRAF QC Sample. A special probability sample described in Naroll (1970b: 910). A subset of the Human Relations Area Files. Also known as the Probability Sample Files (PSF) and the Blue Ribbon Sample.

Human Relations Area Files. A specially indexed set of ethnographic files, much used for hologeistic theory testing; also, the organization that creates them.

⃰Indicated Range. Used on scoreboard tables to demarcate scores within one probable error of the model country—at this time, Norway. If the model country is to be a guide, then the highest priority in allocating scarce resources ought to go to lowering the scores of bad things that are above the Indicated Range, and to raising the scores of good things that are below the Indicated Range.

Instinct. A genetically transmitted liking, wish, desire, or craving, the means of satisfying which must be learned. Thus the only genetic element of an instinct is its end result or goal. If that result is to be achieved, the behavior pattern developed by the organism to achieve that goal must first be learned—and perhaps may not be. Further, an instinctual goal can be overridden or blocked by some other conflicting desire, and so the behavior called for by any given instinct is simply made probable; it is not certain to occur at all.

Interval scale. In mathematical statistics, a mode of measurement with intervals of equal value but no true zero point; if score A is twice score B, A nevertheless does not have twice as much of the thing measured as B. If it is 90 degrees Fahrenheit in New Orleans but only 45 degrees Fahrenheit in Chicago, New Orleans is *not* exactly twice as hot as Chicago. Other kinds of scales are ratio scales, ordinal scales, nominal scales, and dichotomies.

IPSS (International Pilot Study of Schizophrenia). A worldwide (nine-country) comparative study of all kinds of mental illness (not just schizophrenia, although that received the most attention); it is reported in United Nations, World Health Organization (1973).

Kurtosis chance risk. The probability that the kurtosis of the distribution of the scores of the 22 OECD nations be obtained by chance through random sampling error in a sample of 22 taken from an infinitely large and normally distributed universe (see Appendix E). By kurtosis is meant the departure of a curve from normality in that it is either too peaked (too skinny) or else too squat (too fat). As used on the scoreboards, the higher this chance risk, the more confidence we can have in the country chance risk scores and in the indicated and extreme range limits.

Kendall's S. In mathematical statistics, a test for statistical significance based on the variance of Kendall's S, computed by formula (4.3) of Kendall (1962: 55). The value of S itself may be corrected for continuity according to Freeman's (1965: 172) formula; this correction may not be necessary but is conservative, tending to favor the chance hypothesis.

Lagged correlation. A correlation between two characteristics (variables, traits), one measured at an earlier time and another one measured at a later time. If the first is the cause, and the second is the effect, the scientist expects that such correlations will be higher than if both measurements are taken at the same time.

Large-scale society. A culture with cities. Used here instead of "civilized" society because the latter phrase gives offense to many non-European people classed as "uncivilized" (see the complaint by Chilungu, 1976).

Latching bias. The fallacious tendency of the mind to cling stubbornly to an idea once formed, in the face of overwhelming evidence that it is false. See Section 4.5.

Literary scholarship. I use this term to mean the unstructured, uncontrolled essay as a study that relies on documents for its source of data, but unlike archival studies, lacks systematic controls for the counting, the matching, or the latching biases.

Linear regression equation. In mathematical statistics, an analysis of cause/effect relations that assumes that the direction of causality is already known, that a single effect is the result of one or more causes, and that increases in the effect are directly proportionate to increases in any of the causes.

Lineage. The descendants from a common ancestor through intermediate ancestors of a single sex—through men for a patrilineal lineage, through women for a matrilineal lineage.

Linear relationship (linear correlation). In mathematics, a correlation, the scatter diagram of which tends to follow a straight line rather than a curve.

Linguistic memory. In cybernetic theory, the place in which the human mind stores and runs programs for the production of words, phrases, clauses, and sentences, perhaps using sample forms of good and bad examples. However, the meanings of words, phrases, and idioms are not stored here, but in systemic memory.

Linked pair diffusion test. In holocultural method, a solution to Galton's problem that measures the correlation of a trait in its neighbor, thus a spatial autocorrelation.

Logarithm. The logarithm of any given number is given in relationship to a stated base. Call that stated base B, call the number we are interested in X, and call that number's logarithm L. Then the logarithm of X to the base B is defined by the following formula:

$$B^L = X$$

Common logarithms are to the base 10; natural logarithms are to the base 2.71828.

Logarithmic CEV (Coefficient of Evolutionary Variation). The CEV of the logarithms of the measures—used on scoreboards with lognormal distributions.

Logarithmic model variation. The antilogarithm of the probable error of the logarithms of the measures—used on scoreboards with lognormal distributions.

Logarithmic standard deviation. The antilogarithm of the standard deviation of the logarithms of the measures—used on scoreboards with lognormal distributions.

Lognormal distribution. When a group of numbers is such that their logarithms rather than the numbers themselves take the form of the bell curve, they are said to have a lognormal distribution. Sets of measurements of growth or development or evolution often have lognormal distributions. So do some of the scoreboards in this book.

Lurking variable. In social science method, in a simple correlation or association between two variables, the possibility of that correlation resulting from the effect of some third, unmeasured variable. Once a third variable is measured by partial correlations or factor analysis, it is no longer lurking, but instead is out in the open.

Malayalam. The chief language of Kerala in South India, home of the Nayars.

Matched control groups. In experimental design, pairing off members of the experimental and control groups to make them as similar as possible in age, sex, occupation, income, or the like. Random chance then determines which member of the pair is to join the experimental group, which the control. Matching is a method of holding the matched variables constant, so that they do not affect the outcome.

Matching bias. The fallacious tendency of the mind to mistakenly discern cause from effect, or effect from cause, or outcome from origin, or origin from outcome, or antecedent from consequent, or consequent from antecedent, simply by matching salient features of each. Also called *representative heuristic*. See Section 4.5.

Mathematical symbols. (Here is given only the English name of the symbol. See the explanation under that name.)

τ = tau (see under tau-b)
γ = gamma (see under gamma coefficient)
r = correlation
p = probability

Matrilineage. Matrilineal lineage.

Matrilineal descent. A family system in which family membership is traced through mothers only, not through fathers.

Mean. The statistician's standard measure of average; the sum of a set of scores divided by the number of scores in the set.

Median. In mathematical statistics, that score (on a scoreboard, for example) that has as many items (on a scoreboard, as many countries) above as below it. If a scoreboard lists 31 countries, in order, the score of the sixteenth country is the median score: Fifteen countries have lower scores and fifteen other countries have higher scores.

Mensch. In moralnet theory, a real person, or proper human being—one well integrated with his or her moralnets, accepting their values and performing the duties thus implied. From the Yiddish (see Rosten, 1968: 234).

*Model country. The one nation that does best for worldwide scoreboards on the twelve basic meters of seven core values. *The Moral Order* is based on the situation about 1965-1975; during that time, Norway did best, and so it is the model country and fixes the goals for the rest of the world.

*Model score. The score of the model country on worldwide scoreboards.

*Model variation. For national scoreboards covering measures of quality of life, the desired spread of evolutionary variation among the various nations worldwide around the model score. I usually take that spread to be .6745 of the standard deviation of the scores of the OECD countries about 1970—the OECD probable error. There is a presumption that any variation within that range was then merely due to chance—the preponderance of evidence so tilts.

*Moralnet. The largest primary group that serves a given person as a normative reference group (see Section 6.4). Primevally, a person's hunting band was the moralnet. In small-scale societies, people often have no choice of a moralnet; in large-scale societies, they often have many from which to choose. See also normative reference group, primary group, significant others, and social support network.

Multivariate analysis. A method of studying the interrelationships or linkages among three or more variables (traits). Among the leading methods are linear regression, path analysis, multiple and partial correlation, analysis of variance, and factor analysis.

Naive observers or analysts. In a research design, recorders and analysts of data who do not know the theory they are testing. If they do know that theory, they are likely to bias their reports and interpretations for or against it.

Naroll's Exact Test. In mathematical statistics, a measure of chance risk (statistical significance) in R × C tables, analogous to Fisher's Exact Test. It is usually too tedious to compute by hand; it requires a computer program such as ORDMAT, published by the Human Relations Area Files (Details in Naroll, 1974a).

NCALI. National Clearinghouse for Alcohol Information, P. O. Box 2345, Rockville, MD 20852.

Negative-sum game. See Zero-sum game.

*Negotiation Range. Used on the scoreboards to indicate a score neither inside the Indicated Range (with respect to the mean), nor outside the Extreme Range. Whether such a score is evidence of trouble calling for public policy changes is open to legitimate dispute, debate, and bargaining among conflicting interest groups.

Nominal scale. In mathematical statistics, a mode of measurement that divides the things measured into distinct types, without assigning a relative rank or value to each. A dichotomy is a special kind of nominal scale, in which there are only two divisions or classes. Other kinds of scales are ratio scales, interval scales, and ordinal scales.

Normal distribution. See Bell curve.

Normative reference group. The set of other people from whom a person takes social values, and ideas of what is good and bad, right and wrong. Extended family, religious group, and intellectual school of thought are common examples.

Nuclear family. The core family, consisting of one husband, one wife, and their immature children.

Observer. In research design, the one who actually sees or hears the things studied and records them—contrasted with analyst, who uses a codebook to classify the records so that they can be measured statistically.

OECD (Organization for Economic Cooperation and Development). In this book I look at the 22 members it had in 1971: Austria, Belgium, Canada, Denmark, France, Germany (West), Greece, Iceland, Ireland, Italy, Japan, Luxembourg, Netherlands,

Norway, Portugal, Spain, Sweden, Switzerland, Turkey, United Kingdom, United States, and Yugoslavia.

Ordinal polytomy. See Ordinal scale.

Ordinal scale. In mathematical statistics, a mode of measurement made up of a series of ranks, the exact values of which are unequal or unknown. Other kinds of scales are ratio scales, interval scales, nominal scales, and dichotomies.

PAR (Parental Acceptance/Rejection). The warmth of feeling of parents toward children, studied by Rohner and his associates (see Rohner, 1975).

Participant observation. A study of a social or historical situation or event by a reporter who not merely watches what is happening but personally takes part.

Patrilineage. Patrilineal lineage.

Patrilineal descent. A family system in which family membership is traced through fathers only, not through mothers.

Phi coefficient. In mathematical statistics, a measure of correlation in a fourfold contingency table (see Thomas, 1976: 419-423 or almost any other introduction to statistics).

Positive-sum game. See Zero-sum game.

Predicate trait. See Subject trait.

Primary group. That group of other people with which any person habitually lives closely. A family, a set of work mates or school fellows, a soldier's squad or company, and a sailor's shipmates are familiar examples.

Primary observation. A study of a historical or social situation by a scholar who has observed it first hand, directly and personally—rather than from hearsay or from a report written by someone else.

Probable error. In a series of repeated, precise observations of the same phenomenon, that portion of the range of variation equally divided above and below the mean in which exactly half the randomly varying observations may be expected to fall. Since this random variation may be expected to follow the bell curve, that range is exactly 0.6745 of a standard deviation.

*Programmatic memory. In cybernetic theory, it manages plans, decisions, and language; remembered events and stories (tales, myths) fall into it (see Section 6.2).

Prospective study. A study of mental illness in which the subjects are interviewed twice —the second time long after the first—in order to see what changes have taken place in mental health between the two interviews and to relate that change to life events which have transpired in the meantime.

Proxy measure. In social science method, an indirect measure of a societal characteristic that cannot be measured directly. For example, we do not have accurate information on suicide rates from most small-scale societies, but the relative attention given to suicide by ethnographers has been shown to be a valid proxy measure.

PSE (Present State Examination schedule). A psychiatric examination instrument that has been tested worldwide. It is used to diagnose mental illness.

Purpose test. A test of a theory of cause and effect by studying a series of cases in which someone tries to produce the effect by producing the cause, so that the effect happens on purpose. All experiments are purpose tests; the experimenter has an effect in mind and introduces a treatment to produce it. In human affairs, however, not only the students but the cases studied may have purposes. A systematic study of history to look at the success of repeated trials of public policy is also a purpose test.

R × C table. In mathematical statistics, a contingency table in which there are at least three rows or at least three columns. The name comes simply from Row × Column. Table 15.3 is an example.

Random sampling. In research design, a method of choosing cases for study to ensure that chance alone governs that choice. Casual, haphazard choice is not such a device; it is almost certain to contain a systematic bias. Tables of random numbers or dice are commonly used methods of making a random choice.

Range. In mathematical statistics, the difference between the highest score and lowest score on a table. On Table 9.3, the Suicide Scoreboard, for example, the highest score is 33.7, the lowest score is 1.6, and so the range is 32.1.

Ratio scale. In mathematical statistics, a mode of measurement with intervals of equal value, such that if score A is twice score B, then A has twice as much of the thing measured as B. Other kinds of scales are interval scales, ordinal scales, nominal scales and dichotomies.

Raw score. The original count, or original rate, used as a starting point for some kind of transformation. For example, Table 3.4 uses standard scores in which certain raw scores—that is, reported statistical rates—are transformed by subtracting them from the mean and then dividing the difference by the standard deviation.

Receptors. In cybernetic theory, nerves sending messages to the mind about the inner world, the outer world, and the sensorimotor stack.

Ren. A kind of virtue; Chinese people are said to have it when they feel a strong sense of responsibility to their moralnets. A mensch is a person with *ren*.

Replication. The repetition of an experiment or other study to check its findings. Ideally, a hologeistic replication is done on a new sample by a new investigator, using the coding rules of the original study.

Representative heuristic. See Matching bias.

Scale (societal complexity). In cultural theory, the overall cultural and social complexity of a society is sometimes called its scale.

Scoreboard. A table displaying the yardstick or indicator scores of nations around the world. It includes a classification of scores into (1) above the Indicated Range, (2) within the Indicated Range, and (3) below the Indicated Range. These values are here given by taking as boundaries one OECD probable error above and below the score of the model country, Norway. See also Extreme range and Negotiation range.

Secondary description. A study of a historical or social situation by a scholar who has not observed it first hand, but who relies on hearsay or on the written reports of others.

Self-help club. A voluntary association like Alcoholics Anonymous in which victims of some kind of social disorder band together to offer each other friendship and support in a common struggle against a problem they share.

Semantic domain. A general topic or heading or class of concepts, as seen from the point of view of the taxonomist or classifier who studies how such a domain is variously broken up into parts by particular languages. Kinship terms, color terms, and value concepts are examples.

Sensorimotor system. In cybernetic theory, that part of the nervous system which is concerned with measuring the situation outside the mind and/or controlling the response of the body to that situation. The key idea of the Hays-Powers model of the mind is that the sensorimotor system is a single system—at all levels, messages *in* are intimately related to messages *out*. The sensorimotor system is a set of servo controls.

Servo. In cybernetic theory, a servomechanism, or device for controlling something—keeping it at a desired state—by measuring its state, comparing that measurement with some standard or goal, and triggering corrective action if there is a discrepancy. Servos are negative feedback systems, because the feedback is subtracted from the goal, looking for a zero difference. A thermostat connected to a room heater to keep a room above a stated minimum temperature is an example.

Servo stack. See Stack

*****Shallow chance risk.** In contrast to *deep change risk*, the probability of historical accidents affecting national statistical rates from year to year or from country to country.

Significance level. See Chance risk.

Significant others. The set of people whose esteem and values are important to a person—usually that person's moralnet.

Skewness chance risk. The probability that the skewness of the distribution of the scores of the 22 OECD nations would be obtained by chance through random sampling error in a sample of 22 taken from an infinitely large and normally distributed (unskewed) universe (see Appendix E). By skewness is meant lack of symmetry—where scores spread out more widely on one side of the mean than on the other. As used in scoreboards, the higher this chance risk, the more confidence we can have in the country chance risk scores and in the Indicated and Extreme Range limits.

Small-scale society. A culture without cities. Used here as a substitute for "primitive" or "uncivilized" society because these words have often been used contemptuously, and so give offense to many people (see the complaint by Chilungu, 1976).

Smallest space analysis. In mathematical statistics, a kind of multivariate analysis something like factor analysis (Zelman, 1977, is a good example).

*__Snowball.__ Any positive feedback system: a self-reinforcing process consisting of participants and an attribute. The nature of a snowball is such that the more any participant already has of an attribute, the more he is likely to get in the future. Snowballs are also sometimes called vicious circles, upward spirals, or downward spirals.

Social support network. The set of people to whom a person in distress can turn to for advice, comfort, reassurance, and help—usually a subset of that person's moralnet.

*__Socionomics.__ The study of the socionomy—that is, of the general human situation (like economics).

*__Socionomist.__ One who studies the socionomy (like economist).

*__Sociononomy.__ The general human situation, encompassing the position of human society in history; its destiny; its ecological, sociological, political, economic, and ideological situation or status (like economy).

Stack. In cybernetic theory, a system of relating servos or programs in which higher-level elements control lower-level elements by changing their goals.

Standard deviation. The statistician's measure of variation or spread. If x is a raw score, $\bar{x}$ is the mean of all the raw scores, $x' = \bar{x} - x$, and n = the number of raw scores, then the standard deviation is given by the formula:

$$s = \sqrt{(\Sigma x'^2 / n)}$$

in other words, the square root of the average of the squared deviations from the mean. For details, see any introductory textbook on statistics (for example, Thomas, 1976: 76-79). The symbol Σ means "the sum of."

Standard score. In mathematical statistics, if x is the raw score, $\bar{x}$ is the mean score, and s is the standard deviation, then the standard score, z, is given by the formula:

$$z = \frac{x - \bar{x}}{s}$$

for example, Norway's suicide rate in 1973 was 8.6 per 100,000 (x = 8.6). The mean of the twelve suicide scores for Table 3.4 is 13, and the standard deviation 6.41. So Norway's standard score is (8.6 - 13)/6.41 = -4.4/6.41 = -.69.

Statistical significance. See Chance risk.

Stochastic epistemology. The attitude that we cannot know with certainty anything about the world outside the mind, but are able to assess the probability that our mental model of the outside world is accurate.

Studentized. In mathematical statistics, calculating chance risk by using Student's t-distribution rather than the normal or Gaussian distribution.

Study plan. A sketch of a research design to test a theory of the cause or cure of a social problem.

Subculture. A shared way of life, or the social group that shares it, of a group of people who form a part of a cultunit.

Subject trait. The first trait (variable, characteristic) mentioned in an association or correlation of two or more. The second such trait is called a *predicate* trait. The distinction is merely in the order of presentation; it has no theoretical implications of causal direction.

Systemic memory. In cybernetic theory, that part of the memory that remembers basic concepts or ideas corresponding to a dictionary. The idea of *house*—corresponding to the words *casa, maison, spiti, Haus,* and so on—is stored in systemic memory. Systemic memory maintains a model of our inner and outer worlds and colors that model with good and bad feelings as a quick guide through that world. The human moral order may well be grounded in innate feelings about key social concepts like the mother figure and the social band, lodged in systemic memory.

Taravād. Used here to mean a Nayar extended family household. Among the Nayar, the word is also used as the name of the larger matrilineage to which that household belongs, and further, as the name of the matrilineal clan to which the lineage belongs.

Tau-b. In mathematical statistics, an often-used measure of correlation for R × C tables in which many of the columns or rows have more than one case. Thomas (1976: 423-426) explains the statistic. However, his use of chi-square to compute chance risk applies only in cases like his example, where the rows and columns *are not* ranked. Otherwise, I use Kendall's S (1962: 35, formula 3.3) or Naroll's Exact Test (1974a).

Theme. A central organizing idea—or bus—of a culture's value or cognitive system. Many other ideas are linked to such a central one by association. People try to arrange other things so that they fit the theme. Democracy and individual self-reliance are such themes in North American Anglo culture today.

Theoric concept. One of a set of concepts devised by a social scientist or philosopher to explain human behavior. Until recently, scholars used the emic concept of their native language, whatever it was. Many scholars still do, but it frequently leads to misunderstanding. Theoric concepts should be devised in light of the range of variation of emic concepts, in etic terms.

***Theory trust meter.** A device I use to show graphically a standardized measure of confidence in the validity of a theory (see, for example, Figure 11.1). I assume that a theory is one of cause and effect; that it specifies a relationship that, if it in fact holds good, permits someone to control (or master) the effect by means of controlling or mastering the cause. The meter is a report on the state of three kinds of theory tests: (1) Association tests are studies that see whether, in fact, the supposed causes are correlated with the supposed effect. (2) Sequence tests not only measure association, but also test whether the supposed causes tend to precede the supposed effects and so permit prediction from cause to effect. (3) Purpose tests measure association, sequence, and control; they see whether attempts at controlling or mastering supposed effects by means of controlling or mastering supposed causes succeed. Controlled experiments are typical purpose tests. There are four quadrants in each of the three test pie charts; each one measures a different kind of theory test: HCS = holocultural test; HNS = holonational tests; L/I = local or individual test; U.S. = countrywide tests in the United States. In each quadrant: All slices dark = no objective tests of theory found; two slices dark = only one weak test found; one slice dark = two weak tests or one strong test found, no more; no slices dark = at least two tests found, at least one of them strong.

Therapeutic community. A residence home (and so, an artificial family) created for people facing some common problem—like mental illness, alcoholism, drug addiction, or juvenile delinquency.

THINCS (Theoretical Information Control System). A project of the Human Relations Area Files. Propositions are listed and objectively evaluated according to about two dozen elements of the method used in the theory test.

Triangulation. A research strategy that calls for repeatedly testing a given theory by a variety of research methods. Also called *multiple strategy* or the *universalist approach*.

Value. See Core value. An idea of what is good or desirable.

Variation. The extent to which a set of data differ from their mean or average values. Measures of variation used here include standard deviation, range, variance, and Coefficient of Evolutionary Variation (CEV).

Variance. The square of the standard deviation. If the standard deviation of a score-board equals 2, then its variance equals 4.

Victimization surveys. Sample surveys of the public to inquire how many have been victims of crime or other calamity. Crime victimization studies offer a good check on police records.

War, Stress, and Culture Sample (WSC). My 66 society probability holocultural sample, described in Naroll (1970b: 908-910, 917-921).

*Weakened moralnets model. A general theory of social pathology linking twelve proposed causes of moralnet strength with ten proposed consequences of moralnet weakness.

Yardstick. A specific social indicator. One or more yardsticks measuring a given social problem provide the feedback of the Five Steps. For example, male/female salary differential constitutes one yardstick of sex role discrimination.

Zero-sum game. In game theory, a game so arranged that any benefit to one player is exactly compensated for by a corresponding penalty to another; the net benefit to all players, when added up, is exactly 0. Poker and bridge, played for money stakes, in which the stakes and not the scoring points are looked at as the benefits, are zero-sum games. The gains of the winners equal the losses of the losers. A positive-sum game accrues a total net benefit; a negative-sum game accrues a total net cost or loss. Scientific research is a positive-sum game; researchers compete for prestige and professional rewards, but all of them, taken together, gain. Warfare is a negative-sum game; both sides lose in lives and suffering and property before the peace settlement perhaps partially compensates the winner at the expense of the loser.
mmm mmm 12.14 inches

References

Ackerman, Charles.
   1963   Affiliations: Structural Determinants of Differential Divorce Rates. American Journal of Sociology, 69: 13-20.
Adelman, Irma; and Morris, Cynthia Taft.
   1967   Society, Politics, and Economic Development: A Quantitative Approach. Baltimore: Johns Hopkins University Press.
Adler, Leta McKinney.
   1953   The Relationship of Marital Status to Incidence of and Recovery from Mental Illness. Social Forces, 32: 185-194.
Adriani, N.; and Kruyt, Albert C.
   1951   De Bare'e Sprekende Toradja van Midden-Celebes, Tweede deel (Vol. 2). Amsterdam: N. V. Noord-Hollandsche Uitgevers Maatschappij.
Albus, James S.; and Evans, John M., Jr.
   1976   Robot Systems. Scientific American, 234: 76-87.
Alcoholics Anonymous.
   1969   The A. A. Service Manual. New York: Alcoholics Anonymous.
Alcoholics Anonymous.
   1957   Alcoholics Anonymous Comes of Age. New York: Harper.
Alcoholics Anonymous.
   1955   Alcoholics Anonymous. New York: Alcholics Anonymous World Services.
Allardt, Erik.
   1973   About Dimensions of Welfare: An Exploratory Analysis of a Comparative Scandinavian Survey. Research Group for Comparative Sociology. University of Helsinki, Research Report No. 1.
Almond, Gabriel A.; and Coleman, James S., editors.
   1960   The Politics of the Developing Areas. Princeton, N.J.: Princeton University Press.
Alston, William P.
   1963   Religious Belief and Philosophical Thought. New York: Harcourt, Brace & World.
Ammar, S.; and Ledjri, H.
   1972   Les Conditions Familiales de Développement de la Schizophrenie. Paris: Masson.
Andrews, Gavin; Tennant, Christopher; Hewson, Daphne M.; and Vaillant, George E.
   1978   Life Event Stress, Social Support, Coping Style and Risk of Psychological Impairment. Journal of Nervous and Mental Disease, 166: 307-316.
Anthony, Albert S.
   1955   A Cross-Cultural Study of Factors Relating to Male Initiation Rites and Genital Operations. Ph.D. Dissertation, Harvard University.
Apple, Dorrian.
   1956   The Social Structure of Grandparenthood. American Anthropologist, 58: 656-663.
Arkin, Herbert; and Colton, Raymond R.
   1963   Tables for Statisticians. 2nd. ed. College Outline Series. New York: Barnes & Noble.
Asch, Solomon.
   1946   Forming Impressions of Personality. Journal of Abnormal and Social Psychology, 41: 258-290.
Ashford, J. R.; and Lawrence, P. A.
   1976   Aspects of the Epidemiology of Suicide in England and Wales. International Journal of Epidemiology, 5: 33.

Ayres, Barbara.
   1973   Effects of Infant Carrying Practices on Rhythm in Music. Ethos, 1: 387-404.
Bacon, Margaret K.
   1974   The Dependency-Conflict Hypothesis and the Frequency of Drunkenness. Quarterly
           Journal of Studies on Alcohol, 35: 863-876.
Bacon, Margaret K.; Barry, Herbert, III; Buchwald, Charles; and Snyder, Charles.
   1965   A Cross-Cultural Study of Drinking. Quarterly Journal of Studies on Alcohol, Supple-
           ment Number 3.
Bandura, A.; and Walters, R. H.
   1959   Adolescent Aggression. New York: Ronald Press.
Banks, Arthur S.; and Textor, Robert B.
   1963   A Cross-Polity Survey. Cambridge, Mass.: MIT Press.
Barrett, Gerald V.; and Franke, Richard H.
   1970   "Psychogenic" Death: A Reappraisal. Science, 167 (3916): 304-306.
Barry, Herbert, III
   1973   Cross-Cultural Evidence that Dependency Conflict Motivates Drunkenness. Mimeo-
           graph.
Barry, Herbert, III; Bacon, Margaret K.; and Child, Irvin L.
   1957   A Cross-Cultural Survey of Some Sex Differences in Socialization. Journal of Abnormal
           and Social Psychology, 55: 327-332.
Barry, Herbert, III; and Paxson, Leonora M.
   1971   Infancy and Early Childhood: Cross-Cultural Codes 2. Ethnology, 10: 466-508.
Barry, Herbert, III; and Schlegel, Alice, editors.
   1980   Cross-Cultural Samples and Codes. Pittsburgh: University of Pittsburgh Press.
Bateson, Gregory; and Mead, Margaret.
   1942   Balinese Character: A Photographic Analysis. New York: New York Academy of
           Sciences, Special Publication, Vol. 2.
Becker, Wesley C.; Peterson, D. R.; Hellmer, K. A.; Shoemaker, D. J.; and Quoy, H. C.
   1959   Factors in Parental Behavior and Personality as Related to Problem Behavior in Children.
           Journal of Consulting Psychology, 23: 107-118.
Bell, Daniel; Fletcher, Joseph; Bainbridge, William Sims; and Kurtz, Paul.
   1981   A Symposium on the Future of Religion. Free Inquiry, 1: 16-32.
Belo, Jane.
   1956   The Balinese Temper. IN: Personal Character and Cultural Milieu. Douglas Haring,
           editor. Syracuse: Syracuse University Press. pp. 148-174.
Benedict, Ruth.
   1934   Patterns of Culture. New York: Mentor.
Benzon, William L.
   1978   Cognitive Science and Literary Theory. Ph.D. Dissertation, State University of New York,
           Buffalo. Ann Arbor: Xerox University Microfilms No. 78-10602.
Berelson, Bernard; and Steiner, Gary A.
   1964   Human Behavior: An Inventory of Scientific Findings. New York: Harcourt, Brace &
           World.
Berkman, Lisa F.; and Syme, S. Leonard.
   1979   Social Networks, Host Resistance, and Mortality: A Nine-Year Follow-up Study of
           Alameda County Residents. American Journal of Epidemiology, 109: 186-204.
Berlin, Brent; and Kay, Paul.
   1969   Basic Color Terms: Their Universality and Evolution. Berkeley: University of California
           Press.
Bernheim, Ernst.
   1908   Lehrbuch der Historischen Methode und der Geschichtesphilosophie. 6th. ed. Munich:
           Duncker and Humblot.
Bernier, Charles L.; and Yerkey, A. Neil.
   1979   Cogent Communication: Overcoming Reading Overloads. Westport, Conn.: Green-
           wood. pp. 31-45.
Berry, John W.
   1980   Introduction to Methodology. IN: Handbook of Cross-Cultural Psychology, Vol. 2. Harry
           C. Triandis and John W. Berry, editors. Boston: Allyn & Bacon. pp. 1-28.
Blalock, Hubert M., Jr.
   1972   Social Statistics. 2nd. ed. New York: McGraw-Hill.

Blalock, Hubert M., Jr.
    1964 Causal Inferences in Nonexperimental Research. Durham: University of North Carolina Press.
Blitsten, Dorothy R.
    1963 The World of the Family: A Comparative Study of Family Organizations in Their Social and Cultural Settings. New York: Random House.
Bloom, Bernard L.
    1975 Community Mental Health. Monterey, Calif.: Brooks-Cole.
Bloom, V.
    1967 An Analysis of Suicide at a Training Center. American Journal of Psychiatry, 123: 918-925.
Blum, Richard H.
    1969 A Cross-Cultural Study. IN: Society and Drugs. Drugs I: Social and Cultural Observations. Richard H. Blum and associates, editors. San Francisco: Jossey-Bass. pp. 277-292.
Blumberg, Rae L.; and Winch, Robert F.
    1977 The Curvilinear Relation between Societal Complexity and Familial Complexity. IN: Familial Organization: A Quest for Determinants. R. Winch, R. Blumberg, M. Garcia, M. Gordon, and G. Kitson, editors. New York: Free Press. pp. 65-86.
Blumberg, Rae L.; and Winch, Robert R.
    1972 Societal Complexity and Familial Complexity; Evidence for the Curvilinear Hypothesis. American Journal of Sociology, 77: 898-920.
Blumenthal, Monica D.
    1967 Mental Health among the Divorced. Archives of General Psychiatry, 16: 603-680.
Bobrow, Davis B.
    1974 Transitions to Preferred World Futures: Some Design Considerations. University of Minnesota: Center of International Studies. Mimeograph.
Bogue, Donald J.
    1969 Principles of Demography. New York: John Wiley.
Bohannan, Paul.
    1960 Homicide and Suicide in North Kavirondo. IN: African Homicide and Suicide. Paul Bohannan, editor. Princeton, N.J.: Princeton University Press.
Bohrnstedt, George W.
    1980 Social Science Methodology. American Behavioral Scientist, 23: 781-787.
Boissevain, Jeremy.
    1974 Friends of Friends: Networks, Manipulators and Coalitions. New York: St. Martin's Press.
Bolander, Anne-Marie.
    1972 Nordic Suicide Statistics. IN: Suicide and Attempted Suicide. Skandia International Symposia. Stockholm: Nordiska. pp. 57-88.
Bolin, R. K.; Wright, P. E.; Wilkinson, M. N.; and Lindner, C. K.
    1968 Survey of Suicide among Patients on Home Leave from a Mental Hospital. Psychiatric Quarterly, 42: 81-89.
Bonheur, Gaston.
    1963 Qui a Cassé le Vase de Soissons?: L'album de Famille de Tous les Français. Paris: Robert Laffont.
Bonnefille, R.
    1976 Palynological Evidence . . . IN: Earliest Man and Environments in the Lake Rudolf Basin. Yves Coppens et al., editors. Chicago: University of Chicago Press. pp. 421-431.
Boorman, Scott A.; and Levitt, Paul R.
    1980 The Genetics of Altruism. New York: Academic Press.
Booy, D. M.
    1957 Rock of Exile. New York: Devin-Adair.
Borgatta, Edgar F.; and Meyer, Henry J., editors.
    1961 Sociological Theory. New York: Alfred A. Knopf.
Bott, Elizabeth.
    1957 Family and Social Networks. London: Travis Publications.
Botwinick, Jack.
    1978 Aging and Behavior: A Comprehensive Integration of Research Findings. 2nd. ed. New York: Springer.

Boudon, Raymond.
    1967   L'Analyse Mathématique des Faits Sociaux. Paris: Librairie Plon.
Boulding, Elise; Nuss, Shirley A.; Carson, Dorthy Lee; and Greenstein, Michael A.
    1976   Handbook of International Data on Women. New York: Halsted Press.
Bowlby, John.
    1980   Attachment and Loss: Loss, Vol. 3. New York: Basic Books.
Bowlby, John.
    1973   Attachment and Loss: Separation, Vol. 2. New York Basic Books.
Bowlby, John.
    1969   Attachment and Loss: Attachment, Vol. 1. New York: Basic Books.
Bowlby, John.
    1946   Forty-Four Juvenile Thieves: Their Characters and Home Backgrounds. London:
            Vaillier, Tindall & Cox.
Braaten, L. J.; and Darling, C. D.
    1962   Suicidal Tendencies among College Students. Psychiatry Quarterly, 36: 665-692.
Braidwood, Robert J.; Sauer, Jonathan D.; Helbaek, Hans; Mangelsdorf, Paul C.; Coon, Carleton
            S.; Linton, Ralph; Steward, Julian; and Oppenheim, A. Leo.
    1953   Symposium: Did Man Once Live by Beer Alone? American Anthropologist, 55: 515-526.
Braucht, G. Nicholas.
    1979   Interactional Analysis of Suicidal Behavior. Journal of Consulting and Clinical
            Psychology, 47: 653-669.
Breed, W.
    1967   Suicide and Loss in Social Interaction. IN: Essays in Self-Destruction. E. S. Schneidman,
            editor. New York: Science House. pp. 188-202.
Breed, W.
    1966   Suicide, Migration, and Race. Journal of Social Issues, 22: 30-43.
Breed, W.
    1963   Occupational Mobility and Suicide. American Sociological Review, 28: 179-188.
Brim, John A.; and Spain, David H.
    1972   Research Design in Anthropology: Paradigms and Pragmatics in the Testing of
            Hypotheses. New York: Holt, Rinehart & Winston.
Bronfenbrenner, Urie.
    1976   The Disturbing Changes in the American Family. Search, 4: 4-10.
Broude, Gwen J.
    n.d.   Male-Female Relationships in Cross-Cultural Perspective: A Study in Sex and Intimacy.
            Mimeograph.
Broude, Gwen J.
    1981   Male-Female Relationships across Cultures: A Study of Sex and Intimacy. Paper
            presented at meeting of Society for Cross-Cultural Research, Syracuse, New York.
Broude, Gwen J.
    1975   Norms of Premarital Sexual Behavior: A Cross-Cultural Study. Ethos, 3: 381-401.
Broude, Gwen J.; and Green, Sarah J.
    1976   Cross-Cultural Codes on Twenty Sexual Attitudes and Practices. Ethnology, 15: 409-429.
Brown, Elizabeth D.; and Sechrest, Lee.
    1980   Experiments in Cross-Cultural Research. IN: Handbook of Cross-Cultural Psychology,
            Vol. 2. Harry C. Triandis and John W. Berry, editors. Boston: Allyn & Bacon. pp. 297-318.
Brown, George W.; and Harris, Tirril.
    1978a   Social Origins of Depressions. New York: Free Press.
Brown, George W.; and Harris, Tirril.
    1978b   Social Origins of Depression: A Reply. Psychological Medicine, 8: 577-588.
Brown, Judith.
    1963   A Cross-Cultural Study of Female Initiation Rites. American Anthropologist, 65: 837-853.
Buchanan, Francis.
    1807   A Journey from Madras through Mysore, Canara and Malabar, Vol. 1. London: Black,
            Perry & Kingsbury. pp. 345-412.
Buffalo Evening News.
    1968   Buffalo Evening News Almanac and 1968 Fact Book. Buffalo: Buffalo Evening News.

Bullock, Ruth C.; Siegel, Rise; Weissman, Myra; and Paykel, E.S.
1972   The Weeping Wife: Marital Relations of Depressed Women. Journal of Marriage and the Family, 34: 488-495.

Bullough, Vern R.
1976   Sex: Actual Variants in Society and History. New York: John Wiley.

Bunzel, Ruth.
1938   The Economic Organization of Primitive Peoples. IN: General Anthropology. Franz Boas, editor. New York: D.C. Heath. pp. 327-408.

Burgers, J. M.
1975   Causality and Anticipation. Science, 189(4198): 194-198.

Burton, Genevieve; and Kaplan, Howard M.
1968   Marriage Counseling with Alcoholics and Their Spouses—II. The Correlation of Excessive Drinking Behavior with Family Pathology and Social Deteriorations. British Journal of Addiction, 63: 161-170.

Burton, Roger B.; and Whiting, John W. M.
1963   The Absent Father and Cross-Sex Identity. IN: Studies in Adolescence. Robert E. Grinder, editor. New York: Macmillan. pp. 107-117.

Campbell, Angus; Converse, Philip E.; and Rodgers, Willard L.
1976   The Quality of American Life: Perceptions, Evaluations and Satisfactions. New York: Russell Sage Foundation.

Campbell, Donald T.
1981   Comment: Another Perspective on a Scholarly Career. IN: A Volume in Honor of Donald T. Campbell. Marilynn B. Brewer and Barry E. Collins, editors. San Francisco: Jossey-Bass. pp. 476f.

Campbell, Donald T.
1974   Evolutionary Epistemology. IN: The Philosophy of Karl Popper. P. A. Schilpp, editor. La Salle, Ill.: Open Court.

Campbell, Donald T.
1970   Natural Selection as an Epistemological Model. IN: A Handbook of Method in Cultural Anthropology. Raoul Naroll and Ronald Cohen, editors. Garden City, N.Y.: Natural History Press. Reprinted 1973. New York: Columbia University Press. pp. 51-85.

Campbell, Donald T.
1969   Ethnocentrism of Disciplines and the Fish-Scale Model of Omniscience. IN: Interdisciplinary Relationships in the Social Sciences. M. Sherif and C.W. Sherif, editors. Hawthorne, N.Y.: Aldine.

Campbell, Donald T.
1965   Variation and Selective Retention in Sociocultural Evolution. IN: Social Change in Developing Areas. Herbert R. Barringer, George I. Blanksten, and Raymond W. Mack, editors. Cambridge, Mass.: Schenkman. pp. 19-49.

Campbell, Donald T.; and Fiske, Donald W.
1959   Convergent and Discriminant Validation by the Multitrait-Multimethod Matrix. Psychological Bulletin, 56: 81-104.

Caplow, Theodore; and McGee, Reece J.
1958   The Academic Marketplace. New York: Basic Books. pp. 103-105.

Carpenter, Clarence R.
1948   Life in the Trees: The Behavior and Social Relations of Man's Closest Kin. IN: A Reader in General Anthropology. Carleton S. Coon, editor. New York: Henry Holt. pp. 2-44.

Carr, C. J.
1976   Plant Ecological Variation and Pattern in the Lower Omo Basin. Yves Coppens et al., editors. IN: Earliest Man and Environments in the Lake Rudolf Basin. Chicago: University of Chicago Press. pp. 432-467.

Carr-Saunders, A. M.
1922   The Population Problem. Oxford: Clarendon.

Catton, Bruce.
1958   A Stillness at Appomatox. New York: Doubleday.

Caudill, William; and Scarr, Harry.
1962   Japanese Value Orientations and Culture Change. Ethnology, 1: 53-91.

Chekhov, Anton.
    1951 The Three Sisters. IN: Chekhov Plays. Elisaveta Fen, translator. Harmondsworth, Middlesex: Penguin. pp. 247-293.

Chekhov, Anton.
    1929 The Three Sisters. IN: The Works of Anton Chekhov. New York: Walter L. Black. pp. 547-588.

Chilungu, Simeon.
    1976 Issues in the Ethics of Research Method: An Interpretation of the Anglo-American Perspective. Current Anthropology, 17: 457-481.

Chimbos, Peter D.
    1978 Marital Violence. San Francisco: R & E Research Associates.

Clark, Charles L.
    n.d. Snowball Process and Political Development: A Cross-Cultural Study. Manuscript.

Clark, Charles L., editor.
    1981 A Guide to Theories of Economic Development: Cross-National Tests. New Haven, Conn.: Human Relations Area Files.

Clark, J. Cooper, editor.
    1938 Codex Mendoza. 3 vols. London.

Cochran, William.
    1963 Sampling Techniques. 2nd ed. New York: John Wiley.

Cohen, Albert.
    1955 Delinquent Boys: The Culture and the Gang. New York: Free Press.

Cohen, Ronald.
    1967 The Kanuri of Bornu. New York: Holt, Rinehart & Winston.

Cohen, Ronald.
    1961 Marriage Instability among the Kanuri of Northern Nigeria. American Anthropologist, 63: 1231-1249.

Cohen, Ronald; and Naroll, Raoul.
    1970 Method in Cultural Anthropology. IN: A Handbook of Method in Cultural Anthropology. Raoul Naroll and Ronald Cohen, editors. Garden City, N.Y.: Natural History Press. Reprinted 1973. New York: Columbia University Press. p. 5.

Cohen, Yehudi A.
    1969 Ends and Means in Political Control: State Organization and the Punishment of Adultery, Incest, and the Violation of Celibacy. American Anthropologist, 71: 658-687.

Cohen, Yehudi A.
    1964a The Establishment of Identity in a Social Nexus: The Special Case of Initiation Ceremonies and Their Relation to Value and Legal Systems. American Anthropologist, 66: 529-552.

Cohen, Yehudi A.
    1964b The Transition from Childhood to Adolescence: Cross-Cultural Studies of Initiation Ceremonies, Legal Systems, and Incest Taboos. Chicago: Aldine.

Collver, Andrew; and Langlois, Eleanor.
    1962 The Female Labor Force in Metropolitan Areas: An International Comparison. Economic Development and Cultural Change, 10: 367-385.

Cook, Thomas D.; and Campbell, Donald T.
    1979 Quasi-Experimentation. Chicago: Rand McNally.

Cooley, Charles Horton.
    1961 The Social Aspect of Conscience. IN: Sociological Theory. Edgar F. Borgatta and Henry J. Meyer, editors. New York: Alfred A. Knopf. pp. 423-432.

Cooley, William W.; and Lohnes, Paul R.
    1962 Multivariate Procedures for the Behavioral Sciences. New York: John Wiley.

Cooper, Brian; and Sylph, Judith.
    1973 Life Events and the Onset of Neurotic Illness: An Investigation in General Practice. Psychological Medicine, 3: 421-435.

Cooper, John M.
    1963 The Araucanians. IN: Handbook of South American Indians, Vol. 2. Julian H. Steward, editor. New York: Cooper Square.

Corder, B. F.; Ball, B. C.; Halzlip, T. M.; et al.
1976 Adolescent Parricide: A Comparison with Other Adolescent Murder. American Journal of Psychiatry, 133: 957-961.
Cordier, Henri.
1920 Histoire Générale de la Chine. 4 Vols. Paris: Guenther.
Coult, Allan D.
1965 Terminological Correlates of Cross-Cousin Marriage. Bijdragen tot de Taal-, Land- en Volkenkunde, 121: 120-139.
Coult, Allan D.; and Habenstein, Robert W.
1965 Cross-Tabulation of Murdock's World Ethnographic Sample. Columbia: University of Missouri Press.
Creel, Herrlee Glessner, editor.
1948 Literary Chinese by the Inductive Method, Vol. 1. Revised ed. Chicago: University of Chicago Press. First printed 1938.
Cumming, Elaine; and Henry, William E.
1961 Growing Old: The Process of Disengagement. New York: Basic Books.
Cuvelier, F.
1976 La Famille Nourricière de Geel comme Micro-Communauté Thérapeutique. L'Information Psychiatrique, 52: 915-930.
D'Andrade, Roy G.
1966 Sex Difference and Cultural Institutions. IN: The Development of Sex Differences. Eleanor E. Maccoby, editor. Stanford: Stanford University Press. pp. 174-204.
Dalton, George.
1966 Bride Wealth versus Bride Price. American Anthropologist, 68: 732-738.
Dames, Mansel L.
1918 The Book of Duarte Barbosa. London: Hakluyt Society.
Davis, William David.
1971 Societal Complexity and the Nature of Primitive Man's Conception of the Supernatural. Ph.D. Dissertation. Ann Arbor: University Microfilms.
Davis, William N.
1964 A Cross-Cultural Study of Drunkenness. B.A. Thesis. Cambridge, Mass.: Harvard College.
Dawes, R. M.; and Corrigan, B.
1974 Linear Models in Decision-Making. Psychological Bulletin, 81: 95-106.
Demone, Harold W. Jr.; and Kasey, Elizabeth H.
1965 Alcoholic Beverages—Use and Misuse—as a Contributing Factor in Non-Motor Vehicle Accidents. IN: Alcohol and Alcohol Injury: Conference Proceedings. U.S. Department of Health, Education and Welfare. Washington, D.C. Government Printing Office. pp. 21-26.
Denham, Woodrow W.
1971 Energy Relationships and Some Basic Properties of Primate Social Organization. American Anthropologist, 73: 77-95.
Dierauer, Johannes.
1913-1917 Geschichte der Schweizerischen Eidgenossenschaft, Vol. 5. Gotha: Perthes.
Divale, William T.
1971 A Theory of Population Control in Primitive Culture (Tested Cross-Culturally on 462 Societies). M.A. Thesis, California State University, Los Angeles.
Divale, William T.; and Harris, Marvin.
1976 Population, Warfare, and the Male Supremacist Complex. American Anthropologist, 78: 521-538.
Dohrenwend, Bruce P.; and Dohrenwend, Barbara Snell.
1969 Social Status and Psychological Disorder: A Causal Inquiry. New York: Wiley-Interscience.
Dorpat, Theodore L.; Jackson, Joan K.; and Ripley, Herbert S.
1968 Broken Homes and Attempted and Completed Suicides. IN: Suicide. Jack Gibbs, editor. New York: Harper & Row. pp. 170-176.
Dorsey, George Amos.
1903 The Cheyenne. Chicago: Field Museum.
Draguns, Juris K.
1980 Psychological Disorders of Clinical Severity. IN: Handbook of Cross-Cultural Psychology, Vol. 6. Harry C. Triandis and Juris G. Draguns, editors. Boston: Allyn & Bacon. pp. 99-174.

Draper, Patricia.
   1975 !Kung Women: Contrasts in Sexual Egalitarianism in the Foraging and Sedentary Contexts. IN: Toward an Anthropology of Women. Rayna Reiter, editor. New York: Monthly Review Press. pp. 77-109.
Driver, Harold E.
   1973 Cultural Diffusion. IN: Main Currents in Cultural Anthropology. Raoul Naroll and Frada Naroll, editors. New York: Appleton-Century-Crofts. pp. 157-184.
Driver, Harold E.
   1970 Statistical Studies of Continuous Geographical Distribution. IN: A Handbook of Method in Cultural Anthropology. R. Naroll and R. Cohen, editors. Garden City, N.Y.: Natural History Press. Reprinted 1973. New York: Columbia University Press. pp. 620-639.
Driver, Harold E.
   1956 An Integration of Functional Evolutionary and Historical Theory by Means of Correlations. Indiana Publications in Anthropology and Linguistics, Memoir 12: 1-36.
Dublin, Louis I.
   1963 Suicide, A Sociological and Statistical Study. New York: Ronald Press.
Dublin, Louis I.; and Bunzel, B.
   1933 To Be or Not to Be. New York: Smith & Haas.
Du Bois, Cora.
   1961 The People of Alor. 2 vols. New York: Harper Torchbooks.
Duncan, Acheson.
   1959 Quality Control and Industrial Statistics. Revised ed. Homewood, Ill.: Irwin. p. 316.
Duncan, J. W.; and Duncan, G. M.
   1971 Murder in the Family: A Study of Some Homicidal Adolescents. American Journal of Psychiatry, 127: 1498-1502.
Durkheim, Emile.
   1951 Suicide, a Study in Sociology. George Simpson, editor. Glencoe, Ill.: Free Press.
Easterlin, Richard A.
   1974 Does Economic Growth Improve the Human Lot? Some Empirical Evidence. IN: Nations and Households in Economic Growth. Paul A. David and Melvin W. Reder, editors. New York: Academic Press. pp. 89-125.
Eaton, Joseph W; and Weil, Robert J.
   1955 Culture and Mental Disorders: A Comparative Study of Hutterites and Other Populations. New York: Free Press.
Edgerton, J. W.; Bentz, W. K.; and Hollister, W. G.
   1970 III. Demographic Factors and Responses to Stress among Rural People. American Journal of Public Health, 60: 1065-1071.
Edgerton, Robert B.; and Conant, Francis P.
   1964 An East African "Shaming Party." Southwestern Journal of Anthropology, 20: 404-418.
Edmonson, Munro S.
   1957 Kinship Terms and Kinship Concepts. American Anthropologist, 59: 393-433.
Edwards, Griffith.
   1970 Alcoholism: The Analysis of Treatment. IN: Alcohol and Alcoholism. Robert E. Popham, editor. Toronto: University of Toronto Press. pp. 173-178.
Egeland, Janice A.
   1967 Belief and Behavior as Related to Illness. 2 Vols. Ph.D. Dissertation, Yale University.
Eimerl, Sarel; and DeVore, Irven.
   1965 The Primates. New York: Time-Life Books.
Eisenstadt, S. N.
   1956 From Generation to Generation. New York: Free Press of Glencoe.
Electric Power Research Institute.
   1980 Quality of Life: An International Comparison. EPRI Journal, April: 26-31.
Elmer, Elizabeth A.; and Gregg, Grace.
   1967 Developmental Characteristics of Abused Children. Pediatrics, 40: 596-602.
Elwin, Verrier.
   1943 One Hundred Maria Murders. Man in India, 23: 183-235.
Ember, Carol R.
   1975 Residential Variation among Hunter-Gatherers. Behavior Science Research, 10: 199-227.
Ember, Carol R.; Ember, Melvin; and Pasternak, Burton.
   1974 On the Development of Unilineal Descent. Journal of Anthropological Research, 30(2): 69-95.

Ember, Melvin; and Ember, Carol R.
   n.d.   Marriage, Family and Kinship: Comparative Studies of Social Organization. New Haven: HRAF Press. In press.
Ember, Melvin; and Ember, Carol R.
   1979   Male-Female Bonding: A Cross-Species Study of Mammals and Birds. Behavior Science Research, 14: 37-56.
Empey, LaMar T.
   1978   American Delinquency: Its Meaning and Construction. Homewood, Ill.: Dorsey Press.
Empey, LaMar T.; and Erickson, Maynard L.
   1972   The Provo Experiment: Evaluating Community Control of Delinquency. Lexington, Mass.: D.C. Heath.
Empey, LaMar T.; and Lubeck, Steven G.
   1971   The Silverlake Experiment: Testing Delinquency Theory and Community Intervention. Chicago: Aldine.
Esser, P. H.
   1970   Conjoint Family Therapy with Alcoholics—A New Approach. British Journal of Addiction, 64: 275-286.
Etzioni, Amitai; and Dubow, Fredric L.
   1970   Comparative Perspectives: Theories and Methods. Boston: Little, Brown.
Evans-Pritchard, E. E.
   1937   Witchcraft, Oracles and Magic among the Azande. Oxford: Clarendon. pp. 259-350.
Farberow, N. L.; and McEvoy, T.
   1966   Suicide among Patients with Diagnoses of Anxiety Reaction or Depressive Reaction in General Medical and Surgical Hospitals. Journal of Abnormal Psychology, 71: 287-299.
Farberow, N. L.; and Schneidman, E. S., editors.
   1961   The Cry for Help. New York: McGraw-Hill.
Farberow, N. L.; Schneidman, E. S.; and Leonard, C. V.
   1961   Suicide among Schizophrenic Mental Hospital Patients. IN: The Cry for Help. N. L. Farberow and E. S. Schneidman, editors. New York: McGraw-Hill. pp. 78-109.
Farberow, N. L.; Schneidman, E. S.; and Neuringer, C.
   1966   Case History and Hospitalization Factors in Suicides of Neuropsychiatric Hospital Patients. Journal of Mental Disorders, 142: 32-44.
Faron, Louis C.
   1968   The Mapuche Indians of Chile. New York: Holt, Rinehart & Winston.
Fenna, D.; Mix, L.; Schaefer, O.; and Gilbert, J. A. L.
   1971   Ethanol Metabolism in Various Racial Groups. Canadian Medical Association Journal, 105: 472-475.
Feshbach, Seymour.
   1970   Aggression. IN: Carmichael's Manual of Child Psychology, Vol. 2. 3rd. ed. Paul H. Mussen, editor. New York: John Wiley. pp. 159-259.
Field, Peter B.
   1962   A New Cross-Cultural Study of Drunkenness. IN: Society, Culture and Drinking Patterns. D. J. Pittman and C. R. Snyder, editors. New York: John Wiley. pp. 48-74.
Fischer, John L.
   1961   Art Styles as Cultural Cognitive Maps. American Anthropologist, 63: 78-93.
Fisher, Seymour; and Greenberg, Roger P.
   1977   The Scientific Credibility of Freud's Theories and Therapy. New York: Basic Books.
Fjellman, Stephen M.
   1979   Hey, You Can't Do That: A Response to Divale and Harris's "Population, Warfare and the Male Supremacist Complex." Behavior Science Research, 14: 189-200.
Flesch, Rudolf.
   1974   The Art of Readable Writing. New York: Harper & Row.
Fortune, Reo F.
   1939   Arapesh Warfare. American Anthropologist, 41: 22-41.
Fowler, H. W.; and Fowler, F. G.
   1931   The King's English. 3rd. ed. Oxford: Oxford University Press.
Franke, O.
   1961   Geschichte des Chinesischen Reiches. 2nd. ed. 2 Vols. Berlin: De Gruyter.

Freedman, Jonathan.
    1978   Happy People. New York: Harcourt Brace Jovanovich.
Freeman, Linton G.
    1965   Elementary Applied Statistics. New York: John Wiley.
Friedl, Ernestine.
    1975   Women and Men: An Anthropologist's View. New York: Holt, Rinehart & Winston.
Friedl, Ernestine.
    1962   Vasilika: A Village in Modern Greece. New York: Holt, Rinehart & Winston.
Friedlander, K.
    1949   Neurosis and Home Background. IN: The Psychoanalytic Study of the Child. A. Freud,
            editor. New York: International Universities Press.
Friesen, J. W.
    1974   Education and Values in an Indian Community. Alberta Journal of Educational Research,
            20: 146-156.
Fuchs, A.; Gaspari, C.; and Millendorfer, H.
    1977   Makropsychologische Untersuchung der Familie in Europa. Vienna: Studiengruppe für
            Internationale Analysen.
Gallup International Research Institutes.
    1977   Human Needs and Satisfactions: A Global Survey. Summary Volume. Charles F.
            Kettering Foundation and Gallup International Research Institutes.
Gallup, George.
    1976a   Human Needs and Satisfactions: A Global Survey. The Public Opinion Quarterly, 40: 459-
            467.
Gallup, George.
    1976b   What Mankind Thinks about Itself. Reader's Digest (Canadian ed., Montreal). October:
            25-31.
Ganzler, S.
    1967   Some Interpersonal and Social Dimensions of Suicidal Behavior. Dissertation Abstracts,
            28B: 1192-1193.
Gearing, Frederick; and Sangree, Lucinda, editors.
    1979   Toward a Cultural Theory of Education and Schooling. IN: World Anthropology, Part
            Three. The Hague: Mouton. pp. 169-230.
Gearing, Frederick; and Tindale, B. Allen.
    1973   Anthropological Studies of the Education Process. IN: Annual Review of Anthropology,
            Vol. 2. pp. 95-105.
Geary, R. C.; and Pearson, E. S.
    n.d.   Tests of Normality. New Statistical Table No. I. Biometrika Office. London: University
            College.
Geertz, Clifford.
    1970   Ethos, World-View and the Analysis of Sacred Symbols. IN: Man Makes Sense. Selected
            by Eugene Hammel and William S. Simmons. Boston: Little, Brown. pp. 324-338.
Gelles, Richard J.
    1979   Family Violence. Beverly Hills, Calif.: Sage.
Gersten, Joanne C.; Langner, Thomas; Eisenberg, Jeanne G.; and Orzeck, Lida.
    1974   Child Behavior and Life Events. IN: Stressful Life Events: Their Nature and Effects.
            Barbara Dohrenwend and Bruce Dohrenwend, editors. New York: John Wiley. pp.
            159-170.
Gibbs, Jack P.; and Martin, Walter T.
    1964   Status Integration and Suicide: A Sociological Study. Eugene: University of Oregon
            Press.
Gil, David G.
    1974   A Holistic Perspective on Child Abuse and Its Prevention. Journal of Sociology and Social
            Welfare, 2: 110-125.
Gil, David G.
    1971   Violence against Children. Journal of Marriage and the Family, 33: 637-649.
Gil, David G.
    1970   Violence against Children: Physical Child Abuse in the United States. Cambridge, Mass.:
            Harvard University Press.

Gil, David G.
    1968   Incidence of Child Abuse and Demographic Characteristics of Persons Involved. IN: The
            Battered Child. Ray E. Helfer and C. Henry Kempe, editors. Chicago: University of
            Chicago Press. pp. 19-42.
Gilmartin, Kevin J.; Rossi, Robert J.; Lutomski, Leonard S.; and Reed, Donald F. B.
    1979   Social Indicators: An Annotated Bibliography of Current Literature. New York: Garland.
Gladwin, Thomas; and Sarason, Seymour B.
    1953   Truk: Man in Paradise. New York: Wenner Gren.
Glass, G. V; McGaw, Barry; and Smith, Mary Lee.
            1981   Meta-Analysis in Social Research. Beverly Hills, Calif.: Sage.
Gleidman, Lester H.
    1957   Concurrent and Combined Group Treatment of Chronic Alcoholics and Their Wives.
            International Journal of Group Psychotherapy, 7: 414-424.
Glueck, Sheldon; and Glueck, Eleanor T.
    1950   Unravelling Juvenile Delinquency. Cambridge: Harvard University Press.
Goldstein, J. H.
    1975   Aggression and Crimes of Violence. New York: Oxford University Press.
Goodall, Jane.
    1965   Chimpanzees of the Gombe Stream Reserve. IN: Primate Behavior: Field Studies of
            Monkeys and Apes. Irven DeVore, editor. New York: Holt, Rinehart & Winston. pp.
            425-473.
Goode, William J.
    1963   World Revolution and Family Patterns. New York: Free Press.
Goodenough, Ward H.
    1970   Description and Comparison in Cultural Anthropology. Chicago: Aldine.
Goodwin, D. W.; Schulsinger, F.; Moller, N.; Hermansen, L.; Winokur, G.; and Guze, S. B.
    1974   Drinking Problems in Adopted and Non-Adopted Sons of Alcoholics. Archives of
            General Psychiatry, 31: 164-169.
Goodwin, Grenville.
    1942   The Social Organization of the Western Apache. Chicago: University of Chicago Press.
Goody, Jack.
    1976   Production and Reproduction: A Comparative Study of the Domestic Domain. London:
            Cambridge University Press.
Goody, Jack.
    1969   Inheritance, Property, and Marriage in Africa and Eurasia. Sociology, 3: 55-76.
Goody, Jack; Irving, Barrie; and Tahany, Nicky.
    1970   Causal Inferences Concerning Inheritance and Property. Human Relations, 24: 295-314.
Gough, Kathleen.
    1961   Nayar: Central Kerala. IN: Matrilineal Kinship. David M. Schneider and Kathleen Gough,
            editors. Berkeley: University of California Press.
Gough, Kathleen.
    1959   The Nayars and the Definition of Marriage. Journal of the Royal Anthropological Institute,
            89: 23-34.
Grant, James P.
    1978   Disparity Reduction Rates in Social Indicators: A Proposal for Measuring and Targeting
            Progress in Meeting Basic Needs. Washington, D.C.: Overseas Development Council.
Gray, Robert F.
    1960   Sonjo Bride Price and the Question of African "Wife Purchase." American Anthropolo-
            gist, 62: 34-57.
Gregory, Jan.
    1958   Studies of Parental Deprivation in Psychiatric Patients. American Journal of Psychiatry,
            115: 432-443.
Griffis, William E.
    1882   Corea: The Hermit Nation. New York: Scribner's.
Grigson, Sir Wilfred.
    1949   The Maria Gonds of Bastar. London: Oxford University Press.
Gulliver, Philip H.
    1961   Bride Wealth: The Economic versus the Non-Economic Interpretation. American
            Anthropologist, 63: 1098-1100.

Gurr, Ted Robert.
    1972   Politimetrics: An Introduction to Quantitative Macropolitics. Englewood Cliffs, N.J.: Prentice-Hall.
Gusinde, Martin.
    1931   Die Feuerland Indianer, Band 1: Die Selk'nam. Mödling bei Wien: Anthropos.
Ha, Tae Hung.
    1958   Folk Customs and Family Life. Korean Cultural Series, Vol. 3. Seoul: Korea Information Service.
Haas, Michael.
    1970   Dimensional Analysis in Cross-National Research. Comparative Political Studies, 3: 3-35.
Haas, Michael.
    1967   Social Change and Aggressiveness, 1900-1960. IN: Quantitative International Politics: Insights and Evidence. J. David Singer, editor. New York: Free Press. pp. 215-374.
Haas, Michael.
    1964   Some Societal Correlates of International Political Behavior. Ph.D. Dissertation, Stanford University.
Hadden, Kenneth; and DeWalt, Billie.
    1974   Path Analysis: Some Anthropological Examples. Ethnology, 13: 105-128.
Hall, K.R.L.
    1968   Social Organization of the Old World Monkeys and Apes. IN: Primates: Studies in Adaptation and Variability. Phyllis C. Jay, editor. New York: Holt, Rinehart & Winston. pp. 7-31.
Handy, Rollo; and Kurtz, Paul.
    1963   A Current Appraisal of the Behavioral Sciences. Great Barrington, Mass.: Behavioral Research Council.
Harley, John K.
    1963   Adolescent Youths in Peer Groups: A Cross-Cultural Study. Ph.D. Dissertation, Harvard University.
Harris, Marvin.
    1977   Cannibals and Kings: The Origins of Culture. New York: Random House.
Hart, Hornell.
    1948   The Logistic Growth of Political Areas. Social Forces, 26: 397-409.
Hartog, Jan de.
    1966   The Call of the Sea. New York: Atheneum.
Harvard University Computation Laboratory.
    1955   Tables of the Cumulative Binomial Probability Distribution. IN: Annals of the Computation Laboratory of Harvard University, Vol. 35. Cambridge, Mass.: Harvard University Press.
Hays, David G.
    1981   Cognitive Structures. HRAFlex Publication. New Haven, Conn.: Human Relations Area Files.
Hazelton, Lesley.
    1977   Israeli Women: The Reality and the Myths. New York: Simon & Schuster.
Healy, W.; and Bronner, A. F.
    1936   New Light on Delinquency and Its Treatment. New Haven, Conn.: Yale University Press.
Heath, Dwight B.
    1958   Sexual Division of Labor and Cross-Cultural Research. Social Forces, 37: 77-79.
Henderson, Scott; Byrne, D. G.; Duncan-Jones, P.; Adcock, Sylvia; Scott, Ruth; and Steele, G. P.
    1978   Special Bonds in the Epidemiology of Neurosis: A Preliminary Communication. British Journal of Psychiatry, 132: 463-466.
Henderson, Scott; Duncan-Jones, Paul; McAuley, Helen; and Ritchie, Karen.
    1978   The Patient's Primary Group. British Journal of Psychiatry, 132: 74-86.
Herskovits, Melville.
    1967   Dahomey: An Ancient West African Kingdom. 2 Vols. Evanston, Ill.: Northwestern University Press.
Hindelang, Michael J.; Hirschi, Travis, and Weis, Joseph G.
    1981   Measuring Delinquency. Beverly Hills, Calif.: Sage.
Hirschi, Travis.
    1969   Causes of Delinquency. Berkeley: University of California Press.

Hobhouse, L. T.; Wheeler, G. C.; and Ginsberg, M.
   1965   The Material Culture and Social Institutions of the Simpler Peoples. London: Chapman &
          Hall. First printed 1915.
Hockett, Homer Carey.
   1955   The Critical Method in Historical Research and Writing. New York: Macmillan.
Hoebel, E. Adamson.
   1960   The Cheyennes: Indians of the Great Plains. New York: Holt, Rinehart & Winston.
Hofstede, Geert.
   1980   Culture's Consequences. Beverly Hills, Calif.: Sage.
Holan, Lita; and Haakonsen, Solveig.
   1979   Helsestatistik 1977 (Health Statistics 1977). Oslo: Central Bureau of Statistics.
Hollingsworth, I. H.
   1969   Historical Demography. Ithaca, N.Y.: Cornell University Press.
Holmberg, Allan R.
   1969   Nomads of the Long Bow: The Siriono of Eastern Bolivia. Garden City, N.Y.: Natural
          History Press. First printed 1950.
Holmes, Thomas H.; and Rahe, Richard H.
   1967   The Social Readjustment Rating Scales. Journal of Psychosomatic Research, 11: 213-218.
Honigmann, John J.
   1959   The World of Man. New York: Harper.
Hood, Roger; and Sparks, Richard.
   1970   Key Issues in Criminology. New York: McGraw-Hill World University Library.
Horan, Susan J., editor.
   n.d.   A Guide to Theories of Homicide. New Haven, Conn.: Human Relations Area Files. In
          press.
Horan, Susan J.
   1981   Theories of Criminal Homicide. Ph.D. Dissertation, Department of Anthropology, State
          University of N.Y., Buffalo. In preparation.
Horton, Donald.
   1943   The Functions of Alcohol in Primitive Societies: A Cross-Cultural Study. Quarterly
          Journal of Studies on Alcohol, 4: 199-320.
Hourani, George.
   1976   Islamic and Non-Islamic Origins of Mu'tazilite Ethical Rationalism. International Journal
          of Middle East Studies, 7: 59-87.
Hourani, George.
   1956   Ethical Values. Ann Arbor: University of Michigan Press.
Howard, Jane.
   1978   Families. New York: Berkely.
Hsu, Francis L. K.
   1972   Kinship and Ways of Life: An Exploration. IN: Psychological Anthropology. Francis L. K.
          Hsu, editor. Cambridge: Schenkman. pp. 509-567.
Hsu, Francis L. K.
   1971   Psychological Homeostasis. American Anthropologist, 73: 23-44.
Hudgens, Richard W.
   1974   Personal Catastrophe and Depression. IN: Stressful Life Events: Their Nature and
          Effects. Barbara Dohrenwend and Bruce Dohrenwend, editors. New York: John Wiley.
          pp. 119-134.
Hume, David.
   1961   A Treatise of Human Nature. New York: Doubleday. First published 1739-1740.
Humphrey, J. A.
   1978   Role Interference: An Analysis of Suicide Victims, Homicide Offenders, and Non-Violent
          Individuals. Journal of Clinical Psychiatry, 39: 652-655.
Hunter, John E.; Schmidt, Frank L.; and Jackson, Gregg B.
   1982   Meta-Analysis: Cumulating Research Findings across Studies. Beverly Hills, Calif.: Sage.
Hyman, Merton M.
   1981a "Alcoholic," "Unspecified," and "Other Specified" Cirrhosis Mortality: A Study in
          Validity. Journal of Studies on Alcohol, 42: 336-343.

Hyman, Merton M.
  1981b Weighting for Populations at Risk and Standardizing for Age in Alcohol Research. Journal of Studies on Alcohol, 42: 579-593.
Ianni, Francis A. J.; and Reuss-Ianni, Elizabeth.
  1980   What Can Schools Do about Violence? Today's Education, 69: 20G-23G.
Jackson, Lydia.
  1950   Emotional Attitudes toward the Family of Normal, Neurotic, and Delinquent Children, Part I. British Journal of Psychology, 41: 35-51.
Jackson, Royal G.
  1973   A Preliminary Bicultural Study of Value Orientations and Leisure Attitudes. Journal of Leisure Research, 5: 10-23.
Jacobs, Melville; and Stern, Bernhard J.
  1947   Outline of Anthropology. New York: Barnes and Noble.
Jain, Shail.
  1975   Size Distribution of Income: A Compilation of Data. Washington, D.C.: World Bank.
Jay, Phyllis C.
  1968   Primate Field Studies. IN: Primates: Studies in Adaptation and Variability. Phyllis C. Jay, editor. New York: Holt, Rinehart & Winston. pp. 487-503.
Jellinek, E. M.
  1960   The Disease Concept of Alcoholism. New Haven, Conn.: Hillhouse.
Jennings, M. Kent.
  1964   Community Influentials. New York: Free Press.
Jerison, Harry J.
  1973   Evolution of the Brain and Intelligence. New York: Academic Press. pp. 17-25.
Jervis, Robert.
  1976   Perception and Misperception in International Politics. Princeton, N.J.: Princeton University Press.
Johanson, Donald; and Edey, Maitland.
  1981   Lucy, the Beginnings of Mankind. New York: Simon & Schuster.
Johnson, Paul.
  1973   New York Times Book Review, Dec. 30. p. 4.
Johnston, J.
  1972   Econometric Methods. 2nd. ed. New York: McGraw-Hill.
Jones, Maxwell.
  1962   Social Psychiatry: In the Community, in Hospitals, and in Prisons. Springfield, Ill.: Thomas.
Jones, Susan D.; and Singer, J. David.
  1972   Beyond Conjecture in International Politics: Abstracts of Data-Based Research. Itasca, Ill.: F. E. Peacock.
Joseph, Alice; Spicer, Rosamond B.; and Chevsky, Jane.
  1949   The Desert People: A Study of the Papago Indians. Chicago: University of Chicago Press.
Jungermann, Helmut; and Zeeuw, Gerard de, editors.
  1977   Decision Making and Change in Human Affairs. Dordrecht, Holland: Riesel.
Junod, Henri A.
  1912   The Life of a South African Tribe. 2 Vols. Neuchatel: Attinger.
Kagan, Aubrey R.; and Levi, Lennart.
  1974   Health and Environment—Psychosocial Stimuli: A Review. Social Science and Medicine, 8: 225-241.
Kahneman, D.; and Tversky, A.
  n.d.   Intuitive Prediction: Biases and Corrective Procedures. Management Science, In press.
Kahneman, D.; and Tversky, A.
  1973   On the Psychology of Prediction. Psychological Review, 80: 237-251.
Kahneman, D.; and Tversky, A.
  1971   Subjective Probability: A Judgment of Representativeness. Cognitive Psychology, 33: 430-454.
Kang, Gay.
  1981   Evaluation and Modification of the SES Random Error Procedure. Behavior Science Research, 16: 1-26.
Kang, Gay; Horan, Susan; and Reis, Janet.
  1979   Comments on Divale and Harris's "Population, Warfare, and the Male Supremacist Complex." Behavior Science Research, 14: 201-209.

Kaufmann, William J., III
    1979   Galaxies and Quasars. San Francisco: Freeman.
Keiser, R. Lincoln.
    1969   The Vice Lords; Warriors of the Streets. New York: Holt, Rinehart & Winston.
Keller, Mark, editor.
    1974   Second Special Report to the U.S. Congress on Alcohol and Health. National Institute of
            Alcohol and Alcoholism. Washington, D.C.: Department of Health, Education and
            Welfare.
Keller, Mark; and Gurioli, Carel.
    1976   Statistics on Consumption of Alcohol and on Alcoholism, 1976 ed. New Brunswick, N.J.:
            Journal of Studies on Alcohol.
Keller, Mark; and Jellinek, E. M.
    1965   CAAAL Manual. New Brunswick, N.J.: Rutgers Center of Alcohol Studies.
Kelly, Howard A.
    1907   Walter Reed and Yellow Fever. 2nd. ed. New York: McClure.
Kelly, Joan B.; and Wallerstein, Judith S.
    1977   Brief Interventions with Children in Divorcing Families. American Journal of Ortho-
            psychiatry, 47: 23-39.
Kelly, Joan B.; and Wallerstein, Judith S.
    1976   The Effects of Parental Divorce: Experiences of the Child in Early Latency. American
            Journal of Orthopsychiatry, 46: 20-32.
Kelman, Herbert C.
    1977   The Conditions, Criteria and Dialectics of Human Dignity—A Transnational Perspective.
            International Studies Quarterly, 21: 529-552.
Kendall, M. G.
    1962   Rank Correlation Methods. 3rd. ed. London: Griffin.
Kendall, M. G.; and Stuart, A.
    1958   The Advanced Theory of Statistics, Vol. 1. New York: Hafner.
Kennedy, John G.
    1973   Cultural Psychiatry. IN: Handbook of Social and Cultural Anthropology. John J.
            Honigmann, editor. Chicago: Rand McNally. pp. 1119-1198.
Kenny, David A.
    1979   Correlation and Causality. New York: John Wiley.
Key, Wilson Bryan.
    1974   Subliminal Seduction. New York: New American Library.
Kiev, Ari.
    1972   Transcultural Psychiatry. New York: Free Press.
Kissin, Benjamin; Platz, Arthur; and Su, Wen Huey.
    1970   Social and Psychological Factors in the Treatment of Chronic Alcoholism. Journal of
            Psychiatric Research, 8: 13-27.
Kiyama, Hideaki.
    1978   Social Organization of the Eighth Century Japanese Villages. A Statistical Reconstruc-
            tion Based on Contemporary Registration. Ph.D. Dissertation, State University of New
            York, Buffalo.
Kleist, Heinrich von.
    1964   Prinz Friederich von Homburg. Richard Samuel, editor, with the assistance of Dorothea
            Coverlid. Berlin: Schmidt. First printed 1821.
Kluchevsky, V. O.
    1960   A History of Russia, Vol 5. C. J. Hogarth, translator. New York: Russell & Russell.
Kluckhohn, Florence; and Strodtbeck, Fred.
    1961   Variations in Value Orientations. Evanston, Ill.: Peterson.
Knight, R. P.
    1938   The Psychoanalytic Treatment in a Sanitorium of Chronic Addiction to Alcohol. Journal
            of the American Medical Association, 111: 1443.
Knight, R. P.
    1937a   The Dynamics of Chronic Alcohol Addiction. Bulletin of the Menninger Clinic, 1: 233.

Knight, R. P.
  1937b   The Psychodynamics of Chronic Alcoholism. Journal of Nervous Mental Disorders, 86: 538.
Köbben, Andre J. F.
  1967   Cause and Intention. IN: A Handbook of Method in Cultural Anthropology. Raoul Naroll and Ronald Cohen, editors. Garden City, N.Y.: Natural History Press. Reprinted 1973. New York: Columbia University Press. pp. 89-98.
Köbben, Andre J. F.
  1967   Why Exceptions? The Logic of Cross-Cultural Analysis. Current Anthropology, 8: 3-19.
Kotkin, Elizabeth.
  1976   A Review of the Theory and Research on the Child-Abusing Parent. Manuscript. Department of Psychology, State University of New York, Buffalo.
Krauss, Herbert H.
  1970   Social Development and Suicide. Journal of Cross-Cultural Psychology, 1: 159-167.
Krauss, Herbert H.
  1966   A Cross-Cultural Study of Suicide. Ph.D. Dissertation, Northwestern University.
Krauss, Herbert H.; and Krauss, Beatrice J.
  1968   Cross-Cultural Study of the Thwarting-Disorientation Theory of Suicide. Journal of Abnormal Psychology, 73: 353-357.
Krauss, Herbert H.; and Tesser, Abraham.
  1971   Social Contexts of Suicide. Journal of Abnormal Psychology, 78: 222-228.
Kroeber, Alfred L.
  1944   Configurations of Culture Growth. Berkeley: University of California Press.
Kuhn, Alfred.
  1974   The Logic of Social Systems. San Francisco: Jossey-Bass.
Kuhn, Thomas S.
  1962   The Structure of Scientific Revolutions. Chicago: University of Chicago Press.
Kurian, George T.
  1979   The Book of World Rankings. New York: New American Library.
Lambert, William W.; Triandis, Leigh Minturn; and Wolf, Margaret.
  1959   Some Correlates of Beliefs in the Malevolence and Benevolence of Supernatural Beings: A Cross-Cultural Study. Journal of Abnormal and Social Psychology, 58: 162-169.
Lancaster, Jane B.
  1975   Primate Behavior and the Emergence of Human Culture. New York: Holt, Rinehart & Winston.
Langlois, Charles V.; and Seignobos, C.
  1898   Introduction to the Study of History. G. G. Berry, translator. New York: Henry Holt.
Lasswell, Harold; and Holmberg, Allan R.
  1969   Toward a General Theory of Directed Value Accumulation. IN: Political and Administrative Development. Ralph Braibanti, editor. Durham, N. C.: Duke University Press. pp. 354-399.
Lasswell, Harold; and Kaplan, Abraham.
  1950   Power and Society. New Haven, Conn.: Yale University Press.
Laumann, Edward O.
  1973   Bonds of Pluralism: The Form and Substance of Urban Social Networks. New York: John Wiley.
Leacock, Eleanor.
  1954   The Montagnais "Hunting Territory" and the Fur Trades. American Anthropologist, 56 (5), Part 2, Memoir No. 78.
Leakey, Richard E.; and Lewin, Roger.
  1978   People of the Lake: Mankind and Its Beginnings. Garden City, N.Y.: Doubleday.
Ledyard, Patricia.
  1956   Friendly Island. London: Davies.
Lee, Richard Borshay.
  1979   The !Kung San: Men, Women, and Work in a Foraging Society. New York: Cambridge University Press.

Lee, Richard Borshay; and DeVore, Irven, editors.
  1968   Man the Hunter. Chicago: Aldine.
Leeuwe, J. de.
  1970   Society System and Sexual Life. Bijdragen tot de Taal-. Land- en Volkenkunde, 126: 1-36.
Leighton, Alexander H.
  1974   Social Disintegration and Mental Disorder. IN: American Handbook of Psychiatry, Vol. 2.
          2nd ed. Arieto Silvano and Gerald Kaplan, editors. New York: Basic Books. pp. 411-423.
Leighton, Alexander H.
  1959   My Name Is Legion. New York: Basic Books.
Leighton, Alexander H.; Lambo, T. A.; Hughes, C. C.; Leighton, D. C.; Murphy, J. M.; and Macklin,
          D. B.
  1963   Psychiatric Disorders among the Yoruba. Ithaca, N.Y.: Cornell University Press.
Leighton, Dorothea C.; Harding, J. S.; Macklin, D. B.; Macmillan, A. M.; and Leighton, A. H.
  1963   The Character of Danger: Psychiatric Symptoms in Selected Communities. New York:
          Basic Books.
Leonard, C. V.
  1967   Understanding and Preventing Suicide. Springfield, Ill.: Thomas.
Lester, David.
  1977   The Prediction of Suicide and Homicide Rates Cross-Nationally by Means of Stepwise
          Multiple Regression. Behavior Science Research, 12: 61-69.
Lester, David.
  1974   A Cross-Cultural Study of Suicide and Homicide. Behavior Science Research, 9: 307-318.
Lester, David.
  1971   Suicide and Homicide Rates and the Need for Affiliation. Journal of Cross-Cultural Psych-
          ology, 2: 405-406.
Lester, David.
  1970   Suicidal Behavior: A Summary of Research Findings. IN: Crisis Intervention, Supplement
          to Volume 2, no. 3. Buffalo: Suicide Prevention and Crisis Service.
Lester, David.
  1969   Resentment and Dependency in the Suicidal Individual. Journal of General Psych-
          ology. 81: 137-145.
Lester, Gene; and Lester, David.
  1971   Suicide: The Gamble with Death. Englewood Cliffs, N.J.: Prentice-Hall.
Levine, Adeline.
  1982   Love Canal: Science, Politics, and People. Lexington, Mass.: Lexington Books.
LeVine, Robert A.
  1962   Witchcraft and Co-Wife Proximity in Southwestern Kenya. Ethnology, 1: 39-45.
Levinson, David, editor.
  1981   A Guide to Alcoholism Treatment Research. Vol. 1: Behavioral Medicine/Behavior
          Modification. New Haven, Conn.: Human Relations Area Files.
Levinson, David, editor.
  1977a A Guide to Social Theory: Worldwide Cross-Cultural Tests. 5 Vols. New Haven,
          Conn.: Human Relations Area Files.
Levinson, David.
  1977b What Have We Learned from Cross-Cultural Surveys? American Behavioral Scien-
          tist, 20: 757-792.
Levinson, David; and Malone, Martin J.
  1980   Toward Explaining Human Culture: A Critical Review of the Findings of Worldwide
          Cross-Cultural Research. New Haven, Conn.: HRAF Press.
Leys, Simon.
  1977   Chinese Shadows. New York: Viking.
Light, Richard J.
  1973   Abused and Neglected Children in America: A Study of Alternative Policies. Har-
          vard Educational Review, 43: 556-598.
Lindzey, Gardner; and Aronson, Elliot, editors.
  1968   The Handbook of Social Psychology. 2nd. ed. Reading, Mass.: Addison-Wesley.
Liu, Ben-Chieh; and Anderson, Claude F.
  1979   Income, Energy Requirements and the Quality of Life Indicators: An International
          Comparison, 1975. Kansas City: Midwest Research Institute.
Logan, William.
  1887   Malabar. Madras: Government Press.

Lomax, Alan; Erickson, Edwin, E.; Grauer, Victor; Halifax, Joan; Ayres, Barbara; Bartenieff, Irmgard; Paulay, Forrestine; Arensberg, Conrad W.; and Berkowitz, Norman.
    1968   Folk Song Style and Culture. Washington, D.C.: American Association for the Advancement of Science, Publication 88.

Long, John K.
    1904   Voyages and Travels of an Indian Interpreter and Trader. IN: Early Western Travels, 1748-1846, Vol. 2. Reuben G. Thwaites, editor. Cleveland: Arthur H. Clark.

Lönnqvist, J.
    1977   Suicide in Helsinki. Supplement to Acta Psychiatrica Scandinavica.

Lovejoy, C. Owen.
    1981   The Origin of Man. Science, 211(4480): 341-350.

Lowie, Robert.
    1948   Primitive Religion. New York: Liveright. First printed 1924.

Lowie, Robert.
    1947   Primitive Society. New York: Liveright.

Lowie, Robert.
    1935   The Crow Indians. New York: Farrar & Rinehart.

Luepnitz, Deborah A.
    1979   Which Aspects of Divorce Affect Children? The Family Coordinator, 28: 79-85.

Luke, Mary.
    1972   A Crown for Elizabeth. New York: Paperback Library.

Lynch, James J.
    1977   The Broken Heart: The Medical Consequences of Loneliness in America. New York: Basic Books.

Lynn, R.
    1971   Personal and National Character. Oxford: Oxford University Press.

Mackay, Margaret.
    1963   Angry Island. Chicago: Rand McNally.

Mackey, Wade C.
    1980   A Cross-Cultural Analysis of Adult-Child Proxemics in Relation to the Plowman-Protector Complex. Behavior Science Research, 16: 187-223.

Mackey, Wade C.
    1979   Parameters of the Adult Male-Child Bond. Ethnology and Sociobiology, 1: 59-76.

Mackey, Wade C.
    1976   The Adult Male-Child Bond: An Example of Convergent Evolution. Journal of Anthropological Research, 39: 58-73.

Mackey, Wade C.; and Day, Randal D.
    1979   Some Indicators of Fathering Behaviors in the United States: A Cross-Cultural Examination of Adult Male-Child Interaction. Journal of Marriage and the Family, 41: 287-299.

Maddison, David; and Viola, Agnes.
    1968   The Health of Widows in the Year Following Bereavement. Journal of Psychosomatic Research, 12: 297-306.

Maddison, David; and Walker, Wendy L.
    1967   Factors Affecting the Outcome of Conjugal Bereavement. British Journal of Psychiatry, 113: 1057-1067.

Magnus, Philip.
    1964   King Edward the Seventh. New York: Dutton.

Malinowski, Bronislaw.
    1935   Coral Gardens and Their Magic, Vol. 1. New York: American Book Co.

Malinowski, Bronislaw.
    1926   Myth in Primitive Psychology. Westport, Conn.: Negro University Press.

Malinvaud, E.
    1970   Statistical Methods of Econometrics. 2nd. ed. A. Silvey, translator. Amsterdam: North Holland.

Marano, Louis A.
    1982   Windigo Psychosis: The Anatomy of an Emic-Etic Confusion. Current Anthropology, 23: 385-412.

Marano, Louis A.
    1973   A Macrohistoric Trend toward World Government. Behavioral Science Notes, 8: 35-39.

Marris, Peter.
    1974   Loss and Change. London: Routledge & Kegan Paul.
Marsella, Anthony.
    1980   Depressive Experience and Disorder across Cultures. IN: Handbook of Cross-Cul-
            tural Psychology, Vol. 6. Harry C. Triandis and Juris G. Draguns, editors. Boston:
            Allyn & Bacon. pp. 237-289.
Marsella, Anthony.
    1979   Cross-Cultural Studies of Mental Disorders. IN: Perspectives on Cross-Cultural
            Psychology. Anthony Marsella, Roland Tharp and Thomas Ciboroski, editors. New
            York: Academic Press. pp. 233-262.
Martin, F. M.; Brotherston, J.H.F.; and Chave, S.P.W.
    1957   Incidence of Neurosis in a New Housing Estate. British Journal of Preventative
            Social Medicine, 11: 196-202.
Martin, M. Kay; and Voorhies, Barbara.
    1975   Female of the Species. New York and London: Columbia University Press.
Mason, Philip.
    1974   A Matter of Honour. New York: Holt, Rinehart & Winston.
Maxwell, Eleanor Krassen.
    1975   Dynamic Aspects of Ritual Performance: A Resource in Decline? Paper presented
            at the annual meeting of the Gerontological Society, October 26-30, Louisville, Ken-
            tucky.
Maxwell, Robert J.; and Silverman, Philip.
    1970   Information and Esteem: Cultural Considerations in the Treatment of the Aged.
            Aging and Human Development, 1: 361-391.
Mayer, Philip.
    1961   Townsmen or Tribesmen. Cape Town: Oxford University Press.
McClelland, David C.
    1961   The Achieving Society. Princeton, N.J.: Van Nostrand.
McCord, J.
    1978   A Thirty-Year Follow-up of Treatment Effects. American Psychologist, 33: 284-
            289.
McCord, W.; and McCord, J.
    1960   Origins and Alcoholism. Stanford, Calif.: Stanford Universtiy Press.
McCord, W.; McCord, J.; and Zola, I. K.
    1959   Origins of Crime: A New Evaluation of the Cambridge-Somerville Youth Study.
            New York: Columbia University Press.
McGowan, Patrick; and Shapiro, Howard B.
    1973   The Comparitive Study of Foreign Policy: A Survey of Scientific Findings. Beverly
            Hills, Calif.: Sage.
McInnis, Raymond G.; and Scott, James W.
    1975   Social Science Research Handbook. New York: Barnes & Noble. pp. 68-70.
McKim, Fred.
    1947   San Blas: An Account of the Cuna Indians of Panama. Ethnologiska Studier, Vol.
            15.
McMiller, P.; and Ingham, J. G.
    1976   Friends, Confidants and Symptoms. Social Psychiatry, 11: 51-58.
Mead, Margaret.
    1953   Growing up in New Guinea. New York: Mentor.
Mead, Margaret.
    1949   Coming of Age in Samoa. New York: Mentor.
Meeks, Donald E.; and Kelly, Colleen.
    1970   Family Therapy with the Families of Recovering Alcoholics. Quarterly Journal of Studies
            on Alcohol, 31: 399-413.
Menninger, Karl.
    1938   Man against Himself. New York: Hartcourt, Brace and World.
Michod, Richard E.; and Abugov, Robert.
    1980   Adaptive Topography in Family-Structured Models of Kin Selection. Science, 210(4470):
            667-669.

Milbrath, Lester.
   1972   Quality of Life versus Socio-Economic Development. Paper delivered at first international meeting of the Research Committee on Comparative Studies on Local Government and Politics, Catania, September 26-30.
Millay, Edna St. Vincent.
   1922   First Fig. IN: A Few Figs from Thistles: Poems and Sonnets. Edna St. Vincent Millay. New York: Harper. p. 1.
Miller, Delbert C.
   1977   Handbook of Research Design and Social Measurements. 3rd. ed. New York: David McKay. pp. 97-123.
Miller, Peter McC.; and Ingham, J. G.
   1976   Friends, Confidants and Symptoms. Social Psychiatry, 11: 51-58.
Minturn, Leigh; Grosse, Martin; and Haider, Santoah.
   1969   Cultural Patterning of Sexual Beliefs and Behavior. Ethnology, 8: 301-318.
Minturn, Leigh; and Lambert, W. W.
   1964   Mothers of Six Cultures: Antecedents of Child Rearing. New York: John Wiley.
Mintz, Norbett L.; and Schwartz, David T.
   1964   Urban Ecology and Psychosis: Community Factors in the Incidence of Schizophrenia and Manic-Depression among Italians in Greater Boston. Journal of Social Psychiatry, 10: 101-118.
Moore, Frank W., editor.
   1961   Readings in Cross-Cultural Methodology. New Haven, Conn.: HRAF Press.
Moore, George Edward.
   1959   Principia Ethica. Cambridge: Cambridge University Press. First printed 1903.
Moose, J. Robert.
   1911   Village Life in Korea. Nashville: M. E. Church.
Morgan, Ted.
   1980   Maugham: A Biography. New York: Simon & Schuster.
Morgenstern, Oskar.
   1963   On the Accuracy of Economic Observations. 2nd. ed. Princeton, N.J.: Princeton University Press.
Morris, William, editor.
   1969   The American Heritage Dictionary. Boston: Houghton Mifflin.
Morrison, Denton E.; and Henkel, Ramon E., editors.
   1970   The Significance Test Controversy: A Reader. Chicago: Aldine.
Mueller, Daniel P.
   1980   Social Networks: A Promising Direction for Research on the Relationship of the Social Environment to Psychiatric Disorder. Social Sciences and Medicine, 14A: 147-161.
Mueller, Daniel P.; Edwards, Daniel W.; and Yarvis, Richard M.
   1978   Stressful Life Events and Community Mental Health Center Patients. Journal of Nervous and Mental Disease, 166: 16-24.
Mulvihill, Donald; and Tumin, Melvin M.
   1969   Crimes of Violence. A Staff Report Submitted to the National Commission on the Causes and Prevention of Violence. Vols. 11, 12, 13. Washington, D.C.: U. S. Government Printing Office.
Munch, Peter A.
   1971   Crisis In Utopia. New York: Crowell.
Munch, Peter A.
   1970   Economic Development and Conflicting Values: A Social Experiment in Tristan da Cunha. American Anthropologist, 72: 1300-1318.
Munch, Peter A.
   1964   Culture and Superculture in a Displaced Community: Tristan da Cunha. Ethnology, 3: 369-376.
Murdock, George Peter.
   1967   Ethnographic Atlas. Pittsburgh: University of Pittsburgh Press.
Murdock, George Peter.
   1964   Cultural Correlates of the Regulation of Premarital Sex Behavior. IN: Process and Pattern in Culture: Essays in Honor of Julian H. Steward. Robert A. Manners, editor. Chicago: Aldine. pp. 399-410.

Murdock, George Peter.
    1957   World Ethnographic Sample. American Anthropologist, 59: 664-687.
Murdock, George Peter.
    1949   Social Structure. New York: Macmillan.
Murdock, George Peter.
    1940   The Cross-Cultural Survey. American Sociological Review, 5: 361-370.
Murdock, George Peter, editor.
    1937   Studies in the Science of Society: Presented to Albert Galloway Keller. New Haven,
            Conn.: Yale University Press.
Murdock, George Peter; and White, Douglas.
    1969   Standard Cross-Cultural Sample. Ethnology, 8: 329-369.
Murphy, G. E.; and Robins, E.
    1967   Social Factors in Suicide. Journal of the American Medical Association, 199: 303-308.
Myers, Jerome K.; Lindenthal, Jacob J.; and Pepper, Max P.
    1974   Social Class, Life Events, and Psychiatric Symptoms: A Longitudinal Study. IN: Stressful
            Life Events: Their Nature and Effects. Barbara Dohrenwend and Bruce Dohrenwend, ed-
            itors. New York: John Wiley. pp. 191-205.
Myrdal, Gunnar.
    1968   Asian Drama: An Inquiry into the Poverty of Nations. 3 Vols. New York: Pantheon.
Nag, Moni.
    1962   Factors Affecting Fertility in Nonindustrial Societies: A Cross-Cultural Study. Yale Univ-
            sity Publications in Anthropology, 66. New Haven, Conn.: Yale University Press.
Naroll, Maud.
    n.d.   Women's Occupations in Preindustrial Societies. Manuscript.
Naroll, Raoul.
    1981   Foreword: A Cybernetic Model of the Mind. IN: David G. Hays, Cognitive Structures.
            New Haven, Conn.: Human Relations Areas Files, HRAFlex Books, pp. vi-xxxviii.
Naroll, Raoul.
    1980   On Snowballs. Peace Research, 12: 1-6.
Naroll, Raoul.
    1976   Galton's Problem and HRAFLIB. Behavior Science Research, 11: 123-148.
Naroll, Raoul.
    1974a   An Exact Test of Significance for Goodman and Kruskal's Gamma. Behavior Science
            Research, 9: 27-40.
Naroll, Raoul.
    1974b   The Use of Ordinal Statistics in Causal Analysis of Correlations. Social Forces, 53: 251-
            253.
Naroll, Raoul.
    1973   Holocultural Theory Tests. IN: Main Currents in Cultural Anthropology. Raoul Naroll
            and Frada Naroll, editors. New York: Appleton-Century-Crofts.
Naroll, Raoul.
    1971a   Review of Morrison, Denton E. and Henkel, Ramon E., editors: The Significance Test
            Controversy. American Anthropologist, 73: 1437-1439.
Naroll, Raoul.
    1971b   The Double-Language Boundary in Cross-Cultural Surveys. Behavior Science Notes, 6:
            95-102.
Naroll, Raoul.
    1970a   What Have We Learned from Cross-Cultural Surveys? American Anthropologist, 72:
            1227-1288.
Naroll, Raoul.
    1970b   Cross-Cultural Sampling. IN: A Handbook of Method in Cultural Anthropology. Raoul
            Naroll and Ronald Cohen, editors. Garden City, N.Y.: Natural History Press. Reprinted
            1973. New York: Columbia University Press. pp. 889-926.
Naroll, Raoul.
    1970c   The Culture-Bearing Unit in Cross-Cultural Surveys. IN: A Handbook of Method in Cul-
            tural Anthropology. Raoul Naroll and Ronald Cohen, editors. Garden City, New York:
            Natural History Press. Reprinted 1973. N.Y.: Columbia University Press. pp. 721-765.

Naroll, Raoul.
    1970d Data Quality Control in Cross-Cultural Surveys. IN: A Handbook of Method in Cultural
        Anthropology. Raoul Naroll and Ronald Cohen, editors. Garden City, N. Y.: Natural His-
        tory Press. Reprinted 1973. New York: Columbia University Press. pp. 927-945.
Naroll, Raoul.
    1970e Epistemology. IN: A Handbook of Method in Cultural Anthropology. Raoul Naroll and
        Ronald Cohen, editors. Garden City, N.Y.: Natural History Press. Reprinted 1973. New
        York: Columbia University Press. pp. 25-30.
Naroll, Raoul.
    1969   Cultural Determinants and the Concept of the Sick Society. IN: Changing Perspectives in
        Mental Illness. Stanley C. Plog and Robert B. Edgerton, editors. New York: Holt, Rine-
        hart & Winston. pp. 128-155.
Naroll, Raoul.
    1968   Some Thoughts on Comparative Method in Anthropology. IN: Methodology in Social
        Science Research. Hubert M. and Ann B. Blalock, editors. New York: McGraw-Hill. pp.
        236-377.
Naroll, Raoul.
    1967   Imperial Cycles and World Order. Papers, Peace Research Society, 7: 83-101.
Naroll, Raoul.
    1964a A Fifth Solution to Galton's Problem. American Anthropologist, 66: 863-867.
Naroll, Raoul.
    1964b Sobre el Metodo Comparativo de la Antropologia Cultural. Ciencias Politicas y Sociales,
        Mexico City, 10: 681-722.
Naroll, Raoul.
    1962a Data Quality Control: A New Research Technique. New York: Free Press.
Naroll, Raoul.
    1962b How Russians Think. Bucknell Review, 10: 243-262.
Naroll, Raoul
    1956   A Preliminary Index of Social Development. American Anthropologist, 58: 687-715.
Naroll, Raoul.
    1953   Clio and the Constitution: The Influence of the Study of History on the Federal Conven-
        tion of 1787. Ph.D. Dissertation, Department of History, U.C.L.A. Ann Arbor: University
        Microfilms #76-28860.
Naroll, Raoul.
    1952   Sheridan and Cedar Creek: A Reappraisal. Military Affairs, 16: 153-168.
Naroll, Raoul; Bullough, Vern L.; and Naroll, Frada.
    1974   Military Deterrence in History: A Pilot Cross-Historical Survey. Albany: State University
        of New York. pp. xlii-xliii.
Naroll, Raoul; and Cohen, Ronald, editors.
    1970   A Handbook of Method in Cultural Anthropology. Garden City, N. Y.: Natural History
        Press. Reprinted 1973. New York: Columbia University Press.
Naroll, Raoul; Margolis, Enid; Naroll, Frada; Precourt, Walter; and Tatje, Terrence A.
    n.d.   Modes of Exchange, Wealth Concentration and Cultural Evolution. Manuscript.
Naroll, Raoul; Michik, Gary L.; and Naroll, Frada.
    1980   Holocultural Research Methods. IN: Handbook of Cross-Cultural Psychology, Vol 2.
        Harry C. Triandis and John W. Berry, editors. Boston: Allyn & Bacon, pp. 479-521.
Naroll, Raoul; and Naroll, Frada.
    1962   Social Development of a Tyrolean Village. Anthropological Quarterly, 35: 103-120.
Naroll, Raoul; and Wirsing, Rolf.
    1976   Borrowing versus Migration as a Selection Mechanism in Cultural Evolution. Journal of
        Conflict Resolution, 20: 187-212.
Nelson, Walter H.
    1970   The Soldier Kings: The House of Hohenzollern. New York: Putnam.
Neugarten, Bernice L.; and Havinghurst, Robert J.
    1970   Disengagement Reconsidered in a Cross-Cultural Context. IN: Adjustment to Retire-
        ment. R. J. Havinghurst, J. M. A. Munnichs, B. Neugarten and B. Thomae, editors. As-
        sen: Van Gorcum. pp. 138-146.

Newlands, Carol.
  1979   Wotan and Women: A Cross-Cultural Test of the Divale-Harris Population Control Sys-
         tem: Primitive Warfare and Female Infanticide. M. A. Thesis, California State University,
         Hayward.
Newspaper Enterprise Association.
  1972   World Almanac and Book of Facts. New York: Newspaper Enterprise Association.
Nielsen, Caroline C.
  n.d.   Antecedents and Consequences of Parental Acceptance-Rejection. University of Con-
         necticut, Storrs. Manuscript.
Nimkoff, M. F.
  1965   Types of Family and the Social System and the Family. IN: Comparative Family Systems.
         M. F. Nimkoff, editor, Boston: Houghton Mifflin.
Nimkoff, M. F.; and Middleton, Russell.
  1960   Types of Family and Types of Economy. American Journal of Sociology, 56: 215-225.
Nisbett, Richard; and Ross, Lee.
  1980   Human Inference: Strategies and Shortcomings of Social Judgment. Englewood Cliffs,
         N.J.: Prentice-Hall.
Norway, The Central Bureau of Statistics.
  1978   Statistisk Arbok 1978. Oslo: Grondahl.
Nuttall, Ena V.; and Nuttall, Ronald L.
  1971   Effect of Size of Family on Parent-Child Relationships. Proceedings of the 79th annual
         convention of the American Psychological Association, Vol. 6.
Nye, Ivan.
  1958   Family Relationships and Delinquent Behavior. New York: John Wiley.
Ogbu, John U.
  1978   African Bride Wealth and Women's Status. American Ethnologist, 5: 241-262.
Osmond, Marie.
  1969   A Cross-Cultural Analysis of Family Organization. Journal of Marriage and the Family,
         31: 302-310.
Osmond, Marie W.
  1964   Toward Monogamy: A Cross-Cultural Study of Correlates of Type of Marriage. Master's
         Thesis, Department of Anthropology, Florida State University, Tallahassee.
Palmer, Stuart.
  1970   Aggression in Fifty-Eight Nonliterate Societies: An Exploratory Analysis. Annales Inter-
         nationales de Criminologie, 9: 57-69.
Palmer, Stuart.
  1965   Murder and Suicide in Forty Nonliterate Societies. Journal of Criminal Law, Criminology,
         and Police Science, 56: 320-324.
Parents Anonymous.
  1978   Frontiers. Torrance, Calif.: Parents Anonymous.
Parents Anonymous.
  1975   Parents Anonymous Chairperson-Sponsor Manual. Torrance, Calif.: Parents Anonymous.
Parents Anonymous
  1974   Parents Anonymous Charter Development Manual. Torrance, Calif.: Parents Anonymous.
Parkes, Colin Murray.
  1972   Bereavement: Studies of Grief in Adult Life. New York: International Universities Press.
Parkes, Colin Murray.
  1964   Effects of Bereavement on Physical and Mental Health: A Study of the Medical Records of
         Widows. British Medical Journal, 2: 274-279.
Parkin, David.
  1969   Neighbors and Nationals in an African City Ward. Berkeley: University of California
         Press.
Parten, Mildred.
  1950   Surveys, Polls and Samples. New York: Harper.
Paykel, E. S.
  1974   Life Stress and Psychiatric Disorder. IN: Stressful Life Events: Their Nature and Effects.
         Barbara Dohrenwend and Bruce Dohrenwend, editors. New York: John Wiley. pp. 135-
         149.

Paykel, E. S.; Prusoff, B. A.; and Myers, J. K.
    1975   Suicide Attempts and Recent Life Events. Archives of General Psychiatry, 32: 327-333.
Pelto, Pertti J.
    1970   Anthropological Research: The Structure of Inquiry. New York: Harper & Row.
Penick, Bettye K. E.; and Owens, Maurice E. B., III, editors.
            Surveying Crime. Washington, D.C.: National Academy of Sciences.
Perrin, Porter G.
    1950   Writer's Guide and Index to English. Revised ed. Chicago: Scott, Foresman.
Peterfreund, Emanuel; and Schwartz, Jacob T.
    1971   Information, Systems, and Psychoanalysis: An Evolutionary Biological Approach to
            Psychoanalytic Theory. Psychological Issues, Vol. 7, Nos. 1/2, Monograph 25/26. New
            York: International Universities Press.
Polanyi, Michael.
    1970   The Stability of Scientific Theories against Experience. IN: Witchcraft and Sorcery, Se-
            lected Readings. Max Marwick, editor. Baltimore: Penguin. pp. 337-341.
Poole, Lon; and Borchers, Mary.
    1977   Some Common BASIC Programs. 2nd ed. Berkeley: Osborne.
Popper, Karl R.
    1959   The Logic of Scientific Discovery. New York: Basic Books.
Powers, William T.
    1977   Quantitative Analysis of Purposive Systems. Some Spadework at the Foundations of
            Scientific Psychology. Manuscript.
Powers, William T.
    1973   Behavior: The Control of Perception. Chicago: Aldine.
Precourt, Walter E.
    1975   Initiation Ceremonies and Secret Societies as Educational Institutions. IN: Cross-Cultur-
            al Perspectives on Learning. Richard W. Brislin, Stephen Bochner and Walter J. Lonner,
            editors. New York: John Wiley. pp. 231-250.
Prescott, James W.
    1975   Body Pleasure and the Origins of Violence. Bulletin of the Atomic Scientists, 31: 10-20.
Przeworski, Adam; and Teune, Henry.
    1970   The Logic of Comparative Social Inquiry. New York: Wiley-Interscience.
Quinney, Richard.
    1965   Suicide, Homicide and Economic Development. Social Forces, 43: 401-406.
Rachlis, D.
    1969   Suicide and Loss Adjustment in the Aging. New York: American Association of Suicidolo-
            gists.
Rees, W. Dewi; and Lutkins, Sylvia G.
    1967   Mortality of Bereavement. British Medical Journal, 4: 13-16.
Reichenbach, Hans.
    1951   The Rise of Scientific Philosophy. Berkeley: University of California Press.
Reifer, Mary.
    n.d.   The Disengagement Theory: A Cross-Cultural Study. Manuscript.
Retterstøl, Nils.
    1978   Selvmord, Dod og Sorg (Suicide, Death, and Grief). Oslo: Universitetsforlaget.
Retterstøl, Nils.
    1975   Suicide in Norway. IN: Suicide in Different Cultures. Norman L. Farberow, editor. Balti-
            more: University Park Press. pp. 77-94.
Retterstøl, Nils.
    1972   Suicide in Norway. IN: Suicide and Attempted Suicide. Skandia International Symposia.
            Stockholm: Nordiska.
Reynolds, Vernon; and Reynolds, Frances.
    1965   Chimpanzees of the Budungo Forest. IN: Primate Behavior: Field Studies of Monkeys
            and Apes. Irven DeVore, editor. New York: Holt, Rinehart & Winston.
Rin, Hsien; and Lin, Tsung-Yi.
    1962   Mental Illness among Formosan Aborigines as Compared with the Chinese in Taiwan.
            Journal of Mental Science, 108: 134-146.
Robbins, Michael C.; Pelto, Pertti J; and DeWalt, Billie R.
    1972   Climate and Behavior: A Biocultural Study. Journal of Cross-Cultural Psychology, 3:
            331-344.

Roberts, John M.; Arth, Malcolm J.; and Bush, Robert R.
    1959   Games in Cultures. American Anthropologist, 61: 597-605.
Robins, E.; and O'Neal, P.
    1958   Culture and Mental Disorder. Human Organization, 16: 7-11.
Roethlisberger, F. J.; Dickson, W. J.; and Wright, Harold A.
    1939   Management and the Worker. Cambridge, Mass.: Harvard University Press.
Rohner, Evelyn C.
    1980   Perceived Parental Acceptance-Rejection and Children's Personality and Behavioral Dispositions: An Intracultural Test. Behavior Science Research, 15: 81-88.
Rohner, Ronald P.
    n.d.   Enculturative Discontinuity and Adolescent Stress: Worldwide Test of a Hypothesis. Behavior Science Research. In press.
Rohner, Ronald P.
    1976   Sex Differences in Aggression: Phylogenetic and Enculturation Perspectives. Ethos, 4: 57-72.
Rohner, Ronald P.
    1975   They Love Me, They Love Me Not. New Haven, Conn.: HRAF Press.
Rohner, Ronald P.; DeWalt, Billie R.; and Ness, Robert C.
    1973   Ethnographer Bias in Cross-Cultural Research: An Empirical Study. Behavior Science Notes, 8: 275-317.
Rohner, Ronald P.; Naroll, Raoul; Barry, Herbert, III; Divale, William T.; Erickson, Edwin E.; Schaefer, James; and Sipes, Richard.
    1978   Guidelines for Holocultural Research. Current Anthropology, 19: 128-129.
Rohner, Ronald P.; and Rohner, Evelyn C.
    1980   Preface to Special Issue: Worldwide Tests of Parental Acceptance-Rejection Theory. Behavior Science Research, 15: v.
Rohner, Ronald P.; Roll, Samuel; and Rohner, Evelyn C.
    1980   Perceived Parental Acceptance-Rejection and Personality Organization among Mexican and American School Children. Behavior Science Research, 15: 23-39.
Roosens, Eugeen.
    1979   Mental Patients in Town Life. Beverly Hills, Calif.: Sage.
Rosenberg, Shirley Sirota, editor.
    1971   First Special Report to the U. S. Congress on Alcohol and Health from the Secretary of Health, Education and Welfare. National Institute on Alcohol Abuse and Alcoholism.
Rosenblatt, E.; and Greenland, C.
    1974   Female Crimes of Violence. Canadian Journal of Criminology and Corrections, 16: 173-180.
Rosenblatt, Paul C.
    1967   Marital Residence and the Functions of Romantic Love. Ethnology, 6: 471-479.
Rosenblatt, Paul C.
    1966   A Cross-Cultural Study of Child Rearing and Romantic Love. Journal of Personality and Social Psychology, 4: 336-338.
Rosenblatt, Paul C.; Fugita, Stephen; and McDowell, Kenneth V.
    1969   Wealth Transfer and Restrictions on Sexual Relations during Betrothal. Ethnology, 8: 319-328.
Rosenblatt, Paul C.; Walsh, R. Patricia; and Jackson, Douglas A.
    1976   Grief and Mourning in Cross-Cultural Perspective. New Haven, Conn.: HRAF Press.
Rosenthal, Robert.
    1966   Experimental Effects of Behavioral Research. New York: Appleton-Century-Crofts.
Rossi, Peter H.; and Freeman, Howard E.
    1982   Evaluation: A Systematic Approach. 2nd ed. Beverly Hills, Calif.: Sage.
Rossi, Robert J.; and Gilmartin, Kevin J.
    1980   Handbook of Social Indicators. New York: Garland.
Rosten, Leo.
    1968   The Joys of Yiddish. New York: McGraw-Hill.
Roy, Alec.
    1978   Vulnerability Factors and Depression in Women. British Journal of Psychiatry, 133: 106-110.

Rudin, S. A.
 1968   National Motives Predict Psychogenic Death Rates Twenty-Five Years Later. Science,
        160 (3830): 901-903.
Rummel, Rudolph J.
 1970a Applied Factor Analysis. Evanston, Ill.: Northwestern University Press. p. 25.
Rummel, Rudolph J.
 1970b Dimensions of Error in Cross-Cultural Data. IN: A Handbook of Method in Cultural An-
        thropology. Raoul Naroll and Ronald Cohen, editors. Garden City, N. Y.: Natural His-
        tory Press. Reprinted 1973. New York: Columbia University Press. pp. 946-961.
Russell, Bertrand.
 1945   A History of Western Philosophy. New York: Simon & Schuster. pp. 664-674.
Russell, Elbert W.
 1972   Factors of Human Aggression. Behavior Science Notes, 7: 275-312.
Russett, Bruce M.; Alker, Hayward R.; Deutsch, Karl W.; and Lasswell, Harold D.
 1964   World Handbook of Political and Social Indicators. New Haven, Conn.: Yale University
        Press.
Rutter, Michael.
 1972   Maternal Deprivation Reassessed. Harmondsworth, Middlesex: Penguin Books.
Safilios-Rothschild, Constantina.
 1971   A Cross-Cultural Examination of Women's Marital, Educational and Occupational Op-
        tions. Acta Sociologica, 14: 96-113.
Sahlins, M.
 1972   Stone Age Economics. Chicago: Aldine-Atherton.
Sainsbury, J.; Jenkins, J.; and Levey, A.
 1980   The Social Correlates of Suicide in Europe. IN: The Suicide Syndrome. Richard Farmer
        and Steven Hirsch, editors. London: Croon Helm.
Sanday, Peggy R.
 1974   Female Status in the Public Domain. IN: Woman, Culture and Society. M. Z. Rosaldo and
        L. Lamphere, editors. Stanford, Calif.: Stanford University Press. pp. 189-207.
Sanua, Victor D.
 1980   Familial and Sociocultural Antecedents of Psychopathology. IN: Handbook of Cross-Cul-
        tural Psychology, Vol. 6. Harry C. Triandis and Juris C. Draguns, editors. Boston: Allyn
        & Bacon. pp. 175-236.
Satten, J.; Menninger, K. A.; and Mayman, M.
 1960   Murder without Apparent Motive: A Study in Personality Disorganizaiton. American
        Journal of Psychiatry, 117: 48-53.
Saunderson, H. S.
 1894   Notes on Corea and Its People. Journal of the Anthropological Institute of Great Britain
        and Ireland, 24: 299-316.
Sayers, Dorothy L.
 1928   The Unpleasantness at the Bellona Club. New York: Harper.
Schaefer, James M.
 1979   Ethnic Differences in Response to Alcohol. IN: Psychiatric Factors in Drug Abuse. Roy
        W. Pickens and Leonard L. Heston, editors. New York: Grune & Stratton. pp. 219-238.
Schaefer, James M.
 1978   Drunkenness and Culture Stress: A Holoculture Test. IN: Cross-Cultural Approaches to
        the Study of Alcohol. Michael Everett, Jack O. Waddell, and Dwight B. Heath, editors. The
        Hague: Mouton. pp. 287-321.
Schaefer, James M.
 1976   Alcohol Metabolism and Sensitivity Reactions among the Reddis of South India. Alco-
        holism: Clinical and Experimental Research, 2: 61-69.
Schaefer, James M.
 1973   A Hologeistic Study of Family Structure and Sentiment, Supernatural Beliefs, and Drunk-
        enness, Ph.D. Dissertation, State University of New York, Buffalo. Ann Arbor: Univer-
        sity Microfilms No. 73-29131.
Schaller, George B.
 1965a The Behavior of the Mountain Gorilla. IN: Primate Behavior. Irven DeVore, editor. New
        York: Holt, Rinehart & Winston. pp. 324-367.

Schaller, George B.
  1965b Behavioral Comparisons of the Apes. IN: Primate Behavior: Field Studies of Monkeys and Apes. Irven DeVore, editor. New York: Holt, Rinehart & Winston. pp. 474-481.
Schaller, George B.; and Emlen, John T., Jr.
  1963 Observations on the Ecology and Social Behavior of the Mountain Gorilla. IN: African Ecology and Human Evolution. F. Clark Howell and Francois Bourliere, editors. New York: Wenner-Gren.
Schlegel, Alice, editor.
  1977 Sexual Stratification: A Cross-Cultural View. New York: Columbia University Press.
Schlegel, Alice.
  1972 Male Dominance and Female Autonomy. New Haven, Conn.: HRAF Press.
Schneider, David; and Gough, Kathleen, editors.
  1961 Matrilineal Kinship. Berkeley: University of California Press.
Schneider, Pierre B.
  1954 La Tentative de Suicide. Paris: Delachaux & Niestle.
Schopf, J. William.
  1978 The Evolution of the Earliest Cells. Scientific American. Special September Issue on Evolution, 239: 110-138.
Schwartz, Peter; and Ogilvy, James.
  1979 The Emergent Paradigms: Changing Patterns of Thought and Belief. Report No. 7. Menlo Park, Calif.: Values and Lifestyle Program.
Schweizer, Thomas.
  1978a Lineare Strukturmodelle in der Ethnologie: Ein Test von Whiting's Theorie der Pubertäts-riten, Teil 2. Sociologus, 28: 149-173.
Schweizer, Thomas.
  1978b Methodenprobleme des Interkulturellen Vergleichs. Köln: Bohlaw Verlag.
Scientific American.
  1978 Special September Issue on Evolution. Scientific American, 239: 46-231.
Scientific American.
  1977 Cosmology + 1: Readings from Scientific American. With an introduction by Owen Gingerich. San Francisco: Freeman.
Segall, Marshall H.
  1979 Cross-Cultural Psychology: Human Behavior in Global Perspective. Monterey, Calif.: Brooks-Cole.
Service, Elman R.
  1968 War and Our Contemporary Ancestors. IN: War: The Anthropology of Armed Conflict and Aggression. Morton Fried, Marvin Harris and Robert Murphy, editors. New York: Natural History Press.
Shaw, Clifford R.; and McKay, Henry D.
  1969 Juvenile Delinquency and Urban Areas. Revised ed. Chicago: University of Chicago Press. First printed 1942.
Sheehan, Tom.
  1976 Senior Esteem as a Factor of Socioeconomic Complexity. The Gerontologist, 16: 433-440.
Sheils, H. Dean.
  1971 Monogamy and Independent Families: A Research Note Concerning Two Propositions from Macrosociology. Behavior Science Notes, 6: 221-228.
Silk, Joseph.
  1980 The Big Bang: The Creation and Evolution of the Universe. San Francisco: Freeman.
Silverman, Lloyd H.
  1980 Comprehensive Report of Studies Using the Subliminal Psychodynamic Activation Method. Mimeograph.
Silverman, Lloyd H.
  1976 The Unconscious Symbiotic Fantasy as a Ubiquitous Therapeutic Agent. Paper presented at the annual meeting of the American Psychoanalytic Association, Baltimore, May 8.
Silverman, Lloyd H.
  1975a An Experimental Method for the Study of Unconscious Conflict: A Progress Report. British Journal of Medical Psychology, 48: 291-298.
Silverman, Lloyd H.
  1975b On the Role of Laboratory Experiments in the Development of the Clinical Theory of Psychoanalysis; Data on Subliminal Activation of Aggressive and Merging Wishes in Schizophrenia. International Review of Psychoanalysis, 2: 43-64.

Silverman, Lloyd H.
  1972   Drive Stimuation and Psychopathology: On the Conditions under Which Drive-Related External Events Evoke Pathological Reaction. IN: Psychoanalysis and Contemporary Science, Vol. I. R. R. Holt and E. Peterfreund, editors. New York: Macmillan.
Silverman, Lloyd H.
  1967   An Experimental Approach to the Study of Dynamic Propositions in Psychoanalysis. Journal of the American Psychoanalytic Association, 15: 376-403.
Silverman, Lloyd H.; Bronstein, Abbot; and Mendelsohn, Eric.
  1976   The Further Use of the Subliminal Psychodynamic Method for the Experimental Study of the Clinical Theory of Psychoanalysis. Psychotherapy: Theory, Research and Practice, 13: 2-16.
Silverman, Philip; and Maxwell, Robert J.
  1978   How Do I Respect Thee? Let Me Count The Ways: Deference toward Elderly Men and Women. Behavior Science Research, 13: 91-108.
Simmons, Leo W.
  1945   The Role of the Aged in Primitive Society. New Haven, Conn.: Yale University Press.
Simon, Herbert A.
  1955   On a Class of Skew Distribution Functions. Biometrika, 42: 425-440.
Simon, Herbert A.
  1954   Spurious Correlation: A Causal Interpretation. Journal of the American Statistical Association, 49: 467-479.
Singer, Charles.
  1946   Medicine, History of. Encyclopaedia Britannica, Vol. 15: 198. Chicago: Encyclopaedia Britanica.
Singer, J. David; and Small, Melvin.
  1972   The Wages of War: 1816-1965—A Statistical Handbook. New York: John Wiley.
Slovic, P.; and Lichtenstein, S.
  1971   Comparison of Bayesian and Regression Approaches to the Study of Information Processing in Judgment. Organization, Behavior and Human Performance, 6: 649-744.
Sipes, Richard G.
  1973   War, Sports and Aggression: An Empirical Test of Two Rival Theories. American Anthropologist, 75: 64-86.
Skagestad, Peter.
  1981   Hypothetical Realism. IN: Scientific Inquiry and the Social Sciences. Marilynn B. Brewer and Barry E. Collins, editors. San Francisco: Jossey-Bass.
Slater, Mariam K.
  1959   Ecological Factors in the Origin of Incest. American Anthropologist, 61: 1042-1059.
Smail, Lloyd L.
  1953   Analytic Geometry and Calculus. New York: Appleton-Century-Crofts. p. 416.
Smith, Adam.
  1970   The Wealth of Nations, Books I-III. Andrew Skinner, editor. Baltimore: Penguin Books. First printed 1776.
Smith, David M.
  1973   The Geography of Social Well-Being in the United States. New York: McGraw-Hill.
Smith, Hedrick.
  1976   The Russians. New York: Ballantine Books.
Smith, Page.
  1980   The Shaping of America. New York: McGraw-Hill.
Smith, Selwyn M.
  1975   The Battered Child Syndrome. London: Butterworths.
Smith, Selwyn M.; and Hanson, R.
  1975   Interpersonal Relationships and Child-Rearing Practices in 214 Parents of Battered Children. British Journal of Psychiatry, 126: 513-525.
Smith, Selwyn M.; Hanson, R.; and Noble, S.
  1974   Social Aspects of the Battered Baby Syndrome. British Journal of Psychiatry, 125: 568-582.
Smith, Selwyn M.; Hanson R.; and Noble S.
  1973   Parents of Battered Babies. British Journal of Psychiatry, 124: 388-391.
Smith, Selwyn M.; Honigsberger, L.; and Smith, C.
  1973   E.E.G. and Personality Factors in Baby Batterers. British Medical Journal, 2: 20-22.

Snyder, Glenn H.; and Diesing, Paul.
    1977   Conflict among Nations. Princeton, N.J.: Princeton University Press.
Snyder, Richard C.; and Robinson, James A.
    1961   National and International Decision-Making. Report to the Committee on Research for
            Peace. New York: The Institute for International Order.
Sorokin, Pitirim A.
    1937-   Social and Cultural Dynamics. 4 Vols. New York: Bedminster Press.
    1941
Soustelle, Jacques.
    1955   La Vie Quotidienne des Azteques à la Veille de la Conquête Espagnole. Paris: Hachette.
Speck, Frank G.
    1915   The Family Hunting Band as the Basis of Algonkian Social Organization. American An-
            thropologist, 17: 289-305.
Spencer, Judith Alicia.
    1970   Societal Conditions of Monotheism: A Partial Replication of a Study by Guy E. Swanson.
            M.A. Thesis in Anthropology. Columbus: Ohio State University.
Spencer, Paul.
    1965   The Samburu: a Study of Gerontocracy in a Nomadic Tribe. Berkeley and Los Angeles:
            University of California Press.
Spicer, Edward H.
    1971   Persistent Cultural Systems. A Comparative Study of Identity Systems That Can Adapt
            to Contrasting Environments. Science, 174 (4011): 795-800.
Spicer, Edward H.
    1954   Potam: A Yaqui Village in Sonora. American Anthropological Association Memoir, 77.
Spinetta, John. J.; and Rigler, David.
    1972   The Child-Abusing: A Psychological Review. Psychological Bulletin, 77(4): 296-304.
Srole, Leo; Langer, Thomas; Michael, Stanley T.; Kirkpatrick, Price; Opler, Marvin K.; and Rennie,
            Thomas A. C.
    1975   Mental Health in the Metropolis: The Midtown Manhattan Study. Revised and enlarged.
            New York: Harper & Row Torchbooks.
Srole, Leo; Langer, Thomas; Michael, Stanley T.; Kirkpatrick, Price; Opler, Marvin K.;and Rennie,
            Thomas A. C.
    1962   Mental Health in the Metropolis. New York: McGraw-Hill.
Starkey, Sandra Lee.
    1980   The Relationship between Parental Acceptance-Rejection and the Academic Perfor-
            mance of Fourth and Fifth Graders. Behavior Science Research, 15: 67-80.
Stein, William W.
    1974   Modernization and Inequality in Vicos, Peru: An Examination of the "Ignorance of Wo-
            men." Special Study No. 73. Buffalo: Council on International Studies.
Steinmetz, Siegfried.
    1894   Suicide among Primitive Peoples. American Anthropologist, (Old Series) 7: 53-60.
Stephens, William N.
    1972   A Cross-Cultural Study of Modesty. Behavior Science Notes, 7: 1-28.
Stewart, Frank H.
    1977   Fundamentals of Age-Group Systems. New York: Academic Press.
Stoetzel, Jean.
    1948   Une Etude du Budget-Temps de la Femme dans les Agglomerations Urbaines. Population, 3:
            47-62.
Stout, David B.
    1947   San Blas Cuna Acculturation: An Introduction. New York: Viking Fund.
Straus, Murray; Gelles, Richard; and Steinmetz, Suzanne.
    1980   Behind Closed Doors: Violence in the American Family. Garden City, N.Y.: Anchor
            Press-Doubleday.
Strauss, Robert.
    1966   Alcohol. IN: Contemporary Social Problems. 2nd. ed. Robert K. Merton and Robert A.
            Nisbet, editors. New York: Harcourt Brace. pp. 236-280.
Strug, David L.; and Hyman, Merton M.
    1981   Social Networks of Alcoholics. Journal of Studies on Alcohol, 42: 855-844.

Strunk, William, Jr.; and White, E. B.
    1979   The Elements of Style. 3rd. ed. New York: Macmillan.
Sugita, Gempaku.
    1942   Die Anfänge der Holland-Kunde. Koichi Mori, translator. Monumenta Japonica, 5: 144-
            166.
Sutcliffe, Claud R.
    1974   The Effects of Differential Exposure to Modernization on the Value Orientations of Pal-
            estinians. Journal of Social Psychology, 93: 173-180.
Sutherland, Edwin H; and Cressey, Donald R.
    1970   Criminology. 8th ed. Philadelphia: Lippincott.
Swanson, Guy E.
    1960   The Birth of the Gods: The Origin of Primitive Beliefs. Ann Arbor: University of Michigan
            Press.
Sweden, National Central Bureau of Statistics.
    1979   Dodsorsaker 1977. Stockholm: National Central Bureau of Statistics.
Sweden, National Central Bureau of Statistics.
    1978   Statistisk Arsbok for Sverige 1978. Stockholm: National Central Bureau of Statistics.
Swenson, Hugo M.
    1967   Light. IN: The Harper Encyclopedia of Science. James R. Newman, editor. New York:
            Harper. p. 669.
Tabachnick, N.
    1961   Interpersonal Relations in Suicide. Archives of General Psychiatry, 4: 60-69.
Taeuber, Conrad.
    1968   Census. IN: International Encyclopedia of the Social Sciences, Vol. 2. David L. Sills, edit-
            or. New York: Macmillan. pp. 360-365.
Tähkä, Veikko.
    1966   The Alcoholic Personality: A Clinical Study. Helsinki: Finnish Foundation for Alcohol
            Studies.
Tannenbaum, Frank.
    1938   Crime and the Community. New York: Columbia University Press.
Tapp, June L.; and Kohlberg, Lawrence.
    1971   Developing Senses of Law and Justice. Journal of Social Issues, 27: 65-92.
Tatje, Terrence A.; and Naroll, Raoul.
    1970   Two Measures of Societal Complexity. IN: A Handbook of Method in Cultural Anthro-
            pology. Raoul Naroll and Ronald Cohen, editors. Garden City, N.Y.: Natural History
            Press. Reprinted 1973. New York: Columbia University Press. pp. 766-833.
Taylor, Charles Lewis; and Hudson, Michael G.
    1972   World Handbook of Political and Social Indicators. 2nd. ed. New Haven, Conn.: Yale Un-
            iversity Press.
Tchekov, Anton.
    n.d.   The Three Sisters. IN: The Plays of Anton Tchekov. Constance Garnett, translator. New
            York: Random House. pp. 117-185.
Tennant, Christopher; and Bebbington, Paul.
    1978   The Social Causation of Depression: A Critique of the Work of Brown and His Col-
            leagues. Psychological Medicine, 8: 565-575.
Textor, Robert B.
    1967   A Cross-Cultural Summary. New Haven, Conn.: HRAF Press.
Theil, Henri.
    1978   Introduction to Econometrics. Englewood Cliffs, N.J.: Prentice-Hall.
Theil, Henri.
    1971   Principles of Econometrics. New York: John Wiley.
Thomas, David Hurst.
    1976   Figuring Anthopology: First Principles of Probability and Statistics. New York: Holt, Rine-
            hart & Winston.
Thompson, Ellen M.; Paget, Norman W.; Bates, Doris W.; Mesch, Morris; and Putnam, Theodore I.
    1971   Child Abuse: A Community Challenge. Alice E. Glazier, editor. East Aurora, N.Y.: Henry
            Stewart.
Thompson, Laura.
    1950   Culture in Crisis: A Study of the Hopi Indians. New York: Harper.

Thompson, Laura; and Joseph, Alice.
   1944   The Hopi Way. Chicago: University of Chicago Press.
Tiger, Lionel; and Shephner, Joseph.
   1976   Women in the Kibbutz. New York: Harcourt Brace Jovanovich.
Titiev, Mischa.
   1950   The Religion of the Hopi Indians. IN: Ancient Religions. Vergilius Ferm, editor. New York:
          Philosophical Library. pp. 365-378.
Tolstoy. Leo.
   1942   Some Words about War and Peace. IN: War and Peace. Inner Sanctum ed. Leo Tolstoy,
          editor. New York: Simon & Schuster. pp. 1353-1361. (First published in Russian Archive,
          1868).
Toynbee, Arnold J.
   1957   A Study of History, Vols. 7-10. D.C. Somervell abridgement. New York: Oxford Univer-
          sity Press.
Toynbee, Arnold J.
   1939   A Study of History, Vol. 5. London: Oxford University Press.
Travis, Carol.
   1976   Compensatory Education: The Glass Is Half Full. Psychology Today. 10 (4): 73.
Triandis, H. C., editor; with co-editors Lambert, W.; Berry, J. W.; Lonner, W.; Heron, A.; Brislin, R.
          W.; and Draguns, J. C.
   1980   Handbook of Cross-Cultural Psychology. 6 vols. Boston: Allyn & Bacon.
Trice, Harrison; Roman, Paul M. and Belasco, James A.
   1969   Selection for Treatment: A Predictive Evaluation of an Alcoholism Treatment Regimen.
          International Journal of the Addictions, 4: 303-317.
Turnbull, Colin M.
   1972   The Mountain People. New York: Simon and Schuster.
Turner, Victor W.
   1964   A Ndembu Doctor in Practice. IN: Magic, Faith and Healing: Studies in Primitive Psychia-
          try Today. Ari Kiev, editor, New York: Free Press. pp. 230-263.
Tylor, Edward B.
   1889   On a Method of Investigating the Development of Institutions. Journal of the Royal An-
          throp. Inst. of Gr. Britain and Ire., 18: 245-69. Reprinted in Readings in Cross-Cultural
          Methodology. Frank W. Moore, editor. New Haven, Conn.: HRAF Press. pp. 1-25.
Udy, Stanley H., Jr.
   1959   Organization of Work. New Haven, Conn.: HRAF Press.
United Nations, Department of Economic and Social Affairs, Statistical Office.
   1975   Demographic Yearbook, 1974. New York: United Nations.
United Nations, Department of Economic and Social Affairs, Statistical Office.
   1972   Elements of Sample Survey Theory. Studies in Methods Series F/9/Rev.1. New York: Un-
          ited Nations.
United Nations, Department of Economic and Social Affairs, Statistical Office.
   1970   Demographic Yearbook, 1969, 21st issue: Natality Statistics. New York: United Nations.
United Nations, International Labour Office.
   1972   Yearbook of Labour Statistics. Geneva: International Labour Office.
United Nations, World Health Organization.
   1976a World Health Statistics Annual, 1973-1976. Vol. 1: Vital Statistics and Causes of Death.
          Geneva: United Nations.
United Nations, World Health Organization.
   1976b World Health Statistics Annual, 1972. Vol. 3: Health Personnel and Hospital Establish-
          ments. Geneva: United Nations.
United Nations, World Health Organization.
   1973   The International Pilot Study of Schizophrenia, Vol. 1. Geneva: World Health Organiza-
          tion.
United Nations, World Health Organization.
   1962   World Health Statistics Annual, Vols. 1 and 2. Geneva: World Health Organization.
United Nations, World Health Organization.
   1951   Report on the First Session of the Alcoholism Subcommittee on Mental Health. Technical
          Report Series, 42. Geneva: World Health Organization.

United States, Department of Commerce, Bureau of the Census.
  1971   The American Almanac. New York: Grosset & Dunlap.
United States, National Bureau of Standards.
  1953   Tables of Normal Probability Functions. Applied Mathematics Series, No. 35. Washington, D. C.: Government Printing Office.
Unwin, Joseph D.
  1934   Sex and Culture. London: Oxford University Press.
Vaillant, G. C.
  1950   The Aztecs of Mexico. Harmondsworth, Middlesex: Penguin.
Van Doren,Carl.
  1965   The Great Rehearsal. New York: Time. First printed 1948.
Van Gennep, Arnold.
  1960   The Rites of Passage. Monika B. Vizedom and Gabrielle L. Caffee, translators. Chicago: University of Chicago Press.
Vassiliou, George; and Vassiliou, Vasso G.
  1982   Promoting Psychosocial Functioning and Preventing Malfunctioning. Paediatrician, 11: 90-98.
Wade, M. J.
  1980   Kin Selection: Its Components. Science, 210 (4470): 665-667.
Wallace, Harold E. R.; and Whyte, Marion B. H.
  1959   Natural History of the Psychoneuroses. British Medical Journal, 1: 144-148.
Waller, Julian.
  1965   Alcoholic Beverages—Use and Misuse—as a Contributing Factor in Motor Vehicle Accidents. IN: Alcohol and Alcohol Injury: Conference Proceedings. U.S. Department of Health, Education and Welfare. Washington, D. C.: Government Printing Office. pp. 27-34.
Wallerstein, Judith S.; and Kelly, Joan B.
  1977   Divorce Counseling: A Community Service for Families in the Midst of Divorce. American Journal of Orthopsychiatry, 47: 4-22.
Wallerstein, Judith S.; and Kelly, Joan B.
  1976   The Effects of Parental Divorce: Experiences of the Child in Later Latency. American Journal of Orthopsychiatry, 46: 256-260.
Wallerstein, Judith S.; and Kelly, Joan B.
  1975   The Effects of Parental Divorce. Journal of American Academy of Child Psychiatry, 14: 600-616.
Wallerstein, Judith S.; and Kelly, Joan B.
  1974   The Effects of Parental Divorce: The Adolescent Experience. IN: The Child and His Family, Vol. 3. E. Anthony and C. Koupernik, editors. New York: John Wiley.
Warner, W. Lloyd.
  1964   Black Civilization: A Study of an Australian Tribe. New York: Harper Torchbooks. First printed 1937.
Washburn, Sherwood L., editor.
  1961   Social Life of Early Man. Viking Fund Publications in Anthropology, No. 31. New York: Wenner-Gren.
Washburn, Sherwood L.; and Lancaster, C. S.
  1968   The Evolution of Hunting. IN: Man the Hunter. Richard B. Lee and Irven DeVore, editors. Chicago: Aldine. pp. 293-303.
Webb, Eugene J.; Campbell, Donald T.; Schwartz, Richard D.; and Sechrest, Lee.
  1966   Unobtrusive Measures: Nonreactive Research in the Social Sciences. Chicago: Rand McNally.
Webber, Irving L.; Coombs, David W.; and Hollingsworth, J. Selwyn.
  1974   Variations in Value Orientations by Age in a Developing Society. Journal of Genontology, 29: 676-683.
Wellington, Duke of.
  1960   The Penguin Dictionary of Quotations. J. M. and M. J. Cohen, editors. Harmondsworth, Middlesex: Penguin Books. p. 412.
White, Douglas R.; Burton, Michael L.; and Brudner, Lilyan A.
  1977   Entailment Theory and Method: A Cross-Cultural Analysis of the Sexual Division of Labor. Behavior Science Research, 12: 1-23.

Whiting, John W. M.
    1964   The Effects of Climate on Certain Cultural Practices. IN: Explorations in Cultural An-
           thropology: Essays in Honor of George Peter Murdock. Ward H. Goodenough, editor.
           New York: McGraw-Hill. pp. 511-544.
Whiting, John W. M.
    1961   Socialization Process and Personality. IN: Psychological Anthropology: Approaches to
           Culture and Personality. Francis L. K. Hsu, editor. Homewood, Ill.: Dorsey.
Whiting, John W. M.; and Child, Irvin L.
    1953   Child Training and Personality: A Cross-Cultural Study. New Haven, Conn.: Yale Univ-
           sity Press.
Whiting, John W. M.; Kluckhohn, Richard; and Anthony, Albert S.
    1958   The Function of Male Initiation Ceremonies at Puberty. IN: Readings in Social Psy-
           chology. 3rd. ed. Eleanor E. Maccoby, Theodore M. Newcomb, and Eugene L. Hartley,
           editors. New York: Holt, Rinehart, & Winston. pp. 359-370.
Whiting, John W. M.; and Whiting, Beatrice B.
    1975   Aloofness and Intimacy of Husbands and Wives: A Cross-Cultural Study. Ethos, 3: 183-
           207.
Whitt, Hugh P.; Gordon, Charles C.; and Hofley, John R.
    1972   Religion, Economic Development and Lethal Aggression. American Sociological Review,
           37: 193-201.
Whitten, Norman E.; and Wolfe, Alvin W.
    1973   Network Analysis. IN: Handbook of Social and Cultural Anthropology. John J. Honig-
           mann, editor. Chicago: Rand McNally. pp. 717-746.
Whyte, Martin King.
    1978   The Status of Women in Preindustrial Societies. Princeton, N.J.: Princeton University
           Press.
Wilcoxon, Frank.
    1949   Some Rapid Approximate Statistical Procedures. New York: American Cyanamid Co.
Williams, Kenneth P.
    1949   Lincoln Finds a General. New York: Macmillan.
Williams, Neville.
    1967   Elizabeth I, Queen of England. London: Sphere.
Williams, Thomas Rhys.
    1972   Introduction to Socialization: Human Culture Transmitted. St. Louis.: C. V. Mosby.
Williamson, Nancy E.
    1976   Sons or Daughters: A Cross-Cultural Study of Parental Preferences. Beverly Hills, Calif.:
           Sage.
Wilson, David J.
    1981   Of Maize and Men: A Critique of the Maritime Hypothesis of State Origins on the Coast of
           Peru. American Anthropologist, 83: 93-120.
Wilson, Edward, O.
    1975   Sociobiology: The New Synthesis. Cambridge, Mass.: Harvard University Press.
Wilson, G. M.
    1960   Homicide and Suicide among the Joluo of Kenya. IN: African Homicide and Suicide. Paul
           Bohannan, editor. Princeton, N.J.: Princeton University Press. pp. 179-213.
Winch, Robert E.
    1971   The Modern Family. 3rd. ed. New York: Holt, Rinehart & Winston.
Wisse, Jakob.
    1933   Selbstmord und Todesfurcht bei den Naturvölkern. Zutphen: Thieme.
Witkowski, Stanley.
    1978   Ethnographic Field Work: Optimal versus Non-Optimal Conditions. Behavior Science
           Research, 13: 245-254.
Wolfenden, Hugh.
    1954   Population Statistics and Their Compilation. Chicago: University of Chicago Press.
Wolff, P. H.
    1973   Vasomoter Sensitivity to Alcohol in Diverse Mongoloid Populations. American Journal of
           Human Genetics, 25: 193-199.
Wolff, P. H.
    1972   Ethnic Differences in Alcohol Sensitivity. Science (4020), 175: 449-450.

Wolin, Steven J.; Bennett, Linda A.; Noonan, Denise L.; and Teitelbaum, Martha A.
  1980 Disrupted Family Rituals: A Factor in the Intergenerational Transmission of Alcoholism. Journal of Studies on Alcohol, 41: 199-214.
Woodruff, Diana S.
  1978 Sex Is a Factor in Longevity. Buffalo Courier Express, March 13. p. 7.
Wotton, Sir Henry.
  1900 Upon the Death of Sir Albert Morton's Wife. IN: The Oxford Book of English Verse. Arthur Quiller-Couch, editor. Oxford: Oxford University Press. p. 174.
Wright, Quincy.
  1942 A Study of War. 2. Vols. Chicago: University of Chicago Press.
Yablokov, A. V.
  1974 Variability of Mammals. Jayant Honmode, translator; L. Van Allen, editor. Springfield, VA: National Technical Information Service. TT71-58007.
Young, Frank.
  1965 Initiation Ceremonies: A Cross-Cultural Study of Status Dramatization. Indianapolis: Bobbs-Merrill.
Zavalloni, Marisa.
  1980 Values. IN: Handbook of Cross-Cultural Psychology, Vol. 5. Harry C. Triandis and Richard W. Brislin, editors. Boston: Allyn & Bacon. pp. 73-120.
Zborowski, Mark; and Herzog, Elizabeth.
  1952 Life Is with People. New York: International Universities Press.
Zelman, Elizabeth C.
  1977 Reproductive Ritual and Power. American Ethnologist, 4: 714-733.
Zelman, Elizabeth C.
  1974 Women's Rights and Women's Rites: A Cross-Cultural Study of Womanpower and Reproductive Ritual. Ph.D. Dissertation, University of Michigan. Ann Arbor: University Microfilms No. 75-859.
Zern, David.
  1970 The Influence of Certain Child-Rearing Factors upon the Development of a Structured and Salient Sense of Time. Genetic Psychology Monographs, 81: 197-254.
Zern, David.
  1969 The Relevance of Family Cohesiveness as a Determinant of Premarital Sexual Behavior in a Cross-Cultural Sample. Journal of Social Psychology, 78: 3-9.
Zilboorg, Gregory.
  1937 Considerations on Suicide, with Particular Reference to the Young. American Journal of Orthopsychiatry, 7: 15-31.
Zimmerman, Carle C.; and Cervantes, Lucius F.
  1960 Successful American Families. New York: Pageant Press.
Zimmerman, Carle C.; and Cervantes, Lucius F.
  1956 Marriage and the Family. A Text for Moderns. Chicago: Henry Regnery. pp. 91-118.

Acknowledgments

My thanks are due to many helpers:

First of all, to my university, the State University of New York at Buffalo, whose administrators provided the time and facilities with which to do the work. To Presidents Robert Ketter and Steven Sample. To Executive Vice-President Albert Somit. To Academic Vice-Presidents Ronald Bunn and Robert Rossberg. To Deans Myles Slatin, Ira Cohen, Edwin Hollander, Arthur Butler, Kenneth Levy, and John Naylor. To Anthropology Department Chairmen William Stein, Marvin Opler, Erwin Johnson, Frederick Gearing, and A. T. Steegmann.

To the staff of the Lockwood Library at the university, who in eleven years of work as far as I can recall never once failed to fetch a needed title—even if they had to pursue it all over North America or even Western Europe.

To Celia Ehrlich, Susan Horan, Enid Margolis, Frada Naroll, and Maud Naroll, who helped with the research—especially Enid and Susan. To Eloise Benzel, who typed most of the manuscript. To Frada Naroll, who copy-edited it in Buffalo, with help from Enid.

This book has profited immensely from the critiques of those who read the preliminary draft of the manuscript. In response to their suggestions, I revised at least a third of the book. Sara Miller McCune and Mitch Allen at Sage Publications each went over the preliminary draft and offered scores of persuasive comments: Sage is the sixth publishing house I have dealt with and has given me more help on this book than all five of the others put together on the preceding ones. Stephanie Feeney and Lou Marano likewise read the preliminary draft and did not spare me copious frank emendations—and Robert Dentan likewise criticized about three-quarters of it.

For important substantive suggestions, I wish also to thank Kenneth Boulding, Barton Brown, Donald T. Campbell, William Dickens, Bess Kaufman, Robert O. Lagace, Murray Levine, George McCune, Maud Naroll, James M. Schaefer, Richard D. Schwartz, and Marshall Segall.

For helpful information, I have to thank Terry Bellicha, Ronald Cohen, Paul Diesing, David Gissen, Jack Goody, George Hourani, and Timothy J. O'Leary.

Our Scandinavian trip, described in Chapter 3, left us heavily indebted to many kind friends. For guidance to the right people, we are grateful to our friends Lester and Kirsten Milbrath, to Mrs. Bearit Hoie, and to Henry Valens. For sharing generously much wisdom and deep knowledge about Scandinavian vital statistics and the ways of life that underlie them, we were unstintingly helped by Konsulat Lita Holen of Norway's Central Bureau of Statistics; by Professor Nils Retterstøl, Director of Gaustad Hospital; by Prosektor Bjørnar Olaisen, of the Institute of Forensic Medicine at Oslo's Rikshospitalet; by Dr. Anna-Marie Bolander, of Sweden's Statistical Central Office; by Professors Lennart Levi and Aubrey Kagan, of the Stress Research Institute, Karolinska Institut, Stockholm; and Dr. Jan Lindberg, of Stockholm's National Forensic Medicine station. Other courtesies were shown us by Erik B. Tvedt, Dr. Ivan Breenhovd, Dr. Per Haga, Dr. Ruth Ettlinger, Ida Nestvall, and Margereta Mattson. With all this help, the book should be free from error or oversight. But alas, it is very far from that, and for its many failings, there is no one to blame but its author.

The Institute for Cross-Cultural Studies furnished and granted permission to publish the following tables—all copyrighted by the Institute for Cross-Cultural Studies, 4695 Main Street, Amherst, NY 14226. The programming work was done for the Institute by Hilary Shreter and the data input by Celia Ehrlich.

3.2	Unexplained Deaths Scoreboard
7.1	Reported Mental Illness Rate Scoreboard
8.2	Alcohol Consumption Scoreboard
9.3	Suicide Scoreboard
11.4	Child Murder Scoreboard
12.2	Youth Murder Ratio Scoreboard
12.3	Youth Suicide Ratio Scoreboard
13.2	Elders' Suicide Ratio Scoreboard
13.3	Elders' Murder Ratio Scoreboard
14.6	Sex Illiteracy Ratio Scoreboard
14.7	Sex Managerial Ratio Scoreboard
14.8	Sex Earnings Ratio Scoreboard
14.9	Sex Suicide Ratio Scoreboard
14.10	Sex Homicide Ratio Scoreboard
14.11	Sex Accident Ratio Scoreboard
15.8	Extramarital Births Scoreboard
15.9	Divorce Scoreboard
16.2	Frequency of Wars Scoreboard (1816-1965)
16.3	Defense Budgets Scoreboard (1975)
16.4	Civil Disorder Index Scoreboard
16.5	Murder Rate Scoreboard
16.6	Juvenile Criminal Ratio Scoreboard

The data in Table 8.2 are taken by permission from M. Keller and C. Gurioli, *Statistics on Consumption of Alcohol and on Alcoholism*, 1976 edition. Copyright by Journal of Studies on Alcohol, Inc., New Brunswick, NJ 08903.

Figure 10.1, Weak Families Are Linked to Suicide, Homicide, and Crime, is reprinted by permission from "Abbildung 7: Gegenueberstellung eines Indikators fuer sozialpsychologische Belastung . . . ," A. Fuchs, C. Gaspari, and Johan Millendorfer, *Makropsychologische Untersuchung der Familie in*

Name Index

Subject Index

About the Author

RAOUL NAROLL is Distinguished Professor of Anthropology at the State University of New York, Buffalo, and is a world-renowned figure in the field of cultural anthropology. A pioneer in cross-cultural, cross-national, and cross-historical surveys, he has led the development of research in these areas through his eight-year term as President of the Human Relations Area Files and as editor of the HRAF journal, *Behavior Science Research*. Naroll is co-editor of the *Handbook of Method in Cultural Anthropology* (1970), as well as author of several other books and over 100 published articles, reviews, and monographs. A Ph.D. from the University of California at Los Angeles, he has also taught on the faculties of Northwestern University and California State University at Northridge. His field research sites include Germany, Austria, Switzerland, and Greece. The present volume, *The Moral Order*, is the first book of a projected series on the human situation that will describe the progress of mankind toward a stable world political and social order.

Praise for Agile Java

"The most practical, productive, and enjoyable book on programming I've read. Results Driven."

Steve Bartolin, President and CEO, The Broadmoor

"At long last a book that integrates solid beginning lessons in both Java and Test-Driven Development! I know most of the software development apprentices that go through my facility could have avoided the pain of unlearning years of ad hoc programming habits if Jeff's book had been available when they first learned Java."

Steven A. Gordon, Ph.D., Manager,
Arizona State University Software Factory (http://sf.asu.edu/)

"Jeff draws on his exceptionally deep expertise in Java and Agile processes to show us a remarkably powerful approach for building Java programs that are clean, well-structured, and thoroughly tested. Highly recommended! "

Paul Hodgetts, Founder and CEO, Agile Logic, Inc.

"A great way to learn Java. *Agile Java* takes you through not only the basics of the Java language, setup, and tools, but also provides excellent instruction on concepts of test-driven development, refactoring, and Object-Oriented programming. This book is required reading for our engineering team. "

Andrew Masters, President and CIO, 5two8, Inc.

"*Agile Java* is a must-read for anyone developing Java applications. The text contains innovative and insightful ideas on how to write high-quality, extensible Java applications faster and more efficiently than traditional methods. Beginner and experienced developers will learn a tremendous amount from the concepts taught in this book. "

Bret McInnis, Vice President eBusiness Technologies, Corporate Express

Agile Java

Robert C. Martin Series

The mission of this series is to improve the state of the art of software craftsmanship. The books in this series are technical, pragmatic, and substantial. The authors are highly experienced craftsmen and professionals dedicated to writing about what actually works in practice, as opposed to what might work in theory. You will read about what the author has done, not what he thinks you should do. If the book is about programming, there will be lots of code. If the book is about managing, there will be lots of case studies from real projects.

These are the books that all serious practitioners will have on their bookshelves. These are the books that will be remembered for making a difference and for guiding professionals to become true craftsman.

Agile Java™: Crafting Code with Test-Driven Development
Jeff Langr

Working Effectively with Legacy Code
Michael Feathers

UML For Java Programmers
Robert C. Martin

Agile Software Development: Principles, Patterns, and Practices
Robert C. Martin

Agile Software Development with SCRUM
Ken Schwaber and Mike Beedle

Extreme Software Engineering: A Hands on Approach
Daniel H. Steinberg and Daniel W. Palmer

Agile Java
Crafting Code with
Test-Driven Development

Jeff Langr

PRENTICE
HALL
PTR

Prentice Hall Professional Technical Reference

Upper Saddle River, NJ • Boston• Indianapolis • San Francisco
New York • Toronto • Montreal • London • Munich • Paris • Madrid
Capetown • Sydney • Tokyo • Singapore • Mexico City

The publisher offers excellent discounts on this book when ordered in quantity for bulk purchases or special sales, which may include electronic versions and/or custom covers and content particular to your business, training goals, marketing focus, and branding interests. For more information, please contact:

U. S. Corporate and Government Sales
(800) 382-3419
corpsales@pearsontechgroup.com

For sales outside the U. S., please contact:

International Sales
international@pearsoned.com

Visit us on the Web: www.phptr.com

Library of Congress Cataloging Number: 2004114916

ISBN 0-13-148239-4
This product is printed digitally on demand.
First printing, February 2005

In memory of Edmund Langr and Heather Mooney

Contents

About the Author

Jeff Langr is an independent software consultant with a score and more years of development experience. He provides expertise to customers in software development, design, and agile processes through his company Langr Software Solutions (*http://www.LangrSoft.com*).

Langr worked for Uncle Bob Martin for two years at the esteemed Object Mentor, recognized as the premier XP consulting firm. He consulted at and has been employed by several Fortune 500 companies, as well as the obligatory failed dot-com.

Langr's background includes teaching a university course on Java. He has successfully taught hundreds of other professional students in Java, TDD, XP, and object-oriented development. Langr has spoken about software development numerous times at national conferences and local user group meetings.

Langr wrote the Prentice Hall book *Essential Java Style* (Langr2000), a guide for building quality Java code. Five years later you can still find blog entries of people who swear by their dog-eared copy. Several of Langr's articles on Java and TDD have appeared in *Software Development, C/C++ Users Journal,* and various online magazine sites including Developer.com. You can find links to these and other articles at *http://www.langrsoft.com/resources .html.*

He would like to add that he lives for software development, and hopes his love for the craft of building code comes through in Agile Java. Langr resides in Colorado Springs with his wife Kathy and his children Katie, Tim, and Anna.

Foreword

Jeff Langr has written a very interesting Java book in *Agile Java: Crafting Code with Test-Driven Development*. Its purpose is to teach new programmers the Java language, and to do so in the context of the best development approach that he and I know—namely Test-Driven Development (TDD). It's an undertaking of great potential value, and Jeff has done it nicely. It's my pleasure to provide this foreword and to recommend this book.

Agile Java isn't just for rank beginners. It's also a good book for bringing experienced programmers new to the Java language up to speed. It won't replace a certification manual or one of those huge books of "Everything Java." That's not its point. The point of *Agile Java* is to get you up to speed. Better yet, you come up to speed using TDD, which will serve you well in future learning and in your day-to-day work.

The book starts right off with object-oriented concepts and ideas. It helps if you know a bit about objects when you step in, but if you don't, hang on and you should pick up the basic ideas as you go along. Furthermore, every step of the way you'll be using the Test-Driven Development technique. If you haven't tried TDD, it may seem a bit odd at the beginning, but if you're like most of us who have given it a fair try, it will become a frequently-used tool in your kit.

If you already have Java and JUnit set up on your machine, dig right in. If not, be sure to use the "Setting Up" chapter to get your system correctly configured before moving on to the real examples. Once you can compile and run a simple Java program on your machine, you're ready to go.

Jeff asks you to type in the tests and example code, and I would echo that request. The TDD discipline is one that is learned by doing and practicing, not just by reading. You need to develop your own sense of the rhythm of development. Besides, typing in the examples from any programming book is the best way to learn what it has to offer.

In *Agile Java*, Jeff helps you build pieces of two applications. One of these relates to a student information system, the other focuses on playing chess. By the time you have worked through all the chapters, Jeff has introduced you to the basics of Java. Perhaps more importantly, you have met some of the most important deep capabilities, including interfaces, polymorphism, mock objects, reflection, multi-threading, and generics.

I found that Lesson 10, regarding the mathematical features of Java, particularly brought out the way I like to use tests as part of my learning of a new feature of a language or library. It's easy to read about something like BigDecimal and think, "I get it." For a while, I might even really get it. But when I encode my learning as tests, two things happen: First, I learn things about the topic that I would have missed if just reading about it. Writing the code pounds ideas into my thick head a bit better than just reading. Second, the tests record what I've learned as well as my thought process as I learned it. Because I've developed the habit of saving all my test cases, I can refer back to them and quickly refresh my memory. Often I'll even put a book and page reference into the tests as a comment, in case I want to go back later and dig out more.

Lesson 11, regarding I/O, includes a nice example of something I'm not very familiar with. Since I don't work in Java much, and most of the languages I commonly use don't have an equivalent, I'm not familiar with nested classes. Jeff gives a good example of when we would be well-advised to use nested classes, and shows how to use and test them.

As I write this foreword, I'm really getting into the book, because Jeff is taking me where I've not gone before. I like that. Lesson 12 is about Mock Objects, and the first example is one that we agile software developers encounter often: How can we deal in our incremental development with an external API that is fairly well defined but isn't available yet? Jeff shows us how to do this by defining the interface—from the documentation if necessary—and then by building a Mock Object that represents our understanding of what the API will do when we finally get it. Writing tests against our Mock Object gives us tests that we can use to ensure that the API does what we expect when we finally get the real code. An excellent addition to your bag of tricks!

Jeff is an educator, and a darn good one. Jeff wants us to think, and to work! He knows that if you and I are ready to learn, we have to practice: we have to do the work. His chapters have exercises. We are well-advised to think about all of them, and to do the ones that cover topics we aren't familiar with. That's how we'll really hammer these ideas into our heads. Read and study his examples, type them in to drill them into your mind, and then follow his lead as you work the interesting examples. You'll be glad you did.

Agile Java: Crafting Code with Test-Driven Development offers you at least three benefits: You'll learn things about Java that you probably didn't know, even if you're not an absolute beginner. You'll learn how to use test-driven development in a wide range of cases, including some in which you'd probably find difficult to invent on your own. And, through building up your skill, you'll add this valuable technique to your professional bag of tricks.

I enjoyed the book and found it valuable. I think you will, too. Enjoy!

Ron Jeffries
www.XProgramming.com
Pinckney, Michigan
November 2, 2004

Acknowledgments

Many thanks to all of the fantastic developers and learning-to-be developers for their insightful comments on *Agile Java*.

Thanks to Bob Martin of Object Mentor for being a great mentor, ex-employer, and book series editor! Bob's review early on helped guide *Agile Java* to a more concise implementation. I'm exceptionally proud to have my book in the Robert Martin Series. I'm also very honored to have Ron Jeffries contribute kind words on the book.

Jeff Bay of ThoughtWorks did an outstanding job and gave me just what I asked for—brutally honest feedback. Jeff is responsible for providing the stellar exercises at the end of each section.

Many thanks to Steve Arneil, Dave Astels, Tim Camper, Dan D'Eramo, Michael Feathers, Paul Holser, Jerry Jackson, Ron Jeffries, Bob Koss, Torri Lopez, Andrew Masters, Chris Mathews, Jim Newkirk, Wendy and David Peterson, Michael Rachow, Jason Rohman, Tito Velez, and Jeroen Wenting. These reviewers provided extensive feedback on the book.

Special thanks to Paul Petralia and his crew at Prentice Hall for making my experience as smooth as possible.

Once again I thank my sister Christine Langr for providing the cover photo and helping me work through various design questions.

Thanks also go to Jim Condit of San Antonio for the Nerf play and use of his abode, and to my wife Kathy Langr for providing examples (and for again putting up with me throughout the arduous writing process).

Introduction

I am a software craftsman.[1] I have spent much of my software development career trying to quickly build solutions to problems. At the same time I have tried to ensure that my solutions demonstrate carefully crafted code. I strive for perfection in code, yet I know that it is unattainable, particularly with the constant pressure from business to get product out the door. I take modest pride in the code I build daily, yet when I look at the code I wrote the day before, I wonder, "What the heck was I thinking?" This is what keeps the craft challenging to me—the constant desire to figure out how to do things a little better the next time, and with a little less pain than this time.

Agile Java represents a successful approach to learning and mastering Java development. It is based on the way I have learned to best teach programming and to learn new programming languages myself: Using test-driven development (TDD), a technique that introduces a large amount of low-level feedback. This feedback allows you to more quickly see the results of your actions. Using TDD, you will learn how to craft Java code to produce solid object-oriented designs and highly maintainable high-quality systems.

I have used TDD in production systems for over four years and am still amazed at what it does for me. It has improved the quality of my code, it has taught me new things each week, it has made me more productive. I have also created and taught language courses using TDD, both at my own company and at Object Mentor (which continues to teach their language courses with this approach).

Prior to learning TDD, I spent more than fifteen years learning, developing in, and teaching languages the "classic" way—without using tests to drive the development. The student builds and executes example code. The student obtains feedback on what the code is teaching by viewing the output from code execution. While this is a perfectly valid approach, my anecdotal experience is that using it results in less-than-ideal retention of language details.

[1] See [McBreen2000].

1

In contrast, the high volume of rapid feedback in TDD constantly reinforces correct coding and quickly points out incorrect coding. The classic code-run-and-observe approach provides feedback, but at a much slower rate. Unfortunately, it is currently the predominant method of teaching programming.

Others have attempted more innovative approaches to teaching. In the 1990s, Adele Goldberg created a product known as LearningWorks designed for teaching younger students. It allowed a user to directly manipulate visual objects by dynamically executing bits of code. The user saw immediate results from their actions. A recent Java training tool uses a similar approach. It allows the student to execute bits of code to produce visual effects on "live" objects.

The problem with approaches like these is that they are bound to the learning environment. Once you complete the training, you must still learn how to construct your own system from the ground up, without the use of these constrained tools. By using TDD as the driver for learning, you are taught an unbounded technique that you can continue to use in your professional software development career.

Agile Java takes the most object-oriented approach feasible. Part of the difficulty in learning Java is the "bootstrapping" involved. What is the minimum you must learn in order to be able to write classes of some substance?

Most books start by teaching you the prototypical first Java program—the "hello world" application. But it is quite a mouthful: `class Hello { public static void main(String[] args) { System.out.println("hello world"); } }`. This brief program contains at least a dozen concepts that you must ultimately learn. Worse, out of those dozen concepts, at least three are nonobject-oriented concepts that you are better off learning *much* later.

In this book, you will learn the right way to code from the start and come back to fully understand "hello world" later in the book.[2] Using TDD, you will be able to write good object-oriented code immediately. You'll still have a big initial hurdle to get over, but this approach keeps you from having to first understand not-very-object-oriented concepts such as static methods and arrays. You will learn all core Java concepts in due time, but your initial emphasis is on objects.

Agile Java presents a cleaner break from the old way of doing things. It allows you to pretend for a while that there was never a language called C, the syntactical basis for Java that has been around for 30 years. While C is a

---

[2]Don't fret, though: You'll actually start with the "hello world" application in order to ensure you can compile and execute Java code. But you won't have to understand it all until later.

great language, its imprint on Java left a quite a few constructs that can distract you from building good object-oriented systems. Using Agile Java, you can learn the right way of doing things before having to understand these legacies of the Java language.

Who Is This Book For?

I designed Agile Java for new programmers who want to learn Java as their first language. The book can also be effective for programmers familiar with TDD but new to Java, or vice versa. Experienced Java developers may find that going through Agile Java presents them with a new, and I hope better, way of approaching things.

This edition of Agile Java covers Java 2 Standard Edition (J2SE) version 5.0.

Sun has made available dozens of class libraries, or APIs (application programming interfaces), that enhance the core Java language. Some examples: JMS (Java Messaging Service) provides a definition for standard messaging-based solutions. EJBs (Enterprise Java Beans) provide a means of building component-based software for large enterprise solutions. JDBC (Java Data-Base Connectivity) supplies a standard interface for interacting with relational databases. About a dozen of the advanced APIs are collectively known as J2EE (Java 2 Enterprise Edition). Many of the APIs require entire books for comprehensive coverage. There are dozens of books on J2EE.

This book covers only a few of the additional APIs at an introductory level. Technologies that are used pervasively in the majority of enterprise applications, such as logging, JDBC, and Swing, are presented in Agile Java. Some of the information (for example, logging) will teach you all you need to know for most applications. Other lessons (for example, Swing and JDBC) will teach you a basic understanding of the technology. These lessons will provide you with enough to get started and will tell you where to go for more information.

If you are developing mobile applications, you will be using J2ME (Java 2 Micro Edition). J2ME is a version of Java geared toward environments with limited resources, such as cell phones. J2ME has some significant limitations compared to J2SE. This book does not discuss anything specific with respect to J2ME. However, most of the core techniques and concepts of Java development are applicable to the J2ME environment.

In order to use any of these add-on Java technologies, you must first understand the core language and libraries provided in J2SE. Agile Java will help you build that knowledge.

What This Book Is Not

Agile Java is not an exhaustive treatise on every aspect of the Java language. It instead provides an agile approach to learning the language. Rather than giving you all the fish, I teach you how to fish and sometimes where to find the fish. Agile Java will teach you the majority of the core language concepts. Indeed, upon completing the core fifteen lessons, you will be able to produce quality production Java code. However, there are bound to be a few esoteric language features and nuances that I do not cover in the book.

One way to become familiar with the dusty corners of the language is to peruse the Java Language Specification (JLS). The second edition of the language specification is available at *http://java.sun.com/docs/books/jls*. This edition covers versions of Java up to but not including J2SE 5.0. A third edition of the JLS is in the works at the time I write this. You can find a maintenance review version at *http://java.sun.com/docs/books/jls/java_language-3_0-mr-spec.zip*.

For additional understanding of what is in the Java API library, the Java API documentation and actual source code is the best place to go.

Agile Java is not a certification study guide. It will not prepare you for a certification exam. A good book on certification will teach you how to take a test. It will also teach you how to decipher (deliberately) poorly written code that shouldn't have been written that way in the first place. Agile Java will teach you instead how to write professional Java code.

Agile Java doesn't attempt to coddle you. Learning to program is a significant challenge. Programming involves thinking and solving problems—it is not an easy undertaking for idiots or dummies. I've tried to avoid insulting your intelligence in this book. That being said, I have tried to make Agile Java an enjoyable, easy read. It's a conversation between you and me, much like the conversations you will continue to have in your professional development career. It's also a conversation between you and your computer.

TDD Disclaimer

Some developers experienced in TDD will note stylistic differences between their approach and my approach(es) in Agile Java. There are many ways to do TDD. None of these techniques are perfect or ordained as the absolute right way to do things. Do whatever works best for you. Do what makes the most sense, as long as it doesn't violate the basic tenets set forth in Agile Java.

Readers will also find areas in which the code could be improved.[3] Even as a beginning developer, you no doubt will encounter code in Agile Java that you don't like. Let me know. Send in your suggestions, and I may incorporate them in the next edition. And fix your own implementations. *You can improve almost any code or technique.* Do!

After the first lesson in Agile Java, the tests appear wholesale, as if they were coded in one fell swoop. This is not the case: Each test was built assertion by assertion, in much smaller increments than the book can afford to present. Keep this in mind when writing your own code—one of the most important aspects of TDD is taking small, small steps with constant feedback. And when I say small, I mean small! If you think you're taking small steps, try taking even smaller steps.

How to Use This Book

The core of Agile Java is fifteen lessons of about 30 pages each. You will start with baby steps in Java, TDD, and OO. You will finish with a strong foundation for professional Java development.

The core lessons are sequential. You should start at Lesson 1 and complete each lesson before proceeding to the next. Once you have completed the core lessons, you should have a solid understanding of how to build robust Java code.

If you haven't completed the fifteen core lessons, you should not assume you know how to write good Java code! (Even if you have completed the lessons, you're not an expert . . . yet.) Each lesson builds upon the previous lessons. If you stop short of completing the lessons, your lack of full understanding may lead you to construct poor code.

Each lesson starts with a brief overview of the topics to be discussed. The remainder of the lesson is a narrative. I describe each language feature in the text, specified by test code. I demonstrate each feature in a corresponding code implementation. I have interspersed discussions of TDD technique, OO principles, and good development practices in these lessons.

I've supplied three additional lessons to cover a few more Java topics. Two of the lessons present an introduction to Java's tool for user interface development, Swing. These two lessons will provide you with enough information to begin building robust user interface applications in Java. But the bigger in-

---

[3]A constant developer pair would have helped.

tent is to give you some ideas for how to build them using TDD. The third
additional lesson presents an overview for a number of Java topics, things
that most Java developers will want to know.

For the most effective learning experience, you should follow along with
the lessons by entering and executing each bit of test and implementation
code as I present it. While the code is available for downloading (see the next
paragraph), I highly recommend that you type each bit of code yourself. Part
of doing TDD correctly is getting a good understanding of the rhythm involved in going back and forth between the tests and the code. If you just
download the code and execute it, you're not going to learn nearly as much.
The tactile response of the keyboard seems to impart a lot of learning.

However, who am I to make you work in a certain way? You may choose
to download the code from *http://www.LangrSoft.com/agileJava/code*. I've
organized this code by lesson. I have made available the code that is the result of working each lesson—*in the state it exists by the end of the lesson.*
This will make it easier for you to pick up at any point, particularly since
many of the examples carry through to subsequent lessons.

Exercises

Each of the fifteen core lessons in Agile Java has you build bits and pieces of
a student information system for a university. I chose this single common
theme to help demonstrate how you can incrementally build upon and extend existing code. Each lesson also finishes with a series of exercises. Instead
of the student information system, the bulk of the exercises, provided by Jeff
Bay, have you build bits and pieces of a chess application.

Some of the exercises are involved and quite challenging. But I highly recommend that you do every one. The exercises are where the real learning
starts—you're figuring out how to solve problems using Java, without my
help. Doing all of the exercises will give you a second opportunity to let each
lesson sink in.

Conventions Used in This Book

Code flows with the text, in order to make it part of the conversation. If I
refer to code "below," it's the next piece of code as you continue to read;
code "above" appears in recent prior text.

Code (below) appears in a non-proportional font:

```
this.isCode();
```

Smaller portions of a large block of code may appear in **bold**. The **bold** indicates either new code that relates to the current example or code that has particular relevance:

```
class B {
  public void thisIsANewMethod() {
  }
}
```

Code appearing directly in text, such as `this.someCode()`, also appears in a non-proportional font. However, the names of classes, such as CourseSession, appear in the same font as the rest of the text.

I often use ellipses in the code samples. The ellipses indicate code that already exists in a class but is not relevant to the current discussion or example:

```
class C {
  private String interestingVariable;
  ...
  private void someInterestingMethod() {
  }
  ...
```

The dialog in Agile Java alternates between expressing ideas in English and expressing them in code. For example, I may refer to the need to cancel a payroll check or I might choose to say that you should send the `cancel` message to the PayrollCheck object. The idea is to help you start making the necessary connections between understanding requirements and expressing them in code.

Class names are by convention singular nouns, such as Customer. "You use the Customer class to create multiple Customer objects." In the name of readability, I will sometimes refer to these Customer objects using the plural of the class name: "The collection contains all of the Customers loaded from the file system."

New terms initially appear in *italics*. Most of these terms appear in the Glossary (Appendix A).

Throughout Agile Java, you will take specifications and translate them into Java code. In the tradition of agile processes, I present these specifications using informal English. They are requirements, also known as *stories*. A story is a promise for more conversation. Often you will need to continue a dialog with the presenter of the story (sometimes known as the customer) in order to obtain further details on a story. In the case of Agile Java, if a story isn't making sense, try reading a bit further. Read the corresponding tests to see how they interpret the story.

 I have highlighted stories throughout Agile Java with a "story-telling" icon. The icon emphasizes the oral informality of stories.

Your best path to learning the craft of programming is to work with an experienced practitioner. You will discover that there are many "secrets" to programming. Some secrets are basic concepts that you must know in order to master the craft. Other secrets represent pitfalls—things to watch out for. You must bridge these challenges, and remember what you learned, to be a successful Java programmer.

 I've marked such critical points with a bridge icon (the bridge is crossing over the pitfalls). Many of these critical points will apply to development in any language, not just Java.

An Agile Overview

This chapter provides a brief introduction to some of the core concepts in the book, including Java, object-oriented programming, and test-driven development. You will get answers to the following questions:

- What is "agile"?

- What is Java?

- What is object-oriented programming?

- Why OO?

- What is an object?

- What are classes?

- Why UML?

- What is inheritance?

- Why test-driven development?

What Is "Agile?"

This book is called Agile Java. "Agile" is a new catchphrase for describing a bunch of related software development *methodologies*. Loosely defined, a methodology is a process for building software. There are many ways to approach constructing software as part of a team; many of these approaches have been formalized into published methodologies. There are dozens of major processes in use; you may have heard the names of some of them: waterfall, RUP (Rational Unified Process), XP (extreme programming), and Scrum.

Methodologies have evolved as we learn more about how to effectively work. Waterfall is an older approach to building software that promotes copious documentation, rigid up-front (i.e., at the start of the project) definitions of requirements and system design, and division of a project into serialized phases. Its name derives from a diagram that shows progress flowing down from one phase to the next.

9

What Is "Agile?"

While waterfall may be appropriate for some efforts, it has some limitations that can cause severe problems on other software development projects. Using a waterfall process means that you are less able to adapt to change as a project progresses. For these reasons, waterfall is sometimes referred to as a *heavyweight* process. It is heavy because it requires considerable baggage and restricts development teams from being able to rapidly respond to change.

In contrast, *agile* processes, a fairly recent phenomena, are *lightweight* processes. When following an agile process, there is less emphasis on written documentation and on having everything finalized up front. Agile processes are designed around accommodating change. XP is probably the most well-known example of an agile process.

RUP is another very well-known process. Technically RUP is a *process framework*: It supplies a catalog of things you can mix and match in order to create your own customized process. Such a RUP *process instance* can straddle the fence between being a heavyweight and an agile process.

When following any kind of process, heavyweight or agile, you must always do the following things when building software:

- analysis: determine what you need to build by gathering and refining requirements for what the software should do

- planning: figure out how long it will take to build the software

- design: determine how to put together what you are building

- coding: construct the software using one or more programming languages

- testing: ensure that what you built works

- deployment: deliver the software to the environment in which it will be executed and used

- documentation: describe the software for various audiences, including end users who need to know how to use the software and developers who need to know how to maintain the software

- review: ensure, through peer consensus, that the software remains maintainable and retains high quality

If you are not doing all of these things, you are *hacking*—producing code with abandon and no consideration for business needs. Some processes such as XP appear not to promote everything in the above list. In reality, they do, but in a different, kind-of-sideways fashion.

I cover little with respect to methodology in this book. You can find shelves of books devoted to learning about methodologies. Most development teams use a hybrid methodology—they take successful techniques from various published methodologies and adapt them to their own needs. Many development shops do not even acknowledge a methodology at all. But even these shops usually follow some sort of unstated process.

This book is about constructing the software. Agile Java is centered on a technique known as test-driven development, or TDD. TDD is not a methodology itself but a practice that you can use as part of virtually any software development process. TDD derives from XP, where it is one of about a dozen required practices. *You do **not** need to do XP in order to do TDD or in order to use this book!*

I do not discuss XP or other methodologies often in this book. I've centered Agile Java on a technique that will allow you to build and mold your code in an agile fashion. You will learn how to accommodate change in your system via TDD. Even if you are using the most rigid process imaginable, you can still use the techniques in Agile Java to construct high-quality Java code.

What Is Java?

When you hear people refer to Java, they often mean the Java language. The Java language allows you to write instructions, or code, that your computer will interpret in order to execute a software *application,* or *program.* Examples of applications are Microsoft Word, Netscape, and the little clock that runs in the corner of your monitor. *Coding,* or *programming,* is the act of writing programs.

Another thing people mean when they refer to Java is the Java *platform.* The term platform usually indicates an underlying operating system, such as Windows or Unix™, on which you can run applications.[1] Java acts as a platform: It not only defines a language but also gives you a complete environment in which to build and execute your programs. The Java platform acts as a layer between your application and the underlying operating system; it is a mini–operating system in itself. This allows you to write code in a single language and execute it on virtually all major operating systems today.

You will download the Java *software development kit* (SDK), which provides you with three main components:

- a *compiler* (javac)

- a virtual machine, or VM (java)

- a *class library*, or *API* (application programming interface)

[1][WhatIs2004].

What Is Java?

The compiler is a program that reads Java *source files*, ensures they contain valid Java code, and produces *class files*. A source file is a text file that contains the code you type. The class files you generate using the compiler contain *byte codes* that represent the code you typed in. Byte codes appear in a format that the VM can rapidly read and interpret.

The VM (or JVM—Java virtual machine) is a program that executes the code within your class files. The term "virtual machine" derives from the fact that it acts as if it were a complete platform, or operating system, from the standpoint of your Java programs. Your code does not make direct calls to the operating system application programming interface (API), as it might if you were programming directly for Windows in a language such as C or C++.

The Numbers Game

The history of Java contains a handful of significant releases. The first public release of Java (in 1996) was known as Java 1.0. Versions 1.1, 1.2, 1.3, and 1.4 followed, separated by roughly one year each. As of version 1.2, Sun renamed the platform from simply Java to Java 2. With the latest release, Sun chose to embark upon a new numbering scheme, presumably to impart the significance of the release. The version you will learn in this book is formally known as Java 2 Standard Edition 5.0. I will use the abbreviated name J2SE 5.0 throughout the book.

Instead, you write code only in the Java language and use only a set of libraries, known as *class libraries*, or APIs, provided as part of the Java SDK. You might see references to the VM as an *interpreter*, since that is its chief responsibility: The VM interprets the needs of your code and dispatches these needs to the underlying operating system as necessary. The VM is also responsible for allocating and controlling any memory that your code needs.

Java is known as an *object-oriented* programming language. The basic premise of an object-oriented programming language is that you can create abstractions of real-world things, or objects, in code. For example, you can create a Java code representation of a calculator that emulates some of the characteristics and behavior of a real-world calculator.

If you have never programmed before, you are in luck: Object-oriented (OO) programming is much easier to learn from scratch than if you have already learned a non-OO programming language like Cobol or C. If you *have* been tainted by a procedural or declarative language, you may want to read this chapter a few times. Expect that learning OO is not easy; expect to spend a few months before the light bulb in your head stays on all the time without blinking.

This chapter explains the basics of object orientation. Conceptually, OO is reasonably straightforward, but it can take some time for the ideas to sink in, particularly without concrete code examples. Hence, this chapter is brief; instead, you will learn the bulk of OO as you learn to code in Java.

Why OO?

Object-oriented programming has been around for quite some time—since the 1960s—but only during the 1990s did it begin to truly take off in terms of acceptance. Much of what we know about how to program well with objects has been discovered in the past decade. The most important thing we have learned is that OO, done properly, can improve your ability to manage and maintain software applications as they mature and grow.

What Is an Object?

An object is a code-based *abstraction* of some relevant concept. If you are building a payroll system, an object could be a programming representation of a check, an employee's rate classification, or a check printer. It could also be an abstraction of an activity, such as a routing process to ensure that employees are directed to the appropriate processing queue. Abstraction is best defined as "amplification of the essential, elimination of the irrelevant."[2]

A check object might contain many details such as check number, payee, and amount. But the payroll system is not interested in things such as the size and color of the check, so you would not represent these things in payroll code. You might consider them for the check printing system.

There is some value to using objects that have real-world relevancy, but you must be careful not to take the real world too far into your code. As an example, a payroll system might have an employee object, containing details such as an employee ID and his salary. You also want to ensure that you can give raises to an employee. A real-world design might suggest that the code for giving raises belongs elsewhere, but in fact the most appropriate solution in an OO system is for the employee object to execute the code to apply a raise. ("What? An employee giving himself a raise??") In Agile Java, you will discover how to make these sorts of design decisions.

[2][Martin2003].

Figure 1 *Sending a Message*

An object-oriented system should be primarily about behavior. The core concept of OO is that objects send messages to each other in order to effect behavior. One object sends a message to another object to tell it to do something. As a real-world example, I send you a message to you by telling you to lock the front door. In an OO system, a security object sends a message to a door controller object, telling it to secure the door it controls (see Figure 1).

The object being sent the message—the door controller in this example—is known as the *receiver*. The receiver decides what to do with the message. You decide to lock the front door by turning the deadbolt. A different person might have chosen to use the latch. In the OO system, the door controller object might have interacted with a hardware device to activate an electromagnetic lock or to cause an electronic deadbolt to eject.

In either case, the sender of the message is interested only in an abstract concept: that the receiver secure the door. The message sender doesn't care how the door is secured; the details of how that happens is something that only the receiver knows. This is a key concept in OO known as *encapsulation*: Objects should hide unnecessary details from other objects in the system.

The fact that different implementations can be dropped into place without the client knowing or caring which one is going to be used represents another very important OO concept known as *polymorphism*. The security system shouldn't know or care whether the door controller is an electromagnetic lock controller or an electronic deadbolt controller. You will learn about polymorphism in greater detail in one of the lessons.

What Are Classes?

There might be five electromagnetic doors in the building where the security system is deployed, all located in different areas. Each door is thus a separate object with a different physical address. However, all doors share the common behavior of needing to be secured, so they all can be classified similarly. A *class* provides a way of defining commonality for a related grouping of objects. It is a template, or blueprint, for constructing new objects.

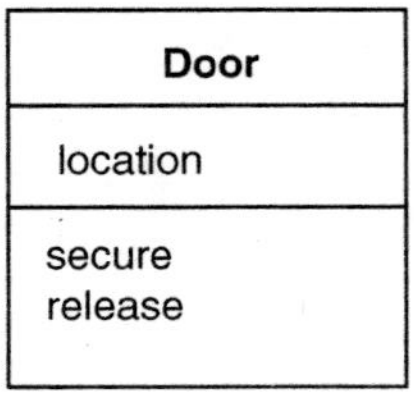

Door
location
secure release

Figure 2   *The Door Class*

The OO security system might define a Door class. The Door class specifies that all Door objects must provide secure and release (unlock) behavior.
Furthermore, each Door object should retain its own location. A picture of
this Door class is shown in Figure 2.

The class box shows the name of the class in the first (topmost) compartment. The second compartment lists the attributes—the information that

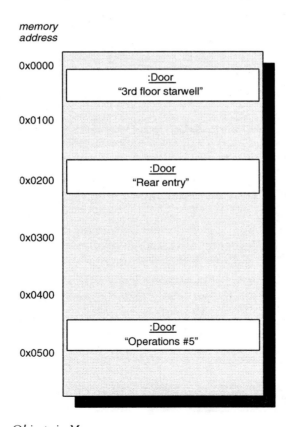

Figure 3   *Door Objects in Memory*

each Door object will store. The third compartment lists the behaviors that each Door object supports—the messages that each door will respond to.

In an object-oriented programming language, you use the Door class as a basis for creating, or *instantiating*, new objects. Each object that you instantiate is allocated a unique area in memory. Any changes you make to an object are exclusive of all other objects in memory.

A *class diagram* is used to represent the structure of an object-oriented system. It shows how classes relate to, or associate with, each other. A class diagram can provide a quick visual understanding of a system. You can also use it as one of the primary indicators of the quality of a system's design.

The basis of all relationships in a class diagram is the association. An association between two classes is formed when one class is *dependent* on the other class or when both classes are dependent on each other. Class *A* is dependent on class *B* if class *A* works only when class *B* is present.

A main reason class A becomes dependent upon class B is that class A sends one or more messages to class B. Since the Security object sends a message to the DoorController object, the Security class is dependent upon the DoorController class.

You show a one-way dependency between two classes with a navigable association (see Figure 4).

Why UML?

This book uses the UML (Unified Modeling Language) standard to illustrate some of the code. The class boxes shown in earlier sections use UML. The UML is the de facto standard for modeling object-oriented systems. The chief benefit of using UML is that it is universally understood and can be used to quickly express design concepts to other developers.

UML itself is not a methodology; it is a diagramming language. It is a tool that can be used to support documenting any kind of object-oriented system. UML can be used on projects using virtually any methodology.

This book will explain the rudiments of the UML it uses. A good place to obtain a better understanding of UML is the book *UML Distilled*, by Martin

Figure 4   *Class Dependency*

Fowler.[3] Also, you can find the latest version of the UML specification online at *http://www.omg.org/technology/documents/formal/uml.htm.*

Most of the UML diagrams in this book show minimal detail. I usually omit attributes, and I only show behaviors when they are particularly relevant. By and large, I intend for the UML to give you a quick pictorial representation of the design of the system. *The UML representation is not the design—it is a model of the design.*[4] The design is the code itself.

To the extent that UML helps you understand the design of the system, it is valuable and worthwhile. Once it begins duplicating information that is more readily understood by reading code, UML becomes a burdensome, expensive artifact to maintain. Use UML judiciously and it will be an invaluable tool for communication.

What Is Inheritance?

A brief discussion of an object-oriented concept known as *inheritance* may help you to understand one of the concepts in the first lesson. Inheritance is a relationship between classes in the system that allows for one class to use another class as a basis for specialization of behavior.

In our real-world example, doors are a class of things that you can shut and open and use as entry/exit points. Beyond that commonality, you can specialize doors: There are automatic doors, elevator doors, bank vault doors, and so on. These are all still doors that open and close, but they each provide a bit of additional specialized behavior.

In your security system, you have the common Door class that specifies secure and release behavior and allows each Door object to store a location. However, you must also support specialty doors that provide additional behaviors and attributes. An AlarmDoor provides the ability to trigger an audible alarm when activated and is also able to operate as a secure door. Since the secure and release behaviors of the AlarmDoor are the same as those in the Door class, the AlarmDoor can designate that it is inheriting from the Door class and need only provide specification for alarm activation.

Inheritance provides the AlarmDoor class with the ability to reuse the secure and release behaviors without having to specify them. For an AlarmDoor object, these behaviors appear as if they were defined in the AlarmDoor class.

[3]See [Fowler2000].
[4][Martin2003/Reeves1992].

Why Test-Driven Development?

Figure 5   *Inheritance*

Note that the relationship between AlarmDoor and Door is also a naviga-ble association. AlarmDoor is dependent upon Door—it cannot exist without Door, since AlarmDoor inherits its code behavior and attributes from Door. UML shows the inheritance relationship as a directional arrow with the ar-rowhead closed instead of opened.

In the first lesson, you'll use inheritance to take advantage of a test frame-work. In a later lesson, you'll learn about inheritance in greater depth.

Why Test-Driven Development?

You will write virtually all code in this book using TDD. TDD is a technique where you specify the system in terms of tests. You write tests prior to (or as) you write the production code; you do not write production code then supply tests after the fact.[5]

TDD is a simple, short-cycled mechanism that you repeat throughout your coding day. Each cycle lasts from seconds to minutes, and consists of the fol-lowing steps:

- Write a specification, in code and in the form of a *unit*[6] *test*.

- Demonstrate test failure (you haven't implemented the specification yet).

---

[5][Langr2001].

[6]The test verifies a functional *unit* of your code. Another term for unit test is *pro-grammer test*.

- Write code to meet the specification.

- Demonstrate test success.

- "Refactor," or rework the code, to ensure that the system still has an optimally clean code base.

That's it. You run all tests against the entire system at all times, ensuring that no new code breaks anything else in the system.

Tests drive several positive aspects of the system:

- *quality*. TDD minimizes the number of defects, since by definition, you test everything in the system. You improve your system's design, since TDD drives you toward more *decoupled* designs—designs where classes are not as heavily dependent upon other classes in the system.

- *documentation of capability*. Each unit test specifies the appropriate use of a production class.

- *malleability*. Having tests in place means that you can continually improve the quality of the code base without fear of breaking something that already works. This can result in lower maintenance costs.

- *consistent pacing*. Since each cycle in TDD is very short, feedback levels are high. You quickly discover if you are going down a rat hole. You learn to maintain a very consistent, sustainable rate of development.

An additional benefit of TDD is that it helps demonstrate the examples in this book. You quickly learn how to translate specifications into test code and how to translate test code into production J2SE 5.0 code.

From a developer's standpoint, TDD is infectious.[7] Most developers who give it an honest try retain it as a valuable tool in their development toolbox. Many of the developers I've talked to about TDD, including some seasoned Java pioneers, say that they never want to go back to the "old way" of doing things. I was first exposed to the idea of always writing tests for code in 1996, when I saw Kent Beck speak at a Smalltalk Solutions conference. My personal reaction was "I'm a programmer, not a tester!" Today, I'm amazed at the value it brings me and the amount by which it improves my development capabilities. I wouldn't do it otherwise.

---

[7][Beck1998].

Setting Up

This section focuses on what you'll need to do in order to get started.

Software You'll Need

IDE or Programmer's Editor

Programming in Java means that you will need to be able to enter source code into your system, compile the source code, and execute the resulting application classes. There are two primary modes of accomplishing this work:

- You can use what is known as an integrated development environment (IDE). An IDE supplies just about everything you'll need to develop in Java in one application. Examples of IDEs include IntelliJ IDEA, Eclipse, Borland JBuilder, and NetBeans.

  I'm currently rebuilding the examples for this book using IntelliJ IDEA, available from JetBrains (*http://www.jetbrains.com*). IDEA does a great job with respect to letting you "work the way you want to work." Its complete support for J2SE 5.0 also arrived sooner than the other IDEs mentioned.

- You can use a programmer's editor. A programmer's editor is an application that allows you to type in code and save it to the file system. It will allow you to configure external tools, such as the Java compiler and VM, that you can execute from within the editor. A programmer's editor typically provides additional support to make the task of programming easier. For example, most programmer's editors recognize other languages enough to provide you with meaningful color schemes (a feature known as syntax highlighting).

  Some of the more popular programmer's editors include emacs, vi, TextPad, UltraEdit, and SlickEdit. My personal choice is TextPad, a $27 editor that you can download from *http://www.textpad.com*. While you could use Windows Notepad (or WordPad) as an editor, you will find that the lack of programming features makes it an ineffective programming tool.

So what is the difference between a programmer's editor and an IDE?

An IDE is often, but not always, limited to a single language. IntelliJ IDEA, JBuilder, and NetBeans specifically target Java, but Microsoft's Visual Studio and Eclipse both provide support for other languages. Modern IDEs know a lot about languages and their class libraries. This knowledge allows the IDEs to provide advanced programming aids such as auto-completion (you type a few letters and the IDE completes what it thought you wanted to type). Modern IDEs also contain sophisticated navigation tools that understand how all your code weaves together. Finally, modern IDEs typically contain a debugger. A debugger is a tool you can use to step through code as it executes. By using a debugger, you can gain a better understanding of what the code does.

In contrast, a programmer's editor is a general-purpose tool that supports editing virtually any kind of program or file. In recent years, programmer's editors have been enhanced to understand more and more about specific languages. However, the level of sophistication remains much lower than an IDE. In order to navigate through code using a programmer's editor, you will typically have to execute text searches. In contrast, IDEs make navigation as simple as a single keystroke. While I know of no programmer's editor that includes a debugger, you can configure most programmer's tools to execute a debugger as an external tool.

Some people find IDEs constricting—you have to work the way the IDE wants you to work. Most IDEs are highly configurable, but you will probably always find something that doesn't work the way you want it to. On the flip side, once you've gotten accustomed to the advanced features that an IDE provides, you'll miss them if you go back to a programmer's editor.

Most of the code in this book was originally constructed under TextPad, since the IDEs generally take a while to support new language versions. You may also find that the IDE you intended to use does not yet support J2SE 5.0. It can take up to a year for vendors to bring their product up to date with the latest Java version.

Agile Java does not assume you use any specific IDE or editor. The few examples in Agile Java that discuss compilation specifics are based upon command-line execution.

If you are using IntelliJ IDEA, Appendix C shows you how to get started with the "Hello World" example shown in this chapter. Appendix C also shows you how to build and run the test-driven examples from Lesson 1. If you're using any other IDE, consult its help documentation for information on configuring it.

Java

You need version 5.0 of the Java 2 SDK (Software Development Kit) in order to run all the examples in Agile Java. If you are running an IDE, it may already include the SDK. I still recommend installing the SDK, as it is wise to learn how to build and execute Java programs exclusive of an IDE.

You can download the SDK from *http://java.sun.com*. You will also want to download the corresponding documentation from the same site. There are installation instructions located at the site to install the SDK that you will want to follow.

Note that you will have the option of downloading either the SDK or the JRE (Java Runtime Environment). You want to download the SDK (which includes the JRE).

The JRE is in essence the JVM. You might download and install the VM if you are interested only in executing Java applications on your system, not in building Java applications. The JVM is supplied separately so that you can ship a minimal set of components with your application when you deploy it to other machines.

After you install the SDK, you will want to extract the documentation, which is a voluminous set of web pages stored in a subdirectory named doc. The best place to extract these is into the directory in which you installed the SDK (under Windows, this might be c:\Program Files\Java\jdk1.5.0). Once you have extracted the docs, you may want to create a shortcut in your web browser to the various index.html files located within. Minimally, you will want to be able to pull up the API documentation, located in the api folder (subdirectory), which is contained directly within the doc folder.

Finally, if you intend to compile and execute Java programs from the command line, you will need to update your path to include the bin directory located directly within the JDK install directory. You will also want to create an environment variable named JAVA_HOME that points to the installation directory of the JDK (if one was not already created by installation of the JDK). Refer to an operating system guide for information on how to set the path and environment variables.

Checking Your Java Installation

You can do a quick sanity check of your installation and configuration. From the command line, execute the command:

```
java -version
```

You should seem something similar to:

```
java version "1.5.0"
Java(TM) 2 Runtime Environment, Standard Edition (build 1.5.0-12345)
Java HotSpot(TM) Client VM (build 1.5.0-12345, mixed mode, sharing)
```

If you instead see something like:

```
'java' is not recognized as an internal or external command, operable program or batch file.
```

Or:

```
java: command not found
```

then you have not set your path correctly. To view the path under Windows, enter the command:

```
path
```

Under Unix, enter:

```
echo $PATH
```

You should see the directory in which you installed Java appear on the path. If you do not, try restarting the shell or command prompt.

If you see a different version of Java, perhaps 1.3 or 1.4, another version of Java appears in the path before the 1.5 version. Try moving your 1.5 install directory to the head of the path.[1]

You will also want to test that you properly set the JAVA_HOME environment variable. Try executing (under Windows):

```
"%JAVA_HOME%"\bin\java -version
```

You should see the same version as before. Under Unix:

```
"$JAVA_HOME/bin/java" -version
```

The quotes handle the possibility that there are spaces in the path name. If you don't get a good result, view the value of the JAVA_HOME environment variable. Unix:

```
echo $JAVA_HOME
```

Windows:

```
echo %JAVA_HOME%
```

---

[1]Windows puts the latest version of Java in the Windows SYSTEM32 directory. You might consider (carefully) deleting this version.

If you can't get past these steps, go no farther! Seek assistance (see the section Still Stuck? at the end of this chapter).

JUnit

You may need to download and install JUnit in order to get started. JUnit is a simple unit-testing framework that you will need in order to do TDD.

Most major IDEs provide direct or indirect support for JUnit. Many IDEs ship with the JUnit product already built in. If you are building and executing Java applications from the command line or as an external tool from a programmer's editor, you will need to install JUnit.

Software You'll
Need

You can download JUnit for free from *http://www.junit.org*. Installation is a matter of extracting the contents of the downloaded zip file onto your hard drive.

Most important, the JUnit zip file contains a file named junit.jar. This file contains the JUnit class libraries to which your code will need to refer in order for you to write tests for your programs.

I built the tests in this book using JUnit version 3.8.1.

Ant

You may also need to download and install Ant. Ant is an XML-based build utility that has become the standard for building and deploying Java projects.

Most major IDEs provide direct or indirect support for Ant. Many IDEs ship with the Ant product already built in. If you are building and executing Java applications from the command line or as an external tool from a programmer's editor, you will want to install Ant.

Ant is available for download at *http://ant.apache.org*. As with JUnit, installation is a matter of extracting the contents of the downloaded zip file onto your hard drive.

You can choose to defer the installation of Ant until you reach Lesson 3, the first use of Ant. This lesson includes a brief introduction to Ant.

If you are not using an IDE with built-in Ant support: You will want to include a reference to the bin directory of your Ant installation in your path statement. Refer to an operating system guide for information on how to set the path. You will also need to create an environment variable named ANT_HOME that points to the installation directory of Ant. Refer to an operating system guide for information on how to set the path and environment variables.

I built the examples in this book using Ant version 1.6.

Does It Work?

Does It Work?

To get started, you will code the "Hello World" program. The hello world program is the prototypical first Java program. When executed, it prints the text "hello world" onto your console. Many programmers venturing into new languages create a hello world program to demonstrate the basic ability to compile and execute code in that new language environment.

The javac Compiler

The basic format of the javac compiler, included in Sun's Java Software Development kit, is

```
javac <options> <source files>
```

javac provides numerous command line options. You can obtain a list of the options by entering the command javac and pressing enter. All options are of course optional. Options precede the name of the source file (or files) being compiled. An example javac command:

```
javac -g:none Hello.java
```

In this command, the text -g:none is an option that tells the compiler to generate no debugging information (information used to help you decipher execution problems).

You can always issue the command:

```
java -version
```

with no source file, to see which version of the Java compiler you are executing.

I include "hello world" here solely as a quick means of feedback. Many of the concepts in it are more advanced topics that you will learn later in the book. This exercise exists to ensure you are able to compile and execute Java programs. For now, type the code below, exactly as it appears, into your IDE or editor.

```java
class Hello {
   public static void main(String[] args) {
     System.out.println("hello world");
   }
}
```

Save this using the filename Hello.java. Case is important in Java. If you save it as hello.java, you may not be able to compile or execute the code.[2]

---

[2]Windows is a little less picky about case. You may find that Windows doesn't always complain about case when it should.

Compiling Hello World

Either use your IDE to compile Hello (if your IDE requires explicit compilation[3]) or compile it from the command line:

```
javac Hello.java
```

See the sidebar for more information about the javac command.

You should be in the directory where you saved Hello.java. If all went well, you will see no messages from the compiler. If you mistyped something, you will likely receive compilation errors. For example, you might see:

```
Hello.java:4: ';' expected
    }
    ^
1 error
```

This specific error means that you forget to type the semicolon (;) at the end of the third line of text.

You might see multiple errors, depending on what you mistyped. Correct any errors and try to compile the file again. If you still have problems, make sure your code looks *exactly* as it appears above. Finally, see the section Still Stuck? at the end of this chapter.

A successful compilation of Hello.java will produce the file Hello.class. Execute a dir or ls command to produce a directory listing and ensure that Hello.class exists. Hello.class is the binary compiled version of the source code—the *class file*. Hello.class is what the Java VM will read and interpret in order to execute the code you typed in Hello.java.

Executing Hello World

To execute the Hello application from the command line, enter:

```
java Hello
```

Make sure that Hello is capitalized as shown.

If you entered the command correctly, you should see the output:

```
hello world
```

[3]Some IDEs require you to explicitly trigger a build. Other IDEs, such as Eclipse, automatically compile the necessary source files each time you save an edit change.

Problems Executing Hello

- If you see:

```
'java' is not recognized as an internal or external command, ...
```

or

```
java: Command not found.
```

then you either have not installed Java or the Java bin directory is not part of your path statement. Refer to the section Checking Your Java Installation for some assistance.
- If you see:

```
Exception in thread "main" java.lang.NoClassDefFoundError: hello (wrong name: Hello) ...
```

then you entered the wrong case, for example:

```
java hello
```

Correct the command and try again.
- If you see:

```
Exception in thread "main" java.lang.NoClassDefFoundError: Hello/class
```

then you entered the .class portion of the name. Correct the command and try again.

Each time you compile the source file, the Java compiler will replace any associated class file that already exists.

Only where pertinent in this book (for example, when I discuss classpath) do I demonstrate use of the javac and java commands. I highly recommend that you familiarize yourself with command-line compilation and execution. The Java compiler and VM work virtually the same across all platforms. If you have difficulty compiling and executing code within your IDE, you will have to refer to the documentation for your IDE.

Still Stuck?

Getting your first Java program compiled and executed can be frustrating, as there are many things that can go wrong. Unfortunately, I can't cover all possibilities in this book. If you are still having trouble, there are wonderful places to go on the web that will provide you with all the help you need. Sun's official Java web site (*http://java.sun.com*) provides you with a wealth of information right from the source.

Another great place to find assistance is the JavaRanch web site at *http://www.javaranch.com*. You'll need to register with a real name in order to use this service. Most of the moderators of the site are particularly helpful and friendly to Java novices. Look for the forum named "Java in General (beginner)" and post your messages there.

As with any public forum, first read the JavaRanch guidelines on posting. The link *http://www.faqs.org/faqs/usenet/primer/part1/* contains a document on etiquette for posting to Usenet. Most of this etiquette applies to virtually any public forum, including JavaRanch. Asking for help in the right way elicits a much better response.

If you're still stuck, I apologize. Please send an email to me at *agileJava@LangrSoft.com*.

Still Stuck?

Lesson 1

Getting Started

Most of the lessons in the first half of Agile Java involve the development of various pieces of a student information system. You will not build a complete system, but you will work on various subsystems that might be part of a complete system.

The student information system involves many different aspects of running a school or university: registration, grades, course scheduling, billing, records, and so on.

In Lesson 1, you will:

- create a simple Java class

- create a test class that exercises the Java class

- use the JUnit framework

- learn about constructors

- refactor the code that you write

This lesson is very detail oriented. I will explicitly describe the steps you should take in doing test-driven development. Future lessons will assume that you are following the cycle of test-driven development in order to produce appropriate tests and code.

Testing

Test-driven development means that you will write tests for virtually every bit of code. It also means that you will write the tests first. The tests are a means of specifying what the code needs to do. After writing the corresponding code, the tests are run to ensure that the code does what the tests specify.

Figure 1.1   *Test and Production Class*

Each class you code will have a corresponding test class. In Figure 1.1, StudentTest is the test class for the production class Student.

StudentTest will have to create objects of class Student, send messages to these objects, and prove that once all the messages have been sent, things are as expected. StudentTest is thus dependent on Student, as shown by the navigable association in the diagram. Conversely, Student is not dependent on StudentTest: The production classes you build should know nothing about the tests written for them.

Design

You design and construct a system based on customer needs, or requirements. Part of the design process is translating the customer requirements into rough ideas or sketches of how the system will be used. For a web-based system, this means designing the web pages that will provide the application's functionality. If you are building "inbetween" software known as middleware, your system will be used by other client software and will interact with other server software. In this case, you will want start by defining the communication points—the *interfaces*—between the other systems and the middleware.

You start by building only high-level designs, not highly detailed specifications. You will continually refine the design as you understand more about the customer needs. You will also update the design as you discover what works well and what doesn't work well in the Java code that you build. The power of object-oriented development can allow you this flexibility, the ability to quickly adapt your design to changing conditions.

Designing the system from the outside in as described above would be a daunting task without complete understanding of the language in which you're going to build it—Java. To get started, you will construct some of the internal building blocks of the system. This approach will get you past the language basics.

The student information system is primarily about students, so as your first task you will abstract that real-world concept into its object-oriented representation. A candidate class might be Student.

Student objects should contain basic information about a student such as name, identification number, and grades. You will concentrate on an even smaller concern first: Create a unique student object that stores the name of the student.

The book icon that appears to the left of the preceding paragraph will appear throughout Agile Java. I will use this icon to designate requirements, or *stories*, that you will build into the student information system. These stories are simple descriptions of what you need to build into the system in order to make the customer happy. You will translate stories into detailed specifications that you realize in the form of tests.

A Simple Test

To represent the initial need to capture student information, start by creating a class that will act as your test case. First, create a new directory or folder on your machine.[1] Then create a file named StudentTest.java in this directory. For the time being, you will save, compile, and execute code out of this single directory. Type the following code into your editor:

```
public class StudentTest extends junit.framework.TestCase {
}
```

Save the file using the file name StudentTest.java.

The two lines of code in StudentTest.java define a class named StudentTest. Everything that comes between the opening and closing braces ({ and }) is part of the definition of StudentTest.

You must designate the class as public in order for the testing framework JUnit to recognize it. I will cover public in more depth later. For now, understand that the public keyword allows other code, including the code in the JUnit framework, to work with the code you write.

The code phrase extends junit.framework.TestCase declares StudentTest to be a subclass of another class named junit.framework.TestCase. This means that StudentTest will acquire, or *inherit*, all the capabilities (behavior) and data (attributes) from a class named junit.framework.TestCase. StudentTest will also be able to add its own behavior and/or attributes. The extends clause also

---

[1]The instructions in this lesson are geared toward command-line use of Java. If you are using an IDE, you will create a class named StudentTest in something called the "default package." If you are prompted for any package name, do not enter anything.

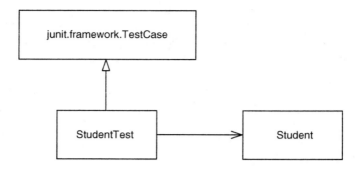

Figure 1.2   *StudentTest Inherits from junit.framework.TestCase*

allows the JUnit user interface to recognize the StudentTest class as something that contains testing methods.

The UML class diagram in Figure 1.2 shows the inheritance relationship between StudentTest and junit.framework.TestCase. StudentTest is now dependent upon both junit.framework.TestCase and Student. Remember that the arrowhead distinguishes between the type of dependency—a closed arrowhead indicates an inheritance relationship.

Your next step is to compile the StudentTest class. In order to do so, you must tell Java where to find any other classes that StudentTest references. Currently this includes only the class junit.framework.TestCase. This class can be found in a packaged format known as a JAR (Java ARchive) file. The JAR file in which junit.framework.TestCase can be found also contains many other classes that comprise the JUnit framework.

I discuss JAR files in more depth in Additional Lesson III. For now, you only need to understand how to tell Java where to find the JUnit JAR file. You do so using the *classpath*.

More on the Classpath

Understanding the classpath can be one of the more confusing aspects of working with Java for beginning developers. For now, you only need a minimal understanding of it.

The classpath is a list of locations separated by semicolons under Windows or colons under Unix. You supply the classpath to both the compiler and the Java VM. A location can be either a JAR file (which contains compiled class files by definition) or a directory that contains compiled class files.

Java depends on the ability to dynamically load other classes when executing or compiling. By supplying a classpath, you provide Java with a list of places to search when it needs to load a specific class.

If you have spaces in your classpath, you may need to surround it with the appropriate quotes for your operating system.

From the command line, you can specify the classpath at the same time that you compile the source file.

```
javac -classpath c:\junit3.8.1\junit.jar StudentTest.java
```

You must specify either the absolute or relative location of the file JUnit. jar;[2] you will find it in the directory where you installed JUnit. This example specifies the absolute location of JUnit.jar.

You should also ensure that you are in the same directory as StudentTest.java.

If you omit the classpath, the Java compiler will respond with an error message:

```
StudentTest.java:1: package junit.framework does not exist
public class StudentTest extends junit.framework.TestCase {
                                 ^
1 error
```

Your IDE will allow you to specify the classpath somewhere in the current project's property settings. In Eclipse, for example, you specify the classpath in the Properties dialog for the project, under the section Java Build Path, and in the Libraries tab.

JUnit

Once you have successfully compiled StudentTest, you can execute it in JUnit. JUnit provides two GUI-based interfaces and a text interface. Refer to the JUnit documentation for further information. The following command will execute the AWT interface[3] against StudentTest.class, using JUnit's class named junit.awtui.TestRunner.

```
java -cp .;c:\junit3.8.1\junit.jar junit.awtui.TestRunner StudentTest
```

---

[2]An absolute location represents the explicit, complete path to a file, starting from the drive letter or root of your file system. A relative location contains a path to a file that is relative to your current location. Example: If StudentTest is in /usr/src/student and JUnit.jar is in /usr/src/JUnit3.8.1, you can specify the relative location as ../JUnit/3.8.1/JUnit.jar.

[3]The AWT is Java's more bare-boned user interface toolkit, in contrast with Swing, which provides more controls and features. The AWT version of the JUnit interface is simpler and easier to understand. To use the Swing version, use the class name junit.swingui.TestRunner instead of junit.awtui.TestRunner. To use the text version, use the class name junit.textui.TestRunner.

You once again specify the classpath, this time using the abbreviated keyword -cp. Not only does the Java compiler need to know where the JUnit classes are, but the Java VM also needs to be able to find these classes at runtime so it can load them up as needed. In addition, the classpath now contains a ., representing the current directory. This is so Java[4] can locate StudentTest.class: If a directory is specified instead of a JAR filename, Java scans the directory for class files as necessary.

The command also contains a single *argument*, StudentTest, which you pass to the junit.awtui.TestRunner class as the name of the class to be tested.

When you execute the TestRunner, you should see a window similar to Figure 1.3.

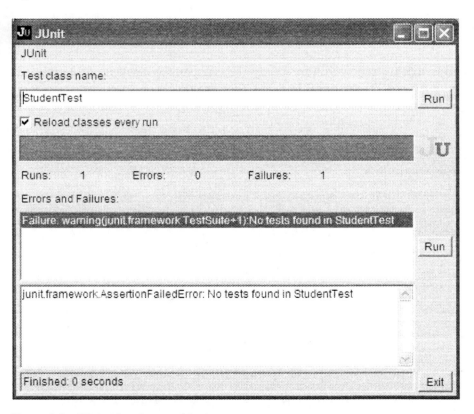

Figure 1.3 *JUnit (showing a red bar)*

---

[4]You'll note I use phrases such as "Java does this" often. This is a colloquial (i.e., lazy) way of saying "The Java virtual machine does this," or "The Java compiler does that." You should be able to determine whether I'm talking about the VM or the compiler from the context.

There really isn't very much to the JUnit interface. I will discuss only part of it for now, introducing the remainder bit by bit as appropriate. The name of the class being tested, StudentTest, appears near the top in an entry field. The Run button to its right can be clicked to rerun the tests. The interface shows that you have already executed the tests once. If you click the Run button (go ahead!), you will see a very quick flash of the red bar[5] spanning the width of the window.

The fact that JUnit shows a red bar indicates that something went wrong. The summary below the red bar shows that there is one (1) failure. The Errors and Failures list explains all the things that went wrong; in this case, JUnit complained because there were "No tests found in StudentTest." Your job as a test-driven programmer will be to first view errors and failures in JUnit and then quickly correct them.

Adding a Test

Edit the source for your StudentTest class to look like the following code:

```
public class StudentTest extends junit.framework.TestCase {
    public void testCreate() {
    }
}
```

The new second and third lines define a *method* within the StudentTest class:

```
public void testCreate() {
}
```

A method is a block of code that will contain any number of code statements. Like the class declaration, Java uses braces to delineate where the method starts and where it ends. All code that appears between method braces belongs to the method.

The method in this example is named testCreate. It is designated as being public, another requirement of the JUnit testing framework.

Methods have two general purposes. First, when Java executes a method, it steps through the code contained within the braces. Among other things, method code can call other methods; it can also modify object attributes. Second, a method can return information to the code that executed it.

The testCreate method returns nothing to the code that invoked it—JUnit has no need for such information. A method that returns no information provides

---

[5]If you are color-blind, the statistics below the bar will provide you with the information you need.

what is known as a void *return type*. Later (see Returning a Value from a Method in this lesson) you will learn how to return information from a method.

The empty pair of parentheses () indicates that testCreate takes no arguments (also known as *parameters*)—it needs no information passed to it in order to do its work.

The name of the method, testCreate, suggests that this is a method to be used for testing. However, to Java, it is just another method name. But for JUnit to recognize a method as a test method, it must meet the following criteria:

Adding a Test

- the method must be declared public,

- the method must return void (nothing),

- the name of the method must start with the word test, in lowercase letters, and

- the method cannot take any arguments ().

Compile this code and rerun JUnit's TestRunner. Figure 1.4 shows that things are looking better.

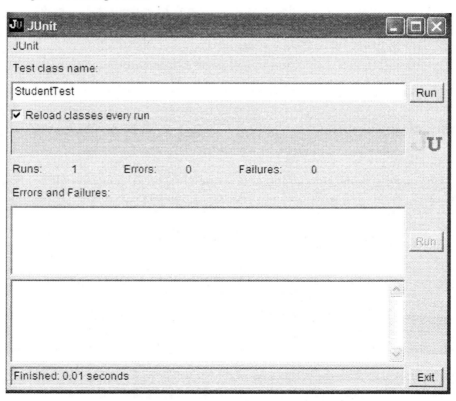

Figure 1.4 *JUnit success (showing a green bar)*

The green bar is what you will always be striving for. For the test class StudentTest, JUnit shows a successful execution of one test method (Runs: 1) and no errors or failures.

Remember that there is no code in testCreate. The successful execution of JUnit demonstrates that an empty test method will always pass.

Creating a Student

Add a single line, or *statement*, to the testCreate method:

```
public class StudentTest extends junit.framework.TestCase {
   public void testCreate() {
      new Student("Jane Doe");
   }
}
```

Creating a Student

You terminate each statement with a semicolon (;).

When the testing framework calls the testCreate method, Java executes this single statement. Once Java executes the statement, it returns control to code in the testing framework that called testCreate.

The statement in testCreate tells Java to create an object of the class type Student:

```
new Student("Jane Doe");
```

You place the new *keyword* before the name of the class to instantiate. You then follow the class name with an *argument list*. The argument list contains information the Student class requires in order to be able to instantiate a Student object. Different classes will need different pieces of information; some classes will not need any information at all. It is up to the designer of the class (you, in this case) to specify what information must be supplied.

The sole argument in this example represents the name of the student, Jane Doe. The value "Jane Doe" is a *string literal*. String literals represent object instances of the predefined Java class java.lang.String. Simply put, string literals are Java's representation of pieces of text.

Soon you will build code for the Student class. At that time, you will specify what to do with this String argument. There are a few things you can do with arguments: You can use them as input data to another operation, you can store them for later use and/or retrieval, you can ignore them, and you can pass them to other objects.

When the Java VM executes the new *operator* in this statement, it allocates an area in memory to store a representation of the Student object. The VM

uses information in the Student class definition to determine just how much
memory to allocate.

Creating the Student Class

Compile the test. You should expect to see problems,[6] since you have only
built the test class StudentTest. StudentTest refers to a class named Student,
which is nowhere to be found—you haven't built it yet!

```
StudentTest.java:3: cannot find symbol
symbol  : class Student
location: class StudentTest
      new Student("Jane Doe");
          ^
1 error
```

Note the position of the caret (^) beneath the statement in error. It indicates that the Java compiler doesn't know what the source text Student represents.

The compile error is expected. Compilation errors are a good thing—they
provide you with feedback throughout the development process. One way
you can look at a compilation error is as your very first feedback after writing a test. The feedback answers the question: Have you constructed your
code using proper Java syntax so that the test can execute?

Simplifying Compilation and Execution

In order to alleviate the tedium of re-executing each of these statements, you may
want to build a batch file or script. An example batch file for Windows:

```
@echo off
javac -cp c:\junit3.8.1\junit.jar *.java
if not errorlevel 1 java -cp .;c:\junit3.8.1\junit.jar junit.awtui.TestRunner StudentTest
```

The batch file does not execute the JUnit test if the compiler returns any compilation errors. A similar script for use under Unix:

```
#!/bin/sh
javac -classpath "/junit3.8.1/junit.jar" *.java
if [ $? -eq 0 ]; then
   java -cp ".:/junit3.8.1/junit.jar" junit.awtui.TestRunner StudentTest
fi
```

[6]You may see different errors, depending on your Java compiler and/or IDE.

Another option under Unix is to use make, a classic build tool available on most systems. However, an even better solution is a tool called Ant. In Lesson 3, you will learn to use Ant as a cross-platform solution for building and running your tests.

To eliminate the current error, create a new class named Student.java. Edit it to contain the following code:

```
class Student {
}
```

Run javac again, this time using a wildcard to specify that all source files should be compiled:

Constructors

```
javac -cp c:\junit3.8.1\junit.jar *.java
```

You will receive a new but similar error. Again the compiler cannot find a symbol, but this time it points to the word new in the source text. Also, the compiler indicates that the symbol it's looking for is a constructor that takes a String argument. The compiler found the class Student, but now it needs to know what to do with respect to the "Jane Doe" String.

```
StudentTest.java:3: cannot find symbol
symbol   : constructor Student(java.lang.String)
location: class Student
        new Student("Jane Doe");
        ^
1 error
```

Constructors

The compiler is complaining that it cannot find an appropriate Student *constructor*. A constructor looks a lot like a method. It can contain any number of statements and can take any number of arguments like a method. However, you must always name a constructor the same as the class in which it is defined. Also, you never provide a return value for a constructor, not even void. You use a constructor to allow an object to be initialized, often by using other objects that are passed along as arguments to the constructor.

In the example, you want to be able to pass along a student name when you instantiate, or construct, a Student object. The code

```
new Student("Jane Doe");
```

implies that there must be a constructor defined in the Student class that takes a single parameter of the String type. You can define such a constructor by editing Student.java so that it looks like this:

```
class Student {
    Student(String name) {
    }
}
```

Compile again and rerun your JUnit tests:

```
javac -classpath c:\junit3.8.1\junit.jar *.java
java -cp .;c:\junit3.8.1\junit.jar junit.awtui.TestRunner StudentTest
```

You should see a green bar.

The constructor currently doesn't do anything with the name String passed to it. It is lost in the ether! Soon, you'll modify the Student class definition to hold on to the name.

Local Variables

So far, when JUnit executes testCreate, Java executes the single statement that constructs a new Student object. Once this statement executes, control returns to the calling code in the JUnit framework. At this point, the object created in testCreate disappears: It had a lifetime only as long as testCreate was executing. Another way to say this is that the Student object is scoped to the testCreate method.

You will want to be able to refer to this Student object later in your test. You must somehow hold on to the memory address of where the Java VM decided to store the Student object. The new operator returns a *reference* to the object's location in memory. You can store this reference by using the *assignment operator*, represented in Java as the equals sign (=). Modify StudentTest:

```
public class StudentTest extends junit.framework.TestCase {
    public void testCreate() {
        Student student = new Student("Jane Doe");
    }
}
```

The statement is now an *assignment* statement: an object or value on the right-hand side of an assignment operator is stored in a reference on the left-hand side of the operator.

When the Java VM executes this statement, it executes the code to the right-hand side of the assignment operator (=) first, creating a Student object in memory. The VM takes note of the actual memory address where it places the new Student object. Subsequently, the VM assigns this address to a reference on the left-hand side, or first half, of the statement.

The first half of the statement creates a *local variable* reference named student of the type Student. The reference will contain the memory address of the Student object. It is local because it will exist only for the duration of the test method. Local variables are also known as *temp variables* or *temporary variables*.

You could have named the variable someStudent, or janeDoe, but in this case, the generic name student will work just fine. See the section Naming Conventions at the end of this lesson for guidelines on how to name your variables.

Local Variables

A conceptual pictorial representation of the student reference and Student object might look something like Figure 1.5.[7] This picture exists only to give you an understanding of what's happening behind the scenes. You need not learn how to create your own such pictures.

Behind the scenes, Java maintains a list of all the variables you define and the memory location to which each variable refers. One of the beauties of Java is that you do not have to explicitly code the mundane details of creating and releasing this memory space. Developers using an older language such as C or C++ expend a considerable amount of effort managing memory.

In Java, you don't have to worry as much about managing memory. But it is still possible to create an application with memory "leaks," where the

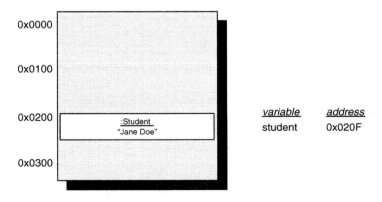

Figure 1.5 *Reference to an Object*

---

[7]The memory addresses are shown in hexadecimal, which is indicated by the "0x" that precedes each number. Lesson 10 includes a discussion of hexadecimal numbers.

application continues to use more and more memory until there is none left. It is also possible to create applications that behave incorrectly because of a poor understanding of how Java manages memory for you. You must still understand what's going on behind the scenes in order to master the language.

I will use the conceptual memory diagrams only in this chapter to help you understand what Java does when you manipulate objects. They are not a standard diagramming tool. Once you have a fundamental understanding of memory allocation, you can for the most part put the nuts and bolts of it out of mind when coding in Java.

Recompile all source files and rerun your test. So far, you haven't written any code that explicitly tests anything. Your tests should continue to pass.

Returning a
Value from
a Method

Returning a Value from a Method

As the next step, you want to ask the Student object created in the test for the student's name.

```
public class StudentTest extends junit.framework.TestCase {
    public void testCreate() {
        Student student = new Student("Jane Doe");
        String studentName = student.getName();
    }
}
```

You now have two statements in testCreate. Each statement is terminated by a semicolon. When the Java VM executes testCreate, it will execute each statement in turn, top to bottom, before returning control to the calling class.

The second statement is another assignment statement, similar to the first statement. In this statement, however, you are not instantiating a new object. Instead, you are sending a message to the Student object, using the student reference assigned to in the previous statement.

The right-hand side of this statement is a message send that asks the Student object for its name. You, as the programmer and class designer of the Student class, are the one who makes the decision about the message name and its arguments. You have decided that the message to which students should respond is called getName and that the message will not need to carry any additional information (arguments).

```
student.getName();
```

You also must specify the message *receiver*—the object to which you want the message sent. To do so, you first specify the object reference, student, followed by a period (.), followed by the message getName(). The parentheses indicate that no arguments are passed along with the message. For this second statement to work, you will need to define a corresponding method in the Student class called getName().

The left hand of the second statement assigns the memory address of this returned String object to a String local variable called studentName. For this assignment to work, you'll need to define the getName() method in Student so that it returns a String object.

You'll see how to build getName() in just a minute.

Compile all source files. The remaining compilation error indicates that the compiler doesn't know about a getName method in the Student class.

Returning a
Value from a
Method

```
StudentTest.java:4: cannot find symbol
symbol  : method getName()
location: class Student
        String studentName = student.getName();
                                      ^
1 error
```

You can eliminate this error by adding a getName method to the Student class definition:

```
class Student {
   Student(String name) {
   }

   String getName() {
   }
}
```

You saw earlier how you can indicate that a method returns nothing by using the void keyword. This getName method specifies instead a return type of String. If you now try to compile Student.java, you receive an error:

```
Student.java:5: missing return statement
   }
   ^
1 error
```

Since the method specifies a return type of String, it needs a return statement that provides a String object to be returned to the code that originally sent the getName message:

```
class Student {
   Student(String name) {
   }

   String getName() {
      return "";
   }
}
```

The `return` statement here returns an empty String object—a String with nothing in it. Compile the code again; you should receive no compilation errors. You are ready to run the test in JUnit again.

Assertions

You now have a complete context for `testCreate`: The first test statement creates a student with a given name, and the second statement asks for the name from the student object. All that you need do now is add a statement that will demonstrate that the student name is as expected—that it is the same as the name passed to the constructor of the student.

```
public class StudentTest extends junit.framework.TestCase {
    public void testCreate() {
        Student student = new Student("Jane Doe");
        String studentName = student.getName();
        assertEquals("Jane Doe", studentName);
    }
}
```

The third line of code (statement) is used to prove, or assert, that everything went well during the execution of the first two statements. This is the "test" portion of the test method. To paraphrase the intent of the third statement: You want to ensure that the student's name is the string literal "Jane Doe". In more general terms, the third statement is an assertion that requires the first argument to be the same as the second.

This third line is another message send, much like the right-hand side of the second statement. However, there is no receiver—to what object is the `assertEquals` message sent? If you specify no receiver, Java assumes that the current object—the object in which the current method is executing—is the receiver.

The class junit.framework.TestCase includes the definition for the method `assertEquals`. Remember that in your class definition for StudentTest, you declared:

```
public class StudentTest extends junit.framework.TestCase {
```

This declaration means that the StudentTest class inherits from junit.framework.TestCase. When you send the message `assertEquals` to the current StudentTest object, the Java VM will attempt to find a definition for `assertEquals` in StudentTest. It will not find one and subsequently will use the definition it finds in junit.framework.TestCase. Once the VM finds the method, it executes it just like any other method.

The important thing to remember is that even though the method is defined in the superclass of StudentTest, it operates on the current StudentTest object. You will revisit this concept of inheritance in Lesson 6.

The third statement also demonstrates how you can pass more than one argument along with a message by using commas to separate each argument. There are two parameters to assertEquals: the String literal "Jane Doe" and the studentName reference you created in the second statement. Both represent objects that will be compared within the assertEquals method. JUnit will use the result of this comparison to determine if the testCreate method should pass or fail. If the string in the memory address referred to by studentName is also "Jane Doe", then the test passes.

Recompile and run your test. JUnit should look something like Figure 1.6.

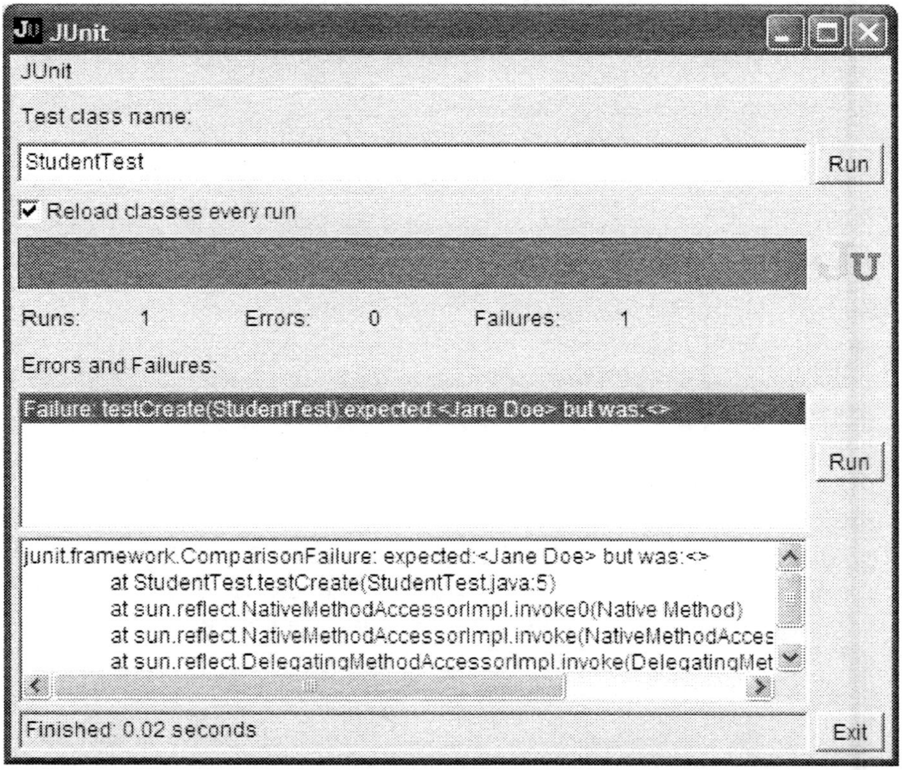

Figure 1.6 *Not Quite Done*

JUnit shows a red bar and indicates one failure. It also tells you what went wrong in the first listbox:

```
Failure: testCreate(StudentTest): expected:<Jane Doe> but was:<>
```

The method failing is `testCreate`, located in the StudentTest class. The problem is that something expected the String literal `"Jane Doe"` but received instead an empty String. Who is expecting this and where? JUnit divulges this information in the second listbox, showing a *walkback* (also known as a *stack trace*) of the code that led up to the failure. The first line of this stack trace indicates that there was a ComparisonFailure, and the second line tells you that the failure occurred at line 5 in StudentTest.java.

Assertions

Use your editor to navigate to line 5 of the StudentTest source code. This will show that the `assertEquals` method you coded is the source of the comparison failure:

```
assertEquals("Jane Doe", studentName);
```

As mentioned before, the `assertEquals` method compares two objects[8] and fails the test if they are not equal. JUnit refers to the first parameter, `"Jane Doe"`, as the *expected* value. The second parameter, the `studentName` variable, references the *actual* value—what you are expecting to also have the value `"Jane Doe"`. The `studentName` reference instead points to an empty String value, since that's what you coded to return from the `getName` method.

Fixing the code is a simple matter—change the `getName` method to return `"Jane Doe"` instead:

```java
class Student {
    Student(String name) {
    }

    String getName() {
        return "Jane Doe";
    }
}
```

Recompile and rerun JUnit. Success! (See Figure 1.7.) There's something satisfying about seeing that green bar. Press the Run button again. The bar should stay green. Things are still good—but not that good. Right now, all students will be named Jane Doe. That's not good, unless you're starting an all-woman school that only accepts people with the name Jane Doe. Read on.

---

[8]Specifically, this example compares a String object to a String variable, or reference. Java *dereferences* the variable to obtain the String object at which it points and uses this for the comparison.

Figure 1.7 *Success!*

Instance Variables

You have built your first test and corresponding class. You used StudentTest to help you build the Student class in an incremental manner. The test can also be used to ensure that any future changes you make don't break something you already did.

Unfortunately, the code isn't quite right. If you were to build more students, they would all respond to the getName message by saying they were Jane Doe. You'll mature both StudentTest and Student in this section to deal with the problem.

You can prove the theory that every Student object will answer the name Jane Doe by elaborating on the testCreate method. Add code to create a second student object:

```
public void testCreate() {
  Student student = new Student("Jane Doe");
  String studentName = student.getName();
  assertEquals("Jane Doe", studentName);

  Student secondStudent = new Student("Joe Blow");
  String secondStudentName = secondStudent.getName();
  assertEquals("Joe Blow", secondStudentName);
}
```

The conceptual picture of the second student in memory is shown in Figure 1.8. Java finds space for the new Student object and stuffs it there. You won't know and shouldn't care where each object ends up. The important thing to get out of the memory diagram is that you now have references to two discrete objects in memory.

Instance Variables

Start JUnit again. If you are running from the command line, start it as a background process (under Unix)[9] or use the start command (under Windows).[10] This will allow JUnit to run as a separate window, returning control to the command line. Whether you are using an IDE or running from the command line, you can keep the JUnit window open. Since JUnit reloads class files that are changed by compilation, you will not need to restart the JUnit GUI each time you make a change.[11]

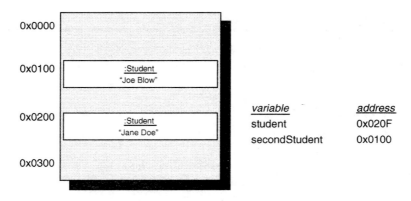

Figure 1.8 *Objects in Memory*

[9]Append an & to the command, under most systems

[10]Prepend the command with the word **start**. For example:

```
start java -cp .;c:\junit3.8.1\junit.jar junit.awtui.TestRunner StudentTest
```

[11]For this to work, ensure that the checkbox labeled "Reload classes every run" is checked in the JUnit GUI.

The test fails:

```
junit.framework.ComparisonFailure: expected:<...oe Blow> but was:<...ane Doe>
```

Sure enough, since getName always returns "Jane Doe", the second assertEquals statement fails.

The problem is that you passed the student name to the constructor of the Student class, but the constructor does nothing with that name. Your code in the Student class is responsible for storing the name if anything is going to be able to refer to the name later.

You want the student's name to be an *attribute* of the student—a piece of information that is kept by the student as long as the student object is around. The most direct way to represent an attribute in Java is by defining it as a *field*, also known as an *instance variable*. You declare a field within the braces that delineate the start and end of a class. A field declaration can appear anywhere within the class as long as it appears outside of the methods defined in that class. But according to convention, you should place field declarations near either the start or the end of the class.

Like a local variable, a field has a type. Define the field myName to be of the type String within the Student class as shown here:

```
class Student {
    String myName;

    Student(String name) {
    }

    String getName() {
        return "Jane Doe";
    }
}
```

In the constructor body, assign the constructor's parameter name to myName:

```
Student(String name) {
    myName = name;
}
```

Finally, return the field from the getName method (instead of the String literal "Jane Doe").

```
String getName() {
    return myName;
}
```

JUnit should still be open, showing the comparison failure and red bar. Rerun the tests by pressing the Run button. The bar should turn green.

Take a look again at the test method:

```java
public void testCreate() {
    Student student = new Student("Jane Doe");
    String studentName = student.getName();
    assertEquals("Jane Doe", studentName);

    Student secondStudent = new Student("Joe Blow");
    String secondStudentName = secondStudent.getName();
    assertEquals("Joe Blow", secondStudentName);
}
```

Summarizing the Test

The test demonstrates, and thus documents, how Student instances can be created with discrete names. To further bolster this assertion, add a line to the end of the test to ensure that you can still retrieve the proper student name from the first student object created:

```java
public void testCreate() {
    Student student = new Student("Jane Doe");
    String studentName = student.getName();
    assertEquals("Jane Doe", studentName);

    Student secondStudent = new Student("Joe Blow");
    String secondStudentName = secondStudent.getName();
    assertEquals("Joe Blow", secondStudentName);

    assertEquals("Jane Doe", student.getName());
}
```

Note that instead of assigning the result of the message send—the result of calling student.getName()—to a local variable, you instead substituted it directly as the second parameter of assertEquals.

Rerun the test (after compiling). The success of the test shows that student and secondStudent refer to two distinct objects.

Summarizing the Test

Let's summarize what the test is supposed to be doing, line by line:

Student student = new Student ("Jane Doe");	Create a student whose name is Jane Doe. Store it locally.
String studentName = student .getName();	Ask for the name of the student and store it in a local variable.
assertEquals("Jane Doe", studentName);	Make sure that the name of the student returned was Jane Doe.

That's a lot of things to know in order to understand a few short lines of code. However, you have already seen the foundation for a large part of Java programming. In well-designed object-oriented Java coding, most statements involve either creating new objects, sending messages to other objects, or assigning object addresses (whether the objects are created via new or are returned from a message send) to an object reference.

Refactoring

One of the main problems in software development is the high cost of maintaining code. Part of the reason is that code quickly becomes "crufty" or messy, as the result of rushed efforts or just plain carelessness. Your primary job in building software is to get it to work, a challenge that you will resolve by writing tests before you write the code. Your secondary job is to ensure that the code stays clean. You do this through two mechanisms:

1. ensure that there is no duplicate code in the system, and

2. ensure that the code is clean and expressive, clearly stating the intent of the code

Throughout Agile Java, you will pause frequently to reflect on the code just written. Anything that does not demonstrate adherence to these two simple rules must be reworked, or *refactored*, immediately. Even within a "perfect" design—an unrealistic goal—the poor implementation of code can cause costly headaches for those trying to modify it.

The more you can continually craft the code as you go, the less likely you are to hit a brick wall of code so difficult that you cannot fix it cheaply. Your rule of thumb should be to never leave the code in a worse state than when you started working on it.

Even within your small example so far, there is some less-than-ideal code. Start on the path to cleaning up the code by taking a look at the test:

```java
public void testCreate() {
    Student student = new Student("Jane Doe");
    String studentName = student.getName();
    assertEquals("Jane Doe", studentName);

    Student secondStudent = new Student("Joe Blow");
    String secondStudentName = secondStudent.getName();
    assertEquals("Joe Blow", secondStudentName);

    assertEquals("Jane Doe", student.getName());
}
```

The first step is to eliminate the unnecessary local variables studentName and secondStudentName. They don't add anything to the understanding of the method and can be replaced with simple queries to the student object, as in the very last `assertEquals`.

When you are done making this change, recompile and rerun your test in JUnit to ensure you haven't broken anything. Your code should look like this:

```
public void testCreate() {
    Student student = new Student("Jane Doe");
    assertEquals("Jane Doe", student.getName());

    Student secondStudent = new Student("Joe Blow");
    assertEquals("Joe Blow", secondStudent.getName());

    assertEquals("Jane Doe", student.getName());
}
```

Refactoring

The second step: It is considered poor programming practice to embed String literals throughout your code. One reason is that the code can be difficult to follow if it is not clear what each String literal represents.

In this example, you also are breaking the rule against code duplication. Each of the two String literals appears twice within the test method. If you change one String, you have to change the other. This is more work, and it also means there is a possibility that you will introduce a defect in your code by changing one and not the other.

One way to eliminate this redundancy (and add a bit of expressiveness to the code) is to replace the String literals with String constants.

```
final String firstStudentName = "Jane Doe";
```

This statement creates a reference named `firstStudentName` of the type String and assigns it an initial value of the String literal `"Jane Doe"`.

The keyword `final` at the beginning of the statement indicates that the String reference cannot be changed—no other object can be assigned to the reference. You are never required to specify `final`, but it is considered good form and helps document the intent that `firstStudentName` is acting as a constant. You will learn other uses for `final` later.

Now that you have declared the constant, you can replace the String literals with it.

```
final String firstStudentName = "Jane Doe";
Student student = new Student(firstStudentName);
assertEquals(firstStudentName, student.getName());
...
assertEquals(firstStudentName, student.getName());
```

Compile and rerun your test to ensure that you haven't inadvertently broken anything.

Apply a similar *refactoring* to the other String literal. In addition, change the local variable name student to firstStudent in order to be consistent with the variable name secondStudent. Between each small change, compile and use JUnit to ensure that you haven't broken anything. When finished, your code should look like this:

```
public void testCreate() {
    final String firstStudentName = "Jane Doe";
    Student firstStudent = new Student(firstStudentName);
    assertEquals(firstStudentName, firstStudent.getName());

    final String secondStudentName = "Joe Blow";
    Student secondStudent = new Student(secondStudentName);
    assertEquals(secondStudentName, secondStudent.getName());

    assertEquals(firstStudentName, firstStudent.getName());
}
```

The final assertEquals proves your understanding of the way Java works rather than the functionality that you are trying to build. You would not likely keep this assertion around in a production system. You may choose to keep it or delete it. If you delete it, make sure you recompile and rerun your test!

Your development cycle is now:

- Write a small test to assert some piece of functionality.

- Demonstrate that the test fails.

- Write a small bit of code to make this test pass.

- Refactor both the test and code, eliminating duplicate concepts and ensuring that the code is expressive.

This cycle will quickly become an ingrained, natural flow of development.

this

Look at the Student class code to see if it can be improved.

```
class Student {
  String myName;

    Student(String name) {
        myName = name;
    }

    String getName() {
        return myName;
    }
}
```

this

The code appears clean, but naming the field `myName` is oh so academic. Show your professionalism by using a better name. A first thought might be to call the field `studentName`. However, that introduces duplication in the form of name redundancy—it's clear that the field represents a student's name, since it is defined in the class Student.

Also, you generally name your `get` methods after the fields, so the redundancy would become very apparent when you coded a statement like:

```
student.getStudentName();
```

How about simply `name`?

The problem with using `name` as the field name is that it clashes with the *formal parameter* name of the Student constructor—both would be called `name`. Try it, though, and see what happens.

```
class Student {
    String name;

    Student(String name) {
        name = name;
    }

    String getName() {
        return name;
    }
}
```

This should pass compilation (you might see a warning). Run your test, however, and it will fail:

```
junit.framework.ComparisonFailure: expected:<Jane Doe> but was:<null>
```

Why? Well, part of the problem is that the Java compiler allows you to name fields the same as formal parameters, or even the same as local variables. When the code is compiled, Java tries to figure out which `name` you meant. The resolution the compiler makes is to use the most locally defined `name`, which happens to be the name of the formal parameter. The statement

```
name = name;
```

thus just results in the object stored in the parameter being assigned to itself. This means that nothing is getting assigned to the instance variable (field) called `name`. Field references that are not assigned an object have a special value of `null`, hence the JUnit message:

```
expected:<Jane Doe> but was:<null>
```

There are two ways to ensure that the value of the formal parameter is assigned to the field: Either ensure both variables have different names or use the Java keyword this to differentiate them. Using this is the most common approach.

The first approach means you must rename either the parameter or the field. Java programmers use many differing conventions to solve this naming issue. One is to rename the formal parameter so that it uses a single letter or is prefixed with an article. For example, name could be renamed to n or aName. Another common choice is to rename the field by prefixing it with an underscore: _name. This makes use of the field stand out like a sore thumb, something that can be very valuable when trying to understand code. There are other schemes, such as prefixing the argument name with the article a or an (aName).

The second approach for disambiguating the two is to use the same name for both, but where necessary refer to the field by prefixing it with the Java keyword this.

```java
class Student {
    String name;

    Student(String name) {
        this.name = name;
    }

    String getName() {
        return name;
    }
}
```

The this keyword represents a reference to the current object—the object for which the code is currently executing. The statement in the above example assigns the value of the formal parameter name to the field name.

Make sure your test now passes after making this change. From now on, remember to recompile after you change the code and before running your tests—there will be few reminders in the rest of the book.

private

Java allows you to access fields of an object, just like you can call a method:

```java
public void testCreate() {
    final String firstStudentName = "Jane Doe";
    Student firstStudent = new Student(firstStudentName);
    assertEquals(firstStudentName, firstStudent.getName());
```

```
final String secondStudentName = "Joe Blow";
Student secondStudent = new Student(secondStudentName);
assertEquals(secondStudentName, secondStudent.getName());

assertEquals(firstStudentName, firstStudent.name);
}
```

If you run this test, it will pass. However, it demonstrates particularly poor object-oriented coding style.

 Do not directly expose fields to other objects.

Suppose you want to design the Student class so that a student's name is *immutable*—it cannot be changed once you've created a Student object. The following test code demonstrates how allowing other objects to access your attributes can be a bad idea:

```
final String firstStudentName = "Jane Doe";
Student firstStudent = new Student(firstStudentName);
firstStudent.name = "June Crow";
assertEquals(firstStudentName, firstStudent.getName());
```

The test shows that Student client code—code that is interacting with the Student object—can directly modify the String stored in the name instance variable. While this doesn't seem like a terrible affront, it eliminates any control you have over clients changing your object's data. If you want to allow client code to change the Student's name, you can create a method for the client to use. For example, you could create a method called setName that takes a new name String as parameter. Within the setName method, you could include code for any additional control you needed.

Make the above change to StudentTest and demonstrate for yourself that the test fails.

To protect your fields—to hide them—you should designate them as private. Change the Student class to hide the name field.

```
class Student {
    private String name;
    ...
```

After doing so, other code that attempts to access the field will not even compile. Since the code in Student test refers to the name field directly:

```
assertEquals(firstStudentName, firstStudent.name);
```

you will receive a compilation error:

```
name has private access in Student
        assertEquals(firstStudentName, firstStudent.name);
                                                    ^
1 error
```

Remove the offending line, recompile, and retest.

The other interest in making fields private is to reinforce the notion of object orientation and encapsulation: An object-oriented system is about behavior, not data. You want to accomplish things by sending messages. You also want to encapsulate implementation details. Perhaps later you want to change the Student class to store both first and last names and change the getName method to return the combined name parts. In that case, code that directly accesses the name field would no longer be valid.

As with any rule, there are exceptions. There are at least a couple legitimate reasons to not designate a field as private. (You'll learn about these much later.)

Naming Conventions

You should have noticed a naming pattern in the Java code you have written so far. Most of the elements in Java that you have already learned about—fields, formal parameters, methods, and local variables—are named in a similar way. This convention is sometimes referred to as *camel case*.[12] When following the camel case naming pattern, you comprise a name, or *identifier*, of words concatenated directly together. You begin each word in the identifier, except for the first word, with a capital letter.

You should name fields using nouns. The name should describe what the field is used for or what it represents, not how it is implemented. Prefixes and suffixes that belie the type of the field are unnecessary and should be avoided. Examples of field names to avoid are firstNameString, trim, and sDescription.

Examples of good field names include firstName, trimmer, description, name, mediaController, and lastOrderPlaced.

Methods are generally either actions or queries: Either you are sending a message to tell an object to do something or you are asking an object for some information. You should use verbs to name action methods. You should also use verbs for query method names. The usual Java convention is to prefix the name of the attribute being retrieved by the word get, as in getNumberOfStudents and getStudent. I will discuss some exceptions to this rule later.

---

[12]Imagine that the letters represent the view of a camel from the side. The upper letters are the humps. For an interesting discussion of the term, see http://c2.com/cgi/wiki?CamelCase. You may hear other names for camel case, such as "mixed case."

Examples of good method names include `sell`, `cancelOrder`, and `isDoorClosed`.

Name classes using *upper camel case*—camel case where the first letter of the identifier is uppercased.[13] You should almost always use nouns for class names—objects are abstractions of things. Do not use plural words for class names. A class is used to create a single object at a time; for example, a Student class can create a Student object. When creating collections of objects, as you will learn to do later, continue to use a nonplural name: StudentDirectory instead of Students. From a StudentDirectory class, you can create a StudentDirectory object. From a Students class, you could create a Students object, but it sounds awkward and leads to similarly awkward code phrases.

Examples of good class names include Rectangle, CompactDisc, LaundryList, and HourlyPayStrategy.

In terms of good object-oriented design, you will find that design impacts the ability to name things. A well-designed class does one thing of importance and only that one thing.[14] Classes generally should not do a multitude of things. For example, if you have a class that cuts paychecks, prints a report of all the checks, and calculates chargebacks to various departments, it would be hard to come up with a name that succinctly describes the class. Instead, break the class up into three separate classes: CheckWriter, PayrollSummaryReport, and ChargebackCalculator.

You can use numbers in an identifier, but you cannot use a number as its first character. Avoid special characters—the Java compiler disallows many of them. Avoid underscores (_), particularly as separators between words. There are exceptions: As mentioned earlier, some developers prefer to prefix their fields with underscores. Also, class constants (to be introduced later) usually include underscores.

Avoid abbreviations. Clarity in software is highly valued. Take the time to type the few extra characters. Doing so is far cheaper than increasing the time it takes for a future reader to comprehend your code. Replace names such as `cust` and `num` with the more expressive `custard` and `numerology`.[15] Modern IDEs provide support for quickly renaming things in your code and for auto-completing things you are typing, so you have no excuse to use cryptic names. Abbreviations are acceptable if you use the abbreviation in common speech, such as `id` or `tvAdapter`.

---

[13]Camel case is thus sometimes called lower camel case to distinguish it from upper camel case.

[14]A guideline known as the Single-Responsibility Principle [Martin2003].

[15]I'll bet you thought they stood for `customer` and `number`. See how easy it is to be led astray?

Remember that Java is case sensitive. This means that stuDent represents a different name than student. It is bad form to introduce this sort of confusion in naming, however.

These naming conventions indicate that there are commonly accepted coding standards for things that aren't necessarily controlled by the compiler. The compiler will allow you to use hideous names that will irritate your fellow developers. Most shops wisely adopt a common standard to be followed by all developers. The Java community has also come to a higher level of agreement on such standards than, say, the C++ community. Sun's coding conventions for Java, located at *http://java.sun.com/docs/codeconv,* is a good, albeit incomplete and outdated, starting point for creating your own coding standards. Other style/standards books exist, including *Essential Java Style* [16] and *Elements of Java Style.*[17]

Whitespace

The layout of code is another area where you and your team should adhere to standards. Whitespace includes spaces, tab characters, form feeds, and new lines (produced by pressing the enter key). Whitespace is required between certain elements and is optional between others. For example, there must be at least one space between the keyword class and the name of the class in a class declaration:

```
class Student
```

And the following spacing is allowable (but avoided):

```
String studentName = student   .   getName();
```

The Java compiler ignores extra whitespace. You should use spaces, tabs, and blank lines to judiciously organize your code. This goes a long way toward allowing easy future understanding of the code.

The examples in this book provide a consistent, solid and generally accepted way of formatting Java code. If your code looks like the examples, it will compile. It will also meet the standards of most Java development shops. You will want to decide on things such as whether to use tabs or spaces for indenting and how many characters to indent by (usually three or four).

[16][Langr2000].
[17][Vermeulen2000].

Exercises

Exercises appear at the end of lesson. Many of the exercises have you build pieces of an application that plays the game of chess. If you are unfamiliar with the rules of chess, you can read them at *http://www.chessvariants .com/d.chess/chess.html.*

1. As with Student, you will start simply by creating a class to represent a pawn. First, create an empty test class named PawnTest. Run JUnit against PawnTest and observe that it fails, since you haven't written any test methods yet.

2. Create a test method named testCreate. Ensure that you follow the correct syntax for declaring test methods.

3. Add code to testCreate that instantiates a Pawn object. Ensure that you receive a compile failure due to the nonexistent class. Create the Pawn class and demonstrate a clean compile.

4. Assign the instantiated Pawn object to a local variable. Ask the pawn for its color. Code a JUnit assertion to show that the default color of a pawn is represented by the string "white". Demonstrate test failure, then add code to Pawn to make the test pass.

5. In testCreate, create a second pawn, passing the color "black" to its constructor. Assert that the color of this second pawn is "black". Show the test failure, then make the test pass. Note: Eliminate the default constructor—require that clients creating Pawn objects pass in the color. The change will impact the code you wrote for Exercise #4.

6. In testCreate, create constants for the Strings "white" and "black". Make sure you rerun your tests.

Lesson 2

Java Basics

In this lesson you will:

- use the numeric type int to count the number of students

- use the Java collection class java.util.ArrayList to store many students

- understand default constructors

- learn how to use the J2SE API documentation to understand how to use java.util.ArrayList

- restrict the java.util.ArrayList collection to contain only Student objects

- create a TestSuite to test more than one class

- learn about packages and the import statement

- understand how to define and use class constants

- use date and calendar classes from the system library

- learn the various types of comments that Java allows

- generate API documentation for your code with javadoc

CourseSession

Schools have courses, such as Math 101 and Engl 200, that are taught every semester. Basic course information, such as the department, the number, the number of credits, and the description of the course, generally remains the same from semester to semester.

A course session represents a specific occurrence of a course. A course session stores the dates it will be held and the person teaching

63

it, among other things. It also must retain an enrollment, or list of students, for the course.

You will define a CourseSession class that captures both the basic course information and the enrollment in the session. As long as you only need to work with the CourseSession objects for a single semester, no two Course Sessions should need to refer to the same course. Once two CourseSession objects must exist for the same course, having the basic course information stored in both CourseSession objects is redundant. For now, multiple sessions is not a consideration; later you will clean up the design to support multiple sessions for a single course.

Create CourseSessionTest.java. Within it, write a test named testCreate. Like the testCreate method in StudentTest, this test method will demonstrate how you create CourseSession objects. A creation test is always a good place to get a handle on what an object looks like just after it's been created.

CourseSession

```java
public class CourseSessionTest extends junit.framework.TestCase {
   public void testCreate() {
      CourseSession session = new CourseSession("ENGL", "101");
      assertEquals("ENGL", session.getDepartment());
      assertEquals("101", session.getNumber());
   }
}
```

The test shows that a CourseSession can be created with a course department and number. The test also ensures that the department and number are stored correctly in the CourseSession object.

To get the test to pass, code CourseSession like this:

```java
class CourseSession {
   private String department;
   private String number;

   CourseSession(String department, String number) {
      this.department = department;
      this.number = number;
   }

   String getDepartment() {
      return department;
   }

   String getNumber() {
      return number;
   }
}
```

So far you've created a Student class that stores student data and a Course-Session class that stores course data. Both classes provide "getter" methods to allow other objects to retrieve the data.

However, data classes such as Student and CourseSession aren't terribly interesting. If all there was to object-oriented development was storing data and retrieving it, systems wouldn't be very useful. They also wouldn't be object-oriented. Remember that object-oriented systems are about modeling behavior. That behavior is effected by sending messages to objects to get them to do something—*not* to ask them for data.

But, you've got to start somewhere! Plus, you wouldn't be able to write assertions in your test if you weren't able to ask objects what they look like.

Enrolling Students

Courses don't earn any revenue for the school unless students enroll in them. Much of the student information system will require you to be able to work with more than one student at a time. You will want to store groups, or collections, of students and later execute operations against the students in these collections.

CourseSession will need to store a new attribute—a collection of Student objects. You will want to bolster your CourseSession creation test so that it says something about this new attribute. If you have just created a new course session, you haven't yet enrolled any students in it. What can you assert against an empty course session?

Modify testCreate so that it contains the **bolded** assertion:

```
public void testCreate() {
    CourseSession session = new CourseSession("ENGL", "101");
    assertEquals("ENGL", session.getDepartment());
    assertEquals("101", session.getNumber());
    assertEquals(0, session.getNumberOfStudents());
}
```

int

The new assertion verifies that the number of students enrolled in a brand-new session should be 0 (zero). The symbol 0 is a *numeric literal* that represents the integer zero. Specifically, it is an integer literal, known in Java as an int.

Add the method getNumberOfStudents to CourseSession as follows:

```
class CourseSession {
    ...
    int getNumberOfStudents() {
        return 0;
    }
}
```

(The ellipses represent the instance variables, constructor code, and getter methods that you have already coded.) The return type of getNumberOf Students is specified as int. The value returned from a method must match the return type, and in this method it does—getNumberOfStudents returns an int. The int type allows variables to be created that store integer values from –2,147,483,648 to 2,147,483,647.

Numbers in Java are not objects like String literals are. You cannot send messages to numbers, although numbers can be passed as parameters along with messages just like Strings can. Basic arithmetic support in Java is provided syntactically; for many other operations, support is provided by system libraries. You will learn about similar non-object types later in Agile Java. As a whole, these non-object types are known as *primitive types*.

You have proved that a new CourseSession object is initialized properly, but you haven't shown that the class can enroll students properly. Create a second test method testEnrollStudents that enrolls two students. For each, create a new Student object, enroll the student, and ensure that the CourseSession object reports the correct number of students.

```
public class CourseSessionTest extends junit.framework.TestCase {
    public void testCreate() {
        ...
    }

    public void testEnrollStudents() {
        CourseSession session = new CourseSession("ENGL", "101");

        Student student1 = new Student("Cain DiVoe");
        session.enroll(student1);
        assertEquals(1, session.getNumberOfStudents());

        Student student2 = new Student("Coralee DeVaughn");
        session.enroll(student2);
        assertEquals(2, session.getNumberOfStudents());
    }
}
```

How do you know that you need a method named enroll, and that it should take a Student object as a parameter? Part of what you are doing in a test method is designing the *public interface* into a class—how developers will interact with the class. Your goal is to design the class such that the needs of developers who want use it are met in as simple a fashion as possible.

The simplest way of getting the second assertion (that the number of students is two) to pass would be to return 2 from the getNumberOfStudents method. However, that would break the first assertion. So you must somehow track the number of students inside of CourseSession. To do this, you will again introduce a field. Any time you know you need information to be stored, you will likely use fields to represent object *state*. Change the CourseSession class to look like this:

```
class CourseSession {
    ...
    private int numberOfStudents = 0;
    ...
    int getNumberOfStudents() {
        return numberOfStudents;
    }

    void enroll(Student student) {
        numberOfStudents = numberOfStudents + 1;
    }
}
```

The field to track the student count is named numberOfStudents, it is private per good practice, and it is of the type int. It is also assigned an *initial value* of 0. When a CourseSession object is instantiated, *field initializers* such as this initialization of numberOfStudents are executed. Field initializers are executed prior to the invocation of code in the constructor.

The method getNumberOfStudents now returns the field numberOfStudents, instead of the int literal 0.

Each time the enroll method is called, you should increment the number of students by one. The single line of code in the enroll method accomplishes this:

```
numberOfStudents = numberOfStudents + 1;
```

The + sign and many other mathematical operators are available for working with variables of the int type (as well as other numeric types to be discussed later). The expression on the right hand side of the = sign takes whatever value is currently stored in numberOfStudents and adds 1 to it. Since the numberOfStudents field appears to the left of the = sign, the resultant value of the right-hand side expression is assigned back into it. Bumping up a variable's value by one, as in this example, is a common operation known as

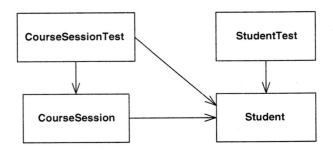

Figure 2.1   *CourseSession and Student Class Diagram*

incrementing the variable. There are other ways to increment a variable that will be discussed later.

It may seem odd that numberOfStudents appears on both sides of the assignment operator. Remember that the Java VM always executes the right hand side of an assignment statement first. It calculates a result using the expression to the right, and assigns this result to the variable on the left.

Note that the enroll method has a return type void, meaning that it returns nothing to the message sender.

The class diagram in Figure 2.1 shows the existing structure of your system so far.

Conceptually, a course session should be able to hold several students. In reality—in the code—the course session holds references to no student objects. It only holds a count of students. Later, when you modify the Course Session class to actually store Student references, the UML diagram will be modified to show that there is a one-to-many relationship between Course Session and Student.

CourseSession depends on Student, since the enroll method can take a Student object as a parameter. In other words, you would not be able to compile the CourseSession class if the Student class did not exist.

Figure 2.1 will be the last class diagram where I show every test class. Since you are doing test-driven development, future diagrams will imply the existence of a test class for each production class, unless otherwise noted.

Initialization

In the last section, you introduced the numberOfStudents field and initialized it to 0. This initialization is technically not required—int fields are initialized to 0 by default. Explicitly initializing a field in this manner, while unnecessary, is useful to help explain the intent of the code.

For now, you have two ways to initialize fields: You can initialize at the field level or you can initialize in a constructor. You could have initialized numberOfStudents in the CourseSession constructor:

```
class CourseSession {
    private String department;
    private String number;
    private int numberOfStudents;

    CourseSession(String department, String number) {
        this.department = department;
        this.number = number;
        numberOfStudents = 0;
    }
    ...
```

There is no hard-and-fast rule about where to initialize. I prefer initializing at the field level when possible—having the initialization and declaration in one place makes it easier to follow the code. Also, as you will learn later in this lesson, you can have more than one constructor; initializing at the field level saves you from duplicate initialization code in each constructor.

You will encounter situations where you cannot initialize code at the field level. Initializing in the constructor may be your only alternative.

Default Constructors

You may have noted that neither of the test classes, StudentTest and Course-SessionTest, contains a constructor. Often you will not need to explicitly initialize anything, so the Java compiler does not require you to define a constructor. If you do not define any constructors in a class,[1] Java provides a default, no-argument constructor. For StudentTest, as an example, it is as if you had coded an empty constructor:

```
class StudentTest extends junit.framework.TestCase {
    StudentTest() {
    }
    ...
}
```

The use of default constructors also implies that Java views constructors as essential elements to a class. A constructor is required in order for Java to initialize a class, even if the constructor contains no additional initialization

---

[1] The Java compiler does allow you to define multiple constructors in a single class; this will be discussed later.

code. If you don't supply a constructor, the Java compiler puts it there for you.

Suites

In the last section, you introduced a second test class, CourseSessionTest. Going forward, you could decide to run JUnit against either CourseSessionTest or StudentTest, depending on which corresponding production class you changed. Unfortunately, it is very possible for you to make a change in the Student class that breaks a test in CourseSessionTest, yet all the tests in StudentTest run successfully.

You could run the tests in CourseSessionTest and then run the tests in StudentTest, either by restarting JUnit each time or by retyping the test class name in JUnit or even by keeping multiple JUnit windows open. None of these solutions is scalable: As you add more classes, things will quickly become unmanageable.

Instead, JUnit allows you to build *suites*, or collections of tests. Suites can also contain other suites. You can run a suite in the JUnit test runner just like any test class.

Create a new class called AllTests with the following code:

```
public class AllTests {
   public static junit.framework.TestSuite suite() {
      junit.framework.TestSuite suite =
         new junit.framework.TestSuite();
      suite.addTestSuite(StudentTest.class);
      suite.addTestSuite(CourseSessionTest.class);
      return suite;
   }
}
```

If you start JUnit with the class name AllTests, it will run all of the tests in both CourseSessionTest and StudentTest combined. From now on, run AllTests instead of any of the individual class tests.

The job of the suite method in AllTests is to build the suite of classes to be tested and return it. An object of the type junit.framework.TestSuite manages this suite. You add tests to the suite by sending it the message addTestSuite. The parameter you send with the message is a *class literal*. A class literal is comprised of the name of the class followed by .class. It uniquely identifies the class, and lets the class definition itself be treated much like any other object.

Each time you add a new test class, you will need to remember to add it to the suite built by AllTests. This is an error-prone technique, as it's easy to forget to update the suite. In Lesson 12, you'll build a better solution: a tool that generates and executes the suite for you.

The code in AllTests also introduces the concept of *static methods*, something you will learn about in Lesson 4. For now, understand that you must declare the suite method as static in order for JUnit to recognize it.

The SDK and java.util.ArrayList

Your CourseSession class tracks the count of students just fine. However, you and I both know that it's just maintaining a counter and not holding onto the students that are being enrolled. For the testEnrollStudents method to be complete, it will need to prove that the CourseSession object is retaining the actual student objects.

One possible solution is to ask the CourseSession for a list of all the enrolled students, then check the list to ensure that it contains the expected students. Modify your test to include the lines shown below in bold.

The SDK and
java.util.ArrayList

```java
public void testEnrollStudents() {
    CourseSession session = new CourseSession("ENGL", "101");

    Student student1 = new Student("Cain DiVoe");
    session.enroll(student1);
    assertEquals(1, session.getNumberOfStudents());
    java.util.ArrayList<Student> allStudents = session.getAllStudents();
    assertEquals(1, allStudents.size());
    assertEquals(student1, allStudents.get(0));

    Student student2 = new Student("Coralee DeVaughn");
    session.enroll(student2);
    assertEquals(2, session.getNumberOfStudents());
    assertEquals(2, allStudents.size());
    assertEquals(student1, allStudents.get(0));
    assertEquals(student2, allStudents.get(1));
}
```

The first line of newly added test code:

```java
java.util.ArrayList<Student> allStudents = session.getAllStudents();
```

says that there will be a method on CourseSession named getAllStudents. The method will have to return an object of the type java.util. ArrayList<Student>, since that's the type of the variable to which the result of getAllStudents is to be assigned. A type appearing in this form—a class name followed by a parameter type within angle brackets (< and >) is known as a *parameterized type*. In the example, the parameter Student of java.util.ArrayList indicates that the java.util.ArrayList is *bound* such that it can only contain Student objects.

The class java.util.ArrayList is one of thousands available as part of the Java SDK class library. You should have downloaded and installed the SDK documentation so that it is available on your machine. You can also browse the documentation online at Sun's Java site. My preference is to have the documentation available locally for speed and accessibility reasons.

Pull up the documentation and navigate to the Java 2 Platform API Specification. You should see something like Figure 2.2.

The Java API documentation will be your best friend, unless you're doing *pair programming*,[2] in which case it will be your second-best friend. It is divided into three frames. The upper left frame lists all the *packages* that are available in the library. A package is a group of related classes.

The lower left frame defaults to showing all the classes in the library. Once a package is selected, the lower left frame shows only the classes contained within that package. The frame to the right that represents the remainder of the page shows detailed information on the currently selected package or class.

Scroll the package frame until you see the package named java.util and select it. The lower left pane should now show a list of *interfaces*, classes, and

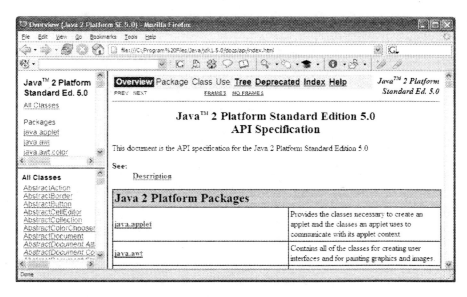

Figure 2.2 *Java 2 Platform API Specification*

[2]A technique whereby members of a development team work in dynamic pairs of developers who jointly construct code.

exceptions. I will explain interfaces and exceptions later. For now, scroll down until you see the class named ArrayList and select it.

The package java.util contains several utility classes that you will use often in the course of Java development. The bulk of the classes in the package support something called the Collections Framework. The Collections Framework is a consistent sublibrary of code used to support standard data structures such as lists, linked lists, sets, and hash tables. You will use collections over and over again in Java to work with groupings of related objects.

The main pane (to the right) shows all of the detailed information on the class java.util.ArrayList. Scroll down until you see the Method Summary. The Method Summary shows the methods implemented in the java.util .ArrayList class. Take a few minutes to read through the methods available. Each of the method names can be clicked on for detailed information regarding the method.

Adding Objects

You will use three of the java.util.ArrayList methods as part of the current exercise: add, get, and size. One of them, size, is already referenced by the test. The following line of code asserts that there is one object in the java.util. ArrayList object.

```
assertEquals(1, allStudents.size());
```

The next line of new code asserts that the first element in allStudents is equal to the student that was enrolled.

```
assertEquals(student, allStudents.get(0));
```

According to the API documentation, the get method returns the element at an arbitrary position in the list. This position is passed to the get method as an index. Indexes are zero-based, so get(0) returns the first element in the list.

Adding Objects

The add method is documented in the Java SDK API as taking an Object as parameter. If you click on the parameter Object in the API docs, you will see that it is actually java.lang.Object.

You might have heard that Java is a "pure" object-oriented language, where "everything is an object."[3] The class java.lang.Object is the mother of all classes defined in the Java system class library, as well as of any class that

---

[3]A significant part of the language is not object-oriented. This will be discussed shortly.

you define, including Student and StudentTest. Every class inherits from java.lang.Object, either directly or indirectly. StudentTest inherits from junit .framework.TestCase, and junit.framework.TestCase inherits from java.lang.Object.

This inheritance from java.lang.Object is important: You'll learn about several core language features that depend on java.lang.Object. For now, you need to understand that String inherits from java.lang.Object, as does Student, as does any other class you define. This inheritance means that String objects and Student objects are also java.lang.Object objects. The benefit is that String and Student objects can be passed as parameters to any method that takes a java.lang.Object as a parameter. As mentioned, the add method takes an instance of java.lang.Object as a parameter.

Even though you can pass any type of object to a java.util.ArrayList via its add method, you don't usually want to do that. In the CourseSession object, you know that you only want to be able to enroll Students. Hence the parameterized type declaration. One of the benefits to restricting the java.util.ArrayList via a parameterized type is that it protects other types of objects from inadvertently being added to the list.

Adding Objects

Suppose someone is allowed to add, say, a String object to the list of students. Subsequently, your code asks for the list of students using getAll Students and retrieves the String object from the list using the get method. When you attempt to assign this object to a Student reference, the Java VM will choke, generating an error condition. Java is a *strongly typed* language, and it will not allow you to assign a String to a Student reference.

The following changes to CourseSession (appearing in bold) will make the test pass:

```java
class CourseSession {
    ...
    private java.util.ArrayList<Student> students =
        new java.util.ArrayList<Student>();
    ...
    void enroll(Student student) {
        numberOfStudents = numberOfStudents + 1;
        students.add(student);
    }

    java.util.ArrayList<Student> getAllStudents() {
        return students;
    }
}
```

A new field, students, is used to store the list of all students. It is initialized to an empty java.util.ArrayList object that is bound to contain only Student

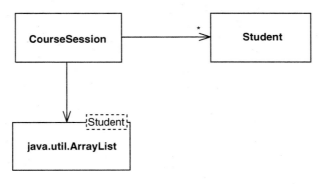

Figure 2.3 *Class Diagram with Parameterized Type*

objects.[4] The `enroll` method adds the student to this list, and the `getAll Students` method simply returns the list.

Figure 2.3 shows how CourseSession is now dependent upon the parameterized type java.util.ArrayList<Student>. Also, the fact that CourseSession is dependent upon zero to many students is shown by the * at the end of the association between CourseSession and Student.

The class diagram in Figure 2.3 is not normal—it really shows the same information twice, in a different fashion. The parameterized type declaration suggests that a single CourseSession has a relationship to a number of Student objects stored in an ArrayList. The association from CourseSession to Student similarly shows a one-to-many relationship.

Incremental Refactoring

Since java.util.ArrayList provides a `size` method, you can just ask the students ArrayList object for its size instead of tracking `numberOfStudents` separately.

```
int getNumberOfStudents() {
   return students.size();
}
```

Make this small refactoring, then recompile and rerun the test. Having the test gives you the confidence to change the code with impunity—if the change doesn't work, you simply undo it and try something different.

---

[4]Due to width restrictions, I've broken the `students` field declaration into two lines. You can type this as a single line if you choose.

Since you no longer return numberOfStudents from getNumberOfStudents, you can stop incrementing it in the enroll method. This also means you can delete the numberOfStudents field entirely.

While you could scan the CourseSession class for uses of numberOfStudents, removing each individually, you can also use the compiler as a tool. Delete the field declaration, then recompile. The compiler will generate errors on all the locations where the field is still referenced. You can use this information to navigate directly to the code you need to delete.

The final version of the class should look like the following code:

```java
class CourseSession {
    private String department;
    private String number;
    private java.util.ArrayList<Student> students =
        new java.util.ArrayList<Student>();

    CourseSession(String department, String number) {
        this.department = department;
        this.number = number;
    }

    String getDepartment() {
        return department;
    }

    String getNumber() {
        return number;
    }

    int getNumberOfStudents() {
        return students.size();
    }

    void enroll(Student student) {
        students.add(student);
    }

    java.util.ArrayList<Student> getAllStudents() {
        return students;
    }
}
```

Objects in Memory

In testEnrollStudents, you send the getAllStudents message to session and store the result in a java.util.ArrayList reference that is bound to the Student class—it can only contain Student objects. Later in the test, after enrolling the second student, allStudents now contains both students—you don't need to ask the session object for it again.

```
public void testEnrollStudents() {
   CourseSession session = new CourseSession("ENGL", "101");

   Student student1 = new Student("Cain DiVoe");
   session.enroll(student1);
   assertEquals(1, session.getNumberOfStudents());
   java.util.ArrayList<Student> allStudents = session.getAllStudents();
   assertEquals(1, allStudents.size());
   assertEquals(student1, allStudents.get(0));

   Student student2 = new Student("Coralee DeVaughn");
   session.enroll(student2);
   assertEquals(2, session.getNumberOfStudents());
   assertEquals(2, allStudents.size());
   assertEquals(student1, allStudents.get(0));
   assertEquals(student2, allStudents.get(1));
}
```

The reason is illustrated in Figure 2.4. The CourseSession object holds on to the students field as an attribute. This means that the students field is available throughout the lifetime of the Course-Session object. Each time the getNumberOfStudents message is sent to the session, a reference to the very same students field is returned. This reference is a memory address, meaning that

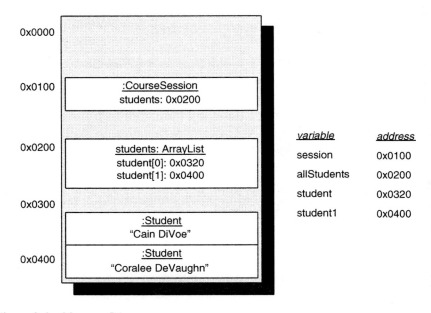

Figure 2.4   *Memory Diagram*

any code using the reference ends up at the same memory location at which the students field is stored.

Packages and the `import` Statement

Packages and
the import
Statement

Up until now, you have been using the *fully qualified* name of the class java.util.ArrayList. The fully qualified name of a class includes its package name (java.util in this example) followed by the class name (ArrayList).

Packages provide a way for developers to group related classes. They can serve several needs: First, grouping classes into packages can make it considerably easier on developers, saving them from having to navigate dozens, hundreds, or even thousands of classes at a time. Second, classes can be grouped into packages for distribution purposes, perhaps to allow easier reuse of modules or subsystems of code.

Third, packages provide *namespaces* in Java. Suppose you have built a class called Student and you purchase a third-party API to handle billing students for tuition. If the third-party software contains a class also named Student, any references to Student will be ambiguous. Packages provide a way to give a class a more unique name, minimizing the potential for class name conflicts. Your class might have a fully qualified name of com .mycompany.studentinfosystem.Student, and the third-party API might use the name com.thirdpartyco.expensivepackage.Student.

I will usually refer to the Java system classes without the package name unless the package is not clear from the class name. For example, I will use ArrayList in place of java.util.ArrayList, and Object instead of java.lang.Object.

Typing java.util.ArrayList throughout code can begin to get tedious, and it clutters the code as well. Java provides a keyword—import—that allows identification of fully qualified class names and/or packages at the source file level. Use of import statements allows you to specify simple class names throughout the remainder of the source file.

Update CourseSessionTest to include import statements as the very first lines in the source file. You can now shorten the phrase extends junit.frame work.TestCase to extends TestCase. You can change the reference defined as java.util.ArrayList<Student> to ArrayList<Student>.

```
import junit.framework.TestCase;
import java.util.ArrayList;

public class CourseSessionTest extends TestCase {
   ...
```

```
    public void testEnrollStudents() {
       CourseSession session = new CourseSession("ENGL", "101");

       Student student1 = new Student("Cain DiVoe");
       session.enroll(student1);
       assertEquals(1, session.getNumberOfStudents());
       ArrayList<Student> allStudents = session.getAllStudents();
       ...
    }
}
```

(Make sure your tests still run! I'll keep reminding you for a while.)

Update AllTests, StudentTest, and CourseSession to use import statements. Your code will look so much cleaner!

The java.lang Package

The String class is also part of the system class library. It belongs to the package named java.lang. So why haven't you had to either use its fully qualified class name (java.lang.String) or provide an import statement?

The Java library contains classes so fundamental to Java programming that they are needed in many, if not all, classes. The classes String and Object are two such classes. The ubiquitous nature of these classes is such that the designers of Java wanted to save you from the nuisance of having to specify an import statement for them everywhere.

If you refer to the String class, then the statement:

```
import java.lang.String;
```

is implicit in each and every Java source file.

When you learn about inheritance (Lesson 6), you will find that every class implicitly extends from the class java.lang.Object. In other words, if a class declaration does not contain an extends keyword, it is as if you coded:

```
class ClassName extends java.lang.Object
```

This is another shortcut provided by the Java compiler.

The Default Package and the **package** Statement

None of the classes you have built—AllTests, StudentTest, Student, Course SessionTest, and CourseSession—specify a package. This means that they go into something called the *default package*. The default package is fine for sample or academic programs. But for any real software development you do, all of your classes should belong to some package other than the default package. In fact, if you place classes in the default package, you will not be able to reference these classes from other packages.

If you are working in a modern IDE, moving a class into a package can be as easy as dragging the class name onto a package name. If you are not working in an IDE, setting up packages and understanding related classpath issues can be somewhat complex. Even if you are working in an IDE, it is important to understand the relationship between packages and the underlying file system directory structure.

Let's try moving your classes into a package named studentinfo. Note that package names are by convention comprised of lowercase letters. While you should still avoid abbreviations, package names can get unwieldy fairly quickly. The judicious use of abbreviations might help keep the package name from being unmanageable.

You should also not start your package names with java or javax, both of which should be used exclusively by Sun.

If your IDE supports moving classes into packages as a simple operation, go ahead and take advantage of it. However, make sure you understand how the classes relate to a package structure, as this will be important when you construct deployable libraries. Consider copying the source files into a different directory structure and following the exercise anyway.

From the directory in which your class files are located, create a new subdirectory called studentinfo. Case is important—ensure that you name this subdirectory using all lowercase letters. If your source files are currently located in c:\source, then you should now have a directory named c:\source\studentinfo. Starting with a Unix directory named /usr/src, you should have a directory named /usr/src/studentinfo.

First carefully delete all of the class files that have been generated. Class files, remember, end with a .class extension. Don't lose all of your hard work—back up your directory if you are unsure about this step. Under Windows, the command:

```
del *.class
```

will suffice. Under Unix, the equivalent command is:

```
rm *.class
```

After deleting the class files, move the five source files (AllTests.java, StudentTest.java, Student.java, CourseSessionTest.java, and CourseSesson .java) into the studentinfo directory. You need to store classes in a directory structure that corresponds to the package name.

The Default
Package and
the package
Statement

Edit each of the five Java source files. Add a `package` statement to each that identifies the class as belonging to the `studentinfo` package. The `package` statement must be the very first statement within a Java class file.

```
package studentinfo;

class Student {
...
```

You should be able to compile the classes from within the `studentinfo` subdirectory.

However, two things will have to change when you run JUnit against AllTests. First, the full name of the class will have to be passed into the TestRunner, otherwise JUnit will not find it. Second, if you are in the `studentinfo` directory, the TestRunner will not be able to find studentinfo.AllTests. You must either go back to the parent directory or, better yet, alter the classpath to explicitly point to the parent directory. The following command shows the altered classpath and the fully qualified test class name.

The setUp Method

```
java -cp c:\source;c:\junit3.8.1\junit.jar junit.awtui.TestRunner studentinfo.AllTests
```

In fact, if you explicitly point to c:\source in the classpath, you can be in any directory when you execute the `java` command. You will also want to use a similar classpath in `javac` compilations:

```
javac -classpath c:\source;c:\junit3.8.1\junit.jar studentinfo\*.java
```

Another way to look at this: The classpath specifies the starting, or "root," directory in which to find any classes that you will use. The class files must be located in the subdirectory of one of the roots that corresponds to the package name. For example, if the classpath is c:\source and you want to include the class com.mycompany.Bogus, then the file Bogus.class must appear in c:\source\com\mycompany.

A package-naming standard is something that your development team will want to agree upon. Most companies name their packages starting with the reverse of their web domain name. For example, software produced by a company named Minderbinder Enterprises might use package names starting with com.minderbinder.

The setUp Method

The test code in CourseSessionTest needs a bit of cleanup work. Note that both tests, `testCreate` and `testEnrollStudents`, instantiate a new CourseSession object and store a reference to it in a local variable named session.

JUnit provides you with a means to eliminate this duplication—a setUp method. If you provide code in this setUp method, JUnit will execute that code prior to executing each and every test method. You should put common test initialization code in this method.

```java
public class CourseSessionTest extends TestCase {
    private CourseSession session;

    public void setUp() {
        session = new CourseSession("ENGL", "101");
    }

    public void testCreate() {
        assertEquals("ENGL", session.getDepartment());
        assertEquals("101", session.getNumber());
        assertEquals(0, session.getNumberOfStudents());
    }

    public void testEnrollStudents() {
        Student student1 = new Student("Cain DiVoe");
        session.enroll(student1);
        ...
    }
}
```

The setUp Method

Caution!

It's easy to make the mistake of coding setUp so that it declares session as a local variable:

```java
public void setUp() {
    CourseSession session =
        new CourseSession("ENGL", "101");
}
```

It is legal to define a local variable with the same name as an instance variable, but it means that the *instance* variable session will not get properly initialized. The result is an error known as a NullPointerException, which you'll learn about in Lesson 4.

In CourseSessionTest, you add the instance variable session and assign to it a new CourseSession instance created in the setUp method. The test methods testCreate and testEnrollStudents no longer need this initialization line. Both test methods get their own separate CourseSession instance.

Even though you could create a constructor and supply common initialization code in it, doing so is considered bad practice. The preferred idiom for test initialization in JUnit is to use the setUp method.

More Refactoring

The method testEnrollStudents is a bit longer than necessary. It contains a few too many assertions that track the number of students. Overall, the method is somewhat difficult to follow.

Instead of exposing the entire list of students to *client* code (i.e., other code that works with CourseSession objects), you can instead ask the Course-Session to return the Student object at a specific index. You currently have no need for the entire list of students as a whole, so you can eliminate the getAll Students method. This also means that you no longer have to test the size of the ArrayList returned by getAllStudents. The test method can be simplified to this:

More
Refactoring

```
public void testEnrollStudents() {
    Student student1 = new Student("Cain DiVoe");
    session.enroll(student1);
    assertEquals(1, session.getNumberOfStudents());
    assertEquals(student1, session.get(0));

    Student student2 = new Student("Coralee DeVaughn");
    session.enroll(student2);
    assertEquals(2, session.getNumberOfStudents());
    assertEquals(student1, session.get(0));
    assertEquals(student2, session.get(1));
}
```

Add the get method to CourseSession and remove the method getAllStudents. This refactoring shows how you can move common code from the test class directly into the production class in order to remove duplication.

```
class CourseSession {

    ...
    ArrayList<Student> getAllStudents() {
      return students;
    }

    Student get(int index) {
        return students.get(index);
    }
}
```

Another significant benefit of this refactoring is that you have hidden a detail of CourseSession that was unnecessarily exposed. You have *encapsulated* the students collection, only selectively allowing the get, add, and size operations to be performed on it.

This encapsulation provides two significant benefits: First, you currently store the list of in an ArrayList. An ArrayList is one specific kind of data structure with certain use and performance characteristics. If you expose this list directly to client code, their code now depends upon the fact that the students are available as an ArrayList. This dependency means that later you cannot easily change the representation of how students are stored. Second, exposing the entire collection means that other classes can manipulate that collection—add new Student objects, remove Student objects, and so on—without your CourseSession class being aware of these changes. The integrity of your CourseSession object could be violated!

Class Constants

It is never a good idea to embed literals directly in code, as mentioned earlier. Declaring a local variable as final, which prevents other code from reassigning its value, is a good idea. The final keyword tells other developers that "I don't intend for you to be able to change the value of this variable."

Idiosyncracies: The Final Keyword

You can mark local object and primitive variables as final:

```
public void testCreate() {
    final String firstStudentName =
        "Jane Doe";
    final Student firstStudent =
        new Student(firstStudentName);
```

You can also mark arguments as final:

```
Student(final String name) {
    this.name = name;
}
```

Doing so can provide you with an additional level of protection from other code in the method that assigns a different value to the local variable or argument. Many developers insist on doing so, and it's not a bad practice.

I choose not to, but I recommend that you try it and see how it helps you. My general reason to mark fields as final is for readability, not protection. As a rule, you should never assign values to arguments. And you should rarely reassign values to local object reference variables. I follow both of these rules and don't feel the need to demonstrate that fact by marking the field as final. Instead, I use final to emphasize the fact that a local declaration is a literal constant and not just an initialized variable. Your mileage may vary.

Frequently you will need more than one class to use the same literal. In fact, if you are doing test-driven development properly, any time you create a literal in code, it is there by virtue of some assertion in a test method against that same literal. A test might say, "assert that these conditions produce an error and that the error message is such-and-such a message." Once this test is written, you then write the production code that produces such-and-such an error message under the right conditions. Now you have code duplication—"such-and-such an error message" appears in both the test and the production code.

While a few duplicated strings here and there may seem innocuous, overlooking the need to refactor out this duplication may prove costly in the future. One possibility is related to the growth of your software. Initially you may only deploy your system to local customers. Later, as your software achieves more success, the business may decide that it needs to deploy the software in another country. You will then need to *internationalize* your software, by deploying it with support for other languages and with consideration for other cultures.

Many software developers have encountered this problem. The software they worked on for months or years has hundreds or thousands of literal Strings strewn throughout the code. It is a major effort to retrofit internationalization support into this software.

As a craftsman of Java code, it is your job to stay vigilant and ensure that duplication is eliminated as soon as you recognize it.[5]

   Replace common literals with class constants.

A class constant is a field that is declared with the static and final keywords. As a reminder, the final keyword indicates that the field reference cannot be changed to point to a different value. The static keyword means that the field is available for use without having to first construct an instance of the class in which it is declared. It also means that there is one and only one field in memory instead of one field for each object created. The following example declares a class constant:

```
class ChessBoard {
    static final int SQUARES_PER_SIDE = 8;
}
```

---

[5]For the problem of duplicated strings, a more robust solution involving *resource bundles* is more appropriate. See Additional Lesson III for a brief discussion of resource bundles.

By convention, class constants appear in uppercase letters. When all letters are uppercase, camel notation is not possible, so the standard is to use underscores to separate words.

You can refer to the class constant by first specifying the class name, followed by the dot (.)operator, followed by the name of the constant.

```
int numberOfSquares =
    ChessBoard.SQUARES_PER_SIDE * ChessBoard.SQUARES_PER_SIDE;
```

You will use class constants already defined in the Java class library in the next section on Dates. Shortly thereafter you will define your own class constant in the CourseSession code.

Dates

If you browse through the J2SE API documentation for the package java.util, you will see several classes that are related to times and dates, including Calendar, GregorianCalendar, Date, TimeZone, and SimpleTimeZone. The Date class provides a simple timestamp mechanism. The other, related classes work together with Date to provide exhaustive support for internationalized dates and for working with components of a timestamp.

Initial versions of Java shipped with the Date class as the sole provider of support for dates and times. The Date class was designed to provide most of the functionality needed. It is a simple implementation: Internally, a date is represented by the number of milliseconds (thousandths of a second) since January 1, 1970 GMT at 00:00:00 (known as the "epoch").

Overloaded Constructors

The Date class provides a handful of constructors. It is possible and often desirable to provide a developer with more than one way to construct new objects of a class type. You will learn how to create multiple constructors for your class in this lesson.

In the Date class, three of the constructors allow you to specify time parts (year, month, day, hour, minute, or second) in order to build a Date object for a specific date and time. A fourth constructor allows you to construct a date from an input String. A fifth constructor allows you to construct a date using the number milliseconds since the epoch. A final constructor, one that takes no parameters, constructs a timestamp that represents "now," the time at which the Date object was created.

There are also many methods that allow getting and setting of fields on the Date, such as setHour, setMinutes, getDate, and getSeconds.

The Date class was not designed to provide support for internationalized dates, however, so the designers of Java introduced the Calendar classes in J2SE 1.1. The intent was for the Calendar classes to supplement the Date class. The Calendar class provides the ability to work with dates by their constituent parts. This meant that the constructors and getters/setters in the Date class were no longer needed as of J2SE 1.1. The cleanest approach would have been for Sun to simply remove the offending constructors and methods.

However, if Sun were to have changed the Date class, large numbers of existing applications would have had to have been recoded, recompiled, retested, and redeployed. Sun chose to avoid this unhappy circumstance by instead *deprecating* the constructors and methods in Date. This means that the methods and constructors are still available for use, but the API developers are warning you that they will remove the deprecated code from the next major release of Java. If you browse the Date class in the API documentation, you will see that Sun has clearly marked the deprecated methods and constructors.

Overloaded
Constructors

In this exercise, you will actually use the deprecated methods. You'll see that their use generates warnings from the compiler. Warnings are for the most part bad—they indicate that you're doing something in code that you probably should not be. There's always a better way that does not generate a warning. As the exercise progresses, you will eliminate the warnings using an improved solution.

 In the student information system, course sessions need to have a start and end date, marking the first and last days of class. You could provide both start and end dates to a CourseSession constructor, but you have been told that sessions are always 16 weeks (15 weeks of class, with a one-week break after week 7). With this information, you decide to design the CourseSession class so that users of the class need only supply the start date—your class will calculate the end date.

Here's the test to be added to CourseSessionTest.

```java
public void testCourseDates() {
    int year = 103;
    int month = 0;
    int date = 6;
    Date startDate = new Date(year, month, date);

    CourseSession session =
        new CourseSession("ABCD", "200", startDate);
```

```
    year = 103;
    month = 3;
    date = 25;
    Date sixteenWeeksOut = new Date(year, month, date);
    assertEquals(sixteenWeeksOut, session.getEndDate());
}
```

You will need an import statement at the top of CourseSessionTest:

```
import java.util.Date;
```

This code uses one of the deprecated constructors for Date. Also of note are the odd-looking parameter values being passed to the Date constructor. Year 103? Month 0?

The API documentation, which should be your first reference for understanding a system library class, explains what to pass in for the parameters. Specifically, documentation for the Date constructor says that the first parameter represents "the year minus 1900," the second parameter represents "the month between 0 and 11," and the third parameter represents "the day of the month between 1-31." So `new Date(103, 0, 6)` would create a Date representation for January 6, 2003. Lovely.

Overloaded Constructors

Since the start date is so critical to the definition of a course session, you want the constructor to require the start date. The test method constructs a new CourseSession object, passing in a newly constructed Date object in addition to the department and course number. You will want to change the instantiation of CourseSession in the setUp method to use this modified constructor. But as an interim, incremental approach, you can instead supply an additional, *overloaded* constructor.

The test finally asserts that the session end date, returned by getEndDate, is April 25, 2003.

You will need to make the following changes to CourseSession in order to get the test to pass:

- Add import statements for java.util.Date, java.util.Calendar, and java.util.GregorianCalendar;

- add a getEndDate method that calculates and returns the appropriate session end date; and

- add a new constructor that takes a starting date as a parameter.

The corresponding production code:

```
package studentinfo;

import java.util.ArrayList;
import java.util.Date;
```

```
import java.util.Calendar;
import java.util.GregorianCalendar;

class CourseSession {
   private String department;
   private String number;
   private ArrayList<Student> students = new ArrayList<Student>();
   private Date startDate;

   CourseSession(String department, String number) {
      this.department = department;
      this.number = number;
   }

   CourseSession(String department, String number, Date startDate) {
      this.department = department;
      this.number = number;
      this.startDate = startDate;
   }
   ...
   Date getEndDate() {
      GregorianCalendar calendar = new GregorianCalendar();
      calendar.setTime(startDate);
      int numberOfDays = 16 * 7 - 3;
      calendar.add(Calendar.DAY_OF_YEAR, numberOfDays);
      Date endDate = calendar.getTime();
      return endDate;
   }
}
```

Overloaded Constructors

As I describe what getEndDate does, try to follow along in the J2SE API documentation for the classes GregorianCalendar and Calendar.

In getEndDate, you first construct a GregorianCalendar object. You then use the setTime[6] method to store the object representing the session start date in the calendar. Next, you create the local variable numberOfDays to represent the number of days to be added to the start date in order to come up with the end date. The appropriate number is calculated by multiplying 16 weeks by 7 days per week, then subtracting 3 days (since the last day of the session is on the Friday of the 16th week).

The next line:

```
calendar.add(Calendar.DAY_OF_YEAR, numberOfDays);
```

sends the add message to the calendar object. The add method in GregorianCalendar takes a field and an amount. You will have to look at the J2SE API documentation for Calendar—in addition to the documentation for Gregorian-Calendar—to fully understand how to use the add method. Gregorian-

[6]Don't use this as a good example of method naming!

Calendar is a *subclass* of Calendar, which means that the way it works is tied tightly to Calendar. The field that represents the first parameter tells the calendar object what you are adding *to*. In this case, you want to add a number to the day of year. The Calendar class defines DAY_OF_YEAR as well as several other class constants that represent date parts, such as YEAR.

The calendar now contains a date that represents the end date of the course session. You extract this date from the calendar using the getTime method and finally return the end date of the course session as the result of the method.

You might wonder if the getEndDate method will work, then, when the start date is close to the end of the year. If that can possibly happen, it's time to write a test for it. However, the student information system you are writing is for a university that has been around for 200 years. No semester has ever begun in one year and ended in the next, and it will never happen. In short, you're not going to need to worry about it . . . yet.

Overloaded
Constructors

The second constructor will be short-lived, but it served the purpose of allowing you to quickly get your new test to pass. You now want to remove the older constructor, since it doesn't initialize the session start date. To do so, you will need to modify the setUp method and testCourseDates. You should also amend the creation test to verify that the start date is getting stored properly.

```
package studentinfo;

import junit.framework.TestCase;
import java.util.ArrayList;
import java.util.Date;

public class CourseSessionTest extends TestCase {
    private CourseSession session;
    private Date startDate;

    public void setUp() {
        int year = 103;
        int month = 0;
        int date = 6;
        startDate = new Date(year, month, date);
        session = new CourseSession("ENGL", "101", startDate);
    }

    public void testCreate() {
        assertEquals("ENGL", session.getDepartment());
        assertEquals("101", session.getNumber());
        assertEquals(0, session.getNumberOfStudents());
        assertEquals(startDate, session.getStartDate());
    }
    ...
```

```
public void testCourseDates() {
    int year = 103;
    int month = 3;
    int date = 25;
    Date sixteenWeeksOut = new Date(year, month, date);
    assertEquals(sixteenWeeksOut, session.getEndDate());
    }
}
```

You can now remove the older constructor from CourseSession. You'll also need to add the getStartDate method to CourseSession:

```
class CourseSession {
    ...
    Date getStartDate() {
        return startDate;
    }
}
```

Deprecation Warnings

The above code will compile and pass the tests, but you will see a warning or note in the compilation output. If you are using an IDE, you might not see the warnings. Find out how to turn on the warnings—you don't want to hide them.

 Eliminate all warnings.

Ignoring a compiler warning is like ignoring a sore tooth—you'll pay for it sooner or later, and it may end up costing you dearly to ignore it for too long.[7]

```
Note: CourseSessionTest.java uses or overrides a deprecated API.
Note: Recompile with -Xlint:deprecation for details.
```

If you are compiling from the command line, you should do just what the message says: Enter the compilation command again, but modify it to include the compilation switch -Xlint:deprecation option.

```
javac -classpath c:\junit3.8.1\junit.jar -Xlint:deprecation *.java
```

The new compile output should look something like this:

```
CourseSessionTest.java:15: warning: Date(int,int,int) in java.util.Date has been deprecated
        startDate = new Date(year, month, date);
            ^
```

---

[7]He writes, as he sits here with a corrupt molar . . .

```
CourseSessionTest.java:43: warning: Date(int,int,int) in java.util.Date has been deprecated
        Date sixteenWeeksOut = new Date(year, month, date);
                               ^
2 warnings
```

If you are running in an IDE, it will have a setting somewhere to allow you to turn warnings on or off. You might already have seen similar deprecation messages, since warnings are usually "on" by default. In any case, the warnings should be disturbing to your craftsperson sensibilities. May they nag at you incessantly. You will soon learn a different way to construct dates that does not result in the warnings.

The test should run just fine. But you have lots of little ugliness in the code that can be cleaned up.

Refactoring

A quick improvement is to remove the unnecessary local variable, endDate, that appears at the end of the method getEndDate in CourseSession. Declaring the temporary variable aided in your understanding of the Calendar class:

```
Date endDate = calendar.getTime();
return endDate;
```

A more concise form is to simply return the Date object returned by the call to getTime.

```
return calendar.getTime();
```

Import Refactorings

The CourseSession class now must import four different classes from the package java.util:

```
import java.util.ArrayList;
import java.util.Date;
import java.util.GregorianCalendar;
import java.util.Calendar;
```

This is still reasonable, but you can see that the list could quickly get out of hand as more system library classes are used. It is also a form of duplication—the package name is duplicated in each import statement. Remember that your primary refactoring job is to eliminate as much duplication as possible.

Java provides a shortcut version of the import statement to declare that you are importing all classes from a specified package:

```
import java.util.*;
```

This form of import is known as a *package import*. The asterisk (*) acts as a wildcard character.

After making this change, you can use any additional classes from the java.util package without having to modify or add to the import statements. Note that there is no runtime penalty for using either this form or the singular class form of the import statement. An import statement merely declares that classes *might* be used in the class file. An import statement does not guarantee that any classes from a package are used in the class file.

There is no consensus about which form is more proper. Most shops use the * form of the import statement either all the time or when the number of import statements begins to get unwieldy. Some shops insist that all classes must be explicitly named in the import statements, which makes it easier to determine the package a class comes from. Modern Java IDEs can enforce the import convention your shop decides on and even switch back and forth between the various forms. An IDE makes the choice of which form to use less significant.

It is possible to import a class or package but not use the class or any classes from the package within your source code. The Java compiler will not warn you about these unnecessary import statements. Most modern IDEs have optimizing facilities that will help you remove them.

Improving Understanding with a Factory Method

The getEndDate method in CourseSession is the most complex method you've written yet. It's about as long as you want your methods to get. Most of the methods you write should be between one and half a dozen lines. Some methods might be between half a dozen and a dozen or so lines. If your methods are regularly this length or even longer, you should work on refactoring them. The primary goal is to ensure that methods can be rapidly understood and maintained.

If your methods are short enough, it will be easy to provide a meaningful, concise name for them. If you are finding it difficult to name a method, consider breaking it up into smaller methods, each of which does only one succinctly nameable thing.

Another bit of duplication and lack of clarity that you should be unhappy with lies in the test method. For the time being, you are using the deprecated Date constructors, a technique that is considerably simpler than using the

Calendar class. However, the code is somewhat confusing because the year has to be specified as relative to 1900, and the months have been numbered from 0 through 11 instead of 1 through 12.

In CourseSessionTest, code a new method called createDate that takes more sensible inputs.

```
Date createDate(int year, int month, int date) {
    return new Date(year - 1900, month - 1, date);
}
```

This will allow you to create dates using a 4-digit year and a number from 1 through 12 for the month.

You can now refactor setUp and testCourseDates to use this utility method. With the introduction of the utility method, defining the local variables year, month, and date adds little to the understanding of the code, since the *factory method*[8] createDate encapsulates some of the confusion. You can eliminate the local variables and embed them directly as parameters in the message send to createDate:

Refactoring

```
public void setUp() {
    startDate = createDate(2003, 1, 6);
    session = new CourseSession("ENGL", "101", startDate);
}
...
public void testCourseDates() {
    Date sixteenWeeksOut = createDate(2003, 4, 25);
    assertEquals(sixteenWeeksOut, session.getEndDate());
}
```

Some of you may be shaking your head at this point. You have done a lot of work, such as introducing local variables, and then you have undone much of that same work shortly thereafter.

Part of crafting software is understanding that code is a very malleable form. The best thing you can do is get into the mindset that you are a sculptor of code, shaping and molding it into a better form at all times. Once in a while, you'll add a flourish to make something in the code stand out. Later, you may find that the modification is really sticking out like a sore thumb, asking for someone to soothe it with a better solution. You will learn to recognize these trouble spots in your code ("code smells," as Martin Fowler calls them.)[9]

---

[8]A method responsible for creating and returning objects. Another, perhaps more concise term, is "creation method."

[9][Wiki2004].

You will also learn that it is cheaper to fix code problems now rather than wait until the code is too intertwined with the rest of the system. It doesn't take long!

    Keep your code clean at all times!

Creating Dates with Calendar

You still receive deprecation warnings each time you compile. Bad, bad. You should get rid of the warnings before someone complains. The benefit of having moved the date creation into a separate method, createDate, is that now you will only have to make a change in one place in your code, instead of two, to eliminate the warnings.

Instead of creating a Date object using the deprecated constructor, you will use the GregorianCalendar class. You can build a date or timestamp from its constituent parts by using the set method defined in Calendar. The API documentation for Calendar lists the various date parts that you can set. The createDate method builds a date by supplying a year, a month, and a day of the month.

```
Date createDate(int year, int month, int date) {
    GregorianCalendar calendar = new GregorianCalendar();
    calendar.clear();
    calendar.set(Calendar.YEAR, year);
    calendar.set(Calendar.MONTH, month - 1);
    calendar.set(Calendar.DAY_OF_MONTH, date);
    return calendar.getTime();
}
```

The GregorianCalendar is a bit more sensible than Date in that a year is a year. If the real year is 2005, you can pass 2005 to the calendar object instead of 105.

You will need to modify the import statements in CourseSessionTest in order to compile and test these changes. The simplest way is to import everything from the java.util package:

```
import java.util.*;
```

Compile and test. Congratulations—no more embarrassing deprecation warnings!

Comments

One part of the `getEndDate` method that could use clarification is the calculation for the number of days to add to the session start date.

```
int numberOfDays = 16 * 7 - 3;
```

To another developer that has to maintain this method, the mathematical expression is not immediately obvious. While the maintainer can probably figure it out in a few minutes, it's far less expensive for you as the original developer to explain what you were thinking.

Java allows you to add free-form explanatory text within the source file in the form of *comments*. The compiler ignores and discards comments encountered when it reads the source file. It is up to you to decide where and when comments are appropriate.

You can add a *single-line comment* to the `numberOfDays` calculation. A single-line comment begins with two forward slashes (//) and continues to the end of the current source line. Anything from the first slash to the end of the line is ignored by the compiler.

```
int numberOfDays = 16 * 7 - 3;  // weeks * days per week - 3 days
```

You can place single-line comments on a separate line:

```
// weeks * days per week - 3 days
int numberOfDays = 16 * 7 - 3;
```

However, comments are notorious for being incorrect or misleading. The above comment is a perfect example of an unnecessary comment. A better solution is to figure out a clearer way to express the code.

 Replace comments with more expressive code.

One possible solution:

```
final int sessionLength = 16;
final int daysInWeek = 7;
final int daysFromFridayToMonday = 3;
int numberOfDays =
    sessionLength * daysInWeek - daysFromFridayToMonday;
```

Hmmm. Well, it's more expressive, but I'm not sure that `daysFromFridayToMonday` expresses exactly what's going on. This should demonstrate that there's not always a perfect solution. Refactoring is not an exact science. That shouldn't stop you from trying, however. Most changes *do* improve the code, and someone (maybe you) can always come along after you and figure out an even better way. For now, it's your call.

Java supplies another form of comment known as a *multiline comment*. A multiline comment starts with the two characters /* and ends with the two characters */. Everything from the beginning slash through to the ending slash is ignored by the compiler.

Note that while multiline comments can nest single line comments, multi-line comments cannot nest other multiline comments.

As an example, the Java compiler allows the following:

```
int a = 1;
/*  int b = 2;
//  int c = 3;
*/
```

while the following code will not compile:

```
int a = 1;
/*  int b = 2;
/*  int c = 3;  */
*/
```

You should prefer single-line comments for the few places that you need to annotate the code. The multiline comment form can then be used for rapidly "commenting out" (turning off the code so that it is not read by the compiler) large blocks of code.

Javadoc Comments

Another use for multiline comments is to provide formatted code documentation that can later be used for automated generation of nicely formatted API documentation. These comments are known as javadoc comments, since there is a javadoc tool that will read your source files, look for javadoc comments, and extract them along with other necessary information in order to build documentation web pages. Sun's documentation for the Java APIs themselves was produced using javadoc.

A javadoc comment is a multiline comment. The distinction is that a javadoc comment starts with /** instead of /*. To the javac compiler, there is no difference between the two, since both start with /* and end with */. The javadoc tool understands the difference, however.

Javadoc comments appear directly before the Java element they are documenting. Javadoc comments can appear before fields, but most typically they are used to document classes and methods. There are rules for how a javadoc comment must be formatted in order to be parsed correctly by the javadoc compiler.

The primary reason for producing javadoc web pages is to document your code for external consumption by other project teams or for public distribution. While you can code javadoc comments for every Java element (fields, methods, classes, etc.), you should only expend the time to produce javadoc comments for things you want to expose. Javadoc comments are intended for telling a client developer how to work with a class.

In a team doing test-driven development, Javadoc comments are of lesser value. If done properly, the tests you produce using test-driven development provide far better documentation on the capabilities of a class. Practices such as pair programming and *collective code ownership*, where developers work on all parts of the system, also minimize the need for producing javadoc comments.

javadoc
Comments

If you code concise, well-named methods, with well-named parameters, the amount of additional text that you should have to write in a Javadoc comment should be minimal. In the absence of text, the Javadoc compiler does a fine job of extracting and presenting the names you chose.

As a brief exercise, provide a Javadoc comment for the CourseSession class—the single-argument constructor—and for one of the methods within the class.

Here are the Javadoc comments I came up with:

```
package studentinfo;

import java.util.*;

/**
 * Provides a representation of a single-semester
 * session of a specific university course.
 * @author Administrator
 */
class CourseSession {
    private ArrayList<Student> students = new ArrayList<Student>();
    private Date startDate;

    CourseSession() {
    }

    /**
     * Constructs a CourseSession starting on a specific date
     *
     * @param startDate the date on which the CourseSession begins
```

```
    */
    CourseSession(Date startDate) {
        this.startDate = startDate;
    }

    /**
     * @return Date the last date of the course session
     */
    Date getEndDate() {
        ...
}
```

Take particular note of the @ keywords in the javadoc comments. When you look at the web pages produced by the Javadoc command, it will be apparent what the Javadoc compiler does with the tagged comments. The Javadoc keywords that you will want to use most frequently are @param, to describe a parameter, and @return, to describe what a method returns.

There are lots of rules and many additional @ keywords in Javadoc. Refer to the Javadoc documentation for further information. The Javadoc documentation can be found in the API documentation for the Java SDK (either online or downloaded), under the tool docs for your platform.

Once you've added these or similar comments to your code, go to the command line. (If you are using an IDE, you may be able to generate the documentation from within the IDE.) You will want to create a new empty directory in which to store the generated docs, so that you can easily delete it when you regenerate the Javadoc. Navigate to this empty directory[10] and enter the following command:

```
javadoc -package -classpath c:\source;c:\junit3.8.1\junit.jar studentinfo
```

The javadoc program will produce a number of .html files and a stylesheet (.css) file. Open the file index.html in a web browser and take a few minutes to see what this simple command has produced (Figure 2.5). Fairly impressive, no?

Well, yes and no. I'm embarrassed by the comments I had you put in for the methods. They really added nothing that the code didn't already state. The @param keyword simply restates information that can be gleaned from the parameter type and name. The @return keyword restates information that can be derived from the method name and return type. If you find a need for @return and @param keywords, try to rename the parameters and the method to eliminate this need.

---

[10] Instead of navigating to the empty directory, you can also redirect the output from the javadoc command using its -d switch.

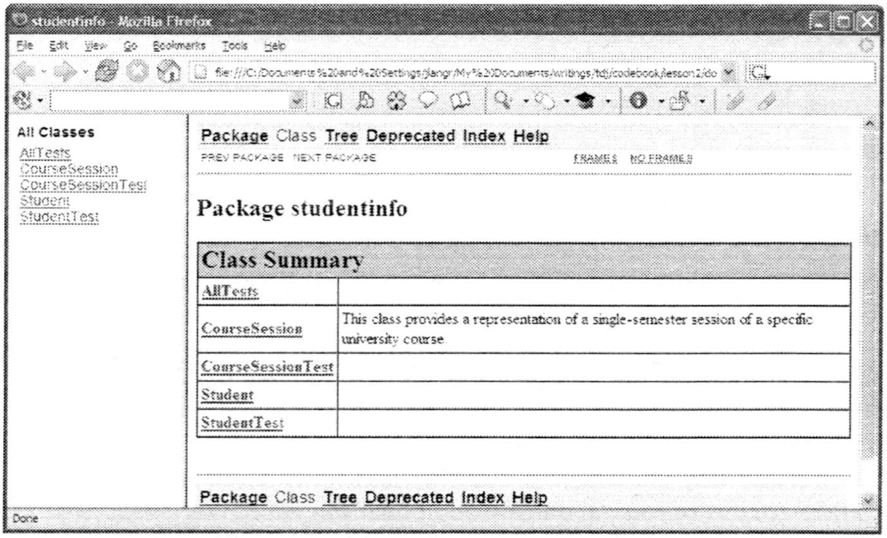

Figure 2.5 *Your Own API Pages*

Remove the comments for the constructor and the methods completely, but leave the comment for the class—it does provide a bit more value to the reader. Then rerun the javadoc command, bring up the web pages again, and see if you feel any useful information was lost. Your opinion may differ.

Exercises

1. Add a test to TestPawn that creates a pawn without a color. Why does this generate a compile error? (Hint: Think about default constructors.) Fix the compiler error by adding a second constructor that constructs a white pawn by default.

2. Make the constants for the two colors static and move them onto the Pawn class.

3. Pawns aren't very useful without a board. Use a test to define a Board class. Assert that the board starts with zero pieces on it. Follow the TDD sequence: Write the smallest test possible. Prove failure with a red bar or a compile error. Incrementally add small bits of code to obtain a clean compile or green bar.

4. Develop code to allow pawns to be added to the board. In a test, add a black and white pawn to the board. Each time you add a pawn, as-

sert that the piece count is correct. Also, each time you add a pawn, obtain a list of pieces from the board and ensure that it contains the expected pawn objects.

5. Write javadoc for each of the production classes and methods you have created so far. Be careful in doing so: Do not duplicate information that your methods already impart! The javadoc should be supplementary information.

6. Move the four tests and classes you have created into a package of their own. Name this package chess. Resolve compilation failures and get to a green bar again. Also, replace fully qualified class names for List and ArrayList by using an import statement.

7. Move TestPawn and Pawn into a package named pieces and resolve any problems discovered along the way.

8. Ensure that nothing other than a Pawn can be added to the board. Try adding a new Integer("7") to the list of pawns and see the resulting compiler error.

9. Create a test suite that runs each test class.

10. Look through the code you have written so far. Ensure there is no duplication anywhere in the code. Remember that the test code is code as well. Use the setUp method if appropriate.

Lesson 3

Strings and Packages

In this lesson, you will:

- learn more about the String class

- learn how characters are represented in Java

- use a system property to ensure platform-independent code

- use StringBuilder objects to dynamically construct strings

- learn how to iterate through a collection to operate on each of its objects

- use System.out to display report output

- organize your classes into packages

- increase your understanding of the access modifiers public and private

Characters and Strings

Strings, or pieces of text, account for up to 50 percent and more of the objects created during the execution of a typical Java application. While Strings are objects, they are made up of sequences of individual characters. Java represents a character as a primitive type known as char. Since a char value is of a primitive type (like an int value), remember that you cannot send messages to it.

Characters

Java includes a char type that represents letters, digits, punctuation marks, diacriticals, and other special characters. Java bases its character set on a standard known as Unicode 4.0 for representation of its characters. The

103

Unicode standard is designed to accommodate virtually all character variations in the major languages of the world. More information regarding the standard can be found at *http://www.unicode.org*.

Java uses two bytes to store each character. Two bytes is 16 bits, which means that Java can represent 2^{16}, or 65,536, characters. While that may seems like a lot, it's not enough to support everything in the Unicode standard. You probably won't need to concern yourself with supporting anything over the two-byte range, but if you do, Java allows you to work with characters as int values. An int is four bytes, so the billions of characters it can support should be sufficient until the Federation requires us to incorporate the Romulan alphabet.

You can represent character literals in Java in a few ways. The simplest form is to embed the actual character between single quotes (tics).

```
char capitalA = 'A';
```

Characters and Strings

Language Tests

While I present most of the code in Agile Java as part of the ongoing student example, I show some Java syntactical details and variations as brief code snippets and assertions. The single-line assertions in this section on characters provide an example. I refer to these as language tests—you write them to learn the language. You might keep them to reinforce your understanding of the language for later use.

You can code these tests wherever you like. I typically code them as separate test methods in the current test class, then delete them once I have an understanding of the element I was working on.

You may choose to create a separate class to contain these "scratch" tests. Ultimately, you might even create a scratch package, suite, and/or project of such tests.

You might get some reuse out of storing these tests: Some of the language tests you build may end up being the basis for utility methods that encapsulate and simplify use of a language feature.

Characters are essentially numerics. Each character maps to a corresponding positive integer from 0 through 65,535. Here is a test snippet that shows how the character 'A' has a numeric value of 65 (its Unicode equivalent).

```
assertEquals(65, capitalA);
```

Not all characters can be directly entered via the keyboard. You can represent Unicode characters using the Unicode escape sequence, \u or \U, followed by a 4-digit hex number.

```
assertEquals('\u0041', capitalA);
```

Additionally, you may represent characters as a 3-digit octal (base 8) escape sequence.

```
assertEquals('\101', capitalA);
```

The highest possible character literal that you may represent as an octal sequence is '\377', which is equivalent to 255.

Most older languages (for example, C) treat characters as single bytes. The most well-known standard for representing characters in a single-byte character set (SBCS), the American Standard Code for Information Interchange (ASCII), is defined by ANSI X3.4.[1] The first 128 characters of Unicode map directly to their ASCII correspondents.

Special Characters

Java defines several special characters that you can use for things such as output formatting. Java represents the special characters with an *escape sequence* that consists of the backslash character (\) followed by a mnemonic. The table below summarizes the char literals that represent these special characters.

Characters and Strings

Carriage return	'\r'
Line feed	'\n'
Tab	'\t'
Form feed	'\f'
Backspace	'\b'

Since the tic character and the backslash character have special meanings with respect to char literals, you must represent them with an escape sequence. You may also escape (i.e., prefix with the escape character \) the double quote character, but you are not required to do so.

Single quote	'\''
Backslash	'\\'
Double quote	'\"'

---

[1]In fact, ASCII is only a true standard for seven of the single byte's eight bits. Characters from 0 through 127 are consistently represented, but there are several competing standards for characters 128 through 255.

Strings

A String object represents a sequence of char values of fixed length. The String class in Java is probably the most frequently used class in any Java application. Even in a small application, thousands of String objects will be created over and over.

The String class supplies dozens of methods. It has special performance characteristics that make it different from most other classes in the system. Finally, even though String is a class like any other class in the system, the Java language provides special syntactical support for working with String objects.

You can construct Strings in a number of ways. Any time you create a new String literal, the Java VM constructs a String object behind the scenes. Here are two ways to construct a String object and assign it to a reference variable:

```
String a = "abc";
String b = new String("abc"); // DON'T DO THIS
```

Avoid the second technique.[2] It creates two String objects, which can degrade performance: First, the VM creates the literal String object "abc". Second, the VM constructs a new String object, passing the literal "abc" to its constructor. Equally as important, it is an unnecessary construct that makes your code more difficult to read.

Since strings are sequences of characters, they can embed special characters. The string literal in the following line of code contains a tab character followed by a line feed character.

```
String z = "\t\n";
```

String Concatenation

You may *concatenate* a string to another string to produce a third string.

```
assertEquals("abcd", "ab".concat("cd"));
```

String concatenation is such a frequent operation in Java that you can use the plus sign (+) as a shortcut for concatenating strings. In fact, most Java concatenations are written this way:

```
assertEquals("abcdef", "abc" + "def");
```

[2][Bloch2001].

Since the result of concatenating two strings together is another string, you can code many + operations to concatenate several strings into a single string.

```
assertEquals("123456", "12" + "3" + "456");
```

In the previous lesson, you used + for addition of integers. Java also allows you to use the plus sign, known as an *operator*, to concatenate strings. Since the + operator has different meanings, depending on what you use it with, it is known as an *overloaded operator*.

String Immutability

As you browse through the Java API documentation for String, you will notice that there are no methods that change a string. You cannot alter the length of a string, nor can you alter any of the characters contained within a string. String objects are thus *immutable*. If you want to perform any manipulations on a string, you must create a new string. For example, when you concatenate two strings using +, the Java VM alters neither string. Instead, it creates a new string object.

Sun designed String to be immutable to allow it to act in a very optimized manner. This optimization is crucial due to the very heavy use of Strings in most applications.

StringBuilder

StringBuilder

Often you will need to be able to construct strings dynamically. The class java.lang.StringBuilder provides this capability. A newly created StringBuilder represents an empty sequence, or collection, of characters. You can add to this collection by sending the append message to the StringBuilder object.

Just as Java overloads the + operator to support both adding int values and concatenating strings, the StringBuilder class overloads the append method to take arguments of any base type. You can pass a character, a String, an int, or other types as arguments to an append message. Refer to the Java API documentation for the list of overloaded methods.

When you finish appending to the StringBuilder, you obtain a concatenated String object from the StringBuilder by sending it the toString message.

 Users of the student information system need to produce a report showing the roster of a course session. For now, a simple text report with just a list of the student names in any order will suffice.

Code the following test in CourseSessionTest. The assertion shows that the report requires a simple header and a footer showing the count of students.

```
public void testRosterReport() {
    session.enroll(new Student("A"));
    session.enroll(new Student("B"));

    String rosterReport = session.getRosterReport();
    assertEquals(
        CourseSession.ROSTER_REPORT_HEADER +
        "A\nB\n" +
        CourseSession.ROSTER_REPORT_FOOTER + "2\n", rosterReport);
}
```

(Remember that testRosterReport uses the CourseSession object created in the setUp method in CourseSessionTest.) Update CourseSession with the corresponding code:

```
String getRosterReport() {
    StringBuilder buffer = new StringBuilder();

    buffer.append(ROSTER_REPORT_HEADER);

    Student student = students.get(0);
    buffer.append(student.getName());
    buffer.append('\n');

    student = students.get(1);
    buffer.append(student.getName());
    buffer.append('\n');

    buffer.append(ROSTER_REPORT_FOOTER + students.size() + '\n');

    return buffer.toString();
}
```

StringBuilder

For each of the two students, you pass a String (the student's name) to append, then you pass a char (line feed) to append. You also append header and footer information to the StringBuilder object stored in buffer. The name buffer implies that the StringBuilder holds on to a collection of characters that will be used later. The line that constructs the footer demonstrates how you can pass a concatenated string as the parameter to the append method.

You defined the getRosterReport method in the CourseSession class. Code within a class can refer directly to static variables. So instead of:

```
CourseSession.ROSTER_REPORT_HEADER
```

the CourseSession code uses:

```
ROSTER_REPORT_HEADER
```

When you learn more about the static keyword in Lesson 4, you will be told to refer to static variables and static methods only by scoping them with the class name (as in CourseSession.ROSTER_REPORT_HEADER), even from within the class they are defined. Doing otherwise obscures the fact that you are using static elements, which can lead to troublesome defects. In the case of class constants, however, the naming convention (UPPERCASE_WITH_UNDERSCORES) makes it explicitly clear that you are referring to a static element. The second, unscoped, form is thus acceptable (although some shops may prohibit it) and is an exception to the rule.

If you look at older Java code, you will see use of the class java.lang.String-Buffer. You interact with a StringBuffer object the same as with a String-Builder object. The distinction between the two is that the StringBuilder class has better performance characteristics. It does not need to support *multi-threaded* applications, where two pieces of code could be working with a StringBuffer simultaneously. See Lesson 13 for a discussion of multithreading.

System Properties

System
Properties

Both the method getRosterReport and its test contain the use of '\n' to represent a line feed in many places. Not only is this duplication, it is not portable—different platforms use different special character sequences for advancing to a new line on output. The solution to this problem can be found in the class java.lang.System. As usual, refer to the J2SE API documentation for a more detailed understanding of the System class.

The System class contains a method named getProperty that takes a system property key (a String) as a parameter and returns the system property value associated with the key. The Java VM sets several system properties upon startup. Many of these properties return information about the VM and execution environment. The API documentation method detail for getProperties shows the list of available properties.

One of the properties is line.separator. According to the Java API documentation, the value of this property under Unix is '\n'. However, under Windows, the value of the property is '\r\n'. You will use the line.separator system property in your code to compensate for the differences between platforms.

The following changes to the test and to CourseSession demonstrate use of the System method getProperty.

Test code:

```
public void testRosterReport()
{
    Student studentA = new Student("A");
```

```
Student studentB = new Student("B");
session.enroll(studentA);
session.enroll(studentB);

String rosterReport = session.getRosterReport();
assertEquals(
    CourseSession.ROSTER_REPORT_HEADER +
    "A" + CourseSession.NEWLINE +
    "B" + CourseSession.NEWLINE +
    CourseSession.ROSTER_REPORT_FOOTER + "2" +
    CourseSession.NEWLINE, rosterReport);
}
```

Production code:

```
class CourseSession {
    static final String NEWLINE =
        System.getProperty("line.separator");
    static final String ROSTER_REPORT_HEADER =
        "Student" + NEWLINE +
        "-----" + NEWLINE;
    static final String ROSTER_REPORT_FOOTER =
        NEWLINE + "# students = ";
    ...
    String getRosterReport() {
        StringBuilder buffer = new StringBuilder();

        buffer.append(ROSTER_REPORT_HEADER);

        Student student = students.get(0);
        buffer.append(student.getName());
        buffer.append(NEWLINE);

        student = students.get(1);
        buffer.append(student.getName());
        buffer.append(NEWLINE);

        buffer.append(ROSTER_REPORT_FOOTER + students.size() + NEWLINE);

        return buffer.toString();
    }
}
```

Looping through All Students

The test method testRosterReport demonstrates how to produce a report for two students. You know that the code to construct the report is written with the assumption that there will be only two students.

You need to produce code that supports an unlimited number of students. To do this, you will modify your test to enroll additional students. Subsequently, you will recognize that the production class contains duplicate code—and the amount of duplication will only get worse—since the same three lines of code are repeated for each student, with the only variance being the index of the student.

What you would like to be able to do is to execute the same three lines of code for *each* of the students in the ArrayList, regardless of how many students the ArrayList contains. There are several ways of doing this in Java. The most straightforward means in J2SE 5.0 is to use a for-each loop.[3]

There are two forms of the for-each loop. The first form, which uses opening and closing braces following the loop declaration, allows you to specify multiple statements as the body of the for-each loop.

```
for (Student student: students) {
    // ... statements here ...
}
```

The second form allows you to define the body as a single statement only, and thus requires no braces:

```
for (Student student: students)
    // ... single statements here;
```

In Lesson 7, you will learn about another kind of for loop that allows you to loop a certain number of times instead of looping through every element in a collection.

The Java VM executes the body of the for loop once for each student in the collection students.

```
String getRosterReport() {
    StringBuilder buffer = new StringBuilder();

    buffer.append(ROSTER_REPORT_HEADER);

    for (Student student: students) {
        buffer.append(student.getName());
        buffer.append(NEWLINE);
    }

    buffer.append(ROSTER_REPORT_FOOTER + students.size() + NEWLINE);

    return buffer.toString();
}
```

A reading of the above for-each loop in English-like prose: Assign each object in the collection students to a reference of the type Student named student and execute the body of the for loop with this context.

[3]Also known as an enhanced for loop.

Looping
through All
Students

Single-Responsibility Principle

 New reports are continually needed in the student information system. You have been told that you must now produce three additional reports. And you can surmise that new reports will continue to be requested. You foresee the need to change the CourseSession class constantly as the reports are added.

One of the most basic design principles in object-oriented programming is that a class should do one thing and do it well. By virtue of doing this one thing, the class should have only one reason to change. This is known as the Single-Responsibility Principle.[4]

 Classes should have only one reason to change.

The one thing CourseSession should be doing is tracking all information pertinent to a course session. Adding the capability to store professor information for the course session is a motivation that is in line with the primary goal of the class. Producing reports such as the roster report, however, is a different motivation for changing the CourseSession class and as such violates the Single-Responsibility Principle.

Create a test class, RosterReporterTest, to demonstrate how a new, separate class named RosterReporter can be used to produce a roster report.

```
package studentinfo;

import junit.framework.TestCase;
import java.util.*;

public class RosterReporterTest extends TestCase {
    public void testRosterReport() {
        CourseSession session =
            new CourseSession("ENGL", "101", createDate(2003, 1, 6));

        session.enroll(new Student("A"));
        session.enroll(new Student("B"));

        String rosterReport = new RosterReporter(session).getReport();
        assertEquals(
            RosterReporter.ROSTER_REPORT_HEADER +
            "A" + RosterReporter.NEWLINE +
            "B" + RosterReporter.NEWLINE +
```

---

[4][Martin2003].

```
        RosterReporter.ROSTER_REPORT_FOOTER + "2" +
        RosterReporter.NEWLINE, rosterReport);
    }

    Date createDate(int year, int month, int date) {
        GregorianCalendar calendar = new GregorianCalendar();
        calendar.clear();
        calendar.set(Calendar.YEAR, year);
        calendar.set(Calendar.MONTH, month - 1);
        calendar.set(Calendar.DAY_OF_MONTH, date);
        return calendar.getTime();
    }
}
```

The method testRosterReport is almost the same as it appeared in CourseSessionTest. The chief differences (highlighted in **bold**):

- You construct an instance of RosterReporter with a CourseSession object as a parameter.

- You now use class constants declared in RosterReporter instead of CourseSession.

- testReport constructs its own CourseSession object.

Single-
Responsibility
Principle

You should also recognize and make note of the duplication—both CourseSessionTest and RosterReporterTest require the createDate method. You will soon refactor this duplication away.

Add the new test to AllTests:

```
package studentinfo;

import junit.framework.TestSuite;

public class AllTests {
    public static TestSuite suite() {
        TestSuite suite = new TestSuite();
        suite.addTestSuite(StudentTest.class);
        suite.addTestSuite(CourseSessionTest.class);
        suite.addTestSuite(RosterReporterTest.class);
        return suite;
    }
}
```

Much of the work of getting the test to pass involves moving the code over from CourseSession. Do this incrementally—don't make any changes to CourseSession or CourseSessionTest until everything is working in RosterReporter.

```
package studentinfo;

import java.util.*;

class RosterReporter {
    static final String NEWLINE =
        System.getProperty("line.separator");
    static final String ROSTER_REPORT_HEADER =
        "Student" + NEWLINE +
        "----" + NEWLINE;
    static final String ROSTER_REPORT_FOOTER =
        NEWLINE + "# students = ";

    private CourseSession session;

    RosterReporter(CourseSession session) {
        this.session = session;
    }

    String getReport() {
        StringBuilder buffer = new StringBuilder();

        buffer.append(ROSTER_REPORT_HEADER);

        for (Student student: session.getAllStudents()) {
            buffer.append(student.getName());
            buffer.append(NEWLINE);
        }

        buffer.append(
            ROSTER_REPORT_FOOTER + session.getAllStudents().size() +
            NEWLINE);

        return buffer.toString();
    }
}
```

The **bold** code in the example above shows the significant differences between RosterReporter and the corresponding code in CourseSession.

To arrive at the code above, first paste the body of getReport from Course-Session directly into the corresponding method in RosterReporter. Then modify the pasted code to request the collection of students from Course-Session by sending the getAllStudents message instead of accessing it directly (since the method no longer executes in CourseSession). Since you removed getAll Students in the previous lesson, you'll just have to add it back to CourseSession.

```
class CourseSession {
    ...
    ArrayList<Student> getAllStudents() {
        return students;
    }
    ...
}
```

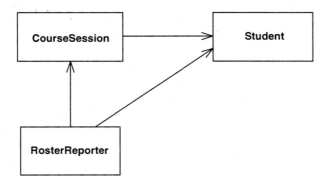

Figure 3.1   *Class Diagram*

Also, in order for code in RosterReporter to be able to send messages to the CourseSession object, it must store a CourseSession reference. You do this by assigning the CourseSession passed to the constructor of Roster-Reporter in the instance variable session.

Next, remove the report-related code from CourseSessionTest and Course-Session. This includes the test method testRosterReport, the production method getRosterReport, and the class constants defined by CourseSession. Rerun all tests.

The current class structure is show in Figure 3.1.

Refactoring

Both CourseSessionTest and RosterReporterTest require the createDate utility method. The code in createDate has nothing to do with course sessions or roster reports; it deals solely with constructing date objects. Including minor utility methods in classes is a mild violation of the Single-Responsibility Principle. You can tolerate small doses of duplication, but in doing so you quickly open the door to excessive, costly duplication in your system. In a larger system, there might be half a dozen methods that construct dates, all with pretty much the same code.

Here the duplication is obvious, since you directly created (and hopefully noted) it. An alternate approach is to not even let the duplication occur: As soon as you recognize that you might be introducing duplicate code, do the necessary refactoring *first* to stave off the potential duplication.

You will create a new test class and production class. You must update AllTests to reference the new test class. The code for all three follows.

```java
// DateUtilTest.java
package studentinfo;

import java.util.*;
import junit.framework.*;

public class DateUtilTest extends TestCase {
    public void testCreateDate() {
        Date date = new DateUtil().createDate(2000, 1, 1);
        Calendar calendar = new GregorianCalendar();
        calendar.setTime(date);
        assertEquals(2000, calendar.get(Calendar.YEAR));
        assertEquals(Calendar.JANUARY, calendar.get(Calendar.MONTH));
        assertEquals(1, calendar.get(Calendar.DAY_OF_MONTH));
    }
}
```

```java
// DateUtil.java
package studentinfo;

import java.util.*;

class DateUtil {
    Date createDate(int year, int month, int date) {
        GregorianCalendar calendar = new GregorianCalendar();
        calendar.clear();
        calendar.set(Calendar.YEAR, year);
        calendar.set(Calendar.MONTH, month - 1);
        calendar.set(Calendar.DAY_OF_MONTH, date);
        return calendar.getTime();
    }
}
```

```java
// AllTests.java
package studentinfo;

import junit.framework.TestSuite;

public class AllTests {
    public static TestSuite suite() {
        TestSuite suite = new TestSuite();
        suite.addTestSuite(StudentTest.class);
        suite.addTestSuite(CourseSessionTest.class);
        suite.addTestSuite(RosterReporterTest.class);
        suite.addTestSuite(DateUtilTest.class);
        return suite;
    }
}
```

Previously, no tests existed for the createDate method, since it was only a utility for use in test classes themselves. When extracting code from one class to a new class, you should always move along any tests that exist into the corresponding new test class. When tests do not exist, you should expend the time to create them. This will maintain the sustainability of your system.

Now that you have created and tested the DateUtil class, you want to update your code to refer to it. At the same time, you want to remove the create-Date method from both CourseSessionTest and RosterReporterTest. One solid approach is to remove the createDate method from both places and recompile. The compiler will tell you precisely which lines of code refer to the nonexistent createDate method.

   Use the compiler to help you refactor code.

Change these lines.

```java
// CourseSessionTest
package studentinfo;

import junit.framework.TestCase;
import java.util.*;

public class CourseSessionTest extends TestCase {
    ...
    public void setUp() {
        startDate = new DateUtil().createDate(2003, 1, 6);
        session = new CourseSession("ENGL", "101", startDate);
    }
    ...
    public void testCourseDates() {
        Date sixteenWeeksOut = new DateUtil().createDate(2003, 4, 25);
        assertEquals(sixteenWeeksOut, session.getEndDate());
    }
}

// RosterReporterTest.java
package studentinfo;

import junit.framework.TestCase;

public class RosterReporterTest extends TestCase {
    public void testRosterReport() {
        CourseSession session =
            new CourseSession("ENGL", "101",
                new DateUtil().createDate(2003, 1, 6));
        ...
    }
}
```

In order to use the createDate utility method, you must construct a DateUtil object each time. In the case of CourseSession test, you construct a DateUtil object twice—a prime candidate for refactoring. You could create an instance variable to hold onto a DateUtil instance. A better solution, however, is to convert the DateUtil to a static method—a method you can call without creating instances of DateUtil. You will learn how to do this in Lesson 4.

System.out

The getReport method returns a String that contains a report of all the students enrolled in a course session. In the production student information system, the String isn't going to be of much use to anyone unless you print it out or display it somewhere. Java provides output facilities to allow you to redirect information to the console, to files, and to other destinations. You will learn about these output facilities in depth in Lesson 11.

In this exercise you will modify the test so that the report displays on the console. It isn't yet a requirement, but sometimes you need to be able to display things for various reasons. The next section goes into some of these reasons.

In the Setup section of this book, you coded and ran a "Hello World" application that printed text to your console. The line of code to print the text on the console was:

```
System.out.println("hello world");
```

Look at the J2SE API documentation for the class named System, located in the package java.lang. You will see that out is a static variable, of the type PrintStream, that represents the standard output stream, also known as std-out or simply "the console." You can directly access this console object using the following static variable reference:

```
System.out
```

Once you have this console object, you may send it a number of messages, including the message println. The println method takes a String (among other things) and writes it to the underlying output stream.

Add a line to RosterReporterTest that displays the report on the console by using System.out:

```
package studentinfo;

import junit.framework.TestCase;

public class RosterReporterTest extends TestCase {
    public void testRosterReport() {
        CourseSession session =
```

```
        new CourseSession("ENGL", "101",
            new DateUtil().createDate(2003, 1, 6));

    session.enroll(new Student("A"));
    session.enroll(new Student("B"));

    String rosterReport = new RosterReporter(session).getReport();
System.out.println(rosterReport);
    assertEquals(
        RosterReporter.ROSTER_REPORT_HEADER +
        "A" + RosterReporter.NEWLINE +
        "B" + RosterReporter.NEWLINE +
        RosterReporter.ROSTER_REPORT_FOOTER + "2" +
        RosterReporter.NEWLINE, rosterReport);
    }
}
```

Rerun your tests. You should see the actual report displayed onscreen. If you are running in an IDE, you may need to use System.err (the standard error output stream, also known as syserr), instead of System.out, in order to view the results.[5]

You'll note that I placed the additional line of code all the way to the left margin. I use this convention to remind me that the code is intended for temporary use. It makes such statements easy to locate and remove.

Revert these changes and rerun all tests once you have finished viewing the output.

Using System.out

The most frequent use of System.out is to post messages to the console in an effort to locate defects in a program. You insert System.out.println statements to display useful information at judicious points in your code. When you execute the application, the output from these *trace statements* can help you understand the flow of messages and data through the objects interacting in the system.

Debuggers are far more sophisticated tools that accomplish the same goal and much more, but simple trace statements can occasionally be a more rapid and effective solution. Also, in some environments it is not feasible to use a debugger.

Regardless, you should find minimal need to debug your code, or even insert trace statements into it, if you do TDD properly. If you do the small

[5]The results might appear in a window named "console."

steps that TDD prescribes, you will introduce very small amounts of code into your application before finding out you have a problem. Instead, the better solution is to discard the small amount of newly introduced code and start again, using even smaller verified steps.

 Build your system in small increments of test and code. Discard an increment and start over with smaller steps if you have a problem.

Most developers do not write console-based applications, although you are probably familiar with many of them. The compiler javac itself is a console-based application. Simple server applications are often coded as console applications so that developers can easily monitor their output.

Refactoring

If you haven't already done so, remove the testReport method from CourseSessionTest and remove the corresponding production code from CourseSession.

The writeReport method is still short, but conceptually it is doing three things. To make understanding even more immediate, you can decompose the code in writeReport into three smaller methods, one each to construct the header, body, and footer of the report:

```
String getReport() {
   StringBuilder buffer = new StringBuilder();
   writeHeader(buffer);
   writeBody(buffer);
   writeFooter(buffer);

   return buffer.toString();
}

void writeHeader(StringBuilder buffer) {
   buffer.append(ROSTER_REPORT_HEADER);
}

void writeBody(StringBuilder buffer) {
   for (Student student: session.getAllStudents()) {
      buffer.append(student.getName());
      buffer.append(NEWLINE);
   }
}

void writeFooter(StringBuilder buffer) {
   buffer.append(
      ROSTER_REPORT_FOOTER + session.getAllStudents().size() + NEWLINE);
}
```

Package Structure

You use packages to arbitrarily group your classes. This grouping of classes, known as the *package structure*, will change over time as your needs change. Initially, your concern will be ease of development. As the number of classes grows, you will want to create additional packages for manageability reasons. Once you deploy the application, your needs may change: You may want to organize the packages to increase the potential for reuse or perhaps to minimize maintenance impact to consumers of the package.

So far, your classes have all ended up in one package, studentinfo. A typical way to start organizing packages is to separate the *user interface*—the part of the application that the end user interacts with—from the underlying classes that represent business objects and infrastructural objects. The RosterReporter class in the previous example could be construed as part of the user interface, as it produces output that the end user will see.

Your next task will be to first move the studentinfo package down a level so that it is in a package named sis.reportinfo. You will then separate the Roster-Reporter and RosterReporterTest classes into their own package named report.

Package Structure

First create a new subdirectory named sis (for "Student Information System") at the same directory level as studentinfo. Beneath this directory, create a new subdirectory named report. Move the studentinfo subdirectory into the sis subdirectory. Move the RosterReporter and RosterReporterTest classes into the report subdirectory. Your directory structure should look something like:

```
source
   |--sis
        |--studentinfo
        |--report
```

Next, you will change the package statements of all your classes. For the packages in the report subdirectory, use this package statement:

```
package sis.report;
```

For the packages in the studentinfo subdirectory, use this package statement:

```
package sis.studentinfo;
```

As you did in Lesson 2, remove all the class files (*.class), then recompile all your code. You will receive several errors. The problem is that the Roster-Reporter and RosterReporterTest classes are now in a separate package from the CourseSession and Student classes. They no longer have appropriate access to the classes in the other package.

Access Modifiers

You have already used the keyword `public` for JUnit classes and methods without an understanding of the full meaning of the keyword, other than that JUnit requires that test classes and methods be declared `public`. You also learned that instance variables can be declared `private` so that objects of other classes cannot access them.

The `public` and `private` keywords are known as *access modifiers*. You use access modifiers to control access to Java elements, including fields, methods, and classes. The access modifiers that are appropriate for a class are different than those that are appropriate for methods and fields.

By declaring a class as `public`, you allow classes in other packages to be able to `import` and refer directly to the class. The JUnit framework classes are located in various packages whose name starts with `junit`. In order for these JUnit classes to be able to instantiate your test classes, you must declare them as `public`.

Neither the CourseSession nor the Student class you built specified an access modifier. In the absence of an access modifier, a class has an access level of *package*, also known as default access. You can refer to a class with package-level access from other classes within the same package; however, classes in a different package cannot refer to the class.

For "safer" programming, the preferred tactic is to start at the most restrictive level and then open up access as needed. Exposing your classes too much can mean that clients can become unnecessarily dependent on the details of how you've put the system together. If you change the details, the clients could break. Also, you open your code up to being corrupted by providing too much access.

 Protect your code as much as possible. Relax access modifiers only when necessary.

The CourseSession and Student classes currently have package-level access. You can keep them at that level until a class in another package requires access to them.

In order to get your code to compile, you will first have to add an `import` statement so that the compiler knows to look in the `studentinfo` package for the Student and CourseSession classes. The modification to RosterReporterTest is shown here:

```
package sis.report;

import junit.framework.*;
import sis.studentinfo.*;

public class RosterReporterTest extends TestCase {
...
```

Add the same import statement to RosterReporter.

The classes in the studentinfo package still have package-level access, so classes in the reports package will not be visible to them. Change the class declaration to be public for Student, CourseSession, and DateUtil, as shown in the example for Student:

```
package sis.studentinfo;

public class Student {
...
```

You will also receive a compilation error for AllTests.java. It no longer recognizes the class RosterReporterTest, since RosterReporterTest has been moved to a different package. For now, comment out that line in AllTests.java:

```
package sis.studentinfo;

import junit.framework.TestSuite;

public class AllTests {
    public static TestSuite suite() {
        TestSuite suite = new TestSuite();
        suite.addTestSuite(StudentTest.class);
        suite.addTestSuite(CourseSessionTest.class);
//      suite.addTestSuite(RosterReporterTest.class);
        suite.addTestSuite(DateUtilTest.class);
        return suite;
    }
}
```

You will soon create a new AllTests for the reports package. Be careful when commenting out code—it's easy to forget why the code is commented out.

After recompiling, you will receive lots of errors for each message sent from the code in the reports package to Student and CourseSession objects. Like classes, the default access level for constructors (and methods) is package. Just as classes need to be public in order to be accessed from outside the package, methods and constructors also must be declared as public. Do so judiciously—you should never make blanket declarations of every method as public.

As a matter of style and organization, you may also want to move public methods so they appear before the non-public methods in the source file. The idea is that a client developer interested in your class will find the public methods—the methods they should be most interested in—first. With IDEs, this organization is not as necessary, as most IDEs provide a better way to organize and navigate through source for a class.

When finished, the production classes in studentinfo should look something like the following.

Student.java:

```java
package studentinfo;

public class Student {
    private String name;

    public Student(String name) {
        this.name = name;
    }

    public String getName() {
        return name;
    }
}
```

Access Modifiers

CourseSession.java:

```java
package studentinfo;

import java.util.*;

/**
 * This class provides a representation of a single-semester
 * session of a specific university course.
 * @author Administrator
 */
public class CourseSession {
    private String department;
    private String number;
    private ArrayList<Student> students = new ArrayList<Student>();
    private Date startDate;

    /**
     * Constructs a CourseSession starting on a specific date
     * @param startDate the date on which the CourseSession begins
     */
    public CourseSession(
            String department, String number, Date startDate) {
        this.department = department;
        this.number = number;
        this.startDate = startDate;
    }
```

```java
    String getDepartment() {
        return department;
    }

    String getNumber() {
        return number;
    }

    int getNumberOfStudents() {
        return students.size();
    }

    public void enroll(Student student) {
        students.add(student);
    }

    Student get(int index) {
        return students.get(index);
    }

    Date getStartDate() {
        return startDate;
    }

    public ArrayList<Student> getAllStudents() {
        return students;
    }

    /**
     * @return Date the last date of the course session
     */
    Date getEndDate() {
        GregorianCalendar calendar = new GregorianCalendar();
        calendar.setTime(startDate);
        final int sessionLength = 16;
        final int daysInWeek = 7;
        final int daysFromFridayToMonday = 3;
        int numberOfDays =
            sessionLength * daysInWeek - daysFromFridayToMonday;
        calendar.add(Calendar.DAY_OF_YEAR, numberOfDays);
        return calendar.getTime();
    }
}
```

DateUtil.java:

```java
package studentinfo;

import java.util.*;

public class DateUtil {
    public Date createDate(int year, int month, int date) {
        GregorianCalendar calendar = new GregorianCalendar();
```

```
    calendar.clear();
    calendar.set(Calendar.YEAR, year - 1900);
    calendar.set(Calendar.MONTH, month - 1);
    calendar.set(Calendar.DAY_OF_MONTH, date);
    return calendar.getTime();
  }
}
```

Where Do the Tests Go?

You have been putting your test classes in the same package as your production classes so far; for example, StudentTest and Student both appear in the same studentinfo package. This is the easiest approach, but not the only one. Another approach is to create an equivalent test package for every production package. For example, you might have a package named test.studentinfo that contains tests for classes in studentinfo.

One advantage of putting the tests in the same package as the production code is that the tests have access to package-level details of the class they test. However, that level of visibility could be construed as a negative: As much as possible, you should design your tests to test a class using its public interface—what it makes publicly available. The more your test requires access to private information, the more tightly *coupled*, or dependent, it becomes to the actual implementation. The tight coupling means that it is more difficult to make modifications to the production class without adversely impacting the test.

You will still find occasion to assert against information from an object that you wouldn't otherwise expose publicly. You may want to combine test and production classes in the same package for that reason. If you find that this scheme results in too many classes in one directory, you can use Java's classpath to your advantage: Create the same directory structure in two different subdirectories and have the classpath refer to both subdirectories.

For example, suppose you compile your classes into c:\source\sis\bin. You can create a second class file location, c:\source\sis\test\bin. Subsequently, you can modify your build scripts (Ant makes this very easy) to compile *only* test classes into the c:\source\sis\test\bin directory. Everything else will compile into c:\source\sis\bin. You can then put both c:\source\sis\bin and c:\source\sis\test\bin on the classpath.

Using this scheme, the class file for Student would end up as c:\source\sis\bin\studentinfo\Student.class, and the class file for StudentTest would end up as c:\source\sis\test\bin\studentinfo\StudentTest.class. Both classes remain in the package studentinfo, yet each is in a separate directory.

Access Modifiers

At this point, everything should compile. Your tests should also run, but don't forget that you commented out RosterReporterTest. It's time to add it back in.

Create a new class named AllTests in the sis.report package. Generally you will want a test suite in each package to ensure that all classes in the package are tested.[6]

```
package sis.report;

import junit.framework.TestSuite;

public class AllTests {
   public static TestSuite suite() {
      TestSuite suite = new TestSuite();
      suite.addTestSuite(RosterReporterTest.class);
      return suite;
   }
}
```

You can now remove the commented-out line from the class student-info.AllTests.

Create a class named AllTests in the sis package by placing its source file in the sis directory. This class will produce the combined test suite that ensures all classes in the application are tested.

```
package sis;

import junit.framework.TestSuite;

public class AllTests {
   public static TestSuite suite() {
      TestSuite suite = new TestSuite();
      suite.addTest(sis.report.AllTests.suite());
      suite.addTest(sis.studentinfo.AllTests.suite());
      return suite;
   }
}
```

Instead of sending the message addTestSuite to the suite, you send the message addTest. As a parameter, you pass along the results of sending the message suite to the appropriate AllTests class. Sending a message to a class instead of to an object will result in a *static method* being called. I will discuss static methods in the next lesson.

You will want to pass sis.AllTests to JUnit in order to run your entire test suite.

---

[6]There are other ways of managing test suites; your IDE may provide some assistance here. Also, refer to Lesson 12 for a dynamic way of gathering tests.

Using Ant

From here on out, I will be using an Ant script to do my compilations, now that I have more than two directories to compile. Ant is a platform-independent tool that allows you to create specifications of how your project should be built and deployed.

If you are using an IDE, you should be able to get it to build your entire codebase easily. Under Eclipse, for example, all of your source code is compiled automatically each time you save changes to Java source.

Regardless of whether or not you are using an IDE, you may want to use Ant in order to obtain IDE and platform independence. Other alternatives are to build a shell script or batch file as I demonstrated in Lesson 1. You can also use one of a number of available make tools. A make tool is a build tool very similar to Ant, but most make tools are very tightly bound to a specific operating system. Few make tools provide the ease of building Java applications that Ant does. Ant is the most effective way of doing builds in Java.

I highly recommend that you learn how to use Ant. Your IDE may suffice for your own personal needs, but it might not be sufficient in a team environment. If you work in a team environment, you will want a standardized way of building and deploying your application. Most development shops have standardized on Ant as a way of ensuring the system is built and deployed consistently and correctly.

See the sidebar "Getting Started with Ant" for a brief overview of using Ant.

Using Ant

Getting Started With Ant

This sidebar will help you obtain a basic understanding of how to work with the Ant build tool.

Most Java IDEs come with Ant support already built in. If you are not using an IDE, you can follow these steps to be able to use Ant for your builds.

- Download the latest version of Ant from http://ant.apache.org.
- Follow the instructions available with the Ant distribution to install Ant. Set the environment variable JAVA_HOME to the directory in which you installed the J2SE 5.0 SDK.
- Update your system's path environment variable to include Ant's bin directory.
- Create a build.xml file in the root directory of your project.

Regardless of whether you are using an IDE or not, you will put together a build.xml file that contains the instructions on how to compile, execute, and/or deploy your application.

Here is a starter build.xml for a project named agileJava.

```xml
<?xml version="1.0"?>

<project name="agileJava" default="junitgui" basedir=".">
  <property name="junitJar" value="\junit3.8.1\junit.jar" />
  <property name="src.dir" value="${basedir}\source" />
  <property name="build.dir" value="${basedir}\classes" />

  <path id="classpath">
    <pathelement location="${junitJar}" />
    <pathelement location="${build.dir}" />
  </path>

  <target name="init">
    <mkdir dir="${build.dir}" />
  </target>

  <target name="build" depends="init" description="build all">
    <javac
        srcdir="${src.dir}" destdir="${build.dir}"
        source="1.5"
        deprecation="on" debug="on" optimize="off" includes="**">
      <classpath refid="classpath" />
    </javac>
  </target>

  <target name="junitgui" depends="build" description="run junit gui">
    <java classname="junit.awtui.TestRunner" fork="yes">
      <arg value="sis.AllTests" />
      <classpath refid="classpath" />
    </java>
  </target>

  <target name="clean">
    <delete dir="${build.dir}" />
  </target>

  <target name="rebuildAll" depends="clean,build" description="rebuild all"/>
</project>
```

Understanding the Sample Build File

Ant allows you to define in XML how to build various *targets* within a *project*. A target has a name and may have one or more other targets as dependencies:

```xml
<target name="rebuildAll" depends="clean,build" />
```

The above line defines a target named rebuildAll. When you execute this target (keep reading), Ant first ensures that the targets named clean and build have been executed.

A target contains a list of commands, or tasks, to execute. The Ant software installation provides a manual describing a large number of tasks that will suffice for most of your needs. If you can't find an appropriate task, you can programmatically create your own.

The clean target contains the single task named delete. In this example, the delete task tells Ant to delete a file system directory with the name provided in quotes.

```
<target name="clean">
  <delete dir="${build.dir}" />
</target>
```

Ant allows you to define properties that provide a construct similar to constants in Java. When the delete task executes, Ant will replace ${build.dir} with the value of the property named build.dir. The property named build.dir is declared in the agileJava Ant script as:

```
<property name="build.dir" value="${basedir}\classes" />
```

This declaration sets the value of build.dir to ${basedir}\classes. The use of ${basedir} is in turn a reference to the property basedir, defined in the project element for the agileJava Ant script:

```
<project name="agileJava" default="junitgui" basedir=".">
```

(The . indicates that basedir is set to the current directory—the directory in which Ant is executed.)

When executing Ant, you can specify a target:

```
ant rebuildAll
```

The default attribute in the project element indicates the target to execute if none is specified. In this example, the junitgui target is the default and gets run if you execute ant with no arguments:

```
ant
```

A list of targets can be obtained by executing:

```
ant -projecthelp
```

This will show main targets—those targets that specify a description attribute.

Using some built-in smarts, Ant executes tasks only when necessary. For example, if you execute the junitgui target, Ant will only run javac compiles against source that has not changed since the last time you executed junitgui. It uses the timestamps of the class files to make this determination.

To summarize the agileJava project, there are three main targets: build, junitgui, and rebuildAll. There are two subtargets, init and clean.

The build target depends on the init target, which ensures that the build output directory (./classes) exists. The build target compiles all sources in the source directory (./source) to the build output directory, using Ant's built-in javac task. The javac task specifies a number of attributes, including the attribute classpath, specified as a nested element of the javac task. The classpath attribute references a path

Using Ant

element by the name classpath; this path element includes the JUnit jar file and the classes directory.

The junitgui target depends on the build target. If the build target succeeds, the junitgui target executes the JUnit GUI using the Java VM, passing in AllTests as the parameter.[7]

The rebuildAll target depends on execution of the clean target, which removes the build output directory, and on the build target.

Refer to the Ant manual for more detailed information. There are also several books available on Ant. One very comprehensive book is *Java Development with Ant.*[8]

Exercises

1. Create a CharacterTest class. Don't forget to add it to the AllSuites class. Observe the zero tests failure. Then add a test named testWhitespace. This test should demonstrate that the new line character, the tab character, and the space character all return true for Character.isWhitespace. Express that other characters return false. Can you find another character that returns true?

2. Java has certain naming restrictions on identifiers—the names you give to methods, classes, variables, and other entities. For example, you cannot use the caret (^) in an identifier name. The Character class contains methods that designate whether or not a character can be used in an identifier. Consult your API documentation to understand these methods. Then add tests to the CharacterTest class to discover some of the rules regarding Java identifiers.

3. Assert that a black pawn's printable representation is the uppercase character 'P', and a white pawn's is the lowercase character 'p'. For the time being, you can accomplish this by adding a second parameter to the Pawn constructor. However, note that this creates a redundancy in representation. You'll improve upon the solution later.

4. (This exercise and Exercise 5 are closely related. You may suspend refactoring until you have completed Exercise 5.) When a client creates a Board object, they should be able to assume that the board is already initialized, with pieces in place. You will need to modify the

---

[7]There is also an optional Ant task named junit that executes a text-based JUnit.
[8][Hatcher2002].

Board tests and code accordingly. Start by changing the assertions on the number of pieces available at time of board creation: There should be 16. Delete testAddPawns; it is not useful in its current form.

5. Add an initialize method to Board. The initialize method should add pawns to create two ranks: a rank for white pawns (the second rank) and a rank for black pawns (the seventh rank). To store a rank, use an ArrayList whose contents are Pawn objects. You declare such a list as ArrayList<Pawn>.

   Add an assertion to **testCreate** that the second rank looks like this: "pppppppp". Assert that the seventh rank looks like this: "PPPPPPPP". Use a StringBuilder and a for loop to gather the printable representation for the pieces in each rank.

   Ensure your solution is as well refactored as you are capable of. Expect a good amount of duplication in adding pawns to the ranks and in other areas of Board. You will learn to eliminate this duplication in later lessons.

6. Assert that the board looks like this at initial setup, with a dot character (a period) representing an empty square (rank 8 is the top row, rank 1 is the bottom row):

Exercises

```
........
PPPPPPPP
........
........
........
........
pppppppp
........
```

   Remember to ensure portability in your tests and in your board-printing method by using the system properties appropriately.

7. If you have implemented your chess board code and tests to this point using String concatenation, change the code to use the StringBuilder class. If you have used StringBuilder as the primary basis for your solution, change your code to use String concatenation. Name some differences in the structure and readability of the code.

8. Modify your test to display the board on the console. Ensure that it appears as expected. If not, correct the test and fix the code.

9. You will need to revisit this code in later exercises to remove even more duplication when they learn about loops and other Java constructs.

10. Create an Ant build file to compile your entire project and run all of your tests with a single command.

Lesson 4

Class Methods and Fields

In this lesson you will:

- refactor an instance method to a class method

- learn about class variables and methods

- use the static import facility

- learn how to use compound assignment and increment operators

- understand what simple design is

- create a utility method

- learn how to judiciously use class methods

- work with the boolean primitive type

- understand why it is important that tests act as documentation

- be exposed to exceptions and stack traces

- learn more about initialization

Class Methods

Objects are a combination of behavior (implemented in Java in terms of methods) and attributes (implemented in Java in terms of fields). Attributes for an object stick around as long as the object sticks around. At any given point in time, an object has a certain *state*, which is the combined snapshot of all its instance variables. For this reason, instance variables are sometimes called state variables.

Action methods in the object may operate on and change attributes of the object. In other words, action methods can alter the object state. *Query methods* return pieces of the object state.

133

Design your methods to either change object state or return information, not both.

Occasionally you will find the need for a method that can take parameters, operate on only those parameters, and return a value. The method has no need to operate on object state. This is known as a utility method. Utility methods in other languages are sometimes called functions. They are *global*: any client code can access them.

Sometimes, having to create an object in order to use a utility method makes little sense. For example, the DateUtil method createDate you coded in Lesson 3 is a simple function that takes month, day, and year integer arguments and returns a Date object. The createDate method changes no other data. Removing the need to construct DateUtil objects will also simplify your code a bit. Finally, since createDate is the only method in DateUtil, there is no other need to construct instances of it.

For these reasons, createDate is a good candidate for being a class method. In this exercise, you will refactor createDate to be a class method in this exercise. Start by changing the test to make a class method call:

```
package sis.studentinfo;

import java.util.*;
import junit.framework.*;

public class DateUtilTest extends TestCase {
    public void testCreateDate() {
        Date date = DateUtil.createDate(2000, 1, 1);
        Calendar calendar = new GregorianCalendar();
        calendar.setTime(date);
        assertEquals(2000, calendar.get(Calendar.YEAR));
        assertEquals(Calendar.JANUARY, calendar.get(Calendar.MONTH));
        assertEquals(1, calendar.get(Calendar.DAY_OF_MONTH));
    }
}
```

You no longer create an instance of DateUtil with the new operator. Instead, to call a class method, you specify the class on which the class method is defined (DateUtil), followed by the dot operator (.), followed by the method name and any arguments (createDate(2000, 1, 1)).

Changes to the DateUtil class itself are similarly minor:

```
package sis.studentinfo;

import java.util.*;

public class DateUtil {
    private DateUtil() {}
```

```
    public static Date createDate(int year, int month, int date) {
        GregorianCalendar calendar = new GregorianCalendar();
        calendar.clear();
        calendar.set(Calendar.YEAR, year);
        calendar.set(Calendar.MONTH, month - 1);
        calendar.set(Calendar.DAY_OF_MONTH, date);
        return calendar.getTime();
    }
}
```

You declare a class method just like a "regular," or instance, method, except that you prefix its declaration with the keyword static.

In addition to making the createDate method static, it's a good idea to make the constructor of DateUtil private. By declaring the constructor as private, only code in the DateUtil class can construct new DateUtil instances. No other code will be able to do so. While it wouldn't be harmful to allow creation of DateUtil objects, keeping clients from doing something nonsensical and useless is a good idea.

Adding the private constructor will also make it simpler for you to pinpoint the nonstatic references to createDate. When you compile your code, methods that create a new DateUtil object will generate compilation errors. For example, the setUp method in CourseSessionTest will fail compilation:

```
public void setUp() {
    startDate = new DateUtil().createDate(2003, 1, 6);
    session = new CourseSession("ENGL", "101", startDate);
}
```

Update it to call createDate statically:

```
public void setUp() {
    startDate = DateUtil.createDate(2003, 1, 6);
    session = new CourseSession("ENGL", "101", startDate);
}
```

Fix the remainder of the failing compilation problems and rerun your tests. You now have a general-purpose utility that may find frequent use in your system.[1]

The class java.lang.Math in the J2SE 5.0 class library supplies many many mathematical functions. For example, Math.sin returns the sine of a double and Math.toRadians converts a double value from degrees to radians. The Math class

Class Methods

---

[1]The utility is not the best-performing one. It is not necessary to create a GregorianCalendar object with each call to createDate. For sporadic use, this is probably just fine. For heavy use—say, creating 10,000 dates upon reading an input file—you'll want to consider caching the calendar object using a class variable (see the next section).

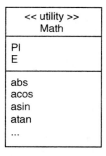

Figure 4.1 *The Math Utility Class*

also provides two standard mathematical constants, Math.PI and Math.E. Since each of the methods in java.lang.Math is a utility class method, it is known as a utility class.

In UML (Figure 4.1), you indicate a utility class using the stereotype «utility». Stereotypes in UML define semantics beyond the limitations of what UML supplies. A utility stereotype specifies that all class behaviors and attributes may be globally accessed.

Normally you <u>underline</u> class behaviors and class attributes in UML. Since the «utility» stereotype declares that *all* methods and attributes in a class are global, you need not underline them.

Class Methods

Static Initialization Blocks

Constructors execute when you create instances of a class. You use constructors for more complex instance initialization.

Occasionally you may need more complex initialization to occur at a class level. You can use a *static initialization block* to accomplish this goal. Code within a static initialization block executes when the Java VM first loads a class.

```
import java.util.Date;
public class St {
   static {
      long now =
         System.currentTimeMillis();
      then = new Date(now + 86400000);
   }
   public static Date then;
}
```

To define a static initialization block, you precede a block of code ({ . . . }) with the keyword static. Place it within a class definition but external to any method or constructor. Virtually any code can appear within a static initialization block, but the block should not throw any exceptions (see Lesson 8).

Class Variables

You will occasionally want to track information about all instances of a class or perform an operation without first creating an instance of an object. As a simplistic example, you might want to track the total number of course sessions. As each CourseSession object is created, you want to bump up a counter. The question is, where should you put this counter? You could provide an instance variable on CourseSession to track the count, but this is awkward: Would all instances of CourseSession have to track the count? How would one CourseSession instance know when others were created so that it could update the count?

You could provide another class, CourseSessionCounter, whose sole responsibility is to track the CourseSession objects created. But a new class seems like overkill for the simple goal you are trying to accomplish.

In Java, you can use *class variables*, as opposed to instance variables, for a solution. Client code can access a class variable without first creating an instance of that class. Class variables have what is known as *static scope*: they exist as long as the class exists, which is pretty much from the time the class is first loaded until your application terminates.

You have already seen class constants in use. Class constants are class variables that you have designated as final.

The following test code (in CourseSessionTest) counts the number of CourseSession instances created:

Class Variables

```java
public void testCount() {
   CourseSession.count = 0;
   createCourseSession();
   assertEquals(1, CourseSession.count);
   createCourseSession();
   assertEquals(2, CourseSession.count);
}

private CourseSession createCourseSession() {
   return new CourseSession("ENGL", "101", startDate);
}
```

(Don't forget to update the setUp method to use createCourseSession.)

To support the test, create a class variable in the CourseSession class named count. You use the static keyword to designate a variable as static in scope. Also add code to CourseSession to update count when a new CourseSession instance is created.

```java
public class CourseSession {
   // ...
   static int count;
```

```
public CourseSession(
        String department, String number, Date startDate) {
    this.department = department;
    this.number = number;
    this.startDate = startDate;
    CourseSession.count = CourseSession.count + 1;
}
// ...
```

You access the class variable count similar to the way you call a class method: First specify the class name (CourseSession), followed by the dot (.) operator, followed by the variable name (count). The Java VM does not create an instance of CourseSession when code accesses the class variable.

As I mentioned, class variables have a different lifetime than instance variables. Instance variables stick around for the lifetime of the object that contains them. Each new CourseSession object that the Java VM creates manages its own set of the instance variables declared in CourseSession. When the VM creates a CourseSession object, it initializes its instance variables.

A class variable, however, comes into existence when the Java VM first loads the containing class—when code that is currently executing first references the class. There is one copy of the class variable in memory. The first time the Java VM loads a class, it initializes its class variables, and that's it. If you need to reset a class variable to an initial state at a later time, you must explicitly initialize it yourself.

Operating on Class Variables with Class Methods

As an experiment, comment out the first line in testCount (the line that reads CourseSession.count = 0). Then run the tests in JUnit. Turn off the checkbox in JUnit that says "Reload classes every run."[2] If you run the tests twice (by clicking the Run button), they will fail, and you should see the actual count go up with each execution of the tests. You may even see the first run of the test fail: Other test methods in CourseSessionTest are creating CourseSession objects, which increments the count variable.

Operating on Class Variables with Class Methods

Just as it is bad form to expose instance variables of your objects directly to prying clients, it is also bad form to expose class variables publicly. The notable exception is the class constant idiom—but there are even good reasons to avoid using class constants that you will learn in Lesson 5.

---

[2]This JUnit switch, when turned on, results in your test classes being physically loaded from disk and reinitialized each time the tests are run in JUnit. If you are running in an IDE such as Eclipse, you may not have control over this JUnit feature.

In addition to being able to use class methods for utility purposes, you can use class methods to operate on static data.

The CourseSession method `testCount` accesses the `count` class variable directly. Change the test code to ask for the count by making a class method call.

```
public void testCount() {
    CourseSession.count = 0;
    createCourseSession();
    assertEquals(1, CourseSession.getCount());
    createCourseSession();
    assertEquals(2, CourseSession.getCount());
}
```

Then add a class method to CourseSession that returns the class variable `count`.

```
static int getCount() {
    return count;
}
```

Class methods can access class variables directly. You should not specify the class name when accessing a class variable from a class method.

The Java VM creates no instances of CourseSession as a result of calling the class method. This means that class methods on CourseSession may not access any of the instance variables that CourseSession defines, such as `department` or `students`.

The test method still refers directly to the `count` class variable, however, since you need it initialized each time the test is run:

```
public void testCount() {
    CourseSession.count = 0;
    ...
```

Operating on
Class Variables
with Class
Methods

Change the code in CourseSessionTest to make a static message send to reset the count:

```
public void testCount() {
    CourseSession.resetCount();
    createCourseSession();
    assertEquals(1, CourseSession.getCount());
    createCourseSession();
    assertEquals(2, CourseSession.getCount());
}
```

Add the `resetCount` method to CourseSession and make the `count` class variable private:

```
public class CourseSession {
    // ...
    private static int count;
    // ...
    static void resetCount() {
```

```
    count = 0;
}

static int getCount() {
  return count;
}
// ...
```

Making the count variable private will point out (when you recompile) any other client code that directly accesses it.

The testCount method, which documents how a client should use the Course-Session class, is now complete and clean. But the CourseSession class itself still accesses the class variable directly in its constructor. Instead of accessing static data directly from a *member* (an instance-side constructor, field, or method), a better approach is to create a class method that you call from the instance side. This is a form of encapsulation that will give you greater control over what happens to the class variable.

Change the CourseSession constructor to send the incrementCount message instead of accessing the class variable directly:

```
public CourseSession(String department, String number, Date startDate) {
    this.department = department;
    this.number = number;
    this.startDate = startDate;
    CourseSession.incrementCount();
}
```

Then add a class method to CourseSession that increments the count. Declare this method as private to prevent other classes from incrementing the counter, which could compromise its integrity:

```
private static void incrementCount() {
    count = count + 1;
}
```

It is possible to access a class method or variable from the instance side of a class without specifying the class name. As an example, you could change the constructor code to the following:

```
public CourseSession(String department, String number, Date startDate) {
    this.department = department;
    this.number = number;
    this.startDate = startDate;
    incrementCount(); // don't do this!
}
```

Even though it will work, avoid doing this. Accessing class methods without using the class name introduces unnecessary confusion in your code and is considered bad form. Is incrementCount a class method or an instance method?

Since it's not possible to tell from looking at the code in the CourseSession constructor alone, the intent is not clear. The expectation that a method is an instance method when it is in reality a class method can lead to some interesting problems.

 Scope a class method call with the class name when invoking the class method from anywhere but another class method on the same class.

Static Import

I just told you to not call class methods from the instance side unless you supply the class name. Doing so obscures where the class method is defined. The same applies for accessing class variables (not including class constants).

Java permits you to muddle things even further. Including a *static import* in a class allows you to use class methods or variables defined in a different class as if they were defined locally. In other words, a static import allows you to omit the class name when referring to static members defined in another class.

There are appropriate uses for static import and inappropriate uses. I'll demonstrate an inappropriate use first. Modify CourseSessionTest:

Static Import

```
// avoid doing this
package sis.studentinfo;

import junit.framework.TestCase;
import java.util.*;
import static sis.studentinfo.DateUtil.*; // poor use of static import

public class CourseSessionTest extends TestCase {
   private CourseSession session;
   private Date startDate;

   public void setUp() {
      startDate = createDate(2003, 1, 6); // poor use of static import
      session = CourseSession.create("ENGL", "101", startDate);
   }
   ...
   public void testCourseDates() {
      // poor use of static import:
      Date sixteenWeeksOut = createDate(2003, 4, 25);
      assertEquals(sixteenWeeksOut, session.getEndDate());
   }
   ...
}
```

A static import statement looks similar to a regular import statement. However, a regular import statement imports one or all classes from a package, while a static import statement imports one or all class members (variables or methods) from a class. The above example imports all class members from the class DateUtil. Since there is only one class method in DateUtil, you could have explicitly imported just that method:

```
import static sis.studentinfo.DateUtil.createDate;
```

If DateUtil were to contain more than one class method with the name createDate (but with different argument lists), or if it also were to contain a class variable named createDate, they would each be statically imported.

Statically importing methods to avoid having to provide a class name in a few spots is lazy and introduces unnecessary confusion. Just where is createDate defined? If you are coding a class that requires quite a few external class method calls (perhaps a couple dozen or more), you might have an excuse to use static import. But a better approach would be to question why you need to make so many static calls in the first place and perhaps revisit the design of the other class.

A similar, potentially legitimate use of static import is to simplify the use of several related class constants that are gathered in a single place. Suppose you've created several report classes. Each report class will need to append new line characters to the output, so each report class will need a NEWLINE constant such as the one currently defined in RosterReporter:

```
static final String NEWLINE = System.getProperty("line.separator");
```

You don't want the duplication of defining this constant in each and every report class. You might create a new class solely for the purpose of holding this constant. Later it might hold other constants such as the page width for any report.

```
package sis.report;

public class ReportConstant {
    public static final String NEWLINE =
        System.getProperty("line.separator");
}
```

Since the NEWLINE constant will be used in a lot of places in a typical report class, you can add a static import to clean up your code a little:[3]

---

[3]You can eliminate the need for the NEWLINE constant entirely in a few other ways. You'll learn about one such technique, using the Java Formatter class, in Lesson 8.

```
package sis.report;

import junit.framework.TestCase;
import sis.studentinfo.*;
import static sis.report.ReportConstant.NEWLINE;

public class RosterReporterTest extends TestCase {
    public void testRosterReport() {
        CourseSession session =
            CourseSession.create(
                "ENGL", "101", DateUtil.createDate(2003, 1, 6));

        session.enroll(new Student("A"));
        session.enroll(new Student("B"));

        String rosterReport = new RosterReporter(session).getReport();
        assertEquals(
            RosterReporter.ROSTER_REPORT_HEADER +
            "A" + NEWLINE +
            "B" + NEWLINE +
            RosterReporter.ROSTER_REPORT_FOOTER + "2" +
            NEWLINE, rosterReport);
    }
}
```

You can make similar changes to the RosterReporter class.

Putting a bunch of constants in a class with no behavior (methods) represents questionable OO design. Classes don't exist in a vacuum; the constants in ReportConstants class may be better off as part of another "normal" Java class, such as a class named Report.

Additional notes on static import:

Static Import

- It is not possible to statically import all members from all classes in a given package in a single statement. That is, you cannot code:

```
import static java.lang.*;  // this does not compile!
```

- If a local method has the same signature as a statically imported method, the local method is called.

Use static imports with prudence. They make it more difficult to understand your classes by obscuring where members are defined. The rule of thumb is to limit use of static imports to things that are both universal and pervasive in your application.

Incrementing

In the `incrementCount` method, you coded:

```
count = count + 1;
```

The right-hand side of the statement is an expression whose value is one plus whatever value that `count` references. On execution, Java stores this new value back into the `count` variable.

Adding a value to a variable is a common operation, so common that Java supplies a a shortcut. The following two statements are equivalent:

```
count = count + 1;
count += 1;
```

The second statement demonstrates *compound assignment*. The second statement adds the value (1) on the right hand side of the compound assignment operator (`+=`) to the value referenced by the variable on the left hand side (`count`); it then assigns this new sum back to the variable on the left hand side (`count`). Compound assignment works for any of the arithmetic operators. For example,

```
rate *= 2;
```

Incrementing

is analogous to:

```
rate = rate * 2;
```

Adding the value 1 to an integer variable, or *incrementing* it, is so common that there is an even shorter cut. The following line uses the *increment operator* to increase the value of `count` by one:

```
++count;
```

The following line uses the *decrement operator* to decrease the value of `count` by one:

```
- -count;
```

You could code either of these examples with plus or minus signs after the variable to increment:

```
count++;
```

```
count- -;
```

The results would be the same. When they are used as part of a larger expression, however, there is an important distinction between the *prefix* operator (when the plus or minus signs appear before the variable) and the *postfix* operator (when the plus or minus signs appear after the variable).

When the Java VM encounters a prefix operator, it increments the variable *before* it is used as part of a larger expression.

```
int i = 5;
assertEquals(12, ++i * 2);
assertEquals(6, i);
```

When the Java VM encounters a postfix operator, it increments the variable *after* it is used as part of a larger expression.

```
int j = 5;
assertEquals(10, j++ * 2);
assertEquals(6, j);
```

Modify the code in CourseSession to use an increment operator. Since you're incrementing count all by itself, and not as part of a larger expression, it doesn't matter whether you use a pre-increment operator or a post-increment operator.

```
private static void incrementCount() {
    ++count;
}
```

Recompile and retest (something you should have been doing all along).

Factory
Methods

Factory Methods

You can modify CourseSession so that it supplies a static-side factory method to create CourseSession objects. By doing so, you will have control over what happens when new instances of CourseSession are created.

Modify the CourseSessionTest method createCourseSession to demonstrate how you will use this new factory method.

```
private CourseSession createCourseSession() {
    return CourseSession.create("ENGL", "101", startDate);
}
```

In CourseSession, add a static factory method that creates and returns a new CourseSession object:

```
public static CourseSession create(
        String department,
        String number,
        Date startDate) {
    return new CourseSession(department, number, startDate);
}
```

Find all other code that creates a CourseSession via new CourseSession(). Use the compiler to your advantage by first making the CourseSession constructor private:

```
private CourseSession(
     String department, String number, Date startDate) {
    // ...
```

Replace the CourseSession constructions you find (there should be one in RosterReporterTest and one in CourseSessionTest) with message sends to the static factory method. With the CourseSession constructor declared as private, no client code (which includes test code) will be able to create an instance of CourseSession directly using a constructor. Clients must instead use the static factory method.

Joshua Kerievsky names the above refactoring "Replace [Multiple[4]] Constructors with Creation Methods."[5] The class methods are the creation methods. The significant benefit is that you can provide descriptive names for creation methods. Since you must name a constructor the same as the class, it cannot always impart enough information for a developer to know its use.

Now that you have a factory method to create CourseSession objects, tracking the total count can be done on the static side, where it belongs. Much of good object-oriented design is about putting code where it belongs. This doesn't mean that you must always start with code in the "right place," but you should move it there as soon as you recognize that there is a better place for it to go. It makes more sense for incrementCount message sends to be made from the static side:

```
private CourseSession(
     String department, String number, Date startDate) {
   this.department = department;
   this.number = number;
   this.startDate = startDate;
}

public static CourseSession create(
     String department,
     String number,
     Date startDate) {
   incrementCount();
   return new CourseSession(department, number, startDate);
}
```

---

[4]Java allows you to code multiple constructors in a class. The descriptive names of creation methods are far more valuable in this circumstance, since they help a client developer determine which to choose.

[5][Kerievsky2004].

Factory Methods

Simple Design

Software development purists will tell you that you could have saved a lot of time by thinking through a complete design in the first place. With enough foresight, you might have figured out that static creation methods were a good idea and you would have put them in the code in the first place. Yes, after considerable experience with object-oriented development, you will learn how to start with a better design.

However, more often than not, the impact of design is not felt until you actually begin coding. Designers who don't validate their design in code frequently produce an overblown system by doing things such as adding static creation methods where they aren't warranted. They also often miss important aspects of design.

The best tactic to take is to keep your code as clean as possible at all times. The rules to keep the design clean are, in order of importance:

- Make sure your tests are complete and always running 100 percent green.

- Eliminate duplication.

- Ensure that the code is clean and expressive.

- Minimize the number of classes and methods.

The code should also have no more design in it than is necessary to support the current functionality. These rules are known as *simple design*.[6]

Simple design will give you the flexibility you need to update the design as requirements change and as you require design improvements. Creating a static factory method from a constructor wasn't all that difficult, as you saw; it is easily and safely done when you follow simple design.

Static Dangers

Using statics inappropriately can create significant defects that can be difficult to resolve. A classic novice mistake is to declare attributes as class variables instead of instance variables.

The class Student defines an instance variable named name. Each Student object should have its own copy of name. By declaring name as static, every Student object will use the same copy of name:

[6][Wiki2004b].

```
package sis.studentinfo;

public class Student {
    private static String name;

    public Student(String name) {
        this.name = name;
    }

    public String getName() {
        return name;
    }
}
```

A test can demonstrate the devastating effect this will have on your code:

```
package sis.studentinfo;

import junit.framework.*;

public class StudentTest extends TestCase {
    ...
    public void testBadStatic() {
        Student studentA = new Student("a");
        assertEquals("a", studentA.getName());
        Student studentB = new Student("b");
        assertEquals("b", studentB.getName());
        assertEquals("a", studentA.getName());
    }
}
```

Using Statics:
Various Notes

The last assertEquals statement will fail, since both studentA and studentB share the class variable name. In all likelihood, other test methods will fail as well.

A mistake like this can waste a lot of your time, especially if you don't have good unit tests. Developers often figure that something as simple as a variable declaration cannot be broken, so the variable declarations are often the last place they look when there are problems.

Revert the Student class to eliminate the keyword static, remove testBadStatic, recompile, and retest.

Using Statics: Various Notes

- Avoid turning an instance method into a class method for the sole sake of making it static. Ensure that either it semantically makes sense or at least one additional class needs access to the class method before doing so.

Garbage Collection

Java tries its best to manage your application's use of memory as it executes. Memory is a precious, limited commodity in most computer systems. Every time your code creates an object, Java must find memory space in which to store the object. If Java did nothing to manage memory, objects put in memory would stay there forever, and you would very quickly use up all available memory.

Java uses a technique known as *garbage collection* to manage your application's memory use. The Java VM tracks your use of all objects; from time to time it runs something known as a *garbage collector* in the background. The garbage collector reclaims objects that it knows you no longer need.

You no longer need an object when no other objects refer to that object. Suppose you create an object within a method and assign it to a local variable (but not to anything else). When the VM completes execution of the method, the object remains in memory, but nothing points to it—the local variable reference is only valid for the scope of the method. At this point, the object is eligible for garbage collection and should disappear the next time the garbage collector runs (if ever—you can never guarantee that the garbage collector will run).

If an instance variable refers to an object, you can give the object up for potential garbage collection by setting the value of the instance variable to null. Or you can wait until the object containing the instance variable is no longer referred to. Once nothing refers to an object, any objects it in turn refers to are also eligible for garbage collection.

If you store an object in a standard collection, such as an ArrayList, the collection holds a reference to the object. The object cannot be garbage collected as long the collection contains it.

Jeff's Rule of
Statics

- Static-side collections (for example, storing an ArrayList object in a class variable) are usually a bad idea. A collection holds a reference to any object added to it. Any object added to a class collection stays there until it is either removed from the collection or until the application terminates. An instance-side collection doesn't have this problem; see the sidebar for a brief overview of how garbage collection works.

Jeff's Rule of Statics

Finally, there is what I immodestly call Jeff's Rule of Statics:

 Don't use statics until you know you *need* to use statics.

The simple rule comes about from observing first Java development efforts. A little knowledge goes a long way. A little knowledge about statics often leads developers to use them rampantly.

My philosophical opposition to overuse of statics is that they are not object-oriented. The more static methods you have in your system, the more procedural it is—it becomes a bunch of essentially global functions operating on global data. My practical opposition is that improper and careless use of statics can cause all sorts of problems, including design limitations, insidious and bizarre defects, and memory leaks.

You will learn when it is appropriate to use statics and when it is not. Make sure that you do not use a static unless you understand why you are doing so.

Booleans

The next small portion of the student information system that you need to build is related to billing students for a semester. For now, the amount that students are billed is based upon three things: whether or not they are in-state students, whether or not they are full-time students, and how many credit hours the students are taking. In order to support billing, you will have to update the Student class to accommodate this information.

Students are either full-time or they are part-time. Put another way, students are either full-time or they are not full-time. Any time you need to represent something in Java that can be only in one of two states—on or off—you can use a variable of the type boolean. For a boolean variable, there are two possible boolean values, represented by the literals true (on) and false (off). The type boolean is a primitive type, like int; you cannot send messages to boolean values or variables.

Create a test method in the StudentTest class named testFullTime. It should instantiate a Student, then test that the student is not full time. Full-time students must have at least twelve credit hours; a newly created student has no credit hours.

```
public void testFullTime() {
    Student student = new Student("a");
    assertFalse(student.isFullTime());
}
```

The assertFalse method is another method StudentTest inherits from junit.framework.TestCase. It takes a single boolean expression as an argument. If the expression represents the value false, then the test passes; otherwise, the test fails. In testFullTime, the test passes if the student is not full-time; that is, if isFullTime returns false.

Add a method named isFullTime to the Student class:

```
boolean isFullTime() {
    return true;
}
```

The return type of the method is boolean. By having this method return true, you should expect that the test fails—the test asserts that isFullTime should return false. Observe the test fail; modify the method to return false; observe the test pass.

 The full-time/part-time status of a student is determined by how many credits worth of courses that the student takes. To be considered full-time, a student must have at least a dozen credits. How does a student get credits? By enrolling in a course session.

The requirement now is that when a student is enrolled in a course session, the student's number of credits must be bumped up. Simplest things first: Students need to be able to track credits, and a newly created student has no credits.

```
public void testCredits() {
    Student student = new Student("a");
    assertEquals(0, student.getCredits());
    student.addCredits(3);
    assertEquals(3, student.getCredits());
    student.addCredits(4);
    assertEquals(7, student.getCredits());
}
```

In Student:

```
package sis.studentinfo;

public class Student {
    private String name;
    private int credits;

    public Student(String name) {
        this.name = name;
        credits = 0;
    }

    public String getName() {
        return name;
    }

    boolean isFullTime() {
        return false;
    }

    int getCredits() {
        return credits;
    }
```

```
    void addCredits(int credits) {
        this.credits += credits;
    }
}
```

The Student constructor initializes the value of the credits field to 0, to meet the requirement that newly created students have no credits. As you learned in Lesson 2, you could have chosen to use field initialization, or to have not bothered, since Java initializes int variables to 0 by default.

Up to this point, the student should still be considered part-time. Since the number of credits is directly linked to the student's status, perhaps you should combine the test methods (but this is a debatable choice). Instead of having two test methods, testCredits and testFullTime, combine them into a single method named testStudentStatus.

```
public void testStudentStatus() {
    Student student = new Student("a");
    assertEquals(0, student.getCredits());
    assertFalse(student.isFullTime());

    student.addCredits(3);
    assertEquals(3, student.getCredits());
    assertFalse(student.isFullTime());

    student.addCredits(4);
    assertEquals(7, student.getCredits());
    assertFalse(student.isFullTime());
}
```

Booleans

Assertion Failure Messages

You can code any JUnit assertion to provide a specialized error message. JUnit displays this message if the assertion fails. While the test itself should be coded well enough to help another developer understand the implication of an assertion failure, adding a message can help expedite understanding. Here's an example:

```
assertTrue(
    "not enough credits for FT status",
    student.isFullTime());
```

In the case of assertEquals, often the default message is sufficient. In any case, try reading the message generated and see if it imparts enough information to another developer.

This test should pass. Now modify the test to enroll the student in a back-breaking five-credit course in order to put them at twelve credits. You can use the assertTrue method to test that the student is now full-time. A test passes if the parameter to assertTrue is true, otherwise the test fails.

```
public void testStudentStatus() {
    Student student = new Student("a");
    assertEquals(0, student.getCredits());
    assertFalse(student.isFullTime());

    student.addCredits(3);
    assertEquals(3, student.getCredits());
    assertFalse(student.isFullTime());

    student.addCredits(4);
    assertEquals(7, student.getCredits());
    assertFalse(student.isFullTime());

    student.addCredits(5);
    assertEquals(12, student.getCredits());
    assertTrue(student.isFullTime());
}
```

The test fails. To make it pass, you must modify the isFullTime method to return true if the number of credits is 12 or more. This requires you to write a conditional. A conditional in Java is an expression that returns a *boolean* value. Change the method isFullTime in Student to include an appropriate expression:

```
boolean isFullTime() {
    return credits >= 12;
}
```

You can read this code as "return true if the number of credits is greater than or equal to 12, otherwise return false."

Refactor isFullTime to introduce a Student class constant to explain what the number 12 means.

```
static final int CREDITS_REQUIRED_FOR_FULL_TIME = 12;
...
boolean isFullTime() {
    return credits >= CREDITS_REQUIRED_FOR_FULL_TIME;
}
```

Now that students support adding credits, you can modify CourseSession to ensure that credits are added to Student objects as they are enrolled. Start with the test:

```
public class CourseSessionTest extends TestCase {
    // ...
    private static final int CREDITS = 3;

    public void setUp() {
        startDate = createDate(2003, 1, 6);
        session = createCourseSession();
    }
```

Booleans

```
    // ...
    public void testEnrollStudents() {
        Student student1 = new Student("Cain DiVoe");
        session.enroll(student1);
        assertEquals(CREDITS, student1.getCredits());
        assertEquals(1, session.getNumberOfStudents());
        assertEquals(student1, session.get(0));

        Student student2 = new Student("Coralee DeVaughn");
        session.enroll(student2);
        assertEquals(CREDITS, student2.getCredits());
        assertEquals(2, session.getNumberOfStudents());
        assertEquals(student1, session.get(0));
        assertEquals(student2, session.get(1));
    }
    // ...
    private CourseSession createCourseSession() {
        CourseSession session =
            CourseSession.create("ENGL", "101", startDate);
        session.setNumberOfCredits(CourseSessionTest.CREDITS);
        return session;
    }
}
```

A few quick changes to CourseSession make this failing test pass:

```
public class CourseSession {
    ...
    private int numberOfCredits;
    ...
    void setNumberOfCredits(int numberOfCredits) {
        this.numberOfCredits = numberOfCredits;
    }

    public void enroll(Student student) {
        student.addCredits(numberOfCredits);
        students.add(student) ;
    }
    ...
```

Tests as Documentation

The test method testStudentStatus ensures that students report the appropriate full-time or part-time status. It also ensures that the Student class correctly adds credits.

What the test does not do is exhaustively test every possibility. The general strategy for testing is to test against 0, 1, many, and any boundary conditions and any exceptional cases. With respect to student credits, the test would ensure that a student with 0, 1, or 11 credits reported as part-time and that a student with 12 or 13 credits reported full-time. It would also test the results of unexpected operations, such as adding negative credits, or adding very high numbers of credits.

Test-driven development takes a slightly different approach. The strategy is similar, but the goals are not quite the same. The tests are not just a means of ensuring that the code is correct. In addition, test-driven design provides a technique for consistently paced development. You learn how to incrementally develop code, getting feedback every few seconds or minutes that you are progressing in a valid direction. Tests are about confidence.

Test-driven development also begins to affect the design of the system you are building. This is deliberate: Test-driven development teaches you how to build systems that can be easily tested. Far too few production systems have testability as a characteristic. With test-driven development, you will learn how to test classes in isolation from other classes in the system. This leads to a system where the objects are not tightly coupled to one another, the leading indicator of a well-design object-oriented system.

Finally, tests document the functionality that your classes provide. When you finish coding, you should be able to review your tests to understand what a class does and how it does it. First, you should be able to view the names of your tests to understand all the functionality that a given class supports. Second, each test should also be readable as documentation on how to use that functionality.

 Code tests as comprehensive specifications that others can understand.

In the case of testStudentStatus, you as the developer have a high level of confidence that the production code for isFullTime is valid. It's only a single line, and you know exactly what that line of code states:

```
return credits >= Student.CREDITS_REQUIRED_FOR_FULL_TIME
```

You might consider the test sufficient and choose to move on, and in doing so you wouldn't be entirely out of line. Again, tests are largely about confidence. The less confident you are and the more complex the code, the more tests you should write.

What about unexpected operations? Won't it destroy the integrity of a Student object if someone sends a negative value for number of credits? Remember, you are the developer building this system. You are the one who will control access to the Student class. You have two choices: you can test for and guard against every possible exceptional condition, or you can use the design of your system to make some assumptions.

In the student information system, the CourseSession class will be the only place where the Student number of credits can be incremented; this is by design. If CourseSession is coded properly, then it will have stored a reasonable number of credits. Since it will have stored a reasonable number of credits, there is theoretically no way for a negative number to be passed to Student. You know that you have coded CourseSession properly because you did it using TDD!

Of course, somewhere some human will have to enter that number of credits for a course session into the system. It is at that point—at code that represents the user interface level—that you must guard against all possibilities. A human might enter nothing, a letter, a negative number, or a $ character. The tests for ensuring that a reasonable positive integer is passed into the system will have to be made at this point.

Once you have this sort of barrier against invalid data, you can consider that the rest of the system is under your control—theoretically, of course. With this assumption, you can remove much of the need to guard the rest of your classes against bad data.

In reality, there are always "holes" that you unwittingly use to drop defects in your code. But a large key to success with test-driven development is to understand its heavy emphasis on feedback. A defect is an indication that your unit tests were not complete enough: You missed a test. Go back and write the missing test. Ensure that it fails, then fix it. Over time you will learn what is important to test and what is not. You will learn where you are investing too much time or too little time on the tests.

Tests as Documentation

I have confidence in testStudentStatus and the corresponding implementation. Where the test is lacking is in its ability to act as documentation. Part of the problem is that you as a developer have too much knowledge about how you have coded the functionality. It helps to find another developer to read the test to see if it describes all of the business rules and boundaries properly. If another developer is unavailable, take a step back and try to look at the test as if you had never seen the underlying code. Does it tell you how to use the class? Does it demonstrate the different scenarios? Does it indicate the constraints or limitations of the code being tested—perhaps by omission?

In this case, perhaps all that is needed is to let the test use the same constant that Student uses. The test becomes a good deal more expressive by virtue of doing so. The boundaries of full-time are now implicit and reasonably well understood.

```
public void testStudentStatus() {
    Student student = new Student("a");
    assertEquals(0, student.getCredits());
    assertFalse(student.isFullTime());
```

```
    student.addCredits(3);
    assertEquals(3, student.getCredits());
    assertFalse(student.isFullTime());

    student.addCredits(4);
    assertEquals(7, student.getCredits());
    assertFalse(student.isFullTime());

    student.addCredits(5);
    assertEquals(Student.CREDITS_REQUIRED_FOR_FULL_TIME,
        student.getCredits());
    assertTrue(student.isFullTime());
}
```

More on Initialization

To support the notion of in-state versus out-of-state students, the Student object needs to store a state that represents where the Student resides. The school happens to be located in the state of Colorado (abbreviation: CO). If the student resides in any other state, or if the student has no state specified (either the student is international or didn't complete the forms yet), then the student is an out-of-state student.

Here is the test:

```
public void testInState() {
    Student student = new Student("a");
    assertFalse(student.isInState());
    student.setState(Student.IN_STATE);
    assertTrue(student.isInState());
    student.setState("MD");
    assertFalse(student.isInState());
}
```

The logic for determining whether a student is in-state will have to compare the String representing the student's state to the String "CO". This of course means you will need to create a field named state.

```
boolean isInState() {
    return state.equals(Student.IN_STATE);
}
```

To compare two strings, you use the equals method. You send the equals message to a String object, passing another String as an argument. The equals method will return true if both strings have the same length and if each string matches character for character. Thus "CO".equals("CO") would return true; "Aa".equals("AA") would return false.

In order for `testInState` to pass, it is important that the state field you create has an appropriate initial value. Anything but "CO" will work, but the empty String ("") will do just fine.

```
package sis.studentinfo;

public class Student {
    static final String IN_STATE = "CO";
    ...
    private String state = "";
    ...
    void setState(String state) {
        this.state = state;
    }
    boolean isInState() {
        return state.equals(Student.IN_STATE);
    }
}
```

You might also consider writing a test to demonstrate what should happen if someone passes a lowercase state abbreviation. Right now, if client code passes in "Co", it will not set the student's status to in-state, since "Co" is not the same as "CO". While that may be acceptable behavior, a better solution would be to always translate a state abbreviation to its uppercase equivalent prior to comparing against "CO". You could accomplish this by using the String method `toUpperCase`.

Exceptions

What if you do not supply an initial value for the state field? In the test, you create a new Student object and immediately send it the message `isInState`. The `isInState` message results in the `equals` message being sent to the state field. Find out what happens if you send a message to an uninitialized object. Change the declaration of the state field to comment out the initialization:

```
private String state; // = "";
```

Then rerun the tests. JUnit will report an error, not a test failure. An error occurs when neither your production code nor your test accounts for a problem. In this case, the problem is that you are sending a message to an uninitialized field reference. The second panel in JUnit shows the problem.

```
java.lang.NullPointerException
    at studentinfo.Student.isInState(Student.java:37)
    at studentinfo.StudentTest.testInState(StudentTest.java:39)
    at sun.reflect.NativeMethodAccessorImpl.invoke0(Native Method)
    ...
```

This is known as a *stack walkback*, or *stack trace*. It provides you with the information on what went wrong, but figuring out the stack trace can take a little bit of detective work. The first line in a stack trace tells you what the problem is. In this case, you got something known as a NullPointerException. A NullPointerException is actually an error object, or *exception*, that is "thrown" by some underlying, problematic code.

The rest of the lines in a stack trace "walk back" through the message sends leading up to the error. Some of the lines refer to classes and methods that you have coded; other lines refer to Java system library code and third-party library code. The easiest way to decipher stack traces is to read down and find the first line of code that you recognize as being "your" code. Then keep reading lines up to the last line that you recognize. This last recognized line is the entry point into your code; you will probably want to dig down from there.

In the above example, the last line to execute was line 37 in Student.java (the line numbers in your code will likely differ). That code was invoked by the message send in StudentTest line 39. So start with StudentTest line 39 in order to follow the trail leading up to the trouble. That should take you to the following line of code:

```
assertFalse(student.isInState());
```

Taking a look at line 37 in Student.java reveals the line of your code that generated the NullPointerException:

```
return state.equals(Student.IN_STATE);
```

A reference that you do not explicitly initialize has a value of `null`. The value `null` represents the unique instance of an object known as the null object. If you send a message to the null object, you receive a NullPointerException. In this line of code, you sent the message `equals` to the uninitialized `state` reference, hence the NullPointerException.

In Lesson 6, you will see how to determine if a field is `null` before attempting to send a message to it. For now, ensure that you initialize String fields to the empty String ("").

Revert your code so that the `state` field is initialized properly. Rerun your tests.

Revisiting Primitive-Type Field Initialization

Only reference-type fields—fields that can point to objects in memory—can be initialized to `null` or have a value of `null`. You cannot initialize a variable of the primitive type to `null`, nor can such a variable ever have a value of `null`.

This includes `boolean` variables and variables of the numeric type (`char` and `int`, plus the rest that you'll learn about in Lesson 10: `byte`, `short`, `long`, `float`, and `double`). Fields of the `boolean` type have an initial value of `false`. Each of the numeric types has an initial value of `0`.

Even though `0` is often a useful initial value for a numeric type, you should explicitly initialize the field to `0` if that represents a meaningful value for the field. For example, explicitly initialize a field to `0` if it represents a counter that will track values starting at `0` when the Java VM instantiates the object. If you are going to explicitly assign a more meaningful value to the field in later execution of the code, then you need not explicitly initialize the field to `0`.

Provide explicit initializations only when necessary. This will help clarify what you, the developer of the code, intend.

Exercises

Exercises

1. Concatenating a new line character to the end of a string has created repetitive code. Extract this functionality to a new utility method on the class util.StringUtil. Mark StringUtil as a utility class by changing its constructor's access privilege to `private`. You will need to move the class constant NEWLINE to this class. Use your compiler to help you determine impacts on other code. Ensure that you have tests for the utility method.

2. Transform your Pawn class into a more generic class named Piece. A Piece is a color plus a name (pawn, knight, rook, bishop, queen, or king). A Piece should be a *value object*: It should have a private constructor and no way to change anything on the object after construction. Create factory methods to return Piece objects based on the color and name. Eliminate the ability to create a default piece.

3. Change BoardTest to reflect the complete board:

```
package chess;

import junit.framework.TestCase;
import util.StringUtil;

public class BoardTest extends TestCase {
    private Board board;

    protected void setUp() {
        board = new Board();
    }
```

```
public void testCreate() {
    board.initialize();
    assertEquals(32, board.pieceCount());
    String blankRank = StringUtil.appendNewLine("........");
    assertEquals(
        StringUtil.appendNewLine("RNBQKBNR") +
        StringUtil.appendNewLine("PPPPPPPP") +
        blankRank + blankRank + blankRank + blankRank +
        StringUtil.appendNewLine("pppppppp") +
        StringUtil.appendNewLine("rnbqkbnr"),
        board.print());
    }
}
```

4. Ensure that a new Board creates sixteen black pieces and sixteen white pieces. Use a class counter on the Piece object to track the counts. Make sure you can run your tests twice without problems (uncheck the "Reload Classes Every Run" box on JUnit and click Run a second time).

5. Create methods isBlack and isWhite on the Piece class (test first, of course).

6. Gather the names of each of your test methods. Put the class name in front of each test name. Show the list to a friend and ask what the methods say about each class.

7. Read over the section on Simple Design again. Does your current chess design follow the patterns of simple design?

Exercises

Lesson 5

Interfaces and Polymorphism

In this lesson you will learn about:

- sorting

- interfaces

- the Comparable interface

- if statements

- enumerated types using enum

- polymorphism

Sorting: Preparation

The school needs a report of all course sessions. You must sort the report first by department, then by course number. This implies that all courses for a given department will be listed together. The groups of departments will be ordered in ascending alphabetical order. Within a department, the sessions will be ordered by course number.

To get started, get a simple report working of all course sessions. Don't worry yet about its order.

```
package sis.report;

import junit.framework.*;
import java.util.*;
import sis.studentinfo.*;
import static sis.report.ReportConstant.NEWLINE;

public class CourseReportTest extends TestCase {
    public void testReport() {
        final Date date = new Date();
```

163

```
CourseReport report = new CourseReport();
report.add(CourseSession.create("ENGL", "101", date));
report.add(CourseSession.create("CZEC", "200", date));
report.add(CourseSession.create("ITAL", "410", date));

assertEquals(
    "ENGL 101" + NEWLINE +
    "CZEC 200" + NEWLINE +
    "ITAL 410" + NEWLINE,
    report.text());
    }
}
```

The report is bare boned, showing simply a course department and number on each line. Currently the report lists sessions in the order in which you added them to the CourseReport object.

The production class, CourseReport, looks similar to RosterReporter:

```
package sis.report;

import java.util.*;
import sis.studentinfo.*;
import static sis.report.ReportConstant.NEWLINE;

public class CourseReport {
    private ArrayList<CourseSession> sessions =
        new ArrayList<CourseSession>();

    public void add(CourseSession session) {
        sessions.add(session);
    }

    public String text() {
        StringBuilder builder = new StringBuilder();
        for (CourseSession session: sessions)
            builder.append(
                session.getDepartment() + " " +
                session.getNumber() + NEWLINE);
        return builder.toString();
    }
}
```

In order to get CourseReport to compile, you'll have to designate the CourseSession methods `getDepartment` and `getNumber` as `public`.

Sorting: Collections.sort

Sorting: Collections.sort

You can sort a list of String objects quite simply, as this language test demonstrates:

```
public void testSortStringsInPlace() {
   ArrayList<String> list = new ArrayList<String>();
   list.add("Heller");
   list.add("Kafka");
   list.add("Camus");
   list.add("Boyle");
   java.util.Collections.sort(list);
   assertEquals("Boyle", list.get(0));
   assertEquals("Camus", list.get(1));
   assertEquals("Heller", list.get(2));
   assertEquals("Kafka", list.get(3));
}
```

The static sort method in the java.util.Collections class takes a list as a parameter and sorts the list *in place*.[1] If you do not want to sort the list in place—if you do not want to modify the original list—you can create a new list and send that list as a parameter to the sort message.

```
public void testSortStringsInNewList() {
   ArrayList<String> list = new ArrayList<String>();
   list.add("Heller");
   list.add("Kafka");
   list.add("Camus");
   list.add("Boyle");
   ArrayList<String> sortedList = new ArrayList<String>(list);
   java.util.Collections.sort(sortedList);
   assertEquals("Boyle", sortedList.get(0));
   assertEquals("Camus", sortedList.get(1));
   assertEquals("Heller", sortedList.get(2));
   assertEquals("Kafka", sortedList.get(3));

   assertEquals("Heller", list.get(0));
   assertEquals("Kafka", list.get(1));
   assertEquals("Camus", list.get(2));
   assertEquals("Boyle", list.get(3));
}
```

The last four assertions verify that the original list remains unmodified.

CourseReport
Test

CourseReportTest

In CourseReportTest, modify the assertion in testReport to ensure that you produce the report in sorted order. Your test data currently takes only the department into account. That's fine for now:

---

[1] The sort method uses a merge sort algorithm that splits the list of elements into two groups, recursively sorts each group, and merges all sorted subgroups into a complete list.

```
assertEquals(
    "CZEC 200" + NEWLINE +
    "ENGL 101" + NEWLINE +
    "ITAL 410" + NEWLINE,
  report.text());
```

The test fails as expected. You should be able to see in JUnit that the sessions are in the wrong order.

To solve the problem, use `Collections.sort` to order the `sessions` list.

```
public String text() {
    Collections.sort(sessions);
    StringBuilder builder = new StringBuilder();
    for (CourseSession session: sessions)
      builder.append(
          session.getDepartment() + " " +
          session.getNumber() + NEWLINE);
    return builder.toString();
}
```

Unfortunately, this will not compile:

```
cannot find symbol
symbol  : method sort(java.util.List<sis.studentinfo.CourseSession>)
location: class java.util.Collections
      Collections.sort(sessions);
             ^
```

The source of the error can be difficult to decipher, even if you are relatively experienced in Java. The problem is that the method declaration for sort requires the objects it sorts to be of the type java.lang.Comparable. (How it does that involves advanced syntax that I will discuss in Lesson 14 on generics.)

Interfaces

Comparable is a type that allows you to compare objects to one another. But you want to compare CourseSession objects, since that's what you bound the variable sessions to. The secret to getting this to work takes advantage of a feature in Java known as *interfaces*. Interfaces allow an object to act as more than one type. You will modify CourseSession to act as a java.lang.Comparable type in addition to being a CourseSession.

Interfaces

Comparable is an *interface* type, not a class type. An interface contains any number of method *declarations*. A method declaration is the *signature* for a method followed by a semicolon. There are no braces and there is no method code. Java defines the type Comparable as follows:

```
public interface Comparable<T> {
    public int compareTo(T o);
}
```

The letter T is a placeholder for the type of objects to be compared. Lesson 14 on generics will explain this concept in further detail. For now, understand that you declare a Comparable reference along with a type. The Java compiler substitutes this type for all occurrences of T in the interface declaration.

Contrast an interface declaration to a class declaration. You declare an interface using the interface keyword, whereas you declare a class using the class keyword. An interface can contain no implementations for any of the methods that it declares.

In UML, you can represent an interface in a number of ways. Figure 5.1 shows one such way.

The goal of the compareTo method is to return a value that indicates whether an object should come before or after another object with respect to ordering. All sort techniques involve comparing only two objects at a time and swapping those two objects if necessary.

For example, a list contains two String objects, "E" and "D", in that order. You want the list sorted in alphabetical order. The Collections method sort would send the compareTo message to the String "E", along with the parameter "D". The compareTo method would return a value that indicates that "D" should appear first in the sort order, before "E". The sort method would then know that it would have to swap the two objects for them to be sorted correctly.

A class can declare that it *implements* an interface. By making this declaration, a class promises to provide implementations for each method declared in the interface. Implementing an interface allows classes to act as more than one type.

Interfaces

The earlier sorting example, the one that actually worked, sorted a collection of String objects. The J2SE API documentation for the String class lists the Comparable interface as one of three implemented interfaces. Implementing the Comparable interface allows String objects to be treated not just as objects of String type but also as objects of Comparable type.

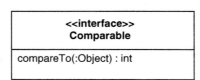

Figure 5.1 *Comparable*

The syntax for implementing interfaces is demonstrated in this bit of code from the actual Java String class:

```
public final class String
    implements java.io.Serializable, Comparable<String>, CharSequence
{
  ...
```

If you look further into the source for the String class, you will find the implementation for the compareTo method that Comparable declares.

For the sort invoked by CourseReport to work, it must be able to send the message compareTo to the objects contained within sessions. The sort method is unaware of the class of objects in the collection, however. It takes each object in turn and tries to assign the object to a variable of the Comparable interface type. When this assignment is successful, the sort can safely send the compareTo message to the object. When the assignment is not successful, Java generates an error.

Why Interfaces

Interfaces are a very powerful and very important feature in Java. Part of the key to solid design in Java is knowing when (and when not) to use interfaces. Used properly, interfaces help you compartmentalize your software to help minimize impacts on other parts of the code.

Interfaces provide higher levels of abstraction. The sort code doesn't need to know any details about the objects it is sorting. It need not know whether it is sorting Student objects, Customer objects, or Strings. All the sort code needs to know is that the objects it is sorting support being compared to other objects. The sort code knows only about this more abstract quality, not any other specifics of the objects it is sorting.

You can view this concept of abstracting sortability as a way to eliminate duplication. Interfaces allow a sort algorithm to operate on objects of different base types. The sort algorithm needs no repetitive code to determine the types of objects it compares.

 Use interfaces to provide abstraction layers in your system and to help remove duplication.

The abstraction layers in your system isolate your code from negative effects. Ideally, you write the sort class once, get it to work perfectly, and then close it off to any future changes. The only detail the sort class has to know about the objects it sorts is that they respond to the compareTo method by returning an int. The classes of those objects can change in other myriad ways, but none of these changes will ever impact your sort code.

You can use interfaces can break dependencies on code that doesn't work or doesn't even exist by writing stub code to meet the specifications of the interface. In Lesson 12, you will learn how to accomplish this using a technique known as mocking. Interfaces are an essential tool for effective testing.

By implementing the Comparable interface, the String class publicizes the fact that Strings can be compared for sort purposes. The String supplies code in the compareTo method to determine how String objects are compared.

In order to get the sort to work for the list of sessions, you must modify CourseSession to implement the Comparable interface.

Implementing Comparable

The job of the compareTo method in the Comparable interface is to indicate which of two objects—the message receiver and the message parameter—should appear first. The code you will supply in compareTo should result in what is known as the *natural*, or default, sort order for CourseSessions. In other words, how do you normally want to sort a collection of CourseSession objects?

The compareTo method must return an int value. If this return value is 0, then the two objects are equal for purposes of sorting. If the return value is negative, then the receiver (the object to which code sends the compareTo message) should come before the parameter in the sort order. If the value is positive, then the parameter should come before the receiver in the sort order.

Implementing
Comparable

The String class implements the compareTo method in order to sort strings in alphabetical order. The following language test demonstrates the values returned from the compareTo method in the three possible scenarios.

```
public void testStringCompareTo() {
    assertTrue("A".compareTo("B") < 0);
    assertEquals(0, "A".compareTo("A"));
    assertTrue("B".compareTo("A") > 0);
}
```

You will need to modify the CourseSession class to implement the Comparable interface and supply a definition for compareTo. An appropriate test to add to CourseSessionTest:

```
public void testComparable()  {
    final Date date = new Date();
    CourseSession sessionA = CourseSession.create("CMSC", "101", date);
```

```
CourseSession sessionB = CourseSession.create("ENGL", "101", date);
assertTrue(sessionA.compareTo(sessionB) < 0);
assertTrue(sessionB.compareTo(sessionA) > 0);

CourseSession sessionC = CourseSession.create("CMSC", "101", date);
assertEquals(0, sessionA.compareTo(sessionC));
}
```

CourseSession must then declare that it implements the Comparable interface. It must also specify a bind type of CourseSession—you want to be able to compare CourseSession objects to CourseSession objects.

```
public class CourseSession implements Comparable<CourseSession> {
...
```

Implementing Comparable

More on this

In the Student compareTo method, the return statement includes the expression this.getDepartment(). As you learned in Lesson 1, the this reference is to the current object. Scoping method calls with this is usually unnecessary, but in this case it helps differentiate the current object and the parameter object.

Another use of the this keyword that you haven't seen is for *constructor chaining*. You can invoke another constructor defined on the same class by using a slightly different form of this:

```
class Name {
   ...
   public Name(String first, String mid, String last) {
      this.first = first;
      this.mid = mid;
      this.last = last;
   }

   public Name(String first, String last) {
      this(first, "", last);
   }
   ...
```

The single statement in the second constructor of Name calls the first constructor. The goal in this example is to pass a default value of the empty string as the middle name.

Such a call to another constructor must appear as the first line of a constructor.

Constructor chaining can be a valuable tool for helping you eliminate duplication. Without chaining, you would need to write a separate method to do common initialization.

Since you bound the implementation of Comparable to the CourseSession, you must define the compareTo method so that it takes a CourseSession as parameter:

```
public int compareTo(CourseSession that) {
    return this.getDepartment().compareTo(that.getDepartment());
}
```

For the compareTo method implementation, you are returning the result of comparing the current CourseSession's department (this.getDepartment()) to the parameter CourseSession object's department (that.getDepartment()).

At this point, both testComparable in CourseSessionTest and testReport in CouseReportTest should pass.

Sorting on Department and Number

You are now able to produce a report that sorts course sessions by their department. You will now enhance the report code to sort sessions by both department and number. You will need to first modify the test to incorporate appropriate data. The following test (in CourseReportTest) adds two new sessions. The test data now includes two sessions that share the same department.

```
package sis.report;

import junit.framework.*;
import java.util.*;
import sis.studentinfo.*;
import static sis.report.ReportConstant.NEWLINE;

public class CourseReportTest extends TestCase {
    public void testReport() {
        final Date date = new Date();
        CourseReport report = new CourseReport();
        report.add(CourseSession.create("ENGL", "101", date));
        report.add(CourseSession.create("CZEC", "200", date));
        report.add(CourseSession.create("ITAL", "410", date));
        report.add(CourseSession.create("CZEC", "220", date));
        report.add(CourseSession.create("ITAL", "330", date));

        assertEquals(
                "CZEC 200" + NEWLINE +
                "CZEC 220" + NEWLINE +
                "ENGL 101" + NEWLINE +
                "ITAL 330" + NEWLINE +
```

```
        "ITAL 410" + NEWLINE,
    report.text());
  }
}
```

In order to determine the proper ordering of these students, your compareTo method will need to first look at department. If the departments are different, that comparison will be sufficient to provide a return value. If the departments are the same, you will have to compare the course numbers.

The if Statement

You use the if statement for conditional branching: If a condition holds true, execute one branch (section) of code, otherwise execute another branch of code. A branch can be a single statement or a block of statements.

Flesh out the CourseSessionTest method testCompareTo by adding tests to represent more complex comparisons:

```
public void testComparable()  {
    final Date date = new Date();
    CourseSession sessionA = CourseSession.create("CMSC", "101", date);
    CourseSession sessionB = CourseSession.create("ENGL", "101", date);
    assertTrue(sessionA.compareTo(sessionB) < 0);
    assertTrue(sessionB.compareTo(sessionA) > 0);

    CourseSession sessionC = CourseSession.create("CMSC", "101", date);
    assertEquals(0, sessionA.compareTo(sessionC));

    CourseSession sessionD = CourseSession.create("CMSC", "210", date);
    assertTrue(sessionC.compareTo(sessionD) < 0);
    assertTrue(sessionD.compareTo(sessionC) > 0);
}
```

The if
Statement

Then update the compareTo method in CourseSession:

```
public int compareTo(CourseSession that) {
    int compare =
        this.getDepartment().compareTo(that.getDepartment());
    if (compare == 0)
        compare = this.getNumber().compareTo(that.getNumber());
    return compare;
}
```

Paraphrased, this code says: Compare this department to the department of the parameter; store the result of the comparison in the compare local variable. *If* the value stored in compare is 0 (if the departments are the same), compare this course number to the parameter's course number and assign the result to compare. Regardless, return the value stored in the compare local variable.

You could have also written the code as follows:

```
public int compareTo(CourseSession that) {
    int compare =
        this.getDepartment().compareTo(that.getDepartment());
    if (compare != 0)
        return compare;
    return this.getNumber().compareTo(that.getNumber());
}
```

If, on the first comparison, the departments are unequal (the result of the comparison is not 0), then that's all that needs to happen. You can stop there and return the result of the comparison. The rest of the code is not executed. This style of coding can be easier to follow. Be cautious, however: In longer methods, multiple returns can make the method more difficult to understand and follow. For longer methods, then, I do not recommend multiple return statements. But the real solution is to have as few long methods as possible.

All tests should pass.

Grading Students

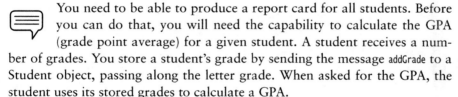 You need to be able to produce a report card for all students. Before you can do that, you will need the capability to calculate the GPA (grade point average) for a given student. A student receives a number of grades. You store a student's grade by sending the message addGrade to a Student object, passing along the letter grade. When asked for the GPA, the student uses its stored grades to calculate a GPA.

You will supply grades as decimal numbers, known in Java as floating-point numbers.

Floating-Point Numbers

Floating-Point Numbers

You are already familiar with the primitive-type int, representing integer values. In addition to integer numerics, Java supports IEEE 754 32-bit single precision binary floating point format numbers, also known as float points, or floats. Java also supports 64-bit double precision floats, also known as doubles.

Table 5.1 *Floating-Point Precision Types*

Type	Range	Example Literals
float	1.40239846e -45f to 3.40282347e + 38f	6.07f 6F 7.0f 7.0f 1.8e5f
double	4.94065645841246544e -324 to 1.79769313486231570e +308	1440.0 6 3.2545e7 32D 0d

Table 5.1 lists the types, the range of values that they support and some examples.

Any numeric literal with a decimal point or any numeric literal with a suffix of f, F, d, or D, is by definition a floating-point number.

Float and double literals may also use scientific notation. Any number with an e or E in the middle is by definition a floating-point number. The double numeric literal 1.2e6 represents 1.2 times 10 to the 6th power, or 1.2×10^6 in standard mathematical notation.

If you do not supply a suffix for a floating-point number, it is by default a double precision float. In other words, you must supply an F or f suffix to produce a single precision float literal. In Agile Java, I will prefer the use of double over float due to its higher precision and the fact that I need not supply a suffix.

Realize, though, that floating-point numbers are approximations of real numbers based on bit patterns. It is not possible to represent all real numbers, since there are an infinite amount of real numbers and only a finite set of possible representations in either 32- or 64-bit precision floats. This means that most real numbers have only an *approximate* floating-point representation.

Floating-Point Numbers

For example, if you execute the following line of code:

```
System.out.println("value = " + (3 * 0.3));
```

the output will be:

```
value = 0.8999999999999999
```

and not the expected value 0.9.

If you use floating-point numbers, you must be prepared to deal with these inaccuracies by using rounding techniques. Another solution is to use the Java class BigDecimal to represent numbers with fractional parts. Agile Java presents BigDecimal in Lesson 10.

Testing Grades

The following test, which you should add to StudentTest, demonstrates a range of possibilities. It starts with the simplest case: The student has received no grades, in which case the student's GPA should be 0. It also tests grade combinations based on applying each of the possible letter grades from A through F.

```
private static final double GRADE_TOLERANCE = 0.05;
...
public void testCalculateGpa() {
    Student student = new Student("a");
    assertEquals(0.0, student.getGpa(), GRADE_TOLERANCE);
    student.addGrade("A");
    assertEquals(4.0, student.getGpa(), GRADE_TOLERANCE);
    student.addGrade("B");
    assertEquals(3.5, student.getGpa(), GRADE_TOLERANCE);
    student.addGrade("C");
    assertEquals(3.0, student.getGpa(), GRADE_TOLERANCE);
    student.addGrade("D");
    assertEquals(2.5, student.getGpa(), GRADE_TOLERANCE);
    student.addGrade("F");
    assertEquals(2.0, student.getGpa(), GRADE_TOLERANCE);
}
```

The assertEquals method calls in this test show three parameters instead of two. Since floating-point numbers are not precise representations of real numbers, there is a possibility that a calculated value may be off from an expected value by a certain amount. For example, were it possible to code:

```
assertEquals(0.9, 3 * 0.3);
```

the test would fail:

```
AssertionFailedError: expected:<0.9> but was:<0.8999999999999999>
```

JUnit provides a third parameter when you need to compare two floating-point values for equality. This parameter represents a *tolerance*: How much can the two floating-point values be off by before JUnit reports an error?

A general rule of thumb is that values should be off by no more than half of the smallest precision you are interested in representing accurately. For example, if you are working with cents (hundredths of a dollar), then you want to ensure that compared amounts are off by no more than half a cent.

You want to accurately express GPAs to tenths of a point; therefore your tolerance should be 5/100 of a point. The above code defines a static constant GRADE_TOLERANCE local to the StudentTest class and uses it as the third parameter to each assertEquals method:

```
assertEquals(2.0, student.getGpa(), GRADE_TOLERANCE);
```

Testing Grades

In order to make the test pass, you will need to change the Student class to store each added grade in an ArrayList.[2] You can then code the getGpa method to calculate the result GPA. To do so, you must first iterate through the list of grades and obtain a grade point total. You then divide this grade point total by the total number of grades to get the GPA.

```java
import java.util.*;
...
class Student {
    private ArrayList<String> grades = new ArrayList<String>();
    ...
    void addGrade(String grade) {
        grades.add(grade);
    }
    ...
    double getGpa() {
        if (grades.isEmpty())
            return 0.0;
        double total = 0.0;
        for (String grade: grades) {
            if (grade.equals("A")) {
                total += 4;
            }
            else {
                if (grade.equals("B")) {
                    total += 3;
                }
                else
                {
                    if (grade.equals("C")) {
                        total += 2;
                    }
                    else {
                        if (grade.equals("D")) {
                            total += 1;
                        }
                    }
                }
            }
        }
        return total / grades.size();
    }
}
```

Testing Grades

The method getGpa starts with an if statement to determine whether or not the list of grades is empty. If there are no grades, the method immediately returns a GPA of 0.0. An if statement that appears at the beginning of a method

---

[2]You could also calculate the GPA as each grade is added.

and returns upon a special condition is known as a *guard clause*. The guard clause in getGpa guards the remainder of the method from the special case where there are no grades. Since you calculate a GPA by dividing by the number of grades, the guard clause eliminates any possibility of dividing by zero.

The method code then uses a for-each loop to extract each grade from the grades collection. The body of the for-each loop compares each grade against the possible letter grades. The body code uses an extension of the if statement known as the if-else statement.

A paraphrasing of the body of the for-each loop: *If* the grade is an A, add 4 to the total,[3] *otherwise*, execute the block of code (or single statement) appearing after the else keyword. In this case, the block of code is itself comprised of another if-else statement: If the grade is a B, add 3 to the total, otherwise execute yet another block of code. This pattern continues until all possibilities are exhausted (an F is ignored, since it adds nothing to the grade total).

Complex if-else statements can be difficult to read because of the many curly braces and repeated indenting. In the circumstance where you have repetitive *nested* if-else statements, you can use a tighter formatting style. Each else-if statement combination goes on the same line. Also, you can eliminate the braces in this example, since the body of each if statement is a single line.

```
double getGpa() {
   if (grades.isEmpty())
      return 0.0;
   double total = 0.0;
   for (String grade: grades) {
      if (grade.equals("A"))
         total += 4;
      else if (grade.equals("B"))
         total += 3;
      else if (grade.equals("C"))
         total += 2;
      else if (grade.equals("D"))
         total += 1;
   }
   return total / grades.size();
}
```

This alternative formatting style makes the getGpa method far easier to read but produces the same results.

[3]You may add int values to doubles with no ill effects. However, mixing int and double values in an expression can cause unintended effects. See Lesson 10 for a discussion of numerics in Java.

Refactoring

The method getGpa is still a bit long and difficult to follow. Extract from it a new method that returns a double value for a given letter grade:

```
double getGpa() {
    if (grades.isEmpty())
        return 0.0;
    double total = 0.0;
    for (String grade: grades)
        total += gradePointsFor(grade);
    return total / grades.size();
}

int gradePointsFor(String grade) {
    if (grade.equals("A"))
        return 4;
    else if (grade.equals("B"))
        return 3;
    else if (grade.equals("C"))
        return 2;
    else if (grade.equals("D"))
        return 1;
    return 0;
}
```

Refactoring

Make sure this compiles and passes the tests. One further change that you can make is to remove the else clauses. A return statement is a flow of control. Once the Java VM encounters a return statement in a method, it executes no more statements within the method.

```
int gradePointsFor(String grade) {
    if (grade.equals("A")) return 4;
    if (grade.equals("B")) return 3;
    if (grade.equals("C")) return 2;
    if (grade.equals("D")) return 1;
    return 0;
}
```

In the gradePointsFor method, as soon as there is a match on grade, the VM executes a return statement and makes no more comparisons.

You'll also note that I put each return on the same line as the corresponding if statement conditional. Normally, you will want to keep the conditional and the body of an if statement on separate lines. In this example, the multiple if statements are repetitive, terse, and visually consistent. The code is easy to read and digest. In other circumstances, jumbling the conditional and body together can result in an unreadable mess.

You can refactor the test itself:

```
public void testCalculateGpa() {
    Student student = new Student("a");
    assertGpa(student, 0.0);
    student.addGrade("A");
    assertGpa(student, 4.0);
    student.addGrade("B");
    assertGpa(student, 3.5);
    student.addGrade("C");
    assertGpa(student, 3.0);
    student.addGrade("D");
    assertGpa(student, 2.5);
    student.addGrade("F");
    assertGpa(student, 2.0) ;
}

private void assertGpa(Student student, double expectedGpa) {
    assertEquals(expectedGpa, student.getGpa(), GRADE_TOLERANCE);
}
```

Enums

J2SE 5.0 introduces the notion of an enumerated type—a type that constrains all possible values to a discrete list. For example, if you implement a class that represents a deck of cards, you know that the only possible suit values are clubs, diamonds, spades, and hearts. There are no other suits. For grades, you know there are only five possible letter grades.

You can define grades as strings, as in the above GPA code, and use String values to represent possible letter grades. While this will work, it has some problems. First, it is easy to make a mistake when typing all the various strings. You can create class constants to represent each letter grade (which we probably should have done in the above code), and as long as all code uses the constants, things are fine.

Even if you have supplied class constants, client code can still pass an invalid value into your code. There is nothing that prevents a user of the Student class from executing this line of code:

```
student.addGrade("a");
```

The results are probably not what you expect—you wrote the code to handle only uppercase grade letters.

You can instead define an enum named Grade. The best place for this, for now, is within the Student class:

```
public class Student {
    enum Grade { A, B, C, D, F };
    ...
```

Using enum results in the declaration of a new type. In this case, you have just created a new type named Student.Grade, since you defined the Grade enum within the Student class. The new enum has five possible values, each representing a named object instance.

Change the test to use the enum instances:

```
public void testCalculateGpa() {
   Student student = new Student("a");
   assertGpa(student, 0.0);
   student.addGrade(Student.Grade.A);
   assertGpa(student, 4.0);
   student.addGrade(Student.Grade.B);
   assertGpa(student, 3.5);
   student.addGrade(Student.Grade.C);
   assertGpa(student, 3.0);
   student.addGrade(Student.Grade.D);
   assertGpa(student, 2.5);
   student.addGrade(Student.Grade.F);
   assertGpa(student, 2.0);
}
```

In the Student class, you will need to change any code that declared a grade to be of the type String to now be of the type Grade. Since the Grade enum is defined within Student, you can refer to it directly (i.e., as Grade instead of Student.Grade).

```
public class Student implements Comparable<Student> {
   enum Grade { A, B, C, D, F };
   ...
   private ArrayList<Grade> grades = new ArrayList<Grade>();
   ...

   void addGrade(Grade grade) {
      grades.add(grade);
   }
   ...
   double getGpa() {
      if (grades.isEmpty())
         return 0.0;
      double total = 0.0;
      for (Grade grade: grades)
         total += gradePointsFor(grade);
      return total / grades.size();
   }
   ...
   int gradePointsFor(Grade grade) {
      if (grade == Grade.A) return 4;
      if (grade == Grade.B) return 3;
      if (grade == Grade.C) return 2;
      if (grade == Grade.D) return 1;
```

```
        return 0;
    }
    ...
}
```

The method gradePointsFor compares the value of the parameter grade to each of the enum values in turn. Each of the enum values represents a unique instance in memory. This allows you to make the comparison using the == operator instead of the equals method. Remember that the == operator is used for comparing two object references: Do the two references point to the same object in memory?

It is no longer possible for a client to pass in an invalid value to the method addGrade. Client code cannot create a new instance of Grade. The five instances specified in the enum declaration within Student are all that exist.

Polymorphism

Overuse of the if statement can quickly turn your code into a high-maintenance legacy that is difficult to follow. A concept known as polymorphism can help structure your code to minimize the need for if statements.

 Student grading is a bit more involved than the above example. You need to support grading for honors students. Honors students are graded on a higher scale. They can earn five grade points for an A, 4 points for a B, 3 points for a C, and 2 points for a D.

A highly refactored test:

```
public void testCalculateHonorsStudentGpa() {
    assertGpa(createHonorsStudent(), 0.0);
    assertGpa(createHonorsStudent(Student.Grade.A), 5.0);
    assertGpa(createHonorsStudent(Student.Grade.B), 4.0);
    assertGpa(createHonorsStudent(Student.Grade.C), 3.0);
    assertGpa(createHonorsStudent(Student.Grade.D), 2.0);
    assertGpa(createHonorsStudent(Student.Grade.F), 0.0);
}

private Student createHonorsStudent(Student.Grade grade) {
    Student student = createHonorsStudent();
    student.addGrade(grade);
    return student;
}

private Student createHonorsStudent() {
    Student student = new Student("a");
    student.setHonors();
    return student;
}
```

The code to resolve this is trivial.

```
private boolean isHonors = false;
// ...
void setHonors() {
    isHonors = true;
}
// ...
int gradePointsFor(Grade grade) {
    int points = basicGradePointsFor(grade);
    if (isHonors)
        if (points > 0)
            points += 1;
    return points;
}

private int basicGradePointsFor(Grade grade) {
    if (grade == Grade.A) return 4;
    if (grade == Grade.B) return 3;
    if (grade == Grade.C) return 2;
    if (grade == Grade.D) return 1;
    return 0;
}
```

. . . but things are becoming unwieldy. Next, suppose you must support a different grading scheme:

```
double gradePointsFor(Grade grade) {
    if (isSenatorsSon) {
        if (grade == Grade.A) return 4;
        if (grade == Grade.B) return 4;
        if (grade == Grade.C) return 4;
        if (grade == Grade.D) return 4;
        return 3;
    }
    else {
        double points = basicGradePointsFor(grade);
        if (isHonors)
            if (points > 0)
                points += 1;
        return points;
    }
}
```

Now the code is getting messy. And the dean has indicated that there are more schemes on the way, in this politically correct age of trying to be everything to everyone. Every time the dean adds a new scheme, you must change the code in the Student class. In changing Student, it is easy to break the class and other classes that depend on it.

You would like to *close* the Student class to any further changes. You know that the rest of the code in the class works just fine. Instead of chang-

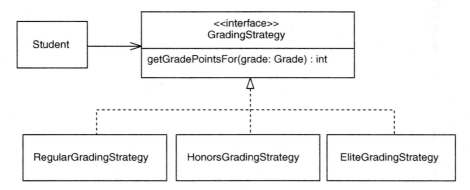

Figure 5.2   *Strategy*

ing the Student class each time the dean adds a new scheme, you want to support the new requirement by extending the system.[4]

 Design your system to accommodate changes through extension, not modification.

You can consider the grading scheme to be a *strategy* that varies based on the type of student. You could create specialized student classes, such as HonorsStudent, RegularStudent, and PrivilegedStudent, but students can change status. Changing an object from being one type to being a different type is difficult.

Instead, you can create a class to represent each grading scheme. You can then assign the appropriate scheme to each student.

You will use an interface, GradingStrategy, to represent the abstract concept of a grading strategy. The Student class will store a reference of the interface type GradingStrategy, as shown in the UML diagram in Figure 5.2. In the diagram, there are three classes that implement the interface: RegularGradingStrategy, HonorsGradingStrategy, and EliteGradingStrategy. The closed-arrow relationship shown with a dashed line is known as the *realizes* association in UML. In Java terms, RegularGradingStrategy implements the GradingStrategy interface. In UML terms, RegularGradingStrategy realizes the GradingStrategy interface.

The GradingStrategy interface declares that any class implementing the interface will provide the ability to return the grade points for a given grade. You define GradingStrategy in a separate source file, GradingStrategy.java, as follows:

Polymorphism

[4][Martin2003], p. 99.

UML and Interfaces

More often than not, UML class diagrams are intended to show the structure of the system—the relations and thus the dependencies between its classes. As such, UML diagrams are best left uncluttered with detail. You should rarely show non-public methods, and often you might show no methods at all in a particular class. Diagram only interesting and useful things.

UML is best used as a simple semipictorial language for expressing some high-level concepts of a system. If you clutter your diagram with every possible detail, you will obscure the important things that you are trying to express.

Representing interfaces in UML is no different. Often it is valuable to show only that a class implements a particular interface. The methods defined in the interface might be generally understood and are also available in the code. UML gives you a visually terse way of showing that a class implements an interface. As an example, you can express the fact that the String method implements the Comparable interface with this UML diagram:

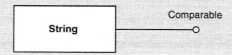

```
package sis.studentinfo;

public interface GradingStrategy {
    public int getGradePointsFor(Student.Grade grade);
}
```

Polymorphism

You represent each strategy with a separate class. Each strategy class implements the GradingStrategy interface and thus provides appropriate code for the getGradePointsFor method.

An interface defines methods that must be part of the public interface of the implementing class. All interface methods are thus public by definition. As such, you need not specify the public keyword for method declarations in an interface:

```
package sis.studentinfo;

public interface GradingStrategy {
    int getGradePointsFor(Student.Grade grade);
}
```

HonorsGradingStrategy:

```
package sis.studentinfo;

public class HonorsGradingStrategy implements GradingStrategy {
    public int getGradePointsFor(Student.Grade grade) {
```

```
      int points = basicGradePointsFor(grade);
      if (points > 0)
         points += 1;
      return points;
   }

   int basicGradePointsFor(Student.Grade grade) {
      if (grade == Student.Grade.A) return 4;
      if (grade == Student.Grade.B) return 3;
      if (grade == Student.Grade.C) return 2;
      if (grade == Student.Grade.D) return 1;
      return 0;
   }
}
```

RegularGradingStrategy:

```
package sis.studentinfo;

public class RegularGradingStrategy implements GradingStrategy {
   public int getGradePointsFor(Student.Grade grade) {
      if (grade == Student.Grade.A) return 4;
      if (grade == Student.Grade.B) return 3;
      if (grade == Student.Grade.C) return 2;
      if (grade == Student.Grade.D) return 1;
      return 0;
   }
}
```

If you're savvy enough to spot the duplication in this code, take the time to refactor it away. You could introduce a BasicGradingStrategy and have it supply a static method with the common code. Or you can wait (only because I said so—otherwise never put off eliminating duplication!): The next lesson introduces another way of eliminating this duplication.

In StudentTest, instead of using setHonors to create an honors student, you send the message setGradingStrategy to the Student object. You pass an Honors-GradingStrategy instance as the parameter.

```
private Student createHonorsStudent() {
   Student student = new Student("a");
   student.setGradingStrategy(new HonorsGradingStrategy());
   return student;
}
```

Note how you were able to make this change in one place by having eliminated all duplication in the test code!

You then need to update the Student class to allow the strategy to be set and stored. Initialize the gradingStrategy instance variable to a RegularGradingStrategy object to represent the default strategy.

```
public class Student {
    ...
    private GradingStrategy gradingStrategy =
        new RegularGradingStrategy();
        ...
    void setGradingStrategy(GradingStrategy gradingStrategy) {
        this.gradingStrategy = gradingStrategy;
    }
    ...
```

The next section, Using Interface References, explains why you can declare both the gradingStrategy instance variable and the parameter to setGradingStrategy as the type GradingStrategy.

Modify the Student code to obtain grade points by sending the gradePointsFor message to the object stored in the gradingStrategy reference.

```
int gradePointsFor(Grade grade) {
    return gradingStrategy.getGradePointsFor(grade);
}
```

Eliminate the instance variable isHonors, its associated setter method, and the method basicGradePointsFor.

Now that the gradePointsFor method does nothing but a simple delegation, you can *inline* its code to the getGpa method. In some cases, single-line delegation methods such as gradePointsFor can provide cleaner, clearer code, but in this case, the gradePointsFor method adds neither. Its body and name say the same thing, and no other code uses the method.

Inline the gradePointsFor method by replacing the call to it (from getGPA) with the single line of code in its body. You then can eliminate the gradePointsFor method entirely.

Polymorphism

```
double getGpa() {
    if (grades.isEmpty())
        return 0.0;
    double total = 0.0;
    for (Grade grade: grades)
        total += gradingStrategy.getGradePointsFor(grade);
    return total / grades.size();
}
```

You now have an extensible, closed solution. Adding a third implementation of GradingStrategy, such as EliteGradingStrategy, is a simple exercise of creating a new class and implementing a single method. The code in Student can remain unchanged—you have closed it to any modifications in grading strategy. Also, you can make future changes to a particular grading strategy exclusive of all other grading strategies.

Using Interface References

The code you implemented in Student uses GradingStrategy as the type for defining both instance variables and parameters:

```
public class Student implements Comparable<Student> {
    ...
    private GradingStrategy gradingStrategy =
        new RegularGradingStrategy();
    ...
    void setGradingStrategy(GradingStrategy gradingStrategy) {
        this.gradingStrategy = gradingStrategy;
    }
```

Even though you create a RegularGradingStrategy object and assign it to the gradingStrategy instance variable, you defined gradingStrategy as being of the type GradingStrategy and not of the type RegularGradingStrategy. Java allows this: A class that implements an interface is of that interface type. A RegularGradingStrategy implements the GradingStrategy interface, so it *is* a GradingStrategy.

When you assign an object to a reference variable of the GradingStrategy interface type, it is still a RegularGradingStrategy object in memory. The client working with a GradingStrategy reference, however, can send only GradingStrategy messages through that reference.

The code in Student doesn't care whether it is passed a RegularGradingStrategy or an HonorsGradingStrategy. The code in the getGpa method can send the getGradePointsFor message to the gradingStrategy reference without having to know the actual type of the instance stored at that reference.

   Always prefer use of an interface type for variables and parameters.

The use of interface types is a cornerstone to implementing systems with good object-oriented design. Interfaces are "walls of abstraction." They allow you to define a means of interacting with an object through an abstraction—something that is unlikely to change. The alternative is to be dependent on a class with concrete details—something that is likely to change.

Why is this important? Because any time you introduce a change to class X, you must recompile and retest all classes that are dependent upon class X. You must also recompile and retest any classes dependent upon *those* classes. Changes to class X in Figure 5.3 could adversely impact both dependent classes A and B.

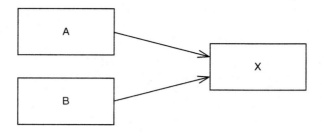

Figure 5.3 *Changes to X Impact Both A and B*

Interfaces *invert* the dependencies so that client classes are dependent upon abstractions.[5] The class that implements the interface is also dependent upon this abstraction. But the client class is no longer dependent upon the concrete, changing class. In Figure 5.4, the interface XAbstraction represents abstract concepts from XImplementation. Classes A and B now communicate to XImplementation objects via this interface. Classes A and B now are dependent upon abstractions only. The XImplementation class depends upon the abstraction as well. No class in Figure 5.4 depends upon implementation details that are likely to change!

When designing object-oriented systems, you want to strive for this dependency arrangement. The more you depend upon concrete types, the more difficult your system is to change. The more you depend upon abstract types (interfaces), the easier your system is to change. By introducing interfaces, you build an abstraction barrier between the client and a concrete server class.

Using Interface References

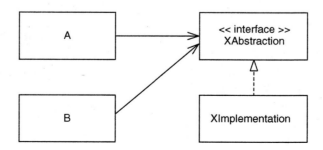

Figure 5.4 *Inverted Dependencies*

---

[5][Martin2003], p. 127.

ArrayList and the List Interface

In earlier lessons, you created ArrayList instances and assigned them to references of the ArrayList type:

```
ArrayList<Student> students = new ArrayList<Student>();
```

The Java API documentation shows that ArrayList implements the List interface. If you browse the documentation for the List interface, you'll see that virtually all messages you had sent to ArrayList instances are defined in List. Thus, you should prefer defining students (in this example) as a List type:

```
List<Student> students = new ArrayList<Student>();
```

The ArrayList class defines a fixed-length array in memory. Its performance characteristics are good unless you are constantly inserting or deleting elements that appear before the end of the list. If your list needs these characteristics, a linked list is the better data structure, since it uses more dynamic memory management. The downside is that accessing elements in a linked list is done by serially traversing the list from the beginning, whereas accessing an element in an array is immediate, since it only needs to calculate an offset from the beginning of the memory block.

Java's implementation of a linked list is provided as java.util.LinkedList. If you use the List reference type throughout your code, you could change the performance characteristics of your application by making a change in one place:

```
List<Student> students = new LinkedList<Student>();
```

For now, go through your source code and change as many references as possible to be an interface type.

Exercises

Exercises

1. Create an enumeration for the two colors. Encapsulate the enumeration so that only the Piece class is aware of its existence. Depending on your implementation, this may require significant refactoring. Note each place you have to change in order to introduce the change—How could you have removed the need for any changes you felt were done twice?

You might consider also creating an enumeration for the piece values. If your code allows you to do so easily, go ahead. You may want to wait until Lesson 6, where you will learn how to associate data with enumeration values.

2. Introduce an enum for each piece. You will want to divorce the piece representation from the piece enum.

3. Create a separate factory method on Piece for each color/piece combination (e.g., createWhitePawn, createBlackRook).

```
package pieces;

import junit.framework.TestCase;

public class PieceTest extends TestCase {
    public void testCreate() {
        verifyCreation(
            Piece.createWhitePawn(), Piece.createBlackPawn(),
            Piece.Type.PAWN, Piece.PAWN_REPRESENTATION);
        verifyCreation(
            Piece.createWhiteRook(), Piece.createBlackRook(),
            Piece.Type.ROOK, Piece.ROOK_REPRESENTATION);
        verifyCreation(
            Piece.createWhiteKnight(), Piece.createBlackKnight(),
            Piece.Type.KNIGHT, Piece.KNIGHT_REPRESENTATION);
        verifyCreation(
            Piece.createWhiteBishop(), Piece.createBlackBishop(),
            Piece.Type.BISHOP, Piece.BISHOP_REPRESENTATION);
        verifyCreation(Piece.createWhiteQueen(), Piece.createBlackQueen(),
            Piece.Type.QUEEN, Piece.QUEEN_REPRESENTATION);
        verifyCreation(Piece.createWhiteKing(), Piece.createBlackKing(),
            Piece.Type.KING, Piece.KING_REPRESENTATION);
        Piece blank = Piece.noPiece();
        assertEquals('.', blank.getRepresentation());
        assertEquals(Piece.Type.NO_PIECE, blank.getType());
    }

    private void verifyCreation(Piece whitePiece, Piece blackPiece,
            Piece.Type type, char representation) {
        assertTrue(whitePiece.isWhite());
        assertEquals(type, whitePiece.getType());
        assertEquals(representation, whitePiece.getRepresentation());

        assertTrue(blackPiece.isBlack());
        assertEquals(type, blackPiece.getType());
        assertEquals(Character.toUpperCase(representation),
            blackPiece.getRepresentation());
    }
}
```

Reduce the createWhite and createBlack methods to a single private factory method that uses an if clause.

4. Write code in Board to return the number of pieces, given the color and piece representation. For example, the below board should return 3 if you ask it for the number of black pawns. Calculate the count on demand (in other words, do not track the counts as you create pieces).

```
. K R . . . . .
P . P B . . . .
. P . . Q . . .
. . . . . . . .
. . . . . n q .
. . . . . p . .
. . . . . . p .
. . . . r k . .
```

5. Create a method to retrieve the piece at a given location. Given an initial board setup, asking for the piece at "a8" returns the black rook. The white king is at "e1".

   Use utility methods defined on the Character class to help convert the individual characters of the location string to numeric indexes. Note: Your board may be flipped; in other words, rank 1 may be at the top and rank 8 at the bottom. Your code will have to invert the rank passed in.

```
R N B Q K B N R 8  (rank 8)
P P P P P P P P 7
. . . . . . . . 6
. . . . . . . . 5
. . . . . . . . 4
. . . . . . . . 3
p p p p p p p p 2
r n b q k b n r 1  (rank 1)
a b c d e f g h
   files
```

Exercises

   In the next exercise, you will create the ability to place pieces on an empty board. Start by adding a test that verifies that a newly instantiated Board object contains no pieces. This will lead you to a bit of refactoring. You may need to replace use of the add method on ArrayList with the set method.

6. Create the code necessary to place pieces at arbitrary positions on the board. Make sure you refactor your solution with earlier code you've written to manage squares.

```
. . . . . . . . 8  (rank 8)
. . . . . . . . 7
. K . . . . . . 6
. R . . . . . . 5
. . k . . . . . 4
. . . . . . . . 3
. . . . . . . . 2
```

```
. . . . . . . . 1  (rank 1)
a b c d e f g h
     files
```

7. In chess programs, determining the relative strength of board positions is pivotal in determining which move to make. Using a very primitive board evaluation function, you will add up the values of the pieces on the board. Calculate this sum by adding 9 points for a queen, 5 points for a rook, 3 points for a bishop, and 2.5 points for a knight. Add 0.5 points for a pawn that is on the same file as a pawn of the same color and 1 point for a pawn otherwise. Remember to count the points for only one side at a time.

```
. K R . . . . . 8
P . P B . . . . 7
. P . . Q . . . 6
. . . . . . . . 5
. . . . . n q . 4
. . . . . p . p 3
. . . . . p p . 2
. . . . r k . . 1
a b c d e f g h
```

For the example shown, black would have a strength of 20, and white would have a strength of 19.5.

Develop your solution incrementally. Start with a single piece on the board. Add pieces to the board one by one, altering your assertions each time. Finally, add the complex scenario of determining if another pawn is in the same file.

8. As you loop through all pieces on the board, assign the strength of each piece to the Piece object itself. For each side (black and white), gather the list of pieces in a collection. Ensure that the collection is sorted in order from the piece with the highest value to the piece with the lowest value.

9. Examine your code for an opportunity to create an interface. Does the system feel cleaner or more cluttered? Be wary of introducing an interface without need—remember that simplicity requires "fewest classes, fewest methods" shortly after "no duplication."

10. Go through the code you have produced so far and look for opportunities to use early returns and guard clauses to simplify your code.

11. Go through the code you have produced so far and ensure that you are using interfaces rather than concrete implementations wherever possible. In particular, examine your usages of collections and ensure you are programming to the interfaces.

Also: While the static import facility can make code more difficult to follow, one appropriate place you can use it is in test code. Test code generally interacts with a single target class. If the target class contains class constants, you can use static import in the test class for these constants. The context should make it clear as to where the constants are defined.

Alter your code to make judicious use of `import static`.

Lesson 6

Inheritance

In this lesson you will learn about:

- switch statements

- maps

- lazy initialization

- inheritance

- extending methods

- calling superclass constructors

- the principle of subcontracting

The `switch` Statement

In the last chapter, you coded methods in HonorsGradingStrategy and RegularGradingStrategy to return the proper GPA for a given letter grade. To do so, you used a succession of if statements. As a reminder, here is what some of the relevant code looks like (taken from HonorsGradingStrategy):

```
int basicGradePointsFor(Student.Grade grade) {
    if (grade == Student.Grade.A) return 4;
    if (grade == Student.Grade.B) return 3;
    if (grade == Student.Grade.C) return 2;
    if (grade == Student.Grade.D) return 1;
    return 0;
}
```

Each of the conditionals in basicGradePointsFor compares a value to a single variable, grade. Another construct in Java that allows you to represent related comparisons is the switch statement:

195

```
int basicGradePointsFor(Student.Grade grade) {
    switch (grade) {
        case A: return 4;
        case B: return 3;
        case C: return 2;
        case D: return 1;
        default: return 0;
    }
}
```

As the target of the switch statement, you specify a variable or expression to compare against. In this example, the target is the grade parameter:

```
switch (grade) {
```

You then specify any number of case labels. Each case label specifies a single enum value. When the Java VM executes the switch statement, it determines the value of the target expression. It compares this value to each case label in turn.

If the target value matches a case label, the Java VM transfers control to the statement immediately following that case label. It skips statements between the switch target and the case label. If the target value matches no case label, the Java VM transfers control to the default case label, if one exists. The default case label is optional. If no default case label exists, the VM transfers control to the statement immediately following the switch statement.

Thus, if the value of the grade variable is Student.Grade.B, Java transfers control to the line that reads:

```
case B: return 3;
```

The Java VM executes this return statement, which immediately transfers control out of the method.

Case Labels Are Just Labels

A case label is just a label. The Java VM uses the case labels only when the Java VM initially encounters the switch statement. Once Java has located the matching case label and transferred control to it, it ignores the remainder of the case labels. Java executes the remainder of the code in the switch statement in top-to-bottom order. Java blissfully ignores the case labels and the default label, through to the end of the switch statement (or until another statement such as return transfers control.)[1]

---

[1]You'll learn more about statements to transfer control in Lesson 7.

The following example demonstrates how the switch statement flows:

```
public void testSwitchResults() {
    enum Score
        { fieldGoal, touchdown, extraPoint,
        twoPointConversion, safety };

    int totalPoints = 0;

    Score score = Score.touchdown;

    switch (score) {
        case fieldGoal:
            totalPoints += 3;
        case touchdown:
            totalPoints += 6;
        case extraPoint:
            totalPoints += 1;
        case twoPointConversion:
            totalPoints += 2;
        case safety:
            totalPoints += 2;
    }
    assertEquals(6, totalPoints);
}
```

The test fails:

```
junit.framework.AssertionFailedError: expected<6> but was<11>
```

Since score was set to Score.touchdown, the Java VM transferred control to the line following the corresponding case label:

```
case touchdown:
    totalPoints += 6;
```

Once Java executed that line, it then executed the next three statements (and ignored the case labels):

Case Labels Are
Just Labels

```
case extraPoint:  // ignored
    totalPoints += 1;
case twoPointConversion:  // ignored
    totalPoints += 2;
case safety:    // ignored
    totalPoints += 2;
```

Total points thus is 6 plus 1 plus 2 plus 2, or 11. Test failure!

You obtain the desired behavior by inserting a break statement at the end of each section of code following a case label:

```
public void testSwitchResults() {
    enum Score
        { fieldGoal, touchdown, extraPoint,
```

```
        twoPointConversion, safety };

    int totalPoints = 0;

    Score score = Score.touchdown;

    switch (score) {
        case fieldGoal:
            totalPoints += 3;
            break;
        case touchdown:
            totalPoints += 6;
            break;
        case extraPoint:
            totalPoints += 1;
            break;
        case twoPointConversion:
            totalPoints += 2;
            break;
        case safety:
            totalPoints += 2;
            break;
    }
    assertEquals(6, totalPoints);
}
```

The break statement is another statement that transfers control flow. It transfers control out of the switch statement to the next statement following. In the example, executing any break statement results in control being transferred to the assertEquals statement.

Multiple case labels can precede a statement appearing within the switch statement:

```
switch (score) {
    case fieldGoal:
        totalPoints += 3;
        break;
    case touchdown:
        totalPoints += 6;
        break;
    case extraPoint:
        totalPoints += 1;
        break;
    case twoPointConversion:
    case safety:
        totalPoints += 2;
        break;
}
```

If score matches either Score.twoPointConversion or Score.safety, the code adds two points to the total.

In addition to switching on enum values, you can switch on char, byte, short, or int values. You cannot, unfortunately, switch on String values.

Your code should not contain a lot of switch statements. Also, it should not contain lots of multiple if statements that accomplish the same goal. Often, you can eliminate switch statements in favor of polymorphic solutions, as in the previous lesson. Your main guides as to whether you should replace switch statements with polymorphism are duplication and frequency/ease of maintenance.

Before continuing, refactor RegularGradingStrategy to use a switch statement instead of multiple if statements.

Maps

Yet another alternative to using a switch statement is to use a map. A map is a collection that provides fast insertion and retrieval of values associated with specific keys. An example is an online dictionary that stores a definition (a value) for each word (key) that appears in it.

Java supplies the interface java.util.Map to define the common behavior for all map implementations. For the report card messages, you will use the EnumMap implementation. An EnumMap is a Map with the additional constraint that all keys must be enum objects.

To add a key-value pair to a Map, you use the put method, which takes the key and value as parameters. To retrieve a value stored at a specific key, you use the get method, which takes the key as a parameter and returns the associated value.

Suppose you need to print an appropriate message on a report card for each student, based on their grade. Add a new class named ReportCardTest to the sis.reports package.

```
package sis.report;

import junit.framework.*;
import sis.studentinfo.*;

public class ReportCardTest extends TestCase {
    public void testMessage() {
        ReportCard card = new ReportCard();
        assertEquals(ReportCard.A_MESSAGE,
                     card.getMessage(Student.Grade.A));
        assertEquals(ReportCard.B_MESSAGE,
                     card.getMessage(Student.Grade.B));
        assertEquals(ReportCard.C_MESSAGE,
```

Maps

```
                        card.getMessage(Student.Grade.C));
        assertEquals(ReportCard.D_MESSAGE,
                        card.getMessage(Student.Grade.D));
        assertEquals(ReportCard.F_MESSAGE,
                        card.getMessage(Student.Grade.F));
    }
}
```

Change the Grade `enum` defined in Student to `public` to make this code compile.

The ReportCard class:

```
package sis.report;

import java.util.*;
import sis.studentinfo.*;

public class ReportCard {
    static final String A_MESSAGE = "Excellent";
    static final String B_MESSAGE = "Very good";
    static final String C_MESSAGE = "Hmmm...";
    static final String D_MESSAGE = "You're not trying";
    static final String F_MESSAGE = "Loser";

    private Map<Student.Grade, String> messages = null;

    public String getMessage(Student.Grade grade) {
        return getMessages().get(grade);
    }

    private Map<Student.Grade, String> getMessages() {
        if (messages == null)
            loadMessages();
        return messages;
    }

    private void loadMessages() {
        messages =
            new EnumMap<Student.Grade, String>(Student.Grade.class);
        messages.put(Student.Grade.A, A_MESSAGE);
        messages.put(Student.Grade.B, B_MESSAGE);
        messages.put(Student.Grade.C, C_MESSAGE);
        messages.put(Student.Grade.D, D_MESSAGE);
        messages.put(Student.Grade.F, F_MESSAGE);
    }
}
```

Maps

The ReportCard class defines an instance variable `messages` as a parameterized Map type. The type parameters are Student.Grade for the key and String for the value. When you construct an EnumMap, you must also pass in the class that represents the enum type of its keys.

The getMessages method uses lazy initialization (see the sidebar) to load the appropriate message strings, which you define as static constants, into a new instance of the EnumMap.

Lazy Initialization

You have learned to initialize fields either where you declared them or within a constructor. Another option is to wait until you first need to use a field and then initialize it. This is a technique known as *lazy initialization*.

Within a getter method, such as getMessages, you first test to see whether or not a field has already been initialized. For a reference instance variable, you test whether or not it is null. If it is null, you do whatever initialization is necessary and assign the new value to the field. Regardless, you return the field as the result of the getter, like you normally would.

The primary use of lazy initialization is to defer the potentially costly operation of loading a field until it is necessary. If the field is never needed, you never expend the cycles required to load it. A minor amount of overhead is required to test the field each time it is accessed. This overhead is negligible for occasional access.

Here, lazy initialization is used as a way of keeping more-complex initialization logic close to the field access logic. Doing so can improve understanding of how the field is initialized and used.

The getMessage method is a single line of code that uses the Map method get to retrieve the appropriate string value for the grade key.

Maps are extremely powerful, fast data structures that you might use frequently in your applications. Refer to Lesson 9 for a detailed discussion of their use.

Inheritance

The code for RegularGradingStrategy and HonorsGradingStrategy contains duplicate logic. The code that you used to derive a basic grade is the same in both classes—both classes contain switch statements with the exact same logic:

```
switch (grade) {
    case A:  return 4;
    case B:  return 3;
    case C:  return 2;
    case D:  return 1;
    default: return 0;
}
```

One solution for eliminating this duplication is to use inheritance. I discussed inheritance briefly in the Agile Java Overview chapter. You can factor the commonality between RegularGradingStrategy and HonorsGradingStrategy into a common class called BasicGradingStrategy. You can then declare the classes RegularGradingStrategy and HonorsGradingStrategy as *subclasses* of BasicGradingStrategy. As a subclass, each of RegularGradingStrategy and BasicGradingStrategy obtain all of the behaviors of BasicGradingStrategy.

You will refactor to an inheritance-based solution in very small increments. The first step is to create a BasicGradingStrategy class:

```
package sis.studentinfo;

public class BasicGradingStrategy {
}
```

Then declare both RegularGradingStrategy and HonorsGradingStrategy as subclasses of BasicGradingStrategy by using the extends keyword. The extends clause must appear before any implements clause.

```
// RegularGradingStrategy.java
package sis.studentinfo;

public class RegularGradingStrategy
    extends BasicGradingStrategy
    implements GradingStrategy {
  public int getGradePointsFor(Student.Grade grade) {
    switch (grade) {
      case A: return 4;
      case B: return 3;
      case C: return 2;
      case D: return 1;
      default: return 0;
    }
  }
}
// HonorsGradingStrategy.java
package sis.studentinfo;

public class HonorsGradingStrategy
    extends BasicGradingStrategy
    implements GradingStrategy {
  public int getGradePointsFor(Student.Grade grade) {
    int points = basicGradePointsFor(grade);
    if (points > 0)
      points += 1;
    return points;
  }

  int basicGradePointsFor(Student.Grade grade) {
    switch (grade) {
```

```
            case A: return 4;
            case B: return 3;
            case C: return 2;
            case D: return 1;
            default: return 0;
        }
    }
}
```

You can now move the common code to a method on the BasicGrading-Strategy *superclass* (also known as the *base class*). First, move the method basicGradePointsFor from HonorsGradingStrategy to BasicGradingStrategy:

```
// HonorsGradingStrategy.java
package sis.studentinfo;

public class HonorsGradingStrategy
      extends BasicGradingStrategy
      implements GradingStrategy {
   public int getGradePointsFor(Student.Grade grade) {
      int points = basicGradePointsFor(grade);
      if (points > 0)
         points += 1;
      return points;
   }
}
```

```
// BasicGradingStrategy.java
package sis.studentinfo;

public class BasicGradingStrategy {
   int basicGradePointsFor(Student.Grade grade) {
      switch (grade) {
         case A: return 4;
         case B: return 3;
         case C: return 2;
         case D: return 1;
         default: return 0;
      }
   }
}
```

Recompile and test.

Even though HonorsGradingStrategy no longer contains the definition for basicGradePointsFor, it can call it just as if it were defined in the same class. This is akin to your ability to call assertion methods in your test classes, because they extend from junit.framework.TestCase. Conceptually, HonorsGradingStrategy is a BasicGradingStrategy, much as a class that implements an interface is of that interface type. Thus HonorsGradingStrategy can use any (nonprivate) method defined in BasicGradingStrategy. (We'll discuss the nonprivate distinction shortly.)

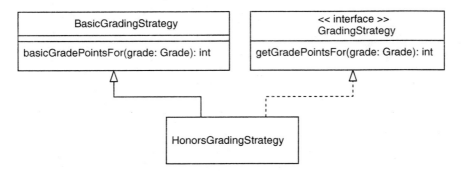

Figure 6.1   *Inheriting from BasicGradingStrategy*

The UML representation of this relationship appears in Figure 6.1.

Next, modify RegularGradingStrategy to reuse the method basicGradePoints-For.

```
package sis.studentinfo;

public class RegularGradingStrategy
     extends BasicGradingStrategy
     implements GradingStrategy {
  public int getGradePointsFor(Student.Grade grade) {
    return basicGradePointsFor(grade);
  }
}
```

Abstract Classes

You could stop here and have a sufficient solution. You could also go one step further and eliminate a bit more duplication by having the superclass BasicGradingStrategy implement the GradingStrategy interface directly. The only problem is, you don't necessarily have an implementation for getGradePointsFor.

Java allows you to define a method as abstract, meaning that you cannot or do not wish to supply an implementation for it. Once a class contains at least one abstract method, the class itself must similarly be defined as abstract. You cannot create new instances of an abstract class, much as you cannot directly instantiate an interface.

Any class extending from an abstract class must either implement all inherited abstract methods, otherwise it too must be declared as abstract.

Change the declaration of BasicGradingStrategy to implement the Grading-Strategy interface. Then supply an abstract declaration for the getGradePointsFor method:

```
package sis.studentinfo;

abstract public class BasicGradingStrategy implements GradingStrategy {
    abstract public int getGradePointsFor(Student.Grade grade);

    int basicGradePointsFor(Student.Grade grade) {
        switch (grade) {
            case A: return 4;
            case B: return 3;
            case C: return 2;
            case D: return 1;
            default: return 0;
        }
    }
}
```

The subclasses no longer need to declare that they implement the GradingStrategy interface:

```
// HonorsGradingStrategy.java
package sis.studentinfo;

public class HonorsGradingStrategy extends BasicGradingStrategy {
    public int getGradePointsFor(Student.Grade grade) {
        int points = basicGradePointsFor(grade);
        if (points > 0)
            points += 1;
        return points;
    }
}

// RegularGradingStrategy.java
package sis.studentinfo;

public class RegularGradingStrategy extends BasicGradingStrategy {
    public int getGradePointsFor(Student.Grade grade) {
        return basicGradePointsFor(grade);
    }
}
```

Extending Methods

A third solution[2] is to recognize that the RegularGradingStrategy is virtually the same as BasicGradingStrategy. The method getGradePointsFor as defined in HonorsGradingStrategy is basically an extension of the method in RegularGradingStrategy—it does what the base class method does, plus a little more. In other words, you can supply a default definition for getGradePointsFor in BasicGradingStrategy that will be extended in HonorsGradingStrategy.

Move the definition for getGradePointsFor from RegularGradingStrategy to BasicGradingStrategy. You should no longer declare BasicGradingStrategy as abstract, since all of its methods supply definitions.

```
// BasicGradingStrategy.java
package sis.studentinfo;

public class BasicGradingStrategy implements GradingStrategy {
    public int getGradePointsFor(Student.Grade grade) {
        return basicGradePointsFor(grade);
    }

    int basicGradePointsFor(Student.Grade grade) {
        switch (grade) {
            case A: return 4;
            case B: return 3;
            case C: return 2;
            case D: return 1;
            default: return 0;
        }
    }
}

// RegularGradingStrategy.java
package sis.studentinfo;

public class RegularGradingStrategy extends BasicGradingStrategy {
}
```

RegularGradingStrategy no longer defines any methods!

(Compile, test.)

Next, change the code in HonorsGradingStrategy to extend the superclass method getGradePointsFor. To extend a method, you define a method with the same name in a subclass. In that subclass method, you call the superclass method to effect its behavior. You supply additional, specialized behavior in the remainder of the subclass method.

[2]Are you getting the picture that there are many ways to skin a cat in Java? All these options allow you to make your code as expressive as possible. It also means that there is no one "perfect" way to implement anything of complexity.

In comparison to extending, Java will let you fully supplant a method's definition with a completely new one that has nothing to do with the original. This is known as *overriding* a method. This is a semantic definition: The Java compiler knows no distinction between overriding and extending; it's all overriding to the compiler. You, on the other hand, recognize an extending method by its call to the superclass method of the same name.

 Prefer extending to overriding.

Your subclass definition should specialize the behavior of the superclass method in some manner, not change it completely.

To explicitly call a method in a superclass, use the super keyword to scope the message send, as shown in bold:

```
package sis.studentinfo;

public class HonorsGradingStrategy extends BasicGradingStrategy {
    public int getGradePointsFor(Student.Grade grade) {
        int points = super.getGradePointsFor(grade);
        if (points > 0)
            points += 1;
        return points;
    }
}
```

When you use the super keyword, the Java VM looks in the superclass to find the corresponding method definition.

Refactoring

The method basicGradePointsFor in BasicGradingStrategy is now superfluous. You can inline it and eliminate the method basicGradePointsFor.

Refactoring

```
package sis.studentinfo;

public class BasicGradingStrategy implements GradingStrategy {
    public int getGradePointsFor(Student.Grade grade) {
        switch (grade) {
            case A: return 4;
            case B: return 3;
            case C: return 2;
            case D: return 1;
            default: return 0;
        }
    }
}
```

Is there any more need for the separate subclass RegularGradingStrategy? There's not much left to it:

```
package studentinfo;

public class RegularGradingStrategy
    extends BasicGradingStrategy {
}
```

You can eliminate this class by changing the gradeStrategy reference in Student to use BasicGradingStrategy as the default.

```
public class Student {
    ...
    private GradingStrategy gradingStrategy =
        new BasicGradingStrategy();
    ...
```

All the work you have done since learning about inheritance has been on the code side only. You have not changed any tests. (I hope you have been running your tests with each incremental change.) You have not changed any behavior; you have only changed the way in which the existing behavior is implemented. The tests in Student for GPA adequately cover the behavior.

However, the tests in Student cover behavior within the context of managing students. You want to additionally provide tests at the unit level. The general rule is to have at least one test class for each production class. You should test each of HonorsGradingStrategy and BasicGradingStrategy individually.

Here is a test for BasicGradingStrategy:

```
package sis.studentinfo;

import junit.framework.*;

public class BasicGradingStrategyTest extends TestCase {
    public void testGetGradePoints() {
        BasicGradingStrategy strategy = new BasicGradingStrategy();
        assertEquals(4, strategy.getGradePointsFor(Student.Grade.A));
        assertEquals(3, strategy.getGradePointsFor(Student.Grade.B));
        assertEquals(2, strategy.getGradePointsFor(Student.Grade.C));
        assertEquals(1, strategy.getGradePointsFor(Student.Grade.D));
        assertEquals(0, strategy.getGradePointsFor(Student.Grade.F));
    }
}
```

A corresponding test for HonorsGradingStrategy:

```
package sis.studentinfo;

import junit.framework.*;

public class HonorsGradingStrategyTest extends TestCase {
    public void testGetGradePoints() {
        GradingStrategy strategy = new HonorsGradingStrategy();
        assertEquals(5, strategy.getGradePointsFor(Student.Grade.A));
        assertEquals(4, strategy.getGradePointsFor(Student.Grade.B));
        assertEquals(3, strategy.getGradePointsFor(Student.Grade.C));
        assertEquals(2, strategy.getGradePointsFor(Student.Grade.D));
        assertEquals(0, strategy.getGradePointsFor(Student.Grade.F));
    }
}
```

Don't forget to add these tests to the suite defined in AllTests.

Enhancing the Grade Enum

The number of basic grade points is information that can be associated directly with the Grade enum. It is possible to enhance the definition of an enum to include instance variables, constructors, and methods, just like any other class type. The main restriction is that you cannot extend an enum from another enum.

Modify the declaration of the Grade enum in the Student class:

```
public class Student {
    public enum Grade {
        A(4),
        B(3),
        C(2),
        D(1),
        F(0);

        private int points;

        Grade(int points) {
            this.points = points;
        }

        int getPoints() {
            return points;
        }
    }
    ...
```

Enhancing the
Grade Enum

You have now associated each named instance of the enum with a parameter. Further, you terminated the list of enum instances with a semicolon. After that semicolon, code in the Grade enum declaration looks just like that in any class type. The parameter associated with each named enum instance is passed to the constructor of Grade. This points parameter is stored in an instance variable named points. You retrieve the points via the getPoints method.

You can now simplify the code in BasicGradingStrategy to:

```
package sis.studentinfo;

public class BasicGradingStrategy implements GradingStrategy {
   public int getGradePointsFor(Student.Grade grade) {
      return grade.getPoints();
   }
}
```

No more switch statement!

Summer Course Sessions

The CourseSession class currently supports only 15-week sessions (with a one-week break) that occur in the spring and fall. The university also needs support for summer sessions. Summer sessions will begin in early June. They last eight weeks with no break.

One solution would be to pass the session length into the CourseSession class, store it, and use it as a multiplier when calculating the session end date.

However, there are many other differences between summer sessions and spring/fall sessions, including differences in maximum class session, credit values, and so on. For this reason, you have chosen to create a new class named SummerCourseSession.

The simplest approach for implementing SummerCourseSession, given what you know, is to have it extend from CourseSession. A SummerCourseSession is a CourseSession with some refinement on the details (see Figure 6.2).

You want to create the SummerCourseSession classes (test and production) in a new package, summer, for organizational purposes.

The test you initially code verifies that SummerCourseSession calculates the course end date correctly:

```
package sis.summer;

import junit.framework.*;
import java.util.*;
import sis.studentinfo.*;
```

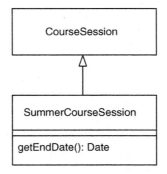

Figure 6.2 *SummerCourseSession Specialization*

```
public class SummerCourseSessionTest extends TestCase {
   public void testEndDate() {
      Date startDate = DateUtil.createDate(2003, 6, 9);
      CourseSession session =
         SummerCourseSession.create("ENGL", "200", startDate);
      Date eightWeeksOut = DateUtil.createDate(2003, 8, 1);
      assertEquals(eightWeeksOut, session.getEndDate());
   }
}
```

Calling Superclass Constructors

An initial noncompiling attempt at an implementation for SummerCourse-
Session follows.

```
// this code does not compile!
package sis.summer;

import java.util.*;
import sis.studentinfo.*;

public class SummerCourseSession extends CourseSession {
   public static SummerCourseSession create(
         String department,
         String number,
         Date startDate) {
      return new SummerCourseSession(department, number, startDate);
   }

   private SummerCourseSession(
         String department,
         String number,
```

```
        Date startDate) {
    super(department, number, startDate);
  }

  Date getEndDate() {
    GregorianCalendar calendar = new GregorianCalendar();
    calendar.setTime(startDate);
    int sessionLength = 8;
    int daysInWeek = 7;
    int daysFromFridayToMonday = 3;
    int numberOfDays =
        sessionLength * daysInWeek - daysFromFridayToMonday;
    calendar.add(Calendar.DAY_OF_YEAR, numberOfDays);
    return calendar.getTime();
  }
}
```

The key things to note are in bold.

First, you want to declare SummerCourseSession as a subclass of Course-Session, so you use the extends keyword in the class declaration.

Second, the constructor for SummerCourseSession makes a call to the superclass constructor that takes the department, course number, and start date as parameters. It does this by using the super keyword. This is similar to a super method invocation.

Third, in order to quickly get things working, you copied the getEndDate method from CourseSession and altered the value of the sessionLength temporary to be 8 instead of 16.

This code will not compile. You should see three compiler errors. The first one you know how to fix:

```
getEndDate() is not public in sis.studentinfo.CourseSession; cannot be accessed from outside
package
        assertEquals(eightWeeksOut, session.getEndDate());
                                           ^
```

Calling Superclass Constructors

Change the definition of getEndDate in CourseSession to public and recompile:

```
public Date getEndDate() {
```

You now receive a different error related to getEndDate:

```
getEndDate() in sis.summer.SummerCourseSession cannot override getEndDate() in
sis.studentinfo.CourseSession; attempting to assign weaker access privileges; was public
    Date getEndDate() {
         ^
```

A subclass method that overrides a superclass method must have equivalent or looser access privileges than a superclass method. In other words, Course-Session's control over the getEndDate method must be tighter than the control of any of its subclasses. If a superclass marks a method as package, a subclass can mark the overridden method as package or public. If a superclass marks a method as public, a subclass must mark the overridden method as public.

The solution is to change getEndDate in SummerCourseSession to be public:

```
public Date getEndDate() {
```

After compiling, you should have two remaining errors that appear similar:

```
CourseSession(java.util.Date) has private access in sis.studentinfo.CourseSession
     super(department, number, startDate);
     ^
startDate has private access in sis.studentinfo.CourseSession
     calendar.setTime(startDate);
                      ^
```

Sure enough, the CourseSession constructor that takes a Date as a parameter is marked private:

```
private CourseSession(
    String department, String number, Date startDate) {
    // ...
```

You made the constructor private in order to force clients to construct Course-Session instances using the class creation method. The problem is, the private access modifier restricts access to the constructor. Only code defined within CourseSession itself can invoke its constructor.

Your intent is to expose the CourseSession constructor to code only in CourseSession itself or code in any of its subclasses. Even if you define a CourseSession subclass in a different package, it should have access to the Course-Session constructor. You don't want to expose the constructor to other classes.

Specifying public access would allow too much access. Non-subclasses in different packages would be able to directly construct CourseSession objects. Package access would not allow subclasses in different packages to access the CourseSession constructor.

Java provides a fourth (and final) access modifier, protected. The protected keyword indicates that a method or field may be accessed by the class in which it is defined, by any other class in the same package, or by any of its subclasses. A subclass has access to anything in its superclass marked as protected, even if you define the subclass in a package other than the superclass.

Change the CourseSession constructor from private to protected:

```
protected CourseSession(
    String department, String number, Date startDate) {
    // ...
```

The compilation error regarding the constructor goes away. You have one remaining error: getEndDate references the private superclass field startDate directly.

```
startDate has private access in sis.studentinfo.CourseSession
    calendar.setTime(startDate);
                   ^
```

You could solve the problem by changing startDate to be a protected field. A better solution is to require that subclasses, like any other class, access the field by using a method.

Change the getStartDate method from package to protected access.

```java
public class CourseSession implements Comparable<CourseSession> {
    ...
    protected Date getStartDate() {
        return startDate;
    }
    ...
```

You must change the code in both CourseSession and SummerCourseSession to use this getter:

```java
// CourseSession.java
public Date getEndDate() {
    GregorianCalendar calendar = new GregorianCalendar();
    calendar.setTime(getStartDate());
    final int sessionLength = 16;
    final int daysInWeek = 7;
    final int daysFromFridayToMonday = 3;
    int numberOfDays =
        sessionLength * daysInWeek - daysFromFridayToMonday;
    calendar.add(Calendar.DAY_OF_YEAR, numberOfDays);
    return calendar.getTime();
}
```

Calling
Superclass
Constructors

```java
// SummerCourseSession.java:
public Date getEndDate() {
    GregorianCalendar calendar = new GregorianCalendar();
    calendar.setTime(getStartDate());
    int sessionLength = 8;
    int daysInWeek = 7;
    int daysFromFridayToMonday = 3;
    int numberOfDays =
        sessionLength * daysInWeek - daysFromFridayToMonday;
    calendar.add(Calendar.DAY_OF_YEAR, numberOfDays);
    return calendar.getTime();
}
```

Since I told you to be lazy and copy the code for getEndDate, note that you had the additional effort of making the change in two places.

In SummerCourseSession, getEndDate makes a call to getStartDate, but getStartDate is not defined in SummerCourseSession. Since the super. scope modifier was not used, Java first looks to see if getStartDate is defined in Summer-CourseSession. It is not, so Java starts searching up the inheritance chain until it finds an accessible definition for getStartDate.

Protected-level access is one step "looser" than package. One minor downside is that it is possible for other classes in the same package to access a protected element (method or field). Usually this is not what you want. There are few good design reasons to make a field accessible to other classes in the same package *and* to subclasses in different packages but not to other classes.

In the case of CourseSession, you want the constructor to be accessible *only* to subclasses, regardless of package, and not to any other classes. There is no way in Java to enforce this restriction.

Refactoring

Time to eliminate the duplicate code you hastily introduced.

The only change between getEndDate as defined in CourseSession and SummerCourseSession is the session length. Define a protected method in CourseSession to return this value:

```
public class CourseSession implements Comparable<CourseSession> {
    ...
    protected int getSessionLength() {
        return 16;
    }
    ...
```

Change getEndDate to call getSessionLength:

```
public Date getEndDate() {
    GregorianCalendar calendar = new GregorianCalendar();
    calendar.setTime(getStartDate());
    final int daysInWeek = 7;
    final int daysFromFridayToMonday = 3;
    int numberOfDays =
        getSessionLength() * daysInWeek - daysFromFridayToMonday;
    calendar.add(Calendar.DAY_OF_YEAR, numberOfDays);
    return calendar.getTime();
}
```

In SummerCourseSession, override the method `getSessionLength`. Summer sessions are 8 weeks, not 16. In this case, overriding is a fine alternative to extending, since you are not changing behavior, only data-related details of the behavior.

```
public class SummerCourseSession extends CourseSession {
  ...
  @Override
  protected int getSessionLength() {
     return 8;
  }
  ...
```

When you override a method, you should precede it with an `@Override` annotation. You use annotations to mark, or annotate, specific portions of code. Other tools, such as compilers, IDEs, and testing tools, can read and interpret these annotations. The Java compiler is the tool that reads the `@Override` annotation.

The compiler ensures that for a method marked as `@Override`, a method with the same name and arguments exists in a superclass. If you screwed up somehow—perhaps you mistyped the method as `getSessionLentgh` instead of `getSessionLength`—the compile fails. You see the message:

`method does not override a method from its superclass`

Java does not require you to add `@Override` annotations to your code. However, they provide valuable documentation for your code as well as protections from simple mistakes. You can read more about annotations in Lesson 15.

You may now remove `getEndDate` from SummerCourseSession. In Figure 6.3, the `getSessionLength` operation appears twice, an indication that the subclass (SummerCourseSession) overrides the superclass (CourseSession) definition. Note that I have preceded each method with access privilege information, something I rarely do. Since normally I *only* display public information in a UML sketch, I prefer to omit the + (plus sign) that indicates a publicly accessible operation.

In this circumstance, however, `getSessionLength` is `protected`, not `public`. Adding the access privilege indicators to the diagram in Figure 6.3 differentiates access between the methods and highlights the relevancy of `getSessionLength`. The UML indicator for `protected` is the pound sign (#).[3]

---

[3]The UML access indicator for private is (-). The indicator for package-level access is (~).

Refactoring

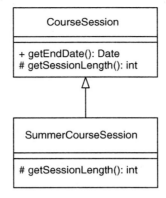

Figure 6.3 *Overriding a Protected Method*

Idiosyncrasies

Since Java does not require you to add @Override annotations to methods, it's easy to forget. (That's one thing a pair developer can be good for.) The @Override annotation is a new J2SE 5.0 feature, so I have my excuse if I've forgotten to use it elsewhere in Agile Java.

You'll note that I do not use @Override on my setUp and tearDown methods, even though the annotation is applicable for these TestCase method overrides. Using @Override would be a good idea (particularly since it's easy enough to spell setUp as setup). But old habits are hard to break. I justify it by saying that it's only test code and the tests will help correct me anyway. Nonetheless, I recommend that you avoid my bad habits.

Most of the logic for determining the end date of a session is fixed. The only variance in the logic between CourseSession and SummerCourseSession is the session length. This variance is represented by the abstraction of a separate method, getSessionLength. The CourseSession class can supply one implementation for getSessionLength, the SummerCourseSession another.

The method getEndDate in CourseSession acts as a template. It supplies the bulk of the algorithm for calculating a session end date. Certain pieces of the algorithm are "pluggable," meaning that the details are provided elsewhere. Subclasses can vary these details. The template algorithm in getEndDate is an example of a design pattern known as Template Method.[4]

---

[4][Gamma1995].

More on Constructors

You call a superclass constructor from a subclass constructor by using the super keyword, as demonstrated earlier. A call to a superclass constructor must appear as the first line in a subclass constructor.

A subclass extends, or builds upon, a superclass. You can think of a subclass object as an outer layer, or shell, around an object of the base class. Before the subclass object can exist, Java must build and properly initialize an object of the superclass. The following language test demonstrates how classes are constructed, using a demo class called SuperClass and its subclass SubClass.

```
// SuperClassTest.java
import junit.framework.TestCase;

public class SuperClassTest extends TestCase {
    public void testConstructorCalls() {
        SuperClass superClass = new SubClass();
        assertTrue(SuperClass.constructorWasCalled);
    }
}

// SuperClass.java
class SuperClass {
    static boolean constructorWasCalled = false;

    SuperClass() {
        constructorWasCalled = true;
    }
}

// SubClass.java
class SubClass extends SuperClass {
    SubClass() {
    }
}
```

More on
Constructors

The Java virtual machine requires every class to have at least one constructor. However, you can code a class without explicitly defining a constructor. If you don't define a constructor Java will automatically generate a default, no-argument constructor.

If you do not provide a super call in a subclass constructor, it is as if Java inserted a call to the no-argument superclass constructor. Even constructors that take parameters call the no-argument superclass constructor by default.

```
// SuperClassTest.java
import junit.framework.TestCase;
```

```
public class SuperClassTest extends TestCase {
    public void testConstructorCalls() {
        SuperClass superClass = new SubClass("parm");
        assertTrue(SuperClass.constructorWasCalled);
    }
}


// SubClass.java
class SubClass extends SuperClass {
    SubClass(String parm) {
    }
}
```

The test constructs a new SubClass instance, passing in a String as a parameter. The parameter information appears in bold. The test then demonstrates that creating a SubClass instance results the execution of the SuperClass no-argument constructor.

Remember, if you *do* supply a constructor with arguments in a class, Java *does not* automatically supply a no-argument constructor. In this situation, any subclass constructors *must* explicitly call a superclass constructor, otherwise you receive a compilation error.

```
// This code will not compile
// SuperClass.java
class SuperClass {
    static boolean constructorWasCalled = false;

    SuperClass(String parm) {
        constructorWasCalled = true;
    }
}


// SubClass.java
class SubClass extends SuperClass {
    SubClass(String parm) {
    }
}
```

The above code generates the following compiler error:

```
SubClass.java: cannot find symbol
symbol  : constructor SuperClass()
location: class studentinfo.SuperClass
    SubClass(String parm) {
                        ^
```

The subclass constructor should probably be:

```
class SubClass extends SuperClass {
    SubClass(String parm) {
        super(parm);
    }
}
```

More on
Constructors

Inheritance and Polymorphism

The class SummerCourseSession inherits from CourseSession. Just as a class that implements an interface is of that interface type, a class that inherits from another is of that superclass type. Therefore, SummerCourseSession is a CourseSession.

Just as you were taught to prefer interface reference types, you should also prefer base class for the reference type. Assign a new SummerCourseSession to a CourseSession reference:

```
CourseSession session = new SummerCourseSession();
```

Even though the session variable is of the type CourseSession, it still refers to a SummerCourseSession in memory.

You defined the method getEndDate in both CourseSession and Summer-CourseSession. When you send the getEndDate message using the session variable, the message is received by a SummerCourseSession object. Java executes the version of getEndDate defined in SummerCourseSession.

The client thinks it is sending a message to a CourseSession, but an object of a class *derived from* CourseSession receives and interprets the message. This is another example of polymorphism.

The Principle of Subcontracting

The client that sends a message to an object using a variable of CourseSession type expects it to be interpreted and acted upon in a certain manner. In test-driven development, unit tests define this "manner." A unit test describes the behavior supported by interacting with a class through its interface. It describes the behavior by first actually effecting that behavior, then by ensuring that any number of *postconditions* hold true upon completion.

For a class to properly derive from CourseSession, it must not change the expectations of behavior. Any postcondition that held true for a test of CourseSession should also hold true for a test executing against a subclass of CourseSession. In general, subclasses should keep or strengthen postconditions. Subclasses should *extend* the behavior of their superclasses, meaning that postconditions should be *added* to tests for the subclass.

What this means for TDD is that you should specify contracts (in the form of unit tests) at the level of the superclass. All subclasses will need to conform

The Principle of Subcontracting

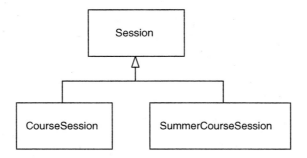

Figure 6.4   *The Session Hierarchy*

to these unit tests. You will build these contracts using a pattern known as Abstract Test.[5]

Technically, there is no compelling reason to make this refactoring. The tests for CourseSession class could retain the contract for both CourseSession and SummerCourseSession. Minor differences do exist, though. The Course-Session class explicitly tracks the number of instances created; this is something the SummerCourseSession class need not do.

Building the Session superclass results in a slightly cleaner and easier to understand hierarchy. Conceptually, a CourseSession seems to be an object at the same hierarchical "level" as a SummerCourseSession.

It's up to you to decide if such a refactoring is worthwhile. If it gives you a simpler solution, go for it. If it creates artificial classes in the hierarchy without any benefit, it's a waste of time.

For the CourseSession example, you will refactor such that both Course-Session and SummerCourseSession inherit from a common abstract super-class, instead of SummerCourseSession inheriting from CourseSession. See Figure 6.4.

Create an abstract test class, SessionTest, that specifies the base unit tests for Session and its subclasses. Move `testCreate`, `testComparable`, and `testEnrollStudents` from CourseSessionTest into SessionTest. These tests represent the contracts that should apply to all Session subclasses.

SessionTest contains an abstract factory method, `createSession`. Subclasses of SessionTest will provide definitions for `createSession` that return an object of the appropriate type (CourseSession or SummerCourseSession).

```
package sis.studentinfo;

import junit.framework.TestCase;
import java.util.*;
import static sis.studentinfo.DateUtil.createDate;
```

[5][George2002].

```java
abstract public class SessionTest extends TestCase {
    private Session session;
    private Date startDate;
    public static final int CREDITS = 3;

    public void setUp() {
        startDate = createDate(2003, 1, 6);
        session = createSession("ENGL", "101", startDate);
        session.setNumberOfCredits(CREDITS);
    }

    abstract protected Session createSession(
        String department, String number, Date startDate);

    public void testCreate() {
        assertEquals("ENGL", session.getDepartment());
        assertEquals("101", session.getNumber());
        assertEquals(0, session.getNumberOfStudents());
        assertEquals(startDate, session.getStartDate());
    }

    public void testEnrollStudents() {
        Student student1 = new Student("Cain DiVoe");
        session.enroll(student1);
        assertEquals(CREDITS, student1.getCredits());
        assertEquals(1, session.getNumberOfStudents());
        assertEquals(student1, session.get(0));

        Student student2 = new Student("Coralee DeVaughn");
        session.enroll(student2);
        assertEquals(CREDITS, student2.getCredits());
        assertEquals(2, session.getNumberOfStudents());
        assertEquals(student1, session.get(0));
        assertEquals(student2, session.get(1));
    }

    public void testComparable()   {
        final Date date = new Date();
        Session sessionA = createSession("CMSC", "101", date);
        Session sessionB = createSession("ENGL", "101", date);
        assertTrue(sessionA.compareTo(sessionB) < 0);
        assertTrue(sessionB.compareTo(sessionA) > 0);

        Session sessionC = createSession("CMSC", "101", date);
        assertEquals(0, sessionA.compareTo(sessionC));

        Session sessionD = createSession("CMSC", "210", date);
        assertTrue(sessionC.compareTo(sessionD) < 0);
        assertTrue(sessionD.compareTo(sessionC) > 0);
    }
}
```

The Principle of Subcontracting

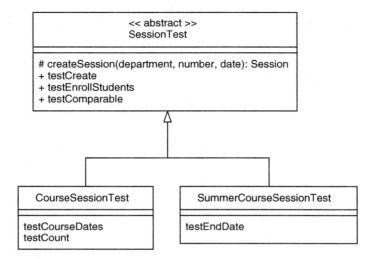

Figure 6.5 *Abstract Test*

You must change the test subclasses, CourseSessionTest and Summer-CourseSessionTest, so they extend from SessionTest. As you work through the example, you may refer to Figure 6.5 as the UML basis for the test reorganization.

Each test subclass will also need to provide the implementation for create-Session.

```
// SummerCourseSessionTest.java
package sis.summer;

import junit.framework.*;
import java.util.*;
import sis.studentinfo.*;

public class SummerCourseSessionTest extends SessionTest {
    public void testEndDate() {
        Date startDate = DateUtil.createDate(2003, 6, 9);
        Session session = createSession("ENGL", "200", startDate);
        Date eightWeeksOut = DateUtil.createDate(2003, 8, 1);
        assertEquals(eightWeeksOut, session.getEndDate());
    }

    protected Session createSession(
            String department,
            String number,
            Date date) {
```

```
        return SummerCourseSession.create(department, number, date);
    }
}
```

In CourseSessionTest, you'll need to change any usages of the createCourseSession method to createSession.

```
// CourseSessionTest.java
package sis.studentinfo;

import junit.framework.TestCase;
import java.util.*;
import static sis.studentinfo.DateUtil.createDate;

public class CourseSessionTest extends SessionTest {
    public void testCourseDates() {
        Date startDate = DateUtil.createDate(2003, 1, 6);
        Session session = createSession("ENGL", "200", startDate);
        Date sixteenWeeksOut = createDate(2003, 4, 25);
        assertEquals(sixteenWeeksOut, session.getEndDate());
    }

    public void testCount() {
        CourseSession.resetCount();
        createSession("", "", new Date());
        assertEquals(1, CourseSession.getCount());
        createSession("", "", new Date());
        assertEquals(2, CourseSession.getCount());
    }

    protected Session createSession(
            String department,
            String number,
            Date date) {
        return CourseSession.create(department, number, date);
    }
}
```

The Principle of Subcontracting

The method testCourseDates creates its own local instance of a CourseSession. The alternative would be to use the CourseSession object created by the setUp method in SessionTest. Creating the CourseSession directly in the subclass test method makes it easier to read the test, however. It would be difficult to understand the meaning of the test were the instantiation in another class. The assertion is closely related to the setup of the CourseSession.

Both CourseSessionTest and SummerCourseSessionTest now provide an implementation for the abstract createSession method.

The most important thing to note is that CourseSessionTest and Summer-CourseSessionTest share all tests defined in SessionTest, since both classes extend from SessionTest. JUnit executes each test defined in SessionTest twice—once for a CourseSessionTest instance and once for a SummerCourse-SessionTest instance. This ensures that both subclasses of Session behave appropriately.

When JUnit executes a method defined in SessionTest, the code results in a call to createSession. Since you defined createSession as abstract, there is no definition for the method in SessionTest. The Java VM calls the createSession method in the appropriate test subclass instead. Code in createSession creates an appropriate subtype of Session, either CourseSession or SummerCourse-Session.

The refactoring of the production classes (I've removed the Java API documentation):

```java
package sis.studentinfo;

import java.util.*;

abstract public class Session implements Comparable<Session> {
    private static int count;
    private String department;
    private String number;
    private List<Student> students = new ArrayList<Student>();
    private Date startDate;
    private int numberOfCredits;

    protected Session(
            String department, String number, Date startDate) {
        this.department = department;
        this.number = number;
        this.startDate = startDate;
    }

    public int compareTo(Session that) {
        int compare =
            this.getDepartment().compareTo(that.getDepartment());
        if (compare != 0)
            return compare;
        return this.getNumber().compareTo(that.getNumber());
    }

    void setNumberOfCredits(int numberOfCredits) {
        this.numberOfCredits = numberOfCredits;
    }

    public String getDepartment() {
        return department;
    }

    public String getNumber() {
        return number;
    }
```

```java
    int getNumberOfStudents() {
        return students.size();
    }

    public void enroll(Student student) {
        student.addCredits(numberOfCredits);
        students.add(student);
    }

    Student get(int index) {
        return students.get(index);
    }

    protected Date getStartDate() {
        return startDate;
    }

    public List<Student> getAllStudents() {
        return students;
    }

    abstract protected int getSessionLength();

    public Date getEndDate() {
        GregorianCalendar calendar = new GregorianCalendar();
        calendar.setTime(getStartDate());
        final int daysInWeek = 7;
        final int daysFromFridayToMonday = 3;
        int numberOfDays =
            getSessionLength() * daysInWeek - daysFromFridayToMonday;
        calendar.add(Calendar.DAY_OF_YEAR, numberOfDays);
        return calendar.getTime();
    }
}
```

The bulk of code in Session comes directly from CourseSession. The method getSessionLength becomes an abstract method, forcing subclasses to each implement it to provide the session length in weeks. Here are CourseSession and SummerCourseSession, each having been changed to inherit from Session:

The Principle of Subcontracting

```java
// CourseSession.java
package sis.studentinfo;

import java.util.*;

public class CourseSession extends Session {
    private static int count;
```

```java
    public static CourseSession create(
        String department,
        String number,
        Date startDate) {
      return new CourseSession(department, number, startDate);
    }

    protected CourseSession(
        String department, String number, Date startDate) {
      super(department, number, startDate);
      CourseSession.incrementCount();
    }

    static private void incrementCount() {
      ++count;
    }

    static void resetCount() {
      count = 0;
    }

    static int getCount() {
      return count;
    }

    protected int getSessionLength() {
      return 16;
    }
}

// SummerCourseSession.java
package sis.summer;

import java.util.*;
import sis.studentinfo.*;

public class SummerCourseSession extends Session {
    public static SummerCourseSession create(
        String department,
        String number,
        Date startDate) {
      return new SummerCourseSession(department, number, startDate);
    }

    private SummerCourseSession(
        String department,
        String number,
        Date startDate) {
      super(department, number, startDate);
    }
```

```
   protected int getSessionLength() {
      return 8;
   }
}
```

All that is left in the subclasses are constructors, static methods, and template method overrides. Constructors are not inherited. Common methods, such as enroll and getAllStudents, now appear only in the Session superclass. All of the fields are common to both subclasses and thus now appear in Session. Also important is that the return type for the create method in SummerCourse-Session and CourseSession is the abstract supertype Session.

The test method testCourseDates appears in both SessionTest subclasses. You could define a common assertion for this test in SessionTest, but what would the assertion be? One simple assertion would be that the end date must be later than the start date. Subclasses would strengthen that assertion by verifying against a specific date.

Another solution would be to assert that the end date is exactly *n* weeks, minus the appropriate number of weekend days, after the start date. The resultant code would have you duplicate the logic from getEndDate directly in the test itself.

Of perhaps more value is adding assertions against the method getSession-Length in the abstract test:

```
public void testSessionLength() {
   Session session = createSession(new Date());
   assertTrue(session.getSessionLength() > 0);
}
```

By expressing postconditions clearly in the abstract class, you are establishing a subcontract that all subclasses must adhere to.

This refactoring was a considerable amount of work. I hope you took the time to incrementally apply the changes.

Exercises

Exercises

1. In the exercises for Lesson 5, you created a method to calculate the strength of a piece based on its type and board position. Modify this method to use a switch statement instead of an if statement.

2. Modify the strength calculation method to use a Map that associates piece types with their base strength value. In order to place double values in Map, you will need to declare the map as Map<Piece.Type,Double>.[6]

[6]Lesson 7 includes a section on wrapper types that explains why this is so.

3. Use lazy initialization to preload the Map of piece type to base-strength value. Note the effect on readability this change has on the code. What factors would drive you to either leave this change in the code or to remove it?

4. Move the point values for the pieces into the piece type enumeration and use a method on the enumeration to get the point value.

5. Move the character representation for a piece onto the Piece.Type enum. Code in Board will still need to manage uppercasing this character for a black piece.

6. You must implement the various moves that a king can make. The basic rule is that a king can move one square in any direction. (For now, we will ignore the fact that neighboring pieces can either restrict such a move or can turn it into a capture.)

7. The code in Board is getting complex. It now manages the mathematics of a grid, it stores pieces, it determines valid moves for pieces (the queen and king, so far), it gathers pieces and determines their strength. By the time you add move logic for the remaining pieces (queen, pawn, rook, bishop, and knight), the class will be very cluttered with conditional logic.

    There are a few ways to break things up. From my viewpoint, there are two main functions of code in Board class. One goal is to implement the 8x8 board using a data structure—a list of lists of pieces. A lot of the code in Board is geared toward navigating this data structure, without respect to the rules of chess. The rest of the code in Board defines the rules of the chess game.

    Break the Board class into two classes: Game, which represents the logic of a chess game, and Board, a simple data structure that stores pieces and understands the grid layout of the board.

    This will be a significant refactoring. Move methods as incrementally as possible, making sure tests remain green with each move. If necessary, create parallel code as you refactor, then eliminate the unnecessary code once everything is working. Make sure you add tests as needed.

    Take this opportunity to begin to encapsulate the implementation details of the data structure of Board. Instead of asking for ranks and adding pieces, have the Game code use the Board method put.

8. A queen can move any number of squares as long as it forms a straight line. Implement this capability on Piece. Note that your initial implementation will require an if statement to determine whether the piece is a queen or a king.

    The solution may involve *recursion*—the ability of a method to call itself. A recursive call is no big deal; it is a method call like any other. But you must be careful to provide a way for the recursion to stop, otherwise you might get stuck in an infinite loop of the method calling itself.

9. Your code to manage moves for kings and queens includes an `if` statement. You can imagine that supporting further moves for pieces will involve a bunch of conditional statements. One way of cleaning things up is to create a Piece hierarchy, with separate subtypes for King, Queen, Bishop, and so on.

    In preparation for creating Piece subclasses, move the method `getPossibleMoves` to the Piece class.

10. Now you are ready to create Piece subclasses. You will note that as you create subclasses for Queen and King, the Piece.Type enum seems redundant. In the next exercise, you'll eliminate this enum. Create Queen and King classes to extend Piece. Move the relevant tests from PieceTest into QueenTest and KingTest. This will force you to move code as well into the new subclasses. Also, create subclasses for the remaining pieces and alter the factory methods accordingly on Piece. Don't worry about coding up the move rules for the other pieces yet.

    Refactor at will. Eliminate duplication. Add tests where tests were missing due to moving methods onto a new class.

11. The final step is to eliminate the need for the Type enum. Since you now have a subclass for each piece, you can move code depending on the type into that sublcass.

    You may need to test the type of the subclass created. Instead of asking each piece for its Piece.Type value, you can simply ask for its class:

    ```
    piece.getClass()
    ```

    You can then compare this to a Class literal:

    ```
    Class expectedClass = Queen.class;
    assertEquals(expectedClass, piece.getClass());
    ```

    You also want to eliminate as much code as possible that asks for the type of an object—that's one of the main reasons for creating the subclasses in the first place. See if you can move any code that looks like `if (piece.getClass().equals(Pawn.class)` into the appropriate class.

Lesson 7

Legacy Elements

In this lesson you will learn about legacy elements of Java. Java is a continually evolving language. The original release of Java was immature with respect to both its language features and its class library. Over the years, Sun has added to the language and class library in attempts to provide a more robust platform. Sun has removed little. The result is that Java contains many features that Sun recommends you no longer use.

J2SE 5.0 introduces many new language elements, some that aspire to replace existing Java elements. As the most relevant example, the designers of Java changed the means of iterating through a collection in 5.0. Previously, the language supported iteration through a combination of the class library and procedural looping constructs. Now, the Java language directly supports iteration with the for-each loop.

In this lesson, you will learn about many Java elements that come from its syntactical grandparent, the C language. These elements are largely procedural in nature but are still necessary in order to provide a fully functional programming language. Nonetheless, most of the time you should be able to use constructs that are more object-oriented instead of the legacy elements in this lesson.

While I downplay the use of these legacy elements, you *must* understand them in order to fully master Java. They remain the underpinnings of the Java language. In many circumstances, you will be forced to use them. And in some cases, they still provide the best solution to the problem at hand.

Some of the legacy elements you will learn about include:

- for, while, and do loops

- looping control statements

- legacy collections

- iterators

- casting

231

- wrapper classes

- arrays

- varargs

Each of these elements, with the exception of varargs, has been around since the advent of Java. The concept of collections, Iterators, and wrapper classes are object-oriented constructs. Everything else derives from the C language. The switch statement that you learned in Lesson 6 is also a legacy element that was derived from C.

Looping Constructs

The for loop as you have learned it provides a means of iterating through a collection and operating on each element.

You will need more general-purpose looping. Perhaps you need to execute a body of code infinitely, loop until some condition is met, or send a message ten times. Java meets these needs with three looping constructs: while, do, and for.

Breaking Up a Student's Name

 Currently, the Student class supports constructing a student with a single string that represents the student's name. You need to modify the Student class so that it can break apart a single string into its constituent name parts. For example, the Student class should be able to break the name string "Robert Cecil Martin" into a first name "Robert," a middle name "Cecil," and a last name "Martin."

The class should also assume that a string with two name parts represents a first and last name and that a string with one name part represents a last name only.

First, modify the existing testCreate method defined in StudentTest:

```
public void testCreate() {
    final String firstStudentName = "Jane Doe";
    Student firstStudent = new Student(firstStudentName);
    assertEquals(firstStudentName, firstStudent.getName());
    assertEquals("Jane", firstStudent.getFirstName());
    assertEquals("Doe", firstStudent.getLastName());
    assertEquals("", firstStudent.getMiddleName());
```

Breaking Up a
Student's Name

```
    final String secondStudentName = "Blow";
    Student secondStudent = new Student(secondStudentName);
    assertEquals(secondStudentName, secondStudent.getName());
    assertEquals("", secondStudent.getFirstName());
    assertEquals("Blow", secondStudent.getLastName());
    assertEquals("", secondStudent.getMiddleName());


    final String thirdStudentName = "Raymond Douglas Davies";
    Student thirdStudent = new Student(thirdStudentName);
    assertEquals(thirdStudentName, thirdStudent.getName());
    assertEquals("Raymond", thirdStudent.getFirstName());
    assertEquals("Davies", thirdStudent.getLastName());
    assertEquals("Douglas", thirdStudent.getMiddleName());
}
```

You'll need to add fields and create getter methods in Student:

```
private String firstName;
private String middleName;
private String lastName;
...
public String getFirstName() {
    return firstName;
}

public String getMiddleName() {
    return middleName;
}

public String getLastName() {
    return lastName;
}
```

The modified Student constructor code shows your *intent* of how to solve the problem:

```
public Student(String fullName) {
    this.name = fullName;
    credits = 0;
    List<String> nameParts = split(fullName);
    setName(nameParts);
}
```

Programming by intention is a useful technique that helps you figure out *what* you need to do before you figure out *how* you are going to do it.[1] It can be viewed as decomposing the problem into smaller abstractions. You can put these abstractions into code before actually implementing the abstractions. Here, you know that you need to split the full name into different parts, but you don't yet know how.

[1][Astels2003], p. 45.

Use programming by intention to break down a problem into a number of smaller goals.

Once you have figured out how to split the string into a list of up to three name parts, the implementation of setName is straightforward. It involves a few if-else statements. Each if conditional tests the number of name parts available in the list of tokens:

```java
private void setName(List<String> nameParts) {
    if (nameParts.size() == 1)
        this.lastName = nameParts.get(0);
    else if (nameParts.size() == 2) {
        this.firstName = nameParts.get(0);
        this.lastName = nameParts.get(1);
    }
    else if (nameParts.size() == 3) {
        this.firstName = nameParts.get(0);
        this.middleName = nameParts.get(1);
        this.lastName = nameParts.get(2);
    }
}
```

The setName code always sets a value into lastName. However, it does not always set the value of firstName or middleName. You will need to ensure that these fields are properly initialized in Student:

```java
private String firstName = "";
private String middleName = "";
private String lastName;
```

The while Loop

As usual, Java gives you several ways to solve the problem of splitting the name. You'll start with a more "classic," more tedious approach. You will loop through each character in the name, looking for space characters, using them to determine where one name part ends and the next name part begins. Later you'll learn a couple of simpler, more-object-oriented solutions.

Breaking Up a Student's Name

The split method needs to take the full name as an argument and return a list of tokens as a result. You will use a while loop to derive each token in turn from the string and add it to the result list.

```java
private List<String> tokenize(String string) {
    List<String> results = new ArrayList<String>();

    StringBuffer word = new StringBuffer();
    int index = 0;
    while (index < string.length()) {
```

```
        char ch = string.charAt(index);
        if (ch != ' ') // prefer Character.isSpace.  Defined yet?
          word.append(ch);
        else
          if (word.length() > 0) {
            results.add(word.toString());
            word = new StringBuffer();
          }
        index++;
      }
      if (word.length() > 0)
        results.add(word.toString());
      return results;
    }
```

You use the while loop to execute a statement or block of code as long as a condition holds true.

In this example, after Java initializes an index counter to 0, it executes the while loop. As long as the index is less than the string length (index < string .length()), Java executes the body of the while loop (all code between the braces following the while conditional).

The body in this example extracts the character at the current index from the string. It tests whether the character is a space (' ') or not. If not, the character is appended to the current StringBuffer instance. If so, and if there are any characters in the current StringBuffer, the contents of the StringBuffer represent a complete word and are added to the results. A new StringBuffer, to represent a new word, is created and assigned to the word reference.

Each time the body of the while loop completes, control is transferred back up to the while loop conditional. Once the conditional returns a false result, the while loop terminates. Control is then transferred to the statement immediately following the while loop body. In the example, the statement immediately following is an if statement that ensures that the last word extracted becomes part of the results.

The modified test should pass.

Refactoring

The setName method is a bit repetitive. You can refactor it by taking advantage of having the name parts in a list that you can manipulate.

```
private void setName(List<String> nameParts) {
  this.lastName = removeLast(nameParts);
  String name = removeLast(nameParts);
  if (nameParts.isEmpty())
    this.firstName = name;
  else {
```

```
        this.middleName = name;
        this.firstName = removeLast(nameParts);
    }
}

private String removeLast(List<String> list) {
    if (list.isEmpty())
        return "";
    return list.remove(list.size() - 1);
}
```

You actually create more lines of code overall with this solution. But you eliminate the duplication and hard-coded indexes rampant in setName. Further, you produce a generic method, removeLast, that later may be a useful abstraction.

The for Loop

Looping using a counter and a limit, as in the previous example, is a common operation. You can more succinctly express this operation by using a variant of the for loop. The for loop allows you to combine three common loop parts into one declaration. Each for loop declaration contains:

- initialization code

- a conditional expression representing whether or not to continue execution of the loop

- an update expression that the Java VM executes each time the loop terminates

You separate each of these three sections in the for loop declaration using a semicolon.

The classic use of a for loop is to execute a body of code a certain number of times. Typically, but not necessarily, the initialization code sets an index to 0, the conditional tests that the index is less than a limit, and the update expression increments the counter by one.

Breaking Up a Student's Name

```
private List<String> split(String name) {
    List<String> results = new ArrayList<String>();

    StringBuffer word = new StringBuffer();
    for (int index = 0; index < name.length(); index++) {
        char ch = name.charAt(index);
        if (!Character.isWhitespace(ch))
            word.append(ch);
```

```
        else
          if (word.length() > 0) {
             results.add(word.toString());
             word = new StringBuffer();
          }
      }
      if (word.length() > 0)
         results.add(word.toString());
      return results;
   }
```

In the for loop example, the initialization code declares index as an int and initializes it to 0. The conditional tests that index is less than the number of characters in the String argument. As long as the condition holds true, Java executes the body of the loop. Subsequent to each time Java executes the loop, Java increments index (index++); it then transfers control back to the conditional. Once the conditional returns false, Java transfers control to the statement following the for loop body.

In the example, Java executes the body of the for loop once for each character in the input string. The index value ranges from zero up to the number of characters in the input string minus one.

Multiple Initialization and Update Expressions in the **for** Loop

Both the initialization and update code sections allow for multiple expressions separated by commas. The countChars method,[2] which returns the number of occurrences of a specified character within a string, shows how you can initialize both the variables i and count to 0.

```
public static int countChars(String input, char ch) {
   int count;
   int i;
   for (i = 0, count = 0; i < input.length(); i++)
     if (input.charAt(i) == ch)
        count++;
   return count;
}
```

The use of the letter i as a for loop index variable is an extremely common idiom. It is one of the few commonly accepted standards that allows you to abbreviate a variable name. Most developers prefer to use i over a full word such as index.

Breaking Up a
Student's Name

---

[2]This method and several other methods in this lesson such as the upcoming method isPalindrome, have nothing to do with the student information system. They are here to help demonstrate some of the lesser-seen nuances of Java syntax.

The following method, isPalindrome, returns true if a string reads backward the same as forward. It shows how you can declare and initialize more than one variable in the initialization code. The method also shows multiple expressions—incrementing forward and decrementing backward—in the update step.

```java
public static boolean isPalindrome(String string) {
    for
        (int forward = 0, backward = string.length() - 1;
         forward < string.length();
         forward++, backward-)
        if (string.charAt(forward) != string.charAt(backward))
            return false;
    return true;
}

// tests
public void testPalindrome() {
    assertFalse(isPalindrome("abcdef"));
    assertFalse(isPalindrome("abccda"));
    assertTrue(isPalindrome("abccba"));
    assertFalse(isPalindrome("abcxba"));
    assertTrue(isPalindrome("a"));
    assertTrue(isPalindrome("aa"));
    assertFalse(isPalindrome("ab"));
    assertTrue(isPalindrome(""));
    assertTrue(isPalindrome("aaa"));
    assertTrue(isPalindrome("aba"));
    assertTrue(isPalindrome("abbba"));
    assertTrue(isPalindrome("abba"));
    assertFalse(isPalindrome("abbaa"));
    assertFalse(isPalindrome("abcda"));
}
```

A local variable that you declare in the initialization code of a for loop is valid only for the scope of the for loop. Thus, in the countChars method, you must declare count prior to the loop, since you return count *after* the for loop.

Java stipulates that "if you have a local variable declaration, each part of the expression after a comma is expected to be a part of that local variable declaration."[3] So while it would be nice to be able to recode countChars to declare i and only initialize count, Java expects the following initialization code to declare both i *and* count.

Breaking Up a Student's Name

```java
// this code will not compile!
public static int countChars(String input, char ch) {
    int count;
    for (int i = 0, count = 0; i < input.length(); i++)
        if (input.charAt(i) == ch)
            count++;
    return count;
}
```

[3][Arnold2000].

But since you already declared `count` before the `for` loop, the Java compiler rejects the attempt:

```
count is already defined in countChars(java.lang.String,char)
```

All three parts of the `for` loop declaration—initialization, conditional, and update expression—are optional. If you omit the conditional, Java executes the loop infinitely. The following `for` statement is a common idiom for an infinite loop:

```
for (;;) {
}
```

A more expressive way to create an infinite loop is to use a `while` loop:

```
while (true) {
}
```

As mentioned, the most common use for `for` loops is to count from 0 up to $n - 1$, where n is the number of elements in a collection. Nothing prohibits you from creating `for` loops that work differently. The `isPalindrome` method shows how you can count upward at the same time as counting downward.

Another language test shows how you can have the update expression do something other than decrement or increment the index:

```
public void testForSkip() {
    StringBuilder builder = new StringBuilder();
    String string = "123456";
    for (int i = 0; i < string.length(); i += 2)
        builder.append(string.charAt(i));
    assertEquals("135", builder.toString());
}
```

The do Loop

The `do` loop works like a `while` loop, except that the conditional to be tested appears at the *end* of the loop body. You use a `do` loop to ensure that the you execute the body of a loop at least once.

In the thirteenth century, Leonardo Fibonacci came up with a numeric sequence to represent how rabbits multiply.[4] The Fibonacci sequence starts with 0 and 1. Each subsequent number in the sequence is the sum of the two preceding numbers in the sequence. The test and code below demonstrate an implementation of the Fibonacci function using a `do` loop.

Breaking Up a
Student's Name

[4][Wikipedia2004]

```
public void testFibonacci() {
    assertEquals(0, fib(0));
    assertEquals(1, fib(1));
    assertEquals(1, fib(2));
    assertEquals(2, fib(3));
    assertEquals(3, fib(4));
    assertEquals(5, fib(5));
    assertEquals(8, fib(6));
    assertEquals(13, fib(7));
    assertEquals(21, fib(8));
    assertEquals(34, fib(9));
    assertEquals(55, fib(10));
}

private int fib(int x) {
    if (x == 0) return 0;
    if (x == 1) return 1;
    int fib = 0;
    int nextFib = 1;
    int index = 0;
    int temp;
    do {
        temp = fib + nextFib;
        fib = nextFib;
        nextFib = temp;
    } while (++index < x);
    return fib;
}
```

Comparing Java Loops

A way exists to code any looping need using any one of the three loop variants. The following test and three methods show three techniques for displaying a list of numbers separated by commas.

```
public void testCommas() {
    String sequence = "1,2,3,4,5";
    assertEquals(sequence, sequenceUsingDo(1, 5));
    assertEquals(sequence, sequenceUsingFor(1, 5));
    assertEquals(sequence, sequenceUsingWhile(1, 5));

    sequence = "8";
    assertEquals(sequence, sequenceUsingDo(8, 8));
    assertEquals(sequence, sequenceUsingFor(8, 8));
    assertEquals(sequence, sequenceUsingWhile(8, 8));
}

String sequenceUsingDo(int start, int stop) {
    StringBuilder builder = new StringBuilder();
    int i = start;
```

Comparing Java
Loops

```
    do {
        if (i > start)
            builder.append(',');
        builder.append(i);
    } while (++i <= stop);
    return builder.toString();
}

String sequenceUsingFor(int start, int stop) {
    StringBuilder builder = new StringBuilder();
    for (int i = start; i <= stop; i++) {
        if (i > start)
            builder.append(',');
        builder.append(i);
    }
    return builder.toString();
}

String sequenceUsingWhile(int start, int stop) {
    StringBuilder builder = new StringBuilder();
    int i = start;
    while (i <= stop) {
        if (i > start)
            builder.append(',');
        builder.append(i);
        i++;
    }
    return builder.toString();
}
```

As this example shows, you will find that one of the loop variants is usually more appropriate than the other two. Here, a for loop is best suited since the loop is centered around counting needs.

If you have no need to maintain a counter or other incrementing variable, the while loop will usually suffice. Most of the time, you want to test a condition each and every time upon entry to a loop. You will use the do loop far less frequently. The need to always execute the loop at least once before testing the condition is less common.

Refactoring

isPalindrome

The isPalindrome method expends almost twice as much effort as necessary to determine whether a string is a palindrome. While normally you shouldn't worry about performance until it is a problem, an algorithm should be clean.

Doing something unnecessarily in an algorithm demonstrates poor understanding of the problem. It can also confuse future developers.

You only need to traverse the string up to its middle. The current implementation traverses the string for its entire length, which means that all or almost all characters are compared twice. A better implementation:

```java
public static boolean isPalindrome(String string) {
    if (string.length() == 0)
        return true;
    int limit = string.length() / 2;
    for
        (int forward = 0, backward = string.length() - 1;
         forward < limit;
         forward++, backward-)
        if (string.charAt(forward) != string.charAt(backward))
            return false;
    return true;
}
```

Fibonacci and Recursion

Java supports *recursive* method calls. A recursive method is one that calls itself. A more elegant solution for the Fibonacci sequence uses recursion:

```java
private int fib(int x) {
    if (x == 0)
        return 0;
    if (x == 1)
        return 1;
    return fib(x - 1) + fib(x - 2);
}
```

Be cautious when using recursion! Make sure you have a way of "breaking" the recursion, otherwise your method will recurse infinitely. You can often use a guard clause for this purpose, as in the fib method (which has two guard clauses).

Looping Control Statements

Looping Control Statements

Java provides additional means for altering control flow within a loop: the continue statement, the break statement, the labeled break statement, and the labeled continue statement.

The **break** Statement

You may want to prematurely terminate the execution of a loop. If the Java VM encounters a break statement within the body of a loop, it immediately transfers control to the statement following the loop body.

The String class defines a trim method that removes blank characters[5] from *both ends* of a String. You will define another String utility that trims blank characters from only the *end* of a String.

```java
public void testEndTrim() {
    assertEquals("", endTrim(""));
    assertEquals("  x", endTrim("  x  "));
    assertEquals("y", endTrim("y"));
    assertEquals("xaxa", endTrim("xaxa"));
    assertEquals("", endTrim(" "));
    assertEquals("xxx", endTrim("xxx       "));
}

public String endTrim(String source) {
    int i = source.length();
    while (-i >= 0)
        if (source.charAt(i) != ' ')
            break;
    return source.substring(0, i + 1);
}
```

The **continue** Statement

When it encounters a continue statement, Java immediately transfers control to the conditional expression of a loop.

 The example calculates the average GPA for part-time students enrolled in a course session. The test, as implemented in SessionTest:

```java
public void testAverageGpaForPartTimeStudents() {
    session.enroll(createFullTimeStudent());

    Student partTimer1 = new Student("1");
    partTimer1.addGrade(Student.Grade.A);
    session.enroll(partTimer1);

    session.enroll(createFullTimeStudent());

    Student partTimer2 = new Student("2");
    partTimer2.addGrade(Student.Grade.B);
    session.enroll(partTimer2);
```

Looping Control Statements

---

[5]It actually removes *whitespace*, which includes space characters as well as tab, new line, form feed, and carriage return characters.

```
    assertEquals(3.5, session.averageGpaForPartTimeStudents(), 0.05);
}

private Student createFullTimeStudent() {
    Student student = new Student("a");
    student.addCredits(Student.CREDITS_REQUIRED_FOR_FULL_TIME);
    return student;
}
```

The implementation (in Session) demonstrates use of the continue statement to skip students that are not part-time.

```
double averageGpaForPartTimeStudents() {
    double total = 0.0;
    int count = 0;
    for (Student student: students) {
        if (student.isFullTime())
            continue;
        count++;
        total += student.getGpa();
    }
    if (count == 0) return 0.0;
    return total / count;
}
```

You can easily rewrite this (and most) uses of continue using if-else statements. Sometimes the use of continue provides the more-elegant, easy-to-read presentation.

Labeled break and continue Statements

The labeled break and continue statements allow you to transfer control when you have more complex nesting.

The first example tests a labeled break. Don't let the interesting declaration of table scare you. List<List<Integer>> declares a list into which you can put lists bound to the Integer type.

```
public void testLabeledBreak() {
    List<List<String>> table = new ArrayList<List<String>>();

    List<String> row1 = new ArrayList<String>();
    row1.add("5");
    row1.add("2");
    List<String> row2 = new ArrayList<String>();
    row2.add("3");
    row2.add("4");

    table.add(row1);
    table.add(row2);
    assertTrue(found(table, "3"));
```

```
      assertFalse(found(table, "8"));
}

private boolean found(List<List<String>> table, String target) {
   boolean found = false;
   search:
   for (List<String> row: table) {
      for (String value: row) {
         if (value.equals(target)) {
            found = true;
            break search;
         }
      }
   }
   return found;
}
```

If you did not associate the search label with the break statement in this example, Java would break out of only the innermost for loop (the one with the expression Integer num: row). Instead, the break statement causes looping to terminate from the search label, representing the outermost loop in this example.

The labeled continue statement works similarly, except the Java VM transfers control to the loop with the label instead of breaking from the loop with the label.

There are few situations where your solution will require labeled break or continue statements. In most cases, you can easily restructure code to eliminate them, either by use of if-else statements or, even better, by decomposition of methods into smaller, more composed methods. Use the labeled statements only when the solution is easier to comprehend.

The Ternary Operator

Lesson 5 introduced the if statement. Often you want to assign a value to a variable or return a value from a method based on the results of an if conditional. For example:

```
String message =
   "the course has " + getText(sessions) + " sessions";
...
private String getText(int sessions) {
   if (sessions == 1)
      return "one";
   return "many";
}
```

For simple conditional expressions that must return a new value, Java provides a shortcut form known as the *ternary operator*. The ternary operator compacts the if-else statement into a single expression. The general form of the ternary operator is:

```
conditional ? true-value : false-value
```

If conditional returns the value true, the result of the entire expression is true-value. Otherwise the result of the entire expression is false-value. Using the ternary operator, you can rewrite the previous code to produce a message as:

```
String message =
    "the course has " + (sessions == 1 ? "one" : "many") + " sessions";
```

If the value of sessions is 1, the parenthesized ternary expression returns the String "one", otherwise it returns "many". This result string is then used as part of the larger string concatenation.

The ternary operator is a holdover from the language C. Do not use the ternary operator as a general replacement for the if statement! The best use of the ternary operator is for simple, single-line expressions like the one shown here. If you have more complex needs, or if the code won't fit on a single line, you're better off using an if statement. Abuse of the ternary operator can result in cryptic code that is more costly to maintain.

Legacy Collections

Prior to the SDK version 1.2, there was no collections "framework" in Java. Java contained two main workhorse collections—java.util.Vector and java.util.Hashtable[6]—that still exist today. The analogous classes in modern Java are respectively java.util.ArrayList and java.util.HashMap. The class java.util.HashMap provides similar functionality as the class java.util.Enum Map, with which you are already familiar. Refer to Lesson 9 for more information on HashMap.

Both Vector and Hashtable are concrete; they implement no common interfaces. They incorporate support for multithreaded programming[7] by default, a choice that often results in unnecessary overhead. Unfortunately, today you will still encounter a large amount of code that uses or requires use of the Vector class.

[6]There were only two other collection classes: BitSit and Stack (a subclass of Vector). Both were minimally useful.

[7]See Lesson 13 for a discussion of multithreaded programming.

Since there were no corresponding interfaces for these classes in the initial versions of Java, you were forced to assign Vector or Hashtable instances to a reference to an implementation class:

```
Vector names = new Vector();
```

With the introduction of the collections framework, Sun retrofitted the Vector class to implement the List interface and the Hashtable class to implement the Map interface. You might for some reason be stuck with continuing to use a Vector or Hashtable. If so, you may be able to migrate to a modern approach by assigning the instance to an interface reference:

```
List names = new Vector();
Map dictionary = new Hashtable();
```

Sun also retrofitted Vector and Hashtable so that they are parameterized types. You can thus code:

```
List<String> names = new Vector<String>();
Map<Student.Grade,String> dictionary =
    new Hashtable<Student.Grade,String>();
```

Iterators

You have learned to use the for-each loop to iterate through each element in a collection. This form of the for loop is a new construct, introduced in J2SE 5.0.

Prior to the for-each loop, the preferred way to iterate through a collection was to ask it for a java.util.Iterator object. An Iterator object maintains an internal pointer to an element in the collection. You can ask an iterator to return the next available element in the collection. After returning an element from the collection, an Iterator advances its internal pointer to refer to the next available element. You can also ask an iterator whether or not there are more elements in a collection.

As an example, rewrite the averageGpaForPartTimeStudents method shown earlier in this lesson to use an Iterator object and a for loop instead of a for-each loop:

Iterators

```
double averageGpaForPartTimeStudents() {
    double total = 0.0;
    int count = 0;

    for (Iterator<Student> it = students.iterator();
         it.hasNext(); ) {
      Student student = it.next();
```

```
        if (student.isFullTime())
            continue;
        count++;
        total += student.getGpa();
    }
    if (count == 0) return 0.0;
    return total / count;
}
```

You usually obtain an Iterator by sending the message iterator to the collection. You assign the Iterator object to an Iterator reference that you bind to the type of object stored within the collection. Here, you bind the Iterator to the type Student, which is what the students collection stores.

The Iterator interface defines three methods: hasNext, next, and remove (which is optional and infrequently needed). The hasNext method returns true if there are any elements remaining in the collection that have not yet been returned. The next method returns the next available element from the collection and advances the internal pointer.

The legacy collections Vector and Hashtable use an analogous technique known as enumeration. The solution is virtually the same, only the names are different. Redefine the students instance variable in Session to be a Vector.

```
package sis.studentinfo;

import java.util.*;

abstract public class Session
      implements Comparable<Session> {
   ...
   private Vector<Student> students = new Vector<Student>();

   double averageGpaForPartTimeStudents() {
      double total = 0.0;
      int count = 0;

      for (Enumeration<Student> it = students.elements();
           it.hasMoreElements(); ) {
         Student student = it.nextElement();
         if (student.isFullTime())
            continue;
         count++;
         total += student.getGpa();
      }
      if (count == 0) return 0.0;
      return total / count;
   }
}
```

Iterators

Instead of asking for an Iterator using the iterator method, you ask for an Enumeration by using the elements method. You test whether there are more elements available using hasMoreElements instead of hasNext. You retrieve the next element using nextElement instead of next. Sun introduced the Iterator in response to many complaints about the unnecessary verbosity of the class name Enumeration and its method names.

Since Vector implements the List interface, you can send a Vector the iterator message to obtain an Iterator instead of an Enumeration.

Revert your Session code to use modern collections and the for-each loop.

Iterators and the **for-each** Loop

The for-each loop construct is built upon the Iterator construct. In order to be able to loop through a collection, the collection must be able to return an Iterator object when sent the iterator message. The for-each loop recognizes whether a collection is iterable or not by seeing if the collection implements the java.lang.Iterable interface.

In this upcoming example, you will modify the Session class to support iterating through its collection of students.

Code the following test in SessionTest:

```
public void testIterate() {
   enrollStudents(session);

   List<Student> results = new ArrayList<Student>();
   for (Student student: session)
      results.add(student);

   assertEquals(session.getAllStudents(), results);
}

private void enrollStudents(Session session) {
   session.enroll(new Student("1"));
   session.enroll(new Student("2"));
   session.enroll(new Student("3"));
}
```

When you compile, you will receive an error, since Session does not yet support the ability to be iterated over.

```
foreach not applicable to expression type
        for (Student student: session)
                  ^
```

You must change the Session class to implement the Iterable interface. Since you want the for-each loop to recognize that it is iterating over a collection containing only Student types, you must bind the Iterable interface to the Student type.

```
abstract public class Session
      implements Comparable<Session>, Iterable<Student> {
// ...
```

Now you only need to implement the iterator method in Session. Since Session merely encapsulates an ArrayList of students, there is no reason that the iterator method can't simply return the ArrayList's Iterator object.

```
public Iterator<Student> iterator() {
   return students.iterator();
}
```

Casting

The need for *casting* of references occurs when *you*, the programmer, know that an object is of a certain type but the compiler couldn't possibly know what the type is. Casting allows you to tell the compiler that it can safely assign an object of one type to a reference of a different type.

Sun's introduction of parameterized types removed much of the need for casting in Java. Prior to J2SE 5.0, since the collection classes in Java did not support parameterized types, everything that went into a collection had to go in as an Object reference, as shown by the signature for the add method in the List interface:

```
public boolean add(Object o)
```

Since everything went *in* as an Object, you could only retrieve it as an Object:

```
public Object get(int index)
```

You, the developer, knew you were stuffing Student objects into a collection, but the collection could only store Object references to the Students. When you went to retrieve the objects from the collection, you knew that the collection stored Student objects. This meant that you typically cast the Object references back to Student references as you retrieved them from the collection.

To cast, precede a target expression with the reference type that you want to cast it to, in parentheses:

```
Student student = (Student)students.get(0);
```

In this example, the target is the result of the entire expression students.get(0). You could have parenthesized the target to be more explicit:

```
(Student)(students.get(0));
```

Note the absence of any spaces between the cast and the target. While you may interject spaces between a cast and its target, the more commonly accepted style specifies no spaces.

It is important to understand that casting does nothing to change the target object. The cast to Student type only creates a new reference to the same memory location. Since this new reference is of type Student, the Java compiler will then allow you to send Student-specific messages to the object via the reference. Without casting, you would only be able to send messages defined in Object to the Student object.

Using parameterized types, there are few reasons to cast object references. If you find yourself casting, determine if there is a way to avoid casting by using parameterized types.

As an exercise, the following test demonstrates the "old way" of iterating through a collection—without a for-each loop and without parameterized types. Note that this code will still work under J2SE 5.0, although you may receive warnings because you are not using the parameterized collection types.

```
public void testCasting() {
    List students = new ArrayList();
    students.add(new Student("a"));
    students.add(new Student("b"));

    List names = new ArrayList();

    Iterator it = students.iterator();
    while (it.hasNext()) {
        Student student = (Student)it.next();
        names.add(student.getLastName());
    }

    assertEquals("a", names.get(0));
    assertEquals("b", names.get(1));
}
```

Casting

Casting Primitive Types

You cannot cast primitive types to reference types or vice versa.

There is another form of casting that you will still need to use in order to convert numeric types. I will discuss numeric conversion in Lesson 10 on mathematics.

Wrapper Classes

 The student system must store student charges in a collection to be totaled later. Each charge is an int that represents the number of cents a student spent on an item.

Remember that primitive types are not objects—they do not inherit from the class java.lang.Object. The java.util.List interface only supplies an add method that takes a reference type as a argument. It does not supply overloaded add methods for each of the primitive types.

In order to store the int charge in a collection, then, you must convert it to an object. You accomplish this by storing the int in a *wrapper* object.

For each primitive type, java.lang defines a corresponding wrapper class.[8]

Type	Wrapper Class
char	Character
byte	Byte
short	Short
int	Integer
long	Long
float	Float
double	Double
boolean	Boolean

Each wrapper class provides a constructor that takes a primitive of the appropriate type as argument. The wrapper stores this primitive and allows for extracting it using a corresponding getter method. In the case of the Integer wrapper, you extract the original int by sending the message intValue to the wrapper.

A test (in StudentTest) for the example:

```
public void testCharges() {
    Student student = new Student("a");
    student.addCharge(500);
    student.addCharge(200);
    student.addCharge(399);
    assertEquals(1099, student.totalCharges());
}
```

[8]The table lists all available primitive types and corresponding wrappers. You will learn more about the unfamiliar types in Lesson 10.

If you had to write the implementation using pre-J2SE 5.0 code, it would look something like this:

```
public class Student implements Comparable {
   ...
   private List charges = new ArrayList();
   ...
   public void addCharge(int charge) {
      charges.add(new Integer(charge));
   }

   public int totalCharges() {
      int total = 0;
      Iterator it = charges.iterator();
      while (it.hasNext()) {
         Integer charge = (Integer)it.next();
         total += charge.intValue();
      }
      return total;
   }
   ...
```

The addCharge method shows how you would wrap the int in an instance of the Integer wrapper class in order to pass it to the add method of the charges collection. When iterating through the collection (in totalCharges), you would have to cast each retrieved Object to the Integer wrapper class. Only then would you be able to extract the original int value through use of the intValue method.

J2SE 5.0 simplifies the code through the use of parameterized types and the for-each loop.

```
public class Student implements Comparable<Student> {
   ...
   private List<Integer> charges = new ArrayList<Integer>();
   ...
   public void addCharge(int charge) {
      charges.add(new Integer(charge));
   }

   public int totalCharges() {
      int total = 0;
      for (Integer charge: charges)
         total += charge.intValue();
      return total;
   }
   ...
```

Wrapper Classes

In addition to allowing you to wrap a primitive, the wrapper classes provide many class methods that operate on primitives. Without the wrapper classes, these methods would have nowhere to go. You have already used the Character class method isWhitespace.

A further simplification of the code comes about from one of the new J2SE 5.0 features, autoboxing.

Autoboxing and Autounboxing

Autoboxing is the compiler's ability to automatically wrap, or "box" a primitive type in its corresponding wrapper class. Autoboxing only occurs when Java can find no method with a matching signature. A signature match occurs when the name and arguments of a message send match a method defined on the class of the object to which the message is being sent. An argument is considered to match if the types match exactly or if the type of the argument is a subtype of the argument type as declared in the method.

As an example, if Box declares a method as:

```
void add(List list) { ... }
```

then any of the following message sends will resolve to this add method:

```
Box b = new Box();
b.add(new List());
b.add(new ArrayList());
```

The second add message send works because ArrayList is a subclass of List.

If Java finds no direct signature match, it attempts to find a signature match based on wrapping. Any method with an Object argument in the appropriate place is a match.

In the addCharge method, the explicit wrapping of the int into an Integer is no longer necessary:

```
public void addCharge(int charge) {
   charges.add(charge);
}
```

It is important for you to understand that the wrapping does occur behind the scenes. Java creates a new Integer instance for each primitive value you wrap.

Autoboxing only occurs on arguments. It would be nice if autoboxing occurred anywhere you attempted to send a message to a primitive. This is not yet a capability, but it would allow expressions like:

```
6.toString() // this does not work
```

Auto*un*boxing occurs when you attempt to use a wrapped primitive anywhere a primitive is expected. This is demonstrated in the following two tests:

```
public void testUnboxing() {
    int x = new Integer(5);
    assertEquals(5, x);
}

public void testUnboxingMath() {
    assertEquals(10, new Integer(2) * new Integer(5));
}
```

The more useful application of autounboxing is when you extract elements from a collection bound to a primitive wrapper type. With both autoboxing and autounboxing, the charge code in Student becomes:

```
public void addCharge(int charge) {
    charges.add(charge);
}

public int totalCharges() {
    int total = 0;
    for (int charge: charges)
        total += charge;
    return total;
}
```

You will learn about addition capabilities of wrapper classes in Lesson 10 on mathematics.

Arrays

I have mentioned arrays several times in this book. An array is a fixed-size, contiguous set of slots in memory. Unlike an ArrayList or other collection object, an array can fill up, preventing you from adding more elements. The only way to add elements to a full array is to create a second larger array and copy all elements from the first array to the second array.

Java provides special syntactical support for arrays. Indirectly, you have been using arrays all along, in the form of the class ArrayList. An ArrayList stores all elements you add to it in a Java array. The ArrayList class also encapsulates the tedium of having to grow the array when you add too many elements.

Arrays

The example here creates a new class named Performance, which CourseSession might use to track test scores for each student. The Performance class allows calculating the average across all tests.

```
package sis.studentinfo;

import junit.framework.*;

public class PerformanceTest extends TestCase {
    private static final double tolerance = 0.005;
    public void testAverage() {
        Performance performance = new Performance();
        performance.setNumberOfTests(4);
        performance.set(0, 98);
        performance.set(1, 92);
        performance.set(2, 81);
        performance.set(3, 72);

        assertEquals(92, performance.get(1));

        assertEquals(85.75, performance.average(), tolerance);
    }
}
```

The Performance class:

```
package sis.studentinfo;

public class Performance {
    private int[] tests;
    public void setNumberOfTests(int numberOfTests) {
        tests = new int[numberOfTests];
    }

    public void set(int testNumber, int score) {
        tests[testNumber] = score;
    }

    public int get(int testNumber) {
        return tests[testNumber];
    }

    public double average() {
        double total = 0.0;
        for (int score: tests)
            total += score;
        return total / tests.length;
    }
}
```

Arrays

You store the scores for the tests in an int array named tests:

```
private int[] tests;
```

This declaration only says that the instance variable tests is of type int[] (you read this as "int array"). The braces are the indicator that this is an array. You use the braces to *subscript*, or index, the array. By subscripting the array, you tell Java the index of the element with which you wish to work.

Java allows you to declare an array with the braces following the variable.

```
private int tests[]; // don't declare arrays this way
```

Avoid this construct. Use of it will brand you as a C/C++ programmer (a fate worse than death in Java circles).

Neither of the two array declarations above allocate any memory. You will receive an error[9] if you reference any of its (nonexistent) elements.

When a Performance client calls setNumberOfTests, the assignment statement initializes the test array.

```
public void setNumberOfTests(int numberOfTests) {
    tests = new int[numberOfTests];
}
```

You allocate an array using the new keyword. After the new keyword, you specify the type (int in this example) that the array will hold and the number of slots to allocate (numberOfTests).

Once you initialize an array, you can set a value into any of its slots. The type of the value must match the type of the array. For example, you can only set int values into an int[].

```
public void set(int testNumber, int score) {
    tests[testNumber] = score;
}
```

The line of code in set assigns the value of score to the slot in the tests array that corresponds to the testNumber. Indexing of arrays is 0-based. The first slot is slot #0, the second slot #1, and so on.

The get method demonstrates accessing an element in an array at a particular index:

```
public int get(int testNumber) {
    return tests[testNumber];
}
```

You can iterate an array like any other collection by using a for-each loop.

```
public double average() {
    double total = 0.0;
    for (int score: tests)
```

Arrays

---

[9]Specifically, a NullPointerException. See Lesson 8 for more information on exceptions.

```
      total += score;
   return total / tests.length;
}
```

The `average` method also shows how you may access the number of elements in an array by using a special variable named `length`.

You can iterate an array using a classic `for` loop:

```
public double average() {
   double total = 0.0;
   for (int i = 0; i < tests.length; i++)
      total += tests[i];
   return total / tests.length;
}
```

You may declare an array as any type, reference or primitive. You might have an instance variable representing an array of Students:

```
private Student[] students;
```

Array Initialization

When you allocate an array, Java initializes its elements to the default value for the type. Java initializes all slots in an array of numerics to `0`, to `false` in an array of booleans, and to `null` in an array of references.

Java provides special array initialization syntax that you can use at the time of array instantiation and/or declaration.

```
public void testInitialization() {
   Performance performance = new Performance();
   performance.setScores(75, 72, 90, 60);
   assertEquals(74.25, performance.average(), tolerance);
}
```

The `setScores` method passes each of the four score arguments into an *array initializer.*

Arrays

```
public void setScores(int score1, int score2, int score3, int score4) {
   tests = new int[] { score1, score2, score3, score4 };
}
```

The array initializer in this example produces an array with four slots, each populated with an `int` value.

A shortcut that you can use as part of an array declaration assignment statement is:

```
int[] values = { 1, 2, 3 };
```

You may terminate the list of values in an array initializer with a comma. The Java compiler ignores the final comma (it does not create an additional slot in the array). For example, the preceding declaration and initialization is equivalent to:

```
int[] values = {
  1,
  2,
  3,
};
assertEquals(3, values.length);
```

I coded the initialization on multiple lines to help demonstrate why this feature might be useful. It allows you to freely add to, remove from, and move elements around in the array initialization. You need not worry about leaving a comma after the last element; you can terminate each element with a comma.

When to Use Arrays

Prefer use of Java reference-type collections over native arrays. Your code will be simpler, closer to pure OO, and more flexible. It is easy to replace an ArrayList with a LinkedList, but it can be very costly to have to replace a native array with a LinkedList.

Some situations will force you into using arrays. Many existing APIs either return arrays or require arrays as arguments.

There are circumstances where arrays are more appropriate. Many mathematical algorithms and constructs (matrices, for example) are better implemented with arrays.

Accessing an element in an array is a matter of knowing which numbered slot it's in, multiplying by the slot size, and adding to some memory offset. The pseudo–memory diagram in Figure 7.1 shows a three-element int array. Java stores the starting location of the array in this example as 0x100. To access the third element of the array (x[2]), Java calculates the new memory location as:

```
0x100 starting address + 2nd slot * 4 bytes per slot
```

Each slot requires four bytes, since it takes four bytes to represent an int.[10] The result is the address 0x108, where the element 55 can be found.

---

[10]Java stores primitive types directly in the array. An array of objects would store a contiguous list of references to *other* locations in memory.

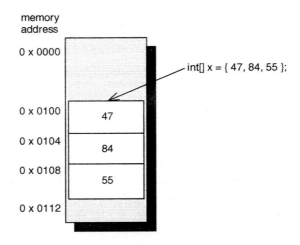

memory
address

0 x 0000

int[] x = { 47, 84, 55 };

0 x 0100   47

0 x 0104   84

0 x 0108   55

0 x 0112

Figure 7.1 *An Array in Memory*

If you need the absolute fastest performance possible, an array provides a performance improvement over a collection class. However, prefer the use of collection classes over arrays. Always measure performance before arbitrarily converting use of a collection class to an array.

 Prefer object-oriented collections over arrays.

Varargs

If you want to pass a variable number of similar-typed arguments to a method, you must first combine them into a collection. The setScores method above is restricted to four test scores; you would like to be able to pass any number of scores into a Performance object. Prior to J2SE 5.0, a standard idiom for doing so was to declare a new array on the fly:

Arrays

```
public void testArrayParm() {
    Performance performance = new Performance();
    performance.setScores(new int[] { 75, 72, 90, 60 });
    assertEquals(74.25, performance.average(), tolerance);
}
```

The setScores method can then store the array directly:

```
public void setScores(int[] tests) {
    this.tests = tests;
}
```

You might try to use the shorter array declaration/initialization syntax:

```
performance.setScores({ 75, 72, 90, 60 }); // this will not compile
```

but Java does not allow it.

J2SE 5.0 allows you to specify that a method takes a variable number of arguments. The arguments must appear at the end of the method argument list and must all be of the same type.

You declare the variability of a parameter with ellipses (...). Programmers familiar with C refer to this as a *varargs* declaration.

```
public void setScores(int... tests) {
   this.tests = tests;
}
```

Method calls to setScores can now have a variable number of test scores:

```
public void testVariableMethodParms() {
   Performance performance = new Performance();
   performance.setScores(75, 72, 90, 60);
   assertEquals(74.25, performance.average(), tolerance);

   performance.setScores(100, 90);
   assertEquals(95.0, performance.average(), tolerance);
}
```

When you execute a Java application, the VM passes command-line arguments to the main method as an array of String objects:

```
public static void main(String[] args)
```

You can declare the main method too as:

```
public static void main(String... args)
```

Multidimensional Arrays

Java also supports arrays of arrays, also known as multidimensional arrays. A classic use of multidimensional arrays is to represent matrices. You can create arrays that have up to 255 dimensions, but you will probably never need more than 3 dimensions. The following language test demonstrates how you allocate, populate, and access a two-dimensional array.

```
// 0 1  2  3
// 4 5  6  7
// 8 9 10 11
public void testTwoDimensionalArrays() {
   final int rows = 3;
   final int cols = 4;
   int count = 0;
```

Arrays

```
    int[][] matrix = new int[rows][cols];
    for (int x = 0; x < rows; x++)
        for (int y = 0; y < cols; y++)
            matrix[x][y] = count++;
    assertEquals(11, matrix[2][3]);
    assertEquals(6, matrix[1][2]);
}
```

You do not need to allocate all dimensions at once. You can allocate dimensions starting at the left, leaving the rightmost dimensions unspecified. Later, you can allocate these rightmost dimensions. In `testPartialDimensions`, the code initially allocates `matrix` as an `int` array of three rows. Subsequently, it allocates each slot in the rows portion of the array to differing-sized `int` arrays of columns.

```
// 0
// 1 2
// 3 4 5
public void testPartialDimensions() {
    final int rows = 3;
    int[][] matrix = new int[rows][];
    matrix[0] = new int[]{ 0 };
    matrix[1] = new int[]{ 1, 2 };
    matrix[2] = new int[]{ 3, 4, 5 };
    assertEquals(1, matrix[1][0]);
    assertEquals(5, matrix[2][2]);
}
```

As shown in `testPartialDimensions`, Java does not restrict you to rectangular multidimensional arrays; you can make them *jagged*.

You can initialize multidimensional arrays using array initialization syntax. The following initialization produces an array that is equivalent to the array initialized by `testPartialDimensions`:

```
int[][] matrix2 = { { 0 }, { 1, 2 }, { 3, 4, 5 } };
```

The Arrays Class

Arrays

Since arrays are not objects, you cannot send messages to them. You can access the variable `length` to determine the size of an array, but Java provides it as special syntax.

The class java.util.Arrays gives you a number of class methods to perform common operations on arrays. Using the Arrays class, you can do the following with a single-dimensional array:

- perform binary searches (which assumes the array is in sorted order) (`binarySearch`)

- sort it (sort)

- convert it to an object that implements the List interface (asList)

- compare it to another single-dimensional array of the same type (equals)

- obtain a hash code (see Lesson 9) (hashCode)

- fill each of its elements, or a subrange of its elements, with a specified value (fill)

- obtain a printable representation of the array (toString)

I'll discuss the equals method in more depth. For more information about the other methods, refer to the Java API documentation for more information on java.util.Arrays.

Arrays.equals

An array is a reference type, regardless of whether you declare it to contain primitives or references. If you create two separate arrays, the Java VM will store them in separate memory locations. This means that comparing the two arrays with == will result in false.

```
public void testArrayEquality() {
    int[] a = { 1, 2, 3 };
    int[] b = { 1, 2, 3 };
    assertFalse(a == b);
}
```

Since an array is a reference, you can compare two arrays using the equals method. But even if you allocate both arrays to exactly same dimensions and populate them with exactly the same contents, the comparison will return false.

```
public void testArrayEquals() {
    int[] a = { 1, 2, 3 };
    int[] b = { 1, 2, 3 };
    assertFalse(a.equals(b));
}
```

You can use the Arrays.equals method to compare the contents, not the memory location, of two arrays.

```
public void testArraysEquals() {
    int[] a = { 1, 2, 3 };
    int[] b = { 1, 2, 3 };
    assertTrue(Arrays.equals(a, b));
}
```

Arrays

Refactoring

Splitting a String

While either the hand-coded while loop or for loop in the Student method split will work, the resulting code is fairly complex. Java provides at least two more ways to break apart String objects into tokens. First, you will learn how to use the StringTokenizer class to break an input string into individual components, or *tokens*. The StringTokenizer class is considered a legacy class, meaning that Sun wants you to supplant its use with something better. That something better is the split method, defined on String. Once you have coded the solution using StringTokenizer, you will recode it to use String.split.

Up until Java 1.4, Sun recommended the StringTokenizer as the solution for tokenizing strings. You will still encounter a lot of code that uses String-Tokenizer; that's why you'll learn it here. In Java 1.4, Sun introduced the regular expressions API. Regular expressions are specifications for pattern-matching against text. A robust, standardized language defines the patterns you can express with regular expressions. The newer String.split method uses a regular expression, making it far more effective than the StringTokenizer solution. For more information about the regular expressions API, see Additional Lesson III.

The constructor for the class java.util.StringTokenizer takes as parameters an input String and a String representing a list of character delimiters. String-Tokenizer then breaks the input String into tokens, allowing you to iterate through each token in turn. The while loop provides the best mechanism for traversing these tokens:

```
private List<String> split(String name) {
   List<String> results = new ArrayList<String>();
   StringTokenizer tokenizer = new StringTokenizer(name, " ");
   while (tokenizer.hasMoreTokens())
     results.add(tokenizer.nextToken());
   return results;
}
```

Sending the message hasMoreTokens to a StringTokenizer returns false once there are no more tokens. The message nextToken returns the next token available. The StringTokenizer code uses the list of delimiters to determine what separates tokens. The example here uses only the space character to delineate tokens.

Splitting a String: `String.split`

The String class contains a `split` method that makes the job of tokenizing a full name even simpler than using StringTokenizer. Using `String.split` would allow you to eliminate your entire `Student.split` method with one line of code.

Here is a stab at the refactoring:

```java
public Student(String fullName) {
    this.name = fullName;
    credits = 0;
    List<String> nameParts = split(fullName);
    setName(nameParts);
}

private List<String> split(String name) {
    return Arrays.asList(name.split(" "));  // this doesn't work!
}

private void setName(List<String> nameParts) {
    this.lastName = removeLast(nameParts);
    String name = removeLast(nameParts);
    if (nameParts.isEmpty())
        this.firstName = name;
    else {
        this.middleName = name;
        this.firstName = removeLast(nameParts);
    }
}

private String removeLast(List<String> list) {
    if (list.isEmpty())
        return "";
    return list.remove(list.size() - 1);
}
```

Part of your goal should be to make changes with as little impact to other code as possible. The single line of code that now appears in your `split` method seems like it should do the trick:

```java
return Arrays.asList(name.split(" "));  // this doesn't work!
```

The `split` method takes a single parameter, the list of characters that represent word boundaries. It returns an array of words. The Arrays class method `asList` takes an array and returns a List representation of that array.

One would think that this line of code would be a suitable replacement for the previous code that constructed the list using StringTokenizer. But it doesn't work. You will receive many JUnit errors indicating that the `remove` call

Refactoring

in your removeLast method now generates something known as an Unsupport-edOperationException.

The problem is in the Arrays method asList. According to the Java API documentation for asList, it returns a list *backed by* the array you pass as parameter. The list is a view onto the array, which does not go away. The list reflects any changes you make to the array.

Since the list is backed by an array, and since you cannot remove elements from an array, Java prohibits the remove call.

A solution that will work is to iterate through the results of split using a for-each loop. As with the StringTokenizer solution, you can add each word to a results array.

```
private List<String> split(String fullName) {
   List<String> results = new ArrayList<String>();
   for (String name: fullName.split(" "))
      results.add(name);
   return results;
}
```

The split method uses a Java feature known as *regular expressions*. A regular expression is a set of syntactical elements and symbols that is used to match text. You have likely used a simple form of regular expression when listing files in a directory. You use the asterisk (*) as a wildcard symbol to match any sequence of characters in a filename. See Additional Lesson III for an overview of the powerful regular expressions feature.

Exercises

1. To see the different loop types in action, code the factorial algorithm (without using recursion). The definition of factorial:

   ```
   if n is 0, n factorial = 1.
   if n is 1, n factorial = 1.
   if n is greater than one, n factorial is 1 * 2 * 3 * ... up to n
   ```

   Code the tests, then create a factorial method using a while loop. Next, modify the same method to pass the tests without using the while keyword, but instead using the C-style for loop. Finally, recode it again using the do-while loop. Notice the changes you must make in order to use the different loop structures. Also note that you only need one loop structure to solve any looping problem.
   a) Why would you prefer one loop structure over the others?
   b) Which is shortest?

c) Which is the most appropriate to this problem? Why?

d) Replace the loop with

```
while (true) {
```

and get the test to pass using the break keyword to end the loop.

2. Demonstrate your understanding of the continue keyword. Create a method to return a string containing the numbers from 1 to *n*. Separate each pair of numbers with a single space. Append an asterisk to the numbers divisible by five. For example, setting *n* to 12 would result in the string:

```
"1 2 3 4 5* 6 7 8 9 10* 11 12".
```

3. a) Break the results of the string from the previous exercise into a Vector of substrings. Split the string on the space character. The string "1 2 3 4 5* 6 7" would split into a Vector containing the strings "1", "2", "3", "4", "5*", "6", and "7".

b) Iterate through the elements of the vector using an Enumeration and recreate the string from Exercise #2.

c) Remove all parameterized type information, note the compiler errors, and correct the code where necessary.

4. In an earlier exercise, you wrote a test to ensure that the list of valid moves for a given piece contained a set of squares. Simplify this assertion to something like:

```
public void testKingMoveNotOnEdge() {
    Piece piece = Piece.createBlackKing();
    board.put("d3", piece);
    assertContains(piece.getPossibleMoves("d3", board),
        "c4", "d4", "e4", "c3", "e3", "c2", "d2", "e2");
}
```

Refactor other tests to use this mechanism.

5. You may have noticed that the chess board you have spent so much time on is really a two-dimensional array of squares. Back up your Board class. Modify Board to use a two-dimensional array as its underlying data structure.

One bit of difficulty you may encounter is due to the fact that client code (such as Game and Pawn) uses the implementation specifics of the board. For this exercise, modify the client code to loop through the ranks and files of the two-dimensional array. This is a less-than-ideal situation: Normally you want to design a solid public interface to your class, one that does not change. When you change the implementation details of the Board class, the Game class should not be affected.

The alternative would be to dynamically convert the Piece two-dimensional array to a List of List of Piece objects each time a client

Exercises

wanted to iterate through it. But the best solution is to not require the client to do the iteration themselves. One sophisticated (and somewhat complex) solution to accomplish this involves the visitor design pattern. See the book *Design Patterns*[11] for further information. For now, exposing the board's underlying two-dimensional array will suffice.

Compare and contrast the two Board versions. Which is easier to read and understand? Which involves the least code?

6. Make the Board class iterable, so that you can access the pieces (not including "no piece" objects) using a for-each loop. A complex solution would involve creating a separate Iterator class that tracks both a rank and file index. A simpler solution would involve looping through the board's matrix and adding each piece to a List object. You could then return the iterator from the List object.

Once you have made the class iterable, go back and change any code that loops through all pieces to use a for-each loop. Look for opportunities to refactor code so that you use the for-each loop as much as possible. For example, if you haven't already, modify your code so that each Piece object stores its current rank and file.

7. Read the javadoc API for the ArrayList class and determine a way to simplify the last example in the chapter—the one that splits the student name and returns a List of name parts. It is possible to recode the split method without the use of a loop at all! Hint: Look at the constructors for ArrayList.

Exercises

[11][Gamma1995].

Lesson 8

Exceptions and Logging

In this lesson you will learn about exceptions and logging. Exceptions in Java are a transfer control mechanism. You generate exceptions to signal problematic conditions in your code. You write code to either acknowledge or handle exceptions that are generated.

Java provides a flexible logging facility that allows you to record information as your application executes. You might choose to log exceptions, interesting occurrences, or events that you want to track.

Things you will learn include:

- the try-catch block

- checked vs. unchecked (runtime) exceptions

- errors vs. exceptions

- the throws clause

- the exception hierarchy

- creating your own exception type

- exception messages

- working with multiple exceptions

- rethrowing exceptions

- working with the stack trace

- the finally block

- the Formatter classes

- the Java logging API

- logging to files

- logging handlers

Exceptions and Logging

269

- logging properties
- logging hierarchies

Exceptions

In Lesson 4, you saw how your code generated a NullPointerException when you did something with a variable that was not properly initialized.

Exceptions are objects that represent exceptional conditions in code. You can create an Exception object and *throw* it. If you are aware that there might be exceptions, you can write code that explicitly deals with, or *catches*, them. Or, you can declare that your code chooses to not deal with exceptions, and let someone else handle the problem.

A thrown exception represents a transfer of control. You may throw an exception at any point in code; other APIs may similarly throw exceptions at any time. The VM may also throw exceptions. From the point the exception is thrown, the Java VM transfers control to the first place that deals with, or catches, the exception. If no code catches the exception, the result is abnormal program termination.[1]

 You will ultimately need to build a user interface that allows for entry of test scores for students in a session. The user interface is where anything can go wrong: a user can type a number that is too large, they can type nothing, or they can type garbage. Your job will be to deal with invalid input as soon as it is typed in.

Test scores typed into the user interface come in as String objects. You will need to convert these strings into ints. To do so, you can use the Integer wrapper class utility method named parseInt. The parseInt method takes a String as a number and attempts to convert it to a number. If successful, parseInt returns the appropriate int. If the source String contains invalid input, the code in parseInt throws a NumberFormatException.

Start with a simple test representing a successful case:

```
package sis.studentinfo;

import junit.framework.TestCase;

public class ScorerTest extends TestCase {
    public void testCaptureScore() {
        Scorer scorer = new Scorer();
        assertEquals(75, scorer.score("75"));
    }
}
```

---

[1]This is not necessarily the case when your application is executing multiple threads. See the lesson on threading.

Get this to pass:

```
package sis.studentinfo;

public class Scorer {
    public int score(String input) {
        return Integer.parseInt(input);
    }
}
```

Then write a second test that shows what happens when invalid input is passed to the score method:

```
public void testBadScoreEntered() {
    Scorer scorer = new Scorer();
    scorer.score("abd");
}
```

This isn't the complete test, but it will demonstrate what happens when code throws an exception. Compile the code and run the tests. JUnit will report an error instead of a test failure. An error means that code within the test (or, of course, code that the test called) generated an exception that was not handled. The exception's stack trace appears in the details window in JUnit, showing that the Integer class generated a NumberFormatException.

You want your test to demonstrate that the score method generates an exception when clients pass invalid input to it. The test case documents a case for which you expect to get an exception. Thus, you want the test to pass if the exception occurs and fail if it does not.

Java provides a construct called a try-catch block that you use to trap exceptions. The standard form of a try-catch block contains two blocks of code. The try block consists of code that might throw an exception. The catch block contains code to execute *if* an exception is generated.

```
public void testBadScoreEntered() {
    Scorer scorer = new Scorer();
    try {
        scorer.score("abd");
        fail("expected NumberFormatException on bad input");
    }
    catch (NumberFormatException success) {
    }
}
```

The code in testBadScoreEntered presents the most common idiom used when testing for exceptions. The try block wraps the score message send, since it is the code that could generate the NumberFormatException. If the code in score generates an exception, the Java VM immediately transfers control from the point the exception was thrown to the catch block.

Exceptions

If execution of the code in score does not raise an exception, control proceeds normally and Java executes the next statement in the try block. In testBadScoreEntered, the next statement is a call to the JUnit method fail. ScorerTest inherits fail (indirectly) from junit.framework.TestCase. Execution of fail immediately halts the test method; the VM executes no more of its code. JUnit reports the test method as a failure. Calling fail is equivalent to calling assertTrue(false) (or assertFalse(true)).

You expect score to generate an exception. If it does not, something has gone wrong, and you want to fail the test. If score does generate an exception, the fail statement is skipped, since the VM transfers control to the catch block.

The catch block is empty. Tests are about the only place where your catch blocks should ever be empty. Normally, you want to deal with a trapped exception somehow. You would do this in the catch block. In this lesson, I will present you with options for managing a caught exception.

In testBadScoreEntered, receiving an exception is a good thing. You document that by naming the NumberFormatException object in the catch clause success. Most code you will encounter will use a generic name for the exception object, such as e. Nothing says that you can't improve on this. Use an exception name to describe why you expect an exception.

The "exception test" represents what other client code will have to deal with. Somewhere in the user interface code, you will have code that you structure very similar to the code in testBadScoreEntered. The test documents the potential for score to generate a NumberFormatException and under what circumstance that potential exists.

Dealing with Exceptions

One tactic for managing exceptions is to catch them as close to the source (the point at which they are generated) as possible. Once you catch an exception, you might be able to provide code that deals with it. Providing code that converts a problem into a legitimate action is a way of encapsulating an exception.

You can also head off the exception. In the Scorer class, you can provide an additional method, isValid, that allows the client to test the validity of the input string. You put the burden on the client to guard against calling score with invalid input.

Dealing with Exceptions

```
// ScorerTest.java
public void testIsValid() {
   Scorer scorer = new Scorer();
```

```
      assertTrue(scorer.isValid("75"));
      assertFalse(scorer.isValid("bd"));
}

// Scorer.java
public boolean isValid(String input) {
   try {
      Integer.parseInt(input);
      return true;
   }
   catch (NumberFormatException e) {
      return false;
   }
}
```

A client first calls isValid. If isValid returns true, the client could safely call the score method. If isValid returns false, the client could apprise the user of the invalid input.

One benefit of using this construct is that the client would not have to code a try-catch block. You want to use exceptions as little as possible to control the flow of your code. By catching an exception as close to the source as possible, you eliminate the need for clients to use try-catch blocks to manage their control flow.

Another possibility would be for the score method to have a try-catch block. When it caught a NumberFormatException, it would return -1 or some other special int value that the client could recognize.

Checked Exceptions

Each course session at the university will have its own web page. After creating a Session object, you can send it a String representing the URL[2] of its web page. Session should create a java.net.URL object using this string. One of the constructors of java.net.URL takes a *properly formed* URL string. To be properly formed, a URL must follow a number of rules for its component parts, such as the protocol name and host name. If you create a java.net.URL with an improperly formed URL, the constructor of java.net.URL throws an exception of type java.net.MalformedURLException.

A simple test in SessionTest sets the URL into the session as a string. The test then retrieves the URL as a java.net.URL object. Finally, the test ensures

[2]Uniform Resource Locator, a pointer to a resource on the World Wide Web.

that the URL object's string representation (toString) is a match for the URL string argument.

```
public void testSessionUrl() {
    final String url = "http://course.langrsoft.com/cmsc300";
    session.setUrl(url);
    assertEquals(url, session.getUrl().toString());
}
```

The code in Session is just a setter and getter:

```
package sis.studentinfo;

import java.util.*;
import java.net.*;

abstract public class Session
        implements Comparable<Session>, Iterable<Student> {
    ...
    private URL url;
    ...
    public void setUrl(String urlString) {
        this.url = new URL(urlString);
    }

    public URL getUrl() {
        return url;
    }
    ...
```

When you compile, however, you will receive an error:

```
unreported exception java.net.MalformedURLException; must be caught or declared to be thrown
            this.url = new URL(urlString);
                       ^
```

Java defines the exception type MalformedURLException as a *checked exception* (as opposed to an *unchecked* exception). A checked exception is an exception that you must explicitly deal with in your code. You may ignore an unchecked exception (such as NumberFormatException), but remember that ignoring an exception may not be safe.

Any code that can generate a checked exception *must be handled by the method in which the code appears*. You handle an exception either by using a try-catch block or by declaring that the method simply propagates the exception to any of *its* callers. To declare that the method propagates the exception (and thus otherwise ignores it), use the throws clause:

Checked Exceptions

```
public void setUrl(String urlString) throws MalformedURLException {
    this.url = new URL(urlString);
}
```

The code phrase `throws MalformedURLException` says that the method `setUrl` can possibly generate an exception. Any code that calls the `setUrl` method must either be enclosed in a `try-catch` block or it must similarly appear in a method that contains an appropriate `throws` clause.

The test itself, then, must either catch MalformedURLException or declare that it throws MalformedURLException. Compile to see for yourself.

```
public void testSessionUrl() throws MalformedURLException {
    final String url = "http://course.langrsoft.com/cmsc300";
    session.setUrl(url);
    assertEquals(url, session.getUrl().toString());
}
```

(Don't forget to add the java.net `import` statement to SessionTest.)

Unless you are specifically expecting to receive an exception as part of your test, simply declare that the test `throws` an exception. Do not enclose the `setUrl` call in a `try-catch` block. You are defining the test. For this test, you are defining a "happy case" in which you know that the URL is valid. Given these two things under your control, an exception should never be thrown during the execution of the test unless something is horribly wrong. You can safely ignore any exceptions for the purpose of such a positive test. In the unlikely event that an exception *is* thrown, JUnit will catch it and fail the test with an error.

You still need a negative test, one that demonstrates what the client will see when there *is* a problem:

```
public void testInvalidSessionUrl() {
    final String url = "httsp://course.langrsoft.com/cmsc300";
    try {
        session.setUrl(url);
        fail("expected exception due to invalid protocol in URL");
    }
    catch (MalformedURLException success) {
    }
}
```

You will need to `import` the MalformedURLException class.

Exception Hierarchy

In order to be able to throw an object as an exception, it must be of type Throwable. The class Throwable is at the root of the exception hierarchy as defined in java.lang. Throwable has two subclasses: Error and Exception.

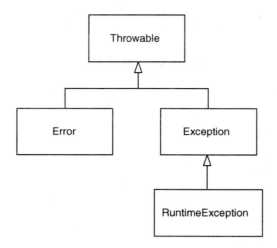

Figure 8.1 *The Exception Hierarchy*

The checked and unchecked exceptions you will work with derive from the class Exception.

Sun reserves the Error class for serious problems that can go wrong with the Java environment itself. Errors are unchecked, and you should not have any usual reason for catching instances of the Error class. Error exception types include things such as OutOfMemoryError and InternalError. You are not expected to write code to recover from any of these situations.

The Exception class is the superclass of all other exception types. Sun defines exceptions generated by the VM or the Java class library as Exception subclasses. Any exceptions that you define should also be Exception subclasses. Subclasses of Exception are sometimes referred to as application exceptions.

Unchecked application exceptions must derive from RuntimeException, which in turn directly subclasses Exception.

Figure 8.1 shows the core of the exception hierarchy.

Creating Your Own Exception Type

Creating Your
Own Exception
Type

You can create and throw an exception object that is of an existing Java exception type. But creating your own custom exception type can add clarity to your application. A custom exception type can also make testing easier.

As mentioned earlier, you want to propagate exceptions for things that you cannot otherwise control in your application. Prefer any approach where you have a means of preventing an exception from being thrown.

One case where exceptions are more appropriate is when a constructor takes a parameter that must be validated, as in the URL example. You could control validation via a static method call (for example, `public static boolean URL.isValid(String url)`). But it is reasonable for a constructor to generate an exception as an alternative to forcing clients to first make a static method call.

 For example, you may want to reject creation of students with more than three parts to their name, as in this test implemented in StudentTest:

```
public void testBadlyFormattedName() {
    try {
        new Student("a b c d");
        fail("expected exception from 4-part name");
    }
    catch (StudentNameFormatException success) {
    }
}
```

The first step toward realizing this test is creating a new Exception subclass. Before extending Exception directly, you should peruse the Exception types that Sun provides in the Java class library. Look for a similar Exception type on which you might want to base yours. In this case, java.lang.IllegalArgumentException is the most appropriate place to start. Create your StudentNameFormatException class as a subclass of IllegalArgumentException:

```
package sis.studentinfo;

public class StudentNameFormatException
    extends IllegalArgumentException {
}
```

That's all you need to do to define the exception type. Your new test should now compile and fail, since you do not yet generate the exception in the code. To make the test pass:

```
public Student(String fullName) {
    this.name = fullName;
    credits = 0;
    List<String> nameParts = split(fullName);
    final int maximumNumberOfNameParts = 3;
    if (nameParts.size() > maximumNumberOfNameParts)
        throw new StudentNameFormatException();
    setName(nameParts);
}
```

The code demonstrates that you create a new Exception object just like any other object:

```
throw new StudentNameFormatException();
```

You throw the exception object using the throw keyword:

```
throw new StudentNameFormatException();
```

Since your class StudentNameFormatException is a subclass of IllegalArgumentException, and since IllegalArgumentException is a subclass of RuntimeException, you do not need to declare the throws clause on the Student constructor.

Note that there is no test class for StudentNameFormatException! The reason is that there is virtually no code that could break. Yes, you could forget to extend from an Exception superclass, but your code would then not compile.

Checked Exceptions vs. Unchecked Exceptions

As the code designer, you may designate StudentNameFormatException as checked or unchecked. There is considerable debate on which to prefer. One argument suggests that checked exceptions cause more trouble than they are worth.[3] One reason is that changing method signatures to add new throws types breaks client code—potentially lots of it!

The reality is that most code can't do anything about most exceptions. Often, the only appropriate place to manage exceptions is at the user interface layer: "Something went horribly wrong in our application; please contact the support desk." An exception generated by code buried deep in the system must trickle out to the user interface code layer. Forcing all intermediary classes to acknowledge this potential problem clutters your code.

A general recommendation is to eliminate the need for clients to deal with exceptions as much as possible. Consider a way of returning a default value that the client can manage as part of normal processing. Or consider instead requiring a client to follow a protocol where they execute some sort of validation. See the example above, where clients of the Scorer class first execute the method isValid.

Some developers promote checked exceptions, claiming that forcing client developers to immediately and always acknowledge exceptions is beneficial. Unfortunately, many developers choose a far worse solution when confronted with checked exception types:

[3][Venners2003].

```
try {
    doSomething();
}
catch (Exception e) {
    // log or do nothing
}
```

Doing nothing within a `catch` block is an anti-pattern known as Empty Catch Clause.[4] Logging the exception is tantamount to doing nothing. There are a few rare cases where Empty Catch Clause is appropriate. But doing nothing means that you are hiding a potentially serious problem that could cause even worse problems down the road.

 Avoid propagating exceptions, but do not create empty `catch` blocks.

Messages

Most exceptions store an associated message. The message is more often than not for developer consumption. Only sometimes is the message appropriate to present to an end user of an application (although the message might be used as the determining basis for an appropriate end user message). You typically use the message for debugging purposes. Often you will record the message in an application log file to help document what caused a problem.[5]

The class Exception allows you to create a new exception object with or without a message. You can retrieve the message from an exception using the method `getMessage`. For an exception object created without a message, `getMessage` returns `null`.

You may want to store an error message within a StudentNameFormatException object that provides more information.

```
public void testBadlyFormattedName() {
    try {
        new Student("a b c d");
        fail("expected exception from 4-part name");
    }
    catch (StudentNameFormatException expectedException) {
        assertEquals(
            "Student name 'a b c d' contains more than 3 parts",
            expectedException.getMessage());
    }
}
```

[4][Wiki2004a].

[5]See the second half of this lesson for a detailed discussion of logging.

Instead of declaring a temporary variable success to hold the exception object, you now declare the variable name as expectedException. Just catching the exception is no longer enough for success; the message stored in expectedException must also be as expected.

The test will fail, since e.getMessage() returns null by default. You must modify the StudentNameFormatException constructor to take a message parameter. The constructor can then call the corresponding superclass constructor directly.

```
package sis.studentinfo;

public class StudentNameFormatException
    extends IllegalArgumentException {
    public StudentNameFormatException(String message) {
        super(message);
    }
}
```

The Student constructor can then put together a message and pass it off to the exception constructor.

```
public Student(String fullName) {
    this.name = fullName;
    credits = 0;
    List<String> nameParts = split(fullName);
    final int maximumNumberOfNameParts = 3;
    if (nameParts.size() > maximumNumberOfNameParts) {
        String message =
            "Student name '" + fullName +
            "' contains more than " + maximumNumberOfNameParts +
            " parts";
        throw new StudentNameFormatException(message);
    }
    setName(nameParts);
}
```

The exception message string does represent duplication between the test and code. You may refactor it now if you choose. Later in this lesson, you will learn how to dynamically construct the message using the String method format. I will refactor the code at that time.

Catching Multiple Exceptions

It is possible for a single line of code to generate more than one exception. Each exception can be of a different exception type. A method that throws more than one exception can list each exception type individually:

```
public void send() throws ObjectStreamException, UnknownHostException
```

If both exceptions derive from the same class, you can instead declare that the method throws an exception of the common supertype:

```
public void send() throws Exception
```

The try-catch block can have multiple catch clauses, each representing an exception that might be thrown.

```
try {
    new Student("a b c d");
}
catch (StudentNameFormatException e) {
    ...
}
catch (NoSuchElementException e) {
    ...
}
```

If code within the try block throws an exception, the Java VM transfers control to the first catch block. If the type of the exception thrown matches the type declared in the catch clause, the VM executes code within that catch block. Otherwise, the VM transfers control to the next catch block, and so on. Once code in a catch block is executed, the VM ignores all other catch blocks.

In the following code, the second catch block catches any exception that is of type Exception. Since all (normal) exceptions extend from Exception, this "catch-all" block will trap any application exception other than Student-NameFormatException, which you already trapped with the first catch block.

```
try {
    new Student("a b c d");
}
catch (StudentNameFormatException e) {
    ...
}
catch (Exception e) {
    ...
}
```

A catch-all is useful for trapping any unexpected exceptions. You should usually include a catch-all only in your top-level class, the one closest to the user interface layer. About the only thing you will be able to do in the catch-all is to log the error and possibly show something to the end user. What you gain is the ability to keep the application from crashing or visibly failing.

Use extreme discretion when introducing a catch-all. If you introduce new code in the try block or in the code it calls, this code can generate a new

Catching
Multiple
Exceptions

exception. The problem is that you might be unaware of the new exception, even if it is a checked exception. Hiding errors is bad.

Rethrowing Exceptions

Nothing prevents you from catching an exception and then throwing it (or another exception) from within the catch block. This is known as *rethrowing* an exception.

A common reason to rethrow an exception is to catch it as close to its source as possible, log it, and then propagate it again. This technique can make it easier to determine the source of a problem.

```
public void setUrl(String urlString) throws MalformedURLException {
    try {
        this.url = new URL(urlString);
    }
    catch (MalformedURLException e) {
        log(e);
        throw e;
    }
}

private void log(Exception e) {
    // logging code.  The second half of this lesson contains more
    // info on logging. For now, this method is empty.
}
```

In the above changes to setUrl, code in the catch block passes the caught exception object to the log method, then rethrows it. A refinement of this technique is to create and throw a new exception of a more application-specific type. Doing so can encapsulate the specific implementation details that caused the exception.

Instead of throwing a MalformedURLException, you want to throw an instance of the application-specific exception type SessionException. Once you have created the exception class:

```
package sis.studentinfo;

public class SessionException extends Exception {
}
```

You can alter test code to reflect the new exception type:

```
public void testSessionUrl() throws SessionException {
    final String url = "http://course.langrsoft.com/cmsc300";
```

Rethrowing
Exceptions

```
      session.setUrl(url);
      assertEquals(url, session.getUrl().toString());
}

public void testInvalidSessionUrl() {
    final String url = "httsp://course.langrsoft.com/cmsc300";
    try {
        session.setUrl(url);
        fail("expected exception due to invalid protocol in URL");
    }
    catch (SessionException success) {
    }
}
```

Finally, you can change the production code to throw the new exception instead.

```
public void setUrl(String urlString) throws SessionException {
    try {
        this.url = new URL(urlString);
    }
    catch (MalformedURLException e) {
        log(e);
        throw new SessionException();
    }
}
```

The downside is that you lose information with this solution: If an exception is thrown, what is the true reason? In a different circumstance, code in the try block might throw more than one kind of exception. Rethrowing the application-specific exception would hide the root cause.

As a solution, you could extract the message from the root exception and store it in the SessionException instance. You would still lose the original stack trace information, however.

In J2SE 1.4, Sun added the ability to the Throwable class to store a root cause. The Throwable class provides two additional constructor forms: one that takes a Throwable as a parameter and another that takes both a message string and a Throwable as a parameter. Sun also added these constructors to the Exception and RuntimeException derivatives of Throwable. You may also set the root cause in the Throwable object after its construction via the method initCause. Later, you can retrieve the Throwable object from the exception by sending it the message getCause.

First, modify testInvalidSessionUrl to extract the cause from the SessionException instance. As part of the test verification, ensure that the cause of the exception is the reason expected.

Rethrowing Exceptions

```
public void testInvalidSessionUrl() {
    final String url = "httsp://course.langrsoft.com/cmsc300";
    try {
        session.setUrl(url);
        fail("expected exception due to invalid protocol in URL");
    }
    catch (SessionException expectedException) {
        Throwable cause = expectedException.getCause();
        assertEquals(MalformedURLException.class, cause.getClass());
    }
}
```

The assertEquals statement ensures that the class of the cause is Malformed-URLException. The code to make this comparison demonstrates some *reflective* capabilities of Java—the ability of the language to dynamically derive information about types and their definitions at runtime. I will explain reflection capabilities in further depth in Lesson 12.

In short, you can send all objects the message getClass, which returns an appropriate class constant. A class constant is a class name followed by .class. MalformedURLException.class is a class constant that represents the Malformed-URLException class.

The test will fail: If no cause is explicitly set, getCause returns null. You will first need to modify SessionException to capture the cause upon construction:

```
package studentinfo;

public class SessionException extends Exception {
    public SessionException(Throwable cause) {
        super(cause);
    }
}
```

You can then change the production code to embed the cause in the SessionException instance.

Rethrowing
Exceptions

```
public void setUrl(String urlString) throws SessionException {
    try {
        this.url = new URL(urlString);
    }
    catch (MalformedURLException e) {
        log(e);
        throw new SessionException(e); // <- here's the change
    }
}
```

Stack Traces

Lesson 4 taught you how to read the exception stack to help decipher the source of an exception.

You can send the stack trace stored within an exception to a print stream or print writer using the printStackTrace method defined in Throwable. One implementation of printStackTrace takes no parameters, printing the stack trace on the system console (System.out) by default. A crude implementation of the log method might do just that.

```
private void log(Exception e) {
   e.printStackTrace();
}
```

(Try it.) For a production system, you will want a more robust logging solution. Sun introduced a logging API in J2SE 1.4; I discuss logging in the second half of this lesson.

The stack trace representation printed by printStackTrace contains information that might be useful for more advanced programming needs. You could parse the stack trace yourself in order to obtain the information, which many developers have done. Or, as of J2SE 1.4, you can send the message getStackTrace to the exception object in order to access the information in already parsed form.

The finally Block

When an exception is thrown, the Java VM immediately transfers control from its point of origin to the first catch block matching the exception type. Java executes no further lines of code within the try block. If no try block exists, the VM immediately transfers control out of the method. You may have the need, however, to ensure that some bit of code *is* executed before control transfers out.

The optional finally block ensures that the Java VM always executes some piece of code, regardless of whether or not an exception was thrown. You may attach a single finally block to the end of a try-catch block.

The prototypical reason for using a finally block is to clean up any local resources. If you have opened a file, the finally block can ensure that the file gets properly closed. If you have obtained a connection to a database, the finally block ensures that the connection is closed.

The finally
Block

```
public static Student findByLastName(String lastName)
      throws RuntimeException {
   java.sql.Connection dbConnection = null;
   try {
      dbConnection = getConnection();
      return lookup(dbConnection, lastName);
   }
   catch (java.sql.SQLException e) {
      throw new RuntimeException(e.getMessage());
   }
   finally {
      close(dbConnection);
   }
}
```

(Note that the example is here for demonstration purposes only. Refer to Additional Lesson III for a brief overview of interacting with databases via JDBC.)

Both the lookup method and the getConnection method can throw an SQL-Exception object. You call the the lookup method after obtaining a connection. If the lookup method subsequently throws an exception, you want to ensure that the database connection gets closed.

If no exception is thrown, Java transfers control to the finally block upon completion of the code in the try block. In the example, the finally block makes a call to close the database connection. If an exception *is* thrown, Java executes code in the catch block. As soon as either the catch block completes or the VM directs control out of the catch block (in the above example, through use of the throw statement), Java executes the finally block, which closes the connection.

If you supply a finally block, the catch block itself is optional. For example, you may not want to attempt to handle an SQL exception from within findBy-LastName. Instead, you declare that findByLastName can throw an SQLException. But you still need to close the connection before the VM transfers control out of findByLastName:

The finally Block

```
public static Student findByLastName(String lastName)
      throws java.sql.SQLException {
   java.sql.Connection dbConnection = null;
   try {
      dbConnection = getConnection();
      return lookup(dbConnection, lastName);
   }
   finally {
      close(dbConnection);
   }
}
```

Under no circumstances should you include a `return` statement within a `finally` block—it will "eat" any exceptions that might have been thrown by the `catch` block. Some developers also promote the more strict notion that you should not `return` from either a `try` block or a `catch` block; instead only `return` after completion of the whole try-catch block.

Refactoring

Creating a string to present to the user often involves concatenating several substrings and printable representations of primitives and objects. The Student constructor provides an example:

```
public Student(String fullName) {
    this.name = fullName;
    credits = 0;
    List<String> nameParts = split(fullName);
    final int maximumNumberOfNameParts = 3;
    if (nameParts.size() > maximumNumberOfNameParts) {
        String message =
            "Student name '" + fullName +
            "' contains more than " + maximumNumberOfNameParts +
            " parts";
        throw new StudentNameFormatException(message);
    }
    setName(nameParts);
}
```

In the Student constructor, you combine five separate elements to form a single string—three substrings, the full name, and a constant representing the maximum number of name parts allowed. You must likewise construct a string in the test method. Concatenations of larger strings, with more embedded information, become very difficult to read and maintain.

The String class supplies a class method named `format`. The `format` method allows you to pass a format String and a variable number of arguments (see the information on varargs in Lesson 7). In return, you receive a string formatted to your needs. A format String contains elements known as *format specifiers*. These specifiers are placeholders for the arguments. A format specifier tells the formatter how to interpret and format each argument. Often, but not always, you will have one format specifier for each argument.

For those of you who are familiar with the language C, Java's String formatting capability derives from a comparable C feature used in functions such as `printf`. The Java implementation is similar but provides more features and safety. Do not assume that a Java format specifier works the same as an equivalent C format specifier.

Start with testBadlyFormattedName and replace the concatenation with a call to format. Also, introduce a class constant for the maximum number of name parts allowed.

```java
public void testBadlyFormattedName() {
    final String studentName = "a b c d";
    try {
        new Student(studentName);
        fail("expected exception from 4-part name");
    }
    catch (StudentNameFormatException expectedException) {
        assertEquals(
            String.format("Student name '%s' contains more than %d parts",
                studentName, Student.MAX_NAME_PARTS),
            expectedException.getMessage());
    }
}
```

The call to format has three arguments: the format string and two format string arguments. Within the format string are two format specifiers: %s and %d. The first format specifier corresponds to the first argument, studentName. The second format specifier corresponds to the second argument, Student.MAX_NAME_PARTS. A format specifier always begins with a percent sign (%) and ends with a conversion. A conversion is a character or character that tells the format method how to interpret the corresponding argument.

The character s, as in %s, indicates a string conversion. When the format method encounters a string conversion in a format specifier, it replaces the format specifier with the corresponding argument. In the test, format replaces %s with the contents of studentName:

Student name 'a b c d' contains more than %d parts

The character d, as in %d, indicates an integral conversion to decimal. In the test, format replaces %d with the value of Student.MAX_NAME_PARTS (which you will set to the int literal 3):

Student name 'a b c d' contains more than 3 parts

Refactoring

The String method format is a utility method that delegates all the work to an instance of the java.util.Formatter class. The Formatter class supplies more than a dozen different conversions, including date conversions and more-sophisticated conversions for numeric values.

One very useful conversion is n, which stands for "new line." If you provide the format specifier %n, the formatter replaces it with the platform-specific line separator (usually "\n" or "\r\n"). This saves you from having to provide code that accesses the system line separator property.

Some of the other things Formatter supports:

- internationalization

- the ability to provide arguments in an order that does not match the order of format specifiers

- sending output incrementally to a StringBuilder or other sink

The API documentation for java.util.Formatter is long and detailed. Refer to it to understand how to use additional conversions or how to work with the additional features of Formatter.

As a final step, you can refactor to introduce a class constant for the error message. The following code also shows the implementation in Student:

```java
// StudentTest.java
public void testBadlyFormattedName() {
    final String studentName = "a b c d";
    try {
        new Student(studentName);
        fail("expected exception from 4-part name");
    }
    catch (StudentNameFormatException expectedException) {
        assertEquals(
            String.format(Student.TOO_MANY_NAME_PARTS_MSG,
                          studentName, Student.MAX_NAME_PARTS),
            expectedException.getMessage());
    }
}

// Student.java
static final String TOO_MANY_NAME_PARTS_MSG =
    "Student name '%s' contains more than %d parts";
...
public Student(String fullName) {
    this.name = fullName;
    credits = 0;
    List<String> nameParts = split(fullName);
    if (nameParts.size() > MAX_NAME_PARTS) {
        String message =
            String.format(Student.TOO_MANY_NAME_PARTS_MSG,
                          fullName, MAX_NAME_PARTS);
```

Refactoring

```
        throw new StudentNameFormatException(message);
    }
    setName(nameParts);
}
```

Logging

In most enterprises, it is valuable to track interesting history as applications execute. The job of *logging* code is to record significant events and data supporting those events. As a developer, it is your job to determine what is relevant enough to track. Once you make this determination, you insert code at judicious points in the application to write the information out to (typically) a log file or files. You later can use the logs to answer questions about performance, problems, and so on.

Figuring out just what to track is the hard part. Currently, you are logging nothing. You lose information on any errors that occur. The lack of relevant problem data can deprive you of the ability to solve problems. Worse, you may not know you have a problem until it is too late (this is one reason to avoid empty catch blocks).

Minimally, you should log all unexpected error conditions (exceptions). You may also want to log critical calculations, execution of troublesome routines, or interesting data. You can also choose to log virtually everything that occurs, such as every time a method executes.

Logging everything, or logging too much, has its problems. Log files can grow at an extreme rate, particularly as use of the system increases. Logging has a minor performance penalty; excessive logging can lead to system slowdown. A worse problem, however, is that if there is too much information being logged, you will not be able to physically analyze the voluminous amount of data. Problems may get lost in the forest. Logging becomes useless. On the code side, logging has a cluttering effect and can bloat your code.

It will be up to you to determine how much to log. In some circumstances, where it is easy for you to deploy updated code (for example, a web application), err on the side of logging too little information. Where it is difficult to update deployed code, err on the side of logging too much information. Having more information will increase your prospects of solving a problem. Err on the side of logging too much information when you know that a section of code has problems or when the code presents a high risk (for example, code that controls critical components).

Logging

Logging in Java

Java supplies complete logging facilities in the package java.util.logging.[6] For an exercise, you will learn to use the logging package to capture exception events. The Student constructor throws an exception. Let's log it. Here is a slightly modified Student constructor with a placeholder for logging.

```java
public Student(String fullName) {
    this.name = fullName;
    credits = 0;
    List<String> nameParts = split(fullName);
    if (nameParts.size() > MAX_NAME_PARTS) {
        String message =
            String.format(Student.TOO_MANY_NAME_PARTS_MSG,
                          fullName, MAX_NAME_PARTS);
        // log the message here
        throw new StudentNameFormatException(message);
    }
    setName(nameParts);
}
```

The first question is how to test that an appropriate message gets logged when you throw the exception. Or should you bother with such a test?

Remember the first rule of testing: Test everything that can possibly break. Logging can definitely break. Take a stab at a test:

```java
public void testBadlyFormattedName() {
    final String studentName = "a b c d";
    try {
        new Student(studentName);
        fail("expected exception from 4-part name");
    }
    catch (StudentNameFormatException expectedException) {
        String message =
            String.format(Student.TOO_MANY_NAME_PARTS_MSG,
                          studentName, Student.MAX_NAME_PARTS);
        assertEquals(message, expectedException.getMessage());
        assertTrue(wasLogged(message));
    }
}

private boolean wasLogged(String message) {
    // ???
}
```

[6]While Java's logging facilities are adequate for most needs, many developers prefer to use the freely available Log4J package (http://logging.apache.org/log4j/docs/).

How do you determined whether or not a message was logged? The method name wasLogged represents the intent of *what* you need to determine. The contents of wasLogged will represent *how* you determine it.

Learning how to test an unfamiliar API such as logging, sometimes involves playing around with the API until you understand how it works. Without this more complete understanding of the API, you may not be able to figure out how to test it. In this exercise, you'll write a bit of "spike" code that provides you with a better understanding of the logging API. Then you'll throw away the spike code, write a test, and write the production code to meet the test specification.

In Student, create an "intention message" in the constructor:

```
public Student(String fullName) {
    this.name = fullName;
    credits = 0;
    List<String> nameParts = split(fullName);
    if (nameParts.size() > MAX_NAME_PARTS) {
        String message =
            String.format(Student.TOO_MANY_NAME_PARTS_MSG,
                          fullName, MAX_NAME_PARTS);
        log(message);
        throw new StudentNameFormatException(message);
    }
    setName(nameParts);
}
```

Then code the log method.

```
private void log(String message) {
    Logger logger = Logger.getLogger(getClass().getName());
    logger.info(message);
}
```

To log a message, you need a Logger object. To obtain a Logger object, you call the Logger factory method getLogger. As a parameter to getLogger, you pass the name of the subsystem within which you are logging. Later in this lesson (in the section entitled Logging Hierarchies), you'll learn more about the relevance of the subsystem name. Passing in the name of the class is typical and will suffice.

If a Logger object with that name already exists, getLogger returns that logger. Otherwise, getLogger creates and returns a new Logger object.

The second line in log calls the Logger method info, passing the message parameter. By using the info method, you request that the message be logged at an informational level. The logging API supports several levels of message log.

The Logger class provides a method that corresponds to each level. From highest to lowest, the levels are severe, warning, info, config, fine, finer, and finest.

Each logger object maintains its own logging level. If you attempt to log a message at a lower level than the logger's level, the logger discards the message. For example, if a logger is set to warning, it logs only severe and warning messages.

You can obtain and set the logging level on a logger using getLevel and setLevel. You represent the logging level with a Level object. The Level class defines a set of Level class constants, one to represent each logging level. The Level class also supplies two additional class constants: Level.ALL and Level.OFF, to designate either logging all messages or logging no messages.

Modify the wasLogged method in StudentTest to return false. Run all your tests. By returning false, you cause testBadlyFormattedName to fail. This failure reminds you that you will need to flesh out the test.

On the console, you should see something like:

```
Apr 14, 2005 2:45:04 AM sis.studentinfo.Student log
INFO: Student name 'a b c d' contains more than 3 parts
```

You have successfully logged a message!

The UML class diagram in Figure 8.2 shows the relationship between Logger and Level. It also includes Logger's relationship to other relevant classes that you will learn about in the upcoming sections.

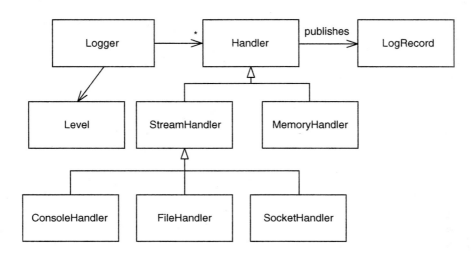

Figure 8.2 *The Logger Hierarchy*

Testing Logging

Now your problem is figuring out how to test the logging. First, however, as I promised, you must throw away the spike code in Student. Discard the log method and update the constructor by removing the call to log.

```java
public Student(String fullName) {
    this.name = fullName;
    credits = 0;
    List<String> nameParts = split(fullName);
    if (nameParts.size() > MAX_NAME_PARTS) {
        String message =
            String.format(Student.TOO_MANY_NAME_PARTS_MSG,
                          fullName, MAX_NAME_PARTS);
        throw new StudentNameFormatException(message);
    }
    setName(nameParts);
}
```

Don't forget that writing code without tests is a good way of getting into trouble. Make sure you specify what you're going to code first.

While you have successfully logged a message, its output went to the console. How are you going to intercept this message for the purpose of writing a test?

The logging facility lets you direct messages to destinations other than the console. You can also direct logging to more than one destination at a time.[7] The Logger stores handler objects that it uses to determine the logging destinations. A handler object is a subclass of java.util.logging.Handler. The class ConsoleHandler represents the behavior of sending output to the console. Most shops prefer to redirect logging output to files, using a FileHandler, so that developers can later peruse the files. You can tell the logger to route messages to alternate destinations by sending it Handler objects.

Unfortunately, you wouldn't be able to write test code that reads a log file, since you haven't learned about Java IO yet (you will in Lesson 11). Instead, you will create a new handler class, TestHandler. Within this handler class, you will trap all messages being logged. You will provide a getter method

[7]The UML diagram in Figure 8.2 shows that a Logger can have multiple Handler objects by using an asterisk (*) at the end of the navigable association between the two classes. The * is a multiplicity indicator. The absence of a multiplicity indicates either 1 or that the multiplicity is uninteresting or irrelevant. The relationship between Logger and Handler is a one-to-many relationship.

that returns the last message that was logged. Once you have built this handler class, you can pass an instance of it to the logger.

For each message you log, the Logger object calls the method publish on the Handler object, passing it a java.util.logging.LogRecord parameter object.

It is the publish method that you will override in your Handler subclass to trap the message being logged. You must also supply definitions for the other two abstract methods in Handler, flush and close. They can be empty.

```
package sis.studentinfo;

import java.util.logging.*;

class TestHandler extends Handler {
   private LogRecord record;

   public void flush() {}
   public void close() {}
   public void publish(LogRecord record) {
      this.record = record;
   }

   String getMessage() {
      return record.getMessage();
   }
}
```

In testBadlyFormattedName, you first obtain the same logger that Student will use. Since both the test and the code in Student pass the Student class name to getLogger, they will both reference the same Logger object. Subsequently, you construct an instance of TestHandler and add it as a handler to the logger.

```
public void testBadlyFormattedName() {
   Logger logger = Logger.getLogger(Student.class.getName());
   TestHandler handler = new TestHandler();
   logger.addHandler(handler);
   ...
}
```

Any messages you log will be routed to the TestHandler object. To prove that Student code indeed logs a message, you can ask the handler for the last message it received.

```
public void testBadlyFormattedName() {
   ...
   final String studentName = "a b c d";
   try {
      new Student(studentName);
      fail("expected exception from 4-part name");
   }
   catch (StudentNameFormatException expectedException) {
      String message =
```

Testing Logging

```
          String.format(Student.TOO_MANY_NAME_PARTS_MSG,
                     studentName, Student.MAX_NAME_PARTS);
       assertEquals(message, expectedException.getMessage());
       assertTrue(wasLogged(message, handler));
   }
}

private boolean wasLogged(String message, TestHandler handler) {
   return message.equals(handler.getMessage());
}
```

On a stylistic note, I prefer coding the test as follows:

```
public void testBadlyFormattedName() {
   Logger logger = Logger.getLogger(Student.class.getName());
   Handler handler = new TestHandler();
   logger.addHandler(handler);

   final String studentName = "a b c d";
   try {
      new Student(studentName);
      fail("expected exception from 4-part name");
   }
   catch (StudentNameFormatException expectedException) {
      String message =
         String.format(Student.TOO_MANY_NAME_PARTS_MSG,
                     studentName, Student.MAX_NAME_PARTS);
      assertEquals(message, expectedException.getMessage());
      assertTrue(wasLogged(message, (TestHandler)handler));
   }
}
```

Instead of assigning the new instance of TestHandler to a TestHandler reference, you assign it to a Handler reference. This can clarify the test, so you understand that the addHandler method expects a Handler as a parameter (and not a TestHandler). The wasLogged method needs to use the getMessage method you created in TestHandler, so you must cast back to a TestHandler reference.

The test should fail, particularly since you should have no production code in Student to meet the specification of the test (you deleted it, correct?). Demonstrate the failure before proceeding. For all you know, the new test code might not do anything, and if you get a green bar, alarms should go off in your head. (It happens. Sometimes it means you forgot to compile your code.) Sticking to the method will help you keep your cool and make fewer mistakes.

Another reason you should have deleted the spike code is that you will produce a better, refactored version this time around. You currently have du-

Testing Logging

plicate code: Both StudentTest and Student include a complex line of code to retrieve a Logger object.

In addition to using a Student class variable for the logger, the modified test inlines the wasLogged method:

```java
public void testBadlyFormattedName() {
   Handler handler = new TestHandler();
   Student.logger.addHandler(handler);

   final String studentName = "a b c d";
   try {
      new Student(studentName);
      fail("expected exception from 4-part name");
   }
   catch (StudentNameFormatException expectedException) {
      String message =
         String.format(Student.TOO_MANY_NAME_PARTS_MSG,
                       studentName, Student.MAX_NAME_PARTS);
      assertEquals(message, expectedException.getMessage());
      assertEquals(message, ((TestHandler)handler).getMessage());
   }
}
```

Here's the resurrected, refactored Student code:

```java
package sis.studentinfo;

import java.util.*;
import java.util.logging.*;

public class Student {
   ...
   final static Logger logger =
      Logger.getLogger(Student.class.getName());
   ...
   public Student(String fullName) {
      this.name = fullName;
      credits = 0;
      List<String> nameParts = split(fullName);
      if (nameParts.size() > MAX_NAME_PARTS) {
         String message =
            String.format(Student.TOO_MANY_NAME_PARTS_MSG,
                          fullName, MAX_NAME_PARTS);
         Student.logger.info(message);
         throw new StudentNameFormatException(message);
      }
      setName(nameParts);
   }
   ...
}
```

Logging to Files

Sun designed the logging facility to allow you to change logging characteristics at runtime. You can quickly route log messages to a file instead of to the console without having to change, recompile, and redeploy code.

The default behavior is to send logging messages to the console. This behavior is not hardcoded somewhere in the Logger class; it is located in an external properties file that you can freely edit.

Browse to the directory in which you installed Java. Within this directory, you should be able to navigate into the subdirectory jre/lib (or jre\lib if you are using Windows). Within this subdirectory you should see the file logging.properties.[8] Edit the file using any editor.

You can use properties files in many circumstances to store values that you may want to change with each execution of an application. Sun chose to allow you the ability to configure logging behavior using a properties file. The layout of a properties file should be self explanatory. Comment lines begin with the pound sign (#). Blank lines are ignored. The remainder of the lines are key-value pairs, like entries in a hash table. Each key-value pair, or property, appears in the form:

```
key = value
```

Several lines down into logging.properties, you should see:

```
# "handlers" specifies a comma separated list of log Handler
# classes. These handlers will be installed during VM startup.
# Note that these classes must be on the system classpath.
# By default we only configure a ConsoleHandler, which will only
# show messages at the INFO and above levels.
handlers= java.util.logging.ConsoleHandler

# To also add the FileHandler, use the following line instead.
#handlers=java.util.logging.FileHandler,java.util.logging.ConsoleHandler
```

Swap the commenting around. Comment out the line that sets handlers to only the ConsoleHandler. Uncomment the line that sets the property handlers to both the FileHandler and the ConsoleHandler. By doing so, you tell the logger to route output to objects of each handler type.

Nearer to the bottom of logging.properties, you will find these lines:

```
java.util.logging.FileHandler.pattern = %h/java%u.log
java.util.logging.FileHandler.limit = 50000
java.util.logging.FileHandler.count = 1
java.util.logging.FileHandler.formatter = java.util.logging.XMLFormatter
```

[8]If you don't have this file, you can create it. Use the bits of content that I demonstrate.

The logging facility uses these lines to determine how the FileHandler works.

The value for the `java.util.logging.FileHandler.pattern` is a pattern for naming the log file. The `%h` and `%u` that currently appear in the pattern are known as fields. The `%h` field tells the FileHandler to store log files in your home directory.

The file handler replaces the `%u` field in the pattern with a unique number. The goal is to avoid the conflict of two log files sharing the same filename.

Rerun your tests and then navigate to your home directory. Under most versions of Windows, you can do so using the command:[9]

```
cd %USERPROFILE%
```

Under most Unix shells you can navigate to your home directory using the command:

```
cd $HOME
```

Within your home directory, you should see a file named `java0.log`. The number `0` is the unique number replacement for the `%u` field.

View the contents of `java0.log`. They should look similar to this:

```
<?xml version="1.0" encoding="windows-1252" standalone="no"?>
<!DOCTYPE log SYSTEM "logger.dtd">
<log>
<record>
  <date>2004-04-15T03:27:05</date>
  <millis>1082021225078</millis>
  <sequence>0</sequence>
  <logger>sis.studentinfo.Student</logger>
  <level>INFO</level>
  <class>sis.studentinfo.Student</class>
  <method>log</method>
  <thread>10</thread>
  <message>Student name 'a b c d' contains more than 3 parts</message>
</record>
</log>
```

It's not the two lines of logging message you expected. Instead, the message appears in XML format.[10] The logging facility allows you attach a different formatter to each handler. A formatter is a subclass of java.util.logging.Formatter; Sun supplies two formatter implementations. SimpleFormat-

---

[9]You must change to the drive on which the user profile is located. You can view the full path of your home directory, including the drive on which it is located, by executing set USERPROFILE.

[10]eXtensible Markup Language. See *http://www.w3.org/XML/*.

ter produces the two log lines you saw earlier. XMLFormatter produces the output you're currently seeing in `java0.log`. You can code your own formatter class to produce log output however you wish.

Find the `java.util.logging.FileHandler.formatter` property in `logging.properties`. Its current value is `java.util.logging.XMLFormatter`. Change the value to `java.util.logging.SimpleFormatter` and rerun your tests.

The contents of `java0.log` should now look the same as the output produced by the ConsoleHandler.

Testing Philosophy for Logging

In the previous section, Logging to Files, you changed logging behavior by modifying the `logging.properties` file. The ability to make dynamic changes using properties files is very powerful and allows your system to remain flexible.

Note that the test you wrote executed regardless of where the logging output went. Your test code instead proved that your code sent a specific message to the logger object. You were able to prove this by inspecting the message sent from the logger to one of its handlers.

However, the destination of logging output is another specification detail, one that needs to be adequately tested. It would be very easy to make invalid changes to the properties file. When the application shipped, those changes would cause serious problems. It is imperative that you test not only your Java code but also how the configuration of the system impacts that code.

You could write JUnit tests to ensure that log files were correctly created.[11] The strategy for the test would be:

1. write out a properties file with the proper data

2. force the logging facility to load this properties file

3. execute code that logs a message

4. read the expected log file and ensure that it contains the expected message

Or you could consider that this test falls into the scenario of what is known as integration testing. (Some shops may refer to this as customer testing, system testing, or acceptance testing.) You have already testing that your unit of code—Student—interacts with the logging facility correctly. Testing

Testing Philosophy for Logging

---

[11] . . . once you learned how to write code that works with files. See Lesson 11.

how the logging facility works in conjunction with dynamic configurations begins to fall outside the realm of unit testing.

Regardless of the semantics—regardless of whether you consider such a test a unit test or not—it is imperative that you test the configuration that you will ship. You might choose to do this manually and visually inspect the log files like you did in the previous section. You might translate the above 4-step strategy into an executable test and call it an integration test. You will want to execute such tests as part of any *regression test* suite. A regression test suite ensures that new changes don't break existing code through execution of a comprehensive set of tests against the entire system.

Logging is a tool for supportability. Supportability is a system requirement, just like any other functional requirement. Testing logging at some level is absolutely required. But should you write a test for each and every log message?

The lazier answer is no. Once you have proved that the basic mechanics of logging are built correctly, you might consider writing tests for additional loggings a waste of time. Often, the only reason you log is so that you as a developer can analyze what the code is doing. Adding new calls to the logger can't possibly break things.

The better answer is yes. It will be tedious to maintain a test for every log message, but it will also keep you from getting into trouble for a few reasons.

Many developers introduce try-catch blocks because the compiler insists upon it, not because they have a specification or test. They don't have a solution for what to do when an exception occurs. The nonthinking reaction by the developer is to log a message from within the catch block. This produces an Empty Catch Clause, effectively hiding what could be a serious problem.

By insisting that you write a test for all logged messages, you don't necessarily solve the problem of Empty Catch Clause. But two things happen: First, you must figure out how to emulate generating the exception in question in order to code the test. Sometimes just going through this process will educate you about how to eliminate the need for an Empty Catch Clause. Second, writing a test elevates the folly of Empty Catch Clause to a higher level of visibility. Such a test should help point out the problem.

Another benefit of writing a test for every logged message is that it's painful. Sometimes pain is a good thing. The pain here will make you think about each and every logging message going into the system. "Do I really need to log something here? What will this buy me? Does it fit into our team's logging strategy?" If you take the care to log only with appropriate answers to these questions, you will avoid the serious problem of overlogging.

Finally, it is possible to introduce logging code that breaks other things. Unlikely, but possible.

Testing
Philosophy for
Logging

More on FileHandler

FileHandler defines more fields, including %t and %g. FileHandler code replaces occurrences of the %t field in the name pattern with the system temporary directory. On Windows, this is usually c:\temp; on Unix, this is usually /tmp.

The FileHandler code replaces occurrences of the %g field with a generation number. You use this field in conjunction with the java.util.logging.File-Handler.count (I'll refer to this as the shortened property-name count) and java.util.logging.FileHandler.limit (limit) properties. The limit property represents how many bytes will be stored in a log file before it reaches its limit. A limit value of 0 means there is no limit. When a log file reaches its limit, the File-Handler object closes it. The count field specifies how many log files that File-Handler cycles through. If the value of count is 1, the FileHandler will reuse the same log file each time it reaches its limit.

Otherwise the FileHandler tracks a generation number. The first log file uses a generation number of 0 in place of the %g field. With a log filename pattern of java%g.log, the first generated log filename is java0.log. Each time a log file reaches capacity, the FileHandler bumps up the generation number and uses this to replace the %g field in the filename pattern. The FileHandler writes subsequent log entries to the log file with this new name. The second log file is java1.log. Once the FileHandler closes count log files, it resets the generation number to 0.

Logging Levels

You may want to log messages for special purposes, such as for timing how long a critical method takes to execute or for introducing "trace" messages that allow you as a developer to follow the flow of execution in the system. You may not want these messages to normally appear in the logs when the application is run in production. Instead, you may need the ability to "turn on" these kinds of messages from time to time without having to recode, recompile, and redistribute the application.

As mentioned earlier, the Java logging API supports seven logging levels: severe, warning, info, config, fine, finer, and finest. You should restrict normal production logging to severe, warning, and info levels. Reserve the other levels for special, ephemeral logging needs.

Suppose you need to log the execution time of the Student method getGpa. You are concerned that it may not perform well under heavy load. Introduce logging messages at the beginning and end of getGpa, using the fine Logger method.

Logging Levels

```
double getGpa() {
    Student.logger.fine("begin getGpa " + System.currentTimeMillis());
    if (grades.isEmpty())
        return 0.0;
    double total = 0.0;
    for (Grade grade: grades)
        total += gradingStrategy.getGradePointsFor(grade);
    double result = total / grades.size();
    Student.logger.fine("end getGpa " + System.currentTimeMillis());
    return result;
}
```

Recompile and rerun your tests.[12] You won't see these new logging messages either on your console or within a log file.

In order to view the logging messages, you must configure the handler to accept messages at the lower logging level. You typically do this within logging.properties. Edit the logging.properties file and make the modifications noted in bold:

```
...
.level= FINE

########################################################
# Handler specific properties.
# Describes specific configuration info for Handlers.
########################################################

# default file output is in user's home directory.
java.util.logging.FileHandler.pattern = %h/java%u.log
java.util.logging.FileHandler.limit = 50000
java.util.logging.FileHandler.count = 1
java.util.logging.FileHandler.level = FINE
java.util.logging.FileHandler.formatter=java.util.logging.SimpleFormatter

# Limit the message that are printed on the console to INFO and above.
java.util.logging.ConsoleHandler.level = INFO
...
```

You designate both the global level (.level) and the FileHandler level (java.util.logging.FileHandler.level) to accept any message logged at a FINE or higher level. The logging facility first ensures that the request level is as high as the global level; if not, it does not send the message to the handler. If the logger sends the message to the handler, the handler similarly determines whether the message should be logged.

In other words, the global should either be the same level or lower than any handler levels. If the reverse is true, no messages will be logged by a

Logging Levels

---

[12]Here I've chosen to take a lazy logging route—no testing—because these are temporary log messages.

handler. For example, if you were to set the global level to INFO and the File-Handler to FINE, the FileHandler would never log any messages.

Rerun the tests one more time and ensure that the timing log messages appear in the log file but not on the console.

Logging Hierarchies

When you retrieve a logger using the Logger class method getLogger, the Logger code returns either a new Logger object or an existing Logger object if the Logger has already created one with the same name. Calling Logger.getLogger (Student.class.getName()) creates a logger with the name "sis.studentinfo.Student". Using this fully qualified class name for a Logger is usually sufficient.

The following language tests shows how getLogger returns the same Logger object when called twice with the same name:

```
public void testLoggingHierarchy() {
    Logger logger = Logger.getLogger("sis.studentinfo.Student");
    assertTrue(logger == Logger.getLogger("sis.studentinfo.Student"));
}
```

The fully qualified name of a class represents a hierarchical relationship. The top level of the hierarchy, or tree, is sis. The next lower level is studentinfo. Each class within studentinfo is a leaf on the tree. You can see this hierarchy more clearly by looking at the directory structure in which Java creates compiled class files.

You can take advantage of this naming hierarchy with respect to logging. The logging facility creates an analogous hierarchy of Logger objects. If you create a logger named sis.studentinfo.Student, its parent is sis.studentinfo. The parent of a logger named sis.studentinfo is named sis. You can demonstrate this by adding to the language test:

```
public void testLoggingHierarchy() {
    Logger logger = Logger.getLogger("sis.studentinfo.Student");
    assertTrue(logger == Logger.getLogger("sis.studentinfo.Student"));

    Logger parent = Logger.getLogger("sis.studentinfo");
    assertEquals(parent, logger.getParent());
    assertEquals(Logger.getLogger("sis"), parent.getParent());
}
```

The benefit of this hierarchy is that you can set logging levels at a higher level. For example, you can set the logging level to Level.ALL at the sis logger. A child logger uses the logging level of its parent if it has none itself.

Additional Notes on Logging

- The logging facility allows you to attach arbitrary filters to a logger or handler. The Filter interface defines one method—isLoggable—which takes a LogRecord as a parameter. Using information in the LogRecord, the job of isLoggable is to return true if the message should be logged or false otherwise. You might code a Filter implementation that ignores log messages over a certain length, for example.

- The logging facility provides support for internationalization. See the Java API documentation for more information and Additional Lesson III for a brief discussion of internationalization in general.

- You may need to change logging properties while the application is already executing. Once you have changed the physical properties file, you can use the LogManager class method readConfiguration to reload the properties file. In order to do so, you will need to represent the properties file as an InputStream. See Lesson 11 for information on how to read files using input streams.

- You learned to modify the logging.properties to define logging characteristics at runtime. You can supply a custom configuration file instead of using the logging.properties file. To do so, set the value of the system property java.util.logging.config.file. One way to do this is on the command line when you start the Java application. For example:

```
java -Djava.util.logging.config.file=sis.properties sis.MainApp
```

- The Logger class provides convenience methods for logging special situations. You can use entering and existing to simplify logging entry to a method and exits from it. You can use the throwing method to simplify logging an exception. Refer to the Java API documentation for Logger for more information.

Exercises

1. Write a test that calls a method named blowsUp. Code the method blowsUp to throw a new RuntimeException with the message "Somebody should catch this!". Run the test. Verify that it fails with an appropriate stack trace.

2. Make the test pass without removing the call to blowsUp. Ensure that the test fails if blowsUp throws no exception.

3. Ensure that the caught exception contains the proper message. Change the message, and see the test fail. Change it back in order to keep the tests passing.

4. Create a test that calls a new method named rethrows. The rethrows method should call blowsUp and catch the exception. It should then wrap the exception in a new RuntimeException and throw it again. Use getCause to ensure that the caught exception contains the original exception.

5. Modify the test to expect a new exception type, SimpleException, when calling the blowsUp method. SimpleException should extend RuntimeException.

6. Which of the following test methods will not compile? Of those that compile, which will pass and which will fail?

```java
public void testExceptionOrder1() {
    try {
        blowsUp();
        rethrows();
        fail("no exception");
    }
    catch (SimpleException yours) {
        fail("caught wrong exception");
    }
    catch (RuntimeException success) {
    }
}

public void testExceptionOrder2() {
    try {
        rethrows();
        blowsUp();
        fail("no exception");
    }
    catch (SimpleException success) {
    }
    catch (RuntimeException failure) {
        fail("caught wrong exception");
    }
}

public void testExceptionOrder3() {
    try {
        blowsUp();
        rethrows();
        fail("no exception");
    }
    catch (RuntimeException success) {
```

Exercises

```
      }
      catch (SimpleException yours) {
         fail("caught wrong exception");
      }
   }

   public void testExceptionOrder4() {
      try {
         blowsUp();
         rethrows();
         fail("no exception");
      }
      catch (RuntimeException fail) {
         fail("exception unacceptable");
      }
      catch (SimpleException yours) {
         fail("caught wrong exception");
      }
      finally {
         return;
      }
   }

   public void testExceptionOrder5() {
      try {
         blowsUp();
         rethrows();
         fail("no exception");
      }
      catch (SimpleException yours) {
         fail("caught wrong exception");
      }
      catch (RuntimeException success) {
      }
   }

   public void testExceptionOrder6() {
      try {
         rethrows();
         blowsUp();
         fail("no exception");
      }
      catch (SimpleException yours) {
         fail("caught wrong exception");
      }
      catch (RuntimeException success) {
      }
   }
   public void testExceptionOrder7() {
      try {
         rethrows();
         blowsUp();
         fail("no exception");
```

```
        }
        catch (SimpleException success) {
        }
        catch (RuntimeException fail) {
            fail("caught wrong exception");
        }
    }

    public void testErrorException1() {
        try {
            throw new RuntimeException("fail");
        }
        catch (Exception success) {
        }
    }

    public void testErrorException2() {
        try {
            new Dyer();
        }
        catch (Exception success) {
        }
    }

    public void testErrorException3() {
        try {
            new Dyer();
        }
        catch (Error success) {
        }
    }

    public void testErrorException4() {
        try {
            new Dyer();
        }
        catch (Throwable success) {
        }
    }

    public void testErrorException5() {
        try {
            new Dyer();
        }
        catch (Throwable fail) {
            fail("caught exception in wrong place");
        }
        catch (Error success) {
        }
    }

    public void testErrorException6() {
        try {
            new Dyer();
```

Exercises

```
      }
      catch (Error fail) {
         fail("caught exception in wrong place");
      }
      catch (Throwable success) {
      }
   }

   public void testErrorException7() {
      try {
         new Dyer();
      }
      catch (Error fail) {
         fail("caught exception in wrong place");
      }
      catch (Throwable success) {
      }
      finally {
         return;
      }
   }

Dyer:
class Dyer {
   Dyer() {
      throw new RuntimeException("oops.");
   }
}
```

7. What compiler error would you expect the following code to generate? Copy it into a test class of your own and make it pass.

```
public void testWithProblems() {
   try {
      doSomething();
      fail("no exception");
   }
   catch (Exception success) {}
}

void doSomething() {
   throw new Exception("blah");
}
```

8. What is wrong with the following commonly seen code?

```
public void doSomething() {
   try {
      complexOperationWithSideEffects();
   } catch (Exception e) {
      e.printStackTrace();
   }
}
```

9. Write a method to log an exception to a given log with the stack trace in reverse order (so that the point of failure is at the tail of the log instead of the head).

10. Create a custom Handler which discards the messages it receives and counts the number of times that messages were logged at various levels of severity. Use a map to store the count by severity.

11. Create a custom log message formatter that you can optionally construct with a CountingLogHandler. If no CountingLogHandler is passed in, the formatter should produce output in the form:

```
LEVEL: message
```

For example:

```
WARNING: watch out
```

If a CountingLogHandler is passed in, each message should show the count for the current level. For example:

```
WARNING: watch out (WARNING total = 1)
```

Make sure you write tests for both circumstances.

Then ensure that the CountingLogHandler uses the custom formatter as its default. Modify the CountingLogHandler to store formatted output in a StringBuilder so that your test can request the complete logging summary.

Finally, edit the logging property file and assign the custom formatter to the ConsoleHandler. Visually ensure that logging messages sent to the ConsoleHandler come out as expected.

Exercises

Lesson 9

Maps and Equality

In this lesson you will learn more about the hash table data structure classes
in Java. You will also learn about the fundamental concept of equality. Understanding these two fundamental, related topics is critical to your ability to
master Java. Yet many developers with years of Java experience do not fully
understand these concepts. Insidious defects and severe performance issues
can arise from this lack of education. Before we start on these important topics, however, you'll learn about logical operators, an equally important topic.

You will learn about:

- logical operators

- hash tables

- equality

- toString

- Map and Set implementations

- Strings and equality

Logical Operators

Suppose you want to execute a line of code only if two separate conditions
both hold true. You can use cascading if statements to guard that line of
code:

```
if (isFullTime)
   if (isInState)
      rate *= 0.9;
```

311

Logical Operators

Using *logical operators*, you can combine multiple conditionals into a single complex boolean expression:

```
if (isFullTime && isInState)
    rate *= 0.9;
```

The double ampersands symbol (&&) is the logical *and* operator. It is a binary operator—it separates two boolean expressions—the operands. If the result of both operands is true, the result of the entire conditional is true. In any other case, the result of the entire conditional is false. Here is the test-driven truth table (TDTT[1]) that represents the possible combinations of the logical *and* operator:

```
assertTrue(true && true);
assertFalse(true && false);
assertFalse(false && true);
assertFalse(false && false);
```

The logical *or* operator (||), also a binary operator, returns true if either one of the two operands returns true or if both operands return true. The logical *or* operator returns false only if both operands are false. The TDTT for logical *or*:

```
assertTrue(true || true);
assertTrue(true || false);
assertTrue(false || true);
assertFalse(false || false);
```

The logical *not* operator (!) is a unary operator that reverse the boolean value of an expression. If the source expression is true, the not operator results in the entire expression returning false, and vice versa. The TDTT:

```
assertFalse(!true);
assertTrue(!false);
```

The logical exclusive-or (*xor*) operator (^) is a less frequently used binary operator that returns false if both operands result in the same boolean value. The TDTT:

```
assertFalse(true ^ true);
assertTrue(true ^ false);
assertTrue(false ^ true);
assertFalse(false ^ false);
```

You can combine multiple logical operators. If you do not provide parentheses, the order of precedence is !, then &&, then ^^, then ||.

---

[1]A fabricated but cute acronym.

Short-Circuiting

The && and || logical operators just shown are known as *short-circuited* logical operators. When the Java VM executes an expression using a short-circuited logical operator, it evaluates the left operand (the expression to the left of the operator) of the expression first. The result of the left operand may immediately determine the result of the entire expression.

In the case of *or* (||), if the left operand is true, there is no need to evaluate the right operand. The entire expression will always be true. The Java VM saves time by executing only half of the expression. With respect to *and* (&&), if the left operand is false, the entire expression will always be false. The Java VM will not evaluate the right operand.

You may have a rare need to always execute both sides of the expression. The code on the right-hand side may do something that you need to always happen. This is poor design. Lesson 4 points out that methods should either effect actions or return information, but not both. Likewise, operands should be viewed as atomic operations that are either commands or queries. You should be able to restructure the code so that the action occurs before executing the complex conditional.

If you still feel compelled to always execute both operands, you can use *non-short-circuited* logical operators. The non-short-circuited *and* operator is a single ampersand (&). The non-short-circuited *or* operator is a single pipe (|).

Note that xor (^) is always non-short-circuited. Java cannot discern the result of an xor expression from only one operand. Refer to the TDTT above to see why.

Hash Tables

 You need to create a student directory to contain students enrolled in the university. The system must allow each student to be assigned a unique identifier, or ID. The system must allow you to later retrieve each student from the directory using its ID.

To build this story, you will create a StudentDirectory class. While you could use an ArrayList to store all students, you will instead use a Map. You learned a bit about maps in Lesson 6. As a reminder, Map is the interface for a data structure that allows elements to be stored and received based on a key. A map is a collection of key-value pairs. You store, or put, an element at a certain key in a map. You later retrieve, or get, that element by supplying the proper key.

In Lesson 6, you learned about the EnumMap implementation of the Map interface. If the keys in a Map are of enum type, you should use an EnumMap. Otherwise you will usually want to use the workhorse implementation of Map, java.util.HashMap. HashMap is a general-use map based on a data structure known as a hash table. Most Map code you encounter will use the HashMap implementation (or the legacy Hashtable implementation—see Lesson 7).

A hash table provides a specific way to implement a map. It is designed for rapid insertion and retrieval.

To build the student directory, start with the test:

```java
package sis.studentinfo;

import junit.framework.*;
import java.io.*;

public class StudentDirectoryTest extends TestCase {
    private StudentDirectory dir;

    protected void setUp() {
        dir = new StudentDirectory();
    }

    public void testStoreAndRetrieve() throws IOException {
        final int numberOfStudents = 10;

        for (int i = 0; i < numberOfStudents; i++)
            addStudent(dir, i);

        for (int i = 0; i < numberOfStudents; i++)
            verifyStudentLookup(dir, i);
    }

    void addStudent(StudentDirectory directory, int i)
            throws IOException {
        String id = "" + i;
        Student student = new Student(id);
        student.setId(id);
        student.addCredits(i);
        directory.add(student);
    }

    void verifyStudentLookup(StudentDirectory directory, int i)
            throws IOException {
        String id = "" + i;
        Student student = dir.findById(id);
        assertEquals(id, student.getLastName());
        assertEquals(id, student.getId());
        assertEquals(i, student.getCredits());
    }
}
```

The test, testStoreAndRetrieve, uses a for loop to construct and insert a number of students into the StudentDirectory. The test verifies, again using a for loop, that each student can be found in the directory using the Student directory method findById.

The StudentDirectory code is brief.

```
package sis.studentinfo;

import java.util.*;

public class StudentDirectory {
    private Map<String,Student> students =
        new HashMap<String,Student>();

    public void add(Student student) {
        students.put(student.getId(), student);
    }

    public Student findById(String id) {
        return students.get(id);
    }
}
```

A StudentDirectory object encapsulates a HashMap, students. When client code invokes the add method, the code in add inserts the student argument into the HashMap. The key for the inserted student is the student's ID.

The ID must be unique. If you put a new value at an ID for which an entry already exists, the old value is replaced.

Later in this lesson, you will revisit hash tables. First, however, you will learn about equality. And before you can learn about equality, you have a story to implement.

Courses

 A Session represents the teaching of a course for a given start date. Most courses are taught once per term. Each course may thus be represented by many Session instances.[2]

Currently the Session class contains the department and number information for the associated course, as well as its number of credits. If there can be multiple sessions of a course, this implementation is inefficient and trouble-

---

[2]This is a small school, so we're ignoring the possibility that there may need to be two separate sections of a session in order to accommodate a large number of students.

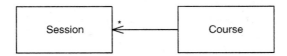

Figure 9.1   *A Course Has Many Sessions*

some, since the course information will be repeated throughout each Session object.

What you want instead is a way of tying many session objects back to a single Course object. The UML diagram in Figure 9.1 shows this many-to-one relationship from Session to a new class named Course.

You will refactor your code to the above relationship. Start by creating a simple Course class that captures the department, number, and number of credits. A simple test declares that department and number are required to create a Course. The department and number combined represent the unique *key* for a Course. Two separate courses cannot have the same department and number.

```
package sis.studentinfo;

import junit.framework.*;

public class CourseTest extends TestCase {
    public void testCreate() {
        Course course = new Course("CMSC", "120");
        assertEquals("CMSC", course.getDepartment());
        assertEquals("120", course.getNumber());
    }
}
```

Course starts out as a simple data object. It contains a constructor and two getters for the key fields.

```
package sis.studentinfo;

public class Course {
    private String department;
    private String number;

    public Course(String department, String number) {
        this.department = department;
        this.number = number;
    }

    public String getDepartment() {
        return department;
    }
```

```
    public String getNumber() {
        return number;
    }
}
```

Refactoring Session

Here's an overview of the steps you'll undertake in this refactoring:

1. Construct session objects using a Course object. Impacts: SessionTest, Session, CourseSessionTest, SummerCourseSessionTest, RosterReporterTest, CourseReportTest.

2. Change the creation methods in CourseSession and SummerCourseSession to take a Course as a parameter.

3. Modify CourseSession and SummerCourseSession constructors to take a Course.

4. Modify the Session constructor to take a Course.

5. Store a Course reference in Session instead of department and number strings.

You will make these changes incrementally. With each change, you'll use the compiler to help you find problems, then run your tests to ensure that you didn't break anything.

Starting in SessionTest:

Currently, the abstract method createSession constructs Session objects using department and number strings:

```
abstract protected Session createSession(
    String department, String number, Date startDate);
```

You want to change this creation method to reflect the need to construct Session objects using a Course object:

```
abstract public class SessionTest extends TestCase {
    ...
    abstract protected Session createSession(
        Course course, Date startDate);
```

This change will necessitate quite a few other changes, but overall it shouldn't take more than 5 minutes to make them. In SessionTest, you will need to change both the setUp method and testComparable. Here's the existing setUp method in SessionTest (I've boldfaced the code that will need to change):

```
public void setUp() {
    startDate = createDate(2003, 1, 6);
    session = createSession("ENGL", "101", startDate);
    session.setNumberOfCredits(CREDITS);
}
```

I've shown the change to setUp here; changes to testComparable are similar:

```
protected void setUp() {
    startDate = new Date();
    session = createSession(new Course("ENGL", "101"), startDate);
    session.setNumberOfCredits(CREDITS);
}
```

Use the compiler to guide you through making these changes. As you fix one problem, the compiler can take you to the next problem to fix.

You will need to change both SummerCourseSessionTest and CourseSessionTest. In the interest of incrementalism, try to make the smallest amount of changes that will get you to a green bar. You can modify both CourseSessionTest and SummerCourseSessionTest without having to touch CourseSession or SummerCourseSession.

Here are the changes to the tests. This time I've included the old lines of code from the previous version of the code and struck them out so you could see the difference line to line. I'll use this approach for the remainder of the refactoring.

```
// CourseSessionTest
...
public class CourseSessionTest extends SessionTest {
    public void testCourseDates() {
        Date startDate = DateUtil.createDate(2003, 1, 6);
        Session session = createSession("ENGL", "200", startDate);
        Session session = createSession(createCourse(), startDate);
        Date sixteenWeeksOut = createDate(2003, 4, 25);
        assertEquals(sixteenWeeksOut, session.getEndDate());
    }

    public void testCount() {
        CourseSession.resetCount();
        createSession("", "", new Date());
        createSession(createCourse(), new Date());
        assertEquals(1, CourseSession.getCount());
        createSession("", "", new Date());
        createSession(createCourse(), new Date());
        assertEquals(2, CourseSession.getCount());
    }

    private Course createCourse() {
        return new Course("ENGL", "101");
    }
```

```
    protected Session createSession(
        String department, String number, Date date) {
        return CourseSession.create(department, number, date);
    }
    protected Session createSession(Course course, Date date) {
        return CourseSession.create(
            course.getDepartment(), course.getNumber(), date);
    }
}

// SummerCourseSessionTest.java
package sis.summer;

import junit.framework.*;
import java.util.*;
import sis.studentinfo.*;

public class SummerCourseSessionTest extends SessionTest {
    public void testEndDate() {
        Date startDate = DateUtil.createDate(2003, 6, 9);
        Session session = createSession("ENGL", "200", startDate);
        Session session =
            createSession(new Course("ENGL", "200"), startDate);
        Date eightWeeksOut = DateUtil.createDate(2003, 8, 1);
        assertEquals(eightWeeksOut, session.getEndDate());
    }

    protected Session createSession(
        String department, String number, Date date) {
        return SummerCourseSession.create(department, number, date);
    }
    protected Session createSession(Course course, Date date) {
        return SummerCourseSession.create(
            course.getDepartment(), course.getNumber(), date);
    }
}
```

Tests should pass at this point. Now modify the Session subclass creation methods to take a Course directly.

```
// CourseSessionTest.java

protected Session createSession(Course course, Date date) {
    return CourseSession.create(
        course.getDepartment(), course.getNumber(), date);
    return CourseSession.create(course, date);
}

// SummerCourseSessionTest.java
protected Session createSession(Course course, Date date) {
    return SummerCourseSession.create(
        course.getDepartment(), course.getNumber(), date);
    return SummerCourseSession.create(course, date);
}
```

This change impacts RosterReporterTest:

```
package sis.report;

import junit.framework.TestCase;
import sis.studentinfo.*;
import static sis.report.ReportConstant.NEWLINE;

public class RosterReporterTest extends TestCase {
    public void testRosterReport() {
        Session session =
            CourseSession.create(
                "ENGL", "101", DateUtil.createDate(2003, 1, 6));
        Session session =
            CourseSession.create(
                new Course("ENGL", "101"),
                DateUtil.createDate(2003, 1, 6));
        ...
    }
}
```

And also CourseReportTest[3]:

```
package sis.report;

import junit.framework.*;
import java.util.*;
import sis.studentinfo.*;
import static sis.report.ReportConstant.NEWLINE;

public class CourseReportTest extends TestCase {
    public void testReport() {
        final Date date = new Date();
        CourseReport report = new CourseReport();
        report.add(CourseSession.create("ENGL", "101", date));
        report.add(CourseSession.create("CZEC", "200", date));
        report.add(CourseSession.create("ITAL", "410", date));
        report.add(CourseSession.create("CZEC", "220", date));
        report.add(CourseSession.create("ITAL", "330", date));
        report.add(create("ENGL", "101", date));
        report.add(create("CZEC", "200", date));
        report.add(create("ITAL", "410", date));
        report.add(create("CZEC", "220", date));
        report.add(create("ITAL", "330", date));
```

---

[3]I've taken some liberties by updating both RosterReporterTest and CourseReportTest with Java features you have learned since originally coding them. For example, the code now assigns a CourseSession object to a Session reference. Doing so will also force you to change to RosterReporter and CourseReport.

```
        assertEquals(
            String.format(
                "CZEC 200%n" +
                "CZEC 220%n" +
                "ENGL 101%n" +
                "ITAL 330%n" +
                "ITAL 410%n"),
            report.text());
    }

    private Session create(String name, String number, Date date) {
        return CourseSession.create(new Course(name, number), date);
    }
}
```

Change the creation methods in CourseSession and SummerCourseSession to take a Course as a parameter, but—for the moment—continue to pass along the department and number to the constructor.

```
// CourseSession.java
public static Session create(
    String department, String number, Date startDate) {
    incrementCount();
    return new CourseSession(department, number, startDate) ;
}
public static Session create(Course course, Date startDate) {
    incrementCount();
    return new CourseSession(
        course.getDepartment(), course.getNumber(), startDate);
}

// SummerCourseSession.java
public static SummerCourseSession create(
    String department, String number, Date startDate) {
    return new SummerCourseSession(department, number, startDate);
}
public static Session create(Course course, Date startDate) {
    return new SummerCourseSession(
        course.getDepartment(), course.getNumber(), startDate);
}
```

Tests pass. Now push the course into the constructor and rerun the tests.

```
// CourseSession.java
public static Session create(Course course, Date startDate) {
    incrementCount();
    return new CourseSession(course, startDate);
}

protected CourseSession(
    String department, String number, Date startDate) {
    super(department, number, startDate);
}
```

```
protected CourseSession(Course course, Date startDate) {
    super(course.getDepartment(), course.getNumber(), startDate);
}

// SummerCourseSession.java
public static Session create(Course course, Date startDate) {
    return new SummerCourseSession(course, startDate);
}

private SummerCourseSession(
        String department, String number, Date startDate) {
    super(department, number, startDate);
}
private SummerCourseSession(Course course, Date startDate) {
    super(course.getDepartment(), course.getNumber(), startDate);
}
```

Tedious? Perhaps. Simple? Each one of the steps in this refactoring is very basic and takes only seconds to execute. Safe? Extremely. The overall time expenditure should only be a few minutes before everything is working. You get to see a green bar several times during the gradual code transformation. The foremost authority on refactoring, Martin Fowler, suggests that you can never run your tests too frequently.[4]

The alternative would be to make the changes all at once and hope they work. You might save a couple of minutes, but there is a likely possibility that you will make a mistake. Correcting the mistake will take you more time than you saved.

You're almost there. Push the Course object into the superclass Session constructor.

```
// CourseSession.java
protected CourseSession(Course course, Date startDate) {
    super(course, startDate);
}

// SummerCourseSession.java
private SummerCourseSession(Course course, Date startDate) {
    super(course, startDate);
}

// Session.java
protected Session(
        String department, String number, Date startDate) {
    this.department = department;
    this.number = number;
    this.startDate = startDate;
}
```

[4][Fowler2000], p. 94.

```
protected Session(Course course, Date startDate) {
    this.department = course.getDepartment();
    this.number = course.getNumber();
    this.startDate = startDate;
}
```

Finally, you can change the Session class to store a Course reference instead of the separate department and number String references.

```
// Session.java
abstract public class Session implements Iterable<Student> {
    private String department;
    private String number;
    private Course course;
    // ...
    protected Session(Course course, Date startDate) {
        this.course = course;
        this.startDate = startDate;
    }

    String getDepartment() {
        return department;
        return course.getDepartment();
    }

    String getNumber() {
        return number;
        return course.getNumber();
    }
    // ...
```

Equality

 In an upcoming lesson, you will build a course catalog. One requirement for the course catalog will be to ensure that duplicate courses are not added to the catalog. Courses are *semantically equal* if they have the same department and course number.

Now that you have a functional Course class, you will want to override the equals method to supply a semantic definition for equality. If you have two Course objects and the department and number fields in both objects contain the same (corresponding) String, comparing the two should return true.

```
// in CourseTest.java:
public void testEquality() {
```

```
    Course courseA = new Course("NURS", "201");
    Course courseAPrime = new Course("NURS", "201");
    assertEquals(courseA, courseAPrime);
}
```

This test fails. Remember from Lesson 1 that the object courseA is a separate object in memory, distinct from courseAPrime. The assertEquals method translates roughly[5] to the underlying lines of code:

```
if (!courseA.equals(courseAPrime))
    fail();
```

In other words, the comparison between two objects in assertEquals uses the equals method defined on the receiver. The receiver is the first parameter, which JUnit refers to as the expected value. The receiver in this example is courseA.

You have not yet defined an equals method in Course. Java therefore searches up the hierarchy chain to find one. The only superclass of Course is the implicit superclass Object. In Object you will find the default definition of equals:

```
package java.lang;
public class Object {
    // ...
    public boolean equals(Object obj) {
        return (this == obj);
    }
    // ...
}
```

The equals implementation in Object compares the reference—the memory location—of the receiver to the reference of the object being passed in.

 If you do not provide a definition for equals in your subclass, you get the default definition, memory equivalence.

Memory equivalence exists if two references point to the exact same object in memory.

You will want to override the equals method in the Course object. The Course definition of equals will override the Object definition of equals. The equals method should return true if the receiver object is semantically equal to the parameter object. For Course, equals should return true if the department and course number of the receiver is equal to that of the parameter Course.

Let's code this slowly, one step at a time. For now, code the equals method in Course to most simply pass the test:

---

[5]The actual code is slightly more involved.

```
@Override
public boolean equals(Object object) {
    return true;
}
```

The `equals` method must match the signature that `assertEquals` expects. The `assertEquals` method expects to call an `equals` method that takes an Object as parameter. If you were to specify that `equals` took a Course object as parameter, the `assertEquals` method would not find it:

```
@Override
public boolean equals(Course course) { // THIS WILL NOT WORK
    return true;
}
```

The `assertEquals` method would instead invoke the Object definition of `equals`.

Add a comparison to the test that should fail (since `equals` always returns true):

```
public void testEquality() {
    Course courseA = new Course("NURS", "201");
    Course courseAPrime = new Course("NURS", "201");
    assertEquals(courseA, courseAPrime);

    Course courseB = new Course("ARTH", "330");
    assertFalse(courseA.equals(courseB));
}
```

Once you see that this test fails, update your `equals` method:

```
@Override
public boolean equals(Object object) {
    Course that = (Course)object;
    return
        this.department.equals(that.department) &&
        this.number.equals(that.number);
}
```

You must first cast the `object` argument to a Course reference so that you can refer to its instance variables. The local variable name you give to the argument helps differentiate between the receiver (`this`) and the argument (`that`). The `return` statement compares `this` Course's department and number to the department and number of `that` Course. If both (`&&`) are equal, the `equals` method returns `true`.

The Contract for Equality

The Java API documentation for the `equals` method in Object provides a list of what defines an equivalence relation between two objects:

Reflexivity:	`x.equals(x)`
Symmetry:	`x.equals(y)` *if-and-only-if (iff)* `y.equals(x)`
Transitivity:	if `x.equals(y)` and `y.equals(z)`, then `x.equals(z)`
Consistency:	`x.equals(y)` returns a consistent value given consistent state
Comparison to null:	`!x.equals(null)`

The above contract should hold true for all non-`null` values of x and y. You can implement each of these rules in your unit test for equality.[6]

```
public void testEquality() {
    Course courseA = new Course("NURS", "201");
    Course courseAPrime = new Course("NURS", "201");
    assertEquals(courseA, courseAPrime);

    Course courseB = new Course("ARTH", "330");
    assertFalse(courseA.equals(courseB));

    // reflexivity
    assertEquals(courseA, courseA);

    // transitivity
    Course courseAPrime2 = new Course("NURS", "201");
    assertEquals(courseAPrime, courseAPrime2);
    assertEquals(courseA, courseAPrime2);

    // symmetry
    assertEquals(courseAPrime, courseA);

    // consistency
    assertEquals(courseA, courseAPrime);

    // comparison to null
    assertFalse(courseA.equals(null));
}
```

[6]A nice set of JUnit extensions, located at *http://sourceforge.net/projects/junit-addons*, provides an automated means of testing the equality contract.

When you run your tests, everything will pass but the final assertion in testEquality. You will receive a NullPointerException: The that argument is null and the equals code attempts to access its fields (department and object). You can add a guard clause to return false if the argument is null:

```
@Override
public boolean equals(Object object) {
    if (object == null)
        return false;
    Course that = (Course)object;
    return
        this.department.equals(that.department) &&
        this.number.equals(that.number);
}
```

You might choose to represent each of the "qualities of equality" (reflexivity, transitivity, symmetry, consistency, and comparison to null) in a separate test. There are differing views on approaches to TDD. Some developers feel that you should structure your code so that each test contains a single assertion.[7] I take the viewpoint that the goal of a test is to prove a single piece of functionality. Doing so may require many assertions/postconditions. In this example, the many assertions you just coded represent a complete contract for a single piece of functionality—equality.

Apples and Oranges

Since the equals method takes an Object as parameter, you can pass anything to it (and the code will still compile). Your equals method should handle this situation:

```
// apples & oranges
assertFalse(courseA.equals("CMSC-120"));
```

Even though the String value matches the department and number of courseA, a Course is not a String. You would expect this comparison to return false. When Java executes the equals method, however, you receive a ClassCast-Exception. The line of the equals method that executes the cast is the cause:

```
@Override
public boolean equals(Object object) {
    if (object == null)
        return false;
    Course that = (Course)object;
```

---

[7][Astels2004].

```
        return
            this.department.equals(that.department) &&
            this.number.equals(that.number);
    }
```

The code attempts to cast the String parameter to a Course reference. This invalid cast generates the ClassCastException.

You need a guard clause that immediately returns false if someone throws an orange at your equals method. The guard clause ensures that the type of the parameter matches the type of the receiver.

```
@Override
public boolean equals(Object object) {
    if (object == null)
        return false;
    if (this.getClass() != object.getClass())
        return false;
    Course that = (Course)object;
    return
        this.department.equals(that.department) &&
        this.number.equals(that.number);
}
```

You learned about the getClass method in Lesson 8. It returns a class constant. For the example comparison that threw the ClassCastException, the class constant of the receiver is Course.class, and the class constant of the parameter is String.class. Class constants are unique—there is only one "instance" of the Class object Course.class. This uniqueness allows you to compare class constants using the operator != (not equal to) instead of comparing them using equals.

Some developers choose to use the instanceof operator. The instanceof operator returns true if an object is an instance of, or subclass of, the target class. Here is the equals method rewritten to use instanceof.

```
@Override
public boolean equals(Object object) {
    if (object == null)
        return false;
    if (!(object instanceof Course))
        return false;
    Course that = (Course)object;
    return
        this.department.equals(that.department) &&
        this.number.equals(that.number);
}
```

You should initially prefer to compare the classes of the receiver and argument, instead of using instanceof. The class comparison only returns true if both objects are of the exact same type. Introduce instanceof later if you need to compare objects irrespective of their position in an inheritance hierarchy. See Lesson 12 for more information on instanceof.

JUnit and Equality

Sometimes I will code equals tests to be a bit more explicit. Instead of saying:

```
assertEquals(courseA, courseB);
```

I'll express the comparison as:

```
assertTrue(courseA.equals(courseB));
```

You should be clear on the fact that assertEquals uses the equals method for reference comparisons. But it can be helpful to explicitly emphasize that fact, and show that the equals method is what you're actually testing.

You may want to compare two references to see if they are the same. In other words, do they point to the same object in memory? You could code this comparison as:

```
assertTrue(courseA == courseB);
```

or as:

```
assertSame(courseA, courseB);
```

You should prefer the second assertion form, since it supplies a better error message upon failure. As before, though, you might choose to explicitly show the == comparison if for purposes of building an equals method test.

Collections and Equality

The student information system will need to create a course catalog that contains all of the Course objects. You will thus need to be able to store a Course in a collection, then verify that the collection contains the object.

```
package sis.studentinfo;

import junit.framework.*;
import java.util.*;

public void testEquality() {
    Course courseA = new Course("NURS", "201");
    Course courseAPrime = new Course("NURS", "201");
    assertEquals(courseA, courseAPrime);
```

```
...
// containment
List<Course> list = new ArrayList<Course>();
list.add(courseA);
assertTrue(list.contains(courseAPrime));
}
```

The contains method defined in ArrayList loops through all contained objects, comparing each to the parameter using the equals method. This test should pass with no further changes. In fact, the test for containment is more of a language test. It tests the functionality of ArrayList, by demonstrating that ArrayList uses the equals method for testing containment. The containment test does not add to the equality contract. Feel free to remove it.

What about using the Course as a key in a HashMap object?

```
public void testEquality() {
    Course courseA = new Course("NURS", "201");
    Course courseAPrime = new Course("NURS", "201");

    // ...

    Map<Course, String> map = new HashMap<Course, String>();
    map.put(courseA, "");
    assertTrue(map.containsKey(courseAPrime));
}
```

The above bit of test demonstrates a Map method, containsKey. This method returns true if a matching key exists in the map. Even though a Map is a collection, just as a List is, this test fails! To understand why, you must understand how the HashMap class is implemented.

Hash Tables

An ArrayList encapsulates an array, a contiguous block of space in memory. Finding an object in an array requires serially traversing the array in order to find an element. The class java.util.HashMap is built around the hash table construct mentioned at the beginning of this lesson. It too is based on a contiguous block of space in memory.

I can pictorially represent a hash table as a bunch of slots (Figure 9.2).

When inserting an element into a hash table, the code rapidly determines a slot for the element by first asking it for its *hash code*. A hash code is simply an integer, ideally as unique as possible. The contract for hash code is based on the definition of equality for a class: If two objects are equal, their hash

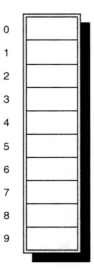

0
1
2
3
4
5
6
7
8
9

Figure 9.2 *A Hash Table with Ten Slots*

code should be equal. If two objects are not equal, then their hash codes are ideally (but not necessarily) unequal.

Once the hash code is available, a bit of arithmetic determines the slot:

```
hash code % table size = slot number
```

(Remember that the modulus operator, %, returns the remainder of the equivalent integer division.) For example, if you insert a Course object into a hash table of size 10 and the hash code value of the course is 65, it would go into the fifth slot:

```
65 % 10 = 5
```

Just as in an array, Java calculates the memory address for the start of a slot using the formula:

```
offset + (slot size * slot number)
```

Figure 9.3 shows a Course element slotted into a hash table.

The hash code is an int that is retrieved by sending the message hashCode to any Object. The class java.lang.Object supplies a default definition of hashCode. It returns a unique number based upon the memory address of the object.

To retrieve an object from a hash table, you recalculate the slot by asking for the object's hashCode again. You can then do the same offset calculation to immediately retrieve the object.

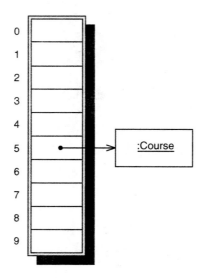

Figure 9.3   *Hash Table with Course in the Fifth Slot*

So what goes in a hashCode method? It must return an int, and as mentioned, two equal objects must return the same hashCode. The simplest, but worst, solution would be to return a constant, such as the number 1.

Collisions

The hash code for an object should be as unique as possible. If two unequal objects return the same hash code, they will resolve to the same slot in the hash table. This is known as a *collision*. The implication of a collision is extra logic and extra time to maintain a list of collided objects. A few solutions for resolving collisions exist. The simplest is manage a list of collided objects for each slot. Figure 9.4 shows a pictorial representation.

Since the possibility of collisions exists, when retrieving an object, the hash table code must also compare the object retrieved from a slot to ensure that it is the one expected. If not, the code must traverse the list of collided objects to find the match.

If all objects were to return the same hashCode, such as 1, then all objects will collide to the same slot in a HashMap. The end result would be that every insertion and deletion would require serially traversing the list of collided

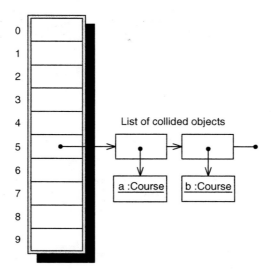

Figure 9.4 *Hash Table Collisions*

objects. This list would include every object inserted. In this degenerate case, you might as well use an ArrayList.

If the hash codes of all objects generate different slots, you have an optimally mapped hash table. Performance is the best possible: All insertions to and retrievals from the table execute in constant time. There is no need to serially traverse a collision list.

An Ideal Hash Algorithm

Java already provides a good hashCode implementation for the class String, which is more often than not the key type for a HashMap. The integral numeric wrapper classes (Integer, Long, Byte, Char, Short) are also often used as a HashMap key; their hash code is simply the number they wrap.

The fields that uniquely identify your object are typically one of these object types (String or numeric). To obtain a decent hash code that satisfies the equality condition, you can simply return the hash code of the unique key. If more than one field is used to represent the unique key, you will need to devise an algorithm to generate the hash code.

The following code, to be added to the Course class, generates a hashCode based on arithmetically combining the hashCodes of department and number. Hash code algorithms typically use prime numbers. The use of primes tends to give better distribution when combined with the modulus operation against the table size.

```
@Override
public int hashCode() {
    final int hashMultiplier = 41;
    int result = 7;
    result = result * hashMultiplier + department.hashCode();
    result = result * hashMultiplier + number.hashCode();
    return result;
}
```

The tests should pass once you implement this hashCode method.[8] Separate the hash code tests into a new test method that will enforce the complete contract for hashCode.

```
public void testHashCode() {
    Course courseA = new Course("NURS", "201");
    Course courseAPrime = new Course("NURS", "201");

    Map<Course, String> map = new HashMap<Course, String>();
    map.put(courseA, "");
    assertTrue(map.containsKey(courseAPrime));

    assertEquals(courseA.hashCode(), courseAPrime.hashCode());
    // consistency
    assertEquals(courseA.hashCode(), courseA.hashCode());
}
```

The test proves that two semantically equal courses produce the same hash code. It also demonstrates consistency. The return value from hashCode is the same (consistent) with each call to it, as long as the key values for the courses do not change.

The part of the test that demonstrates stuffing the Course into a hash map can be removed, since the contract assertions for hashCode are all that is required. The final set of equality and hash code contract tests:

```
public void testEquality() {
    Course courseA = new Course("NURS", "201");
    Course courseAPrime = new Course("NURS", "201");
    assertEquals(courseA, courseAPrime);

    Course courseB = new Course("ARTH", "330");
    assertFalse(courseA.equals(courseB));

    // reflexivity
    assertEquals(courseA, courseA);
```

---

[8]This algorithm was obtained from the example at *http://mindprod.com/jgloss/hashcode.html*.

```
    // transitivity
    Course courseAPrime2 = new Course("NURS", "201");
    assertEquals(courseAPrime, courseAPrime2);
    assertEquals(courseA, courseAPrime2);

    // symmetry
    assertEquals(courseAPrime, courseA);

    // consistency
    assertEquals(courseA, courseAPrime);

    // comparison to null
    assertFalse(courseA.equals(null));

    // apples & oranges
    assertFalse(courseA.equals("CMSC-120"));
}
public void testHashCode() {
    Course courseA = new Course("NURS", "201");
    Course courseAPrime = new Course("NURS", "201");

    assertEquals(courseA.hashCode(), courseAPrime.hashCode());
    // consistency
    assertEquals(courseA.hashCode(), courseA.hashCode());
}
```

These tests contain a good amount of code! Again, consider JUnit-addons (see footnote 6 above) as a way of automatically enforcing equality and hash code contracts. If you choose to not use JUnit-addons, make sure you refactor to eliminate duplication when writing these tests.

A Final Note on hashCode

    If you code an equals method for a class, also code a hashCode method.

In the absence of hashCode, the compiler won't complain, and you may not encounter any problems. However, unexpected behavior will likely result if you put objects of that class into a hash table based collection (the class java.util.Set also uses a hash table implementation). Figuring out that there is a missing hashCode method can waste a considerable amount of time. Get in the habit of coding hashCode if you code equals!

If performance is a consideration, you may want to write unit tests for the hash code. One technique is to load a HashSet with a large number of elements, testing the performance to ensure that the insertions execute in a reasonable time. If not, the hash table probably managed a high number of collisions.

```java
public void testHashCodePerformance() {
    final int count = 10000;
    long start = System.currentTimeMillis();
    Map<Course, String> map = new HashMap<Course, String>();
    for (int i = 0; i < count; i++) {
        Course course = new Course("C" + i, "" + i);
        map.put(course, "");
    }
    long stop = System.currentTimeMillis();
    long elapsed = stop - start;
    final long arbitraryThreshold = 200;
    assertTrue("elapsed time = " + elapsed,
        elapsed < arbitraryThreshold);
}
```

There are many ways to test performance, but the above test provides a simple, adequate mechanism. The class java.lang.System contains a static method, currentTimeMillis, that returns the milliseconds representing the current time stamp. Before starting, you store the current timestamp in a local variable (start). You execute the desired code *n* times using a for loop. When the loop completes, you capture the timestamp (stop). You obtain the elapsed time by subtracting the start time from the stop time. The assertion ensures that the loop completed in a reasonable amount of time (arbitraryThreshold).

The assertTrue method call contains a String as its first parameter. The String gets printed by JUnit as part of the error message only if the assertion fails. In this example, the failure will show how long the loop actually took to execute.

You may want to isolate performance tests in a separate suite. You will still want to run them regularly (perhaps daily, or after you have completed a significant task). The nature of performance tests makes them slow, however, so you may not want the constant negative impact to the performance of your functional unit test suite.

If you find you need more comprehensive unit testing, either build your own framework by eliminating duplication or consider a tool such as Junit-Perf.[9] JUnit itself contains some rudimentary hooks to help you with repetitive testing.

To demonstrate the usefulness of the example performance test, change the hashCode implementation in Course to return a constant number:

```java
@Override
public int hashCode() {
    return 1;
}
```

[9] See *http://www.clarkware.com/software/JUnitPerf.html.*

Even with only 10,000 entries into the HashMap, the test should fail miserably. Revert the hashCode to its previous form; the test should now pass.

Another technique for testing hashCode is to ensure that the variance that a number of hash codes produces is reasonably high. The variance is a measure of how spread out a distribution of numbers is. You calculate the variance as the average of the squared deviation of each number from the mean.

The problem with both of these testing techniques is that they are based on arbitrary measures of what is acceptable. As a developer, you can determine the value of this kind of testing and choose to defer it until you can pinpoint a true performance problem to the hash table.

Minimally, you should at least write enough tests to prove that the contract for hashCode holds true.

More on Using HashMaps

Like a list, you will often want to iterate through the contents of a hash table. Your needs may include iterating through only the keys, through only the values or through both simultaneously.

In Lesson 6, you built a ReportCard class. You used ReportCard to store a map of grades to corresponding messages for printing on a report card. As a reminder, here is the source for ReportCard:

```
package sis.report;

import java.util.*;
import sis.studentinfo.*;

public class ReportCard {
    static final String A_MESSAGE = "Excellent";
    static final String B_MESSAGE = "Very good";
    static final String C_MESSAGE = "Hmmm...";
    static final String D_MESSAGE = "You're not trying";
    static final String F_MESSAGE = "Loser";

    private Map<Student.Grade, String> messages = null;

    public String getMessage(Student.Grade grade) {
        return getMessages().get(grade);
    }

    private Map<Student.Grade, String> getMessages() {
        if (messages == null)
            loadMessages();
        return messages;
    }
```

More on Using
HashMaps

```
    private void loadMessages() {
        messages =
            new EnumMap<Student.Grade, String>(Student.Grade.class);
        messages.put(Student.Grade.A, A_MESSAGE);
        messages.put(Student.Grade.B, B_MESSAGE);
        messages.put(Student.Grade.C, C_MESSAGE);
        messages.put(Student.Grade.D, D_MESSAGE);
        messages.put(Student.Grade.F, F_MESSAGE);
    }
}
```

The following three new tests for ReportCard demonstrate how to iterate through each of the three possibilities. (These are unnecessary tests, and act more like language tests.) Each of the three tests show different but valid testing approaches.

```
package sis.report;

import junit.framework.*;
import sis.studentinfo.*;
import java.util.*;

public class ReportCardTest extends TestCase {
    private ReportCard card;

    protected void setUp() {
        card = new ReportCard();
    }

    public void testMessage() {
        // remove declaration of card since it is declared in setUp
        ...
    }

    public void testKeys() {
        Set<Student.Grade> expectedGrades = new HashSet<Student.Grade>();
        expectedGrades.add(Student.Grade.A);
        expectedGrades.add(Student.Grade.B);
        expectedGrades.add(Student.Grade.C);
        expectedGrades.add(Student.Grade.D);
        expectedGrades.add(Student.Grade.F);

        Set<Student.Grade> grades = new HashSet<Student.Grade>();
        for (Student.Grade grade: card.getMessages().keySet())
            grades.add(grade);
        assertEquals(expectedGrades, grades);
    }
}
```

The first test, testKeys, provides one technique for ensuring that you iterate through all expected values in a collection. You first create a set and populating it with the objects (grades in this example) you expect to receive. You then create a secondary set and add to it each element that you iterate through. After iteration, you compare the two sets to ensure that they are equal.

Perhaps you remember sets from grade school. (Remember Venn diagrams?) If not, no big deal. A set is an unordered collection that contains unique elements. If you attempt to add a duplicate element to a set, the set rejects it. In Java, the java.util.Set interface declares the behavior of a set. The class java.util.HashSet is the workhorse implementation of the Set interface. The HashSet class compares objects using `equals` to determine if a candidate object is a duplicate.

Based on your understanding of how a hash table works, it should be clear that you cannot guarantee that its keys will appear in any specific order. It should also be clear that each key is unique. You cannot have two entries in a hash table with the same key. As such, when you send the message `keySet` to a HashMap object, it returns the keys to you as a set.

As shown in `testKeys`, you iterate a Set much as you iterate a List, using a `for-each` loop.

In contrast, the values in a hash table can be duplicates. For example, you might choose to print the same message ("get help") for a student with a D or an F. A HashMap thus cannot return the values as a Set. Instead, it returns the values as a java.util.Collection.

Collection is an interface implemented by both HashSet and ArrayList. The Collection interface declares basic collection functionality, including the abilities to add objects to a collection and obtain an iterator from a collection. The Collection interface does not imply any order to a collection, so it does not declare methods related to indexed access as does the List interface. Both java.util.Set and java.util.List interfaces extend the Collection interface.

```
public void testValues() {
    List<String> expectedMessages = new ArrayList<String>();
    expectedMessages.add(ReportCard.A_MESSAGE);
    expectedMessages.add(ReportCard.B_MESSAGE);
    expectedMessages.add(ReportCard.C_MESSAGE);
    expectedMessages.add(ReportCard.D_MESSAGE);
    expectedMessages.add(ReportCard.F_MESSAGE);

    Collection<String> messages = card.getMessages().values();
    for (String message: messages)
        assertTrue(expectedMessages.contains(message));
    assertEquals(expectedMessages.size(), messages.size());
}
```

The test, `testValues`, uses a slightly different technique. You again create a Set to represent expected values, then add to it each possible value. You obtain the hash table values by sending the message values to the HashMap object.

As you iterate through the values, you verify that the list of expected values contains each element. The contains method uses the equals method to determine if the collection includes an object. Finally, you must also test the size of the secondary set to ensure that it does not contain more elements than expected.

The third test, testEntries, shows how you can iterate through the keys and associated values (the maps) simultaneously. If you send the message entrySet to a HashMap, it returns a Set of key-value pairs. You can iterate through this set using a for-each loop. For each pass through the loop you get a Map.Entry reference that stores a key-value pair. You can retrieve the key and value from a Map.Entry by using the methods getKey and getValue. The Map.Entry is bound to the same key type (Student.Grade in the example) and value type (String) as the HashMap object.

```
public void testEntries() {
    Set<Entry> entries = new HashSet<Entry>();

    for (Map.Entry<Student.Grade,String> entry:
            card.getMessages().entrySet())
        entries.add(
            new Entry(entry.getKey(), entry.getValue()));

    Set<Entry> expectedEntries = new HashSet<Entry>();
    expectedEntries.add(
        new Entry(Student.Grade.A, ReportCard.A_MESSAGE));
    expectedEntries.add(
        new Entry(Student.Grade.B, ReportCard.B_MESSAGE));
    expectedEntries.add(
        new Entry(Student.Grade.C, ReportCard.C_MESSAGE));
    expectedEntries.add(
        new Entry(Student.Grade.D, ReportCard.D_MESSAGE));
    expectedEntries.add(
        new Entry(Student.Grade.F, ReportCard.F_MESSAGE));

    assertEquals(expectedEntries, entries);
}
```

You need to test that the for-each loop iterates over all the entries. You can create a secondary set of expected entries, like in the previous tests, and compare this expected set to the set populated by iteration. To the expected set you need to add the appropriate key-value entries, but unfortunately, Map.Entry is an interface. No concrete class to store a key-value pair is available to you.

Instead, you will create your own Entry class to store a key-value pair. The process of iteration will instantiate Entry objects and add them to the "actuals" set. Also, you will populate the expected set with Entry objects. You can then compare the two sets to ensure that they contain equal Entry objects.

```java
class Entry {
    private Student.Grade grade;
    private String message;
    Entry(Student.Grade grade, String message) {
        this.grade = grade;
        this.message = message;
    }

    @Override
    public boolean equals(Object object) {
        if (object.getClass() != this.getClass())
            return false;
        Entry that = (Entry)object;
        return
            this.grade == that.grade &&
            this.message.equals(that.message);
    }

    @Override
    public int hashCode() {
        final int hashMultiplier = 41;
        int result = 7;
        result = result * hashMultiplier + grade.hashCode();
        result = result * hashMultiplier + message.hashCode();
        return result;
    }
}
```

The class Entry is a quick-and-dirty class used solely for testing. I therefore chose to write no tests for it. The Entry class contains an equals method and its companion method hashCode. Since this is a quick-and-dirty test class, I might have chosen to omit the hashCode method, but a successful test requires it. Try running the tests without hashCode, and make sure you understand why the test fails without it.

Additional Hash Table and Set Implementations

The package java.util includes several additional classes that implement the Map and Set interfaces. I'll briefly overview some of these. Consult the Java API documentation for the package java.util for more details on their use.

EnumSet

You learned about EnumMap in Lesson 6. The EnumSet class works a little differently. It is defined as an abstract class. You create an instance of an (unnamed) EnumSet subclass by calling one of almost a dozen EnumSet class methods. I summarize these factory methods in Table 9.1.

Using EnumSet, you can simplify the ReportCardTest method testKeys (above) as follows:

```
public void testKeys() {
    Set<Student.Grade> expectedGrades =
        EnumSet.allOf(Student.Grade.class);
    Set<Student.Grade> grades =
        EnumSet.noneOf(Student.Grade.class);
    for (Student.Grade grade: card.getMessages().keySet())
        grades.add(grade);
    assertEquals(expectedGrades, grades);
}
```

TreeSet and TreeMap

A TreeSet maintains the order of its elements based on their natural sorting order (that you define using Comparable) or a sort order you define using a Comparator object. A TreeMap maintains the order of its keys in a similar manner. As an example, you might choose to ensure that the report card messages stay ordered by student grade. You pay for this behavior. Instead of

Table 9.1 *EnumSet Factory Methods*

Method	Description
allOf	creates an EnumSet using all possible elements of the specified enum type
complementOf	creates an EnumSet as the complement of another EnumSet—i.e., the new EnumSet contains all enum instances not contained by the source EnumSet
copyOf (+1 variant)	creates an EnumSet using elements from an existing collection
noneOf	creates an empty EnumSet of the specified type
of (+4 variants)	creates an EnumSet with up to five different initial values
range	

almost immediate insertion and retrieval time, as you expect when using a HashMap or HashSet, operation times increase logarithmically as the size of the collection increases.

LinkedHashSet and LinkedHashMap

A LinkedHashSet maintains the order of its elements chronologically: It remembers the order in which you inserted elements. It does so by maintaining a linked list behind the scenes. Its performance is comparable to that of HashSet: add, contains, and remove all execute in constant time but with slightly more overhead. Iterating against a LinkedHashSet can actually execute faster than iterating against a regular HashSet. The Map analog is Linked-HashMap.

IdentityHashMap

An IdentityHashMap uses reference equality (==) to compare keys instead of equality (equals). You would use this Map implementation if you needed keys to represent unique instances. This class is not a general-purpose map implementation since it violates the contract that Maps should compare keys using equals.

toString

You have seen how you can send the toString message to a StringBuilder object in order to extract its contents as a String.

The toString method is one of the few methods that the Java designers chose to define in java.lang.Object. Its primary purpose is to return a printable (String) representation of an object. You could use this printable representation as part of an end-user application, but don't. The toString method is more useful for developers, to help in debugging or deciphering a JUnit message.

You want objects of the Course class to display a useful string when you print them out in a JUnit error message. One way would be to extract its elements individually and produce a concatenated string. Another way is to use the toString method.

```
public void testToString() {
    Course course = new Course("ENGL", "301");
    assertEquals("ENGL 301", course.toString());
}
```

Since toString is inherited from Object, you get a default implementation that fails the test:

```
expected: <ENGL 301> but was: <studentinfo.Course@53742e9>
```

This is the implementation that passes the test:

```
@Override
public String toString() {
    return department + " " + number;
}
```

Many IDEs will display objects in watch or inspection windows by sending them the toString message. JUnit uses toString to display an appropriate message upon failure of an assertEquals method. If you code:

```
assertEquals(course, new Course("SPAN", "420"));
```

then JUnit will now display the following ComparisonFailure message:

```
expected: <ENGL 301> but was: <SPAN 420>
```

You can concatenate an object to a String by using the + operator. Java sends the toString message to the object in order to "convert" it to a String object. For example:

```
assertEquals("Course: ENGL 301", "Course: " + course);
```

The default implementation of toString is rarely useful. You will probably want to supply a more useful version in most of your subclasses. If you only use the toString implementation for the purpose of debugging or understanding code, writing a test is not necessary.

In fact, toString's definition is often volatile. It depends upon what a developer wants to see as a summary string at a given time. Creating an unnecessary toString test means that you have made the production class a little harder to change.

One of the main reason you write tests is to allow you to change code with impunity, without fear. For each test that is missing, your confidence in modifying code diminishes. Writing tests enables change. The irony is that the more tests you have, the more time-consuming it will be to make changes.

You should never use the difficulty of maintaining tests as an excuse to not write tests. But you should also not write tests for things that are unnecessary to test. You should also code your tests so that they are as resistant as possible to change. Finding the right balance is a matter of experience and good judgment.

Ultimately, it's your call. My usual recommendation is to start out with more tests than necessary. Cut back only when they become a problem that you can't fix through other means.

Strings and Equality

The String class is optimized for heavy use. In most applications, the number of String objects created vastly outweighs the number of any other type being created.

The current version of the Java VM provides a set of command-line switches to turn on various types of profiling. You can enter:

```
java -agentlib:hprof=help
```

at the command line for further details.[10]

I ran a heap profile against the JUnit run of the current suite of almost 60 tests. The Java VM created about 19,250 objects in the fraction of the second required to run the tests. Out of those objects, over 7,100 were String objects. The object count for the next most frequently instantiated type was around 2,000. Counts dropped off dramatically after that.

These numbers demonstrate the key role that the String class plays in Java. String objects will account for a third to over a half of all objects created during a typical application execution. As such, it is critical that the String class perform well. It is also critical that the creation of so many strings does not bloat the memory space.

To minimize the amount of memory used, the String class uses a literal pool. The main idea is that if two String objects contain the same characters, they share the same memory space (the "pool"). The String literal pool is an implementation of a design pattern called Flyweight.[11] Flyweight is based on sharing and is designed for efficient use of large numbers of fine-grained objects.

To demonstrate:

```
String a = "we have the technology";
String b = "we have the technology";
assertTrue(a.equals(b));
assertTrue(a == b);
```

[10]This feature is not guaranteed to be part of future versions of Java.
[11][Gamma1995].

Exercises

The strings a and b are semantically equal (.equals): Their character content is the same. The string references also have memory equivalence (==): They point to the same String object in memory.

Because of this optimization, as a beginning Java programmer it is easy to think you should compare String objects using ==.

```
if (name == "David Thomas")
```

But this is almost always a mistake. It is possible for two strings to contain the same characters but not be stored in the same memory location. This occurs because Java cannot optimize Strings that are constructed through the use of StringBuilder or concatenation.[12]

Compare Strings using equals, not ==.

```
String c = "we have";
c += " the technology";
assertTrue(a.equals(c));
assertFalse(a == c);
```

This test passes. The Java VM stores c in a different memory location than a.

You might be able to compare String objects using == in certain controlled circumstances in your code. Doing so can provide a boost in performance. However, you should use == for a String comparison only as a performance optimization and document it as such with explicit comments. Being clever and using memory equivalence comparisons for String in other circumstances is a great way to invite insidious bugs that are difficult to track down.

Exercises

1. Create a String literal using the first two sentences of this exercise. You will create a WordCount class to parse through the text and count the number of instances of each word. Punctuation should not appear in the word list, either as part of a word or as a separate "word." Use a map to store the frequencies. The WordCount class should be able to return a set of strings, each showing the word and its frequency. Track the frequency without respect to case. In other

---

[12]When compiled, code using the + for String concatenation translates to equivalent code that uses the StringBuffer class.

words, two words spelled the same but with different case are the same word. Hint: You can use the regular expression \W+ in conjunction with the String split method in order to extract the words from the String.

2. Create a class, Name, that declares a single string field. Create an equals method on the class that uses the string for comparisons. Do not create a hashCode method. Build a test that verifies the contract of equality for Name.

3. Create a Set<Name> object that contains a variety of Name objects, including new Name("Foo"). Verify that the Set contains method returns false if you ask the Set whether or not it contains the Name("Foo") instance. Show that if you create:

    ```
    Name foo = new Name("Foo");
    ```

    the set *does* contain foo.

4. Modify the test for Name (see the previous question) to pass only if the list *does* contain new Name("Foo").

Lesson 10

Mathematics

In this lesson you will learn about the mathematical capabilities of Java. Java is designed as a multipurpose language. In addition to standard, general-purpose arithmetic support, Java supports a small number of more-advanced math concepts such as infinity. Support is provided through a mixture of Java language features and library classes.

Java supplies a wide range of floating point and integral numerics in both fixed and arbitrary precision form. The representation of numerics and related functions in Java generally adheres to IEEE standards. In some cases, you can choose to use either algorithms designed for speed or algorithms whose results strictly adhere to published standards.

Topics:

- BigDecimal
- additional integral types and operations
- numeric casting
- expression evaluation order
- NaN (Not a Number)
- infinity
- numeric overflow
- bit manipulation
- java.lang.Math
- static imports

BigDecimal

The class java.math.BigDecimal allows you to do arbitrary-precision decimal (base 10) floating-point arithmetic. This means that arithmetic with BigDecimal works like you learned in grade school. The BigDecimal class provides a comprehensive set of arithmetic methods and extensive control over rounding. A BigDecimal object represents a decimal number of arbitrary precision, meaning that you decide the number of significant digits it will contain. It is immutable—you cannot change the number that a BigDecimal stores.

The most frequent use of BigDecimal is in financial applications. Financial applications often require you to accurately account for money down to the last hundredth of a cent or even at more granular levels.

Floating-point numbers, as implemented by the Java primitive types float and double, do not allow every number to be represented exactly as specified. This is because it is not mathematically possible to represent certain decimal numbers (such as 0.1) using binary.[1] BigDecimal *can* exactly represent every number.

There are two major downsides to using BigDecimal. First, hardware normally optimizes binary floating-point operations, but BigDecimal's decimal floating point is implemented in software. You may experience poor performance when doing extremely heavy math calculations with BigDecimal.

Second, there is no mathematical operator support for BigDecimal. You must execute common operations such as addition and multiplication via method calls. The requisite code is wordy and thus tedious to write and read.

Using BigDecimal

The student information system must maintain an account of charges and credits for each student. The first test demonstrates the ability of an Account to track a balance based on applied charges and credits.

```
package sis.studentinfo;

import java.math.BigDecimal;
import junit.framework.*;

public class AccountTest extends TestCase {
    public void testTransactions() {
        Account account = new Account();
```

[1]See *http://www.alphaworks.ibm.com/aw.nsf/FAQs/bigdecimal.*

```
        account.credit(new BigDecimal("0.10"));
        account.credit(new BigDecimal("11.00"));
        assertEquals(new BigDecimal("11.10"), account.getBalance());
    }
}
```

Big Decimal

The preferred way to construct a new BigDecimal is to pass a String to its constructor. The String contains the value you want the BigDecimal to represent. You could also pass a `double`, but it may not precisely represent the number you expect, due to the nature of floating-point representation in Java.[2] As a result, the BigDecimal may not precisely represent the number you expect.

You may also construct BigDecimal objects from other BigDecimal objects. This allows you to directly use an expression returning a BigDecimal as the constructor parameter.

The Account implementation:

```
package sis.studentinfo;

import java.math.BigDecimal;

public class Account {
    private BigDecimal balance = new BigDecimal("0.00");

    public void credit(BigDecimal amount) {
        balance = balance.add(amount);
    }

    public BigDecimal getBalance() {
        return balance;
    }
}
```

BigDecimal objects are immutable. Sending an `add` message to a BigDecimal does not alter it. Instead, the `add` method takes the argument's value and adds it to the value the BigDecimal stores. The `add` method then creates and returns a *new* BigDecimal object with this sum. In the Account implementation, the result of sending the `add` message to `balance` is a new BigDecimal object. You must reassign this new object to `balance` in order to maintain the total.

BigDecimal provides a full complement of methods to represent arithmetic operations. They include `abs`, `add`, `divide`, `max`, `min`, `multiply`, `negate`, and `subtract`. Additional methods help you to manage scaling and to extract values as different types from a BigDecimal.

---

[2]See the Java Glossary entry at *http://mindprod.com/jgloss/floatingpoint.html* for a discussion of floating-point representation.

Scale

In `testTransactions`, the assertion expects the result to be a BigDecimal with value "11.10"—with two places after the decimal point. In contrast, you would expect the result of an equivalent Java `float` or `double` operation to be "11.1". Adding such an assertion:

```
assertEquals(new BigDecimal("11.1"), account.getBalance());
```

fails the test.

The number of digits in the fractional part represents the *scale* of the number. When one does arithmetic operations on BigDecimal numbers, the result is a new BigDecimal whose scale is the larger between the receiving BigDecimal and the parameter BigDecimal. For example:

```
assertEquals(new BigDecimal("5.300"),
    new BigDecimal("5.000").add(new BigDecimal("0.3")));
```

That is, the scale as the result of adding a 1-scale number to a 3-scale number is 3.

Division and Rounding

When dividing numbers, the result often contains a larger number of fractional digits than either the divisor or the dividend. By default, BigDecimal does not expand the scale of the result to this larger amount; instead, it restricts it to the larger of the dividend and divisor scales. You can also explicitly define a new scale for the result.

 Constraining the scale means that Java may need to round the result of a division operation. Java provides eight different rounding modes. You are probably most familiar with the rounding mode that corresponds to `BigDecimal.ROUND_HALF_UP`. This mode tells BigDecimal to round the result up if the distance toward the nearest neighbor is greater than or equal to 0.5, and to round it down otherwise. For example, 5.935 would round up to the 2-scale number 5.94, and 5.934 would round down to 5.93.

For an account, you must be able to capture the average transaction amount. A test demonstrates this need:

```
public void testTransactionAverage() {
  Account account = new Account();
  account.credit(new BigDecimal("0.10"));
  account.credit(new BigDecimal("11.00"));
  account.credit(new BigDecimal("2.99"));
  assertEquals(new BigDecimal("4.70"), account.transactionAverage());
}
```

The modified Account class:

```
package sis.studentinfo;

import java.math.BigDecimal;

public class Account {
    private BigDecimal balance = new BigDecimal("0.00");
    private int transactionCount = 0;

    public void credit(BigDecimal amount) {
        balance = balance.add(amount);
        transactionCount++;
    }

    public BigDecimal getBalance() {
        return balance;
    }

    public BigDecimal transactionAverage() {
        return balance.divide(
            new BigDecimal(transactionCount), BigDecimal.ROUND_HALF_UP);
    }
}
```

Review the Java API documentation for details on the other seven rounding modes.

More on Primitive Numerics

To this point, you have learned about the numeric primitive types int, double, and float. You have learned about the basic arithmetic operators, the increment/decrement operators for int, and compound assignment.

Other Integer Types

You have been using the int type for integer numerics. There are other integer types available, each representing different sizes available in which to store numbers of that type. Table 10.1 lists all integral types, their size, and the range of values that they support.

The char type is also a numeric type. Refer to Lesson 3 for more information on char.

You usually express numeric literals as decimal, or base 10, numbers. Java also allows you to represent them in hexadecimal (base 16) or octal (base 8).

You prefix hexadecimal literals with 0x.

Integer Math

Table 10.1 *Integer Types*

Type	Size	Range	Example Literals
byte	8 bits	-128 to 127	0 24
char	16 bits	0 to 65535	17 'A' '%' \u0042 \062
short	16 bits	-32768 to 32767	1440 0x1AFF
int	32 bits	-2,147,483,648 to 2,1477,483,647	-1440525 0x41F0 083
long	64 bits	-9223372036854775808 to 9223372036854775807	-90633969363693 77L 42

```
assertEquals(12, 0xC);
```

You prefix octal literals with 0:

```
assertEquals(10, 012);
```

Integral literals are by default of int type. You can force an integral literal to be a long by suffixing it with the letter L. The lowercase letter l can also be used, but prefer use of an uppercase L, since the lowercase letter is difficult to discern from the number 1.

Integer Math

Let's revisit the code in the class Performance (from Lesson 7) that calculates the average for a series of tests.

```
public double average() {
   double total = 0.0;
   for (int score: tests)
      total += score;
   return total / tests.length;
}
```

Suppose the total local variable had been declared as an int instead of a double, which is reasonable since each test score is an int. Adding an int to an int returns another int.

```
public double average() {
   int total = 0;
   for (int score: tests)
      total += score;
   return total / tests.length;
}
```

This seemingly innocuous change will break several tests in Performance Test. The problem is, dividing an int by an int also returns an int. Integer division always produces integer results; any remainders are discarded. The following two assertions demonstrate correct integer division:

```
assertEquals(2, 13 / 5);
assertEquals(0, 2 / 4);
```

If you need the remainder while doing integer division, use the *modulus* operator (%).

```
assertEquals(0, 40 % 8);
assertEquals(3, 13 % 5);
```

Numeric Casting

Java supports numeric types of different ranges in value. The float type uses 32 bits for its implementation and expresses a smaller range of numbers than does double, which uses 64 bits. The integral primitive types—char, byte, short, int, and long—each support a range that is different from the rest of the integral primitive types.

You can always assign a variable of a smaller primitive type to a larger primitive type. For example, you can always assign a float reference to a double reference:

```
float x = 3.1415f;
double y = x;
```

Behind the scenes, this assignment implicitly causes a type conversion from float to double.

Going the other way—from a larger primitive type to a smaller—implies that there might be some loss of information. If a number stored as a double is larger than the largest possible float, assigning it to a float would result in the truncation of information. In this situation, Java recognizes the possible loss of information and forces you to cast so that you explicitly recognize that there might be a problem.

**Expression
Evaluation
Order**

If you attempt to compile this code:

```
double x = 3.1415d;
float y = x;
```

you will receive a compiler error:

```
possible loss of precision
found   : double
required: float
float y = x;
          ^
```

You must cast the double to a float:

```
double x = 3.1415d;
float y = (float)x;
```

You may want to go the other way and cast from integral primitives to floating-point numbers in order to force noninteger division. A solution to the above problem of calculating the average for a Performance is to cast the dividend to a double before applying the divisor:

```
public double average() {
   int total = 0;
   for (int score: tests)
      total += score;
   return (double)total / tests.length;
}
```

As an added note: When it builds an expression that uses a mix of integral and float values, Java converts the result of the expression to an appropriate float value:

```
assertEquals(600.0f, 20.0f * 30, 0.05);
assertEquals(0.5, 15.0 / 30, 0.05);
assertEquals(0.5, 15 / 30.0, 0.05);
```

Expression Evaluation Order

The order of evaluation in a complex expression is important. The basic rules:

- Java evaluates parenthesized expressions first, from innermost parentheses to outermost parentheses.

- Certain operators have higher precedence than others; for example, multiplication has a higher precedence than addition.

- Otherwise, expressions are evaluated from left to right.

You should use parentheses in particularly complex expressions, since the precedence rules can be difficult to remember. In fact, some of them are counterintuitive. Parenthesizing is worth the effort to ensure that there is no misunderstanding about how an expression will be evaluated. Just don't go overboard with the parentheses—most developers should be familiar with the basic precedence rules.

 Use parentheses to simplify understanding of complex expressions.

Here are a few examples of how precedence affects the result of an expression:

```
assertEquals(7, 3 * 4 - 5);     // left to right
assertEquals(-11, 4 - 5 * 3);   // multiplication before subtraction
assertEquals(-3, 3 * (4 - 5));  // parentheses evaluate first
```

When in doubt, write a test!

NaN

 If no test scores exist, the average for a Performance should be zero. You haven't yet written a test for this scenario. Add the following brief test to PerformanceTest.

```
public void testAverageForNoScores() {
    Performance performance = new Performance();
    assertEquals(0.0, performance.average());
}
```

If you run this, oops! You get a NullPointerException. That can be solved by initializing the integer array of tests defined in Performance to an empty array:

```
private int[] tests = {};
```

When rerunning the tests, you get a different exception:

```
junit.framework.AssertionFailedError: expected:<0.0> but was:<NaN>
```

NaN is a constant defined on both the java.lang.Float and java.lang.Double classes that means "Not a Number."

If there are no scores, tests.length() returns 0, meaning you are dividing by zero in this line of code:

```
return total / tests.length;
```

Infinity

When it works with integers, Java throws an ArithmeticException to indicate that you are dividing by zero. With floating-point numbers, you get NaN, which *is* a legitimate floating-point number.

Fix the problem by checking the number of test scores as the very first thing in average.

```java
public double average() {
    if (tests.length == 0)
        return 0.0;
    int total = 0;
    for (int score: tests)
        total += score;
    return (double)total / tests.length;
}
```

NaN has some interesting characteristics. Any boolean comparisons against NaN always result in false, as these language tests demonstrate:

```java
assertFalse(Double.NaN > 0.0);
assertFalse(Double.NaN < 1.0);
assertFalse(Double.NaN == 1.0);
```

You might *want* the average method to return NaN. But how would you write the test, since you cannot compare NaN to any other floating-point number? Java supplies the isNaN static method, defined on both Float and Double, for this purpose:

```java
public void testAverageForNoScores() {
    Performance performance = new Performance();
    assertTrue(Double.isNaN(performance.average()));
}
```

Infinity

The java.lang.Float class provides two constants for infinity: Float.NEGATIVE_INFINITY and Float.POSITIVE_INFINITY. The class java.lang.Double provides corresponding constants.

While integral division by zero results in an error condition, double and float operations involving zero division result in the mathematically correct infinity value. The following assertions demonstrate use of the infinity constants.

```java
final float tolerance = 0.5f;
final float x = 1f;

assertEquals(
    Float.POSITIVE_INFINITY, Float.POSITIVE_INFINITY * 100, tolerance);
```

```
assertEquals(Float.NEGATIVE_INFINITY,
    Float.POSITIVE_INFINITY * -1, tolerance);

assertEquals(Float.POSITIVE_INFINITY, x / 0f, tolerance);
assertEquals(Float.NEGATIVE_INFINITY, x / -0f, tolerance);
assertTrue(Float.isNaN(x % 0f));

assertEquals(0f, x / Float.POSITIVE_INFINITY, tolerance);
assertEquals(-0f, x / Float.NEGATIVE_INFINITY, tolerance);
assertEquals(x, x % Float.POSITIVE_INFINITY, tolerance);

assertTrue(Float.isNaN(0f / 0f));
assertTrue(Float.isNaN(0f % 0f));

assertEquals(
    Float.POSITIVE_INFINITY, Float.POSITIVE_INFINITY / x, tolerance);
assertEquals(
    Float.NEGATIVE_INFINITY, Float.NEGATIVE_INFINITY / x, tolerance);
assertTrue(Float.isNaN(Float.POSITIVE_INFINITY % x));

assertTrue(
    Float.isNaN(Float.POSITIVE_INFINITY / Float.POSITIVE_INFINITY));
assertTrue(
    Float.isNaN(Float.POSITIVE_INFINITY % Float.POSITIVE_INFINITY));
assertTrue(
    Float.isNaN(Float.POSITIVE_INFINITY / Float.NEGATIVE_INFINITY));
assertTrue(
    Float.isNaN(Float.POSITIVE_INFINITY % Float.NEGATIVE_INFINITY));
assertTrue(
    Float.isNaN(Float.NEGATIVE_INFINITY / Float.POSITIVE_INFINITY));
assertTrue(
    Float.isNaN(Float.NEGATIVE_INFINITY % Float.POSITIVE_INFINITY));
assertTrue(
    Float.isNaN(Float.NEGATIVE_INFINITY / Float.NEGATIVE_INFINITY));
assertTrue(
    Float.isNaN(Float.NEGATIVE_INFINITY % Float.NEGATIVE_INFINITY));
```

Numeric Overflow

When working with integral variables, you must be careful to avoid overflow, which can create incorrect results.

For each numeric type, Java provides constants representing its range. For example, the constants Integer.MAX_VALUE and Integer.MIN_VALUE represent the largest $(2^{31} - 1)$ and smallest (-2^{31}) values an int can have, respectively.

Java will internally assign the results of an expression to an appropriately large primitive type. The example test shows how you can add one to a byte at its maximum value (127). Java stores the result of the expression as a larger primitive value.

```
byte b = Byte.MAX_VALUE;
assertEquals(Byte.MAX_VALUE + 1, b + 1);
```

But if you attempt to assign the result of an expression that is too large back to the `byte`, the results are probably not what you expected. The following test passes, showing that adding 1 to a byte at maximum value results in the smallest possible byte:

```
byte b = Byte.MAX_VALUE;
assertEquals(Byte.MAX_VALUE + 1, b + 1);
b += 1;
assertEquals(Byte.MIN_VALUE, b);
```

The result is due to the way Java stores the numbers in binary. Any additional significant bits are lost in an overflow condition.

Floating-point numbers overflow to infinity.

```
assertTrue(Double.isInfinite(Double.MAX_VALUE * Double.MAX_VALUE));
```

Floating-point numbers can also underflow—that is, have a value too close to zero to represent. Java makes these numbers zero.

Bit Manipulation

Java supports bit-level operations on integers. Among myriad other uses, you might use bit manipulation for mathematical calculations, for performance (some mathematical operations may be faster using bit shifting), in encryption, or for working with a compact collection of flags.

Binary Numbers

Your computer ultimately stores all numbers internally as a series of bits. A bit is represented by a binary, or base 2, number. A binary number is either 0 or 1. The following table on top of page 381 counts in binary from 0 through 15.

The table also shows the hexadecimal ("hex") representation of each number. Java does not allow you to use binary literals, so the easiest way to understand bit operations is to represent numbers with hexadecimal (base 16) literals. Each hex digit in a hex literal represents four binary digits.

Java Binary Representation

Java represents an `int` as 32 binary digits. The leading bit indicates whether the `int` is positive (0) or negative (1). Java stores positive integers as pure bi-

Decimal	Binary	Hex	Decimal	Binary	Hex
0	0	0x0	8	1000	0x8
1	1	0x1	9	1001	0x9
2	10	0x2	10	1010	0xA
3	11	0x3	11	1011	0xB
4	100	0x4	12	1100	0xC
5	101	0x5	13	1101	0xD
6	110	0x6	14	1110	0xE
7	111	0x7	15	1111	0xF

nary—each binary digit adds into a positive sum. Negative integers are stored in *two's complement* form. To obtain the two's complement representation of a number, take its positive binary representation, invert all binary digits, and add 1.

For example, the number 17 is represented in two's complement as:

0000_0000_0000_0000_0000_0000_0001_0001[3]

The number -17 is represented in two's complement as:

1111_1111_1111_1111_1111_1111_1110_1111

Logical Bit Operations

Java contains four logical operators that allow you to manipulate bits: bit-and, bit-or, negation, and bit-xor (exclusive-or). A truth table defines how each logical bit operator works, by specifying the results for all possible bit pairings.

The bit-and, bit-or, and bit-xor logical operators operate on two integers; they are therefore referred to as binary operators. The negation operator operates on a single integer and is thus a unary operator.

To execute a binary logical operation, Java compares all corresponding bits from each of the two numbers involved. When doing a bitwise-and operation on two 32-bit integers, then, this means that 32 individual bit-ands

---

[3]I have added underscores for readability.

take place. To execute a unary logical operation against an integer, Java negates each bit in the integer individually.

You can perform logical bit operations against two integers of type int or smaller. However, Java internally translates integers declared as smaller than int—byte, short, and char—to type int before the bit operation takes place.

The bit-and operator (&) is also known as bitwise multiplication. If both bits are 1, bitwise multiplication returns a 1; otherwise it returns a 0. The following TDTT demonstrates bit-and.

```
assertEquals(0, 0 & 0);
assertEquals(0, 0 & 1);
assertEquals(0, 1 & 0);
assertEquals(1, 1 & 1);
```

The bit-or operator (|) is also known as bitwise addition. If both bits are 0, bitwise addition returns a 0; otherwise it returns a 1. The following TDTT demonstrates bit-or.

```
assertEquals(0, 0 | 0);
assertEquals(1, 0 | 1);
assertEquals(1, 1 | 0);
assertEquals(1, 1 | 1);
```

The xor (exclusive-or) operator (^) is also known as bitwise difference. If both bits are the same, bitwise difference returns 0; otherwise it returns a 1. The following TDTT demonstrates xor.

```
assertEquals(0, 0 ^ 0);
assertEquals(1, 0 ^ 1);
assertEquals(1, 1 ^ 0);
assertEquals(0, 1 ^ 1);
```

The logical negation operator (~) flips all bits in the integer so that 0s become 1s and 1s become 0s.

```
int x = 0x7FFFFFF1;         //0111_1111_1111_1111_1111_1111_1111_0001
assertEquals(0x8000000E, ~x); //1000_0000_0000_0000_0000_0000_0000_1110
```

Java supports the use of compound assignment with logical bit operators. Thus, x &= 1 is equivalent to x = x & 1.

Using Bit-And, Bit-Or and Negation

If you have a series of related flags (boolean values) to represent, you can use an integer variable to compactly represent them. A less-efficient alternative would be to define each as a separate boolean variable or as an array of booleans. Each bit in the integer represents a different flag. Thus, you could represent eight flags in a single byte. For example, the binary value 00000001 would mean that the first flag is on and all other flags are off. The binary value 00000101 would mean that the first and third flags are on and all other flags are off.

To set the values of each flag, you first define a *mask* for each binary position. The mask for the first position is 00000001 (decimal 1), the mask for the second position is 00000010 (decimal 2), and so on. Setting a value is done using bit-or, and extracting a value is done using bit-and.

 You need to be able to set four yes-no flags on each student: Does the student reside on campus, is the student tax-exempt, is the student a minor, and is the student a troublemaker? You have 200,000 students and memory is at a premium.

```
public void testFlags() {
    Student student = new Student("a");
    student.set(
        Student.Flag.ON_CAMPUS,
        Student.Flag.TAX_EXEMPT,
        Student.Flag.MINOR);
    assertTrue(student.isOn(Student.Flag.ON_CAMPUS));
    assertTrue(student.isOn(Student.Flag.TAX_EXEMPT));
    assertTrue(student.isOn(Student.Flag.MINOR));

    assertFalse(student.isOff(Student.Flag.ON_CAMPUS));
    assertTrue(student.isOff(Student.Flag.TROUBLEMAKER));

    student.unset(Student.Flag.ON_CAMPUS);
    assertTrue(student.isOff(Student.Flag.ON_CAMPUS));
    assertTrue(student.isOn(Student.Flag.TAX_EXEMPT));
    assertTrue(student.isOn(Student.Flag.MINOR));
}
```

You should normally prefer explicit query methods for each flag (isOnCampus, isTroublemaker, etc.). The above approach may be preferable if you have a large number of flags and more dynamic needs.

The relevant code in Student follows.

```
public enum Flag {
    ON_CAMPUS(1),
    TAX_EXEMPT(2),
    MINOR(4),
    TROUBLEMAKER(8);

    private int mask;

    Flag(int mask) {
        this.mask = mask;
    }
}

private int settings = 0x0;
...
```

```
public void set(Flag... flags) {
   for (Flag flag: flags)
      settings |= flag.mask;
}

public void unset(Flag... flags) {
   for (Flag flag: flags)
      settings &= ~flag.mask;
}

public boolean isOn(Flag flag) {
   return (settings & flag.mask) == flag.mask;
}

public boolean isOff(Flag flag) {
   return !isOn(flag);
}
```

Each flag is an enum constant, defined by the Flag enum located in Student. Each enum instantiation passes an integer representing a mask to the constructor of Flag. You store the flags in the int instance variable settings. You explicitly initialize this variable to all 0s to demonstrate intent.

The set method takes a variable number of Flag enum objects. It loops through the array and applies the Flag's mask to the settings variable by using a bit-or operator.

The unset method loops through Flag enum objects and bit-ands the negation of the Flag's mask to the settings variable.

A demonstration of how the bit-or operation sets the correct bit:

Flag.MINOR	0100
settings	0000
settings = settings | Flag.MINOR	0100
Flag.ON_CAMPUS	0001
settings | Flag.ON_CAMPUS	0101

The isOn method bit-ands a Flag's mask with the settings variable.

settings	0000
Flag.MINOR	0100
settings & Flag.MINOR	0000
settings & Flag.MINOR == Flag.MINOR	false
settings = settings | Flag.MINOR	0100
settings & Flag.MINOR	0100
settings & Flag.MINOR == Flag.MINOR	true

Finally, a demonstration of the use of negation in the unset method:

```
settings                         0101

~Flag.MINOR                      1011

settings & ~Flag.MINOR           0001
```

Using bit operations to store multiple flags is a classic technique that comes from a need to squeeze the most possible information into memory. It is not normally recommended or needed for most Java development, since an array or other collection of boolean values provides a clearer, simpler representation.

Using Xor

The xor operator has the unique capability of being reversible.

```
int x = 5;             // 101
int y = 7;             // 111
int xPrime = x ^ y;    // 010
assertEquals(2, xPrime);
assertEquals(x, xPrime ^ y);
```

You can also use xor as the basis for *parity checking*. Transmitting data introduces the possibility of individual bits getting corrupted. A parity check involves transmitting additional information that acts like a checksum. You calculate this checksum by applying an xor against all data sent. The receiver executes the same algorithm against the data and checksum. If checksums do not match, the sender knows to retransmit the data.

The parity check is binary: A stream of data has either even parity or odd parity. If the number of 1s in the data is even, parity is even. If the number of 1s in the data is odd, the parity is odd. You can use xor to calculate this parity. Here is a simple stand-alone test:

```
public void testParity() {
   assertEquals(0, xorAll(0, 1, 0, 1));
   assertEquals(1, xorAll(0, 1, 1, 1));
}

private int xorAll(int first, int... rest) {
   int parity = first;
   for (int num: rest)
      parity ^= num;
   return parity;
}
```

Xoring an even number of 1s will always result in an even parity (0). Xoring an odd number of 1s will always result in an odd parity (1).

The reason this works: Xoring is the same as adding two numbers, then taking modulus of dividing by 2. Here is an extension of the truth table that demonstrates this:

```
0 ^ 0 = 0        (0 + 0) % 2 = 0

0 ^ 1 = 1        (0 + 1) % 2 = 1

1 ^ 0 = 1        (1 + 0) % 2 = 1

1 ^ 1 = 1        (1 + 1) % 2 = 0
```

Dividing mod 2 tells you whether a number is odd (1) or even (0). When you add a string of binary digits together, only the 1 digits will contribute to a sum. Thus, taking this sum modulus 2 will tell you whether the number of 1 digits is odd or even.

Take this one level further to calculate a checksum for any integer. The job of the ParityChecker class is to calculate a checksum for a byte array of data. The test shows how corrupting a single byte within a datum results in a different checksum.

```
package sis.util;

import junit.framework.*;

public class ParityCheckerTest extends TestCase {
    public void testSingleByte() {
        ParityChecker checker = new ParityChecker();
        byte source1 = 10;   // 1010
        byte source2 = 13;   // 1101
        byte source3 =  2;   // 0010

        byte[] data = new byte[] { source1, source2, source3 };

        byte checksum =  5;  // 0101

        assertEquals(checksum, checker.checksum(data));

        // corrupt the source2 element
        data[1] = 14;        // 1110

        assertFalse(checksum == checker.checksum(data));
    }
}
```

ParityChecker loops through all bytes of data, xoring each byte with a cumulative checksum. In the test, I lined up the binary translation of each decimal number (source1, source2, and source3). This allows you to see how the checksum of 5 is a result of xoring the bits in each column.

```
package sis.util;

public class ParityChecker {
    public byte checksum(byte[] bytes) {
        byte checksum = bytes[0];
        for (int i = 1; i < bytes.length; i++)
            checksum ^= bytes[i];
        return checksum;
    }
}
```

A simple xor parity check will not catch all possible errors. More-complex schemes involve adding a parity bit to each byte transmitted in addition to the a parity byte at the end of all bytes transmitted. This provides a matrix scheme that can also pinpoint the bytes in error.

Bit Shifting

Java provides three operators for shifting bits either left or right.

To shift bits left or right, and maintain the sign bit, use the bit shift left (<<) or bit shift right (>>) operators.

A bit shift left moves each bit one position to the left. Leftmost bits are lost. Rightmost bits are filled with zeroes.

For example, shifting the bit pattern 1011 one position to the left in a 4-bit unsigned number would result in 0110. Some annotated Java examples:

```
                       //    101 = 5
assertEquals(10, 5 << 1);  //   1010 = 10
assertEquals(20, 5 << 2);  //  10100 = 20
assertEquals(40, 5 << 3);  // 101000 = 40
assertEquals(20, 40 >> 1);
assertEquals(10, 40 >> 2);
                           // ... 1111 0110 = -10
assertEquals(-20, -10 << 1); // ... 1110 1100 = -20
assertEquals(-5, -10 >> 1);  // ... 1111 1011 = -5
```

You'll note that bit shifting left is the equivalent of multiplying by powers of 2. Bit shifting right is the equivalent of dividing by powers of 2.

The unsigned bit shift right shifts all bits irrespective of the sign bit. Rightmost bits are lost, and the leftmost bits (including the sign bit) are filled with 0.

```
assertEquals(5, 10 >>> 1);
assertEquals(2147483643, -10 >>> 1);
    // 1111_1111_1111_1111_1111_1111_1111_0110 = -10
    // 0111_1111_1111_1111_1111_1111_1111_1011 = 2147483643
```

Note that an unsigned bit shift right always results in a positive number.

Bit shifting has uses in cryptography and in graphical image manipulation. You can also use bit shifting for some mathematical operations, such as dividing or multiplying by powers of 2. Only do so if you need extremely fast performance, and then only if your performance tests show you that the math is the performance problem.

BitSet

The Java API library includes the class java.util.BitSet. It encapsulates a vector of bits and grows as needed. BitSet objects are mutable—its individual bits may be set or unset. You can bit-and, bit-or, or bit-xor one BitSet object to another. You can also negate a BitSet. One of its few benefits is that it supports bit operations for numbers larger than the capacity of an int.

java.lang.Math

The class java.lang.Math provides a utility library of mathematical functions. It also provides constant definitions Math.E, for the base of the natural log, and Math.PI, to represent pi. These constants are double quantities that provide fifteen decimal places.

The Java API library also contains a class named java.lang.StrictMath, which provides bit-for-bit adherence to accepted standard results for the functions. For most purposes, Math is acceptable and also results in better performance.

I summarize the functions provided by the Math class in the following table. Refer to the Java API documentation for complete details on each function.

Method Name(s)	Functionality
abs	absolute value; overloaded for all primitive numeric types
max, min	maximum and minimum value
acos, asin, atan	arc cosine, arc sine, arc tangent
cos, sin, tan	cosine, sine, tangent
atan2	convert (x, y) coordinates to polar
ceil, floor, round	ceiling, floor, and rounding capabilities

Method Name(s)	Functionality
exp	e raised to a power
log	natural log
pow	x raised to y
sqrt	square root
random	random from 0.0 to 1.0
rint	closest int value for a double
toDegrees, toRadians	convert between degrees and radians
IEEERemainder	IEEE 754 remainder for double operation x / y

A method to calculate the hypotenuse of a right triangle provides a simple example. (The hypotenuse is the side opposite the right angle.)

```
// util.MathTest.java:
package util;

import junit.framework.*;

public class MathTest extends TestCase {
    static final double TOLERANCE = 0.05;

    public void testHypotenuse() {
        assertEquals(5.0, Math.hypotenuse(3.0, 4.0), TOLERANCE);
    }
}

// in util.Math:
package util;

import static java.lang.Math.*;

public class Math {
    public static double hypotenuse(double a, double b) {
        return sqrt(pow(a, 2.0) + pow(b, 2.0));
    }
}
```

The pow function is used to square the sides a and b. The hypotenuse method then sums these squares and returns the square root of the sum using sqrt.

Pervasive use of the Math class gives you a justifiable reason for using the static import facility introduced in Lesson 4. Code with a lot of Math method calls otherwise becomes a nuisance to code and read.

I've named the utility class Math, like the java.lang.Math class. While this is a questionable practice (it may introduce unnecessary confusion), it demonstrates that Java can disambiguate the two.

Numeric Wrapper Classes

As you saw in Lesson 7, Java supplies a corresponding wrapper class for each primitive type: Integer, Double, Float, Byte, Boolean, and so on. The primary use of the wrapper class is to convert primitives to object form so that they can be stored in collections.

The wrapper classes for the numeric types have additional uses. You learned earlier in this lesson that each numeric wrapper class provides a MIN_VALUE and MAX_VALUE constant. You also saw how the Float and Double classes provide constants for Not a Number (NaN) and infinity.

Printable Representations

The class Integer provides static utility methods to produce printable representations of an int in hex, octal, and binary form.

```
assertEquals("101", Integer.toBinaryString(5));
assertEquals("32", Integer.toHexString(50));
assertEquals("21", Integer.toOctalString(17));
```

The Java library includes general-purpose methods to produce a proper String for any radix (base). The following assertion shows how to get the trinary (base 3) String for an int.

```
assertEquals("1022", Integer.toString(35, 3));
```

Converting Strings to Numbers

In Lesson 8, you learned that the method Integer.parseInt takes a String and parses it to produce the corresponding int value. You typically use the parseInt method to convert user interface input into numeric form. All characters in the input String must be decimal digits, except for the first character, which may optionally be a negative sign. If the String does not contain a parseable integer, parseInt throws a NumberFormatException.

An additional form of parseInt takes a radix, representing the base of the input string, as the second parameter. The method valueOf operates the same as parseInt, except that it returns a new Integer object instead of an int.

Each of the corresponding numeric wrapper classes has a parsing method. For example, you may convert a String to a double using Double.parseDouble, or to a float using Float.parseFloat.

The parseInt method can accept only decimal input. The decode method can parse an input string that might be in hex or octal, as these assertions show:

```
assertEquals(253, Integer.decode("0xFD"));
assertEquals(253, Integer.decode("0XFD"));
assertEquals(253, Integer.decode("#FD"));
assertEquals(15, Integer.decode("017"));
assertEquals(10, Integer.decode("10"));
assertEquals(-253, Integer.decode("-0xFD"));
assertEquals(-253, Integer.decode("-0XFD"));
assertEquals(-253, Integer.decode("-#FD"));
assertEquals(-15, Integer.decode("-017"));
assertEquals(-10, Integer.decode("-10"));
```

Random Numbers

The class Math provides the method random to return a pseudorandom double between 0.0 and 1.0. A number in this range may be all you need. The generated number is not truly random—the elements of a sequence of pseudorandom numbers are only approximately independent from each other.[4] For most applications, this is sufficient.

The class java.util.Random is a more comprehensive solution for generating pseudorandom numbers. It produces pseudorandom sequences of booleans, bytes, ints, longs, floats, Gaussians, or doubles. A pseudorandom sequence generator is not purely random; it is instead based upon an arithmetical algorithm.

You can create a Random instance with or without a *seed*. A seed is essentially a unique identifier for a random sequence. Two Random objects created with the same seed will produce the same sequence of values. If you create a Random object without explicitly specifying a seed, the class uses the system clock as the basis for the seed.[5]

You could create a simulation of coin flips through repeated use of the nextBoolean method on Random. A true value would indicate heads and a false

---

[4]http://en.wikipedia.org/wiki/Pseudo-random_number_generator.

[5]Which means that if you construct two Random objects and the construction happens to execute in the same nanosecond, you get the same sequence in both. In earlier versions of Java, the Random constructor used the current system time in milliseconds. This increased granularity significantly increased the likelihood of two Random objects having the same sequence.

value would indicate tails. The below test shows use of the seed value to produce two identical pseudorandom coin-flip sequences.

```java
public void testCoinFlips() {
   final long seed = 100L;
   final int total = 10;
   Random random1 = new Random(seed);
   List<Boolean> flips1 = new ArrayList<Boolean>();
   for (int i = 0; i < total; i++)
      flips1.add(random1.nextBoolean());

   Random random2 = new Random(seed);
   List<Boolean> flips2 = new ArrayList<Boolean>();
   for (int i = 0; i < total; i++)
      flips2.add(random2.nextBoolean());

   assertEquals(flips1, flips2);
}
```

The methods `nextInt`, `nextDouble`, `nextLong`, and `nextFloat` work similarly. An additional version of `nextInt` takes as a parameter a maximum value, such that the
method always returns a number from 0 through the maximum value.

Testing Random Code

There are a few ways to write unit tests against code that must use random
sequences. One way is to provide a subclass implementation of the Random
class and substitute that for the Random class used in the code. The substitute Random class will provide a known sequence of values. This technique
is known as *mocking* the Random class. I will cover mocking in considerable
depth later.

 In Lesson 8, you provided your own logging Handler class solely
for purposes of testing. This was also a form of mocking.

You must assign passwords to students so they can access their accounts
online. Passwords are eight characters long. Each character of the password
must fall in a certain character range.

```java
package sis.util;

import junit.framework.*;

public class PasswordGeneratorTest extends TestCase {
   public void testGeneratePassword() {
      PasswordGenerator generator = new PasswordGenerator();
      generator.setRandom(new MockRandom('A'));
      assertEquals("ABCDEFGH", generator.generatePassword());
```

```
        generator.setRandom(new MockRandom('C'));
        assertEquals("CDEFGHIJ", generator.generatePassword());
    }
}
```

The test method `testGeneratePassword` sets the `random` variable into the Password-Generator class to point to an instance of MockRandom. The MockRandom class extends from the Random class. The Java API documentation explains how to properly extend the Random class by overriding the method `next(int bits)` to return a random number based on a bit sequence. All other methods in the Random class are based on this method.

The *mock* implementation takes an `int` representing a starting character value as a parameter to its constructor. It uses this to calculate an initial value for the random sequence and stores it as `i`. The initial value is a number relative to the lowest valid character in the password. Its `next(int bits)` method simply returns and then increments the value of `i`.

```
package sis.util;

import junit.framework.*;

public class PasswordGeneratorTest extends TestCase {
    ...
    class MockRandom extends java.util.Random {
        private int i;
        MockRandom(char startCharValue) {
            i = startCharValue - PasswordGenerator.LOW_END_PASSWORD_CHAR;
        }
        protected int next(int bits) {
            return i++;
        }
    }
}
```

MockRandom is defined completely within PasswordGeneratorTest. It is a *nested class* of PasswordGenerator. You can directly instantiate Mock-Random from within PasswordGeneratorTest, but not from any other class. There are additional kinds of nested classes, each kind with its own nuances. In Lesson 11, you will learn about nested classes in depth. Until then, use them with caution.

The implementation of PasswordGenerator follows.

```
package sis.util;

import java.util.*;
```

Random
Numbers

```java
public class PasswordGenerator {
    private String password;
    private static final int PASSWORD_LENGTH = 8;
    private Random random = new Random();

    static final char LOW_END_PASSWORD_CHAR = 48;
    static final char HIGH_END_PASSWORD_CHAR = 122;

    void setRandom(Random random) {
        this.random = random;
    }

    public String generatePassword() {
        StringBuffer buffer = new StringBuffer(PASSWORD_LENGTH);
        for (int i = 0; i < PASSWORD_LENGTH; i++)
            buffer.append(getRandomChar());
        return buffer.toString();
    }

    private char getRandomChar() {
        final char max = HIGH_END_PASSWORD_CHAR - LOW_END_PASSWORD_CHAR;
        return (char)(random.nextInt(max) + LOW_END_PASSWORD_CHAR);
    }

    public String getPassword() {
        return password;
    }
}
```

Note that if the package-level setRandom method is not called, the random instance variable keeps its initialized value of a legitimate java.util.Random instance. Since MockRandom meets the contract of java.util.Random, you can substitute an instance of MockRandom for Random for purposes of testing.

The goal of testGeneratePassword is to prove that the PasswordGenerator class can generate and return a random password. The test does not need to re-prove the functionality inherent in the Random class, but the test does need to prove that a PasswordGenerator object interacts with a Random instance (or subclass instance) through its published interface, nextInt(int max). The test must also prove that PasswordGenerator uses the nextInt return value properly. In this example, PasswordGenerator uses the nextInt return value to help construct an 8-character String of random values.

Java supplies an additional random class, java.util.SecureRandom, as a standards-based, cryptographically strong pseudorandom number generator.

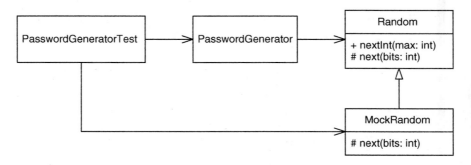

Figure 10.1 *Mocking the Random Class*

Exercises

1. Create a test demonstrating the immutability of a BigDecimal. Add a second BigDecimal to the first and show that the first still has the original value.

2. Create one BigDecimal using the value `"10.00"` and another using the value `"1"`. Show they are not equal. Use multiplication and scale to create a new BigDecimal from the second so that it equals the first. Now reverse the transformation, starting from 10.00, and get back to 1.

3. Show that `0.9` and `0.005 * 2.0` are not equal with floats. To what precision are they equal? With doubles?

4. Why won't the following compile? What are two ways it can be fixed?

```
public class CompilerError {
    float x = 0.01;
}
```

5. Write a brief spike program to discover the decimal value of `0xDEAD`. How could you recode the literal in octal?

6. Find as many interesting variations of NaN and Infinity calculations as you can.

7. Challenge: Can you find ways in which the wrappers such as Float act differently than the corresponding primitive?

8. Create a method (test first, of course) that takes a variable number of `int` values. Code it to return only numbers in the list that are divisible by 3. Code it twice: The first time, use only the modulus (%) operator.

The second time, use the division (/) operator and the multiplication operator if necessary, but not the % operator. Test against the sequence of integers from 1 through 10.

9. Change the chess code to use casting where appropriate. Eliminate the need for the toChar method on the Board class.

10. Which of the following lines will compile correctly? Why?

```
float x = 1;
float x = 1.0;
float x = (int)1.0;
```

11. What is the value of (int)1.9?

12. What is the value of Math.rint(1.9)?

13. When using Math.rint, how is rounding performed? Is 1.5 equal to 1 or 0? How about 2.5?

14. What are the final values of the following expressions, assuming x is 5 and y is 10 and x and y are both ints? Flag the lines that wouldn't compile, as well. What are the values of x and y afterward? (Consider each expression to be discrete—i.e., each expression starts with the values of x and y at 5 and 10.)

```
x * 5 + y++ * 7 / 4
++x * 5 * y++
x++ * 5 * ++y
++x + 5 * 7 + y++
++y++ % ++x++
x * 7 == 35 || y++ == 0     // super tricky
++x * ++y
x++ * y++
true && x * 7
x * 2 == y- || ++y == 10    // super tricky
x * 2 == -y || ++y == 10    // super tricky
```

15. Using only the << operator, convert 17 into 34.

16. What is the decimal value of ~1?

17. Demonstrate the difference between >> and >>>. Is there a difference between the two for positive numbers? For negative numbers?

18. Create a function which uses Math.random to generate a random integer from 1 through 50. How will you go about testing your function? Can you test it perfectly? How confident can you get that your code works?

19. Create a list of numbers from 1 to 100. Use a Random generator to randomly swap elements of the list around 100 times. Write a test that

does a reasonable verification: Ensure that the list size remains the same and that two numbers were swapped with each call to the swapper.

20. Show that the next `double` is not the same between a Random seeded with 1 and a Random with no seed. Can you make a test that absolutely proves that this is true?

21. Challenge: Swap two numbers without a temporary variable by using the xor operator.

22. Challenge: Programmatically demonstrate the number of bits required to store each integral type (`char`, `byte`, `short`, `int`, `long`). Hint: Use shift operators. Remember that signed types require an extra bit to store the sign.

Lesson 11

IO

In this lesson you will learn about the input-output (IO) facilities of Java. IO refers to anything that transfers data to or from your application. IO in Java is wonderfully complete, wonderfully complex, and reasonably consistent. You might use Java's IO capabilities to write reports to files or to read user input from the console.

In this lesson, you will learn about:

- organization of the stream classes

- character streams versus byte streams

- the File class

- data streams

- redirecting System.in and System.out

- object streams

- random access files

- nested classes

Organization

The java.io package contains dozens of classes to manage input and output using data streams, serialization, and the file system. Understanding the organization and naming strategy of the classes in the package will help you minimize the otherwise overwhelming nature of doing IO in Java.

Java IO is based upon the use of *streams*. A stream is a sequence of data that you can write to or read from. A stream may have a source, such as the console, or a destination, such as the file system. A stream with a source is an input stream; a stream with a destination is an output stream.

Java further distinguishes its streams by the format of the data they carry. Java contains character streams and byte streams. You use character streams to work with 2-byte (16-bit) Unicode character data. Java classes with Reader (input) and Writer (output) in their names are character streams. You use character streams to work with human-readable text.

Byte streams work with 8-bit binary data. Byte stream classes have the word Input or Ouput in their name. You normally use byte streams for working with nontext data such as image files or compiled byte codes.

Low-level Java streams support basic concepts such as reading or writing single bytes at a time. Were you able to work only with low-level streams, you would be forced to write tedious, repetitive code. Java supplies a number of higher-level streams that simplify your work by providing aggregate and additional functionality. These higher level streams are known as *wrapper* streams.

A wrapper stream object contains a reference to, or *wraps*, a low-level stream object. You interact with the wrapper stream. It in turn interacts with the wrapped low-level stream that does the dirty work.

Take a look at the java.io package, which contains a set of interfaces and classes to define the basic building blocks for IO. You will note that it is crowded—Java's IO facilities are complete but complex. The package includes specific stream implementations, including filtered, buffered, piped, and object streams.

In addition to the stream classes, the java.io package provides a set of classes to manipulate the underlying file system.

Character Streams

In Lesson 3, you created the RosterReporter class to write a report of students enrolled in a course session. You wrote the report to a string, then printed the report using System.out. Here is the existing RosterReporter class:

```
package sis.report;

import java.util.*;
import sis.studentinfo.*;
import static sis.report.ReportConstant.NEWLINE;
```

```
class RosterReporter {
    static final String ROSTER_REPORT_HEADER =
        "Student" + NEWLINE +
        "----" + NEWLINE;
    static final String ROSTER_REPORT_FOOTER =
        NEWLINE + "# students = ";

    private Session session;

    RosterReporter(Session session) {
        this.session = session;
    }

    String getReport() {
        StringBuilder buffer = new StringBuilder();

        writeHeader(buffer);
        writeBody(buffer);
        writeFooter(buffer);

        return buffer.toString();
    }

    void writeHeader(StringBuilder buffer) {
        buffer.append(ROSTER_REPORT_HEADER);
    }

    void writeBody(StringBuilder buffer) {
        for (Student student: session.getAllStudents()) {
            buffer.append(student.getName());
            buffer.append(NEWLINE);
        }
    }

    void writeFooter(StringBuilder buffer) {
        buffer.append(
            ROSTER_REPORT_FOOTER + session.getAllStudents().size() +
            NEWLINE);
    }
}
```

Currently the RosterReporter class builds a string representing the entire report. Another class using RosterReporter would take this string and send it to a desired destination—the console, a file, or perhaps the Internet. Thus, you write every character in the report twice—first to the String, then to a final destination. With a larger report, the receiver of the report may experience an unacceptable delay while waiting for the entire report to be produced.

A preferable solution would involve writing each character directly to a stream that represents the ultimate destination. This also means that you wouldn't need to store the entire report in a large string buffer, something that has the potential to cause memory problems.

 You have been told to make the student information system flexible. Initially the system must be able to write reports to either the console or to local files. To meet this requirement, you will first update the RosterReporter class to write directly to a character stream. First, you will need to update the test.

Character Streams

```
package sis.report;

import junit.framework.TestCase;
import sis.studentinfo.*;
import static sis.report.ReportConstant.NEWLINE;
import java.io.*;

public class RosterReporterTest extends TestCase {
    public void testRosterReport() throws IOException {
        Session session =
            CourseSession.create(
                new Course("ENGL", "101"),
                DateUtil.createDate(2003, 1, 6));

        session.enroll(new Student("A"));
        session.enroll(new Student("B"));

        Writer writer = new StringWriter();
        new RosterReporter(session).writeReport(writer);
        String rosterReport = writer.toString();

        assertEquals(
            RosterReporter.ROSTER_REPORT_HEADER +
            "A" + NEWLINE +
            "B" + NEWLINE +
            RosterReporter.ROSTER_REPORT_FOOTER + "2" +
            NEWLINE, rosterReport);
    }
}
```

To use Java's IO classes, you must import the package java.io. Many IO operations can generate an exception. You'll need to declare that the test method throws an IOException.

You want the RosterReporter to write its report to a Writer object provided by the client. The class java.io.Writer is the base abstraction for character streams. For purposes of testing, you can create an object of the Writer subclass StringWriter. When you send the message toString to a StringWriter, it returns a String of all characters written to it.

Note the improvement to the design. Instead of *asking* the RosterReporter object for a report (getReport), you are *telling* it to write a report (writeReport).

In RosterReporter, like RosterReporter test, you will need to add an import statement and throws clauses to methods that perform IO operations. (Instead of believing me, the better approach is to code this without the throws clauses and let the compiler tell you what to do.)

```
package sis.report;

import java.util.*;
import sis.studentinfo.*;
import static sis.report.ReportConstant.NEWLINE;
import java.io.*;

class RosterReporter {
    static final String ROSTER_REPORT_HEADER =
        "Student" + NEWLINE +
        "----" + NEWLINE;
    static final String ROSTER_REPORT_FOOTER =
        NEWLINE + "# students = ";

    private Session session;
    private Writer writer;

    RosterReporter(Session session) {
        this.session = session;
    }

    void writeReport(Writer writer) throws IOException {
        this.writer = writer;
        writeHeader();
        writeBody();
        writeFooter();
    }

    private void writeHeader() throws IOException {
        writer.write(ROSTER_REPORT_HEADER);
    }

    private void writeBody() throws IOException {
        for (Student student: session.getAllStudents())
            writer.write(student.getName() + NEWLINE);
    }

    private void writeFooter() throws IOException {
        writer.write(
            ROSTER_REPORT_FOOTER + session.getAllStudents().size() +
            NEWLINE);
    }
}
```

In writeHeader, writeBody, and writeFooter, you have replaced calls to the String-Builder method append with calls to the Writer method write. Also, previously the code passed a StringBuilder from method to method. Now you have a Writer instance variable. By not passing the same pervasive variable to every method, you can eliminate some duplication.

Watch your tests pass, then make the following refactorings to take advantage of Java String formatting.

```
package sis.report;

import java.util.*;
import sis.studentinfo.*;
import java.io.*;

class RosterReporter {
    static final String ROSTER_REPORT_HEADER = "Student%n----%n";
    static final String ROSTER_REPORT_FOOTER = "%n# students = %d%n";

    private Session session;
    private Writer writer;

    RosterReporter(Session session) {
        this.session = session;
    }

    void writeReport(Writer writer) throws IOException {
        this.writer = writer;
        writeHeader();
        writeBody();
        writeFooter();
    }

    private void writeHeader() throws IOException {
        writer.write(String.format(ROSTER_REPORT_HEADER));
    }

    private void writeBody() throws IOException {
        for (Student student: session.getAllStudents())
            writer.write(String.format(student.getName() + "%n"));
    }

    private void writeFooter() throws IOException {
        writer.write(
            String.format(ROSTER_REPORT_FOOTER,
                          session.getAllStudents().size()));

    }
}
```

The requisite changes to the test:

```
package sis.report;

import junit.framework.TestCase;
import sis.studentinfo.*;
import java.io.*;

public class RosterReporterTest extends TestCase {
    public void testRosterReport() throws IOException {
        Session session =
            CourseSession.create(
                new Course("ENGL", "101"),
                DateUtil.createDate(2003, 1, 6));

        session.enroll(new Student("A"));
        session.enroll(new Student("B"));

        Writer writer = new StringWriter();
        new RosterReporter(session).writeReport(writer);
        String rosterReport = writer.toString();

        assertEquals(
            String.format(RosterReporter.ROSTER_REPORT_HEADER +
                        "A%n" +
                        "B%n" +
                        RosterReporter.ROSTER_REPORT_FOOTER, 2),
            rosterReport) ;
    }
}
```

Writing to a File

You will now need to update RosterReporter to be able to take a filename as a parameter. The test will need to make sure that the report is properly written to an operating system file.

First, you will refactor RosterReporterTest to create a setUp method and an assertion method assertReportContents. By doing so, you will set the stage to quickly add a new test, testFiledReport, that uses these common methods and thus introduces no duplication.

Within assertReportContents, you can modify the assertion to obtain the number of expected students from the session object. You will need to change getNumberOfStudents in Session from package to public.

The refactored RosterReporterTest:

```
package sis.report;

import junit.framework.TestCase;
import sis.studentinfo.*;
import java.io.*;
```

```
public class RosterReporterTest extends TestCase {
    private Session session;

    protected void setUp() {
        session =
            CourseSession.create(
                new Course("ENGL", "101"),
                DateUtil.createDate(2003, 1, 6));

        session.enroll(new Student("A"));
        session.enroll(new Student("B"));
    }

    public void testRosterReport() throws IOException {
        Writer writer = new StringWriter();
        new RosterReporter(session).writeReport(writer);
        assertReportContents(writer.toString());
    }

    private void assertReportContents(String rosterReport) {
        assertEquals(
            String.format(RosterReporter.ROSTER_REPORT_HEADER +
                          "A%n" +
                          "B%n" +
                          RosterReporter.ROSTER_REPORT_FOOTER,
                          session.getNumberOfStudents()),
            rosterReport);
    }
}
```

The new test, testFiledReport, calls an overloaded version of writeReport. This second version of writeReport takes a filename instead of a Writer as a parameter.

```
public void testFiledReport() throws IOException {
    final String filename = "testFiledReport.txt";
    new RosterReporter(session).writeReport(filename);

    StringBuffer buffer = new StringBuffer();
    String line;

    BufferedReader reader =
        new BufferedReader(new FileReader(filename));
    while ((line = reader.readLine()) != null)
        buffer.append(String.format(line + "%n"));
    reader.close();

    assertReportContents(buffer.toString());
}
```

After calling writeReport, the test uses a BufferedReader to read the contents of the report file into a buffer. The test then passes the buffer's contents to the assertReportContents method.

A BufferedReader is a Reader subclass that can wrap another reader. Remember that you use Reader objects to read from character streams. The test constructs a BufferedReader with a FileReader as a parameter. A FileReader is a character-based input stream that can read data from a file. You construct a FileReader using a filename.

Writing to a File

You could read the file's contents by directly using a FileReader instead of a BufferedReader. However, a BufferedReader is more efficient since it buffers characters as it reads. In addition, BufferedReader supplies the method readLine to help you simplify your code. The readLine method returns a logical line of input from the wrapped stream, using the system property "line.separator" to delineate lines.

The new method in RosterReporter:

```
void writeReport(String filename) throws IOException {
    Writer bufferedWriter =
        new BufferedWriter(new FileWriter(filename));
    try {
        writeReport(bufferedWriter);
    }
    finally {
        bufferedWriter.close();
    }
}
```

The writeReport method creates a FileWriter using the filename passed to it. It wraps the FileWriter in a BufferedWriter. The method then passes the writer to the existing writeReport method (which takes a PrintWriter as a parameter).

A finally block ensures that the PrintWriter is always closed, regardless of whether writeReport threw an exception or not. You must remember to close file resources, otherwise you may encounter locked file problems. Also, buffered information will not appear in the file until you close the Writer. You can also use the Writer method flush to force the Writer to write its contents to the destination.

Notice that you were able to add functionality to the existing Roster-Reporter class without modifying a single line of its code. You simply added a new method. Achieving this ideal happens more often if you strive to ensure that your code maintains an optimal design at all times. Prefer the use of abstractions in your code.

java.io.File

The File class is not a stream-based class. Instead of working with streams, the File class provides you with an interface into the file and directory structure of your underlying file system. It contains a number of file-based utilities, such as the ability to delete files and to create temporary files.

When writing tests that work with files, you want to ensure that you have a clean environment for testing. You also want to ensure that you leave things the way they were when the test completes. With respect to testFiled-Report, this means that you need to delete any existing report file as the first step in the test and delete the created report file as the last step in the test.

```java
public void testFiledReport() throws IOException {
    final String filename = "testFiledReport.txt";
    try {
        delete(filename);

        new RosterReporter(session).writeReport(filename);

        StringBuffer buffer = new StringBuffer();
        String line;

        BufferedReader reader =
            new BufferedReader(new FileReader(filename));
        while ((line = reader.readLine()) != null)
            buffer.append(String.format(line + "%n"));
        reader.close();

        assertReportContents(buffer.toString());
    }
    finally {
        delete(filename);
    }
}

private void delete(String filename) {
    File file = new File(filename);
    if (file.exists())
        assertTrue("unable to delete " + filename, file.delete());
}
```

The delete method uses the File class to accomplish its goals. It creates a File object by passing a filename to its constructor. It calls the exists method to determine whether the file can be found in the file system. Finally, it calls the delete method, which returns true if the file system successfully removed the file, false otherwise. A file system might not be able to delete a file if it is locked or has its read-only attribute set, among other reasons.

Table 11.1 *java.io.File methods by category*

Category	Methods
temporary file creation	createTempFile
empty file creation	createNewFile
file manipulation	delete, deleteOnExit, renameTo
file and path name queries	getAbsoluteFile, getAbsolutePath, getCanonicalFile, getCanonicalPath, getName, getPath, toURI, toURL
classification	isFile, isDirectory
attribute query/manipulation	isHidden, lastModified, length, canRead, canWrite, setLastModified, setReadOnly
directory query/manipulation	exists, list, listFiles, listRoots, mkdir, mkdirs, getParent, getParentFile

I have categorized most of the functionality of the class java.io.File in Table 11.1.

Byte Streams and Conversion

Java represents standard input (stdin) and standard output (stdout) with stream objects stored in System.in and System.out, respectively. System.in refers to an InputStream, while System.out refers to a PrintStream. A PrintStream is a specialized OutputStream that simplifies writing objects of various types.

Both System.in and System.out are byte streams, not character streams. Remember that Java uses the multibyte character set Unicode, while most operating systems use a single-byte character set.

The java.io package provides a means of converting between byte streams and character streams. The class InputStreamReader wraps an InputStream and converts each byte read into an appropriate character. The conversion uses your platform system's default encoding scheme (as understood by Java) by default; you may also supply a decoding class that defines the mapping. In a similar fashion, the class OutputStreamWriter wraps an output stream, converting each character to a single byte.

The predominant use for InputStreamReader and OutputStreamWriter is to map between Java's character streams and stdin/stdout. Reader and Writer subclasses allow you to work with input and output on a line-by-line basis.

 Do not send messages directly to System.in and System.out.

Referring to Reader and Writer abstract classes instead allows for quick redirecting to a different medium (e.g., files), and also makes for easier testing.

A Student User Interface

 In this section, you will write a very simple console-based user interface (UI). The UI will allow an end user of the student information system to create student objects. You will prompt the user with a simple menu that either drives the addition of a new student or allows the user to terminate (exit) the application.

There are many ways to approach development of a user interface through TDD. The following test, implemented in the class StudentUITest, presents one solution. I have broken the listing into three parts for clarity. The first part shows the core test method, testCreateStudent.

```
package sis.ui;

import junit.framework.*;
import java.io.*;
import java.util.*;
import sis.studentinfo.*;

public class StudentUITest extends TestCase {
    static private final String name = "Leo Xerces Schmoo";

    public void testCreateStudent() throws IOException {
        StringBuffer expectedOutput = new StringBuffer();
        StringBuffer input = new StringBuffer();
        setup(expectedOutput, input);
        byte[] buffer = input.toString().getBytes();

        InputStream inputStream = new ByteArrayInputStream(buffer);
        BufferedReader reader =
            new BufferedReader(new InputStreamReader(inputStream));

        OutputStream outputStream = new ByteArrayOutputStream();
        BufferedWriter writer =
            new BufferedWriter(new OutputStreamWriter(outputStream));
```

```
        StudentUI ui = new StudentUI(reader, writer);
        ui.run();

        assertEquals(
            expectedOutput.toString(),
            outputStream.toString());
        assertStudents(ui.getAddedStudents());
    }

    private String line(String input) {
        return String.format("%s%n", input);
    }
    ...
}
```

The test creates two StringBuffers. One will hold expected output—what the console application displays—and the other will hold the input that a user (the test, in this case) types in. The setup method explicitly populates each of these:

```
private void setup(StringBuffer expectedOutput, StringBuffer input) {
    expectedOutput.append(StudentUI.MENU);
    input.append(line(StudentUI.ADD_OPTION));
    expectedOutput.append(StudentUI.NAME_PROMPT);
    input.append(line(name));
    expectedOutput.append(line(StudentUI.ADDED_MESSAGE));
    expectedOutput.append(StudentUI.MENU);
    input.append(line(StudentUI.QUIT_OPTION));
}
```

The setup method can be viewed as presenting a script to which the system must adhere. The buffer appends are intertwined to emulate the interaction between system output and user input. This natural flow should aid you in understanding the script. First, the user interface presents the user with a menu:

```
expectedOutput.append(StudentUI.MENU);
```

The user responds to the menu by first typing the option to add a student, then pressing enter.

```
input.append(line(StudentUI.ADD_OPTION));
```

The line method is a utility method that appends an end-of-line string to an input string. The remainder of the setUp method represents the expected sequence of events between the system presenting some text (expectedOutput.append) and the user entering a response (input.append).

The code in testCreateStudent creates an InputStream by wrapping a Byte-ArrayInputStream around the bytes from the input StringBuffer. It then creates an InputStreamReader, wrapped with a BufferedReader, to convert incoming bytes to characters.

Similarly, the test creates and wraps a ByteArrayOutputStream with an OutputStreamWriter that will convert characters to bytes. A BufferedWriter wraps the OutputStreamWriter.

You pass these two streams, reader and writer, to the constructor of Student-UI after setup executes. The UI is told to run and should continually present a menu of options until the user chooses to quit.

A Student User Interface

After the UI completes processing, an assertion verifies that the application produced correct output. The assertion compares the contents of the ByteArrayOutputStream to the contents of the expectedOutput StringBuffer.

Finally, the test calls assertStudents to ensure that the list of students created and stored in the UI instance is as expected.

```
private void assertStudents(List<Student> students) {
    assertEquals(1, students.size());
    Student student = students.get(0);
    assertEquals(name, student.getName());
}
```

To verify the example user "script" coded in the setup method, assertStudents must ensure that the StudentUI object added only one student and that this student's data (its name) is as expected.

The entire StudentUI implementation appears below. To build this class test-first and very incrementally, you should start with an even simpler set of unit tests. First, ensure that the menu is presented and that the user can immediately quit the application. Then add functionality to support adding students. Start with assertions against the user interface flow, then add the assertion to ensure that a student object was created. A more complete test than this would ensure that multiple students could be created.

```
package sis.ui;

import java.io.*;
import java.util.*;
import sis.studentinfo.*;

public class StudentUI {
    static final String MENU = "(A)dd or (Q)uit?";
    static final String ADD_OPTION = "A";
    static final String QUIT_OPTION = "Q";
    static final String NAME_PROMPT = "Name: ";
    static final String ADDED_MESSAGE = "Added";

    private BufferedReader reader;
    private BufferedWriter writer;
    private List<Student> students = new ArrayList<Student>();
```

```
    public StudentUI(BufferedReader reader, BufferedWriter writer) {
        this.reader = reader;
        this.writer = writer;
    }

    public void run() throws IOException {
        String line;
        do {
            write(MENU);
            line = reader.readLine();
            if (line.equals(ADD_OPTION))
                addStudent();
        } while (!line.equals(QUIT_OPTION));
    }

    List<Student> getAddedStudents() {
        return students;
    }

    private void addStudent() throws IOException {
        write(NAME_PROMPT);
        String name = reader.readLine();

        students.add(new Student(name));
        writeln(ADDED_MESSAGE);
    }

    private void write(String line) throws IOException {
        writer.write(line, 0, line.length());
        writer.flush();
    }

    private void writeln (String line) throws IOException {
        write(line);
        writer.newLine();
        writer.flush();
    }
}
```

Testing the Application

The student user interface represents an actual application that someone might want to execute and interact with. You will need to provide a main method so that they can start the application. Currently, in order to execute the application, you would need to construct a student UI with System.in and System.out appropriately wrapped, then call the run method.

You can simplify the main method by encapsulating this work in the Student-UI class itself. This may or may not be an appropriate tactic—if you only have one user interface class, it's fine. But if you have a dozen related UI classes, each controlling a portion of the user interface, you'd be better off constructing the console wrappers in a single class.

For this example, let's make the main method as simple as possible. You can do this by redirecting console input and output using the System methods setIn and setOut instead of wrapping the input and output streams in buffered streams. You must wrap the ByteArrayOutputStream in a PrintStream in order to call setOut.

```
public void testCreateStudent() throws IOException {
    StringBuffer expectedOutput = new StringBuffer();
    StringBuffer input = new StringBuffer();
    setup(expectedOutput, input);
    byte[] buffer = input.toString().getBytes();

    InputStream inputStream = new ByteArrayInputStream(buffer);
    OutputStream outputStream = new ByteArrayOutputStream();

    InputStream consoleIn = System.in;
    PrintStream consoleOut = System.out;
    System.setIn(inputStream);
    System.setOut(new PrintStream(outputStream));
    try {
        StudentUI ui = new StudentUI();
        ui.run();

        assertEquals(
            expectedOutput.toString(),
            outputStream.toString());
        assertStudents(ui.getAddedStudents());
    }
    finally {
        System.setIn(consoleIn);
        System.setOut(consoleOut);
    }
}
```

You want to make sure you reset System.in and System.out by using a try-finally statement.

The new constructor for StudentUI must use an InputStreamReader to wrap stdin in a BufferedReader and an OutputStreamWriter to wrap stdout in a BufferedWriter.

```
public StudentUI() {
    this.reader =
        new BufferedReader(new InputStreamReader(System.in));
    this.writer =
        new BufferedWriter(new OutputStreamWriter(System.out));
}
```

After demonstrating that the test passes, you can now write a main method that kicks off the application.

```
public static final void main(String[] args) throws IOException {
    new StudentUI().run();
}
```

There are two trains of thought on this. First, it is possible to write a test against the main method, since you can call it like any other method (but you must supply an array of String objects that represent command-line arguments):

```
StudentUI.main(new String[] {});
```

The other testing philosophy is that the main method is virtually unbreakable. It is one line of code. You will certainly run the application from the command line at least once to ensure it works. As long as the main method does not change, it can't break, in which case you do not necessarily need a test against the main method.

The choice is yours as to whether to test main or not. Regardless, you should strive to minimize the main method to a single line. Refactor code from the main method into either static or instance-side methods. Create utility classes to help you manage command-line arguments. Test the code you move out of main.

I hope you've noticed that testing this simple console-based user interface required a good amount of code. Were you to write more of the console application, the work would simplify as you built utility methods and classes to help both testing and production coding.

Data Streams

You can write Java primitive data directly to a DataOutputStream. DataOutputStream is an example of a filtered stream. A filtered stream *wraps* another stream to either provide additional functionality or to alter the data along the way. The base filtered stream classes are FilteredOutputStream, FilteredInputStream, FilteredWriter, and FilteredReader.

The filter in DataOutputStream provides methods to output each Java primitive type: writeBoolean, writeDouble, and so on. It also provides the writeUTF method to output a String.

CourseCatalog

The student information system requires a CourseCatalog class to store a list of all available course sessions. CourseCatalog will be responsible for persisting basic course information (department, course number, start date, and number of credits) to a file so that the application can be restarted without any data loss.

The CourseCatalog provides a load method that reads all Session objects from a DataOutputStream into a collection. It also provides a store method to write the collection to a DataOutputStream.

```
package sis.studentinfo;

import junit.framework.*;
import java.util.*;
import java.io.*;

public class CourseCatalogTest extends TestCase {
    private CourseCatalog catalog;
    private Session session1;
    private Session session2;
    private Course course1;
    private Course course2;

    protected void setUp() {
        catalog = new CourseCatalog();
        course1 = new Course("a", "1");
        course2 = new Course("a", "1");

        session1 =
            CourseSession.create(
                course1, DateUtil.createDate(1, 15, 2005));
        session1.setNumberOfCredits(3);

        session2 =
            CourseSession.create(
                course2, DateUtil.createDate(1, 17, 2005));
        session2.setNumberOfCredits(5);

        catalog.add(session1);
        catalog.add(session2);
    }

    public void testStoreAndLoad() throws IOException {
        final String filename = "CourseCatalogTest.testAdd.txt";
        catalog.store(filename);
        catalog.clearAll();
        assertEquals(0, catalog.getSessions().size());
        catalog.load(filename);
```

```
        List<Session> sessions = catalog.getSessions();
        assertEquals(2, sessions.size());
        assertSession(session1, sessions.get(0));
        assertSession(session2, sessions.get(1));
    }

    private void assertSession(Session expected, Session retrieved) {
        assertNotSame(expected, retrieved);
        assertEquals(expected.getNumberOfCredits(),
            retrieved.getNumberOfCredits());
        assertEquals(expected.getStartDate(), retrieved.getStartDate());
        assertEquals(expected.getDepartment(), retrieved.getDepartment());
        assertEquals(expected.getNumber(), retrieved.getNumber());
    }
}
```

CourseCatalog

The test loads a couple courses into the catalog, calls the store method, clears the catalog, and then calls the load method. It asserts that the catalog contains the two courses initially inserted.

The code other than load and store in CourseCatalog is trivial:

```
package sis.studentinfo;

import java.util.*;
import java.io.*;

public class CourseCatalog {
    private List<Session> sessions =
        new ArrayList<Session>();

    public void add(Session session) {
        sessions.add(session);
    }

    public List<Session> getSessions() {
        return sessions;
    }

    public void clearAll() {
        sessions.clear();
    }
    // ...
}
```

The store method creates a DataOutputStream by wrapping a FileOutput-Stream. It first writes an int that represents the number of course sessions to be stored. The method then loops through all sessions, writing the start date, number of credits, department, and course number for each.

```
public void store(String filename) throws IOException {
    DataOutputStream output = null;
    try {
```

```
    output =
        new DataOutputStream(new FileOutputStream(filename));
    output.writeInt(sessions.size());
    for (Session session: sessions) {
        output.writeLong(session.getStartDate().getTime());
        output.writeInt(session.getNumberOfCredits());
        output.writeUTF(session.getDepartment());
        output.writeUTF(session.getNumber());
    }
}
finally {
    output.close();
}
}
```

You'll need to create a getter method in Session to return the number of credits:

```
public int getNumberOfCredits() {
    return numberOfCredits;
}
```

The load method creates a DataInputStream by wrapping a FileInputStream. It reads the count of sessions to determine how many sessions are stored in the file. Using counts in this manner is preferred to the alternative, which is to anticipate an end-of-file exception with each read operation against the file.

The load method assumes that the session being read is a CourseSession, not a SummerCourseSession or other Session subclass. If the CourseCatalog needed to support more than one type, you would need to store the type of Session. The type information would allow code in the load method to know what class to instantiate when reading each object.

```
public void load(String filename) throws IOException {
    DataInputStream input = null;
    try {
        input = new DataInputStream(new FileInputStream(filename));
        int numberOfSessions = input.readInt();
        for (int i = 0; i < numberOfSessions; i++) {
            Date startDate = new Date(input.readLong());
            int credits = input.readInt();
            String department = input.readUTF();
            String number = input.readUTF();
            Course course = new Course(department, number);
            Session session =
                CourseSession.create(course, startDate);
            session.setNumberOfCredits(credits);
            sessions.add(session);
        }
    }
    finally {
        input.close();
    }
}
```

Both load and store methods ensure that the associated data streams are closed by use of a finally block.

Advanced Streams

Piped Streams

You use piped streams for a safe I/O-based data communication channel between different threads. Piped streams work in pairs: Data written to a piped output stream is read from a piped input stream to which it is attached. The piped stream implementations are PipedInputStream, PipedOutputStream, PipedReader, and PipedWriter. Refer to Lesson 13 for more information on multithreading.

SequenceInputStream

You can use a SequenceInputStream to allow a collection of input sources to act as a single input stream. The collection of sources is ordered; when one source is fully read, it is closed and the next stream in the collection is opened for reading.

Pushback Streams

The primary use of pushback streams (PushbackInputStream and Pushback-Reader) is for lexical analysis programs such as a tokenizer for a compiler. They allow data to be put back onto a stream as if it had not yet been read by the stream.

StreamTokenizer

The primary use of StreamTokenizer is also in parsing applications. It acts similarly to StringTokenizer. Instead of returning only strings from the underlying stream, however, a StreamTokenizer returns the type of the token in addition to the value. A token type may be a word, a number, an end-of-line marker, or an end-of-file marker.

Object Streams

Java provides the capability to directly read and write objects from and to streams. Java can write an object to an object output stream by virtue of *serializing* it. Java serializes an object by converting it into a sequence of bytes.

The ability to serialize objects is the basis for Java's RMI (Remote Method Invocation) technology. RMI allows objects to communicate with other objects on remote systems as if they were local. RMI in turn provides the basis for Java's EJB (Enterprise Java Bean) technology for component-based computing.

You write and read objects using the classes ObjectOutputStream and ObjectInputStream. As a quick demonstration, the following code is a rewrite of the the methods store and load in the CourseCatalog class. The modified code uses object streams instead of data streams.

Object Streams

```
public void store(String filename) throws IOException {
    ObjectOutputStream output = null;
    try {
        output =
            new ObjectOutputStream(new FileOutputStream(filename));
        output.writeObject(sessions);
    }
    finally {
        output.close();
    }
}

public void load(String filename)
        throws IOException, ClassNotFoundException {
    ObjectInputStream input = null;
    try {
        input = new ObjectInputStream(new FileInputStream(filename));
        sessions = (List<Session>)input.readObject();
    }
    finally {
        input.close();
    }
}
```

The test remains largely unchanged.

```
public void testStoreAndLoad() throws Exception {
    final String filename = "CourseCatalogTest.testAdd.txt";
    catalog.store(filename);
    catalog.clearAll();
    assertEquals(0, catalog.getSessions().size());
    catalog.load(filename);

    List<Session> sessions = catalog.getSessions();
    assertEquals(2, sessions.size());
    assertSession(session1, sessions.get(0));
    assertSession(session2, sessions.get(1));
}
```

The throws clause on the test method signature must change, since the load method now throws a ClassNotFoundException. Within the context of this example, it doesn't seem possible for a ClassNotFoundException to be generated. You store a List of Session objects and immediately read it back, and both java.util.List and Session are known to your code. An exception could be thrown, however, if another application with no access to your Session class were to read the objects from the file.

When you run the test, you should receive an exception:

```
java.io.NotSerializableException: studentinfo.CourseSession
```

In order to write an object to an object stream, its class must be *serializable*. You mark a class as serializable by having it implement the interface java.io.Serializable. Most of the classes in the Java system class library that you would expect to be serializable are already marked as such. This includes the String and Date classes as well as all collection classes (HashMap, ArrayList, and so on). But you will need to mark your own application classes:

```
abstract public class Session
     implements Comparable<Session>,
               Iterable<Student>,
               java.io.Serializable { ...
```

Don't forget the Course class, since Session encapsulates it:

```
public class Course implements java.io.Serializable { ...
```

When you mark the abstract superclass as serializable, all its subclasses will also be serializable. The Serializable interface contains no method definitions, so you need not do anything else to the Session class.

An interface that declares no methods is known as a *marker interface*. You create marker interfaces to allow a developer to explicitly mark a class for a specific use. You must positively designate a class as capable of being serialized. The Serializable marker is intended as a safety mechanism—you may want to prevent certain objects from being serialized for security reasons.

Transient

Course sessions allow for enrollment of students. However, you don't want the course catalog to be cluttered with student objects. Suppose, though, that a student has enrolled early, before the catalog was created. The setUp method in CourseCatalogTest enrolls a student as an example:

```
protected void setUp() {
    catalog = new CourseCatalog();
    course1 = new Course("a", "1");
    course2 = new Course("a", "1");

    session1 =
        CourseSession.create(
            course1, DateUtil.createDate(1, 15, 2005));
    session1.setNumberOfCredits(3);

    session2 =
        CourseSession.create(
            course2, DateUtil.createDate(1, 17, 2005));
    session2.setNumberOfCredits(5);
    session2.enroll(new Student("a"));

    catalog.add(session1);
    catalog.add(session2);
}
```

If you run your tests, you again receive a NotSerializableException. The course session now refers to a Student object that must be serialized. But the Student class does not implement java.io.Serializable.

Instead of changing Student, you can indicate that the list of students in Session is to be skipped during serialization by marking them with the transient modifier.

```
abstract public class Session
        implements Comparable<Session>,
                    Iterable<Student>,
                    java.io.Serializable {
    ...
    private transient List<Student> students = new ArrayList<Student>();
```

The list of students will not be serialized in this example. Your tests will now pass.

Serialization and Change

Serialization makes it easy to persist objects. Too easy, perhaps. There are many implications to declaring a class as Serializable. The most significant issue is that when you persist a serialized object, you export with it a definition of the class as it currently exists. If you subsequently change the class definition, then attempt to read the serialized object, you will get an exception.

To demonstrate, add a name field to Session.java. This creates a new version of the Session class. Don't worry about a test; this is a temporary "spike," or experiment. You will delete this line of code in short time. Also, *do not run any tests*—doing so will ruin the experiment.

```
abstract public class Session
      implements Comparable<Session>,
                 Iterable<Student>,
                 java.io.Serializable {
   private String name;
   ...
```

Your last execution of tests persisted an object stream to the file named CourseCatalogTest.testAdd.txt. The object stream stored in this file contains Session objects created using the older definition of Session without the name field.

Then create an entirely new test class, studentinfo.SerializationTest:

```
package sis.studentinfo;

import junit.framework.*;

public class SerializationTest extends TestCase {
   public void testLoadToNewVersion() throws Exception {
      CourseCatalog catalog = new CourseCatalog();
      catalog.load("CourseCatalogTest.testAdd.txt");
      assertEquals(2, catalog.getSessions().size());
   }
}
```

The test tries to load the persisted object stream. *Execute only this test.* Do not execute your AllTests suite. You should receive an exception that looks something like:

```
testLoadToNewVersion(studentinfo.SerializationTest)
   java.io.InvalidClassException: studentinfo.Session;
   local class incompatible:
      stream classdesc serialVersionUID = 5771972560035839399,
      local class serialVersionUID = 156127782215802147
```

Java determines compatibility between the objects stored in the output stream and the existing (local) class definition. It considers the class name, the interfaces implemented by the class, its fields, and its methods. Changing any of these will result in incompatibility.

Transient fields are ignored, however. If you change the declaration of the name field in Session to transient:

```
private transient String name;
```

SerializationTest will then pass.

Serial Version UID

The InvalidClassException you received referred to a serialVersionUID for both the stream's class definition and the local (current Java) class definition. In order to determine whether the definition of a class has changed, Java generates the serialVersionUID based on the class name, interfaces implemented, fields, and methods. The serialVersionUID, a 64-bit long value, is known as a *stream unique identifier*.

You can choose to define your own serialVersionUID instead of using the one Java generates. This may give you some ability to better control version management. You can obtain an initial serialVersionUID by using the command-line utility serialver or you can assign an arbitrary value to it. An example execution of serialver:

```
serialver -classpath classes studentinfo.Session
```

You optionally specify the classpath, followed by the list of classes for which you wish to generate a serialVersionUID.

Remove the name field from Session. Rebuild and rerun your entire test suite. Add a serialVersionUID definition to Session. At the same time, add back the name field.

```
abstract public class Session
    implements Comparable<Session>,
               Iterable<Student>,
               java.io.Serializable {
    public static final long serialVersionUID = 1L;
    private String name;
    ...
```

Then run only SerializationTest. Even though you've added a new field, the version ID is the same. Java will initialize the name field to its default value of null. If you change the serialVersionUID to 2L and rerun the test, you will cause the stream version (1) to be out of synch with the local class version (2).

Creating a Custom Serialized Form

Your class may contain information that can be reconstructed based on other data in the class. When you model a class, you define its attributes to represent the logical state of every object of that class. In addition to those attributes, you may have data structures or other fields that cache dynamically computed information. Persisting this dynamically calculated data may be slow and/or a grossly inefficient use of space.

 Suppose you need to persist not only the course sessions but also the students enrolled in each session. Students carry a large amount of additional data, and they are already being persisted elsewhere. You can traverse the collection of course sessions and persist only the unique identifier for each student to the object stream.[1] When you load this compacted collection, you can execute a lookup to retrieve the complete student object and store it in the course session.

To accomplish this, you will define two methods in Session, writeObject and readObject. These methods are hooks that the serialization mechanism calls when reading and writing each object to the object stream. If you don't supply anything for these hooks, default serialization and deserialization takes place.

First, change the test in CourseCatalogTest to ensure that the enrolled student was properly persisted and restored.

```java
public void testStoreAndLoad() throws Exception {
    final String filename = "CourseCatalogTest.testAdd.txt";
    catalog.store(filename);
    catalog.clearAll();
    assertEquals(0, catalog.getSessions().size());
    catalog.load(filename);

    List<Session> sessions = catalog.getSessions();
    assertEquals(2, sessions.size());
    assertSession(session1, sessions.get(0));
    assertSession(session2, sessions.get(1));

    Session session = sessions.get(1);
    assertSession(session2, session);
    Student student = session.getAllStudents().get(0);
    assertEquals("a", student.getLastName());
}
```

Make sure that the students field in Session is marked as transient. Then code the writeObject definition for Session:

```java
private void writeObject(ObjectOutputStream output)
      throws IOException {
   output.defaultWriteObject();
   output.writeInt(students.size());
   for (Student student: students)
      output.writeObject(student.getLastName());
}
```

[1] We have a small school. We don't admit anyone with the same last name as another student, so you can use that as your unique identifier.

Object Streams

The first line of writeObject calls the method defaultWriteObject on the stream. This will write every nontransient field to the stream normally. Subsequently, the code in writeObject first writes the number of students to the stream, then loops through the list of students, writing each student's last name to the stream.

```
private void readObject(ObjectInputStream input)
    throws Exception {
  input.defaultReadObject();
  students = new ArrayList<Student>();
  int size = input.readInt();
  for (int i = 0; i < size; i++) {
    String lastName = (String)input.readObject();
    students.add(Student.findByLastName(lastName));
  }
}
```

On the opposite end, readObject first calls defaultReadObject to load all nontransient fields from the stream. It initializes the transient field students to a new ArrayList of students. It reads the number of students into size and iterates size times. Each iteration extracts a student's last name from the stream. The code looks up and retrieves a Student object using this last name and stores the Student in the students collection.

In real life, the findByLastName method might involve sending a message to a student directory object, which in turn retrieves the appropriate student from a database or another serialization file. For demonstration purposes, you can provide a simple implementation that will pass the test:

```
public static Student findByLastName(String lastName) {
  return new Student(lastName);
}
```

Serialization Approaches

For classes whose definitions are likely to change, dealing with serialization version incompatibility issues can be a major headache. While it is possible to load serialized objects from an older version, it is difficult. Your best tactics include:

- minimizing use of serialization

- maximizing the number of transient fields

- identifying versions with serialVersionUID

- defining a custom serialization version

When you serialize an object, you are exporting its interface. Just as you should keep interfaces as abstract and unlikely to change as possible, you should do the same with serializable classes.

Random Access Files

Instead of loading and storing the complete course catalog each time you execute the application, you can dynamically interact with the catalog by implementing it as a *random access file*. A random access file allows you to quickly seek to specific positions in the file and either read from or write to that position.

It would be possible to create a fully featured object database in Java using random access files. The forthcoming example code is a starting point.

In Lesson 9, you created a StudentDirectory class. You implemented the class to to store student objects in a HashMap, using the student's ID as a key.

 Now you need to ensure that your student directory supports the tens of thousands of students enrolling at the university. Further, you must persist the directory to the file system in order to secure the data. It is imperative that retrieving students from the directory executes rapidly. A retrieval must execute in constant time—the amount of time to access a student should not vary depending on where the student appears in the file.

You will implement the student directory using a simple indexed file system. You will store student records in a data file and unique ids (identifiers) for each student in an index file. As you insert a serialized student into the data file, you will record its id, position, and length in the index file. The index file will be small compared to the data file size. It can be quickly loaded into memory and written out when the data file is closed.[2]

The example code is the most involved in this book so far. If you take it a test and method at a time, you shouldn't have much trouble understanding it. Building the tests and code from scratch is a bit more of a challenge. The UML is shown in Figure 11.1.

And here is the code. I'll explain the interesting parts of it after the code listing for each class.

---

[2]There is a bit of risk in not persisting the indexes as you add Students. You could mitigate this risk by writing the data length within the data file itself as well. Doing so would allow you to re-create the index file by traversing through the data file.

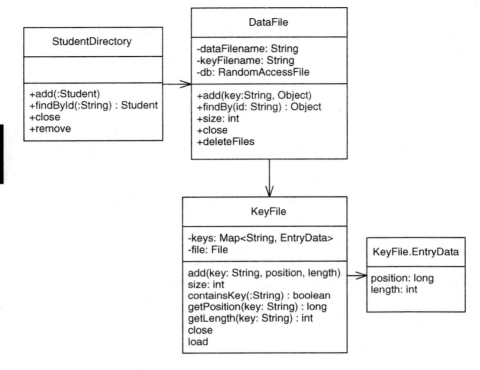

Figure 11.1 *The Student Directory*

The Student Directory

```
package sis.studentinfo;

import junit.framework.*;
import java.io.*;

public class StudentDirectoryTest extends TestCase {
   private StudentDirectory dir;

   protected void setUp() throws IOException {
      dir = new StudentDirectory();
   }

   protected void tearDown() throws IOException {
      dir.close();
      dir.remove();
   }
```

```
        public void testRandomAccess() throws IOException {
            final int numberOfStudents = 10;
            for (int i = 0; i < numberOfStudents; i++)
                addStudent(dir, i);
            dir.close();

            dir = new StudentDirectory();
            for (int i = 0; i < numberOfStudents; i++)
                verifyStudentLookup(dir, i);
        }

    void addStudent(StudentDirectory directory, int i)
            throws IOException {
        String id = "" + i;
        Student student = new Student(id);
        student.setId(id);
        student.addCredits(i);
        directory.add(student);
    }

    void verifyStudentLookup(StudentDirectory directory, int i)
            throws IOException {
        String id = "" + i;
        Student student = dir.findById(id);
        assertEquals(id, student.getLastName());
        assertEquals(id, student.getId());
        assertEquals(i, student.getCredits());
    }
}
```

The most significant new addition to StudentDirectoryTest appears in testRandomAccess. When it adds the students to the directory, the test closes it. It then creates a new directory instance to be used for the student lookups. By doing this, the test demonstrates at least some notion of persistence.

An additional performance test might be worthwhile to demonstrate that a lookup into the directory takes the same amount of time regardless of where it appears in the file. Additions of students to the directory should also execute in constant time.

```
package sis.studentinfo;

import java.io.*;
import sis.db.*;

public class StudentDirectory {
    private static final String DIR_BASENAME = "studentDir";
    private DataFile db;

    public StudentDirectory() throws IOException {
        db = DataFile.open(DIR_BASENAME);
    }
```

```
public void add(Student student) throws IOException {
    db.add(student.getId(), student);
}

public Student findById(String id) throws IOException {
    return (Student)db.findBy(id);
}

public void close() throws IOException {
    db.close();
}

public void remove() {
    db.deleteFiles();
}
}
```

In contrast, most of the StudentDirectory class has changed. The Student-Directory class now encapsulates a DataFile instance to supply directory functionality. It provides a few additional specifics, including the key field to use (the student id) and the base filename for the data and key files. Beyond that, the class merely delegates messages to the DataFile object.

sis.db.DataFileTest

```
package sis.db;

import junit.framework.*;
import java.io.*;
import sis.util.*;

public class DataFileTest extends TestCase {
    private static final String ID1 = "12345";
    private static final String ID2 = "23456";
    private static final String FILEBASE = "DataFileTest";

    private DataFile db;
    private TestData testData1;
    private TestData testData2;

    protected void setUp() throws IOException {
        db = DataFile.create(FILEBASE);
        assertEquals(0, db.size());

        testData1 = new TestData(ID1, "datum1a", 1);
        testData2 = new TestData(ID2, "datum2a", 2);
    }
```

```
protected void tearDown() throws IOException {
    db.close();
    db.deleteFiles();
}

public void testAdd() throws IOException {
    db.add(ID1, testData1);
    assertEquals(1, db.size());

    db.add(ID2, testData2);
    assertEquals(2, db.size());

    assertTestDataEquals(testData1, (TestData)db.findBy(ID1));
    assertTestDataEquals(testData2, (TestData)db.findBy(ID2));
}

public void testPersistence() throws IOException {
    db.add(ID1, testData1);
    db.add(ID2, testData2);
    db.close();

    db = DataFile.open(FILEBASE);
    assertEquals(2, db.size());

    assertTestDataEquals(testData1, (TestData)db.findBy(ID1));
    assertTestDataEquals(testData2, (TestData)db.findBy(ID2));

    db = DataFile.create(FILEBASE);
    assertEquals(0, db.size());
}

public void testKeyNotFound() throws IOException {
    assertNull(db.findBy(ID2));
}

private void assertTestDataEquals(
        TestData expected, TestData actual)  {
    assertEquals(expected.id, actual.id);
    assertEquals(expected.field1, actual.field1);
    assertEquals(expected.field2, actual.field2);
}

static class TestData implements Serializable {
    String id;
    String field1;
    int field2;
    TestData(String id, String field1, int field2) {
        this.id = id;
        this.field1 = field1;
        this.field2 = field2;
    }
}
}
```

sis.db.DataFile-
Test

DataFileTest shows that you create a new DataFile using the static factory method create. The create method takes the name of the DataFile as its parameter.

The test also shows that you insert objects into a DataFile by using the add method, which takes a unique key and associated object as parameters. To retrieve objects, you send the message findBy, passing with it the unique id of the object to be retrieved. If the object is not available, DataFile returns null.

Persistence is tested by closing a DataFile and creating a new instance using the static factory method open.[3] The distinction between open and create is that create will delete the data file if it already exists, while open will reuse an existing data file or create a new one if necessary.

Note that the object returned by the findBy method requires a cast! This suggests that DataFile is a candidate for implementing as a parameterized type. (See Lesson 14 for more information on parameterized types.)

Static Nested Classes and Inner Classes

DataFileTest needs to show that DataFile can persist an object and retrieve that object at a later time. In order to write such a test, it's best to use a class that you can guarantee no one else will change. You could use a Java system library class such as String, but they change with new releases of Java. Instead, the better solution is to create a test class solely for use by DataFileTest.

The class TestData is defined as a *nested* class of DataFileTest; that is, it is completely contained within DataFileTest. There are two kinds of nested classes: inner classes and static nested classes. The chief distinction is that inner classes have access to the instance variables defined within the enclosing class. Static nested classes do not.

Another distinction is that inner classes are completely encapsulated by the enclosing class. Since inner classes can refer to instance variables of the enclosing class, it makes no sense for other code to be able to create instances of an instance inner class. While Java technically allows you to refer to an

---

[3]Technically the test does not *prove* disk persistence. You could have implemented a solution that stored objects in a static-side collection. However, the point of the test is not to protect you from being dishonest and coding a foolish solution. The test instead demonstrates the expected behavior. If you're not convinced, however, there's nothing that prohibits you from writing a test to ensure that the object is actually stored in a disk file. It's just a lot more complex, and probably unnecessary.

Class Names for Nested Classes

When you compile a class or interface, the compilation unit is named by taking the class name and appending a .class file extension. For example, the Course class compiles to Course.class.

When compiling a class containing a nested class, Java names the compilation unit for the inner class by first using the containing class name, followed by the dollar sign ($), then the nested class name.

For example, the DataFileTest class creates two compilation units: DataFileTest.class and DataFileTest$TestData.class.

When you copy class files or put them in a JAR file (see Additional Lesson III) for distribution, don't forget to include all the nested classes.

inner class from external code, it's a bit of trickery that I'm not going to show you here—don't do it!

Static nested classes, on the other hand, can be used by external code as long as the access specifier is not private. You have already used the static nested class Entry in order to iterate key-value pairs in a Map object. You referred to this class as Map.Entry, since you used it in a code context other than Map.

So the first reason to declare a nested class as static is to allow other classes to use it. You could declare the class as a top-level (i.e., non-nested) class, but you may want to tightly couple it to the containing class. For example, Map.Entry is tightly bound to Map, since it makes no sense for the Entry class to exist in the absence of Map.

The second reason to declare a nested class as static is to allow it to be serialized. You cannot serialize inner class objects, since they must have access to the instance variables of the enclosing class. In order to make it work, the serialization mechanism would have to capture the fields of the enclosing class. Yuck.

Since you need to persist TestData objects, you must make the class serializable. If TestData is to be a nested class, you must declare it as static.

sis.db.DataFile

```
package sis.db;

import java.util.*;
import java.io.*;
import sis.util.*;
```

```
public class DataFile {
    public static final String DATA_EXT = ".db";
    public static final String KEY_EXT = ".idx";

    private String dataFilename;
    private String keyFilename;

    private RandomAccessFile db;
    private KeyFile keys;

    public static DataFile create(String filebase) throws IOException {
        return new DataFile(filebase, true);
    }

    public static DataFile open(String filebase) throws IOException {
        return new DataFile(filebase, false);
    }

    private DataFile(String filebase, boolean deleteFiles)
            throws IOException {
        dataFilename = filebase + DATA_EXT;
        keyFilename = filebase + KEY_EXT;

        if (deleteFiles)
            deleteFiles();
        openFiles();
    }

    public void add(String key, Object object) throws IOException {
        long position = db.length();

        byte[] bytes = getBytes(object);
        db.seek(position);
        db.write(bytes, 0, bytes.length);

        keys.add(key, position, bytes.length);
    }

    public Object findBy(String id) throws IOException {
        if (!keys.containsKey(id))
            return null;

        long position = keys.getPosition(id);
        db.seek(position);

        int length = keys.getLength(id);
        return read(length);
    }

    public int size() {
        return keys.size();
    }
```

```
public void close() throws IOException {
   keys.close();
   db.close();
}

public void deleteFiles() {
   IOUtil.delete(dataFilename, keyFilename);
}

private Object read(int length) throws IOException {
   byte[] bytes = new byte[length];
   db.readFully(bytes);
   return readObject(bytes);
}

private Object readObject(byte[] bytes) throws IOException {
   ObjectInputStream input =
      new ObjectInputStream(new ByteArrayInputStream(bytes));
   try {
      try {
         return input.readObject();
      }
      catch (ClassNotFoundException unlikely) {
         // but write a test for it if you must
         return null;
      }
   }
   finally {
      input.close();
   }
}

private void openFiles() throws IOException {
   keys = new KeyFile(keyFilename);
   db = new RandomAccessFile(new File(dataFilename), "rw");
}

private byte[] getBytes(Object object) throws IOException {
   ByteArrayOutputStream byteStream = new ByteArrayOutputStream();
   ObjectOutputStream outputStream =
      new ObjectOutputStream(byteStream);
   outputStream.writeObject(object);
   outputStream.flush();
   return byteStream.toByteArray();
}
}
```

The DataFile class is the core part of the solution. It demonstrates use of a RandomAccessFile object, which you store in the instance variable db (short for database, one of the small number of abbreviations I use). You create a RandomAccessFile object by passing in a File object and a String declaring the mode in which you wish to access the RandomAccessFile.

RandomAccessFile provides four modes: "r" (read-only), "rw" (read and write access), "rws" (read-write with synchronous data/metadata updates), and "rwd" (read-write with synchronous data updates). The synchronous updates ensure that updates to the file are safely written to the underlying storage device. Without using them, you could conceivably lose data in a system crash. The "rws" option ensures persistence of both content and metadata (information such as the last modified timestamp for the file), while the "rwd" option only ensures updates of the content.

Here we chose the "rw" option, since you want to be able to both read data from and write data to the data file. The other read-write options incur additional overhead but may be necessary to maintain data integrity.

You use the seek method to rapidly move an internal file pointer to any location within the underlying file. The getFilePointer method (not used here) returns the current position of the file pointer. The length method returns the total number of bytes in the file. Like other IO classes, RandomAccessFile supplies many read and write methods to extract and store data.

RandomAccessFile does not directly support storing objects. In order to persist an object to the RandomAccessFile, you must first convert it to a byte array. To convert an object to bytes, the getBytes method wraps a ByteArrayOutputStream in an ObjectOutputStream. This means that any objects written to the ObjectOutputStream are piped to the underlying ByteArrayOutputStream. You can extract the bytes from an ByteArrayOutputStream by sending it the toByteArray message.

To read an object from the RandomAccessFile, you must do the opposite. Create a byte array of the appropriate length and use the method readFully to populate the bytes from the RandomAccessFile. Wrap the populated byte array in a ByteArrayInputStream, which you then wrap in an ObjectInputStream. Reading from the ObjectInputStream will reconstitute the persisted object using the underlying bytes.

sis.db.KeyFileTest

```
package sis.db;

import junit.framework.*;
import java.io.*;
import java.util.*;
import sis.util.*;
```

```
public class KeyFileTest extends TestCase {
   private static final String FILENAME = "keyfiletest.idx";
   private static final String KEY = "key";
   private static final long POSITION = 1;
   private static final int LENGTH = 100;

   private KeyFile keyFile;

   protected void setUp() throws IOException {
      TestUtil.delete(FILENAME);
      keyFile = new KeyFile(FILENAME);
   }

   protected void tearDown() throws IOException {
      TestUtil.delete(FILENAME);
      keyFile.close();
   }

   public void testCreate() {
      assertEquals(0, keyFile.size());
   }

   public void testAddEntry()  {
      keyFile.add(KEY, POSITION, LENGTH) ;

      assertEquals(1, keyFile.size());
      assertTrue(keyFile.containsKey(KEY));
      assertEquals(POSITION, keyFile.getPosition(KEY));
      assertEquals(LENGTH, keyFile.getLength(KEY));
   }

   public void testReopen() throws IOException {
      keyFile.add(KEY, POSITION, LENGTH);
      keyFile.close();

      keyFile = new KeyFile(FILENAME);
      assertEquals(1, keyFile.size());
      assertEquals(POSITION, keyFile.getPosition(KEY));
      assertEquals(LENGTH, keyFile.getLength(KEY));
   }
}
```

KeyFileTest demonstrates the ability to add keys (unique ids) to a KeyFile. A key is stored with the position of the associated data in the DataFile object as well as with the length of that data. The data position and length can be retrieved from the KeyFile using the unique key.

The third test, testReopen, ensures that you can create a new KeyFile object using the name of an existing key file. The KeyFile object must load the already-persisted key data.

sis.db.KeyFile

```java
package sis.db;

import java.util.*;
import java.io.*;

class KeyFile {
    private Map<String, EntryData> keys =
        new HashMap<String, EntryData>();
    private File file;

    KeyFile(String filename) throws IOException {
        file = new File(filename);
        if (file.exists())
            load();
    }

    void add(String key, long position, int length) {
        keys.put(key, new EntryData(position, length));
    }

    int size() {
        return keys.size();
    }

    boolean containsKey(String key) {
        return keys.containsKey(key);
    }

    long getPosition(String key) {
        return keys.get(key).getPosition();
    }

    int getLength(String key) {
        return keys.get(key).getLength();
    }

    void close() throws IOException {
        ObjectOutputStream stream =
            new ObjectOutputStream(new FileOutputStream(file));
        stream.writeObject(keys);
        stream.close();
    }

    void load() throws IOException {
        ObjectInputStream input = null;
        try {
            input = new ObjectInputStream(new FileInputStream(file));
            try {
```

```
                keys = (Map<String, EntryData>)input.readObject();
            }
            catch (ClassNotFoundException e) {
            }
        }
        finally {
            input.close();
        }
    }

    static class EntryData implements Serializable {
        private long position;
        private int length;

        EntryData(long position, int length) {
            this.position = position;
            this.length = length;
        }

        private long getPosition() {
            return position;
        }

        private int getLength() {
            return length;
        }
    }
}
```

KeyFile stores the key information using a Map named keys. This Map object maps the key to a serializable static nested class, EntryData, which contains the data position and length. When closed, the KeyFile writes the entire Map to the file by using an ObjectOutputStream. It loads the entire Map when opened.

sis.util.IOUtilTest

```
package sis.util;

import junit.framework.*;
import java.io.*;

public class IOUtilTest extends TestCase {
    static final String FILENAME1 = "IOUtilTest1.txt";
    static final String FILENAME2 = "IOUtilTest2.txt";

    public void testDeleteSingleFile() throws IOException {
        create(FILENAME1);
```

```
        assertTrue(IOUtil.delete(FILENAME1));
        TestUtil.assertGone(FILENAME1);
    }

    public void testDeleteMultipleFiles() throws IOException {
        create(FILENAME1, FILENAME2);
        assertTrue(IOUtil.delete(FILENAME1, FILENAME2));
        TestUtil.assertGone(FILENAME1, FILENAME2);
    }

    public void testDeleteNoFile() throws IOException {
        TestUtil.delete(FILENAME1);
        assertFalse(IOUtil.delete(FILENAME1));
    }

    public void testDeletePartiallySuccessful() throws IOException {
        create(FILENAME1);
        TestUtil.delete(FILENAME2);
        assertFalse(IOUtil.delete(FILENAME1, FILENAME2));
        TestUtil.assertGone(FILENAME1);
    }

    private void create(String... filenames) throws IOException {
        for (String filename: filenames) {
            TestUtil.delete(filename);
            new File(filename).createNewFile();
        }
    }
}
```

The most interesting aspect of IOUtilTest is that it contains four test methods, each testing the same IOUtil method delete. Each test proves a typical scenario. There are probably many more tests possible. It's up to you to decide whether you have enough tests to give you the confidence you need in your code.

 Err in the direction of too many tests instead of too few.

sis.util.IOUtil

```
package sis.util;

import java.io.*;

public class IOUtil {
    public static boolean delete(String... filenames) {
        boolean deletedAll = true;
```

```
        for (String filename: filenames)
            if (!new File(filename).delete())
                deletedAll = false;
        return deletedAll;
    }
}
```

The delete method uses varargs to allow you to delete multiple files in a single method call. It returns true only if all files were successfully deleted.

sis.util.TestUtil

```
package sis.util;

import junit.framework.*;
import java.io.*;

public class TestUtil {
    public static void assertGone(String... filenames) {
        for (String filename: filenames)
            Assert.assertFalse(new File(filename).exists());
    }

    public static void delete(String filename) {
        File file = new File(filename);
        if (file.exists())
            Assert.assertTrue(file.delete());
    }
}
```

Only tests use code in the TestUtil class. Since TestUtil does not extend from junit.framework.TestCase, it does not have instance access to any assert methods. However, the class junit.framework.Assert defines the assert methods as class methods, allowing you to access them anywhere.

Other things you will need to do:

- Make the GradingStrategy implementation types and Student serializable.

- Add an id field and associated getter/setter methods to the Student class.

- Update the AllTests suite classes.[4]

---

[4]Having to remember to add the classes is asking for trouble. In Lesson 12, you'll learn how to use Java's reflections capabilities to dynamically build test suites.

Exercises

Developing the Solution

In this example, I started by trying to implement StudentDirectory through the single test you see in StudentDirectoryTest, testRandomAccess. As often happens, the task of building functionality for StudentDirectory represented a large step. As I stubbed out the methods in StudentDirectory, it led me to the task of building the DataFile class. This meant my work on Student-DirectoryTest was temporarily put on hold. Similarly, after I started to work on DataFile, I found it easier to encapsulate the key functionality to a class named KeyFile.

As I progressed in developing the solution, I was constantly reevaluating the design at hand. My general strategy is to sketch an initial design going from the "outside" and moving in. In other words, I determine how client code wants to be able to use a class and base its design on that interface. If necessary, I sketch out the high-level structure and work on some of the "inner" details. No matter how I work, I find that the design is usually in a state of flux. Implementing inner details sometimes impacts the surrounding classes, and vice versa.

Changes to the design are normal. The outermost interface remains fairly stable, but the details change frequently. Few of the design changes are major—it's more like pushing small bits of code from here to there, constantly honing and improving the design.

Doing an initial design can still be very valuable. Just don't invest much time in the details. The important parts of the design to get right are the interface points—where does your code have to interact with other code in the system? Beyond that, the pieces in the middle are under your control. You'll craft a better system by letting the implementation guide your design.

Exercises

1. Create a test to write the text of this exercise to the file system. The test should read the file back in and make assertions about the content. Ensure that you can run the test multiple times and have it pass. Finally, make sure that there are no leftover files when the test finishes, even if an exception is thrown.

2. (hard) Create a timing test to prove that using a Buffered class is important for performance. The test can loop through various sizes of

file, creating character data in sizes growing by a factor of 10, calling a method coded to write using the basic character-at-a-time methods, then wrapping the writer in a buffered output stream and writing it again until a 5x performance gain is reached. What is the threshold at which a buffered writer is a significant performance gain?

3. Create and test a utility class called MyFile. This class should wrap a File object, taking a string filename as its constructor argument. It should have methods for retrieving the content of the file as a String or as a List of lines. It should also have a method for writing either a String or a List of Strings. Read and write operations should encapsulate opening and closing the file—clients should not have to close the file themselves.

   Ensure that the read methods fail with a specific unchecked exception type if the file doesn't exist. Similarly, the write methods should fail if the file does exist. Provide delete and overwrite methods, and you will have built a well-tested utility class that you can place in your toolbox.

4. Further adventures in utility classes: Create a Dir class that encapsulates a File object that in turn represents an actual file system directory. Design the class so that it is functional only when mapped to an existing directory. Provide a method named ensureExists to create the directory if it does not exist. The constructor should throw an exception if the directory name is the same as an existing file. Finally, provide a method that returns a list of MyFile objects in the directory and throws an exception if the directory has not been created yet.

5. Code a test that shows the use of a ByteArrayOutputStream to capture an exception and dump the stack trace into a string. Code it with and without an OutputStreamWriter. In both the character version and the byte version, use buffered readers and writers.

6. Modify the chess application to allow you to save the board positions to a text file and read them back in. Provide two choices—a serialized object of type Board or a textual representation as shown in the earlier exercises.

7. In Additional Lesson III, you will learn the preferred Java technique for cloning, or creating a copy of, an object. Until you learn this technique, you can implement cloning using object serialization and deserialization to duplicate objects. Your implementation will be a "poor man's" clone that you should not use in production systems.

8. Create an instance inner class for Dir, named Attributes, that encapsulates two directory attributes: Is the directory read-only and is it hidden? The Dir class should return an instance of this object if

requested. Demonstrate (through failure to compile) that the test cannot instantiate this object.

9. Change the Dir.Attributes inner class to a static nested class and change the code and test so they still work. What are the implications? Show that the test can instantiate a Dir.Attributes class. Does this design make sense?

10. In the exercises for Lesson 10, you wrote code to programmatically determine the size of each primitive integral type. Now, write code to determine the base size of *all* primitive types by using a data stream.

Lesson 12

Reflection and Other Advanced Topics

In terms of learning enough Java to be able to tackle most problems, you're just about there! This chapter presents some advanced Java topics as well as a few important odds and ends that haven't made their way into your student information system.

You will learn about:

- additional mocking techniques

- anonymous inner classes

- reflection

- adapters

- instance initializers

- the class Class

- the dynamic proxy mechanism

Mock Objects Revisited

In Lesson 10, you created a mock class to force the behavior of a random number generator. The mock class you built extended from the class java.util.Random. You built the mock class as a nested class within the test. Since the mock class was used solely by the test, it was beneficial to include the mock code directly within the test class. In this lesson, you'll learn an even more succinct technique: embedding the mock class completely within a test method.

425

You might need to use mock objects if your code must interact with an external API. You typically have little control over the external code or the results an API returns. Writing tests against such code often results in breakage due to changing results from the API. Also, the API might communicate with an external resource that is not always available. Such an API introduces a bad dependency that mocks can help you manage.[1]

Ensure that you have a dependency issue before introducing mocks.

The student Account class needs to be able to handle transfers from an associated bank account. To do so, it must interact with ACH (automated clearing house) software from Jim Bob's ACH Shop. The ACH software publishes an API specification. Another bad dependency: We haven't licensed or installed the actual software yet! But you need to start coding now in order to be able to ship working software soon after the actual code is licensed and delivered.

Mock Objects Revisited

The test itself is small.

```
package sis.studentinfo;

import java.math.BigDecimal;
import junit.framework.*;

public class AccountTest extends TestCase {
    static final String ABA = "102000012";
    static final String ACCOUNT_NUMBER = "194431518811";

    private Account account;

    protected void setUp() {
        account = new Account();
        account.setBankAba(ABA);
        account.setBankAccountNumber(ACCOUNT_NUMBER);
        account.setBankAccountType(Account.BankAccountType.CHECKING);
    }
    // ...
    public void testTransferFromBank() {
        account.setAch(new com.jimbob.ach.JimBobAch()); // uh-oh

        final BigDecimal amount = new BigDecimal("50.00");
        account.transferFromBank(amount);

        assertEquals(amount, account.getBalance());
    }
}
```

---

[1][Langr2003].

Debiting an account requires the bank's ABA (routing) number, the account number, and the type of account. You can populate this required account information using the setUp method.

The test method, testTransferFromBank, creates a new JimBobAch object and passes it into the Account object. Uh-oh; you don't have the JimBobAch class yet, so the code won't even compile. You'll solve this problem shortly with a mock class.

The remainder of the test sends the transferFromBank message to the account, then asserts that the account balance increased to the correct amount.

So how will you solve the problem of the nonexistent JimBobAch class? You *do* have just about everything else you need. Jim Bob ACH Company has supplied you with the API documentation.

The Jim Bob ACH Interface

The API documentation, which has been supplied to you in PDF form, includes the interface definition that the class JimBobAch implements. It also includes the definition for the related data classes. You can take the Jim Bob ACH code and for the time being copy it into your system. Enter this code into the directory structure ./com/jimbob/ach within your source directory. (You would probably be able to paste it directly from the PDF document.)

When you receive the actual API library from Jim Bob and company, ensure that it matches what you have before deleting your temporary copy.

```
// com.jimbob.ach.Ach
package com.jimbob.ach;

public interface Ach {
    public AchResponse issueDebit(AchCredentials credentials, AchTransactionData data);
    public AchResponse markTransactionAsNSF(AchCredentials credentials, AchTransactionData data,
String traceCode);
    public AchResponse refundTransaction(AchCredentials credentials, AchTransactionData data,
String traceCode);
    public AchResponse issueCredit(AchCredentials credentials, AchTransactionData data);
    public AchResponse voidSameDayTransaction(AchCredentials credentials, AchTransactionData
data, String traceCode);
    public AchResponse queryTransactionStatus(AchCredentials credentials, AchTransactionData
data, String traceCode);
}

// com.jimbob.ach.AchCredentials
package com.jimbob.ach;
```

```
public class AchCredentials {
    public String merchantId;
    public String userName;
    public String password;
}

// com.jimbob.ach.AchTransactionData
package com.jimbob.ach;

import java.math.BigDecimal;

public class AchTransactionData {
    public String description;
    public BigDecimal amount;
    public String aba;
    public String account;
    public String accountType;
}

// com.jimbob.ach.AchResponse
package com.jimbob.ach;

import java.util.*;

public class AchResponse {
    public Date timestamp;
    public String traceCode;
    public AchStatus status;
    public List<String> errorMessages;
}

// com.jimbob.ach.AchStatus
package com.jimbob.ach;

public enum AchStatus {
    SUCCESS, FAILURE;
}
```

The Jim Bob ACH Interface

For now, you are interested only in the Ach interface method named issueDebit. You must send the issueDebit message to a JimBobAch object in order to withdraw money from the bank account. The message takes an AchCredentials object and an AchTransactionData object as parameters. Note the questionable practice of exposing the instance variables directly in these two classes. Unfortunately, when you deal with third-party vendor software, you get what you get.

The issueDebit method returns an AchResponse object upon completion. This response data indicates whether or not the debit succeeded by using an AchStatus enum value.

The Mock Class

You don't have the actual JimBobAch class, but you can create a mock class that implements the same Ach interface as the JimBobAch class. Your test will work with this mock object.

The MockAch class below implements the Ach interface. The only ACH service that concerns you for now is the issueDebit method; you implement the other methods as stubs, returning null to satisfy the compiler. You code the issueDebit method to ensure that the parameters passed to it are as expected. If the parameters are valid,[2] you construct an AchResponse object, populating it with the data that the test expects to see.

```
package sis.studentinfo;

import java.util.*;
import com.jimbob.ach.*;
import junit.framework.Assert;

class MockAch implements Ach {
    public AchResponse issueDebit(
        AchCredentials credentials, AchTransactionData data) {
        Assert.assertTrue(
            data.account.equals(AccountTest.ACCOUNT_NUMBER));
        Assert.assertTrue(data.aba.equals(AccountTest.ABA));

        AchResponse response = new AchResponse();
        response.timestamp = new Date();
        response.traceCode = "1";
        response.status = AchStatus.SUCCESS;
        return response;
    }

    public AchResponse markTransactionAsNSF(AchCredentials credentials,
        AchTransactionData data,
        String traceCode) {
        return null;
    }
    public AchResponse refundTransaction(AchCredentials credentials,
        AchTransactionData data,
        String traceCode) {
        return null;
    }
    public AchResponse issueCredit(AchCredentials credentials,
        AchTransactionData data) {
        return null;
```

[2]You should also ensure that the AchCredentials object is as expected; I'm omitting the check here because of space considerations.

```
    }
    public AchResponse voidSameDayTransaction(
            AchCredentials credentials,
            AchTransactionData data,
            String traceCode) {
        return null;
    }
    public AchResponse queryTransactionStatus(AchCredentials credentials,
            AchTransactionData data, String traceCode) {
        return null;
    }
}
```

The Mock Class

Note that this solution creates a two-way dependency, as shown in Figure 12.1. AccountTest class creates MockAch, meaning the test class is dependent upon MockAch. MockAch is dependent upon AccountTest since Mock-Ach refers to the ACCOUNT_NUMBER and ABA class constants from AccountTest. Two-way dependencies are generally not a good thing, but in some cases such a tight coupling is acceptable. The test requires the mock, and the mock is useful only in close concert with the test.

Now back to testTransferFromBank. In it, you originally wrote code to instantiate the nonexistent JimBobAch class. Instead, you can now create a Mock-Ach instance and pass that into the Account object:

```
public void testTransferFromBank() {
    // acount.setAch(new com.jimbob.ach.JimBobAch());
    account.setAch(new MockAch());

    final BigDecimal amount = new BigDecimal("50.00");
    account.transferFromBank(amount);

    assertEquals(amount, account.getBalance());
}
```

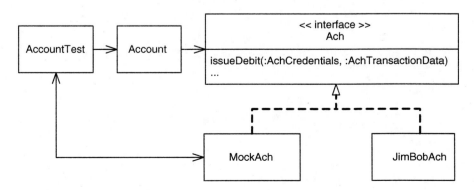

Figure 12.1 *Mocking the Ach Interface*

The Account Class Implementation

Here is the updated Account class implementation:

```
package sis.studentinfo;

import java.math.BigDecimal;
import com.jimbob.ach.*;

public class Account {
    private BigDecimal balance = new BigDecimal("0.00");
    private int transactionCount = 0;
    private String bankAba;
    private String bankAccountNumber;
    private BankAccountType bankAccountType;
    private Ach ach;

    public enum BankAccountType {
        CHECKING("ck"), SAVINGS("sv");
        private String value;
        private BankAccountType(String value) {
            this.value = value;
        }
        @Override
        public String toString() {
            return value;
        }
    }

    public void credit(BigDecimal amount) {
        balance = balance.add(amount);
        transactionCount++;
    }

    public BigDecimal getBalance() {
        return balance;
    }

    public BigDecimal transactionAverage() {
        return balance.divide(
            new BigDecimal(transactionCount), BigDecimal.ROUND_HALF_UP);
    }

    public void setBankAba(String bankAba) {
        this.bankAba = bankAba;
    }

    public void setBankAccountNumber(String bankAccountNumber) {
        this.bankAccountNumber = bankAccountNumber;
    }
```

The Account
Class
Implementation

```
   public void setBankAccountType(
         Account.BankAccountType bankAccountType) {
      this.bankAccountType = bankAccountType;
   }

   public void transferFromBank(BigDecimal amount) {
      AchCredentials credentials = createCredentials();

      AchTransactionData data = createData(amount);

      Ach ach = getAch();
      AchResponse achResponse = ach.issueDebit(credentials, data);

      credit(amount);
   }

   private AchCredentials createCredentials() {
      AchCredentials credentials = new AchCredentials();
      credentials.merchantId = "12355";
      credentials.userName = "sismerc1920";
      credentials.password = "pitseleh411";
      return credentials;
   }

   private AchTransactionData createData(BigDecimal amount) {
      AchTransactionData data = new AchTransactionData();
      data.description = "transfer from bank";
      data.amount = amount;
      data.aba = bankAba;
      data.account = bankAccountNumber;
      data.accountType = bankAccountType.toString();
      return data;
   }

   private Ach getAch() {
      return ach;
   }

   void setAch(Ach ach) {
      this.ach = ach;
   }
}
```

Account allows clients to pass it an Ach reference that it then stores. In the production system, your client code that constructs an Account will pass the Account a JimBobAch object. In the test, your code passes a MockAch object to the Account. In either case, Account doesn't know and doesn't care which concrete type it is sending the issueDebit message to.

While testTransferFromBank now passes, it is difficult to see exactly why. The mock class is in another source file, so to figure out what's going on, you must flip between the two class definitions. This isn't totally unacceptable, but you can improve upon things. One solution would be to include the mock definition as a nested class. Another would be to set up the mock directly within the test method, using an anonymous inner class.

Anonymous Inner Classes

Lesson 11 discussed the distinction between static nested classes and inner classes. A third type of nested class is the *anonymous inner class*. An anonymous inner class allows you to dynamically define unnamed class implementations within a method body.

Understanding the syntax and nuances of anonymous inner classes can be daunting. But once you understand anonymous inner classes, your use of them can make your code more concise and easy to understand.

Take the body of the MockAch class (i.e., all the method definitions) and insert it as the first line of code in testTransferFromBank. Immediately preceding all that code, add the line:

```
Ach mockAch = new Ach() {
```

Then terminate the mock Ach method definitions with a closing brace and semicolon. The transformed test:[3]

```
public void testTransferFromBank() {
    Ach mockAch = new Ach() {
        public AchResponse issueDebit(
                AchCredentials credentials, AchTransactionData data) {
            Assert.assertTrue(
                data.account.equals(AccountTest.ACCOUNT_NUMBER));
            Assert.assertTrue(data.aba.equals(AccountTest.ABA));

            AchResponse response = new AchResponse();
            response.timestamp = new Date();
            response.traceCode = "1";
            response.status = AchStatus.SUCCESS;
            return response;
        }
        public AchResponse markTransactionAsNSF(
                AchCredentials credentials,
                AchTransactionData data,
                String traceCode) {
            return null;
        }
        public AchResponse refundTransaction(AchCredentials credentials,
                AchTransactionData data,
```

[3]You'll need to import com.jimbob.ach and java.util to get this to compile.

Instance Initializers

In Lesson 4 you learned about static initialization blocks. Java allows you to use instance initialization blocks, which are also known as instance initializers.

Within an anonymous inner class, you cannot create a constructor. Since the anonymous inner class has no name, you wouldn't be able to supply a name for its constructor! Instead, you can use an instance initialization block.

```java
Expirable t = new Expirable() {
  private long then;
  {
    long now = System.currentTimeMillis();
    then = now + 86400000;
  }

  public boolean isExpired(Date date) {
    return date.getTime() > then;
  }
};
```

Instance initializers are rarely used within top-level classes. Prefer either constructor or field-level initialization. However, you might use instance initializers to eliminate duplication if you have multiple constructors that must execute common setup code.

```java
        String traceCode) {
      return null;
    }
    public AchResponse issueCredit(AchCredentials credentials,
        AchTransactionData data) {
      return null;
    }
    public AchResponse voidSameDayTransaction(
        AchCredentials credentials,
        AchTransactionData data,
        String traceCode) {
      return null;
    }
    public AchResponse queryTransactionStatus (
        AchCredentials credentials,
        AchTransactionData data, String traceCode) {
      return null;
    }
};

account.setAch(mockAch);

final BigDecimal amount = new BigDecimal("50.00");
account.transferFromBank(amount);

assertEquals(amount, account.getBalance());
}
```

Anonymous
Inner Classes

The line of code:

```
Ach mockAch = new Ach() {
```

creates a reference named mockAch of the interface type Ach. The right-hand side instantiates an Ach object using new. But Ach is an interface—how can you instantiate an interface?

Java is allowing you to dynamically provide an implementation for the Ach interface and at the same time create an instance with that implementation. You provide the implementation in a block of code immediately after the constructor call (new Ach()) but before the semicolon that terminates the statement.

The implementation supplied in the block is of Ach type, but it has no specific class name. It is *anonymous*. You can send messages to this object, store it, or pass it as a parameter, just as you might with an object of a named Ach implementation such as MockAch.

Make sure that your tests pass, but don't delete MockAch just yet.

As you've seen, anonymous inner classes can be useful when building mocks for testing purposes. Swing applications (see Additional Lesson I) and multithreading (see Lesson 13) often make heavy use of anonymous inner classes.

Admittedly, it's still a bit difficult to follow what's going on in testTransferFromBank. The test method is now long and cluttered. The next section on adapters shows how to improve on things.

Adapters

Adapters

Overusing anonymous inner classes can actually make code harder to follow. Your goal should be to keep methods short, even test methods. The long anonymous inner class implementation in testTransferFromBank means that you will probably need to scroll in order to get the big picture of what the method is doing.

You can create an *interface adapter class* that provides an empty implementation for the Ach interface. Modify the MockAch class to supply an empty definition for the issueDebit method.

```
package sis.studentinfo;

import java.util.*;
import com.jimbob.ach.*;
import junit.framework.Assert;
```

```
class MockAch implements Ach {
    public AchResponse issueDebit(
            AchCredentials credentials, AchTransactionData data) {
        return null;
    }
    public AchResponse markTransactionAsNSF(AchCredentials credentials,
            AchTransactionData data,
            String traceCode) {
        return null;
    }
    public AchResponse refundTransaction(AchCredentials credentials,
            AchTransactionData data,
            String traceCode) {
        return null;
    }
    public AchResponse issueCredit(AchCredentials credentials,
            AchTransactionData data) {
        return null;
    }
    public AchResponse voidSameDayTransaction(
            AchCredentials credentials,
            AchTransactionData data,
            String traceCode) {
        return null;
    }
    public AchResponse queryTransactionStatus(AchCredentials credentials,
            AchTransactionData data, String traceCode) {
        return null;
    }
}
```

Back in AccountTest, change the instantiation from new Ach() to new MockAch(). Remove the method implementations for everything but issueDebit.

```
public void testTransferFromBank() {
    Ach mockAch = new MockAch() {
        public AchResponse issueDebit(
                AchCredentials credentials, AchTransactionData data) {
            Assert.assertTrue(
                data.account.equals(AccountTest.ACCOUNT_NUMBER));
            Assert.assertTrue(data.aba.equals(AccountTest.ABA));

            AchResponse response = new AchResponse();
            response.timestamp = new Date();
            response.traceCode = "1";
            response.status = AchStatus.SUCCESS;
            return response;
        }
    };

    account.setAch(mockAch);
```

```
final BigDecimal amount = new BigDecimal("50.00");
account.transferFromBank(amount);

assertEquals(amount, account.getBalance());
}
```

You are still creating an anonymous inner class. An anonymous inner class can either implement an interface or subclass another class. This code demonstrates the latter. Here, you use the MockAch class as an adapter to hide the methods that your mock doesn't need to worry about. Now you can include the relevant mock code in a reasonably brief test method.

Accessing Variables from the Enclosing Class

You need an additional test, testFailedTransferFromBank, to define what happens when the bank rejects the debit request. The test and mock are going to be very similar to testTransferFromBank. The student's balance should not change on a failed transfer, so the test assertion must change. The status returned from the mock in the AchResponseData object must be AchStatus.FAILURE.

Because the mocks will be almost exactly the same, you want a way to create both of them without introducing duplicate code. You want to be able to phrase the new test as follows:[4]

```
public void testFailedTransferFromBank() {
    account.setAch(createMockAch(AchStatus.FAILURE));
    final BigDecimal amount = new BigDecimal("50.00");
    account.transferFromBank(amount);
    assertEquals(new BigDecimal("0.00"), account.getBalance());
}
```

The existing test, testTransferFromBank, can use the same construct.

```
public void testTransferFromBank() {
    account.setAch(createMockAch(AchStatus.SUCCESS));
    final BigDecimal amount = new BigDecimal("50.00");
    account.transferFromBank(amount);
    assertEquals(amount, account.getBalance());
}
```

Anonymous inner class objects are just objects. They can be created in a separate method and returned like any other object.

[4]You may also want the Account code to throw an exception if the ACH debit fails. I avoided the exception here for simplicity reasons.

```
// THIS WON'T COMPILE!
private Ach createMockAch(AchStatus status) {
    return new MockAch() {
        public AchResponse issueDebit(
            AchCredentials credentials, AchTransactionData data) {
            Assert.assertTrue(
                data.account.equals(AccountTest.ACCOUNT_NUMBER));
            Assert.assertTrue(data.aba.equals(AccountTest.ABA));

            AchResponse response = new AchResponse();
            response.timestamp = new Date();
            response.traceCode = "1";
            response.status = status;
            return response;
        }
    };
}
```

Accessing Variables from the Enclosing Class

Class Names for Anonymous Inner Classes

When it compiles a class containing an anonymous inner class, Java uses a similar rule for naming the compilation unit as its rule for anonymous nested classes that are not anonymous. Java uses the dollar sign ($) to separate the class names.

A slight problem: An anonymous inner class has no name! Java provides a simple solution, numbering anonymous inner classes using a counter starting at 1. It then uses this number as the nested inner class name portion of the compilation unit name.

For example, the AccountTest class creates two compilation units: AccountTest.class and AccountTest$1.class.

I'll repeat my warning from last chapter: When you copy class files or put them in a JAR file for distribution, don't forget to include all the nested classes.

However, this code won't compile. You will see the message:

```
local variable status is accessed from within inner class; needs to be declared final
```

Anonymous inner classes are inner classes. By the definition you learned in Lesson 11, an inner classes has access to the instance variables (and methods) of the enclosing class.

An anonymous inner class does *not* have access to local variables. The status parameter is analogous to a local variable because it is accessible only to code in the createMockAch method.

According to the compiler error, however, you can get around this limitation by declaring the status parameter as final.

```
private Ach createMockAch(final AchStatus status)
```

After you do this, your code should compile but your tests will not pass.

Why must you define the variable as final? Remember that by declaring a variable as final, you are declaring that its value cannot be changed after it has been set.

An instance of an anonymous inner class can exist outside of the method in which it is declared. In our example, the createMockAch method instantiates a new anonymous inner class and returns it from the method it will be used by the calling test methods

Local variables do not exist once a method has finished executing! Nor do parameters—all parameters to methods are copies of the arguments passed by the calling code.[5] If an anonymous inner class was able to access local variables, the value of the local variable could be destroyed by the time the code in the anonymous inner class actually executed. This would, of course, be a bad thing.

To get your tests to pass, insert the code in Account so that you credit only successful transfers.

```
public void transferFromBank(BigDecimal amount) {
    AchCredentials credentials = createCredentials();
    AchTransactionData data = createData(amount);
    Ach ach = getAch();
    AchResponse achResponse = ach.issueDebit(credentials, data);
    if (achResponse.status == AchStatus.SUCCESS)
        credit(amount);
}
```

With a bit of refactoring, this method simplifies to:

```
public void transferFromBank(BigDecimal amount) {
    AchResponse achResponse =
        getAch().issueDebit(createCredentials(), createData(amount));
    if (achResponse.status == AchStatus.SUCCESS)
        credit(amount);
}
```

Tradeoffs

Earlier, I mentioned that it is a good thing to be able to see the mock behavior right in the test itself. Then I had you extract the mock definition to a separate method in order to eliminate the duplication that was impending with the addition of another test method that needed a similar mock. This was at a cost of some expressiveness, although it's reasonably clear what the code

---

[5]For a further discussion, see Additional Lesson III, which talks about call by value.

```
account.setAch(createMockAch(AchStatus.SUCCESS));
```

is doing.

Which is worse? Duplication or code that is hard to follow? The answer isn't always clear cut. The question often engenders debate. From my perspective, duplicate code is usually more troublesome than difficult-to-read code. You don't often need to choose one over the other, but when you do, eliminating duplication is a safer route. By eliminating duplicate code, you reduce the cost of maintenance efforts—you avoid having to make changes in more than one place. You also minimize the risk of making a change in one place but forgetting to make it in another place.

Reflection

Reflection

You've seen how the use of the Object method getClass allows you to determine the type of an object at runtime. This is known as reflective capability—the ability of code to examine information about the code itself; that is, to *reflect* on itself. Another term used for reflection capabilities is *metadata*.

JUnit uses reflection heavily to gather the information it needs to be able to run your tests. You supply a test class file to JUnit to be tested. JUnit uses reflection to determine whether or not your class file inherits from junit.framework.TestCase, rejecting it if it does not. JUnit also uses reflection to obtain a list of methods in a test class. It then iterates these methods, executing only those that pass its criteria for being a test method:

- The method name must start with the word "test," in lowercase letters.

- The return type of the method must be void.

- The method must not take any parameters.

So far, you have been telling JUnit which classes you want tested. This allows you to run only the tests that you specify. A problem with this approach is that it is easy to forget to add your test class to a suite. You might end up skipping critical tests!

Another approach is to have Java scan through all the classes in your classpath, gather the classes that are legitimate test classes, and execute only those. The benefit is that you don't have to maintain the suites in code. No tests will be left behind. The only downside is that there may be tests, such as performance tests, that you don't want run all the time. However, you can write additional code to bypass such tests if necessary.

Using JUnit Code

Fortunately, JUnit supplies a mechanism that will help you gather the test classes on the classpath. How would you know that? First, you might have run JUnit and observed that it has the capability to gather a list of all test classes. Following up on that, you could have perused the source distributed with JUnit and seen that it has a class named junit.runner.ClassPathTest-Collector.

You will create a class named SuiteBuilder to gather all test classes. A simple first test for SuiteBuilder would ensure that SuiteBuilderTest itself was returned in the list of test classes found on the classpath.

Using JUnit
Code

```
package sis.testing;

import junit.framework.*;
import java.util.*;

public class SuiteBuilderTest extends TestCase {
    public void testGatherTestClassNames() {
        SuiteBuilder builder = new SuiteBuilder();
        List<String> classes = builder.gatherTestClassNames();
        assertTrue(classes.contains("testing.SuiteBuilderTest"));
    }
}
```

The interesting part of the test is that it binds the list to the String type—not the Class type. When you look at the source for ClassPathTestCollector, you will note that it returns an Enumeration of Strings, each representing the class name. We'll go along with that for now and see if it causes any problems later.

```
package sis.testing;

import java.util.*;
import junit.runner.*;
import junit.framework.*;

public class SuiteBuilder {
    public List<String> gatherTestClassNames() {
        TestCollector collector = new ClassPathTestCollector() {
            public boolean isTestClass(String classFileName) {
                return super.isTestClass(classFileName);
            }
        };
        return Collections.list(collector.collectTests());
    }
}
```

The ClassPathTestCollector is declared as abstract, so you *must* extend it in order to instantiate it. Interestingly, there are no abstract methods contained within, meaning you are not required to override any of ClassPathTest-Collector's methods. You *will* want to override the method isTestClass:

```
protected boolean isTestClass(String classFileName) {
    return
        classFileName.endsWith(".class") &&
        classFileName.indexOf('$') < 0 &&
        classFileName.indexOf("Test") > 0;
}
```

The Class Class

The query method isTestClass concerns itself only with the class filenames, not with the structure of the classes themselves. The conditional states that if a filename ends in a .class extension, does not contain a $ (i.e., it does not represent a nested class), and contains the text "Test," then it is a test class.

You might recognize that this definition could cause problems: What if a file with a .class extension is not a valid class file? What if the class name contains the text "Test" but is not a test class? The last condition is highly likely. Your own code for the student information system contains the class util.TestUtil, which is not a TestCase subclass.

You're not going to worry about these problems (yet) since your test doesn't (yet) concern itself with any of these cases. For now, your implementation code in getTestClassNames overrides isTestClass and simply calls the superclass method to use its existing behavior. This is unnecessary, but it acts as a placeholder and reminder when you are ready to take care of the other concerns.

The last line of gatherTestClassNames sends the message collectTests to the ClassPathTestCollector. Somewhere along the way, collectTests indirectly calls isTestClass. The return type of collectTests is java.util.Enumeration. You can use the java.util.Collections utility method list to transform the Enumeration into an ArrayList. You will get an unchecked warning, since ClassPathTestCollector uses raw collections—collections not bound to a specific type.

The Class Class

Let's tackle the likely concern that a class with the word "Test" in its name is not a junit.framework.TestCase subclass. A test for this case would need to specify a class that the SuiteBuilder can attempt to gather and then reject. You might consider using an existing class that you have already coded for the student information system, such as TestUtil.

However, you do not want to depend on the existence or stability of existing classes. Someone making a valid change to TestUtil, or deleting it, would unwittingly break SuiteBuilderTest tests. You instead will create dummy test classes expressly for the use of SuiteBuilderTest. Start by creating the class NotATestClass in the new package sis.testing.testclasses.

```
package sis.testing.testclasses;
public class NotATestClass {}
```

NotATestClass does not extend junit.framework.TestCase, so it should not be recognized as a test class. Add an assertion to your test method.

```
public void testGatherTestClassNames() {
    SuiteBuilder builder = new SuiteBuilder();
    List<String> classes = builder.gatherTestClassNames();
    assertTrue(classes.contains("testing.SuiteBuilderTest"));
    assertFalse(classes.contains("testing.testclasses.NotATestClass"));
}
```

The relevant code in SuiteBuilder:[6]

```
public List<String> gatherTestClassNames() {
    TestCollector collector = new ClassPathTestCollector() {
        public boolean isTestClass(String classFileName) {
            if (!super.isTestClass(classFileName))
                return false;
            String className = classNameFromFile(classFileName);    // 1
            Class klass = createClass(className);                    // 2
            return TestCase.class.isAssignableFrom(klass);           // 3

        }
    };
    return Collections.list(collector.collectTests());
}

private Class createClass(String name) {
    try {
        return Class.forName(name);
    }
    catch (ClassNotFoundException e) {
        return null;
    }
}
```

The additional constraint implemented in SuiteBuilder is that a class filename must represent a compilation unit that extends from TestCase. There

---

[6]Note use of the variable name klass to represent a Class object. You can't use class, since Java reserves it for defining classes only. Some developers use the single character c (not recommended), others clazz.

are three steps involved. The following descriptions correspond to the commented lines of code in gatherTestClassNames.

1. Translate the directory-based filename into a class name, for example from "testing/testclasses/NotATestClass" to "testing.testclasses.NotATestClass." The ClassPathTestCollector method classNameFromFile accomplishes this task.

2. Create a Class object from the class name. In createClass, the static method call of forName, defined on Class, does this. The forName method throws a ClassNotFoundException if the String object you pass to it does not represent a class that can be loaded by Java. For now, you can return null from createClass if this occurs, but you will need to write a test to cover this possibility.

3. Determine whether the class is a subclass of TestCase. To do so, you will use a method on the class java.lang.Class, which provides metadata about a class definition. The Class method isAssignableFrom takes as a parameter a Class object and returns true if it is possible to assign an instance of the parameter (klass, in the above code) to a reference of the receiving class type (junit.framework.TestCase).

Take a brief look at the Java API documentation for java.lang.Class. It contains methods such as getMethods, getConstructors, and getFields that you can use to derive most of the information you need about a compiled Java class.

Building the Suite

The next step is to construct a TestSuite object to be passed to the Swing test runner. The code to do this is simple: iterate through the results of gatherTestClassNames, create the corresponding Class object for each test class name, and add it to the suite. The test seems to be straightforward: Ensure that the suite contains the expected test classes.

```
public void testCreateSuite() {
    SuiteBuilder builder = new SuiteBuilder() {
        public List<String> gatherTestClassNames() {
            List<String> classNames = new ArrayList<String>();
            classNames.add("testing.SuiteBuilderTest");
            return classNames;
        }
    };

    TestSuite suite = builder.suite();
    assertEquals(1, suite.testCount());
    assertTrue(contains(suite, testing.SuiteBuilderTest.class));
}
```

I used a mock instead of letting the suite method gather all classes normally. Otherwise, gatherTestClassNames would return the entire list of classes on the classpath. This list would include all other tests in the student information system. You would have no definitive way to prove that the suite method was doing its job.

Determining whether or not a class is included in a TestSuite is not as trivial as you might expect. A test suite can either contain test case classes or other test suites. Figure 12.2 shows this design, known as a composite.[7] The filled-in diamond represents a *composition* relationship between TestSuite and Test. A TestSuite is composed of Test objects.

To determine if a class is contained somewhere within a suite, you must traverse the entire hierarchy of suites. The contains method here uses recursion, since contains calls itself when encountering a suite within the current suite.

```
public boolean contains(TestSuite suite, Class testClass) {
   List testClasses = Collections.list(suite.tests());
   for (Object object: testClasses) {
      if (object.getClass() == TestSuite.class)
         if (contains((TestSuite)object, testClass))
            return true;
      if (object.getClass() == testClass)
         return true;
   }
   return false;
}
```

All that is left is for you to create a TestRunner class. TestRunner will use the SuiteBuilder to construct a suite. It will then execute the Swing test runner using this suite. There are no tests—you'll exercise the code as part of

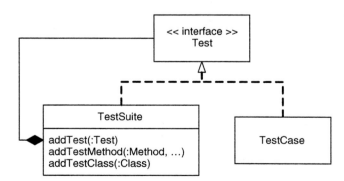

Figure 12.2 *JUnit Composite Design*

[7][Gamma1995].

continually running JUnit. Writing tests for this code would be possible but difficult. The way you constructed SuiteBuilder, however, means that the TestRunner code is so small, it's almost breakproof.

```
package sis.testing;

public class TestRunner {
    public static void main(String[] args) {
        new junit.swingui.TestRunner().run(TestRunner.class);
    }

    public static junit.framework.Test suite() {
        return new SuiteBuilder().suite();
    }
}
```

You'll want to add a target to your build script that executes testing.TestRunner:

```
<target name="runAllTests" depends="build">
  <java classname="testing.TestRunner" fork="yes">
    <classpath refid="classpath" />
  </java>
</target>
```

When you run all the tests, however, you get about half a dozen failures.

Class Modifiers

The problem is that SessionTest, an abstract class, contains a number of definitions for test methods. The methods are intended to be executed as part of SessionTest subclasses; thus, you did not previously add SessionTest to a suite. You need to modify SuiteBuilder to ignore abstract classes.

Create a test class that is abstract and extends from TestCase.

```
package sis.testing.testclasses;

abstract public class AbstractTestClass
        extends junit.framework.TestCase {
    public void testMethod() {}
}
```

Then modify the test to ensure that it isn't collected.

```
public void testGatherTestClassNames() {
    SuiteBuilder builder = new SuiteBuilder();
    List<String> classes = builder.gatherTestClassNames();
    assertTrue(classes.contains("testing.SuiteBuilderTest"));
```

Class Modifiers

```
    assertFalse(classes.contains("testing.testclasses.NotATestClass"));
    assertFalse(
        classes.contains("testing.testclasses.AbstractTestClass"));
}
```

Run the test and ensure that it fails. Only then should you go on to correct the code in SuiteBuilder. You are following a testing pattern: If you release code that fails either in production or in an acceptance test (a customer-defined test that exercises code from an end user's standpoint), it means that it was inadequately unit-tested. Your job is to add the missing test code and ensure that it fails for the same reason that the acceptance test failed[8].

 Never depend solely on one level of testing. Ensure you have a layer above unit testing to ferret out "holes" in your unit tests.

Now that you've seen the test fail, you can add code to Suite-Builder that corrects the defect:

```
public List<String> gatherTestClassNames() {
    TestCollector collector = new ClassPathTestCollector() {
        public boolean isTestClass(String classFileName) {
            if (!super.isTestClass(classFileName))
                return false;
            String className = classNameFromFile(classFileName);
            Class klass = createClass(className);
            return
                TestCase.class.isAssignableFrom(klass) &&
                isConcrete(klass);
        }
    };
    return Collections.list(collector.collectTests());
}

private boolean isConcrete(Class klass) {
    if (klass.isInterface())
        return false;
    int modifiers = klass.getModifiers();
    return !Modifier.isAbstract(modifiers);
}
```

If a type (Class represents both interface and class types) is an interface, it is not concrete. You can determine that using the Class method isInterface.

The isConcrete method also uses the Class method getModifiers. The method getModifiers returns an int that embeds a list of flags, each corresponding to a possible class modifier.[9] Some of the modifiers you have seen include abstract, static, private, protected, and public. A utility class java.lang.reflect.Modifier

---

[8][Jeffries2001], p. 163.

[9]Methods and fields also have modifiers and use the same int-flag construct.

(you'll need to add an appropriate import statement to SuiteBuilder) contains a number of static query methods to help you determine the modifiers that are set within the modifiers int.

You can now delete all of your AllTests classes!

Dynamic Proxy

J2SE version 1.3 introduced a new class, java.lang.reflect.Proxy, that allows you to construct *dynamic proxy classes*. A dynamic proxy class allows you to dynamically—at runtime—implement one or more interfaces.

The *proxy* pattern is one of the more useful patterns identified in the book *Design Patterns*.[10] A proxy is a stand-in; a proxy object stands in for a real object. In a proxy pattern implementation, client objects think they are interacting with the real object but are actually interacting with a proxy.

Figure 12.3 shows the proxy pattern in the context of distributed object communication. A ServiceImplementation class resides on a separate machine in a separate process space from the Client class. In order for a Client to interact with a ServiceImplementation, some low-level communications must take place. Suppose Client must send the message submitOrder to a ServiceImplementation. This Java message send must be translated to a data stream that can be transmitted over the wire. On the server side, the data

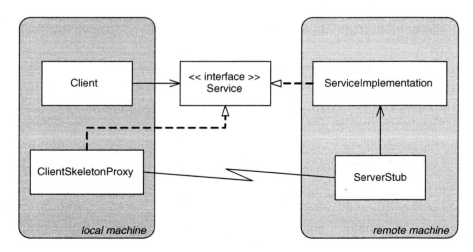

Figure 12.3 *Distributed Communication Using a Proxy*

[10][Gamma1995].

stream must be reconstituted into a Java message to be sent to the ServiceImplementation object.

You want the code in Client to be able to work with the code in ServiceImplementation as if it were executing in the same local Java VM process. Neither the code in Client nor the code in ServiceImplementation should have to be concerned with the nuts and bolts of the remote communication.

The solution is to have the ServiceImplementation class implement a Service interface that a client-side class, ClientSkeletonProxy, also implements. A Client object can then interact with a ClientSkeletonProxy through this interface, thinking that it is interacting with the real ServiceImplementation. Thus, the ClientSkeletonProxy is a stand-in, or proxy, for the real ServiceImplementation. The ClientSkeletonProxy takes incoming requests and collaborates with a ServerStub on the remote machine to do the low-level communication. The ServerStub takes incoming data transmissions and translates them into calls against the ServiceImplementation. (You might recognize that implementing this solution in Java is heavily dependent upon the use of reflection.)

In Java, this proxy scheme is the basis of a technology known as Remote Method Invocation (RMI). RMI, in turn, is the basis of the Enterprise Java Beans (EJB) technology for component-based distributed computing.[11]

Proxies have many other uses, including techniques known as lazy load, copy on write, pooling, caching, and transactional markup. You will code a transparent security mechanism using a proxy.

In a Java proxy implementation, the proxy implements the same interface as the real object. The proxy intercepts messages sent to a client; after processing a message, the proxy often delegates it to the real, or *target*, object. You can imagine that maintaining proxies can become tedious if a proxy class must implement the same interface as the target class. For every method you add to an interface, you must provide both the real implementation and the proxy implementation. Fortunately, the dynamic proxy in Java eliminates the need for you to explicitly implement every interface method within the proxy class.

A Secure Account Class

 You need to be able to restrict access to certain Account methods based on the permissions that the client has. A client should have either read-only or update access. A client with update access can use

---

[11]EJB is a part of the J2EE (Java 2 Enterprise Edition) platform.

any method defined on Account. A client with read-only access can use only methods that don't change an account's state.

You could add code to the Account class, passing in a user's classification when the account is created. To each restricted method, you would add code that would check the user classification and throw an exception if the user did not have the proper access rights. Security-related code would quickly clutter your Account class, obscuring its business logic. You would be violating the Single-Responsibility Principle![12]

Instead, you will externalize the security restrictions into a proxy class. The Account class itself will remain almost completely untouched! We are going for the open-closed principle[13] here—building new functionality by adding new code, not by modifying existing code.

The use of proxies often calls for factories. The UML diagram in Figure 12.4 shows the complete solution for the security proxy, including the use of the class AccountFactory to return an instance of a SecureProxy. The client can think that it is interacting with a real Account, but it is instead interacting with a proxy that is able to respond to the same messages.

A Secure Account Class

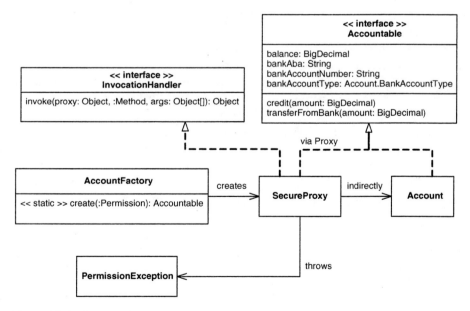

Figure 12.4 *Security Proxy*

[12][Martin2003], p. 95.

[13][Martin2003], p. 99.

The AccountFactory class uses the dynamic proxy class Proxy to create the SecureProxy object. SecureProxy does not directly implement Accountable; instead, the Proxy class sets SecureProxy up to capture all incoming messages and redirect each to the InvocationHandler interface method invoke.

Building the Secure Account Solution

The starting point is AccountFactoryTest, a test class that exercises the various combinations of permissions and methods. The test class contains two test methods: testReadOnlyAccess ensures that all account methods can be called normally by a user with update permission, and testUpdateAccess ensures that exceptions are thrown when a user with read-only access attempts to execute a secure method.

Building the
Secure Account
Solution

```
package sis.studentinfo;

import java.math.*;
import java.util.*;
import java.lang.reflect.*;
import junit.framework.*;

import sis.security.*;

public class AccountFactoryTest extends TestCase {
    private List<Method> updateMethods;
    private List<Method> readOnlyMethods;

    protected void setUp() throws Exception {
        updateMethods = new ArrayList<Method>();
        addUpdateMethod("setBankAba", String.class);
        addUpdateMethod("setBankAccountNumber", String.class);
        addUpdateMethod("setBankAccountType",
            Account.BankAccountType.class);
        addUpdateMethod("transferFromBank", BigDecimal.class);
        addUpdateMethod("credit", BigDecimal.class);

        readOnlyMethods = new ArrayList<Method>();
        addReadOnlyMethod("getBalance");
        addReadOnlyMethod("transactionAverage");
    }

    private void addUpdateMethod(String name, Class parmClass)
            throws Exception {
        updateMethods.add(
            Accountable.class.getDeclaredMethod(name, parmClass));
    }
```

```
    private void addReadOnlyMethod(String name) throws Exception {
        Class[] noParms = new Class[] {};
        readOnlyMethods.add(
            Accountable.class.getDeclaredMethod(name, noParms));
    }

    public void testUpdateAccess() throws Exception {
        Accountable account = AccountFactory.create(Permission.UPDATE);
        for (Method method: readOnlyMethods)
            verifyNoException(method, account);
        for (Method method: updateMethods)
            verifyNoException(method, account);
    }

    public void testReadOnlyAccess() throws Exception {
        Accountable account = AccountFactory.create(Permission.READ_ONLY);
        for (Method method: updateMethods)
            verifyException(PermissionException.class, method, account);
        for (Method method: readOnlyMethods)
            verifyNoException(method, account);
    }

    private void verifyException(
            Class exceptionType, Method method, Object object)
            throws Exception {
        try {
            method.invoke(object, nullParmsFor(method));
            fail("expected exception");
        }
        catch (InvocationTargetException e) {
            assertEquals("expected exception",
                exceptionType, e.getCause().getClass());
        }
    }

    private void verifyNoException(Method method, Object object)
            throws Exception {
        try {
            method.invoke(object, nullParmsFor(method));
        }
        catch (InvocationTargetException e) {
            assertFalse(
                "unexpected permission exception",
                PermissionException.class == e.getCause().getClass());
        }
    }

    private Object[] nullParmsFor(Method method) {
        return new Object[method.getParameterTypes().length];
    }
}
```

The test demonstrates some additional features of the Java reflection API.

In the test, you create two collections, one for read-only methods and one for update methods. You populate both read-only and update collections in the setUp method with java.lang.reflect.Method objects. Method objects represent the individual methods defined within a Java class and contain information including the name, the parameters, the return type, and the modifiers (e.g., static and final) of the method. Most important, once you have a Method object and an object of the class on which the method is defined, you can dynamically execute that method.

You obtain Method objects by sending various messages to a Class object. One way is to get an array of all methods by sending getDeclaredMethods to a Class. The class will return all methods directly *declared* within the class. You can also attempt to retrieve a specific method by sending the Class the message getDeclaredMethod, passing along with it the name and the list of parameter types. In the above code, the line:

```
Accountable.class.getDeclaredMethod(name, parmClass)
```

demonstrates use of getDeclaredMethod.

The test testReadOnlyAccess first uses the AccountFactory to create an object—the proxy—that implements the Accountable interface. The parameter to the create method is a Permission enum:

```
package sis.security;

public enum Permission {
    UPDATE, READ_ONLY
}
```

You derive the Accountable interface by extracting all public method signatures from the Account class:

```
package sis.studentinfo;

import java.math.*;

public interface Accountable {
    public void credit(BigDecimal amount);
    public BigDecimal getBalance();
    public BigDecimal transactionAverage();
    public void setBankAba(String bankAba);
    public void setBankAccountNumber(String bankAccountNumber);
    public void setBankAccountType(
        Account.BankAccountType bankAccountType);
    public void transferFromBank(BigDecimal amount);
}
```

You'll need to modify the Account class definition to declare that it implements this interface:

```
public class Account implements Accountable {
```

Which it already does—no further changes to Account are required.

Once testReadOnlyAccess has an Accountable reference, it loops through the lists of update methods and read-only methods.

```
for (Method method: updateMethods)
    verifyException(PermissionException.class, method, account);
for (Method method: readOnlyMethods)
    verifyNoException(method, account);
```

**Building the
Secure Account
Solution**

For each update method, testReadOnlyAccess calls verifyException to ensure that an exception is thrown when method is invoked on account. The test also ensures that each read-only method can be called without generating security exceptions.

The method verifyException is responsible for invoking a method and ensuring that a SecurityException was thrown. The line of code that actually calls the method:

```
method.invoke(object, nullParmsFor(method));
```

To execute a method, you send a Method object the invoke message, passing along with it the object on which to invoke the method plus an Object array of parameters. Here, you use the utility method nullParmsFor to construct an array of all null values. It doesn't matter what you pass the methods. Even if a method generates a NullPointerException or some other sort of exception, the test concerns itself only with PermissionException:

```
package sis.security;

public class PermissionException extends RuntimeException {
}
```

The method verifyException expects the invoke message send to generate an InvocationTargetException, not a PermissionException. If the underlying method called by invoke throws an exception, invoke wraps it in an Invocation-TargetException. You must call getCause on the InvocationTargetException to extract the original wrapped exception object.

The use of reflection in the test was not necessary. If this was not a lesson on reflection, I might have had you implement the test in some other nondynamic manner.

The job of the AccountFactory class is to create instances of classes that implement the Accountable interface.

```
package sis.studentinfo;

import java.lang.reflect.*;
```

```
import sis.security.*;

public class AccountFactory {
    public static Accountable create(Permission permission) {
        switch (permission) {
            case UPDATE:
                return new Account();
            case READ_ONLY:
                return createSecuredAccount();
        }
        return null;
    }

    private static Accountable createSecuredAccount() {
        SecureProxy secureAccount =
            new SecureProxy(new Account(),
                "credit",
                "setBankAba",
                "setBankAccountNumber",
                "setBankAccountType",
                "transferFromBank");

        return (Accountable)Proxy.newProxyInstance(
            Accountable.class.getClassLoader(),
            new Class[] { Accountable.class },
            secureAccount);
    }
}
```

The use of a factory means that the client is isolated from the fact that a security proxy even exists. The client can request an account and, based on the Permission enum passed, AccountFactory creates either a real Account object (Permission.UPDATE) or a dynamic proxy object (Permission.READ_ONLY). The work of creating the dynamic proxy appears in the method createSecuredAccount.

The class SecureProxy is the dynamic proxy object that you will construct. It could act as a secure proxy for any target class. To construct a Secure-Proxy, you pass it the target object and a list of the methods that must be secured. (The list of methods could easily come from a database lookup. A security administrator could populate the contents of the database through another part of the SIS application.)

The second statement in createSecuredAccount is the way that you set up the SecureProxy object to act as a dynamic proxy. It's an ugly bit of code, so I'll repeat it here with reference numbers:

```
return (Accountable)Proxy.newProxyInstance(    // 1
    Accountable.class.getClassLoader(),        // 2
    new Class[] { Accountable.class },         // 3
    secureAccount);                            // 4
```

Line 1 invokes the Proxy factory method newProxyInstance. This method is not parameterized, thus it returns an Object. You must cast the return value to an Accountable interface reference.

The first parameter to newProxyInstance (line 2) requires the *class loader* for the interface class. A class loader reads a stream of bytes representing a Java compilation unit from some source location. Java contains a default class loader, which reads class files from a disc file, but you can create custom class loaders that read class files directly from a database or from a remote source, such as the internet. In most cases you will want to call the method getClassLoader on the Class object itself; this method returns the class loader that originally loaded the class.

The second parameter (line 3) is an array of interface types for which you want to create a dynamic proxy. Behind the scenes, Java will use this list to dynamically construct an object that implements all of the interfaces.

The type of the final parameter (line 4) is InvocationHandler, an interface that contains a single method that your dynamic proxy class must implement in order to intercept incoming messages. You pass your proxy object as this third parameter.

The SecureProxy Class

SecureProxyTest:

```
package sis.security;

import java.lang.reflect.*;
import junit.framework.*;

public class SecureProxyTest extends TestCase {
    private static final String secureMethodName = "secure";
    private static final String insecureMethodName = "insecure";
    private Object object;
    private SecureProxy proxy;
    private boolean secureMethodCalled;
    private boolean insecureMethodCalled;

    protected void setUp() {
        object = new Object() {
            public void secure() {
                secureMethodCalled = true;
            }
            public void insecure() {
                insecureMethodCalled = true;
            }
```

```
    };
    proxy = new SecureProxy(object, secureMethodName);
  }

  public void testSecureMethod() throws Throwable {
    Method secureMethod =
      object.getClass().getDeclaredMethod(
        secureMethodName, new Class[]{});
    try {
      proxy.invoke(proxy, secureMethod, new Object[]{});
      fail("expected PermissionException");
    }
    catch (PermissionException expected) {
      assertFalse(secureMethodCalled);
    }
  }

  public void testInsecureMethod() throws Throwable {
    Method insecureMethod =
      object.getClass().getDeclaredMethod(
        insecureMethodName, new Class[]{});
    proxy.invoke(proxy, insecureMethod, new Object[]{});
    assertTrue(insecureMethodCalled);
  }
}
```

Some of the code in SecureProxyTest is similar to that of AccountFactory-Test. Some refactoring of common test code is probably a good idea. The main distinction between the two tests is that AccountFactoryTest needs to ensure that all methods defined on the Accountable interface are covered properly. SecureProxyTest instead works with a pure test-class definition.

The setUp method uses an anonymous inner class construct to define a new unnamed class with two methods, secure and insecure. All that these methods do is set a corresponding boolean instance variable if they are called. The second statement in the setUp method creates a SecureProxy object by passing in its target object—the anonymous inner class instance—along with the name of the method to be secured for testing purposes.

The test testSecureMethod first looks up the correct Method object on the anonymous class. The test then passes this Method object, along with the proxy instance and an empty parameter list, to the invoke method on the proxy object. Normally you would never call the invoke method directly, but there's no reason you can't do so for purposes of testing.

```
proxy.invoke(proxy, secureMethod, new Object[]{});
```

The test testSecureMethod uses the expected exception testing idiom, looking for a PermissionException. It also ensures that the secure method was never called. The test testInsecureMethod ensures that the insecure method *was* called.

Finally, here is SecureProxy:

```java
package sis.security;

import java.lang.reflect.*;
import java.util.*;

public class SecureProxy implements InvocationHandler {
    private List<String> secureMethods;
    private Object target;

    public SecureProxy(Object target, String... secureMethods) {
        this.target = target;
        this.secureMethods = Arrays.asList(secureMethods);
    }

    public Object invoke(Object proxy, Method method, Object[] args)
            throws Throwable {
        try {
            if (isSecure(method))
                throw new PermissionException();
            return method.invoke(target, args);
        }
        catch (InvocationTargetException e) {
            throw e.getTargetException();
        }
    }

    private boolean isSecure(Method method) {
        return secureMethods.contains(method.getName());
    }
}
```

The SecureProxy Class

SecureProxy stores the target object and the list of methods to be secured in its constructor. It implements the sole method in InvocationHandler, invoke. Any messages sent to the proxy get routed to the invoke method. As you saw in the test, the invoke method takes three parameters: the proxy object itself, the method being called, and the parameters to the method.[14] It's up to you to interpret the incoming information.

In SecureProxy, your interpretation is to look up the method name to see if it is in the list of secure methods. If so, you throw a PermissionException. If not, you delegate the message to the target by calling invoke on the incoming Method object.

That's it!! Your tests should pass.

---

[14]If it has not been apparent until now, primitive parameters are autoboxed into object references.

Problems With Reflection

As you've seen, you can do some very cool things using reflection. Reflection is almost essential for some applications. JUnit currently depends heavily upon reflection. Many other Java technologies require the use of reflection, including EJBs and JavaBeans. Reflection can allow you to accomplish tasks that would otherwise be virtually impossible to do in Java. However, you should approach the use of reflection with caution.

First, code using reflection can be hard to decipher and debug. Modern IDEs, such as Eclipse, go a long way toward helping you easily navigate a system. Eclipse, for example, allows you to find all references to a class or a method. It cannot, however, as effectively find code that uses reflection to create the class or method call you are interested in. Reflection introduces a hole in your code's traceability!

Code that uses reflection executes considerably slower than equivalent code that does not use it. When you introduce reflection code that will be used frequently or on a large scale, profile it to ensure that it executes in a timely fashion.

Finally, when you use reflection, you code can exhibit defects that you might have otherwise caught at compile time. You must ensure that you code defensively, for example by dealing with the ClassNotFoundException that could be thrown by Class.forName.

  Don't use reflection for the sake of using reflection.

This is Jeff's Rule of Statics (from Lesson 4) applied to reflection.

Exercises

1. Use an anonymous inner class of type Comparable to sort the chess-board positions that you created in an earlier exercise.

2. When you debug, you will often find that a toString method doesn't provide you with enough information. At times like this, it may be handy to have a utility method to expose, or "dump," information that is more internal.

   Create an object-dumper utility class that takes an object and lists every field name on the object and the current dump of those objects, recursively, using a hierarchical output format. Do not traverse into classes from java or javax packages. The utility should be able to display private fields. Mark static fields as such. For simplicity's sake, ignore fields from any superclass.

3. Yet another clone exercise: Implement another version of the poor man's clone, this time using reflection operations. Obtain a Constructor object from the source object's class. Call newInstance to create the new object and copy each field's values from the source object to the new object. The class being cloned will need to provide a no-argument constructor. Build support for a shallow copy only.

Exercises

4. Create a Proxy class that delegates to the original object for every method it defines, except for toString. When the proxy receives the toString message, it delegates to the object dumper instead. The target object will need to implement an interface type that defines toString, since proxies work off an interface.

Lesson 13

Multithreading

This chapter presents the most difficult core Java technology to understand and master: multithreading. So far, you have been writing code to run in a single *thread* of execution. It runs serially, start to finish. You may have the need, however, to *multithread*, or execute multiple passages of code simultaneously.

You will learn about:

- suspending execution in a thread
- creating and running threads by extending Thread
- creating and running threads by implementing Runnable
- cooperative and preemptive multitasking
- synchronization
- BlockingQueue
- stopping threads
- wait and notify methods
- locks and conditions
- thread priorities
- deadlocks
- ThreadLocal
- the timer classes
- basic design principles for multithreading

Multithreading

Many multithreading needs are related to building responsive user interfaces. For example, most word processing applications contain an "autosave" function. You can configure the word processor to save your documents every x minutes. The autosave executes automatically on schedule without needing your intervention. A save may take several seconds to execute, yet you can continue work without interruption.

The word processor code manages at least two threads. One thread, often referred to as the foreground thread, is managing your direct interaction with the word processor. Any typing, for example, is captured by code executing in the foreground thread. Meanwhile, a second, background thread is checking the clock from time to time. Once the configured number of minutes has elapsed, the second thread executes the code in the save function.

On a multiple-processor machine, multiple threads can actually run simultaneously, each thread on a separate processor. On a single-processor machine, threads each get a little slice of time from the processor (which can usually only execute one thing at a time), making the threads appear to execute simultaneously.

Learning to write code that runs in a separate thread is fairly simple. The challenge is when multiple threads need to share the same resource. If you are not careful, multithreaded solutions can generate incorrect answers or freeze up your application. Testing multithreaded solutions is likewise complex.

Search Server

A server class may need to handle a large number of incoming requests. If it takes more than a few milliseconds to handle each request, clients who make the request may have to wait longer than an acceptable period of time while the server works on other incoming requests. A better solution is to have the server store each incoming request as a search on a *queue*. Another thread can then take searches from the queue in the order they arrived and process them one at a time. This is known as the active object pattern;[1] it decouples the method request from the actual execution of the method. See Figure 13.1. All relevant search information is translated into a *command object* for later execution.

[1][Lavender1996].

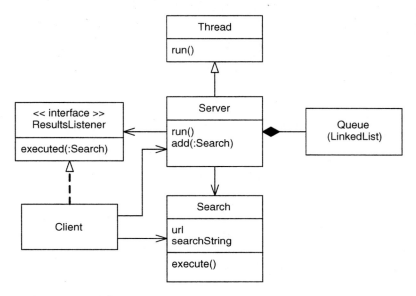

Figure 13.1 *Active Object*

You will build a simple web search server. The server will take a search object consisting of a URL and a search string as a request. As it searches the URL, the server will populate the search object with the number of times the string was found in the document at the URL.

Note: If you're not connected to the Internet, the search test will not execute properly. This is corrected in short time—the section entitled Less Dependent Testing shows how to modify the test to execute against local URLs.

The Search Class

The simplest approach to creating a search server is to follow the Single-Responsibility Principle and first design a class that supports a single search. Once it works, you can concern yourself with the multithreading needs. The benefit is that in keeping each search as a separate object, you have fewer concerns with respect to shared data.

The SearchTest class tests a few possible cases:

```
package sis.search;

import junit.framework.TestCase;
import java.io.*;
```

```
public class SearchTest extends TestCase {
    private static final String URL = "http://www.langrsoft.com";
    public void testCreate() throws IOException {
        Search search = new Search(URL, "x");
        assertEquals(URL, search.getUrl());
        assertEquals("x", search.getText());
    }

    public void testPositiveSearch() throws IOException {
        Search search = new Search(URL, "Jeff Langr");
        search.execute();
        assertTrue(search.matches() >= 1);
        assertFalse(search.errored());
    }

    public void testNegativeSearch() throws IOException {
        final String unlikelyText = "mama cass elliott";
        Search search = new Search(URL, unlikelyText);
        search.execute();
        assertEquals(0, search.matches());
        assertFalse(search.errored());
    }

    public void testErroredSearch() throws IOException {
        final String badUrl = URL + "/z2468.html";
        Search search = new Search(badUrl, "whatever");
        search.execute();
        assertTrue(search.errored());
        assertEquals(FileNotFoundException.class,
            search.getError().getClass());
    }
}
```

The Search
Class

The implementation a:

```
package sis.search;

import java.net.*;
import java.io.*;
import sis.util.*;

public class Search {
    private URL url;
    private String searchString;
    private int matches = 0;
    private Exception exception = null;

    public Search(String urlString, String searchString)
            throws IOException {
        this.url = new URL(urlString);
        this.searchString = searchString;
    }
```

```java
   public String getText() {
      return searchString;
   }
   public String getUrl() {
      return url.toString();
   }
   public int matches() {
      return matches;
   }
   public boolean errored() {
      return exception != null;
   }
   public Exception getError() {
      return exception;
   }

   public void execute() {
      try {
         searchUrl();
      }
      catch (IOException e) {
         exception = e;
      }
   }

   private void searchUrl() throws IOException {
      URLConnection connection = url.openConnection();
      InputStream input = connection.getInputStream();
      BufferedReader reader = null;
      try {
         reader = new BufferedReader(new InputStreamReader(input));
         String line;
         while ((line = reader.readLine()) != null)
            matches += StringUtil.occurrences(line, searchString);
      }
      finally {
         if (reader != null)
            reader.close();
      }
   }
}
```

The method searchUrl in Search uses a the class java.net.URL to obtain a java.net.URLConnection object. A URLConnection is used to establish communication between the client and the actual URL. Once you send the openConnection message to a URLConnection, you can send the message getInputStream to obtain an InputStream reference. The remainder of the method uses Java IO code (see Lesson 11) to search the file.

Currently, searchUrl invokes the StringUtil method occurrences to count the number of matches within each line read from the input stream. Here are StringUtilTest and StringUtil.

```java
// StringUtilTest.java
package sis.util;

import junit.framework.*;

public class StringUtilTest extends TestCase {
    private static final String TEXT = "this is it, isn't it";
    public void testOccurrencesOne() {
        assertEquals(1, StringUtil.occurrences(TEXT, "his"));
    }
    public void testOccurrencesNone() {
        assertEquals(0, StringUtil.occurrences(TEXT, "smelt"));
    }
    public void testOccurrencesMany() {
        assertEquals(3, StringUtil.occurrences(TEXT, "is"));
        assertEquals(2, StringUtil.occurrences(TEXT, "it"));
    }
    public void testOccurrencesSearchStringTooLarge() {
        assertEquals(0, StringUtil.occurrences(TEXT, TEXT + "sdfas"));
    }
}
```

```java
// StringUtil.java
package sis.util;

public class StringUtil {
    static public int occurrences(String string, String substring) {
        int occurrences = 0;
        int length = substring.length();
        final boolean ignoreCase = true;
        for (int i = 0; i < string.length() - substring.length() + 1; i++)
            if (string.regionMatches(ignoreCase, i, substring, 0, length))
                occurrences++;
        return occurrences;
    }
}
```

Another solution would be to use Java's regular expression (regex) API. See Additional Lesson III for a discussion of regex.

Less Dependent Testing

If you're unfortunate enough to not be connected to the Internet on your computer, you're probably grousing about your inability to execute ServerTest at all. You will now rectify this situation by changing the search

Less Dependent
Testing

URLs to file URLs.[2] This also means you can write out test HTML files to control the content of the "web" pages searched.

```
package sis.search;

import junit.framework.TestCase;
import java.io.*;
import java.util.*;
import sis.util.*;

public class SearchTest extends TestCase {
   public static final String[] TEST_HTML = {
      "<html>",
      "<body>",
      "Book: Agile Java, by Jeff Langr<br />",
      "Synopsis: Mr Langr teaches you<br />",
      "Java via test-driven development.<br />",
      "</body></html>"};

   public static final String FILE = "/temp/testFileSearch.html";
   public static final String URL = "file:" + FILE;

   protected void setUp() throws IOException {
      TestUtil.delete(FILE);
      LineWriter.write(FILE, TEST_HTML);
   }

   protected void tearDown() throws IOException {
      TestUtil.delete(FILE);
   }
   // ...
```

You will need the LineWriter utility; here is the test and production source.

```
// LineWriterTest.java
package sis.util;

import junit.framework.*;
import java.io.*;

public class LineWriterTest extends TestCase {
   public void testMultipleRecords() throws IOException {
      final String file = "LineWriterTest.testCreate.txt";
      try {
         LineWriter.write(file, new String[] {"a", "b"});

         BufferedReader reader = null;
         try {
            reader = new BufferedReader(new FileReader(file));
            assertEquals("a", reader.readLine());
            assertEquals("b", reader.readLine());
```

[2]Another solution would involve installing a local web server, such as Tomcat.

```
                    assertNull(reader.readLine());
                }
                finally {
                    if (reader != null)
                        reader.close();
                }
            }
            finally {
                TestUtil.delete(file);
            }
        }
    }

// LineWriter.java
package sis.util;

import java.io.*;

public class LineWriter {
    public static void write(String filename, String[] records)
            throws IOException {
        BufferedWriter writer = null;
        try {
            writer = new BufferedWriter(new FileWriter(filename));
            for (int i = 0; i < records.length; i++) {
                writer.write(records[i]);
                writer.newLine();
            }
        }
        finally {
            if (writer != null)
                writer.close();
        }
    }
}
```

Less Dependent Testing

The good part is that the changes to SearchTest are not very invasive. In fact, none of the test methods need change. You are adding setup and teardown methods to write HTML to a local file and subsequently delete that file

---

Initialization Expressions

The method searchUrl contains the code:

```
String line;
while ((line = reader.readLine()) != null)
```

The parentheses should help you understand this code. First, the result of reader.read-Line() is assigned to the line reference variable. The value of the line reference is compared to null to determine whether or not the while loop should terminate.

each time a test completes. You are also changing the URL to use the file protocol instead of the http protocol.

The bad part is that the Search class must change. To obtain an InputStream from a URL with a file protocol, you must extract the path information from the URL and use it to open the stream as a FileInputStream. It's not a significant change. The minor downside is that you now have a bit of code in your production system that will probably only be used by the test.

```
private void searchUrl() throws IOException {
    InputStream input = getInputStream(url);
    BufferedReader reader = null;
    try {
        reader = new BufferedReader(new InputStreamReader(input));
        String line;
        while ((line = reader.readLine()) != null)
            matches += StringUtil.occurrences(line, searchString);
    }
    finally {
        if (reader != null)
            reader.close();
    }
}

private InputStream getInputStream(URL url) throws IOException {
    if (url.getProtocol().startsWith("http")) {
        URLConnection connection = url.openConnection();
        return connection.getInputStream();
    }
    else if (url.getProtocol().equals("file")) {
        return new FileInputStream(url.getPath());
    }
    return null;
}
```

One other thing you want to consider is that you are no longer exercising the portion of of the code that deals with an http URL. The best approach is to ensure that you have adequate coverage at an *acceptance test*[3] level. Acceptance tests provide a level of testing above unit testing—they test the system from an end user's standpoint. They are executed against as live a system as possible and should not use mocks. For the search application, you would certainly execute acceptance tests that used live web URLs.

---

[3]There are many different nomenclatures for different types of testing. Acceptance tests are the tests that signify that the system meets the acceptance criteria of the customer to whom it's delivered. You may hear these tests referred to as customer tests.

The Server

ServerTest:

```java
package sis.search;

import junit.framework.*;
import sis.util.*;

public class ServerTest extends TestCase {
    private int numberOfResults = 0;
    private Server server;
    private static final long TIMEOUT = 3000L;
    private static final String[] URLS = {
        SearchTest.URL, SearchTest.URL, SearchTest.URL };       // 1

    protected void setUp() throws Exception {
        TestUtil.delete(SearchTest.FILE);
        LineWriter.write(SearchTest.FILE, SearchTest.TEST_HTML);

        ResultsListener listener = new ResultsListener() {      // 2
            public void executed(Search search) {
                numberOfResults++;
            }};

        server = new Server(listener);
    }

    protected void tearDown() throws Exception {
        TestUtil.delete(SearchTest.FILE);
    }

    public void testSearch() throws Exception {
        long start = System.currentTimeMillis();
        for (String url: URLS)                                  // 3
            server.add(new Search(url, "xxx"));
        long elapsed = System.currentTimeMillis() - start;
        long averageLatency = elapsed / URLS.length;
        assertTrue(averageLatency < 20);                        // 4
        assertTrue(waitForResults());                           // 5
    }

    private boolean waitForResults() {
        long start = System.currentTimeMillis();
        while (numberOfResults < URLS.length) {
            try { Thread.sleep(1); }
            catch (InterruptedException e) {}
            if (System.currentTimeMillis() - start > TIMEOUT)
                return false;
        }
        return true;
    }
}
```

The test first constructs a list of URL strings (line 1).

The setup method constructs a ResultsListener object (line 2). You pass this object as a parameter when constructing a new Server instance.

Your test, as a client, will only be to pass search requests to the server. In the interest of responsiveness, you are designing the server so the client will not have to wait for each request to complete. But the client will still need to know the results each time theserver gets around to processing a search. A frequently used mechanism is a *callback*.

The term callback is a holdover from the language C, which allows you to create pointers to functions. Once you have a function pointer, you can pass this pointer to other functions like any other reference. The receiving code can then *call back* to the function located in the originating code, using the function pointer.

In Java, one effective way to implement a callback is to pass an anonymous inner class instance as a parameter to a method. The interface Results-Listener defines an executed method:

The Server

```
package sis.search;

public interface ResultsListener {
    public void executed(Search search);
}
```

In testSearch, you pass an anonymous inner class instance of ResultsListener to the constructor of Server. The Server object holds on to the ResultsListener reference and sends it the executed message when the search has completed execution.

Callbacks are frequently referred to as listeners in Java implementations. A listener interface defines methods that you want called when something happens. User interface classes frequently use listeners to notify other code when an event occurs. For example, you can configure a Java Swing class with a event listener that lets you know when a user clicks on the button to close a window. This allows you to tie up any loose ends before the window actually closes.

In the test, you use the ResultsListener instance simply to track the total number of search executions that complete.

Once you create a Server object, you use a loop (line 3) to iterate through the list of URLs. You use each URL to construct a Search object (the search text is irrelevant). In the interest of demonstrating that Java rapidly dispatches each request, you track the elapsed execution time to create and add a search to the server. You use a subsequent assertion (line 4) to show that the average latency (delay in response time) is an arbitrarily small 20 milliseconds or less.

Since the server will be executing multiple searches in a separate thread, the likelihood is that the code in the JUnit test will complete executing before the searches do. You need a mechanism to hold up processing until the searches are complete—until the number of searches executed is the same as the number of URLs searched.

Waiting in the Test

The assertion at line 5 in the ServerTest listing calls the waitForResults method, which will suspend execution of the current thread (i.e., the thread in which the test is executing) until all search results have been retrieved. The timeout value provides an arbitrary elapsed time after which waitForResults should return false and cause the assertion to fail.

```
private boolean waitForResults() {
    long start = System.currentTimeMillis();
    while (numberOfResults < URLS.length) {
        try { Thread.sleep(1); }
        catch (InterruptedException e) {}
        if (System.currentTimeMillis() - start > TIMEOUT)
            return false;
    }
    return true;
}
```

The waitForResults method executes a simple loop. Each time through, the body of the loop pauses for a millisecond, then makes a quick calculation of elapsed time to see if it's passed the timeout limit. The pause is effected by a call to the static Thread method sleep. The sleep method takes a number of milliseconds and idles the currently executing thread for that amount of time.[4]

Since sleep can throw a checked exception of type InterruptedException, you can choose to enclose it in a try-catch block. It is possible for one thread to interrupt another, which is what would generate the exception. But thread interruptions are usually only by design, so the code here shows one of the rare cases where it's acceptable to ignore the exception and provide an empty catch block.

The looping mechanism used in waitForResults is adequate at best. The wait/notify technique, discussed later in this lesson (see Wait/Notify), provides the best general-purpose mechanism of waiting for a condition to occur.

---

[4]The thread scheduler will wait *at least* the specified amount of time and possibly a bit longer.

Creating and Running Threads

The Server class needs to accept incoming searches and simultaneously process any requests that have not been executed. The code to do the actual searches will be executed in a separate thread. The main thread of Server, in which the remainder of the code executes, must spawn the second thread.

Java supplies two ways for you to initiate a separate thread. The first requires you to extend the class java.lang.Thread and provide an implementation for the run method. Subsequently, you can call the start method to kick things off. At that point, code in the run method begins execution in a separate thread.

A second technique for spawning threads is to create an instance of a class that implements the interface java.lang.Runnable:

```
public interface Runnable {
    void run();
}
```

You then construct a Thread object, passing the Runnable object as a parameter. Sending the message start to the Thread object initiates code in the run method. This second technique is often done using anonymous inner class implementations of Runnable.

It is important that you distinguish between a *thread*, or thread of execution, and a *Thread* object. A thread is a control flow that the thread scheduler manages. A Thread is an object that manages information about a thread of execution. The existence of a Thread object does not imply the existence of a thread: A thread doesn't exist until a Thread object starts one, and a Thread object can exist long after a thread has terminated.

For now, you'll use the first technique to create a thread and have the Server class extend from Thread. Thread itself implements the Runnable interface. If you extend Thread, you will need to override the run method in order for anything useful to happen.

```
package sis.search;

import java.util.*;

public class Server extends Thread {
    private List<Search> queue = new LinkedList<Search>();  // flaw!
    private ResultsListener listener;

    public Server(ResultsListener listener) {
        this.listener = listener;
        start();
    }
```

Creating and
Running
Threads

```
public void run() {
   while (true) {
      if (!queue.isEmpty())
         execute(queue.remove(0));
      Thread.yield();
   }
}

public void add(Search search) {
   queue.add(search);
}

private void execute(Search search) {
   search.execute();
   listener.executed(search);
}
}
```

**Creating and
Running
Threads**

The Server class defines two fields: a ResultsListener reference and a LinkedList of Search objects, named queue. A flaw exists in the declaration of the queue reference—it is not "thread safe"! For now, your test will likely execute successfully, but the flaw could cause your application to fail. In the section Synchronized Collections in this chapter, you will learn about this thread safety issue and how to correct it.

The java.util.LinkedList class implements the List interface. Instead of storing elements in a contiguous block of memory, as in an ArrayList, a linked list allocates a new block of memory for each element you add to it. The individual blocks of memory thus will be scattered in memory space; each block contains a link to the next block in the list. See Figure 13.2 for a conceptual memory picture of how a linked list works. For collections that require frequent removals or insertions at points other than the end of the list, a LinkedList will provide better performance characteristics than an ArrayList.

The queue reference stores the incoming search requests. The linked list in this case acts as a *queue* data structure. A queue is also known as a first-in, first-out (FIFO) list: When you ask a queue to remove elements, it removes the oldest item in the list first. The add method in Server takes a Search parameter and adds it to the *end* of the queue. So in order for the LinkedList to act as a queue, you must remove Search objects from the *beginning* of the list.

The constructor of Server kicks off the second thread (often called a *worker* or *background* thread) by calling start. The run method is invoked at this point. The run method in Server is an infinite loop—it will keep executing until some other code explicitly terminates the thread (see Stopping Threads

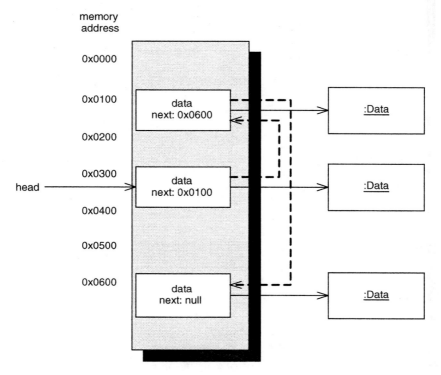

Figure 13.2   *A Conceptual View of a Linked List*

in this chapter) or until the application in which it is running terminates (see Shutting Down in this chapter). When you run ServerTest in JUnit, the background thread will keep executing even after all the JUnit tests have completed. It will stop only when you close the JUnit window.

The body of the loop first checks whether the queue is empty. If not, the code removes and executes the first element in the queue. Regardless, the code then calls the Thread method yield. The yield method potentially allows other threads the opportunity to get some time from the processor before the background thread picks up again. The next section on cooperative and preemptive multitasking discusses why the yield might be necessary.

The execute method delegates the actual search to the Search object itself. When the search completes, the ResultsListener reference is sent the message executed with the Search object as a parameter.

You can represent the flow of messages in a successful search using a UML sequence diagram (Figure 13.3). The sequence diagram is a dynamic view of your system in action. It shows the ordered message flow between objects. I

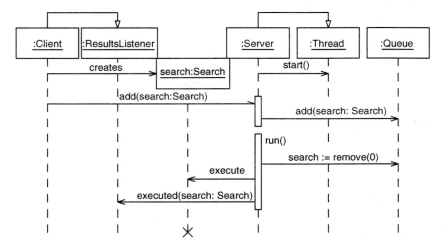

Figure 13.3   *Sequence Diagram for the Active Object Search*

find that sequence diagrams can be a very effective means of communicating how a system is wired together with respect to various uses.[5]

In a sequence diagram, you show object boxes instead of class boxes. The dashed line that emanates vertically downward from each box represents the object's lifeline. An "X" at the bottom of the object lifeline indicates its termination. The Search object in Figure 13.3 disappears when it is notified that a search has been completed; thus, its lifeline is capped off with an "X."

You represent a message send using a directed line from the sending object's lifeline to the receiver. Messages flow in order from top to bottom. In Figure 13.3, a Client object sends the first message, creates. This special message shows that the Client object is responsible for creation of a Search object. Note that the Search object starts farther down; it is not in existence until this point.

After the first message send, the Client sends add(Search) to the Server object. This message send is conceptually asynchronous—the Client need not wait for any return information from the Server object.[6] You use a half-arrowhead to represent asynchronous message sends. When it receives this add message, the Server's add method passes the Search object off to the queue. You represent the execution lifetime of the add method at the Server object using an *activation*—a thin rectangle laid over the object lifeline.

---

[5]Sequence diagrams sometimes are not the best way of representing complex parallel activity. A UML model that is perhaps better suited for representing multithreaded behavior is the *activity diagram*.

[6]The way we've implemented it, the message send is synchronous, but since the operation is immediate and returns no information you can represent it as asynchronous.

Meanwhile, the Server thread has sent the message start to its superclass (or, more correctly, to itself). The run method overridden in Server begins execution. Its lifetime is indicated by an activation on the Server object's lifeline. Code in the run method sends the message remove(0) to the Queue to obtain and remove its first Search element. Subsequently the run method sends the message execute to the Search object and notifies the ResultsListener (via executed) when execute completes.

Cooperative and Preemptive Multitasking

In a single-processor environment, individual threads each get a slice of time from the processor in which to execute. The question is, how much time does each thread get before another thread takes over? The answer depends upon many things, including which operating system you are using to run Java and your particular JVM implementation.

Most modern operating systems (including Unix variants and Windows) use *preemptive multitasking*, in which the operating system (OS) interrupts the currently executing thread. Information about the thread is stored, and the OS goes on to provide a slice of time to the next thread. In this environment, all threads will eventually get some attention from the thread scheduler.

The other possibility is that the operating system manages threads using *cooperative multitasking*. Cooperative multitasking depends on thread code behaving well by yielding time to other threads frequently. In a cooperative threading model, one poorly written thread could hog the processor completely, preventing all other threads from doing any processing. Threads may yield time by explicitly calling the yield method, by sleeping, when blocking (waiting) on IO operations, and when they are suspended, to mention a few ways.

In the Server class, the while loop in the run method calls the yield method each time through the loop to allow other threads the opportunity to execute.[7]

```
public void run() {
    while (true) {
        if (!queue.isEmpty())
            execute(queue.remove(0));
        Thread.yield();
    }
}
```

[7] You may experience significant CPU usage when executing this code, depending on your environment. The yield method may effectively do nothing if there are no other threads executing. An alternative would be to introduce a sleep of a millisecond.

Synchronization

One of the biggest pitfalls with multithreaded development is dealing with the fact that threads run in *nondeterministic* order. Each time you execute a multithreaded application, the threads may run in a different order that is impossible to predict. The most challenging result of this nondeterminism is that you may have coded a defect that surfaces only once in a few thousand executions, or once every second full moon.[8]

Two threads that are executing code do not necessarily move through the code at the same rate. One thread may execute five lines of code before another has even processed one. The thread scheduler interleaves slices of code from each executing thread.

Also, threading is not at the level of Java statements, but at a lower level of the VM operations that the statements translate down to. Most statements you code in Java are *non-atomic*: The Java compiler might create several internal operations to correspond to a single statement, even something as simple as incrementing a counter or assigning a value to a reference. Suppose an assignment statement takes two internal operations. The second operation may not complete before the thread scheduler suspends the thread and executes a second thread.

All this code interleaving means that you may encounter *synchronization* issues. If two threads go after the same piece of data at the same time, the results may not be what you expect.

 You will modify the sis.studentinfo.Account class to support withdrawing funds. To withdraw funds, the balance of the account must be at least as much as the amount being withdrawn. If the amount is too large, you should do nothing (for simplicity's and demonstration's sake). In any case, you never want the account balance to go below zero.

```
package sis.studentinfo;
// ...
public class AccountTest extends TestCase {
   // ...
   private Account account;

   protected void setUp() {
      account = new Account();
      // ...
   }
   // ...
```

[8]The subtle gravitational pull might cause electrostatic tides that slow the processor for a picosecond.

```
    public void testWithdraw() throws Exception {
       account.credit(new BigDecimal("100.00"));
       account.withdraw(new BigDecimal("40.00"));
       assertEquals(new BigDecimal("60.00"), account.getBalance());
    }

    public void testWithdrawInsufficientFunds() {
       account.credit(new BigDecimal("100.00"));
       account.withdraw(new BigDecimal("140.00"));
       assertEquals(new BigDecimal("100.00"), account.getBalance());
    }
    // ...
}
```

The withdraw method:

```
package sis.studentinfo;
// ...
public class Account implements Accountable {
    private BigDecimal balance = new BigDecimal("0.00");
    // ...
    public void withdraw(BigDecimal amount) {
       if (amount.compareTo(balance) > 0)
          return;
       balance = balance.subtract(amount);
    }
    // ...
}
```

A fundamental problem exists with the withdraw method in a multithreaded environment. Suppose two threads attempt to withdraw $80 from an account with a $100 balance at the same time. One thread should succeed; the other thread should fail. The end balance should be $0. However, the code execution could interleave as follows:

Thread 1	Thread 2	Bal
amount.compareTo(balance) > 0		100
	amount.compareTo(balance) > 0	100
balance = balance.subtract(amount)		20
	balance = balance.subtract(amount)	-60

The second thread tests the balance after the first thread has approved the balance but before the first thread has subtracted from the balance. Other execution sequences could cause the same problem.

You can write a short test to demonstrate this problem.

```
package sis.studentinfo;

import junit.framework.*;
import java.math.BigDecimal;

public class MultithreadedAccountTest extends TestCase {
    public void testConcurrency() throws Exception {
        final Account account = new Account();
        account.credit(new BigDecimal("100.00"));

        Thread t1 = new Thread(new Runnable() {
            public void run() {
                account.withdraw(new BigDecimal("80.00"));
            }});
        Thread t2 = new Thread(new Runnable() {
            public void run() {
                account.withdraw(new BigDecimal("80.00"));
            }});

        t1.start();
        t2.start();
        t1.join();
        t2.join();

        assertEquals(new BigDecimal("20.00"), account.getBalance());
    }
}
```

Creating
Threads with
Runnable

There's definitely some code redundancy in this method. After you understand what the method is doing, make sure you refactor it to eliminate the duplication.

Creating Threads with Runnable

The method testConcurrency introduces two new things. First, it shows how you can create a thread by passing it an instance of the Runnable interface. Remember that the Runnable interface defines the single method run. The test constructs an anonymous inner class instance of Runnable for each thread. Note that the code in the run methods does not execute until the start methods are called.

The second new thing in testConcurrency is the use of the Thread method join. When you send the message join to a thread, execution in the current thread halts until that thread completes. The code in testConcurrency first waits until t1 completes, then t2, before the test can proceed.

When you execute JUnit, testConcurrency will in all likelihood pass. In a small method, where everything executes quickly, the thread scheduler will probably allot enough time to a thread to execute the entire method before moving on to the next thread. You can force the issue by inserting a pause in the withdraw method:

```
public void withdraw(BigDecimal amount) {
    if (amount.compareTo(balance) > 0)
        return;
try { Thread.sleep(1); }
catch (InterruptedException e) {}
    balance = balance.subtract(amount);
}
```

You should now see a red bar.

Synchronized

Semantically, you want all of the code in withdraw to execute atomically. A thread should be able to execute the entire withdraw method, start to finish, without any other thread interfering. You can accomplish this in Java through use of the synchronized method modifier.

```
public synchronized void withdraw(BigDecimal amount) {
    if (amount.compareTo(balance) > 0)
        return;
    balance = balance.subtract(amount);
}
```

This implementation of synchronization in Java is known as *mutual exclusion*. Another way you can refer to the code protected by mutual exclusion is as a *critical section*.[9] In order to ensure that the withdraw code executes mutually exclusively, Java places a lock on the object in which the thread's code is executing. While one thread has a lock on an object, no other thread can obtain a lock on that object. Other threads that try to do so will block until the lock is released. The lock is released when the method completes execution.

Java uses a concept known as monitors to protect data. A monitor is associated with each object; this monitor protects the object's instance data. A monitor is associated with each class; it protects the class's static data. When you acquire a lock, you are acquiring the associated monitor; only one thread can acquire a lock at any given time.[10]

[9][Sun2004].

[10]http://www.artima.com/insidejvm/ed2/threadsynch2.html.

You should always try to lock the smallest amount of code possible, otherwise you may experience performance problems while other threads wait to obtain a lock. If you are creating small, composed methods as I've repetitively recommended, you will find that locking at the method level suffices for most needs. However, you can lock at a smaller atomicity than an entire method by creating a synchronized block. You must also specify an object to use as a monitor by enclosing its reference in parentheses after the synchronized keyword.

The following implementation of withdraw is equivalent to the above implementation.

```
public void withdraw(BigDecimal amount) {
    synchronized(this) {
        if (amount.compareTo(balance) > 0)
            return;
        balance = balance.subtract(amount);
    }
}
```

A synchronized block requires the use of braces, even if it contains only one statement.

You can declare a class method as synchronized. When the VM executes a class method, it will obtain a lock on the Class object for which the method is defined.

Synchronized Collections

As I hinted earlier, the Server class contains a flaw with respect to the declaration of the queue as a LinkedList.

```
public class Server extends Thread {
    private List<Search> queue = new LinkedList<Search>();  // flaw!
```

When you work with the Java 2 Collection Class Framework with classes such as ArrayList, LinkedList, and HashMap, you should be cognizant of the fact that they are not thread-safe—the methods in these classes are not synchronized. The older collection classes, Vector and Hashtable, are synchronized by default. However, I recommend you *do not* use them if you need thread-safe collections.

Instead, you can use utility methods in the class java.util.Collections to enclose a collection instance in what is known as a synchronization wrapper. The synchronization wrapper obtains locks where necessary on the target collection and delegates all messages off to the collection for normal processing. Modify the Server class to wrap the queue reference in a synchronized list:

```
public class Server extends Thread {
   private List<Search> queue =
      Collections.synchronizedList(new LinkedList<Search>());
   // ...
   public void run() {
      while (true) {
         if (!queue.isEmpty())
            execute(queue.remove(0));
         Thread.yield();
      }
   }

   public void add(Search search) throws Exception {
      queue.add(search);
   }
   // ...
}
```

Adding the synchronization wrapper doesn't require you to change any code that uses the queue reference.

Using a bit of analysis, it doesn't seem possible for there to be a synchronization problem with respect to the queue. The add method inserts to the end of the list; the run loop removes from the beginning of the queue only if the queue is not empty. There are no other methods that operate on the queue. However, there is a slim possibility that portions of the add and remove operations will execute at the same time. This concurrency could corrupt the integrity of the LinkedList instance. Using the synchronization wrappers will eliminate the defect.

BlockingQueue

A promising API addition in J2SE 5.0 is the concurrency library of classes, located in the package java.util.concurrent. It provides utility classes to help you solve many of the issues surrounding multithreading. While you should prefer use of this library, its existence doesn't mean that you don't need to learn the fundamentals and concepts behind threading.[11]

Since queues are such a useful construct in multithreaded applications, the concurrency library defines an interface, BlockingQueue, along with five

---

[11]The importance of learning how multiplication works before always using a calculator to solve every problem is an analogy.

specialized queue classes that implement this interface. Blocking queues implement another new interface, java.util.Queue, which defines queue semantics for collections. Blocking queues add concurrency-related capabilities to queues. Examples include the ability to wait for elements to exist when retrieving the next in line and the ability to wait for space to exist when storing elements.

You can rework the Server class to use a LinkedBlockingQueue instead of a LinkedList.

BlockingQueue

```
package sis.search;

import java.util.concurrent.*;

public class Server extends Thread {
    private BlockingQueue<Search> queue =
        new LinkedBlockingQueue<Search>();
    private ResultsListener listener;

    public Server(ResultsListener listener) {
        this.listener = listener;
        start();
    }

    public void run() {
        while (true)
            try {
                execute(queue.take());
            }
            catch (InterruptedException e) {
            }
    }

    public void add(Search search) throws Exception {
        queue.put(search);
    }

    private void execute(Search search) {
        search.execute();
        listener.executed(search);
    }
}
```

The LinkedBlockingQueue method put adds an element to the end of the queue. The take method removes an element from the beginning of the queue. It also waits until an element is available in the queue. The code doesn't look very different from your original implementation of Server, but it is now thread-safe.

Stopping Threads

A testing flaw still remains in ServerTest. The thread in the Server class is executing an infinite loop. Normally, the loop would terminate when the Server itself terminated. When running your tests in JUnit, however, the thread keeps running until you close down JUnit itself—the Server run method keeps chugging along.

The Thread API contains a stop method that would appear to do the trick of stopping the thread. It doesn't take long to read in the detailed API documentation that the stop method has been deprecated and is "inherently unsafe." Fortunately, the documentation goes on to explain why and what you should do instead. (Read it.) The recommended technique is to simply have the thread die on its own based on some condition. One way is to use a boolean variable that you initialize to true and set to false when you want the thread to terminate. The conditional in the while loop in the run method can test the value of this variable.

Stopping
Threads

You will need to modify the ServerTest method tearDown to do the shutdown and verify that it worked.

```
protected void tearDown() throws Exception {
    assertTrue(server.isAlive());
    server.shutDown();
    server.join(3000);
    assertFalse(server.isAlive());
    TestUtil.delete(SearchTest.FILE);
}
```

Remember, the tearDown method executes upon completion of each and every test method, regardless of whether or not an exception was thrown by the test. In tearDown, you first ensure that the thread is "alive" and running. You then send the message shutDown to the server. You've chosen the method name shutDown to signal the server to stop.

You then wait on the server thread by using the join method, with an arbitrary timeout of 3 seconds. It will take some time for the thread to terminate. Without the join method, the rest of the code in tearDown will likely execute before the thread is completely dead. Finally, after you issue the shutDown command to the Server, you ensure that its thread is no longer alive. The isAlive method is defined on Thread and Server is a subclass of Thread, so you can send the message isAlive to the Server instance to get your answer.

Since the Server class now uses a LinkedBlockingQueue, you cannot use a boolean flag on the run method's while loop. The LinkedBlockingQueue take method *blocks*—it waits until a new object is available on the queue. It would wait forever if you left JUnit running.

One way you could get the LinkedBlockingQueue to stop waiting would be to put a special Search object on the queue, one that signifies that you're done. Each time you take an object from the queue, you would need to check to see if it was the special Search object and terminate the run method if it was.

Another way to stop LinkedBlockingQueue from waiting is to interrupt the thread by sending it the interrupt message, which generates an Interrupted-Exception. If you catch an InterruptedException, you can then break out of the infinite while loop. Here is the implementation of this approach:

```
public class Server extends Thread {
    // ...
    public void run() {
        while (true)
            try {
                execute(queue.take());
            }
            catch (InterruptedException e) {
                break;
            }
    }
    // ...
    public void shutDown() throws Exception {
        this.interrupt();
    }
}
```

 Wait/Notify

Wait/Notify

Java provides a mechanism to help you coordinate actions between two or more threads. Often you need to have one thread wait until another thread has completed its work. Java provides a mechanism known as wait/notify. You can call a wait method from within a thread in order to idle it. Another thread can wake up this waiting thread by calling a notify method.

An example? Let's rock! A clock—tic-toc!

 In this example, you'll build a clock class suitable for use in a clock application. A user interface (UI) for the clock application could display either a digital readout or an analog representation, complete with hour, minute, and second hands. While the UI is busy creating output that the user sees, the actual Clock class can execute a separate thread to constantly track the time. The Clock thread will loop indefinitely. Every second, it will wake up and notify the user interface that the time has changed.

The UI class implements the ClockListener interface. You pass a ClockListener reference to a Clock object; the clock can call back to this listener with the changed time. With this listener-based design, you could replace an analog clock interface with a digital clock interface and not have to change the clock class (see Figure 13.4).

The tough part is going to be writing a test. Here's a strategy:

- Create a mock ClockListener that stores any messages it receives.

- Create the Clock instance, passing in the mock object.

- Start the clock up and wait until five messages have been received by the mock.

- Ensure that the messages received by the ClockListener, which are date instances, are each separated by one second.

The test below performs each of these steps. The tricky bit is getting the test to wait until the mock gets all the messages it wants. I'll explain that part, but I'll let you figure out the rest of the test, including the verification of the tics captured by the test listener.

```
package sis.clock;

import java.util.*;
import junit.framework.*;
```

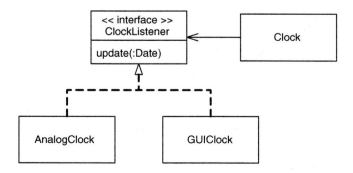

Figure 13.4 *A Clock Listener*

```
public class ClockTest extends TestCase {
    private Clock clock;
    private Object monitor = new Object();              // 1

    public void testClock() throws Exception {
        final int seconds = 5;
        final List<Date> tics = new ArrayList<Date>();
        ClockListener listener = new ClockListener() {
            private int count = 0;
            public void update(Date date) {
                tics.add(date);
                if (++count == seconds)
                    synchronized(monitor) {             // 2
                        monitor.notifyAll();            // 3
                    }
            }
        };
        clock = new Clock(listener);
        synchronized(monitor) {                         // 4
            monitor.wait();                             // 5
        }
        clock.stop();
        verify(tics, seconds);
    }

    private void verify(List<Date> tics, int seconds) {
        assertEquals(seconds, tics.size());
        for (int i = 1; i < seconds; i++)
            assertEquals(1, getSecondsFromLast(tics, i));
    }

    private long getSecondsFromLast(List<Date> tics, int i) {
        Calendar calendar = new GregorianCalendar();
        calendar.setTime(tics.get(i));
        int now = calendar.get(Calendar.SECOND);
        calendar.setTime(tics.get(i - 1));
        int then = calendar.get(Calendar.SECOND);
        if (now == 0)
            now = 60;
        return now - then;
    }
}
```

Wait/Notify

After the test creates the Clock instance, it waits (line 5). You can send the wait message to *any* object—wait is defined in the class Object. You must first obtain a lock on that same object. You do so using either a synchronized block (line 4) or synchronized method, as mentioned above. In the test, you use an arbitrary object stored in the monitor field (line 1) as the object to lock and wait on.

What does the test wait for? In the mock listener implementation, you can store a count variable that gets bumped up by 1 each time the update(Date) method is called. Once the desired number of messages is received, you can tell the ClockTest to stop waiting.

From an implementation standpoint, the test thread waits until the listener, which is executing in another thread, says to proceed. The listener says that things can proceed by sending the notifyAll message to *the same object the test is waiting on* (line 3). In order to call notifyAll, you must first obtain a lock against the monitor object, again using a synchronized block.

But . . . wait! The call to wait was in a synchronized block, meaning that no other code can obtain a lock—including the synchronized block wrapping the notifyAll method—until the synchronized block exits. Yet it won't exit until the waiting is done, and the waiting isn't done until notifyAll is called. This would seem to be a Catch-22 situation.

The trick: Behind the scenes, the wait method puts the current thread on what is called a "wait set" for the monitor object. It then *releases all locks* before idling the current thread. Thus when code in the other thread encounters the synchronized block wrapping the notifyAll call, there is no lock on the monitor. It can then obtain a lock (line 2). The notifyAll call requires the lock in order to be able to send its message to the monitor.

You may want to go over the discussion of wait/notify a few times until it sinks in.

Here is the ClockListener interface and the Clock class implementation:

Wait/Notify

```
// sis.clock.ClockListener
package sis.clock;

import java.util.*;

public interface ClockListener {
    public void update(Date date);
}

// sis.clock.Clock
package sis.clock;

import java.util.*;

public class Clock implements Runnable {
    private ClockListener listener;
    private boolean run = true;

    public Clock(ClockListener listener) {
        this.listener = listener;
        new Thread(this).start();
```

```
    }

    public void stop() {
        run = false;
    }

    public void run() {
        while (run) {
            try { Thread.sleep(1000); }
            catch (InterruptedException e) {}
            listener.update(new Date());
        }
    }
}
```

The run method in Clock uses the simple technique of testing a boolean flag, run, each time through a while loop to determine when to stop. The stop method, called by the test after its waiting is complete, sets the run boolean to false.

There is a flaw in the Clock implementation. The run method sleeps for *at least* a full second. As I noted earlier, a sleep call may take a few additional nanoseconds or milliseconds. Plus, creating a new Date object takes time. This means that it's fairly likely that the clock could skip a second: If the last time posted was at 11:55:01.999, for example, and the sleep plus additional execution took 1,001 milliseconds instead of precisely 1,000 milliseconds, then the new time posted would be 11:55:03.000. The clock UI would show 11:55:01, then skip to 11:55:03. In an analog display, you'd see the second hand jump a little bit more—not that big a deal in most applications. If you run enough iterations in the test, it will almost certainly fail.

Here's an improved implementation:

```
public void run() {
    long lastTime = System.currentTimeMillis();
    while (run) {
        try { Thread.sleep(10); }
        catch (InterruptedException e) {}
        long now = System.currentTimeMillis();
        if ((now / 1000) - (lastTime / 1000) >= 1) {
            listener.update(new Date(now));
            lastTime = now;
        }
    }
}
```

Could you have written a test that would have uncovered this defect consistently? One option for doing so might include creating a utility class to return the current milliseconds. You could then mock the utility class to force a certain time.

The test for Clock is a nuisance. It adds 5 seconds to the execution time of your unit tests. How might you minimize this time? First, it probably doesn't matter if the test proves 5 tics or 2. Second, you might modify the clock class (and test accordingly) to support configurable intervals. Instead of 1 second, write the test to demonstrate support for hundredths of a second (like a stopwatch would require).

Additional Notes on wait and notify

The Object class overloads the wait method with versions that allow you to specify a timeout period. A thread you suspend using one of these versions of wait idles until another thread notifies it or until the timeout period has expired.

Under certain circumstances, it is possible for a *spurious wakeup* to occur—one that you did not trigger by an explicit notification! This is rare, but if you use wait and notify in production code, you need to guard against this condition. To do so, you can enclose the wait statement in a while loop that tests a condition indicating whether or not execution can proceed. The Java API documentation for the wait method shows how you might implement this.

In a test, you could create a do-while loop that called the verify method each time through. If the verify method were to then fail, you would execute wait again. I view this as an unnecessary complexity for a test. The worst case of not guarding against the unlikely spurious wakeup would be that the test would fail, at which time you could rerun it.

While notifyAll wakes up *all* threads that are waiting if there is more than one, the notify method chooses an arbitrary thread to be woken up. In most circumstances you will want to use notifyAll. However, in some situations you will want to wake up only a single thread. An example is a *thread pool*.

The search server currently uses a single thread to process incoming requests. Clients eventually get the results of their search in an asynchronous fashion. While this may be fine for a small number of requests, clients could end up waiting quite a while if a number of other clients have requested searches ahead of them.

You might consider spawning each search request off in a new, separate thread as it arrives. However, each Java thread you create and start carries with it significant overhead costs. Creating one thread for each of thousands of search requests would result in severe performance problems. The Java thread scheduler would spend more time context-switching between threads than it would processing each thread.

A thread pool collects an arbitrary, smaller number of worker Thread objects that it creates and starts running. As a search comes in, you pass it off to the pool. The pool adds the work to the end of a queue, then issues a notify message. Any worker thread that has completed its work checks the queue for any pending tasks. If no tasks are available, the worker thread sits in an idle state by blocking on a wait call. If there are idle threads, the notify message will wake up one of them. The awakened worker thread can then grab and process the next available piece of work.

Locks and Conditions

J2SE 5.0 introduces a new, more flexible mechanism for obtaining locks on objects. The interface java.util.concurrent.locks.Lock allows you to associate one or more conditions with a lock. Different types of locks exist. For example, the ReadWriteLock implementation allows one thread to write to a shared resource, while allowing multiple threads to read from the same resource. You can also add fairness rules to a reentrant lock to do things like allow threads waiting the longest to obtain the lock first. Refer to the API documentation for details.

The listing of ClockTest shows how you would replace the use of synchronization with the new lock idiom.

```
package sis.clock;

import java.util.*;
import java.util.concurrent.locks.*;

import junit.framework.*;

public class ClockTest extends TestCase {
    private Clock clock;
    private Lock lock;
    private Condition receivedEnoughTics;

    protected void setUp() {
        lock = new ReentrantLock();
        receivedEnoughTics = lock.newCondition();
    }

    public void testClock() throws Exception {
        final int seconds = 2;
        final List<Date> tics = new ArrayList<Date>();
        ClockListener listener = createClockListener(tics, seconds);
```

```
        clock = new Clock(listener);
        lock.lock();
        try {
            receivedEnoughTics.await();
        }
        finally {
            lock.unlock();
        }
        clock.stop();
        verify(tics, seconds);
    }

    private ClockListener createClockListener(
            final List<Date> tics, final int seconds) {
        return new ClockListener() {
            private int count = 0;
            public void update(Date date) {
                tics.add(date);
                if (++count == seconds) {
                    lock.lock();
                    try {
                        receivedEnoughTics.signalAll();
                    }
                    finally {
                        lock.unlock();
                    }
                }
            }
        };
    }
    ...
}
```

The modified and slightly refactored implementation of ClockTest uses a ReentrantLock implementation of the Lock interface. A thread interested in accessing a shared resource sends the message lock to a ReentrantLock object. Once the thread obtains the lock, other threads attempt to lock the block until the first thread releases the lock. A thread releases the lock by sending unlock to a Lock object. You should always ensure an unlock occurs by using a try-finally block.

The shared resource in ClockTest is the Condition object. You obtain a Condition object from a Lock by sending it the message newCondition (see the setUp method). Once you have a Condition object, you can block on it by using await. As with the wait method, code in await releases the lock and suspends the current thread.[12] Code in another thread signals that the condition has been met by sending the Condition object the message signal or signalAll.

[12]Which suggests you may not need to enclose an await call in a try-finally block. Don't risk it—you can't guarantee that something won't go awry with the code in await.

Coupled with the use of Condition objects, the idiom shown in ClockTest effectively replaces the classic wait/notify scheme.

Thread Priorities

Threads can specify different priority levels. The scheduler uses a thread's priority as a suggestion for how often the thread should get attention. The main thread that executes has a default priority assigned to it, Thread.NORM_PRIORITY. A priority is an integer, bounded by Thread.MIN_PRIORITY on the low end and Thread.MAX_PRIORITY on the high end.

You might use a lower priority for a thread that executes in the background. In contrast, you might use a higher priority for user interface code that needs to be extremely responsive. Generally, you will want to deviate from NORM_PRIORITY only by small amounts, such as +1 and −1. Deviating by large amounts can create applications that perform poorly, with some threads dominating and others starving for attention.

Every thread (other than the main thread) starts with the same priority as the thread that spawned it. You can send a thread the message setPriority to specify a different priority.

The following snippet of code from the Clock class shows how you might set the priority for the clock to a slightly lower value.

```
public void run() {
    Thread.currentThread().setPriority(Thread.NORM_PRIORITY - 1);
    long lastTime = System.currentTimeMillis();
    while (run) {
        try { Thread.sleep(10); }
        catch (InterruptedException e) {}
        long now = System.currentTimeMillis();
        if ((now / 1000) - (lastTime / 1000) >= 1) {
            listener.update(new Date(now));
            lastTime = now;
        }
    }
}
```

Note use of the currentThread static method, which you can always call to obtain the Thread object that represents the thread that is currently executing.

Deadlocks

If you are not careful in coding multithreaded applications, you can encounter deadlocks, which will bring your system to a screeching halt. Suppose you have an object *alpha* running in one thread and an object *beta* running in another thread. *Alpha* executes a synchronized method (which by definition holds a lock on *alpha*) that calls a synchronized method defined on *beta*. If at the same time *beta* is executing a synchronized method, and this method in turn calls a synchronized method on *alpha*, each thread will wait for the other thread to relinquish its lock before proceeding. Deadlock![13]

Solutions for resolving deadlock:

1. Order the objects to be locked and ensure the locks are acquired in this order.

2. Use a common object to lock.

ThreadLocal

You may have a need to store separate information along with each thread that executes. Java provides a class named ThreadLocal that manages creating and accessing a separate instance, per thread, of any type.

When you interact with a database through JDBC,[14] you obtain a Connection object that manages communication between your application and the database. It is not safe for more than one thread to work with a single connection object, however. One classic use of ThreadLocal is to allow each thread to contain a separate Connection object.

However, you've not learned about JDBC yet. For your example, I'll define an alternate use for ThreadLocal.

In this example, you'll take the existing Server class and add logging capabilities to it. You want each thread to track when the search started and when it completed. You also want the start and stop message pairs for a search to appear together in the log. You could store a message for each event (start and stop) in a common thread-safe list stored in Server. But if several threads were to add messages to this common list, the messages would interleave. You'd probably see all the start log events first, then all the stop log events.

---

[13][Arnold2000].

[14]The Java DataBase Connectivity API. See Additional Lesson III for further information.

To solve this problem, you can have each thread store its own log messages in a ThreadLocal variable. When the thread completes, you can obtain a lock and add all the messages at once to the complete log.

First, modify the Server class to create a new thread for each Search request. This should boost the performance in most environments, but you do want to be careful how many threads you let execute simultaneously. (You might experiment with the number of searches the test kicks off to see what the limits are for your environment.) You may want to consider a thread pool as mentioned in the section Additional Notes on wait and notify.

```
private void execute(final Search search) {
    new Thread(new Runnable() {
        public void run() {
            search.execute();
            listener.executed(search);
        }
    }).start();
}
```

Thread/Local

Ensure that your tests still run successfully. Next, let's refactor ServerTest—significantly. You want to add a new test that verifies the logged messages. The current code is a bit of a mess, and it has a fairly long and involved test. For the second test, you will want to reuse most of the nonassertion code from testSearch. The refactored code also simplifies a bit of the performance testing.

Here is the refactored test that includes a new test, testLogs.

```
package sis.search;

import junit.framework.*;
import java.util.*;
import sis.util.*;

public class ServerTest extends TestCase {
    // ...
    public void testSearch() throws Exception {
        long start = System.currentTimeMillis();
        executeSearches();
        long elapsed = System.currentTimeMillis() - start;
        assertTrue(elapsed < 20);
        waitForResults();
    }

    public void testLogs() throws Exception {
        executeSearches();
        waitForResults();
        verifyLogs();
    }
```

ThreadLocal

```
private void executeSearches() throws Exception {
    for (String url: URLS)
        server.add(new Search(url, "xxx"));
}

private void waitForResults() {
    long start = System.currentTimeMillis();
    while (numberOfResults < URLS.length) {
        try { Thread.sleep(1); }
        catch (InterruptedException e) {}
        if (System.currentTimeMillis() - start > TIMEOUT)
            fail("timeout");
    }
}

private void verifyLogs() {
    List<String> list = server.getLog();
    assertEquals(URLS.length * 2, list.size());
    for (int i = 0; i < URLS.length; i += 2)
        verifySameSearch(list.get(i), list.get(i + 1));
}

private void verifySameSearch(
        String startSearchMsg, String endSearchMsg) {
    String startSearch = substring(startSearchMsg, Server.START_MSG);
    String endSearch = substring(endSearchMsg, Server.END_MSG);
    assertEquals(startSearch, endSearch);
}

private String substring(String string, String upTo) {
    int endIndex = string.indexOf(upTo);
    assertTrue("didn't find " + upTo + " in " + string,
        endIndex != -1);
    return string.substring(0, endIndex);
}
}
```

The method testLogs executes the searches, waits for them to complete, and verifies the logs. To verify the logs, the test requests the complete log from the Server object, then loops through the log, extracting a pair of lines at a time. It verifies that the search string (the first part of the log message) is the same in each pair of lines.[15]

The modifications to the Server class:

```
package sis.search;

import java.util.concurrent.*;
import java.util.*;
```

---

[15]See Lesson 8 for an in-depth discussion of Java logging and a discussion of whether or not it is necessary to test logging code.

```
public class Server extends Thread {
    private BlockingQueue<Search> queue =
        new LinkedBlockingQueue<Search>();
    private ResultsListener listener;
    static final String START_MSG = "started";
    static final String END_MSG = "finished";

    private static ThreadLocal<List<String>> threadLog =
        new ThreadLocal<List<String>>() {
            protected List<String> initialValue() {
                return new ArrayList<String>();
            }
        };
    private List<String> completeLog =
        Collections.synchronizedList(new ArrayList<String>());
    // ...
    public List<String> getLog() {
        return completeLog;
    }

    private void execute(final Search search) {
        new Thread(new Runnable() {
            public void run() {
                log(START_MSG, search);
                search.execute();
                log(END_MSG, search);
                listener.executed(search);
                completeLog.addAll(threadLog.get());
            }
        }).start();
    }

    private void log(String message, Search search) {
        threadLog.get().add(
            search + " " + message + " at " + new Date());
    }
    // ...
}
```

ThreadLocal

You declare a ThreadLocal object by binding it to the type of object you want stored in each thread. Here, threadLog is bound to a List of String objects. The threadLog ThreadLocal instance will internally manage a List of String objects for each separate thread.

You can't simply assign an initial value to threadLog, since each of the List objects it manages need to be initialized. Instead, ThreadLocal provides an initialValue method that you can override. The first time each thread gets its ThreadLocal instance via threadLog, code in the ThreadLocal class calls the initialValue method. Overriding this method provides you with the opportunity to consistently initialize the list.

ThreadLocal defines three additional methods: get, set, and remove. The get and set methods allow you to access the current thread's ThreadLocal instance. The remove method allows you to remove the current thread's Thread-Local instance, perhaps to save on memory space.

In the search thread's run method, you call the log method before and after executing the search. In the log method, you access the current thread's copy of the log list by calling the get method on threadLog. You then add a pertinent log string to the list.

Once the search thread completes, you want to add the thread's log to the complete log. Since you've instantiated completeLog as a synchronized collection, you can send it the addAll method to ensure that all lines in the thread log are added as a whole. Without synchronization, another thread could add its log lines, resulting in an interleaved complete log.

The Timer Class

 You want to continually monitor a web site over time to see if it contains the search terms you specify. You're interested in checking every several minutes or perhaps every several seconds.

The test testRepeatedSearch in SearchSchedulerTest shows the intent of how this search monitor should work: Create a scheduler and pass to it a search plus an interval representing how often to run the search. The test mechanics involve waiting for a set period of time once the scheduler has started and then verifying that the expected number of searches are executed within that time.

```
package sis.search;

import junit.framework.*;
import sis.util.*;

public class SearchSchedulerTest extends TestCase {
   private int actualResultsCount = 0;

   protected void setUp() throws Exception {
      TestUtil.delete(SearchTest.FILE);
      LineWriter.write(SearchTest.FILE, SearchTest.TEST_HTML);
   }

   protected void tearDown() throws Exception {
      TestUtil.delete(SearchTest.FILE);
   }

   public void testRepeatedSearch() throws Exception {
      final int searchInterval = 3000;
```

```
Search search = new Search(SearchTest.URL, "xxx");

ResultsListener listener = new ResultsListener() {
    public void executed(Search search) {
        ++actualResultsCount;
    }};

SearchScheduler scheduler = new SearchScheduler(listener);
scheduler.repeat(search, searchInterval);

final int expectedResultsCount = 3;
Thread.sleep((expectedResultsCount - 1) * searchInterval + 1000);

scheduler.stop();
assertEquals(expectedResultsCount, actualResultsCount);
    }
}
```

The Timer Class

The SearchScheduler class, below, uses the java.util.Timer class as the basis for scheduling and executing searches. Once you have created a Timer instance, you can call one of a handful of methods to schedule TimerTasks. A TimerTask is an abstract class that implements the Runnable interface. You supply the details on what the task does by subclassing TimerTask and implementing the run method.

In SearchScheduler, you use the method scheduleAtFixedRate, which you pass a TimerTask, a delay before start of 0 milliseconds, and an interval (currently specified by the test) in milliseconds. Every *interval* milliseconds, the Timer object wakes up and sends the run message to the task. This is known as fixed-rate execution.

When you use fixed-rate execution,[16] the Timer does its best to ensure that tasks are run every *interval* milliseconds. If a task takes longer than the interval, the Timer tries to execute tasks more tightly together to ensure that they finish before each interval is up. You can also use one of the delayed-rate execution methods, in which the case the interval from the end of one search to the next remains consistent.

You can cancel both timers and timer tasks via the cancel method.

```
package sis.search;

import java.util.*;

public class SearchScheduler {
    private ResultsListener listener;
    private Timer timer;
```

---

[16][Sun2004b].

```
public SearchScheduler(ResultsListener listener) {
    this.listener = listener;
}

public void repeat(final Search search, long interval) {
    timer = new Timer();
    TimerTask task = new TimerTask() {
        public void run() {
            search.execute();
            listener.executed(search);
        }
    };
    timer.scheduleAtFixedRate(task, 0, interval);
}

public void stop() {
    timer.cancel();
}
}
```

Thread
Miscellany

Thread Miscellany

Atomic Variables and `volatile`

Java compilers try to optimize as much code as possible. For example, if you assign an initial value to a field outside of a loop:

```
private String prefix;
void show() throws Exception {
    prefix = ":";
    for (int i = 0; i < 100; i++) {
        System.out.print(prefix + i);
        Thread.sleep(1);
    }
}
```

the Java compiler *may* figure that the value of the prefix field is fixed for the duration of the show method. It *may* optimize the code to treat the use of prefix within the loop as a constant. Java thus *may not* bother reading the value of prefix with each iteration through the loop. This is an appropriate assumption, as long as no other code (in a multithread execution) updates the value of prefix at the same time. But if another thread does modify prefix, code in the loop here may never see the changed value.[17]

---

[17]The actual behavior may depend on your compiler, JVM, and processor configuration.

You can force Java to always read a fresh value for a field by enclosing access to it in a synchronized block. Java uses this awareness that the code could be executing in multiple threads to ensure that it always gets the latest value for all fields contained within. Another way to get Java to read a fresh value is to declare the field as volatile. Doing so essentially tells the compiler that it cannot optimize access to the field.

When you use a shared boolean variable as the conditional for a thread's run loop, you may want to declare the boolean variable as volatile. This will ensure that the while loop reads the updated value of the boolean each time through the loop.

A related consideration is how Java treats common access to fields accessed from multiple threads. Java guarantees that reading or writing a variable—with the exception of a long or double variable—is *atomic*. This means that the smallest possible operation against the variable is to read or write its entire value. It is not possible for one thread to write a portion of the variable while another thread is writing another portion, which would corrupt the variable.

Thread Information

As mentioned earlier, you can obtain the Thread object for the currently executing thread by using the Thread static method currentThread. The Thread object contains a number of useful methods for obtaining information about the thread. Refer to the Java API documentation for a list of these getter and query methods. Additionally, using setName and getName, you can set and retrieve an arbitrary name for the thread.

Shutting Down

The main thread in an executing application is by default a *user thread*. As long as there is at least one active user thread, your application will continue to execute. In contrast, you can explicitly designate a thread as a *daemon thread*. If all user threads have terminated, the application will terminate as well, even if daemon threads continue to execute.

The ThreadTest example demonstrates this behavior with respect to user threads. The code executing in main runs in a user thread. Any threads spawned inherit the execution mode (user, or daemon) of the thread that spawned them, so thread t in the example is a user thread.

```
public class ThreadTest {
    public static void main(String[] args) throws Exception {
        Thread t = new Thread() {
```

```
        public void run() {
            while (true)
                System.out.print('.');
        }
    };
    t.start();
    Thread.sleep(100);
    }
}
```

When you execute ThreadTest, it will not stop until you force termination of the process (Ctrl-c usually works from the command line).

Setting a Thread object to execute as a daemon thread is as simple as sending it the message setDaemon with a parameter value of true. You must set the thread execution mode prior to starting the thread. Once a thread has started, you cannot change its execution mode.

```
public class ThreadTest {
    public static void main(String[] args) throws Exception {
        Thread t = new Thread() {
            public void run() {
                while (true)
                    System.out.print('.');
            }
        };
        t.setDaemon(true);
        t.start();
        Thread.sleep(100);
    }
}
```

You can forcibly exit an application, regardless of whether any user threads remain alive or not, by calling the System static method exit. (The Runtime class has an equivalent method.)

```
public class ThreadTest {
    public static void main(String[] args) throws Exception {
        Thread t = new Thread() {
            public void run() {
                while (true)
                    System.out.print('.');
            }
        };
        t.start();
        Thread.sleep(100);
        Runtime.getRuntime().exit(0);
        //System.exit(0);  // this will also work
    }
}
```

The exit method requires you to pass it an int value. This value represents the application return code, which you can use to control shell scripts or batch files.

In many applications, such as Swing applications, you will not have control over other threads that are spawned. Swing itself executes code in threads. More often than not, threads end up being initiated as user threads. Accordingly, you may need to use the exit method to terminate a Swing application.

Managing Exceptions

When a run method throws an (unchecked[18]) exception, the thread in which it is running terminates. Additionally, the exception object itself disappears. You may wish to capture the exception, as ServerTest.testException suggests.

```
public void testException() throws Exception {
    final String errorMessage = "problem";
    Search faultySearch = new Search(URLS[0], "") {
        public void execute() {
            throw new RuntimeException(errorMessage);
        }
    };
    server.add(faultySearch);
    waitForResults(1);
    List<String> log = server.getLog();
    assertTrue(log.get(0).indexOf(errorMessage) != -1);
}

private void waitForResults() {
    waitForResults(URLS.length);
}

private void waitForResults(int count) {
    long start = System.currentTimeMillis();
    while (numberOfResults < count) {
        try { Thread.sleep(1); }
        catch (InterruptedException e) {}
        if (System.currentTimeMillis() - start > TIMEOUT)
            fail("timeout");
    }
}
```

The test uses a mock override of the Search execute method to simulate a RuntimeException being thrown. Your expectation is that this exception will

---

[18]Since the Runnable run method signature declares no exceptions, you cannot override it to throw any checked exceptions.

be logged to the Server as a failed search. Here is the Server class implementation:

```
private void execute(final Search search) {
    Thread thread = new Thread(new Runnable() {
        public void run() {
            log(START_MSG, search);
            search.execute();
            log(END_MSG, search);
            listener.executed(search);
            completeLog.addAll(threadLog.get());
        }
    });
    thread.setUncaughtExceptionHandler(
        new Thread.UncaughtExceptionHandler() {
            public void uncaughtException(Thread th, Throwable thrown) {
                completeLog.add(search + " " + thrown.getMessage());
                listener.executed(search);
            }
        }
    );
    thread.start();
}
```

After creating the thread object, but before starting it, you can set an *uncaught exception handler* on the thread. You create an uncaught exception handler by implementing the method uncaughtException. If the thread throws an exception that is not caught, the uncaughtException method is called. Java passes uncaughtException both the thread and throwable objects.

Thread Groups

Thread groups provide a way to organize threads into arbitrary groups. A thread group can also contain other thread groups, allowing for a containment hierarchy. You can control all threads contained in a thread group as a unit. For example, you can send the message interrupt to a thread group, which will in turn send the interrupt message to all threads contained within the hierarchy.

In *Effective Java*, Joshua Bloch writes that thread groups "are best viewed as an unsuccessful experiment, and you may simply ignore their existence."[19] They were originally designed to facilitate security management in Java but never satisfactorily fulfilled this purpose.

Prior to J2SE 5.0, one useful purpose for thread groups was to monitor threads for uncaught exceptions. However, you can now fulfill this need by

[19][Bloch 2001].

creating an UncaughtExceptionHandler for a thread (see the previous section, Managing Exceptions).

Atomic Wrappers

Even simple arithmetic operations are not atomic. As of J2SE 5.0, Sun supplies the package java.util.concurrent.atomic. This package includes a dozen Atomic wrapper classes. Each class wraps a primitive type (int, long, or boolean), a reference, or an array. By using an atomic wrapper, you guarantee that operations on the wrapped value are thread safe and work against an up-to-date value (as if you had declared the field volatile).

Here is an example use:

```
AtomicInteger i = new AtomicInteger(50);
assertEquals(55, i.addAndGet(5));
assertEquals(55, i.get());
```

Exercises

Refer to the Java API documentation for further details.

Summary: Basic Design Principles for Synchronization

- Avoid it. Introduce synchronization only when necessary.

- Isolate it. Cluster synchronization needs into a single-responsibility class that does as little as possible. Ensure that as few clients as possible interact with a synchronized class. Ensure that as few methods as possible interact with shared data.

- Shared, or "server," classes should provide synchronization instead of depending on clients to synchronize properly.

- If a server class has not provided synchronization, consider writing a "wrapper" class that adds synchronization and delegates all messages to the server class.

- Use the synchronization class library located in java.util.concurrent.

Exercises

1. Create an AlarmClock class. A client can submit a single event and corresponding time. When the time passes, the AlarmClock sends an alarm to the client.

2. Eliminate the wait loop in AlarmClockTest (from the previous exercise) by using wait and notify.

3. Modify the alarm clock to support multiple alarms (if it doesn't already). Then add the ability to cancel an alarm by name. Write a test that demonstrates the ability to cancel the alarm. Then analyze your code and note the potential for synchronization issues. Introduce a pause in the production code to force the issue and get your test to fail. Finally, introduce synchronization blocks or modify methods to be synchronized as necessary to fix the problem.

4. Change the run method in AlarmClock to use a timer to check for alarms every half-second.

Lesson 14

Generics

I introduced you to parameterized types in Lesson 2. This lesson covers parameterized types, or generics, in depth. You will learn the many rules behind creating parameterized types. Creating parameterized types is probably tied with multithreading as the most complex topic in core Java programming.

You will learn about:

- creating parameterized types

- multiple type parameters

- the erasure scheme

- upper bounds (extends)

- wildcards

- generic methods

- lower bounds (super)

- additional bounds

- raw types

- checked collections

Parameterized Types

You generally develop a collection so that it can contain objects of any type. However, in most cases, collections are useful only if you constrain them to hold objects of a single (set of) types: a list of students, a words-to-definitions map, and so on. You could consider this to be the Single-Responsibility

Principle applied to collections: Collections should hold one kind of thing and one kind of thing only. You rarely want your student list to contain a stray professor. And if you included a word-to-picture entry in your map, it would create significant headaches for your dictionary application.

Sun originally developed the base collection classes in Java's class library to support storing and returning objects of any type (i.e., Object or any subclass). This meant that you could add a String object to a collection intended to store Student objects. While this sounds like an unlikely mistake, pulling an object of an unexpected type out of a collection is a frequent source of application defects. The reason is that code that stores objects into the collection is often distant from code that retrieves objects from the collection.

With the advent of J2SE 5.0, Sun introduced the concept of *parameterized types*, also known as generics. You can now associate, or *bind*, a collection instance to a specific type. You can specify that an ArrayList can only hold Student objects. Under earlier Java versions, you would receive a ClassCastException error at runtime when retrieving a String inadvertently stored in the ArrayList. Now, with parameterized types, you receive a compilation error at the point where code attempts to insert a String in the list.

Collection
Framework

Collection Framework

Sun has parameterized all collection classes in the Collections Framework. A simple language-based test demonstrates a simple use of the parameterized type ArrayList:

```
final String name = "joe";
List<String> names = new ArrayList<String>();    // 1
names.add(name);                                  // 2
String retrievedName = names.get(0);              // 3
assertEquals(name, retrievedName);
```

Both the implementation class ArrayList and the interface List are bound to the String class (line 1). You can add String objects to name (2). When retrieving from name and assigning to a String reference (3), you need not cast to String.

If you attempt to insert an object of any other type:

```
names.add(new Date()); // this won't compile!
```

the compiler will present you with an error:

```
cannot find symbol
symbol  : method add(java.util.Date)
```

```
location: interface java.util.List<java.lang.String>
     names.add(new Date()); // this won't compile!
   ^
```

Multiple Type Parameters

If you look at the API documentation for java.util.List and java.util
.ArrayList, you will see that they are declared as List<E> and ArrayList<E>,
respectively. The <E> is known as the *type parameter list*. The List interface
and ArrayList class declarations each contain a single type parameter in the
type parameter list. Therefore you must supply a single bind type when using
List or ArrayList in your code.[1]

The class HashMap represents a collection of key-value pairs. A key can
be of one type and the value could be another. For example, you might store
an appointment book in a HashMap, where the key is a Date and the value is
a String description of an event occurring on that date.

```
final String event = "today";
final Date date = new Date();
Map<Date, String> events = new HashMap<Date, String>();
events.put(date, event);
String retrievedEvent = events.get(date);
assertEquals(event, retrievedEvent);
```

The Map interface and HashMap class are declared as Map<K,V> and
HashMap<K,V>, respectively. You must supply two bind types when using
these—one for the key (K) and one for the value (V).

Creating
Parameterized
Types

Creating Parameterized Types

You will develop a parameterized MultiHashMap. A MultiHashMap is similar to a HashMap, except that it allows you to associate multiple values with
a given key. Let's expand on the calendar example: Some people lead particularly interesting lives, in which two events might occur on one day.

A few starter tests will get you off the ground. Remember that you should
be developing incrementally, one test method and one assertion at a time.

---

[1]You are not required to supply any bind types; however, this is not recommended.
See the section in this lesson entitled Raw Types.

```
package sis.util;

import junit.framework.*;
import java.util.*;

public class MultiHashMapTest extends TestCase {
    private static final Date today = new Date();
    private static final Date tomorrow =
        new Date(today.getTime() + 86400000);
    private static final String eventA = "wake up";
    private static final String eventB = "eat";

    private MultiHashMap<Date,String> events;
    protected void setUp() {
        events = new MultiHashMap<Date,String>();
    }

    public void testCreate() {
        assertEquals(0, events.size());
    }

    public void testSingleEntry() {
        events.put(today, eventA);
        assertEquals(1, events.size());
        assertEquals(eventA, getSoleEvent(today));
    }

    public void testMultipleEntriesDifferentKey() {
        events.put(today, eventA);
        events.put(tomorrow, eventB);
        assertEquals(2, events.size());
        assertEquals(eventA, getSoleEvent(today));
        assertEquals(eventB, getSoleEvent(tomorrow));
    }

    public void testMultipleEntriesSameKey() {
        events.put(today, eventA);
        events.put(today, eventB);
        assertEquals(1, events.size());
        Collection<String> retrievedEvents = events.get(today);
        assertEquals(2, retrievedEvents.size());
        assertTrue(retrievedEvents.contains(eventA));
        assertTrue(retrievedEvents.contains(eventB));
    }

    private String getSoleEvent(Date date) {
        Collection<String> retrievedEvents = events.get(date);
        assertEquals(1, retrievedEvents.size());
        Iterator<String> it = retrievedEvents.iterator();
        return it.next();
    }
}
```

Creating
Parameterized
Types

The method getSoleEvent is of some interest. After retrieving the events collection stored at a date using the Map method get, you must ensure that it contains only one element. To retrieve the sole element, you can create an iterator and return the first element it points to. You must bind the Iterator object to the same type that you bound the collection to (String in this example).

From an implementation standpoint, there is more than one way to build a MultiHashMap. The easiest is to use a HashMap where each key is associated with a collection of values. For this example, you will define MultiHashMap to encapsulate and use a HashMap.

In order to support the existing tests, the implementation of MultiHashMap is simplistic. Each method size, put, and get will delegate to the encapsulated HashMap:

```java
package sis.util;

import java.util.*;

public class MultiHashMap<K,V> {
   private Map<K,List<V>> map = new HashMap<K,List<V>>();

   public int size() {
      return map.size();
   }

   public void put(K key, V value) {
      List<V> values = map.get(key);
      if (values == null) {
         values = new ArrayList<V>();
         map.put(key, values);
      }
      values.add(value);
   }

   public List<V> get(K key) {
      return map.get(key);
   }
}
```

The put method first extracts a list from map using the key passed in. If there is no entry at the key, the method constructs a new ArrayList bound to the value type V and puts this list into map. Regardless, value is added to the list.

Like HashMap, the type parameter list contains two type parameters, K and V. Throughout the definition for MultiHashMap, you will see these symbols where you might expect to see type names. For example, the get method returns V instead of, say, Object. Each use of a type parameter symbol within the type declaration is known as a *naked type variable*.

At compile time, each occurrence of a naked type variable is replaced with the appropriate type of the corresponding type parameter. You'll see how this actually works in the next section, Erasure.

In the definition of the `map` field (highlighted in bold), you construct a HashMap object and bind it to <K,List<V>>. The key for `map` is the same type and the one to which the key of MultiHashMap is bound (K). The value for `map` is a List bound to type V—the value type to which the MultiHashMap is bound.

Bind parameters correspond to type parameters. The test contains this instantiation of MultiHashMap in its `setUp` method:

```
events = new MultiHashMap<Date,String>();
```

The Date type corresponds to the type parameter K, and the String type corresponds to the type parameter V. Thus, the embedded `map` field would be a HashMap<Date,List<String>>—a hash map whose key is bound to a date and whose value is bound to a list of strings.

Erasure

There is more than one way that Sun might have chosen to implement support for parameterized types. One possible way would have been to create a brand-new type definition for each type to which you bind a parameterized class. In binding to a type, each occurrence of a naked type variable in the source would be replaced with the bind type. This technique is used by C++.

For example, were Java to use this scheme, binding MultiHashMap to <Date,String> would result in the following code being created behind the scenes:

```java
// THIS ISN'T HOW JAVA TRANSLATES GENERICS:
package sis.util;

import java.util.*;

public class MultiHashMap<Date,String> {
    private Map<Date,List<String>> map =
        new HashMap<Date,List<String>>();

    public int size() {
        return map.size();
    }

    public void put(Date key, String value) {
        List<String> values = map.get(key);
```

```
      if (values == null) {
         values = new ArrayList<String>();
         map.put(key, values);
      }
      values.add(value);
   }

   public List<String> get(Date key) {
      return map.get(key);
   }
}
```

Binding MultiHashMap to another pair of types, such as <String,String>, would result in the compiler creating another version of MultiHashMap. Using this scheme could potentially result in the compiler creating dozens of class variants for MultiHashMap.

Java uses a different scheme called *erasure*. Instead of creating separate type definitions, Java erases the parameterized type information to create a single equivalent type. Each type parameter is associated with a constraint known as its *upper bound*, which is java.lang.Object by default. Client bind information is erased and replaced with casts as appropriate. The MultiHashMap class would translate to:

Erasure

```
package sis.util;

import java.util.*;

public class MultiHashMap {
   private Map map = new HashMap();

   public int size() {
      return map.size();
   }

   public void put(Object key, Object value) {
      List values = (List)map.get(key);
      if (values == null) {
         values = new ArrayList();
         map.put(key, values);
      }
      values.add(value);
   }

   public List get(Object key) {
      return (List)map.get(key);
   }
}
```

Knowing how parameterized types work behind the scenes is critical to being able to understand and use them effectively. Java contains a number of restrictions on the use of parameterized types that exist because of the erasure scheme. I'll discuss these limitations throughout this chapter. Each possible scheme for implementing generics has its downsides. Sun chose the erasure scheme for its ability to provide ultimate backward compatibility.

Upper Bounds

As mentioned, every type parameter has a default upper bound of Object. You can constrain a type parameter to a different upper bound. For example, you might want to supply an EventMap class, where the key must be bound to a Date type—either java.util.Date or java.sql.Date (which is a subclass of java.util.Date). A simple test:

```
package sis.util;

import junit.framework.*;
import java.util.*;

public class EventMapTest extends TestCase {
    public void testSingleElement() {
        EventMap<java.sql.Date,String> map =
            new EventMap<java.sql.Date,String>();
        final java.sql.Date date =
            new java.sql.Date(new java.util.Date().getTime());
        final String value = "abc";
        map.put(date, value);

        List<String> values = map.get(date);
        assertEquals(value, values.get(0));
    }
}
```

The EventMap class itself has no different behavior, only additional constraints on the type parameter K:

```
package sis.util;

public class EventMap<K extends java.util.Date,V>
    extends MultiHashMap<K,V> {
}
```

You use the extends keyword to specify the upper bound for a type parameter. In this example, the K type parameter for EventMap has an upper bound of java.util.Date. Code using an EventMap must bind the key to a java.util.Date or a subclass of java.util.Date (such as java.sql.Date). If you attempt to do otherwise:

```
EventMap<String,String> map = new EventMap<String,String>();
```

you will receive compile-time errors:

```
type parameter java.lang.String is not within its bound
EventMap<String,String> map = new EventMap<String,String>();
          ^
type parameter java.lang.String is not within its bound
EventMap<String,String> map = new EventMap<String,String>();
                                                    ^
```

The compiler replaces naked type variables in generated code with the upper bound type. This gives you the ability to send more specific messages to naked type objects within the generic class.

You want the ability to extract all event descriptions from the EventMap for events where the date has passed. Code the following test in Event-MapTest.

```
public void testGetPastEvents() {
    EventMap<Date,String> events = new EventMap<Date,String>();
    final Date today = new java.util.Date();
    final Date yesterday =
        new Date(today.getTime() - 86400000);
    events.put(today, "sleep");
    final String descriptionA = "birthday";
    final String descriptionB = "drink";
    events.put(yesterday, descriptionA);
    events.put(yesterday, descriptionB);
    List<String> descriptions = events.getPastEvents();
    assertTrue(descriptions.contains(descriptionA));
    assertTrue(descriptions.contains(descriptionB));
}
```

Upper Bounds

Within EventMap, you can presume that objects of type K are Date objects:

```
package sis.util;

import java.util.*;

public class EventMap<K extends Date,V>
    extends MultiHashMap<K,V> {
    public List<V> getPastEvents() {
        List<V> events = new ArrayList<V>();
        for (Map.Entry<K,List<V>> entry: entrySet()) {
            K date = entry.getKey();
            if (hasPassed(date))
                events.addAll(entry.getValue());
        }
        return events;
    }

    private boolean hasPassed(K date) {
        Calendar when = new GregorianCalendar();
```

```
    when.setTime(date);
    Calendar today = new GregorianCalendar();
    if (when.get(Calendar.YEAR) != today.get(Calendar.YEAR))
        return when.get(Calendar.YEAR) < today.get(Calendar.YEAR);
    return when.get(Calendar.DAY_OF_YEAR) <
        today.get(Calendar.DAY_OF_YEAR);
  }
}
```

In order to accomplish this, you'll have to add a method to Multi-HashMap to return the entrySet from the encapsulated map:

```
protected Set<Map.Entry<K,List<V>>> entrySet() {
    return map.entrySet();
}
```

The entrySet method returns a set bound to the Map.Entry type. Each Map.Entry object in the Set is in turn bound to the key type (K) and a list of the value type (List<V>).

Wildcards

Sometimes you'll write a method where you don't care about the type to which a parameter is bound. Suppose you need a utility method that creates a single string by concatenating elements in a list, separating the printable representation of each element with a new line. The StringUtilTest method testConcatenateList demonstrates this need:

```
package sis.util;

import junit.framework.*;
import java.util.*;

public class StringUtilTest extends TestCase {
    ...
    public void testConcatenateList() {
        List<String> list = new ArrayList<String>();
        list.add("a");
        list.add("b");

        String output = StringUtil.concatenate(list);

        assertEquals(String.format("a%nb%n"), output);
    }
}
```

In the StringUtil method concatenate, you will append each list element's string representation to a StringBuilder. You can get the string representation of any object, provided by the toString method, without knowing or caring about its type. Thus, you want to be able to pass a List that is bound to any type as the argument to concatenate.

You might think that you can bind the list parameter to Object:

```
// this won't work
public static String concatenate(List<Object> list) {
   StringBuilder builder = new StringBuilder();
   for (Object element: list)
     builder.append(String.format("%s%n", element));
   return builder.toString();
}
```

By binding list to Object, you constrain it to hold objects only of type Object—and not of any Object subclasses. *You cannot assign a List<String> reference to a List<Object> reference.* If you could, client code could add an Object to list using the List<Object> reference. Code that then attempted to extract from list using the List<String> reference would unexpectedly retrieve an Object.

Instead, Java allows you to use a *wildcard* character (?) to represent any possible type:

```
package sis.util;

import java.util.*;

public class StringUtil {
   ...
   public static String concatenate(List<?> list) {
      StringBuilder builder = new StringBuilder();
      for (Object element: list)
         builder.append(String.format("%s%n", element));
      return builder.toString();
   }
}
```

Within the concatenate method body, you cannot use the ? directly as a naked type variable. But since list can contain any type of object, you can assign each of its elements to an Object reference in the for-each loop.

Additionally, you can constrain a wildcard to an upper bound using the extends clause.

 For a second string utility method, you need to be able to concatenate a list of numerics, whether they are BigDecimal objects or Integer objects. Several tests drive out the minor differences between decimal output and integral output:

```
public void testConcatenateFormattedDecimals() {
    List<BigDecimal> list = new ArrayList<BigDecimal>();
    list.add(new BigDecimal("3.1416"));
    list.add(new BigDecimal("-1.4142"));

    String output = StringUtil.concatenateNumbers(list, 3);
    assertEquals(String.format("3.142%n-1.414%n"), output);
}

public void testConcatenateFormattedIntegers() {
    List<Integer> list = new ArrayList<Integer>();
    list.add(12);
    list.add(17);

    String output = StringUtil.concatenateNumbers(list, 0);
    assertEquals(String.format("12%n17%n"), output);
}
```

The implementation in StringUtil:

```
public static String concatenateNumbers(
        List<? extends Number> list, int decimalPlaces) {
    String decimalFormat = "%." + decimalPlaces + "f";
    StringBuilder builder = new StringBuilder();
    for (Number element: list) {
        double value = element.doubleValue();
        builder.append(String.format(decimalFormat + "%n", value));
    }
    return builder.toString();
}
```

Implications of Using Wildcards

You'll need to import java.math.* to get the above code to compile.

The declaration of the list parameter in concatenateNumbers specifies that it is a List bound to either Number or a subclass of Number. The code in concatenateNumbers can then assign each element in list to a Number reference.

Implications of Using Wildcards

The downside of using a wildcard on a reference is that you cannot call methods on it that take an object of the type parameter. For example, suppose you create a pad utility method that can add an element n times to the end of a list.

```
package sis.util;

import java.util.*;
import junit.framework.*;
```

```
public class ListUtilTest extends TestCase {
    public void testPad() {
        final int count = 5;
        List<Date> list = new ArrayList<Date>();
        final Date element = new Date();
        ListUtil.pad(list, element, count);
        assertEquals(count, list.size());
        for (int i = 0; i < count; i++)
            assertEquals("unexpected element at " + i,
                element, list.get(i));
    }
}
```

The pad method declares the list parameter to be a List that can be bound to any type:

```
package sis.util;

import java.util.*;

public class ListUtil {
    public static void pad(List<?> list, Object object, int count) {
        for (int i = 0; i < count; i++)
            list.add(object);
    }
}
```

Implications of
Using Wildcards

The error you receive indicates that the compiler doesn't recognize an appropriate add method.

```
cannot find symbol
symbol   : method add(java.lang.Object)
location: interface java.util.List<?>
         list.add(object);
             ^
```

The problem is that the wildcard ? designates an unknown type. Suppose that the List is bound to a Date:

```
List<Date> list = new ArrayList<Date>();
```

Then you attempt to pass a String to the pad method:

```
ListUtil.pad(list, "abc", count);
```

The pad method doesn't know anything about the specific type of the object being passed in, nor does it know anything about the type to which the list is bound. It can't guarantee that a client isn't trying to subvert the type safety of the list. Java just won't allow you to do this.

There is still a problem even if you specify an upper bound on the wildcard.

```
public static void pad(
    List<? extends Date> list, Date date, int count) {
  for (int i = 0; i < count; i++)
    list.add(date);  // this won't compile
}
```

The problem is that a client could bind the list to java.sql.Date:

```
List<java.sql.Date> list = new ArrayList<java.sql.Date>();
```

Since java.util.Date is a superclass ofjava.sql.Date, you cannot add it to a list that is constrained to hold only objects of type java.sql.Date or a subclass of java.sql.Date. Due to erasure, Java has no way of figuring out whether or not a given operation is safe, so it must prohibit them all. The general rule of thumb is that you can use bounded wildcards only when reading from a data structure.

Generic Methods

How *do* you solve the above problem? You can declare the pad method as a *generic method*. Just as you can specify type parameters for a class, you can specify type parameters that exist for the scope of a method:

```
public static <T> void pad(List<T> list, T object, int count) {
  for (int i = 0; i < count; i++)
    list.add(object);
}
```

The compile can extract, or infer, the type for T based on the arguments passed to pad. It uses the most specific type that it can infer from the arguments. Your test should now pass.

Generic method type parameters can also have upper bounds.

You will need to use generic methods when you have a dependency between an argument to a method and either another argument or the return type. Otherwise, you should prefer the use of wildcards. In the pad method declaration, the object parameter's type is dependent upon the type of the list parameter.

Wildcard Capture

The technique of introducing a generic method to solve the above problem is known as wildcard capture. Another example is a simple method that swaps the elements of a list from front to back.

```
public void testWildcardCapture() {
    List<String> names = new ArrayList<String>();
    names.add("alpha");
    names.add("beta");
    inPlaceReverse(names);
    assertEquals("beta", names.get(0));
    assertEquals("alpha", names.get(1));
}

static void inPlaceReverse(List<?> list) {
    int size = list.size();
    for (int i = 0; i < size / 2; i++) {
        int opposite = size - 1 - i;
        Object temp = list.get(i);
        list.set(i, list.get(opposite));
        list.set(opposite, temp);
    }
}
```

The wildcard capture involves calling a new generic method, swap:

```
public void testWildcardCapture() {
    List<String> names = new ArrayList<String>();
    names.add("alpha");
    names.add("beta");
    inPlaceReverse(names);
    assertEquals("beta", names.get(0));
    assertEquals("alpha", names.get(1));
}

static void inPlaceReverse(List<?> list) {
    int size = list.size();
    for (int i = 0; i < size / 2; i++)
        swap(list, i, size - 1 - i);
}

private static <T> void swap(List<T> list, int i, int opposite) {
    T temp = list.get(i);
    list.set(i, list.get(opposite));
    list.set(opposite, temp);
}
```

By doing so, you are giving the wildcard a name.

Super

Upper-bounded wildcards, which you specify using extends, are useful for *reading from* a data structure. You can support *writing to* a data structure using lower-bounded wildcards.

You want to be able to create a new MultiHashMap from an existing MultiHashMap. The new map is a subset of the existing map.

You obtain this subset by applying a filter to the values in the existing MultiHashMap. The test shown here creates a multimap of meetings. A meeting can be a one-time event or it can be recurrent. You want to create a new multimap that consists only of meetings that occur on Mondays.

Further, the original meetings multimap consists of java.sql.Date objects. Perhaps it was directly loaded from a database application. You want the new multimap to consist of java.util.Date objects.

```java
public void testFilter() {
    MultiHashMap<String,java.sql.Date> meetings=
        new MultiHashMap<String,java.sql.Date>();

    meetings.put("iteration start", createSqlDate(2005, 9, 12));
    meetings.put("iteration start", createSqlDate(2005, 9, 26));
    meetings.put("VP blather", createSqlDate(2005, 9, 12));
    meetings.put("brown bags", createSqlDate(2005, 9, 14));

    MultiHashMap<String,java.util.Date> mondayMeetings =
        new MultiHashMap<String,java.util.Date>();
    MultiHashMap.filter(mondayMeetings, meetings,
        new MultiHashMap.Filter<java.util.Date>() {
            public boolean apply(java.util.Date date) {
                return isMonday(date);
            }
        });

    assertEquals(2, mondayMeetings.size());
    assertEquals(2, mondayMeetings.get("iteration start").size());
    assertNull(mondayMeetings.get("brown bags"));
    assertEquals(1, mondayMeetings.get("VP blather").size());
}

private boolean isMonday(Date date) {
    Calendar calendar = GregorianCalendar.getInstance();
    calendar.setTime(date);
    return calendar.get(Calendar.DAY_OF_WEEK) == Calendar.MONDAY;
}

private java.sql.Date createSqlDate(int year, int month, int day) {
    java.util.Date date = DateUtil.createDate(year, month, day);
    return new java.sql.Date(date.getTime());
}
```

You can use lower-bounded wildcards on the MultiHashMap filter method to allow transforming from java.sql.Date values to java.util.Date values. In the implementation, the target argument of the filter method is a MultiHashMap whose value type (V) has a *lower bound* of V. This is expressed as ? super V. This means that the value type (V) of the target MultiHashMap can be the same as V or a supertype of V. The meetings example works because java.util.Date is a supertype of java.sql.Date.

```
...
public class MultiHashMap <K,V> {
   private Map<K, List<V>> map = new HashMap<K, List<V>>();
   ...
   public interface Filter<T> {
      boolean apply(T item);
   }

   public static <K,V> void filter(
         final MultiHashMap<K, ? super V> target,
         final MultiHashMap<K, V> source,
         final Filter<? super V> filter) {
      for (K key : source.keys()) {
         final List<V> values = source.get(key);
         for (V value : values)
            if (filter.apply(value))
               target.put(key, value);
      }
   }
}
```

Additional Bounds

It is possible to specify additional bounds, or more than one type, in an extends clause. While the first constraint can be either a class or interface, subsequent constraints must be interface types. For example:

```
public static
   <T extends Iterable&Comparable<T>> void iterateAndCompare(T t)
```

By using additional bounds, you are constraining the parameter passed to implement more than one interface. In the example, the object passed in must implement both the Iterable and Comparable interfaces. This is not normally something you want to do; additional bounds were introduced largely to solve issues of backward compatibility (see below).

If a method requires that an object behave as two different types, it intends for that method to do two different kinds of things to that object. In most cases, this will be a violation of the Single-Responsibility Principle, which is as applicable to methods as it is to classes. There will always be exceptions, of course, but before using additional bounds for this reason, see if you can decompose the method in question.

The more legitimate reason to use additional bounds is demonstrated by code in the Collections class. The Collections class contains static utility methods for operating on collection objects; it includes a method named max that returns the largest element in a collection. Under earlier versions of Java, the signature of max was:

```
public static Object max(Collection c)
```

The passed-in collection could hold any type of object, but the max method depended upon the collection holding objects that implemented the Comparable interface. An initial stab at a solution using generics could insist that the collection hold Comparable objects:

```
public static
    <T extends Comparable<? super T>> T max(Collection<? extends T> c)
```

Paraphrased, this signature says: max takes a collection of objects of any type and that that type must implement the Comparable interface, which in turn must be bound to the type or supertype of elements stored in the collection. The problem is that after erasure, this results in a different signature for the max method:

```
public static Comparable max(Collection c)
```

Instead of returning an Object reference, max would now return a Comparable reference. The change in signature would break existing compiled code that used the max method, killing compatibility. Using additional bounds effectively solves the problem:

```
public static
    <T extends Object&Comparable<? super T>>
    T max(Collection<? extends T> c)
```

Per J2SE specification, a type variable gets erased to its leftmost bound—Object in this example, and not Comparable. The max method now returns an Object reference but also defines the additional constraint that the collection objects must implement the appropriate Comparable interface.

Raw Types

If you work with an existing system, written in J2SE 1.4 or earlier, it will use collection classes that do not support parameterization. You'll have plenty of code such as:

```
List list = new ArrayList();
list.add("a");
```

You can still use this code under J2SE 5.0. When you use a generic type without binding it to a type parameter, you refer to the type as a *raw type*. The use of raw types is inherently not typesafe: You can add objects of any type to a raw collection and encounter runtime exceptions when retrieving an object of unexpected type. This is the fundamental reason why Sun introduced parameterized types.

Any such unsafe operation is met with a warning by the compiler. Using the default compiler options, the above two lines of code that add to a raw ArrayList result in the following compiler message:

```
Note: Some input files use unchecked or unsafe operations.
Note: Recompile with -Xlint:unchecked for details.
```

Do what the message says and recompile using the VM switch -Xlint:unchecked:

```
javac -source 1.5 -Xlint:unchecked *.java
```

Under Ant, supply an additional nested element on the javac task:

```
<target name="build" depends="init" description="build all">
 <javac
     srcdir="${src.dir}" destdir="${build.dir}"
     source="1.5"
     deprecation="on" debug="on" optimize="off" includes="**">
   <classpath refid="classpath" />
   <compilerarg value="-Xlint:unchecked"/>
 </javac>
</target>
```

Recompiling will present you with more specific details on the source of each unchecked warning:

```
warning: [unchecked] unchecked call to add(E) as a member of the raw type java.util.List
     list.add("a");
         ^
```

The Java compiler will generate an unchecked warning whenever it cannot guarantee the type safety of an operation on a parameterized type. If you are developing on an existing 1.4 or older application, you'll likely receive gobs of warnings. While it may not be possible or desirable to fix all the warnings at once, you should never treat warnings lightly. If you modify a section of legacy code, attempt to introduce generic types. You should be extremely leery of warnings that arise from any new code that you add.

Checked Collections

Suppose you're working with legacy code. In fact, most systems you encounter will include code written for older versions of Java. This is the reality of Java development. I still encounter systems that make pervasive use of Vector and Hashtable—even though Sun recommended use of collections framework classes (List/ArrayList, etc.) instead as of Java 1.2. That was over six years ago!

You will likely encounter raw collections for some time coming. You can quickly add some time safety to your code by using a checked wrapper. Suppose your existing mess of a system creates a list intended to hold Integer wrapper objects:

```
List ages = new ArrayList();
```

Elsewhere in the code, in a method nested a few classes away, another bozo developer adds a new line of code:

```
ages.add("17");
```

And even further away, code in another class is responsible for extracting age values from the collection:

```
int age = ((Integer)ages.get(0)).intValue();
```

Oops! That line of legacy code results in a ClassCastException, since the first element in ages is a String, not an Integer. Sure, you will find the problem "real soon now," but you will have wasted valuable time in the process.

The best solution would be to parameterize references to ages in each of the three classes in question. Then the second developer wouldn't even be able to compile the code that inserts a string. But changing those classes might be beyond your control or there might be dozens of affected classes and not three.[2]

Sun introduced a new set of methods to the Collections class that can help solve this problem with type safety. These methods create *checked wrapper* objects. A checked wrapper object delegates off to the actual collection object, much like the unmodifiable and synchronized wrappers. A checked wrapper ensures that an object passed to the collection is of the appropriate type, preventing inappropriate objects from being inserted into the collection.

Using a checked collection will at least constrain the exception to the point of error. In other words, the code that adds the bad data will generate

---

[2]And of course none of those dozens of classes will have tests. The vast majority of legacy systems have no tests.

the exception, not the code that attempts to extract it. This will make for quicker debugging efforts. You can make the change in one place:

```
List ages = Collections.checkedList(new ArrayList(), Integer.class);
```

When the Java VM executes this line of code, you receive an exception:

```
java.lang.ClassCastException: Attempt to insert class java.lang.String element into collection
with element type class java.lang.Integer
```

A language unit test demonstrates this in toto:

```
public void testCheckedCollections() {
   List ages =
      Collections.checkedList(new ArrayList(), Integer.class);
   try {
      ages.add("17");
      fail("expected ClassCastException on invalid insert");
   }
   catch (ClassCastException success) {
   }
}
```

Checked Collections

Checked collections are not at all magical. The first argument to checkedList is the ArrayList object you are creating; it is bound to the Integer type. The second argument is a Class reference to the Integer type. Each time you invoke the add method, it uses the class reference to determine whether or not the passed parameter is of that type. If not, it throws a ClassCastException.

Checked wrappers require the redundancy of having to pass in a type (Integer.class) reference in addition to specifying a bind type (<Integer>). This is required because of erasure: the bind type information is not available to the list object at runtime. You can encapsulate unchecked wrappers in your own parameterized types, but you will then need to require clients to pass in the Class reference.

The Collection class provides checked collection wrappers for the types Collection, List, Map, Set, SortedMap, and SortedSet.

Even if you are writing J2SE 5.0 code, using checked collections can protect you from loose and fast developers beyond your sphere of influence. Some cowboy and cowgirl developers enjoy subverting the rules whenever they can. In the case of parameterized types, Java lets them.

You can cast an object of a parameterized type to a raw type. This allows you to store an object of any type in the collection. You will receive a compilation warning, but you can ignore the warning. Do so at your own peril. The results will generally be disastrous. This sort of strategy falls under the category of "don't do that!"

Using checked collections in 5.0 code can help solve this problem. The exceptions thrown will come from the sneaky code, letting you pinpoint the source of trouble.

Arrays

You cannot create arrays of bounded parameterized types:

```
List<String>[] names = new List<String>[100]; // this does not compile
```

Attempting to do so generates the compilation error:

```
arrays of generic types are not allowed
```

Again, the problem is that you could easily assign the parameterized type reference to another type reference. You could then add an inappropriate object, causing a ClassCastException upon attempted extraction:

```
// this does not compile
List<String>[] namesTable = new List<String>[100];
Object[] objects = (Object[])namesTable;
List<Integer> numbers = new ArrayList<Integer>();
numbers.add(5);
objects[0] = numbers;
String name = namesTable[0].get(0); // would be a ClassCastException
```

Java does allow you to create arrays of parameterized types that are unbounded (i.e., where you use only the wildcard character ?):

```
public void testArrays() {
    List<?>[] namesTable = new List<?>[100];
    Object[] objects = (Object[])namesTable;
    List<Integer> numbers = new ArrayList<Integer>();
    numbers.add(5);
    objects[0] = numbers;
    try {
        String name = (String)namesTable[0].get(0);
    }
    catch (ClassCastException expected) {
    }
}
```

The chief distinction is that you must acknowledge the potential for problems by casting, since the List is a collection of objects of unknown type.

Additional Limitations

Due to the erasure scheme, an object of a parameterized type has no information on the bind type. This creates a lot of implications about what you can
and cannot do.

You cannot create new objects using a naked type variable:

```
package util;

import java.util.*;

public class NumericList<T extends Number> {
   private List<T> data = new ArrayList<T>();

   public void initialize(int size) {
      data.clear();
      T zero = new T(0);  // does not compile!
      for (int i = 0; i < size; i++)
         data.add(zero);
   }
}
```

This code generates the compile error:

```
unexpected type
found   : type parameter T
required: class
      T zero = new T(0);
                   ^
```

Erasure means that a naked type variable erases to its upper bound, Number in this example. In most cases, the upper bound is an abstract class such
as Number or Object (the default), so creating objects of that type would not
be useful. Java simply prohibits it.

You can cast to a naked type variable, but for the same reason, it is not
often useful to do so. You cannot use a naked type variable as the target of
the instanceof operator.

You can use type variables in a generic static method. But you cannot use
the type variables defined by an enclosing class in static variables, static
methods, or static nested classes. Because of erasure, there is only one class
definition that is shared by all instances, regardless of the type to which they
are bound. The class definition is created at compile time. This means that
sharing static elements wouldn't work. Each client that binds the parameterized type to something different would expect to have the static member constrained to the type they specified.

Reflection

The reflection package has been retrofitted to support providing parameter information for parameterized types and methods. For example, you can send the message getTypeParameters to a class in order to retrieve an array of TypeParameter objects; each TypeParameter object provides you with enough information to be able to reconstruct the type parameters.

To support these changes, Sun altered the Java byte code specification. Class files now store additional information about type parameters. Most significant, the Class class has been modified to be a parameterized type, Class<T>. The following assignment works:

```
Class<String> klass = String.class;
```

If you're interested in how you might use this, take a look at the source for the CheckedCollection class. It's a static inner class of java.util.Collections.

The reflection modifications provide you with information on the *declaration* of parameterized types and methods. What you will *not* get from reflection is information about the binding of a type variable. If you bind an ArrayList to a String, that information is not known to the ArrayList object because of the erasure scheme. Thus reflection has no way of providing it to you. It would be nice to be able to code

```
public class MultiHashMap<K,V> {
    ...
    public Class<V> getKeyType() {
        return V.class; // this will not work!
    }
}
```

but it just won't work.

Final Notes

As you've seen, knowing how the erasure scheme works is key to being able to understand and implement parameterized types. From a client perspective, using parameterized types is relatively easy and imparts the significant benefit of type safety. From the perspective of a developer creating parameterized types, it can be a fairly complex adventure.

If you find yourself struggling with how to understand or define a parameterized type, distill the definition and sample use of the parameterized type into its erased equivalent. Also, take a look at some of the uses in the J2SE 5.0 source code. The collections framework classes and interfaces, such as Map and HashMap, provide some good examples. For more complex examples, take a look at java.util.Collections.

Exercises

1. Create a new parameterized collection type—a Ring. A Ring is a circular list that maintains knowledge of a current element. A client can retrieve and remove the current element. The Ring must support advancing or backing up the current pointer by one position. The method add adds an element after the current element. The Ring class should support client iteration through all elements, starting at the current pointer, using for-each. The Ring class should throw appropriate exceptions on any operation that is invalid because the ring is empty.

   Do *not* use another data structure to store the ring (e.g., a java.util.LinkedList). Create your own link structure using a nested node class. Each node, or entry, should contain three things: the data element added, a reference to the next node in the circle, and a reference to the previous node in the circle.

Exercises

Lesson 15

Assertions and Annotations

J2SE 5.0 introduced a new facility known as annotations. Annotations are a metaprogramming facility that allow you to mark code with arbitrarily defined tags. The tags (generally) have no meaning to the Java compiler or runtime itself. Instead, other tools can interpret these tags. Examples of tools for which annotations might be useful include IDEs, testing tools, profiling tools, and code-generation tools.

In this lesson you will begin to build a testing tool, similar to JUnit, based upon Java's annotation capabilities. The testing tool, like JUnit, will need to allow developers to specify assertions. Instead of coding assertion methods, you will learn to use Java's built-in assertion capability.

You will learn about:

- assertions

- annotations and annotation types

- retention policies for annotations

- annotation targets

- member-value pairs

- default values for annotation members

- allowable annotation member types

- package annotations

- compatibility considerations for annotations

Assertions

You have been using assert methods defined as part of the JUnit API. These assert methods, defined in junit.framework.Assert, throw an AssertionFailed-Error when appropriate.

535

Java supports a similar assertion feature that you can turn on or off using a VM flag. An assertion statement begins with the keyword assert. It is followed by a conditional; if the conditional fails, Java throws a RuntimeException of type AssertionError. You can optionally supply a message to store in the AssertionError by following the conditional with a colon and the String message. An example:

```
assert name != null : "name is required";
```

Without the message:

```
assert name != null;
```

Assertions are disabled by default. When assertions are disabled, the VM ignores assert statements. This prevents assert statements from adversely affecting application performance. To turn assertions on:

```
java -ea MainClass
```

or, more explicitly:

Assertions

```
java -enableassertions MainClass
```

Both of these statements will enable assertions for all your code but not for the Java library classes. You can turn assertions off using -da or -disableassertions. To turn assertions on or off for system classes, use -enablesystemassertions (or -esa) or -disablesystemassertions (or -dsa).

Java allows you to enable or disable assertions at a more granular level. You can turn assertions on or off for any individual class, any package and all its subpackages, or the default package.

For example, you might want to enable assertions for all but one class in a package:

```
java -ea:sis.studentinfo... -da:sis.studentinfo.Session SisApplication
```

The example shown will enable assertions for all classes in sis.studentinfo with the exception of Session. The ellipses means that Java will additionally enable assertions for any subpackages of sis.studentinfo, such as sis.studentinfo .ui. You represent the default package with just the ellipses.

Assertions are disabled/enabled in the order in which they appear on the java command line, from left to right.

The assert Statement vs. JUnit Assert Methods

JUnit was built in advance of the Java assertion mechanism, which Sun introduced in J2SE version 1.4. Today, JUnit could be rewritten to use the assertion mechanism. But since use of JUnit is very entrenched, such a JUnit rewrite would be a major undertaking for many shops. Also, the junit.framework.Assert methods supplied by JUnit are slightly more expressive. The assertEquals methods automatically provide an improved failure message.

When doing test-driven development, you will always need an assertion-based framework. The use of tests in TDD is analogous to design by contract (referred to as the subcontracting principle in Lesson 6). The assertions provide the preconditions, postconditions, and invariants. If you are not doing TDD, you might choose to bolster the quality of your system by introducing assert statements directly in the production code.

Sun recommends against using assertions as safeguards against application failure. For example, one potential use would be to check parameters of public methods, failing if client code passes a null reference. The downside is that the application may no longer work properly if you turn off assertions. For similar reasons, Sun recommends that you do not include code in assertions that produces side effects (i.e., code that alters system state).

Nothing prohibits you from doing so, however. If you have control over how your application is executed (and you should), then you can ensure that the application is always initiated with assertions enabled properly.

The chief value of Java's assert keyword would seem to be as a debugging aid. Well-placed assert statements can alert you to problems at their source. Suppose someone calls a method with a null reference. Without a protective assertion, you might not receive a NullPointerException until well later in the execution, far from the point where the reference was set. Debugging in this situation can be very time consuming.

You also could use assertions to help build a TDD tool in place of JUnit. In the exercise in this chapter, you will use assertions to begin building such a framework.

Annotations

You have already seen some examples of built-in *annotations* that Java supports. In Lesson 2 you learned how you can mark a method as @deprecated, meaning that the method is slated for eventual removal from the public interface of a class. The @deprecated annotation is technically not part of the Java language. Instead, it is a tag that the compiler can interpret and use as a basis for printing a warning message if appropriate.[1]

You have also seen examples of javadoc tags, annotations that you embed in javadoc comments and that you can use to generate Java API documentation web pages. The javadoc.exe program reads through your Java source files, parsing and interpreting the javadoc tags for inclusion in the web output.

Also, in Lesson 9, you learned how you could use the @Override tag to indicate that you believed you were overriding a superclass method.

You can also build your own annotation tags for whatever purpose you might find useful. For example, you might want the ability to mark methods with change comments:

```
@modified("JJL", "12-Feb-2005")
public void cancelReservation() {
   // ...
}
```

Subsequently, you could build a tool (possibly an Eclipse plug-in) that would allow you to view at a glance all the change comments, perhaps sorted by initials.

You could achieve equivalent results by insisting that developers provide structured comments that adhere to a standard format. You could then write code to parse through the source file, looking for these comments. However, the support in Java for custom annotation types provides significant advantages.

First, Java validates annotations at compile time. It is not possible to introduce a misspelled or incorrectly formatted annotation. Second, instead of having to write parse code, you can use reflection capabilities to quickly gather annotation information. Third, you can restrict annotations so that they apply to a specific kind of Java element. For example, you can insist that the @modified tag applies only to methods.

Building a Testing Tool

Building a Testing Tool

In this lesson, you will build a testing tool similar to JUnit. I'll refer to this tool as TestRunner, since that will be the primary class responsible for executing the tests. The tool will be text-based. You will be able to execute it from Ant. Technically, you don't have to build a

---

[1] @deprecated existed in the Java language from its early days and long before Sun introduced formalized annotations support. But it works just like any other compiler-level annotation type.

testing tool using TDD, because it's not intended to be production code. But there's nothing that says you *can't* write tests. We will.

JUnit requires a test class to extend from the class junit.framework.Test-Case. In TestRunner you will use a different mechanism than inheritance: You will use Java annotations to mark a class as a test class.

Getting started is the toughest part, but using Ant can help. You can set up an Ant target to represent the user interface for the test. If not all of the tests pass, you can set things up so that the Ant build fails, in which case you will see a "BUILD FAILED" message. Otherwise you will see a "BUILD SUC-CESSFUL" message.

TestRunnerTest

The first test in TestRunnerTest, singleMethodTest, goes up against a secondary class SingleMethodTest defined in the same source file. SingleMethodTest provides a single empty test method that should result in a pass, as it would in JUnit.

So far you need no annotations. You pass a reference to the test class, TestRunnerTest.class, to an instance of TestRunner. TestRunner can assume that this parameter is a test class containing only test methods.

To generate test failures, you will use the assert facility in Java, described in the first part of this lesson. Remember that you must enable assertions when executing the Java VM; otherwise, Java will ignore them.

TestRunnerTest

Here is TestRunnerTest.

```
package sis.testing;

import java.util.*;
import java.lang.reflect.*;

public class TestRunnerTest {
    public void singleMethodTest() {
        TestRunner runner = new TestRunner(SingleMethodTest.class);

        Set<Method> testMethods = runner.getTestMethods();
        assert 1 == testMethods.size() : "expected single test method";

        Iterator<Method> it = testMethods.iterator();
        Method method = it.next();

        final String testMethodName = "testA";
        assert testMethodName.equals(method.getName()) :
            "expected " + testMethodName + " as test method";
        runner.run();
        assert 1 == runner.passed() : "expected 1 pass";
        assert 0 == runner.failed() : "expected no failures";
    }
```

```
    public void multipleMethodTest() {
        TestRunner runner = new TestRunner(MultipleMethodTest.class);
        runner.run();

        assert 2 == runner.passed() : "expected 2 pass";
        assert 0 == runner.failed() : "expected no failures";

        Set<Method> testMethods = runner.getTestMethods();
        assert 2 == testMethods.size() : "expected single test method";

        Set<String> methodNames = new HashSet<String>();
        for (Method method: testMethods)
            methodNames.add(method.getName());

        final String testMethodNameA = "testA";
        final String testMethodNameB = "testB";

        assert methodNames.contains(testMethodNameA):
            "expected " + testMethodNameA + " as test method";
        assert methodNames.contains(testMethodNameB):
            "expected " + testMethodNameB + " as test method";
    }
}

class SingleMethodTest {
    public void testA() {}
}

class MultipleMethodTest {
    public void testA() {}
    public void testB() {}
}
```

TestRunner

The second test, multipleMethodTest, is a bit of a mess. To create it, I duplicated the first test and modified some of the details. It screams out for refactoring. The problem is that as soon as you extract a common utility method
in TestRunnerTest, the TestRunner class will assume it's a test method and attempt to execute it. The solution will be to introduce an annotation that you
can use to mark and distinguish test methods.

TestRunner

First, let's go over the initial implementation of TestRunner.

```
package sis.testing;

import java.util.*;
import java.lang.reflect.*;
```

```
class TestRunner {
   private Class testClass;
   private int failed = 0;
   private Set<Method> testMethods = null;

   public static void main(String[] args) throws Exception {
      TestRunner runner = new TestRunner(args[0]);
      runner.run();
      System.out.println(
         "passed: " + runner.passed() + " failed: " + runner.failed());
      if (runner.failed() > 0)
         System.exit(1);
   }

   public TestRunner(Class testClass) {
      this.testClass = testClass;
   }
   public TestRunner(String className) throws Exception {
      this(Class.forName(className));
   }

   public Set<Method> getTestMethods() {
      if (testMethods == null)
         loadTestMethods();
      return testMethods;
   }

   private void loadTestMethods() {
      testMethods = new HashSet<Method>();
      for (Method method: testClass.getDeclaredMethods())
         testMethods.add(method);
   }

   public void run() {
      for (Method method: getTestMethods())
         run(method);
   }

   private void run(Method method) {
      try {
         Object testObject = testClass.newInstance();
         method.invoke(testObject, new Object[] {})²;
      }
      catch (InvocationTargetException e) {
         Throwable cause = e.getCause();
         if (cause instanceof AssertionError)
            System.out.println(cause.getMessage());
         else
            e.printStackTrace();
         failed++;
```

---

²You can use the slightly-more-succinct idiom new Object[0] in place of new Object[] {}.

```
        }
        catch (Throwable t) {
            t.printStackTrace();
            failed++;
        }
    }

    public int passed() {
        return testMethods.size() - failed;
    }

    public int failed() {
        return failed;
    }
}
```

If you're having a bit of trouble understanding the run(Method) method, refer to Lesson 12 for a discussion of reflection. The basic flow in the run method is:

- Create a new instance of the test class. This step assumes a no-argument constructor is available in the test class.

- invoke the method (passed in as a parameter) using the new test class instance and an empty parameter list.

- If the invoke message send fails, extract the cause from the thrown InvocationTargetException; the cause should normally be an AssertionError. Java throws an AssertionError when an assert statement fails.

TestRunner

TestRunner supplies two constructors. One takes a Class object and for now will be used from TestRunnerTest only. The second constructor takes a class name String and loads the corresponding class using Class.forName. You call this constructor from the main method, which provides a bit of user interface for displaying test results.

The main method in turn gets the class name from the Ant target:

```
<target name="runAllTests" depends="build" description="run all tests">
  <java classname="sis.testing.TestRunner" failonerror="true" fork="true">
    <classpath refid="classpath" />
    <jvmarg value="-enableassertions"/>
    <arg value="sis.testing.TestRunnerTest" />
  </java>
</target>
```

There are a few interesting things in the runAllTests target:

- You specify failonerror="true" in the java task. If running a Java application returns a nonzero value, Ant considers the execution to have resulted in an error. The build script terminates on an error. Using the System.exit command (see the `main` method in TestRunner) allows you to terminate an application immediately and return the value passed as a parameter to it.

- You specify `fork="true"` in the `java` task. This means that the Java application executes as a separate process from the Java process in which Ant executes. The pitfall of not forking is that the Ant build process itself will crash if the Java application crashes.

- You pass the test name to TestRunner using a nested `arg` element.

- You pass the argument `enableassertions` to the Java VM using a nested `jvmarg` element.

The @TestMethod Annotation

In order to be able to refactor tests, you must be able to mark the test methods so that other newly extracted methods are not considered tests. The `@TestMethod` annotation precedes the method signature for each method you want to designate as a test. Annotate the two test methods (`singleMethodTest` and `multipleMethodTest`) in TestRunnerTest with `@TestMethod`. Also annotate the three additional test methods in the miniclasses (SingleMethodTest and Multiple-MethodTest) used by the TestRunnerTest tests.

```java
package sis.testing;

import java.util.*;
import java.lang.reflect.*;

public class TestRunnerTest {
    private TestRunner runner;
    private static final String methodNameA = "testA";
    private static final String methodNameB = "testB";

    @TestMethod
    public void singleMethodTest() {
        runTests(SingleMethodTest.class);
        verifyTests(methodNameA);
    }

    @TestMethod
    public void multipleMethodTest() {
        runTests(MultipleMethodTest.class);
        verifyTests(methodNameA, methodNameB);
    }
```

```
      private void runTests(Class testClass) {
          runner = new TestRunner(testClass);
          runner.run();
      }

      private void verifyTests(String... expectedTestMethodNames) {
          verifyNumberOfTests(expectedTestMethodNames);
          verifyMethodNames(expectedTestMethodNames);
          verifyCounts(expectedTestMethodNames);
      }

      private void verifyCounts(String... testMethodNames) {
          assert testMethodNames.length == runner.passed() :
              "expected " + testMethodNames.length + " passed";
          assert 0 == runner.failed() : "expected no failures";
      }

      private void verifyNumberOfTests(String... testMethodNames) {
          assert testMethodNames.length == runner.getTestMethods().size() :
              "expected " + testMethodNames.length + " test method(s)";
      }

      private void verifyMethodNames(String... testMethodNames) {
          Set<String> actualMethodNames = getTestMethodNames();
          for (String methodName: testMethodNames)
              assert actualMethodNames.contains(methodName):
                  "expected " + methodName + " as test method";
      }

      private Set<String> getTestMethodNames() {
          Set<String> methodNames = new HashSet<String>();
          for (Method method: runner.getTestMethods())
              methodNames.add(method.getName());
          return methodNames;
      }
  }

class SingleMethodTest {
  @TestMethod public void testA() {}
}

class MultipleMethodTest {
  @TestMethod public void testA() {}
  @TestMethod public void testB() {}
}
```

The @TestMethod Annotation

The @TestMethod annotation may appear after any method modifiers such as public or static. The annotation must appear before the signature of the method (which starts with the return type of the method).

To declare the @TestMethod annotation type, you create what looks a lot like an interface declaration:

```
package sis.testing;
public @interface TestMethod {}
```

The only difference between an interface declaration and an annotation type declaration is that you put an "at" sign (@) before the keyword interface in an interface declaration. There can be space between @ and interface, but the convention is to abut the two.

The code will now compile and you can execute your tests, but you will see at least one IllegalAccessException stack trace. The code in TestRunner still treats every method as a test method, including the private methods you just extracted. The reflection code in TestRunner is unable to invoke these private methods. It's time to introduce code in TestRunner to look for the @TestMethod annotations:

```
private void loadTestMethods() {
    testMethods = new HashSet<Method>();
    for (Method method: testClass.getDeclaredMethods())
        if (method.isAnnotationPresent(TestMethod.class))
            testMethods.add(method);
}
```

One line of code is all it takes. You send the message isAnnotationPresent to the Method object, passing in the type (TestMethod.class) of the annotation. If isAnnotationPresent returns true, you add the Method object to the list of tests.

Now the test executes but returns improper results:

```
runAllTests:
    [java] passed: 0 failed: 0
```

You're expecting to see two passed tests but no tests are registered—the isAnnotationPresent method is always returning false.

Retention

The java.lang.annotations package includes a *meta*-annotation type named @Retention. You use meta-annotations to annotate other annotation type declarations. Specifically, you use the @Retention annotation to tell the Java compiler how long to retain annotation information. There are three choices, summarized in Table 15.1.

As explained by the table, if you don't specify an @Retention annotation, the default behavior means that you probably won't be able to extract informa-

Table 15.1 *Annotation Retention Policies*

RetentionPolicy enum	Annotation Disposition
RetentionPolicy.SOURCE	Discarded at compile time
RetentionPolicy.CLASS (default)	Stored in the class file; can be discarded by the VM at runtime
RetentionPolicy.RUNTIME	Stored in the class file; retained by the VM at runtime

tion on the annotation at runtime.[3] An example of RetentionPolicy.CLASS is the @Override annotation discussed in Lesson 9.

You will have the most need for RetentionPolicy.RUNTIME so that tools such as your TestRunner will be able to extract annotation information from their target classes. If you build tools that work directly with source code (for example, a plug-in for an IDE such as Eclipse), you can use RetentionPolicy.SOURCE to avoid unnecessarily storing annotation information in the class files. An example use might be an @Todo annotation used to mark sections of code that need attention.

To get reflection code to recognize @TestMethod annotations, you must modify the annotation type declaration:

```
package sis.testing;

import java.lang.annotation.*;

@Retention(RetentionPolicy.RUNTIME)
public @interface TestMethod {}
```

Your two TestRunnerTest tests should now pass:

```
runAllTests:
    [java] passed: 2 failed: 0
```

Annotation Targets

You have designed the @TestMethod annotation to be used by developers to mark test methods. Annotations can modify many other *element types*: types (classes, interfaces, and enums), fields, parameters, constructors, local vari-

---

[3]The VM may choose to retain this information.

ables, and packages. By default, you may use an annotation to modify any element. You can also choose to constrain an annotation type to modify one *and only one* element type. To do so, you supply an @Target meta-annotation on your annotation type declaration.

Since you didn't specify an @Target meta-annotation for @TestMethod, a developer could use the tag to modify any element, such as a field. Generally no harm would be done, but a developer could mark a field by accident, thinking that he or she marked a method. The test method would be ignored until someone noticed the mistake. Adding an @Target to an annotation type is one more step toward helping a developer at compile time instead of making him or her decipher later troubles.

Add the appropriate @Target meta-annotation to @TestMethod:

```
package sis.testing;

import java.lang.annotation.*;

@Retention(RetentionPolicy.RUNTIME)
@Target(ElementType.METHOD)
public @interface TestMethod {}
```

The parameter to @Target must be an ElementType enum, defined in java.lang.annotation. This enum supplies constants corresponding to the element types that an annotation type can modify: TYPE, FIELD, METHOD, PARAMETER, CONSTRUCTOR, LOCAL_VARIABLE, ANNOTATION_TYPE, and PACKAGE. There are special considerations for annotations with a target of ElementType.PACKAGE. See the section Package Annotations later in this lesson for more information.

To demonstrate what @Target does for your annotation types, modify TestRunnerTest. Instead of marking a method with @TestMethod, mark a field instead:

```
// ...
public class TestRunnerTest {
    private @TestMethod TestRunner runner;

    @TestMethod
    public void singleMethodTest() {
    // ...
```

When you compile, you should see an error similar to the following:

```
annotation type not applicable to this kind of declaration
private @TestMethod TestRunner runner;
        ^
```

Remove the extraneous annotation, recompile, and rerun your tests.

Annotation Targets

Skipping Test Methods

From time to time, you may want to bypass the execution of certain test methods. Suppose you have a handful of failing methods. You might want to concentrate on getting a green bar on one failed method at a time before moving on to the next. The failure of the other test methods serves as a distraction. You want to "turn them off."

In JUnit, you can skip a method by either commenting it out or by renaming the method so that its signature does not represent a test method signature. An easy way to skip a test method is to precede its name with an X. For example, you could rename testCreate to XtestCreate. JUnit looks for methods whose names start with the word test, so it will not find XtestCreate.

You do not want to make a habit of commenting out tests. It is poor practice to leave methods commented out for any duration longer than your current programming session. You should avoid checking in code with commented-out tests. Other developers won't understand your intent. My first inclination when I see commented-out code, particularly test code, is to delete it.

Commenting out test methods is risky. It is easy to forget that you have commented out tests. It can also be difficult to find the tests that are commented out. It would be nice if JUnit could warn you that you've left tests commented out.

**Modifying
TestRunner**

A similar problem exists for your new TestRunner class. The simplest way of bypassing a test would be to remove its @TestMethod annotation. The problem with doing that is the same as the problem with commenting out a test. It's easy to "lose" a test in a system with any significant number of tests.

For this exercise, you will make the necessary modifications to TestRunner to ignore designated methods. You will create a new annotation type, @Ignore, and change code in TestRunner to recognize this annotation. The @Ignore annotation will allow developers to supply a parameter with a text description of why the test is being skipped. You will modify TestRunner to print these descriptions.

Modifying TestRunner

Add a new test method, ignoreMethodTest, to TestRunnerTest. It will go up against a new test class, IgnoreMethodTest, which contains three methods marked with @TestMethod. One of the test methods (testC) is additionally marked @Ignore. You must verify that this test method is not executed.

```
package sis.testing;

import java.util.*;
import java.lang.reflect.*;

public class TestRunnerTest {
   private TestRunner runner;
   // ...
   @TestMethod
   public void ignoreMethodTest() {
      runTests(IgnoreMethodTest.class);
      verifyTests(methodNameA, methodNameB);
   }
   // ...
}

// ...
class IgnoreMethodTest {
   @TestMethod public void testA() {}
   @TestMethod public void testB() {}

   @Ignore
   @TestMethod public void testC() {}
}
```

The @Ignore annotation declaration looks a lot like the @TestMethod declaration.

Modifying
TestRunner

```
package sis.testing;

import java.lang.annotation.*;

@Target(ElementType.METHOD)
@Retention(RetentionPolicy.RUNTIME)
public @interface Ignore {}
```

To get your tests to pass, make the following modification to TestRunner.

```
package sis.testing;

import java.util.*;
import java.lang.reflect.*;

class TestRunner {
   ...
   private void loadTestMethods() {
      testMethods = new HashSet<Method>();
      for (Method method: testClass.getDeclaredMethods())
         if (method.isAnnotationPresent(TestMethod.class) &&
             !method.isAnnotationPresent(Ignore.class))
            testMethods.add(method);
   }
   ...
}
```

Single-Value Annotations

 The `@Ignore` annotation is a *marker* annotation—it marks whether a method should be ignored or not. You merely need to test for the presence of the annotation using `isAnnotationPresent`. Now you need developers to supply a reason for ignoring a test. You will modify the `@Ignore` annotation to take a reason String as a parameter.

To support a single parameter in an annotation type, you supply a member method named `value` with an appropriate return type and no parameters. Annotation type member methods cannot take any parameters.

```
package sis.testing;

import java.lang.annotation.*;

@Target(ElementType.METHOD)
@Retention(RetentionPolicy.RUNTIME)
public @interface Ignore {
    String value();
}
```

Mark one of the methods in IgnoreMethodTest with just `@Ignore`. Do not supply any parameters:

```
class IgnoreMethodTest {
    @TestMethod public void testA() {}
    @TestMethod public void testB() {}
    @Ignore()
        @TestMethod public void testC() {}
}
```

Note that `@Ignore` is a shortcut for `@Ignore()`.

When you compile, you will see an error message:

```
annotation testing.Ignore is missing value
    @Ignore
    ^
```

The compiler uses the corresponding annotation type declaration to ensure that you supplied the proper number of parameters.

Change the test target class, IgnoreMethodTest, to supply a reason with the `@Ignore` annotation.

```
public class TestRunnerTest {
    public static final String IGNORE_REASON1 = "because";
    // ...
}
class IgnoreMethodTest {
    @TestMethod public void testA() {}
```

```
@TestMethod public void testB() {}
@Ignore(TestRunnerTest.IGNORE_REASON1)
   @TestMethod public void testC() {}
}
```

Rerun your tests. They pass, so you haven't broken anything. But you also want the ability to print a list of the ignored methods. Modify the test accordingly:

```
@TestMethod
public void ignoreMethodTest() {
   runTests(IgnoreMethodTest.class);
   verifyTests(methodNameA, methodNameB);
   assertIgnoreReasons();
}

private void assertIgnoreReasons() {
   Map<Method, Ignore> ignoredMethods = runner.getIgnoredMethods();
   Map.Entry<Method, Ignore> entry = getSoleEntry(ignoredMethods);
   assert "testC".equals(entry.getKey().getName()):
      "unexpected ignore method: " + entry.getKey();
   Ignore ignore = entry.getValue();
   assert IGNORE_REASON1.equals(ignore.value());
}

private <K, V> Map.Entry<K, V> getSoleEntry(Map<K, V> map) {
   assert 1 == map.size(): "expected one entry";
   Iterator<Map.Entry<K, V>> it = map.entrySet().iterator();
   return it.next();
}
```

You return the ignored methods as a collection of mappings between Method objects and the "ignored reason" string. Since you expect there to be only one ignored method, you can introduce the utility method getSoleEntry to extract the single Method key from the Map. In my excitement over figuring out how to use generics (see Lesson 14), I've gone a little overboard here and made getSoleEntry into a generic method that you could use for any collection. There's no reason you couldn't code it specifically to the key and value types of the map.

Now make the necessary changes to TestRunner to get it to store the ignored methods for later extraction:

```
package sis.testing;

import java.util.*;
import java.lang.reflect.*;

class TestRunner {
   // ...
   private Map<Method, Ignore> ignoredMethods = null;
   // ...
```

Single-Value
Annotations

```
private void loadTestMethods() {
    testMethods = new HashSet<Method>();
    ignoredMethods = new HashMap<Method, Ignore>();
    for (Method method: testClass.getDeclaredMethods()) {
        if (method.isAnnotationPresent(TestMethod.class))
            if (method.isAnnotationPresent(Ignore.class)) {
                Ignore ignore = method.getAnnotation(Ignore.class);
                ignoredMethods.put(method, ignore);
            }
            else
                testMethods.add(method);
    }
}

public Map<Method, Ignore> getIgnoredMethods() {
    return ignoredMethods;
}
// ...
}
```

You can send the getAnnotation method to any element that can be annotated, passing it the annotation type name (Ignore.class here). The getAnnotation method returns an annotation type reference to the actual annotation object. Once you have the annotation object reference (ignore), you can send messages to it that are defined in the annotation type interface.

You can now modify the text user interface to display the ignored methods.

A TestRunner
User Interface
Class

A TestRunner User Interface Class

At this point, the main method is no longer a couple of simple hacked-out lines. It's time to move this to a separate class responsible for presenting the user interface.

Since TestRunner is a utility for test purposes, as I mentioned earlier, tests aren't absolutely required. For the small bit of nonproduction user interface code you'll write for the test runner, you shouldn't feel compelled to test first. You're more than welcome to do so, but I'm not going to here.

The following listing shows a refactored user interface class that prints out ignored methods. About the only thing interesting in it is the "clever" way I return the number of failed tests in the System.exit call. Why? Why not? It's more succinct than an if statement, it doesn't obfuscate the code, and it returns additional information that the build script or operating system could use.

```
package sis.testing;

import java.lang.reflect.*;
import java.util.*;
```

```
public class TestRunnerUI {
   private TestRunner runner;

   public static void main(String[] args) throws Exception {
      TestRunnerUI ui = new TestRunnerUI(args[0]);
      ui.run();
      System.exit(ui.getNumberOfFailedTests());
   }

   public TestRunnerUI(String testClassName) throws Exception {
      runner = new TestRunner(testClassName);
   }

   public void run() {
      runner.run();
      showResults();
      showIgnoredMethods();
   }

   public int getNumberOfFailedTests() {
      return runner.failed();
   }

   private void showResults() {
      System.out.println(
         "passed: " + runner.passed() +
         " failed: " + runner.failed());
   }

   private void showIgnoredMethods() {
      if (runner.getIgnoredMethods().isEmpty())
         return;

      System.out.println("\nIgnored Methods");
      for (Map.Entry<Method, Ignore> entry:
            runner.getIgnoredMethods().entrySet()) {
         Ignore ignore = entry.getValue();
         System.out.println(entry.getKey() + ": " + ignore.value());
      }
   }
}
```

Array Parameters

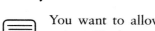 You want to allow developers to provide multiple separate reason strings. To do so, you can specify String[] as the return type for the annotation type member value. An @Ignore annotation can then contain multiple reasons by using a construct that looks similar to an array initializer:

```
@Ignore({"why", "just because"})
```

Here's the updated annotation type declaration:

```
package sis.testing;

import java.lang.annotation.*;

@Target(ElementType.METHOD)
@Retention(RetentionPolicy.RUNTIME)
public @interface Ignore {
    String[] value();
}
```

If you only need to supply a single string for an annotation type member
with a return type of String[], Java allows you to eliminate the array-style initialization. These annotations for the current definition of @Ignore are equivalent:

```
@Ignore("why")
@Ignore({"why"})
```

You will need to modify TestRunnerTest to support the change to Ignore.

```
package sis.testing;

import java.util.*;
import java.lang.reflect.*;

public class TestRunnerTest {
    public static final String IGNORE_REASON1 = "because";
    public static final String IGNORE_REASON2 = "why not";
    ...

    @TestMethod
    public void ignoreMethodTest() {
        runTests(IgnoreMethodTest.class);
        verifyTests(methodNameA, methodNameB);
        assertIgnoreReasons();
    }

    private void assertIgnoreReasons() {
        Map<Method, Ignore> ignoredMethods = runner.getIgnoredMethods();
        Map.Entry<Method, Ignore> entry = getSoleEntry(ignoredMethods);
        assert "testC".equals(entry.getKey().getName()):
            "unexpected ignore method: " + entry.getKey();
        Ignore ignore = entry.getValue();
        String[] ignoreReasons = ignore.value();
        assert 2 == ignoreReasons.length;
        assert IGNORE_REASON1.equals(ignoreReasons[0]);
        assert IGNORE_REASON2.equals(ignoreReasons[1]);
    }
    ...
}
```

Array Parameters

```
class SingleMethodTest {
    @TestMethod public void testA() {}
}

class MultipleMethodTest {
    @TestMethod public void testA() {}
    @TestMethod public void testB() {}
}

class IgnoreMethodTest {
    @TestMethod public void testA() {}
    @TestMethod public void testB() {}

    @Ignore({TestRunnerTest.IGNORE_REASON1,
            TestRunnerTest.IGNORE_REASON2})
        @TestMethod public void testC() {}
}
```

Multiple Parameter Annotations

You may want annotations to support multiple parameters. As an example, suppose you want developers to add their initials when ignoring a test method. A proper annotation might be:

```
@Ignore(reasons={"just because", "and why not"}, initials="jjl")
```

Now that you have more than one annotation parameter, you must supply *member-value pairs*. Each member-value pair includes the member name, which must match an annotation type member, followed by the equals (=) sign, followed by the constant value for the member.

The second member-value pair in the above example has initials as a member name and "jjl" as its value. In order to support this annotation, you must modify the @Ignore annotation type declaration to include initials as an additional member. You must also rename the value member to reasons. Each key in an annotation member-value pair must match a member name in the annotation type declaration.

```
package sis.testing;

import java.lang.annotation.*;

@Target(ElementType.METHOD)
@Retention(RetentionPolicy.RUNTIME)
public @interface Ignore {
    String[] reasons();
    String initials();
}
```

556 ASSERTIONS AND ANNOTATIONS

You can specify member-value pairs in any order within an annotation. The order need not match the member order of the annotation type declaration.

Here are the corresponding modifications to TestRunnerTest:

```
package sis.testing;
// ...
public class TestRunnerTest {
    // ...
    public static final String IGNORE_INITIALS = "jjl";
    // ...
    private void assertIgnoreReasons() {
        Map<Method, Ignore> ignoredMethods = runner.getIgnoredMethods();
        Map.Entry<Method, Ignore> entry = getSoleEntry(ignoredMethods);
        assert "testC".equals(entry.getKey().getName()):
            "unexpected ignore method: " + entry.getKey();
        Ignore ignore = entry.getValue();
        String[] ignoreReasons = ignore.reasons();
        assert 2 == ignoreReasons.length;
        assert IGNORE_REASON1.equals(ignoreReasons[0]);
        assert IGNORE_REASON2.equals(ignoreReasons[1]);
        assert IGNORE_INITIALS.equals(ignore.initials());
    }
    // ...
}

class IgnoreMethodTest {
    @TestMethod public void testA() {}
    @TestMethod public void testB() {}

    @Ignore(
        reasons={TestRunnerTest.IGNORE_REASON1,
         TestRunnerTest.IGNORE_REASON2},
        initials=TestRunnerTest.IGNORE_INITIALS)
    @TestMethod public void testC() {}
}
```

You do not need to make modifications to TestRunner. You will need to make a small modification to TestRunnerUI to extract the reasons and initials properly from the Ignore object.

```
private void showIgnoredMethods() {
    if (runner.getIgnoredMethods().isEmpty())
        return;

    System.out.println("\nIgnored Methods");
    for (Map.Entry<Method, Ignore> entry:
            runner.getIgnoredMethods().entrySet()) {
        Ignore ignore = entry.getValue();
        System.out.printf("%s: %s (by %s)",
            entry.getKey(),
```

Multiple
Parameter
Annotations

```
        Arrays.toString(ignore.reasons()),
        ignore.initials());
    }
}
```

Default Values

 The reason for ignoring a test method is likely to be the same most of the time. Most often, you will want to temporarily comment out a test while fixing other broken tests. Supplying a reason each time can be onerous, so you would like to have a default ignore reason. Here's how you might reflect this need in a TestRunner test:

```
@TestMethod
public void ignoreWithDefaultReason() {
    runTests(DefaultIgnoreMethodTest.class);
    verifyTests(methodNameA, methodNameB);
    Map<Method, Ignore> ignoredMethods = runner.getIgnoredMethods();
    Map.Entry<Method, Ignore> entry = getSoleEntry(ignoredMethods);
    Ignore ignore = entry.getValue();
    assert TestRunner.DEFAULT_IGNORE_REASON.
        equals(ignore.reasons()[0]);
}

class DefaultIgnoreMethodTest {
    @TestMethod public void testA() {}
    @TestMethod public void testB() {}
    @Ignore(initials=TestRunnerTest.IGNORE_INITIALS)
        @TestMethod public void testC() {}
}
```

You will need to define the constant DEFAULT_IGNORE_REASON in the TestRunner class to be whatever string you desire:

```
class TestRunner {
    public static final String DEFAULT_IGNORE_REASON =
        "temporarily commenting out";
    // ...
```

You can supply a default value on any annotation type member. The default must be a constant at compile time. The new definition of @Ignore includes a default value on the reasons member. Note use of the keyword default to separate the member signature from the default value.

```
package sis.testing;

import java.lang.annotation.*;

@Target(ElementType.METHOD)
@Retention(RetentionPolicy.RUNTIME)
```

```
public @interface Ignore {
    String[] reasons() default TestRunner.DEFAULT_IGNORE_REASON;
    String initials();
}
```

Additional Return Types and Complex Annotation Types

In addition to String and String[], an annotation value can be a primitive, an enum, a Class reference, an annotation type itself, or an array of any of these types.

The following test (in TestRunnerTest) sets up the requirement for an @Ignore annotation to include a date. The Date type will be an annotation; its members each return an int value.

```
@TestMethod
public void dateTest() {
    runTests(IgnoreDateTest.class);
    Map<Method, Ignore> ignoredMethods = runner.getIgnoredMethods();
    Map.Entry<Method, Ignore> entry = getSoleEntry(ignoredMethods);
    Ignore ignore = entry.getValue();
    sis.testing.Date date = ignore.date();
    assert 1 == date.month();
    assert 2 == date.day();
    assert 2005 == date.year();
}

class IgnoreDateTest {
    @Ignore(
            initials=TestRunnerTest.IGNORE_INITIALS,
            date=@Date(month=1, day=2, year=2005))
        @TestMethod public void testC() {}
}
```

The annotation in IgnoreDateTest is known as a *complex annotation*—an annotation that includes another annotation. @Ignore includes a member, date, whose value is another annotation, @Date.

The definition of the sis.testing.Date annotation type:

```
package sis.testing;

public @interface Date {
    int month();
    int day();
    int year();
}
```

The @Ignore annotation type can now define a date member that returns a testing.Date instance:

```
package sis.testing;

import java.lang.annotation.*;

@Target(ElementType.METHOD)
@Retention(RetentionPolicy.RUNTIME)
public @interface Ignore {
    String[] reasons() default TestRunner.DEFAULT_IGNORE_REASON;
    String initials();
    Date date();
}
```

Since the Date annotation type is only used as part of another annotation, it does not need to specify a retention or a target.

You may not declare a recursive annotation type—that is, an annotation type member with the same return type as the annotation itself.

To get your tests to compile and pass, you'll also need to modify IgnoreMethodTest and DefaultIgnoreMethodTest:

```
class IgnoreMethodTest {
    @TestMethod public void testA() {}
    @TestMethod public void testB() {}

    @Ignore(
        reasons={TestRunnerTest.IGNORE_REASON1,
                 TestRunnerTest.IGNORE_REASON2},
        initials=TestRunnerTest.IGNORE_INITIALS,
        date=@Date(month=1, day=2, year=2005))
    @TestMethod public void testC() {}
}

class DefaultIgnoreMethodTest {
    @TestMethod public void testA() {}
    @TestMethod public void testB() {}
    @Ignore(initials=TestRunnerTest.IGNORE_INITIALS,
            date=@Date(month=1, day=2, year=2005))
    @TestMethod public void testC() {}
}
```

Package Annotations

Suppose you want the ability to designate packages as testing packages. Further, you want your testing tool to run "performance-related" tests separately from other tests. In order to accomplish this, you can create an annotation whose target is a package. A test for this annotation:[4]

```
@TestMethod
public void packageAnnotations() {
    Package pkg = this.getClass().getPackage();
    TestPackage testPackage = pkg.getAnnotation(TestPackage.class);
    assert testPackage.isPerformance();
}
```

You extract annotation information from the Package object like you would from any other element object. You can obtain a Package object by sending the message getPackage to any Class object.

The annotation declaration is straightforward:

```
package sis.testing;

import java.lang.annotation.*;

@Target(ElementType.PACKAGE)
@Retention(RetentionPolicy.RUNTIME)
public @interface TestPackage {
    boolean isPerformance() default false;
}
```

Package Annotations

However, the question is, Where does a package annotation go? Would it go before the package statement in every source file that belongs to the package? Or before just one of them? Or is it stored elsewhere?

Java limits you to at most one annotated package statement per package. This means that you can't just place an annotation before the package statement in an arbitrary source file.

The answer depends on which compiler you are using. Sun recommends a specific scheme that is based on a file system. Other compiler vendors may choose a different scheme. They may have to if the compile environment is not based on a file system.

The Sun scheme requires you to create a source file named package-info.java in the source directory that corresponds to the package you want to annotate. Sun's Java compiler reads this pseudo–source file but produces no visible class files as output. (In fact, it is not possible to include a hyphen [-] in a class name.) This file should include any package annotations, followed by the appropriate package statement. You should not include anything else in package-info.java.

Here's what package-info.java might look like in the sis.testing package:

```
@TestPackage(isPerformance=true) package sis.testing;
```

[4]Note use of the variable name pkg, since package is a keyword.

Compatibility Considerations

Sun has, as much as possible, designed the annotations facility to support changes to an annotation with minimal impact on existing code. This section goes through the various modification scenarios and explains the impact of each kind of change to an annotation type.

When you add a new member to an annotation type, provide a default if possible. Using a default will allow code to continue to use the compiled annotation type without issue. But this *can* cause a problem if you try to access the new member. Suppose you access the new member from an annotation compiled using the annotation type declaration *without* the new member. If no default exists on the new member, this will generate an exception.

If you remove an annotation type member, you will obviously cause errors on recompilation of any likewise annotated sources. However, any existing class files that use the modified annotation type will work fine until their sources are recompiled.

Avoid removing defaults, changing the return type, or removing target elements with existing annotation types. These actions all have the potential to generate exceptions.

If you change the retention type, the behavior is generally what you would expect. For example, if you change from RUNTIME to CLASS, the annotation is no longer readable at runtime.

When in doubt, write a test to demonstrate the behavior!

Additional Notes on Annotations

Additional Notes on Annotations

- An annotation with no target can modify any Java element.

- In an annotation type declaration, the only parameterized type that you can return is the Class type.

- The @Documented meta-annotation type lets you declare an annotation type to be included in the published API generated by tools such as javadoc.

- The @Inherited meta-annotation type means that an annotation type is inherited by all subclasses. It will be returned if you send getAnnotation to a method or class object but not if you send getDeclaredAnnotations.

- You cannot use null as an annotation value.

- You can modify an element only once with a given annotation. For example, you cannot supply two @Ignore annotations for a test method.

- In order to internally support annotation types, Sun modified the Arrays class to include implementations of toString and hashCode for Arrays.

Summary

Annotations are a powerful facility that can help structure the notes you put into your code. One of the examples that is touted the most is the ability to annotate interface declarations so that tools can generate code from the pertinent methods.

The chief downside of using annotations is that you make your code dependent upon an annotation type when your code uses it. Changes to the annotation type declaration could negatively impact your code, although Sun has built in some facilities to help maintain binary compatibility. You also must have the annotation type class file present in order to compile. This should not be surprising: An annotation type is effectively an interface type.

Again, the rule of thumb is to use annotation types prudently. An annotation type is an interface and should represent a stable abstraction. As with any interface, ensure that you have carefully considered the implications of introducing an annotation type into your system. A worst-case scenario, where you needed to make dramatic changes to an annotation type, would involve a massive search and replace[5] followed by a compile.

Exercises

1. Using the RingTest and Ring classes from the previous lesson, introduce an assert into the add method that rejects a null argument. Make sure you write a test! Don't forget to enable assertions before running your tests.

---

[5]For the time being, IDEs might not provide sophisticated support for manipulating and navigating annotations. You may need to resort to search and replace (or compile, identify, and replace) to effect a major change. Integrated IDE support for annotations should emerge quickly. The support in IDEA is already at a level I would consider acceptable.

2. Create an annotation @Dump. This annotation can be applied to any field in a class. Then create a ToStringer class which, when passed an object, will spit out a dump of each field that has been marked for use in the toString method.

3. Modify the dump annotation to allow for sorting the fields by adding an optional order parameter. The order should be a positive integer. If a field is not annotated, it should appear last in the list of fields.

4. Add another parameter for dump called quote, which should be a boolean indicating whether or not to surround the value with quotes. This is useful for objects whose toString representation might be empty or have leading or trailing spaces.

5. Add an outputMethod field to the @Dump annotation. This specifies the method for toStringer to use in order to get a printable representation of the field. Its value should default to toString. This is useful for when you have an object with a toString representation you cannot change, such as an object of a system class type.

6. Change the outputMethod annotation to outputMethods and have it support a String array of method names. The ToString code should construct a printable representation of the object by calling each of these method names in order and concatenating the results. Separate each result with a single space. (You might consider adding another annotation to designate the separator character.)

Exercises

Additional Lesson I

Swing, Part 1

Swing is Java's standard library for cross-platform GUI (graphical user interface) development. The Swing API provides a rich feature set, allowing you to construct sophisticated user interfaces. Using Swing, you can construct applications that allow the user to interact through basic controls[1] such as push buttons, entry fields, and list boxes or using advanced controls such as tables, trees, and drag & drop.

This chapter introduces Swing. It is an overview that shows you the basics: how to construct simple applications using some of the more common widgets. By no means does this chapter encompass everything about Swing. In fact, it only scratches the surface. Authors have devoted entire books, and even multiple volumes, to the topic.

Learning the basics of Swing, however, will provide you with a foundation for understanding how the rest of it works and how to go about finding more information. Once you have learned how to build a table widget using a table model, for example, learning how to build a tree widget using a tree model is easy. The Java API documentation usually provides sufficient information about how to use a widget. For more complex widgets, including the tree model and things such as sophisticated widget layouts, the Java API documentation often has a link to a good Sun tutorial on the topic.

More important, in this chapter you will learn various approaches to and philosophies about how to test Swing applications. Developers often view testing Swing applications as a difficult proposition and decide instead to forgo it. As a result, Swing code is frequently an untested, poorly designed mess.

This chapter is as much about ideas for testing Swing as it is about Swing itself. Testing Swing applications can be difficult, but that isn't an excuse to

---

[1]Also known as widgets or components, controls are elements of graphical user interfaces that either present information or allow end users some aspect of control over their interaction with the user interface.

not do so. There are huge benefits to having well-tested, well-designed user interface code.

There are two different aspects of design for user interfaces. The Java you design and code to construct the user interface is the aspect you will concern yourself with in this chapter. Another aspect of design is the aesthetic and functional quality of the user interface—its look and feel.

The look and feel represents requirements—how does an end user need to interact with the application? The customer, or perhaps a user interface design expert working with the customer, should derive and present these requirements to the development team. Many shops involve members of the development team in the GUI design as well. The format in which the customer presents requirements to the developers could be screen snapshots, crude drawings, or various formalized diagrams.

You will learn about:

- Swing application design

- panels and frames

- buttons and action listeners

- lists and list models

- Swing layouts: BorderLayout, GridLayout, FlowLayout, BoxLayout, GridBagLayout

Swing

Swing is not your only choice for GUI development, but it is available to you "out of the box." The Eclipse IDE was built using SWT (Standard Widget Toolkit), an API that you could also choose to use for your applications.

Swing is actually built atop another Java API known as AWT (Abstract Window Toolkit). Sun introduced AWT with the first version of Java as the sole means for producing GUIs. It consisted of a small number of widgets that at the time were guaranteed to be available on all platforms supported by Java. This "lowest common denominator" design decision allowed you to build cross-platform GUI applications but restricted your expressiveness with respect to GUI design.

AWT is known as a heavyweight GUI framework. Java tightly couples each AWT control to an equivalent control directly supported by the operating system. The operating system manages each AWT control.

Swing, which was introduced a few years after AWT, is, in contrast, a lightweight GUI framework. Swing eliminates the lowest common denominator problem by creating controls that use heavyweight controls as a "shell." Swing components inherit from AWT components. They add custom rendering and interaction code so that they act and look far more sophisticated than the controls supported by all operating systems.

You can attach a look and feel to your Swing application so that it mimics a specific operating system. For example, you can tell Java to render your Swing controls so that they look like Motif controls or like Windows controls.

Getting Started

 You will build a simple Swing application that presents a lists of courses to the end user. It will also allow the user to add new courses.

As you learn Swing, you might start with spike solutions—bits of code that demonstrate how Swing should work. Once you get these spikes working, you will go back and figure out how to test the Swing code. This chapter sometimes presents its material in this fashion: I will demonstrate how to code something in Swing, then supply code that shows how to test it.

Most applications, whether they use Swing or not, initiate with a *frame*. A frame is a top-level window with a title bar and border by default. The frame is largely drawn by and under the control of your operating system. Within Java, the Swing frame class is javax.swing.JFrame. Building an initial application in Java is as simple as constructing a JFrame, setting its size, and making it visible.

Create the class Sis (short for Student Information System).

```
package sis.ui;

import javax.swing.*;

public class Sis {
    static final int WIDTH = 350;
    static final int HEIGHT = 500;

    public static void main(String[] args) {
        new Sis().show();
    }

    public void show() {
        JFrame frame = new JFrame();
        frame.setSize(WIDTH, HEIGHT);
        frame.setVisible(true);
    }
}
```

Getting Started

Figure 1 *A Frame Window*

The definition for Sis includes a main method to allow you to execute the application from the command line. About the only things you ever want to do in a main method are to construct a new instance and call a single method on it. You may first need to call a method to parse the command-line arguments. If your main method is more involved, you need to refactor. Resist adding any real logic to main—main is usually not comprehensively tested.

Compile and execute Sis. You should see a simple frame window (see Figure 1). Experiment with this window and note that you can do things such as size it, minimize it, or close it like any other windowed application. You may also want to experiment with the setSize and setVisible messages to see how they impact the frame. Try omitting either or both message sends.

The only problem is that when you close this window, the Java process does not terminate. Behind the scenes, Swing creates user threads. Exiting the main method does not result in the termination of these user threads. See the section Shutting Down in Lesson 13 for a discussion of user threads and daemon threads.

You can tell the JFrame to terminate the Java process by telling it to exit on close:

```
package sis.ui;

import javax.swing.*;

public class Sis {
    static final int WIDTH = 300;
    static final int HEIGHT = 200;

    public static void main(String[] args) {
        new Sis().show();
    }
```

```
  void show() {
     JFrame frame = new JFrame();
     frame.setSize(WIDTH, HEIGHT);
     frame.setDefaultCloseOperation(JFrame.EXIT_ON_CLOSE);
     frame.setVisible(true);
  }
}
```

Now that you understand what it takes to build a frame, you can toss this code away and write a couple of tests. You will want to refer to the Java API documentation to see what kinds of queries you can send to a JFrame object. The tests show that you can inspect each piece of information you use to initialize the frame. You can also query whether or not the frame is visible.

```
package sis.ui;

import junit.framework.*;
import javax.swing.*;

public class SisTest extends TestCase {
   private Sis sis;
   private JFrame frame;

   protected void setUp() {
      sis = new Sis();
      frame = sis.getFrame();
   }

   public void testCreate() {
      final double tolerance = 0.05;
      assertEquals(Sis.HEIGHT, frame.getSize().getHeight(), tolerance);
      assertEquals(Sis.WIDTH, frame.getSize().getWidth(), tolerance);
      assertEquals(JFrame.EXIT_ON_CLOSE,
                   frame.getDefaultCloseOperation());
   }

   public void testShow() {
      sis.show();
      assertTrue(frame.isVisible());
   }
}
```

The code that meets this test ends up slightly different than the spike code:

```
package sis.ui;

import javax.swing.*;

public class Sis {
   static final int WIDTH = 300;
   static final int HEIGHT = 200;

   private JFrame frame = new JFrame();
```

```
public static void main(String[] args) {
    new Sis().show();
}

Sis() {
    frame.setSize(WIDTH, HEIGHT);
    frame.setDefaultCloseOperation(JFrame.EXIT_ON_CLOSE);
}

void show() {
    frame.setVisible(true);
}

JFrame getFrame() {
    return frame;
}
}
```

When you run the test, you will see the frame window display on screen, because the test instantiates Sis. Resist embedding such tests that pop up windows. It is very distracting and will slow down your tests considerably. You will learn techniques later that eliminate the need to render the user interface while running tests. For now, a test or two that pops up windows *might* be considered acceptable.

The frame window does not disappear even after the test completes. This is a bigger distraction that you can fix. In your test's tearDown method, tell the application to close:

```
public class SisTest extends TestCase {
    ...
    protected void tearDown() {
        sis.close();
    }
    ...
}
```

Close the application by having it dispose of the frame window:

```
package sis.ui;

import javax.swing.*;

public class Sis {
    ...
    private JFrame frame = new JFrame();
    ...
    void close() {
        frame.dispose();
    }
}
```

View First or Model First?

When developing a user interface, the question often arises of which to approach first: building the model or building the view? There is no right answer. It depends on your comfort level and ultimately on the approach you derive the most success from.

In the core 15 lessons of Agile Java, you learned to build Java classes in the absence of a user interface or place in a larger system. In reality, you will find that context often changes your design. Application needs may significantly impact the public interface of model classes.

I've been most successful when I've designed a system "application first." Each time I've built model classes in isolation, I've been forced to alter their behavior considerably when attempting to drop them into an application.

Even though I center the development of a system around its application classes, I do so with the view and its needs clearly in mind. And in reality, I rarely develop any of a system "first." I've found it far more effective to bounce around between the various layers, using tests and their results as my guide.

Swing Application Design

Designing a Swing application revolves around the organization of responsibilities germane to any application based on a user interface. These responsibilities include displaying information, managing input, modeling the business logic, and managing the application flow.

The terminology for these responsibilities is reasonably standard. A *view* displays things to the end user. The JFrame object in Sis is a view object. A *controller* manages input from the end user via the keyboard, mouse, or other device. A view may interact with one or more *models*, also known as domain objects. For example, code in the Sis application will need to interact with model objects of type Course and Student. Finally, the *application* coordinates models, views, and controllers. The application is responsible for the sequencing of a user's experience.

There are many ways to approach building Swing applications. You might hear different terms for these responsibilities. You might also encounter terms that imply various overlaps and combinations of the responsibilities. For example, Swing classes themselves often combine view and controller logic. (In fact, when you hear me refer to view in this chapter, I usually mean the combination of view and controller.) Nonetheless, the core responsibilities always exist. In this lesson, we will see where TDD takes us in terms of design—I've not forced any rigid design on the development of your example.

Swing
Application
Design

For the example, you will initially code the view portion of the Sis application. Per the Single-Responsibility Principle, the only code you should have in a view class is code responsible for displaying and arranging the user interface. A significant benefit of organizing the code this way is that you can execute the panel as a stand-alone application. This allows you to concentrate on developing the look, or *layout*, of the user interface.

In contrast, many Swing applications do not follow this rule. The view class in these applications is cluttered with other interactions. For example, the view class might send a message to a model class that in turn accesses data from the database. It is virtually impossible to display the view in isolation—that is, without executing the entire application. This design results in a significantly decreased rate of layout development. Often, you can access the view in question only by traversing a number of other application screens.

Panels

A JFrame envelopes a content pane—a place where you put visual content. A content pane object is a *container* of type java.awt.Container. You add other components to a container, including things such as list boxes, text, and containers themselves. In Swing, the workhorse container class is JPanel. Like JFrame, the JPanel class is a view class, used only for display purposes.

Panels

You may have noticed the package and naming convention. Swing components all begin with the letter J (JFrame, JPanel, JList, and so on); their containing package is javax.swing or a subpackage of javax.swing. The package java.awt (or a subpackage thereof) contains AWT classes. AWT class names do not use a prefix.

Your first piece of relevant user interface will be to display the text "Courses:" to the end user. You could directly embed this text in the JFrame's content pane. A better approach is to build up a second container consisting of the text, then embed this container in the content pane. To do so, you will create a JPanel subclass that displays text to the end user. You will then embed this JPanel in the JFrame's content pane.

Here is the spike for the JPanel:

```
package sis.ui;

import javax.swing.*;
import java.awt.*;
```

```
public class CoursesPanel extends JPanel {
    public static void main(String[] args) {
        show(new CoursesPanel());
    }

    private static void show(JPanel panel) {
        JFrame frame = new JFrame();
        frame.setSize(100, 100);
        frame.setDefaultCloseOperation(JFrame.EXIT_ON_CLOSE);
        frame.getContentPane().add(panel); // 1
        frame.setVisible(true);
    }

    public CoursesPanel() {
        JLabel label = new JLabel("Courses:");
        add(label);
    }
}
```

The spike uses a main method containing a bit of "driver" code to allow you to manually test the panel. If you were to code a second panel class, you would be compelled to refactor this driver code into a common utility class.

Within the constructor of CoursesPanel, you create a new JLabel object. A JLabel is a widget that displays text to an end user. You specify the text via the constructor of JLabel. In order for the JLabel to be displayed, you must add it to the JPanel using the add method.

CoursesPanel does not define add, nor does the JPanel class from which CoursesPanel extends. You must traverse the inheritance hierarchy up to the class java.awt.Container in order to find the definition for add. It makes sense for add to belong there: You add other components, including JPanel objects, to Container objects.

Following is the inheritance hierarchy for CoursesPanel.

```
Object
  |
  |-java.awt.Component
       |
       |-java.awt.Container
            |
            |-javax.swing.JComponent
                 |
                 |-javax.swing.JPanel
                      |
                      |-sis.ui.CoursesPanel
```

Everything in Swing sits atop the AWT framework. Everything is a Component. All Swing components (JComponent objects) are also containers. JPanel and CoursesPanel are therefore containers.

Panels

Figure 2 *A JPanel*

In order to display a panel, you can add it to the content pane of a JFrame. The line marked 1 in the show method of CoursesPanel accomplishes this.

Compile and execute the CoursesPanel spike. The result should look like Figure 2.

What should a test for CoursesPanel prove? For now, the only significant thing that CoursesPanel does is to present a label to the user. The test should thus ensure that the panel contains a label with the correct text:

```
package sis.ui;

import junit.framework.*;
import javax.swing.*;
import java.awt.*;

public class CoursesPanelTest extends TestCase {
    public void testCreate() {
        CoursesPanel panel = new CoursesPanel();
        JLabel label = getLabel(panel);
        assertEquals(CoursesPanel.LABEL_TEXT, label.getText());
    }

    private JLabel getLabel(JPanel panel) {
        for (Component component: panel.getComponents())
            if (component instanceof JLabel)
                return (JLabel)component;
        return null;
    }
}
```

Panels

The job of the method getLabel is to take as its parameter a JPanel and return the first JLabel object encountered within the JPanel. Since a JPanel is a Container, you can ask it for the list of components it contains using the getComponents message. Each element contained within the list is of type java.awt.Component. You must test the type of each element using instanceof to determine if it is a JLabel. You must also cast the matching element in order to return it as a JLabel type.

The use of instanceof suggests that perhaps a better approach works to determine if a component exists. For now, the technique will suffice until you have to test for a second type of component—or a second label.

Is this test necessary? The answer is debatable. You will always manually execute a Swing application from time to time to take a look, even if you were to write thousands of automated tests. In doing so, you will quickly determine whether or not a specific component appears.

One could also ask the opposite question: *Is this test sufficient?* Not only could you test that the widget appeared in the window but you could also test that it was presented in the appropriate font and appeared at the correct coordinates.

My view is that the test may be mild overkill, but it's not a difficult test to write. I would rather expend the effort than find out the hard way that someone accidentally changed the JLabel text in one of 200 screens. Positioning-based layout tests (tests that prove where the label appears onscreen) are another matter. They are notoriously difficult to write and even more difficult to maintain. A bit of aesthetic distress is not usually a barrier to successful application execution.

More important is that you write tests for any dynamic user interface capabilities. For example, you might allow the application to change the color of text when the user presses a button. You will want to write a test to ensure that this action and reaction works as you expect.

The CoursesPanel class differs from the spike only in that it defines a class constant representing the label text.

```
package sis.ui;

import javax.swing.*;
import java.awt.*;

public class CoursesPanel extends JPanel {
   static final String LABEL_TEXT = "Courses";
   ...
   public CoursesPanel() {
      JLabel label = new JLabel(LABEL_TEXT);
      add(label);
   }
}
```

In the Sis application, you want CoursesPanel to represent the main view. The modified SisTest uses a similar mechanism to that in CoursesPanelTest to prove that the content pane contains a CoursesPanel instance.

```
package sis.ui;

import junit.framework.*;
import javax.swing.*;
import java.awt.*;
```

```
public class SisTest extends TestCase {
    ...
    public void testCreate() {
        final double tolerance = 0.05;
        assertEquals(Sis.HEIGHT, frame.getSize().getHeight(), tolerance);
        assertEquals(Sis.WIDTH, frame.getSize().getWidth(), tolerance);
        assertEquals(JFrame.EXIT_ON_CLOSE,
                     frame.getDefaultCloseOperation());
        assertTrue(containsCoursesPanel(frame));
    }

    private boolean containsCoursesPanel(JFrame frame) {
        Container pane = frame.getContentPane();
        for (Component component: pane.getComponents())
            if (component instanceof CoursesPanel)
                return true;
        return false;
    }
    ...
}
```

You're already familiar with how to get a frame to include and show a panel. You wrote virtually the same code in the "driver" for CoursesPanel.

```
package sis.ui;

import javax.swing.*;

public class Sis {
    ...
    Sis() {
        frame.setSize(WIDTH, HEIGHT);
        frame.setDefaultCloseOperation(JFrame.EXIT_ON_CLOSE);
        frame.getContentPane().add(new CoursesPanel());
    }
    ...
}
```

The tests pass.

Refactoring

In the course of building this example for the book, I coded the Sis constructor to include the statement that makes the frame visible. Michael Feathers reminded me that constructors are for initialization only. It's a bit of a stretch, I countered, but you could consider displaying the window as part of its initialization. To which he replied, using wisdom from Ron Jeffries, that a constructor has a lot of nerve doing something it isn't asked to do.

I listened to the voices of these two and fixed the deficiency. However, I still consider that GUI widget and layout construction is simple initialization. Putting panels within a frame is layout initialization. While you could conceivably separate this layout initialization from object initialization, there is little value in doing so. A JPanel subclass with uninitialized contents is of little use. Forcing clients to make an additional call to initialize its layout is redundant.

Separating the setVisible statement from the constructor is of potential value, however. In the case of SisTest, doing so allowed for a separate initialization test that doesn't force the frame to be rendered. In production systems, it's often valuable to initialize a frame behind the scenes, later controlling its visibility separately.

Ultimately the decision is somewhat arbitrary and thus academic. With regards to CoursesPanel, a future requirement may require a developer to create a CoursesPanel subclass. Putting initialization code in a separate method makes it easier to override or extend the initialization functionality. Yet you want to avoid designing for future what-ifs (that often never come). It's just as easy to wait and make the change down the road—if necessary.

An acceptable compromise is to consider simple design rule #3 and extract initialization to a private method for readability purposes:

```
public CoursesPanel() {
    createLayout();
}

private void createLayout() {
    JLabel label = new JLabel(LABEL_TEXT);
    add(label);
}
```

Refactoring

The code in SisTest.containsCoursesPanel is very similar in form to that in CoursesPanelTest.getLabel. Both methods loop through the components in a container and test for a match.

The duplicate code is a problem that will only get worse. Adding buttons, list boxes, or other component types will require a new method for each type. Additionally, suppose you have two labels on a panel. The current code will grab only the first label.

One solution is to provide a name for each component. You can then loop through the list of subcomponents until you find a matching name. This solution requires a little more management overhead in your view class, but it makes testing easier. It also can make aggregate operations on components easier, as you'll see later.

All component and container classes inherit from java.awt.Component. In this class you will find the methods setName and getName that respectively take and return a String object.

Starting with the code in SisTest:

```
public void testCreate() {
    final double tolerance = 0.05;
    assertEquals(Sis.HEIGHT, frame.getSize().getHeight(), tolerance);
    assertEquals(Sis.WIDTH, frame.getSize().getWidth(), tolerance);
    assertEquals(JFrame.EXIT_ON_CLOSE,
                 frame.getDefaultCloseOperation());
    assertNotNull(getComponent(frame, CoursesPanel.NAME));
}

private Component getComponent(JFrame frame, String name) {
    Container container = frame.getContentPane();
    for (Component component: container.getComponents())
        if (name.equals(component.getName()))
            return component;
    return null;
}
```

The corresponding changes to CoursesPanel:

```
package sis.ui;
...
public class CoursesPanel extends JPanel {
    static final String NAME = "coursesPanel";
    ...
    public CoursesPanel() {
        setName(NAME);
        createLayout();
    }
}
```

Refactoring

Part of the secret to eliminating duplication is to push toward use of abstractions. For example, the new getComponent method deals in terms of abstract components instead of the concrete type CoursesPanel. Pushing the code in CoursesPanelTest in this direction leads to:

```
package sis.ui;
...
public class CoursesPanelTest extends TestCase {
    public void testCreate() {
        CoursesPanel panel = new CoursesPanel();
        JLabel label =
            (JLabel)getComponent(panel, CoursesPanel.LABEL_NAME);
        assertEquals(CoursesPanel.LABEL_TEXT, label.getText());
    }

    private Component getComponent(Container container, String name) {
        for (Component component: container.getComponents())
            if (name.equals(component.getName()))
```

```
        return component;
     return null;
   }
}

// in CoursesPanel:
...
public class CoursesPanel extends JPanel {
   static final String LABEL_NAME = "coursesLabel";
...
   private void createLayout() {
      JLabel label = new JLabel(LABEL_TEXT);
      label.setName(LABEL_NAME);
      add(label);
   }
}
```

At this point, the getComponent methods are different only by the first line. For lack of a better place, move them into a new class as class methods and refactor. Here is the code for the resulting class, sis.ui.Util, as well as for the modified test classes:

```
// sis.ui.Util
package sis.ui;

import java.awt.*;
import javax.swing.*;

class Util {
   static Component getComponent(Container container, String name) {
      for (Component component: container.getComponents())
         if (name.equals(component.getName()))
            return component;
      return null;
   }

   static Component getComponent(JFrame frame, String name) {
      return getComponent(frame.getContentPane(), name);
   }
}
// sis.ui.SisTest
public void testCreate() {
   final double tolerance = 0.05;
   assertEquals(Sis.HEIGHT, frame.getSize().getHeight(), tolerance);
   assertEquals(Sis.WIDTH, frame.getSize().getWidth(), tolerance);
   assertEquals(JFrame.EXIT_ON_CLOSE,
              frame.getDefaultCloseOperation());
   assertNotNull(Util.getComponent(frame, CoursesPanel.NAME));
}

// sis.ui.CoursesPanelTest
public void testCreate() {
   CoursesPanel panel = new CoursesPanel();
```

Refactoring

```
        JLabel label =
            (JLabel)Util.getComponent(panel, CoursesPanel.LABEL_NAME);
        assertEquals(CoursesPanel.LABEL_TEXT, label.getText());
    }
```

The new method calls are a bit more unwieldy. One reason is the new need to cast. You'll refactor when or if casting duplication becomes apparent. But the short-term solution is a vast improvement—you've eliminated method-level duplication that otherwise would become rampant in short time.

More Widgets

The SIS application should allow users to add new courses. To support this, CoursesPanel can contain a couple of entry fields in which the user may type the course department and course number. The user should be able to click an "Add" button that adds a new course, created using the entered department and number, to the list.

The test for the view:

```
package sis.ui;

import junit.framework.*;
import javax.swing.*;
import java.awt.*;
import static sis.ui.CoursesPanel.*;

public class CoursesPanelTest extends TestCase {
    public void testCreate() {
        CoursesPanel panel = new CoursesPanel();
        JLabel label =
            (JLabel)Util.getComponent(panel, LABEL_NAME);
        assertEquals(LABEL_TEXT, label.getText());

        JList list =
            (JList)Util.getComponent(panel, COURSES_LIST_NAME);
        assertEquals(0, list.getModel().getSize());

        JButton button =
            (JButton)Util.getComponent(panel, ADD_BUTTON_NAME);
        assertEquals(ADD_BUTTON_TEXT, button.getText());

        JLabel departmentLabel =
            (JLabel)Util.getComponent(panel, DEPARTMENT_LABEL_NAME);
        assertEquals(DEPARTMENT_LABEL_TEXT, departmentLabel.getText());

        JTextField departmentField =
            (JTextField)Util.getComponent(panel, DEPARTMENT_FIELD_NAME);
        assertEquals("", departmentField.getText());
```

```
        JLabel numberLabel =
            (JLabel)Util.getComponent(panel, NUMBER_LABEL_NAME);
        assertEquals(NUMBER_LABEL_TEXT, numberLabel.getText());

        JTextField numberField =
            (JTextField)Util.getComponent(panel, NUMBER_FIELD_NAME);
        assertEquals("", numberField.getText());
    }
}
```

The qualified class constants were getting a bit unwieldy, so I decided to do a static import of the CoursesPanel class. In this case, there is little possibility for confusion about the origin of the class constants.

The role of new component types JButton, JTextField, and JList should be apparent. Code for most of the assertions against the new widgets is similar to the previously coded test for the label.

The assertion against the JList object is different. It proves that the JList on a newly constructed CoursesPanel is empty. You can determine how many elements a JList contains by first obtaining its model, then asking the model for its size. A JList uses a model object to contain its data. You will learn more about list models in the upcoming section, List Models.

The modified view class:

```
package sis.ui;

import javax.swing.*;
import java.awt.*;

public class CoursesPanel extends JPanel {
    static final String NAME = "coursesPanel";
    static final String LABEL_TEXT = "Courses";
    static final String LABEL_NAME = "coursesLabel";
    static final String COURSES_LIST_NAME = "coursesList";
    static final String ADD_BUTTON_TEXT = "Add";
    static final String ADD_BUTTON_NAME = "addButton";
    static final String DEPARTMENT_FIELD_NAME = "deptField";
    static final String NUMBER_FIELD_NAME = "numberField";
    static final String DEPARTMENT_LABEL_NAME = "deptLabel";
    static final String NUMBER_LABEL_NAME = "numberLabel";
    static final String DEPARTMENT_LABEL_TEXT = "Department";
    static final String NUMBER_LABEL_TEXT = "Number";

    public static void main(String[] args) {
        show(new CoursesPanel());
    }

    private static void show(JPanel panel) {
        JFrame frame = new JFrame();
        frame.setSize(300, 200);
```

```
        frame.setDefaultCloseOperation(JFrame.EXIT_ON_CLOSE);
        frame.getContentPane().add(panel); // 1
        frame.setVisible(true);
    }

    public CoursesPanel() {
        setName(NAME);
        createLayout();
    }

    private void createLayout() {
        JLabel label = new JLabel(LABEL_TEXT);
        label.setName(LABEL_NAME);

        JList list = new JList();
        list.setName(COURSES_LIST_NAME);

        JButton addButton = new JButton(ADD_BUTTON_TEXT);
        addButton.setName(ADD_BUTTON_NAME);

        int columns = 20;

        JLabel departmentLabel = new JLabel(DEPARTMENT_LABEL_TEXT);
        departmentLabel.setName(DEPARTMENT_LABEL_NAME);

        JTextField departmentField = new JTextField(columns);
        departmentField.setName(DEPARTMENT_FIELD_NAME);

        JLabel numberLabel = new JLabel(NUMBER_LABEL_TEXT);
        numberLabel.setName(NUMBER_LABEL_NAME);

        JTextField numberField = new JTextField(columns);
        numberField.setName(NUMBER_FIELD_NAME);

        add(label);
        add(list);
        add(addButton);
        add(departmentLabel);
        add(departmentField);
        add(numberLabel);
        add(numberField);
    }
}
```

More Widgets

The tests should pass. You should see a window similar to that in Figure 3 when you compile and execute the view class.

The user interface is a mess. You'll rectify this in the upcoming section entitled Layout. Also, nothing that would seem to be a JList appears in the window. One reason is that you have added no elements to the list—it is empty. You'll fix this in time as well.

Even with only seven widgets, you've written a good amount of tedious code to test and build the user interface. Let's see what we can do to tighten it up.

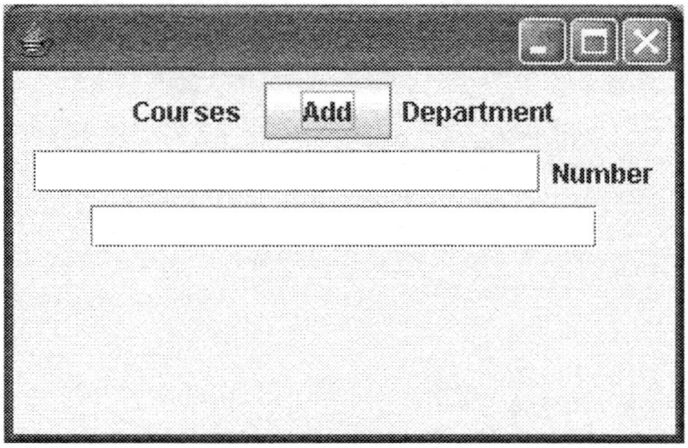

Figure 3

Refactoring

The getComponent method calls require casts. For example:

```
JTextField numberField =
    (JTextField)Util.getComponent(panel, NUMBER_FIELD_NAME);
```

Since you must retrieve two text fields from the panel, you have two lines of code with the same cast. This is a form of duplication that you can eliminate, using convenience methods that both eliminate the cast and make the code clearer.

The separate utility class Util contains the getComponent method. However, it is perhaps more appropriate for CoursesPanel to have this responsibility, since a panel is a container of components.

The following listing shows a highly refactored CoursesPanelTest. Some of the changes to CoursesPanelTest will necessitate changes in CoursesPanel—see the listing after this one.

```
package sis.ui;

import junit.framework.*;
import javax.swing.*;
import java.awt.*;
import static sis.ui.CoursesPanel.*;

public class CoursesPanelTest extends TestCase {
    private CoursesPanel panel;

    protected void setUp() {
        panel = new CoursesPanel();
```

Refactoring

```
    }

    public void testCreate() {
        assertLabelText(COURSES_LABEL_NAME, COURSES_LABEL_TEXT);
        assertEmptyList(COURSES_LIST_NAME);
        assertButtonText(ADD_BUTTON_NAME, ADD_BUTTON_TEXT);
        assertLabelText(DEPARTMENT_LABEL_NAME, DEPARTMENT_LABEL_TEXT);
        assertEmptyField(DEPARTMENT_FIELD_NAME);
        assertLabelText(NUMBER_LABEL_NAME, NUMBER_LABEL_TEXT);
        assertEmptyField(NUMBER_FIELD_NAME);
    }

    private void assertLabelText(String name, String text) {
        JLabel label = panel.getLabel(name);
        assertEquals(text, label.getText());
    }

    private void assertEmptyField(String name) {
        JTextField field = panel.getField(name);
        assertEquals("", field.getText());
    }

    private void assertEmptyList(String name) {
        JList list = panel.getList(name);
        assertEquals(0, list.getModel().getSize());
    }

    private void assertButtonText(String name, String text) {
        JButton button = panel.getButton(name);
        assertEquals(text, button.getText());
    }
}
```

Refactoring

While some of these refactorings eliminate duplication, technically not all of them do. However, those refactorings that do not eliminate duplication help improve readability. First, even though only one list needs to be verified, creating assertEmptyList more clearly states the intent. Second, extracting assertButtonText allows the entire body of testCreate to contain single-line, simple, consistently phrased assertion statements.

Each of the new assertion methods contains two implicit tests. First, if no component with the given name exists within the panel, a NullPointerException will be thrown, failing the test. Second, if the component is not of the expected type, a ClassCastException will be thrown, also failing the test. If this implicitness bothers you, feel free to add additional assertions (e.g. assertNotNull), but I don't view them as necessary.

The new assertion methods are very general purpose. When (or if) you add a second panel to the SIS application, you can refactor the assertion methods to a common test utility class. You might choose to move them to a junit.framework.TestCase subclass that all panel test classes inherit.

In most systems, Swing code and associated test code is excessive and repetitive. Take the time up front to do these refactorings. You will significantly minimize the amount of redundancy and overall code in your system.

You can refactor component creation in CoursesPanel in a similar manner. The following listing shows new component creation methods in addition to the get methods required by the test.

```java
package sis.ui;

import javax.swing.*;
import java.awt.*;

public class CoursesPanel extends JPanel {
    static final String NAME = "coursesPanel";
    static final String COURSES_LABEL_TEXT = "Courses";
    static final String COURSES_LABEL_NAME = "coursesLabel";
    ...
    private void createLayout() {
        JLabel coursesLabel =
            createLabel(COURSES_LABEL_NAME, COURSES_LABEL_TEXT);

        JList coursesList = createList(COURSES_LIST_NAME);
        JButton addButton =
            createButton(ADD_BUTTON_NAME, ADD_BUTTON_TEXT);

        int columns = 20;
        JLabel departmentLabel =
            createLabel(DEPARTMENT_LABEL_NAME, DEPARTMENT_LABEL_TEXT);
        JTextField departmentField =
            createField(DEPARTMENT_FIELD_NAME, columns);
        JLabel numberLabel =
            createLabel(NUMBER_LABEL_NAME, NUMBER_LABEL_TEXT);
        JTextField numberField =
            createField(NUMBER_FIELD_NAME, columns);

        add(coursesLabel);
        add(coursesList);
        add(addButton);
        add(departmentLabel);
        add(departmentField);
        add(numberLabel);
        add(numberField);
    }

    private JLabel createLabel(String name, String text) {
        JLabel label = new JLabel(text);
        label.setName(name);
        return label;
    }

    private JList createList(String name) {
        JList list = new JList();
```

```
        list.setName(name);
        return list;
    }

    private JButton createButton(String name, String text) {
        JButton button = new JButton(text);
        button.setName(name);
        return button;
    }

    private JTextField createField(String name, int columns) {
        JTextField field = new JTextField(columns);
        field.setName(name);
        return field;
    }

    JLabel getLabel(String name) {
        return (JLabel)Util.getComponent(this, name);
    }

    JList getList(String name) {
        return (JList)Util.getComponent(this, name);
    }

    JButton getButton(String name) {
        return (JButton)Util.getComponent(this, name);
    }

    JTextField getField(String name) {
        return (JTextField)Util.getComponent(this, name);
    }
}
```

Button Clicks and ActionListeners

When you click a Swing button, some action should take place. When you click on the Add button in CoursesPanel, you want a new course to show up in the list of courses. Code to accomplish this will require three steps:

1. Read the contents of the course department and course number text fields.

2. Create a new Course object using the course department and course number text.

3. Put the Course object in the model for the courses list.

Adding a new course with these steps is a mixture of user interface responsibility and business logic. Remember, you want CoursesPanel to be a more or less dumb class that just shows information to the user. Clicking a button is a controller event, one that you can respond to with an action. The details of the action—the business logic—does not belong in CoursesPanel.

For now, you still need to write a test for the view class. Code in the panel class still needs to tell "someone" to take action when a user clicks the Add button. The panel test will prove that clicking on an Add button triggers some action—an action that has yet to be defined.

You can wire a button click to an action method by using a callback. Java supplies the interface java.awt.event.ActionListener for this purpose. To implement ActionListener, you code the action method actionPerformed. Code in actionPerformed should do whatever you want to happen when someone clicks the button.

After defining an ActionListener class, you can assign an instance of it to the button. When a user clicks the button, logic in JButton calls back to the actionPerformed method on the ActionListener object.

```
package sis.ui;

import junit.framework.*;
import javax.swing.*;
import java.awt.*;
import java.awt.event.*;
import static sis.ui.CoursesPanel.*;

public class CoursesPanelTest extends TestCase {
   private CoursesPanel panel;
   private boolean wasClicked;

   protected void setUp() {
      panel = new CoursesPanel();
   }
   ...
   public void testAddButtonClick() {
      JButton button = panel.getButton(ADD_BUTTON_NAME);

      wasClicked = false;
      panel.addCourseAddListener(new ActionListener() {
         public void actionPerformed(ActionEvent e) {
            wasClicked = true;
         }
      });

      button.doClick();
      assertTrue(wasClicked);
   }
}
```

Button Clicks and ActionListeners

You will usually want to implement listeners as anonymous inner classes. Here, the sole job of the ActionListener is to ensure that the actionPerformed method gets called when the button is clicked. The JButton class provides the method doClick to emulate a user clicking on a button.

CoursesPanel must supply a new method, addCourseAddListener. This method simply attaches the ActionListener callback object to the JButton object. Some production client using CoursesPanel will be responsible for defining this callback and passing it to the view. The view remains blissfully ignorant of any business logic.

```
package sis.ui;

import javax.swing.*;
import java.awt.*;
import java.awt.event.*;

public class CoursesPanel extends JPanel {
    ...
    private JButton addButton;
    ...
    private void createLayout() {
        ...
        addButton = createButton(ADD_BUTTON_NAME, ADD_BUTTON_TEXT);
        ...
    }

    void addCourseAddListener(ActionListener listener) {
        addButton.addActionListener(listener);
    }
    ...
}
```

List Models

You must change addButton to be a field and not a local variable for this to work.

The method addCourseAddListener is a single line of code. For view code other than layout, this is your ideal. If you find yourself putting while loops, if statements, or other convoluted logic in your view class, stop! It likely contains business or application logic that you should represent elsewhere.

List Models

You have gotten the view to represent part of the equation: Tell "someone" to do "something" when the user clicks Add. You know that the result of clicking Add should be that the courses panel shows a new course. You want your view class to treat these as two discrete operations; you'll implement logic elsewhere to connect the two.

The view should allow client code to pass a Course object and, as a result, display the course object. It doesn't care how the Course object comes into being. Add a new test to CoursesPanelTest:

```
package sis.ui;

import junit.framework.*;
import javax.swing.*;
import java.awt.*;
import java.awt.event.*;
import sis.studentinfo.*;
import static sis.ui.CoursesPanel.*;

public class CoursesPanelTest extends TestCase {
    ...
    public void testAddCourse() {
        Course course = new Course("ENGL", "101");
        panel.addCourse(course);
        JList list = panel.getList(COURSES_LIST_NAME);
        ListModel model = list.getModel();
        assertEquals("ENGL 101", model.getElementAt(0).toString());
    }
    ...
}
```

The test sends the addCourse message to the CoursePanel. It then extracts the underlying model of the JList. A list model is a collection class that notifies the JList when something in the collection changes.

The JList view needs to show a useful representation of the objects contained in the model. To do so, JList code sends the toString message to each object in the model. The final line in the test asserts that the printable representation of the first object in the model is the concatenated department and course number.

List Models

```
package sis.ui;

import javax.swing.*;
import java.awt.*;
import java.awt.event.*;
import sis.studentinfo.*;

public class CoursesPanel extends JPanel {
    ...
    private DefaultListModel coursesModel = new DefaultListModel();
    ...
    private void createLayout() {
        JLabel coursesLabel =
            createLabel(COURSES_LABEL_NAME, COURSES_LABEL_TEXT);

        JList coursesList = createList(COURSES_LIST_NAME, coursesModel);
        ...
```

```
      }
      ...
      void addCourse(Course course) {
          coursesModel.addElement(course);
      }
      ...
      private JList createList(String name, ListModel model) {
          JList list = new JList(model);
          list.setName(name);
          return list;
      }
  }
```

A list model is a class that implements the interface javax.swing.List-Model. For JList objects, you will normally use the ListModel implementation class DefaultListModel. Interestingly, the ListModel interface declares no interface methods for adding elements. DefaultListModel does (addElement). You will want to declare the model reference (coursesModel) as being of the implementation type DefaultListModel and not of the interface type ListModel.

In the CoursesPanel method createList, you now pass a ListModel reference to the JList as you construct it. The addCourse method takes the Course passed to it and stuffs it into the model.

Use of **toString**

I mentioned in Lesson 9 that you should not depend upon the toString method for production code. A toString method is generally more useful for developer-related debugging activities. A developer might need to change Course output from the form:

List Models

ENGL 101

to something like:

[Course:ENGL,101]

The modified string would be inappropriate for the CoursesPanel user interface view. Another conflict can arise if two different views must show Course information in different formats.

In either case, you can and should introduce a display adapter class that wraps each course and provides the toString definition needed. You store these adapter objects in the JList model.

 The user now wants to see a hyphen between each department and course number in the list. Modify the test to require this new display format:

```
public void testAddCourse() {
    Course course = new Course("ENGL", "101");
    panel.addCourse(course);
    JList list = panel.getList(COURSES_LIST_NAME);

    ListModel model = list.getModel();
    assertEquals("ENGL-101", model.getElementAt(0).toString());
}
```

A simple implementation of the adapter class is to have it subclass Course and override the definition of toString.

```
package sis.ui;

import sis.studentinfo.*;

class CourseDisplayAdapter extends Course {
    CourseDisplayAdapter(Course course) {
        super(course.getDepartment(), course.getNumber());
    }

    @Override
    public String toString() {
        return String.format(
            "%s-%s", getDepartment(), getNumber());
    }
}
```

The CoursesPanel addCourse method must change:

```
void addCourse(Course course) {
    coursesModel.addElement(new CourseDisplayAdapter(course));
}
```

Later, when you need to write code to obtain a Course selected in the list box, you'll need to extract the target Course from its adapter.

The Application

The Application

Now that the view is in place, you can specify how the application should use it. It's time to tie things together.[2] Here's a new SisTest method, testAddCourse.

---

[2]Depending on your mindset, you might have found it easier to have started building from the application and driven down into the view. Even while I was constructing the view, I had in mind how I wanted the application to tie things together.

```
package sis.ui;

import junit.framework.*;
import javax.swing.*;
import java.awt.*;
import sis.studentinfo.*;

public class SisTest extends TestCase {
    ...
    public void testAddCourse() {
        CoursesPanel panel =
            (CoursesPanel)Util.getComponent(frame, CoursesPanel.NAME);
        panel.setText(CoursesPanel.DEPARTMENT_FIELD_NAME, "MATH");
        panel.setText(CoursesPanel.NUMBER_FIELD_NAME, "300");

        JButton button = panel.getButton(CoursesPanel.ADD_BUTTON_NAME);
        button.doClick();

        Course course = panel.getCourse(0);
        assertEquals("MATH", course.getDepartment());
        assertEquals("300", course.getNumber());
    }
}
```

The test drives the application from the perspective of an end user. It's almost an acceptance test.

First, the test sets values into the department and course number fields. It then emulates a click of the Add button using the button method click. In order to ensure that the application is behaving correctly, the tests asks the embedded CoursesPanel to return the first Course in its list.

You'll need to add a couple of methods to CoursesPanel to support the test:

The Application

```
package sis.ui;
...
public class CoursesPanel extends JPanel {
    ...
    Course getCourse(int index) {
        Course adapter =
            (CourseDisplayAdapter)coursesModel.getElementAt(index);
        return adapter;
    }
    ...
    void setText(String textFieldName, String text) {
        getField(textFieldName).setText(text);
    }
}
```

Since a CourseDisplayAdapter extends from Course, you can assign the extracted adapter object to a Course reference to return.

Code changes to Sis (including a few minor refactorings):

```
package sis.ui;

import javax.swing.*;
import java.awt.event.*;
import sis.studentinfo.*;

public class Sis {
    ...
    private CoursesPanel panel;
    ...

    public Sis() {
        initialize();
    }

    private void initialize() {
        createCoursesPanel();

        frame.setSize(WIDTH, HEIGHT);
        frame.setDefaultCloseOperation(JFrame.EXIT_ON_CLOSE);
        frame.getContentPane().add(panel);
    }
    ...
    void createCoursesPanel() {
        panel = new CoursesPanel();
        panel.addCourseAddListener(
            new ActionListener() {
                public void actionPerformed(ActionEvent e) {
                    addCourse();
                }
            }
        );
    }

    private void addCourse() {
        Course course =
            new Course(
                panel.getText(CoursesPanel.DEPARTMENT_FIELD_NAME),
                panel.getText(CoursesPanel.NUMBER_FIELD_NAME));
        panel.addCourse(course);
    }
}
```

The Sis class ties together the action listener and the ability to add a course to the panel. Most of the code should look familiar—it is the client code you built in tests for CoursesPanel.

You'll need to add the getText method to CoursesPanel:

```
String getText(String textFieldName) {
    return getField(textFieldName).getText();
}
```

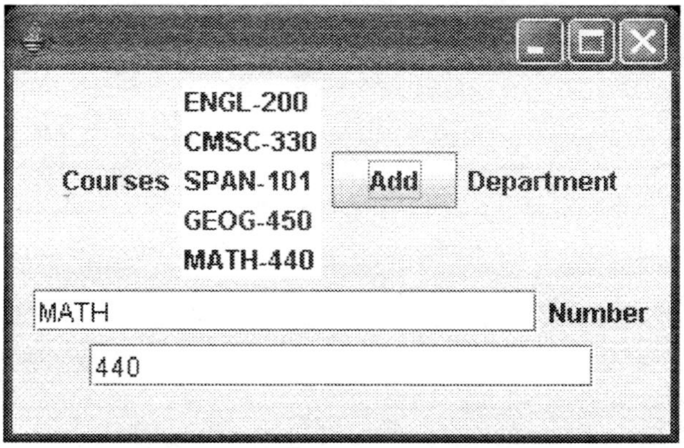

Figure 4

You can now run Sis as a stand-alone application and experiment with adding courses. The screen shot in Figure 4 shows Sis after a user has entered five courses. It's still a mess!

Layout

The user interface for the Sis application is so poorly laid out that it's confusing to the end user. The problem is that by default, Swing lays out components to flow from left to right, in the order you add them to a container. When insufficient room remains to place a component on a "line," Swing wraps it, just like a word in a word processor. The component appears to the left side of the panel below the current line.

In Figure 4, the first line consists of four widgets: the "Courses" label, the list of courses, the Add button, and the "Department" label. The second line consists of the department field, the "Number" label, and the course number field.

Resize the window and make it as wide as your screen. Swing will redraw the widgets. If your screen is wide enough, all of the components should flow from left to right on a single line.

Swing provides several alternate layout mechanisms, each in a separate class, to help you produce aesthetically pleasing user interfaces. Swing refers to these classes as *layout managers*. You can associate a different layout manager with each container. The default layout manager, java.awt.FlowLayout, is not very useful if you want to create a professional-looking user interface.

Getting a view to look "just right" is an incremental, taxing exercise. You will find that mixing and matching layouts is an easier strategy than trying to stick to a single layout for a complex view.

An alternative to hand-coding layouts is to use a tool. Many IDEs provide GUI (view) composition tools that allow you to visually edit a layout. Using a tool can reduce the tedium of trying to get a user interface to be perfect.

You will learn to use a few of the more-significant layout mechanisms in an attempt to make CoursesPanel look good. Little of this work requires you to test first. Instead, you should test last. Make a small change, compile, run your tests, execute CoursesPanel as a stand-alone application, view the results, react!

GridLayout

You'll start with a simply understood but usually inappropriate layout, Grid-Layout. A GridLayout divides the container into equal-sized rectangles based on the number of rows and columns you specify. As you add components to the container, the GridLayout puts each in a cell (rectangle), moving from left to right, top to bottom (by default). The layout manager resizes each component to fit its cell.

Make the following changes in CoursesPanel:

```
private void createLayout() {
    JLabel coursesLabel =
        createLabel(COURSES_LABEL_NAME, COURSES_LABEL_TEXT);

    JList coursesList = createList(COURSES_LIST_NAME, coursesModel);
    addButton =
        createButton(ADD_BUTTON_NAME, ADD_BUTTON_TEXT);
    int columns = 20;
    JLabel departmentLabel =
        createLabel(DEPARTMENT_LABEL_NAME, DEPARTMENT_LABEL_TEXT);
    JTextField departmentField =
        createField(DEPARTMENT_FIELD_NAME, columns);
    JLabel numberLabel =
        createLabel(NUMBER_LABEL_NAME, NUMBER_LABEL_TEXT);
    JTextField numberField =
        createField(NUMBER_FIELD_NAME, columns);

    int rows = 4;
    int cols = 2;
    setLayout(new GridLayout(rows, cols));
```

Layout

```
     add(coursesLabel);
     add(coursesList);
     add(addButton);
     add(new JPanel());
     add(departmentLabel);
     add(departmentField);
     add(numberLabel);
     add(numberField);
}
```

You assign a layout manager to the panel by sending it the message setLayout. In createLayout, you send the message setLayout to the CoursesPanel object, passing it a GridLayout instance.

The result of executing CoursesPanel using the GridLayout is shown in Figure 5.

The coursesLabel ends up in the upper left rectangle. The coursesList, the second component to be added, is in the upper right rectangle. The Add button drops down to the second row of rectangles, and is followed by an empty JPanel to fill the next rectangle. Each of the final two rows displays a label and its corresponding field.

Since each rectangle must be the same size, GridLayout doesn't have a lot of applicability in organizing "typical" interfaces with lots of buttons, fields, lists, and labels. It does have applicability if, for example, you are presenting a suite of icons to the end user. GridLayout does contain additional methods to improve upon its look, but you will usually want to use a more-sophisticated layout manager.

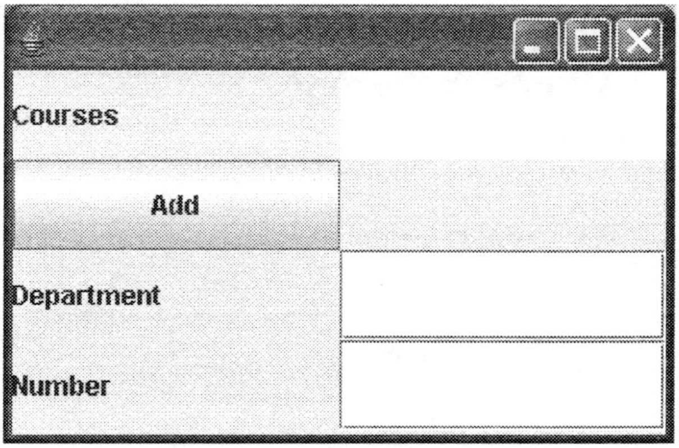

Layout

Figure 5

BorderLayout

BorderLayout is a simple but effective layout manager. BorderLayout allows you to place up to five components within the container: one each at the compass points north, east, south, and west and one to fill the remainder, or center (see Figure 6).

For CoursesPanel, you will replace the GridLayout with a BorderLayout. Your BorderLayout will use three of the available areas: north, to contain the "Courses" Label; center, to contain the list of courses; and south, to contain the remainder of the widgets. You will organize the southern, or "bottom," widgets in a subpanel that uses a separate layout manager.

The createLayout method already is overly long, at close to 30 lines. Courses-Panel is a simple interface so far. Imagine a sophisticated panel with several dozen widgets. Unfortunately, it is common to encounter Swing code that does all of the requisite initialization and layout in a single method. Developers create panels within panels, they create and initialize components and place them in panels, they create layouts, and so on.

A more effective code composition is to extract the creation of each panel into a separate method. This not only makes the code far more readable but also provides more flexibility in rearranging the layout. I've refactored the code in CoursesPanel to reflect this cleaner organization.

```
private void createLayout() {
    JLabel coursesLabel =
        createLabel(COURSES_LABEL_NAME, COURSES_LABEL_TEXT);

    JList coursesList = createList(COURSES_LIST_NAME, coursesModel);
```

Layout

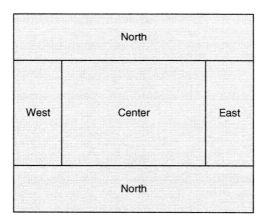

Figure 6 *A Border Layout Configuration*

```
        setLayout(new BorderLayout());

        add(coursesLabel, BorderLayout.NORTH);
        add(coursesList, BorderLayout.CENTER);
        add(createBottomPanel(), BorderLayout.SOUTH);
    }

    JPanel createBottomPanel() {
        addButton = createButton(ADD_BUTTON_NAME, ADD_BUTTON_TEXT);

        JPanel panel = new JPanel();
        panel.setLayout(new BorderLayout());

        panel.add(addButton, BorderLayout.NORTH);
        panel.add(createFieldsPanel(), BorderLayout.SOUTH);

        return panel;
    }

    JPanel createFieldsPanel() {
        int columns = 20;
        JLabel departmentLabel =
            createLabel(DEPARTMENT_LABEL_NAME, DEPARTMENT_LABEL_TEXT);
        JTextField departmentField =
            createField(DEPARTMENT_FIELD_NAME, columns);
        JLabel numberLabel =
            createLabel(NUMBER_LABEL_NAME, NUMBER_LABEL_TEXT);
        JTextField numberField =
            createField(NUMBER_FIELD_NAME, columns);

        int rows = 2;
        int cols = 2;

        JPanel panel = new JPanel();
        panel.setLayout(new GridLayout(rows, cols));
        panel.add(departmentLabel);
        panel.add(departmentField);

        panel.add(numberLabel);
        panel.add(numberField);

        return panel;
    }
```

Layout

The code in the CoursesPanel constructor sets its layout to a new instance of BorderLayout. It puts the label on the north (top) side of the panel and the list in the center of the panel. It puts the result of the method createBottomPanel, another JPanel, on the south (bottom) side of the panel (see Figure 7) The benefit of putting the list in the center is that it will expand as the frame window expands. The other widgets retain their original size.

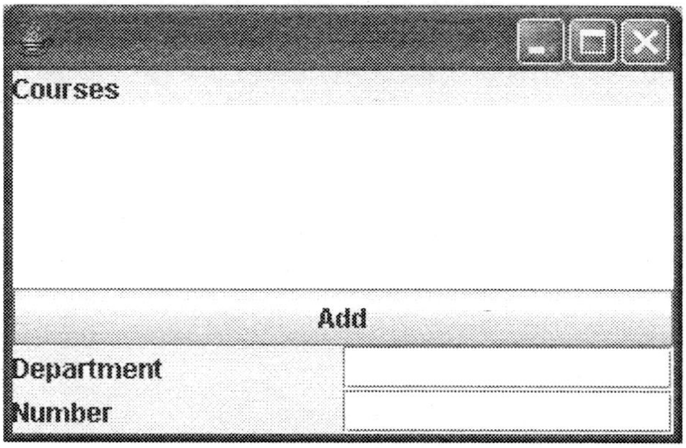

Figure 7

The code in createBottomPanel creates a JPanel that also uses a BorderLayout to organize its components. It places the Add button north and the resulting JPanel from createFieldsPanel south. The createFieldsPanel uses a GridLayout to organize the department and course number labels and fields. The result (Figure 7) is a considerable improvement but is still not good enough. Again, make sure you experiment with resizing the frame window to see how the layout reacts.

A Test Problem

If you rerun your tests, you now get three NullPointerException errors. How can that be, since you neither changed logic nor added/removed any components?

When you investigate the stack trace for the NullPointerException, you should discover that some of the get methods to extract a component from a container are failing. The problem is that the Util method getComponent only looks at components directly embedded within a container. Your layout code now embeds containers within containers (JPanels within JPanels). The code in getComponent ignores Components that have been added to subpanels.

The Util class doesn't have any tests associated with it. At this point, to help fix the problem and enhance your test coverage, you need to add appropriate tests. UtilTest contains three tests that should cover most expected circumstances:

```
package sis.ui;

import junit.framework.*;
import javax.swing.*;
import java.awt.*;
```

```
public class UtilTest extends TestCase {
    private JPanel panel;

    protected void setUp() {
        panel = new JPanel();
    }

    public void testNotFound() {
        assertNull(Util.getComponent(panel, "abc"));
    }

    public void testDirectlyEmbeddedComponent() {
        final String name = "a";
        Component component = new JLabel("x");
        component.setName(name);
        panel.add(component);
        assertEquals(component, Util.getComponent(panel, name));
    }

    public void testSubcomponent() {
        final String name = "a";
        Component component = new JLabel("x");
        component.setName(name);

        JPanel subpanel = new JPanel();
        subpanel.add(component);

        panel.add(subpanel);

        assertEquals(component, Util.getComponent(panel, name));
    }
}
```

Layout

The third test, testSubcomponent, should fail for the same reason your other
tests are failing. To fix the problem, you will need to modify getComponent. For
each component in a container, you will need to determine whether or not
that component is a container (using instanceof). If so, you will need to traverse all of that subcontainer's components, repeating the same process for
each. The most effective way to accomplish this is to make recursive calls to
getComponent.

```
static Component getComponent(Container container, String name) {
    for (Component component: container.getComponents()) {
        if (name.equals(component.getName()))
            return component;
        if (component instanceof Container) {
            Container subcontainer = (Container)component;
            Component subcomponent = getComponent(subcontainer, name);
```

```
        if (subcomponent != null)
            return subcomponent;
    }
}
return null;
}
```

Your tests should all pass with this change.

BoxLayout

The BoxLayout class allows you to lay your components out on either a horizontal or vertical axis. Components are not wrapped when you resize the container; also, components do not grow to fill any area. The bottom panel, which must position an Add button and the fields subpanel vertically, one atop the other, is an ideal candidate for BoxLayout.

```
JPanel createBottomPanel() {
    addButton = createButton(ADD_BUTTON_NAME, ADD_BUTTON_TEXT);

    JPanel panel = new JPanel();
    panel.setLayout(new BoxLayout(panel, BoxLayout.PAGE_AXIS));

    panel.add(Box.createRigidArea(new Dimension(0, 6)));
    addButton.setAlignmentX(Component.CENTER_ALIGNMENT);
    panel.add(addButton);
    panel.add(Box.createRigidArea(new Dimension(0, 6)));
    panel.add(createFieldsPanel());

    panel.setBorder(BorderFactory.createEmptyBorder(8, 8, 8, 8));

    return panel;
}
```

Layout

You must pass an instance of the panel to the constructor of BoxPanel and a constant indicating the direction in which to lay out components. The constant PAGE_AXIS by default represents a top-to-bottom, or vertical, orientation. The other option is LINE_AXIS, which represents horizontal orientation by default.[4]

You can create invisible "rigid areas" to separate components with whitespace. These rigid areas retain a fixed size even when the container is resized.

---

[4]You can change the orientation by sending applyComponentOrientation to the container. Older versions of BoxLayout supported only explicit X_AXIS and Y_AXIS constants. The newer constants allow for dynamic reorganization, perhaps to support internationalization needs.

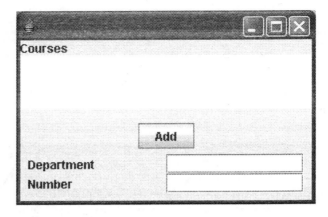

Figure 8 *Using BoxLayout*

The class method createRigidArea takes a Dimension object as a parameter. A Dimension is a width (0 in this example) by a height (6).

You may want to align each component with respect to the axis. In the example, you center the Add button around the vertical axis by sending it the message setAlignmentX with the parameter Component.CENTER_ALIGNMENT.

A final tweak is to supply an invisible border around the entire panel. The BorderFactory class can provide several types of borders that you can pass to the panel's setBorder method. Creating an empty border requires four parameters, each representing the width of the spacing from the outside edge of the panel. Other borders you can create include beveled borders, line borders, compound borders, etched borders, matte borders, raised beveled borders, and titled borders. Take a look at the Java API documentation and experiment with the effects that using different borders produces.

The code now produces an effective, but not quite perfect, layout. See Figure 8.

GridBagLayout

To fine-tune a layout, you will be forced to work with GridBagLayout, a highly configurable but more complex layout manager. GridBagLayout is similar to GridLayout in that it lets you organize components in a grid of rectangles. However, GridBagLayout gives you far more control. First, each rectangle is not fixed in size—it is generally sized according to the default, or "preferred" size of the component it contains. Components can span multiple rows or columns.

GridBagLayout

The modified `createFieldsPanel` code shows how to lay out labels and fields using a GridBagLayout. (The code in the method presumes that you have statically imported `java.awt.GridBagConstraints.*`.)

```java
JPanel createFieldsPanel() {
   GridBagLayout layout = new GridBagLayout();

   JPanel panel = new JPanel(layout);
   int columns = 20;
   JLabel departmentLabel =
      createLabel(DEPARTMENT_LABEL_NAME, DEPARTMENT_LABEL_TEXT);
   JTextField departmentField =
      createField(DEPARTMENT_FIELD_NAME, columns);
   JLabel numberLabel =
      createLabel(NUMBER_LABEL_NAME, NUMBER_LABEL_TEXT);
   JTextField numberField =
      createField(NUMBER_FIELD_NAME, columns);

   layout.setConstraints(departmentLabel,
      new GridBagConstraints(
         0, 0,  // x, y
         1, 1,  // gridwidth, gridheight
         40, 1, // weightx, weighty
         LINE_END, //anchor
         NONE, // fill
         new Insets(3, 3, 3, 3), // top-left-bottom-right
         0, 0)); // padx, ipady
   layout.setConstraints(departmentField,
      new GridBagConstraints(1, 0, 2, 1, 60, 1,
         CENTER, HORIZONTAL,
         new Insets(3, 3, 3, 3), 0, 0));
   layout.setConstraints(numberLabel,
      new GridBagConstraints(0, 1, 1, 1, 40, 1,
         LINE_END, NONE,
         new Insets(3, 3, 3, 3), 0, 0));
   layout.setConstraints(numberField,
      new GridBagConstraints(1, 1, 2, 1, 60, 1,
         CENTER, HORIZONTAL,
         new Insets(3, 3, 3, 3), 0, 0));

   panel.add(departmentLabel);
   panel.add(departmentField);
   panel.add(numberLabel);
   panel.add(numberField);

   return panel;
}
```

GridBagLayout

After creating a GridBagLayout and setting it into the panel, you call the method `setConstraints` on the layout for each widget to add. The `setConstraints` method takes two parameters: a Component object and a GridBagConstraints object. A GridBagConstraints object contains several constraints for the Component object. This table very briefly summarizes the constraints (see the API documentation for complete details):

gridx/gridy	The cell at which to begin drawing the component. The upper left cell is 0, 0.
gridwidth/gridheight	The amount of rows or columns the component should span. The default value is 1 for each, meaning that a component takes a single cell.
weightx/weighty	The weighting constraint is used to determine how much of the additional space is allocated to a component if space remains after laying out all the components in a row or column.
anchor	The anchor constraint is used to determine how it is placed within the cell if a component is smaller than its display area. The default is GridBagConstraints.CENTER.
fill	The fill constraint specifies how the component should grow to fill the display area if a component is smaller than its display area. Values are NONE (don't resize), HORIZONTAL, VERTICAL, and BOTH.
insets	Uses an Insets object to specify the space between a component and the edges of its display area.
ipadx/ipady	Specifies how much space to add to the minimum size of a component.

GridBagLayout

Each of the fields in GridBagConstraints is public. You can construct a GridBagConstraints object with no parameters, then set individual fields as necessary. Or, as in the listing for createFieldsPanel, you can specify every possible constraint using the alternate GridBagConstraints constructor.

The best tactic is to sketch, on paper or whiteboard, a grid representing how you want the output to look. Use the gridx/gridy and gridwidth/gridheight constraints to determine the relative sizes and positions of the components. Then concentrate on the anchor and fill aspects of each component. Code the layout to these sketched specifications and modify if necessary. You can then experiment with the insets and weightx/weighty constraints (and occasionally the ipadx/ipadx constraints) to tweak the spacing between components.

Obviously there is a lot of redundancy in createFieldsPanel. The following code is modestly refactored.

```
JPanel createFieldsPanel() {
   GridBagLayout layout = new GridBagLayout();

   JPanel panel = new JPanel(layout);
   int columns = 20;

   addField(panel, layout, 0,
      DEPARTMENT_LABEL_NAME, DEPARTMENT_LABEL_TEXT,
      DEPARTMENT_FIELD_NAME, columns);
   addField(panel, layout, 1,
      NUMBER_LABEL_NAME, NUMBER_LABEL_TEXT,
      NUMBER_FIELD_NAME, columns);

   return panel;
}

private void addField(
   JPanel panel, GridBagLayout layout, int row,
   String labelName, String labelText,
   String fieldName, int fieldColumns) {

   JLabel label = createLabel(labelName, labelText);
   JTextField field = createField(fieldName, fieldColumns);

   Insets insets = new Insets(3, 3, 3, 3); // top-left-bottom-right
   layout.setConstraints(label,
      new GridBagConstraints(
         0, row,  // x, y
         1, 1,   // gridwidth, gridheight
         40, 1, // weightx, weighty
         LINE_END, //anchor
         NONE, // fill
         insets, 0, 0)); // padx, ipady
   layout.setConstraints(field,
      new GridBagConstraints(1, row,
         2, 1, 60, 1, CENTER, HORIZONTAL,
         insets, 0, 0));

   panel.add(label);
   panel.add(field);
}
```

GridBagLayout

The onerous nature of such code should drive you in the direction of extreme refactoring. Consider replacing repetition in the construction of GridBagConstraints objects by using a simplified utility constructor. If you need to represent more than a couple of fields and associated labels, consider representing each pair using a data class. You can then represent the entire set of fields in a table, iterating through it to create the layout.

Figure 9 shows a layout that is getting close to being acceptable. Resize it to see how the field components fill to their display area.

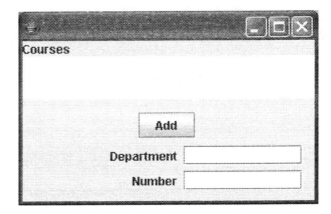

Figure 9   *Using GridBagLayout*

As of Java 1.4, Sun introduced the SpringLayout class. This layout manager is primarily designed for the use of GUI composition tools. The basic concept of SpringLayout is that you define a layout by tying the edges of components together using constraints known as springs.

In CoursesPanel, you might create a spring to attach the west (left) edge of the department text field to the east (right) edge of the department label. The spring object attaching the two components is a fixed five pixels in size. Another spring might attach the east edge of the department text field to the east side of the panel itself, also separated by a spring of fixed length. As the panel grows in width, the department text field would grow accordingly.

Creating a SpringLayout by hand is fairly easy for a panel with only a few components. It can also be incredibly frustrating and difficult for a more complex layout. In most cases, you will want to leave the job to a layout tool.

Moving Forward

Moving Forward

You've only scratched the surface of Swing! In the next chapter, you'll tighten up the look and the feel of CoursesPanel with some fine-tuning. I'll then run through a few more generally useful Swing topics.

Additional Lesson II

Swing, Part 2

In the last lesson you learned how to build a basic Swing application, using panels, labels, buttons, text fields, and lists. You also learned how to use Swing's layout managers for enhancing the look of your user interface (UI).

In this chapter, you will learn about:

- Scroll panes

- Borders

- Setting text in the title bar

- Icons

- Keyboard support

- Button mnemonics

- Required fields

- Keyboard listeners

- The Swing Robot class

- Field edits and document filters

- Formatted text fields

- Tables

- Mouse listeners

- Cursors

- SwingUtilities methods `invokeAndWait` and `invokeLater`

Miscellaneous Aesthetics

In this section you'll learn how to enhance the look of the existing Courses-Panel.

JScrollPane

If you add more than a few courses using sis.ui.Sis, you'll note that the JList shows only some of them. To fix this problem, you can wrap the JList in a scroll pane. The scroll pane acts as a viewport onto the list. When the list's model contains more information than can be displayed given the current JList size, the scroll pane draws scroll bars. The scroll bars allow you to move the viewport either horizontally or vertically to reveal hidden information.

The bold code in this listing for the CoursesPanel adds a scroll pane. You can specify whether you want to show scroll bars always or only as needed using either setVerticalScrollBarPolicy or setHorizontalScrollBarPolicy. I find it more aesthetically pleasing to always show the vertical scroll bar.

```
private void createLayout() {
    JLabel coursesLabel =
        createLabel(COURSES_LABEL_NAME, COURSES_LABEL_TEXT);

    JList coursesList = createList(COURSES_LIST_NAME, coursesModel);
    JScrollPane coursesScroll = new JScrollPane(coursesList);
    coursesScroll.setVerticalScrollBarPolicy(
        ScrollPaneConstants.VERTICAL_SCROLLBAR_ALWAYS);

    setLayout(new BorderLayout());

    add(coursesLabel, BorderLayout.NORTH);
    add(coursesScroll, BorderLayout.CENTER);
    add(createBottomPanel(), BorderLayout.SOUTH);
}
```

Borders

The courses list and associated labels directly abut the edge of the panel. You can use a *border* to create a buffer area between the edges of the panel and any of its components.

```
private void createLayout() {
    JLabel coursesLabel =
        createLabel(COURSES_LABEL_NAME, COURSES_LABEL_TEXT);

    JList coursesList = createList(COURSES_LIST_NAME, coursesModel);
    JScrollPane coursesScroll = new JScrollPane(coursesList);
```

```
        coursesScroll.setVerticalScrollBarPolicy(
            ScrollPaneConstants.VERTICAL_SCROLLBAR_ALWAYS);

        setLayout(new BorderLayout());

        final int pad = 6;
        setBorder(BorderFactory.createEmptyBorder(pad, pad, pad, pad));

        add(coursesLabel, BorderLayout.NORTH);
        add(coursesScroll, BorderLayout.CENTER);
        add(createBottomPanel(), BorderLayout.SOUTH);
    }
```

You can use the BorderFactory class to create one of several different border types. Most of the borders are for decorative purposes; the empty border is the exception. You can also combine borders using createCompoundBorder. The reworked createLayout method demonstrates the use of a few different border types.

```
private void createLayout() {
    JList coursesList = createList(COURSES_LIST_NAME, coursesModel);
    JScrollPane coursesScroll = new JScrollPane(coursesList);
    coursesScroll.setVerticalScrollBarPolicy(
        ScrollPaneConstants.VERTICAL_SCROLLBAR_ALWAYS);

    setLayout(new BorderLayout());

    final int pad = 6;
    Border emptyBorder =
        BorderFactory.createEmptyBorder(pad, pad, pad, pad);
    Border bevelBorder =
        BorderFactory.createBevelBorder(BevelBorder.RAISED);
    Border titledBorder =
        BorderFactory.createTitledBorder(bevelBorder, COURSES_LABEL_TEXT);
    setBorder(BorderFactory.createCompoundBorder(emptyBorder,
                                    titledBorder));

    add(coursesScroll, BorderLayout.CENTER);
    add(createBottomPanel(), BorderLayout.SOUTH);
}
```

The use of a titled border eliminates the need for a separate JLabel to represent the "Courses:" text. The elimination of the JLabel will break testCreate in CoursesPanelTest—did you remember to make this change by testing first?

Adding a Title

No text appears in the SIS frame window's titlebar. Rectify this by updating testCreate in SisTest:

```
public void testCreate() {
    final double tolerance = 0.05;
    assertEquals(Sis.HEIGHT, frame.getSize().getHeight(), tolerance);
    assertEquals(Sis.WIDTH, frame.getSize().getWidth(), tolerance);
    assertEquals(JFrame.EXIT_ON_CLOSE,
                 frame.getDefaultCloseOperation());
    assertNotNull(Util.getComponent(frame, CoursesPanel.NAME));
    assertEquals(Sis.COURSES_TITLE, frame.getTitle());
}
```

JFrame supplies constructors that allow you to pass in titlebar text. The code in Sis:

```
public class Sis {
    ...
    static final String COURSES_TITLE = "Course Listing";
    private JFrame frame = new JFrame(COURSES_TITLE);
    ...
}
```

Icons

The final aesthetic element you'll add is an icon for the window. By default, you get the cup-o-Java icon, which appears as a mini-icon in the titlebar and when you minimize the window. Since the icon is part of the titlebar, it falls under the control of the frame window.

A test can simply ask for the icon from a frame by sending it the message getIconImage. The method, implemented in java.awt.Frame, returns an object of type java.awt.Image. The code in testCreate asserts that the icon retrieved from the SIS frame is the same as one explicitly loaded by name. Both the test and the sis.ui.Sis code will use a common utility method to load the image: ImageUtil.create.

```
public void testCreate() {
    final double tolerance = 0.05;
    assertEquals(Sis.HEIGHT, frame.getSize().getHeight(), tolerance);
    assertEquals(Sis.WIDTH, frame.getSize().getWidth(), tolerance);
    assertEquals(JFrame.EXIT_ON_CLOSE,
                 frame.getDefaultCloseOperation());
    assertNotNull(Util.getComponent(frame, CoursesPanel.NAME));
    assertEquals(Sis.COURSES_TITLE, frame.getTitle());

    Image image = frame.getIconImage();
    assertEquals(image, ImageUtil.create("/images/courses.gif"));
}
```

Create the class ImageUtilTest in the sis.util package. There are several ways to write a test against the create method. The best way would be to dynamically generate an image using a collection of pixels and write it out to disk. After the create method loaded the image, you could assert that the pixels in the loaded image were the same as the original pixel collection. Unfortunately, this is an involved solution, one that is best solved using an API that eases the dynamic creation of images.

A simpler technique is to allow the test to assume that a proper image already exists on disk under a recognized filename. The test can then simply assert that the image load was successful by ensuring that the loaded image is not null. The image must appear on the classpath.[1]

```
package sis.util;

import junit.framework.*;
import java.awt.*;

public class ImageUtilTest extends TestCase {
    public void testLoadImage() {
        assertNull(ImageUtil.create("/images/bogusFilename.gif"));
        assertNotNull(ImageUtil.create("/images/courses.gif"));
    }
}
```

This may seem weak, but it will provide an effective solution for now. You must ensure that the image courses.gif continues to stay in existence throughout the lifetime of the project. Instead of using an image file assocciated with the SIS project, you might consider creating an image explicitly used for testing purposes.

Java provides several different ways to load and manipulate images. You will use the most direct.

```
package sis.util;

import javax.swing.*;
import java.awt.*;

public class ImageUtil {
    public static Image create(String path) {
        java.net.URL imageURL = ImageUtil.class.getResource(path);
        if (imageURL == null)
            return null;
        return new ImageIcon(imageURL).getImage();
    }
}
```

Miscellaneous Aesthetics

---

[1] I've modified the build.xml Ant script for this section to copy any file in src/images into classes/images each time a compile takes place. This allows you to quickly remove the entire contents of the classes directory without having to worry about retaining any images.

The class Class defines the method getResource. This method allows you to locate resources, including files, regardless of whether the application is loaded from a JAR file, individual class files, or some other source such as the Internet.[2] The result of calling getResource is a URL—the unique address of the resource.

Once you have a proper URL, you can pass it to the ImageIcon constructor to obtain an ImageIcon object. You can use ImageIcon objects for various purposes, such as decorating buttons or labels. Since the Frame class requires an Image object, not an ImageIcon, here you use the getImage method to produce the return value for create.

Note that the image filename passed to getResource is /images/courses.gif—a path that uses a leading slash. This indicates that the resource should be located starting from the root of each classpath entry. Thus, if you execute classes from the directory c:\swing2\classes, you should put courses.gif in c:\swing2\classes\images. If you execute classes by loading them from a JAR file, it should contain courses.gif with a relative path of images.

Here are the changes to the initialize method in the Sis class.

```
private void initialize() {
    createCoursesPanel();

    Image image = ImageUtil.create("/images/courses.gif");
    frame.setIconImage(image);

    frame.setSize(WIDTH, HEIGHT);
    frame.setDefaultCloseOperation(JFrame.EXIT_ON_CLOSE);
    frame.getContentPane().add(panel);
}
```

You now have an acceptably pleasing interface—at least from a visual standpoint. The revised layout is shown in Figure 1.

Feel

The visual appearance of the interface is important, but more important is its "feel." The feel of an application is what a user experiences as he or she interacts with it. Examples of elements relevant to the feel of an application include:

---

[2]Technically, the image is loaded using the class loader as that of the Class object on which you call getResource. For applications that do not use a custom class loader, using the class loader of the ImageUtil class will work just fine.

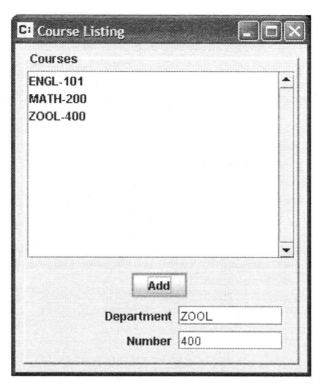

Figure 1 *A Good Look*

- ability to effect all behaviors using either the keyboard or the mouse
- tabbing sequence—can the user visit all text fields in the proper order and are irrelevant items omitted from the tab sequence?
- field limits—is the user restricted from entering too many characters?
- field constraints—is the user restricted from entering inappropriate data into a field?
- button activation—are buttons deactivated when their use is inappropriate?

It is possible to address both the look and feel at the same time. In the last section, you decorated the list of courses with a scroll pane. This improved the look of the interface and at the same time provided the "feel" to allow a user to scroll the list of courses when necessary.

Feel

Keyboard Support

One of the primary rules of GUIs is that a user must be able to completely control the application using either the keyboard or the mouse. Exceptions exist. Using the keyboard to draw a polygon is ineffective, as is entering characters using the mouse. (Both are of course possible.) In such cases, the application developer often chooses to bypass the rule. But in most cases it is extremely inconsiderate to ignore the needs of a keyboard-only or mouse-only user.

By default, Java supplies most of the necessary support for dual keyboard and mouse control. For example, you can activate a button by either clicking on it with the mouse or tabbing to it and pressing the space bar.

Button Mnemonics

An additional way you can activate a button is using an Alt-key combination. You combine pressing the Alt key with another key. The other key is typically a letter or number that appears in the button text. You refer to this key as a *mnemonic* (technically, a device to help you remember something; in Java, it's simply a single-letter shortcut). An appropriate mnemonic for the Add button is the letter A.

The mnemonic is a view class element. The specifications for the mnemonic remain constant with the view's appearance. Therefore the more appropriate place to test and manage the mnemonic is in the view class.

In CoursesPanelTest:

```
public void testCreate() {
    assertEmptyList(COURSES_LIST_NAME);
    assertButtonText(ADD_BUTTON_NAME, ADD_BUTTON_TEXT);
    assertLabelText(DEPARTMENT_LABEL_NAME, DEPARTMENT_LABEL_TEXT);
    assertEmptyField(DEPARTMENT_FIELD_NAME);
    assertLabelText(NUMBER_LABEL_NAME, NUMBER_LABEL_TEXT);
    assertEmptyField(NUMBER_FIELD_NAME);

    JButton button = panel.getButton(ADD_BUTTON_NAME);
    assertEquals(ADD_BUTTON_MNEMONIC, button.getMnemonic());
}
```

In CoursesPanel:

```
public class CoursesPanel extends JPanel {
    ...
    static final char ADD_BUTTON_MNEMONIC = 'A';
    ...
    JPanel createBottomPanel() {
        addButton = createButton(ADD_BUTTON_NAME, ADD_BUTTON_TEXT);
```

```
    addButton.setMnemonic(ADD_BUTTON_MNEMONIC);
    ...
    return panel;
  }
  ...
}
```

After seeing your tests pass, execute sis.ui.Sis as an application. Enter a course department and number, then press Alt-A to demonstrate use of the mnemonic.

Required Fields

A valid course requires both a department and course number. However, sis.ui.Sis allows you to omit either or both, yet still press the Add button. You want to modify the application to disallow this circumstance.

One solution would be to wait until the user presses Add, then ensure that both department and course number contain a nonempty string. If not, then present a message pop-up that explains the requirement. While this solution will work, it creates a more annoying user experience. Users don't want continual interruption from message pop-ups. A better solution is to proactively disable the Add button until the user has entered information in both fields.

You can monitor both fields and track when a user enters information in them. Each time a user presses a character, you can test the field contents and enable or disable the Add button as appropriate.

Managing enabling/disabling of the Add button is an application characteristic, not a view characteristic. It involves business-related logic, as it is based on the business need for specific data. As such, the test and related code belongs not in the panel class, but elsewhere.

Another indicator that the code does not belong in the view class is that you have interaction between two components. You want the controller to notify other classes of an event (keys being pressed) and you want those other classes to tell the view what to present (a disabled or enabled button) under certain circumstances. These are two separate concerns. You don't want logic in the view trying to mediate things.

To solve the bigger problem, however, it is easier to provide tests against CoursesPanel that prove each of the two smaller occurences. A first test ensures that a listener is notified when keys are pressed. A second test ensures that CoursesPanel can enable and disable buttons.

Start with a test (in CoursesPanelTest) for enabling and disabling buttons:

```
public void testEnableDisable() {
    panel.setEnabled(ADD_BUTTON_NAME, true);
    JButton button = panel.getButton(ADD_BUTTON_NAME);
    assertTrue(button.isEnabled());

    panel.setEnabled(ADD_BUTTON_NAME, false);
    assertFalse(button.isEnabled());
}
```

The code in CoursesPanel is a one-line reactive method—no logic:

```
void setEnabled(String name, boolean state) {
    getButton(name).setEnabled(state);
}
```

The second test shows how to attach a keystroke listener to a field:

```
public void testAddListener() throws Exception {
    KeyListener listener = new KeyAdapter() {};
    panel.addFieldListener(DEPARTMENT_FIELD_NAME, listener);
    JTextField field = panel.getField(DEPARTMENT_FIELD_NAME);
    KeyListener[] listeners = field.getKeyListeners();
    assertEquals(1, listeners.length);
    assertSame(listener, listeners[0]);
}
```

A KeyAdapter is an abstract implementation of the KeyListener interface that does nothing. The first line in the test creates a concrete subclass of KeyAdapter that overrides nothing. After adding the listener (using addField-Listener) to the panel, the test ensures that the panel properly sets the listener into the text field. The code in CoursesPanel is again trivial:

```
void addFieldListener(String name, KeyListener listener) {
    getField(name).addKeyListener(listener);
}
```

The harder test is at the application level. A listener in the Sis object should receive messages when a user types into the department and number fields. You must prove that the listener's receipt of these messages triggers logic to enable/disable the Add button. You must also prove that various combinations of text/no text in the fields results in the appropriate state for the Add button.

A bit of programming by intention in SisTest will provide you with a test skeleton:

```
public void testKeyListeners() throws Exception {
    sis.show();

    JButton button = panel.getButton(CoursesPanel.ADD_BUTTON_NAME);
    assertFalse(button.isEnabled());
    selectField(CoursesPanel.DEPARTMENT_FIELD_NAME);
    type('A');
```

Feel

```
    selectField(CoursesPanel.NUMBER_FIELD_NAME);
    type('1');
    assertTrue(button.isEnabled());
}
```

The test ensures that the button is disabled by default. After typing values into the department and number fields, it verifies that the button is enabled. The trick, of course, is how to select a field and emulate typing into it. Swing provides a few solutions. Unfortunately, each requires you to render (make visible) the actual screen. Thus the first line in the test is a call to the show method of Sis.

The solution I'll present involves use of the class java.awt.Robot. The Robot class emulates end-user interaction using the keyboard and/or mouse. Another solution requires you to create keyboard event objects and pass them to the fields using a method on java.awt.Component named dispatchEvent.

You can construct a Robot object in the SisTest setUp method. (After building this example, I noted persistent use of the CoursesPanel object, so I also refactored its extraction to setUp.)

```
public class SisTest extends TestCase {
    ...
    private CoursesPanel panel;
    private Robot robot;

    protected void setUp() throws Exception {
        ...
        panel = (CoursesPanel)Util.getComponent(frame, CoursesPanel.NAME);
        robot = new Robot();
    }
```

The selectField method isn't that tough:

```
private void selectField(String name) throws Exception {
    JTextField field = panel.getField(name);
    Point point = field.getLocationOnScreen();
    robot.mouseMove(point.x, point.y);
    robot.mousePress(InputEvent.BUTTON1_MASK);
    robot.mouseRelease(InputEvent.BUTTON1_MASK);
}
```

After obtaining a field object, you can obtain its absolute position on the screen by sending it the message getLocationOnScreen. This returns a Point object—a coordinate in Cartesian space represented by an x and y offset.[3] You can send this coordinate as an argument to Robot's mouseMove method.

Feel

---

[3]The upper left corner of your screen has an (x, y) coordinate of $(0, 0)$. The value of y increases as you move down the screen. For example, you would express two pixels to the right and one pixel down as $(2, 1)$.

Subsequently, sending a mousePress and mouseRelease message to the Robot results in a virtual mouse-click at that location.

The type method is equally straightforward:

```
private void type(int key) throws Exception {
    robot.keyPress(key);
    robot.keyRelease(key);
}
```

The code in Sis adds a single listener to each text field. This listener waits on keyReleased events. When it receives one, the listener calls the method setAddButtonState. The code in setAddButtonState looks at the contents of the two fields to determine whether or not to enable the Add button.

```
public class Sis {
    ...
    private void initialize() {
        createCoursesPanel();
        createKeyListeners();
        ...
    }
    ...
    void createKeyListeners() {
        KeyListener listener = new KeyAdapter() {
            public void keyReleased(KeyEvent e) {
                setAddButtonState();
            }
        };
        panel.addFieldListener(CoursesPanel.DEPARTMENT_FIELD_NAME,
                               listener);
        panel.addFieldListener(CoursesPanel.NUMBER_FIELD_NAME, listener);

        setAddButtonState();
    }

    void setAddButtonState() {
        panel.setEnabled(CoursesPanel.ADD_BUTTON_NAME,
            !isEmpty(CoursesPanel.DEPARTMENT_FIELD_NAME) &&
            !isEmpty(CoursesPanel.NUMBER_FIELD_NAME));
    }

    private boolean isEmpty(String field) {
        String value = panel.getText(field);
        return value.equals("");
    }
}
```

Note that the last line in createKeyListeners calls setAddButtonState in order to set the Add button to its default (initial) state.

The code in testKeyListeners doesn't represent all possible scenarios. What if the user enters nothing but space characters? Is the button properly disabled if one of the two fields has data but the other does not?

You could enhance testKeyListeners with these scenarios. A second test shows a different approach, one that directly interacts with setAddButtonState. This test covers a more complete set of circumstances.

```
public void testSetAddButtonState() throws Exception {
    JButton button = panel.getButton(CoursesPanel.ADD_BUTTON_NAME);
    assertFalse(button.isEnabled());

    panel.setText(CoursesPanel.DEPARTMENT_FIELD_NAME, "a");
    sis.setAddButtonState();
    assertFalse(button.isEnabled());

    panel.setText(CoursesPanel.NUMBER_FIELD_NAME, "1");
    sis.setAddButtonState();
    assertTrue(button.isEnabled());

    panel.setText(CoursesPanel.DEPARTMENT_FIELD_NAME, " ");
    sis.setAddButtonState();
    assertFalse(button.isEnabled());

    panel.setText(CoursesPanel.DEPARTMENT_FIELD_NAME, "a");
    panel.setText(CoursesPanel.NUMBER_FIELD_NAME, "  ");
    sis.setAddButtonState();
    assertFalse(button.isEnabled());
}
```

The test fails. A small change to isEmpty fixes things.

```
private boolean isEmpty(String field) {
    String value = panel.getText(field);
    return value.trim().equals("");
}
```

Field Edits

When you provide an effective user interface, you want to make it as difficult as possible for users to enter invalid data. You learned that you don't want to interrupt users with pop-ups when requiring fields. Similarly, you want to avoid presenting pop-ups to tell users they have entered invalid data.

A preferred solution involves verifying and even modifying data in a text field as the user enters it. As an example, a course department must contain only uppercase letters. "CMSC" is a valid department, but "Cmsc" and "cmsc" are not. To make life easier for your users, you can make the department text field automatically convert each lowercase letter to an uppercase letter as the user types it.

Feel

The evolution of Java has included several attempts at solutions for dynamically editing fields. Currently, there are at least a half dozen ways to go about it. You will learn two of the preferred techniques: using JFormattedTextField and creating custom DocumentFilter classes.

You create a custom filter by subclassing javax.swing.text.DocumentFilter. In the subclass, you override definitions for any of three methods: insertString, remove, and replace. You use these methods to restrict invalid input and/or transform invalid input into valid input.

As a user enters or pastes characters into the text field, the insertString method is indirectly called. The replace method gets invoked when a user first selects existing characters in a text field before typing or pasting new characters. The remove method is invoked when the user deletes characters from the text field. You will almost always need to define behavior for insertString and replace, but you will need to do so only occasionally for remove.

Once you have defined the behavior for the custom filter, you attach it to a text field's document. The document is the underlying data model for the text field; it is an implementation of the interface javax.swing.text.Document. You obtain the Document object associated with a JTextField by sending it the message getDocument. You can then attach the custom filter to the Document using setDocumentFilter.

Testing the Filter

How will you test the filter? You could code a test in CoursesPanel that uses the Swing robot (as described in the Required Fields section). But for the purpose of testing units, the robot is a last-resort technique that you should use only when you must. In this case, a DocumentFilter subclass is a stand-alone class that you can test directly.

In some cases, you'll find that Swing design lends itself to easy testing. For custom filters, you'll have to do a bit of legwork first to get around a few barriers.

UpcaseFilterTest appears directly below. The individual test method testInsert is straightforward and easy to read, the result of some refactoring. In testInsert, you send the message insertString directly to an UpcaseFilter instance. The second argument to insertString is the column at which to begin inserting. The third argument is the text to insert. (For now, the fourth argument is irrelevant, and I'll discuss the first argument shortly).

Inserting the text "abc" at column 0 should generate the text "ABC". Inserting "def" at position 1 (i.e., before the second column) should generate the text "ADEFBC".

```
package sis.ui;

import javax.swing.*;
import javax.swing.text.*;
import junit.framework.*;

public class UpcaseFilterTest extends TestCase {
    private DocumentFilter filter;
    protected DocumentFilter.FilterBypass bypass;
    protected AbstractDocument document;

    protected void setUp() {
        bypass = createBypass();
        document = (AbstractDocument)bypass.getDocument();
        filter = new UpcaseFilter();
    }

    public void testInsert() throws BadLocationException {
        filter.insertString(bypass, 0, "abc", null);
        assertEquals("ABC", documentText());

        filter.insertString(bypass, 1, "def", null);
        assertEquals("ADEFBC", documentText());
    }

    protected String documentText() throws BadLocationException {
        return document.getText(0, document.getLength());
    }

    protected DocumentFilter.FilterBypass createBypass() {
        return new DocumentFilter.FilterBypass() {
            private AbstractDocument document = new PlainDocument();
            public Document getDocument() {
                return document;
            }
            public void insertString(
                    int offset, String string, AttributeSet attr) {
                try {
                    document.insertString(offset, string, attr);
                }
                catch (BadLocationException e) {}
            }
            public void remove(int offset, int length) { }
            public void replace(int offset,
                    int length, String string, AttributeSet attrs) { }
        };
    }
}
```

The setup is considerably more involved than the test itself.

If you look at the javadoc for insertString, you'll see that it takes a reference of type DocumentFilter.FilterBypass as its first argument. A filter bypass is essentially a reference to the document that ignores any filters. After you transform data in insertString, you must call insertString on the filter bypass. Otherwise, you will create an infinite loop!

The difficulty with respect to testing is that Swing provides no direct way to obtain a filter bypass object. You need the bypass in order to test the filter.

The solution presented above is to provide a new implementation of DocumentFilter.FilterBypass. This implementation stores a concrete instance of an AbstractDocument (which implements the Document interface) known as a PlainDocument. To flesh out the bypass, you must supply implementations for the three methods insertString, remove, and replace. For now, the test only requires you to implement insertString.

The insertString method doesn't need to take a bypass object as its first parameter, since it is defined in the filter itself. Its job is to call the document's insertString method directly (i.e., without calling back into the DocumentFilter). Note that this method can throw a BadLocationException if the start position is out of range.

Once you have a DocumentFilter.FilterBypass instance, the remainder of the setup and test is easy. From the bypass object, you can obtain and store a document reference. You assert that the contents of this document were appropriately updated.

The test (UpcaseFilterTest) contains a lot of code. You might think that the robot-based test would have been easier to write. In fact, it would have. However, robots have their problems. Since they take control of the mouse and keyboard, you have to be careful not to do anything else while the tests execute. Otherwise you can cause the robot tests to fail. This alone is reason to avoid them at all costs. If you must use robot tests, find a way to isolate them and perhaps execute them at the beginning of your unit-test suite.

Also, the test code for the second filter you write will be as easy to code as the corresponding robot test code. Both filter tests would require the documentText and createBypass methods as well as most of the setUp method.

Coding the Filter

You're more than halfway done with building a filter. You've completed the hard part—writing a test for it. Coding the filter itself is trivial.

```
package sis.ui;

import javax.swing.text.*;

public class UpcaseFilter extends DocumentFilter {
    public void insertString(
        DocumentFilter.FilterBypass bypass,
```

```
         int offset,
         String text,
         AttributeSet attr) throws BadLocationException {
      bypass.insertString(offset, text.toUpperCase(), attr);
   }
}
```

When the filter receives the insertString message, its job in this case is to convert the text argument to uppercase, and pass this transformed data off to the bypass.

Once you've demonstrated that your tests all still pass, you can now code the replace method. The test modifications:

```
...
public class UpcaseFilterTest extends TestCase {
   ...
   public void testReplace() throws BadLocationException {
      filter.insertString(bypass, 0, "XYZ", null);
      filter.replace(bypass, 1, 2, "tc", null);
      assertEquals("XTC", documentText());

      filter.replace(bypass, 0, 3, "p8A", null);
      assertEquals("P8A", documentText());
   }
   ...
   protected DocumentFilter.FilterBypass createBypass() {
      return new DocumentFilter.FilterBypass() {
         ...
         public void replace(int offset,
               int length, String string, AttributeSet attrs) {
            try {
               document.replace(offset, length, string, attrs);
            }
            catch (BadLocationException e) {}
         }
      };
   }
}
```

The test shows that the replace method takes an additional argument. The third parameter represents the number of characters to be replaced, starting at the position represented by the second argument. The production code:

```
package sis.ui;

import javax.swing.text.*;

public class UpcaseFilter extends DocumentFilter {
   ...
   public void replace(
      DocumentFilter.FilterBypass bypass,
      int offset,
```

```
        int length,
        String text,
        AttributeSet attr) throws BadLocationException {
        bypass.replace(offset, length, text.toUpperCase(), attr);
    }
}
```

UpcaseFilter is complete. You need not concern yourself with filtering re-moval operations when uppercasing input.

Attaching the Filter

You have proved the functionality of UpcaseFilter as a standalone unit. To prove that the department field in CoursesPanel transforms its input into up-percase text, you need only demonstrate that the appropriate filter has been attached to the field.

Should the code in CoursesPanel attach the filters to its fields, or should code in Sis retrieve the fields and attach the filters? Does the test belong in SisTest or in CoursesPanelTest? A filter is a combination of business rule and view functionality. It enforces a business constraint (for example, "Depart-ment abbreviations are four uppercase characters"). A filter also enhances the feel of the application by making it easier for the user to enter only valid information.

Remember: Keep the view class simple. Put as much business-related logic in domain (Course) or application classes (Sis). The filter representation of the business logic is very dependent upon Swing. The filters are essentially plug-ins to the Swing framework. You don't want to make the domain class dependent upon such code. Thus, the only remaining choice is the applica-tion class.

The code in SisTest:

Feel

```
public void testCreate() {
    ...
    CoursesPanel panel =
        (CoursesPanel)Util.getComponent(frame, CoursesPanel.NAME);
    assertNotNull(panel);
    ...
    verifyFilter(panel);
}

private void verifyFilter(CoursesPanel panel) {
    DocumentFilter filter =
        getFilter(panel, CoursesPanel.DEPARTMENT_FIELD_NAME);
    assertTrue(filter.getClass() == UpcaseFilter.class);
}
```

```
   private DocumentFilter getFilter(
       CoursesPanel panel, String fieldName) {
     JTextField field = panel.getField(fieldName);
     AbstractDocument document = (AbstractDocument)field.getDocument();
     return document.getDocumentFilter();
   }
   ...
}
```

The code in Sis:

```
private void initialize() {
   createCoursesPanel();
   createKeyListeners();
   createInputFilters();
   ...
}
...
private void createInputFilters() {
   JTextField field =
      panel.getField(CoursesPanel.DEPARTMENT_FIELD_NAME);
   AbstractDocument document = (AbstractDocument)field.getDocument();
   document.setDocumentFilter(new UpcaseFilter());
}
```

A Second Filter

You also want to constrain the number of characters in both the department and course number field. In fact, in most applications that require field entry, you will want the ability to set field limits. You can create a second custom filter, LimitFilter. The following code listing shows only the production class. The test, LimitFilterTest (see the code at*http://www.LangrSoft.com/agileJava/code/*) contains a lot of commonality with UpcaseFilterTest that you can factor out.

```
package sis.ui;

import javax.swing.text.*;

public class LimitFilter extends DocumentFilter {
   private int limit;

   public LimitFilter(int limit) {
      this.limit = limit;
   }

   public void insertString(
       DocumentFilter.FilterBypass bypass,
       int offset,
       String str,
       AttributeSet attrSet) throws BadLocationException {
     replace(bypass, offset, 0, str, attrSet);
   }
```

```
    public void replace(
        DocumentFilter.FilterBypass bypass,
        int offset,
        int length,
        String str,
        AttributeSet attrSet) throws BadLocationException {
      int newLength =
        bypass.getDocument().getLength() - length + str.length();
      if (newLength > limit)
        throw new BadLocationException(
            "New characters exceeds max size of document", offset);
      bypass.replace(offset, length, str, attrSet);
    }
}
```

Note the technique of having insertString delegate to the replace method. The other significant bit of code involves throwing a BadLocationException if the replacement string is too large.

Building such a filter and attaching it to the course number field is easy enough. You construct a LimitFilter by passing it the character length. For example, the code snippet new LimitFilter(3) creates a filter that prevents more than three characters.

The problem is that you can set only a single filter on a document. You have a couple of choices. The first (bad) choice is to create a separate filter for each combination. For example, you might have filter combinations Upcase-LimitFilter and NumericOnlyLimitFilter. A better solution involves some form of abstraction—a ChainableFilter. The ChainableFilter class subclasses Document-Filter. It contains a sequence of individual filter classes and manages calling each in turn. The code available at *http://www.LangrSoft.com/agileJava/code/* for this lesson demonstrates how you might build such a construct.[4]

Feel

JFormattedTextField

Another mechanism for managing field edits is to use the class javax.swing.JFormattedTextField, a subclass of JTextField. You can attach formatters to the field to ensure that the contents conform to your specification. Further, you can retrieve the contents of the field as appropriate object types other than text.

You want to provide an effective date field for the course. This date represents when the course is first made available in the system. Users must enter the date in the format mm/dd/yy. For example, 04/15/02 is a valid date.

---

[4]The listing does not appear here for space reasons.

The test extracts the field as a JFormattedTextField, then gets a formatter object from the JFormattedTextField. A formatter is a subclass of javax.swing.JFormattedTextField.AbstractFormatter. In verifyEffectiveDate, you expect that the formatter is a DateFormatter. The DateFormatter in turn wraps a java.text.SimpleDateFormat instance whose format pattern is MM/dd/yy.[5]

The final part of the test ensures that the field holds on to a date instance. When the user clicks Add, code in sis.ui.Sis can extract the contents of the effective date field as a java.util.Date object.

```
private void verifyEffectiveDate() {
   assertLabelText(EFFECTIVE_DATE_LABEL_NAME,
      EFFECTIVE_DATE_LABEL_TEXT);

   JFormattedTextField dateField =
      (JFormattedTextField)panel.getField(EFFECTIVE_DATE_FIELD_NAME);
   DateFormatter formatter = (DateFormatter)dateField.getFormatter();
   SimpleDateFormat format = (SimpleDateFormat)formatter.getFormat();
   assertEquals("MM/dd/yy", format.toPattern());
   assertEquals(Date.class, dateField.getValue().getClass());
}
```

Code in CoursesPanel constructs the JFormattedTextField, passing a SimpleDateFormat to its constructor. The code sends the message setValue to dateField in order to supply the Date object in which to store the edited results.

```
JPanel createFieldsPanel() {
   GridBagLayout layout = new GridBagLayout();

   JPanel panel = new JPanel(layout);
   int columns = 20;

   addField(panel, layout, 0,
      DEPARTMENT_LABEL_NAME, DEPARTMENT_LABEL_TEXT,
      createField(DEPARTMENT_FIELD_NAME, columns));

   addField(panel, layout, 1,
      NUMBER_LABEL_NAME, NUMBER_LABEL_TEXT,
      createField(NUMBER_FIELD_NAME, columns));

   Format format = new SimpleDateFormat("MM/dd/yy");
   JFormattedTextField dateField = new JFormattedTextField(format);
   dateField.setValue(new Date());
   dateField.setColumns(columns);
   dateField.setName(EFFECTIVE_DATE_FIELD_NAME);
```

[5]The capital letter M is used for month, while the lowercase letter m is used for minutes.

```
addField(panel, layout, 2,
   EFFECTIVE_DATE_LABEL_NAME, EFFECTIVE_DATE_LABEL_TEXT,
   dateField);

return panel;
}
```

If you execute the application with these changes, you will note that the effective date field allows you to type invalid input. When you leave the field, it reverts to a valid value. You can override this default behavior; see the API documentation for JFormattedTextField for the alternatives.

A design issue now exists. The code to create the formatted text field is in CoursesPanel and the associated test is in CoursesPanelTest. This contrasts with the goal I previously stated to manage edits at the application level!

You want to completely separate the view and application concerns. A solution involves the single responsibility principle. It will also eliminate some of the duplication and code clutter that I've allowed to fester in CoursesPanel and Sis.

A Field object is a data object whose attributes describe the information necessary to be able to create Swing text fields. A field is implementation-neutral, however, and has no knowledge of Swing. A FieldCatalog contains the collection of available fields. It can return a Field object given its name.

The CoursesPanel class needs only contain a list of field names that it must render. The CoursesPanel code can iterate through this list, asking a FieldCatalog for the corresponding Field object. It can then send the Field object to a factory, TextFieldFactory, whose job is to return a JTextField. The factory will take information from the Field object and use it to add various constraints on the JTextField, such as formats, filters, and length limits.

The code for the new classes follows. I also show the code in CoursesPanel that constructs the text fields.

```
// FieldCatalogTest.java
package sis.ui;

import junit.framework.*;
import static sis.ui.FieldCatalog.*;

public class FieldCatalogTest extends TestCase {
   public void testAllFields() {
      FieldCatalog catalog = new FieldCatalog();

      assertEquals(3, catalog.size());
```

```java
            Field field = catalog.get(NUMBER_FIELD_NAME);
            assertEquals(DEFAULT_COLUMNS, field.getColumns());
            assertEquals(NUMBER_LABEL_TEXT, field.getLabel());
            assertEquals(NUMBER_FIELD_LIMIT, field.getLimit());

            field = catalog.get(DEPARTMENT_FIELD_NAME);
            assertEquals(DEFAULT_COLUMNS, field.getColumns());
            assertEquals(DEPARTMENT_LABEL_TEXT, field.getLabel());
            assertEquals(DEPARTMENT_FIELD_LIMIT, field.getLimit());
            assertTrue(field.isUpcaseOnly());

            field = catalog.get(EFFECTIVE_DATE_FIELD_NAME);
            assertEquals(DEFAULT_COLUMNS, field.getColumns());
            assertEquals(EFFECTIVE_DATE_LABEL_TEXT, field.getLabel());
            assertSame(DEFAULT_DATE_FORMAT, field.getFormat());
        }
    }

// FieldCatalog.java
package sis.ui;

import java.util.*;
import java.text.*;

public class FieldCatalog {

    public static final DateFormat DEFAULT_DATE_FORMAT =
        new SimpleDateFormat("MM/dd/yy");

    static final String DEPARTMENT_FIELD_NAME = "deptField";
    static final String DEPARTMENT_LABEL_TEXT = "Department";
    static final int DEPARTMENT_FIELD_LIMIT = 4;

    static final String NUMBER_FIELD_NAME = "numberField";
    static final String NUMBER_LABEL_TEXT = "Number";
    static final int NUMBER_FIELD_LIMIT = 3;

    static final String EFFECTIVE_DATE_FIELD_NAME = "effectiveDateField";
    static final String EFFECTIVE_DATE_LABEL_TEXT = "Effective Date";

    static final int DEFAULT_COLUMNS = 20;

    private Map<String,Field> fields;

    public FieldCatalog() {
        loadFields();
    }

    public int size() {
        return fields.size();
    }
```

Feel

```
    private void loadFields() {
        fields = new HashMap<String,Field>();

        Field fieldSpec = new Field(DEPARTMENT_FIELD_NAME);
        fieldSpec.setLabel(DEPARTMENT_LABEL_TEXT);
        fieldSpec.setLimit(DEPARTMENT_FIELD_LIMIT);
        fieldSpec.setColumns(DEFAULT_COLUMNS);
        fieldSpec.setUpcaseOnly();

        put(fieldSpec);

        fieldSpec = new Field(NUMBER_FIELD_NAME);
        fieldSpec.setLabel(NUMBER_LABEL_TEXT);
        fieldSpec.setLimit(NUMBER_FIELD_LIMIT);
        fieldSpec.setColumns(DEFAULT_COLUMNS);

        put(fieldSpec);

        fieldSpec = new Field(EFFECTIVE_DATE_FIELD_NAME);
        fieldSpec.setLabel(EFFECTIVE_DATE_LABEL_TEXT);
        fieldSpec.setFormat(DEFAULT_DATE_FORMAT);
        fieldSpec.setInitialValue(new Date());
        fieldSpec.setColumns(DEFAULT_COLUMNS);

        put(fieldSpec);
    }

    private void put(Field fieldSpec) {
        fields.put(fieldSpec.getName(), fieldSpec);
    }

    public Field get(String fieldName) {
        return fields.get(fieldName);
    }
}

// TextFieldFactoryTest.java
package sis.ui;

import javax.swing.*;
import javax.swing.text.*;
import java.util.*;
import java.text.*;
import junit.framework.*;
import sis.util.*;

public class TextFieldFactoryTest extends TestCase {
    private Field fieldSpec;
    private static final String FIELD_NAME = "fieldName";
    private static final int COLUMNS = 1;

    protected void setUp() {
        fieldSpec = new Field(FIELD_NAME);
```

Feel

```
      fieldSpec.setColumns(COLUMNS);
   }

   public void testCreateSimpleField() {
      final String textValue = "value";
      fieldSpec.setInitialValue(textValue);

      JTextField field = TextFieldFactory.create(fieldSpec);

      assertEquals(COLUMNS, field.getColumns());
      assertEquals(FIELD_NAME, field.getName());
      assertEquals(textValue, field.getText());
   }

   public void testLimit() {
      final int limit = 3;
      fieldSpec.setLimit(limit);

      JTextField field = TextFieldFactory.create(fieldSpec);

      AbstractDocument document = (AbstractDocument)field.getDocument();
      ChainableFilter filter =
         (ChainableFilter)document.getDocumentFilter();
      assertEquals(limit, ((LimitFilter)filter).getLimit());
   }

   public void testUpcase() {
      fieldSpec.setUpcaseOnly();

      JTextField field = TextFieldFactory.create(fieldSpec);

      AbstractDocument document = (AbstractDocument)field.getDocument();
      ChainableFilter filter =
         (ChainableFilter)document.getDocumentFilter();
      assertEquals(UpcaseFilter.class, filter.getClass());
   }

   public void testMultipleFilters() {
      fieldSpec.setLimit(3);
      fieldSpec.setUpcaseOnly();

      JTextField field = TextFieldFactory.create(fieldSpec);

      AbstractDocument document = (AbstractDocument)field.getDocument();
      ChainableFilter filter =
         (ChainableFilter)document.getDocumentFilter();

      Set<Class> filters = new HashSet<Class>();
      filters.add(filter.getClass());
      filters.add(filter.getNext().getClass());

      assertTrue(filters.contains(LimitFilter.class));
      assertTrue(filters.contains(UpcaseFilter.class));
   }
```

```
    public void testCreateFormattedField() {
        final int year = 2006;
        final int month = 3;
        final int day = 17;
        fieldSpec.setInitialValue(DateUtil.createDate(year, month, day));
        final String pattern = "MM/dd/yy";
        fieldSpec.setFormat(new SimpleDateFormat(pattern));

        JFormattedTextField field =
            (JFormattedTextField)TextFieldFactory.create(fieldSpec);

        assertEquals(1, field.getColumns());
        assertEquals(FIELD_NAME, field.getName());

        DateFormatter formatter = (DateFormatter)field.getFormatter();
        SimpleDateFormat format = (SimpleDateFormat)formatter.getFormat();
        assertEquals(pattern, format.toPattern());
        assertEquals(Date.class, field.getValue().getClass());
        assertEquals("03/17/06", field.getText());

        TestUtil.assertDateEquals(year, month, day,
            (Date)field.getValue()); // a new utility method
    }
}

// TextFieldFactory.java
package sis.ui;

import javax.swing.*;
import javax.swing.text.*;

public class TextFieldFactory {
    public static JTextField create(Field fieldSpec) {
        JTextField field = null;

        if (fieldSpec.getFormat() != null)
            field = createFormattedTextField(fieldSpec);
        else {
            field = new JTextField();
            if (fieldSpec.getInitialValue() != null)
                field.setText(fieldSpec.getInitialValue().toString());
        }

        if (fieldSpec.getLimit() > 0)
            attachLimitFilter(field, fieldSpec.getLimit());

        if (fieldSpec.isUpcaseOnly())
            attachUpcaseFilter(field);

        field.setColumns(fieldSpec.getColumns());
        field.setName(fieldSpec.getName());
        return field;
    }
```

Feel

```
    private static void attachLimitFilter(JTextField field, int limit) {
       attachFilter(field, new LimitFilter(limit));
    }

    private static void attachUpcaseFilter(JTextField field) {
       attachFilter(field, new UpcaseFilter());
    }

    private static void attachFilter(
          JTextField field, ChainableFilter filter) {
       AbstractDocument document = (AbstractDocument)field.getDocument();
       ChainableFilter existingFilter =
          (ChainableFilter)document.getDocumentFilter();
       if (existingFilter == null)
          document.setDocumentFilter(filter);
       else
          existingFilter.setNext(filter);
    }

    private static JTextField createFormattedTextField(Field fieldSpec) {
       JFormattedTextField field =
          new JFormattedTextField(fieldSpec.getFormat());
       field.setValue(fieldSpec.getInitialValue());
       return field;
    }
}


// CoursesPanelTest.java
...
public void testCreate() {
    assertEmptyList(COURSES_LIST_NAME);
    assertButtonText(ADD_BUTTON_NAME, ADD_BUTTON_TEXT);

    String[] fields =
       { FieldCatalog.DEPARTMENT_FIELD_NAME,
         FieldCatalog.NUMBER_FIELD_NAME,
         FieldCatalog.EFFECTIVE_DATE_FIELD_NAME };
    assertFields(fields);

    JButton button = panel.getButton(ADD_BUTTON_NAME);
    assertEquals(ADD_BUTTON_MNEMONIC, button.getMnemonic());
}

private void assertFields(String[] fieldNames) {
    FieldCatalog catalog = new FieldCatalog();
    for (String fieldName: fieldNames) {
       assertNotNull(panel.getField(fieldName));
       // can't compare two JTextField items for equality,
       // so we must go on faith here that CoursesPanel
       // creates them using TextFieldFactory
       Field fieldSpec = catalog.get(fieldName);
```

```
            assertLabelText(fieldSpec.getLabelName(), fieldSpec.getLabel());
        }
    }
    ...

    // CoursesPanel.java
    ...
    JPanel createFieldsPanel() {
        GridBagLayout layout = new GridBagLayout();

        JPanel panel = new JPanel(layout);
        int i = 0;
        FieldCatalog catalog = new FieldCatalog();

        for (String fieldName: getFieldNames()) {
            Field fieldSpec = catalog.get(fieldName);
            addField(panel, layout, i++,
                    createLabel(fieldSpec),
                    TextFieldFactory.create(fieldSpec));
        }

        return panel;
    }

    private String[] getFieldNames() {
        return new String[]
            { FieldCatalog.DEPARTMENT_FIELD_NAME,
              FieldCatalog.NUMBER_FIELD_NAME,
              FieldCatalog.EFFECTIVE_DATE_FIELD_NAME };
    }

    private void addField(
            JPanel panel, GridBagLayout layout, int row,
            JLabel label, JTextField field) {
        ...
        panel.add(label);
        panel.add(field);
    }
    ...
```

Feel

Notes:

- TestUtil.assertDateEquals is a new utility method whose implementation should be obvious.

- I finally moved the DateUtil class from the sis.studentinfo package to the sis.util package. This change impacts a number of existing classes.

- You must also edit Sis and CoursesPanel (and tests) to remove constants and code for constructing filters/formatters. See *http://www.LangrSoft.com/agileJava/code/* for full code.

- The Field class, which is omitted from these listings, is a simple data class with virtually no logic.

- You'll want to update the Course class to contain the new attribute, effective date.

Tables

The CoursesPanel JList shows a single string for each Course object. This presentation is adequate because you only display two pieces of data: the department and course number. Adding the new effective date attribute to the summary string, however, would quickly make the list look jumbled. The JList control, in fact, works best when you have only a single piece of data to represent per row in the list.

A JTable is a very effective control that allows you to present each object as a sequence of columns. A JTable can look a lot like a spreadsheet. In fact, JTable code and documentation uses the same terms as spreadsheets: rows, columns, and cells.

The JTable class gives you a considerable amount of control over look and feel. For example, you can decide whether or not you want to allow users to edit individual cells in the table, you can allow the user to rearrange the columns, and you can control the width of each column.

For this exercise, you'll replace the JList with a JTable. The best place to start is to create the data model that will underly the JTable. Just as you inserted Course objects into a list model for the JList, you will put Course objects into a model that you attach to the JTable.

Creating the JTable model is slightly more involved. The JList was able to get a printable representation by sending the toString message to each object it contained. The JTable must treat each attribute for a given object separately. For every cell it must display, the JTable sends the message getValueAt to the model. It passes the row and column representing the current cell. The getValueAt method must return a string to display at this location.

There would be no easy way for the model to figure out what attribute you want to display for a given column. As such, you must provide a model implementation yourself. You must supply the getValueAt method in this implementation, as well as two other methods: getRowCount and getColumnCount. To enhance the look and feel of the table, you will likely implement other methods. The test below, CoursesTableModelTest, shows that the model implements the method getColumnName to return a text header for each column.

```
package sis.ui;

import junit.framework.*;
import sis.studentinfo.*;
import sis.util.*;
import java.util.*;

public class CoursesTableModelTest extends TestCase {
    private CoursesTableModel model;

    protected void setUp() {
        model = new CoursesTableModel();
    }

    public void testCreate() {
        assertEquals(0, model.getRowCount());
        assertEquals(3, model.getColumnCount());
        FieldCatalog catalog = new FieldCatalog();

        Field department =
            catalog.get(FieldCatalog.DEPARTMENT_FIELD_NAME);
        assertEquals(department.getShortName(), model.getColumnName(0));

        Field number = catalog.get(FieldCatalog.NUMBER_FIELD_NAME);
        assertEquals(number.getShortName(), model.getColumnName(1));

        Field effectiveDate =
            catalog.get(FieldCatalog.EFFECTIVE_DATE_FIELD_NAME);
        assertEquals(effectiveDate.getShortName(),
                        model.getColumnName(2));
    }

    public void testAddRow() {
        Course course = new Course("CMSC", "110");

        course.setEffectiveDate(DateUtil.createDate(2006, 3, 17));

        model.add(course);

        assertEquals(1, model.getRowCount());
        final int row = 0;
        assertEquals("CMSC", model.getValueAt(row, 0));
        assertEquals("110", model.getValueAt(row, 1));
        assertEquals("03/17/06", model.getValueAt(row, 2));
    }
}
```

Tables

The test presents another use for the FieldCatalog—returning an appropriate column header for each field. It uses a new Field attribute with the more abstract concept of a "short name," an abbreviated name for use in constrained display spaces. You'll need to update Field and FieldCatalog/FieldCatalogTest to supply this new information.

The easiest way to build a table model is to subclass javax.swing.table.AbstractTableModel. You then need only supply definitions for getValueAt, getRowCount, and getColumnCount. You will want to store a collection of courses in the model. You'll need a method (add) that allows adding a new Course to the model.

You can also choose to work with javax.swing.table.DefaultTableModel. Sun provided this concrete implementation to make your job a bit simpler. However, DefaultTableModel requires that you organize your data first (in the form of either Vector objects or Object arrays) and then pass it to the model. It's almost as easy, and ultimately more effective, to create your own AbstractTableModel subclass.

```java
package sis.ui;

import javax.swing.table.*;
import java.text.*;
import java.util.*;
import sis.studentinfo.*;

class CoursesTableModel extends AbstractTableModel {
    private List<Course> courses = new ArrayList<Course>();
    private SimpleDateFormat formatter =
        new SimpleDateFormat("MM/dd/yy");
    private FieldCatalog catalog = new FieldCatalog();
    private String[] fields = {
        FieldCatalog.DEPARTMENT_FIELD_NAME,
        FieldCatalog.NUMBER_FIELD_NAME,
        FieldCatalog.EFFECTIVE_DATE_FIELD_NAME };

    void add(Course course) {
        courses.add(course);
        fireTableRowsInserted(courses.size() - 1, courses.size());
    }

    Course get(int index) {
        return courses.get(index);
    }

    public String getColumnName(int column) {
        Field field = catalog.get(fields[column]);
        return field.getShortName();
    }

    // abstract (req'd) methods: getValueAt, getColumnCount, getRowCount
    public Object getValueAt(int row, int column) {
        Course course = courses.get(row);
        String fieldName = fields[column];
        if (fieldName.equals(FieldCatalog.DEPARTMENT_FIELD_NAME))
            return course.getDepartment();
        else if (fieldName.equals(FieldCatalog.NUMBER_FIELD_NAME))
            return course.getNumber();
```

```
        else if (fieldName.equals(FieldCatalog.EFFECTIVE_DATE_FIELD_NAME))
            return formatter.format(course.getEffectiveDate());
        return "";
    }

    public int getColumnCount() {
        return fields.length;
    }

    public int getRowCount() {
        return courses.size();
    }
}
```

Note the subtle redundancies that abound. The table must contain a list of fields you are interested in displaying. In getValueAt, you obtain the field name at the column index provided. You use this name in a pseudo–switch statement to determine which Course getter method to call. A shorter bit of code would involve a switch statement:

```
switch (column) {
    case 0: return course.getDepartment();
    case 1: return course.getNumber();
    case 2: return formatter.format(course.getEffectiveDate());
    default: return "";
}
```

While it is acceptable, I dislike the disconnect between the column number and the attribute. Changes to the columns or their order can easily result in errors. (At least your tests would catch the problem.) But see the sidebar for a discussion of the solution I present.

You will, of course, need to make a few more changes to get the JTable working. In CoursesPanelTest:

```
public void testCreate() {
    assertEmptyTable(COURSES_TABLE_NAME);
    assertButtonText(ADD_BUTTON_NAME, ADD_BUTTON_TEXT);
    ...
}

public void testAddCourse() {
    Course course = new Course("ENGL", "101");
    panel.addCourse(course);
    JTable table = panel.getTable(COURSES_TABLE_NAME);
    CoursesTableModel model = (CoursesTableModel)table.getModel();
    assertSame(course, model.get(0));
}

private void assertEmptyTable(String name) {
    JTable table = panel.getTable(name);
    assertEquals(0, table.getModel().getRowCount());
}
```

Domain Maps

The implementation of getValueAt contains significant redundancy. You test the selected field name against each possible field name in order to obtain the corresponding attribute from the Course object. A more radical solution is to implement your domain objects as hash tables. The hash table key is the attribute name. You would set the value in the Course like this:

```
course.set(DEPARTMENT_FIELD_NAME, "CMSC");
```

And you would retrieve the value like this:

```
String courseName = (String)course.get(DEPARTMENT_FIELD_NAME);
```

or

```
String courseName = course.getString(DEPARTMENT_FIELD_NAME);
```

The code in getValueAt becomes very succinct:

```
Course course = courses.get(row);
return course.get(fields[column]);
```

This solution can greatly diminish the redundancy in your system, but it introduces other concerns. First is the decreased readability when you attempt to follow the code or debug it. Also, the solution would require casting, either at the point of call or embedded within a bunch of utility methods such as getString, getDate, and getInt.

In CoursesPanel:

```
static final String COURSES_TABLE_NAME = "coursesTable";
...
private void createLayout() {
   JTable coursesTable = createCoursesTable();
   JScrollPane coursesScroll = new JScrollPane(coursesTable);
   coursesScroll.setVerticalScrollBarPolicy(
      ScrollPaneConstants.VERTICAL_SCROLLBAR_ALWAYS);
   ...
}

private JTable createCoursesTable() {
   JTable table = new JTable(coursesTableModel);
   table.setName(COURSES_TABLE_NAME);
   table.setShowGrid(false);
   table.setSelectionMode(ListSelectionModel.SINGLE_SELECTION);
   return table;
}

void addCourse(Course course) {
   coursesTableModel.add(course);
}

Course getCourse(int index) {
   return coursesTableModel.get(index);
}
```

Tables

You can remove the class CourseDisplayAdapter and any references to the old courses list.

Make sure you take a look at the Java API documentation for JTable and the various table model classes. The JTable class contains quite a bit of customization capabilities.

Feedback

Part of creating a good user experience is ensuring that you provide plenty of feedback. Sun has already built a lot of feedback into Swing. For example, when you click the mouse button atop a JButton, the JButton repaints to appear as if it were physically depressed. This kind of information reassures the user about his or her actions.

The Sis application lacks a pertinent piece of feedback: When the user enters one of the filtered or formatted text fields, how does he or she know what they're expected to type? The user will eventually discover the constraints they are under. But he or she will waste some time as they undergo guesswork, trial, and error.

You can instead provide your users with helpful information ahead of time. Several options exist:

- Put helpful information in the label for the field. Generally, though, there is not enough screen real estate to do so.

- Provide a separate online help window that describes how the application works.

- As the user moves the mouse over fields, display a small pop-up rectangle with relevant information. This is known as hover help, or tool tips. All modern applications such as Internet Explorer provide tool tips as you hover your mouse over toolbar buttons.

- As the user moves the mouse over fields, display relevant information in a status bar at the bottom of the window.

For this exercise, you will choose the last option and create a status bar.

Unfortunately, for mouse-based testing, you must usually render (display) the user interface in order to test it. The reason is that components do not have established sizes until they are rendered. You can again use the Swing robot to help you write your tests. Note that the setUp in this test uses a couple of Swing utility methods that I will display in subsequent listings.

Feedback

```
package sis.ui;

import junit.framework.*;
import javax.swing.*;
import java.awt.*;
import sis.util.*;

public class StatusBarTest extends TestCase {
    private JTextField field1;
    private JTextField field2;
    private StatusBar statusBar;
    private JFrame frame;

    protected void setUp() {
        field1 = new JTextField(10);
        field2 = new JTextField(10);
        statusBar = new StatusBar();

        JPanel panel = SwingUtil.createPanel(field1, field2, statusBar);
        frame = SwingUtil.createFrame(panel);
    }

    protected void tearDown() {
        frame.dispose();
    }

    public void testMouseover() throws Exception {
        final String text1 = "text1";
        final String text2 = "text2";

        statusBar.setInfo(field1, text1);
        statusBar.setInfo(field2, text2);

        Robot robot = new Robot();

        Point field1Location = field1.getLocationOnScreen();

        robot.mouseMove(field1Location.x - 1, field1Location.y - 1);
        assertEquals("", statusBar.getText().trim());

        robot.mouseMove(field1Location.x + 1, field1Location.y + 1);
        assertEquals(text1, statusBar.getText());
        Point field2Location = field2.getLocationOnScreen();

        robot.mouseMove(field2Location.x + 1, field2Location.y + 1);
        assertEquals(text2, statusBar.getText());
    }
}
```

Conceptually, providing status information is a common need for all of your application's windows. Instead of cluttering each window with additional code, you can encapsulate the status concept in a separate class.

StatusBar

A StatusBar is a JLabel with additional functionality. You can associate an information String with each text field by sending setInfo to a Status object.

The test extracts the location of the first field, then moves the mouse to an arbitrary position outside this field. The status bar should show nothing; the first assertion proves that. The test then moves the mouse over the field, then ensures that the status bar contains the expected text. The test finally asserts that the status bar text changes to TEXT2 when the mouse is over the second field.

The SwingUtil class extracts common code used to create a simple panel and a frame for testing:

```
package sis.util;

import javax.swing.*;

public class SwingUtil {
    public static JPanel createPanel(JComponent... components) {
        JPanel panel = new JPanel();
        for (JComponent component: components)
            panel.add(component);
        return panel;
    }

    public static JFrame createFrame(JPanel panel) {
        JFrame frame = new JFrame();
        frame.getContentPane().add(panel);
        frame.setDefaultCloseOperation(JFrame.EXIT_ON_CLOSE);
        frame.setSize(300, 300);
        frame.setVisible(true);
        return frame;
    }
}
```

Feedback

In StatusBar, the job of setInfo is to add a mouse listener to the text field. The listener reacts to mouse entry and mouse exit events. When a user moves the mouse atop the text, listener code displays the associated information. When a user moves the mouse away from the text field, listener code clears the status bar.

```
package sis.ui;

import java.awt.event.*;
import java.util.*;
import javax.swing.*;

public class StatusBar extends JLabel {
    private final static String EMPTY = " ";
```

```
    public StatusBar() {
        super(EMPTY);
        setBorder(BorderFactory.createLoweredBevelBorder());
    }

    public void setInfo(final JTextField textField, final String text) {
        textField.addMouseListener(
            new MouseAdapter() {
                public void mouseEntered(MouseEvent event) {
                    setText(text);
                }

                public void mouseExited(MouseEvent event) {
                    setText(EMPTY);
                }
            });
    }
}
```

The test for StatusBar passes. Now you must attach the status bar to CoursesPanel. How will you test this? Your test for CoursesPanel could use the robot again. But it would be easier to ensure that each text field has been attached to the status bar.

Update the test in CoursesPanelTest. The assertion declares a new intent: A StatusBar object should be able to return the informational text for a given text field. It also suggests that the informational text should come from the field spec object, obtained from the field catalog.

```
private void assertFields(String[] fieldNames) {
    StatusBar statusBar =
      (StatusBar)Util.getComponent(panel, StatusBar.NAME);

    FieldCatalog catalog = new FieldCatalog();
    for (String fieldName: fieldNames) {
        JTextField field = panel.getField(fieldName);
        Field fieldSpec = catalog.get(fieldName);

        assertEquals(fieldSpec.getInfo(), statusBar.getInfo(field));
        assertLabelText(fieldSpec.getLabelName(), fieldSpec.getLabel());
    }
}
```

Feedback

This will not compile because you have not implemented getInfo. Note also that you will need to associate a component name with the status bar. Here are the changes to StatusBarTest and StatusBar:

```
// StatusBarTest
...
public void testInfo() {
    statusBar.setInfo(field1, "a");
```

```
        assertEquals("a", statusBar.getInfo(field1));
    }
    ...

    // StatusBar
    package sis.ui;

    import java.awt.event.*;
    import java.util.*;
    import javax.swing.*;

    public class StatusBar extends JLabel {
        public static final String NAME = "StatusBar";
        private final static String EMPTY = " ";
        private Map<JTextField,String> infos =
            new IdentityHashMap<JTextField,String>();

        public StatusBar() {
            super(EMPTY);
            setName(NAME);
            setBorder(BorderFactory.createLoweredBevelBorder());
        }

        public String getInfo(JTextField textField) {
            return infos.get(textField);
        }

        public void setInfo(final JTextField textField, String text) {
            infos.put(textField, text);
            textField.addMouseListener(
                new MouseAdapter() {
                    public void mouseEntered(MouseEvent event) {
                        setText(getInfo(textField));
                    }

                    public void mouseExited(MouseEvent event) {
                        setText(EMPTY);
                    }
                });
        }
    }
}
```

You must also add a field, getter, and setter to Field. You'll need to modify FieldCatalog to populate each field with a pertinent informational string:

```
...
static final String DEPARTMENT_FIELD_INFO =
    "Enter a 4-character department designation.";
static final String NUMBER_FIELD_INFO =
    "The department number should be 3 digits.";
static final String EFFECTIVE_DATE_FIELD_INFO =
    "Effective date should be in mm/dd/yy format.";
...
```

```
private void loadFields() {
    fields = new HashMap<String,Field>();

    Field fieldSpec = new Field(DEPARTMENT_FIELD_NAME);
    ...
    fieldSpec.setInfo(DEPARTMENT_FIELD_INFO);

    put(fieldSpec);

    fieldSpec = new Field(NUMBER_FIELD_NAME);
    ...
    fieldSpec.setInfo(NUMBER_FIELD_INFO);

    put(fieldSpec);

    fieldSpec = new Field(EFFECTIVE_DATE_FIELD_NAME);
    ...
    fieldSpec.setInfo(EFFECTIVE_DATE_FIELD_INFO);

    put(fieldSpec);
}
```

Finally, the code in CoursesPanel to make it all work for the student information system:

```
private Status status;

private void createLayout() {
    ...
    add(coursesScroll, BorderLayout.CENTER);
    add(createBottomPanel(), BorderLayout.SOUTH);
}

JPanel createBottomPanel() {
    JLabel statusBar = new JLabel(" ");
    statusBar.setBorder(BorderFactory.createLoweredBevelBorder());
    status = new Status(statusBar);

    JPanel panel = new JPanel();
    panel.setLayout(new BorderLayout());
    panel.add(statusBar, BorderLayout.SOUTH);
    panel.add(createInputPanel(), BorderLayout.CENTER);
    return panel;
}

JPanel createFieldsPanel() {
    GridBagLayout layout = new GridBagLayout();

    JPanel panel = new JPanel(layout);
    int i = 0;
    FieldCatalog catalog = new FieldCatalog();
```

Feedback

```
for (String fieldName: getFieldNames()) {
    Field fieldSpec = catalog.get(fieldName);
    JTextField textField = TextFieldFactory.create(fieldSpec);
    status.addText(textField, fieldSpec.getLabel());
    addField(panel, layout, i++,
            createLabel(fieldSpec),
            textField);
}

return panel;
}
```

If you execute sis.ui.Sis as a stand-alone application, you should now see something like Figure 2. I rested the mouse pointer above the department field when I captured this screen image.

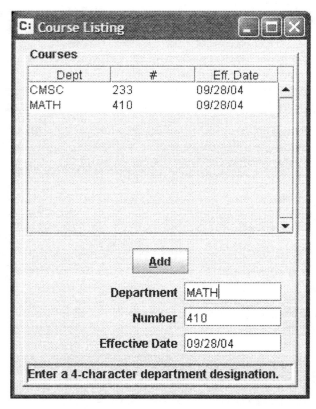

Figure 2 *The Completed Look*

Responsiveness

In the Sis method addCourse, insert a deliberate wait of three seconds. This wait might emulate the time required to verify and insert the Course object into the database.

```
private void addCourse() {
   Course course =
      new Course(
         panel.getText(FieldCatalog.DEPARTMENT_FIELD_NAME),
         panel.getText(FieldCatalog.NUMBER_FIELD_NAME));
try { Thread.sleep(3000); } catch (InterruptedException e) {}
   JFormattedTextField effectiveDateField =
      (JFormattedTextField)panel.getField(
         FieldCatalog.EFFECTIVE_DATE_FIELD_NAME);
   Date date = (Date)effectiveDateField.getValue();
   course.setEffectiveDate(date);

   panel.addCourse(course);
}
```

Execute the application. Enter a department and course number and press Add. You should experience a 3-second delay. During that time, you cannot do anything else with the user interface! For an end user, this is a frustrating experience, since there is no feedback about why the application is not responding.

As an application developer, you can do two things with respect to responsiveness: First, provide feedback to the user that they should wait patiently for a short period. Second, ensure that the user is able to do other things while waiting.

Feedback comes in the form of a "wait" cursor. Windows represents a wait cursor using an hourglass. Some Unix desktops represent a wait cursor using a clock. You should provide an hourglass for any operation that does not immediately return control to the user.

Responsiveness

```
private void addCourse() {
   frame.setCursor(Cursor.getPredefinedCursor(Cursor.WAIT_CURSOR));
   try {
      Course course =
         new Course(
            panel.getText(FieldCatalog.DEPARTMENT_FIELD_NAME),
            panel.getText(FieldCatalog.NUMBER_FIELD_NAME));
try { Thread.sleep(3000); } catch (InterruptedException e) {}
      JFormattedTextField effectiveDateField =
         (JFormattedTextField)panel.getField(
            FieldCatalog.EFFECTIVE_DATE_FIELD_NAME);
```

```
        Date date = (Date)effectiveDateField.getValue();
        course.setEffectiveDate(date);

        panel.addCourse(course);
    }
    finally {
        frame.setCursor(Cursor.getDefaultCursor());
    }
}
```

The finally block is essential! Otherwise, any unnoticed or abnormal return from addCourse will burden the user with an hourglass as a pointer.

Providing a wait cursor is an adequate and necessary response for any prolonged wait period. But the real solution is to ensure that the user does not have to wait. The threshold is a half a second: You should spawn a slow operation off in another thread if it is going to take any longer. In the example shown here, I've separated the behind-the-scenes operation of adding the course from the code that updates the user interface. I've also disabled the Add button until the thread completes.

```
// THIS IS AN INADEQUATE SOLUTION!
private void addCourse() {
    Thread thread = new Thread() {
        public void run() {
            panel.setEnabled(CoursesPanel.ADD_BUTTON_NAME, false);
            Course course = basicAddCourse();
            panel.addCourse(course);
            panel.setEnabled(CoursesPanel.ADD_BUTTON_NAME, true);
        }
    };
    thread.start();
}

private Course basicAddCourse() {
try { Thread.sleep(3000); } catch (InterruptedException e) {}
    Course course =
        new Course(
            panel.getText(FieldCatalog.DEPARTMENT_FIELD_NAME),
            panel.getText(FieldCatalog.NUMBER_FIELD_NAME));
    JFormattedTextField effectiveDateField =
        (JFormattedTextField)panel.getField(
            FieldCatalog.EFFECTIVE_DATE_FIELD_NAME);
    Date date = (Date)effectiveDateField.getValue();
    course.setEffectiveDate(date);
    return course;
}
```

Responsiveness

A subtle but real problem exists with this code. It is not thread-safe! Since Swing uses a separate thread known as an event dispatch thread, it is possible for a user to click the Add button before the panel is completely updated. The user might see unexpected results.

You can rectify this by executing statements to update the user interface in the event dispatch thread. The class javax.swing.SwingUtilities contains two methods, invokeLater and invokeAndWait, to allow this. Each method takes a Runnable object that defines the code to execute in the event dispatch thread. You use invokeLater when you can allow the run method to execute asynchronously (when you don't need to "hold up" activities on the user interface). In our example, you want to use invokeAndWait, which results in the run method being executed synchronously.

Here's how addCourse might look using invokeAndWait:

```
private void addCourse() {
   Thread thread = new Thread() {
      public void run() {
         panel.setEnabled(CoursesPanel.ADD_BUTTON_NAME, false);
         try {
            final Course course = basicAddCourse();
            SwingUtilities.invokeAndWait(new Runnable() {
               public void run() {
                  panel.addCourse(course);
                  panel.setEnabled(CoursesPanel.ADD_BUTTON_NAME, true);
               }
            });
         }
         catch (Exception e) {}
      }
   };
   thread.start();
}
```

The big downside is that this change will break the SisTest method testAddCourse. The test presumes that clicking on Add will block until the course has been added to the panel. As a quick fix, you can have the test wait until elements appear in the panel's table.

```
public void testAddCourse() {
   ...
   JButton button = panel.getButton(CoursesPanel.ADD_BUTTON_NAME);
   button.doClick();

   while (panel.getCourseCount() == 0)
      ;
   Course course = panel.getCourse(0);
   assertEquals("MATH", course.getDepartment());
   assertEquals("300", course.getNumber());
   TestUtil.assertDateEquals(2006, 3, 17, course.getEffectiveDate());
}
```

The change requires a small addition to CoursesPanel:

```
int getCourseCount() {
    return coursesTableModel.getRowCount();
}
```

Remaining Tasks

You've invested a considerable amount of code in this simple interface. Yet it's far from complete. Here is a list of some of the things you might consider coding to complete the interface:

- Clear the text fields when the user presses Add.

- Add a constraint that prevents the user from entering duplicate courses. You would code the logic to check for duplicates in CourseCatalog.

- Add delete button to remove courses. You might allow the user to select multiple rows for deletion.

- Add an update button to make edits to existing courses.

- Install the ability to sort the data in each column.

- Add a numeric filter to limit the user to entering only digits for the course number.

- Set each column width depending upon the average or maximum width of its contents.

- Add a hook that selects the contents of each field as the user tabs or clicks into it. This allows the user to replace the field's contents by simply typing.

- Add mouseover help. As the user moves the mouse over each field, show summary information in either the status bar or in a small pop-up "tool tip."

- Add keyboard help. Respond to the F1 key by popping up help. (Obviously this is more involved and requires an understanding of how to build a help subsystem.)

- Replace the department and/or course number fields with a drop-down list (JComboBox).

- Add interaction with the preferences subsystem (see Additional Lesson III) to allow the application to "remember" the last position of each window.

I've no doubt left a few features off this list. Building a robust, sophisticated user interface is a lot of work. The absence of any of these features will severely cripple the effectiveness of your application. However, rather than you as a developer trying to figure out what you need, you should treat each of these features as customer requirements. Your customer team needs a qualified expert to design and detail the specifications for the user interface.[6]

Final Notes

A large number of Swing books exist. Many are very thick, suggesting that there is quite a bit to learn about Swing. Indeed, there is. In these short two chapters you have only scratched the surface of Swing.

However, you have seen the basics of how to construct Swing applications. You would be able to build a decent interface with this small bit of information. No doubt you will want to learn about more complex Swing topics, such as tree widgets and drag & drop. A bit of searching should provide you with what you need to know. As always, the Java API documentation is the best place to start. Often the API documentation will lead you to a Sun tutorial on the topic.

I hope you've learned the more important lesson in these two Swing chapters: how to approach building a Swing application using TDD. Unit-testing Swing is often viewed as too difficult, and many shops choose to forgo it altogether. Don't succumb to the laziness: The frequent result of not testing Swing code is the tendency for Swing classes to bloat with easily testable application or model code.

Looking at the resultant view class, CoursesPanel, you should have noticed that it is very small and simple. Other than layout, there is little complexity in the class; it does almost nothing. TDD or not, that is always the

---

[6]This person can be a developer acting in the role of UI expert for the customer team. Do not, however, underestimate the importance of this role. Most developers, even those who have read a book or two on the topic, don't have a clue how to create an effective user experience.

design goal in a user-interface application: to keep the application and/or business logic out of the view.

Using TDD has pushed you toward this goal. The basic rule of TDD is to test everything that can't possibly break. One way to interpret this rule is "test everything that you can and redesign everything else so it can't possibly break." TDD has led you to create a small view class with very simple, discrete methods that you can easily test. You've also created dumb "reactive" methods that simply delegate their work to another trusted class. These methods can't break.

The shops that choose to not test their user interface classes always regret it. Business logic creeps into the application; application and business logic creeps into the view. The view code becomes a cluttered conglomerate of various responsibilities. Since tests aren't written for the view, a considerable amount of code goes untested. The defect rate rises.

Worse, the human tendency toward laziness takes over. Since no tests for the view exist, a developer often figures that the easiest way to get out of testing is to stuff the code into the view. "Yeah, creating a new class is a pain, and so is creating a new test class, so I'll just dump all the code in this mother Swing class." Doing so is a slippery slope that quickly degrades your application.

In these past two chapters, you've learned some additional guidelines and techniques for building Swing applications using TDD:

- Ensure that your design separates application, view, and domain logic.

- Break down design even further by considering the Single-Responsibility Principle.

- Eliminate the otherwise excessive redundancies in Swing (e.g., use common methods to create and extract fields).

- Use listeners to test abstract reactions of the view (e.g., to ensure that clicking a button results in some action being triggered).

- Use mock classes to avoid Swing rendering.

- Don't test layout.

- Use the Swing robot, but only as a last resort.

Swing was not designed with unit-level testing in mind. Figuring out how to test Swing is a problem-solving exercise. Dig through the various Swing classes to find what you need. Sometimes they'll supply the hooks to help you test; other times they won't. You may need to think outside the box to figure out how to test things!

Additional Lesson III

Java Miscellany

This chapter provides a handful of Java odds and ends. The primary goal of this chapter is twofold:

- It will present you with an overview of some very involved APIs that can take entire books to cover adequately.

- It will discuss a few core Java odds and ends that didn't fit elsewhere in *Agile Java*.

You will learn about:

- JARs

- the finalize method

- regular expressions

- JDBC

- internationalization

- call by reference versus call by value

- Java periphery: quick overviews of various other Java APIs, with pointers to more information

JARs

When you learned about the Java classpath in Lesson 1, you learned to add class folders (or directories) to your classpath. A class folder contains discrete class files that Java looks for when it needs to load a class.

Your classpath can include *JARs* in addition to, or instead of, class folders. A JAR (Java ARchive) is a single file that collects Java class files and other

653

resources needed at runtime. You can create JARs using the jar command-line utility executable supplied in your Java bin directory. You can also create JARs using Ant.

An understanding of JARs is absolutely essential to being able to work in any production Java environment. The usage of JARs falls under the category of deployment, so the discussion of JARs didn't have an appropriate place earlier in the book.

The jar utility combines class files and other resources (such as images or property files) into a single file with an extension of .jar. The utility creates JARs as ZIP files, a file format you are likely familiar with. A ZIP file uses a standard compression algorithm to reduce the overall space requirements.

There are many reasons to use JARs:

- Deployment speed. Transferring or installing a few files is considerably faster than transferring or installing thousands of files.

- Compression. Disk requirements are smaller; smaller files are downloaded faster.

- Security. When working in secure environments, you can attach a digital signature to a JAR.

- Pluggability. You can organize JARs around reuse interests. JARs can be components or complete API sets.

- Versioning. You can attach vendor and version information to JARs.

- Simplified execution. You can designate a JAR to be "Java executable." A user of the JAR does not need to know an entry class name.

JARs are the basis for deploying classes to a web server or enterprise Java installation.

To create a JAR for the SIS application, first navigate to the classes directory. Then execute:

JARs

```
jar cvf sis.jar *
```

In the above jar command, the options cvf (c, v, and f) tell the JAR command to create a new JAR, to provide verbose output (not necessary but useful), and to use a filename of sis.jar. The * at the end of the command tells the jar program to archive all files in the current directory and all subdirectories. You can execute the command jar with no arguments to display a brief summary of the command and its proper usage.

After executing the jar cvf command, you should have a file named sis.jar. Under Windows, you can open this JAR using WinZip. Under any platform, you can use the jar command to list the contents of the JAR.

```
jar tvf sis.jar
```

The only difference in the command is the option t (list table of contents) instead of c. You should see output similar to this:

```
   0 Mon Aug 02 23:25:36 MDT 2004 META-INF/
  74 Mon Aug 02 23:25:36 MDT 2004 META-INF/MANIFEST.MF
 553 Sat Jul 24 10:41:28 MDT 2004 A$B.class
 541 Sat Jul 24 10:41:28 MDT 2004 A.class
1377 Sat Jul 24 10:41:28 MDT 2004 AtomicLong.class
   0 Sat Jul 24 10:41:28 MDT 2004 com/
   0 Sat Jul 24 10:41:28 MDT 2004 com/jimbob/
   0 Sat Jul 24 10:41:28 MDT 2004 com/jimbob/ach/
 486 Sat Jul 24 10:41:28 MDT 2004 com/jimbob/ach/Ach.class
 377 Sat Jul 24 10:41:28 MDT 2004 com/jimbob/ach/AchCredentials.class
 516 Sat Jul 24 10:41:28 MDT 2004 com/jimbob/ach/AchResponse.class
1164 Sat Jul 24 10:41:28 MDT 2004 com/jimbob/ach/AchStatus.class
 ...
```

You can extract files from the JAR using the command option x (i.e., jar xvf).

Once you have added classes to a JAR, you can add the JAR to your classpath. Java will dig into the JAR file to look for classes it needs to load. For example, suppose you deploy sis.jar to the directory /usr/sis. You can execute the SIS application using the command:

```
java -cp /usr/sis/sis.jar sis.ui.Sis
```

In order for Java to find a class within a JAR, its path information must match the package information. To locate the class com.jimbob.ach.Ach, Java must be able to find an entry in the JAR with the complete pathname com/jimbob/ach/Ach.class. In the jar tvf listing, I've shown this entry in bold.

If you were a directory higher when you were creating the JAR, the path information in the JAR file might be:

```
 486 Sat Jul 24 10:41:28 MDT 2004 sis/com/jimbob/ach/Ach.class
```

Java would not match up this entry with the class com.jimbob.ach.Ach.

The jar utility adds a manifest file, META-INF/MANIFEST.MF, to the ZIP file. The manifest file contains information about the contents of the JAR (i.e., meta-information).

One use for the manifest file is to indicate a "main" class. If you specify a main class, you can initiate an application by providing only the JAR name.

JARs

You can accomplish this by first creating a separate manifest file with the contents:

```
Main-Class: sis.ui.Sis
```

Make sure you include a blank line as the last line of this file! Otherwise Java may not recognize the manifest entry.

When you create the JAR, specify the manifest file using the command:

```
jar cvmf main.mf sis.jar *
```

The m option stands for manifest, of course. If you look at the file MANIFEST.MF in sis.jar, it should look something like this:

```
Manifest-Version: 1.0
Created-By: 1.5.0 (Sun Microsystems Inc.)
Main-Class: sis.ui.Sis
```

You can now initiate the SIS application using the simplified command:

```
java -jar sis.jar
```

You can manipulate JARs (and ZIP files) programmatically. Java supplies a complete API in the package java.util.zip to help you accomplish this. The java.util.zip package contains tools to both read and write JARs. This allows you to write unit tests against JAR operations about as simply as if you were testing against text files.

Regular Expressions

A regular expression, also known as a regex or regexp, is a string containing a search pattern. The regular expression language is a fairly standardized language for pattern-matching specifications. Other languages such as Perl and Ruby provide direct support for regular expressions. Programmers' editors such as TextPad and UltraEdit allow you to search file text using regular expressions. Java supplies a set of class libraries to allow you to take advantage of regular expressions.

You might have used a wildcard character ('*') to list files in a directory. Using the wildcard tells the ls or dir command to find all matching files, assuming that the * can expand into any character or sequence of characters. For example, the DOS command dir *.java lists every file with a .java extension.

The regular expression language is similar in concept but far more powerful. In this section, I'll introduce you to regular expressions using a few simple examples. I'll show you how to take advantage of regular expressions in your Java code. I'll suggest how you might approach testing Java code that uses regular expressions. But a complete discussion of regular expressions is way out of the scope of this book. Refer to the end of this section for a few sites that provide regular expression tutorials and information.

Splitting Strings

Back in Lesson 7, you used the String method split to break a full name into discrete name parts. You passed a String containing a single blank character to split:

```
for (String name: fullName.split(" "))
```

The split method takes a regular expression as its sole argument.[1] The split method breaks the receiving string up when it encounters a match for the regular expression.

Suppose you try to split the string "Jeffrey Hyman"[2] with three spaces separating the first and last name. You want the results to be the strings "Jeffrey" and "Hyman", but a passing language test represents the actual results:

```
public void testSplit() {
    String source = "Jeffrey   Hyman";
    String expectedSplit[] = { "Jeffrey", "", "", "Hyman" };
    assertTrue(
        java.util.Arrays.equals(expectedSplit, source.split(" ")));
}
```

In other words, there are four substrings separated by spaces. Two of those substrings are the empty string (""): The first blank character separates "Jeffrey" from an empty string, the second blank character separates the first empty string from a second empty string, and the third blank character separates the second empty string from "Hyman".

You instead want to split the names around any *groupings* of whitespace characters. Using the Java API documentation for the class java .util.regex.Pattern as your guide, you should be able to figure out that the construct \s matches a single whitespace character (tab, new line, form feed, space, or carriage return). Under the section Greedy Quantifiers in the API doc, you'll note that X+ means that a match is found when the construct X occurs at least one time.

Regular
Expressions

---

[1] An overloaded version of split takes a limit on the number of times the pattern is applied.

[2] Aka Joey Ramone. Gabba gabba hey.

Combining the two ideas, the regular expression string \s+ will match on sequences with one or more whitespace characters.

I've moved the name-splitting code from the Student class and into a class called sis.studentinfo.Name. You can find the complete code for NameTest and Name at *http://www.LangrSoft.com/agileJava/code*. The listings below of NameTest and Name show only relevant or new material.

```java
// NameTest.java
public void testExtraneousSpaces() {
    final String fullName = "Jeffrey    Hyman";
    Name name = createName(fullName);
    assertEquals("Jeffrey", name.getFirstName());
    assertEquals("Hyman", name.getLastName());
}

private Name createName(String fullName) {
    Name name = new Name(fullName);
    assertEquals(fullName, name.getFullName());
    return name;
}

// Name.java
private List<String> split(String fullName) {
    List<String> results = new ArrayList<String>();
    for (String name: fullName.split(" "))
        results.add(name);
    return results;
}
```

The test method testExtraneousSpaces will not pass given the current implementation in Name.split. Using the new pattern you learned about, you can update the split method to make the tests pass:

```java
private List<String> split(String fullName) {
    List<String> results = new ArrayList<String>();
    for (String name: fullName.split("\\s+"))
        results.add(name);
    return results;
}
```

Regular Expressions

The backslash character ('\') represents the start of an escape sequence in Java strings. Thus, the regular expression \s+ appears as \\s+ within the context of a String.

Since \s matches *any* whitespace character, change the test to demonstrate that additional whitespace characters are ignored.

```java
public void testExtraneousWhitespace() {
    final String fullName = "Jeffrey    \t\t\n \r\fHyman";
    Name name = createName(fullName);
    assertEquals("Jeffrey", name.getFirstName());
    assertEquals("Hyman", name.getLastName());
}
```

Replacing Expressions in Strings

Many applications must capture a phone number from the user. People enter phone numbers in myriad ways. The best place to start is to strip all nondigits (parentheses, hyphens, letters, whitespace, and so on) from the phone number. This is very easy to do using regular expressions. Using a U.S. 10-digit phone number as an example:

```
public void testStripPhoneNumber() {
   String input = "(719) 555-9353 (home)";
   assertEquals("7195559353", StringUtil.stripToDigits(input));
}
```

The corresponding production code:

```
public static String stripToDigits(String input) {
   return input.replaceAll("\\D+", "");
}
```

The replaceAll method takes two arguments: a regular expression to match on and a replacement string. The expression \D matches any *non*digit character. The convention in the regular expression language is that the lowercase version of a construct character is used for positive matches and the uppercase version is used for negative matches. As another example, \w matches a "word" character: any letter, digit, or the underscore ('_') character. The uppercase construct, \W, matches any character that is not a word character.

The Pattern and Matcher Classes

You can use a JTextPane as the basis for a Swing-based text editor application. The JTextPane allows you to apply styles to sections of text. Many text editors provide the ability to search and highlight all strings matching a pattern. You'll want to build a class that can manage text searches against the underlying text.

Here's a test that demonstrates a small bit more of the regular expressions language.

```
package sis.util;

import junit.framework.TestCase;

import java.util.regex.*;

public class RegexTest extends TestCase {
   public void testSearch() {
      String[] textLines =
         { "public class Test {",
           "public void testMethod() {}",
           "public void testNotReally(int x) {}",
```

```
                    "public void test() {}",
                    "public String testNotReally() {}",
                    "}" };
        String text = join(textLines);

        String testMethodRegex =
            "public\\s+void\\s+test\\w*\\s*\\(\\s*\\)\\s*\\{";
        Pattern pattern = Pattern.compile(testMethodRegex);
        Matcher matcher = pattern.matcher(text);
        assertTrue(matcher.find());
        assertEquals(text.indexOf(textLines[1]), matcher.start());
        assertTrue(matcher.find());
        assertEquals(text.indexOf(textLines[3]), matcher.start());
        assertFalse(matcher.find());
    }

    private String join(String[] textLines) {
        StringBuilder builder = new StringBuilder();
        for (String line: textLines) {
            if (builder.length() > 0)
                builder.append("\n");
            builder.append(line);
        }
        return builder.toString();
    }
}
```

The regular expression in `testMethodRegex` looks pretty tough. They can get much worse! The regular expression above doesn't handle the possibility of a static or abstract modifier.[3] The double backslashes in the regular expression don't help matters.

Breaking the pattern down into its constructs makes it pretty straightforward. I'll step through each construct, left to right in the expression:

public\\s+void\\s+test\\w*\\s*\\(\\s*\\)\\s*\\{

match the text "public"	public
match one or more whitespace characters	\\s+
match the text "void"	void
match one or more whitespace characters	\\s+
match the text "test"	test

[3]Perhaps regex isn't the best tool for this job.

match zero or more word characters	\\w*
	An asterisk indicates that there may be any number of the preceding construct (including 0).
match zero or more whitespace characters	\\s*
match a left parenthesis	\\(
	You must escape parenthesis characters and brace characters.
match one or more whitespace characters	\\s*
match a right parenthesis	\\)
match zero or more whitespace characters	\\s*
match a left brace	\\{

A regular expression string is free-format, unproven text. You must compile it first using the Pattern class method compile. A successfully compiled regular expression string returns a Pattern object. From a Pattern object, you can obtain a Matcher for a given input String. Once you have a Matcher object, you can send it the find message to get it to locate the next matching *subsequence* (the substring of the input String that matches the regular expression). The find method returns true if a match was found, false otherwise.

The Matcher instance stores information about the last found subsequence. You can send the Matcher object the messages start and end to obtain the indexes that delineate the matched subsequence. Sending the message group to the Matcher returns the matching subsequence text.

In addition to triggering a find, you can send the message matches to the Matcher. This returns true if and only if the entire input string matches the regular expression. You can also send lookingAt, which returns true if the start of the input string (or the entire string) matches the regular expression.

For More Information

As you've seen, testing regular expressions is extremely simple—the assertions compare only String objects. This brief section should have given you

Regular
Expressions

enough information about regular expressions to be able to dig further into Java's support for it. The API documentation for the class java.util.regex.Pattern is the best place to start.

The regular expression language is a bit more involved. Knowing how patterns match against text is necessary to understanding how to write an appropriate regular expression.

The Sun tutorial on regular expressions at the web page *http:// java.sun.com/docs/books/tutorial/extra/regex/* supplies information on a few additional regular expression topics. You may also want to visit

http://www.regular-expressions.info/
http://www.javaregex.com/

Cloning and Covariance

Java allows you the ability to *clone*, or make a copy of, an object. You might find it surprising that cloning is only rarely a useful thing to do. In my numerous years of professional Java development, I've only seen a few needs for cloning. Therefore, I'm relegating cloning to a brief overview in this final section.

Unfortunately, cloning is often misunderstood and poorly implemented. If you have more sophisticated cloning needs than this simple example demonstrates, I refer you *Effective Java*[4] for an excellent discussion of the many issues related to cloning.

As an example, let's provide cloning capability for the simple class Course. The test is straightforward:

Cloning and
Covariance

```
public void testClone() {
    final String department = "CHEM";
    final String number = "400";
    final Date now = new Date();
    Course course = new Course(department, number);
    course.setEffectiveDate(now);
    Course copy = course.clone();
    assertFalse(copy == course);
    assertEquals(department, copy.getDepartment());
    assertEquals(number, copy.getNumber());
    assertEquals(now, copy.getEffectiveDate());
}
```

[4][Bloch2001].

Even though clone is defined on the class Object, the test won't compile. Object defines the clone method as protected. You must override the clone method in the Course subclass and make it public. The clone method is defined in Object as:

```
protected native Object clone() throws CloneNotSupportedException;
```

The native keyword in the signature indicates that the method is not implemented in Java but instead in the JVM.

To be able to clone an object, its class must implement the Cloneable interface. Cloneable is a marker interface—it doesn't define clone, as you might expect. Instead, its goal is to prevent clients from cloning a class that was not explicitly designed to be cloneable.

The implementation in Course:

```
package sis.studentinfo;
...
public class Course implements java.io.Serializable, Cloneable {
    private String department;
    private String number;
    private Date effectiveDate;
    ...
    @Override
    public Course clone() {
        Course copy = null;
        try {
            copy = (Course)super.clone();
        }
        catch (CloneNotSupportedException impossible) {
            throw new RuntimeException("unable to clone");
        }
        return copy;
    }
}
```

The first thing you might notice is that the clone method returns an object of the type Course—not Object, as defined in the superclass. This is a capability of Java known as *covariance*. Covariance is the ability of a subclass method to return an object that is a subclass of the superclass return type. Cloning is the canonical example for covariance in Java.

The core of the clone method is the call to the superclass clone method. You always want to call the superclass clone method. The clone method as implemented in Object (in the VM actually) performs a bitwise copy of the contents of the object. This means that it copies values for every field defined on the class. References are copied as well, but the objects they refer to are not copied. For example, for the effectiveDate field in Course, both the original and the clone refer to the same Date object.

Cloning and Covariance

The default clone behavior, in which references are copied but not the objects to which they point, is known as a *shallow clone*. If you want a *deep clone*—a copy where the contained objects are copied also—you must implement the details yourself in the clone method.

The call to super.clone can throw a CloneNotSupportedException. This is what requires your class to implement the Cloneable marker interface.

JDBC

The vast majority of business-oriented applications access relational databases such as Oracle, MySQL, Sybase, SQL Server, and DB2. Applications require information to be available and dependable from execution to execution—to be *persistent*. A relational database[5] provides an application-independent means of storing and accessing that information.

A relational database is comprised of tables. A table is a matrix of rows and columns. A column is an attribute. A row is a collection of column values. For example, a student table might have columns ID, name, and city. A row exists in the database for each student. A representation of a student table appears in Table 1. In the table, there are two rows and thus two students: Schmoo, living in the city of Pueblo, and Caboose, living in the city of Laurel.

The language SQL (Structured Query Language) allows you to store and retrieve information from any relational database. SQL, for the most part, is standard across database implementations. An SQL statement to access student records from an Oracle database will work for accessing student records from Sybase (with perhaps minor modifications). In Java, you use an API called JDBC (Java DataBase Connectivity) to interact with the database.

JDBC

Table 1 *A Student Table with Two Rows*

ID	Name	City
221-44-4400	Schmoo	Pueblo
234-41-0001	Caboose	Laurel

[5]You may hear the term DBMS—database management system—to refer to the software that manages the database. An RDBMS is a relational DBMS.

JDBC allows you to establish connections to the database and execute SQL against it.

The need for database interaction is so commonplace that many Java products exist to simplify it. Enterprise Java Beans (EJBs), Hibernate, and JDO are three of the more popular attempts to simplify Java persistence. JDBC is the foundation of many of these tools. As is often the case, you are better off learning how the foundation works before considering use of a higher-level tool. Doing so will give you a better understanding of what the tools are doing. You may even find that a custom, highly refactored JDBC implementation is the better solution.

In this brief section, I'll demonstrate how to write simple JDBC tests and code to interact with a database. Just like Swing, entire books and many good web sites on JDBC exist. You will want to consult additional resources for more details on JDBC. You will also want to consult additional resources on SQL. I will provide only minimal explanation about the SQL in this section.

The examples in this section are written to interact with MySQL, a database freely available at *http://www.mysql.com*. Most of the examples are applicable to any other database. However, some of the code details for connecting to the database will differ. Also, a few of the "getting started" tests make presumptions about the availability of test structures within the database.

You will also need a JDBC *driver* for MySQL (see *http://dev .mysql.com/downloads/connector/j/3.0.html*). A driver is a Java library that meets Sun's JDBC interface specification. Your code always interacts with the same Sun-supplied JDBC interface methods, regardless of the database or database driver vendor. The database driver implementation adapts JDBC API calls to the specific requirements of the database itself.

Connecting to a Database

Perhaps the most difficult aspect of interacting with databases is establishing a connection to them. Installing MySQL always creates a database named test that you can access. Your first test will ensure that you can access the database test.

Make sure you have installed the MySQL JDBC driver and added it to your classpath. Note that you won't need the driver on the classpath to compile, but you will need it to execute.

```
package sis.db;

import junit.framework.TestCase;
import java.sql.*;
```

JDBC

```
public class JdbcAccessTest extends TestCase {
    public void testConnection() throws SQLException {
        JdbcAccess access = new JdbcAccess("test");
        Connection connection = null;
        try {
            connection = access.getConnection();
            assertFalse(connection.isClosed());
        }
        finally {
            connection.close();
        }
    }
}
```

The test is simple enough. Create a JdbcAccess instance using the database name test. Request a connection from the access object and verify that the connection is open (not closed). Make sure the connection gets closed by using a `finally` block.

A couple of comments: First, the test itself throws SQLException. You'll want to quickly encapsulate SQLException—you want as few classes as possible to even know that you are using JDBC.

  Isolate knowledge of JDBC in your system to one class.

Second, you will not usually want client code to request its own connection object. A common problem in many systems is that the client code forgets to close the connection. Clients open more and more connections. Ultimately, the system crashes when it becomes unable to supply any more connections. For now, writing a test to prove the ability to establish a connection allows you to proceed incrementally. You probably won't want to publicize `getConnection`.

```
package sis.db;

import java.sql.*;

public class JdbcAccess {
    private String database;

    public JdbcAccess(String database) {
        this.database = database;
    }

    Connection getConnection() throws SQLException {
        try {
            Class.forName("com.mysql.jdbc.Driver");
        } catch (Exception cause) {
            throw new SQLException(cause.getMessage());
        }
```

```
        String url = "jdbc:mysql://localhost/" + database;
        return DriverManager.getConnection(url);
    }
}
```

The implementation of getConnection in JdbcAccess involves two steps: first, load the JDBC driver class. Second, establish a connection by passing a database URL to the DriverManager class method getConnection.

The suggested technique for loading the driver is to use reflection. You pass a String representing the name of the class to the Class forName class method. Some drivers require you to send newInstance to actually create a driver instance.[6] But there's no reason you couldn't directly create a new instance of it:

```
Connection getConnection() throws SQLException {
    new com.mysql.jdbc.Driver();
    String url = "jdbc:mysql://localhost/" + database;
    return DriverManager.getConnection(url);
}
```

The original reason for suggesting the use of reflection is flexibility. Using Class.forName, you could load the driver class name from a property file or pass it in via a system property (see Properties in this chapter). You would then have the flexibility to change the driver at a later time without changing code. In reality, changing drivers doesn't happen that frequently, and you'll probably have to revisit your code anyway if you do.[7]

When you call Class.forName (or when you first reference and instantiate the class), the static initializer in the Driver class is invoked. Code in the static initializer is responsible for registering the driver with the DriverManager. The DriverManager maintains a list of all registered drivers and selects a suitable one based on the URL when getConnection gets called.

Another means of specifying one or more drivers is to supply class names using the system property jdbc.drivers. Refer to the Properties section later in this chapter for information on how to set this property.

The organization of information in the database URL is specific to the driver vendor. It usually follows a few conventions, such as starting with the word jdbc followed by a subprotocol string (mysql in this case; it's often the vendor name). You separate elements in the URL using colons (:). In MySQL, you follow the subprotocol with a reference to the server (localhost here—your machine) and the database name.

JDBC

---

[6]MySQL does not. Check your driver documentation. Or you can be lazy and always call newInstance.

[7]Of course, the need to support a second driver is reason enough to eliminate the hard-coded class reference.

The end result of calling getConnection is a java.sql.Connection object. You'll need a connection in order to execute any SQL statements.

Connections are scarce resources. You will be able to create only a limited number of connections. Further, establishing a new connection is costly from a performance standpoint. *Connection pools* allow you to maintain a number of always-open connections. A client requests a connection from the pool, uses it, then relinquishes the connection so it can return to the pool. Some JDBC implementations support connection pools directly; others do not. For purposes of these exercises and for simple, single-client access, connection pools are not necessary.

Executing Queries

The second test demonstrates executing SQL statements.

```
package sis.db;

import junit.framework.TestCase;
import java.sql.*;

public class JdbcAccessTest extends TestCase {
    private JdbcAccess access;

    protected void setUp() {
        access = new JdbcAccess("test");
    }
    ...
    public void testExecute() throws SQLException {
        access.execute("create table testExecute (fieldA char)");
        try {
            assertEquals("fieldA",
                access.getFirstRowFirstColumn("desc testExecute"));
        }
        finally {
            access.execute("drop table testExecute");
        }
    }
}
```

You cannot assume the existence of any tables in the test database, so testExecute creates its own. The SQL statement "create table testExecute (fieldA char)" creates a table named testExecute with one char (character) column named fieldA.

The proof that the table was created is via a method named getFirstRowFirstColumn. The query desc testExecute returns a description of the testExecute table. The SQL command desc is short for describe. A desc command returns one row for each column that it describes. The first column in each row is the name of the column.

As a final measure, the test removes the testExecute table by using the SQL command drop table.

A slightly refactored JdbcAccess shows the new methods execute and get-FirstRowFirstColumn. The refactoring eliminates some code duplication. It also eliminates processing duplication by ensuring that the driver instance only gets loaded once. Both the execute and getFirstRowFirstColumn methods obtain and relinquish their own connection. This alleviates the client from that responsibility.

```
package sis.db;

import java.sql.*;

public class JdbcAccess {
   private String url;
   ...
   public void execute(String sql) throws SQLException {
      Connection connection = getConnection();
      try {
         Statement statement = connection.createStatement();
         statement.execute(sql);
      }
      finally {
         close(connection);
      }
   }

   private void close(Connection connection) throws SQLException {
      if (connection != null)
         connection.close();
   }

   Connection getConnection() throws SQLException {
      if (url == null) {
         loadDriver();
         url = "jdbc:mysql://localhost/" + database;
      }
      return DriverManager.getConnection(url);
   }

   private void loadDriver() throws SQLException {
      try {
         Class.forName("com.mysql.jdbc.Driver");
      } catch (Exception cause) {
         throw new SQLException(cause.getMessage());
      }
   }

   public String getFirstRowFirstColumn(String query)
         throws SQLException {
      Connection connection = getConnection();
```

```
    try {
        Statement statement = connection.createStatement();
        ResultSet results = statement.executeQuery(query);
        results.next();
        return results.getString(1);
    }
    finally {
        close(connection);
    }
  }
}
```

You need a Statement object in order to execute SQL. You obtain a Statement object from a Connection by sending it createStatement. Once you have a Statement, you can either use the execute method to invoke SQL statements where you expect no results to come back or executeQuery to invoke SQL statements and subsequently obtain results. To execute or executeQuery, you pass the SQL string as an argument.

Results return in the form of a ResultSet object. A ResultSet is very similar to an Iterator. It maintains an internal pointer to the current row. You advance this pointer, which initially points to nothing, by sending the message next to the ResultSet. The method next returns true until the internal pointer moves past the last row. You access columns from the current row by either column name or column index. Various methods exist for obtaining column values, each differing by the type of data stored in each column. The Result-Set method getString returns character data, for example, and the method getInt returns an int value.

The code in getFirstRowFirstColumn advances the pointer to the first row returned from executeQuery by calling results.next(). The getFirstRowFirstColumn method returns the value of the first column by sending getString to the ResultSet using its index, 1, as an argument. Column indexes start at 1 in JDBC, not 0.

Prepared Statements

Often you will want to execute the same statement numerous times in an application, different only perhaps by key information. For example, the SIS application requires rapid student lookups based on student identification (ID) number.

Since you pass an SQL statement in the form of a String, the statement must be compiled before the database can execute it. Compiling the statement ensures that it follows valid SQL syntax. Compilation takes enough execution time that it can cause performance problems. (Profile, as always, to be sure that you have poor performance.) To speed things up, you can create a PreparedStatement object using an SQL string. A PreparedStatement compiles the SQL once and stores this compiled version for later, more rapid use.

You can insert placeholders in the SQL string in the form of question marks ('?'). Later, you bind values to these placeholders. An appropriate SQL string for the student lookup might be:

```
select id, name from testQueryBy where id = ?
```

For each student lookup, you bind a value to the question mark by using set methods. The method statement.setString(1, "boo") would bind the value 'boo' to the first (and only) question-mark argument.

```java
public void testQueryBy() throws SQLException {
    drop("testQueryBy");
    access.execute(
        "create table testQueryBy (id varchar(10), name varchar(30))");
    PreparedStatement statement = null;

    try {
        access.execute("insert into testQueryBy values('123', 'schmoe')");
        access.execute(
            "insert into testQueryBy values('234', 'patella')");

        statement =
         access.prepare("select id, name from testQueryBy where id = ?");

        List<String> row = access.getUnique(statement, "234");
        assertEquals("234", row.get(0));
        assertEquals("patella", row.get(1));

        row = access.getUnique(statement, "123");
        assertEquals("123", row.get(0));
        assertEquals("schmoe", row.get(1));
    }
    finally {
        statement.close();
        drop("testQueryBy");
    }
}

private void drop(String tableName) {
    try {
        access.execute("drop table " + tableName);
    }
    catch (SQLException ignore) {
        // exception thrown if table doesn't exist; we don't care
    }
}
```

Since the point of using PreparedStatement is client efficiency, you do not want to close the connection each time you execute a query against the PreparedStatement. In this case, you will have to trust that client code closes out the connection when it is done using the PreparedStatement.

The implementation:

```
public PreparedStatement prepare(String sql) throws SQLException {
    Connection connection = getConnection();
    return connection.prepareStatement(sql);
}

public List<String> getUnique(
        PreparedStatement statement, String... values)
        throws SQLException {
    int i = 1;
    for (String value: values)
        statement.setString(i++, value);
    ResultSet results = statement.executeQuery();
    results.next();

    List<String> row = new ArrayList<String>();
    ResultSetMetaData metadata = results.getMetaData();
    for (int column = 1; column <= metadata.getColumnCount(); column++)
        row.add(results.getString(column));
    return row;
}
```

From a ResultSet, you can extract metadata. The ResultSetMetaData object supplies useful information about the results returned: number of columns, data type for each column, value for each column, and so on. The implementation of getUnique obtains the number of columns using getColumnCount and uses this to iterate through all the column values.

Metadata is also available at the database level. You can send the message getMetaData to a Connection object. In return you receive a DatabaseMetaData object populated with a wealth of information about the database and drivers, including tables and columns, versions, driver limitations, and database limitations.

JDBC Application Design

There are dozens of ways to implement persistence using JDBC in an application. As mentioned earlier, you can use a tool that sits atop JDBC or even supplants it. Or, following TDD, you can grow a similar tool using the philosophy of zero duplication. By being vigilant about squashing duplication, you can quickly build a tool to meet your needs. Unlike a third-party tool, yours will be flexible enough to change rapidly based on demand.

You can use the example above as a starting point for your own tool. The JdbcAccess class should end up being the only place in which you interact with the JDBC API. Most of the remainder of the application is blissfully ignorant of the fact that JDBC is the persistence mechanism. If you choose to supplant JDBC with an object-oriented database down the road, replacement work is minimal.

You can create mapping objects to translate between database columns and domain attributes. You can accomplish this using code generation (which is preferable) or reflection. It is even possible to store everything in String format in the database and do type translation a layer up from JdbcAccess. This can help keep JdbcAccess simple: It provides access methods that return generic lists of lists of strings (rows of columns, each of which are strings).

SQL statements contain rampant duplication. It is fairly easy to code a SQL generator class that builds SQL statements using information available from the database (the database metadata).

Internationalization

A significant amount of software product gets deployed to all corners of the globe. No longer can you get away with developing an application for only your home language. Some localities, such as Quebec, require all software to execute in two or more languages. Success in the global marketplace hinges on the ability to sell your software in many countries using many different languages.

Building software so that it supports different languages and cultures is known as *internationalization*, or *i18n*[8] in shorthand. Preparing software for delivery to a single locale is known as *localization*. A *locale* is a region. Geography, culture, or politics can define locales.

Retrofitting a large, existing application to support multiple languages can be expensive. This might lead you to believe that you must internationalize your application from the outset of development. Perhaps. Extreme adherence to the "no duplication" rule can leave you with a design that supports a rapid transition to internationalized software. Nonetheless, building a foundation for internationalization *can* make things easier. You can justify these building blocks because they do help eliminate duplication.

 Use internationalization mechanisms to help eliminate duplication and position you to localize your application.

[8]Count the number of letters between the first and last letters of internationalization.

Resource Bundles

String literals embedded directly within code cause problems. Most significant, they create duplication. If a literal appears in production code and if you've been testing everything like you should, some test will duplicate that same literal. Also, the meaning of the literal is not always clear. In Agile Java, I had you extract String literals to class constants. Both the test and production code can refer to the same constant. The name of the constant imparts meaning.

Still, having to maintain a bunch of class constants is painful. Consider also the needs of the international application. The ideal solution involves extracting all literals to a common file. When you must deploy the software to a different locale, you provide a new file that contains the translated text.

Instances of the Java class java.util.ResourceBundle manage interaction with locale-specific resource files. To internationalize your software, you'll update all code to ask a ResourceBundle for a localized message String.

Using a ResourceBundle is pretty easy. You obtain a ResourceBundle by calling the creation method getBundle, passing it the name of the bundle. You then work with the ResourceBundle like a map—you pass it a key, it gives you a localized object in return.

Testing use of a ResourceBundle is another matter. You want to ensure that you can read a given property and its value from a ResourceBundle. But you can't presume that a key and certain value already exists in the resource file. The easiest solution would be to write out a small file with a known key and value. The problem is, you don't want to overwrite the resource file that the rest of your application requires.

```
package sis.util;

import junit.framework.TestCase;

import java.io.IOException;

public class BundleTest extends TestCase {
    private static final String KEY = "someKey";
    private static final String VALUE = "a value";
    private static final String TEST_APPEND = "test";
    private static final String FILENAME =
        "./classes/sis/util/" + Bundle.getName() + "Test.properties";
    private String existingBundleName;

    protected void setUp() {
        TestUtil.delete(FILENAME);
        existingBundleName = Bundle.getName();
        Bundle.setName(existingBundleName + TEST_APPEND);
    }

    protected void tearDown() {
        Bundle.setName(existingBundleName);
```

```
      TestUtil.delete(FILENAME);
   }

   public void testMessage() throws IOException {
      writeBundle();
      assertEquals(VALUE, Bundle.get(KEY));
   }

   private void writeBundle() throws IOException {
      LineWriter writer = new LineWriter();
      String record = String.format("%s=%s", KEY, VALUE);
      writer.write(FILENAME, record);
   }
}
```

The test carefully manages a test resource file using setUp and tearDown. It interacts with a class you will create named sis.util.Bundle to retrieve the name of the existing bundle. The test stores the existing resource file base name, then tells Bundle to use a new base name. Only the test will recognize this base name. The test itself (testMessage) writes to the test resource file. Each entry in the resource file is a key-value pair separated by an equals sign (=).

The assertion in testMessage calls the get method on the Bundle class to retrieve a localized resource. Finally, the tearDown method resets Bundle to use the original base name.

```
package sis.util;

import java.util.ResourceBundle;

public class Bundle {
   private static String baseName = "Messages";
   private static ResourceBundle bundle;

   static String getName() {
      return baseName;
   }

   static void setName(String name) {
      baseName = name;
      bundle = null;
   }

   public static String get(String key) {
      if (bundle == null)
         loadBundle();
      return (String)bundle.getString(key);
   }

   private static void loadBundle() {
      bundle = ResourceBundle.getBundle("sis.util." + getName());
   }
}
```

The method `loadBundle` obtains a ResourceBundle instance by base name. The base name is similar to a fully qualified class name. Presume that you have a resource file with a fully qualified path name of ./classes/sis/util/ Messages.properties. Also presume that the directory ./classes appears on the classpath. In order for `getBundle` to locate this resource file, the base name must be "sis.util.Messages".

Once you have a ResourceBundle object, you can send it a few different messages to extract localized resources. The message `getString` returns localized text.

Once you've implemented the Bundle class, you would replace occurrences of literals in your application to use its `get` method. You will end up with a potentially large file of key-value pairs. If the file size makes management of the resource file unwieldy, consider partitioning it into multiple resource bundles.

Localization

Suppose you must deploy your application to Mexico. You would send your resource file to a translator for localization. The translator's job is to return a new file of key-value pairs, replacing the base value (perhaps English) with a Spanish translation.

(In reality, the translator will probably need to interact with you or someone else who understands the application. The translator will often require contextual information because of multiple word meanings. For example, your translator may need to know whether "File" is a verb or a noun.)

You must name the file that the translator returns to you according to the specific Locale. A locale is a language, a country (which is optional), and a variant (also optional; it is rarely used). For deployment to Mexico, the language is Spanish, indicated by "es" (español). The country is "MX" (Mexico). To come up with a resource file name, you append these bits of locale information to the base name, using underscores ('_') as separators. The Mexican-localized file name for the base name "Messages" is "Messages_es_MX.properties".

You can request a complete list of locales supported on your platform using the Locale class method `getAvailableLocales`. Code and execute this ugly bit of code:

```
for (Locale locale: Locale.getAvailableLocales())
  System.out.println(String.format("%s %s: use '_%s%s'",
    locale.getDisplayLanguage(), locale.getDisplayCountry(),
    locale.getLanguage(),
    (locale.getCountry().equals("") ? "" : "_" + locale.getCountry())));
```

The output from executing this code snippet will give you appropriate extensions to the base name.

Here is BundleTest, modified to include a new test for Mexican localization:

```
package sis.util;

import junit.framework.TestCase;
import java.io.IOException;
import java.util.Locale;

public class BundleTest extends TestCase {
    private static final String KEY = "someKey";
    private static final String TEST_APPEND = "test";
    private String filename;
    private String existingBundleName;

    private void prepare() {
        TestUtil.delete(filename);
        existingBundleName = Bundle.getName();
        Bundle.setName(existingBundleName + TEST_APPEND);
    }

    protected void tearDown() {
        Bundle.setName(existingBundleName);
        TestUtil.delete(filename);
    }

    public void testMessage() throws IOException {
        filename = getFilename();
        prepare();
        final String value = "open the door";
        writeBundle(value);
        assertEquals(value, Bundle.get(KEY));
    }

    public void testLocalizedMessage() throws IOException {
        final String language = "es";
        final String country = "MX";
        filename = getFilename(language, country);
        prepare();

        Locale mexican = new Locale(language, country);
        Locale current = Locale.getDefault();
        try {
            Locale.setDefault(mexican);
            final String value = "abre la puerta";
            writeBundle(value);
            assertEquals(value, Bundle.get(KEY));
        }
        finally {
            Locale.setDefault(current);
```

```
        }
    }

    private void writeBundle(String value) throws IOException {
        LineWriter writer = new LineWriter();
        String record = String.format("%s=%s", KEY, value);
        writer.write(getFilename(), record);
    }

    private String getFilename(String language, String country) {
        StringBuilder builder = new StringBuilder();
        builder.append("./classes/sis/util/");
        builder.append(Bundle.DEFAULT_BASE_NAME);
        builder.append("Test");
        if (language.length() > 0)
            builder.append("_" + language);
        if (country.length() > 0)
            builder.append("_" + country);
        builder.append(".properties");
        return builder.toString();
    }

    private String getFilename() {
        return getFilename("", "");
    }
}
```

BundleTest requires refactoring to support the changes to the test resource filename format. You cannot use the setUp method to delete the test resource file, since its name must change. I renamed setUp to prepare (an adequate name at best). The prepare method assumes that the field filename is populated with the appropriate test resource filename.

The new test, testLocalizedMessage, writes test data to a file using a name encoded with the language and country. The test creates a Locale object using the same language and country. It then obtains the current (default) Locale so that the test can reset the Locale to this default when it completes. As the final preparation before testing the Bundle.get method, the test sets the default locale to the newly created Mexican Locale object.

Setting a Locale is a global change. Any code that might need to be internationalized can request the current Locale so that it knows what to do. Most of the time, this is handled for you. In the case of ResourceBundle, you don't need to do anything. To load a bundle, you supply only the base name. Code in ResourceBundle retrieves the default Locale and combines information from it with the base name to create a complete resource file name.

Formatted Messages

Entries in resource files may contain substitution placeholders. For example:

```
dependentsMessage=You have {0} dependents, {1}. Is this correct?
```

The value for dependentsMessage contains two *format elements:* {0} and {1}. Code that loads this string via a ResourceBundle would use a MessageFormat object to replace the format elements with appropriate values. The following language test demonstrates:

```
public void testMessageFormat() {
   String message = "You have {0} dependents, {1}. Is this correct?";

   MessageFormat formatter = new MessageFormat(message);
   assertEquals(
      "You have 5 dependents, Señor Wences. Is this correct?",
      formatter.format(message, 5, "Señor Wences"));
}
```

In older code using MessageFormat, you might see the arguments wrapped in an Object array:

```
formatter.format(new Object[] {new Integer(5), "Señor Wences"})
```

Why not just use the java.util.Formatter class? The reason is that the MessageFormat scheme predates the Formatter class, which Sun introduced in Java 5.0.

A more interesting reason for using the MessageFormat scheme is to take advantage of the ChoiceFormat class. This can eliminate the need to code additional if/else logic in order to supply format element values. The classic example shows how to manage formatting of messages that refer to numbers. We want to present a friendlier message to Señor Wences, and telling him that he has "one dependents" is unacceptable.[9]

Using ChoiceFormat is a bit of a bear. You first create a mapping of numeric ranges to corresponding text. You refer to the ranges, expressed using an array of doubles, as limits. You express the corresponding text, or formats, in an array of strings.

```
double[] dependentLimits = { 0, 1, 2 };
String[] dependentFormats =
   { "no dependents", "one dependent", "{0} dependents" };
```

The numbers in the limits array are ranges. The final element in the limits array represents the low end of the range—two dependents and up, in this case. For two dependents, the ChoiceFormat would apply the corresponding format string "{0} dependents", substituting the actual number of dependents for {0}.

Using these limits and formats, you create a ChoiceFormat object:

```
ChoiceFormat formatter =
   new ChoiceFormat(dependentLimits, dependentFormats);
```

[9]No doubt he would have responded indignantly, "Tell it to the hand."

A message string might have multiple format elements. Only some of the format elements might require a ChoiceFormat. You must create an array of Format objects (Format is the superclass of ChoiceFormat), substituting null where you have no need for a formatter.

```
Format[] formats = { formatter, null };
```

You can then create a MessageFormat object and set the array of formats into it:

```
MessageFormat messageFormatter = new MessageFormat(message);
messageFormatter.setFormats(formats);
```

You're now able to use the MessageFormat as before. The entire process is shown in the language test testChoiceFormat.

```
public void testChoiceFormat() {
    String message = "You have {0}, {1}. Is this correct?";
    double[] dependentLimits = { 0, 1, 2 };
    String[] dependentFormats =
        { "no dependents", "one dependent", "{0} dependents" };

    ChoiceFormat formatter =
        new ChoiceFormat(dependentLimits, dependentFormats);

    Format[] formats = { formatter, null };

    MessageFormat messageFormatter = new MessageFormat(message);
    messageFormatter.setFormats(formats);

    assertEquals(
        "You have one dependent, Señor Wences. Is this correct?",
        messageFormatter.format(new Object[] { 1, "Señor Wences" }));

    assertEquals(
        "You have 10 dependents, Señor Wences. Is this correct?",
        messageFormatter.format(new Object[] { 10, "Señor Wences" }));
}
```

ternationalization

Interaction with ChoiceFormat can be even more complex. Refer to the Java API documentation for the class.

Note that the format strings should come from your ResourceBundle.

Other Areas to Internationalize

The formatting of numbers, dates, and currencies can vary depending upon the locale. Display numbers using separators every three digits in order to make them more readable. The separators are commas (,) in the United States, while some other localities use periods (.). Dates in the United States often appear in month-day-year order, separated by slashes or hyphens. Dates elsewhere may appear in a different order, such as year-month-day.

The classes java.text.NumberFormat, java.util.Calendar, and java.text .DateFormat and their subclasses, support the use of Locale objects. Your code that works with these classes should request instances using factory methods. Your code should not directly instantiate these classes, otherwise you will not get the default Locale support. For example, to obtain a SimpleDateFormat instance with support for the default locale:

```
DateFormat formatter = SimpleDateFormat.getDateInstance();
```

The Calendar class also allows you to manage time zones.

Various layout managers in Java supply support for different axis orientation. Some non-Western cultures orient text so that it reads from top to bottom instead of left to right. For example, the BoxLayout class allows you to organize components within a container around a LINE_AXIS. Each Locale contains a java.awt.ComponentOrientation object; this object defines whether text reads from right to left or left to right (Western) and whether lines are horizontal (Western) or vertical. At runtime, then, the BoxLayout obtains the ComponentOrientation in order to determine whether LINE_AXIS corresponds to the x axis or the y axis.

Other languages require the use of different character sets. Since Java uses Unicode, you generally don't have to concern yourself with the different character sets. However, if you need to sort text elements, you will have to work with collation sequences. The class java.text.RuleBasedCollator provides the basis for this support. The API documentation for this class contains a good overview of collation in Java.

Call by Reference versus Call by Value

Much ado is made over whether Java uses "call by reference" or "call by value." These classic software development phrases describe how a language manages the passing of arguments to functions (perhaps in C) or methods. The terminology (or people's interpretations of the terminology) is not necessarily important. What's important is that you understand how Java manages the passing of arguments.

Call by value means that the called function[10] makes a copy of an argument behind the scenes. Code in the function operates on the copy. The implication is that any changes made to the argument are discarded when the

Call by Reference versus Call by Value

---

[10]I use the term "function" in these general definitions to imply that this is not necessarily how Java does it.

function completes execution. The reason is because changes are not actually made to the argument but to its local copy. The copy of the argument has only method scope.

Call by reference means that the function works on the same physical argument that was passed in. Any changes to the argument are retained.

Java is entirely call by value. If you pass an int to a method, the method operates on a copy of the int. If you pass an object reference to a method, the method operates on a copy of the *reference—not a copy of the object itself.* I'll demonstrate both of these statements in code.

Understanding call by value with respect to primitives is easy enough. Here's a test to show you how the method's copy of the primitive gets discarded.

```java
public void testCallByValuePrimitives() {
    int count = 1;
    increment(count);
    assertEquals(1, count);
}

private void increment(int count) {
    count++;
}
```

Even though the increment method changes the value of count, the change is to a local copy. The local copy disappears upon exit of the increment method. Code in testCallByValuePrimitives remains oblivious to any of these shenanigans.

Remember that a reference is a pointer—an address of an object's location in memory. The called method copies this address, creating a new pointer that refers to the same memory location. If you assign a new memory address (i.e., a different object) to the reference within the called method, this new address is discarded when the method completes.

Code in the called method can send messages to the object pointed at by the reference. These message sends *can* effect permanent changes in the object.

In testCallByValueReferences, shown following this paragraph, code creates a customer with an ID of 1. The test then calls the method incrementId. The first line of code in incrementId grabs the existing ID from the customer, adds 1 to this number, and sets the sum back into the customer. The second line in incrementId creates a new Customer object and assigns its address to the customer argument reference. You don't want to do this![11] The assignment is discarded when incrementId completes. The test finally verifies that the customer ID is 2, not 22.

Call by Reference versus Call by Value

---

[11] You might consider declaring all your arguments as final. Attempts to assign to the argument will result in compile failure. My ingrained habits prevent me from doing this consistently.

```
public void testCallByValueReferences() {
    Customer customer = new Customer(1);
    incrementId(customer);
    assertEquals(2, customer.getId());
}

private void incrementId(Customer customer) {
    customer.setId(customer.getId() + 1);
    customer = new Customer(22); // don't do this
}

class Customer {
    private int id;
    Customer(int id) { this.id = id; }
    void setId(int id) { this.id = id; }
    public int getId() { return id; }
}
```

Java Periphery

Java gives you a number of mechanisms to help your application interact with the local operating environment.

Properties

A small hash table of system properties is always available from any point in your application. This table contains useful information, including things about your Java environment and your operating system. You can obtain the entire set of properties using the java.lang.System method `getProperties`:

```
Properties existingProperties = System.getProperties();
```

The java.util.Properties class extends the old java.util.Hashtable class. It adds a number of management methods and utility methods. The management methods help you do things such as load a set of properties from a file. The utility methods simplify access to the hash table.

The API documentation for the java.lang.System class method `getProperties` shows the list of predefined properties. Some of the more useful properties include:

`java.class.path`	value of the Java classpath[12]
`java.io.tmpdir`	the default temp file path

[12]You can set this property to a new value, but it has no effect on the current Java execution. The Java VM does not reread this value. If you think you need to change the classpath, you may need to build a custom class loader instead.

file.separator	the file separator ('/' under Unix; '\' under Windows)
path.separator	the separator between entries in a path (':' under Unix; ';' under Windows)
line.separator	the line separator ('\n' under Unix; '\r\n' under Windows)
user.home	the current user's home directory
user.dir	the current working directory

Using these properties, you can code your application to execute on different operating systems without change.

You retrieve the value of a single system property using the System class method getProperty:

```
assertEquals("1.5.0-beta3", System.getProperty("java.version"));
```

System properties are global. You can access them from anywhere in your code.

You can add your own global properties to the list of system properties. Generally, a database is a better place for this sort of information. Your main reason to use properties should be to dynamically alter small pieces of information from one application execution to the next. For example, your deployed application may need to execute in "kiosk" mode most of the time, looping and occupying the full screen without borders or a title bar. During development, you may want to be able to switch rapidly back and forth between execution modes.

You can accomplish this dynamism in a number of ways. You could put a mode setting flag into a database, but having to modify data in a database can slow you down. You could pass the information as command line arguments and manage it in your main method. But you might not need the information until later in your application; what do you do with it until then?

You can add your property to the system properties programmatically:

```
System.setProperty("kioskMode", "loopFullscreen");
```

Or, as you saw with logging in Lesson 8, you can set the property as a VM argument:

```
java -DkioskMode=noloopFullscreen sis.Sis
```

If a property is not set, getProperty returns null. You can provide a default value to getProperty to be returned if the property is not set. A language test shows how this works:

```
public void testGetPropertyWithDefault() {
    Properties existingProperties = System.getProperties();
    try {
        System.setProperties(new Properties()); // removes all properties
        assertEquals(
            "default", System.getProperty("noSuchProperty", "default"));
    }
    finally {
        System.setProperties(existingProperties);
    }
}
```

Property Files

One technique you will encounter in many shops and many applications is the use of property files. A property file is similar to a resource file; it is a collection of key-value pairs in the form key=value. Developers often use property files as a quick-and-dirty catchall for configurable values. Things such as class names of drivers, color schemes, and boolean flags end up in property files.

One driving force is the need to change certain values as software moves from a production environment into a test environment, an integration environment, or a production environment. For example, your code might need to connect to a web server. The web server name you use for development will differ from the web server name for production.

I recommend that you minimize your use of property files or at least minimize the entries that go in them. Property file entries are disjointed from your application; they represent a bunch of global variables arbitrarily clustered together. You should prefer instead to carefully associate configurable values with the classes they impact. The better way to do this is through the use of a database.

 Keep any property files small and simple or, better yet, eliminate them. Resist adding new entries.

If you must use property files, the Properties class contains methods for loading from an input stream that is either in key-value text format or in XML format. Do not try to dynamically update this file from your executing application. Instead, consider the Preferences API, discussed in the next section.

Preferences

For critical information that you must retain from application execution to execution, you should use a database or other trustworthy persistence mechanism. However, you often want the ability to quickly and simply store various bits of noncritical information. Usually this is in the area of user trivialities: preferred colors, window positioning, recently visited web sites, and so on. Were any of this information lost, it would be a nuisance to a user but would not prevent him or her from accurately completing work.

The Java Preferences API supplies a simple local persistence scheme for this data. PersistentFrameTest (shown after the next paragraph) demonstrates. The first test, testCreate, shows that the first time a frame is created, it uses default window positions. The test testMove moves a frame, then closes it. The test shows that subsequent frames use the last position of any Persistent-Frame.

In order for PersistentFrameTest to work more than once, the setUp method sends the message clearPreferences to the frame. This method ensures that the PersistentFrame object uses default window placement settings.

```java
package sis.ui;

import junit.framework.*;
import java.awt.*;
import java.util.prefs.BackingStoreException;

import static sis.ui.PersistentFrame.*;

public class PersistentFrameTest extends TestCase {
    private PersistentFrame frame;

    protected void setUp() throws BackingStoreException {
        frame = new PersistentFrame();
        frame.clearPreferences();
        frame.initialize();
        frame.setVisible(true);
    }

    protected void tearDown() {
        frame.dispose();
    }

    public void testCreate() {
        assertEquals(
            new Rectangle(
                DEFAULT_X, DEFAULT_Y, DEFAULT_WIDTH, DEFAULT_HEIGHT),
            frame.getBounds());
    }

    public void testMove() {
        int x = 600;
        int y = 650;
        int width = 150;
        int height = 160;
        frame.setBounds(x, y, width, height);
```

```
            frame.dispose();

            PersistentFrame frame2 = new PersistentFrame();
            frame2.initialize();
            frame2.setVisible(true);
            assertEquals(
                new Rectangle(x, y, width, height), frame2.getBounds());
        }
    }
```

The implementation in PersistentFrame:

```
package sis.ui;

import javax.swing.*;
import java.awt.*;
import java.awt.event.*;
import java.util.prefs.*;

public class PersistentFrame extends JFrame {
    static final int DEFAULT_X = 100;
    static final int DEFAULT_Y = 101;
    static final int DEFAULT_WIDTH = 300;
    static final int DEFAULT_HEIGHT = 400;

    private static final String X = "x";
    private static final String Y = "y";
    private static final String WIDTH = "width";
    private static final String HEIGHT = "height";

    private Preferences preferences =
        Preferences.userNodeForPackage(this.getClass());          // 1

    public void initialize() {
        int x = preferences.getInt(X, DEFAULT_X);                 // 2
        int y = preferences.getInt(Y, DEFAULT_Y);
        int width = preferences.getInt(WIDTH, DEFAULT_WIDTH);
        int height = preferences.getInt(HEIGHT, DEFAULT_HEIGHT);

        setBounds(x, y, width, height);

        setDefaultCloseOperation(JFrame.EXIT_ON_CLOSE);
        addWindowListener(new WindowAdapter() {
            public void windowClosed(WindowEvent e) {
                saveWindowPosition();
            }
        });
    }

    private void saveWindowPosition() {
        Rectangle bounds = getBounds();

        preferences.putInt(X, bounds.x);                          // 3
        preferences.putInt(Y, bounds.y);
```

Java Periphery

```
      preferences.putInt(WIDTH, bounds.width);
      preferences.putInt(HEIGHT, bounds.height);
      try {
         preferences.flush();                                    // 4
      }
      catch (BackingStoreException e) {
         // not crucial; log message
      }
   }

   // for testing
   void clearPreferences() throws BackingStoreException {
      preferences.clear();
      preferences.flush();
   }
}
```

You create a Preference object by passing a class name to one of two Preferences factory methods, userNodeForPackage or systemNodeForPackage, corresponding to the user and system trees of preference data. You might use the system preferences tree for application-specific information, such as the location of a properties file. You might use the user preferences tree for user-specific information, such as color choices.

Java stores preferences in trees that are analogous to file system directory tree structures. Depending on the platform (and specific implementation), the actual storage location of preferences could be an operating system registry, the file system, a directory server, or a database.

The PersistentFrame class uses the user preferences tree (see line 1). The frame initialization code attempts to read the preferences for the frame's bounds[13] (starting at line 2). Each call to getInt can contain a default value to use if no corresponding preference data exists.

When the frame gets closed (by client code that invokes the dispose method or by other means), code in saveWindowPosition stores the current bounds of the frame using the Preferences API. You must flush the preferences object (line 4) to force a write to the persistent store. In addition to putInt (line 3) the Preferences class supplies other methods to support storing various types of data: String, boolean, byte[], double, float, and long.

The Preferences API provides methods for writing data to and reading data from a file in XML format.

---

[13]A Rectangle object specifies the bounds of a window. The (x, y) coordinate represent its origin, or upper-left corner. The height and width represent the extent of the window in pixels.

System Environment

On rare occasions, you'll need to know information about your operating environment that the predefined system properties does not provide. Unix and Windows operating systems have environment variables, yet again a key-value pair scheme. From a command-line prompt, you view the environment variables using the command set.[14] From within Java, the System class provides two getEnv methods to help you retrieve these environment variables and their values.

```
Map<String,String> env = System.getenv();
for (Map.Entry entry: env.entrySet())
   System.out.printf("%s->%s%n", entry.getKey(), entry.getValue());

System.out.println(System.getenv("SystemRoot")); // Unix: try "SHELL"
```

Avoid depending on system environment variables. It will make it more difficult to port your application to another platform. Almost no environment variables are common between Windows and Unix. If you feel compelled to create your own system-wide environment variables, try to use the Java properties mechanism instead.

Executing Other Applications

You may on rare occasion need to kick off another operating system process. For example, you may want your application to bring up the system calculator application (calc.exe under Windows). Java will allow you to execute separate processes, but doing so is something you should avoid. It will usually tie you to a single operating system. In most cases you will then need to maintain conditional logic if you must handle multiple platforms.

There are two ways to create and execute separate processes under Java. The older technique requires you to obtain the singleton[15] instance of java.lang.Runtime using its class method getRuntime. You can then pass a command-line string along with optional arguments to the exec method. J2SE 5.0 introduced a ProcessBuilder class that replaces this technique. You create a ProcessBuilder using the command-line string, then initiate the process by sending start to the ProcessBuilder object.

Java Periphery

[14]This works under Windows and under many Unix shells.

[15]The Runtime class is designed so that there can only be a *single* instance of Runtime in an executing Java application, therefore Runtime is an example of the *singleton* design pattern.

You will not see a console window when executing the new process. It is possible, but slightly tricky, to capture output from or siphon input to the new process. Java redirects the three standard IO streams (stdin, stdout, and stderr) to Java streams so that you can work with them. Usually you'll only need to capture output; that's what we'll concentrate on here.

The trickiness to capturing output comes from the fact that the buffer size of the operating system may be small. You must promptly manage data coming from each output stream. If you do not, your application is likely to hang as it executes.

```java
package sis.util;

import junit.framework.TestCase;
import java.util.*;

public class CommandTest extends TestCase {
   private static final String TEST_SINGLE_LINE = "testOneLine";
   private static final String TEST_MULTIPLE_LINES = "testManyLines";
   private static final String TEST_LOTS_OF_LINES = "testLotsLines";
   private static Map<String, String> output =
      new HashMap<String, String>();
   private static final String COMMAND =             // 1
      "java " +
      "-classpath \"" + System.getProperty("java.class.path") + "\" " +
      "sis.util.CommandTest %s";
   private Command command;

   static {                                           // 2
      output.put(TEST_SINGLE_LINE, "a short line of text");
      output.put(TEST_MULTIPLE_LINES, "line 1\\nline 2\\");
      output.put(TEST_LOTS_OF_LINES, lotsOfLines());
   }

   static String lotsOfLines() {
      final int lots = 1024;
      StringBuilder lotsBuffer = new StringBuilder();
      for (int i = 0; i < lots; i++)
         lotsBuffer.append("" + i);
      return lotsBuffer.toString();
   }

   public static void main(String[] args) {           // 3
      String methodName = args[0];
      String text = output.get(methodName);
      // redirected output:
      System.out.println(text);
      System.err.println(text);
   }

   public void testSingleLine() throws Exception {
      verifyExecuteCommand(TEST_SINGLE_LINE);
   }
```

```
    public void testMultipleLines() throws Exception {
        verifyExecuteCommand(TEST_MULTIPLE_LINES);
    }

    public void testLotsOfLines() throws Exception {
        verifyExecuteCommand(TEST_LOTS_OF_LINES);
    }

    private void verifyExecuteCommand(String text) throws Exception {
        command = new Command(String.format(COMMAND, text));
        command.execute();
        assertEquals(output.get(text), command.getOutput());
    }
}
```

CommandTest uses itself as the very command to test. Line 1 constructs a java command line to execute sis.util.CommandTest as a stand-alone application. It obtains the appropriate classpath by querying the system property java.class.path. The main method (line 3) supplies the code for the application.

The main method simply writes lines of output to stderr (System.err) and stdout (System.out). It uses a single argument, an arbitrary string that corresponds to a test method name, to determine what lines to write. The lines come from a map populated using a static initializer (line 2).

The Command class appears next. In line 1, you create a ProcessBuilder object using the command string. The ProcessBuilder start method kicks off the corresponding operating system process. Lines 4 and 6 show how you can extract the streams corresponding to stderr and stdout. Once you've obtained these streams, you can use them to capture output using a BufferedReader (see the collectOutput method at line 7). The trick to making all this work is to ensure that the process of collecting output executes in simultaneous threads, otherwise you run the risk of blocking or losing output. Thus, the code in collectErrorOutput (line 3) and collectOutput (line 5) creates and starts new Thread objects. After initiating the threads, code in execute waits until the process completes, using the Process method waitFor (line 2).

```
package sis.util;

import java.io.*;

public class Command {
    private String command;
    private Process process;
    private StringBuilder output = new StringBuilder();
    private StringBuilder errorOutput = new StringBuilder();

    public Command(String command) {
        this.command = command;
    }

    public void execute() throws Exception {
```

```java
        process = new ProcessBuilder(command).start();      // 1
        collectOutput();
        collectErrorOutput();
        process.waitFor();                                   // 2
    }

    private void collectErrorOutput() {                      // 3
        Runnable runnable = new Runnable() {
            public void run() {
                try {
                    collectOutput(process.getErrorStream(),  // 4
                                  errorOutput);
                } catch (IOException e) {
                    errorOutput.append(e.getMessage());
                }
            }
        };
        new Thread(runnable).start();
    }

    private void collectOutput() {                           // 5
        Runnable runnable = new Runnable() {
            public void run() {
                try {
                    collectOutput(process.getInputStream(),  // 6
                                  output);
                } catch (IOException e) {
                    output.append(e.getMessage());
                }
            }
        };
        new Thread(runnable).start();
    }

    private void collectOutput(                              // 7
            InputStream inputStream, StringBuilder collector)
            throws IOException {
        BufferedReader reader = null;
        try {
            reader =
                new BufferedReader(new InputStreamReader(inputStream));
            String line;
            while ((line = reader.readLine()) != null)
                collector.append(line);
        }
        finally {
            reader.close();
        }
    }

    public String getOutput() throws IOException {
        return output.toString();
    }
```

```
    public String getErrorOutput() throws IOException {
        return output.toString();
    }

    public String toString() {
        return command;
    }
}
```

Avoid use of command-line redirection (> and <) or piping (|)—these will be considered part of the command input string and will not be appropriately handled by the operating system.

The ProcessBuilder class allows you to pass new environment variables and values to the new process. You can also change the current working directory under which the process executes.

One thing that ProcessBuilder provides that the Runtime.exec technique does not is the ability to merge the stdout and stderr streams. Console applications often interweave these: You might get a prompt or other output message that comes from stdout, then an error message from stderr, then a stdout prompt, and so on. If stdout and stderr are separated into two streams, there is no way to determine the original chronological sequencing of the combined output. See the API documentation for details on how to control this feature.

 Avoid use of things such as getEnv and ProcessBuilder that introduce dependencies on your operating environment.

What Else Is There?

Java contains many more advanced topics that most developers will rarely have a need for. There are also dozens upon dozens of additional APIs that you may need to consider. This section briefly mentions some of these topics and APIs.

Custom Class Loaders

When you access a class for the first time, the Java VM uses one of three default class loaders to load the class for use. The first class loader Java uses is the bootstrap class loader. The bootstrap class loader looks in the system JAR files rt.jar and i18n.jar to find Java classes from the core Java API library. If Java does not find the class, it then looks in the Java extension directory, ./lib/ext under the JRE installation directory. If necessary, Java finally uses the directories on your classpath to load the class.

You can create additional custom class loaders. A custom *class loader* can load a class from an alternate location. It might load a class from a database, from a web site, from an FTP site, or from dynamically created byte codes.

For further information, refer to the article "Create a Custom Java 1.2-Style Classloader" by Ken McCrary at *http://www.javaworld.com/java-world/jw-03-2000/jw-03-classload.html*. For more-up-to-date information, start with the API documentation for the class java.lang.ClassLoader.

Weak References

Java's garbage collection scheme manages reclaiming memory for objects that you're done with. But what if you want to write an application that monitors memory use? In order to monitor an object, you must hold a reference to it. As long as your monitor application retains such a reference, the garbage collector cannot reclaim the object in question.

You might also want to implement a caching scheme. A cache loads frequently accessed objects. But since the cache data structure must (by definition) refer to cached objects, the garbage collector can never consider them for reclamation. You must write complex additional code to manage removing objects from the cache from time to time. Otherwise your cache will continue to grow until you get an out-of-memory error.

To help with these and other problems, Java lets you use *weak references*. A weak reference to an object does not count for purposes of garbage collection. The garbage collector will reclaim any object with weak references but no strong references.

Java supplies three levels of weak references, in order from weakest to strongest:[16] phantom, weak, and soft. A phantom reference can be used for special cleanup processing after object finalization. A weak reference results in the referred object being removed when garbage is collected. A soft reference results in the referred object being removed only when the garbage collector determines that memory is really needed.

The class java.util.WeakHashMap is a Map implementation with weak keys. Refer to its API documentation for further details.

Refer to the Java API documentation for the package java.lang.ref for more information on the various weak reference types.

What Else Is There?

The finalize Method

In Lesson 4, you learned a bit about garbage collection. Java automatically collects unused objects—ones that no other objects refer to. Once in a while, you may find the need to accomplish something when an object is garbage collected. To do so, you might consider defining a finalize method:

---

[16][JavaGloss2004b].

```
protected void finalize() throws Throwable {
   try {
      // do some cleanup work
   }
   finally {
      super.finalize();
   }
}
```

The garbage collector calls the finalize method against any objects that it collects.

The problem is that you cannot guarantee that finalize ever gets called. Even when the Java VM shuts down—when your application exits—finalize might not get called. This means that you should never write code in finalize that must execute. Closing file or database connections in a finalize method is not a good idea—chances are that these resources will never be released.

If you think you need a finalize method, try to find a way to redesign your code. Or consider the use of phantom references as an alternative. If you do implement finalize, it is a good idea to ensure that you always call the super-class finalize method (as shown in the above bit of code).

Instrumentation

Using Java instrumentation capabilities, you can add informational byte codes to Java class files. This information can be used to aid in logging messages, profiling method execution times, or building code coverage tools. The goal is to allow you to insert such information in a manner that does not alter the functionality of the existing application.[17]

To use instrumentation, you implement the ClassFileTransformer interface. You register this implementation at the java command line using the -javaagent switch. As the class loader attempts to load a class, it calls the transform method in your ClassFileTransformer implementation. The goal of the transform method is to return a byte array representing the replacement class file.

Refer to the Java API documentation for the package java.lang.instrument for more information.

Management

The Management API allows you to monitor and manage the Java VM. It also allows for some management of the OS under which the VM is executing. The Management API allows you to do things such as compare perfor-

[17]Java's instrumentation API is an example of a scheme known as *aspect-oriented programming*.

mance characteristics of the garbage collector, determine the number of processors available, monitor memory usage, monitor threads, or to monitor class loading from an external perspective.

Refer to the API documentation for the package java.lang.management for more information.

Networking

The java.net package supplies several classes to help you build network applications. This package provides support for low-level communications, based on the universal concept of a bidirectional communication mechanism known as a socket. Sockets allow you access to the TCP/IP protocol. Sockets are the underpinning of most host-to-host communication.

The java.net package also provides a number of higher-level APIs centered on web programming and URLs (Universal Resource Locators).

For more information, refer to the API documentation for the package java.net.

NIO

Java NIO ("New I/O") is an advanced, high-performance facility for input-output operations. If you need to boost your performance for mass data transfers, you many want to consider NIO. While Sun has retrofitted many of the java.io streams to use NIO, you may want to directly interact with the NIO API for the fastest possible data transfers.

NIO is not stream based. You instead use channels, which are similar to streams in that they are sources and sinks for data. A buffer contains chunks of data that channels read from and write to. The main speed gain in NIO comes from the use of direct buffers. Normally, data is copied between Java arrays and VM buffers. Direct buffers are allocated directly within the VM and allow your code to directly access them. This avoids the need for expensive copy operations.[18]

NIO is nonblocking. Normally when you execute an I/O operation, calling code is blocked—it must wait until the operation completes. Using nonblocking I/O, your code can continue to execute even if a read or write operation is taking place. You can use nonblocking socket channels as the foundation for socket servers. This increases the scalability of the socket server and simplifies the management of incoming connections and requests. Blocking I/O

[18][Travis2002], pp. 2–3.

requires the judicious use of multithreading, while NIO allows you to manage all incoming requests in a single thread.

Conceptually, NIO is more complex than the standard java.io library. The tradeoff is worth it if performance is paramount. In the case of socket servers, NIO is definitely the way to go. For most other needs, the standard I/O library will suffice.

For more information, refer to the Sun NIO document at *http://java .sun.com/j2se/1.4.2/docs/guide/nio/index.html.*

JNI

The Java Native Interface (JNI) is your hook to the outside world. You might need to interact with a hardware API written in C, or perhaps you might need to call operating system routines that go beyond the capabilities of Java. Using JNI, you can call libraries (DLLs in Windows and sos in Unix) written in other languages including C++ and C.

For more information, the Sun tutorial is a good place to start (but it may be somewhat out of date): *http://java.sun.com/docs/books/tutorial/ native1.1/stepbystep/index.html.*

As with any Java technology that allows you to interact with external resources, minimize your use of JNI in order to maximize your potential for cross-platform deployment.

RMI

Remote Method Invocation (RMI) is an API that allows you to call methods on Java objects that execute in the context of another Java VM. The other VM can be on the same machine or on a remote machine. RMI is the basis for the distributed component-based computing used in EJBs (Enterprise Java Beans).

RMI uses the proxy design pattern. A client object can interact with a server method located on another machine by working through its public interface. In reality, the client interacts with a client-side stub. The stub takes a Java message and translates it into serialized objects that can be sent across the wire. The stub interacts with a server-side skeleton, the job of which is to take those object streams and translate them into a method call against the actual server class.

You generate the stub and skeleton Java source using the RMI compiler rmic, located in your Java bin directory.

Using RMI keeps your clients from having to build remote communication code. As far as your client code knows, it is interacting with just another Java object in the same virtual machine. Network limitations will inherently slow your application, however, so you must still design your application with the high overhead of RMI in mind. The primary design goal for distributed applications is to minimize the amount of distributed processing—don't distribute your objects unless you must![19]

Beans

You use JavaBeans, not to be confused with Enterprise Java Beans (EJBs), for building pluggable GUI components. You might build a new Java stoplight GUI control that you want to sell to Java GUI developers. The stoplight Java-Bean is a Java class like any other. But in order for developers to load and use your stoplight control in tools such as JBuilder, it must adhere to JavaBeans specifications.

To be a visual JavaBean, a class must inherit from java.awt.Component and must be serializable. It must expose its information using accessor methods that follow the standard Java naming convention (e.g. getName to return the value of the field name). The ability of tools to gather bean information based on knowledge of these conventions is known as introspection. A bean has a related BeanInfo class that provides relevant bean metadata. Beans communicate with other beans using an event mechanism.

For more information, the best place to start is the Sun tutorial at *http://java.sun.com/docs/books/tutorial/javabeans/*.

Security

Security in Java is easily a topic for a whole book. The J2SE security API, located in various packages starting with the name java.security, includes classes for things that include certificate management, key store management, policy files, encryption/decryption algorithms, and access control lists.

The Java security model is based on the concept of a *sandbox*, a customizable virtual place. In the sandbox, Java programs can execute without adverse impact to the underlying system or its users.

The core J2SE security API grows with each new release of Java. For full information on what's available, refer to the Java API and release documentation.

What Else Is There?

J2EE

The Java 2 Platform Extended Edition (J2EE) is a collection of various enterprise-level APIs. J2EE can allow you to create scalable component-based applications.

---

[19][Fowler 2003a], p. 89.

Often when people refer to J2EE, they specifically mean Enterprise Java Beans (EJBs). EJBs are components. The goal of EJBs is to eliminate the need for an application developer to re-create deployment, security, transaction, and persistence services. An EJB application server such as BEA's WebSphere, IBM's WebLogic, or JBoss is a container that provides these services for EJBs.

J2EE is heavily weighted toward XML as the common data language. Four APIs center on XML: the Java API for XML Processing (JAXP), the Java API for XML-based RPC (remote procedure calls) (JAX-RPC), SOAP with Attachments API for Java (SAAJ), and the Java API for XML Registries (JAXR).

Another set of J2EE APIs centers on Web development. The Java Servlet API is the basis for web applications. JavaServer Pages (JSPs) simplify the presentation layer for web applications. The JSP Standard Tag Library (JSTL) provides common custom tags to simplify writing JSPs. JavaServer Faces gives you a framework for simplifying the development of the model and application facets of a web application.

Various other J2EE APIs support transactions, resource connections, and security. The Java Message Service (JMS) provides an interface for asynchronous message needs.

Scads of books exist on J2EE. The J2EE tutorial available at *http://java.sun.com/j2ee/download.html* is as good a place as any to start. Before you leap into the extremely complex world of J2EE, ensure that you have justified your decision from the standpoints of functionality need, cost of development, complexity requirements, performance need, and scalability needs. Many shops invested heavily in J2EE, only to find that they didn't need most of the things it provides. Often you will find that your own custom implementation provides all you need, is vastly simpler, and is a far more flexible solution.

More?

Dozens more Java APIs exist. They support various things such as image manipulation, speech, applets, cryptography, shared data, telephony, accessibility, and automatic web installation.

Java is an entrenched technology that will not go away anytime soon. The evidence is the fact that for virtually every computing need, a Java API for it exists. The best place to start is Sun's Java site, *http://java.sun.com*. Beyond that, the world is a haystack with many needles. Use Google to find them!

 Go fish!

Appendix A

An Agile Java Glossary

This appendix lists key terms. Most terms that appear in the text of *Agile Java* in *italicized form* appear here.

Each definition is brief but should provide you with a good idea what a given term means. Refer to the index in order to locate occurrences of the term within *Agile Java*. The context should provide you with a more robust understanding of a specific term.

abstract   representing concepts as opposed to concrete, specific details

acceptance test   a test that demonstrates functional behavior; also known as a functional test or customer test

access modifier   a keyword that identifies the level of exposure of a Java element to other code

action method   a method that effects an action, usually altering the state of an object

activation   a UML construct that represents the lifetime of a method in a sequence diagram

actual value   in an assertEquals statement, the expression or value that you are testing. The actual value immediately follows the expected value.

agile   a term for a body of lightweight processes; an agile process centers around the idea that requirements will change as a project progresses

annotation   a construct that allows you to embed descriptive information for Java elements in source code. An annotation is verified against an interface specification by the compiler.

anonymous inner class   an unnamed class that is dynamically defined within a method body

API   application programming interface

application   a computer-based system that provides value to humans or other systems

701

application programming interface the published specification for other classes with which your code can interact

argument an element that is passed to a method. Informal use of the term can indicate either one of the list of actual arguments passed in a method call or the formal parameters listed in the method's signature

argument list the list of values or references passed to a method

array initializer an initialization construct that allows provision of a set of initial values for elements in an array

assignment the act of storing the result of an expression in a field or variable

assignment operator the equals sign (=); used as part of an assignment

atomic an operation that executes as a single indivisible unit

attribute a general object-oriented term for a characteristic of an object. You define attributes on a class.

autoboxing automatically enclosing a primitive with its corresponding wrapper type

autounboxing automatically extracting a primitive from its corresponding wrapper type

bind to supply a type for a parameterized class

boolean a type that represents two possible values: `true` and `false`

bound having supplied a type for a parameterized class

block (n.) a section of code enclosed between braces; (v.) to wait until some other operation has completed

border a buffer area between the edges of a container and any of its components

byte codes the programming operations and other relevant information contained in a class file

callback the technique of passing a function as a parameter so that the receiver can message to it

camel case the mixed-case naming scheme preferred for Java identifiers

cast to tell the compiler that you want to convert the type of a reference; to narrow a numeric value to a smaller type

catch to trap a thrown exception

checked exception an exception that your code must explicitly acknowledge

checked wrapper   a collection wrapper that ensures that objects stored in the collection are of the appropriate type

class   a template for creating objects; a class defines behavior and attributes

class constant   a reference to a fixed value that can be accessed irrespective of creating object instances

class diagram   a UML model that shows class detail and the static relationship between classes

class file   a file containing code that has been compiled from source code

class library   a collection of useful classes provided by a vendor or another developer as an API

class literal   a value that represents the sole instance of a class

class loader   code that dynamically reads a stream of bytes representing a Java compilation unit from some source location and converts it to a usable class

class variable   a variable defined on a class that can be accessed without using an instance of the class

classpath   a list of directories or JAR files that Java uses for compilation and execution

client   a class, or code in general, that interacts with a specific target class. The target class may be referred to as a server class.

clone   to create a copy of an object

close   to design a class so that it needs no further modification despite future changes

coding   the act of writing programs

collective code ownership   a team philosophy that allows anyone to modify any portion of the system

collision   when two elements hash to the same location in a hash table

compiler   an application that transforms source code into a binary form that a platform can understand and execute

command object   an object that captures information in order to be able to effect specific behavior at a later time

comment   a free-form annotation of code that is ignored by the compiler

complex annotation   an annotation that includes another annotation

compound assignment   a shortcut form of assignment that presumes that the variable being assigned to is also the target of the first operation in the right-hand expression

composition　an association between classes whereby objects of one class are composed of objects of another class

concatenate　append

connection pool　a group of shared database connections

constructor　a block of code that allows you to provide statements to initialize an object. Invoking a constructor using the new operator results in the creation of an object.

constructor chaining　calling one constructor from another

container　a component that can contain other components

controller　a class responsible for managing input from the end user

cooperative multitasking　a multithreading scheme in which the individual threads are responsible for yielding time to allow other threads to execute

couple　to increase dependencies between classes

covariance　the ability for a subclass to vary the return type of an overridden method

critical section　see "mutual exclusion"

customer test　see :acceptance test

daemon thread　a secondary thread; an application can terminate regardless of whether or not daemon threads are active

declaration　the point at which something is defined

decouple　to minimize dependencies between classes

decrement　to subtract (usually one) from a value

decrement operator　--. A unary operator that subtracts 1 from the operand

default package　the unnamed package; classes that are defined without a package statement end up in the default package

dependency　a relationship between two classes (or any two entities) where one requires the existence of the other

dependency inversion　designing class associations so that classes are dependent upon abstractions instead of concrete implementations

deprecated　Java code intended for eventual removal from a class library

dereference　to navigate to a memory location based on the memory address stored in a reference

derived class　see "subclass"

deserialize　to "reconstitute" an object from a sequence of bytes

design by contract   a design technique that requires programmers to create a contract for how their software is expected to behave. See precondition, post-condition, and invariant.

driver   with respect to JDBC, an API that meets Sun's specification for interfacing with a database

dynamic proxy class   a class that allows you to implement one or more interfaces at runtime

element   a Java construct that an annotation can possibly annotate: a class, enum, interface, method, field, parameter, constructor, or local variable

encapsulation   hiding implementation specifics from clients; a core object-oriented concept

erasure   the scheme chosen by Sun to implement parameterized types; it refers to the fact that parameterized type information is erased to its upper bounds

escape sequence   a sequence of characters within a String or character literal that maps to a single character. An escape sequence begins with the character \. Escape sequences allow you to represent characters that you may not be able to type directly.

exception   an object that encapsulates error information

expected value   in an assertEquals statement, the value you expect to receive when comparing to an actual result. The expected value immediately precedes the actual value.

factory method   a method responsible for constructing and returning objects

field   the Java implementation of an attribute. A field minimally specifies a type and name for a characteristic of a class

field initializer   a code expression used to provide an initial value for a field or local variable

formal parameter   a named argument listed in a method or constructor signature

format elements   substitution parameters in a resource defined in a resource bundle

format specifier   a placeholder for substitution values within a format string; defines the transformation from value to output string

frame   a top-level window

fully qualified   indicates that a class name contains its complete package information

garbage collection   the VM process of reclaiming memory that is no longer needed

garbage collector   the code that is responsible for garbage collection

generic method   a method that can be parameterized with one or more type parameters

generics   parameterized types

global   available to any interested client

guard clause   a code construct that defines an early return from a method in the event of an exceptional condition

hacking   informal: creating software with abandon. Originally, hacking was a positive term; modern use of the term (including its use in *Agile Java*) is usually pejorative

hash code   an integer generated by a hashing algorithm that is used as the key for locating elements in a hash table

hash table   a fixed-size collection that determines the location of its elements using a hash code

heavyweight   refers to a process that emphasizes written, up-front documentation and discourages deviation from an initial plan

i18n   Internationalization

identifier   the name given to a Java element, such as a field, method, or class

immutable   unchangeable. A class is immutable if its attributes cannot be altered. An immutable object is also known as a value object

implement   to provide code details. When you implement an interface, you supply concrete definitions for the methods it declares

increment   to add (usually 1) to a value

increment operator ++.   A unary operator that adds 1 to the operand

inherit   to extend from a base class

inheritance   a relationship between two classes where one class (known as the subclass or derived class) specializes the behavior of another class (known as the superclass or base class)

initial value   the value that a field or local variable has at the time of declaration

inline   to embed previously externalized code into a method body; i.e., to eliminate the need for a method call by moving the target method's code into the calling method

instance variable   see field

instantiate   to create an object

interface   general: the point of communication between two things, such as two systems or two classes; Java: a construct that allows you to define method specifications, but no implementation details

interface adapter class   a class that transforms an externally defined interface into one that is more useful in the context of the current system

internationalize   to code a system such that it can supports deployment to different localities

interpreter   an application that reads and executes compiled code; see also virtual machine

invariant   an assertion that must always hold true while executing code; see also design by contract

invert   to turn upside-down; used in the context of dependency inversion

jagged array   an array of arrays where each subarray can vary in size

JAR   Java ARchive

Java archive   a class container; implemented using the ZIP file format

layout   the arrangement of components in a user interface

layout manager   a class that can aid in arranging components in a user interface

lazy initialization   a programming technique whereby you do not provide an initial value for a field until it is used for the first time

lightweight   refers to a process that emphasizes adaptation over adherence to plan

linked list   a serial data structure that adds new elements by dynamically allocating memory. Elements of a linked list must refer to other elements by storing one or more references to them.

local variable   a variable defined within the body of a method

locale   a region that is defined by perhaps geography, culture, or politics

localize   to prepare an internationalized application for delivery to a locale

log   to record

logical operator   an operator that returns a boolean value

lower bound   a constraint that requires a wildcard to be a supertype of the specified class

marker annotation   an annotation that provides no arguments

marker interface   an interface with no method declarations; allows programmers to signal intent for a class

member   a constructor, field, or method defined on the instance side of a class

member-value pair   a key and corresponding value supplied in an annotation

memory equivalence   when two object references are equal—i.e., they point to the same object in memory

metadata   data about data

method   a unit of code that helps define the behavior of a class. A return type, name, and argument list uniquely define a method. A method consists of a number of statements

methodology   a process for building software

mnemonic   a single-letter shortcut for activating a button

mock object   an object used for creating context to aid in verifying assertions against target code. Loosely used, a mock is any object that substitutes for production code to aid in testing

model   a class that contains application or business logic

modulus   an operator that returns the remainder of a division operation

multiline comment   a comment that can span multiple source lines; you start a multiline comment with /* and end it with */

multithreaded   having the ability to execute certain code sections at the same time as other sections

mutual exclusion   a form of synchronization in which a section of code has exclusive attention from the Java VM while it executes

naked type variable   a use of a type parameter symbol within a type declaration

namespace   a namespace implies the ability to define unique names, such that entities with the same base name do not clash with one another. In Java, this is accomplished through the use of package names

nested   embedded within

nested class   a class defined within another class

nondeterministic   having the potential to return different results each time when given the same inputs and initial state

numeric literal   a code instance of a number, such as an integer or a floating-point number

object   an entity that has identity, type, and state; objects are created from classes

object-oriented   based on the concepts of classes and objects

operator   a special token or keyword recognized by the compiler. An operator takes action against one or more values or expressions

overload   to supply multiple definitions for a method or constructor. You vary the definitions by their argument list (or possibly their return value; see covariance)

overloaded operator   an operator that has different meanings depending on the context in which it is used

override   to provide a replacement definition for a method already defined in a superclass

package   an arbitrary collection of classes, defined either for deployment or organizational purposes

package import   a form of the import statement that indicates that any of the classes in the specified package might be used in the class

package structure   the current state of package organization

pair programming   a development technique in which two developers actively program at a single workstation

parameter   informally, another name for an argument

parameterized type   a class to which you can bind one or more classes; doing so supplies additional constraints on the types of object that the class can interact with

persistent   existing from application execution to execution

platform   an underlying system on which applications can be run

polymorphism   the ability of objects to supply variant behaviors, in response to a message, based on their type. Seen from the opposite direction, the ability of clients to send a message to an object without an awareness or concern for which object actually receives the message

postcondition   an assertion that must hold true after executing code; see also design by contract

postfix operator   a unary operator that appears after the target it operates on

precondition   an assertion that must hold true prior to executing code; see also design by contract

preemptive multitasking   a multithreading scheme in which the operating system (or virtual machine) is responsible for interrupting and scheduling threads

prefix operator   a unary operator that appears before the target it operates on

primitive type   non-object types in Java. Numeric types and the `boolean` type are primitive types

process framework   a foundation for creating and customizing a process tailored to your needs

process instance   a specific customization of a process framework

program   the body of code that comprises an application; often used interchangeably with the term "application"

programmer test   see "unit test"

programming   see "coding"

programming by intention   a programming technique whereby you first specify your intent for a solution (i.e., the general steps involved) before implementing it (i.e., providing the detailed code)

project   the related things that make up an effort

proxy   a stand-in. A proxy object is an object that might filter or control access to the object it stands in for. To a client, a proxy is indistinguishable from the real thing

public interface   the methods of a class that are exposed to any other client class

query method   a method that returns information to a client but does not alter the state of the object

queue   a serial data structure that returns the eldest object when a client requests an object from it Also known as a first-in-first-out (FIFO) data structure

random access file   a logical interpretation of a file that allows you to quickly seek to specific positions in the file and read from or write to that position

raw type   an unbound parameterized type

realizes   implements

receiver   the object to which a message is sent, directly or indirectly, as the result of a method call

recursive   calling oneself; sending a message to the same method that is currently executing

refactor   to transform code; by definition, refactoring should not change the behavior of code

refactoring   (n.) a code transformation; (v.) the act of applying transforms to code

reference   a memory address; a variable that points to an object

reflective   of or dealing with reflection

reflection   the capability in Java that allows you to dynamically derive information about types and their definitions at runtime

regression test   a test that ensures that the existing application still works after changes have been applied

regular expression   a set of syntactical elements and symbols that is used to match text

resource bundle   a collection of resources such as message strings; allows an application to dynamically load said resources by name. A resource bundle is usually an external file.

rethrow   to catch and subsequently throw the same or another exception object

return type   indicates the class of object that a method must provide to the caller

runtime   refers to the scope of execution of a program; i.e., when it is running

sandbox   a customizable virtual Java place that defines boundaries for security purposes

scale   the number of digits to the right of the decimal point in a decimal number

scope   the lifetime of an object or variable; the sphere of influence it has

seed   a number used as the basis for determining a pseudorandom number sequence

semantic equality   when two objects are considered the same based on arbitrary criteria as supplied by a programmer. In Java, you use the `equals` method to define semantic equality

serializable   a class whose objects can be serialized; arbitrarily designated by a programmer

serialize   to convert an object to a sequence of bytes

server   a class or group of classes that provides a service to clients

singleton   a class that is coded to disallow creation of more than one instance of itself

signature   the information that uniquely identifies a method: its return type, name, and list of argument types

simple design   an approach to design that values testing, elimination of duplication, and code expressiveness. Simple design rules result in positive emergent behavior in code.

single-line comment   a comment that begins with //; an end-of-line character terminates the comment

software development kit   a bundle of applications and utilities designed to help developers build and execute custom applications

source file   a file containing code as typed by a programmer

spurious wakeup   an unexpected activation of an idling thread

stack trace   the execution summary that an exception generates. A stack trace shows, in reverse order, the chain of message sends leading up to a problem

stack walkback   see "stack trace"

state   a snapshot of what an object looks like at a current point in time, represented by the values in its attributes

statement   a line of Java code, terminated by a semicolon

static import   an import form that allows you to use class methods or variables defined in a different class as if they were defined locally

static initialization block   a block of code that executes when a class is first loaded by the VM

static method   a method you can invoke without first instantiating the class on which it is defined

static scope   having existence for the lifetime of a class

story   an informally stated requirement; a promise of further conversation

strategy   an algorithm; a variant way of accomplishing a task

stream   a sequence of data that you can write to or read from

string literal   a code instance of a String object, represented by text enclosed in double quotation marks

strongly typed   a characteristic of a programming language whereby variables and constants must be associated with a specific data type

subclass   the specialized class in an inheritance relationship

subscript   an index representing a position within an array

suite   a collection of unit tests

synchronization   the coordination of simultaneously executing threads to avoid data contention

target   the subject of desire; the object being operated on; in Ant, a process you want to execute

TDTT   test-driven truth table

temp variable   see "local variable"

temporary variable   see "local variable"

ternary operator   an operator that allows you to represent an if-else statement as an expression

test-driven   designed by virtue of programming specification tests prior to coding the corresponding implementation

test-driven truth table (TDTT)   a series of assertions to demonstrate the results for all possible combinations of bitwise and logical operators

token   an individual text component delineated by specially designated text characters

tolerance   the acceptable margin of error when comparing two floating-point quantities

thread   a Java unit of execution. A Java process may contain multiple threads, each of which can be executing simultaneously with the others

thread pool   a group of reusable threads

throw   to generate an exception; a transfer control mechanism

trace statements   code inserted in your application to allow you to monitor its behavior as it executes

two's complement   an scheme used for internal representation of negative integers. To obtain the two's complement representation of a number, take its positive binary representation, invert all binary digits, and add 1

type parameter list   in a parameterized type, the list of arguments that you must bind to

uncaught exception handler   a hook that allows you to trap executions thrown from a thread

upper camel case   a Java identifier naming scheme; camel case in which the first letter of the identifier is upper case

unary operator   an operator that has a single target

unchecked exception   an exception that does not require code to explicitly acknowledge it

unit test   a body of code that verifies the behavior of a target class (i.e., a unit); also known as a programmer test

upper bound   the constraint attached to a type parameter

user interface   the means with which a human interacts with an application

user thread   the main thread in an executing application; the existence of an active user thread sustains application execution

varargs   a variable number of arguments

view   a class responsible for displaying things to an end user

VM   virtual machine

virtual machine   an application that executes and manages custom programs. A virtual machine interacts with an underlying operating system as necessary; also referred to as an interpreter

walkback   see "stack trace"

weak reference   a reference that does not count for purposes of garbage collection

whitespace   space, tab, new line, form feed, and carriage return characters (collectively)

wildcard   a substitution character (?) in a type argument (for a parameterized type) that represents any possible type

wrapper   an object that contains another object or value. In Java, wrapper objects are used to contain primitives so that they can be used as objects

Appendix B

Java Operator Precedence Rules

The table in this appendix lists the complete set of operators.[1] Operators grouped on the same line have the same precedence. The table orders precedence groups from highest to lowest. In contrast with the binary operators + and -, the unary operators + and - are used in conjunction with a numeric literal or variable to express whether it is positive or negative.

postfix	`[] . () ++ -`
unary	`++ - + -`
creation, cast	`new (class)reference`
multiplicative	`* / %`
additive	`+ -`
shift	`<< >> >>>`
relational	`< > >= <= instanceof`
equality	`== !=`
and	`&`
exclusive or	`^`
inclusive or	`|`
conditional and	`&&`
conditional or	`||`
ternary (conditional)	`?:`
assignment	`= += -= *= /= %= >>= <<= >>>= &= ^= |=`

[1][Arnold 2000].

715

Appendix C

Getting Started with IDEA

This appendix demonstrates how to build and execute the "Hello World" application using IntelliJ IDEA. Before you attempt to use a sophisticated IDE such as IDEA, you should first learn how to do command-line compilation, execution, and testing of Java code. Learning these fundamentals will ensure that you can use Java on any platform you encounter.

IDEA

IDEA is a Java IDE built by a Czech company called JetBrains. IDEA has been one of the driving forces behind Java-specific intelligent features in an IDE. Many of the valuable features sported by other Java IDEs appeared first in IDEA. IDEA is also an open tool, meaning that third-party vendors and individual developers can enhance its capabilities by writing plug-ins for it.

I've used IDEA for several years, alternating between it and Eclipse as my primary IDEs (the choice my client often makes). One thing I've noted about IDEA is that it promotes the notion of least surprise: Generally, if you want to do something, IDEA does it and in a way you might expect or hope for.

IDEA also happened to support all of the new features of J2SE 5.0 well before Eclipse, in time for me to write this appendix before my deadline.

You can obtain the latest version of IDEA from the JetBrains web site at *http://www.jetbrains.com*. The version I used at the time of writing this appendix was IntelliJ IDEA 4.5.1. Follow the instructions at the site for downloading and installing IDEA. You should have already installed Java before bothering to install IDEA.

The installation program walks you through a number of questions regarding how you want IDEA configured. In general, you can go along with the defaults and just hit the Next button.

The following instructions are intended to be a brief introduction to getting started with IDEA, not a comprehensive user's guide. If you need more information, refer to the help supplied with IDEA or contact JetBrains support. Expect that the instructions shown in this appendix should not change dramatically in the near future, barring any significant changes from JetBrains.

The Hello Project

Start IDEA once you have installed it. IDEA will show you the dialog shown in Figure C.1.

The "Hello World" project will be throwaway. Change the text untitled to hello in the **Name** field. As you type the project name, note that the directory specified in the **Project file location** field changes automatically. You may want to make a note of the location so that you are aware of where it is in your file system.[1] Click the Next button. You will see the dialog shown in Figure C.2.

If you see nothing listed in the Project JDK field or if you do not see a version of Java that is 1.5 (5.0) or later, click the Configure button. Use the Configure JDK to add (+) new JDKs as necessary. You will need to know the installation location of J2SE 5.0.

Ensure you have selected a J2SE 5.0 JDK and click Next. Continue to click Next, accepting the defaults for each panel. Click the Finish button when IDEA first makes it available to you.

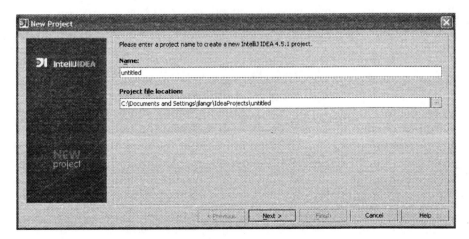

Figure C.1

[1]IDEA saves information on recently opened projects, so usually you will not need to worry about the location.

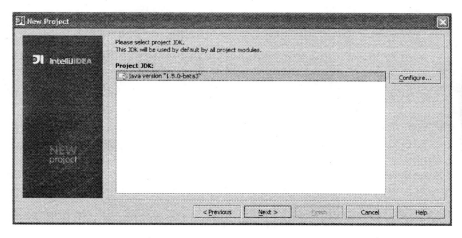

Figure C.2

The initial project screen, shown in Figure C.3, is spartan. A tab marked Project appears in the upper left corner, oriented vertically. Click this tab to open the Project tool window (see Figure C.4).

Select the top entry in the hierarchy tree—the first entry named **hello**. This is the project. The next entry below, also **hello**, is the module. Simple projects you build usually will need to contain only one module.

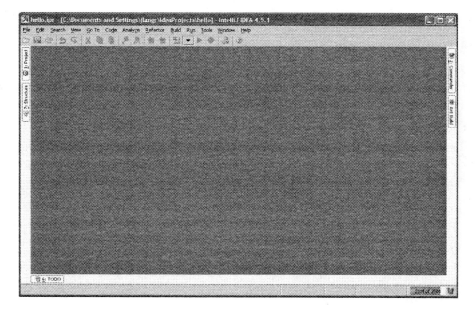

Figure C.3

The Hello Project

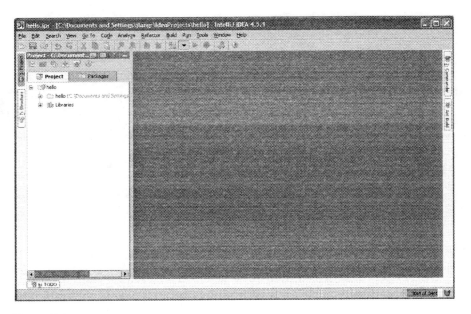

Figure C.4

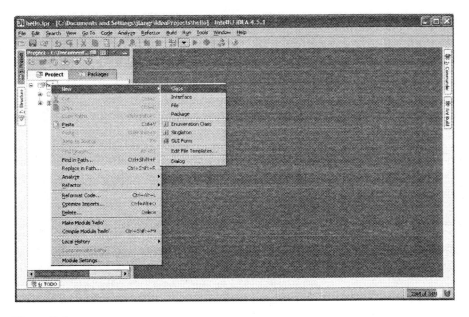

Figure C.5

Click your right mouse button after selecting the hello project in order to bring up the project context menu. The first entry in this menu is New; select it. You should see a screen that looks like Figure C.5.

Click the menu item Class. When prompted for a class name, enter Hello. Make sure you enter the class name with the correct case! You should see an editor with a starting definition for the class Hello (see Figure C.6).

In the Hello.java editor window, change the code to reflect the Hello code as originally presented in Chapter II, Setting Up:

```
class Hello {
   public static void main(String[] args) {
      System.out.println("hello world");
   }
}
```

The Project tool window to the left now shows the expanded project hierarchy. Beneath the **src** entry, you see your new class **Hello** listed. Right-click this class entry to bring up the context menu. See Figure C.7.

Click the menu entry Run "Hello.main()", third from the bottom of the menu. Note that you can press the key combination Ctrl+Shift+F10 as an alternative to using the menu. You need not save your source files before attempting to run programs—IDEA saves them for you automatically.

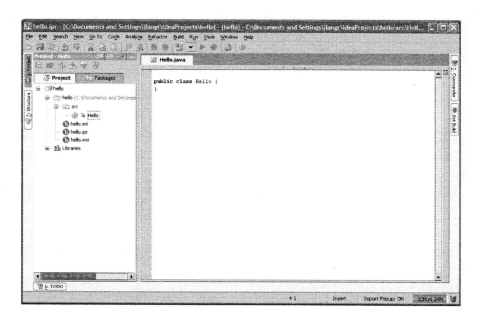

Figure C.6

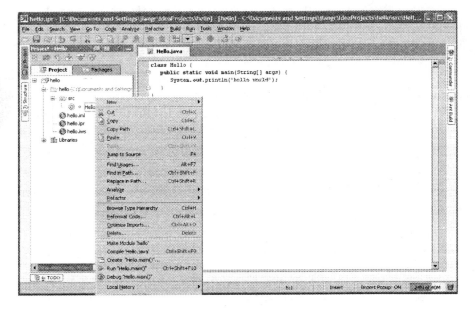

Figure C.7

IDEA might present you with a dialog asking whether or not you want to create an output directory. If so, simply click Yes.

A Compile Progress dialog should appear briefly. Before IDEA can execute your program, it must compile it to ensure there are no problems. The first time you compile, it may take a little longer; subsequent runs should begin more quickly.[2] Presuming that you have no compile errors, you should see an output window at the bottom of IDEA (see Figure C.8).

Success!

Next, you'll change the source code to deliberately contain errors in order to see how IDEA deals with them.

Change the source code in the Hello.java editor to something that should generate an error. Here's one possibility:

```java
class Hello {
    public static void main(String[] args) {
        xxxSystem.out.println("hello world");
    }
}
```

---

[2]The slow initial compilation appears to occur each time you start IDEA.

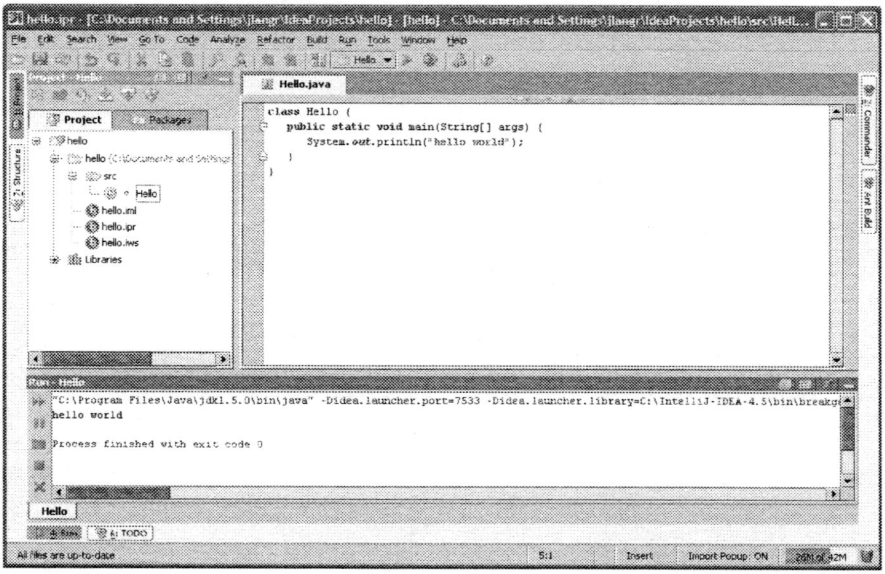

Figure C.8

Observe that off to the right, there are a couple of visual indicators telling you that the code has problems. In the upper right corner of the editor a small square will appear; it will be red. It was green until you mucked up the code. Below this square, you will see one or or more thin red lines. These lines indicate the problem spots in the code. You can hold your mouse over a line to see the error message. You can click on the line to navigate to the problem spot.

Try running Hello again and see what happens. Since you've already executed Hello one time, you can quickly execute it again using one of at least two ways: either press the Shift-F10 key combination or click the Run arrow (a green arrow pointing right, like the play button on a CD player). The Run arrow is located on the toolbar beneath the menu and above the Hello.java editor.

Instead of seeing the Run tool window with the correct output, you see the Messages tool window (Figure C.9). This window presents you with a complete list of error messages. Off to the left are various icons that help you manage the messages. Hold your mouse over any one of the icons for a second or so to see a tool tip that explains the icon's use.

If you double-click a specific error message in the Messages tool window, IDEA will put the text cursor on the specific location in Hello.java that contains the error. Correct the error and re-run Hello.

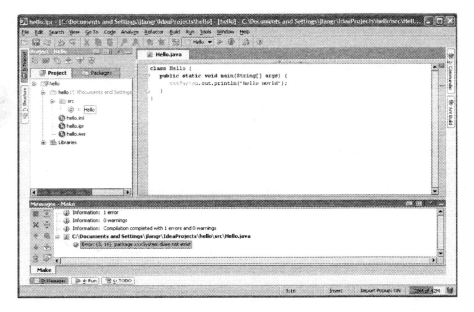

Figure C.9

Running Tests

This section walks you through the first part of Lesson 1, in which you create a StudentTest class and a corresponding Student class. The goal of this section is to show you how to effectively do test-driven development in IDEA.

Start by creating a new project. Click on the File menu, then click New Project. IDEA will present you with the same series of dialogs as when you created the **hello** project. This time, type the name of the project as lesson1. Then follow the same steps as when you created the **hello** project—keep clicking Next. When you click Finish, IDEA gives you the opportunity to open the project in a new frame. Select Yes.

Before you enter code, you will need to change some project settings. From the Project tools window, select the Project (lesson1). Right-click to bring up the context menu and select Module Settings.

You should see the Paths dialog, shown in Figure C.10.

First, you must configure the lesson1 module to recognize the J2SE 5.0 language level (if it doesn't already). Near the bottom of the dialog is a drop-down list marked Language level for project (effective on restart). The paren-

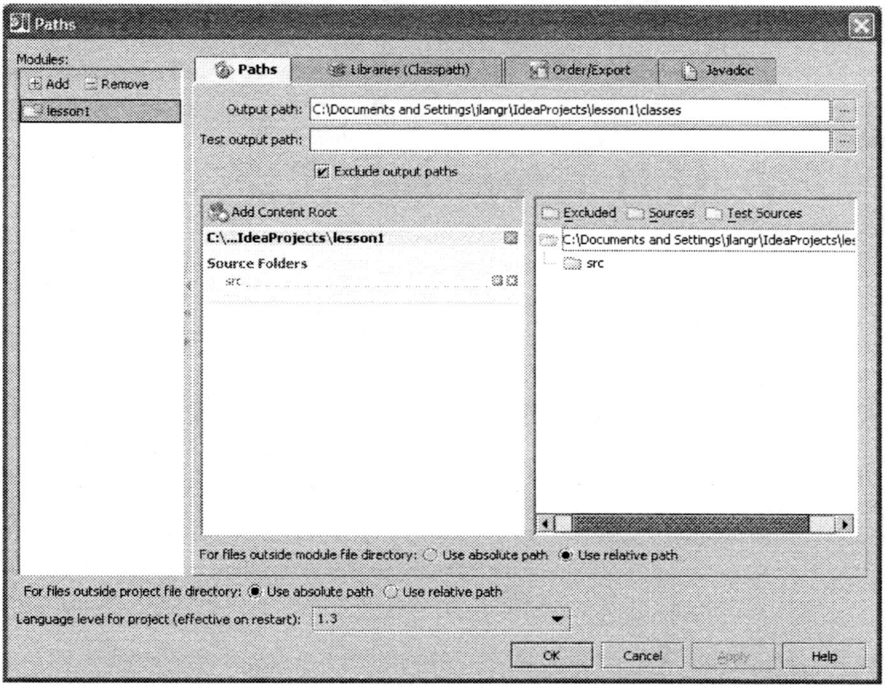

Figure C.10

thesized comment suggests that you'll need to exit IDEA and restart it for changes to be effective.[3] You'll do this shortly. Now, click on the drop-down list to expose the selection list. Choose the entry that indicates version 5.0.

Next, you must specify where the module can find the JUnit JAR file. (If you're not sure what this means, refer to Lesson 1 as well as Chapter II on setting up.) Click on the tab marked Libraries (Classpath) (it appears at the top of the Paths dialog). Your Paths dialog should look like the screen snapshot shown in Figure C.11.

Currently the **Paths** dialog shows that you have no libraries (JAR files) on your classpath. Click the button Add Jar/Directory. You will see a Select Path dialog. Navigate to the directory in which you installed JUnit, select junit.jar, and click OK. You should be back at the Paths dialog.

Click OK to close the Paths dialog. Exit IDEA, then restart IDEA. Make sure you completely exit IDEA—close the hello project frame if it remains open.

---

[3]While some of the new features of J2SE 5.0 will work, others will not do so until you restart.

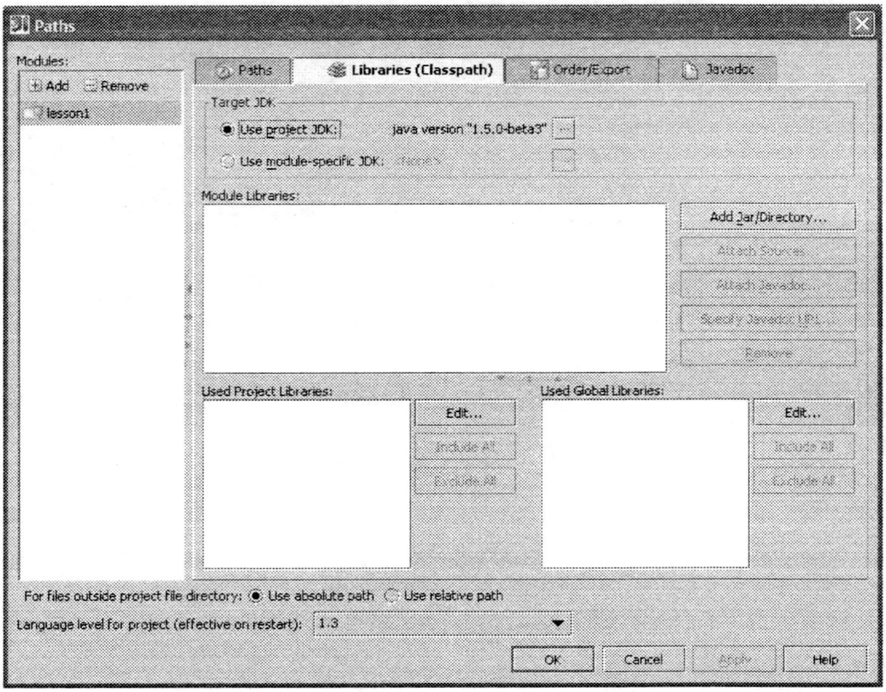

Figure C.11

IDEA will probably reopen with the hello project, not the **lesson1** project. If it does so, select File→Close Project from the menu. Then click File→Reopen and select the lesson1 project from the list of recently opened projects. If the lesson1 project does not appear, click File→Open Project. You will then need to navigate to the directory in which you created the project. If you accepted the defaults, under Windows this directory is probably C:\Documents and Settings\userName\IdeaProjects\lesson1, where userName is your Windows login name.

Once you have reopened lesson1, right-click in the Project tool window. Select New→Class from the context menu. For the class name, enter StudentTest. In the StudentTest.java editor, enter the initial code from Lesson 1 for the StudentTest class:

```
public class StudentTest extends junit.framework.TestCase {
}
```

From the Project tool window tree, right-click and select Run "StudentTest". Create an output directory if asked to do so. You should see something like the window in Figure C.12.

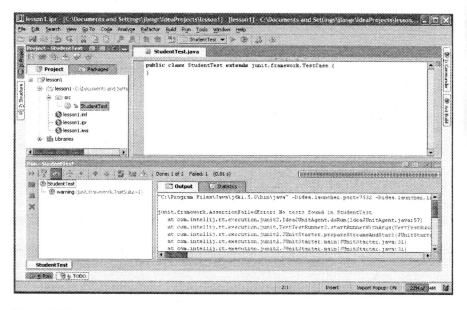

Figure C.12

The pane in the lower right quadrant shows output from the test run. This is JUnit output—IDEA has integrated JUnit directly into the IDE.

If you can't see enough of the output, drag the slider bar up. The slider bar appears just above the Run tool window and separates the top half of IDEA from the bottom half. Move the mouse slowly over the slider until you see a double-headed north-south arrow, then click and drag.

Make sure you're following along with the directions in Lesson 1 as you proceed. As expected, the Output window shows a failure, since you have defined no tests in StudentTest. Modify the StudentTest code:

```
public class StudentTest extends junit.framework.TestCase {
   public void testCreate() {
   }
}
```

Rerun (Shift-F10). Now, instead of a red bar and an error in the Output window, you see a green bar and two lines of output. The first line shows the actual java command passed to the operating system. The second line says that the "Process finished with exit code 0." Good. You demonstrated failure, corrected the problem, then demonstrated success.

Next, the fun part. Modify the StudentTest code again:

```
public class StudentTest extends junit.framework.TestCase {
    public void testCreate() {
        new Student("Jane Doe");
    }
}
```

You should see red indicators to the right. The class name Student appears in red. You can hold the mouse over any red for more information. If you click on the class name Student, you will see a little light bulb to the left of the line after a short delay. Click on the light bulb. See Figure C.13.

The light bulb represents the "intention actions" tool. It presents you with a list of actions that you can effect. As an alternative to clicking the light bulb, you can bring up the list of actions using the Alt-Enter key combination. IDEA builds the intention actions list based on what it thinks you want to do. In this case you can select the only entry in the list, Create Class "Student". When asked for a package, just click OK.

Figure C.14 shows that you now have two editors, StudentTest.java and Student.java. You can bring up either one by clicking on its tab.

The intention actions tool is one of many ways in which IDEA reduces the amount of code you must type. You have a Student class with a bunch of the relevant code already filled in. The generated class code is currently in "template" mode—you can press tab to move through various relevant

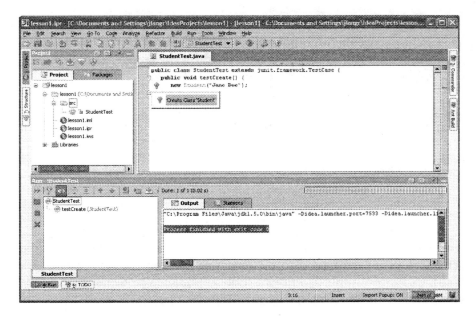

Figure C.13

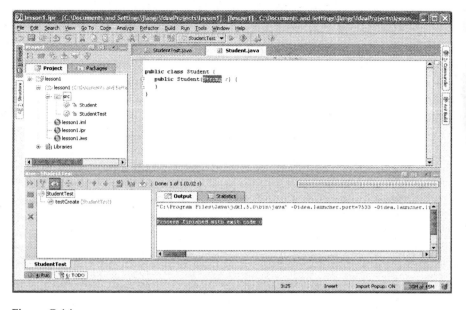

Figure C.14

fields. This gives you the opportunity to replace template code with your specifics. Tab to the argument field and replace the argument name s with name. Tab again or press the Esc key to exit template mode.

You should see no red indicators. Rerun and ensure you see green results from JUnit.

Continue with the remainder of the Lesson 1 exercise. Take advantage of the various intention actions as IDEA presents them to you. Experiment with alternate ways of effecting things. If you've been leaning toward mouse-directed options, try the key combinations to see if they help you go faster. And vice versa! Dig through the menus available and see if you can effect actions from there.

Taking Advantage of IDEA

IDEA, like most modern IDEs, is full of many time-saving features. It behooves you to learn how to master your IDE. The difference between a novice using only the basic features versus an expert taking full advantage of the IDE can be measured in weeks over the lifetime of a one-year project.

Code Completion

One valuable feature is code completion, which I'll also refer to as auto-completion. When you begin typing things that IDEA can recognize, such as class names, package names, and keywords, click Ctrl-Space. IDEA will do one of three things: It may say "No suggestions," it may automatically complete the text you began typing, or it may bring up a list of selections to choose from. You can navigate to the selection using the cursor (arrow) keys and press Enter or you can click on the desired selection. IDEA will finish your typing based on this selection.

Pressing the Enter key results in the new text being inserted at the current location. If you instead press the Tab key, the new text will replace any text immediately to the right.

Get in the habit of pressing Ctrl-Space after typing two or three significant characters. I press it all the time. You may be surprised at what IDEA is able to figure out about your intentions.

IDEA provides two additional kinds of code completion: Smart Type and Class Name. These are more sophisticated tools triggered by alternate keystrokes. Refer to the IDEA help system for more information (Help→Help Topics).

Navigation

One of the most significant strengths of using an IDE such as IDEA is the ease with which you can navigate through Java code. Click on the Go To menu. The size of this menu suggests how flexible this feature is. Click on the Class selection from the Go To menu. Type the three letters Stu. Pause. You will see a drop-down list of appropriate classes to choose from.

Class navigation is basic but important. More valuable is the ability to navigate from directly within code. Open the StudentTest class. From the line that reads new Student("Jane Doe");, click on the class name Student. Then press the Ctrl-b key combination (b for "browse," I suppose). Pressing Ctrl-b is equivalent to selecting the menu option Go To→Declaration.

IDEA will navigate directly into the Student constructor. You can return to your previous edit location by using the key combination Ctrl-Shift-Backspace. Learning all these navigation shortcuts will save you considerable time. I've watched programmers, even recently, use inferior tools. They waste several minutes every hour in manually navigating through a list of classes and scrolling through large amounts of code.

Searching is another form of navigation. IDEA understands Java and how it all fits together, making searches far more effective. Suppose you want to find all code that invokes a certain method. Using a programmer's editor, you can do only text searches against code. Suppose you're trying to find all client classes that call a method named getId. There might be other classes that implement getId; the text searches will report uses against these classes as well.

But IDEA can use its Java smarts to help you find only the usages you're interested in. As an example: In the Student class, click on the constructor. Right-click and select Find Usages from the context menu. Click OK when presented with the Find Usages dialog. The Find tool window will appear at the bottom of IDEA. As with the Messages tool window, you can double-click an entry in the find results to navigate directly to it.

Refactoring

Another important capability is the built-in refactoring support. IDEA automates a number of refactorings that allow you to quickly and safely transform your code. Take a look at all the entries in the Refactor menu to get an idea of the things you can do.

The simplest and perhaps most valuable refactoring appears first—Rename, also effected by Shift-F6. In a few keystrokes, you can safely change the name of a method. This means that IDEA also changes any other code that calls the method to reflect the new name. It also shows you the proposed rename before it applies it to your code. This allows you to back out if you recognize a problem with the potential refactoring.

I use the Rename refactoring all the time. Rather than waste a lot of time coming up with the "perfect" method or class name, I'll often go with a name I know to be inferior. This allows me to immediately get moving. After coding a little, a better name usually suggests itself. A quick Shift-F6 and I'm on my way. Sometimes I might change a method name more than a couple of times before I'm satisfied.

Code Analysis

IDEA supplies you with a code analysis feature known as the code inspector (Analyze→Inspect Code). You execute code inspection on demand against a single source file or the entire project. The inspector looks for problem spots in your code, including things such as unused methods or variables or empty catch blocks. The list of options includes over 300 categorized entries. You pick and choose what you're interested in: individual entries or groups of related entries or both.

Taking
Advantage of
IDEA

The inspection can take a bit of time to execute. When an inspection completes, the inspector presents you with a tree showing all the results. Each result is a detailed explanation of the problem or potential problem in your code. From a detailed explanation, you can click to navigate to the corresponding trouble spot. When possible, IDEA will give you the option to automatically correct the problem.

IDEA may report dozens or hundreds of entries that you may not think are problems. It's up to you and your team to decide the items that are relevant. Some items are not problems at all. But virtually everything on the list can point to the potential for trouble in certain environments or circumstances.

The practice of TDD can mitigate most of these concerns. In *Agile Java*, you've learned to build things incrementally and not always to an overly robust expectation. You can "get away" with things that would be deemed unacceptable in the absence of good testing.

Relax. Some others might consider the style in *Agile Java* to be fast and loose. Certainly there is always room for improvement in my code. But I don't worry about it as much when doing TDD.

I consider the bulk of code I come across difficult to understand and maintain. Blindly adhering to standards can seem like a good idea, but often it can lead you to waste considerable time for little gain. If you instead look to the simple design goals of testability, elimination of duplication, and code expressiveness, you will rarely go wrong.

Agile Java References

[Arnold2000] Arnold, K.; Gosling, J.; Holmes, D. *The Java Programming Language (3e)*. Sun Microsystems, 2000.

[Astels2003] Astels, Dave. *Test-Driven Development: A Practical Guide.* Pearson Education, 2003.

[Astels2004] Astels, Dave. "One Assertion Per Test." *http://www.artima .com/weblogs/viewpost.jsp?thread=35578.*

[Beck1998] Beck, Kent; Gamma, Erich. *"Test Infected: Programmers Love Writing Tests." http://members.pingnet.ch/gamma/junit.htm.*

[Bloch2001] *Effective Java Programming Language Guide.* Addison-Wesley, 2001.

[Fowler2000] Fowler, Martin. *Refactoring: Improving the Design of Existing Code.* Addison-Wesley, 2000.

[Fowler2003] Fowler, Martin. *UML Distilled: A Brief Guide to the Standard Object Modeling Language.* 3rd ed. Addison-Wesley, 2003.

[Fowler2003a] Fowler, Martin. *Patterns of Enterprise Application Architecture.* Addison-Wesley, 2003.

[Gamma1995] Gamma, Erich; Helm, Richard; Johnson, Ralph; Vlissides, John. *Design Patterns.* Addison-Wesley, 1995.

[George2002] George, Eric. "Testing Interface Compliance with Abstract Test" *http://www.placebosoft.com/abstract-test.html.*

[Hatcher2002] Hatcher, Eric; Loughran, Steve. *Java Development with Ant.* Manning Publications Company, August 2002.

[Heller1961] Heller, Joseph. *Catch-22.* Dell Publishing, 1961.

[JavaGloss2004a] Green, Roedy. "Java Glossary: float." *http://mindprod .com/jgloss/floatingpoint.html.*

[JavaGloss2004b] Green, Roedy, "Java Glossary: weak references." *http:// mindprod.com/jgloss/weak.html.*

[Jeffries2001] Jeffries, R.; Anderson, A.; Hendrickson, C. *Extreme Programming Installed.* Addison-Wesley, 2001.

[Kerievsky2004] Kerievsky, Joshua. *Refactoring to Patterns.* Addison-Wesley, 2004.

[Langr2000] Langr, Jeff. *Essential Java Style.* Prentice Hall PTR, 2000.

[Langr2001] Langr, Jeff. "Evolution of Test and Code Via Test-First Design." *http://www.objectmentor.com/resources/articles/tfd.pdf.*

[Langr2003] Langr, Jeff. "Don't Mock Me." *http://www.LangrSoft.com/articles/mocking.html.*

[Lavender1996] Lavender, R. Greg; Schmidt, Douglas C. "An Object Behavioral Pattern for Concurrent Programming." *http://citeseer.ist.psu.edu/lavender96active.html.*

[Link2003] Link, Johannes. *Unit Testing in Java: How Tests Drive the Code.* Morgan Kaufmann, 2003.

[Martin2003] Martin, Robert. *Agile Software Development: Principles, Patterns, and Practices.* Prentice Hall, 2003.

[Massol2004] Massol, Vincent. *JUnit in Action.* Manning Publications, 2004.

[McBreen2000]   McBreen, Pete. *Software Craftmanship.* Addison-Wesley, 2001.

[Rainsberger2005] Rainsberger, J. B. *JUnit Recipes.* Manning Publications, 2005.

[Sun2004] *[Java] Reference Glossary. http://java.sun.com/docs/glossary.html.*

[Travis2002] Travis, Gregory M. *JDK 1.4 Tutorial.* Manning Publications, 2002.

[Venners2003] Venners, Bill; Eckel, Bruce. "The Trouble with Checked Exceptions: A Conversation With Anders Hejlsberg, Part II." *http://www.artima.com/intv/handcuffs.html.*

[Vermeulen2000] Vermeulen, Allan, et al. *The Elements of Java Style.* Cambridge University Press, 2000.

[WhatIs2004] "platform." *http://www.whatis.com.*

[Wiki2004] "CodeSmell." *http://c2.com/cgi/wiki?CodeSmell.*

[Wiki2004a] "EmptyCatchClause." *http://c2.com/cgi/wiki?EmptyCatchClause.*

[Wiki2004b] "SimpleDesign" and "XpSimplicityRules," *http://c2.com/cgi/wiki?SimpleDesign* and *http://c2.com/cgi/wiki?XpSimplicityRules.*

[Wikipedia2004] *http://en.wikipedia.org/wiki/Java_programming_language.*

Index

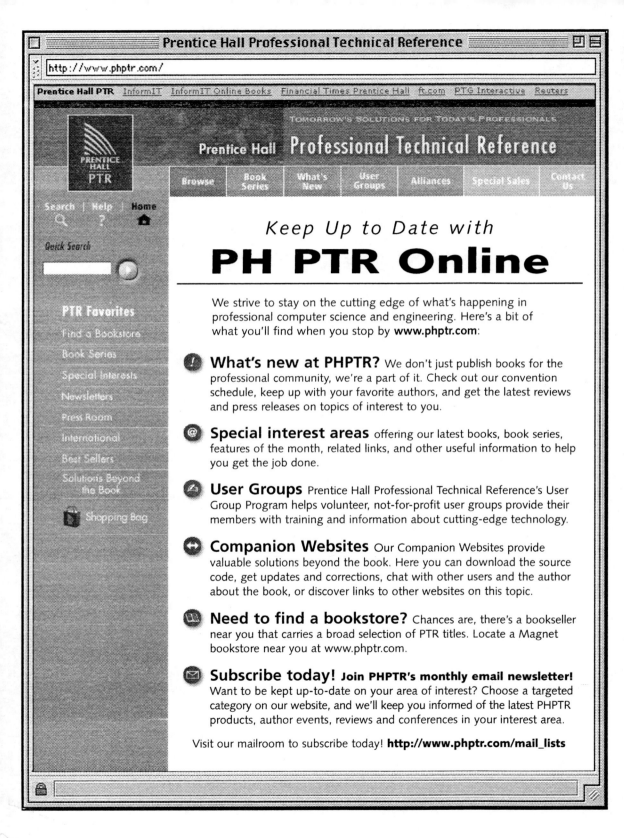

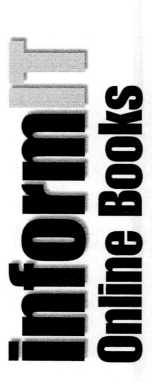

informIT